ADVANCED ACCOUNTING

concepts & practice

9TH EDITION

ARNOLD J. PAHLER

San Jose State University

Australia · Canada · Mexico · Singapore · Spain · United Kingdom · United States

Advanced Accounting: Concepts and Practice, Ninth Edition
Arnold J. Pahler

VP/Editorial Director:
Jack W. Calhoun

Publisher:
Rob Dewey

Acquisitions Editor:
Matt Filimonov

Developmental Editor:
Craig Leonard

Marketing Manager:
C. Kislack

Production Editor:
Robert Dreas

Manager of Technology, Editorial:
Vicky True

Technology Project Editor:
Robin K. Browning

Web Coordinator:
Scott Cook

Manufacturing Coordinator:
Doug Wilke

Production House:
Cover to Cover Publishing, Inc.

Printer:
Quebecor World
Versailles, Kentucky

Art Director:
Chris A. Miller

Internal Designer:
Beckmeyer Design
Cincinnati, Ohio

Cover Designer:
Beckmeyer Design
Cincinnati, Ohio

Cover Images:
© Getty Images

Printed in the United States of America
1 2 3 4 5 07 06 05 04

Student Edition: ISBN 0-324-23353-1

Library of Congress Control Number:
2004113252

For more information about our products, contact us at:

Thomson Learning Academic
Resource Center
1-800-423-0563

Thomson Higher Education
5191 Natorp Boulevard
Mason, OH 45040
USA

Asia (including India)
Thomson Learning
5 Shenton Way
#01-01 UIC Building
Singapore 068808

Australia/New Zealand
Thomson Learning Australia
102 Dodds Street
Southbank, Victoria 3006
Australia

Canada
Thomson Nelson
1120 Birchmount Road
Toronto, Ontario
M1K 5G4
Canada

Latin America
Thomson Learning
Seneca, 53
Colonia Polanco
11560 Mexico
D.F.Mexico

UK/Europe/Middle East/Africa
Thomson Learning
High Holborn House
50/51 Bedford Row
London WC1R 4LR
United Kingdom

Spain (including Portugal)
Thomson Paraninfo
Calle Magallanes, 25
28015 Madrid, Spain

Dedication

To my family, Anne, Laura, and Brett

Arnold J. Pahler

Preface

OVERVIEW

Since the publication of the previous edition in 2002, the *major* accounting change concerning Advanced Accounting topics, by far, was the FASB's issuance in 2003 of *Interpretation No. 46*, "Consolidation of Variable Interest Entities" (an interpretation of *ARB No. 51*, "Consolidated Financial Statements"). *FIN 46* was issued as a result of Enron Corporation's improper consolidation practices that (1) came to light in 2001 and (2) ultimately led to the implosion and demise in 2002 of the then Big 5 and once highly respected and mighty public accounting firm of Arthur Andersen & Co.

FIN 46 has resulted in a large number of companies having to consolidate many previously "off-balance sheet" entities. *FIN 46* sets forth entirely new concepts and complex rules to determine whether consolidation of entities that are *not* majority-owned (in the traditional sense of stock ownership) is appropriate. We discuss *FIN 46* in detail in Chapter 3.

Other overall changes for the ninth edition are as follows:

> We updated the text for other new FASB and GASB pronouncements as well (none of which were major).
> We added some *Internet assignments* (identified with an icon), challenging cases (to promote critical thinking), and challenging financial analysis problems (to broaden students' perspectives). These changes are consistent with the recent restructuring of the CPA examination content.
> Ethics situations and questions were moved into the chapters for more visibility and ease of use.
> The end-of-chapter Self-Study Questions in the Eighth Edition were moved into the chapters at various points and renamed as Check Points, so that students could more easily self-assess comprehension at periodic intervals.
> To streamline the text, we shortened the number of chapters from 31 to 26. (Some of the chapters were combined and some of the chapters were moved into appendices.)
> To shorten the text, all appendices (19 of them totaling roughly 150 pages) except Appendix 6A were moved from the text to the publisher's web page for downloading as .pdf files. (Many instructors omit most of these topics anyway due to time constraints.)

In the remainder of this preface, we (1) list the new professional standards incorporated, (2) further explain the general design and features of this text, (3) cover the chapter-by-chapter changes from the Eighth Edition to the Ninth Edition, (4) outline student-oriented features, (5) summarize the supplements available with this text (including how they may be readily obtained), and (6) acknowledge others for their review contributions with this edition.

I. NEW ACCOUNTING STANDARDS

We incorporate the following new accounting standards in the Ninth Edition:

> FASB *Interpretation No. 46*, "Consolidation of Variable Interest Entities," an interpretation of *ARB No. 51* (as revised in December 2003).
> FASB *Statement No. 150*, "Accounting for Certain Financial Instruments with Characteristics of both Liabilities and Equity" (2003).
> FASB *Statement No. 147*, "Acquisitions of Certain Financial Institutions" (2002).
> GASB *Statement No. 45*, "Accounting and Financial Reporting by Employers for Postemployment Benefits Other Than Pension Plans" (2004).

II. CONSOLIDATIONS AND BUSINESS COMBINATIONS APPROACH

Two unique aspects of this text in the *consolidated financial statements* and *business combinations* sections (Chapters 1–11) are:

1. It uses **internal expansion** (Chapters 1–3) as a stepping stone to **external expansion** (Chapters 4–6) and
2. It does *not* carry forward the *purchase method* accounting complexities (Chapters 4–6) into the intercompany transactions section (Chapters 8–10).

Thus this sequential approach used for the consolidations topic is one of going from the *simplest situation* to the most *complex situation* in a step-by-step manner for the five major consolidation concepts, as shown below.

1. The **general concept of consolidating** using a *created* subsidiary—in **Chapter 1.**
2. The **accounting for a parent's investment** using a *created* subsidiary—in **Chapter 2.**
3. The **concept of a noncontrolling interest** using a *partially owned* ***created*** subsidiary (and whether to use the *parent company concept* or the *economic unit concept*, both of which are currently allowed under GAAP)—in **Chapter 3.**

   As in the Eighth Edition, we place primary emphasis on the *parent company concept* (by far, the more widely used concept in practice) because the FASB continues its lengthy debate of whether to only allow one of these methods.
4. The **concept of changing the basis of accounting** (*purchase accounting*) for an *acquired* business (the most complex of the five concepts)—in **Chapters 4–6.**
5. The **procedures to eliminate intercompany transactions** using a *created* subsidiary—in **Chapters 8–10.**

This sequence enables these five major concepts to be learned separately in a progressive fashion (which makes it easier for students) rather than having to learn several of them simultaneously, as handled by other advanced accounting texts.

Additional Reasons for Use of Created Subsidiaries Approach

Further reasons for the use of the created subsidiaries approach and the full separation of the five major concepts are discussed in the following three paragraphs.

Most Subsidiaries Are *Created*—Not *Acquired*

Aside from the pedagogical advantage, the initial emphasis on *created* subsidiaries better reflects actual business expansion practices. The vast majority of *existing subsidiaries* were *not* acquired but were **created** by their parent companies. Consequently, we treat *external expansion* as only one facet of preparing consolidated statements—*not* as an integral part around which the consolidations area is structured.

IMA-FEI Study Supports Treating Consolidation as a Separate Issue from External Expansion

In a major Institute of Management Accountants/Financial Executive Institute joint research project, completed in 1994, two findings support this emphasis. The study found that (1) preparing consolidated financial statements is one of the most important of 15 accounting skills and knowledge areas deemed vital as "the essence of management" to corporate entry-level accountants, but that (2) accounting for external expansion (*purchase accounting*) is *not* one of these 15 skills.

Partially Owned *Created Subsidiaries* Discussed Separately from *Acquired Subsidiaries*

To introduce major concepts on a full step-by-step basis, we discuss noncontrolling interest situations first in the relatively simple situation in which the parent *creates* a partially owned subsidiary. Accordingly, Chapter 3 is a logical extension of Chapters 1 and 2, both of which deal with 100%-owned *created subsidiaries*. Noncontrolling interest situations involving *acquired subsidiaries* are discussed in Chapter 6, thus enabling the emphasis in that chapter to be entirely on the *change in basis of accounting* concept.

III. EMPHASIZING THE *EQUITY METHOD* OVER THE *COST METHOD*

Significant diversity of opinion exists among advanced accounting faculty as to (1) how much emphasis should be placed on the *equity method* versus the *cost method* and (2) whether to use the *full equity method* or the *partial equity method* in dealing with unrealized intercompany profit. We have tried different degrees of emphasis in this regard over the prior eight editions. Based on feedback from students and adopting instructors over the years, we have settled on the emphasis described in the following two paragraphs.

Predominant Use of the Equity Method

Chapters 2–11 use the *equity method* of accounting for the parent's investment. Because the *cost method* is widely used in practice, however, we also illustrate it in Chapter 2 (comparing it to the *equity method*) and Appendix 3A (for a noncontrolling interest ownership situation).

Use of Both the *Full Equity Method* and the *Partial Equity Method* in Self-Contained Modules in Chapters 9–10

In the intercompany transactions section (Chapters 9–10), instructors have the option of using either (1) the *full equity method* (**Module 1**) or (2) the *partial equity method* (**Module 2**) in dealing with unrealized intercompany profit. For the *full equity method*, we achieve the results desired under the *full equity method* by having the *selling entity* book a deferral entry in its general ledger (as opposed to having the parent adjust its Equity in Net Income of Subsidiary account for any unrealized intercompany profit). This alternative procedure has two significant advantages over the procedure of adjusting the parent's Equity in Net Income of Subsidiary account. First, it enables unrealized intercompany profit to be dealt with in a more straightforward and simpler manner that is far more readily understood by students—regardless of whether the transfer is *downstream* or *upstream*. Second, it requires no separate adjustment to the noncontrolling interest amounts (determined in the basic elimination entry as shown in Chapter 3) on upstream sales from a partially owned subsidiary, which simplifies matters for students.

Discussion of Intercompany Transactions Using *Created Subsidiaries* (Chapters 8–10) Instead of *Acquired Subsidiaries*

As briefly mentioned earlier, the textual material and illustrations in Chapters 8–10 (intercompany transactions) are based on *created subsidiaries* instead of *acquired subsidiaries*. We believe intercompany transaction topics are difficult enough for students to learn without the burden of introducing the carryforward of the change in basis of accounting issue that arises with *external expansion*. Accordingly, the *purchase method procedures* are largely contained in Chapters 4–6.

Furthermore, substantially all of the consolidation problems in Chapters 8–10 are based on *created subsidiaries.* (A few of the problems, however, are labeled as "comprehensive" and involve the additional complexity of either *purchased subsidiaries* so that instructors have the flexibility of integrating these situations into the intercompany transactions topics if they desire.)

IV. Chapter-by-Chapter Changes

The following is an outline of the more significant changes made to the content from the Eighth Edition to the Ninth Edition:

Chapter 1 Wholly Owned Subsidiaries: At Date of Creation

> Added a provocative Internet research assignment (Exercise 1-2).

> Added two real-world financial analysis problems (one of which deals with the interesting theoretical question of whether to consolidate the assets and liabilities of a company's pension plan trust fund).

Chapter 2 Wholly Owned Subsidiaries: Postcreation Periods

> Added a real world case (involving a non-GAAP Enron accounting practice).

> Added a unique consolidation problem (Problem 2-5).

Chapter 3 Partially Owned Created Subsidiaries and Variable Interest Entities: Postcreation Periods

> Moved the *cost method* discussion to Appendix 3A.

> Added a comprehensive summary illustration comparing the *parent company concept* with the *economic unit concept.*

> Added a detailed discussion of FASB *FIN 46*, "Variable Interest Entities."

Chapter 4 Introduction to Business Combinations

> Made several clarifications.

> Updated the historical development of accounting for goodwill capsule at the end of the chapter.

Chapter 5 The Purchase Method: At Date of Acquisition—100% Ownership

> Moved the *acquisition of assets* module to Appendix 5A.

> Added a discussion of the FASB's proposed change to the treatment of merger costs (proposed in September 2004).

Chapter 6 The Purchase Method: Postacquisition Periods and Partial Ownerships

> In light of the staggering goodwill impairment write-downs that have occurred so shortly after the business combination, added a discussion concerning the wisdom of reporting goodwill, which can lose its value virtually overnight, as an asset.

> Moved the discussion of the Consolidated Statement of Cash Flows and Consolidated Earnings Per Share to Chapter 11.

Chapter 10 Intercompany Fixed Asset Transfers and Bond Holdings

> Shortened and moved the Intercompany Bond Holding material (Chapter 11 in the Eighth Edition) to the end of Chapter 10.

Chapter 11 Changes in a Parent's Ownership Interest, Cash Flow Statement, and EPS

> Moved the Indirect and Reciprocal Holdings material (Chapter 13 in the Eighth Edition) to Appendix 11B.

Chapter 13 International Accounting Standards and Translating Foreign Currency Transactions

> Centralized material from Chapters 15 and 16 of the Eighth Edition in this new chapter, enabling international accounting to be given greater emphasis and visibility for AACSB accreditation purposes. Moved the material on "Going International" to Appendix 13A.
> Added a discussion of the FASB's short-term convergence project with the IASB.

Chapter 16 Translating Foreign Currency Statements: The Temporal Method & the Functional Currency Concept

> Moved Chapter 20 of the Eighth Edition, "Evaluating the Validity of the Functional Currency Concept" to Appendix 16B.

Chapter 17 Interim Period Reporting

> Added a discussion of the FASB's proposed new rules (12/03) on accounting changes and error changes.

Chapter 18 Securities and Exchange Commission Reporting

> Added a discussion of Regulation G (non-GAAP Earnings Disclosures).
> Added several recent enforcement actions.

Chapter 22 Partnerships: Liquidations

> Added a discussion of the 2002 collapse of the then Big 5 accounting firm Andersen.

Chapter 23 Estates and Trusts

> Made revisions to reflect the *new estate tax rules* enacted by Congress in 2001.

Chapter 24 Governmental Accounting: Basic Principles and the General Fund

> Updated for new GASB standards.

Chapter 26 Not-for-Profit Organizations: Introduction and Private NPOs

> Moved the discussion of Public NPOs (Chapter 31 of the Eighth Edition) to Appendix 26B and 26C.

V. Features Common to Multiple Chapters

> An **international focus** is fully integrated into each topic. Capsules of international GAAP are included for the consolidation and foreign currency topics so that students can place U.S. GAAP in perspective relative to GAAP around the world. The capsules are:
> > Foreign Consolidation Practices (Ch. 1)
> > Widespread Use of Parent-Company-Only Statements Overseas (Ch. 2)

  - > Manner of Presenting the Noncontrolling Interest in the Balance Sheet in Foreign Countries (Ch. 3)
  - > Foreign Goodwill Accounting Practices (Ch. 4)
  - > Worldwide Translation Practices (Ch. 15)
- > Numerous **articles from journals** and financial newspapers and magazines are included to heighten student interest.
- > Numerous **Cases-in-Point** are presented (as set off boxes) so that students can relate better to the real world.
- > In-depth discussions of **income tax issues** are set forth in five appendices.
- > A wealth of **discussion cases** and **financial analysis problems** are provided to stimulate thinking and develop research and writing skills. These assignments fit in with the content changes that have recently been made to the CPA examination.

VI. STUDENT-ORIENTED FEATURES

The following features in the Ninth Edition are designed to heighten students' interest and make the text easy to read and use:

1. A list of **key learning objectives** to accompany the **topic outline** preceding each chapter.
2. A literary, anecdotal, personal growth, or humorous **chapter-opening quotation** for each chapter.
3. A **chapter overview** introducing each chapter.
4. Inclusion of numerous **relevant articles** from *Newsweek* and *The Wall Street Journal*, so that students can better relate the material to current events.
5. Use of **roman numerals** to distinguish major chapter sections so that students can easily find chapter topics.
6. Extensive use of boldface type for key terms and key concepts.
7. Convenient ***vertical format* for consolidation worksheets** that uses a plus-and-minus scheme consistent with Excel® **spreadsheet software.**
8. Clearly marked **review points** for major illustrations.
9. **Check point questions** (with answers) interspersed within each chapter for periodic self-assessment of concept comprehension.
10. **Demonstration problems and solutions** in key consolidation chapters (Chapters 5 and 6).
11. **End-of-chapter review sections** for each chapter that include (a) a summary of key points and (b) a glossary of new terms.
12. **Descriptive overviews** of all exercises, problems, cases, financial analysis problems, and personal situations.
13. Placement of *cases*, *financial analysis problems*, and *personal situations* in a readily identifiable section called "Thinking Critically."
14. Placement of virtually all **chapter appendix material** on the publisher's web site to lighten the book.
15. **Checklist of key figures** for both exercises and problems at the rear of the book for easy reference.
16. Use of **marginal icons** to identify either (a) Internet research assignments or (b) problems that can be worked using the spreadsheet software models.
17. **Display of dates** in the assignment material in a more graphic manner (12/31/05 rather than December 31, 2005) for quicker recognition.
18. An author-prepared **study guide** that has (a) chapter highlights, (b) completion statements, (c) true-or-false questions, (d) multiple-choice questions, (e) problems, and (f) consolidation worksheet templates and translation worksheet templates.
19. Publisher's web page for this text—***student* section (http://pahler.swlearning.com)**, with the following downloadable items: (a) new pronouncement updates, (b) Excel spreadsheet models, (c) chapter appendices (other than Appendix 6A which is in the text), and (d) several useful accounting links.

VII. ANCILLARIES

The following ancillaries are available to adopting instructors in the following manner:

> **Hardcopy:** Solutions Manual, Instructor's Manual/Test Bank, and Study Guide.
> **Instructor's Resource CD ROM** (ISBN 0-324-23567-4): Solutions Manual, Instructor's Manual/Test Bank, Examview Testing Software, PowerPoint Slides, Excel Spreadsheet Models, Excel Solutions to roughly 60 consolidation and translation problems, and spreadsheet software models. Examview Testing Software allows you to customize exams.
> **South-Western's web site—Instructor Section (http://pahler.swlearning.com):** Solutions Manual, Instructor's Manual/Test Bank, PowerPoint Slides, Excel Spreadsheet Models, and Excel Solutions to roughly 60 consolidation and translation problems.

Details about these updated ancillaries, all written and revised solely by the author, are as follows:

1. **Solutions Manual** (ISBN 0-324-23571-2)
   To assist instructors in evaluating and selecting assignment materials, the Solutions Manual contains a description of each exercise, problem, case, financial analysis problem, and personal situation. The **relative difficulty** and **estimated time for completion** of the assignment materials are also included.
2. **Instructor's Resource Manual and Test Bank** (ISBN 0-324-23572-0)
   The manual is divided into five parts:
   > Part I consists of course coverage considerations.
   > Part II contains master lists of both (1) **teaching transparencies** for lectures and **problem solution transparencies** that accompany the text and (2) the personal situation assignments.
   > Part III is an **instructor's introduction to the spreadsheet software models** that are provided free to instructors and students (in an Excel version).
   > Part IV contains **teaching-related materials for each individual chapter**. The materials consist of teaching suggestions (including additional items of current interest to students), descriptions of assignment material (including level of difficulty and estimated times), and a list of transparencies provided.
   > Part V is a **test bank** for each chapter of the text. The test bank is highly accessible as a result of grouping items by subtopics within each chapter. (It is also available as a ***computerized* test bank**, Examview Testing Software, which is easy to install and use.)
3. **Excel Spreadsheet Software Models**
   Available free to adopting instructors, these spreadsheet models in PC format are compatible with Excel (version 5.0 or higher) software. Approximately 60 problems from the text can be worked on the computer using these spreadsheets, in 16 class-tested models for 15 chapters. Each model has its own on-screen instructions that are displayed above the worksheet area. Each problem that can be worked using one of the models is identified with a spreadsheet icon in the margin of the book. Also, electronic solutions—available at the web site (**http://pahler.swlearning.com**) for downloading as well as available on CD ROM—to virtually all of these problems are available so that instructors wishing to review them in class using computer projection panels can do so.

   To give students the opportunity to design a model of their own, program some macros for their model, and create logic functions for their model, an assignment containing detailed instructions is provided in Chapter 2 (Problem 2-8). We also have included an assignment in Chapter 9 containing detailed instructions (Problem 9-7) on how to automate the entire consolidation process when intercompany transactions exist.
4. **PowerPoint Slides**
   PowerPoint teaching transparencies exist (approximately 900 in total) for instructor lectures. These transparencies contain substantial clip art and other graphics for the purpose of keeping students interested in the topics presented.

5. **Study Guide (with Selected Working Paper Templates)** (ISBN 0-324-23570-4)
   The Study Guide contains approximately 70 study items per chapter grouped into (a) chapter highlights, (b) completion statements, (c) true-or-false statements, (d) *conceptual* multiple-choice questions, (e) *application* multiple-choice questions, and (f) problems (for Chapters 2, 5, 6, and 10). The study guide also contains 17 *working paper templates* for working (a) consolidation problems in Chapters 2 through 10 and (b) foreign currency translation problems in Chapters 15 and 16.

Thomson/South-Western World Wide Web Site

A wealth of additional accounting links, resources, and information can also be found through the South-Western accounting web site. Go to **http://www.swlearning.com** and select "accounting" from the pull-down menu of companion web sites.

Please contact your local Thomson/South-Western representative for more information and discount packaging options for all ancillaries available for sale.

VIII. ACKNOWLEDGMENTS

I am very grateful to the following instructors who reviewed the major changes for this edition:

Peter A. Aghimien, Indiana University South Bend
Harry Howe, SUNY at Geneseo
Ronald Lombardi, Rutgers University
Mallory McWilliams, San Jose State University
Linda Tauber, CUNY—Lehman College
Charles A. Tritischler (Emeritus), Purdue University
David E. Wallin, The Ohio State University

I, of course, assume full responsibility for any shortcomings in these chapters.

I express appreciation to the American Institute of Certified Public Accountants, the Financial Accounting Standards Board, the Governmental Accounting Standards Board, and the Government Finance Officers Association for their permission to quote material from their pronouncements and various other publications.

I also express my appreciation to the many partners and managers of the Big 4 international accounting firms to whom I made numerous inquiries concerning current accounting issues and practices.

Arnold J. Pahler

Brief Contents

Appendices

Available on the South-Western Web Site http://pahler.swlearning.com

Contents

part one

I

Consolidated Financial Statements: Internal Expansion Issues

chapter

1

Wholly Owned Subsidiaries: At Date of Creation

Character cannot be developed in ease and quiet. Only through experience of trial and suffering can the soul be strengthened, vision cleared, ambition inspired, and success achieved.

HELEN KELLER

LEARNING OBJECTIVES

To Understand

> **The business reasons for choosing between the *subsidiary* and *branch* forms of organization.**
> **The way to create (incorporate) a subsidiary.**
> **The concept and purpose of consolidated financial statements.**
> **The way to prepare a consolidated balance sheet.**
> **The major conceptual issues pertaining to consolidated statements.**
> **The basic reporting standards for consolidated statements.**

TOPIC OUTLINE

I. *Subsidiary* versus *Branch/Division* Form of Organization
   PRACTITIONER PERSPECTIVE: *Perseverance: Accountant Metcalf Knows Firsthand Give and Take of Taxes*
II. Creating (Incorporating) a Subsidiary
III. Consolidated Statements: The Concept
   ENRON PERSPECTIVE: *Enron's Stunning Collapse Pressured the FASB to Act*
IV. Consolidated Statements: Conceptual Issues
V. Consolidated Statements: *Current* Reporting Standards
   INTERNATIONAL PERSPECTIVE: *Foreign Consolidation Practices*
VI. Disclosures Required
   APPENDIX 1A: The Basics of Branch/Division Accounting

Appendices can be found at http://www.pahler.swlearning.com

CHAPTER OVERVIEW

A substantial portion of the subject matter of advanced accounting concerns businesses that expand their operations or diversify into new fields. A business may expand or diversify in one of two ways: **internal expansion** and **external expansion.**

Internal Expansion

Internal expansion may be accomplished by constructing or leasing additional facilities, most often for use in the same line of business in which the entity currently operates. Many companies have dramatically increased revenues by expanding in this manner.

CASE IN POINT

Spectacular Growth from *Internal* Expansion

Walt Disney's revenues increased from $1.5 billion in 1984 to $26 billion in 2003—virtually all this growth was the result of *internal* expansion. [IBM, Kmart, and Wal-Mart ($245 billion of revenues in 2003 for Wal-Mart) are also renowned for having dramatically increased revenues by *internal* expansion.]

Before expanding in this way, management must decide whether to organize the new operation as (1) a **subsidiary** (a separate legal entity)[1] or (2) a **branch** or **division** (an extension of the existing legal entity).

Subsidiary Form of Organization

When the subsidiary form of organization is used, the relationship between the existing company and the newly created company is called a **parent-subsidiary** relationship. Because a subsidiary is a separate legal entity, it must keep its own records (a "stand-alone" basis). Thus a **decentralized accounting** system is used.

Branch or Division Form of Organization

When the branch or division form of organization is used, the relationship between the two operations is called a **home office–branch/division** relationship. The record-keeping system for a branch or division can be either (1) **decentralized accounting** (as subsidiaries use) or (2) **centralized accounting** whereby all transactions pertaining to the branch or division are recorded in the home office's general ledger (usually in separate accounts so that separate operating statements can be prepared for each location).

External Expansion

External expansion takes place when two existing businesses **combine into a unified larger business.** A significant percentage of business combinations occurs among companies in unrelated fields, enabling the expanding company to diversify its product lines. Much of the growth of ITT and General Electric was due to external expansion.

Focusing Initially on *Internal* Expansion

This chapter and Chapters 2 and 3 deal exclusively with *internal* expansion. Chapters 4 through 7 deal with *external* expansion. By discussing *internal* expansion first, we address basic financial

[1] Creating a subsidiary is not always done in connection with internal expansion. Sometimes subsidiaries are created "on paper only" for income tax or legal and related purposes. For example, Enron Corp. created roughly 1,000 subsidiaries for the sole purpose of minimizing U.S. income taxes.

reporting standards for multilocation operations in the much simpler of the two areas, resulting in a step-by-step learning approach. Furthermore, most expansion that occurs is *internal* expansion (although *external* expansion is usually more noticeable because it gets far more headlines in the financial press).[2] For instance, more than 600 subsidiaries of U.S. companies were created in Ireland alone in the last 30 years, whereas virtually no U.S. firms expanded externally in Ireland. See the following Cases in Point for two specific company examples.

CASES IN POINT

Major Subsidiaries of Intel Corporation, the World's Largest Computer Chip Manufacturer

	CREATED	ACQUIRED
Intel Japan	X	
Intel France	X	
Intel United Kingdom	X	
Intel Germany	X	
Intel Hong Kong	X	
Intel Canada	X	
Intel Brazil	X	
Shiva Corporation		X
Level One Communications		X

Major Subsidiaries of Seagate Technology, One of the World's Largest Disk Drive Manufacturers

	CREATED	ACQUIRED
Seagate China	X	
Seagate Singapore	X	
Seagate Thailand	X	
Seagate Germany	X	
Seagate Cayman Islands	X	
Seagate Scotland	X	
Seagate Japan	X	
Seagate Magnetics		X
Conner Peripherals, Inc.		X
Seagate Philippines	X	

Note: Seagate has 55 subsidiaries—40 were created, and 15 were acquired.

Although we initially compare the *subsidiary* form of organization with the *branch/division* form of organization, we then deal solely with the *subsidiary* form. The *branch/division* form is discussed in detail in the Appendix at the end of this chapter.

In the United States, some of our largest companies (such as General Electric) have hundreds of subsidiaries. In China, a sprawling conglomerate named Gitic has more than 1,000 subsidiaries.

When a parent-subsidiary relationship is established, the first financial reporting issue from the parent's perspective is deciding whether to present (1) separate company financial statements for both the parent and the subsidiary or (2) consolidated statements (**as though** *one* company exists instead of *two*). Most of this chapter discusses this issue. Additional reporting issues (ranging from simple to complex) are discussed in this and later chapters.

When a parent has one or more subsidiaries, it is common to refer to all the entities collectively as the **group** or the *consolidated group*. Occasionally, we use these terms.

Start-Up Costs

Regardless which form of organization is chosen, expenses incurred by the subsidiary or the branch ***before*** it formally opens for business are start-up costs. An operating loss incurred for a period of time ***after*** the formal opening is *not* considered a start-up cost.

Start-up costs must be expensed as incurred, as required by AICPA *Statement of Position 98-5*, "Reporting on the Costs of Start-Up Activities" (issued in 1998).

[2] Two of the findings of a major Institute of Management Accountants/Financial Executive Institute research project completed in 1994 were that (1) preparing consolidated financial statements was one of eight accounting and knowledge skill areas deemed most important for corporate entry-level accountants and (2) accounting for *external* expansion (purchase accounting) was *not*. These eight skills were deemed "the essence of management." In discussing the relative importance of these two areas with many corporate controllers in the electronics industry in the "Silicon Valley" region of Northern California, the consensus was that preparing consolidated statements is far more important than accounting for *external* expansion.

I. *Subsidiary* versus *Branch/Division* Form of Organization

In referring to the new operation established by an extension of the existing legal entity, we use the lone term *branch* rather than the dual terms *branch* and *division,* even though *division* is used in business as frequently as *branch.* Using only the term *branch* also is consistent with the Internal Revenue Code terminology for all such outlying locations.

Limiting Legal Liability Exposure

A major consideration in selecting the form of organization for the new operation is deciding whether to insulate the existing operation from the new (and therefore highly uncertain) operation so that if something adverse happens at the new one, the problem can be contained and *not* have a spillover effect on the existing operation. **This limits the existing operation's potential loss exposure to the amount it has invested in the new operation.** Accordingly, some businesses have a policy of forming a separate subsidiary—that is, a separate legal entity with limited liability—for each new state or country into which they expand. This strategy is *not* foolproof, however; sometimes the corporate shield of the parent is pierced. See, for example, the Case in Point.

CASE IN POINT

Perhaps the best example of this is Union Carbide Corporation, whose plant in Bhopal, India, exploded in 1984, killing approximately 4,000 people within hours. Possibly to preserve its image as a good corporate citizen, the *parent* company paid $470 million to the Indian government in 1989 to settle claims, far in excess of the assets available at the *subsidiary* level. In 2002, the Indian government stated that the death toll had risen to 14,410 as those sickened by the gas later died.

In the motion picture industry, each newly conceived movie is assigned to either a newly created or dormant subsidiary, partly for limiting the investor's exposure. (Recall the unfortunate helicopter crash several years ago during the filming of *Twilight Zone* that resulted in the deaths of several people and subsequent multimillion dollar lawsuits alleging negligence.) When the accounting for a movie has been completed (usually three to five years after filming and showing), that particular subsidiary (which over time becomes dormant) may be used again for a new movie.

Even the U.S. international public accounting firms (partnerships) insulate their *foreign operations* from their *domestic operations.* See the Case in Point.

CASE IN POINT

Liquidators in Singapore trying to mop up in the aftermath of the spectacular collapse of Barings PLC sought nearly $2.5 billion from Coopers & Lybrand and Deloitte & Touche in a lawsuit that contained detailed allegations of negligence in connection with their respective audits of Barings PLC for 1992–1994. Barings, England's oldest merchant bank (nearly 200 years old), collapsed in 1995 as a result of incurring a $1.3 billion loss from trading Japanese financial futures (derivatives) in Singapore.

When the lawsuit was filed, spokespersons for both Coopers & Lybrand and Deloitte & Touche stated that the U.S. operations of each accounting firm were immune to the liabilities of their respective Singapore operations.

Subsidiary Creditors Beware

Some subsidiaries obtain credit from vendors partly by referring to the parent's strong financial condition and asserting that the parent stands behind its subsidiaries. Often such assertions prove to be hot air.

Ring Around the Subsidiary

Sometimes a company experiencing or anticipating expected operating difficulties in one of its divisions or segments will effectively incorporate those specific operations (involves transferring certain assets and liabilities to a newly created subsidiary). The purpose is to wall off the corporation's remaining assets so that they are protected from future creditors of the newly created subsidiary in the event of a potential bankruptcy filing by the newly created subsidiary.

CASE IN POINT

Bankruptcy Court to Determine if PG&E Corp. Acted Illegally

In 2001 Pacific Gas and Electric Company (one of California's two colossal utilities and a subsidiary of PG&E Corporation) filed for bankruptcy protection after multi-billion-dollar operating losses in 2000 and the first quarter of 2001. This was the third largest bankruptcy filing in U.S. history.

Creditors of Pacific Gas and Electric Company (who were owed roughly $14 billion) argued in court that the fencing off of PG&E Corporations's National Energy Group in the second half of 2000 was for the primary purpose of protecting certain PG&E Corporation assets from them and thus was illegal.

Considering Income Taxes

When a company expands into foreign countries, income taxes become an important consideration (discussed more fully in Appendix 13A). Foreign tax authorities can examine in great detail the books and records of a *branch* or *subsidiary*; however, the *subsidiary* form of organization greatly limits the foreign taxing authorities' ability to examine data concerning the *parent* because all aspects of the overseas unit's operations are contained at the *subsidiary* level—a separate legal entity.

Another consideration is that the Internal Revenue Service **taxes as current income the earnings of *overseas branches*** but in most situations **taxes earnings of foreign *subsidiaries* when the parent receives dividends** in the United States—a major concern for companies expanding in foreign countries that grant "tax holidays" (very low income tax rates, if any) to entice foreign investment.[3] Possibly for these reasons, along with the legal insulation consideration, IBM's extensive foreign expansion was the result of creating *subsidiaries—not branches*. On the other hand, because foreign tax considerations were not an issue, both Kmart's and Wal-Mart's extensive domestic expansions resulted from creating *branches—not subsidiaries*.

Carving Up an Entity to Save State Income Taxes

Many existing companies have restructured themselves into a parent and one or more subsidiaries so that they can report more income in low-income tax states rather than in a high-income tax state. Such restructurings, although neither *internal* nor *external* expansion, also show how tax considerations can weigh heavily in determining an entity's organization structure.

The Wall Street Journal infrequently publishes an article that profiles an accountant. We present such an article (in the Practitioner Perspective) because of its uniqueness manifest by the extraordinary perseverance that one individual had in becoming a successful accountant.

Retaining Patent and Copyright Protection

Many developing foreign countries have virtually no patent or copyright law protection. The transfer of these items to a *foreign subsidiary* results in the total loss of protection. If the *branch* organization form were used, however, the patents and copyrights remain subject to U.S. laws. Accordingly, many domestic companies use the *branch* form of organization.

To retain patent and copyright protection and to obtain the legal liability advantages associated with the subsidiary organization form, many companies transfer these technology rights to a *domestic subsidiary* created solely for the purpose of establishing a *branch* in the foreign country.

[3] Under the Internal Revenue Code, "when received" means (1) when the dividend is *declared*—if the parent is on the *accrual basis* for tax reporting purposes or (2) when the dividend is *received in cash*—if the parent is on the *cash basis* for tax reporting purposes.

Practitioner Perspective

Perseverance: Accountant Metcalf Knows Firsthand Give and Take of Taxes

Robert Metcalf was a teenage showoff. So when he and his friends went to the reservoir for a swim, he made a spectacular dive to impress the girls.

He hit a rock. He awoke a quadriplegic.

That was 42 years ago. Today, Mr. Metcalf is a CPA with 550 tax clients, practicing law and selling securities on the side. Each spring he works furiously, making enough money to spend the rest of the year indulging his passions for travel, wine making and ancient languages.

Though inspiring in its own right, his story is a parable for the evolving values of the business world. Affirmative action is under attack; no one seems to know the difference between a moral workplace and a politically correct one. At a time like this, it's comforting to find proof that the entrepreneurial economy can create a profitable opportunity for someone with a sharp mind, an iron constitution, a little marketing savvy and the right help early in the effort.

Bob Metcalf was born in a workaday world, riding with his father in the cab of a truck hauling Packards from Detroit to Chicago. His mother was a hairdresser. He liked boxing.

The accident, when he was 18, threw him not only into bed but into a deep depression. But it was 1953, in the midst of the polio scourge, and rehabilitation was in its ascendancy. A specialist gave the former pugilist the pep talk of a lifetime. Mr. Metcalf entered a publicly subsidized rehab institution, where he remained until past his 20th birthday.

Soon he was in City College of San Francisco (with a wheelchair and tuition paid for by his family, the Easter Seals and, once again, the U.S. Treasury). As a freshman he took Spanish II, organic chemistry and political science; those were the courses offered in ground-floor classrooms.

Ultimately he landed at Golden Gate College to study accounting, a field in which he had precisely no personal interest. "What's to like?" he says. "I had to make a living."

He put out his shingle as a tax man in 1961, recruiting 10 clients in his first year. His biggest problem, alas, was numbers—writing them down and tallying them up. Clumsily clutching a pencil, he could scrawl on a scratch pad or peck an adding machine, but his legibility and accuracy were low. He compensated with fanatical rechecking and by reading his notes into a tape recorder when the client had left.

Still, he lacked the temperament for accounting creativity. To him the Tax Code was a system of rules; the rules were complex because taxes were progressive, which swelled the U.S. Treasury with money to be spent in the public interest.

His by-the-book mindset became a virtue. Believe it or not, a huge segment of the working populace doesn't view the Tax Code as mainly an obstacle to wealth. Mr. Metcalf found that many clients engaged a tax professional simply for the assurance that they were paying neither too much nor too little tax.

"He doesn't try to cut corners to get us a tax break," says one long-time client, Jean M. F. Dubois, a property appraiser in Los Gatos. "I never have to worry that I'll get stuck with an audit."

But he was still a quadriplegic accountant, so he spent years in night school for a law degree—his way of trying to overcome the disadvantages he faced in the marketplace.

"I've got to be better than the average accountant," he told himself. Whether it's a disability or anything else that hinders you in the business or professional world, "you've got to be head and shoulders above the average," he says, "because you're starting out with a disadvantage." As a lawyer he could offer estate planning to his tax clients (eventually adding a sideline in mutual funds).

In the early 1970s, as his practice grew, Mr. Metcalf hired Mindy Meyers, one of his part-time tape transcribers, as his full-time assistant. While interviewing clients he and Ms. Meyers carried on a banter calculated to display their familiarity with the intricacies of the code—and their commitment to operating within the rules.

Transcribing gave way in 1980 to his first desktop computer, an ungainly $15,000 contraption. Soon track balls and drag-down menus supplanted the unrelenting keystroke demands of the DOS world. He installed a signal splitter between two monitors, allowing clients to watch the process unfold on a screen facing them from above his desk—another small marketing touch. He supplemented his arsenal with speed-dialers, speaker phones and the availability of instant tax research through a Triple Check Income Tax Service franchise.

(continued)

Practitioner Perspective, continued

He quotes the law in Hebrew and Greek. He reels off aphorisms from Churchill, Santayana, "Richard II" and Henny Youngman. He looks arrestingly youthful for 60 years (perhaps from his organic diet and love of wine). The guy should be a state court judge, or a talking head on a Sunday morning news show.

His politics, however, are all wrong for 1995. Though a case study in the meritocracy of the market economy, Bob Metcalf is a tainted hero by today's standards because he overcame adversity with help from taxpayer money.

"I'm very grateful for what the taxpayers and the Congress have done for me," he says. But for the country, the investment was profitable. "For many years I've been a net contributor to the national Treasury. I don't resent that at all."

Source: Thomas Petzinger, Jr., "Accountant Metcalf Knows Firsthand Give and Take of Taxes," *The Wall Street Journal*, August 11, 1995, p. B1.

Meeting Foreign Country Local Ownership Requirements

Some foreign countries prohibit foreign investment within them unless local citizens own some portion of the operation. This automatically eliminates the use of the *branch* organization form. The only way to share ownership is to use the *subsidiary* organization form, whereby local citizens can own stock (sometimes only 10% but often as high as 51%). For instance, China requires 50% local ownership. Several years ago, IBM closed its *subsidiary* in India rather than give up a major portion of its ownership as newly enacted local legislation required.

Creating a Perception of Separateness

Often an entity creates a *subsidiary* to market a new product or enter a new field. The following are examples:

1. **General Motors Corporation's** 1982 creation of Saturn Corporation (with $4.7 billion of initial capitalization) to give the Saturn car a separate identity.
2. **Syntex Corporation's** 1993 creation of Hamilton Pharmaceuticals Ltd., solely to market Syntex's own generic form of naproxen, an anti-inflammatory drug developed by Syntex, whose patent protection expired in 1993. It would have been potentially confusing to consumers if Syntex were selling both the original and the generic brand (which differ considerably in price).
3. **Silicon Graphic Corporation's** 1994 creation of DreamWorks SKG to enhance Silicon's ability to cultivate business from the entertainment industry.
4. **Hewlett-Packard's** 1999 creation of Apollo to sell Hewlett-Packard's new, less than $100 "Apollo" printers, enabling H-P to better protect its high-prestige brand name even while selling in the low end of the market.

Breaking Up to Shake Things Up and Achieve Better Focusing

Sometimes an entity will reorganize itself so that managers can focus more clearly on the areas for which they are responsible. For example, in 2002, Tyco International (one of the biggest acquirers in the 1990s) announced plans to split itself into *four* separately traded companies.

Getting Around Importing Restrictions

Sometimes a *subsidiary* can do what a *parent cannot*. For example, federal trade restrictions imposed by the Carter administration in 1979 made it illegal for U.S. companies to import oil from Iran. In practice, *foreign subsidiaries* of U.S. companies purchase nearly 25% of Iran's oil production, most of which is marketed in Europe and Japan.

Getting Around Union Requirements

In the motion picture industry, each of the numerous union guilds (for actors, directors, screenwriters, etc.) has provisions requiring a movie company that hires a guild member (say, a director) to use guild directors for all its movies. To get around this limitation, thousands of *subsidiaries* have been created to cover all possible variations that occur. Thus a subsidiary can be created for use only in situations in which, for example, the director *is* a guild member but the actors and screenwriter are *not*. After the subsidiary becomes dormant, it can be used again in this situation.

Changing the *Existing* Organizational Structure

Companies often change their organizational structures for various reasons, some of which we now discuss.

Incorporating a Segment into a Subsidiary to Avoid Being Responsible for Collecting State Sales Taxes

Borders Group Inc. created Borders Online Inc. as a subsidiary in 1998 to handle Internet sales. As a result, although Borders Group operates bookstores in all but 10 states, Borders Online is responsible for collecting sales taxes in only two states (the two in which it has physical presence)—*not* 40 states.

Incorporating a Division into a Subsidiary for Spin-off Purposes

Companies often divest one of their operating *divisions* by first incorporating the division and then spinning the *subsidiary* off to its shareholders (in a stock-for-stock exchange).

CASES IN POINT

Citigroup (created in 1998 with the mega-merger of Citicorp and Travelers Insurance Group) announced plans in 2002 to spin off major parts of its Travelers insurance business.

General Motors Corporation incorporated its auto-parts division into Delphi Automotive Systems and announced plans in 1998 to spin the subsidiary off to shareholders in 1999 so that GM would be substantially *less* vertically integrated.

Compaq Computer Corporation spun off its AltaVista search engine division into a wholly owned subsidiary in 1999, so that it could sell shares in the company to profit from investor's appetite for Internet stocks.

Liquidating Subsidiaries into Divisions

Sometimes having separate subsidiaries proves to be troublesome and confusing to customers. Consequently, companies often simplify or streamline operations by liquidating *subsidiaries* into *divisions*. This is done by using the *statutory merger* procedure discussed in Chapter 4.

CASES IN POINT

A few years ago, **Sun Microsystems Inc.** abandoned its "planet" company structure by liquidating its five semi-autonomous operating subsidiaries in favor of seven more traditional, product-oriented divisions.

Created in 1991, Sun's planets—as the operating companies were known—were an attempt to promote some degree of competition and independence among Sun's software, computer systems, and microprocessor groups (SunSoft, Javasoft, Sun Micro Computer, Sun Micro Electronics, and Sun Service).

But the structure created internal strife, along with redundancies and a perception among some customers that Sun was a conglomerate of independent companies.

A few years ago, **Sony Pictures Entertainment Inc.**, citing the need to be more efficient in its moviemaking operations, announced that it was folding its Tristar Pictures subsidiary into its sister company Columbia Pictures.

II. CREATING (INCORPORATING) A SUBSIDIARY

The remainder of this chapter deals with accounting for created 100%-owned *subsidiaries*. Accounting for newly created *branches* is discussed in the Appendix at the end of this chapter.

Incorporating the New Operation

The creation (formation) of a subsidiary merely involves obtaining a **corporate charter** from the state (or country) in which the subsidiary is being formed, paying incorporation fees, and investing some capital in the newly formed company. Because the subsidiary is a separate legal entity, it must (1) have its own board of directors and officers (often the same individuals serving as officers and directors for the company that formed it) and (2) maintain its own books and records (as mentioned earlier).

Creating the Parent-Subsidiary Relationship

Virtually all "created" subsidiaries (as opposed to "acquired" subsidiaries resulting from *external* expansion) are 100% owned by the parent company. However, a parent-subsidiary relationship can exist with less than 100% ownership, so long as **more than** 50% of the outstanding common stock is owned. Subsidiaries **less than 100% owned** present special reporting problems for the voting interest *not* owned by the parent (called the *noncontrolling interest*); they are introduced in Chapter 3.

Recording the Parent's Initial Capital Investment

Assume that on December 31, 2005, Parrco (the parent) invested $60,000 cash in Subbco (its newly created subsidiary), with the subsidiary issuing 1,000 shares of its $5 par value common stock to the parent. The entries to record this transaction follow:

PARRCO'S BOOKS (THE PARENT)

Investment in Subbco	60,000	
Cash		60,000

SUBBCO'S BOOKS (THE SUBSIDIARY)

Cash	60,000	
Common Stock (1,000 shares).		5,000
Additional Paid-in Capital		55,000

Note that at the creation date, Subbco's assets of $60,000 equal Parrco's investment in Subbco; thus **Subbco's assets are the economic resources that underlie Parrco's investment in Subbco.** In Chapter 2, we discuss a subsidiary with liabilities, in which case its **net assets** (Total Assets – Total Liabilities) underlie the parent's investment in the subsidiary.

CHECK POINT

The economic resources that (normally) underlie the parent's investment in a subsidiary are the subsidiary's

a. Assets.
b. Assets, net of liabilities.
c. Equity.
d. Noncurrent assets.

Answer: b

ETHICS

Creating a Subsidiary to Lay Off Employees

Your employer is planning on a sizeable downsizing, which will result in substantial employee layoffs. The president asks you, the controller, to take steps to create a new subsidiary. The employees to be laid off will be transferred to the new subsidiary, become employees for one day, and then be terminated. The subsidiary will then cease its legal existence. By having the subsidiary become the terminator, the parent's state unemployment tax rate will not be increased (a significant rate increase would occur if the parent were the terminator).

Questions

Would you comply with the president's instructions? What might be the legal ramifications if the taxing authorities subsequently uncover this practice? If the president asked someone else to create the subsidiary (such as the vice-president of finance) and you found out this person had complied with the president's instructions, would you place an anonymous call to the state agency or department in charge of collecting unemployment taxes to inform them of this practice?

Creating a Parent Company to Allow for Expansion

When a company wants to diversify into areas prohibited by its corporate charter, it can transform itself into a subsidiary. Procedurally, a new corporate entity having different charter provisions is created to serve as the parent company, and this new entity issues common stock in exchange for the first entity's outstanding common stock. The parent can then expand into the prohibited areas. This has occurred most notably in the banking and the savings and loan industries.

Furthermore, in these industries, the parent is usually a **holding company**, an entity that has no operations of its own but only investments in one or more subsidiaries. For instance, Citigroup is a bank holding company that has nearly 30 subsidiaries (almost all having been *created* instead of *acquired)*, one of which is Citibank, N.A. (the largest U.S. bank).

III. CONSOLIDATED STATEMENTS: THE CONCEPT

Consolidated statements, which have been used in the United States for nearly a century, refer to the financial statements that a parent company produces when its financial statements and those of a subsidiary are added together in a manner that portrays the resulting financial statements **as if they represent a single company.**

The idea is to disregard the separate legal entity status of each company and instead portray both as a **single economic entity** in light of one entity controlling the other entity—**regardless of the fact that each entity maintains its own separate records and prepares its own separate financial statements.** Consequently, consolidated statements are **pro forma** or "as-if" statements.

The accompanying Business Perspective concerning Enron Corporation shows the importance of presenting consolidated statements.

The Parent's Power to Liquidate the Subsidiary into a Branch

A supporting argument for presenting consolidated statements is that a parent usually has the power to liquidate a *subsidiary* into a *branch* at any time using the **statutory merger** provisions in state corporation laws. Thus a subsidiary's legal entity status can be taken away easily (its corporate charter is canceled) with the result that the remaining legal entity, the **parent** (which takes title to the subsidiary's assets and assumes responsibilities for the subsidiary's liabilities), is the economic entity.

Consolidated statements are extremely important because they constitute the **general-purpose financial statements** of companies having one or more subsidiaries—that is, the statements to be furnished to a parent's stockholders when a parent-subsidiary relationship exists.

Enron Perspective

Enron's Stunning Collapse Pressured the FASB to Act

In late 2001, the stunning collapse and unforeseen Chapter 11 bankruptcy filing of Enron Corp., the giant energy trading company based in Houston and the seventh largest U.S. company, gave rise to (1) scores of federal cabinet-level and Securities and Exchange Commission (SEC) investigations (which led to criminal charges being filed against Enron, its officers, and its outside supposedly independent auditor), congressional hearings, and class-action civil lawsuits, (2) calls for much tougher and more comprehensive consolidation rules concerning "special purpose entities" (SPEs), (3) restructuring the oversight of the public accounting profession (as a result of passage of the Sarbanes-Oxley Act of 2002), (4) the federal indictment of Andersen in 2002 and its sudden implosion immediately thereafter.

In a nutshell, the Enron meltdown created the biggest crisis investors have had since the 1929 stock market crash. In the several months following Enron's bankruptcy filing, the spillover effect was widespread, with a multitude of companies experiencing substantial declines in their stock prices as investors became nervous about any company that appears to have Enron-type accounting practices.

The Biggest Bankruptcy Filing Ever

The bankruptcy filing by Enron and its 13 major subsidiaries is the largest in corporate history (Enron listed roughly $50 billion in consolidated assets and $13 billion in consolidated liabilities in its filing). Enron, with 20,000 employees and 3,500 subsidiaries and affiliates, reported $139 billion of revenues for 2001. For the year preceding its bankruptcy filing, Enron's stock price fell from $85 per share to $.26 per share, wiping out roughly $63 billion of stock market capitalization.

The stock price decline reflected investor skiddishness and loss of confidence in the company caused by (1) big third-quarter 2001 losses, (2) restatements of earnings for the first two quarters of 2001 as well as the years 1997–2000, and (3) revelations that some of its employees participated in partnerships designed to keep debt off the balance sheet but which produced still more losses.

The Key Issue—Consolidation of Its SPEs

Enron's collapse began when it announced in October 2001 (to nearly everyone's surprise) that its equity was being reduced by $1.2 billion (of which roughly 50% applied to prior years). Specifically, Enron began consolidating several limited partnerships that Enron had (1) created years earlier and (2) reported substantial profits on transactions with those partnerships. These partnerships had never met the key condition necessary for nonconsolidation, which was that at least 3% of the total capital of each partnership (both debt and equity) had to be from independent outside investors.

Immediately, one of the major credit rating companies reduced Enron's credit rating to the lowest level of investment grade. This credit rating decrease resulted in a substantial amount of this off-balance-sheet debt becoming due and payable by Enron. Because Enron was *not* liquid, it could *not* repay this debt. Accordingly, Enron filed for bankruptcy protection—even though its listed assets were roughly four times its listed liabilities at the time of the filing.

Restatements of Previously Reported Earnings

As a result of having to consolidate these limited partnerships, Enron restated downward its previously reported earnings for calendar years 1997–2000 by $586 million or 20% (which restatement *increased* previously reported debt by $628 million at the end of 2000).

It Could Have Been Avoided

The Enron debacle dramatized the need for comprehensive and meaningful consolidation rules. The entire episode probably would never have occurred if (1) tougher consolidation rules concerning SPEs had existed and (2) Enron's outside auditing firm had done a better job of evaluating "substance versus form." Whether to consolidate SPEs is the troublesome part of the FASB's current project on consolidation policy, which has dragged on since 1993.

Enron Perspective, continued

Unfortunately, the FASB's attempts in the period 1993–2001 to toughen its consolidation rules were unsuccessful because of strong opposition from corporations bent on keeping debt off the balance sheet through the use of SPEs. In 2003, the FASB issued tougher consolidation rules concerning SPEs (including increasing the 3% requirement to 10%). Regrettably, it was a case of too little too late.

These new consolidation rules are in *FASB Interpretation No. 46*, which are discussed in Chapter 3.

Before discussing the many conceptual issues and the detailed requirements of the current accounting standards, we briefly illustrate the general idea of consolidated statements. Recall from our earlier example that the parent created a subsidiary on December 31, 2005, by making a $60,000 cash investment. Let us further assume that Subbco's only other transaction on December 31, 2005, was to purchase a parcel of land costing $12,000 cash. Subbco's balance sheet at December 31, 2005, is shown in Illustration 1-1, along with Parrco's separate balance sheet at that date.

Issuing *Un*consolidated Statements

If consolidated statements were *not* required to be furnished (contrary to current practice), Parrco would publish its separate "unconsolidated" balance sheet (more commonly referred to as a **parent-company-only statement**) as shown in the top section of Illustration 1-1. In most instances, Parrco would also include in its financial statement notes the separate balance sheet of Subbco to show what economic resources underlie Parrco's investment in Subbco.

Later in the chapter and in Chapter 3, we discuss infrequently encountered situations for which it is inappropriate to furnish consolidated statements. In such situations, the *parent-company-only statements* constitute the *general-purpose financial statements*.

ILLUSTRATION 1-1 SEPARATE COMPANY STATEMENTS

Parrco
Balance Sheet—Unconsolidated
As of December 31, 2005

ASSETS		LIABILITIES AND EQUITY	
Cash	$ 58,000	Payables and accruals	$150,000
Receivables	52,000	Long-term debt	250,000
Inventory	90,000	Total Liabilities	$400,000
Investment in Subbco	**60,000**	Common stock, $1 par	$ 10,000
Land	220,000	Add'l paid-in capital	190,000
Buildings and equipment	500,000	Retained earnings	100,000
Accumulated depreciation	(280,000)	Total Equity	$300,000
	$ 700,000		$700,000

Subbco
Balance Sheet
As of December 31, 2005

ASSETS		EQUITY	
Cash	$48,000	Common stock	$ 5,000
Land	12,000	Add'l paid-in capital	55,000
	$60,000		$60,000

Presenting Consolidated Statements: Two Possible Reporting Approaches

If consolidated financial statements were required to be furnished, the consolidated balance sheet could be presented in one of two manners:

1. A **disaggregated,** "layered" reporting **format.**
2. An **aggregated,** "unlayered" reporting **format.**[4]

The *Disaggregated* Format

In the disaggregated format, the subsidiary's assets and liabilities are shown separately from the parent's assets and liabilities in a **layered manner** (also referred to as a **tiered, stacked,** or **"pancake"** manner). This reporting format makes sense when a parent has a subsidiary in a *different* line of business, such as when a manufacturing company has a captive finance subsidiary (as is the case for the Big Three auto companies).[5]

By presenting the assets and liabilities of such subsidiaries in a layered manner, the consolidated balance sheet shows exactly what assets and liabilities exist at the subsidiary level and how much they contribute to the parent. Ford Motor Company uses this manner of reporting, showing an automotive category and a financial services category in both its consolidated balance sheet and its consolidated income statement. Ford classifies the automotive category as to *current* and *noncurrent* but *not* the financial services category (the usual case for finance subsidiaries). This disaggregated manner of reporting is shown in Illustration 1-2.

Review Points for Illustration 1-2. Note the following:

1. The effect of presenting consolidated statements is to substitute the subsidiary's assets (Cash of $48,000 and Land of $12,000) for the parent's Investment in Subbco account that totals $60,000, as shown in Illustration 1-1.

ILLUSTRATION 1-2 CONSOLIDATED BALANCE SHEET: DISAGGREGATED FORMAT

Parrco
Consolidated Balance Sheet—Disaggregated Format
As of December 31, 2005

ASSETS		LIABILITIES AND EQUITY	
Cash	$ 58,000	Payables and accruals	$150,000
Receivables	52,000	Long-term debt	250,000
Inventory	90,000	Total Liabilities	$400,000
Land	220,000	Common stock, $1 par	$ 10,000
Buildings and equipment	500,000	Add'l paid-in capital	190,000
Accumulated depreciation	(280,000)	Retained earnings	100,000
	$ 640,000	Total Equity	$300,000
ASSETS OF SUBSIDIARY			
Cash	$ 48,000		
Land	12,000		
	$ 60,000		
Total Assets	$ 700,000	Total Liabilities and Equity	$700,000

Note: If the subsidiary had liabilities, its liabilities would also be shown separately.

[4] The *aggregated* versus *disaggregated* terminology is used in various FASB publications (for example, see *Reporting Disaggregated Information about a Business Enterprise,* a proposed standard published in 1996 and finalized in 1997).

[5] A captive finance subsidiary is a company whose business purpose is to provide financing solely to its *parent's* customers.

2. Subbco's equity is *not* reported in the consolidated balance sheet because, from a consolidated perspective, its issued stock is *not* outstanding—it is held internally. Thus the Investment in Subbco is treated as "treasury stock," which must be *subtracted* from or offset against Subbco's equity. (Recall from intermediate accounting that treasury stock purchases are shown as a *reduction* of equity.)
3. When a *subsidiary* is in a *different* line of business from that of the *parent*, the disaggregated (layered) format is often used. If companies have too many subsidiaries in unrelated lines of business (in relation to the line of business of the parent and its remaining subsidiaries), however, they shy away from this format. In practice, the *aggregated* (unlayered) format is much more prevalent than the *disaggregated* (layered) format.

The *Aggregated* Format

In aggregated consolidated statements, the individual accounts of the parent and the subsidiary are summed, thus presenting only one amount for each asset, liability, and income statement account. This manner of reporting is shown in Illustration 1-3.

Review Points for Illustration 1-3. Note the following:

1. The substitution effect mentioned for Illustration 1-2 also occurs in Illustration 1-3. Here, however, each company's Cash and Land accounts have been summed together (shown in boldface for emphasis).
2. When a parent and subsidiary are in the *same* line of business, the aggregated format is almost always used because financial statement users have not expressed any significant desire for the disaggregated format in such situations.

Shortcomings of the *Aggregated* Reporting Format

The aggregated format makes the most sense if the parent and the subsidiary are in the *same* line of business. In these cases, the asset composition and liability structure of the two entities are *not* radically different. However, many situations exist in which (1) the two entities are in totally *unrelated* industries and (2) the asset composition and liability structures *are* radically different. For example, when a manufacturing parent has a bank, savings and loan, or insurance subsidiary, it is not uncommon for (1) the parent to have roughly a 60–40% debt-to-equity ratio and (2) the subsidiary to have roughly a 95–5% debt-to-equity ratio. Such disparities make it somewhat difficult to analyze or use an aggregated balance sheet. Later in this chapter we discuss the aggregated format of reporting in more detail.

ILLUSTRATION 1-3 CONSOLIDATED BALANCE SHEET: AGGREGATED FORMAT

Parrco
Consolidated Balance Sheet—Aggregated Format
As of December 31, 2005

ASSETS		LIABILITIES AND EQUITY	
Cash	**$106,000**	Payables and accruals	$150,000
Receivables	52,000	Long-term debt	250,000
Inventory	90,000	Total Liabilities	$400,000
		Common stock, $1 par	$ 10,000
Land	**232,000**	Add'l paid-in capital	190,000
Buildings and equipment	500,000	Retained earnings	100,000
Accumulated depreciation	(280,000)	Total Equity	$300,000
Total Assets	$ 700,000	Total Liabilities and Equity	$700,000

CHECK POINT

In a *disaggregated* consolidated balance sheet, the subsidiary's assets are

a. Netted against the subsidiary's liabilities and shown as a net amount.
b. Not included.
c. Shown separately.
d. Summed with the parent's assets.

Answer: c

Effecting a Consolidation: The Mechanical Procedures

To prepare consolidated statements, accountants use a working paper called a **consolidation worksheet** because **a general ledger is *not* kept for the "consolidated reporting entity."** However, the consolidation worksheets are just as much a part of the books and records of the parent company as its general ledger—especially because the consolidated statements derived therefrom are the general-purpose financial statements. Thus the consolidation worksheets are much more important than other types of working papers (such as analyses and schedules).

The worksheet used to accomplish the consolidation of Parrco's and Subbco's balance sheets at December 31, 2005, **into the *aggregated* format shown in Illustration 1-3** is presented in Illustration 1-4.

Review Points for Illustration 1-4. Note the following:

1. Conceptually, the entry shown in the Debit and Credit columns of the worksheet merely reclassifies the Investment in Subbco account—**a treasury stock holding from a consolidated**

ILLUSTRATION 1-4 CONSOLIDATION WORKSHEET AT DATE OF CREATION (BALANCE SHEET ONLY)

Parrco and Subsidiary (Subbco)
Consolidation Worksheet as of December 31, 2005

	PARRCO	SUBBCO	CONSOLIDATION ENTRIES DR.			CR.	CONSOLIDATED
Balance Sheet							
Cash	58,000	48,000					106,000
Receivables	52,000						52,000
Inventory	90,000						90,000
Investment in Subbco	**60,000**				1	**60,000**	–0–
Land	220,000	12,000					232,000
Buildings and equipment	500,000						500,000
Accumulated depreciation	(280,000)						(280,000)
Total Assets	700,000	60,000				60,000	700,000
Payables and accruals	150,000						150,000
Long-term debt	250,000						250,000
Parrco:							
Common stock, $1 par	10,000						10,000
Add'l paid-in capital	190,000						190,000
Retained earnings	100,000						100,000
Subbco:							
Common stock, $5 par		**5,000**	**5,000**	1			–0–
Add'l paid-in capital		**55,000**	**55,000**	1			–0–
Total Liabilities & Equity	700,000	60,000	60,000				700,000
Proof of debit and credit postings			*60,000*			*60,000*	

Explanation of entry:

1 To eliminate accounts having reciprocal balances.

perspective—to Subbco's equity section. Consequently, it is commonly said that this entry "eliminates" the account balances that are *not* presented in the consolidated balance sheet—namely the Investment in Subbco account on the parent's books and the Common Stock and APIC accounts on the subsidiary's books. Eliminating these accounts **achieves the desired substitution** of Subbco's assets (which underlie the parent's investment) for Parrco's Investment account.

2. In practice, such worksheet entries are called *consolidation entries*—as contrasted with *general ledger adjusting entries.* **Because consolidated amounts are *not* maintained in a general ledger, worksheet entries are never posted to a general ledger.** Hereafter, all *worksheet entries* are so labeled (as shown at the left margin) and are shaded to differentiate them from *general ledger* entries.

WORKSHEET ENTRY ONLY

3. **For ease of reference only,** we refer to this particular consolidation entry, **which is made in all consolidations,** as **the basic elimination entry.** In later chapters, other types of consolidation entries that relate to various types of transactions that a parent and subsidiary may have with each other (such as inventory sales, lending transactions, and leasing transactions) are encountered—all of which are called *intercompany transactions.*
4. In this example, the $60,000 *debit* balance in the Investment in Subbco account equals the sum of the $5,000 *credit* balance in the subsidiary's Common Stock account and the $55,000 *credit* balance in the subsidiary's Additional Paid-in Capital account. These three accounts have what are called *reciprocal balances.* In practice, they are usually referred to as either the **reciprocal accounts** or the **intercompany accounts.** In later chapters, you will see numerous other types of intercompany accounts that arise from intercompany transactions.
5. If the Investment in Subbco balance were *not* eliminated (reclassified to equity) in consolidation, **Subbco's assets would be double counted** because Subbco's individual assets are included in the consolidated totals. Thus consolidated assets would be $760,000 instead of $700,000 (the proper amount).
6. By eliminating Subbco's Common Stock account and Additional Paid-in Capital account, only Parrco's equity—**the equity of external shareholders to the consolidated entity**—is reported in the consolidated column.
7. As shown in Chapter 2 in consolidation worksheets that include income statements, this reciprocal relationship between the parent's Investment account and the subsidiary's equity accounts may or may not be maintained in future periods, depending on how the parent subsequently accounts for its investment in the subsidiary (discussed in Chapter 2).

CHECK POINT

Consolidation entries are

a. Recorded in the parent's general ledger.
b. Posted only to the consolidation worksheet.
c. Recorded in the consolidated entity's general ledger.
d. Reversed at the beginning of the following year.

Answer: b

Consolidated Statements—Are They Used by Governments?

The Federal Government

In 1997, the federal government had to begin preparing consolidated financial statements that were subject to an annual independent audit by the Government Accountability Office. This requirement is pursuant to the 1994 Government Management Reform Act, one of a series of recent laws passed to inject more private-sector practices into the federal bureaucracy.

Unfortunately, the audit results for each subsequent fiscal year were an unmitigated disaster. The GAO, which was *not* able to express an opinion on the consolidated statements, found that significant financial systems weaknesses, problems with fundamental record keeping, incomplete documentation, and weak internal controls, including computer controls, prevent the government from accurately reporting a large portion of its assets, liabilities, and costs. Furthermore, **trillions of dollars of liabilities pertaining to social security are omitted.**

State and Local Government

In 1999, the Governmental Accounting Standards Board (GASB) issued a financial reporting standard that requires the preparation of consolidated financial statements (referred to as "government-wide" financial statements) for *external* financial reporting by state and local governments. This manner of reporting is in addition to the *fund-based* reporting system. We discuss this relatively new standard in Chapters 24 and 25.

IV. CONSOLIDATED STATEMENTS: CONCEPTUAL ISSUES

Many conceptual issues concerning consolidated statements exist. For discussion purposes, we separate these issues into (1) those that can apply to 100%-owned created subsidiaries in which no intercompany transactions take place (other than dividend payments) and (2) all other situations.

Conceptual Issues That Can Exist for 100%-Owned Created Subsidiaries— No Intercompany Transactions Assumed

When the parent-subsidiary relationship results from the parent's creation of a 100%-owned subsidiary and when no intercompany transactions occur between the parent and the subsidiary, only a few major conceptual issues can exist:

1. **Appropriateness of consolidating.** Is it appropriate to present consolidated statements in view of the fact that each company is a separate legal entity? The alternative is to present the separate company financial statements of the parent and the subsidiary, something *not* very practical for companies having numerous (exceeding 100 in some cases) subsidiaries.
2. **Potential for users to draw misleading inferences.** Does it make sense to show one combined amount for cash when restrictions exist on the transferability of cash within the consolidated group? For example, to protect creditors, federal and state laws restrict the ability of banks, savings and loans, and insurance subsidiaries to transfer cash to a parent or other subsidiaries.

ETHICS

Let's Shaft the Subsidiary's Creditors

Subbco is a financially healthy, 100%-owned subsidiary of Pubbco, which, in contrast, has serious financial problems (liabilities exceed the fair market value of its assets). On 4/1/06, Pubbco liquidated Subbco into a division under allowable provisions of state corporation law. On 8/15/06, Pubbco filed for bankruptcy protection under Chapter 11 of the federal bankruptcy statutes.

Questions

1. What are the ramifications of this liquidation to Subbco's unsecured creditors? Do these creditors have any legal redress?
2. Why might Pubbco have liquidated Subbco?
3. Was liquidating Subbco into a division ethical in this situation?
4. In retrospect, what precautions should Subbco's unsecured creditors have taken in dealing with Subbco?

Would the parent's bondholders be misled into thinking all the cash is available for liquidation of the bond indebtedness? Could this problem be eliminated by requiring extensive disclosures in notes to the consolidated statements regarding restrictions on asset transferability?

3. **Appropriateness of consolidating a subsidiary in a different line of business.** Would consolidated financial statements be understandable and meaningful if the subsidiary were in an entirely *different* industry from that of the parent, thereby **having a radically different (1) asset composition, (2) debt-to-equity structure, and (3) income statement format**? Some claim that the activities of *finance subsidiaries* (the most controversial area of the unrelated businesses issue) would be *submerged* if they are consolidated instead of being disclosed in a note to the financial statements if not consolidated. On the other hand, consolidated statements do present the big picture. If consolidation is required, should the *disaggregated* format be mandatory to clearly set out these different industries? If the *aggregated* format is allowed, should industry segment information disclosures be required in notes to the consolidated statements?
4. **Appropriateness of consolidating foreign subsidiaries.** Should subsidiaries located in foreign countries be consolidated, even though they are exposed to several unique risks not faced by domestic subsidiaries? Such risks include (1) government seizure or confiscation of assets following political upheaval (as was done in Cuba, Iran, and Peru, for example) and (2) currency exchange restrictions (the subsidiary's inability to pay dividends to the parent).

CASE IN POINT

In 2002, Argentina imposed controls on capital *outflows* through the use of multitiered restrictions on the *outflow* of funds.

5. **Appropriateness of consolidating domestic subsidiaries having "blocked funds."** Should domestic subsidiaries that are prohibited from distributing their earnings to their parents be consolidated? Should guidelines be established for these situations, or should management use its best judgment? Would disclosure of these restrictions in the consolidated statements be sufficient?
6. **Minimum ownership level and conditions.** What level of ownership or other conditions must exist to require consolidation? Would it make sense to consolidate a subsidiary that is *not* 100% owned? What if the investee is *not* majority owned? For instance, some foreign companies are only 49% owned by U.S. companies, with local citizens required to own the remaining 51%; however, U.S. companies effectively manage such units just as if they were majority or 100% owned.

The accounting profession's current rules governing consolidated statements in light of these conceptual issues are discussed later. Our purpose here was merely to acquaint you with these basic issues.

Major Conceptual Issues Existing for Other Situations

Many additional conceptual issues arise when (1) the parent and subsidiary have intercompany transactions in which one party reports a profit or loss on the transaction, (2) the subsidiary is *less than* 100% owned or controlled by means other than common stock ownership, and (3) the subsidiary was *acquired* instead of *created*. These issues are addressed in later chapters.

V. CONSOLIDATED STATEMENTS: *CURRENT* REPORTING STANDARDS

Before discussing the U.S. consolidation rules, it is useful to present a brief list of some consolidation practices that exist internationally to place our U.S. rules in perspective relative to those of

International Perspective

Foreign Consolidation Practices

International Accounting Standards

The London-based International Accounting Standards Board (formed in 1973) issues international accounting standards. Compliance with its standards, however, is *voluntary*.

International Accounting Standard 27, "Consolidated Financial Statements and Accounting for Investments in Subsidiaries" (issued in 1987), is *similar* to the consolidation rules of the FASB and the SEC because it has **control** as the basis for consolidation. *IAS 27 differs* from the FASB's rules, however, in that it allows *more* exemptions from consolidation.

The GAAP of most foreign countries also differs significantly from *IAS 27*. Even in the European Union (EU), where member countries must abide by its Seventh Company Directive that requires consolidated reporting, the member countries have diverse consolidation rules because of the options and elections permitted under the Seventh Directive. Selected examples of this worldwide diversity follow:

Canada. All subsidiaries must be consolidated; consolidation ceases only when control is lost.

France. A subsidiary is excluded from consolidation if it is (1) in a dissimilar line of business from that of the parent and consolidation would be misleading, (2) insignificant, and (3) unable to prepare its statements on a timely basis.

Germany. A subsidiary may be excluded from consolidation if (1) it is immaterial, (2) the parent's right to control subsidiary assets or management is seriously impaired, (3) unreasonable expense or delays would be incurred, and (4) the investment is held solely for resale purposes.

Italy. Only listed companies need prepare consolidated statements. Even so, they are furnished as supplements to the parent company's separate statements.

Japan. A subsidiary may be excluded from consolidation if (1) consolidation would be misleading and (2) it is insignificant (not meeting a 10% size test). Consolidated statements are deemed supplementary information, which need be filed only with the government; accordingly, they are not widely disseminated to stockholders.

United Kingdom. A subsidiary may be excluded from consolidation if (1) it is immaterial, (2) severe long-term restrictions substantially impede the parent's exercise of its rights over management or subsidiary assets, (3) the investment is held exclusively with the intent to resell it (providing it was never previously consolidated), and (4) it is so dissimilar in nature that a true and fair view would not result (this exception is rarely allowed).

other countries. Accordingly, please refer to the International Perspective on page 20. The U.S. consolidation rules are more demanding than the consolidation rules of the foreign countries listed.

The Purpose and Presumption of Consolidated Statements

Recall that the result of the consolidation process is to present financial statement information as if the group were a single company with one or more branches. Consequently, a presumption exists that consolidated statements are more meaningful, useful, and necessary for a fair presentation than are separate statements.

The Requirement to Consolidate All Controlled Entities

All controlled entities must be consolidated. Thus consolidation is the rule, *not* the exception. This rule makes consolidated statements the *general-purpose financial statements* of companies having one or more majority-owned subsidiaries.

Once a subsidiary is consolidated, it must continue to be consolidated until the parent either (1) sells the subsidiary or (2) loses control.[6] One event that causes a parent to lose control occurs when a subsidiary files for bankruptcy protection; in such situations, **the bankruptcy court effectively controls the subsidiary.**

CHECK POINT

In the absence of other factors, a parent usually does *not* consolidate a subsidiary that

a. Has been *sold* under a contract of sale—closing of sale not yet consummated.
b. Is *expected to be sold* within one year.
c. Control of which is expected to be temporary.
d. Is in a different line of business and is located in a foreign country.
e. Is reporting such large losses that the subsidiary is no longer viewed as a going concern.
f. None of the above.

Answer: f

The Meaning of Control

An entity that has the ability to elect a majority of the board of directors of another entity has control over it. **Control** enables a parent company to do as it pleases with the subsidiary's assets—as the parent can do with its own assets. Thus the parent can (1) direct the subsidiary to expand, contract, or distribute cash to the parent, (2) establish the subsidiary's financing structure (*debt* versus *equity* levels), (3) enforce its will on the subsidiary's management by having the power to hire and fire it, and (4) set compensation levels for the subsidiary's management.

In the FASB's February 1999 exposure draft, "Consolidated Financial Statements: Purpose and Policy," control is explicitly defined as:

> The ability of an entity to direct the policies and management that guide the ongoing activities of another entity so as to increase its benefits and limit its losses from that other entity's activities. For purposes of consolidated financial statements, control involves decision-making ability that is not shared with others.[7]

The Two Types of Control

One entity can attain either **legal control** (control by *legal* means) or **effective control** (control by *nonlegal* means) over another entity. Ownership of a majority of the subsidiary's outstanding voting shares gives the parent *legal control* because it has the legal right to elect a majority of the board of directors (a right that is enforceable by law). *Effective control* occurs when a majority of the board of directors can be elected by means other than by having legal control. Thus situations exist in which *50% or less* ownership may result in control.

Delayed Discussion of Effective Control Situations and Loss of Control Situations

We delay until Chapter 3 a discussion of situations in which (1) one entity effectively controls another entity even though it owns *50% or less* of the outstanding voting shares (such situations have become fairly widespread in the last 25 years in the United States practice) and (2) one entity owns *more than 50%* of the outstanding voting shares but has lost control (recall the earlier example of

[6] Prior to the issuance of FASB *Statement No. 144,* "Accounting for the Impairment or Disposal of Long-Lived Assets" (in 2001), an exception to the requirement to consolidate all controlled subsidiaries existed for *"when control was likely to be **temporary.**" FAS 144* eliminated that exception.

[7] *Proposed Statement of Financial Accounting Standards*, "Consolidated Financial Statements: Purpose and Policy" (Norwalk: Financial Accounting Standards Board, 1999), par. 6a.

a subsidiary that has filed for bankruptcy protection). Thus all consolidation illustrations in Chapters 1 and 2 assume that *legal control* exists.

Our government officials evidently do not fully understand the concept of control, as the following Case in Point reveals.

CASE IN POINT

Does the Government Understand the Concept of Control?

In 1995 the federal government, by an executive order, prohibited all trade by U.S. companies with Iran (this is above and beyond the executive order issued in 1979 mentioned earlier). The executive order also applies to foreign subsidiaries of U.S. companies. Government officials stated, however, that foreign subsidiaries of U.S. companies can continue buying Iranian oil, providing that those subsidiaries are autonomous and *not* controlled, run, or directed by U.S. companies.

What If the Parent Chooses *Not* to Exercise Its Powers?

When a parent has a "hands-off" decentralized operating philosophy, its status as a controlling entity is unchanged. Thus consolidation is still required.

Restrictions of Control Powers

A subsidiary *can* still be consolidated if the parent's control powers are restricted—depending on the severity and expected length of the restriction (a judgment call). Two examples of restrictions are (1) a foreign government's prohibiting a foreign-owned subsidiary from paying dividends and (2) regulatory authorities' prohibiting a domestic bank or savings and loan subsidiary from paying dividends until the subsidiary's financial condition improves.

CHECK POINT

Legal control always exists when a subsidiary is

a. Wholly owned.
b. More than 50% owned.
c. More than 50% owned or wholly owned.
d. Effectively controlled.

Answer: c

A Highly Controversial Issue: Whether to Consolidate *Non*homogeneous Subsidiaries

Prior to 1987, the consolidation rules permitted a parent *not* to consolidate a subsidiary in a different line of business from that of the parent (commonly referred to as the *nonhomogeneity exception*). Beginning in the 1960s, many businesses began to be more diverse and complex. For example, many companies previously considered nonfinancial in the scope of their operations diversified into financial services (financing, insurance, leasing, investment banking, and real estate).

The liabilities carried by unconsolidated financial subsidiaries had become enormous, contributing greatly to the growing "off-balance-sheet financing" controversy. Practice had become quite diverse. Some companies consolidated such subsidiaries; others did not.

In 1987 the FASB eliminated the homogeneity exception.[8] The requirement to consolidate these subsidiaries has drastically changed the reported assets, liabilities, and resulting financial analysis

---

[8] This rule change was implemented as a result of the issuance of *Statement of Financial Accounting Standard No. 94*, "Consolidation of All Majority-owned Subsidiaries" (Stamford: Financial Accounting Standards Board, 1987). This pronouncement amended *Accounting Research Bulletin No. 51*, "Consolidated Financial Statements" (issued in 1951), the governing pronouncement at the time.

ratios of many companies. For example, Ford Motor Company, which did *not* consolidate its *financial services* subsidiary prior to 1987, reported *financial services* assets and liabilities of $189 billion and $177 billion, respectively, in its consolidated balance sheet at the end of 2003—compared with *automotive* assets and liabilities of $95 billion and $88 billion, respectively.

The consolidation of nonhomogeneous subsidiaries is controversial. To look at the pros and cons of this issue, we (1) present the major criticisms of the 1987 rule and (2) discuss the shortcomings that existed under the pre-1987 rule. In this chapter, *balance sheet issues* are examined; *income statement issues* are examined in Chapter 2.

Criticisms of and Problems with the Consolidation of Subsidiaries in Diverse Lines of Business

The requirement to consolidate subsidiaries in unrelated businesses has *not* been overwhelmingly accepted by financial statement preparers and users. Many believe that this rule should be repealed, and some of their reasons follow:

1. The fundamental nature of the business is *not* clearly evident. For example, General Motors, now fully consolidated, looks like a *finance company* with a *car division* instead of a *car company* with a *finance division.* When GMAC (GM's *finance subsidiary*) was reported as an investment as a result of *not* being consolidated, the magnitude of the *finance* receivables and payables did *not* swamp the *automobile* accounts.
2. The debt-to-equity ratio on a *consolidated basis,* which often is far *higher* than on an *unconsolidated basis,* usually is *not* used by (1) lenders because they extend credit on an *entity-by-entity basis* or (2) the parent's stockholders because they perceive the subsidiary as a service, and they are concerned with the parent's ratio. The consolidated debt-to-equity ratio becomes even more irrelevant when the subsidiary has substantial debt that is *not* guaranteed by the parent.
3. The financial ratios produced are *not* industry oriented. Thus valid comparisons cannot be made with the financial ratios of competing entities.
4. Financial analysis is now much more difficult for analysts who prefer to evaluate a group on a *disaggregated* basis. (See Chapter 12 for a discussion of *disaggregated* reporting, its shortcomings, and its advantages.)

Criticisms of and Problems with the *Non*consolidation of Subsidiaries in Diverse Lines of Business

The pre-1987 practice of allowing the exclusion of unrelated businesses also had its share of criticisms and reporting problems.[9]

1. Critics claimed that it did *not* portray a comprehensive representation of the economic entity—especially when the subsidiary's operations were functionally related to the parent, such as for a captive finance (credit or leasing) subsidiary that effectively purchased the parent's receivables.
2. The parent's debt-to-equity ratio (a *leverage* ratio) was usually much *lower* when captive finance subsidiaries were *excluded,* thus not presenting the true capital structure of the economic entity. Also, *liquidity* ratios were often significantly *higher* than under consolidated reporting.
3. The business relationship of the subsidiary to the parent was *not* always disclosed.
4. Condensed balance sheet information required to be disclosed for unconsolidated subsidiaries (pursuant to *APB Opinion No. 18,* "The Equity Method of Accounting") ranged from a *complete set of financial statements to one-line disclosures of total assets and total equity,* with information on the subsidiary's long-term debt ranging from complete to nonexistent. The subsidiary's intercompany receivable (or payable) was *not* disclosed in a uniform manner; it was either shown *separately* or *combined* with the subsidiary's equity.

---

[9] For a fuller discussion, see Martin L. Gosman and Philip E. Meyer, "*SFAS No. 94*'s Effect on Liquidity Disclosure," *Accounting Horizons*, March 1992, pp. 88–100; James B. Heian and James B. Thies, "Consolidation of Finance Subsidiaries: $230 Billion in Off-Balance-Sheet Financing Comes Home to Roost," *Accounting Horizons*, March 1989, pp. 1–9; and Joseph C. Rue and David E. Tosh, "Should We Consolidate Finance Subsidiaries?" *Management Accounting*, April 1987, pp. 45–50.

5. The parent reported its equity in the subsidiary's net income in diverse manners, such as (1) a component of consolidated revenues, (2) a separate line item in *arriving at* operating income, (3) a separate line item *below* operating income (either before tax or net of tax), or (4) a net against the parent's interest expense.
6. Collection costs relating to receivables were effectively shifted to captive subsidiaries formed to buy the parent's receivables, enabling parent companies to report *higher* operating income.

Conformity of Accounting Policies

When different accounting methods are permitted for the same type of transactions or events, the subsidiary *need not* use the same method the parent uses. For example, the parent could use the first-in, first-out method for inventory costing, and the subsidiary could use the last-in, first-out method.

If a foreign subsidiary uses an accounting method *not* allowed under U.S. reporting standards (GAAP), the subsidiary's financial statements must be *restated* to U.S. GAAP *before* consolidation (and *before* translation into U.S. dollars, as explained in Chapter 15).

VI. Disclosures Required

Fiscal Periods Do Not Conform

A subsidiary's financial statements must cover the same period as the parent's financial statements—unless it is *not* practical to achieve conformity. If conformity is *not* practical, disclosure is necessary of (1) that fact, (2) the reasons that it is not practical, (3) the period covered by the subsidiary's statements, and (4) any material and unrecognized events occurring during the "gap" period.

In the vast majority of instances, conformity occurs because (1) parents and their subsidiaries have the *same* fiscal year-end and (2) the ability to send financial statements over telephone lines enables subsidiaries to submit financial information on a timely basis. When a parent allows a subsidiary to have a fiscal year-end *different* from its own, the subsidiary's financial information will be from *two different fiscal years* to cover the same period as the parent's financial information (a fact that need *not* be disclosed).

Check Point

A parent *cannot* consolidate a subsidiary that

a. Is in an unrelated line of business.
b. Is in a foreign country.
c. Has a different year-end.
d. Has filed for bankruptcy protection.

Answer: d

Consolidation Procedures

As we discuss in detail in later chapters, all intercompany transactions between a parent and its subsidiaries are eliminated (undone) in preparing consolidated statements. Thus the consolidated results are *as if* none of the intercompany transactions had occurred. A disclosure that intercompany transactions have been eliminated must be made. In brief, intercompany transactions are eliminated because, from a consolidated perspective, they are **internal transactions**—only transactions with third parties outside the consolidated entity can be reported in the consolidated statements.

To illustrate, assume that (1) Parrco lent $6,000 to Subbco during 2005 and (2) the $6,000 has *not* been repaid at year-end. In consolidation at year-end, the following consolidation entry is made:

WORKSHEET ENTRY ONLY

Intercompany Payable	6,000	
Intercompany Receivable		6,000

If the loan were interest bearing, the Intercompany Interest Income and Intercompany Interest Expense accounts would also be eliminated in consolidation as follows:

WORKSHEET ENTRY ONLY

Intercompany Interest Income	400	
Intercompany Interest Expense		400

Neither entry affects the group net income or equity, but the effects on the gross array of accounts can be dramatic in some instances. How to "undo" more complex intercompany transactions for consolidated reporting purposes is discussed in Chapters 8 through 10.

Industry Segments and Foreign Geographic Areas

Because of the limitations of consolidated statements, disclosure of segment and related information is mandatory. The specific disclosure requirements are set forth in FASB *Statement of Financial Accounting Standard No. 131,* "Disclosures about Segments of an Enterprise and Related Information" (which was issued in 1997 and superseded an earlier segment reporting standard). It requires specified information on industry segments and foreign operations to be presented as *supplementary information* to the consolidated statements.[10] This pronouncement, which is discussed at length in Chapter 12, imposes extensive public reporting requirements on companies with diversified or foreign operations.

Restrictions on a Subsidiary's Ability to Transfer Funds to the Parent

A reader of consolidated statements is entitled to presume that cash can be freely transferred within the consolidated group unless he or she is informed otherwise. When a subsidiary *cannot* distribute some or all of its earnings to its parent, the ramification is that it may limit the parent's ability to (1) pay dividends to its stockholders or (2) pay for its corporate expenses.

The Securities and Exchange Commission's Disclosure Rules Concerning Restrictions

When a subsidiary of a publicly owned company is restricted from transferring funds to its parent in the form of cash dividends, loans, or advances (such as the result of borrowing arrangements, regulatory restraints, or foreign government actions), the SEC requires disclosure of (1) the nature of the restriction and (2) the amounts of restricted net assets for consolidated subsidiaries. In general, however, disclosure is required only if the **restricted net assets** of all subsidiaries (including any unconsolidated subsidiaries) **exceed 25% of consolidated net assets.**[11]

---

[10] The term *supplementary information* has a precise meaning in accounting and auditing literature. It refers to GAAP–required information to be included with the historical cost basis financial statements.

[11] Rule 4-08 (e) of Article 4 (Rules of General Application) of Regulation S-X.

ETHICS

Suspicious Upstream Cash Transfers—What's an Auditor to Do?

You are the outside auditor for a parent and its subsidiary. The subsidiary is a financial institution, which regulatory authorities have prohibited from paying dividends until its financial condition improves. During the audit, you notice several unusually large cash payments from the subsidiary to the parent to pay for management services. You suspect that these payments are dividends in disguise.

Questions

1. What audit procedures would you perform to determine whether these cash payments are bona fide?
2. If you conclude that these payments are illegal, should you report them to the appropriate regulatory authorities? If not, what would you do?

Bank subsidiaries, savings and loan subsidiaries, and insurance subsidiaries usually have significant fund transferability restrictions imposed by law or regulatory agencies, thereby usually requiring such disclosures.

CHECK POINT

A subsidiary is unable to distribute dividends because of restrictions imposed by regulatory authorities. The parent should always

a. Consolidate the subsidiary anyway.
b. *Not* consolidate the subsidiary and present the subsidiary's condensed financial statements in a note.
c. *Not* consolidate the subsidiary and explain why.
d. Use its judgment in determining whether to consolidate the subsidiary.

Answer: d

END-OF-CHAPTER REVIEW

Summary of Key Points

1. Consolidated statements (which can be in a **disaggregated** or **aggregated** format) constitute the **general-purpose financial statements** for reporting to stockholders.
2. The **purpose of consolidated statements** is to present a single set of financial statements as if the parent and its subsidiaries were a **single company** having one or more divisions; the separate legal entity status of each company within the consolidated group is disregarded.
3. The result of the consolidation process is the **substitution** of the subsidiary's assets and liabilities for the Investment in Subsidiary account on the parent's books.
4. Consolidation entries are **worksheet entries**—never to be posted to the general ledger—because a general ledger is *not* kept for the consolidated entity.
5. U.S. GAAP requires that all subsidiaries be consolidated unless **control** is lacking.
6. **Control** over a subsidiary means that the parent can use the subsidiary's assets in the same manner as its own assets.
7. The normal means of control is ownership of *more than* 50% of the outstanding voting shares (**legal control**).

8. Control can exist when *50% or fewer* of the voting shares of an entity are owned (**effective control**). Also, control *may not* exist even though *more than* 50% of the voting shares are owned.

9. All **intercompany receivables and payables** must be eliminated (offset against each other) in consolidation.

10. Significant cash transfer restrictions placed on a subsidiary must be disclosed in notes to the consolidated statements.

Glossary of New Terms

Aggregated format A format that does *not* display the subsidiary's financial statement accounts separately in the consolidated statements.

Branch (division) An extension of an existing legal entity.

Centralized accounting A system in which the transactions for a branch are recorded in the home office's general ledger.

Consolidation The process of combining the financial statements of a parent and one or more subsidiaries to present financial position and results of operations as though the separate companies were a single company with one or more divisions or branches.

Consolidation worksheet A working paper or spreadsheet in which the financial statements of a parent and its subsidiaries are consolidated using consolidation entries.

Corporate charter A document issued by a state or country that grants legal entity status to a business being incorporated.

Decentralized accounting A system in which a subsidiary or branch maintains its own general ledger.

Disaggregated format A format that displays the subsidiary's financial statement accounts separately in the consolidated statements in a "layered" manner.

Effective control The ability to control an entity by means other than majority ownership (legal control).

External expansion The expansion of a business by combining with another existing business.

General-purpose financial statements The financial statements used for reporting to stockholders.

Group (consolidated group) A manner of referring to a parent and its subsidiaries collectively.

Holding company An entity that has no operations of its own but only investments in one or more subsidiaries.

Home office The headquarters office of the legal entity that establishes a branch.

Intercompany accounts (reciprocal accounts) Accounts in different general ledgers for which the *debit* balance in one account (or set of accounts) equals the *credit* balance in the other account (or set of accounts). In parent-subsidiary relationships, the Investment in Subsidiary account on the parent's books can be maintained so that its balance equals the sum of the Common Stock, Additional Paid-in Capital, and Retained Earnings accounts on the subsidiary's books.

Internal expansion The expansion of a business by constructing or leasing additional facilities at an existing or outlying location.

Legal control The ability to control an entity by ownership of *more than* 50% of the entity's outstanding voting shares.

Net assets The difference between an entity's assets and liabilities.

Parent A company that controls another company (usually achieved by direct or indirect ownership of *more than* 50% of the voting interest).

Parent-company-only statements The unconsolidated financial statements of a parent company.

Pro forma A manner of presenting financial information on an "as-if" basis.

Statutory merger A legal term referring to the loss of a *subsidiary's* corporate legal entity status by canceling the subsidiary's corporate charter. The *parent* takes title to the *subsidiary's* assets and assumes responsibility for the subsidiary's liabilities. Thus the *subsidiary* is *transformed* into a branch.

Subsidiary A company controlled by another company (usually resulting from direct or indirect ownership of *more than* 50% of the voting interest).

ASSIGNMENT MATERIAL

Review Questions

1. What are the advantages of the *subsidiary* organization form?
2. What are the advantages of the *branch/division* organization form?
3. Does establishing a subsidiary always legally insulate the parent's operations from the subsidiary's operations?
4. How can a company expand into an industry prohibited by its corporate charter?
5. What is a *holding company*?
6. What underlies the parent's Investment account?
7. What is the concept of consolidated statements?
8. What does the term *general-purpose financial statements* mean?
9. What two types of consolidated balance sheets can be issued? When does it make most sense to use each type?
10. Is a general ledger maintained for the consolidated reporting entity? Why or why not?
11. How important are *consolidation worksheets* relative to the parent's general ledger?
12. Are *consolidation elimination entries* posted to a general ledger? Why or why not?
13. What is the definition of the term *intercompany transaction*?
14. What does *intercompany accounts* mean?
15. What do *reciprocal balances* and *reciprocal accounts* mean? In a parent-subsidiary relationship, what are the reciprocal accounts?
16. What would be the reporting results if the reciprocal accounts were *not eliminated* in consolidation?
17. What is the formal name for a *consolidation worksheet*?
18. How are many of the limitations of consolidated statements overcome?
19. What is the usual condition for *control* by one entity over another entity?
20. What does having control enable a parent to do?
21. What does the term *nonhomogeneity exception* mean?
22. What are the exceptions to the general rule requiring consolidation of all subsidiaries?
23. What types of disclosures typically accompany consolidated statements?

Exercises

E 1-1 **Subsidiary or Branch: Choose Wisely** Each item in the left-hand column represents various corporate objectives in connection with establishing a new foreign operation. To the right of these items is a list of possible forms of organization.

Corporate Objectives

1. To legally insulate the new operation.
2. To minimize paying U.S. income taxes on the foreign operation's earnings.
3. To pay U.S. taxes currently on the foreign operation's earnings.
4. To restrict the ability of foreign tax authorities to examine the U.S. operation's records.
5. To have complete ownership of the foreign operation.
6. To share ownership of the foreign operation with local foreign citizens.
7. To retain patent protection.
8. To retain patent protection and to legally insulate the new operation.
9. To retain patent protection and to minimize paying U.S. income taxes on the foreign operation's earnings.
10. To retain patent protection, to legally insulate the new operation, and to minimize paying U.S. income taxes on the foreign operation's earnings.

Possible Forms of Organization

A. U.S. subsidiary.
B. Foreign subsidiary.
C. Branch.
D. U.S. subsidiary having a foreign branch.
E. Foreign subsidiary having a foreign branch.

Required For each corporate objective, which of the possible choices in the right-hand column accomplishes that objective? If an objective has *more than one* possible answer, your first choice should be the one that accomplishes the objective in the simplest manner.

E 1-2 **Internet Research Assignment: Aggregated or Disaggregated?** Using the Internet, find General Motor Corporation's most recent annual financial statements.

Required Determine if GM presents its consolidated balance sheet and consolidated income statement on an *aggregated* or *disaggregated* basis.

E 1-3 **Consolidation Theory**

1. Which item does *not* occur as a result of the consolidation process?
   a. The parent's equity is decreased.
   b. The parent's Investment account disappears.
   c. The subsidiary's equity disappears.
   d. The subsidiary's net assets are substituted for the parent's Investment account.
2. Which of the following items is *false* concerning the consolidation process?
   a. The entry made in consolidation is essentially a reclassification entry.
   b. The parent's Investment account is reported as a long-term treasury stock investment in the noncurrent asset section of the consolidation balance sheet.
   c. The entry made in consolidation accomplishes a substitution process.
   d. A double counting of the subsidiary's net assets is avoided.
3. Which of the following items is *true* concerning the consolidation process?
   a. The subsidiary's equity is combined with the parent's equity.
   b. The *disaggregated* reporting format is automatically achieved.

c. The entry made in consolidation is posted to the parent's general ledger.
d. A pro forma presentation is achieved.

E 1-4 Consolidation Rules

1. A parent normally consolidates a *created* subsidiary that
   a. Is a captive finance subsidiary created to furnish financing to the parent's retail customers.
   b. Is expected to be sold in the very near future.
   c. Is in an entirely different line of business.
   d. Is located in a developing country.
   e. Is described by items *a* through *d*.

2. Which of the following is an *acceptable* reason for excluding a subsidiary from consolidation?
   a. The subsidiary's assets equal its liabilities.
   b. Currency transfer restrictions prevent the subsidiary from paying dividends.
   c. The subsidiary has substantial intercompany inventory sales to its parent.
   d. The parent presents the subsidiary's separate financial statements in the parent's annual report.

3. Which of the following statements is *true*?
   a. The *disaggregated* reporting format is *not* allowed.
   b. The parent and subsidiary must have the *same* year-end to be consolidated.
   c. A subsidiary *need not* be consolidated if the parent requires the subsidiary to reinvest all its earnings and not pay any dividends.
   d. The *aggregated* reporting format is acceptable for a subsidiary in a completely different line of business than the parent.

E 1-5 Consolidation Worksheet Entries The following accounts exist on the separate company financial statements of a parent and its newly created subsidiary at the end of 2006:

	Parent's Books	Subsidiary's Books
Investment in subsidiary	$400,000	
Intercompany receivable	50,000	
Common stock		$ 100,000
Additional paid-in capital		300,000
Intercompany payable		50,000
Assest (in total)		1,000,000
Liabilities (in total)		600,000

Assume that the subsidiary has not yet commenced operations and therefore has no income statement account activity for 2006.

Required What are the consolidation entry(ies) at 12/31/06? What is substituted for the parent's investment account in the consolidation process?

E 1-6 Consolidation Worksheet Entries On 4/1/06, Piltco created Siltco as a 100%-owned subsidiary. Piltco made a cash investment of $500,000 by purchasing 1,000 shares of Siltco's $5 par value common stock. For 2006, Siltco reported net income of $66,000 and declared no dividends. At 12/31/06, the carrying amount of Piltco's investment in Siltco was the initial investment of $500,000.

Required

1. What is the required consolidation entry as of 12/31/06?
2. Should Siltco's retained earnings at year-end be reported in the consolidated balance sheet? Why or why not? If so, how?

E 1-7 Intercompany Receivables and Payables At 12/31/06, Plethora had the following receivables and payables with its subsidiaries, all of which are consolidated except Sebco:

	Receivables	Payables
Advance (long term) to Sabco	$100,000	
Interest receivable from Sebco	20,000	
Interest payable to Sibco		$ 30,000
Long-term receivable from Sobco	400,000	
Intercompany payable to Subco		55,000
Long-term payable to Subco		600,000

Required

1. In the consolidated balance sheet at 12/31/06, what net amount should Plethora report as being receivable from its subsidiaries?
2. Repeat requirement 1 for payables instead of receivables.

THINKING CRITICALLY

Cases

C 1-1 **Lending to a *Parent*: Extra Caution Needed?** Pyne Inc. is the parent of Syne Inc., a 100%-owned subsidiary created many years ago. Pyne is a holding company in the process of issuing debenture bonds to the public through an investment banking firm (the underwriter). The bond proceeds will be lent to Syne under a lending agreement having the same interest rate and repayment terms of the bond offering (this use of proceeds information is disclosed in the bond offering prospectus).

Required

1. What financial statements do you think should be provided to potential bond investors for their review before buying the bonds? Why?
2. Can you think of any special concerns that potential bond investors should have because of the existence of the *parent-subsidiary* form of organization instead of a *home office–branch* form of organization?

C 1-2 **Lending to a *Subsidiary*: Extra Caution Needed?** Poma Inc. is the parent of Soma Inc., a 100%-owned subsidiary created many years ago. A bank is considering making a loan to Soma, which is financially strong. Poma will *not* be guaranteeing the loan.

Required

1. Would the *consolidated* financial statements or the *subsidiary's* separate financial statements (or both) be useful to the bank? Why?
2. If the parent were to file for bankruptcy under Chapter 7 of the bankruptcy statutes (the *liquidation* chapter), would the parent's creditors have a legal claim against the subsidiary's assets—either on a parity with the subsidiary's creditors or a higher priority than the subsidiary's creditors—in settling creditor claims? Why or why not?
3. Can you think of two major special restrictions the bank might insist on to protect the loan to Soma because of its subsidiary status?

C 1-3 ***Foreign* Subsidiary with Currency Transfer Restrictions: Is This Really Any Big Deal?** Pilla has a 100%-owned foreign subsidiary, Silla. The foreign government recently imposed currency transfer restrictions on all local companies owned by foreign corporations. Accordingly, Silla *cannot* declare any dividends.

Required

1. What reporting issue does this restriction raise?
2. What factors are relevant in deciding how to resolve this issue?
3. What reporting issue is raised for parent-company-only statements that Pilla must issue to its major lender?

C 1-4 **How to Save Taxes and Distribute Foreign Earnings** Pisa Company is forming a foreign subsidiary in a country having a high tax rate (relative to the United States). The foreign country's laws will make it difficult for the subsidiary to pay dividends.

Required How might the parent avoid these problems in setting up the capital structure of the subsidiary?

Financial Analysis Problems

FAP 1-1 **The Social Security "Trust" Fund: Real or Imaginary—Will a Consolidated Perspective Reveal the Truth?** Around the year 2010, the "baby-boom" generation (those born shortly after World War II—roughly 70 million people) will begin reaching retirement age. Accordingly, in a single decade, a 30% increase in the number of citizens eligible for social security retirement benefits will occur. As a result, the ratio of workers to retirees will *decrease* markedly. Consequently, the government must either (1) increase social security taxes significantly between 2010 and 2030 or (2) increase social security taxes prior to 2010 and set aside the additional taxes collected in a trust fund (to be invested until needed).

In 1983, the federal government chose the latter course. Consequently, it abandoned the "pay-as-you-go" system used for nearly a half century. (Under that system, social security taxes collected equaled the benefits that were paid out each year.) The excess FICA taxes collected and put into the trust fund each year are commonly referred to as the surplus (approximately $160 billion for 2003). At the end of 2003, the Social Security Trust Fund totaled approximately $1.5 trillion. (This amount is expected eventually to increase to over $2 trillion.) The Social Security Administration has invested the funds in U.S. Treasury bonds.

Required

1. Taking a *consolidated* perspective, what conclusions would you draw?
2. Why would an agency of the federal government purchase Treasury bonds from the U.S. Treasury Department? (*Hint:* You need to know what the Treasury Department does with the money received.) The Web site for the U.S. Government's 2003 consolidated financial statements is **http://www.gao.gov/special.pubs/03frusg.pdf.**
3. What conclusion would you draw if the $1.5 trillion had been lent to *private* corporations?

The following requirements are optional—check with your instructor.

4. Assume that you are 27 years old and will earn $50,000 a year for 40 years and have $3,100 of social security taxes withheld each year (withholding rate of 7.65% – 1.45% for Medicare = 6.20%; $50,000 × 6.20% = $3,100). Your employer will match this amount. Using an ordinary annuity table, how much would you have accumulated after 40 years assuming that you had invested the $6,200 yourself and earned 5% on your investment each year?
5. Using an *ordinary annuity* table and the future value amount calculated in requirement 4, how much would you be able to withdraw each year if you planned to live 10 years, 20 years, and 30 years beyond age 67?
6. What will be your *actual* social security benefits beginning at age 67 (use the social security calculator on the web site of the Social Security Administration).
7. If the government allowed you to opt out of social security and invest on your own, would you?
8. If all individuals were required to invest on their own (and had the same annual salary), how much would be invested in total at any point in time (assume 100 million full-time workers in the economy)?

FAP 1-2 **Real Estate Transaction Involving Controlled Entities** Pye Inc. owns 100% of *both* Sye Savings and Loan and Tye Realty. Tye owns several parcels of undeveloped land on the outskirts of Phoenix, Arizona. On 4/1/06, Tye sold its Hidden Valley parcel to Dymo Development for $16 million. Tye had purchased this parcel two years before for $5 million.

Dymo made a cash down payment of $4 million to Tye and issued a $12 million, 10% promissory note for the balance. Dymo, which is thinly capitalized (at $30,000), borrowed $4 million from Sye Savings and Loan to make the $4 million cash down payment. Under current GAAP, the minimum down payment needed to recognize profit on a real estate sale is 25%. Pye, Sye, and Tye are audited by the same firm of certified public accountants, Lowe, Price, and Sells.

Required

1. May Pye report this $11 million profit in its 2006 consolidated statements?
2. If your answer to requirement 1 is ***no***, what amounts would be reported in (1) the consolidated *income statement* and (2) the consolidated *balance sheet*?

FAP 1-3 **Whether to Consolidate a Company's Pension Trust Fund** Many companies have employee pension plans. Such companies set aside money each year in their pension trust funds to be invested. When a company disburses cash to a pension trust fund, the company *reduces* its pension liability. Companies having pension plans must disclose extensive information regarding pension plan assets, pension plan obligations, and other pension plan matters in their notes to the financial statements (as required under *FAS 87*, "Employers' Accounting for Pensions").

A pension trust fund's activities are limited to making investments and paying pensions to retirees. Pension plan trust funds invariably have minimal liabilities, all of which pertain to administering the pension trust fund. Thus a pension trust fund does *not* report the present value of either the *projected benefit obligation* or the *accumulated benefit obligation* to the employees that are covered by the plan. Accordingly, the excess of pension trust fund *assets* over pension trust fund *liabilities* is called *Net Assets Held in Trust for Members* in the balance sheet of the pension trust fund. A pension trust fund has no income statement—instead, it presents a "Statement of Activity" that for the most part summarizes the items that increase and decrease the net assets during the year (for the most part, these items are the cash receipts and disbursements for the year).

Required

1. Using the Internet, find General Motors Corp.'s latest annual financial report (**http://www.gm.com**). Note that the financial statements are described as consolidated. Determine if GM consolidated the *balance sheet* of its employee pension trust fund at year-end—in addition to having consolidated the financial statements of its several subsidiaries. Explain what factors led you to your conclusion.
2. What are the total assets of the company's pension trust fund?
3. Calculate GM debt to equity ratio *with* and *without* consolidation of the pension trust fund. (For simplicity, assume that the pension trust fund has *zero liabilities*.) If you were a potential lender, would the difference between the two ratios matter to you?
4. If GM had not debited the pension liability account when it transferred money to the pension trust fund, what other account might it have made sense to *debit*? What might be an advantage of this approach?
5. What consolidation entry is necessary to consolidate the pension plan trust fund at the end of the year? (For simplicity, assume that the pension trust fund has *zero liabilities*.) If GM had *debited* the account you came up with in requirement 4 when it transferred cash to the pension plan trust fund, what would be the worksheet entry to consolidate the pension trust fund?
6. Assuming consolidation of the pension plan trust fund, how should the pension trust fund *assets* (virtually all of which are investments in stocks and bonds) be reported in the *consolidated* balance sheet?
7. Assume that Debtco Inc. has filed for Chapter 7 bankruptcy protection, which will result in the sale of its assets, settlement of its liabilities to the extent possible, and going out of business. Debtco has (a) liabilities of $75 million, (b) assets of $45 million (at liquidation value), and (c) a 100% funded pension plan that has $25 million of assets (and zero liabilities). In the settlement of its claims, will Debtco's creditors receive $.60 on the dollar ($45 million/$75 million) and the pension plan employees 100% on the dollar or would creditors and pension plan employees each receive $.70 on the dollar ($70 million/$100 million)? If the pension plan were *over*funded by $5 million, who would receive the $5 million? If the pension plan were *under*funded by $20 million (only $5 million of assets exist), what would the bankruptcy court do?
8. What arguments can be made *for* and *against* consolidating the pension trust fund's balance sheet?
9. Which presentation best reflects *economic reality*—consolidated or unconsolidated?
10. Which presentation makes more sense to you—consolidated or unconsolidated?

FAP 1-4 **Subsidiary's Purchase of Some of Parent's Stock to Save U.S. Income Taxes** Perlex, which is low on cash, desires to buy back $1 million of its own outstanding common stock. Perlex has a very profitable Irish subsidiary (Irelex), however, that has accumulated substantial profits, $1 million of which Perlex would like to have remitted to the United States. If Perlex instructs Irelex to pay dividends, Perlex will incur substantial U.S. income taxes (because Ireland's corporate income tax rate of 12% is so much *lower* than the U.S. income tax rate of 35%). Accordingly, Perlex created a

Swiss subsidiary (Swerlex), which borrowed the equivalent of $1 million (at 4% interest) from Irelex. Swerlex used the money to acquire $1 million of Perlex's outstanding common stock (10% of the total shares outstanding). Assume that these transactions occurred on the first day of the year.

Required Are any consolidation entries needed at year-end as a result of these two transactions? If so, what are they?

Personal Situations: Interpersonal Skills

PS 1-1 **Interpersonal Skills: Does It Do Any Good to Express Anger?** As accountants move higher within organizations, they usually assume supervisory responsibilities over certain employees. Occasionally, the performance of these employees will not be to the accountant's satisfaction. Sometimes poor performance occurs when deadlines are tight and everyone is working substantial amounts of overtime—situations in which the likelihood of becoming upset and expressing anger is high.

Required

1. If a supervisor expresses anger, what probably is the intended effect on the employee?
2. What most likely will be the unintended effect on the working relationship?
3. What might be an alternative and better emotion for one to feel and possibly express when things go wrong?
4. What do you think studies have shown as to the long-term effect on individuals who continually become angry when things go wrong?

chapter

2

Wholly Owned Subsidiaries: Postcreation Periods

My father taught me to not do anything that could not be put on the front page of a newspaper. I have never known a better human being than my Dad.
WARREN BUFFET

LEARNING OBJECTIVES

To Understand:

> The *cost method* of valuing a parent's investment in a subsidiary.

> The *equity method* of valuing a parent's investment in a subsidiary.

> The way to prepare a *full* set of consolidated statements at reporting dates *subsequent* to a subsidiary's creation.

> The way to present a parent's *separate* financial statements in notes to the consolidated statements when required.

TOPIC OUTLINE

I. Methods for Valuing Investments in Common Stock

II. Subsidiary Dividends: An Intercompany Transaction to Be Eliminated

III. Methods for Valuing a Parent's Investment and Preparing Consolidated Statements

MODULE 1: *The Cost Method*

MODULE 2: *The Equity Method*

IV. Presenting Parent-Company-Only Statements in Notes to the Consolidated Statements

INTERNATIONAL PERSPECTIVE: *Widespread Use of Parent-Company-Only Statements Overseas*

V. The *Equity Method* of Valuing a Parent's Investment: Total Investment Loss Situations

APPENDIX 2A: The Trial Balance Worksheet Technique

Appendices can be found at http://www.pahler.swlearning.com

CHAPTER OVERVIEW

For periods subsequent to a subsidiary's creation, consolidated statements are prepared at each financial reporting date. The consolidation entries at these future dates depend on how the parent values its investment in the subsidiary *after* the initial investment.

Any company that makes an investment must decide how to value that investment at future reporting dates. For investments in common stock of controlled subsidiaries, two valuation methods have evolved: the *cost method* and the *equity method*. These valuation methods, which are at the opposite ends of the conceptual spectrum, are explained in this chapter.[1]

Because the carrying value of a parent's investment differs under the *cost method* and the *equity method* at postcreation financial reporting dates, the basic *elimination* entry at these dates will differ slightly under each of the methods as to both (1) amounts and (2) certain accounts. We explain the consolidation procedures peculiar to each valuation method.

Use of Modules

In this chapter, we present the *cost method* and the *equity method* in two self-contained independent modules. Each module stands on its own when read in conjunction with the nonmodule textual matter. The *cost method* module is the easier of the two, and it can serve as a stepping stone to the *equity method* module. **The *cost method* is *not* illustrated after Chapter 3.**

If time does *not* permit assigning both modules, only the *equity method* should be assigned.

The Big Picture

From a **consolidated reporting perspective**, however, it does *not* matter which method a parent uses to value its investment in a subsidiary because the Investment in Subsidiary account is *always* eliminated in preparing consolidated statements. **The key point is that all the consolidated amounts are the *same* no matter which method a parent uses to account for its investment in a subsidiary.** Thus valuing investments in subsidiaries is usually **an *internal* reporting issue—*not* an *external* reporting issue.**

Most publicly owned banks and savings and loans must also present the parent company's separate statements (**parent-company-only statements**) in a note to the consolidated statements. We discuss the very detailed disclosures required in this note by the Securities and Exchange Commission (SEC), which has certain regulatory powers over these entities.

I. METHODS FOR VALUING INVESTMENTS IN COMMON STOCK

The current rules for valuing *all* corporate investments in common stocks can be depicted as follows:

Ownership Ranges and Governing Pronouncements

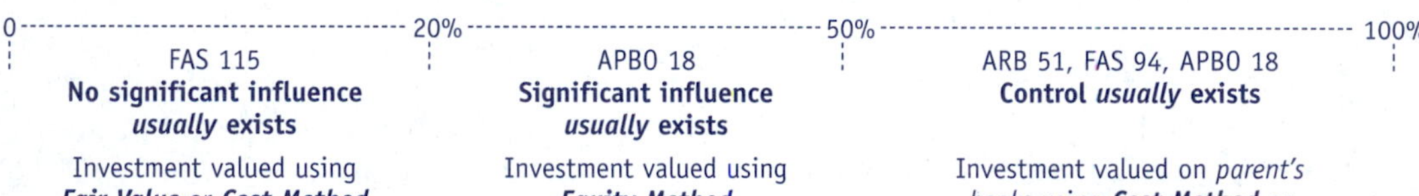

[1] Both of these methods are used for **income tax–reporting** purposes. The Internal Revenue Code, however, uses the terms *cash basis* (instead of *cost method*) and *accrual basis* (instead of *equity method*) because it addresses the area from the perspective of the taxable income to be reported on the parent's investment—not the manner of determining the tax basis of the parent's investment (which is the "other side of the coin"). In most cases, the *cash basis* is required, with the *accrual basis* required only for certain types of foreign income characterized as *passive income*. Income tax issues pertaining to consolidated statements are discussed in appendices to Chapters 3 (for *domestic* subsidiaries) and 16 (for *foreign* subsidiaries).

The "no significant influence" and "significant influence" situations are discussed in *intermediate accounting* texts. The "control" situations are the subject matter of this chapter. Guidance on how to apply the *cost method* and the *equity method* on the *parent's books* is set forth in Accounting Principles Board *Opinion No. 18*, "The Equity Method of Accounting for Investments in Common Stock." If control exists, consolidation is mandatory—making it irrelevant from a *consolidated perspective* which valuation method the parent uses on its books. If the parent issues *parent-company-only statements* (either separately or in notes to the consolidated statements), however, it is quite a relevant issue (as discussed later).

Loss of Control Situations

Occasionally, a parent loses control over a subsidiary (such as when the subsidiary files for bankruptcy protection). Thus the subsidiary *cannot* be consolidated. These situations are discussed in Chapter 3 in the section dealing with *unconsolidated subsidiaries*.

CHECK POINT

A parent *cannot* consolidate a subsidiary when which of the following is true for the parent?

a. It uses the *equity method* of accounting.
b. It uses the *cost method* of accounting.
c. It is unable to do as it pleases with the subsidiary's assets.
d. It allows the subsidiary to operate freely and independently of the parent.

Answer: c

II. SUBSIDIARY DIVIDENDS: AN INTERCOMPANY TRANSACTION TO BE ELIMINATED

In practice, *parents* commonly require *subsidiaries* to pay dividends periodically so that the *parent* has sufficient cash to pay dividends to its shareholders. The *parent* can use the cash received from a *subsidiary* for any purpose, however, including creating or acquiring *additional* subsidiaries (*new* investments).

When a subsidiary *declares* a dividend, an *intercompany transaction* occurs—**a transaction that occurs only within the consolidated entity.** The following entries are made (assuming the dividend is *paid* on the *declaration date*):

Parent's Books			**Subsidiary's Books**		
Cost Method:					
Cash	4,000		Dividends *Declared*	4,000	
Dividend *Income*		4,000	Cash		4,000
Equity Method:					
Cash	4,000		Dividends *Declared*	4,000	
Investment in Subsidiary . .		4,000	Cash		4,000

Thus regardless of which method the parent uses to account for its investment, the cash transferred to the parent does *not* leave the *consolidated entity* as a result of the transfer—the *consolidated* cash balance is the same *before* and *after* the transfer.

Dividends Declared but *Not* Yet Paid

Sometimes a subsidiary's dividend is *not* paid on the declaration date. Thus between the *declaration date* and the *dividend payment date*, the *parent* has an Intercompany Dividend *Receivable* balance, and the *subsidiary* has an Intercompany Dividend *Payable* balance. These two intercompany account balances (which have a *reciprocal* relationship) are *extinguished* upon payment of the dividend. If these accounts exist at a financial reporting date, however, they must be eliminated in consolidation.

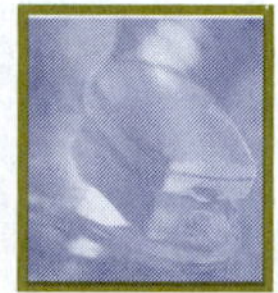

CHECK POINT

Which account is *not* debited or credited under the *cost method* when the subsidiary reports profits and distributes them?

a. Dividends Receivable.
b. Dividend Income.
c. Investment in Subsidiary.
d. Cash.

Answer: c

A Dividend Is One of Many Types of Intercompany Transactions

A dividend declared by a subsidiary is *not* a dividend from the *consolidated group* to the *parent's stockholders*. It is only one of many types of intercompany transactions that can occur. (Other types of intercompany transactions are discussed extensively in Chapters 8–11.)

The Need to Eliminate *All* Intercompany Transactions

Recall from Chapter 1 that *all* intercompany transactions (*including* any related open intercompany *receivable* and *payable* balances) are eliminated in consolidation because they are **internal transactions** (taking place entirely within the consolidated group)—as contrasted with **external transactions** (taking place entirely with outside unrelated parties). Recall further from Chapter 1 that **only transactions and balances with entities *outside the consolidated entity* are reported in the consolidated statements.**

Eliminating the *Subsidiary's* Dividends *Declared* on the Worksheet

Recall from Chapter 1 that from a *consolidated* perspective, a *subsidiary's* outstanding common stock is treated as *not* being outstanding (just as *treasury stock* is treated). Thus it is illogical and inconsistent to add a *subsidiary's* dividends declared to the *parent's* dividends declared in the statement of retained earnings. Consequently, in preparing the consolidated *statement of retained earnings*, the balance in the *subsidiary's* Dividends Declared account is eliminated. **Thus a *subsidiary's* dividends are *not* summed with the *parent's* dividends on the consolidation worksheet.** (Likewise, the offsetting *credit* made by the parent at the dividend declaration date is also eliminated in consolidation.)

III. METHODS FOR VALUING A PARENT'S INVESTMENT AND PREPARING CONSOLIDATED STATEMENTS

Fundamental to addressing the way to value a parent's investment in a subsidiary is the issue of determining what to report as the parent's income on the parent's investment in the subsidiary. Two choices are possible: the parent must report (1) the **dividends** received from the subsidiary (the *distributed* earnings) or (2) the subsidiary's **earnings** (includes both *distributed* and *undistributed* earnings). This is the essential difference between the *cost method* and the *equity method*.

SECTION 1 OF MODULE 1: THE PARENT'S GENERAL LEDGER ENTRIES—*COST METHOD*

The Way the *Cost Method* Works

Under the *cost method,* the parent's investment income is limited to dividends it receives from the subsidiary. Thus **the parent reports investment income only when the subsidiary declares dividends.** In years in which the subsidiary declares a dividend, the parent credits its Dividend Income account—with the offsetting debit being to Dividends Receivable (or the Cash account if it is paid the same day). Because the parent reports only the subsidiary's dividends as its investment income, it ignores the subsidiary's earnings and losses. Consequently, the carrying value of the parent's investment remains constant—unless an impairment of value occurs.[2]

Impairment of Value

If the subsidiary reports losses, these too are ignored—unless they result in reducing the subsidiary's equity to below the carrying value of the parent's investment. In such cases, **if serious doubt exists as to realization of the investment, a permanent write-down** is made. The result of a write-down is the establishment of a **new cost basis**—the investment *cannot* be written back up to original cost if the subsidiary later reports profits.

Determining the Amount of a Write-Down

When an impairment of value has occurred, the amount to which the investment should be written down under the *cost method* is largely a judgment call. Writing down the investment to the book value of the subsidiary's net assets certainly is a justifiable possibility. FASB *Statement No. 144*, "Accounting for the Impairment or Disposal of Long-Lived Assets" is *not* applicable to investments in common stock. However, the guidance in that pronouncement applied to this situation also justifies a valuation based on using the *present value* of estimated expected future cash flows.

The Rationale of the *Cost Method*

The general idea of the *cost method* is that income on the parent's investment should be recognized only to the extent that it has been realized. Because it ignores the subsidiary's reported earnings results and focuses instead on dividends, the cost method produces a **conservative** (although usually unrealistic) **carrying value** for profitable subsidiaries.

Critique of the *Cost Method*

The *cost method* makes sense only when conservatism is warranted. Such conservatism may be appropriate when realization of the subsidiary's undistributed earnings is in doubt. The most common such situation is an instance when a foreign subsidiary is unable to pay cash dividends because of (1) government-imposed currency transfer restrictions (often to support the value of the local currency) or (2) the foreign country's banks continually having a very limited number of dollars available for the subsidiary to purchase to pay dividends.

A major criticism of the *cost method* is that the *parent* (by having control) can manipulate the *subsidiary's* dividend policy to report income at the *parent level* as it pleases. For example, a *parent* could require the *subsidiary* to pay dividends only in years in which the *parent* has losses or depressed earnings on its own separate operations. As shown later, however, this is *not* an issue if the

---

[2] An exception to this general statement occurs in the case of *liquidating dividends*, something that may happen with an *acquired* subsidiary (as opposed to a *created* subsidiary), as discussed in Chapter 6.

subsidiary's financial statements are consolidated with those of the *parent* (the typical situation). Thus **the *parent* can manipulate only its own book net income—*not* the consolidated net income.**

Illustration 2-1 shows the entries under the *cost method*.

Review Points for Illustration 2-1. Note the following:

1. The amount to which the Investment account is written *down* establishes a **new cost basis,** which may *not* be written back up.
2. No write-down was made at the end of 2008, even though the $70,000 loss for 2008 would certainly raise the issue of whether the original $100,000 investment could be recovered at the end of 2008. We assumed here that management concluded that the $100,000 was (a) fully recoverable at the end of 2008 and (b) *not* fully recoverable at the end of 2009.
3. If management believed the subsidiary could be sold at the end of 2009 for, say, $80,000, then only a $20,000 write-down (instead of $55,000) would have been made.
4. How the Investment account is carried on the parent's books is irrelevant from a consolidated perspective because the Investment account is *always* eliminated in consolidation.

ILLUSTRATION 2-1 THE *COST METHOD*

I. General Ledger Activity

	INVESTMENT IN SUBSIDIARY— COST METHOD (Debit)	(Credit)	SUBSIDIARY'S EQUITY
Initial capital investment	$100,000		$100,000
2006 Net income			35,000
2006 Dividends declared			(15,000)
Balances, 12/31/06	$100,000		$120,000
2007 Net income			40,000
2007 Dividends declared			(50,000)
Balances, 12/31/07	$100,000		$110,000
2008 Net loss			(70,000)
Balances, 12/31/08	$100,000		$ 40,000
2009 Net income		55,000[a]	5,000
Balances, 12/31/09	$ 45,000		$ 45,000

[a] This assumes that the *parent* concluded that the recoverability of its investment was in substantial doubt, thus warranting a *permanent* write-down. The write-down could have been any amount; here we assumed that it should be to the amount of the *subsidiary's* net assets.

II. General Ledger Journal Entries

2006		
Dividends Receivable	15,000[a]	
Dividend Income (*from Subbco*)		15,000
2007		
Dividends Receivable	50,000[a]	
Dividend Income (*from Subbco*)		50,000
2008		
No entry.		
2009		
Loss on Investment (*in Subbco*)	55,000	
Investment in Subsidiary		55,000
To write down the investment as a result of concluding that its value has been permanently impaired.		

[a] When the dividend is paid, Cash is *debited* and Dividends Receivable is *credited*.

Illustration 2-2 summarizes the accounting under the *cost method*.

CHECK POINT

Under the *cost method*, cash dividends received from a *created* subsidiary should always be recorded as

a. Dividend income.
b. An *addition* to the parent's share of the subsidiary's profits.
c. A *deduction* from the parent's share of the subsidiary's profits.
d. A *deduction* from the Investment account.

Answer: a

SECTION 2 OF MODULE 1: PREPARING CONSOLIDATED STATEMENTS—*COST METHOD*

In preparing consolidated statements at dates subsequent to the creation date, it also is necessary to prepare (1) a *consolidated income statement* and (2) a *consolidated statement of retained earnings*.

Three-Tier Articulation Format of the Consolidation Worksheet

These two additional statements can be readily prepared on the *same* worksheet used to prepare the *consolidated balance sheet*. By arranging the statements on the worksheet in a certain sequence, however, the three statements can be made to readily articulate with one another. To do so, we place (1) the income statement *first*, (2) the statement of retained earnings *second*, and (3) the balance sheet *last*.

Articulation results because (1) the net income line of the *income statement* ties into the net income line in the *statement of retained earnings* (in *all five* amount columns) and (2) the *ending* balance line in the *statement of retained earnings* ties into the retained earnings line in the *balance*

ILLUSTRATION 2-2 SUMMARY OF THE *COST METHOD*

Subsidiary's Earnings:	
Increases Investment account	No
Report as investment income	No
Subsidiary's Losses:	
Decreases Investment account	No[a]
Report as investment loss	No[a]
Subsidiary's Dividends Declared:	
Reduces Investment account	No
Report as dividend income	Yes
Investment account may be written *back up* after a *write-down*	No
Investment account's carrying value normally equals the subsidiary's net assets	No
Event That Impacts the Parent's Retained Earnings:	
Earnings and losses	No
Dividend declarations	Yes

[a] Unless the *parent* concludes that serious doubt exists as to recoverability of the investment.

sheet (in *all five* amount columns). At this point, you may want to familiarize yourself with the format of such a consolidation worksheet (see page 44).

Consolidation Worksheet Procedures: Subsidiary Does *Not* Declare Any Dividends

As long as no impairment write-down has been made, the basic *elimination* entry is always the same as the basic elimination entry used at the subsidiary's creation date. With the initial investment being $60,000 (as shown in Chapter 1), that entry is as follows:

WORKSHEET ENTRY ONLY

Common Stock	5,000	
Additional Paid-in Capital.	55,000	
Investment in Subsidiary		60,000

Recall from Chapter 1 that the purpose of this entry is to *substitute* the subsidiary's assets and liabilities for the Investment in Subsidiary account.

If the subsidiary (1) has *not* declared any dividends during the current period and (2) has no other intercompany transactions during the current period, no additional *consolidation entries* are necessary.

Illustration 2-3 shows the consolidation worksheet as of December 31, 2006 (the *first* year subsequent to the creation date), assuming that (1) the parent (*Parrco*) uses the *cost method,* (2) the subsidiary (*Subbco*) **declared no dividends** during 2006, and (3) Subbco had no other intercompany transactions during 2006.

Review Points for Illustration 2-3 (*subsidiary did **not** declare dividends*). Note the following:

1. When a subsidiary does *not* declare any dividends and has no other intercompany transactions, preparing the consolidated *income statement* and the consolidated *statement of retained earnings* is simple. In both of these statements, the parent's amounts are merely summed with the subsidiary's related amounts.
2. Thus Subbco's *beginning* and *ending* retained earnings were added to Parrco's *beginning* and *ending* retained earnings, respectively, to obtain the *beginning* and *ending* consolidated retained earnings amounts. **This result *always* occurs for subsidiaries *created* by the parent.** (For *acquired* subsidiaries [discussed in Chapter 6], however, it does *not* hold true.)
3. If the *subsidiary* had declared dividends of $24,000 (equal to its 2006 net income), its retained earnings at year-end would be zero. Consequently, the *parent* would report (1) net income of $74,000 (the *same* as the *consolidated* net income) and (2) retained earnings of $123,000 (the *same* as the *consolidated* retained earnings).

Consolidation Worksheet Procedures: Subsidiary *Does* Declare Dividends

As stated in Section II, the Dividend Income account on the parent's books under the *cost method* must be eliminated in consolidation because it results from an *intercompany transaction.*

Eliminating the *Parent's* Dividend *Income* on the Worksheet

On the worksheet, the sales, cost of sales, and expenses of both companies are summed (as before). The parent's Dividend Income account, however, is "eliminated" (prevented from being reported in the Consolidated column). Eliminating the Dividend Income account in consolidation (1) prevents *partial* or *complete* double counting of the subsidiary's earnings in the consolidated column and (2) requires a *debit* posting.

This elimination is accomplished using a separate consolidation entry, which we call the **intercompany dividend elimination entry**. The other half of the consolidation entry (the *credit* posting)

ILLUSTRATION 2-3 *COST METHOD*: FIRST YEAR SUBSEQUENT TO DATE OF CREATION

Subsidiary Did *Not* Declare Dividends

PARRCO AND SUBBCO
Consolidation Worksheet as of December 31, 2006

	PARRCO	SUBBCO	CONSOLIDATION ENTRIES DR.			CR.	CONSOLIDATED
Income Statement							
Sales	600,000	234,000					834,000
Cost of sales	(360,000)	(110,000)					(470,000)
Expenses	(190,000)	(100,000)					(290,000)
Dividend income *(from Subbco)*	**-0-**						**-0-**
Net Income	50,000	24,000					74,000
Statement of Retained Earnings							
Balances, 1/1/06	100,000	-0-					100,000
+ Net income	50,000	24,000					74,000
– Dividends declared	(51,000)	-0-					(51,000)
Balances, 12/31/06	99,000	24,000					123,000
Balance Sheet							
Cash	61,000	15,000					76,000
Accounts receivable	75,000	37,000					112,000
Inventory	110,000	55,000					165,000
Investment in Subbco	**60,000**				**1**	**60,000**	**-0-**
Land	220,000	30,000					250,000
Buildings and equipment	500,000	150,000					650,000
Accumulated depreciation	(320,000)	(13,000)					(333,000)
Total Assets	706,000	274,000				60,000	920,000
Payables and accruals	157,000	70,000					227,000
Long-term debt	250,000	120,000					370,000
Common stock, $1 par	10,000						10,000
Additional paid-in capital	190,000						190,000
Common stock, $5 par		**5,000**	**5,000**	**1**			**-0-**
Additional paid-in capital		**55,000**	**55,000**	**1**			**-0-**
Retained earnings	99,000	24,000					123,000
Total Liabilities & Equity	706,000	274,000	60,000				920,000
Proof of debit and credit postings			*60,000*			*60,000*	

Explanation of entry:
1 The basic elimination entry.

is made in the retained earnings section of the worksheet. Thus *both* the *credit* on the *parent's books* and the *debit* on the *subsidiary's books* are eliminated in consolidation.

Comprehensive Illustration

The Intercompany Dividend Elimination Entry

We now assume that the *subsidiary* (1) *declared* dividends at year-end and (2) *paid* the dividends in the *following* year. Thus the *parent* has an **intercompany dividend receivable** (rather than more cash) at the end of the year of declaration. Using assumed dividend amounts, the *consolidation* entries at assumed consolidation dates are as follows:

WORKSHEET ENTRY ONLY

	Consolidation Date December 31, 2006		December 31, 2007	
Common Stock	5,000		5,000	
Additional Paid-in Capital	55,000		55,000	
Investment in Subsidiary		60,000		60,000

WORKSHEET ENTRY ONLY

	Consolidation Date			
	December 31, 2006		December 31, 2007	
Dividend Income *(from Subbco)*	4,000		12,000	
Dividends Declared		4,000		12,000
Intercompany Dividend Payable	4,000		12,000	
Intercompany Dividend Receivable		4,000		12,000

The *Nonimpact* of the Intercompany Dividend Elimination Entry on the Consolidated Balance Sheet

The Intercompany Dividend elimination entry has no effect on ending Retained Earnings because the *debit* amount is carried forward from the *income statement* to the net income line in the *statement of retained earnings* section of the worksheet. **Thus the entry has a "wash" effect on the ending retained earnings.** Note that the entry serves a twofold purpose:

1. To prevent the dividend income recorded by the *parent* from appearing in the Consolidated column so as to prevent partially double counting the *subsidiary's* net income.
2. To prevent the *subsidiary's* dividends from being added to the *parent's* dividends in arriving at the *consolidated* dividends declared.

Illustrations 2-4 and 2-5 show the consolidation worksheets as of December 31, 2006 (the *first* year subsequent to the creation date), and December 31, 2007 (the *second* year subsequent to the creation date), assuming that the parent uses the *cost method.*

Review Points for Illustrations 2-4 and 2-5. Note the following:

1. The *parent's* retained earnings include **only those earnings of the subsidiary that *have* been distributed to the parent in the form of dividends.**
2. If the *subsidiary* had declared dividends *equal to* net income each year, the *parent's* net income would equal the *consolidated* net income each year. Likewise, the *parent's* retained earnings at each year-end would equal *consolidated* retained earnings at each year-end.
3. The *debit* amount carried forward from the net income line in the *income statement* to the net income line in the *statement of retained earnings* eliminates the dividend income included in the parent's net income. Thus the effect on the net income line in the *statement of retained earnings* is identical to the effect on the net income line in the *income statement:* To enable all of the subsidiary's income to be added to the parent's income from its own separate operations.

Concluding Comments on the *Cost Method*

The *cost method* involves minimal bookkeeping by the parent because it is *not* necessary to record the subsidiary's earnings on the parent's books under the *cost method.* Entries are necessary only when the subsidiary declares dividends. In practice, the *cost method* is widely used because of its simplicity and minimal work in (1) accounting for the parent's investment and (2) preparing consolidated statements.

ILLUSTRATION 2-4 *COST METHOD*: FIRST YEAR SUBSEQUENT TO DATE OF CREATION

Subsidiary *Did* Declare Dividends

PARRCO AND SUBBCO
Consolidation Worksheet as of December 31, 2006

			CONSOLIDATION ENTRIES				
	PARRCO	SUBBCO	DR.			CR.	CONSOLIDATED
Income Statement							
Sales	600,000	234,000					834,000
Cost of sales	(360,000)	(110,000)					(470,000)
Expenses	(190,000)	(100,000)					(290,000)
Dividend income *(from Subbco)*	**4,000**		**4,000**	2			**–0–**
Net Income	54,000	24,000	4,000				74,000
Statement of Retained Earnings							
Balances, 1/1/06	100,000	–0–					100,000
+ Net income	54,000	24,000	4,000				74,000
– Dividends declared	**(51,000)**	**(4,000)**			2	**4,000**	**(51,000)**
Balances, 12/31/06	103,000	20,000	4,000			4,000	123,000
Balance Sheet							
Cash	61,000	15,000					76,000
Accounts receivable	75,000	37,000					112,000
Interco. dividend receivable	**4,000**				3	**4,000**	**–0–**
Inventory	110,000	55,000					165,000
Investment in Subbco	**60,000**				1	**60,000**	**–0–**
Land	220,000	30,000					250,000
Buildings and equipment	500,000	150,000					650,000
Accumulated depreciation	(320,000)	(13,000)					(333,000)
Total Assets	710,000	274,000				64,000	920,000
Payables and accruals	157,000	70,000					227,000
Interco. dividend payable		**4,000**	**4,000**	3			**–0–**
Long-term debt	250,000	120,000					370,000
Common stock, $1 par	10,000						10,000
Additional paid-in capital	190,000						190,000
Common stock, $5 par		**5,000**	**5,000**	1			**–0–**
Additional paid-in capital		**55,000**	**55,000**	1			**–0–**
Retained earnings	103,000	20,000	4,000			4,000	123,000
Total Liabilities & Equity	710,000	274,000	68,000			4,000	920,000
Proof of debit and credit postings			*68,000*			*68,000*	

Explanation of entries:

1 The basic *elimination* entry.
2 The intercompany dividend *elimination* entry.
3 The intercompany receivable and payable *elimination* entry.

ILLUSTRATION 2-5 *COST METHOD*: SECOND YEAR SUBSEQUENT TO DATE OF CREATION

Subsidiary *Did* Declare Dividends

PARRCO AND SUBBCO
Consolidation Worksheet as of December 31, 2007

	PARRCO	SUBBCO	CONSOLIDATION ENTRIES DR.			CR.	CONSOLIDATED
Income Statement							
Sales	710,000	282,000					992,000
Cost of sales	(390,000)	(130,000)					(520,000)
Expenses	(210,000)	(120,000)					(330,000)
Dividend income *(from Subbco)*	**12,000**		**12,000**	2			**–0–**
Net Income	122,000	32,000	12,000				142,000
Statement of Retained Earnings							
Balances, 1/1/07	103,000	20,000					123,000
+ Net income	122,000	32,000	12,000				142,000
– Dividends declared	**(85,000)**	**(12,000)**			2	**12,000**	**(85,000)**
Balances, 12/31/07	140,000	40,000	12,000			12,000	180,000
Balance Sheet							
Cash	56,000	41,000					97,000
Accounts receivable	82,000	45,000					127,000
Interco. dividend receivable	**12,000**				3	**12,000**	**–0–**
Inventory	140,000	82,000					222,000
Investment in Subbco	**60,000**				1	**60,000**	**–0–**
Land	220,000	30,000					250,000
Buildings and equipment	500,000	150,000					650,000
Accumulated depreciation	(360,000)	(26,000)					(386,000)
Total Assets	710,000	322,000				72,000	960,000
Payables and accruals	160,000	90,000					250,000
Interco. dividend payable		**12,000**	**12,000**	3			**–0–**
Long-term debt	210,000	120,000					330,000
Common stock, $1 par	10,000						10,000
Additional paid-in capital	190,000						190,000
Common stock, $5 par		**5,000**	**5,000**	1			**–0–**
Additional paid-in capital		**55,000**	**55,000**	1			**–0–**
Retained earnings	140,000	40,000	12,000			12,000	180,000
Total Liabilities & Equity	710,000	322,000	84,000			12,000	960,000
Proof of debit and credit postings			*84,000*			*84,000*	

Explanation of entries:

1 The basic *elimination* entry.

2 The intercompany dividend *elimination* entry.

3 The intercompany receivable and payable *elimination* entry.

SECTION 1 OF MODULE 2: THE PARENT'S GENERAL LEDGER ENTRIES—*EQUITY METHOD*

How the *Equity Method* Works

Under the *equity method,* the parent's investment income is deemed to be the subsidiary's earnings—**whether or not they are distributed.** Procedurally, the parent's interest in a subsidiary's earnings is reflected as an *upward* adjustment of the Investment in Subsidiary account; the parent effectively has *more* capital invested in the subsidiary.[3] Increasing the carrying value of the Investment in Subsidiary account is somewhat analogous to updating a bank savings passbook for interest earned that one leaves invested in the bank. The offsetting *credit* is reported as investment income in the parent's income statement (the account Equity in Net Income of Subsidiary is used).

Subsidiary's Losses

If the subsidiary reports **losses,** the carrying value of the parent's investment account is **decreased,** and **the parent records an investment loss on its income statement** (the account Equity in Net Loss of Subsidiary is used).

Subsidiary's Dividends

Cash dividends declared by the subsidiary (which can easily be paid the same day in parent-subsidiary relationships) are treated as a **liquidation of the investment**—the parent has *less* capital invested in the subsidiary than *before* the dividend declaration. Accordingly, cash dividends are *credited* to the Investment in Subsidiary account **at the declaration date,** and the offsetting *debit* is made to the Dividends Receivable account (or the Cash account if paid the same day as declared). Reducing the carrying value of the Investment account for dividends is somewhat analogous to withdrawing a portion of the interest that has been accumulated in a savings account.

The Rationale of the *Equity Method*

The general idea of the *equity method* is that the earnings generated by the subsidiary "belong" to the parent. Accordingly, those earnings should be "accrued" on the parent's books (an asset)—even though the accrued asset (given an appropriate descriptive name in accordance with its substance) is **unrealized** in nature.

When the subsidiary distributes some or all of its earnings to the parent (as dividends), the parent has **realized** those earnings (cash goes up and the accrued asset goes down).

Critique of the *Equity Method*

Note that as a result of these procedures, the carrying value of the investment always equals the subsidiary's net assets—**the economic resources underlying the parent's investment.** Thus the *equity method* reflects in the Investment in Subsidiary account the *increase* or *decrease* in the subsidiary's net assets based on **the economic activity** (earnings and distributions) **occurring at the subsidiary** as determined under the *accrual basis.* Consequently, the *equity method* perfectly matches reporting earnings and losses based on the economic transactions and events affecting the subsidiary.

Distinguishing between *Adjusted Carrying Value* and *Market Value*

The valuation of the parent's investment in a subsidiary under the *equity method* is only as good as the accounting practices and estimates the subsidiary uses. Furthermore, the valuation produced

[3] The result is as if the parent had instructed the subsidiary to pay a *cash dividend* equal to its net income and the parent had then made an *additional cash investment* equal to the cash dividend it received.

under the *equity method* is *not* necessarily the *market value* of the subsidiary's common stock—the parent may be able to sell its common stock investment at more or less than the *carrying value*.[4]

Illustration 2-6 shows how the *carrying value* of the Investment account for a 100%-owned created subsidiary is adjusted under each method for several years of assumed earnings, losses, and dividends.

Review Points for Illustration 2-6. Note the following:

1. Under the *equity method*, the Investment account's carrying value parallels the subsidiary's reported equity—this *always* occurs when the subsidiary's equity is **positive** (*negative* situations are discussed later).
2. How the Investment account is carried on the parent's books is irrelevant from a consolidated perspective because the Investment account is *always* eliminated in consolidation.

ILLUSTRATION 2-6 THE *EQUITY* METHOD

I. General Ledger Activity

	INVESTMENT IN SUBSIDIARY—EQUITY METHOD (Debit)	INVESTMENT IN SUBSIDIARY—EQUITY METHOD (Credit)	SUBSIDIARY'S EQUITY
Initial capital investment	$100,000		$100,000
2006 Net income	35,000		35,000
2006 Dividends declared		15,000	(15,000)
Balances, 12/31/06	$120,000		$120,000
2007 Net income	40,000		40,000
2007 Dividends declared		50,000	(50,000)
Balances, 12/31/07	$110,000		$110,000
2008 Net loss		70,000	(70,000)
Balances, 12/31/08	$ 40,000		$ 40,000
2009 Net income	5,000		5,000
Balances, 12/31/09	$ 45,000		$ 45,000

II. General Ledger Journal Entries

	EQUITY METHOD	
2006		
Investment in Subsidiary	35,000	
Equity in Net Income (of Subbco)		35,000
Dividends Receivable	15,000[a]	
Investment in Subsidiary		15,000
2007		
Investment in Subsidiary	40,000	
Equity in Net Income (of Subbco)		40,000
Dividends Receivable	50,000[a]	
Investment in Subsidiary		50,000
2008		
Equity in Net Loss (of Subbco)	70,000	
Investment in Subsidiary		70,000
2009		
Investment in Subsidiary	5,000	
Equity in Net Income (of Subbco)		5,000

[a] When the dividend is paid, Cash is *debited* and Dividends Receivable is *credited*.

[4] The concept of lower of cost or market is generally *not* applied to subsidiaries. An exception exists for an *unconsolidated, partially owned subsidiary* in which the common stock shares *not* owned by the parent are actively traded on a stock exchange (discussed in Chapter 3). For 100%-owned subsidiaries, such trading *cannot* occur, and accordingly, no ready market price exists.

Check Point

Which account is *not* used under the *equity method*?

a. Dividends Receivable.
b. Dividend Income.
c. Equity in Net Income of Subsidiary.
d. Investment in Subsidiary.

Answer: b

Illustration 2-7 summarizes the accounting under the *equity method.*

Check Point

Under the *equity method,* cash dividends received from a *created* subsidiary should always be recorded as

a. Dividend income.
b. An *addition* to the parent's share of the subsidiary's profits.
c. A *deduction* from the parent's share of the subsidiary's profits.
d. A *deduction* from the Investment account.

Answer: d

Advantages of the *Equity Method*

In addition to more closely reflecting the probable *market value* of the investment (which could be significantly more or less than the equity method *carrying value*), the following are other advantages of the *equity method:*

1. **It provides built-in self-checking features in the consolidation process.** As shown shortly, the *equity method* provides two useful self-checking features in preparing consolidated statements (the

ILLUSTRATION 2-7 SUMMARY OF THE *EQUITY METHOD*

Subsidiary's Earnings:	
Increases Investment account	Yes
Report as investment income	Yes
Subsidiary's Losses:	
Decreases Investment account	Yes[a]
Report as investment loss	Yes
Subsidiary's Dividends Declared:	
Reduces Investment account	Yes
Report as dividend income	No
Investment account may be written *back up* after a *write-down*	Yes
Investment account's *carrying value* normally equals the subsidiary's net assets	Yes[b]
Event That Impacts the *Parent's* Retained Earnings:	
Earnings and losses	Yes
Dividend declarations	No

[a] The Investment in Subsidiary account can (1) be written down to a zero balance or (2) become a *negative* balance (classified as a liability in the parent's separate statements) when the parent is obligated to invest additional funds into the subsidiary (as discussed later in the section The Equity Method of Valuing a Parent's Investment: Total Investment Loss Situations).

[b] This equality usually does *not* exist for "acquired" subsidiaries (as shown in Chapters 5 and 6).

consolidated net income and the *consolidated* retained earnings amounts always equal the *parent's* net income and *parent's* retained earnings amounts, respectively), which can make the consolidation effort easier. Under the *cost method,* no such features exist.

2. **It enables parent-company-only (PCO) statements to articulate with the consolidated statements.** Often PCO statements must be presented either (1) in a condensed manner in a note to the consolidated statements or (2) separately (uncondensed) for reporting to a parent's creditor pursuant to a loan agreement requirement. We discuss the importance of this articulation later.
3. **It enables PCO statements to be used more meaningfully internally.** To the extent that PCO statements are used for internal management purposes, they are usually meaningful only if investments in subsidiaries are accounted for under the *equity method.* Under the *cost method,* such statements can become of limited usefulness.
4. **It facilitates financial analysis.** By tracking the amount invested (including the reinvestment of the subsidiary's undistributed earnings), meaningful return-on-investment (ROI) calculations can be made readily. Using the amounts produced by the *cost method* usually gives artificial and nonmeaningful percentages (recall that the *parent* controls the *subsidiary's* dividend policy). Accordingly, if the *cost method* is used, meaningful ROI percentages can be obtained only by using amounts as if the *equity method* were being used instead. Illustration 2-8 shows how the ROI percentages can be (1) greatly different for the two methods and (2) arbitrarily determined under the *cost method* (the amounts used in the illustration are from Illustrations 2-1 and 2-6).
5. **It achieves a "one-line consolidation."** When a subsidiary is *not* consolidated and is reported under the *equity method,* the *equity method* is often viewed as a *one-line consolidation.* This happens because the subsidiary's earnings are reported on one line in the parent's income statement (using the Equity in Net Income of Subsidiary account[5]) instead of the subsidiary's sales, cost of sales, and expenses.

ILLUSTRATION 2-8 PARENT'S ANNUAL[a] RETURN-ON-INVESTMENT (AROI) CALCULATIONS

		COST METHOD		EQUITY METHOD	
2006:	Net Income / Beginning Investment	$15,000 / $100,000	= 15%	$35,000 / $100,000	= 35%
2007:	Net Income / Beginning Investment	$50,000 / $100,000	= 50%	$40,000 / $120,000	= 33%
2008:	Net Income / Beginning Investment	$-0- / $100,000	= 0%	$(70,000) / $110,000	= (64)%
2009:	Net Income / Beginning Investment	$(55,000) / $100,000	= (55)%	$5,000 / $40,000	= 12%

Source of these dollar amounts: Illustrations 2-1 and 2-6.

	Cost Method		Equity Method
Average *annual* return on investment (AROI) (4 years)	2.5%		4%
Internal rate of return		1.9%[b]	

[a] Some texts call these calculations the *"accounting" return on investment.* We use the more descriptive term *annual.*

[b] Using the following actual and assumed cash flows:

Initial investment	$(100,000)
End of Year 1 (dividends)	15,000
End of Year 2 (dividends)	50,000
End of Year 3	-0-
End of Year 4 (Assumes the subsidiary was sold at this time for an amount equal to the book value of its net assets)	45,000

Note: Some view the internal rate of return (IRR) as the most reliable indicator of an investment's "true" profitability. However, the IRR calculation (which covers four years and *cannot* tell anything regarding any *particular* year's profitability) can be compared only to the *average* of the AROIs—*not* to the AROI for an *individual* year. Thus the IRR and the AROI calculations serve entirely different purposes.

[5] The analogy is to an income statement that displays only a net income amount and none of the elements it comprises, that is, sales, cost of sales, expenses, gains, and losses.

Likewise in the parent's balance sheet, one account (the Investment in Subsidiary account[6]) is reported instead of the individual assets and liabilities of the subsidiary. Thus the amounts for both net income and retained earnings reported to the parent's stockholders are *identical* whether the subsidiary is consolidated or not.

Therefore, the only difference between furnishing the parent's stockholders (1) unconsolidated statements reflecting the equity method and (2) consolidated statements is the manner of presenting amounts (gross or net) pertaining to the subsidiary within the income statement and balance sheet furnished to these stockholders.

SECTION 2 OF MODULE 2: PREPARING CONSOLIDATED STATEMENTS—*EQUITY METHOD*

In preparing consolidated statements at dates subsequent to the creation date, it is also necessary to prepare (1) a *consolidated income statement* and (2) a *consolidated statement of retained earnings.*

Three-Tier Articulation Format of the Consolidation Worksheet

These two additional statements can be readily prepared on the *same* worksheet used to prepare the consolidated balance sheet. By arranging the statements on the worksheet in a certain sequence, however, the three statements can be made to readily articulate with one another. To do so, we place (1) the income statement *first,* (2) the statement of retained earnings *second,* and (3) the balance sheet *last.*

Articulation results because (1) the net income line of the *income statement* ties into the net income line in the *statement of retained earnings* (in *all five* amount columns) and (2) the *ending* balance line in the *statement of retained earnings* ties into the retained earnings line in the *balance sheet* (in *all five* amount columns). At this point, you may want to familiarize yourself with the format of such a consolidation worksheet (see page 54).

Consolidation Worksheet Procedures: Subsidiary Does Not Declare Any Dividends

The amounts used in the basic elimination entry at each consolidation date can be readily obtained by updating an analysis of the *parent's* Investment account. Recall from Chapter 1 that this analysis shows the **reciprocal relationship** between the *parent's* investment account and the *subsidiary's* equity accounts.

Such an analysis is presented in Illustration 2-9, which shows and assumes $24,000 of earnings and *no dividends* declared by Subbco for the year subsequent to its creation date of December 31, 2005. Also shown there is the basic elimination entry (as derived from the updated analysis) required in consolidation as of December 31, 2006 (*one* year after the subsidiary's *creation date*).

Review Points for Illustration 2-9 (*subsidiary did **not** declare dividends*). Note the following:

1. **The *debit* to the *Equity in Net Income* account.** Summing the sales, cost of sales, and expenses of both entities *without* eliminating the *Equity in Net Income* account would *double count* all of the subsidiary's net income in the Consolidated column.

---

[6] The analogy is to a balance sheet that shows only the stockholders' equity, not the assets and liabilities, the net of which equals the stockholders' equity.

ILLUSTRATION 2-9 PREPARING AND UPDATING THE ANALYSIS OF THE PARENT'S INVESTMENT ACCOUNT

	PARENT'S INVESTMENT ACCOUNT	=	SUBSIDIARY'S EQUITY ACCOUNTS COMMON STOCK	+	ADDITIONAL PIC	+	RETAINED EARNINGS
Balances, Dec. 31, 2005	$60,000		$5,000		$55,000		$ -0-
+ Equity in net income	24,000						24,000
– Dividends	-0-						-0-
Balances, Dec. 31, 2006	$84,000		$5,000		$55,000		$24,000

The Basic *Elimination* Entry

WORKSHEET ENTRY ONLY

	CONSOLIDATION AS OF DECEMBER 31, 2006	
Common Stock	5,000	
Additional Paid-in Capital	55,000	
Equity in Net Income (*of Subbco*)	24,000	
Investment in Subbco		84,000

2. **Eliminating the subsidiary's *ending* retained earnings balance.** Unlike the Common Stock account balance and Additional Paid-in Capital account balance, which are both eliminated by *debits* that are *equal to* their respective *end-of-year* balances, the *end-of-year* Retained Earnings balance is *not* debited using its *end-of-year* balance of $24,000. In this illustration **in which the subsidiary's *beginning* retained earnings balance is zero,** the subsidiary's *ending* retained earnings is automatically eliminated in consolidation as a result of the carryforward process from the net income line in the *income statement.*
3. **The necessity of eliminating the subsidiary's *ending* retained earnings balance.** The *subsidiary's* ending retained earnings balance must be eliminated because the identical amount is also included in the *parent's* ending retained earnings balance. Thus double counting is prevented.

Illustration 2-10 shows the consolidation worksheet as of December 31, 2006 (*one* year after the subsidiary's *creation date*), using the preceding basic *elimination* entry.

Review Points for Illustration 2-10. Note the following:

1. **The *first* built-in checking feature.** The *consolidated* net income is the same as the *parent's* net income.
2. **The *second* built-in checking feature.** The *consolidated* retained earnings amounts are the same as the *parent's* retained earnings.
3. **The reciprocal relationship.** As in Chapter 1, *all* of the *subsidiary's* equity accounts (the *total* of which is the *reciprocal balance* to the *parent's* Investment account) have been eliminated.

Consolidation Worksheet Procedures: Subsidiary Declares Dividends

If a *subsidiary* declares dividends, the *subsidiary's* Dividends Declared account must be eliminated in consolidation (as was done under the *cost method*). Illustration 2-11 shows an analysis of the *parent's* investment account using assumed amounts for earnings and dividends of Subbco for the two years subsequent to its creation date of December 31, 2005. Also shown there is the basic *elimination* entries (as derived from the updated analysis) required in consolidation as of December 31, 2006 (*one* year after the *subsidiary's* creation date) and December 31, 2007 (*two* years after the *subsidiary's* creation).

ILLUSTRATION 2-10 *EQUITY METHOD*: FIRST YEAR SUBSEQUENT TO DATE OF CREATION

Subsidiary Did *Not* Declare Dividends

PARRCO AND SUBBCO
Consolidation Worksheet as of December 31, 2006

	PARRCO	SUBBCO	CONSOLIDATION ENTRIES DR.			CR.	CONSOLIDATED
Income Statement							
Sales	600,000	234,000					834,000
Cost of sales	(360,000)	(110,000)					(470,000)
Expenses	(190,000)	(100,000)					(290,000)
Equity in net income *(of Subbco)*	**24,000**		**24,000**	1			**-0-**
Net Income	74,000	24,000	24,000				74,000
Statement of Retained Earnings							
Balances, 1/1/06	100,000	-0-					100,000
+ Net income	74,000	24,000	➤ 24,000				74,000
– Dividends declared	(51,000)	-0-					(51,000)
Balances, 12/31/06	123,000	24,000	24,000				123,000
Balance Sheet							
Cash	61,000	15,000					76,000
Accounts receivable	75,000	37,000					112,000
Inventory	110,000	55,000					165,000
Investment in Subbco	**84,000**				1	**84,000**	**-0-**
Land	220,000	30,000					250,000
Buildings and equipment	500,000	150,000					650,000
Accumulated depreciation	(320,000)	(13,000)					(333,000)
Total Assets	730,000	274,000				84,000	920,000
Payables and accruals	157,000	70,000					227,000
Long-term debt	250,000	120,000					370,000
Common stock, $1 par	10,000						10,000
Additional paid-in capital	190,000						190,000
Common stock, $5 par		**5,000**	**5,000**	1			**-0-**
Additional paid-in capital		**55,000**	**55,000**	1			**-0-**
Retained earnings	123,000	24,000	➤ 24,000				123,000
Total Liabilities & Equity	730,000	274,000	84,000				920,000
Proof of debit and credit postings			84,000			84,000	

Explanation of entry:

1 The basic *elimination* entry.

Review Points for Illustration 2-11. Note the following:

1. **The *credit* to the Dividends Declared account.** This *credit* posting eliminates an account balance created as a result of an intercompany transaction. Recall that all intercompany transaction generated balances must be eliminated in consolidation.
2. **The effect on the subsidiary's statement of retained earnings.** The combination of (1) the *direct* postings to the analysis of retained earnings (for the *beginning* balance and dividends declared) and (2) the *carryforward* from the income statement to the net income line in the analysis of retained earnings results in eliminating *all* the balances in the subsidiary's statement of retained earnings. Thus the Consolidated column reports only the *parent's* amounts.
3. **The effect on the balance sheet.** The total of the eliminations in the analysis of retained earnings is then carried forward to the retained earnings line in the balance sheet. This carryforward process results in eliminating the subsidiary's *end-of-year* retained earnings balance—as though a *debit* amount equal to the year-end balance had been directly posted to this account.

ILLUSTRATION 2-11 PREPARING AND UPDATING THE ANALYSIS OF THE PARENT'S INVESTMENT ACCOUNT

	PARENT'S INVESTMENT ACCOUNT	=	SUBSIDIARY'S EQUITY ACCOUNTS: COMMON STOCK	+	ADDITIONAL PIC	+	RETAINED EARNINGS
Balances, Dec. 31, 2005	$ 60,000		$5,000		$55,000		$ -0-
+ Equity in net income	24,000						24,000
– Dividends	(4,000)						(4,000)
Balances, Dec. 31, 2006	$ 80,000		$5,000		$55,000		$ 20,000
+ Equity in net income	32,000						32,000
– Dividends	(12,000)						(12,000)
Balances, Dec. 31, 2007	$100,000		$5,000		$55,000		$ 40,000

The Basic *Elimination* Entry

WORKSHEET ENTRY ONLY

	CONSOLIDATION DATE: DECEMBER 31, 2006		DECEMBER 31, 2007	
Common Stock	5,000		5,000	
Additional Paid-in Capital	55,000		55,000	
Retained Earnings, 1/1/06 and 1/1/07	-0-		20,000	
Equity in Net Income (of Subbco)	24,000		32,000	
Dividends Declared		4,000		12,000
Investment in Subbco		80,000		100,000

Note: **The analysis is a powerful tool.** In later chapters, we show how it can be expanded to readily handle more involved aspects of consolidations.

Illustrations 2-12 and 2-13 show the consolidation worksheets as of December 31, 2006 (*one* year after the *creation date*), and December 31, 2007 (*two* years after the *creation date*), using the preceding basic elimination entries.

Review Points for Illustrations 2-12 and 2-13. Note the following:

1. The *debit* amount carried forward from the net income line in the *income statement* to the net income line in the *statement of retained earnings* eliminates the subsidiary income included in the parent's net income. Thus the effect on the net income line in the *statement of retained earnings* is identical to the effect on the net income line in the *income statement:* to enable all of the subsidiary's income to be added to the parent's income from its own separate operations.
2. The consolidated net income and consolidated retained earnings amounts are identical to the parent's amounts.

CHECK POINTS

On 4/1/05, Pitco *created* Sitco by investing $100,000 cash. For 2005, Sitco reported net income of $17,000 and declared and paid cash dividends of $7,000. What is the *carrying value* of Pitco's investment in Sitco at 12/31/05?

	Cost Method	Equity Method
a.	$100,000	$110,000
b.	$110,000	$117,000
c.	$100,000	$117,000
d.	$93,000	$117,000

Answer: a

ILLUSTRATION 2-12 *EQUITY METHOD*: FIRST YEAR SUBSEQUENT TO DATE OF CREATION

Subsidiary *Did* Declare Dividends

PARRCO AND SUBBCO
Consolidation Worksheet as of December 31, 2006

	PARRCO	SUBBCO	CONSOLIDATION ENTRIES DR.			CR.	CONSOLIDATED
Income Statement							
Sales	600,000	234,000					834,000
Cost of sales	(360,000)	(110,000)					(470,000)
Expenses	(190,000)	(100,000)					(290,000)
Equity in net income *(of Subbco)*	**24,000**		**24,000**	1			**-0-**
Net Income	74,000	24,000	24,000				74,000
Statement of Retained Earnings							
Balances, 1/1/06	100,000	-0-					100,000
+ Net income	74,000	24,000	24,000				74,000
– Dividends declared	**(51,000)**	**(4,000)**			1	**4,000**	**(51,000)**
Balances, 12/31/06	123,000	20,000	24,000			4,000	123,000
Balance Sheet							
Cash	61,000	15,000					76,000
Accounts receivable	75,000	37,000					112,000
Interco. dividend receivable	**4,000**				2	**4,000**	**-0-**
Inventory	110,000	55,000					165,000
Investment in Subbco	**80,000**				1	**80,000**	**-0-**
Land	220,000	30,000					250,000
Buildings and equipment	500,000	150,000					650,000
Accumulated depreciation	(320,000)	(13,000)					(333,000)
Total Assets	730,000	274,000				84,000	920,000
Payables and accruals	157,000	70,000					227,000
Interco. dividend payable		**4,000**	**4,000**	2			**-0-**
Long-term debt	250,000	120,000					370,000
Common stock, $1 par	10,000						10,000
Additional paid-in capital	190,000						190,000
Common stock, $5 par		**5,000**	**5,000**	1			**-0-**
Additional paid-in capital		**55,000**	**55,000**	1			**-0-**
Retained earnings	123,000	20,000	24,000			4,000	123,000
Total Liabilities & Equity	730,000	274,000	88,000			4,000	920,000
Proof of debit and credit postings			*88,000*			*88,000*	

Explanation of entries:

1 The basic *elimination* entry.

2 The intercompany receivable and payable *elimination* entry.

Assume the same information as in the previous Check Point, but the dividend was declared on December 31, 2005, and paid two days later. What is the investment's *carrying value*?

Answer: a

ILLUSTRATION 2-13 *EQUITY METHOD*: SECOND YEAR SUBSEQUENT TO DATE OF CREATION

Subsidiary *Did* Declare Dividends

PARRCO AND SUBBCO
Consolidation Worksheet as of December 31, 2007

	PARRCO	SUBBCO	CONSOLIDATION ENTRIES DR.			CR.	CONSOLIDATED
Income Statement							
Sales	710,000	282,000					992,000
Cost of sales	(390,000)	(130,000)					(520,000)
Expenses	(210,000)	(120,000)					(330,000)
Equity in net income *(of Subbco)*	**32,000**		**32,000**	1			**-0-**
Net Income	142,000	32,000	32,000				142,000
Statement of Retained Earnings							
Balances, 1/1/07	123,000	20,000	**20,000**	1			123,000
+ Net income	142,000	32,000	32,000				142,000
– Dividends declared	**(85,000)**	**(12,000)**			1	**12,000**	**(85,000)**
Balances, 12/31/07	180,000	40,000	52,000			12,000	180,000
Balance Sheet							
Cash	56,000	41,000					97,000
Accounts receivable	82,000	45,000					127,000
Interco. dividend receivable	**12,000**				2	**12,000**	**-0-**
Inventory	140,000	82,000					222,000
Investment in Subbco	**100,000**				1	**100,000**	**-0-**
Land	220,000	30,000					250,000
Buildings and equipment	500,000	150,000					650,000
Accumulated depreciation	(360,000)	(26,000)					(386,000)
Total Assets	750,000	322,000				112,000	960,000
Payables and accruals	160,000	90,000					250,000
Interco. dividend payable		**12,000**	**12,000**	2			**-0-**
Long-term debt	210,000	120,000					330,000
Common stock, $1 par	10,000						10,000
Additional paid-in capital	190,000						190,000
Common stock, $5 par		**5,000**	**5,000**	1			**-0-**
Additional paid-in capital		**55,000**	**55,000**	1			**-0-**
Retained earnings	180,000	40,000	52,000			12,000	180,000
Total Liabilities & Equity	750,000	322,000	124,000			12,000	960,000
Proof of debit and credit postings			*124,000*			*124,000*	

Explanation of entries:

1 The basic *elimination* entry.
2 The intercompany receivable and payable *elimination* entry.

On 5/1/05, Paxco *created* Saxco by investing $500,000 cash. Saxco reported a highly unexpected $230,000 loss for 2005. For 2006 Saxco reported a $10,000 profit, which was far below expectations. What is or could be an appropriate *carrying value* of Paxco's investment in Saxco at 12/31/06?

	Cost Method	**Equity Method**
a.	$270,000 or $500,000	$270,000
b.	$270,000 or $500,000	$280,000
c.	$280,000 or $500,000	$280,000
d.	$270,000 or $500,000	$510,000

Answer: b

IV. PRESENTING PARENT-COMPANY-ONLY STATEMENTS IN NOTES TO THE CONSOLIDATED STATEMENTS

In the United States, consolidated statements have primacy relative to parent-company-only statements. PCO statements, when presented, are usually in a condensed form in notes to the consolidated statements; they are usually presented only if required by the Securities and Exchange Commission.

Special Rules for Certain Holding Companies

Many U.S. banks and savings and loans are subsidiaries of **holding companies**. A holding company has no operations of its own—only investments in other companies that have operations. Concerning banks, federal law and bank regulations impose certain restrictions on transactions between a bank holding company and a bank subsidiary that is a federally insured depository institution.

The major restriction is that such a bank subsidiary may pay cash dividends to its parent company only if certain capital levels (as determined by the regulatory agency) are maintained. Thus a portion of a bank subsidiary's stockholders' equity (net assets) may be restricted. As discussed in Chapter 1, the SEC requires all publicly owned companies (all industries) to disclose such restrictions if the *subsidiary's restricted* net assets exceed 25% of *consolidated* net assets.

The SEC's 25% Test for Presenting Parent-Company-Only Statements

When the **restricted net assets** of all subsidiaries of a bank holding company exceed **25% of *consolidated* net assets**, the SEC's rules also require that the notes to the consolidated statements include PCO **condensed financial statements**.[7] These rules also apply to savings and loan holding companies.

The Exclusive Use of the *Equity Method*

In presenting PCO statements in the notes to the consolidated statements, bank holding companies and savings and loan holding companies report their investments in their subsidiaries using the *equity method*. Consequently, the PCO retained earnings amount and the PCO total stockholder's equity amount agree with consolidated retained earnings and consolidated total stockholders' equity amounts, respectively. Thus the statements articulate with each other.

As the accompanying International Perspective shows, PCO statements are accorded a different stature overseas.

ETHICS

Bankruptcy on the Horizon—Start Draining the Subsidiary

Poes Inc. owns 100% of the outstanding common stock of Soes Inc. Soes has a growing number of liability suits against it, which could very well force it into financial distress or bankruptcy, in which case the parent would most likely lose its entire investment. Accordingly, during the past three years, Poes had Soes pay huge cash dividends, which has reduced Soes' retained earnings from $280 million to $80 million.

Questions

1. Are creditors, existing claimants, and potential claimants being treated fairly?
2. May a subsidiary legally pay dividends to its parent right up to the time it files for bankruptcy?
3. If you were an existing supplier to Soes, would you continue to grant credit? What precautions might you take to put your company in a more secure position relative to existing and potential lawsuit claimants?

[7] Rule 9-06 of Article 9 ("Bank Holding Companies") of Regulation S-X. Even though the title of Article 9 indicates that it applies only to bank holding companies, the SEC considers it applicable to savings and loan holding companies as well.

International Perspective

Widespread Use of Parent-Company-Only Statements Overseas

In many foreign countries, PCO statements are on a level higher than or equal to the consolidated statements—but not to their exclusion. The practices for selected countries follow:

France. A full set (not condensed) of PCO statements must be published separately (not just in a note to the consolidated statements). These statements are usually included in the annual report containing the consolidated statements.

Italy. PCO statements are the statutory-required statements, whereas the consolidated statements are presented as additional disclosures to the PCO statements.

Japan. PCO statements (uncondensed) are the required statements for reporting to creditors and stockholders. Consolidated statements are supplementary.

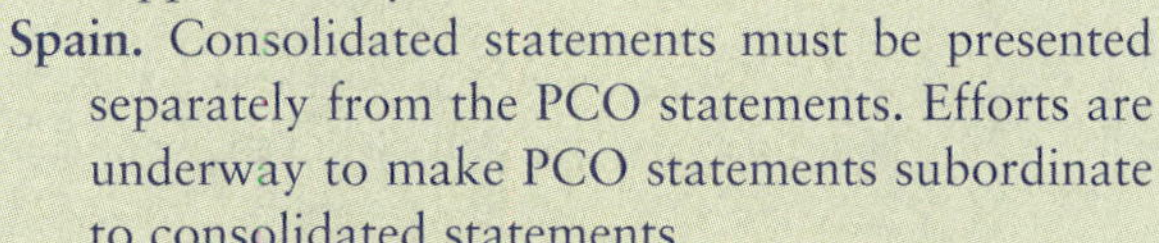

Spain. Consolidated statements must be presented separately from the PCO statements. Efforts are underway to make PCO statements subordinate to consolidated statements.

United Kingdom. At a minimum, a parent company's separate balance sheet (uncondensed) must be presented with the consolidated statements.

Why Exclusive Use of the *Equity Method*?

The SEC requires the use of the equity method because such articulation is considered essential. The use of the cost method is incongruous with the consolidated statements. Furthermore, state laws regarding dividend distributions clearly provide that they are to be based on the parent's retained earnings—*not* consolidated retained earnings. Accounting for the investment under the equity method avoids any possible confusion that investors might otherwise experience as to the amount of retained earnings available for dividend distribution.

Virtually all bank holding companies and savings and loan holding companies are publicly owned and thus are subject to the SEC's reporting requirements. Consequently, holding companies of banks and savings and loans use the equity method almost exclusively.[8] To put matters in further perspective, these publicly owned holding companies—approximately 800 banks and 250 savings and loans—control the vast majority of bank and savings and loan assets in the United States.

The SEC's Dividend Income Disclosure Rule

In presenting the PCO condensed income statement, the SEC's rules require separate display of cash dividends received from all subsidiaries. Because the *equity method* is used in the PCO condensed statements, the parent's equity interest in the **undistributed earnings** of the subsidiaries is shown on a separate line in the PCO condensed income statement.

V. The *Equity Method* of Valuing a Parent's Investment: Total Investment Loss Situations

If the *subsidiary* reports losses to the extent that it exhausts its equity and its equity becomes negative (properly called a *stockholder's deficiency*), the *parent's* Investment account is automatically

[8] Inquiries to audit partners of the Big Four accounting firms that specialize in auditing these institutions uniformly stated that the bank holding companies and the savings and loan holding companies account for these investments in the parent's books using the *equity method*—they do *not* account for them using the *cost method* and merely convert to the *equity method* for presenting PCO statements in the notes to the consolidated statements.

written down to zero when the *subsidiary's* stockholder's equity becomes *zero*. (For a real world Case in Point read about Euro Disney below.)

Unlike individuals who invest in corporate stocks, however, a parent can lose *more than* it has invested, depending on whether it has obligated itself to make additional investments in the subsidiary. Frequently, subsidiaries cannot obtain certain types of credit unless the parent will *guarantee* that indebtedness. Consequently, the parent often guarantees some or all of the debt of its subsidiaries.

The Parent *Is* Obligated to Invest Additional Funds

If the *subsidiary* has a stockholder's deficiency *and* **the parent is obligated to invest additional funds in the subsidiary** in the event that the *subsidiary* is unable to pay creditors, the *parent* must recognize a liability on its books equal to the subsidiary's stockholder's deficiency. Mechanically, rather than using a separate liability account, the parent's Investment in Subsidiary account can be allowed to become a *negative* amount, which is classified as a *liability* in the parent's separate balance sheet. The offsetting debit is recorded in the parent's income statement (using the Equity in Net Loss of Subsidiary account). **Thus *no* stoppage occurs in the application of the *equity method*.**

The Parent Is *Not* Obligated to Invest Additional Funds

If the *subsidiary* has a stockholder's deficiency and the *parent* is *not* obligated to invest additional funds, the *parent* cannot lose more than it has invested. Thus it **stops applying the *equity method*** when the Investment account balance reaches *zero*. If the *subsidiary* subsequently reports profits, the parent **waits until the subsidiary's stockholder's deficiency is eliminated before resuming application of the *equity method*.** See the following Case in Point.

Illustration 2-14 is a continuation of Illustration 2-6 for three additional years to show total investment loss situations.

CASE IN POINT

Disney Suspends Use of the Equity Method of Accounting for Euro Disney[a]

Several years ago, Walt Disney Company stopped recording Euro Disney's losses on its books since its investment in Euro Disney had been written down to zero at that point using the equity method of accounting.

[a] Although Disney is not a parent company of Euro Disney (owning only 49% of the voting shares), the principle involved is the same as when a parent company writes down to zero its investment in a subsidiary.

End-of-Chapter Review

Summary of Key Points

1. Parent companies may account for investments in subsidiaries using the **equity method** or the **cost method**—the consolidated amounts are the same regardless of which method is used.

2. Under the **cost method** (which is overly conservative), the carrying value of the investment is *not* adjusted unless the subsidiary **incurs losses** to such an extent that the carrying value of the investment is permanently **impaired**. Also, the subsidiary's **dividends** constitute the parent's **investment income**.

3. Under the **equity method**, the carrying value of the investment is automatically adjusted for the subsidiary's **economic activity** so that the Investment account balance is always in a **reciprocal relationship** with the subsidiary's equity accounts. Also, the subsidiary's **earnings are accrued** on the parent's books and constitute the parent's **investment income**.

4. A subsidiary's dividends are **not** summed with the parent's retained earnings in consolidation—they are eliminated.

ILLUSTRATION 2-14 COMPARISON OF THE EQUITY AND COST METHODS: CONTINUED FROM ILLUSTRATIONS 2-1 AND 2-6

Parent *Has* Guaranteed *All* of the Subsidiary's Debt—
***No* Temporary Discontinuance of the Equity Method**

	INVESTMENT IN SUBSIDIARY				SUBSIDIARY'S EQUITY
	COST METHOD		EQUITY METHOD		
Balances, 12/31/09 (from Illustration 2-1 on page 41 and Illustration 2-6 on page 49)	$45,000		$45,000		$ 45,000
2010 Net loss $(75,000)		$45,000[a]		75,000	(75,000)
Balances, 12/31/10	$ -0-			$30,000[b]	$(30,000)
2011 Net income—$22,000			22,000		22,000
Balances, 12/31/11	$ -0-			$ 8,000[b]	$ (8,000)
2012 Net income—$12,000			12,000		12,000
Balances, 12/31/12	$ -0-		$ 4,000		$ 4,000

[a] This assumes that the parent concluded that the recoverability of its investment was in substantial doubt, thus warranting a *permanent* write-down.

[b] This *credit* balance is classified as a liability in the parent's separate financial statements.

Parent Has *Not* Guaranteed Any of the Subsidiary's Debt—
Temporary Discontinuance of the Equity Method

	INVESTMENT IN SUBSIDIARY				SUBSIDIARY'S EQUITY
	COST METHOD		EQUITY METHOD		
Balances, 12/31/09 (from Illustration 2-1 on page 41 and Illustration 2-6 on page 49)	$45,000		$45,000		$ 45,000
2010 Net loss—$(75,000)		$45,000[a]		45,000	(75,000)
Balances, 12/31/10	$ -0-		$ -0-		$(30,000)
2011 Net income—$22,000					22,000
Balances, 12/31/11	$ -0-		$ -0-		$ (8,000)
2012 Net income—$12,000			4,000[b]		12,000
Balances, 12/31/12	$ -0-		$ 4,000		$ 4,000

[a] This assumes that the parent concluded that its recoverability of its investment was in substantial doubt, thus warranting a *permanent* write-down at this time.

[b] This amount is the difference between (1) the 2010 unrecognized loss of $(30,000) and (2) the sum of the net income reported for 2011 and 2012, which totals $34,000 ($22,000 + $12,000).

5. The subsidiary's **undistributed earnings** account for the difference between the amounts reported under the equity and cost methods for (a) the investment's carrying value and (b) the parent's retained earnings.
6. In presenting PCO statements in notes to the consolidated statements, the use of the **equity method** results in **articulation with the consolidated statements**—a result *not* achieved using the **cost method.**
7. In determining the maximum amount of dividends that can **legally be paid** under state laws, parents refer to their *own* retained earnings—which under the *equity method* is the same as the *consolidated* retained earnings.
8. Under the ***equity method*** a parent that is **obligated to invest additional funds** in a subsidiary reports a **liability to the subsidiary** to the extent that the subsidiary has a stockholder's **deficiency.**

Glossary of New Terms

Cost method A method of accounting for certain common stock investments whereby the *carrying value* of the investment is *never* changed unless it is believed to be *permanently* impaired (or *liquidating dividends* occurs, as discussed in Chapter 6). The only income reported on the investment is from dividends declared by the subsidiary.

Equity method A method of accounting for certain common stock investments whereby the *carrying value* of the investment is adjusted for the subsidiary's earnings, losses, and dividends.

Assignment Material

Review Questions

1. What are the general rules for valuing all corporate investments in common stocks?
2. What is the *general idea* of the *equity method*? The *cost method*?
3. To what is the *equity method* analogous? The *cost method*?
4. What *income statement* account is used under the *equity method*? The *cost method*?
5. How are *dividends* treated under the *equity method*? The *cost method*?
6. Does a subsidiary's *dividend declaration* or *actual dividend payment* impact the carrying value of the investment under the *equity method*? The *cost method*?
7. Does a subsidiary's *dividend declaration* or *actual dividend payment* impact the parent's retained earnings under the *equity method*? The *cost method*?
8. Why must the consolidated amounts be the *same* regardless of whether the parent uses the *equity method* or the *cost method*?
9. Can a parent lose *more* than it has invested in a subsidiary? Explain.
10. Can a parent's investment account be *written back up* after it has been written down?
11. Why are a subsidiary's dividends *not* reported in the consolidated statement of retained earnings?
12. What are the two *built-in checking features* under the *equity method*?
13. What are the *advantages* of the *equity method*? The *cost method*?
14. Would it be a good idea for the FASB to require the use of *only* the *equity method* or the *cost method* (and to eliminate the other method)? Why?
15. Does the IRS use either the *equity method* or the *cost method*? Explain.
16. How are PCO *statements* generally presented when required by the SEC?
17. What are some of the *detailed disclosures* the SEC requires in PCO income statements?
18. Legally, is the maximum amount of dividends that a parent can pay determined by referring to the *parent's* retained earnings or the *consolidated* retained earnings?
19. If a parent has *discontinued* applying the *equity method* because of the subsidiary's losses, when would it start applying the *equity method* again?
20. How is a *negative balance* in the parent's Investment account reported in the parent's separate balance sheet? Why?

Exercises

E 2-1 **Investment Valuation: Cost or Equity** On 6/1/05, Pyco created Syco by investing $300,000 cash. Syco reported the following items:

	Net Income (Loss)	Dividends Declared
2005	$ 45,000	$15,000
2006	(60,000)	20,000[a]

[a] Paid in the first quarter of 2006 (which was profitable).

Required What is the investment's carrying value at 12/31/06 under the *cost method*? Under the *equity method*?

E 2-2 **Journal Entries: Cost or Equity** A 100%-owned subsidiary reported the following amounts:

	Net Income (Loss)	Dividends Declared
2005	$140,000	$80,000[a]
2006	(90,000)	–0–

[a] Of this amount, $60,000 was paid in 2005 and $20,000 was paid in early 2006.

Required What are the general ledger entries for 2005 and 2006 under the *cost method*? The *equity method*?

E 2-3 **Conceptualizing Consolidated Amounts** For 2005, a parent and subsidiary reported the following amounts from their own *separate* operations:

	Parent[a]	Subsidiary
Net income	$200,000	$50,000
Dividends declared	140,000	30,000[b]

[a] Excludes earnings and dividends relating to subsidiary.

[b] Of this amount, $20,000 was paid in 2005 and $10,000 was paid on 1/2/06.

Required
1. What is the consolidated net income for 2005?
2. What amount is reported as dividends in the 2005 consolidated statement of retained earnings?

E 2-4 **Consolidated Dividends** During 2005, Pixcor declared dividends of $100,000, and its 100%-owned subsidiary, Sixcor, declared dividends of $40,000 ($30,000 was paid in 2005 and $10,000 was paid on 1/1/06).

Required What amount is reported as dividends in the consolidated statement of retained earnings for 2005? Why?

E 2-5 **Consolidation Entries: Cost or Equity** Pelco created Selco, a 100%-owned subsidiary, several years ago. For 2005, Selco reported net income of $80,000 and declared and paid cash dividends of $50,000. At 12/31/05, Selco's equity accounts were as follows:

Common stock	$100,000
Additional paid-in capital	400,000
Retained earnings	240,000

Required
1. What entry(ies) was (were) made in consolidation at the end of 2005 if Pelco uses the *cost method*?
2. Repeat requirement 1 but assume the use of the *equity method*.

E 2-6 **Investment Valuation: Cost or Equity—All Debt Guaranteed** On 4/1/05, Pote Inc. formed Sote Inc. by investing $600,000 cash. Pote guaranteed *all* of Sote's debt. Sote reported the following items:

	Net Income (Loss)	Dividends Declared
2005	$(650,000)	$ -0-
2006	770,000	40,000[a]

[a] Paid on 1/3/07.

At 12/31/05, Pote doubted that it could recover but $200,000 of its initial investment.

Required
1. What is the investment's carrying value at 12/31/05 and 2006 under the *cost method*? The *equity method*?
2. What amount did Pote report in its income statement for each year?

E 2-7 **Investment Valuation: Equity or Cost—No Debt Guaranteed** Use the information in Exercise 2-6, but assume that Pote has guaranteed *none* of Sote's debt.

E 2-8 **Investment Valuation: Cost or Equity—Some Debt Guaranteed** On 5/1/07, Potu Inc. created Sotu Inc. by investing $100,000 cash. Potu has guaranteed $50,000 of Sotu's debt. Sotu subsequently reported the following items:

	Net Income (Loss)	Dividends Declared
2007	$(160,000)	$ -0-
2008	290,000	40,000[a]

[a] Of this amount, $25,000 was paid in 2008 and $15,000 was paid on 1/2/09.

At 12/31/07, Potu seriously doubted that it could recover but $30,000 of its initial investment.

Required
1. What is the investment's carrying value at 12/31/07 and 12/31/08 under the *cost method*? The *equity method*?
2. How much did the parent report in its income statement for each year?

E 2-9 **(Module 1 only) Mini Review: Consolidation (no worksheet): *Cost Method*** The following six accounts appear on the *separate company financial statements* (as opposed to a *trial balance*) of Partex and its 100%-owned subsidiary, Sartex (created in 2001), at the end of 2007:

	Partex	Sartex
Dividend income (from Sartex)	$ 40,000	
Investment in subsidiary	200,000	
Common stock	100,000	$ 20,000
Additional paid-in capital	400,000	180,000
Retained earnings	660,000	90,000
Dividends declared	(123,000)	(40,000)
Additional information:		
Retained earnings at 1/1/07	$ 610,000	$ 144,000

Required
1. What consolidation entries are required at 12/31/07?
2. What is the consolidated retained earnings amount at 12/31/07?
3. What amount is reported as dividends in the consolidated statement of retained earnings for 2007?
4. What is the subsidiary's net income for 2007?

E 2-10 **(Module 2 only) Mini Review: Consolidation (no worksheet): *Equity Method*** The following six accounts appear on the *separate company financial statements* (as opposed to a *trial balance*) of a parent and its 100%-owned subsidiary (created in 2001) at the end of 2007:

	Paymor	Saymor
Equity in net income (of subsidiary)	$ 33,000	
Investment in subsidiary	480,000	
Common stock	50,000	$ 10,000
Additional paid-in capital	250,000	340,000
Retained earnings	550,000	130,000
Dividends declared	(64,000)	(11,000)
Additional information:		
Retained earnings at 1/1/07	$494,000	

Required

1. What consolidation entries are required at 12/31/07?
2. What is the consolidated retained earnings amount at 12/31/07?
3. What amount is reported as dividends in the consolidated statement of retained earnings for 2007?
4. What is the consolidated net income for 2007?

Problems

P 2-1* **(Module 1 only) Consolidation Worksheet: *Cost Method*** The comparative financial statements of Pane Inc. and its 100%-owned subsidiary, Sill Inc. (created six years ago), follow:

	Pane Inc.		
	Cost Method[a]	Equity Method[b]	Sill Inc.
Income Statement (2006)			
Sales	$ 400,000	$ 400,000	$ 225,000
Cost of sales	(210,000)	(210,000)	(120,000)
Expenses	(140,000)	(140,000)	(80,000)
Dividend income (from Sill)	20,000		
Equity in net income (of Sill)		25,000	
Net Income	$ 70,000	$ 75,000	$ 25,000
Statement of Retained Earnings			
Balances, 1/1/06	$ 150,000	$ 205,000	$ 55,000
+ Net income	70,000	75,000	25,000
– Dividends declared	(40,000)	(40,000)	(20,000)
Balances, 12/31/06	$ 180,000	$ 240,000	$ 60,000
Balance Sheet (as of 12/31/06)			
Cash	$ 35,000	$ 35,000	$ 30,000
Accounts receivable, net	65,000	65,000	45,000
Intercompany receivable	15,000	15,000	
Inventory	190,000	190,000	70,000
Investment in subsidiary	50,000	110,000	
Property and equipment	370,000	370,000	180,000
Accumulated depreciation	(160,000)	(160,000)	(40,000)
Total Assets	$ 565,000	$ 625,000	$ 285,000
Payables and accruals	$ 135,000	$ 135,000	$ 70,000
Intercompany payable			15,000
Long-term debt	150,000	150,000	90,000
Common stock	100,000	100,000	50,000
Retained earnings	180,000	240,000	60,000
Total Liabilities and Equity	$ 565,000	$ 625,000	$ 285,000

[a] Use this column for working the problem under the *cost method,* as called for in this problem.

[b] Use this column for working the problem under the *equity method,* as called for in Problem 2-2.

Required

1. Prepare all consolidation entries as of 12/31/06.

*The financial statement information presented for problems accompanied by asterisks is also provided on Model 2 (filename: MODEL02) at the http://pahler.swlearning.com website, allowing the problem to be worked on the computer.

2. Prepare a consolidation worksheet at 12/31/06.
3. What is the maximum *additional* cash dividend the parent can declare ($180,000 or $240,000) if cash were available?

P 2-2* **(Module 2 only) Consolidation Worksheet:** ***Equity Method*** Use the information provided in Problem 2-1 but assume that the parent uses the *equity method.*

Required

1. Analyze the parent's Investment account for 2006 (work backward to do so).
2. Prepare all consolidation entries as of 12/31/06.
3. Prepare a consolidation worksheet at 12/31/06.

P 2-3* **(Module 1 only) Consolidation Worksheet:** ***Cost Method*** The comparative financial statements of Pylo Inc. and its 100%-owned subsidiary, Sylo Inc. (created seven years ago), follow:

	Pylo Inc.		
	Cost Method[a]	**Equity Method**[b]	**Sylo Inc.**
Income Statement (2006)			
Sales	$ 700,000	$ 700,000	$ 250,000
Cost of sales	(430,000)	(430,000)	(130,000)
Expenses	(170,000)	(170,000)	(90,000)
Dividend income (from Sylo)	10,000		
Equity in net income (of Sylo)		30,000	
Net Income	$ 110,000	$ 130,000	$ 30,000
Balance Sheet (as of 12/31/06)			
Cash	$ 45,000	$ 45,000	$ 40,000
Accounts receivable, net	95,000	95,000	55,000
Inventory	170,000	170,000	75,000
Investment in subsidiary	50,000	130,000	
Property and equipment	280,000	280,000	175,000
Accumulated depreciation	(120,000)	(120,000)	(25,000)
Total Assets	$ 520,000	$ 600,000	$ 320,000
Payables and accruals	$ 140,000	$ 140,000	$ 70,000
Long-term debt	300,000	300,000	120,000
Common stock	10,000	10,000	50,000
Retained earnings	70,000	150,000	80,000
Total Liabilities and Equity	$ 520,000	$ 600,000	$ 320,000
Dividends declared in 2006	$ 90,000	$ 90,000	$ 10,000

[a] Use this column for working the problem under the cost method, as called for in this problem.
[b] Use this column for working the problem under the equity method, as called for in Problem 2-4.

Required

1. Prepare all consolidation entries as of 12/31/06.
2. Prepare a consolidation worksheet at 12/31/06.
3. What is the maximum dividend the parent can declare ($70,000 or $150,000) if cash were available?

P 2-4* **(Module 2 only) Consolidation Worksheet:** ***Equity Method*** Use the information provided in Problem 2-3 but assume that the parent uses the *equity method.*

1. Analyze the parent's Investment account for 2006 (work backward to do so).
2. Prepare all consolidation entries as of 12/31/06.
3. Prepare a consolidation worksheet at 12/31/06.

P 2-5 **Consolidation Worksheet: Equity Method**

Parrco and Subbco
Consolidation Worksheet as of December 31, 2006
(Subbco's *fourth year* of operations)

	PARRCO	SUBBCO	CONSOLIDATION ENTRIES DR.	CONSOLIDATION ENTRIES CR.	CONSOLIDATED
Income Statement					
Sales	600,000	240,000			840,000
Cost of sales	(360,000)	(110,000)			(470,000)
Expenses	(190,000)	(100,000)			(290,000)
	,000				,000
Net Income	,000	30,000			,000
Statement of Retained Earnings					
Balances, 1/1/06	,000				,000
+ Net income	,000	30,000			,000
– Dividends declared	(40,000)	(10,000)			,000
Balances, 12/31/06	,000	,000			,000
Balance Sheet					
Cash	60,000	15,000			75,000
Accounts receivable	70,000	37,000			107,000
Interco. dividend rec.	10,000				,000
Inventory	110,000	55,000			165,000
Investment in Subbco	,000				,000
Land	220,000	36,000			256,000
Buildings and equipment	500,000	150,000			650,000
Accumulated depreciation	(320,000)	(13,000)			(333,000)
Total Assets	,000	280,000		,000	,000
Payables and accruals	230,000	20,000			250,000
Interco. dividend pay.		10,000			,000
Long-term debt	150,000	80,000			230,000
Common stock, no par	200,000				200,000
Common stock, $1 par		5,000			,000
Additional paid-in capital		55,000			,000
Retained earnings	,000	110,000			,000
Total Liabilities & Equity	,000	280,000	,000	,000	,000
Proof of debit and credit postings			*,000*	*,000*	

Explanation of entries:

Required Complete the worksheet assuming that the parent uses the *equity method.*

P 2-6 **Comprehensive Review: Consolidation Entries—*Cost Method and Conversion to Equity Method*** The following accounts are as they appear on the *separate company financial statements* of Pifo Inc. and its 100%-owned subsidiary, Sifo Inc. (created in 2001), at *the end of 2006:*

	Pifo Inc.	Sifo Inc.
Dividend income (from Sifo)	$ 14,000	
Dividends receivable	7,000	
Investment in subsidiary	200,000	
Dividends payable	30,000	$ 7,000
Common stock	50,000	30,000
Additional paid-in capital	450,000	170,000
Retained earnings	330,000	51,000
Dividends declared	(120,000)	(14,000)
Additional information:		
Reported net income (loss) for 2006	$ 150,000	$(23,000)

Required

1. What consolidation entries, given these data, are required at the end of 2006?
2. What is the consolidated net income amount?
3. What did the parent earn from its own separate operations?
4. What is the consolidated retained earnings amount?
5. What amount is reported as dividends in the consolidated statement of retained earnings for 2006?

(Requirements 6, 7, and 8 can be assigned if both modules are covered.)

6. If Pifo used the *equity method* instead of the *cost method,* what would be its retained earnings balance at the end of 2006?
7. What *general ledger* entry would the parent make at 12/31/06 to convert to the *equity method*? **Guidance:** First try to make the entry to convert the balance sheet only; then try the entry that converts all three financial statements.
8. If Pifo used the *equity method* instead of the *cost method,* what consolidation entries would it make at the end of 2006?

P 2-7 **Comprehensive Review: Consolidation Entries—*Equity Method* and Conversion to *Cost Method*** The following accounts are as they appear on the *separate company financial statements* of Pufa Inc. and its 100%-owned subsidiary, Sufa Inc. (created in 2001), at *the end of 2006:*

	Pufa Inc.	Sufa Inc.
Equity in net loss of subsidiary	$ (49,000)	
Dividends receivable	6,000	
Investment in subsidiary	660,000	
Dividends payable	20,000	$ 6,000
Common stock	300,000	20,000
Additional paid-in capital	100,000	380,000
Retained earnings	500,000	260,000
Dividends declared	(80,000)	(24,000)
Additional information:		
Retained earnings at 1/1/06	$400,000	

Required

1. What consolidation entries, given these data, are required at the end of 2006?
2. What is the consolidated net income amount?
3. What did the parent earn from its own separate operations?
4. What is the consolidated retained earnings amount?
5. What amount is reported as dividends in the consolidated statement of retained earnings for 2006?

(Requirements 6, 7, and 8 can be assigned if both modules are covered.)

6. If Pufa used the *cost method* instead of the *equity method,* what would be its retained earnings balance at the end of 2006?
7. What *general ledger* entry would the parent make at 12/31/06 to convert to the *cost method*? **Guidance:** First try to make the entry to convert the balance sheet only; then try the entry that converts all three financial statements.
8. If the parent used the *cost method* instead of the *equity method,* what consolidation entries would it make at the end of 2006?

Spreadsheet Integration Problem

P 2-8 **Creating a Consolidation Template and Two Keystroke Macros (Stored Instructions)** Employers expect accounting graduates to be able to (1) create accounting models containing macros and (2) use models created by others. Accordingly, this assignment gives you programming experience in (1) creating a model and (2) creating two specific keystroke macros (stored instructions that can be automatically executed instantly at the touch of a key). These two macros are highly useful in reviewing a newly created model to detect bugs in programmed formulas.

You should use one of the leading spreadsheet programs such as EXCEL or Lotus 1-2-3. Refer to an EXCEL or Lotus 1-2-3 manual for particulars about creating and naming macros (so that you can execute your macros by pressing a letter of the alphabet after holding down either the Control key or the Alt key, depending on which spreadsheet program you use).

Required

1. Prepare a consolidation model (complete with formulas) for the trial balance consolidation worksheet shown in Appendix 2A. Use an appropriate format (such as the "Accounting" format of EXCEL) with zero decimal places. You may abbreviate account descriptions and omit the *vertical* lines. To code your consolidation entries, program a three-character-wide column immediately to the *right* of the Debit column; do likewise for the Credit column. Program formulas in the Income Statement column as well as the Balance Sheet and Retained Earnings columns. (All amounts in the Debit and Credit columns must be **"absolute"**—no amounts can be shown in *parentheses.*)
2. Program a keystroke macro (a stored instruction) to convert your model from your, selected format to a format that will display your formulas (**Excel: Tools, Options, View Formulas, OK**). Include in this macro instructions to change column widths as necessary to fully display the formulas you programmed.
3. Program a macro to *reverse* the macro you programmed in requirement 2 (to go back to your selected format).
4. Program a logic formula (=IF function for EXCEL and @IF function for Lotus 1-2-3) for (a) the cell containing the $142,000 balancing debit in the Income Statement Debit column and (b) the cell to its immediate right. Thus your model must be able to accommodate a loss situation (in which you now balance in the *Credit* column instead of the *Debit* column. (To test this second logic formula, create a *loss* by *decreasing* the parent's Sales account by $200,000 to see whether you are now balancing in the Credit column with a $58,000 amount.) To create your logic function using EXCEL, use the **Insert, Function** [or the *fx* icon on the standard tool bar]. *Single* click on **Logical** (top of dialog box in Office 2000). Then *double click* on **If** (bottom portion of dialog box in Office 2000). Then follow the prompts (be sure to press the **OK** button when you are done). Note that an IF logic function has *three* parts (*commas* separate the three parts in the formula): (1) an argument concerning a *condition,* (2) a command to insert a defined amount (or zero) if the condition is *true*, and (3) a command to insert a defined amount (or zero) if the condition is *false*. An example of an IF logic formula is as follows: IF(K40>J40, K40–J40,0).
5. Program either a logic function or a formula in the Retained Earnings column so that the $142,000 net income in the income statement is extended to the Retained Earnings column. (This logic function or formula should also be able to accommodate a *loss* situation—a *loss* amount must appear in the Retained Earnings column *in parentheses.*) Accordingly, check out your solution as you did in requirement 4.
6. **Printing instructions.** *First*, print a copy of your model (in *landscape* layout—not *picture* layout) that does *not* display any formulas. *Second*, print a copy of your model (in *landscape* layout) that *does* display the formulas (first use the **File, Page Setup, Sheets**, place X in box command, so that your Excel column letters and row numbers are printed [enables your formulas and logic functions to be verified]). Third, print out your recorded macro instructions in Visual Basic Language (use the *Edit* command).

THINKING CRITICALLY

Cases

C 2-1 **My Goodness: *Not* Disclosing an Accounting Method!** The notes to the consolidated statements do *not* disclose the parent's manner of accounting for its investments in its numerous subsidiaries, *all* of which are consolidated.

Required

1. Should the company's outside auditors mention this omission in their audit report or qualify their opinion on the consolidated statements?
2. Would your answer change if the parent had changed its method of accounting for its investment?

C 2-2 ***Cost Method:* Assessing Impairment of Value: Time to Bite the Bullet?** Sebco, a 100%-owned created subsidiary of Pebco, has *total* stockholder's equity of $300,000, which is $200,000 below the parent's *initial* capital investment of $500,000. Pebco uses the *cost method* to account for its investment in Sebco.

Required How would you go about assessing whether an impairment in value has occurred and whether a write-down is appropriate? In the absence of an outright offer from a potential buyer, what analysis would you perform to support an assumption or contention that the subsidiary probably could be sold to a willing buyer for at least $500,000?

C 2-3 ***Cost Method:* Maybe the Parent Can Write Its Investment Back Up!** Ponn Inc. owns 100% of Sonn's outstanding common stock. In 2006, Ponn, which uses the *cost method,* wrote down to zero its $1,000,000 investment in Sonn because of Sonn's severe ongoing concern problems. In 2007, Sonn had a remarkable recovery, and its stockholder's equity at the end of 2007 was $1,500,000. Ponn now wishes to write the investment *back up* to $1,000,000.

Required

1. Under what circumstances, if any, could Ponn write the investment back up to its original cost of $1,000,000 and still comply with GAAP?
2. What account did the parent *debit* when it wrote the investment *down* to zero? What account would the parent *credit* to write the investment *back up* to $1,000,000?
3. Can you think of two ways that would result in the Investment account being valued at $1,500,000 in accordance with GAAP?

C 2-4 ***Cost Method:* Reformatting the Consolidation Worksheet So That Consolidation Entries Are Unnecessary** Accountants often find shortcuts to save time and therefore accomplish tasks in a more efficient manner. The *cost method* lends itself to such a shortcut.

Required Reformat the accounts on the consolidation worksheet (*cost method* used by the parent) in Illustration 2-5 so that it is *not* necessary to post to the consolidation worksheet either (1) the *basic* elimination entry or (2) the *intercompany dividend* elimination entry.

C 2-5 ***Equity Method:* Reformatting the Consolidation Worksheet So That Elimination Entries Are Unnecessary**

Required Perform Case 2-4 but for the *equity method* rather than the *cost method*—use Illustration 2-13.

C 2-6 **Do We Need Both Valuation Methods?** Because the parent's investment is eliminated in consolidation, it would appear that no sound reason exists for allowing use of both the *cost method* and the *equity method.*

Required Why doesn't the FASB eliminate one of these two methods?

C 2-7 **Spin Away** Paxco spun off its wholly owned subsidiary, Saxco, by distributing the Saxco stock it owned to Paxco's shareholders. At the time, Paxco's investment had a *carrying value* of $3 million and a *fair value* of $1 million.

Required What is the parent's general ledger entry?

C 2-8 **Theory Review: "Give Me 10"** Ten valuation bases exist in accounting.

Required

1. Can you name the 10 valuation bases?
2. Can you give an example of an asset or liability for each valuation basis?

C 2-9 **Investee's Ownership in Investor's Stock Which Has Appreciated in Value** Penron (publicly owned) owns (1) 25% of the common stock of a Talrex and (2) 100% of the common stock of

Senron. Each investee company purchased common stock of Penron at the beginning of the current year. By year-end, each investee company had a $100,000 unrealized gain (reported in earnings) as a result of the increase in the market price of Penron's common stock during the year. Penron uses the *equity method* for both of these investments.

Required

1. How should the 25%-owned entity's gain impact Penron's income statement for the year? *(The solution manual explains what Enron did in this situation.)*
2. How should the 100%-owned subsidiary's gain be reported in consolidation?

Financial Analysis Problems

FAP 2-1 **How Much Can the Parent Legally Pay in Cash Dividends?** Selected account balances at 12/31/06 for Pitticorp and its 100%-owned banking subsidiary, Sittibank, are as follows:

	Pitticorp	Sittibank	Consolidated
Cash	$300,000	$250,000	$550,000
Investment in Sittibank (under the equity method)	440,000		
Retained earnings	500,000	400,000	500,000

Required

1. How much of a cash dividend could Pitticorp legally declare on its outstanding common stock?
2. Repeat requirement 1 but first revise the amounts given to reflect use of the *cost method* instead of the equity method.
3. Repeat requirement 1 but also assume that federal bank regulators have imposed *upstream* cash transfer restrictions that prevent Sittibank from paying any dividends until its stockholder's equity has become a much higher percentage of total assets.
4. What disclosure should be made in the consolidated statements regarding intercompany upstream cash transfer restrictions by the banking regulators? What purpose would it serve?
5. If the parent had $1,000,000 in cash instead of $300,000, do you think the disclosure in requirement 4 would still be needed? Why or why not?

FAP 2-2 **How Much Did the Parent Really Earn on Its Investment?** Presto Inc. created Seco Inc. on 1/1/06 by investing $1,000,000 cash. Information regarding Seco follows:

	Net Income	Dividends Declared
2006	$200,000	$ -0-
2007	300,000	400,000
2008	330,000	130,000

Seco's earnings occurred evenly throughout each year except for 2007 when $250,000 of income was earned in the *first* six months. Seco's dividends were declared and paid at the *end* of each year.

Required

1. What is the parent's annual return on investment (AROI) for each year under the *equity method*? Use the *beginning* investment balances for this requirement—*not* the *average* balances.
2. Repeat requirement 1 but use the *cost method.*
3. Which method depicts the parent's *true* annual return on investment for 2007? Why?
4. Calculate the AROI *internal rate of return* (IRR). What assumption must you make to do so?
5. Repeat the AROI calculation for 2007 under the *equity method* but assume that $200,000 of the dividends was declared and paid on 1/1/07 and $200,000 was declared and paid on 12/31/07.
6. Repeat the calculation for 2007 under the *equity method* but assume that the entire $400,000 of dividends was declared and paid on 6/30/07.
7. Repeat the calculation for 2006 under the *equity method* using the average investment balance. Is the correct annual return on investment this percentage or the percentage in requirement 1? Why?

FAP 2-3 ***Cost Method:* Reporting the Sale of a Subsidiary Can Be Tricky!** On 4/1/06, Parba Inc. sold its 100%-owned subsidiary, Sarba Inc., for $700,000 cash. Sarba, which was created on 1/1/04 with Parba's $1,000,000 equity investment, reported the following results of operations since inception:

		Net Loss
2004		$ (22,000)
2005		(78,000)
		$(100,000)
2006 (1/1 through 3/31):		
Sales	$ 400,000	
Costs and expenses	(510,000)	(110,000)
		$(210,000)

Parba used the *cost method* and had *never* written down in value the cost of its investment. Sarba, which was in the same line of business as Parba, has always been consolidated.

Required

1. What is Parba's entry to record Sarba's sale?
2. What amount should be reported for the loss on the sale of Sarba in Parba's 2006 financial statements customarily sent to stockholders?
3. Would this loss be reported as a loss on discontinued operations? Why or why not?
4. What consolidation entry, if any, should be made at 12/31/06 relating to Sarba?

Personal Situations: Ethics and Interpersonal Skills

PS 2-1 **Interpersonal Skills: Who Is Right?** You are having a dispute with your supervisor, with whom you have a significant personality conflict, as to the proper way to apply the *equity method* of accounting.

Required In resolving this issue, what is far more important than *who* is right?

chapter

3

Partially Owned Created Subsidiaries and Variable Interest Entities

There is only one good and that is knowledge.
There is only one evil and that is ignorance.
ARISTOTLE

LEARNING OBJECTIVES

To Understand

> The various concepts that exist for dealing with a noncontrolling interest.
> The way to handle a noncontrolling interest in preparing consolidated statements.
> The way to value a parent's Investment account when a *wholly owned* or *partially owned* subsidiary is *not* consolidated.
> The way to control an entity *other than* by owning a majority voting interest.
> The way earnings of *domestic* groups are taxed.

TOPIC OUTLINE

I. Consolidation Methods for Partially Owned Created Subsidiaries
INTERNATIONAL PERSPECTIVE: *Manner of Presenting the Noncontrolling Interest in the Balance Sheet in Foreign Countries*
II. Unconsolidated Subsidiaries
III. Consolidation of Variable Interest Entities (VIEs) (no majority voting ownership exists)
APPENDIX 3A: The Cost Method
APPENDIX 3B: Consolidated U.S. Income Taxes: Domestic Subsidiaries Only

Appendices can be found at http://www.pahler.swlearning.com

CHAPTER OVERVIEW

In partial ownership situations (which occur less frequently than 100% ownership situations), the voting shares *not* owned by the parent are referred to formally as the **noncontrolling interest.** (In practice, these small owners are usually referred to collectively as the *minority interest.*)

This chapter discusses the basic issues associated with reflecting a noncontrolling interest in a subsidiary in the consolidated statements. Additional, more complex issues arise when one entity "acquires" (in a business combination) a majority voting interest in another entity; we discuss these issues in Chapter 6. For brevity, we hereafter use the abbreviation **NCI** for *noncontrolling interest* in most instances and **CI** for *controlling interest* in limited instances.

Occasionally, consolidating a subsidiary is no longer appropriate, which raises the issue of how to value the parent's Investment account in the statements that it issues to its stockholders (its *general-purpose financial statements*). Such statements could be either (1) parent-company-only statements (when the parent has only one subsidiary) or (2) consolidated statements (when other subsidiaries exist and *are* consolidated). Accordingly, we discuss when the parent may use (1) the *equity method,* (2) the *cost method,* and (3) the *fair value* (market value) *method.*

Beginning in the early 1980s, a very small number of companies designed novel ways to justify *not* consolidating entities that substantively were subsidiaries. We address (1) the *substance* versus *form* aspects of these situations and (2) the ways the Financial Accounting Standards Board (FASB) has responded to this *effective* versus *legal* control issue.

Creating a subsidiary raises an issue as to whether the investment income recorded on the parent's books relating to the subsidiary (the Equity in Net Income account under the *equity method* or the Dividend Income account under the *cost method*) will be taxed at the parent level. The *cost method* is discussed in Appendix 3A of this chapter.

The financial statement implications of this tax issue for *domestic* subsidiaries, which we discuss in this chapter's Appendix 3B, represent a relatively simple area. This tax issue for *foreign* subsidiaries, which we discuss in Appendix 16A, is a much more involved area.

I. Consolidation Methods for Partially Owned Created Subsidiaries

Many reasons exist as to why a subsidiary is *not* 100% owned. Recall from Chapter 1, for instance, that some foreign countries require local citizens to own a percentage of a foreign company's subsidiary. Another instance is when a parent sells a portion of its common stock holdings in a subsidiary to obtain needed cash.

CASE IN POINT

Sears, Roebuck and Co. had its 100%-owned Allstate Corporation subsidiary complete a primary initial public offering of 19.9% of the Allstate common shares held by Sears. This partial disposal a few years ago raised $2.29 billion of needed cash for Sears. It also increased the Noncontrolling Interest account in Sears' consolidated balance sheet from $300 million to $2.3 billion.

Conceptual Issues

When a subsidiary is partially owned, two basic issues arise:

1. **Whether to report the NCI:** Should the noncontrolling interest (NCI) in the subsidiary's net assets and net income be reported in the consolidated statements? The debate concerns the use of (1) the **full consolidation** method (using 100% of the subsidiary's account balances) or (2) the **proportional consolidation** method (using, say, 75% of the subsidiary's account balances).

2. **How to report the NCI:** If the NCI is presented in the consolidated statements (as it does only under *full consolidation*), how should it be reported? Several conceptual treatments exist.

Conceptual Issue 1: Proportional or Full Consolidation?

Proportional Consolidation (*Not* Permitted under GAAP)

Under the **proportional consolidation concept**, the parent consolidates only its ownership in each of the items in the subsidiary's financial statements. In other words, for a 75%-owned subsidiary, we multiply the cash, accounts receivable, sales, and so forth by 75% to arrive at the amounts to include in the consolidation. Under this method, accounting for the NCI in the consolidated statements is *not* necessary because it is *not* reported there. The rationale underlying *proportional consolidation* is summarized as follows:

1. The consolidated statements should be merely an extension of the parent's statements.
2. In *substance* (although not as a *legality*), the parent has a percentage interest in each of the subsidiary's assets, liabilities, revenues, costs and expenses, gains, and losses.

In recent years, *proportional consolidation* has become one of several methods to account for investments in real estate partnerships and construction joint ventures. Moreover, it has been advocated increasingly for consolidated statements.[1] However, proportional consolidation has never been permitted in the United States—only *full consolidation* is allowed.

Full Consolidation (Required under GAAP)

Under the *full consolidation method*, the parent consolidates the entire amount of each of the subsidiary's individual asset, liability, and income statement accounts with those of the parent company. Because the subsidiary is only partially owned, however, the additional amounts consolidated constitute the NCI. Therefore, the NCI in (1) the subsidiary's net assets (Assets – Liabilities) and (2) the subsidiary's net income are both *reported as separate items in the consolidated statements*. The rationale underlying *full consolidation* is summarized as follows:

1. Legally, the parent does *not* have a separable percentage in each individual asset, liability, and income statement account of the subsidiary. Its ownership interest is a percentage of the net assets and net income *as a whole*.
2. The parent controls *all* of the subsidiary even though its ownership is less than 100%.
3. The purpose of consolidated statements is to present financial information *as if* the parent and the subsidiary were a single company.

Conceptual Issue 2: Manner of Reporting the NCI under Full Consolidation

Two concepts exist for reporting the NCI in the consolidated statements under the full consolidation method: (1) the **parent company concept** and (2) the **economic unit concept.**[2] We now discuss both of these concepts.

Current GAAP

The current accounting consolidation rules (*Accounting Research Bulletin No. 51* as modified by FASB *Statement No. 94*) permit use of either (1) the *parent company concept* or (2) the "nonpure" form of the *economic unit concept* (in which amounts are *not* imputed for goodwill identifiable

---

[1] Perhaps the strongest argument in favor of proportional consolidation is proposed by Harold Bierman, Jr., "Proportionate Consolidation and Financial Analysis," *Accounting Horizons*, December 1992, pp. 5–17.

[2] Prior to 1991, these concepts were referred to in the accounting literature as *theories*. Furthermore, the *economic unit concept* was called the *entity theory*. In this chapter, we use the same terminology used in the applicable FASB documents issued in the 1990s, which is more accurate and descriptive.

with the noncontrolling interest when a subsidiary has been acquired). Both of these concepts pertain to **consolidation *procedures*—**not **consolidation *policies*.**

The Parent Company Concept

Under the *parent company concept*, consolidated reporting is merely a different manner of reporting the parent's financial position and results of operations. Accordingly, the **reporting format emphasizes the interests of the controlling shareholders** (the parent's shareholders).

For the balance sheet, the subsidiary's assets and liabilities are viewed as **merely being substituted** for the parent's Investment in Subsidiary account. Consequently, the stockholders' equity in the *parent-company-only statements* is also the stockholders' equity in the *consolidated statements*. For the income statement, the subsidiary's sales, costs and expenses, gains, and losses are viewed as merely being substituted for the parent's investment income reported in the parent's income statement.

The purpose of these multiline substitutions for the single-line items in the parent's balance sheet and the parent's income statement is to make the parent's financial statements more informative to the parent's stockholders. Therefore, the NCI is presented in the consolidated statements in a somewhat suppressed manner as follows:

1. **In the consolidated balance sheet (*outside* equity).** The NCI in the subsidiary's net assets is treated as an outside interest and is shown *outside* the stockholders' equity section—**in the aggregate**—in one of the following two ways:
   a. **Between liabilities and stockholders' equity.** This presentation reflects the unique nature of the NCI. It is an equity interest but not of the parent company, which is the reporting entity.
   b. **Among liabilities.** This presentation has little or no supporting theory. If the NCI is insignificant and a separate classification is unwarranted, however, this classification is used.
2. **In the consolidated income statement.** The NCI in the subsidiary's net income is shown as a *deduction* in the consolidated income statement in arriving at the consolidated net income. For example, assuming that a 75%-owned subsidiary had net income of $32,000 for the year, the NCI deduction is $8,000 (25% of $32,000) and is presented as follows:

	Consolidated Income Statement
Sales	$ 992,000
Cost of sales	(520,000)
Expenses	(330,000)
NCI in net income	(8,000)[a]
Net Income (consolidated)	$ 134,000

[a] Theoretically, the NCI amount should be reported as a separate line item in the income statement (*below* income tax expense). If the NCI amount is insignificant, however, companies usually lump the NCI amount in with *operating expenses* or *other income and expense* (both of which are shown *above* income tax expense).

3. **In the consolidated statement of changes in stockholders' equity.** Because the NCI is presented *outside* the equity section in the consolidated balance sheet, **all amounts in the consolidated statement of changes in stockholders' equity pertain solely to the controlling interests.**

The Economic Unit Concept

Under the *economic unit concept*, consolidated reporting is viewed as providing information about a group of legal entities (the parent and its subsidiaries) under the control of a single management. Therefore, the assets, liabilities, sales, costs and expenses, gains, and losses of the individual legal entities are the assets, liabilities, revenues, costs and expenses, gains, and losses of the consolidated entity. Accordingly, **no special emphasis is given to the controlling interest**, even though the noncontrolling stockholders' ownership interest relates solely to the ownership in the subsidiary. Because the controlling and noncontrolling interests are viewed as being of the same nature, **they are treated the same way in the consolidated statements.**

For the balance sheet, the stockholders' equity in the *parent's* statements is *not* the stockholders' equity in the *consolidated* statements because the *consolidated* stockholders' equity *includes* the NCI. Likewise, the *parent's* net income is *not* the *consolidated* net income. The *consolidated* net income is the combined net incomes of all companies within the group (exclusive of the parent's investment income on investments in subsidiaries).

Consequently, the NCI is presented in the consolidated statements as follows:

1. **In the consolidated balance sheet (*inside* equity).** The NCI in the subsidiary's net assets is shown—**in the aggregate**—as a separate category *inside* the stockholders' equity section.
2. **In the consolidated income statement.** The NCI in the subsidiary's net income is shown as **an apportionment of the consolidated net income** in one of the following ways (assuming that a 75%-owned subsidiary had net income of $32,000 for the year):

	Consolidated Income Statement[a]	
	Dual Emphasis Format	Single Emphasis Format
Sales	$ 992,000	$ 992,000
Cost of sales	(520,000)	(520,000)
Expenses	(330,000)	(330,000)
Net Income (consolidated)	$ 142,000	$ 142,000
Net income accruing to the NCI	$ 8,000	(8,000)
Net income accruing to the CI	$ 134,000	$ 134,000

[a] These formats are displayed in paragraph 107 of the FASB's October 16, 1995, Exposure Draft on Consolidation Policies and Procedures (not yet finalized).

3. **In the consolidated statement of stockholders' equity.** To illustrate the manner of reporting for this statement, we (1) use the preceding $134,000 and $8,000 apportioned income amounts, (2) assume that, for the year, the parent declared dividends of $85,000 and the subsidiary declared dividends of $12,000, $3,000 of which was paid to the NCI (25% of $12,000), and (3) assume the subsidiary had total stockholders' equity of $80,000 at the beginning of the year, $20,000 of which accrues to the NCI (25% of $80,000). The NCI is presented as follows:

Consolidated Statement of Changes in Stockholders' Equity

Subsidiary's Equity[a]		Noncontrolling Interest	+	Controlling Interest: Common Stock	+	Controlling Interest: Retained Earnings	=	Total Stockholders' Equity
$ 80,000	Balances, 1/1/07	$20,000		$200,000		$117,000		$337,000
32,000	+ Net income	8,000				134,000		142,000
(12,000)	- Dividends	(3,000)				(85,000)		(88,000)
$100,000	Balances, 12/31/07	$25,000		$200,000		$166,000		$391,000

[a] Shown for informational purposes only.

The key point here is that the amounts reported in the Retained Earnings column *exclude* any amounts accruing to the NCI.

Which Concept Is Correct?

Whether the *parent company concept* or the *economic unit concept* is correct depends on whether the reporting entity is considered to have changed as a result of the consolidation process—a purely subjective judgment. The NCI shareholders do *not* influence the parent's operating policies. Thus the consolidated statements are of no benefit whatsoever to these shareholders. This group is entitled only to the financial statements of the partially owned subsidiary.[3]

[3] For a *created* subsidiary, the format of the consolidation worksheet and the consolidation entries are the same whether the *parent company concept* or the *economic unit concept* is used.

On the Horizon

In October 2001, the FASB issued an exposure draft titled "Accounting for Financial Instruments with Characteristics of Liabilities, Equity, or Both." Under this exposure draft, the NCI must be classified as *equity*.

The manner of presenting the NCIs in the balance sheet is mixed in foreign countries as shown in the International Perspective.

International Perspective

Manner of Presenting the Noncontrolling Interest in the Balance Sheet in Foreign Countries

Presented Outside Stockholders' Equity	Presented Inside Stockholders' Equity	Not Specified
Canada	Australia	France
Italy	Germany	Japan
The Netherlands (below equity)		United Kingdom
Spain (below equity)		

International Accounting Standard 27, "Consolidated Financial Statements and Accounting for Investments in Subsidiaries" (1987):

> Minority [noncontrolling] interests should be presented in the consolidated balance sheet separately from liabilities and the parent shareholders' equity.

Note: When the manner of classifying the NCI is prescribed, *full consolidation, not proportional consolidation,* is being used. A review of international accounting materials relating to these countries revealed that none of them allows *proportional consolidation.*

Consolidation Worksheet: Manner of Establishing the NCI in the Balance Sheet

The existence of an NCI adds an additional slight complexity to the consolidation process. To show worksheet techniques available to reflect the NCI in a subsidiary's net assets in the consolidated balance sheet, assume that Subbco is a 75%-owned subsidiary that reported the following balances at December 31, 2007 (for simplicity, we assume *no-par* common stock):

Common stock (no par)	$ 60,000
Retained earnings	40,000
	$100,000

The NCI in Subbco's net assets is thus $25,000 (25% of $100,000). The $25,000 could be established in the Consolidated column of the worksheet in either of the following two ways:

1. **The residual technique.** Under this technique, only the parent's interest in Subbco's common stock and retained earnings is eliminated. The amounts *not* eliminated are extended into the Consolidated column. Consequently, these extended amounts for each of the subsidiary's equity accounts must be summed to obtain the amount to report for the NCI in the net assets. This technique is as shown here:

	Parrco	Subbco	Consolidation Entries Dr.	Consolidation Entries Cr.	Consolidated
Investment in Subbco	75,000			75,000(1)	-0-
Subbco Company:					
Common stock		60,000	45,000(1)		15,000 NCI
Retained earnings		40,000	30,000(1)		10,000 NCI
					25,000

2. **The nonresidual technique.** Under this technique, 100% of each of Subbco's equity accounts is eliminated. Consequently, a single amount is established for the NCI in the subsidiary's net assets. This technique is as shown here:

	Parrco	Subbco	Consolidation Entries Dr.	Consolidation Entries Cr.	Consolidated
Investment in Subbco	75,000			75,000(1)	-0-
NCI in net assets				25,000(1)	25,000
Subbco Company:					
Common stock		60,000	60,000(1)		-0-
Retained earnings		40,000	40,000(1)		-0-

In illustrating the preparation of consolidation worksheets under both the *cost method* and the *equity method,* we use the *nonresidual* technique.

Refer to Illustration 3-1 for a summary of these consolidation theories and concepts.

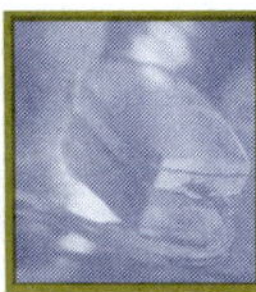

Check Point

An amount for NCI in net assets of subsidiary is reported under which concept?

	Economic Unit	Parent Company	Proportionate
a.	Yes	Yes	Yes
b.	No	Yes	Yes
c.	No	No	Yes
d.	No	Yes	No
e.	Yes	Yes	No

Answer: e

ILLUSTRATION 3-1 SUMMARY OF CONSOLIDATION THEORIES AND CONCEPTS FOR PARTIALLY OWNED SUBSIDIARIES

	Proportional Consolidation	Full Consolidation: Parent Company Concept	Full Consolidation: Economic Unit Concept
U.S. GAAP	No	Yes	Yes
Consolidates 100% of subsidiary's individual account balances	No	Yes	Yes
Manner of classifying NCI in subsidiary's net assets	n/a	*Outside* Con. St. Equity	*Inside* Con. St. Equity
NCI in net income is displayed as a separate line item in the consolidated income statement	No	Yes	Yes
Consolidated net income is defined as: Parent's net income	Yes[a]	Yes ($134,000 on page 77)	No
Combined *separate* earnings of parent and subsidiary (*before* NCI in net income is subtracted)			Yes ($142,000 on page 78)
Used almost exclusively in practice	n/a	Yes	No
FASB is proposing exclusive use of	No	No	Yes

[a] The consolidated net income is the *same* amount as reported under the *parent company concept*—however, the detail line item amounts in the consolidated income statement differ.

The *Equity Method*

When the parent uses the *equity method* of accounting, the additional complexity of an NCI can be easily handled by slightly modifying the parent's analysis of the Investment account to include the NCI. Even in later chapters when more complexities are introduced, the inclusion of the NCI in the analysis of the Investment account minimizes the consolidation effort.

Modifying the Analysis of the Investment Account

Illustration 3-2 shows the way that the analysis of the Investment account can be expanded at the date of a subsidiary's creation to accommodate the NCI. In this illustration, we assume that (1) Subbco was created on December 31, 2005, (2) the parent (Parrco) invested $45,000 cash for a 75% equity interest, (3) outside investors invested $15,000 cash for a 25% equity interest, and (4) Subbco issued no par common stock (thus the Additional Paid-in Capital account is *not* needed).

Illustration 3-2 also shows the basic *elimination* entry made to consolidate Subbco at December 31, 2005. Because of the simplicity of this situation, we do *not* show a consolidation worksheet at this date of creation. We do so shortly at December 31, 2007 (two years later).

Updating the Expanded Analysis of the Investment Account

Assume that Subbco subsequently reported the following items for 2006 and 2007:

	Net Income (Loss)	Dividends Declared
2006	$24,000	$ 4,000
2007	32,000	12,000

Under the *equity method* of accounting, the parent records its share of these amounts. The expanded analysis of the Investment account is updated as shown in Illustration 3-3. This illustration also shows the basic elimination entry used in consolidation at each year-end; the amounts were readily obtained from the updated analysis.

Illustration 3-4 shows a consolidation worksheet as of December 31, 2007, using the related basic elimination entry shown in Illustration 3-3.

Review Points for Illustration 3-4. Note the following:

1. The same equalities and control features that existed for 100%-owned subsidiaries exist for partially owned subsidiaries. That is, the net income and retained earnings amounts in the Consolidated column are the *same* as the comparable items in the Parrco column.

ILLUSTRATION 3-2 MODIFYING THE ANALYSIS OF THE INVESTMENT ACCOUNT TO INCLUDE THE NONCONTROLLING INTEREST

					SUBSIDIARY'S EQUITY ACCOUNTS		
	NONCONTROLLING INTEREST (25%)	+	PARENTS INVESTMENT ACCOUNT	=	COMMON STOCK	+	RETAINED EARNINGS
Balances, 12/31/05	$15,000		$45,000		$60,000		$-0-

The Basic *Elimination* Entry at December 31, 2005 (using the amounts in the above analysis)

WORKSHEET ENTRY ONLY

Common Stock	60,000	
Investment in Subbco		45,000
NCI in Net Assets		15,000

ILLUSTRATION 3-3 UPDATING THE ANALYSIS OF THE INVESTMENT ACCOUNT

	NONCONTROLLING INTEREST (25%)	+	PARENTS INVESTMENT ACCOUNT	=	SUBSIDIARY'S EQUITY ACCOUNTS COMMON STOCK	+	RETAINED EARNINGS
Balances, 12/31/05	$15,000		$45,000		$60,000		
+ Equity in net income:							
To parent (75%)			18,000				$18,000
To NCI (25%)	6,000						6,000
– Dividends:							
To parent (75%)			(3,000)				(3,000)
To NCI (25%)	(1,000)						(1,000)
Balances, 12/31/06	$20,000		$60,000		$60,000		$20,000
+ Equity in net income:							
To parent (75%)			24,000				24,000
To NCI (25%)	8,000						8,000
– Dividends:							
To parent (75%)			(9,000)				(9,000)
To NCI (25%)	(3,000)						(3,000)
Balances, 12/31/07	$25,000		$75,000		$60,000		$40,000

The Basic *Elimination* Entry
(using the amounts in the above analysis)

WORKSHEET ENTRY ONLY

	CONSOLIDATION DATE DECEMBER 31, 2006		DECEMBER 31, 2007	
Common Stock	60,000		60,000	
Retained Earnings, 1/1/06 and 1/1/07	–0–		20,000	
Equity in Net Income	18,000		24,000	
NCI in Net income	6,000		8,000	
Dividends Declared		4,000		12,000
Investment in Subsidiary		60,000		75,000
NCI in Net Assets		20,000		25,000

2. The $25,000 reported for the NCI in Subbco's net assets at year-end can be proven by multiplying Subbco's total stockholders' equity of $100,000 by the NCI ownership percentage ($100,000 × 25% = $25,000).
3. If Parrco were required to furnish a consolidated statement of changes in stockholders' equity (a GAAP requirement for publicly owned entities), it would appear as follows:

Consolidated Statement of Changes in Stockholders' Equity

	Noncontrolling Interest[a]	+	Controlling Interest Common Stock	+	Add'l PIC	+	Retained Earnings	=	Total Stockholders' Equity
Balances, 1/1/07	$20,000		$10,000		$190,000		$117,000		$337,000
+ Net income	8,000						134,000		142,000
– Dividends	(3,000)						(85,000)		(88,000)
Balances, 12/31/07	$25,000		$10,000		$190,000		$166,000		$391,000

[a] This column appears only under the economic *unit concept.*

4. The $3,000 of dividends paid to the NCI was eliminated in consolidation so that it would *not* be summed with dividends paid by the parent—just as dividends paid by a subsidiary to its parent are also *not* reported as dividends in the consolidated statement of retained earnings (as illustrated in Chapter 2). (Note that this $3,000 of dividends is reported in the noncontrolling interest column in the statement in review point 3—*not* in the retained earnings column.)
5. The consolidated statement of retained earnings reflects amounts that pertain to the interests of the controlling shareholders only.

ILLUSTRATION 3-4 THE EQUITY METHOD: SECOND YEAR SUBSEQUENT TO DATE OF CREATION

Parrco and Subbco
Consolidation Worksheet as of December 31, 2007

	PARRCO	75% OWNED SUBBCO	CONSOLIDATION ENTRIES DR.			CR.	CONSOLIDATED
Income Statement (2007)							
Sales	710,000	282,000					992,000
Cost of sales	(390,000)	(130,000)					(520,000)
Expenses	(210,000)	(120,000)					(330,000)
Equity in net income (of Subbco)	24,000		24,000	1			-0-
Net Income	134,000	32,000	24,000				142,000[a]
NCI in net income			**8,000**	1			**(8,000)**
CI in net income			32,000				134,000
Statement of Retained Earnings[b]							
Balances, 1/1/07	117,000	20,000	20,000	1			117,000
+ Net income	134,000	32,000	32,000				134,000
– Dividends declared	(85,000)	(12,000)			1	12,000	(85,000)
Balances, 12/31/07	166,000	40,000	52,000			12,000	166,000
Balance Sheet							
Cash	77,000	31,000					108,000
Accounts receivable	84,000	43,000					127,000
Inventory	140,000	82,000					222,000
Investment in Subbco	75,000				1	75,000	-0-
Land	220,000	30,000					250,000
Buildings and equipment	500,000	150,000					650,000
Accumulated depreciation	(360,000)	(26,000)					(386,000)
Total Assets	736,000	310,000				75,000	971,000
Liabilities	370,000	210,000					580,000
NCI in net assets					1	**25,000**	**25,000[c]**
Common stock	10,000						10,000
Add'l paid-in capital	190,000						190,000
Common stock		60,000	60,000	1			-0-
Retained earnings	166,000	40,000	52,000			12,000	166,000
Total Liabilities and Equity	736,000	310,000	112,000			37,000	971,000
Proof of debit and credit postings			112,000			112,000	

[a] Recall that the consolidated net income is $142,000 under the *economic unit concept.*

[b] Recall that the consolidated statement of retained earnings **includes only amounts that accrue to the controlling interest.**

[c] This amount is reported (1) *outside* stockholders' equity under the *parent company concept* and (2) *inside* stockholders' equity under the *economic unit concept.*

Explanation of entry:

1 The basic *elimination* entry.

CHECK POINT

How are dividends paid to NCI shareholders reported in the *consolidated statements*?

a. They reduce the amount reported as NCI in the subsidiary's net income in the consolidated income statement.

b. They reduce the amount reported as NCI in the subsidiary's net assets in the consolidated balance sheet.

c. They are included in dividends declared in the consolidated statement of retained earnings.

d. They are combined with expenses in the consolidated income statement.

Answer: b

II. UNCONSOLIDATED SUBSIDIARIES

Recall from Chapter 1 that the only reason for *not* consolidating a subsidiary[4] is lack of control. [In 2001, the FASB eliminated a previously allowed exception for *when control was likely to be temporary* (see *FAS144*, "Accounting for the Impairment or Disposal of Long- Lived Assets).]

Lack (loss) of control situations occur, for example, when (1) a subsidiary has filed for bankruptcy protection (the bankruptcy judge then controls the subsidiary) and (2) a subsidiary is placed under severe operating restrictions. Examples of severe operating restrictions are (1) a foreign government–imposed prohibition on paying dividends whereby the foreign government effectively owns the subsidiary and (2) a foreign government's involvement in the day-to-day operations of the foreign subsidiary.

When a subsidiary is justifiably *not* consolidated, the parent must determine how to value its Investment account because this account (instead of being eliminated in consolidation) is now reported in the financial statements the parent issues to its stockholders (those financial statements being the parent's *general-purpose financial statements*). These financial statements could be either (1) the parent's statements *alone* or (2) consolidated statements if the parent has other subsidiaries that are consolidated.

The factors that determine how to value the parent's Investment account in these statements are (1) whether the parent can exert *significant influence* (a condition for using the *equity method*) and (2) whether unowned shares in partial ownership situations are *publicly traded*.[5]

Investment Valuation Methods

Depending on the circumstances, the parent uses the *cost method*, the *equity method*, or the *fair value method*. When a parent has the option to use only the *equity method* (allowed only if the parent *can* exert significant influence) or the cost method, the parent usually focuses on the particular circumstances that resulted in nonconsolidation and decides accordingly.

Wholly Owned Subsidiary Justifiably *Not* Consolidated: Cost and Equity Methods Allowed

In these situations, the *cost method* can always be used. In contrast, the *equity method* is permitted *only* if the parent is able to exert *significant influence*, which is the rationale underlying its required use if an investor has *significant influence* but not *control* (typically 20%–50% ownership situations).

ETHICS

Does Company Loyalty Include Filing a False Corporate Tax Return?

Your employer has asked you to file a false corporate income tax return.

Questions

1. If you comply and the IRS discovers the filing of a false return, what could be the consequences to you? (The instructor's solution manual describes what happened to Georgia Pacific Corporation and its employees who were responsible for filing such a return.)
2. If you do *not* comply and are fired for not cooperating, what legal recourse might you have? (The instructor's solution manual describes what happened to one such accountant.)

[4] Technically, when control is lacking, it may be incorrect to refer to the relationship between the two companies as a *parent-subsidiary relationship*, a term that conjures images of control of the one entity by the other. *Investor-investee* may be more appropriate. In practice and in the accounting literature, however, *parent* and *subsidiary* are used as a matter of convenience in these situations.

[5] These rules concerning how to value the parent's Investment account in *non*consolidation situations also apply to situations in which the parent issues *parent-company-only statements* **in addition to consolidated statements.**

Partially Owned and *Non*publicly Traded Subsidiary Justifiably *Not* Consolidated: Cost and Equity Methods Allowed

In these situations, the rules are the same as when the unconsolidated subsidiary is 100% owned as explained above.

Partially Owned and Publicly Traded Subsidiary Justifiably *Not* Consolidated: Equity and Fair Value Methods Allowed

In these situations, the *cost method* is *not* permitted. Instead, the *equity method* or the *fair value method* must be used. However, the fair value method, which is allowed pursuant to FASB *Statement No. 115*, "Accounting for Certain Investments in Debt and Equity Securities," can be used **only if the fair value is readily determinable** (using a quoted market price).

When the *fair value method* is used, keep in mind that an equity investment in a subsidiary is usually intended as a long-term investment. Thus an equity investment in an unconsolidated subsidiary that is accounted for at fair value is classified in the *available-for-sale* category described in *FAS 115*—not the *trading* category. Unrealized gains and losses on *available-for-sale securities* are excluded from earnings and reported in *Other Comprehensive Income* until realization occurs.

Loss of Control Situations

In these situations, the *cost method* is the predominant method used because realization of the subsidiary's future earnings usually is the critical issue. Accordingly, the conservatism of the cost method (report no investment income until dividends have been received) is usually more appropriate.

Illustration 3-5 summarizes the methods allowed for the various types of nonconsolidation situations.

CHECK POINT

Puntex is currently taking steps to sell its 100%-owned subsidiary. Which of the following should *most likely* be used to value the investment in the general-purpose financial statements that Puntex issues to its stockholders?

a. The *net realizable value.*
b. The *cost method* or the *equity method,* as most appropriate.
c. Only the *equity method.*
d. Only the *cost method.*
e. The *fair value method.*
f. The subsidiary must be consolidated.

Answer: f

ILLUSTRATION 3-5 SUMMARY OF THE USE OF *COST* AND *EQUITY METHODS* WHEN A SUBSIDIARY IS *NOT* CONSOLIDATED

Reason for Not Consolidating	Significant Influence Exists	Wholly Owned *or* Partially Owned & *Not* Publicly Traded	Partially Owned & Publicly Traded
Loss of control	Yes	Cost[a] or equity	Fair value or equity
Loss of control	No	Cost[a]	Fair value

[a] The carrying value under the *cost method* must be adjusted downward if the fair value of the investment is below the *cost method* carrying value. Thus the *cost method* is effectively a lower-of-cost-or-market method.

CHECK POINT

A foreign government has forcibly taken over Potter's 100%-owned overseas subsidiary. Which of the following should most likely be used in valuing the investment in the general-purpose financial statements that Potter issues to its stockholders?

a. The *cost method*.
b. The *equity method*.
c. The *equity method* or *net realizable value*.
d. The *cost method* or net *realizable value*.
e. The lower of the *cost method* or *net realizable value*.
f. The *net realizable value*.

Answer: e

III. CONSOLIDATION OF VARIABLE INTEREST ENTITIES (VIEs) (NO MAJORITY VOTING OWNERSHIP EXISTS)

Recall that having a controlling financial interest in a subsidiary ***by means of having a majority voting interest*** gives the parent company the equitable and legal right to the *majority* (or *all* if 100%-owned) of the subsidiary's future *profits*. Likewise, the parent will suffer the *majority* of the adverse consequences of the subsidiary's future *losses* (to the extent of the parent's investment and any guarantees of the subsidiary's debt). Finally, the parent can make all decisions concerning the subsidiary's operating, investing, and financing activities. These rights and economic exposures are the basic characteristics of possessing a controlling financial interest. Thus the *parent* is the ***primary beneficiary*** of the *subsidiary*.

Occasionally, an analysis of the ***voting interests*** is *not* effective in determining whether a controlling financial interests exists because (1) the entity does not have adequate equity capital at risk or (2) the equity instruments do not have the normal equity characteristics that provide its holders with a potential controlling financial interest.

The FASB's New Consolidation Rules for VIEs (issued in 2003)

Infrequently, an enterprise that does *not* own a majority of the voting equity interests of another entity is involved with that entity as a result of contractual, ownership, or other pecuniary interest (or combination of interests). In most of these "involvement" situations, consolidation of the latter entity is required for a fair presentation. The concepts of risks, rewards, decision-making ability, and primary beneficiary (as discussed in the preceding paragraph) are the basis for the FASB's new consolidation rules for these involvement situations. In a nutshell, the FASB's intent is to require consolidation of any entity in which another entity bears the majority (over 50%) of the risks and/or rewards of ownership.

Issuance of *FAS Interpretation No. 46*

The FASB issued these new rules in January 2003 (and amended them in December 2003) in *FAS Interpretation No. 46*, "Consolidation of Variable Interest Entities" (an interpretation of *Accounting Research Bulletin No. 51*, "Consolidated Financial Statements," which was issued in 1951). The *FIN 46* rules are more comprehensive and much tougher than the previous consolidation rules for these involvement situations.

The Accounting Impact of Enron's Shenanigans

FIN 46 was issued in response to the spectacular collapse and bankruptcy filing (in late 2001) of Enron Corporation, which had improperly concealed nearly $600 million of losses and billions of dollars of Enron-backed debt in its unconsolidated partnerships. These partnerships were created as special-purpose entities (SPEs), which are explained shortly. Interestingly enough, the improper nonconsolidation of Enron's partnerships occurred because Enron knowingly did *not* follow the then existing consolidation rules—*not* because the existing consolidation rules were too weak. Nevertheless, the FASB decided the timing was right to (1) thoroughly reexamine its existing fragmented rules for these situations and (2) strengthen those rules. The result is a tougher, more cohesive set of rules that are more "principles-based" that emphasize *substance* over *form*—as opposed to being "rules-based" (a check-the-box for compliance approach). Consequently, the effect of these new rules is to require consolidation in far more situations than previously required. Practitioners are finding that the new rules are extremely difficult to interpret and apply (producing substantial frustration and consternation).

Variable Interest Entities and Variable Interests Defined

A **variable interest entity** (VIE) is defined as an entity that is ***subject to consolidation*** according to the provisions of *FIN Interpretation 46*. An entity is subject to consolidation if certain conditions (explained shortly) exist. Thus an entity that has a **variable interest** in a VIE—***an interest that changes with changes in the VIE's net assets***—must determine if it must consolidate the VIE. When two or more unrelated entities each have a variable interest in a VIE, only the entity that is determined to be the **primary beneficiary** must consolidate the VIE.

Background Information Regarding VIE Situations (*no* majority voting ownership exists)

Beginning in the late 1970s, numerous "variable interest relationships" were created in which an entity would receive benefits and/or be exposed to risks similar to those received from a having a majority ownership interest—even though the entity either (1) does *not* have a majority ownership interest or (2) has *no* voting interest whatsoever. These situations generally occur as a result of contractual arrangements, such as options, leases, guarantees of asset recovery values, and guarantees of debt repayments. In some instances, the contractual arrangement exists simultaneously with a less than majority ownership in the VIE. Many ways exist in which one entity can have a variable interest in another entity even though neither a majority nor any of the other entity's voting shares are owned. Some of these variable interests are quite simple; others are quite complex. Experts in this area say "each particular variable interest situation has its own DNA."

Special-Purpose Entities (SPEs)

In a high percentage of these VIE situations, an entity sponsors the creation of another entity that is legally structured to serve a specific, predetermined, limited purpose. Because of the narrow scope of their operations, these sponsored entities are called special-purpose entities (SPEs). Thus most VIEs are SPEs. SPEs can be in the form of a corporation, a partnership, a trust, or some other legal entity. SPEs can serve valid business purposes and involve several types of transactions. In many situations (mostly involving *securitizations*, which are discussed in Intermediate Accounting texts), the use of SPEs is highly desirable because their use enable companies to raise capital at a lower interest rate than otherwise possible. This lower interest rate occurs because the SPE's lenders are better protected because they have a claim against specific assets (which are transferred to the SPE by the sponsor as opposed to being a general creditor of the transferor if no SPE were used). The same advantage can be obtained by creating an SPE to purchase assets that are to be leased back to the SPE's sponsor. SPEs are expensive to set up and maintain. Therefore, SPE activities usually occur on a large scale so that the impact of the reduced interest rate more than offsets the costs involved.

Consolidation of "Qualifying" SPEs is Prohibited (a *FIN 46* scope exception)

In the 1980s, many financial institutions began securitizing portions of their receivables by means of sponsoring the creation of SPEs to purchase the sponsor's receivables. Typically, these SPEs are thinly capitalized such that the SPE's equity may be only 5% of total assets, with the remainder being debt. Typically, the sponsor has no ownership in the SPE. These SPEs hold trillions of dollars of assets

If the transfer of a financial institution's receivables to an SPE meets the sales recognition criteria of *FAS 140,* "Accounting for Transfers and Servicing of Financial Assets and Extinguishments of Liabilities" *(the criteria center on the surrender of control over the transferred assets)*, the transferor reports a gain or loss on the sale, and the SPE is called a qualifying SPE (QSPE). If the transfer of the assets does *not* meet the *FAS 140* sales recognition criteria, however, the transaction is *not* treated as a sale, and the money received by the transferor from the SPE is reported as a loan. (Recall that the topic of determining whether the transfer of receivables is, in substance, a (1) sale of the receivables or (2) a secured borrowing is a topic of Intermediate Accounting.) ***FAS 140*** **(paragraph 46) prohibits transferors from consolidating a QSPE** (essentially because the transferor is deemed to *not* have a significant risk exposure or reward potential). For this reason, QSPEs are excluded from the scope of *FIN 46*.

Simple Examples of Variable Interest Situations

Before discussing the FASB's rules regarding consolidation of VIEs in detail, we present two relatively simple, straightforward examples (one of which involves an SPE) to show some of the various contractual manners in which variable interests can occur.

Reward-Based Example—Involvement with An Entity that Is *Not* an SPE

Patco Inc. owns 40% of the outstanding common stock of Techie Inc., a privately owned, high-technology start-up company. Patco has a call option to acquire the remaining 60% of Techie's outstanding common stock at any time during the next three years for $5 million cash. The option contract places Patco in the position of being able to have the right to 100% of Techie's future profits—just as if Patco owns 100% of Techie's common stock. Thus Patco possesses one of the characteristics of having a controlling financial interest. Accordingly, Patco is the primary beneficiary of Techie and must consolidate Techie.

Risk-Based Example—Involvement with an SPE

Patco Inc. owns none of Speco Inc.'s outstanding common stock. Patco sells assets having a book value of $70 million to Speco for $100 million cash. Patco sponsored the creation of Speco specifically for this transaction. Speco is prohibited from having any other operating activities (under the legal documents that created Speco). Thus Speco *is* an SPE. To finance the purchase of assets from Patco, Speco (1) raised $5 million cash from equity investors (other than Patco) and (2) borrowed $95 million from a bank. Patco has guaranteed Speco's equity investment in the event of losses. Furthermore, Patco has guaranteed Speco's bank debt to the extent of nonpayment by Speco. Thus Patco has considerable risk exposure just as if Patco had an actual equity investment in Speco. Consequently, Patco possesses one of the characteristics of having a controlling financial interest. Accordingly, Patco is the primary beneficiary of Speco and must consolidate Techie.

Potential Variable Interests

The following listing consists of some potential variable interests:

> Subordinated loans made to a VIE (thus other "senior" lenders to the VIE have priority as to repayment).

> Equity interests in a VIE (less than a majority voting interest) that are at risk.
> Guarantees to a VIE's lenders or equity holders (which thus reduce the true risk of those parties).
> Written put options on a VIE's assets (the potential obligation to buy certain of a VIE's assets if the option holder exercises the option). Such an option protects the VIE's debt or equity holders from incurring losses.
> Forward contracts on purchases and sales.

All of a VIE's liabilities may be variable interests because a decrease in the fair value of the VIE's assets could be so high that all of the liabilities would absorb that decrease. However, senior debt instruments with *fixed* interest rates would usually not, by themselves, make the holder the VIE's primary beneficiary.

FASB's Rules to Determine if an Entity is a VIE

In general, an entity is subject to consolidation pursuant to the provisions of *FIN 46* if, by design[6] (the way in which an entity is structured), *any* of the following three conditions exists:

1. The total equity investment at risk is *not* sufficient to permit the entity to finance its activities without additional **subordinated financial support**. Subordinated financial support is defined as *variable interests that will absorb some or all of an entity's expected losses*,[7] which would exist if an entity guarantees another entity's debt amounts, asset recovery amounts, or equity at risk. ***In general, the equity at risk is deemed sufficient if it is at least 10% of total assets.*** (In some cases, however, the equity at risk may have to be *higher than* 10% to be sufficient; in other cases, equity of *less than* 10% could be sufficient if the entity can demonstrate through qualitative analysis or quantitative analysis [or a combination of both] that it is sufficient.)
2. The holders of the equity investment at risk (as a group) lack any of the following three characteristics: (A) the ability to make decisions about an entity's activities through voting rights or similar rights, (B) the obligation to absorb the entity's expected losses, and (C) the right to receive the expected residual returns of the entity.
3. Certain disproportionalities exist among the equity investors (such as certain equity investors possessing voting rights that are not proportional to their obligation to share the VIE's losses).

Determining the VIE's Primary Beneficiary

The primary beneficiary of a VIE must consolidate the VIE. The primary beneficiary is the entity that will (1) absorb a majority ***(greater than 50%)*** of the VIE's expected losses and/or (2) receive a majority ***(greater than 50%)*** of the VIE's expected residual returns. If one entity will absorb a majority of the a VIE's expected *losses* and another entity will receive a majority of that VIE's expected *residual returns*, the *former* must consolidate the VIE. Thus expected *losses* are given more weight than expected residual *returns* in determining the primary beneficiary.

Potential for Erroneously Determined Multiple Primary Beneficiaries

By definition, a VIE can have only *one* primary beneficiary. In practice, however, *two* (or more) entities may each conclude that it is a VIE's primary beneficiary. This odd result (which is inconsistent

---

[6] An entity under the control of its equity investors that originally was *not* a VIE does *not* become a VIE because of operating losses.

[7] The terms "expected losses" and "expected residual returns" as used in *FIN 46* do *not* refer to projected income statement amounts in the customary sense of those terms. Instead, FIN 46 defines these terms as "amounts derived from expected cash flows as described in *FASB Concepts Statement No. 7*, "Using Cash Flow Information and Present Value in Accounting Measurements" (issued in 2000). These calculations usually involve determining estimated cash flows that must be probability weighted and discounted to present value. ***Expected losses*** are derived from the portion of possible cash flows that are *less than* the overall expected cash flows. ***Expected residual returns*** are derived from the portion of possible cash flows that are *greater than* overall expected cash flows. Thus the determination of whether the VIE's equity is sufficient to cover "expected losses" is based on "worst case" assumptions (looking at only those estimated cash flow scenarios in which the estimates are *less than* the expected cash flows that are derived from the assets). This analysis requires complex estimates and judgments that could vary significantly from one entity to another. An illustration of these calculations is beyond the scope of this text.

ETHICS

Me Go to Jail—I Only Followed GAAP

Assume that you are the controller of Enrox. Several top Enrox executives, including yourself, are defendants in a stockholder lawsuit that alleges Enrox overstated its earnings for its latest year.

The heart of the lawsuit is that (1) the revenue recognition accounting rules followed by Enrox were extremely weak accounting standards and (2) the financial statements did *not* reflect a fair presentation of economic reality.

Assume also that in response to recent negative publicity regarding these revenue recognition rules, the FASB recently proposed new stricter revenue recognition rules. If Enrox, had followed the proposed new rules, its earnings would have been substantially lower.

Questions

1. Is following GAAP an adequate legal defense?
2. What do you think will be the judge's instructions to the jury concerning the following of GAAP?

with the notion of control) can occur when (1) one or more of the variable interest holders has incomplete information about the VIE's other variable interest holders or (2) different variable interest holders make different judgments about their variable interests.

If No Primary Beneficiary Exists—No Consolidation

If none of a VIE's variable interest holders has a majority of either the VIE's expected losses or expected residual returns, the VIE has no primary beneficiary. Accordingly, the VIE is *not* consolidated. Obviously, this situation occurs when risks and rewards related to the VIE's assets or activities are sufficiently dispersed among the variable interest holders. Of course, each variable interest holder still must account for its rights and obligations related to the assets in the VIE (which might involve application of the *equity method* of accounting).

Information Needed to Assess If a Variable Interest Holder Is the Primary Beneficiary

To reach a conclusion based on complete facts, a variable interest holder needs to know the expected losses and expected residual returns (*quantitative* considerations) and other characteristics (*qualitative* considerations) associated with (1) its own variable interests (as well as those of its related parties, if any), (2) the VIE's other variable interests holders (and their related parties, if any), and (3) the VIE itself. In practice, some situations are relatively simple to evaluate (such as the examples given earlier), while others are quite difficult to assess.

When to Determine If an Entity Is the Primary Beneficiary

The primary beneficiary assessment is performed upon an entity's initial involvement with a VIE. Subsequently, the occurrence of the following "triggering events" (events likely to cause a change in the primary beneficiary) require a reassessment by the variable interest holders:

1. A change in the VIE's governing documents or contractual arrangements among the parties with interests in the VIE that results in reallocating between the existing primary beneficiary and other unrelated parties (a) the rights to absorb the VIE's expected losses or (b) the right to receive the expected residual returns.
2. The primary beneficiary sells or reduces its interest in the VIE.
3. The primary beneficiary's interest is diluted by the issuance of new interests.

Consolidation Procedures for VIEs

The detailed procedures to consolidate VIEs are similar in most all respects to the consolidation procedures used to consolidate a business acquired in a business combination (discussed in Chapters 4–6 and 8–10). The major points are:

1. **Eliminating the Primary Beneficiary Interests in the VIE.** Any interest that the primary beneficiary has in the VIE that is represented by an asset (such as an *equity investment*; a *loan receivable*; or the *carrying value of a call option on unowned, outstanding common shares* of the VIE) is eliminated in consolidation.
2. **Reporting the VIE's Assets and Liabilities.** The VIE's assets and reportable liabilities are initially reported in consolidation at their ***fair values***—*not* their *book values*.
3. **Reporting Goodwill.** In most cases, goodwill is reported in consolidation of a VIE for any excess of (1) the sum of (a) the *fair value* of the consideration paid, (b) the primary beneficiary's *reported amounts* of any previously held interests, and (c) the *fair value* of the newly consolidated liabilities, over (2) the sum of (d) the *fair value* of the newly consolidated assets and (e) the *reported amount* of identifiable assets that the primary beneficiary transferred to the VIE. (If the VIE is *not* a business [defined in Appendix C of *FIN 46*], however, the excess is reported as an ***extraordinary loss***.)
4. **Extinguishing "Negative Goodwill."** When an excess exists of the items in (2) over the items in (1) in item 3 above (sometimes loosely thought of as "negative goodwill" or a "bargain purchase element" [*the intent here is to convey the sense of a "liability" on the primary beneficiary's books*]), that excess is to be dealt with using the required asset allocation procedures set forth in paragraphs 44 and 45 of ***FAS 141***, "Business Combinations," (discussed in Chapter 5). If not fully extinguished in the allocation process, the residual amount is reported as an ***extraordinary gain***.
5. **Reporting the Noncontrolling Interest.** The noncontrolling interest in a VIE is initially reported at ***fair value*** (usually reported at ***book value*** in consolidation of a business acquired in business combination).
6. **Eliminating Intercompany Transactions.** The primary beneficiary must apply paragraphs 6–15 *of Accounting Research Bulletin No. 51*, "Consolidation Policy," which address consolidation procedures, the elimination of intercompany balances and transactions, the allocation of intercompany profits and losses to noncontrolling interests, and income tax considerations—all of which are discussed in Chapter 8. Certain items eliminated must be attributed to the *primary beneficiary*—not the *noncontrolling interest* in the consolidated statements.

Illustrations of Consolidation Entries

The consolidation entry for the primary beneficiary depends on the particular type of involvement situation. We illustrate two situations.

Consolidation Entry for a Call Option and 40%-Ownership Situation

Assume the following information:

1. Patco Inc. owns 40% of the outstanding common stock of Techie Inc., a privately owned high-technology start-up company. (Patco acquired these shares in 2005.)
2. On December 31, 2006, Patco paid $400,000 to purchase a call option that enables Patco to acquire the remaining 60% of Techie's outstanding common stock at any time through 2009.
3. On December 31, 2006, Patco assessed that it was the primary beneficiary of Techie and thus must consolidate Techie's financial statements.
4. At December 31, 2006, Techie's stockholders' equity accounts are as follows:

Common stock	$ 500,000
Retained earnings	(200,000)
Total Stockholders' Equity	$ 300,000

5. The carrying value of Patco's 40% investment in Techie is $120,000 (using the mandatory *equity method* of accounting [Techie's total stockholder's equity of $300,000 × 40% = $120,000]).
6. At December 31, 2006, the only asset or liability of Techie that is *over*- or *under*valued is land, which is *under*valued by $25,000.

Patco's consolidation entry at December 31, 2006, to consolidate Techie's balance sheet at that date (the date that Patco became the primary beneficiary) is as follows:

WORKSHEET ENTRY ONLY

Common Stock	500,000	
Land (adjustment to fair value)	25,000	
Goodwill	390,000	
Retained Earnings		200,000
Investment in Techie (the 40% interest)		120,000
Contract Value of Call Option		400,000
Noncontrolling Interest (assumed fair value of $325,000 [$300,000 + $25,000] × 60%)		195,000

Consolidation Entry for a Guarantee of Debt Situation

Assume that (1) Patco owns none of Valco's outstanding common stock, (2) Patco has guaranteed all of the debt of Valco, (3) Valco has total liabilities of $970,000 and total stockholders' equity of $30,000 ($30,000 *for common stock* and zero for *retained earnings*), and (4) Valco's expected losses are $150,000. Because Patco effectively would have to absorb 80% of the Valco's expected losses ($120,000/$150,000), Patco would be the primary beneficiary and make the following consolidation entry at December 31, 2006, if the guarantee were made on that date:

WORKSHEET ENTRY ONLY

Common Stock	$30,000	
Noncontrolling Interest in Net Assets (presuming that the *fair value* is equal to *book value*)		$30,000

Disclosures Required When Involved with a VIE

The following disclosures are required for ***primary beneficiaries*** (that do *not* hold a majority voting interest):

1. The VIE's nature, purpose, size, and activities.
2. The carrying amount and classification of consolidated assets that are collateral for the VIE's obligations.
3. Lack of recourse if creditors (or beneficial interest holders) of a consolidated VIE have no recourse to the *general credit* of the primary beneficiary.

The following disclosures are required for ***nonprimary beneficiary*** entities that have a significant interest in a VIE:

1. The nature of its involvement with the VIE and the date that involvement began.
2. The VIE's nature, purpose, size, and activities.
3. The entity's maximum exposure to loss as a result of its involvement with the VIE.

Cisco's Disclosures Regarding Its Interests in VIEs

The following VIE disclosures are from Cisco Systems, Inc.'s 2003 annual report:

> In April 2001, the Company entered into a commitment to provide convertible debt funding of approximately $84 million to Andiamo Systems Inc. ("Andiamo"), a storage switch developer. This debt will be convertible into approximately 44% of the equity in Andiamo, subject to certain terms and conditions. In connection with this investment, the Company obtained a call option that provided the company the right to purchase Andiamo. . . . The Company also entered

into a commitment to provide non-convertible debt funding to Andiamo of approximately $100 million. . . .

As of July 26, 2003, the Company has invested $84 million in the convertible debt and $76 million in non-convertible debt. Substantially all of the investment in Andiamo has been expensed as research and development costs, as if such expenses constituted the development costs of the Company.

The Company has evaluated its debt investment in Andiamo and has determined that Andiamo is a variable interest entity under FIN 46. The Company has concluded that it is the primary beneficiary as defined by FIN 46, and, as a result, the Company is required to consolidate Andiamo beginning the first day of the first quarter of fiscal 2004. . . .

FIN 46 will require the Company to account for Andiamo as if it had consolidated it since the Company's initial investment in April 2001. . . .

In the ordinary course of business, the Company has investments in other privately held companies and provides structured financing to certain customers. . . . which may be considered variable interest entities. The Company has evaluated its investments in these other privately held companies and structured financings and has determined that there will be no material impact on its operating results or financial condition upon the adoption of FIN 46.

Closing Comments Regarding VIEs

FIN 46 is exceedingly complex. It has no illustrative examples. Nor has the FASB issued (or announced plans) to issue an implementation guide. The large CPA firms are having difficulty in trying to give proper and consistent guidance to their clients on how to implement *FIN 46*.

Our purpose here is to merely give you an overview of the breadth and far-reaching impact of *FIN 46*—not an in-depth understanding of its detailed procedures, which would probably require two full chapters of explanation.

END-OF-CHAPTER REVIEW

Summary of Key Points

1. Under the **proportionate consolidation method**, no amounts relating to the NCI are presented in the consolidated statements.

2. Under current GAAP, partially owned subsidiaries must be **fully consolidated**—not *proportionally* consolidated.

3. Under the **parent company concept**, (a) the NCI in the subsidiary's net income is shown **as a deduction** in arriving at consolidated net income, and (b) the NCI in the subsidiary's net assets is presented **outside** the consolidated stockholders' equity section.

4. Under the **economic unit concept**, (a) the NCI in the subsidiary's net income is shown as **an apportionment** of the combined earnings of both companies (the consolidated net income), and (b) the NCI in the subsidiary's net assets is presented **inside** the consolidated stockholders' equity section.

5. **Dividends paid to NCI shareholders** are never reported in the consolidated statement of retained earnings as declared dividends.

6. The consolidated statement of retained earnings includes **only amounts accruing to the controlling interest**. (Thus the *parent company concept* applies under the umbrella of the *economic unit concept* in this statement.)

7. If a subsidiary is *not* consolidated, a parent may value its Investment account using either (1) the **equity method** (only if significant influence exists), (2) the **cost method** (but not if unowned shares are publicly traded), or (3) the **fair market value** (**required whenever the unowned shares are publicly traded and the parent does *not* use the *equity method***).

8. Occasionally, an entity must consolidate another entity even though *less than* a majority of that entity's common stock (or none) is owned. These are "involvement" situations and arise as a result of contractual, ownership, or other pecuniary interests (such as a guarantee of an entity's debt).

9. The *primary beneficiary* of a *variable interest entity* must consolidate the *variable interest entity*.

10. The *primary beneficiary* of a VIE is the entity that (1) must absorb the majority (over 50%) of the VIE's *expected losses* or (2) will receive the majority (over 50%) of the VIE's *expected residual returns*. (Expected losses trump expected residual returns in this determination.)

Glossary of New Terms

Controlling interest (CI) The interest of the shareholders of a parent company of a partially owned subsidiary in the combined earnings of the parent and the subsidiary.

Economic unit concept The GAAP concept pertaining to how the assets and liabilities of a partially owned subsidiary and the related NCI in the subsidiary's earnings and net assets should be valued and reported in consolidated statements. A new reporting entity is deemed to exist as a result of the consolidation process. The NCI therefore *is* treated as an equity interest of the consolidated reporting entity. (The need to address this valuation and reporting issue is more frequently encountered in *external expansion* [acquisitions] than in *internal expansion* in which a subsidiary is created.)

Expected losses and **Expected residual returns** Amounts derived from expected cash flows that are discounted and weighted using estimated probabilities of occurrence.

Noncontrolling interest (NCI) The interest of the shareholders of a partially owned subsidiary, other than the parent, in the subsidiary's earnings, losses, and net assets.

Parent company concept A concept concerning the valuation and reporting of the assets and liabilities of a partially owned subsidiary and the related noncontrolling shareholders' interest in the subsidiary's earnings and net assets in consolidated statements. The parent company is deemed the consolidated reporting entity. The NCI therefore is *not* treated as an equity interest of the consolidated reporting entity.

Primary beneficiary The entity that must consolidate a variable interest entity under *FIN 46*.

Proportional consolidation concept A concept concerning the valuation and reporting of a partially owned subsidiary's assets and liabilities and the related NCI in the subsidiary's earnings and net assets in consolidated statements. Only the parent's proportionate interest in each of the subsidiary's assets, liabilities, revenues, and costs and expenses are reported in consolidation. Thus no amounts are reported for the NCI in the consolidated statements.

Subordinated financial support Variable interests that will absorb some or all of an entity's expected losses.

Variable interest Interests in an entity as a result of contractual, ownership, or other pecuniary interests that change with the changes in the fair value of the entity's net assets.

Variable interest entity An entity that is subject to consolidation according to the provisions of *FIN 46*.

ASSIGNMENT MATERIAL

Review Questions

1. What is the *proportional consolidation* method?

2. What are the arguments for *full* consolidation?

3. Which concepts fit under *full consolidation*?

4. What are the three theoretical ways to classify the NCI in the balance sheet?

5. How is *consolidated net income* defined under the *parent company* concept? Under the *economic unit* concept?

6. How are dividends paid to a subsidiary's NCI shareholders treated for consolidated reporting purposes?

7. When a subsidiary is *not* consolidated, what factors are relevant in deciding between the equity and cost methods?

8. When is the *equity method not* allowed in reporting an investment in an unconsolidated subsidiary?

9. When is the *cost method not* allowed in reporting an investment in an unconsolidated subsidiary?

10. When is the *fair market value* used to value an investment in a subsidiary?

11. When might an entity have to consolidate another entity even though the *first* entity does not own a majority of the outstanding voting common stock of the *second* entity?

12. In general, an equity investment below what percentage of the entity's total assets is deemed insufficient to permit the entity to finance its activities without subordinated financial support?

13. What is meant by the term "expected" losses under *FIN 46*?

14. Must all VIEs have a primary beneficiary? Why or why not?

15. When does an entity assess whether it is the primary beneficiary of a VIE?

16. What events could trigger a change in a VIE's primary beneficiary?

17. In what way is consolidating a VIE the same as consolidating a partially owned subsidiary that was acquired in a business combination?

18. **Computers and Spreadsheets:** What is the difference between "linking" and "consolidating" as those terms are used in EXCEL?

Exercises

E 3-1 **Partially Owned Subsidiaries: Consolidated Net Income** Pila Inc. owns 80% of Sila Inc. For 2006, Sila reported net income of $55,000 and declared dividends of $15,000. Pila reported $100,000 from its own separate operations exclusive of its investment income from Sila.

Required

1. What is the consolidated net income under the *parent company* concept?
2. What is the consolidated net income under the *economic unit* concept?
3. What is Pila's investment income under the *equity method*? The *cost method*?

E 3-2 **Partially Owned Subsidiaries: Consolidation Entries** Information for a 70%-owned created subsidiary for 2006 follows:

Common stock (year-end)	$20,000
Retained earnings, 1/1/06	$80,000
Net income	$40,000
Dividends declared	$30,000

Required

1. Prepare an analysis of the parent's investment for 2006, assuming that the parent uses the *equity* method.
2. Prepare the consolidation entry(ies) required at 12/31/06.

E 3-3 **Partially Owned Subsidiaries: Concepts** The following items were obtained at the end of 2006 from the financial statements of a 75%-owned created subsidiary:

Dividends declared	$ 40,000
Net income	84,000
Common stock	200,000
Additional paid-in capital	100,000
Retained earnings, 1/1/06	144,000

In addition, the parent declared and paid dividends of $90,000 in 2006.

Required What is the amount for each of the following items?

a. The parent's year-end investment balance under the *equity method.*
b. The amount reported in the consolidated statements for the NCI in the subsidiary's net assets.
c. The amount reported in the consolidated statements for the NCI in the subsidiary's net income.
d. The amount reported for dividends declared in the 2006 consolidated statement of retained earnings.

E 3-4 Partially Owned Subsidiaries: Consolidation Entries Use the information in Exercise 3-3.

Required Prepare all consolidation entries at year-end if the parent uses the *equity method.*

E 3-5 Unconsolidated Subsidiaries: Intended Disposal Pynco is currently taking steps to sell Synco, its subsidiary for which it has, as a minimum, *significant influence.* Use the following choices to answer the questions.

a. Unconsolidated—the cost method.

b. Unconsolidated—the equity method.

c. Unconsolidated—the fair value method.

d. Unconsolidated—the cost method or the equity method, as most appropriate.

e. Unconsolidated—the equity method or the fair value method.

f. Unconsolidated—the cost method or the fair value method.

g. The subsidiary must be consolidated.

How should Synco be reported in Pynco's general-purpose financial statements that Pynco issues to its stockholders if Synco is

Required

1. A wholly owned subsidiary.
2. A partially owned subsidiary—the unowned shares *are* publicly traded.
3. A partially owned subsidiary—the unowned shares are *not* publicly traded.

E 3-6 Unconsolidated Subsidiaries: Currency Restrictions A foreign government has imposed *severe* dividend payment restrictions on Prell's 100%-owned foreign subsidiary. Consequently, consolidation is *no longer* appropriate.

Required

1. If Prell *can* exercise significant influence how should the investment be valued in the general-purpose financial statements that Prell issues to its stockholders?
   a. The *cost method.*
   b. The *equity method.*
   c. The *cost method* or the *equity method,* as most appropriate.
   d. The *equity method* or the *fair value method.*
   e. The *cost method* or the *fair value method.*
2. Use the information in Question 1 but assume that Prell *cannot* exercise significant influence.
3. Use the information in Question 1 but assume that (a) Prell *can* exercise significant influence, (b) it owns 80% of the voting shares, and (c) the unowned shares are *not* publicly traded.
4. Use the information in Question 1 but assume that (a) Prell *can* exercise significant influence, (b) it owns 80% of the voting shares, and (c) the unowned shares *are* publicly traded.

E 3-7 **Variable Interest Entities** Both Entity A and Entity B have a variable interest in Vixco, a variable interest entity. Entity A is entitled to receive a majority of Vixco's ***expected residual returns.*** Entity B is obligated to absorb a majority of Vixco's ***expected losses.***

Required Which entity, if any, must consolidate Vixco?

E 3-8 **Variable Interest Entities** Entity A, Entity B, and Entity C each have a variable interest in Vixco, a variable interest entity. Their respective interests in Vixco's *expected residual returns* and *expected losses* are 45%, 30%, and 25%.

Required Which entity must consolidate Vixco?

Problems

P 3-1* **Consolidation Worksheet: Equity Method** The comparative financial statements of Pane Inc. and its 60%-owned subsidiary, Sill Inc. (created six years ago), follow:

	Pane Inc.		
	Cost Method[a]	Equity Method[b]	Sill Inc.
Income Statement (2006)			
Sales	$ 400,000	$ 400,000	$ 225,000
Cost of sales	(210,000)	(210,000)	(120,000)
Expenses	(140,000)	(140,000)	(80,000)
Dividend income (from Sill)	12,000		
Equity in net income (of Sill)		15,000	
Net Income	$ 62,000	$ 65,000	$ 25,000
Statement of Retained Earnings			
Balances, 1/1/06	$ 150,000	$ 183,000	$ 55,000
+ Net income	62,000	65,000	25,000
– Dividends declared	(40,000)	(40,000)	(20,000)
Balances, 12/31/06	$ 172,000	$ 208,000	$ 60,000
Balance Sheet (as of 12/31/06)			
Cash	$ 47,000	$ 47,000	$ 30,000
Accounts receivable, net	65,000	65,000	45,000
Intercompany receivable	15,000	15,000	
Inventory	190,000	190,000	70,000
Investment in subsidiary	30,000	66,000	
Property and equipment	370,000	370,000	180,000
Accumulated depreciation	(160,000)	(160,000)	(40,000)
Total Assets	$ 557,000	$ 593,000	$ 285,000
Payables and accruals	$ 135,000	$ 135,000	$ 70,000
Intercompany payable			15,000
Long-term debt	150,000	150,000	90,000
Common stock	100,000	100,000	50,000
Retained earnings	172,000	208,000	60,000
Total Liabilities and Equity	$ 557,000	$ 593,000	$ 285,000

[a] Use this column to work the problem under the *cost method,* which is called for in Problem 3A-1 in Appendix 3A.

[b] Use this column to work the problem under the *equity method,* which is called for in this problem.

Assume that the parent uses the *equity method.*

Required

1. Prepare an analysis of the Investment account for 2006.
2. Prepare all consolidation entries as of 12/31/06.
3. Prepare a consolidation worksheet at 12/31/06.

*The financial statement information presented for problems accompanied by asterisks is also provided on Model 3 (filename: MODEL03) at the **http://pahler.swlearning.com** Web Site, allowing the problem to be worked on the computer.

P 3-2* **Consolidation Worksheet: *Equity* Method** The comparative financial statements of Pylo Inc. and its 90%-owned subsidiary, Sylo Inc. (created seven years ago), follow:

	Pylo Inc.		
	Cost Method[a]	Equity Method[b]	Sylo Inc.
Income Statement (2006)			
Sales	$ 700,000	$ 700,000	$ 250,000
Cost of sales	(430,000)	(430,000)	(130,000)
Expenses	(170,000)	(170,000)	(90,000)
Dividend income (from Sylo)	9,000		
Equity in net income (of Sylo)		27,000	
Net Income	$ 109,000	$ 127,000	$ 30,000
Balance Sheet (as of 12/31/06)			
Cash	$ 49,000	$ 49,000	$ 40,000
Accounts receivable, net	95,000	95,000	55,000
Inventory	170,000	170,000	75,000
Investment in subsidiary	45,000	117,000	
Property and equipment	280,000	280,000	175,000
Accumulated depreciation	(120,000)	(120,000)	(25,000)
Total Assets	$ 519,000	$ 591,000	$ 320,000
Payables and accruals	$ 140,000	$ 140,000	$ 70,000
Long-term debt	300,000	300,000	120,000
Common stock	10,000	10,000	50,000
Retained earnings	69,000	141,000	80,000
Total Liabilities and Equity	$ 519,000	$ 591,000	$ 320,000
Dividends declared in 2006	$ 90,000	$ 90,000	$ 10,000

[a] Use this column to work the problem under the *cost method,* as called for in Problem 3A-2 in Appendix 3A.

[b] Use this column to work the problem under the *equity method,* as called for in this problem.

Assume that the parent uses the *equity method* of accounting.

Required

1. Prepare an analysis of the investment for 2006.
2. Prepare all consolidation entries as of 12/31/06.
3. Prepare a consolidation worksheet at 12/31/06.

P 3-3 **Partially Owned Subsidiaries: Equity or Cost—Other Objective Format Used on the CPA Examination** The following (1) eight account balances and (2) statements of retained earnings were obtained from the *separate company statements* of Pya Inc. and its 90%-owned created subsidiary, Sya Inc. (Pya's only subsidiary), at the end of 2006:

			Answers	
Item	Pya Inc.	Sya Inc.	Equity Method	Cost Method
Accounts				
1 Equity in net income (of Sya)	$ 36,000		______	______
2 Dividend income (from Sya)			______	______
3 Cash	77,000	$ 11,000	______	______
4 Intercompany receivable	18,000		______	______
5 Investment in subsidiary	225,000		______	______
6 Dividends payable	20,000	10,000	______	______
7 Common stock	1,000	5,000	______	______
8 Additional paid-in capital	299,000	95,000	______	______
Statements of Retained Earnings				
9 Retained earnings, 1/1/06	$395,000	$120,000	______	______
10 + Net income	115,000	40,000	______	______
11 − Dividends declared	(80,000)	(10,000)	______	______
12 Retained earnings, 12/31/06	$430,000	$150,000	______	______

Item	Pya Inc.	Sya Inc.	Answers: Equity Method	Answers: Cost Method
Additional Items (to be calculated)				
13 Pya's investment income from Sya—if the *cost method* were used instead of the *equity method*. . .	______		______	______
14 Noncontrolling interest in net income			______	
15 Noncontrolling interest in net assets.			______	
16 Consolidated net income—*Parent company concept*			______	
17 Consolidated net income—*Economic unit concept*			______	
18 The earnings from Pya's own *separate* operations			______	

When Sya was created (in 2001), 10% of the common shares it issued were sold to other private investors. For 2006, Pya had $79,000 of net income from its own separate operations—*excluding* its investment income relating to Sya.

1. How is each of the preceding 13 items reported in Pya's 2006 consolidated statements? Use the following list of possible answer codes in the answer columns:
   a. Report at the amount shown in Pya's separate statements.
   b. Report at the amount shown in Sya's separate statements.
   c. Report at the **sum of** the amounts shown in Pya's and Sya's separate statements.
   d. Report at **less than** the sum of the amounts shown in Pya's and Sya's separate statements.
   e. Do **not** report this item in the consolidated statements.
   f. Create this item in the consolidation process.
   g. Do **not** report this item in the consolidated statements or in either Pya's or Sya's separate statements.
2. For items 14 through 18, calculate the amount that would appear in the 2006 consolidated statements.

THINKING CRITICALLY

Cases

C 3-1 **Partially Owned Subsidiaries: "If I Made the Rules"** Pax Inc. owns 51% of the outstanding common stock of Sax Inc. Rax Inc. owns the other 49% of Sax. The separate company income statements for 2006, excluding any income recorded under the equity or cost methods, follow (in thousands):

	Pax Inc.	Rax Inc.	Sax Inc.
Revenues	$ 2,000	$ 2,000	$ 300
Costs and expenses	(1,800)	(1,800)	(200)
Net Income	$ 200	$ 200	$ 100

Required

1. Show the four possible manners of reporting that Pax could use to present its 2006 income statement to its shareholders.
2. Repeat requirement 1 for Rax.
3. If you were one of the seven FASB members, for which manner of reporting would you vote? Why?

C 3-2 **Rules or Judgment: Which is Better?** The accounting standards setters continually face the issue of whether to include detailed rules in their standards or to allow companies and their outside auditors to use judgment. Such is the case in the issue of whether an entity should be consolidated.

Required

1. What are the arguments for allowing judgment?
2. What are the arguments for having detailed rules?

3. What has been the direction of the standards setters in this respect since the FASB's establishment in 1973? Why do you think this is so?

C 3-3 **FASB versus SEC Rules: How to Live with a Double Standard** You are a CPA who audits both Privex, a privately owned parent company, and Publex, a publicly owned parent company. Assume that the SEC's consolidation rules are slightly more stringent than the FASB's consolidation rules as to (1) when consolidation is required and (2) what detailed disclosures are required.

Required

1. If Privex follows only the FASB consolidation rules, would you still be able to give an unqualified "clean" opinion on Privex's financial statements?
2. If your answer was yes, how comfortable do you feel giving unqualified opinions using two different reporting standards?
3. What do you think CPAs commonly do in such situations?

C 3-4 **Walks, Talks, and Looks Like a Duck: Is It One?** Platt Inc. and Dee Ziner, Platt's head of research and development, formed Secrex Inc., which will perform research and development. Secrex issued 5,000 shares of common stock to Ziner, who is now Secrex's president. (Ziner is no longer employed by Platt.) Platt lent $400,000 to Secrex for initial working capital in return for a note receivable that can be converted at will into 95,000 shares of Secrex's common stock. Platt also granted Secrex a line of credit of $1,000,000.

Required

1. Is consolidation appropriate?
2. What would Platt accomplish with this arrangement?
3. For this question only, assume that consolidating Secrex is *not* appropriate. What serious reporting issue exists regarding Platt's separate financial statements?

C 3-5 **Trust Your Instincts!** On 1/1/06, Phonex, Inc. created a business trust (a trust is *not* a legal entity). Also on that date, the trust issued $1,000,000 of Trust Preferred Securities (TPS) in exchange for $1,000,000. The money was immediately lent to Phonex at 10% all in accordance with the terms of the TPS.

Required

1. Is consolidation appropriate?
2. What would Phonex accomplish with this arrangement?
3. How would this arrangement be treated for *income tax reporting* purposes? (Could Phonex file a *consolidated income tax return* with the Trust?)

Personal Situations: Interpersonal Skills

PS 3-1 **Interpersonal Skills: Leadership—Is Vision Enough?** You recently became an officer in your college accounting club. You have some good ideas as to how the club could be run more effectively and be more fun.

Required What else usually must accompany vision for leadership to be effective?

part two

Consolidated Financial Statements: External Expansion Issues

chapter 4

Introduction to Business Combinations

In the long run, we shape our lives and shape ourselves. The process never dies. And the choices we make are ultimately our own responsibility.

ELEANOR ROOSEVELT

LEARNING OBJECTIVES

To Understand

- The legal and business environment in which business combinations occur.
- The *change* in the basis of accounting concept.
- The nature of and controversy surrounding goodwill.
- The business reasons for acquiring *assets* versus *common stock*.
- The organizational forms that can be used for the acquired business *after* the combination.
- The basic tax considerations in business combinations.

TOPIC OUTLINE

BUSINESS PERSPECTIVE: *Unlikely Hero: A Persistent Accountant Brought New Era's Problems to Light*

I. The Desire to Merge

II. The Attempted Takeover

III. The Manner of Accounting for Business Combinations

IV. The Goodwill Controversy

V. Acquiring Assets versus Common Stock

INTERNATIONAL PERSPECTIVE: *Foreign Goodwill Accounting Practices*

VI. The Resulting Organization Form of the *Acquired* Business

HISTORICAL PERSPECTIVE: *A Capsule History of Accounting for Goodwill*

APPENDIX 4A: Income Tax Considerations

Appendices can be found at http://www.pahler.swlearning.com

CHAPTER OVERVIEW

This chapter deals with *external expansion*, whereby one company expands by combining with another existing company. Bringing together two separate businesses under common ownership is known as a *business combination*. Most of the problems of *internal expansion* are *not* encountered in external expansion; only the assessment of the prospects of an existing business is involved. If the assessment is favorable, efforts to combine the businesses can be made. Most business combinations are completed in far less time than it would take to develop a new product, build manufacturing facilities to produce it, and then successfully market it. Often the newly acquired business produces a profit from the start. The management of the newly acquired business may be retained, and no new competitor is introduced into the field.

We discuss the FASB's relatively new financial reporting standards for *business combinations* and *goodwill*.

Purchase Investigations

Some acquisitions are spectacularly successful, producing fortunes for the acquirer. The most famous example is Microsoft's acquisition of Seattle Computer Products (the owner of the DOS operating system) for $50,000 in 1980. Often, however, companies wish they had never acquired certain businesses either because (1) expected synergies did *not* materialize or (2) material adverse financial information was purposely concealed by the target company prior to the combination date. See the Cases in Point.

CASES IN POINT

Cendant Corp. Makes Record $2.8 Billion Settlement Because of Undiscovered Accounting Irregularities

In 2000 Cendant Corp. (created by the 1998 merger of CUC International and HFS Inc.) made a $2.8 billion settlement with disgruntled shareholders after suffering $19 billion in stock market capitalization losses resulting from an undiscovered fraud scheme at HFS Inc. This is the largest settlement of a shareholder suit to date.

3COM Corp. Pays $259 Million Because of Undiscovered Accounting Irregularities

In 2000, 3COM Corp. (in the second largest settlement of a shareholder suit) paid $259 million as a result of the true financial condition of U.S. Robotics being concealed when 3COM acquired U.S. Robotics in 1997.

Accordingly, acquirers customarily conduct precombination "purchase investigations" of the target company by either (1) outside CPA firms or (2) their own internal accountants. These investigations are designed to uncover any hidden "skeletons in the closet" (material undisclosed financial information such as improper revenue recognition practices, unrecorded liabilities, and undisclosed related-party transactions).

Occasionally an intended business combination is aborted because a purchase investigation discovers major accounting irregularities or other hidden adverse material financial information. Thus an inquisitive accountant conducting a purchase investigation can add substantial value to an acquirer.

Unfortunately, purchase investigation discoveries that result in an acquirer backing out of an intended purchase are never published in the financial press. Accordingly, interviews with those who conduct such investigations are generally nonexistent. A few years ago, however, *The Wall Street Journal* interviewed an accountant employed in the *nonprofit sector* who displayed remarkable inquisitiveness and persistence in questioning one of his employer's investments. Even though the situation was *not* a purchase investigation involving a possible business combination, the qualities displayed by the accountant are those needed in performing purchase investigations. See the accompanying Business Perspective.

Business Perspective

Unlikely Hero: A Persistent Accountant Brought New Era's Problems to Light

As a hero, Albert J. Meyer is an unlikely figure: a mild-mannered, chess-playing accountant who teaches business at a tiny Christian college in a Michigan farming community.

But investigators for the Securities and Exchange Commission and others say that Mr. Meyer, 44 years old, is exactly that: He persevered for nearly two years, despite efforts to discourage him, and eventually blew the lid off a massive case of alleged fraud.

The target of Mr. Meyer's persistence was the Foundation for New Era Philanthropy, which authorities believe was operating a scam that sucked in hundreds of individuals and organizations (including Mr. Meyer's own college) and took in up to $200 million on the promise of a double-your-money return.

It was purely accidental that Mr. Meyer stumbled upon New Era in the first place. He and his wife, Melenie, 39, moved to bucolic Spring Arbor, Mich., from their native South Africa four years ago. "We wanted the excitement of being in another country," he says, "but not the excitement of being in 30 minutes of traffic jams." Devout Baptists, they also wanted to find a close-knit Christian community in which to bring up their three sons.

Mr. Meyer took a tenure-track job teaching accounting at Spring Arbor College, but because the college had only three accounting majors at the time, he worked part-time in the business office, balancing the college's books.

It was in this job that Mr. Meyer found a $294,000 bank transfer, dated July 8, 1993, from Spring Arbor to a foundation called the Heritage of Values Foundation Inc. The word "Heritage" caught his eye, reminding him of fallen TV evangelist Jim Bakker and his Heritage USA theme park. "It was the play on those words," Mr. Meyer recalls. "I guess I'm a cynic."

He dashed to the library to look up Heritage of Values and realized it wasn't connected to the Bakker scam, but could find nothing else. The next day, he approached Janet M. Tjepkema, the college's vice president for business affairs, and told her he felt compelled to query the transfer.

Mr. Meyer says Ms. Tjepkema told him Heritage of Values was connected to a consultant who had introduced the college to New Era and that the money was earmarked for New Era.

He rushed to the library again, but was unable to find anything on New Era. When he returned to campus, "I could sense annoyance" from administrators, he says. "I was biting the hand that was feeding us."

For most of the time that it took Mr. Meyer to amass financial documents and to help bring the alleged scam to light, he worked alone at night and on weekends, with his wife as his only sounding board. He also told a few students, saying, "This is what auditing is all about. This is a real-life case study."

He telephoned all over the country and amassed three thick files of correspondence, with labels like "Ponzi-File: If it quacks like a duck, walks like a duck and looks like a duck, could it really be a duck?" He operated quietly at first, fearing that, as an untenured foreigner on a temporary work visa, he might lose his job.

But Mr. Meyer also tried—repeatedly—to warn Spring Arbor. The associate business professor attempted to rally faculty colleagues, called administrators, sent a cautionary letter to Glenn E. White, the trustees' chairman, and alerted the college's president, Allen Carden.

While most of the faculty eventually came to agree with Mr. Meyer, the administrators never did, and by April, he had begun to sense a coldness that led him to avoid social situations such as Spring Arbor's annual staff appreciation dinner.

At one point, Mr. Meyer thought he had succeeded in persuading the college not to trust New Era. In a mid-March meeting with President Carden and Neil E. Veydt, vice president for planning and advancement, he was told that the college was prepared to plunk down $1 million—but hadn't sent it yet. "As I walked out, I thought, 'That's it, I'm saving the college money,' I was over the moon," he says.

Then he learned that administrators had ignored his advice and sent the money—part of a $1.5 mil-

Business Perspective, continued

lion New Era investment that Spring Arbor (which has only a $6 million endowment) now stands to lose.

"I couldn't believe it. I said, 'OK, if I'm not able to protect them, I'll protect anyone else I can. I will become a crusader,' " he says.

He began to identify with the sleuth in "Scoundrels & Scalawags," a book about Charles Ponzi's turn-of-the-century pyramid scheme in Boston. "By this time . . . I felt that I would have to carry the whole burden of exposing Ponzi," he says.

Mr. Meyer might have kept working inconspicuously, but on March 15, he received tenure. In the tenure letter, the college saluted him for his "strong Christian faith" and for "outstanding qualities that exemplify the kind of faculty members needed at Spring Arbor College." The next day, Mr. Meyer told his wife he was going to "test the limits of tenure."

She knew he wasn't kidding; he's never done anything halfway. He didn't simply play chess: He competed in the national U.S. Open tournament. He didn't simply cut down on TV-watching in his house: He gave away the television. "He's a very focused guy," his wife says. "He's a pit bull. He never daydreams. He's always thinking about things and working things out."

Mr. Meyer launched a full-scale attack on New Era, believing he was the only person who fully understood what was happening, and knowing he would never be able to face faculty members if he backed off. He contacted some of the institutions that had invested money in New Era, including Wheaton College in Illinois and the Moody Bible Institute in Chicago. When they ignored him, he went to the Internal Revenue Service and the American Institute of Certified Public Accountants, among others.

"I spoke to so many people who said, 'Yes, yes, yes, you might be right,' but they didn't do anything because it's a burden," he says.

It was his letter to the SEC last month that prompted the SEC to start investigating New Era, setting off the chain of events that led to the collapse of New Era.

Mr. Meyer says he is "overwhelmed" that the alleged New Era scam is as big as it now appears. "I actually earned my salary," he says, returning to one of his sources of motivation: his sense of obligation to employers and to his host country. "I always count the credit hours—what the students pay, what they pay me, and am I earning $2 or $3 for every $1 I'm being paid? I have to pay my way . . . I'm a visitor," he says.

The campus's reaction has been mixed. Just two weeks before the scandal broke, Dr. Carden assured the Spring Arbor community of the trustees' "business savvy" and warned faculty members that "a healthy skepticism" was commendable, but a "crusading zeal" was often "counterproductive."

Dr. Carden said in an interview Tuesday that he was "not going to give up hope" of recovering the $1.5 million that Spring Arbor stands to lose, but said he believed the college had "acted in an appropriate fashion."

But late Wednesday, Mr. Meyer received a letter from Dr. Carden that said, "I believe you did something heroic. You followed your professional instincts when many of us believed you to be wrong." Ms. Tjepkema, Dr. Carden, Mr. White, Mr. Veydt and Wheaton College couldn't be reached for comment Thursday.

And faculty members and students are showing their support for Mr. Meyer. Former student Virgie Ammerman-Warner says, "I think it's great that he went on. Some people would have sat back and said, 'If my bosses aren't going to support me, I'm not going to go any further.'

"But he didn't. He went anyway," she says.

Source: Barbara Carton, "Unlikely Hero: A Persistent Accountant Brought New Era's Problems to Light," *The Wall Street Journal*, May 19, 1995, p. B1.

I. THE DESIRE TO MERGE

Terminology

In the business community, business combinations are referred to as *mergers* and *acquisitions*. The company whose business is being sought is often called the **target company**. The company attempting to acquire the target company's business is referred to as the **acquiring company**. The legal agreement that specifies the terms and provisions of the business combination is known as the *acquisition*, *purchase*, or *merger agreement*. For simplicity, we refer to this legal agreement as the **acquisition agreement**. The process of trying to acquire a target company's business is often called a **takeover attempt**. Business combinations can be categorized as vertical, horizontal, or conglomerate. **Vertical combinations** take place between companies involved in the same industry but at different levels—for example, a tire manufacturer and a tire distributor. **Horizontal combinations** take place between companies that are competitors at the same level in a given industry—two tire manufacturers, for example. **Conglomerate combinations** involve companies in totally unrelated industries—such as a tire manufacturer and an insurance company. These categories of business combination have no bearing on how the combination is recorded for financial reporting purposes.

Legal Restrictions on Business Combinations

Before discussing business combinations any further, we should note that certain combinations are prohibited. Section 7 of the Clayton Act (1914) prohibits any business combination in which "the effect of such acquisition may be substantially to lessen competition or tend to create a monopoly." The Justice Department and the Federal Trade Commission, the two federal agencies with antitrust jurisdiction, enforce this law. See the Cases in Point for some notable examples.

CASES IN POINT

U.S. Justice Department Prevailed over Microsoft's Plan to Acquire Intuit for $2.1 Billion

Microsoft Corp. abandoned its effort to acquire Intuit Inc. (which dominates the personal-finance software market with its highly popular QUICKEN program) after the U.S. Justice Department filed an antitrust suit seeking an injunction to block the planned combination. The Justice Department claimed that the merger would give Microsoft total dominance over the burgeoning market for personal-finance software.

U.S. Federal Trade Commission Blocked a $4.4 Billion Merger

The Federal Trade Commission blocked Staples Inc.'s acquisition of Office Depot Inc.

U.S. Justice Department and Department of Defense Blocked an $8.4 Billion Merger

Lockheed Martin Corp. scrapped its yearlong effort to buy Northrop Grumman because it was faced with a protracted battle with the Justice Department and the Department of Defense.

Even when the government does *not* challenge a proposed business combination before it is consummated, it can later issue a *divestiture order* requiring the acquiring company to dispose of its acquired business. If the acquiring company appeals the order, the courts may or may not uphold it.

Although the Clayton Act apparently applies only to horizontal and vertical combinations, the regulatory agencies have challenged certain conglomerate combinations too. For the most part, these challenges have not been successful, and companies expanding externally into unrelated fields generally have no problem complying with the Clayton Act. Many companies obtain a legal opinion on the application of this law to each contemplated business combination *before* taking steps that lead to consummation.

Are *Large* Mergers Bad by Definition?

Many observers believe that certain mergers should be prohibited simply because of their size, even though they would not reduce competition or create a monopoly. Their concern is that huge combinations concentrate economic power in fewer hands, which is deemed undesirable. The courts and the governmental agencies have taken the position in recent years, however, that *mergers are not bad merely because they are large.* As a result, virtually all of the 25 largest business combinations in U.S. history have occurred in the last 20 years.

Which Party Is in Power?

Up until 1992, the political party in the White House greatly influenced the zeal with which governmental agencies interpreted and enforced antitrust laws. In general, fewer combinations between competing companies were challenged under Republican administrations than under Democratic administrations because of differing philosophies. This did not hold true, however, during the eight years of the Clinton administration (1993–2000). See the Cases in Point for some examples of notable mergers during this period that consumer groups strongly opposed.

CASES IN POINT

U.S. Federal Trade Commission Allows $81 Billion Merger of U.S.'s No. 1 and No. 2 Oil Companies

In 1999, the Federal Trade Commission reviewed but allowed the $81 billion merger of Exxon Corp. and Mobil Corp. This merger was the largest in a series of consolidations that occurred in the industry in the 1990s.

AOL-Time Warner's $147 Billion Merger Was Opposed by Four Leading Consumer Groups

In January 2000, the merger of AOL and Time Warner (the largest U.S. merger to date) was allowed—despite petitions that four leading U.S. consumer groups filed with the federal government in an attempt to block this merger.

The Prevalence of Business Combinations

External expansion is a major vehicle for corporate growth. The number of business combinations occurring in a given year is largely a function of the state of the economy: Merger activity is usually *low* during recessionary periods and *high* during boom periods when companies tend to accumulate healthy amounts of cash. Excess cash *not* used for dividends must be reinvested. (Of course, the alternative is to distribute the excess cash as dividends and allow the *stockholders* to diversify individually.) Stock market prices tend to rise during a boom, enabling acquiring companies that use stock (instead of cash) as consideration to issue fewer shares of its stock to acquire another company.

From 1992 to 2001—The Largest Wave of Mergers and Acquisitions Ever

Prior to 1992, worldwide mergers and acquisitions never exceeded more than $600 billion per year. Since that time, corporate marriages have occurred at a frenetic pace, with eight consecutive record years occurring. For 2000 (the largest year), the total value of announced mergers worldwide was roughly $3 trillion ($1.75 trillion for the United States). Topping the list was AOL's $147 billion acquisition of Time Warner in 2000. In the last ten years, the 50 largest U.S. companies were involved in roughly 6,000 mergers or acquisitions.

Bigger Is Better

This merger and acquisition frenzy of the 1990s, which dwarfs that of all other historical periods, has occurred most notably in the telecommunications, entertainment, banking, automobile, and oil industries. For example, Cisco Systems Inc.'s astonishing growth was fueled largely as a result of its 71 acquisitions between 1993 and 2000. In 2000, Cisco (created in 1988) became the second most valuable company in the U.S. (based on stock market capitalization)—edging out General Electric Co. and behind only software behemoth Microsoft Corp. The thinking is that being bigger is not only better but essential in a global economy.

The consequences of all these mergers are considerable. In the banking industry, for example, mergers and acquisitions were primarily responsible for the number of banks declining by 36% from approximately 14,500 in 1984 to roughly 9,000 in 2003. The Exxon-Mobil merger was heavily criticized by environmental groups because they feared it would create a double-loud lobbying voice for the notion that global warming (thought to be caused by burning fossil fuels) is unsubstantiated. One environmental group stated, "Economically, they may think this marriage is made in heaven. Ecologically, we think this marriage is bad for the heavens as well as the Earth."[1]

Although many business combinations involve two large companies, most combinations involve a large company combining with a small company. Often such combinations enable a small company to expand more rapidly than would be possible with its existing resources.

The Impetus for Business Combinations

Much of the impetus for business combinations comes from the belief that the results will produce (1) substantial cost savings through economies of scale (the reason given for the high number of recent bank mergers) or (2) synergies so that the combined entity will be more of a force than are the two entities alone.

Much of the impetus also comes, however, from the belief that high asset returns and growth rates exist in other businesses—what could be called the *greener pastures syndrome*. As a result, capital is redeployed; the less-desirable companies are sold and the presumed emerging "stars" are bought.

Many Combinations Fall Flat

Bringing together two companies through a business combination is *not* without risks. As many as 40% of all acquired businesses do *not* achieve their projected sales and profit growth (in retrospect, buyers find that they paid far too much). In many instances, the merger destroys much value. When managements attempt to diversify, they often find that they *cannot* manage a new business that they know nothing about any better than they could manage businesses with which they are familiar. (See the Cases in Point for some notable examples.)

CASES IN POINT

Sony Corporation's Costly Foray into Hollywood

In 1994, Sony Corporation took a staggering $2.7 billion write-off on its $5 billion 1989 acquisition of Columbia Pictures, one of the largest losses ever recognized on an attempt to diversify. Analysts attributed the loss to mismanagement.

AT&T Corp.'s Costly Foray into Electronic

In 1996, AT&T spun off NCR Corp. by distributing shares of the company to holders of AT&T stock. AT&T had acquired NCR in 1991 for $7.5 billion in a hostile takeover. Under AT&T's five-year ownership, NCR bled a staggering $3 9 billion of losses, as customers fled and costs skyrocketed out of control.

America Online's 2001 Merger with Time-Warner Has Been a Mega Disappointment

In 2002 (one year after the record $147 billion merger), AOL Time Warner took a $99 billion goodwill impairment charge against earnings, resulting in the largest annual loss ever reported by a corporation. Major management shakeups were announced. Of the $147 billion purchase price, nearly $130 billion was assigned to goodwill.

---

[1] Robert Reno, "Mindless Merger Mania," *The San Jose Mercury News*, December 15, 1998, p. 6B.

The New Bureaucracy

Often the target company's top management and key employees become both frustrated at having to work within the acquiring company's newly imposed operating procedures and resentful of the unwanted involvement in daily operations. Many of them simply leave the firm rather than continue under the new management—draining the company of leadership and talent needed to remain competitive. Often major operating losses result. (This is most notable in the electronics industry.)

Diversification That Resulted in Retrenchment

When the major U.S. oil companies became flush with cash in the 1970s as a result of rising oil prices, many of them feared the day when the world's oil reserves would run out, so they began diversifying heavily into other industries. Within a few years, however, they had sold or shut down most of the acquired operations.

Because their vast operations simply became unmanageable, conglomerates created in the 1960s and 1970s began in the 1980s to dispose of many of the companies they had so eagerly acquired (General Electric Co. alone disposed of more than 200 subsidiaries during the 1980s). In the 1990s, more and more diversified companies shed units so that they could concentrate on their core businesses. Thus the days of the conglomerate or highly diversified company may be passing. (See the Case in Point below.)

CASE IN POINT

Sears, Roebuck and Co. Returns to Its Merchandising Roots

In the 1980s, Sears, Roebuck and Co. tried to build a financial services empire on the shoulders of its huge retailing business by acquiring a savings and loan, the Coldwell Banker real estate brokerage, and the Dean Witter stockbrokerage. It also introduced the Discover credit card. From 1990 to 1995, however, Sears discarded all these units, as well as its Allstate Insurance subsidiary. As a result, Sears now manages only its retailing business.

Some firms try to diversify within their own industry by filling out a product line. Although such endeavors would seem to be much less risky than diversifying into totally unrelated fields, they often have the same unfortunate consequences. (See the Case in Point below.)

CASE IN POINT

Novell Corporation Sells WordPerfect and Quattro Pro

In late 1995, Novell Corporation announced that it would sell its WordPerfect and Quattro Pro programs, acquired in 1994 in an attempt to go head to head with Microsoft in the sale of application "suites." In doing so, Novell stated that it would concentrate instead on the networking programs that were its foundation. The problem with WordPerfect was that it rapidly lost most of its market share to Microsoft by fall 1995 as a result of fierce competition. Thus it virtually imploded. In 1996, Novell sold WordPerfect for $124 million, roughly one-eleventh of Novell's $1.4 billion purchase price.

Split-Ups: Business Combination Reversals

Rather than selling certain units to focus on the core business, some entities split the business into distinct independent companies. Doing so acknowledges that the vision of *synergy*—the term used for decades to justify all manner of mergers and most recently to explain the wave of big media industry deals—was *not* achieved. (See the Case in Point on page 110.)

Many of the takeover attempts began when a bidder recognized that a company's stock was selling at a depressed level (in relation to the value of the business) precisely because of management's

CASE IN POINT

AT&T Split Itself into *Three* Companies

In a move to allow it to focus on long-distance communications and aggressive competition from the Baby Bells, AT&T in 1996 split itself into *three* independent publicly traded companies: a communication services company (a highly profitable operation that prior to the planned split-up provided 80% of AT&T's annual sales and 60% of its profits), a communication equipment company (Lucent Technology), and a computing company. Thus AT&T jettisoned its ailing computing operation, the bulk of which it acquired from NCR Corporation for $7.48 billion in 1991 (an acquisition that was a huge disappointment in light of NCR's subsequent performance).

Note: In 1995, IT&T Corporation also split itself into *three* independent publicly traded companies.

inability to effectively oversee diversified operations. In this common scenario, discussed in the next section, one segment of the company begins to experience operating losses, which leads to a significant drop in the price of the stock as investors begin to lose confidence in the entire company. This situation makes the company a potential takeover candidate. After buying the company's stock at a fraction of its value, thus gaining management control, the acquirer can then sell off the various divisions at a substantial profit (called a *breakup*).

II. The Attempted Takeover

Preventing a Takeover Attempt

Because business combinations are so prevalent, many managements fearing a potential takeover have taken defensive steps (colloquially known as *shark repellant*) to make it more difficult for an acquiring company to effect a takeover. Some of the more routine steps involve requesting stockholders to approve such articles of incorporation, charter, and bylaw provisions as the following:

1. **Elimination of cumulative voting.** Under cumulative voting, each stockholder has as many votes as the number of shares owned multiplied by the number of directors to be elected. Thus a potential acquiring company with a relatively small holding of common stock could obtain representation on the board of directors. Many companies have reincorporated in Delaware, which does *not* require cumulative voting.
2. **Use of staggered terms for directors.** If directors have staggered terms, changes in the composition of the board of directors occur more slowly, making it impossible for a successful suitor to gain control of the board upon either consummation of the business combination or winning a proxy contest.
3. **Adoption of supermajority provisions.** For votes on *statutory mergers* and acquisitions of assets (specific types of business combinations that are discussed in detail later in the chapter), imposing a stipulated percentage in excess of a simple majority (80% is commonly used) makes a takeover by either of these types of business combinations more difficult.
4. **Authorization of blank-check preferred stock.** Such authorization enables management to place the preferred stock privately in friendly hands. Typically, the owners of the preferred stock have either (1) the right to approve any proposed merger or sale of assets or (2) multiple voting rights (such as three votes for each vote of common stock).

Steps Leading to a Business Combination

Few business activities match the excitement that can be generated by an attempt to acquire a target company's business. Often an acquiring company must operate in strict secrecy until the last possible moment to avoid attracting the attention of other companies that might be interested in acquiring the business. Such secrecy minimizes the possibility of a bidding war. (Some companies, as a matter of policy, immediately cease their takeover efforts if a bidding war starts; the presumption here is that the successful bidder would probably wind up paying too much.) The acquiring company may start purchasing the common stock of the target company slowly, over a period of time, until it owns just under 5% of the target company's common stock (5% ownership requires public disclosure). Such secrecy also affects the target company: If it opposes the takeover, its management has *less* time in which to take defensive actions.

The Friendly Approach

In theory, a business combination should involve only the *acquiring company* and the stockholders of the *target company*. In its simplest terms, the *target company's* stockholders must decide whether to accept the *acquiring company's* offer. In evaluating the offer, the stockholders consider the recommendation of their directors and management. Because of this, most *acquiring companies* attempt to obtain a favorable recommendation from the directors and management of the target company before they present the offer to its stockholders. The usual procedure for this involves negotiating an acquisition agreement with the *target company's* management. If successful, and if the *target company's* directors also approve the agreement, the offer is then submitted to the *target company's* stockholders for their approval or rejection. This sequence of events is characterized as a "friendly" takeover attempt.

This approach of first making a proposal to management is also referred to as the *bearhug* tactic because the threat of making an offer directly to the shareholders looms in the background.

The Refusal to Be Friendly

Less-friendly situations occur when (1) the acquiring company does *not* seek the approval of the *target company's* directors and its management, (2) the *target company's* directors and management refuse to negotiate an acquisition agreement, and (3) negotiations do *not* result in an offer that the *target company's* directors and management believe is in the best interests of the *target company's* stockholders. The *acquiring company* must then present its offer directly to the stockholders of the *target company* without the approval of its directors and management. These cases are characterized as "unfriendly" takeover attempts. Some companies have a policy of pursuing a target company *only* if the takeover can be done on a friendly basis.

Resorting to the Tender Offer

An offer made by an *acquiring company* directly to the target company's stockholders is known as a **tender offer**, commonly known as a *takeover bid*. Under a tender offer, the acquiring company requests that the *target company's* stockholders give up their shares in exchange for cash or securities. The usual features of a tender offer are the following:

1. It is made in newspapers.
2. The *offering price* substantially *exceeds* the current *market price* of the target company's common stock.
3. The offer must be accepted by a certain specified date, usually in the near future (such as 30 days).
4. The acquiring company reserves the right to withdraw the offer if a specified number of shares are *not* tendered. (If *more than* the specified number of shares are tendered, the acquiring company reserves the right to reject such excess shares.)

Because the stockholders send their shares to a financial institution, which holds the shares in a fiduciary capacity until the expiration date of the offer, the shares are said to have been *tendered*—not sold. At the expiration date and provided that the minimum number of shares have been tendered, the acquiring company then pays for the tendered shares.

ETHICS

Ethics: Yes, You Can—No, You Can't After All

In the 1980s, the savings and loan (S&L) regulatory agencies encouraged strong S&Ls to acquire financially failing S&Ls. The regulators allowed the acquirers to treat goodwill as an asset for regulatory purposes. In 1990, Congress passed S&L bailout legislation, which contained provisions that prohibited counting goodwill as an asset after 1994 for regulatory purposes.

As a result of massive subsequent write-offs of goodwill for regulatory purposes, many S&Ls did *not* have sufficient capital for regulatory purposes. Consequently, the S&L regulators forced the closure of these S&Ls, and stockholders lost their entire investment.

Questions

1. Did the federal government act ethically?
2. Do you think that the stockholders of these closed S&Ls would be able to recover damages from the federal government?

Statutes Governing Tender Offers

Federal Statutes

In 1968, in response to the wave of takeovers in the 1960s, Congress passed the Williams Act, which provides for federal regulation of tender offers. The avowed purpose of the law, which the Securities and Exchange Commission (SEC) enforces, is to protect the target company's shareholders by requiring the bidder to furnish detailed disclosures to the target company and its stockholders. Some believe that the Williams Act should be abolished entirely, allowing a return to the pre-1968 open-market takeover environment. Others believe that the act should be tougher.

State Statutes

Since 1968, almost all states have passed legislation ostensibly to provide further protection to stockholders of the target company. For the most part, these statutes require more detailed disclosures than the federal statutes. Furthermore, most of them do not permit a tender offer to be made until 20 days after the initial public disclosure, whereas the federal requirement is only five days. A great controversy has developed over whether these state laws are really essential to protect the stockholders or whether they merely favor the in-state targets over out-of-state bidders because the additional disclosures and waiting period give the target company extra time to thwart the takeover bid if it desires. The constitutionality of these laws may be questioned on the grounds that they interfere with interstate commerce and that federal statutes preempt state statutes. Until 1987, the courts generally declined to enforce these laws for these reasons. As a result, bidding companies routinely filed suits (at the public announcement of their takeover bids) seeking injunctions against the enforcement of these laws. In 1987, the United States Supreme Court for the first time upheld a state law (Indiana) regulating corporate takeovers. Since that decision, more than 30 states have modified their takeover statutes, primarily by adopting provisions similar to those in the Indiana statute.

Defensive Tactics During Takeover Attempts

The board of directors of a target company may authorize management to take aggressive action to try to prevent a takeover. A common defensive action is to file lawsuits against the acquiring company on various grounds relating to probable violation of antitrust laws, violation of state takeover laws, and violation of securities laws pertaining to public disclosures. Even if a lawsuit by itself is *not* successful, it entangles the acquiring company in legal proceedings and usually gives management more time to fight the takeover attempt.

Prior to the 1980s, these **legalistic defenses** were reasonably successful and were often referred to as *showstoppers* (a defense that stops a bidder dead in its tracks). Beginning in the 1980s, however, legalistic defenses lost much of their effectiveness, as courts began taking the position that the stockholders must decide on such attempts. As a result, other types of defensive tactics emerged, most of which are considered **financial defenses.** The following list summarizes the major financial defenses.

1. **The "scorched earth" (or "selling the crown jewels") defense.** When a bidder's primary interest in a target company is one or more prized segments, management may sell those segments to make itself less attractive as a target. A variation of this tactic is the *lock-up option*, whereby a friendly company is granted the option to acquire the prized segment in the event the takeover succeeds.
2. **Adding a fair price amendment to the corporate charter.** Some tender offers are two-tiered offers, whereby cash—for example, $100 per share—is offered for just over 50% of the target company's outstanding common stock, but a lower amount— for example, $80 per share—is offered for the remaining shares. Individuals who tender their shares early receive an extra premium of $20 per share. Fair price amendments are designed to ensure that *all* stockholders receive an equivalent price for their shares. Sometimes the *second tier* of the offer consists of noncash consideration, such as common or preferred stock and notes, making the *first tier* of the offer even more attractive.

   Critics of *two-tiered* offers claim that such offers are coercive and place enormous pressure on stockholders to tender their shares promptly to avoid a lower price on the *second tier*.
3. **Making a self-tender offer.** When the bidder's offer is deemed unfairly low, the target company may make a higher tender offer to a large percentage of its shareholders, called a *self-tender offer*. This tactic is usually paired with the "selling the crown jewels" defense, which raises money from which to pay for the shares acquired in the self-tender offer.

   Many self-tender offers are *two-tiered* tender offers, thus having the same supposed coercive effect as hostile tender offers that are *two tiered*. (Of course, fair price amendments are worded so that they do *not* apply to *two-tiered self-tender* offers.)
4. **The recapitalization defense.** When an increased debt load is likely to make the acquisition unattractive to the acquiring company, the target company may try to boost its debt and use the proceeds to pay a huge one-time dividend to its shareholders, thereby shrinking its equity drastically. (This tactic has the same effect on the debt-to-equity ratio as the self-tender offer.)
5. **The Pac-Man defense.** When the target company is fairly large relative to the acquiring company, it may attempt to acquire the acquiring company.
6. **The mudslinging defense.** When the acquiring company offers stock instead of cash, the target company's management may try to convince the stockholders that the stock would be a bad investment. In some takeover attempts, the fierce attacks on the integrity and ability of the acquiring company's management (in light of certain past transactions and recent performance) put the acquiring company on the defensive to such a degree that it abandoned its takeover attempts. Many target companies hire private investigators to discover embarrassing information that would discredit the management of the hostile bidder.
7. **The defensive acquisition tactic.** When a major reason for an attempted takeover is the target company's favorable cash position, the target company may try to rid itself of this excess cash by attempting a takeover of its own. Such action may also result in a combined business that the initial acquiring company is not interested in acquiring. For example, acquiring a *competitor* of the initial acquiring company creates antitrust issues that would probably derail the takeover attempt with prospective litigation.
8. **The leveraged buyout defense.** When management desires to own the business, it may arrange to buy out the stockholders using the company's assets to finance the deal. (This increasingly common tactic is discussed later in the chapter and in Chapter 7.)
9. **Adopting a "poison pill" provision.** Although many variations exist, the common procedure is to grant the company's stockholders—excluding shares owned by the acquiring company—the right to purchase additional common shares of the company (or of an acquiring company) at bargain prices (typically at 50% of the market price of the stock). The rights usually become exercisable (or *triggered*) when an "unfriendly" acquiring company acquires 20% of the common stock or makes a bid to acquire 30% of the common stock. The purpose of the provision is to make the acquisition prohibitively expensive to the unfriendly company (or make it suffer unwanted dilution of its own shares if the rights pertain to its own common stock). The

provision customarily enables the company to redeem the rights if it chooses to complete a friendly merger. A 1985 Delaware Supreme Court decision upheld the right of managements to use the "poison pill" defenses without shareholder approval. Since then, this tactic has become widely used (both during takeover attempts and to prevent future takeover attempts). Approximately 200 of the *Fortune* 500 companies have adopted poison pill provisions.

10. **Paying "greenmail."** When a bidder acquires perhaps 10–20% of the target company's stock, the company may agree to purchase these stockholdings at a premium, allowing the bidder (most commonly called a *corporate raider*) to walk away with a hefty profit (on the condition that it not buy any stock in the future).

Defensive Tactics: Whose Interest Is Served?

Sometimes turning down an offer or even refusing to negotiate results in the acquiring company's making a higher offer. This is clearly in the best interest of the target company's stockholders. In some cases, however, such management actions are self-serving; managers oppose the takeover because they want to remain top executives of an independent company rather than become top executives of a small part of a much larger company—or they fear the loss of their jobs. In some instances, management's actions in defending against takeover attempts are irresponsible, especially when their stockholders are overwhelmingly tendering their shares and thereby accepting the offer.

The preceding examples make evident that more and more stockholders of target companies file lawsuits against their managers and directors alleging one of two things: (1) misuse of corporate resources in resisting takeover attempts (in a great number of instances, millions have been spent fighting the takeover attempt) or (2) violation of their fiduciary duty to stockholders by refusing to negotiate for the highest price possible. For the most part, the courts have been reluctant to find managements and directors guilty of these charges. Some companies attempt to protect their directors from such potential actions by dissatisfied stockholders by having the stockholders require the board of directors (through an amendment to the articles of incorporation) to consider factors other than the value and type of consideration offered when determining whether to accept an offer. Such factors might include the economic effects the takeover would have on employees and communities in which the target company operates.

In the late 1980s, financial circles and congressional committees extensively debated whether these widespread defensive tactics were (1) really necessary to protect stockholders (presumably from *voluntarily* selling their stock at a higher price) or (2) nothing more than self-serving management entrenchment devices that should be legally banned or at least voted on annually by the stockholders because of the changing composition of the stockholders from year to year. Congress, however, has enacted no federal legislation.

Proxy Contests

In recent years, several factors (poison pills and increased state antitakeover legislation) have weakened the case for making tender offers. As a result, many acquiring companies have turned to **proxy contests** (often called *proxy wars*) to obtain control instead of making a direct purchase. In a proxy contest, both management and the acquirer solicit votes from the target company's stockholders for their respective proposed slates of directors.

In theory, the proxy system appears to be a superior way to obtain control of a target company because the insurgents can have their people (who will approve a proposed merger) placed on the board *without* having to buy *more than* 50% of the company to obtain control. In practice, however, the proxy system is extremely inefficient, and it gives management several built-in advantages over challengers. For example, *management* has full access to the corporate treasury to pay for its proxy solicitation effort (which can cost up to $10 million), but the *acquirer* must use its own funds. Obtaining lists of shareholders, although easy for management, is quite difficult for challengers (who often have to go through the courts). Tracking down stockholders is often impossible when brokers hold the stock in a street name. In most cases, managements win these proxy contests. The most famous recent proxy contest was in 1988 when Carl Icahn (once referred to as the most feared corporate raider in America) sought control of Texaco Inc., but incumbent management narrowly won.

The Debate over Takeovers

During the period 1982 through 1999, mergers and acquisitions, divestitures, breakups, leveraged buyouts, buybacks, and recapitalizations (collectively called *restructurings*) reached a record high in terms of the value of the transactions. The sheer magnitude of the restructurings during this period raises questions as to whether all this restructuring is good or bad for the country.

Some observers contend that restructuring results in (1) many companies becoming overleveraged; (2) substantial disruption of the job market, with a consequent major adverse social impact on the communities affected; and (3) inordinate enrichment of the investment bankers and lawyers who are paid seemingly huge sums for their services ($100 million on a $2 billion deal is not uncommon) and who therefore are highly motivated to continually "put companies into play."

Others contend that restructuring is revitalizing our industry in response to fierce foreign competition by simplifying or "streamlining" corporations that have become too large and too complicated to be efficient, enabling managers to be in closer touch with production workers, customers, and stockholders.

The Debate from a Historical Perspective

Four distinct periods of financial restructurings have occurred in the last 100 years: (1) the *horizontal* combinations near the turn of the century, (2) the *vertical* combinations of the 1920s, (3) the *conglomerate* combinations of the 1960s, and (4) most recently in the 1980s the *leveraged reorganizations* that undid many of the conglomerate combinations of the 1960s. (The 1990s may ultimately be considered a distinct period of mostly horizontal combinations.) Why do financial restructurings occur so frequently? Many contend that periodic waves of restructurings are necessary in an economy based on capitalism to force the business sector to adapt to economic and technological change (the invisible hand of Adam Smith at work that makes for a more productive and competitive economy).

Leveraged Buyouts

A different kind of takeover of an existing business is a **leveraged buyout (LBO)**. The typical LBO involves a group of investors that buys out an existing ownership using an extremely high percentage of debt to pay for the acquisition. The target company's assets are used as collateral to secure the loans. Such buyouts—in which the buyer is a group of investors rather than an existing business—are not combinations of two existing businesses. The new basis of accounting issue (discussed next) pertains, however, to LBOs as well as to combinations. We discuss LBOs in Chapter 7.

III. THE MANNER OF ACCOUNTING FOR BUSINESS COMBINATIONS

In 2001, after six years of research, study, trial-balloons, and heated debates with corporate managements, the FASB greatly simplified the business combination rules by issuing FASB *Statement No. 141*, "Business Combinations." *FAS 141* superseded the heavily criticized, complex, and time-consuming-to-interpret *Accounting Principles Board Opinion No. 16*, "Business Combinations."[2]

Only the Purchase Method Is Permitted

FAS 141 eliminated the previously allowed "pooling of interests" method, thus requiring only the "purchase method" to be used in recording business combinations. Under the *purchase method*,

[2] Prior to the issuance of *FAS 141*, the Division of Corporate Finance of the Securities and Exchange Commission would often spend 40% of their time in some months responding to inquiries from companies as to whether a proposed business combination would satisfy the intricate criteria needed to obtain the *pooling of interests* accounting treatment.

two things occur: (1) a *change in basis* (**from *book value* to *current value***) is effected for the acquired business's assets and liabilities (based on the acquirer's acquisition cost), and (2) goodwill bought and paid for is recognized (reported as an *asset* in the *combined* balance sheet). *Neither* of these things occurs under the now prohibited *pooling of interest* method. Accordingly, enormous financial reporting differences occur between these two methods.

The Rationale for Allowing Only One Method

The FASB eliminated the *pooling of interests method* because it (1) provided less-relevant information to investors than the *purchase method* (by ignoring the values exchanged in a business combination transaction), (2) did *not* provide investors with the information needed to assess the subsequent performance of an investment and compare it with the performance of other companies, (3) was generally *not* permitted by (a) other major industrialized countries or (b) international accounting standards. (Corporate managements absolutely loved the *pooling of interests method* because acquiring companies would report much higher postcombination earnings under this method—they fought hard to keep *APBO 16* intact but lost.)

Achieving Conformity with International Accounting Standards

FAS 141 brought U.S. business combination rules into substantial agreement with (1) international accounting standards *(International Accounting Standard 22* issued by the International Accounting Standards Committee) and (2) business combination standards used by virtually all other major industrialized countries. See Chapter 13 for a discussion of global efforts currently being made to internationalize *all* accounting standards, so as to ultimately achieve a "World GAAP."

The Purchase Method

The Underlying Concept

The underlying concept of the *purchase method* is that **one company has acquired the business of another company and a sale has occurred.** Unlike the *pooling of interests method,* any type of consideration—namely, cash, bonds, preferred stock, and common stock—may be given for *purchase accounting treatment.*

The Accounting Result: A Change in Basis of Accounting Occurs, and Goodwill Is Reported

When a combination is reported as a purchase, the acquiring company's cost (the value of the consideration given for the acquired business) must be allocated to the individual assets acquired. The result is to revalue the acquired business's assets to their *current values*. Consequently, a ***new basis* of accounting** is established. (As explained and illustrated in Chapter 5, the target company's *liabilities* are also revalued to their *current values* in this cost allocation process.)

In an economy experiencing inflation, the acquiring company usually pays an amount in excess of the *book value* of the net assets of the acquired business. If this excess relates to assets other than land (a nondepreciable asset), future income statements reflect higher depreciation and amortization charges and lower earnings.

To the extent that the acquiring entity's cost exceeds the *current value* of the acquired entity's identifiable net assets, **goodwill** arises and must be periodically tested for impairment. (How to test goodwill for impairment is discussed in Chapter 6.)

CHECK POINT

Under *purchase accounting*, the following occurs:

a. Only the target company's *assets* are revalued to the *current values.*

b. Both the target company's *assets* and *liabilities* are revalued to their *current values.*

c. The *assets* of both combining companies are revalued to their *current values*.
d. The *assets* and *liabilities* of both combining companies are revalued to their *current values*.
e. Only the target company's *liabilities* are revalued to their *current values*.

Answer: b

Comprehensive Illustration

The Purchase Method

To illustrate the different reporting results under each method, assume the following information:

1. On December 31, 2006, Parrco Company issued 5,000 shares of its no-par value common stock having a fair market value of $20 per share ($100,000 total fair value) in exchange for *all* of the outstanding common stock of Subbco Company.
2. Subbco Company's net assets of $60,000 at *book value* have a *current value* of $88,000. The $28,000 *under*valuation (which is relevant only under the *purchase method*) pertains to the following accounts:

Inventory	$ 4,000
Land	8,000
Equipment	16,000
	$28,000

3. Under the purchase method, $12,000 of goodwill was paid for ($100,000 Fair Value of Common Stock Issued – $88,000 Current Value of Subbco Company's Net Assets).

Each company's financial statements *immediately before* the combination and the combined statements that Parrco Company would issue for the year ended December 31, 2006, are shown in Illustration 4-1.

ILLUSTRATION 4-1 REPORTING RESULTS: PURCHASE METHOD

	Parrco Company	Subbco Company Book Amounts	Subbco Company Current Values	Combined Purchase Method (*new* basis)
Income Statement (2006)				
Sales	$ 500,000	$ 210,000		$ 500,000
Cost of sales	(330,000)	(140,000)		(330,000)
Expenses	(120,000)	(60,000)		(120,000)
Net Income	$ 50,000	$ 10,000		$ 50,000
Balance Sheet (as of 12/31/06)				
Cash	$ 118,000	$ 15,000	$ 15,000	$ 133,000
Accounts receivable	52,000	23,000	23,000	75,000
Inventory	90,000	42,000	46,000	**136,000**
Land	220,000	30,000	38,000	**258,000**
Buildings and equipment, net	220,000	150,000	166,000	**386,000**
Goodwill			12,000	**12,000**
Total Assets	$ 700,000	$ 260,000	$300,000	$1,000,000
Liabilities	$ 400,000	$ 200,000	$200,000	$ 600,000
Common stock	200,000	40,000	100,000	300,000[a]
Retained earnings	100,000	20,000		100,000
Total Liabilities & Equity	$ 700,000	$ 260,000	$300,000	$1,000,000

[a] $200,000 + $100,000 (5,000 shares × $20 fair market value) = $300,000.

Note: Under the ***pooling of interests*** method, no revaluation of the *acquired company's* assets and liabilities to *current value* occurs. Instead, *book values* are carried forward. Also, no goodwill is reported.

Most accountants agree with the fundamental concept of the *purchase method*, except for the treatment of goodwill. Many accountants and corporate executives believe that goodwill should *not* be shown as an asset of the acquiring company but should be charged to the equity section of the acquiring company at the acquisition. Their reasoning is that the acquiring entity has, in substance, given up some of its equity with the hope of recouping it in subsequent years through the acquired company's superior earnings (which may or may not materialize).

CHECK POINT

Under *purchase accounting*, the following occurs:

a. Goodwill *may* or *may not* be reported in the combined balance sheet.
b. Goodwill is *always* reported in the combined balance sheet.
c. Goodwill is *never* reported in the combined balance sheet.
d. Goodwill, if paid for, is *expensed* at the combination date.
e. Goodwill, if paid for, is charged directly to *stockholders' equity* at the combination date.

Answer: a

IV. THE GOODWILL CONTROVERSY

Goodwill is perhaps the most unique of all intangibles because, unlike other types of intangibles (and tangibles), **it is *not* separable from the business and thus *cannot* be sold apart from the business as a whole**. In general, goodwill represents an existing or perceived future capability to achieve superior earnings. Goodwill has been a controversial issue for more than a century, and the controversy has heated up in the last few years because goodwill is becoming a much larger percentage of business combination purchase prices and consequently of assets and equity than ever before (in many cases exceeding equity).

The magnitude of the goodwill issue may best be exemplified by the savings and loan industry, in which billions of dollars of nonexistent goodwill (using the superior earnings concept) was created in the 1980s by merging near-bankrupt savings and loans with healthier ones at virtually no out-of-pocket costs to the healthy institution. If goodwill had been eliminated from the balance sheet of thrifts in this industry in 1990, the industry's nearly $40 billion of equity would have been reduced to $10 billion. Even Congress recognized that goodwill is a dubious asset for this industry when it passed legislation in 1990 phasing out the inclusion of goodwill as an asset for *regulatory purposes* (used to assess whether an institution has insufficient capital that may trigger seizure and closure by the federal regulators).

Conceptual Issues

The conceptual issues for goodwill are as follows:

1. **Should goodwill—either purchased or internally generated—be reported as an asset?** The accounting alternatives are (1) capitalizing it or (2) charging it to equity (either directly or through the income statement).
2. **If goodwill is reported as an asset, how should its valuation be determined subsequent to the date it is recorded as an asset?** The accounting alternatives are to (1) treat goodwill as a permanent asset, (2) amortize it systematically, or (3) write it down when its value has been impaired.

A capsule history of accounting for goodwill in the United States appears at the end of the chapter on pages 128–130. This history allows you to see the many approaches that have been used in accounting for goodwill during the last century. Goodwill is such a difficult issue because, if properly maintained, it can last forever. For example, many—but certainly not all—leading name brands of the 1920s (Steinway pianos, Gold Medal flour, Colgate toothpaste) are still the leading name brands 70 years later.[3] On the other hand, poor management can result in a loss of value over time or even overnight.For example, Perrier had a virtual stranglehold over the U.S. imported bottled water market until it had to issue a recall in 1990 when traces of benzene, a suspected carcinogen, were found in some bottles after a worker forgot to change a filter. Nearly a year after the recall, Perrier's sales were still down 40% from pre-recall levels. (Consumers had a chance to try other brands, many of which were less expensive, and found no essential difference.)

A Balance Sheet Phrase More Descriptive than Goodwill

Possibly a more descriptive and useful phrase than *goodwill* is as follows:

> Amount paid in a business combination for the estimated future superior earnings that management hopes will materialize in the belief that it can run the acquired business as well as or better than the previous owners and their management.

Accounting for Goodwill in the United States

As stated earlier, U.S. GAAP requires goodwill to be capitalized and periodically tested for impairment.

Concern for U.S. Firms Because of Foreign Competition

Some investment bankers and analysts believe that in acquisitions and mergers, U.S. firms are at a disadvantage relative to foreign bidders domiciled in countries that can immediately charge goodwill to stockholders' equity. In our opinion, this is *not* a valid assertion because the way that goodwill is treated does *not* affect the cash flows of an acquisition. Accordingly, investors should be able to correctly reinterpret accounting reports in terms of economic information. To the extent that foreign bidders can deduct goodwill for income tax-reporting purposes over a significantly *shorter life* than allowed under U.S. tax laws, however, they *do* have an advantage over U.S. firms.

The International Perspective on page 120 describes the way certain foreign countries deal with goodwill.

U.S. Tax Rules Concerning the Deductibility of Goodwill

Historically, goodwill has *not* been tax deductible. In 1991, the General Accounting Office (GAO) recommended to Congress, however, that the tax code be amended to allow goodwill (as well as other purchased intangible assets) to be deducted to eliminate the continuous, costly, and counterproductive legal warfare between the Internal Revenue Service and corporate taxpayers on this issue. Consequently, in a historic shift of position, Congress changed the tax rules (in 1993) so that goodwill and other purchased intangibles are now deductible over 15 years. (Goodwill purchased in a business combination *prior* to this legislation, however, is *not* tax deductible until the acquired business is sold.)

CHECK POINT

Which of the following statements is *true* regarding goodwill under U.S. GAAP?

a. Goodwill paid for in a business combination must be amortized to income over its expected useful life.

b. Internally generated amounts to create or maintain goodwill can be capitalized if specified criteria are met.

c. Goodwill paid for in a business combination may be either reported as an asset or expensed at the combination date.

---

[3] David N. Martin, "Romancing the Brand," *Amacon* (New York: 1989), p. 19.

d. Goodwill paid for in a business combination may be either reported as an asset or charged to stockholders' equity at the combination date.
e. In most cases, goodwill is effectively treated as a permanent asset and need *not* be tested periodically for impairment.
f. It can only arise and be recorded as an asset as a result of a business combination.

Answer: f

V. Acquiring Assets versus Common Stock

Usually of major importance to the acquiring company is the type of property it will *receive* in exchange for the type of consideration it *gives* to the target company or its shareholders. In practice, some classic blunders have been made (one of which we describe shortly) as a result of receiving the wrong type of property.

Types of Property That May Be Received in Exchange for the Consideration Given

A business may be acquired in one of two ways, by acquiring the target company's (1) assets or (2) outstanding common stock from the stockholders.

1. **Acquiring *assets*.** Assume that the *agreed-upon value* of the target company's assets is $7 million and that the *current value* of the target company's liabilities is $5 million. When it acquires

International Perspective

Foreign Goodwill Accounting Practices

Substantial diversity exists among foreign countries as to the treatment of goodwill for both financial and tax-reporting purposes, as evidenced by the practices of the following countries:

United Kingdom. Goodwill is immediately charged to stockholders' equity, thus bypassing the income statement. To avoid the drastic reduction or elimination of equity that can occur under this practice, a recent trend is to separate "brand names" from goodwill and report brand names as an asset. No tax deduction is allowed for goodwill. When companies of *comparable size* merge, they do *not* have to recognize goodwill.

Japan. Goodwill is capitalized and amortized to income over no more than 5 years. Goodwill is tax deductible over 5 years.

Germany. Capitalizing goodwill in stock-based deals is an option; if capitalized, it must be amortized over 4 years unless it is systematically amortized over the benefiting years. Goodwill is tax deductible over 15 years.

The Netherlands. Goodwill is usually charged to stockholders' equity at the acquisition date, thereby bypassing the income statement. An acceptable alternative practice is to allow amortization over 5–10 years. Goodwill is tax deductible over five years.

Canada. Goodwill is capitalized and amortized to income over no more than 40 years. Seventy-five percent of goodwill is tax deductible.

The International Accounting Standards Committee (IASC). The IASC, a London-based organization attempting to develop world GAAP, has issued *International Accounting Standard 22*, (last revised in 1998). *IAS 22* requires goodwill to be capitalized and amortized over not more than *five* years—unless persuasive evidence exists that a longer useful life is appropriate. (The IASC and its successor organization, the International Accounting Standards Board [IASB] is discussed in more detail in Chapter 13.)

the target company's assets, the acquiring company has the option to either give consideration of (1) $7 million or (2) give $2 million and to assume responsibility for paying the target company's $5 million of liabilities. (The latter option is most common.)

2. **Acquiring *common stock*.** The acquiring company must purchase *more than* 50% of the target company's outstanding common stock to be considered a business combination. With an ownership interest of *more than* 50%, the acquiring company can control the target company.

Reasons for Acquiring Assets versus Common Stock

Many circumstances and factors affect the determination of whether to obtain the target company's *assets* or *common stock* in exchange for the consideration given. Here are some of the more common items:

1. **Unrecorded liabilities.** A major concern of a buyer contemplating acquiring common stock is whether the target company has unrecorded liabilities, such as accounts payable omissions and inadequate or unrecognized accruals. **If *common stock* is obtained for the consideration given, the buyer inherits responsibility for the unrecorded liabilities.** By acquiring *assets*, however, the acquiring company can best insulate itself from responsibility for these contingencies, inasmuch as a welldrafted acquisition agreement pertaining to the acquisition of assets can clearly specify those liabilities for which the acquiring company assumes responsibility. One of the major pitfalls for acquiring companies in the 1980s was unrecorded other postretirement benefits (primarily the obligations to pay for retirees' medical costs not covered by Medicare), which were being accounted for on the *"pay-as-you-go" (cash) basis* and were estimated to be between $300 billion and $1 trillion for all U.S. corporations as of 1990. (*FAS 106*, "Employers' Accounting for Postretirement Benefits Other Than Pensions," eliminated this grossly deficient reporting practice by requiring companies to convert to the *accrual basis*.)

CASE IN POINT

A $600 Million Oversight

Probably the most unfortunate omission of an unrecognized liability in an acquisition was the 1987 acquisition of Uniroyal for $1 billion, which stuck the buyer with unrecorded benefits estimated to be as high as $600 million.

2. **Contingent liabilities.** When the acquisition of *common stock* is contemplated, a full understanding of *contingent* liabilities is often of far more importance than the risk posed by *unrecorded* liabilities. Some of the types of *contingent* liabilities that are usually of major concern and thus investigated are as follows:

   Open years for income taxes. Assessing the likelihood of possible IRS tax and penalty assessments for years prior to the business combination date that the IRS has not yet examined is also customary.

   Litigation in process and unasserted claims. Inquiring of the seller's legal counsel about litigation in process and potential unasserted claims is customary. See the Case in Point.

CASE IN POINT

A $1.5 Billion Contingency That Materialized

Probably the most unfortunate materialization of an unknown contingency occurred as a result of the 1967 acquisition of Ruberoid Co. by GAF Corp. Ruberoid was an asbestos manufacturer. Subsequent to that acquisition, GAF (and its successor G-1 Holdings) incurred $1.5 billion in asbestos liability claims and costs, even though Ruberoid earned a total of just $1 million in the three decades after the merger.

3. **Nontransferability of contracts.** If the target company's contracts, leases, franchises, or operating rights *cannot* be transferred through the sale of assets, common stock must be acquired.
4. **Ease of transfer.** Transferring *stock certificates* is easier than transferring *assets*. The transfer of *assets* may require the preparation of separate bills of sale for each asset or class of asset; also, state laws concerning bulk sales must be observed.
5. **Unwanted facilities or segments.** If the acquiring company does not wish to acquire all of the target company's assets, the acquisition of *assets* allows the acquiring company to obtain only those assets it desires. (To arrange for the acquisition of its *common stock*, the target company could dispose of the unwanted assets, but it may *not* always be feasible to do so in the time specified in the acquisition agreement.)
6. **Access to the *target company's* cash.** If the *acquiring company* offers cash as consideration and the *target company* has substantial cash and short-term investment assets, the acquisition of *assets* makes the *target company's* cash and short-term investment assets available to the *acquiring company* to either help replenish its cash or repay loans obtained to finance the acquisition. In effect, the acquisition can be partially paid for using the funds of the *target company*. If *common stock* were acquired, however, the *target company*'s cash and short-term investment assets would *not* be available to the *acquiring company*, except to the extent that the *target company* (as a subsidiary and a separate legal entity) could pay dividends to the *acquiring company* (as the parent).
7. **Eliminating the *target company's* labor union.** If the *target company* has a labor unit that the acquiring company does *not* want to inherit, it can avoid the union only by acquiring *assets* and then hiring all new employees to run the newly acquired operation.
8. **Tax factors.** Sometimes tax factors play an important role in deciding whether to acquire *assets* or *common stock*. For example, goodwill is effectively tax deductible only if *assets* are acquired. We discuss some of the other tax ramifications in Appendix 4A.

Sometimes a potential problem *cannot* be avoided merely by acquiring *assets* instead of *common stock*. For example, a buyer would inherit liabilities for toxic waste cleanup (estimated to be $500 billion for the 10,000 toxic waste sites identified by the Environmental Protection Agency)—regardless of whether it acquires *assets* or *common stock*. As a result of the growing awareness of the contingent liabilities associated with toxic waste sites (General Motors, for instance, has 140 toxic waste sites designated by the EPA as requiring urgent attention), environmental attorneys are now routinely hired to comb company records and inspect waste sites before consummation of a proposed deal. Consequently, many proposed deals are either (1) abandoned because of the magnitude of the potential problems found or (2) revised to have a drastically reduced offering price. (One prominent New York City–based law firm that specializes in takeover work now employs more than 20 environmental attorneys.)

CHECK POINT

A reason for acquiring a target company's *outstanding common stock* rather than the target company's *assets* is:

a. Goodwill is never reported.
b. The *target company* has substantial contingent liabilities.
c. The *target company* has a labor union that the *acquiring company* does *not* wish to inherit.
d. The *acquiring company* wants to avoid having to revalue the *target company's* assets and liabilities to their *current values*.
e. The *target company* is a party to an important contract that *cannot* be assigned.
f. Goodwill will be amortized over 40 years rather than 5–10 years.
g. The target company has a toxic waste dump that will have to be cleaned up.

Answer: e

VI. THE RESULTING ORGANIZATION FORM OF THE *ACQUIRED* BUSINESS

Accounting for business combinations focuses on **how the *acquiring company* initially records the transaction that brings about the combination.** The detailed accounting entries for the *acquiring company* require substantial explanation under the *purchase method*; these are discussed and illustrated in detail in Chapter 5. The entries made by the *target company*, on the other hand, are quite simple. The following discussion is general in nature so that an overall understanding of the organizational effects of business combinations can be grasped.

Acquisition of *Assets*

When the target company's *assets* are acquired, these assets (and any liabilities assumed) are recorded in the *acquiring company's* general ledger. The newly acquired operation is usually referred to as a *division.* For example, Punn Company acquired all the assets and assumed all the liabilities of Sunn Company by giving cash as the consideration. Each company makes the following entries (in condensed format):

Punn Company (the *acquiring company*)				**Sunn Company (the *target company*)**		
Assets	xxx[a]		←	Assets		xxx
Liabilities		xxx[a]	←	Liabilities	xxx	
Cash		xxx	→	Cash	xxx	
				Gain *(if cash exceeds book value of net assets)*		xxx
				Loss *(if cash is less than book value of net assets)*	xxx	

[a] The assets acquired and liabilities assumed are recorded at their current values based on the purchase price. (This is discussed further in Chapter 5.)

Creating a Subsidiary to Acquire the Assets

In some cases, the *acquiring company* creates a subsidiary to effect the acquisition of the *target company's assets.* This creation occurs in situations in which it is *not* possible, practicable, or desirable to acquire the target company's *common stock,* but it is desirable to operate the acquired business as a separate legal entity insulated from the existing operations of the acquiring company.

Removal of Records

The *target company* must pack its records (including its general ledger) and remove them from the location of the business that was sold.

Subsequent Courses of Action for the Target Company

If *all* its assets are disposed of and all its liabilities are assumed, the *target company's* remaining assets consist solely of the consideration received from the *acquiring company.* At this point, the *target company* (still a separate legal entity) is referred to as a **nonoperating company** because it has no operating business—but only passive assets. The *target company* then has *three* courses of action:

1. Continue as a nonoperating company.
2. Use the assets to enter a new line of business.
3. Distribute the assets to its shareholders. (This option is the one most commonly selected.)

If it chooses option 3, the *target company* becomes a **shell company** because it has no operating business and no assets. It still is a separate legal entity, however, until steps are taken to have its charter withdrawn (such withdrawal is usually done).

Acquiring Rights to the Target Company's Name

The *acquiring company* usually specifies in the acquisition agreement that in addition to *assets*, it is acquiring the exclusive right to the *target company's* corporate name. Accordingly, if the *target company* intends to remain in business (either as a nonoperating company or as an operating company in a *new* line of business), it must make a corporate name change. This avoids any future confusion that might arise between, as in the earlier example, the acquirer's *Sunn Division* and the target *Sunn Company*.

Tax Treatment on Any Gain by the Target Company

The *target company* is taxed on any gain resulting from the sale of its assets only if the transaction is a taxable combination. (Taxable versus nontaxable combinations are discussed later in Appendix 4A.)

CHECK POINT

When a target company's *assets* are acquired, which of the following is *true*:

a. The target company becomes a *subsidiary*.
b. The target company automatically becomes a *shell corporation*.
c. Liabilities may or may *not* be assumed by the acquiring company.
d. A stock-for-stock exchange must be effected.
e. The target company can take steps to go out of business.
f. The target company can enter into a new line of business.
g. The target company becomes a *division*.
h. The assets acquired become a *division* of the acquiring company.

Answers: c, e, f, h

Acquisition of *Common Stock*

As discussed in Chapter 1, a company owning *more than* 50% of the outstanding common stock of another company is referred to as the *parent* of that company. Conversely, a company whose outstanding common stock is *more than* 50% owned by another company is referred to as a *subsidiary* of that company. A *subsidiary* (as opposed to a division) is a separate legal entity that must maintain its own general ledger. Accordingly, the *subsidiary's* operations must be accounted for on a *decentralized basis*. The acquisition of the outstanding *common stock* of the target company is a personal transaction involving the *acquiring company* and the target company's shareholders. For the *target company*, the only change is that the company's ownership is concentrated in the hands of significantly fewer stockholders, or even one stockholder if 100% of the outstanding common stock has been acquired. Consequently, only the *acquiring company* (the parent) must make an entry relating to the business combination.

Assuming that Punn Company acquired *more than* 50% of the outstanding common stock of Sunn Company, the relationship is depicted as follows:

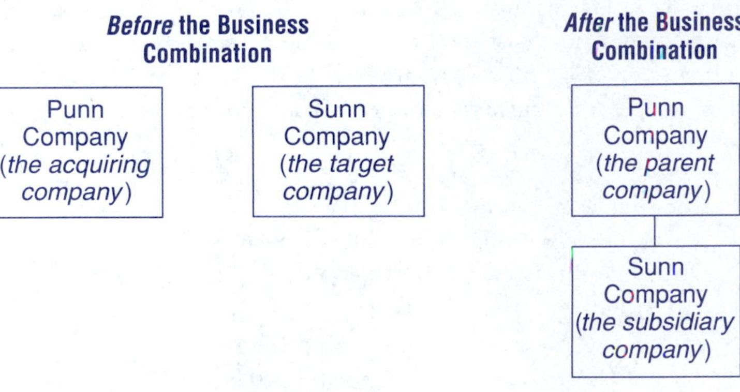

Cash-for-Stock Exchange

If the acquiring company gives cash as consideration for the *target company's* outstanding common stock it makes the following entry:

Investment in Subsidiary	XXX	
Cash		XXX

Stock-for-Stock Exchange

If the acquiring company gives *common stock* as consideration for the *target company's* outstanding common stock, it is necessary to understand what is known as the *exchange ratio*. The **exchange ratio** is the number of common shares to be issued by the *acquiring company* for each outstanding common share of the *target company* to be surrendered. Say that the acquiring company will issue 30,000 shares and the target company has 10,000 shares outstanding, all of which are to be exchanged. This produces a 3:1 exchange ratio. Note that the number of shares to be issued by the acquiring company first has to be calculated by dividing the price the acquiring company is willing to pay for the target company (say, $1,200,000) by the *market price per share* of the *acquiring company's* common stock (say, $40 per share), producing the number of shares to be issued (30,000). The exchange ratio is usually set forth in the acquisition agreement.

If the *acquiring company* issues 30,000 shares of common stock to effect the business combination, the *acquiring company* makes the following entry:

Investment in Subsidiary	XXX	
Common Stock (30,000 × Par Value)		XXX
Additional Paid-in Capital		XXX

CHECK POINT

When a target company's outstanding *common stock* is acquired, which of the following is *true*:

a. Common stock must be the consideration given by the acquiring company.
b. A stock-for-stock exchange always takes place.
c. Liabilities are never directly assumed by the acquiring company.
d. A *home office-division* relationship results.
e. A *parent-division* relationship results.
f. A *parent-subsidiary* relationship results.
g. Cash must be the consideration given by the acquiring company.
h. A shell corporation eventually results.

Answers: c, f

Statutory Mergers

A third common way to effect a business combination is the **statutory merger**, in which the *target company's* equity securities are retired and the target's corporate existence is terminated. **These steps can take place only *after* the parent-subsidiary relationship is formed.** *This* can be depicted as follows:

***Before* the Business Combination**		***After* the Business Combination**
Punn Company (*the acquiring company*)	Sunn Company (*the target company*)	Punn Company (*the surviving company*)

The *target company's* assets and liabilities are transferred to the *acquiring company*. Because the *acquiring company* is the only surviving legal entity, the *target company* is said to have been "merged" into the acquiring company. Because these combinations take place pursuant to state laws, they are called *statutory mergers.* The state statutory merger laws have two primary requirements:

1. The board of directors of each company must approve the plan of proposed merger before the plan can be submitted to the shareholders of each company.
2. The required percentage (usually anywhere from a simple majority to 80%) of the voting power of each company must approve the plan of proposed merger.

The result of a statutory merger is as though the *acquiring company* had acquired directly the *target company's* assets and the *target company* had then ceased its legal existence. The reasons for using this roundabout manner to acquire a target company's assets are explained in the following paragraphs.

Forcing Out Dissenting Shareholders

In most cases in which the *acquiring company* acquires *common stock,* it desires 100% of the *target company's* outstanding common stock. In some of these situations, this outcome may be unlikely because some of the *target company's* shareholders object to the business combination and refuse to sell their shares. If the *acquiring company* acquires the required percentage of outstanding shares to approve a statutory merger, however, it can force out the dissenting shareholders by taking the necessary steps to liquidate the *target company.* In some tender offers, the *acquiring company* clearly specifies that once it obtains the required ownership percentage, it intends to effect a statutory merger with the *target company* if all the *target company's* shareholders do *not* accept the offer. This message means "tender your shares *now* or be forced out *later.*"

In these cases, the business combination technically occurs when the *acquiring company* acquires *more than* 50% of the *target company's* outstanding common stock, creating a parent-subsidiary relationship. Thus the statutory merger takes place after the business combination date, a process that normally can be completed within 30 to 60 days after approval of the plan of merger.

When the statutory merger subsequently becomes effective, entries are made (1) to transfer the *target company's* assets and liabilities to the *acquiring company* and (2) to close out the equity accounts in the *target company's* general ledger. In addition, it is necessary to make a settlement with the target company's *dissenting stockholders* (who did not tender their shares). State laws pertaining to statutory mergers generally provide that *dissenting shareholders* have the right to receive (in cash) the fair value of their shares as of the day before shareholder approval of the merger. Such value may have to be established through a judicial determination as provided under state law if the *dissenting shareholders* and the *acquiring company* cannot agree on the value of these shares.

Forcing Out Shareholders Who Cannot Be Located

The company acquiring common stock in a takeover cannot always locate all the *target company's* shareholders; in most publicly held companies, a small number of shareholders simply cannot be found. When the *acquiring company* desires 100% ownership notwithstanding, it may take the statutory merger route to liquidate these interests in the *target company.*

Acquiring Assets Indirectly

In unfriendly takeover attempts, the *acquiring company* is prevented from acquiring the assets directly from the *target company* because the directors' refusal of the offer prevents the target company's shareholders from voting on it. The *acquiring company* must then make a tender offer to the shareholders. If the *acquiring company* acquires the required percentage of outstanding shares through the tender offer and does *not* wish to maintain a parent-subsidiary relationship, it can then take the necessary steps to liquidate the *target company* via a statutory merger.

CHECK POINT

A *statutory merger* can occur if and only if:

a. Common stock was acquired.
b. Assets were acquired.

c. Common stock was issued as consideration by the acquiring company.
d. Cash was given as consideration by the acquiring company.
e. A *parent-subsidiary* relationship exists.
f. A *home office-division* relationship exists.
g. It is desirable to force out dissenting shareholders of the target company.
h. The target company has shareholders who *cannot* be located.

Answers: a, e

Holding Companies

Infrequently, two companies (generally of comparable size) combine in such a manner that **a new corporate entity is established that controls the operations of both combining companies.** This occurs when (1) the existing name of each corporation would *not* indicate the scope of operations of the combined business or (2) it is desired to have the top-level corporation operate as a **holding company.** A holding company has no revenue-producing operations of its own, only investments in subsidiaries. To illustrate, assume that Punn Company and Sunn Company wish to combine. They form Integrated Technology Company, which issues its stock for the stock of Punn Company and Sunn Company. Punn and Sunn are now subsidiaries of Integrated Technology Company. This is depicted as follows:

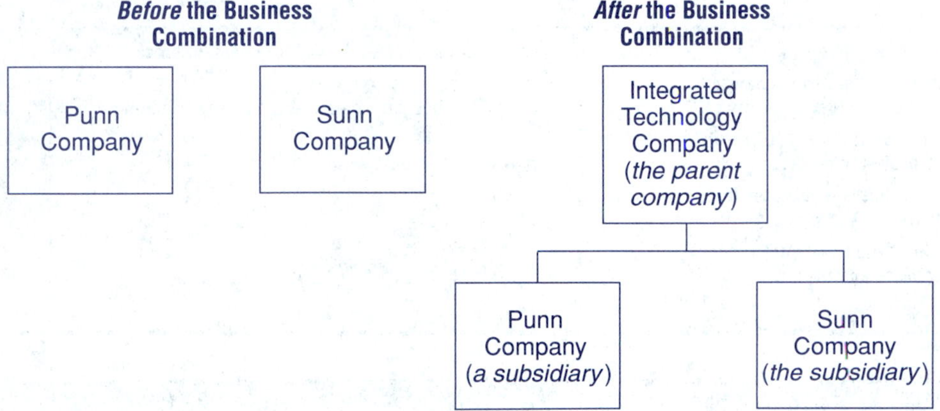

Statutory Consolidation

More infrequent than forming a holding company is the formation of a **statutory consolidation,** in which a *new* legal entity takes over the assets and assumes the liabilities of each of the combining companies. **The combining companies simultaneously cease their separate corporate existences.** Because the new entity is the *only* surviving legal entity, the combining companies are said to have been "consolidated" into the new corporation. Because these combinations take place pursuant to state laws, they are called *statutory consolidations.* The primary requirements of the state *statutory consolidation* laws are the same as those for *statutory mergers.*

For example, assume that Punn Company and Sunn Company agree to combine using a *statutory consolidation.* The surviving company is Integrated Technology Company. This is depicted as follows:

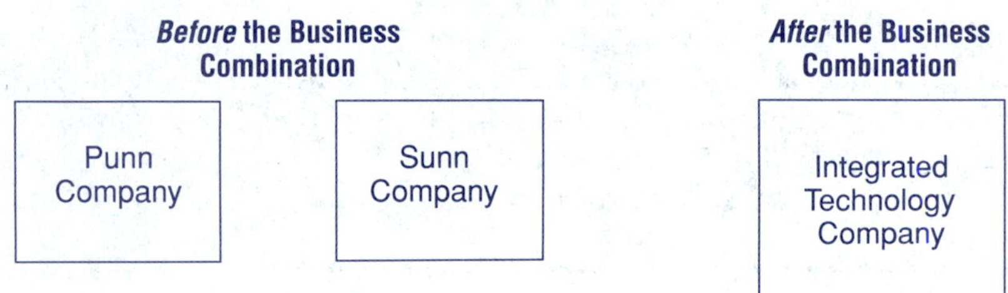

CHECK POINT

The difference between a *statutory consolidation* (SC) and a *statutory merger* (SM) is that:

a. A *holding company* is created in an SC but *not* in an SM.
b. A new entity is created in an SC but *not* in an SM.
c. An existing entity ceases its existence in an SM but *not* in an SC.
d. A *shell company* is created in an SM but *not* in an SC.
e. Both the *acquiring company* and the *target company* cease their existence in an SC but *not* in an SM.
f. An SC results in *two* surviving entities, whereas an SM results in *one* surviving entity.

Answers: b, e

Summary Comparison of Business Combinations

Illustration 4-2 presents the interrelationships of the various topics discussed to this point.

ILLUSTRATION 4-2 SUMMARY COMPARISON OF ACQUIRING ASSETS VERSUS COMMON STOCK

	Purchase Method	
Consideration given may be.	Cash, bonds, preferred stock or common stock	
Property received in exchange for the consideration given.	Common stock held by target company's shareholders	Assets of target company
Asset account(s) used to record the property received.	Investment in Subsidiary	Various assets
Change in basis of accounting occurs for the property received	Yes	Yes
Resulting organizational form of business acquired	Subsidiary	Branch/Division

Historical Perspective

A Capsule History of Accounting for Goodwill

Accounting for goodwill has been studied and debated since about 1880. Through the years, it has evolved from a state of "anything goes" to the restrictive, arbitrary, and uniform accounting requirements of *APB Opinion Nos. 16* and *17*, issued in 1970. No accounting topic has inspired more diversely held views (and fiercely strong views) than goodwill. Consequently, students must not simply memorize the rules of the current pronouncements; they must also understand how and why we have arrived at the present rules from what was tried in the past and rejected. And as their predecessors have done, they must continually question the logic and practicality of these rules and their current application.

Prior to 1917 The entire cost of an acquisition in excess of book value is treated as goodwill. Accountants favor charging goodwill to stockholders' equity at the acquisition date. There is no support for charging goodwill to income, either through amortization or in a lump sum.

1917 The American Institute of Accountants, the predecessor to the AICPA, "recommends" that goodwill be shown as a reduction to stockholders' equity (if it is not already charged to capital).

1918–1929 Companies begin capitalizing internally generated goodwill. (Amounts range from advertising costs to arbitrary estimates of the value of the goodwill.) Many abuses result.

Historical Perspective, continued

1930–1944 Recording as goodwill only purchased goodwill becomes the prevalent thinking. Permanent retention of goodwill as an asset and periodically amortizing it to earnings, retained earnings, or additional paid-in capital become acceptable practice (in addition to immediately charging these to capital). Accounting writers begin advocating the analysis of the cost in excess of book value.

1944 *Accounting Research Bulletin No. 24* is issued. It states that only historical cost should be used to value goodwill. Arbitrary write-ups and capitalization of start-up costs as goodwill are thus banned. The door is left open for companies to capitalize advertising costs as goodwill.

1945 The Securities and Exchange Commission (SEC) begins encouraging companies to amortize goodwill if they have been using the permanent retention treatment.

1953 *Accounting Research Bulletin No. 43* is issued. It prohibits charging goodwill to stockholders' equity immediately after acquisition. The discretionary write-downs of goodwill are banned—a loss of value must take place for a write-down or write-off.

1968 *Accounting Research Study No. 5*, "Accounting for Goodwill" (written by two senior partners of Arthur Andersen and Co.), is issued. The study concludes that goodwill is *not* an asset and should be charged to stockholders' equity at the time of the acquisition.

1968–1970 A fierce and heated debate takes place within the accounting profession concerning accounting for business combinations and the related issue of goodwill.

1970 *APBO 16* and *17* are issued, the first by a vote of 12 to 6 and the second by a vote of 13 to 5. As a result, (1) goodwill can arise only from a business combination; (2) the cost in excess of book value must be analyzed; (3) goodwill existing as of October 31, 1970, *need not* be amortized to income; (4) goodwill arising after that date must be amortized to income over no more than 40 years; and (5) if goodwill loses its value, it must be written off to income as an extraordinary charge. (The positions of the various opposing factions of the APB are so strongly held that, with a two-thirds majority required for passage, many members cannot talk to one another for three months after the vote. One of the largest CPA firms seriously considers not supporting these pronouncements in its practice but decides to continue to work within the profession to bring about needed changes.)

1971 The APB's handling of the business combinations and goodwill issues (in which strong positions were taken only to be withdrawn because of pressure from client companies) ultimately leads to the demise of the APB and the establishment of the FASB in 1973.

1971–1980 Goodwill becomes a dead issue.

1981 A crisis develops in the savings and loan (S&L) industry because of high interest rates. More than a thousand S&L associations become financially distressed—many actually exhausting their net worths and thus facing bankruptcy—and are forced to merge with stronger ones. Seeking ways to report *higher* earnings, the acquiring firms take advantage of a quirk in *APBO 16* and account for these arranged, regulatory mergers as *purchases* (rather than as *poolings of interests*, the usual practice for such mergers). Consequently, billions of dollars of goodwill are reported as being amortized over 30 to 40 years. (The offsetting loan discount is credited to income over 10 to 12 years.)

Undaunted by the peculiarity (some would say absurdity) that companies facing bankruptcy could possibly possess goodwill, auditors of these acquiring companies allow this reporting of artificial income without exception. *Form* prevails over *substance*.

1983 In response to public criticism of the reporting of artificial income in the S&L industry, the FASB amends *APBO 17* in FASB *Statement No. 72*, "Accounting for Certain Acquisitions of Banking or Thrift Institutions." It requires much *shorter* lives for goodwill (10 to 12 years)—but only for that portion of goodwill attributable to the acquired financial institution having an excess of liabilities over assets on a fair value basis.

Some S&Ls rush through their mergers to beat the effective date of the pronouncement, which is retroactive only to September 30, 1982. The auditors of these firms give unqualified ("clean") opinions on the financial statements presented under the *old* rules as well as those presented under the *new* rules—deeming all the statements to "present fairly."

(continued)

Historical Perspective, continued

Analyzing and understanding the financial statements of such S&Ls become quite difficult. (Perplexed investors ask their stockbrokers, "What are the 'real' earnings?")

1983–1985 Scores of companies that went on acquisition binges in the 1970s begin disposing of hundreds of previously acquired companies due to their operating problems and unprofitability.

Billions of dollars of unamortized goodwill (most companies were choosing a 40-year life) must be written off.

1985 The staff of the SEC issues *Staff Accounting Bulletin No. 42A*, which states that the *maximum* amortization life for goodwill that it will accept for financial institutions is 25 years.

1985–1986 A congressional committee headed by Rep. John Dingell holds hearings on the conduct of the accounting profession because of the rising number of collapses, corporate failures and abuses, and alleged auditing failures among large financial institutions.

1986–1987 The accounting profession explores ways to enhance public confidence in itself.

1989 The S&L industry, which reported a $12.1 billion loss for 1988, continues to report approximately $38 billion of goodwill (about 75% of its net worth at book value).

Congress passes the most expensive taxpayer bailout in U.S. history by approving a $306 billion rescue bill for the S&L industry. The bill requires them to maintain "real capital" equal to at least 3% of total assets—with goodwill to be *excluded* from capital after 1994. (Goodwill may be considered part of capital up to 1.5% until then.) Prior to the bill's passage, the S&L industry attempted to have goodwill counted as part of capital to its fullest extent.

1991 The SEC confirms that it is reducing its allowable life for goodwill in acquisitions involving high-technology companies because the technology may become quickly outmoded. In many cases, the SEC allows only *three* years.

1992 Since 1970, goodwill has become a much *higher* percentage of total assets and equity. Many believe that the FASB should reexamine this issue.

In late 1992, the FASB added accounting for the impairment of goodwill to its project on impairment of long-lived assets and intangibles.

1994 The Financial Accounting Policy Committee of the Association for Investment Management and Research (AIMR), the professional association of financial analysts, issues the report "Financial Reporting in the 1990s and Beyond." It recommends that purchased goodwill be written off at the date it is acquired because (1) it depicts value only at a particular date and (2) its presence on the balance sheet is of no significant use in estimating an entity's future cash flows or gauging the entity's value. (The FASB acknowledges that this document is an important summary of how financial analysts use financial statements and how they would like to see financial reporting evolve.)

1995 The FASB completes its impairment project with the issuance of *FAS 121*. Unfortunately, the impairment of goodwill is addressed only for limited situations in which related long-lived assets are impaired (as discussed in Chapter 5).

1996 The FASB adds to its agenda a project to reconsider (1) the accounting for business combinations and (2) the treatment of goodwill created in acquisitions accounted for as purchases.

1997 The FASB begins deliberating the business combination and goodwill issues.

2001 *FAS 141* and *142* are issued (superseding *APBO 16* and *17*, respectively). Goodwill becomes subject to *periodic impairment testing*—amortization is no longer allowed.

2002–2003 Numerous companies write off tens of billions of goodwill ($99 billion for AOL alone).

Source: A major portion of the capsule history prior to 1970 is based on Research Monograph No. 80, *Goodwill in Accounting: A History of the Issues and Problems*, by Hugh P. Hughes (Atlanta: Georgia State University, 1982).

End-of-Chapter Review

Summary of Key Points

1. The acquiring company must use the **purchase method** of accounting.

2. The *purchase method* treats the combination as a purchase of the target company's business, whereby the target company's assets (and liabilities) are to be **reported at the acquiring company's cost**, which is based essentially on the **fair value of the consideration given.**
3. Under the purchase method, a **change in basis of accounting** occurs for the acquired business's assets and liabilities.
4. An **excess of cost over the current value** of the acquired company's net assets is treated as **goodwill.** The opposite situation results in a **bargain purchase element.**
5. **Goodwill** must be reported as an asset and must be **tested periodically** for possible impairment. (Goodwill *cannot* be amortized to earnings.)
6. Many important factors must be considered in deciding whether to acquire the target company's **assets** or outstanding **common stock.**
7. Deciding whether *assets* or *common stock* shares are acquired has no bearing on the accounting treatment: Only the resulting **organizational form** of the acquired business differs.
8. In a **statutory merger,** the acquired company (once it becomes a *subsidiary* after its common stock is acquired) is merged into the *parent*—**only one legal entity survives.**
9. In a **statutory consolidation,** both the acquirer and the acquired company are merged into a newly created corporation (the sole surviving entity).

Glossary of New Terms

Acquiring company A company attempting to acquire the business of another company.

Acquisition agreement The legal agreement that specifies the terms and provisions of a business combination.

Conglomerate combination A business combination that takes place between companies in *unrelated* industries.

Exchange ratio The number of common shares issued by the *acquiring company* in exchange for each outstanding common share of the *target company.*

Goodwill In a purchase business combination, the *acquiring company's* cost in excess of the *current value* of the *target company's* net assets.

Holding company A company that has no revenue-producing operations of its own, only investments in subsidiaries.

Horizontal combination A business combination that occurs between companies involved as competitors at the same level in a given industry.

Leveraged buyout (LBO) Investors and management buy a controlling interest in a company, financing the purchase by borrowing from a financial institution and using the company's own assets as collateral.

Nonoperating company A company that has no operations of its own—only *passive* assets.

Pooling of interests method A formerly allowed but now prohibited method of accounting for a business combination whereby the assets of the acquired business are carried forward to the combined corporation at their historically recorded amounts. A *fusion of equity interests* is deemed to have occurred as opposed to a *sale.*

Proxy contest A system whereby both management and an opposing group solicit votes from the stockholders concerning proposed slates of directors or another issue such as a proposed change to the company's charter.

Purchase method A method of accounting for a business combination whereby the assets and liabilities of the acquired business are valued at their *current values* based on the consideration given by the acquiring company. A *sale* is deemed to have occurred.

Shell company A corporation that has no assets or liabilities.

Statutory consolidation A legal term referring to a specific type of business combination in which a new corporation is formed to carry on the businesses of *two* predecessor corporations that are liquidated.

Statutory merger A legal term referring to a specific type of business combination in which a newly acquired *target company* is liquidated into a *division* at the time of the business combination.

Takeover attempt The process of trying to acquire the business of a *target company.*

Target company The company whose business a company is seeking to acquire.

Tender offer An offer made by an acquiring company directly to the stockholders of the *target company*, whereby the *target company's* stockholders are requested to give up their common shares in exchange for the consideration offered by the *acquiring company*.

Vertical combination A business combination that takes place between companies involved at different levels in a given industry.

ASSIGNMENT MATERIAL

Review Questions

1. What is the difference between horizontal, vertical, and conglomerate combinations?
2. How does the *purchase method* contrast with the *pooling of interests method* of accounting?
3. Why is the acquisition agreement so important in determining the ultimate accounting method used in recording a business combination?
4. What is the treatment accorded goodwill?
5. What types of consideration can be given under *purchase accounting*?
6. What types of assets can the acquiring company obtain in business combinations?
7. What various organization forms can result from a business combination?
8. What is the difference between *centralized* and *decentralized* accounting systems?
9. How is the selling entity's gain or loss computed on the disposition of the seller's assets?

Exercises

E 4-1 **Structuring the Business Combination** The nine choices listed A through I pertain to how a business combination is structured. From these choices, select the appropriate answer for questions 1–13 that follow the choices.

a. Acquisition of assets
b. Acquisition of common stock
c. Statutory merger
d. Statutory consolidation
e. Purchase accounting
f. Pooling of interests accounting
g. Taxable transaction (appendix-related)
h. Nontaxable (tax-deferred) transaction (appendix-related)
i. None of the above

More than one choice may be appropriate for some of the questions.

1. The *acquiring company* does *not* want to be responsible for the *target company's* unrecorded postretirement benefit obligations.
2. The *acquiring company* does *not* want to be responsible for the *target company's* potential unrecorded liabilities pertaining to toxic waste site cleanups.

3. The *target company's* contracts and leases are *not* transferable.
4. The legal existence of only the *target company* is to be terminated.
5. The legal existence of the *acquiring company* and the *target company* is to be terminated.
6. The *target company* desires to continue in business as a *nonoperating* company.
7. The *target company's* directors have turned down the *acquiring company's* offer.
8. The *acquiring company* will have to force out a small minority of *dissenting stockholders* of the *target company.*
9. A *holding company* is to be formed.
10. The *acquiring company* desires to issue *preferred stock* as consideration.

Optional Questions (Appendix 4A-Related)

11. The *target company*'s stockholders desire a cash deal that *maximizes* the after-tax dollars they will receive.
12. The acquiring company does *not* want to be responsible for taxes at the corporate level.
13. The *value of the consideration* exceeds the *tax basis* of the target company's underlying property.

Answers:
1. a **2.** i **3.** b **4.** c **5.** d **6.** a **7.** b **8.** c **9.** i **10.** e **11.** e, b, g **12.** a, g **13.** g (from buyer's perspective), h (from seller's perspective)

E 4-2 **Terminology** Indicate the appropriate term or terms for each of the following:

1. The expansion of a business by constructing a manufacturing facility.
2. A business combination in which a company acquires one of its *suppliers.*
3. A business combination in which a company acquires one of its *competitors.*
4. A business combination in which a company acquires businesses to diversify its product lines.
5. The broad terms used to refer to business combinations.
6. A business combination in which the *target company's* corporate existence is terminated in conjunction with the transfer of assets and liabilities to the *acquiring company.*
7. A business combination in which a *new* corporation is formed to acquire the businesses of *two* existing corporations.
8. The method of accounting for business combinations as set forth in *FAS 141.*
9. The *two* types of assets that can be acquired in a business combination.
10. The expansion of a business by acquiring an *existing* business.
11. An acquired business that maintains its *separate legal existence.*
12. An acquiring business that acquires *common stock* of the acquired business, the latter maintaining its separate legal existence.
13. An acquired business that *ceases* to be a separate legal entity but continues to use a separate general ledger.
14. The primary type of consideration given in a business combination that is accounted for as a *purchase.*

E 4-3 **Acquisition of Assets** Pertex acquired *all* of Sertex's assets in a business combination that did *not* qualify for pooling of interests treatment. Pertex paid $800,000 *cash.* The *book value* of Sertex's net assets is $600,000, and their *current value* is $750,000.

Required Explain the general accounting procedures that Pertex must follow in recording the acquisition of the assets.

E 4-4 **Divestiture Accounting: Sale of Common Stock** Phaco acquired *all* of Shaco's outstanding common stock from Shaco's shareholders by issuing *common stock*.

Required Explain in general how Shaco should account for this change in ownership of its outstanding common stock.

E 4-5 **Divestiture Accounting: Sale of Assets** Panco acquired *all* of Sanco's *assets* by issuing *common stock* (and assuming Sanco's liabilities).

Required Explain in general how Sanco should account for this transaction.

E 4-6 **Statutory Merger and Statutory Consolidation** Parrco is considering a merger or consolidation with Sarrco. Both methods of acquisition are being considered under applicable corporate statutory law. Parrco is the *larger* of the two corporations and, in reality, is acquiring Sarrco.

Required Discuss the meaning of the terms *merger* and *consolidation* as used in corporate law with particular emphasis on the legal difference between the two.

E 4-7 **Basic Understanding of the Nature of Goodwill** Shelley and Brett are children who live one street apart. Shelley has saved $100, and Brett has saved $250. Each child desires to open a lemonade stand on his or her own front lawn. Each invests $100 in the business, using $75 to buy a table, a chair, a pitcher, and a stirrer. Each uses the remaining $25 to purchase supplies (lemons, sugar, paper cups). Shelley lives on a street with many other children; Brett does not. After one year in business, Shelley made a profit of $60, but Brett made a profit of only $20. Each withdraws from the business the profits made and spends the money on personal items. On the first day of the second year of business, the two children meet for lunch and discuss business. Shelley indicates that she is willing to sell her business if the price is right. Brett wants to make more money than his business now generates; he knows that Shelley's lemonade stand sells much more lemonade than his does. Brett offers to buy Shelley's business; she knows that she has a far better business location than Brett does.

Brett and Shelley agree on a purchase price of $130, with $100 for the purchase of equipment and supplies. Brett pays the remaining $30 in anticipation of being able to make substantial profits in the future above and beyond what would be considered average (goodwill). Brett is entitled to use Shelly's site for only two years.

Required

1. How much capital was invested in each separate business just *before* Brett acquired Shelley's business?
2. How much capital is invested in each separate business location just *after* Brett acquired Shelley's business?
3. How much money does each child have after Brett acquired Shelley's business?
4. Considering that the children had a combined capital of $350 just *prior to* the commencement of their businesses and distributed and spent their profits for year 1, how can they now have more capital than they started with? (Combine the answers to requirements 2 and 3 to arrive at their total capital.)
5. What amounts will appear in Brett's income statements for the next two years (for his *second* business) assuming that Brett has:
   a. The *same* cash inflows Shelly had?
   b. The same cash flows he had for his *first* business (superior earnings did *not* materialize)?

Problems

P 4-1 **Comprehensive: Acquisition of *Assets* for *Cash*** PBX Company acquired *all* the *assets* of Sprint Company by assuming responsibility for all of its liabilities and paying $1,500,000 cash. Information with respect to Sprint at the date of combination follows:

	Book Value	Current Value
Cash	$ 10,000	$ 10,000
Accounts receivable, net (including $30,000 due from PBX Company)	90,000	90,000
Inventory	200,000	200,000
Land	400,000	500,000
Buildings and equipment	2,500,000	1,600,000
Accumulated depreciation	(1,200,000)	
Total Assets	$ 2,000,000	$2,400,000
Accounts payable and accruals	$ 300,000	$ 300,000
Long-term debt	800,000	800,000
Total Liabilities	$ 1,100,000	$1,100,000
Common stock, $1 par value	$ 100,000	
Additional paid-in capital	500,000	
Retained earnings	300,000	
Total Stockholders' Equity	$ 900,000	$1,300,000
Total Liabilities and Stockholders' Equity	$ 2,000,000	$2,400,000

Required

1. Does the acquisition appear to be a horizontal, vertical, or conglomerate type of combination?
2. Would the transaction be accounted for as a *purchase* or a *pooling of interests*?
3. Is PBX Company the *parent company* of Sprint Company? Why or why not?
4. Is Sprint Company a *subsidiary*? Why or why not?
5. Is Sprint Company a legal entity *after* the transaction has been consummated?
6. How should the newly acquired operation be referred to?
7. Prepare the journal entry that Sprint Company makes on the date of the combination. Assume a 40% income tax rate.
8. Prepare a balance sheet for Sprint Company *after* recording the entry in requirement 7.
9. What options are available to Sprint Company *after* the business combination?
10. What is Sprint's book value in total and per share *after* the business combination?
11. What is the most likely market price of Sprint Company's common stock *immediately after* the transaction? (How would your answer change if Sprint planned to liquidate and distribute cash to its stockholders one year from now?)
12. Prepare the entry—in condensed form—that PBX would make, assuming that it uses *centralized* accounting.
13. Why did PBX pay $1,500,000 for a company whose net assets are worth only $1,300,000?
14. How could PBX have determined the current value of Sprint's assets and liabilities?
15. Tax questions based on the Appendix (optional):
    a. What is the treatment for *tax-reporting* purposes?
    b. From your answer in requirement 15a, what is PBX's *tax basis* of the land, buildings, and equipment it obtained?

P 4-2 **Comprehensive: Acquisition of *Common Stock* for *Cash*** Assume the same information as in Problem 4-1 except that PBX Company acquired *all* the outstanding common stock of Sprint Company rather than acquiring all Sprint's assets and assuming all its liabilities.

Required Respond to requirements 2–10 in Problem 4-1. Then continue with the following requirements:

11. Prepare the entry that PBX makes to record the combination.
12. Where is the goodwill that PBX paid for recorded?
13. Tax questions based on the Appendix (optional):
    a. What is the treatment for *tax-reporting* purposes?
    b. If the combination is taxable, who is taxed?
    c. Do the selling shareholders have a taxable *gain* or a taxable *loss*?
    d. Assuming the selling shareholders were all initial founders of Sprint, calculate their taxable gain or loss in total.
    e. In what asset does PBX have a *tax basis*?
    f. How much is its *tax basis* in this asset?
    g. Does the *tax basis* of Sprint's land, buildings, and equipment change?

P 4-3 **Comprehensive: Acquisition of *Common Stock* for *Common Stock*** Assume the same information as provided in Problem 4-1 except that PBX Company gave as consideration 50,000 shares of its $10 par value common stock (of which 950,000 shares are already outstanding) having a market value of $30 per share for all the outstanding common stock of Sprint Company.

Required Respond to requirements 2–10 in Problem 4-1. Then continue with the following requirements:

11. Prepare the entry that PBX makes to record the combination.
12. What is the exchange ratio used in the transaction?
13. Tax questions based on the Appendix (optional):
    a. What is the probable treatment for *tax-reporting* purposes?
    b. In what asset does PBX Company have a *tax basis*?
    c. How much is its *tax basis* in this asset?
    d. Nick Tymer acquired 3,000 shares of Sprint's common stock for $34,000 (shortly *before* the announcement of the business combination). What is his *tax basis* of the PBX shares he received in the exchange?
    e. Did Tymer gain from his investment?

THINKING CRITICALLY

Cases

C 4-1 **Limiting Legal Liability and Consistency** Pentex is having merger discussions with Sentex. All of Pentex's business acquisitions to date have been acquisitions of *common stock* resulting in parent-subsidiary relationships. Pentex prefers to legally insulate each of its acquired businesses from all other operations. Sentex has been and still is involved as a defendant in several lawsuits. As a result, Pentex plans to acquire Sentex's *assets* to insulate itself from any current or potential legal entanglements.

Required

1. How could Pentex achieve the objective of insulating the business of Sentex?
2. Is the consistency principle violated as a result of acquiring *assets*? Why or why not?

C 4-2 **How Much to Pay for an Accounting Practice** The practitioner of an accounting sole proprietorship is retiring and is planning to sell the practice, which grosses $100,000 per year and nets $60,000.

Required How much would you be willing to pay to acquire this practice?

C 4-3 ***Accounting* versus *Tax* Treatment** (Appendix-related) Pineco plans to embark on a business acquisition program to diversify its product lines. The controller is unclear about whether the *tax treatment* determines the accounting treatment or whether the *accounting treatment* determines the *tax treatment*.

Required How would you advise the controller?

Financial Analysis Problems

FAP 4-1 **Determining Financial Reporting Impact of a Merger under the *Purchase Method* (Debt Ratio and Return on Investment)** PDQ Inc. is contemplating a business combination with Sprint Inc. on 1/1/06. Selected information follows:

1. PDQ will issue 10,000 shares of its $1 par value common stock to Sprint in exchange for 100% of Sprint's *assets*.
2. PDQ will assume *all* of Sprint's *liabilities*.

3. PDQ will account for Sprint's operations as a *decentralized division* to be evaluated as a profit center.

4. Other financial information:

	PDQ	Sprint
Book Values		
Assets	$3,000,000	$1,300,000
Liabilities	2,000,000	1,000,000
Current Values		
Assets	4,000,000	1,700,000
Liabilities	2,000,000	1,000,000
Current market price of common stock	$80	$35
Common stock shares outstanding	40,000	20,000

5. The expected future annual net income of the acquired business is

Under pooling of interests accounting	$90,000
Under purchase accounting	80,000

6. For 2005, PDQ reported $150,000 of net income, *all* of which was distributed as dividends at the end of 2005.

Required

1. Calculate the issuing company's debt-to-equity ratio:
   a. Before the combination.
   b. After the combination on a consolidated basis.
2. Calculate PDQ's return on equity (ROE) for 2005.
3. Calculate the issuing company's expected annual return on its investment (AROI) in Sprint for 2006.
4. Calculate PDQ's expected ROE for 2006 (combined earnings of both operations) assuming that PDQ expects to earn $150,000 for 2006 from its own separate operations.

FAP 4-2 **Determining if a True Loss Occurred** On 1/1/06, Pyco Company acquired 100% of Syco Company (which was *privately owned*) for $50 million of consideration when Pyco's common stock had a *fair value* of $50 per share. Immediately before the combination, Pyco had (1) total stockholders equity of $20 million and (2) 3,000,000 common shares outstanding.

Of the $50 million purchase price, $40 million was assigned to goodwill. None of Syco's recorded assets or liabilities were over- or undervalued on 1/1/06.

On 12/31/07 (two years later), Pyco wrote off the entire $40 million of goodwill as a result of performing an impairment review. At that time, Pyco's common stock had a fair value of $5 per share.

Required

Determine how much investors gained or lost under each of the following four scenarios.

a. Pyco used $50 million of cash that **it had accumulated** to acquire Syco.
b. Pyco borrowed $50 million cash **from a bank** to acquire Syco.
c. Pyco issued $50 million of common stock (1,000,000 shares) **to the public** to obtain cash to acquire Syco.
d. Pyco issued $50 million of common stock (1,000,000 shares) **to Syco's stockholders** to acquire Syco.

FAP 4-3 **Applying Finance Concepts to Evaluate Profitability: Accounting for Goodwill—ASSUMES GAAP REQUIRES GOODWILL TO BE AMORTIZED** Cork City Batters is a major league baseball team formed 11 years ago. Operations quickly reached expected levels. In each of Years 8, 9, and 10, the team reported net income of approximately $1,000,000. (For simplicity, ignore income taxes.)

At the end of Year 10, the team was sold to a partnership formed with capital of $5,000,000. The purchase price was $4,000,000. The remaining $1,000,000 is needed for working capital purposes. For simplicity, assume that (1) the initial capital of the team, when formed, was $1; (2) all earnings for the 10 years had been distributed to the owners by the end of the tenth year; (3) assets therefore equaled liabilities at the time of sale; and (4) none of the recorded assets or liabilities are over- or undervalued.

As the partnership's accountant, you assigned the $4,000,000 to goodwill having a four-year life, inasmuch as the partnership's plans were to own the team for four to six years. (The partners believed that the goodwill should be recovered over the minimum period.) The income statement for Year 11 follows:

Revenues	$ 8,600,000
Expenses (excluding goodwill)	(7,000,000)
Subtotal	$ 1,600,000
Goodwill amortization	(1,000,000)
Net Income	$ 600,000

The players' union and management are currently negotiating a new contract for Year 12. Management and the players' union are in wide disagreement as to the team's true profitability. At issue is the validity of the goodwill amortization. Management contends that the 12% return on investment for Year 11 ($600,000 ÷ $5,000,000) is not excessive, and, therefore, no pay raises are appropriate.

Additional Information and Assumptions

1. The decision to form the partnership and acquire the baseball team was based on the high rate of return calculated using the internal rate of return method. The calculation produced an estimated annual return on capital exceeding 30% for the six years that the partnership expected to exist. (The calculation included an estimate that the team would be sold for a minimum of $4,000,000 at the end of Year 16.)
2. Revenues and income from operations are expected to remain constant through Year 16.
3. Cash is to be distributed to partners at the end of each year equal to net income.
4. At the end of each year, 11 through 14, an additional $1,000,000 cash is to be distributed to partners as a return *of* capital.
5. The partnership sells the team at the end of Year 16 for $4,000,000. (At the end of Years 11, 12, 13, and 14, a group of outside investors had offered to buy the team for $4,500,000.)
6. All cash on hand at the end of Year 16 was distributed to the partners, and the partnership was dissolved.
7. GAAP requires goodwill to be amortized (**this assumption is contrary to the requirements of *FAS 142***).

Required

1. Before completing requirements 2 through 7, assess whether management's position is reasonable.
2. Using the reported or assumed net income for Years 12 through 16, calculate the partners' annual return on investment (AROI). (For simplicity, ignore the impact of each year's earnings in determining the capital balances to be used in the denominator. In other words, use the *beginning* capital balances for the denominator for each year rather than an *average* capital balance.) Also, calculate an average of the ROIs for the six years.
3. Assuming that revenues and income from operations occurred as expected through the end of Year 16 when the team was sold for $4,000,000, how accurately did the AROI calculations in requirement 2 portray the economics of what transpired? Why?

Guidance Questions

As the partnership's accountant, you should be able to explain the following to the partners:

a. The reason that the AROI for Year 11 (and almost every year thereafter) is so greatly different from the more than 30% initial projected return on capital.

b. Whether the partners really earned twice as much on their capital in Year 14, in terms of return on investment, as in Year 12.

4. Calculate the internal rate of return (IRR) from the perspective of the partners from the time the partnership was formed until it was dissolved. (Use $5,000,000 as the initial cash outflow.)

Spreadsheet Integration Note: You may readily obtain this answer using the IRR function available in the EXCEL spreadsheet program. You merely need to set up a cash flow table *and then* program the IRR function with the cell cursor located in the cell in which you want your answer to appear. To access the IRR function using EXCEL, use either (1) the **Insert/functions command** or (2) the "Paste Function" icon on the standard tool bar (f_x). Select the FINANCIAL category in the *left* dialog box and then select the *IRR* function in the *right* dialog box. Once you have selected the *IRR* function, merely follow the prompts.

5. Why does the IRR answer in requirement 4 differ from the AROI answers in requirement 2? (*Hint:* The fact that the IRR considers the time value of money is *not* the reason.) Which result portrays the economic reality of what transpired during these six years?

6. How does the methodology of the IRR differ from the methodology used in *lease accounting* in which the implicit interest rate (IIR) is encountered?

7. Given that none of the team's recorded assets or liabilities were under- or overvalued at the acquisition date, to what else might the $4,000,000 (or some portion of it) be assigned?

FAP 4-4 **Financial Analysis Problem 4-3 with Changed Assumption** Use the information in Financial Analysis Problem 4-3 except assume that the team's value is zero at the end of Year 16; that is, the team is disbanded, cash on hand is distributed to the partners, and the partnership is dissolved. This happened because the city closed its ballpark at the end of Year 16 to make room for a new freeway. The closing was voted on and passed in Year 15. Through the end of Year 14, the team could have been sold at any time for the partnership's purchase price of $4,000,000. Once the decision to build the new freeway was made, no other investors were interested in buying the team.

Required

1. Repeat requirement 4 of Financial Analysis Problem 4-3 under the new assumption. (Round your IRR answer to the nearest number with no decimal places; for example, 18.92% becomes 19%. Lump your dollar, rounding differences into Year 16.)

2. Starting with both the IRR percentage calculated in requirement 1 and the $5,000,000 beginning capital balance of the partners, determine for Year 11 how much of the $1,600,000 cash distribution to the partners is assumed to be

a. Net income under the IRR method (a return *on* capital).

b. Return of the initial capital investment of $5,000,000 (a recovery *of* capital). Repeat for Years 12 through 16 using (1) the same IRR percentage and (2) the *beginning-of-year* capital balance, as reduced by the prior year's return *of* capital. (Round all amounts to the nearest thousand and include any rounding error in Year 16.) Use the following format (omit 000s):

				Cash Flow Deemed to Be	
Year	Internal Rate of Return	Beginning (unrecovered) Capital Balance	Cash Flow Returned to Partners	A Return *on* Investment (net income)	A Return *of* Investment (recovery of capital)
11		$5,000	$1,600		

Spreadsheet Integration Note: You can simplify the preceding calculations by putting the format on an electronic spreadsheet, programming *three* simple formulas, and duplicating these formulas for subsequent years.

3. Using the net income amounts calculated in requirement 2 (and the cash distributions to the partners), prepare a T-account analysis of the partners' capital account by year from inception through dissolution of the partnership. (Omit 000s.)

4. Supply the missing amounts for the following tables:
   a. As reported by the partnership's accountant:

	Year					
	11	12	13	14	15	16
Operating income before goodwill expense	$ 1,600					
Goodwill expense	(1,000)					
Net Income	$ 600					
Beginning capital	$ 5,000					
Annual return on investment	12%					

   b. As assumed in the internal rate of return method:

	Year					
	11	12	13	14	15	16
Operating income before goodwill expense	$ 1,600					
Goodwill expense						
Net Income						
Beginning capital	$ 5,000					
Annual return on investment						

5. Why does the IRR answer in requirement 1 differ from the AROI percentages calculated in requirement 4a?
6. Does the IRR method assume amortization of goodwill? How can you determine this?
7. Which section in requirement 4 reflects the economic reality of what transpired in these six years? Explain the reasoning behind your answer.
8. If no accounting rules existed concerning goodwill, how would you account for goodwill looking into the future?

FAP 4-5 **Calculating the Amount to Be Paid for Goodwill** On 1/1/06, Pointer Inc. entered into negotiations with the management of Setter Inc. to acquire Setter. Information concerning Setter follows:

	Book Value	Current Value
Total assets	$2,600,000[a]	$3,000,000
Stockholders' equity	600,000	1,000,000
Net income for 2005	250,000	
Average net income for 2005, 2004, and 2003	250,000	

[a] Land is undervalued by $300,000, and equipment having a 10-year life is undervalued by $100,000.

The average return on equity for this industry is 15%. Pointer's management is confident that Setter will be able to continue to earn $250,000 per year indefinitely.

Required

1. Calculate the goodwill that Setter possesses.
2. How much should Pointer pay for goodwill?
3. Should the amount of goodwill calculated for Setter be discounted to its present value? Why? If so, what discount rate should be used?
4. Considering the amount you calculated that Setter should pay for goodwill, what is Pointer's expected annual return on investment for 2006?
5. What life should be assigned to the goodwill?

chapter

5

The Purchase Method: At Date of Acquisition—100% Ownership

The main ingredient of good leadership is good character. This is because leadership involves conduct, and conduct is determined by values. You may call these values by many names. "Ethics," "morality," and "integrity" come to mind. But this much is clear: Values are what makes us who we are.

GENERAL H. NORMAN SCHWARZKOPF

LEARNING OBJECTIVES

To Understand

> The way to calculate the acquirer's *cost* of an acquisition.

> The way to *allocate* the acquirer's cost to the various *tangible* and *intangible* assets and liabilities of the acquired business.

> The way to prepare consolidated statements for a 100%-owned acquired subsidiary at the date of acquisition.

> The difference between *non-push-down* and *push-down* accounting.

> The way to apply the purchase method when control is achieved as a result of purchasing several *blocks of stock* over time.

TOPIC OUTLINE

I. The Essence of the Purchase Method
II. Determining the *Cost* of the Acquired Business
III. The Relationship of *Cost* to the *Current Value* of the Acquired Business's *Net Assets*
IV. The Irrelevance of the Acquired Business's *Book Values* for Consolidated Reporting Purposes
V. Preparing Consolidated Statements at the Acquisition Date
VI. Additional Assignment of Cost (Allocation) Issues
VII. The *Push-Down Basis* of Accounting: A Brief Look
VIII. Step (Piecemeal) Acquisitions Resulting in 100% Ownership
APPENDIX 5A: Acquiring *All* of the Assets
APPENDIX 5B: Recording Deferred Taxes at the Acquisition Date

Appendices can be found at http://www.pahler.swlearning.com

CHAPTER OVERVIEW

Chapter 4 introduced the *purchase method* of accounting for business combinations. The *purchase method* can be applied to either ***form*** of business combination, the *acquisition of assets* and the *acquisition of common stock*; with either, the results of reporting operations and the financial position of the combined businesses are the *same*. Acquisition of *less than* 100% of the common stock requires some additional considerations that are *not* relevant in situations in which *all* of the common stock is acquired. Discussion of these more involved situations is delayed until Chapter 6.

Regardless of whether the acquisition is achieved by acquiring *common stock* or *assets* (the *form* of the acquisition), the consolidated financial statement amounts are always the *same*—both at the date of acquisition and for dates and periods subsequent to it. This chapter deals only with achieving purchase accounting results *at* the acquisition date. In Chapter 6, we discuss achieving purchase accounting results for dates and periods *subsequent to* the acquisition date.

The form of all acquisitions is either the acquisition of (1) the target company's ***assets*** (usually includes the assumption of *liabilities* as well) or (2) the target company's ***outstanding common stock***. In this chapter, we illustrate the acquisition of *common stock*. In Appendix 5A, we illustrate the acquisition of *assets*.

I. THE ESSENCE OF THE PURCHASE METHOD

The underlying concept of the *purchase method* is that one entity has purchased the business of another entity—that is, **a sale has been consummated.** The acquiring entity records at its cost the *assets* or *common stock* acquired. The cost is based essentially on **the value of the consideration given.**

Goodwill Situations

If the acquirer's *cost* is *above* the *current value* of the target company's *net assets*, goodwill exists and must be evaluated periodically for possible impairment. Thus **goodwill is determined in a *residual* manner.** The target company's *current value* is determined by valuing the company's tangible assets, identifiable intangible assets, and liabilities at their *current values*, which may involve qualified appraisers.

Bargain Purchase Element [BPE] ("Negative Goodwill") Situations

In the far less frequent circumstances in which the acquiring company's *cost* is *below* the *current value* of the target company's *net assets*, a bargain purchase element exists and must be allocated against the current value of *certain noncurrent assets*. If the bargain purchase element is so great that it reduces the applicable noncurrent assets to zero, the remaining amount is recognized as an *extraordinary gain* (in most instances).

The purchase method parallels accounting for the acquisition of individual assets—that is, *historical cost* is used. Consequently, some assets and liabilities of the enlarged business are recorded at their *historical cost* (the assets and liabilities of the *acquiring* company), whereas some assets and liabilities of the enlarged business (the assets and liabilities of the *acquired* business) are reported at their *current values* as of the acquisition date. These *current values* become the acquiring company's *historical cost*. From the date of acquisition, the income of the acquired business is combined with the income of the acquiring company. **The *acquired* business's preacquisition earnings are never combined with the preacquisition earnings of the *acquiring* company.**

CHECK POINT

Which of the following is the appropriate basis for valuing fixed assets acquired in a business combination accounted for as a purchase carried out by exchanging cash for *common stock*?

a. Historic cost.
b. Book value.
c. Cost plus any excess of *purchase price* over *book value* of asset acquired.
d. Fair value.

Answer: d

The purchase method can be neatly addressed by two questions:

1. What is the cost of the acquired business to the acquiring business?
2. What specifically is acquired for the cost incurred?

The rest of the chapter discusses the procedures for answering these questions, in addition to the procedures for presenting the financial statements of the enlarged business.

II. DETERMINING THE COST OF THE ACQUIRED BUSINESS

The cost of the acquired business equals the sum of the following:

1. The *fair value* **of the consideration given.**
2. The **direct costs** incurred in connection with the acquisition, excluding costs of registering with the Securities and Exchange Commission (SEC) any securities given as consideration by the acquiring company.
3. The *fair value* **of any contingent consideration** given subsequent to the acquisition date.

Each of these areas is discussed in the three following sections.

The *Fair Value* of the Consideration Given

The following three types of consideration may be given in any business combination:

1. **Cash or other assets.** Cost is the amount of cash or the fair value of other assets given.
2. **Debt.** Cost is the present value of the debt issued, determined by applying the provisions of *APB Opinion No. 21*, "Interest on Receivables and Payables."
3. **Equity securities.** Cost is the fair value of the *equity securities issued.* If the fair value of the *property acquired* is more clearly evident than the fair value of the *equity securities issued*, however, the fair value of the *property acquired* is used to determine cost.

As a practical matter, when *equity securities issued* are identical to the acquiring company's outstanding publicly traded securities, the fair value of the equity securities given is readily determinable and is almost always used to determine cost. (An example of an exception is a common stock that is *thinly traded.*) If the acquiring company's equity securities are *not* publicly traded or a new class of stock is issued, obtaining an appraisal of either (1) the fair value of the *equity securities issued* (usually obtainable from an investment banker) or (2) the *property acquired* is usually necessary, the second alternative being preferable.

CHECK POINT

In a business combination accounted for as a purchase, costs of registering equity securities to be issued by the acquiring company are a (an)

a. Expense of the combined company for the period in which the costs were incurred.
b. Direct addition to stockholders' equity of the combined company.
c. Reduction of the otherwise determinable fair value of the securities.
d. Addition to goodwill.

Answer: c

Direct Costs

Costs and expenses incurred that are *directly traceable* to the acquisition may be capitalized as part of the cost of the acquisition. Examples of capitalizable and noncapitalizable items follow:

	Capitalizable	Noncapitalizable
Legal fees	X	
Investment banker advising fees	X	
Accounting fees (such as for a purchase investigation)	X	
Finders' fees	X	
Travel costs	X	
General expenses (pro rata)		X
Salary and overhead of an internal acquisitions department		X
Costs and fees pertaining to the issuance or registration of debt or equity securities (including investment banker underwriting fees)		X[a]

[a] If an *equity security*, additional paid-in capital is charged; if a *debt security*, debt issuance costs are charged (to be amortized over the life of the debt).

CHECK POINT

A business combination is accounted for appropriately as a purchase. Which of the following should be deducted in determining the combined corporation's net income for the current period?

	Direct Costs of Acquisition	General Expenses Related to Acquisition
a.	Yes	No
b.	Yes	Yes
c.	No	Yes
d.	No	No

Answer: c

Contingent Consideration

Contingent consideration is often used as a compromise when the buyer and seller disagree on the purchase price or the form of consideration to be given, or both. Contingent consideration may be divided into two mutually exclusive categories: contingencies (1) whose outcomes *are* currently determinable and (2) whose outcomes are *not* currently determinable.

Contingencies Whose Outcomes *Are* Currently Determinable

If it can be determined beyond a reasonable doubt at the acquisition date that the outcome of the contingency will be such that the contingent consideration will have to be paid, the fair value of the additional consideration should be recorded at that time as part of the cost of the acquired business. Relatively few contingencies fall into this category.

ETHICS

Gambling—A Surefire Way to Become an Embezzler?

The author knows of two former CPA employees of a Big Four accounting firm (both very bright and talented individuals) who (1) went to work for separate companies in industry at controllership positions, (2) were making very respectable salaries (along with stock options), (3) began gambling (evidently because life was not exciting enough for them), and (4) embezzled money to feed their gambling addiction. Each eventually stole nearly $1,500,000, each was caught, and each was sentenced to a federal penitentiary for eight years. In both cases, their spouses (who became sole providers for the children) divorced them, and their employers recovered one-half of the family's remaining personal assets (the spouses retaining the other half). Thus each professional had largely achieved the good ("yuppie") life.

Question
Would you be willing to throw it all away merely for some extra excitement in your life?

Contingencies Whose Outcomes Are *Not* Currently Determinable

If it *cannot* be determined beyond a reasonable doubt at the acquisition date that the contingent consideration will have to be paid, it should be disclosed but *not* recorded as a liability or shown as outstanding securities until it is determinable beyond a reasonable doubt. This **"determinable beyond a reasonable doubt"** criterion of FASB *Statement No. 141*, "Business Combinations," is more demanding than the "probable" criterion set forth in FASB *Statement No. 5*, "Accounting for Contingencies," which applies only to loss and gain contingencies, as shown below.

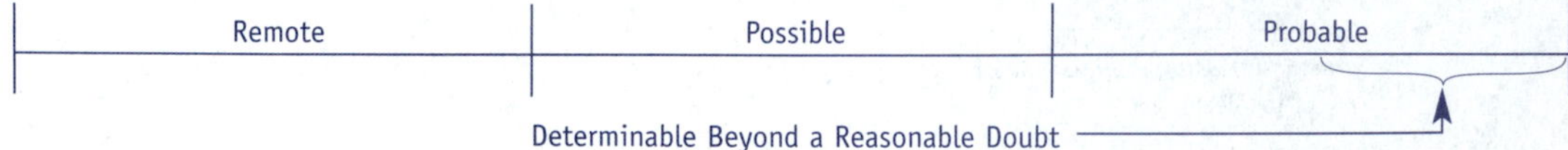

Contingencies that are *not* currently determinable can be divided into two categories:

1. **Contingencies based on *other than* security prices.** This type of contingency is often based on sales or earnings goals for the acquired business. It is commonly used when the *target company* or its *shareholders* want to protect themselves from selling out too cheaply in the event that the acquired business later realizes the potential they believe it possesses and when the *buyer* wants to protect itself from paying too much in the event that the acquired business does *not* realize such potential. Contingent consideration is the compromise whereby an additional amount of consideration is given to the *seller(s)* at a later date if the acquired business achieves certain agreed-upon sales or earnings levels within a specified period of time. Later, when the contingency is resolved and any additional consideration is distributable, **the current value of the additional consideration is added to the acquiring company's cost of the acquired business.** (Usually adding the current value increases the amount of goodwill.)
2. **Contingencies based on security prices.** This type of contingency is common when the target company or its shareholders receive as consideration the acquiring company's *equity securities*, which must be held for a certain period of time. In this situation, the target company or its shareholders want protection in the event the market price of the securities at the expiration of the holding period is *below* their market price at the *acquisition date*. The acquiring company must issue an additional number of securities if the market price at the end of the holding period is *below* the market price that existed on the *acquisition date*. The result brings the total value of the holdings of the target company or its shareholders at that time up to the total value existing on the *acquisition date*. If additional securities are later issued, the current value of the additional consideration is added to the acquiring company's cost of the acquired business. The amount previously recorded for securities issued at the date of acquisition should simultaneously be reduced, however, to the lower current value of those securities. **The net effect of this procedure is *not* to increase the cost of the acquired business above what was recorded at the acquisition date.** The rationale is that the initial recorded cost represents the amount that would

have been paid for the business in a straight cash transaction. Illustration 5-1 gives an example of the accounting entries for this type of contingency.

III. THE RELATIONSHIP OF *COST* TO THE *CURRENT VALUE* OF THE ACQUIRED BUSINESS'S *NET ASSETS*

Once the cost of the acquired business is determined, the next step in purchase accounting is to determine the *current value* of its assets and liabilities. Assume that the assets have a *current value* of $288,000 and the liabilities have a *current value* of $200,000. The $88,000 difference between the two is the *current value* of the net assets. This *current value* is then multiplied by the acquiring company's ownership interest in the acquired business (always 100% when *assets* are acquired or when *all* of the *outstanding common stock* is acquired) to obtain the acquiring company's ownership interest in the *current value* of the net assets. This amount is then compared with the *cost* of the acquisition to determine whether *goodwill* exists (the most common situation) or a *bargain purchase element* is present. This process can be expressed in a formula applicable to all combinations, as well as the preceding example, as shown in Illustration 5-2.

Review Points for Illustration 5-2. Note the following:

1. Both goodwill and bargain purchase elements are determined in a ***residual manner***.
2. When a bargain purchase element is present, its amount must be allocated to certain noncurrent assets (reducing their current values) to the extent possible. The adjusted amounts then become the current values for financial reporting purposes.

ILLUSTRATION 5-1 AN EXAMPLE OF CONTINGENT CONSIDERATION BASED ON SECURITY PRICES

Pine Inc. acquires the business of Spruce Inc. (Whether it acquires *assets* or *common stock* is irrelevant.) The total consideration Pine pays is $1,000,000 worth of its $5 par value common stock. The market price of Pine's common stock on the acquisition date is $50 per share; thus 20,000 shares are issued at that time. A condition of the purchase is that the common stock issued be held by the seller for *two* years. If, at the end of two years, the *market price* of the common stock is *below* $50 per share, an appropriate additional number of shares must be issued so that the total value of the issued shares equals $1,000,000. Two years later, the *market price* of Pine's common stock is $40 per share. Thus, $1,000,000 divided by $40 per share equals 25,000 shares. Because 20,000 shares have already been issued, an additional 5,000 shares are issued at that time.

Entry at the acquisition date:

Cost of Acquired Business[a] (20,000 shares × $50 market price)	1,000,000	
Common Stock (20,000 shares × $5 par)		100,000
Additional Paid-in Capital		900,000
To record the issuance of 20,000 shares of $5 par value common stock.		

Entries required two years later:

Cost of Acquired Business[a] (5,000 shares × $40 market price)	200,000	
Common Stock (5,000 shares × $5 par)		25,000
Additional Paid-in Capital		175,000
To record the issuance of 5,000 shares of $5 par value common stock as additional consideration.		
Additional Paid-in Capital	200,000	
Cost of Acquired Business[a]		200,000
To reflect the reduction in value of the previously issued shares from $50 per share to $40 per share.		

Note that the effect of the entries recorded two years after acquisition is to debit Additional Paid-in Capital for $25,000 and credit Common Stock for $25,000. Thus there is no effect on the cost of the acquired business *as initially recorded on the acquisition date.*

[a] Later in the chapter, more descriptive account titles are used: "Investment in Subsidiary" when *common stock* is acquired and "Investment in Division" when *assets* are acquired.

ILLUSTRATION 5-2 RELATIONSHIP OF TOTAL COST TO THE CURRENT VALUE OF THE ACQUIRED BUSINESS'S NET ASSETS

	Cost	–	Acquiring Company's Ownership Interest in *Current Value* of Net Assets	=	Goodwill (Bargain Purchase) Element
Goodwill situation	$100,000	–	$88,000[a]	=	$12,000
Bargain purchase element situation	$83,000	–	$88,000[a]	=	$(5,000)

[a] Assume that assets have a current value of $288,000, liabilities have a current value of $200,000, and either *assets* or all of the outstanding *common stock* was acquired.

Accounting for Goodwill

When the acquiring company's cost is *higher than* the acquirer's ownership interest in the current value of the acquired business's net assets, the excess amount is considered **goodwill.** Note that goodwill is a residually determined amount. It is reported in the financial statements as an asset of the enlarged, combined business. Its carrying value must be evaluated ***at least annually*** for possible impairment of value (using a ***fair value test***, which is discussed in Chapter 6). If and when impairment occurs, a write-down is made and recognized in earnings.

Goodwill versus Covenants Not to Compete

Prior to August 1993, goodwill was *not* deductible for income tax-reporting purposes. Accordingly, acquiring companies often tried to include in the acquisition agreement a tax-deductible feature known as a *covenant not to compete.* Covenants not to compete are intangible assets similar to goodwill. Such covenants prevent the target company or certain of its key shareholders or employees from reentering the same line of business for a specified period of time. Because goodwill is *now* tax deductible, this built-in incentive favoring the assignment of part of the purchase price to covenants not to compete instead of goodwill no longer exists. Furthermore, both goodwill and covenants not to compete are tax deductible over 15 years. Thus no incentive exists to assign part of the purchase price to one versus the other as might otherwise exist if each had a *different life* for *tax-reporting* purposes.

Tax Rules for Determining Goodwill

In allocating the purchase price of a business between *depreciable* and *nondepreciable* assets for *tax-reporting* purposes, the amount allocated to goodwill must be calculated in a residual manner (termed the *residual method of allocation*). Thus goodwill is determined in the same manner for both *financial reporting* and *tax reporting.*

Accounting for Bargain Purchase Elements

When the acquiring company's cost is *below* the acquirer's ownership interest in the current value of the acquired business's net assets, a **bargain purchase element** exists. Bargain purchase elements are treated arbitrarily under the provisions of *FAS 141*. First, the bargain purchase element must be treated as a *reduction* of the *current values* assigned to certain *noncurrent assets* acquired. Five specific assets are excluded because their *fair values* are generally more certain than those of the *nonexcluded* assets.[1] If the bargain purchase element is so large that the applicable noncurrent as-

[1] The *five* specific assets *excluded* are (1) financial assets *other than* those accounted for by the *equity method* of accounting, (2) assets to be disposed of by sale, (3) deferred tax assets, (4) prepaid assets relating to employee benefit plans, and (5) any other current assets.

sets are reduced to *zero* (such reduction rarely, if ever, happens), any remaining credit is reported *in earnings* as an *extraordinary gain*.[2]

The rationale for attempting to eliminate the bargain purchase element is that the values assigned to the net assets as a whole should *not* exceed the purchase price paid. Under historical cost-based accounting, the purchase price constitutes cost. Were it not for this requirement, managements would have the opportunity to seek or use the highest possible appraisals for the assets to obtain the highest possible bargain purchase element. The high (artificial) bargain purchase element could then be amortized to income over a relatively short period of time in comparison with time periods assigned to the *noncurrent assets*. Thus, substantial opportunity for manipulating income would exist.

Because bargain purchase elements arise most frequently when the acquired business has recently experienced operating losses, this treatment results in a conservative valuation of the *noncurrent assets* other than long-term investments in marketable securities. This treatment makes sense; such *noncurrent assets* acquired from a company experiencing operating losses are subject to greater realization risks than otherwise would be the case if the target company had *not* experienced operating losses.

To illustrate the manner of allocating a bargain purchase to the appropriate assets, assume a $5,000 bargain purchase element. Assume further that the only noncurrent assets of the acquired business are land and buildings and equipment. The $5,000 bargain purchase element is allocated to these accounts based on their relative current values as follows:

Appropriate Noncurrent Assets	Current Value	Percentage to Total		Bargain Purchase Element		Percentage Times Bargain Purchase Element	Adjusted Current Value
Land	$ 40,000	20%	×	$5,000	=	$1,000	$ 39,000
Buildings and equipment . . .	160,000	80%	×	5,000	=	4,000	156,000
	$200,000	100%				$5,000	$195,000

Key Review Point

The presence of a bargain purchase element clearly suggests that the assets are worth more *individually* than as part of a *going business*. If this were true, the previous owners of the acquired business would have been better off to liquidate the company by selling its *individual* assets than by selling the business as a *whole*. Because they did *not* do this, the initially determined current values must be *overstated* to the extent of the bargain purchase element.

"Negative Goodwill"

As noted in paragraph B187 of *FAS 141*, some accountants refer to an excess of *current value* over *cost* as *negative goodwill* rather than as a bargain purchase element. We point this term out only because you may encounter it in practice.

CHECK POINT

Patro Inc. acquired 100% of the *outstanding common stock* of Satro Inc. at a total cost of $200,000. Satro's net assets have a book value of $160,000 and a current value of $210,000. In the consolidated financial statements, which of the following would be reported?

a. Goodwill of $10,000.
b. A deferred credit of $10,000.

---

[2] In the event that *contingent consideration based on earnings* exists (discussed earlier), however, an amount equal to the *lesser of* (1) the *maximum* amount of contingent consideration or (2) the unextinguished BPE, is reported ***as if it were a liability*** until the contingency is resolved. This amount is later recognized *in earnings* as an *extraordinary gain*—but only to the extent that it is *not* needed to absorb any additional consideration paid when the contingency is resolved.

c. Goodwill of $40,000.
d. None of the above.

Answer: d. The $10,000 bargain purchase element normally would be extinguished.

IV. THE IRRELEVANCE OF THE ACQUIRED BUSINESS'S *BOOK VALUES* FOR CONSOLIDATED REPORTING PURPOSES

For future reporting purposes, the *book values* of the acquired business's various assets and liabilities as of the combination date become irrelevant to the acquiring company, inasmuch as a *new basis of accounting* occurs under the purchase method. By comparing the *current value* of the net assets to their *book value*, however, we determine by how much the *net assets* are under- or overvalued. For example, assume that the acquiring company's *cost* is $100,000 and the net assets of the acquired business have a *current value* of $88,000 and a *book value* of $60,000. The formula shown in Illustration 5-2 can be modified slightly to display this information by separating the acquiring company's ownership interest in the *current value* of the net assets into the acquirer's interest in (1) the *book value* of the net assets and (2) the amount of the *under-* or *overvaluation* of the net assets:

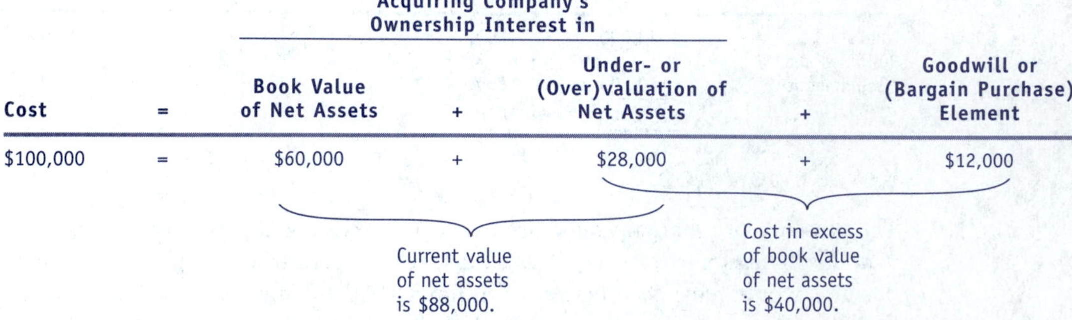

		Acquiring Company's Ownership Interest in				
Cost	=	**Book Value of Net Assets**	+	**Under- or (Over)valuation of Net Assets**	+	**Goodwill or (Bargain Purchase) Element**
$100,000	=	$60,000	+	$28,000	+	$12,000

Current value of net assets is $88,000.

Cost in excess of book value of net assets is $40,000.

This additional information concerning the amount by which the net assets are under- or overvalued is *not* necessary to record the combination, regardless of whether it takes the form of acquiring *assets* or *common stock*. When *common stock* is acquired, however, we must have this additional information to prepare consolidated financial statements. The remainder of this chapter deals with recording business combinations and preparing combined and consolidated statements as of the date of the business combination and at subsequent dates. In an economy that has experienced inflation over many years, the net assets of an acquired business are usually *undervalued*. Accordingly, we will continue under this assumption.

Acquisition of *Assets*

When *assets* are acquired, the procedures to record the business combination and to prepare financial statements reflecting the enlarged, combined operations are *not* complicated. This is because **the assets acquired and liabilities assumed are recorded directly by the acquiring company in its own general ledger** (or in the general ledger of a newly established *division*) **at their *current values*.** We discuss and illustrate this manner of acquisition in Appendix 5A.

Acquisition of *Common Stock*

When *common stock* is acquired, the procedures used to record the business combination are also relatively simple. The procedures to prepare financial statements reflecting the enlarged, combined operations *are* somewhat involved, however, because **the acquired subsidiary continues to account for its assets and liabilities using its recorded *book values*.** Stated differently, the parent does *not* directly record the acquired business's assets and liabilities in its *own* general ledger. The only account in which the parent records the cost of the acquired business is called *Investment in Subsidiary*. As a result, the parent must deal with the **amount of the under- or overvaluation in preparing financial statements that reflect the enlarged, combined operations.**

V. PREPARING CONSOLIDATED STATEMENTS AT THE ACQUISITION DATE

Recording the Acquisition

When *common stock* is acquired, the acquiring company charges its cost to an account called *Investment in Subsidiary*. Assuming that the value of the consideration given by the acquiring company (hereafter referred to as the *parent company*) is $90,000 and *direct costs* incurred are $10,000 (that may be properly added to the cost of the acquisition), the entry to record the acquisition is as follows, assuming that $90,000 cash is the consideration given:

Investment in Subsidiary	100,000	
Cash		100,000

The following entry assumes that 1,000 shares of $1 par value common stock (having a *market value* of $90,000) are the consideration given:

Investment in Subsidiary	100,000	
Common Stock (1,000 shares × $1 par).		1,000
Additional Paid-in Capital		89,000
Cash		10,000

Note that if the common stock issued is registered with the SEC, the following additional entry is made for the *additional direct costs incurred to register the common stock*:

Additional Paid-in Capital.	xxx	
Cash		xxx

CHECK POINT

Page Inc. acquired 100% of Sage Inc.'s *outstanding common stock* at a total cost of $100,000. Sage's net assets have a book value of $60,000 and a current value of $90,000. In the parent's general ledger, how much would be shown in the Goodwill account?

a. $–0–
b. $10,000
c. $30,000
d. $40,000

Answer: a. The $10,000 of goodwill is in the parent's Investment account.

Additional Issues for Acquired Subsidiaries

When *common stock* is acquired and the purchase method of accounting is used, two issues that do not exist for *created* subsidiaries do exist concerning *acquired* subsidiaries:

1. **Manner of revaluing the assets and liabilities of a subsidiary acquired in a purchase transaction.** An internal issue, solely concerning the mechanics of preparing consolidated statements,

is determining whether the assets and liabilities of a subsidiary acquired in a purchase transaction should be revalued to their current values in (a) the *subsidiary's general ledger* or (b) the *consolidation process* (on the consolidation worksheet).

2. **Manner of presenting subsidiary's *separate* financial statements.** If a subsidiary acquired in a purchase transaction issues *separate* financial statements (perhaps because of a loan agreement requirement), on what basis should its assets and liabilities be reported—its *historical cost* or *current values* based on the parent's cost?

Push-Down Accounting

In 1983, the SEC staff issued *Staff Accounting Bulletin No. 54*. This bulletin requires that **when a subsidiary acquired in a purchase transaction issues *separate* financial statements, such statements shall reflect the *new basis* of accounting.** In other words, the assets and liabilities must be revalued to their *current values*. Thus the new basis of accounting is "pushed down" to the subsidiary. **This pronouncement applies only to publicly owned companies.** The manner of implementing the **push-down basis of accounting** is shown briefly on pages 164–165 and discussed in detail in Chapter 7.

The Consolidation Worksheet

Unless the business combination occurs on the *last day* of the parent's reporting year (which rarely happens), preparing consolidated financial statements as of the acquisition date is *not* necessary. They are illustrated in the worksheets in this chapter for instructional purposes only.

The balance sheet is the only financial statement of the subsidiary that can be consolidated with the parent's financial statement as of the acquisition date. This understanding follows from a fundamental concept of the purchase method: **The parent company can report to its stockholders only the operations of the subsidiary that occur *subsequent to* the acquisition date.** Combining the *future* income statements of a parent and a subsidiary is discussed in Chapter 6.

The *Non-Push-Down* Basis of Accounting: The Subsidiary Retains the *Historical Cost Basis* of Its Assets and Liabilities

The **non-push-down basis of accounting** holds that the subsidiary *cannot* revalue its assets and liabilities to their *current values* merely because its outstanding common stock has changed hands and has become concentrated in the hands of significantly fewer stockholders or even a single one.

The obvious question, then, is this: How are the subsidiary's assets and liabilities revalued to their *current values* as required under the purchase method of accounting? The answer requires an understanding of the major conceptual elements of the parent's cost of the investment as reflected in its Investment in Subsidiary account.

The Major Conceptual Elements of Investment Cost

The cost of the investment as recorded on the parent's books must be separated into its major conceptual elements. We do this separation by analyzing the relationship among the *cost*, the *current value* of the subsidiary's net assets, and the *book value* of the subsidiary's net assets as shown earlier in the chapter. Assume the following information:

1. Parrco Company acquired 100% of Subbco Company's *outstanding common stock* on January 1, 2006, by paying $100,000 cash.
2. Cost $100,000
3. *Current value* of net assets $88,000
4. *Book value* of net assets ($260,000 – $200,000) $60,000
5. The *current values* of Subbco's assets and liabilities are assumed to equal their *book values*, except for the following assets:

	Book Value	Current Value	Undervaluation
Inventory	$ 42,000	$ 46,000	$ 4,000
Land	32,000	40,000	8,000
Buildings and equipment	144,000[a]	160,000	16,000
			$28,000

[a] Net of $56,000 accumulated depreciation.

Accordingly, $28,000 of the cost in excess of the book value of the net assets is attributable to these assets. The remaining $12,000 of cost in excess of the book value represents *goodwill*.

Thus the cost of the investment may be considered to comprise three major elements:

1. **The book value element.** The parent's ownership interest in the subsidiary's recorded net assets at their *book value* (100% of $60,000)	$ 60,000
2. **The under- or (over)valuation of net assets element.** The parent's ownership interest in the subsidiary's excess of the *current value* of the subsidiary's net assets over their *book value* (100% of $28,000)	28,000
3. **The goodwill element.** The parent's *cost* in excess of the *current value* of the subsidiary's net assets ($100,000 – $88,000)	12,000
Cost of the Investment	$100,000

The $28,000 difference between the *current value* of the subsidiary's net assets and their *book value* is included in the parent's Investment account. When the subsidiary's financial statements are consolidated with those of the parent, this $28,000 difference is reclassified from the Investment account to the specific assets with which it has been identified. (In this situation, $4,000 is identified with *undervalued* inventories, $8,000 with *undervalued* land, and $16,000 with *undervalued* equipment.) The parent accounts for the individual items that make up this difference in the same manner that the subsidiary accounts for the specific undervalued assets. Specifically, the following occurs:

1. The subsidiary continues to depreciate its assets at their historical cost as though the business combination had *never* occurred.
2. The parent amortizes to its future income that portion of its cost in excess of book value that is attributable to depreciable or amortizable assets (in this example, $4,000 pertaining to the inventory and $16,000 pertaining to the equipment). The $4,000 amount relating to inventory is amortized to income as the subsidiary sells its inventory. The $16,000 amount relating to the equipment is amortized to income using the same remaining life that the subsidiary uses to depreciate its historical cost.

In other words, depreciation and amortization of the subsidiary's assets take place on *two* sets of books instead of just *one* set, as when assets are acquired. These amortization procedures on the parent company's books are necessary to charge the combined operations with the current value of the assets acquired because the assets were *not* revalued on the subsidiary's books. In substance, the net effect on the enlarged business as a whole is the same *as though* the subsidiary had revalued its assets to their *current values* (push-down accounting).

CHECK POINT

Pax Inc. acquired 100% of the *outstanding common stock* of Sax Inc. in exchange for cash. The *acquisition price* exceeds the *fair value* of the net assets. How should Pax determine the amounts to be reported for Sax's inventories and long-term debt in its consolidated statements?

	Inventories	Long-Term Debt
a.	Fair value	Sax's carrying amount
b.	Fair value	Fair value

c. Sax's carrying amount Fair value
d. Sax's carrying amount Sax's carrying amount

Answer: b

Comprehensive Illustration

Separating the Cost of the Investment into Its Major Conceptual Elements

Separating the cost of the investment into its major conceptual elements is possible for all common stock investments, regardless of the price the parent paid, the *current value* of the net assets, or the *book value* of the net assets. Many possible relationship combinations between these three items can be shown. To show how the cost is separated into its major conceptual elements for various possible relationship combinations, Illustration 5-3 shows *four* selected situations.

Review Points for Illustration 5-3. Note the following:

1. In situation A, only *one* major conceptual element exists because *cost* equals *current value* and *current value* equals *book value.*
2. In situation B, all *three* major conceptual elements exist. If the cost of the investment had been $12,000 less, no goodwill element and only *two* major conceptual elements would have existed.
3. In situation C, all *three* major conceptual elements exist, but the parent has a *negative* balance instead of a *positive* balance for its under- or (over)valuation of net assets element. This *negative* balance is identified with depreciable assets and is amortized in future periods to the parent's income statement, as are the *positive* balances in situations B and D, which are identified with depreciable assets.

Displaying the Major Conceptual Elements by Their Components

The analysis of the parent's cost by its major conceptual elements can be expanded to display the *components* of (1) the book value element and (2) the under- or (over)valuation of net assets element. This expanded analysis can be used as the source of two entries that consolidate the parent's financial statements with those of the subsidiary. The preparation of consolidated financial statements has always been an involved process. The use of this expanded analysis of the cost of the investment, which displays the components of the major conceptual elements, however, substantially

ILLUSTRATION 5-3 THE MAJOR CONCEPTUAL ELEMENTS OF THE COST OF THE INVESTMENT

	Net Assets of Subsidiary			Separation of Cost into Its Major Conceptual Elements						
Situation	Current Value (1) (Given)	Book Value (2) (Given)	Under- or (Over)valuation (3) (1)−(2)	Cost (4) (Given)	=	Book Value Element (5) (2)	+	Under- or (Over)valuation of Net Assets Element (6) (3)	+	Goodwill (Bargain Purchase) Element (7) (Residual)
A	$60,000	$60,000		$ 60,000	=	$60,000				
B	88,000	60,000	$ 28,000	100,000	=	60,000	+	$ 28,000	+	$12,000
C	50,000	60,000	(10,000)	55,000	=	60,000	+	(10,000)	+	5,000
D	80,000	60,000	20,000	75,000	=	60,000	+	20,000	+	(5,000)[a]

[a] This bargain purchase element must be allocated to the extent possible to *certain noncurrent assets.* If *all* of it is allocated thus, the amounts in the column to the left *decrease* by $5,000, and no deferred credit remains. (See Illustration 5-4, in which *all* of it is allocated to the appropriate noncurrent assets.)

simplifies the consolidation procedures. The procedures for expanding the analysis are explained below using situation B of Illustration 5-3, in which *cost* is *above current value* and *current value* is *above book value.*

Separating the Book Value Element

The *book value* element is easily separated into its components by multiplying the parent's ownership interest by the balance in each of the subsidiary's individual capital accounts—Common Stock, Additional Paid-in Capital, and Retained Earnings—as of the acquisition date. Subbco Company's capital accounts as of the acquisition date are as follows:

Common stock (no par)	$10,000
Retained earnings	50,000
Total Stockholders' Equity	$60,000

Because we assume that Parrco Company acquires 100% of Subbco Company's outstanding common stock, the $60,000 *book value* element comprises these two components.

Separating the Under- or (Over)valuation of Net Assets Element

As stated previously, the parent accounts for the components of the under- or (over)valuation element—*not* for the total difference as a lump sum. Thus, the under- or (over)valuation of net assets element can be thought of as comprising the following three components:

Inventory	$ 4,000
Land	8,000
Equipment	16,000
Total Undervaluation of Net Assets	$28,000

The Goodwill Element and the Bargain Purchase Element

No separation is needed for goodwill, which is a residual amount accounted for as a lump sum. When a bargain purchase element exists, the initial credit must be allocated as much as possible to *noncurrent assets other than long-term investments in marketable securities.* Any remaining bargain purchase element is amortized to income in future periods.

Recapping the Conceptual Elements

The analysis of the investment cost in situation B of Illustration 5-3 is shown below by the major conceptual elements and their components:

	Analysis of Investment Cost	
	By the Major Conceptual Elements	By the Components of the Major Conceptual Elements
Book value element:		
Common stock		$ 10,000
Retained earnings		50,000
Total	$ 60,000	$ 60,000
Under- or (over)valuation of net assets element:		
Inventory		$ 4,000
Land		8,000
Equipment		16,000
Total	28,000	$ 28,000
Goodwill element	12,000	$ 12,000
Cost	$100,000	$100,000

Illustration 5-4 displays the major conceptual elements for the situations in Illustration 5-3 by their components.

ILLUSTRATION 5-4 THE MAJOR CONCEPTUAL ELEMENTS AND THEIR COMPONENTS

			Book Value Element			+	Under- or (Over) Valuation of Net Assets Element					+	Goodwill
Situation from Illustration 5-3	**Cost**	=	**Common Stock**	+	**Retained Earnings**	+	**Inventory**	+	**Land**	+	**Equipment**	+	**(Bargain Purchase) Element**
A	$ 60,000	=	$10,000	+	$50,000								
B	$100,000	=	$10,000	+	$50,000	+	$4,000	+	$ 8,000	+	$ 16,000	+	$12,000
C	$ 55,000	=	$10,000	+	$50,000	+					(10,000)	+	5,000
D	$ 75,000	=	$10,000	+	$50,000	+	$2,000	+	$12,000	+	$ 6,000	+	$ (5,000)
									(1,000)[a]		(4,000)[a]		5,000[a]
	$ 75,000	=	$10,000	+	$50,000	+	$2,000	+	$11,000	+	$ 2,000	+	$ -0-

[a] The allocation process illustrated on page 149 using **relative fair values** (of $40,000 and $160,000) is used.

Review Points for Illustration 5-4. Note the following:

1. In situation A, in which only the *book value* element exists, the parent has completed accounting for its investment under the purchase method of accounting. No additional accounting procedures are necessary because no other major conceptual elements exist.
2. In situations B and D, in which the *current value* of the net assets *exceeds* their *book value* and the parent pays *more than* the *book value* of the net assets, the amount applicable to the equipment is amortized to the parent's future income over the remaining life of these assets, using the *same* remaining life that the subsidiary uses to depreciate these items. The amount determined for inventory is amortized in the following year, assuming the subsidiary sells its inventory. The amount determined for the land is *not* amortized because land is never depreciated. When the land is *sold,* the amount determined for it is charged to income at that time, thereby *reducing* the *gain* or *increasing* the *loss* that otherwise would be reported. In summary, the parent accounts for each individual component in a manner consistent with the way the subsidiary accounts for its historical cost. Goodwill is periodically evaluated for impairment (as discussed in detail in Chapter 6).
3. In situation C, in which the *current value* of the net assets is *below* their *book value*, the parent has *credit* amounts instead of *debit* amounts to amortize to its subsequent in come statements. Otherwise, the procedures are the same as those in point 2 above. The amortization partially offsets the depreciation expense recorded on the subsidiary's books from the viewpoint of combined operations.

CHECK POINT

On 4/1/06, Place Inc. paid $400,000 for 100% of the issued and *outstanding common stock* of Show Inc. in a transaction properly accounted for as a purchase. Show's assets and liabilities on 4/1/06 are as follows:

Cash	$ 40,000
Inventory	120,000
Property and equipment (net of accumulated depreciation of $160,000).	240,000
Liabilities	(90,000)

On 4/1/06, the *current value* of Show's inventory was $95,000, and Show's property and equipment (net) had a *current value* of $280,000. What is the amount of goodwill as a result of the business combination?

a. $-0-
b. $25,000

c. $75,000
d. $90,000

Answer: c

Splitting the Cost of the Investment to Simplify the Consolidation Process

Once the cost of the parent's investment has been broken down as shown in Illustration 5-4, the future consolidation procedures can be simplified by splitting the cost into (1) the *book value* element and (2) the *cost in excess of book value* elements. For situation B of Illustration 5-4, the split is as follows:

Investment in Subsidiary:	
Book value element	$60,000
Excess cost elements	40,000

The individual components within each category will be tracked *outside the general ledger* in *supporting schedules* and used in preparing consolidation entries. For this situation, the *supporting schedules* at the acquisition date are as follows:

I. BOOK VALUE ELEMENT:

Total	=	Common Stock	+	Retained Earnings
$60,000	=	$10,000	+	$50,000

II. EXCESS COST ELEMENTS:

		Undervaluation of Net Assets Element						
Total	=	**Inventory**	+	**Land**	+	**Equipment**	+	**Goodwill Element**
$40,000	=	$4,000	+	$8,000	+	$16,000	+	$12,000

Comprehensive Illustration

Most Commonly Encountered Situation

Acquisition of Common Stock When

- > Assets Are *Undervalued*
- > Goodwill Exists

Using the preceding information, the following consolidation entries are used to (1) eliminate the Investment account balance, (2) eliminate the subsidiary's equity accounts (which have a *reciprocal relationship* to the parent's book value element), (3) revalue the subsidiary's *undervalued* assets to their *current values*, and (4) report goodwill as a separate account:

WORKSHEET ENTRY ONLY

THE BASIC *ELIMINATION* ENTRY

Common Stock	10,000	
Retained Earnings	50,000	
Investment in Subsidiary		60,000

THE EXCESS COST *RECLASSIFICATION* ENTRY

Inventory	4,000	
Land	8,000	
Equipment	16,000	
Goodwill	12,000	
Investment in Subsidiary		40,000

Illustration 5-5 shows the consolidation worksheet as of the acquisition date using the preceding entries. In addition, the following accumulated depreciation *elimination* entry is needed to recognize that a **new cost basis has been established for the subsidiary's fixed assets** for consolidated reporting purposes:

WORKSHEET ENTRY ONLY

THE ACCUMULATION DEPRECIATION *ELIMINATION* ENTRY

Accumulated Depreciation	56,000	
Buildings and Equipment		56,000

Review Points for Illustration 5-5. Note the following:

1. The parent's *investment cost* in excess of the *book value* of the subsidiary's net assets becomes clear in the consolidation process. The excess is effectively reclassified to the balance sheet accounts with which it has been identified.
2. The amounts in the Consolidated column are composed of (a) the *parent's* items based on *book values* and (b) the *subsidiary's* items based on the *current value* of those items as of the acquisition date.
3. The *Investment in Subsidiary* account and the subsidiary's *equity accounts* are eliminated in consolidation and have a *zero balance* in the consolidated column.

ILLUSTRATION 5-5 THE ACQUISITION OF COMMON STOCK (NON-PUSH-DOWN ACCOUNTING USED BY SUBSIDIARY)

PARRCO COMPANY AND SUBBCO COMPANY
Consolidation Worksheet as of January 1, 2006

	PARRCO COMPANY	SUBBCO COMPANY[a]	CONSOLIDATION ENTRY DR.			CR.	CONSOLIDATED
Balance Sheet							
Cash	18,000	15,000					33,000
Accounts receivable, net	52,000	27,000					79,000
Inventory	90,000	42,000	4,000	2			136,000
Investment in subsidiary:							
Book value element	60,000				1	60,000	–0–
Excess cost elements	40,000				2	40,000	–0–
Land	220,000	32,000	8,000	2			260,000
Buildings and equipment	500,000	200,000	16,000	2	3	56,000	660,000
Accumulated depreciation	(280,000)	(56,000)	56,000	3			(280,000)
Goodwill			12,000	2			12,000
Total Assets	700,000	260,000	96,000			156,000	900,000
Liabilities	400,000	200,000					600,000
Parrco Company:							
Common stock	10,000						10,000
Add'l paid-in capital	190,000						190,000
Retained earnings	100,000						100,000
Subbco Company:							
Common stock		10,000	10,000	1			–0–
Retained earnings		50,000	50,000	1			–0–
Total Liabilities and Equity .	700,000	260,000	60,000				900,000
Proof of debit and credit postings			156,000			156,000	

[a] The amounts in this column reflect the historical cost basis that applied to the previous owners.

Explanation of entries:
1 The basic *elimination* entry.
2 The excess cost *reclassification* entry.
3 The accumulated depreciation *elimination* entry.

Demonstration Problem: Acquisition of *Common Stock*

On 6/30/06, Pane Inc. acquired 100% of Sill Inc.'s outstanding common stock by issuing 20,000 shares of its $1 par value common stock (having a market price of $30 per share). Pane incurred legal and accounting fees of $75,000, of which $25,000 pertained to registering the shares issued with the SEC. If Sill's sales for the two years ended 6/30/08 exceed $8 million, then Pane must issue an additional 4,000 shares of common stock to Sill's former owners. The balances in the capital accounts of the subsidiary as of the acquisition date are as follows:

Common Stock	$ 40,000
Retained Earnings	360,000
	$400,000

All of Sill's assets and liabilities had a *current value* equal to their *book value*, except the following:

	Book Value	Current Value
Land	$150,000	$270,000
Long-term debt, 8%	200,000	230,000

Sill had $20,000 of goodwill on its books as of the acquisition date that Sill's management believes is fully realizable. Of the $75,000 incurred for legal and accounting fees, $33,000 was paid by 6/30/06, and charged to a Deferred Charges account pending consummation of the acquisition. The remaining $42,000 has *not* been paid or accrued.

Required

1. Prepare the entry to record the acquisition.
2. Prepare an expanded analysis of the investment account.
3. Prepare the consolidation entries at 6/30/06.

Solution to Demonstration Problem

1.

Investment in Sill Inc.		
(20,000 shares × $30 market price)	600,000	
Common Stock (20,000 shares × $1 par)		20,000
Additional Paid-in Capital		580,000
To record issuance of common stock.		

Investment in Sill Inc..	50,000	
Additional Paid-in Capital	25,000	
Deferred Charges.		33,000
Accrued Liabilities		42,000
To record direct acquisition costs of $50,000 and $25,000 cost of registering common stock.		

No entry would be made pertaining to the contingent consideration at this time. Disclosure would be made in the notes to the financial statements.

2.

	Parent's Investment Account— Book Value	=	Book Value Element: Subsidiary's Equity Accounts: Common Stock	+	Retained Earnings
Balances, 6/30/06	$400,000		$40,000		$360,000

	Parent's Investment Account— Excess Cost	=	Under- or (Over)Valuation of Net Assets Element: Land	+	Old Goodwill	+	L-T Debt	+	Goodwill Element
Balances, 6/30/06	$250,000		$120,000		$(20,000)		$(30,000)		$180,000

3. The basic *elimination* entry:

Common Stock	40,000	
Retained Earnings	360,000	
Investment in Subsidiary		400,000

The excess cost *reclassification* entry:

Land	120,000	
Goodwill (new)	180,000	
Goodwill (old)		20,000
Long-Term Debt		30,000
Investment in Subsidiary		250,000

VI. Additional Assignment of Cost (Allocation) Issues

Under- or Overvalued *Receivables*

For simplicity, the previous discussions and illustrations dealt only with certain under- and overvalued *nonfinancial* assets. Sometimes receivables are under- or overvalued. For our purposes, receivables can be generally categorized as follows:

1. **Accounts receivable (noninterest bearing).** The *current value* of accounts receivable (using *present value* procedures) is usually so close to their *book value*—because of the relatively short period until collection of the receivable—that the difference is often ignored in the interest of practicality.
2. **Notes receivable—*floating* interest rate.** The *current value* of notes receivable that have a *floating* interest rate (changes *with* market conditions) *always* equals the *book value.*
3. **Notes receivable—*fixed* interest rate.** If a note receivable has a *fixed* interest rate that differs from the interest rate existing at the acquisition date, the *present value* of the note does *not* equal its *book value*. Consequently, the difference between *present value* and *book value* must be reflected as one of the components of the **under- or (over)valuation of net assets element** in the conceptual analysis of the Investment in Subsidiary account. An *undervalued* note means that the subsidiary's net assets are *undervalued*; an *overvalued* note means that the net assets are *overvalued*.

Reporting Fixed Rate Notes Receivable at Their Present Value

To illustrate, assume that on the acquisition date of January 1, 2006, the subsidiary has a 12% note receivable having a *face amount* of $100,000 and a maturity date of December 31, 2007 (*two* years from now). If the *current* interest rate is 10%, the *present value* of the bonds is calculated as follows:

Present value of $100,000 *principal* payment due 12/31/07 ($100,000 × .82645)	$ 82,645
Present value of *two* $12,000 *interest* payments due at the end of 2006 and 2007 ($12,000 × 1.73554)	20,825
Total	$103,470

Accordingly, the note receivable is *undervalued*, meaning the subsidiary's net assets are *undervalued*. (The high *fixed* interest rate of 12% in relation to the *current* interest rate of 10% means that the receivable appears *smaller* than it really is—from a *current value* perspective.)

The $3,470 difference between the note's *book value* ($100,000) and the note's *present value* ($103,470) is reflected as **an *individual component* of the under- or (over) valuation of the net assets element.** If consolidated statements are prepared as of the acquisition date, the note is reported in the Consolidated column at its *present value* of $103,470 because the $3,470 amount is *debited* to the Notes Receivable account in consolidation:

CONSOLIDATION AT 1/1/06 (THE ACQUISITION DATE)

	Parrco Company	Subbco Company	Consolidation Entries Dr.	Consolidation Entries Cr.	Consolidated
Notes receivable		100,000	3,470		103,470

Subsequent Treatment of the Difference

The $3,470 amount is **analogous to a *premium* and is amortized out of the Investment account to *reduce* interest income** over the next *two* years using the *interest method* of amortization. For 2006 and 2007, interest income is reported at 10% of the note's *carrying value* at the *beginning* of the year (rather than at 12% of the $100,000 *book value*). Interest income would be reported as follows:

	2006	2007	Total
Cash collection	$ 12,000	$ 12,000	$24,000
Amortization out of the Investment account	(1,650)	(1,820)	(3,470)
Total	$ 10,350	$ 10,180	$20,530
Proof:			
Carrying value at *beginning* of year	$103,470	$101,820	
Current interest rate at acquisition date	10%	10%	
Interest Income	$ 10,350	$ 10,180	$20,530

In Chapter 6, we show in detail how to amortize amounts out of the Investment account.

Under- or Overvalued Liabilities

As with *receivables,* only *long-term payables* usually need be evaluated as under- or overvalued. Conceptually, under- or overvalued *liabilities* are treated in the same manner as under- or overvalued *receivables*, except that (1) the effect of subsequent amortizations on the income statement is the *opposite* since we are now on the *other side of the balance sheet* and (2) the income statement account affected for subsequent amortizations is Interest *Expense—not* Interest *Income.*

For liabilities, however, note that (1) an *undervalued* liability means the subsidiary's net assets are *overvalued* and (2) an *overvalued* liability means the net assets are *undervalued.* For example, assume that a subsidiary has 8% bonds payable outstanding at the acquisition date. If the *current* interest rate is 12%, the *present value* of the liability is *below* its *book value*, meaning the liability is *overvalued* and the subsidiary net assets are *undervalued.* (The low *fixed* interest rate of 8% in relation to the *current* interest rate of 12% means that the liability appears *larger* than it really is—from a *current value* perspective.)

Consequently, an *overvalued* liability causes (1) a *debit* to be posted to its account in consolidation and (2) *debits* to be posted to Interest Expense in future periods in the amortization process (***increasing* interest expense**). Likewise, an *undervalued* liability causes (1) a *credit* to be posted to its account in consolidation and (2) *credits* to be posted to Interest Expense in future periods in the amortization process (***decreasing* interest expense**).

Intangible Assets *Other Than Goodwill*

Even though goodwill *is* an intangible asset, the term *intangible asset* in the following discussion refers to intangible assets *other than goodwill.* As was the case prior to the issuance of *FAS 141*, an acquired entity's intangible assets must be identified. An intangible asset must be recognized as an asset apart from goodwill if it meets *either* of the following two conditions—***both of which are new criteria imposed by FAS 141***:

1. **It arises from *contractual* or *legal rights*** (regardless of whether those rights are *transferable* or *separable* from the acquired entity).
2. **It does *not* arise from contractual or legal rights but is *separable*** (capable of being separated or divided from the acquired entity and sold, transferred, licensed, rented, or exchanged (whether by itself or with a related asset or liability). No intent to do so must exist.

Examples of intangible assets that meet either of the preceding criteria (paragraph 14A of *FAS 141* lists 29 examples) are as follows:

	Meets *Contractual-Legal* Criterion	Meets *Separability* Criterion
A. Contract-based:		
Licensing and royalty agreements	X	
Employment contracts	X	
Use rights (such as broadcasts, drilling, water, and timber cutting)	X	
B. Technology-based:		
Patented technology	X	
Unpatented technology		X
Trade secrets (formulas, processes, and recipes)	X	
Databases		X
Computer software and mask works	X	
C. Marketing-related:		
Trademarks and tradenames	X	
Noncompetition agreements	X	
D. Customer-related:		
Customer contracts	X	
Customer lists		X
E. Artistic-based:		
Video and audiovisual material	X	
Plays, operas, books, musical compositions, photographs	X	

Examples of intangibles that do *not* meet either of the preceding two criteria are (1) an assembled workforce, (2) nonunion status or strong labor relations, (3) on-going training programs, and (4) market presence. Such items are effectively subsumed into goodwill.

Valuation of *Recognized* Intangible Assets

Recognized intangible assets that have *limited* useful lives are subsequently accounted for differently from those having *indefinite* lives (as prescribed by *FASB Statement No. 142*, "Goodwill and Other Intangible Assets" (which was issued concurrently with *FAS 141*):

1. **Limited-useful-life intangible assets.** The assigned fair value (less any residual value) is amortized over their estimated useful lives using (1) an amortization method that reflects ***the pattern in which the intangible asset's economic benefits are consumed or otherwise used up*** or (2) the ***straight-line method*** (allowed only if the consumption pattern *cannot* be reliably determined). Regardless that these assets are amortized, they are subject to impairment testing (under FASB *Statement No. 144*, "Accounting for the Impairment or Disposal of Long-Lived Assets") if circumstances indicate impairment has occurred.
2. **Indefinite-life intangible assets.** Some intangible assets, such as trademarks and broadcast licenses, may have ***indefinite lives.*** Accordingly, such intangibles will (1) *not* be amortized subsequent to the acquisition date and (2) be subject to an *annual* (or more often if certain "triggering events" occur) impairment test (under FASB *Statement No. 142*, "Goodwill and Other Intangible Assets").

Acquired Research and Development in Process—Expensed Immediately

In the high-technology industry, it is common to assign a major portion of the acquisition cost to "research and development (R&D) in process." Because R&D costs must be expensed as incurred (whether incurred internally or acquired in a business combination), any amount assigned to R&D in process must be expensed immediately after the acquisition occurs. (For federal income tax-reporting purposes, however, this amount must be capitalized as a Section 197 intangible and amortized to income over 15 years.)

CASE IN POINT

When This Practice Began

In 1995, IBM Corporation acquired Lotus Development Corporation. Of the $3 billion purchase price, $1.8 billion was assigned to "purchased in-process research and development included in the value of software products still in the development stage and *not* considered to have reached technological feasibility state." This $1.8 billion was expensed in the quarter in which the acquisition was consummated. Since that time, this treatment has become overwhelmingly popular.

Companies have a high incentive to assign as much of the purchase price as possible to R&D in process because it reduces dollar-for-dollar the amount that otherwise would be assigned to goodwill and be charged to future income statements in the event that a future impairment write-down occurs. The general thinking is that investors will tend to ignore a large "one-time" acquired R&D in-process charge to income in the year of an acquisition. (One study found that in 10 recent sizeable high technology mergers, the R&D in-process write-offs ranged from 78% to 100% of the purchase price.)

On the Horizon

As this book goes to print, the FASB has tentatively decided to require capitalization of acquired R&D in-process.

Goodwill

Recall from Chapter 4 that the residually determined amount for goodwill is *not* amortized. It is instead subject to an annual (or more often if certain "triggering events" occur) *impairment test.*

The Goodwill Impairment Test

For purposes of testing goodwill for impairment, goodwill must be appropriately assigned to one or more "reporting units" at the acquisition date. A reporting unit is the level at which goodwill is tested for impairment. If the impairment test results reveal that goodwill is impaired, it must be written down (establishing a new cost basis)—no subsequent reversals are allowed. The impairment loss is charged to earnings. In chapter 6, we discuss the impairment test in more detail.

Financial Statement Presentation of Goodwill

Goodwill must be reported as a separate line item in the *statement of financial position.* The amount of any goodwill impairment loss must be reported ***as a separate line in the income statement*** before the subtotal ***Income from Continuing Operations*** (unless associated with a discontinued operation, in which case it is reported *net of tax* in that category).

"Old Goodwill"

Sometimes an acquired business has unamortized goodwill on its books at the acquisition date. In determining the current value of the net assets, this "old goodwill" is assumed to always have a zero value under the requirements of *FAS 141*. In the conceptual analysis of the Investment account, old goodwill is treated as an overvalued asset in the under- or (over)valuation of net assets element. This allows the goodwill that the parent was willing to pay for to be properly shown as a single amount. Otherwise, goodwill is considered to comprise two amounts. Assuming that old goodwill of $3,000 exists at the acquisition date and new goodwill is calculated to be $10,000, the consolidation worksheet section pertaining to these accounts appears as follows:

			Consolidation Entries		
	Parrco Company	Subbco Company	Dr.	Cr.	Consolidated
Goodwill (old)		3,000		3,000(2)	-0-
Goodwill (new).			10,000(2)		10,000

See Illustration 5-6 for a graphic depiction of accounting for all acquired intangibles and goodwill.

On the Horizon—Expensing Merger-Related Costs as They Occur

In late 2004, the FASB *proposed* a new standard that will require companies to expense merger-related costs as they happen, rather than charging to them a liability account that was established at the combination date. This action will stop the long-time abuse of overestimating the merger-related liability at the business combination date and then taking the excess amount to income in subsequent periods, thereby making postcombination periods appear to be more favorable than they otherwise would appear.

This change will level the playing field for restructuring costs, whether they are incurred to restructure (1) an *acquired* operating activity or (2) an *existing* operating activity.

VII. THE *PUSH-DOWN BASIS* OF ACCOUNTING: A BRIEF LOOK

As stated earlier, the push-down basis of accounting is discussed in detail in Chapter 7.[3] Obviously, accounting for the target company's assets and liabilities on only one set of books is much simpler than the two sets of books involved in the non-push-down basis of accounting. Push-down accounting is simple to apply. It merely requires **adjusting the subsidiary's assets and liabilities to their** current values **at the acquisition date.** Goodwill paid for is also recorded on the subsidiary's books. For the example used in this chapter, which had $40,000 of cost in excess of the subsidiary's book value of $60,000, the general ledger entries on the subsidiary's books are as follows:

Inventory	4,000	
Land	8,000	
Buildings and Equipment	16,000	
Revaluation Capital[a]		28,000
To adjust assets to current values.		
Goodwill	12,000	
Revaluation Capital[a]		12,000
To reflect goodwill.		

[a] Recall from intermediate accounting that capital is always shown by *source*.

[3] The CPA examination began including questions about push-down accounting in 1992.

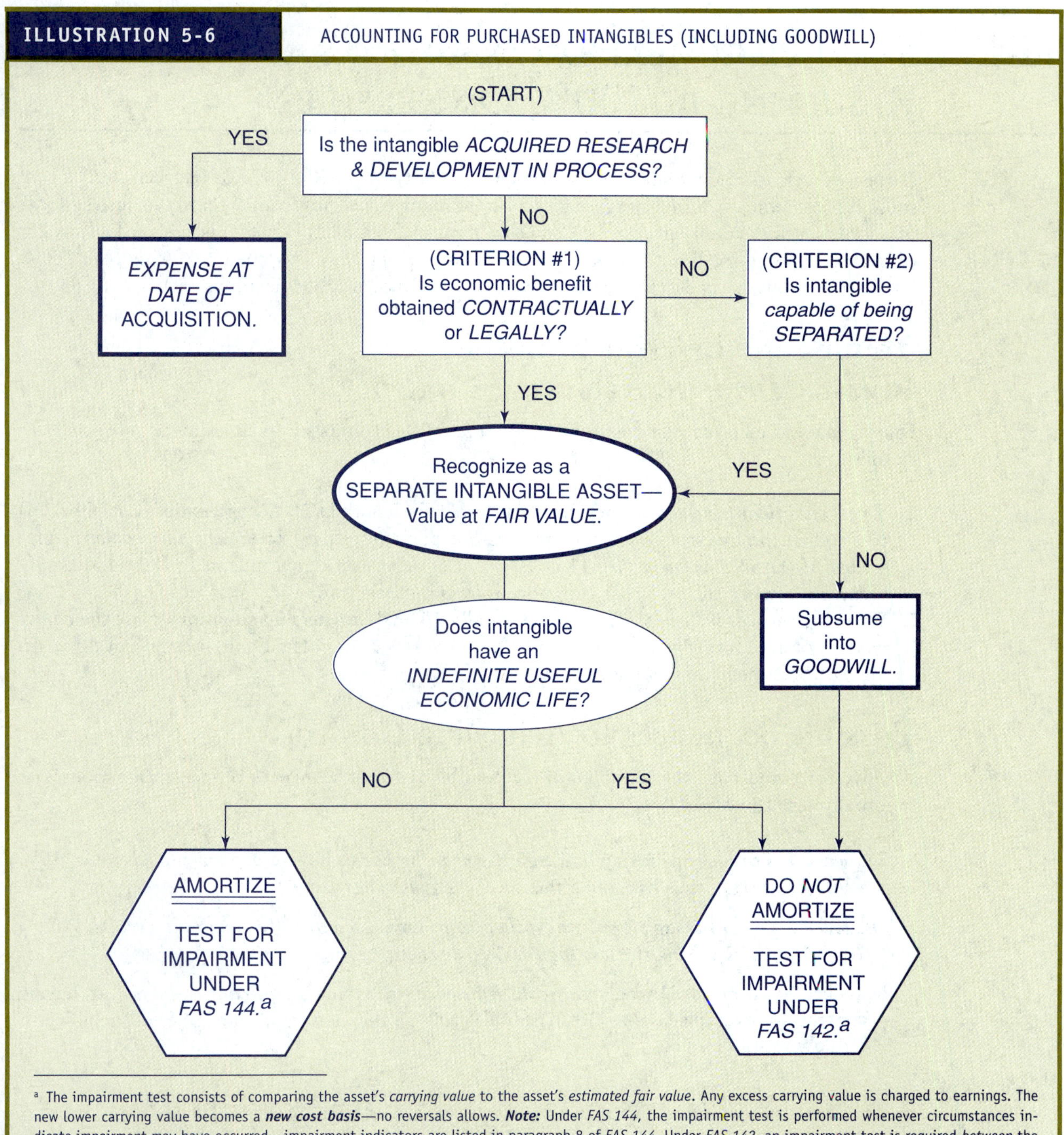

ILLUSTRATION 5-6 ACCOUNTING FOR PURCHASED INTANGIBLES (INCLUDING GOODWILL)

[a] The impairment test consists of comparing the asset's *carrying value* to the asset's *estimated fair value*. Any excess carrying value is charged to earnings. The new lower carrying value becomes a ***new cost basis***—no reversals allows. ***Note:*** Under *FAS 144*, the impairment test is performed whenever circumstances indicate impairment may have occurred—impairment indicators are listed in paragraph 8 of *FAS 144*. Under *FAS 142*, an impairment test is required *between* the annual impairment testing dates if circumstances indicate that impairment has occurred—impairment indicators are listed in paragraph 28 of *FAS 142*.

Consequently, push-down accounting achieves the same results **as if the target company's assets had been acquired** as shown earlier. The only difference is that the acquired business is accounted for as a **subsidiary**—which has the Common Stock, Retained Earnings, and Revaluation Capital equity accounts—instead of as a **division**—which has the lone Home Office Capital account. Note also that the subsidiary's equity accounts now total $100,000 and in total have a **reciprocal balance** to the parent's Investment in Subsidiary account, which has a $100,000 balance at the acquisition date. Subsequently, the reciprocal balance relationship is maintained under the *equity method* but not under the *cost method*.

VIII. Step (Piecemeal) Acquisitions Resulting in 100% Ownership

Earlier we discussed only situations in which one entity acquired 100% of another entity's outstanding common stock in a *single* transaction. In many cases, however, an entity acquires *blocks* of another entity's common stock in *a series of steps* over time until control is achieved as a result of having acquired the last block of stock (for example, acquiring 5%, then 25%, and then 70%). Such acquisitions are called both **step acquisitions** and **piecemeal acquisitions.**

Valuing the Investment in the Investee *Prior* to Achieving *Control*

Until *control* is achieved, the *investor* (not yet a *parent*) accounts for its investment in the *investee* as follows:

1. **When *significant influence* does *not* exist (typically less than 20% ownership):** Use either (1) *cost* (when the investee's common stock is *not* publicly traded) or (2) the *fair value*, as prescribed by FASB *Statement No. 115*, "Accounting for Certain Investments in Debt and Equity Securities" (when the investee's common stock *is* publicly traded).
2. **When *significant influence does* exist (typically 20–50% ownership situations):** Use the *equity method* of accounting as prescribed in APB *Opinion No. 18*, "The Equity Method of Accounting for Investments in Common Stock."

Possible Sequences to Achieving *Control*

An investor could have the following *three* possible types of sequences of step transactions that eventually result in *control*:

Sequence 1: From *never* having had *significant influence* to having *control* (for example, 10% + 90% = 100%), thus bypassing the 20–50% ownership range.

Sequence 2: From having *significant influence* to having *control* (for example, 30% + 70% = 100%), thus bypassing the *less than* 20% ownership range.

Sequence 3: From *not* having *significant influence*, to having *significant influence*, to having control (for example, 10% + 30% + 60% = 100%), thus *not* bypassing either of the previous two ownership ranges.

Unique Aspects Associated with Each Possible Sequence

Each of the three possible sequences used to achieve control has a unique accounting aspect during the period *before* control is obtained. Furthermore, it is necessary to discuss these aspects *before* we discuss procedures to be followed when control *is* obtained.

Sequence 1: From *Never* Having Had *Significant Influence* to Having *Control* (10% + 90% = 100%)

In this situation, when the earlier investment (1) is carried at *fair value* (pursuant to the requirements of *FAS 115*), (2) is classified as an "available-for-sale" security pursuant to *FAS 115*, and (3) has an *unrealized* holding gain or loss (which is to be **excluded from *earnings* and reported in *other comprehensive income* [net of tax] until realized,** pursuant to *FAS 115*), the issue arises of what to do with the unrealized holding gain or loss when control is obtained. Two concepts exist in this regard.

Parent Company Concept (PCC)

Under this concept (introduced in Chapter 3), **the unrealized gain or loss is *reversed* at the date that control is obtained**—thus *changing* the *carrying value* of the Investment account (*fair value*) back to the parent's *historical cost basis*.

Economic Unit Concept (EUC)

Under this concept (also introduced in Chapter 3), the unrealized gain or loss is *recognized in earnings* at the date that control is obtained—thus *not* changing the *carrying value* of the Investment account (*fair value*) back to the parent's *historical cost basis*.

Sequence 2: From Having *Significant Influence* to Having *Control* (30% + 70% = 100%)

In this situation, the investor has had to account for its earlier investment using the *equity method* of accounting. In doing so, the investor will have (1) analyzed the cost of this earlier investment and determined individual components thereof (one component that usually exists is goodwill) and (2) amortized a portion of its investment cost to income, if appropriate.

Thus *immediately prior* to acquiring the block of stock that results in control, the analysis of the parent's earlier investment may show that a "layer" exists as to goodwill and other under- or overvalued assets of the investee. If one or more additional blocks of stock are acquired and control does *not* result, additional layers also will exist.

Sequence 3: From *Not* Having *Significant Influence*, to Having *Significant Influence*, to Having *Control* (10% + 30% + 60% = 100%)

The only difference between this situation and Sequence 2 is that the investor had to deal with changing accounting principles to the *equity method* when it achieved *significant influence* and thus established a layer at that time. We do *not* demonstrate how to do this because it would repeat a topic discussed in intermediate accounting.

Determining the Purchase Price (Cost of the Acquisition): *Parent Company Concept*

Under the *parent company concept*, the parent's purchase price (the *cost* of the acquisition) in *all* three sequences is determined by summing together (1) the *carrying value* of the Investment account *immediately prior* to acquiring the block of stock that results in control (except that in Sequence 1, an adjustment is first made for any *market value* holding gain or loss reversal as explained earlier) and (2) the cost of the block of stock that results in control.

Determining the Purchase Price (Cost of the Acquisition): *Economic Unit Concept*

Under the *economic unit concept*, the parent's purchase price (the *cost* of the acquisition) in all three sequences is determined by (1) adjusting the *carrying value* of the previously owned stock to its *fair value* as of the acquisition date (a technique that results in recognizing a holding gain or loss in earnings) and (2) adding that adjusted carrying value to the cost of acquiring the block of stock that results in control.

Determining Goodwill and the Components of the Investment Account

Under *all* three sequences, two concepts (PCC and EUC) exist concerning how to procedurally determine at the date control is obtained (1) goodwill (when it exists) and (2) any other components of the parent's Investment account (when the subsidiary's assets and/or liabilities are under- or overvalued).

Parent Company Concept

Under this concept, layers that exist for goodwill and these other components *immediately prior* to the date control is obtained are added to the layer that results from obtaining control. Thus **cumulative amounts** are determined for goodwill and any other Investment account components as of the control date. These procedures are usually referred to as the **"step-by-step" method.**

Economic Unit Concept

Under this approach, layers that exist for goodwill and these other components *immediately prior* to the date control is obtained **are *not* carried forward and used in any way.** They are purged. Thus goodwill and any other components are recalculated on a "fresh" basis at the date of control using the fair values at that date. These procedures are usually referred to as the **"date-of-latest-purchase"** method.

Which Concept Is GAAP for Each of the Three Sequences?

We indicate below the current GAAP status of both the *parent company concept* and the *economic unit concept*. (Current GAAP is set forth in *Accounting Research Bulletin No. 51*, "Consolidated Financial Statements," paragraph 10.)

	Sequence		
	1[a]	2	3
Current GAAP	PCC & EUC	PCC	PCC
FASB's 1995 *proposed* GAAP[b]	EUC	EUC	EUC

[a] The treatment of any unrealized gain or loss in this situation is *not* specifically addressed in any official accounting pronouncement. The AICPA's technical hotline personnel, however, recommend use of PCC.

[b] The portion of the FASB's consolidation project dealing with *consolidation procedures* is currently on hold. Thus the FASB may not follow through with this proposal.

We now illustrate the way we determine goodwill and any other Investment account components for Sequence 2 situations under the PCC approach.

Comprehensive Illustration

Analyzing the Investment Account for a Step Acquisition—Significant Influence Period Existed

Assume the following block acquisition information:

			Information Relating to Investee		
					Undervaluation of Net Assets Element[a]
Ownership Percentage Acquired	Date Block Was Acquired	Investor's Cost	Common Stock	Retained Earnings	Equipment
30%	January 1, 2006	$ 55,000	$10,000	$ 60,000	$80,000
	+ 2006 net income			40,000	
	– 2006 dividends declared			(10,000)	
10%	January 1, 2007	$ 21,000	$10,000	$ 90,000	$60,000
	+ 2007 net income (6 mo.)			20,000	
	– 2007 dividends declared			-0-	
60%	July 1, 2007	$140,000	$10,000	$110,000	$30,000
100%					

[a] For simplicity, we assume that the *entire* undervaluation of net assets relates to equipment owned by the investee.

In Illustration 5-7, we use the above information to show the analysis of the Investment account through the date that control was obtained.

Comparison to the Economic Unit Concept

Under the EUC, the parent's $83,000 investment carrying value at June 30, 2007 is adjusted upward by $10,333 to its fair value of $93,333. (Cost of last block of $140,000/60% = $233,333 total fair value of stock; $233,333 – $140,000 = $93,333). The amount assignable to the equipment component is $30,000, which is 100% of its undervaluation at this date—this amount is $8,000 *lower* than under PCC. The residually determined amount for goodwill is $83,333—this amount is $18,333 *higher* than under PCC. These differences net out to $10,333 ($18,333 – $8,000) and result from the $10,333 fair value adjustment ($93,333 – $83,000).

END-OF-CHAPTER REVIEW

Summary of Key Points

1. The total cost of an acquisition is the sum of (1) the **fair value** of the consideration given, (2) any **direct costs** clearly **traceable** to the acquisition, and (3) the fair value of any **contingent consideration.**

ILLUSTRATION 5-7 STEP ACQUISITION: ANALYSIS OF INVESTMENT ACCOUNT— *PARENT COMPANY CONCEPT* (STEP-BY-STEP METHOD)

Ownership Percentage Acquired		Investor's Cost	=	Book Value Element: Common Stock	+	Book Value Element: Retained Earnings	+	Under- or (Over) Valuation of Net Assets Element: Equipment	+	Goodwill Element[d]
	Assigned Life:							4 Yrs.		Indefinite
30%	**Block Purchase—1/1/06**	$ 55,000		$ 3,000[a]		$ 18,000[b]		$ 24,000[c]		$ 10,000
	+ Equity in net income (30% of $40,000)	12,000				12,000				
	– Dividends (30% of $10,000).	(3,000)				(3,000)				
	– Amortization ($24,000/4)	(6,000)						(6,000)[e]		
30%	Balances, 12/31/06.	$ 58,000		$ 3,000		$ 27,000		$ 18,000		$ 10,000
10%	**+ Block purchase—1/1/07**	21,000		1,000		9,000		6,000[f]		5,000
	Balances, 1/1/07	$ 79,000		$ 4,000		$ 36,000		$ 24,000		$ 15,000
	+ Equity in net income for 6 mo. (40% of $20,000)	8,000				8,000				
	– Dividends (40%).	–0–				–0–				
	– Amortization:									
	Block 1 ($24,000/4 × 1/2 yr.). . .	(3,000)						(3,000)[e]		
	Block 2 ($6,000/3 × 1/2 yr.) . . .	(1,000)						(1,000)[e]		
40%	Balances, 6/30/07.	$ 83,000		$ 4,000		$ 44,000		$ 20,000		$ 15,000
60%	**+ Block purchase—7/1/07**	140,000		6,000		66,000		18,000[g]		50,000
100%	Balances, 7/1/07 **Date of control** . . .	**$223,000**		**$10,000**		**$110,000**		**$38,000**		**$65,000**

[a] Calculated at 30% of $10,000. (Subsequent additions to this column are based on ownership percentages and *book values*.)

[b] Calculated at 30% of $60,000. (Subsequent additions to this column are based on ownership percentages and *book values*.)

[c] Calculated at 30% of $80,000 of undervaluation at this date.

[d] All additions to this column are determined *residually*.

[e] A remaining life of four years from the initial acquisition date is used to amortize equipment. Thus the $6,000 of equipment from the *second* block purchase has a 3-year life.

[f] Calculated at 10% of the $60,000 of *undervaluation* at this date.

[g] Calculated at 60% of the $30,000 of *undervaluation* at this date.

2. The acquisition of either *assets* or *common stock* results in a **revaluation** of the assets and liabilities of the acquired business to their **current values.**

3. When **assets are acquired,** the acquired assets and assumed liabilities are recorded at their current values **directly in the books of the acquiring company** (which may require the creation of a new general ledger at the division level if **decentralized accounting** is used).

4. When **common stock is acquired,** the revaluation to current values is done by making adjustments to the subsidiary's book values **in the consolidation process (non-push-down accounting).** The alternative is to have the subsidiary **adjust its general ledger accounts (push-down accounting).**

5. Under the **non-push-down basis of accounting,** the amounts reported by the subsidiary are wholly irrelevant from the perspective of the parent.

6. In a **step acquisition,** the parent's **cost of the acquisition** under the *parent company concept* is the sum of (1) the **carrying value of the earlier investments** at the date on which control is obtained and (2) the cost of the block of stock that resulted in control.

7. In a **step acquisition** in which the **step-by-step method** is used, the amounts assigned to under- or overvalued assets are based on the **fair values on the date that each block of stock was acquired.** Thus "layering" occurs. (This method is currently *permitted* in Sequence 1 situations and *required* in Sequence 2 and 3 situations.)

8. In a **step acquisition** in which the **date of latest purchase method** is used, the amounts assigned to under- or overvalued assets are based on the **fair values on the date that control is obtained.** At this date, balances identified with the earlier investments are discarded. Thus no "layering" occurs. (This method is (1) currently allowed only in Sequence 1 situations and (2) the FASB's *proposed required GAAP* for *all* step acquisitions.)

Glossary of New Terms

Bargain purchase element The amount by which the cost of the investment is *below* the current value of an acquired business's net assets.

Contingent consideration Consideration that must be paid if certain future conditions are satisfied.

Date of latest purchase method The procedure under the *economic unit concept* whereby the cost of each block of stock is analyzed using the fair values existing on the date that control was obtained.

Goodwill The amount by which the *cost* of the investment is *above* the *current value* of an acquired business's net assets.

Non-push-down basis of accounting The subsidiary retains its *historical cost basis* in accounting for its assets and liabilities. (Adjustments to *current values* are made in the *consolidation process.*)

Push-down basis of accounting The subsidiary's assets and liabilities are adjusted to their *current values* in the *general ledger* based on the parent's cost.

Step acquisition An acquisition in which blocks of an investee company's outstanding common stock are acquired over time until the ownership level results in control over the investee.

Step-by-step method The procedure under the *parent company concept* whereby the cost of each block of stock is analyzed using the fair values existing on the date that each block was acquired.

Assignment Material

Review Questions

1. What is the essence of the *purchase method* of accounting?

2. What two basic questions must be answered with respect to the purchase method of accounting?

3. What types of consideration can the acquiring entity give in a business combination?
4. When is it preferable in recording a business combination to use the *fair value* of the *equity securities* issued instead of the *current value* of the *net assets* of the acquired business?
5. How should *direct costs* incurred in a business combination be treated?
6. What is contingent consideration, and how should it be accounted for?
7. What are the three major conceptual elements into which the cost of an investment could possibly be separated?
8. In which situations would only one major conceptual element exist? In which situation would only two major conceptual elements exist?
9. What is the purpose of separating the cost of the investment into the individual components of the major conceptual elements?
10. Why is there no separate account for goodwill on the parent company's books under *non-push-down accounting*?
11. If the acquiring entity's cost *equals* or is *more than* the target company's net assets at book value, can it be said that the acquirer purchased the target's retained earnings?
12. Under *non-push-down accounting*, why are the subsidiary's reported amounts deemed not relevant?
13. What are the two criteria for recognizing an acquired entity's *intangible assets*?
14. How are *limited-life intangible assets* other than goodwill subsequently accounted for?
15. How are *indefinite-life intangible assets* other than goodwill subsequently accounted for?
16. How is *goodwill* determined?
17. How is *goodwill* accounted for in subsequent periods?
18. How is *goodwill* reported in the financial statements?
19. In *step acquisitions* in which the investor has *never* had significant influence, what unique aspect must be dealt with at the date control is obtained?
20. In *step acquisitions*, does "layering" of goodwill occur in the consolidated balance sheet?
21. In *step acquisitions*, how are the excess cost components of an investor's Investment account as determined for the *earlier acquisitions* dealt with when control is achieved?
22. **Computers and Spreadsheets:** In what three ways can spreadsheet cells be "linked" as that term is used in EXCEL?

Exercises

E 5-1 **Recording Acquisition of Common Stock for Cash and Stock** Purl Inc. acquired 100% of the outstanding common stock of Surl Inc. for $2,300,000 cash and 10,000 shares of its common stock ($2 par value), which was traded at $40 per share at the acquisition date.

Required Prepare the entry to record the business combination.

E 5-2 **Recording Direct Costs** Assume the same information provided in Exercise 5-1. In addition, assume that Purl incurred the following direct costs:

Legal fees for preparing the acquisition agreement	$ 47,000
Accounting fees for the purchase investigation	17,000
Travel expenses for meetings held with Surl management	8,000
Legal fees for registering the common stock issued with the SEC	32,000
Accounting fees for the review of unaudited financial statements and other data included in the registration statement	16,000
SEC filing fees	4,000
	$124,000

Prior to the consummation date, $103,000 had been paid and charged to a Deferred Charges suspense account pending consummation of the acquisition. The remaining $21,000 has *not* been paid or accrued.

Required Prepare the journal entry to record the business combination and the direct costs.

E 5-3 **Contingent Consideration: Future Sales** Poly Inc. acquired 100% of the outstanding common stock of Soly Inc. for $1,000,000 cash. If Soly's cumulative sales for the three years subsequent to the acquisition date exceed $10,000,000, the additional cash of $200,000 is to be paid to Soly's former shareholders.

Required Prepare the entry to record the business combination. Explain the accounting treatment of the contingent consideration. What is the entry if Soly's cumulative sales exceed $10,000,000?

E 5-4 **Contingent Consideration: *Existing* Security Price to Be Maintained** Palco Inc. acquired 100% of Salco Inc.'s outstanding common stock by issuing 80,000 shares of its common stock ($10 par value), which had a *market value* of $40 per share at the acquisition date. If the *market value* of Palco's common stock falls *below* $40 per share two years after the acquisition date, Palco must issue additional shares at that time to Salco's former shareholders so that the *total value* of the shares issued *equals* $3,200,000.

Required *Note:* You may want to review paragraphs 29 and 30 of *FAS 141* before solving.

1. Prepare the entry to record the business combination. Explain the accounting treatment of the contingent consideration.
2. Assume that the *market value* of Palco's common stock is $32 per share two years later. Prepare the entry to record the additional shares issued.

E 5-5 **Contingent Consideration: *Higher* Security Price to Be Attained** Phota Inc. acquired 100% of Sota Inc.'s outstanding common stock by issuing 60,000 shares of its common stock ($5 par value), which had a *market value* of $50 per share as of the acquisition date. If the *market value* of Phota's common stock is *not* at least $70 per share two years *after* the acquisition date, additional shares must be issued to Sota's former shareholders so that the *total value* of the shares issued equals $4,200,000.

Required *Note:* Review paragraphs 29 and 30 of *FAS 141* before solving.

1. Prepare the entry to record the business combination. Explain the accounting treatment of the contingent consideration.
2. Assume that the market value of Phota's common stock is $60 per share two years later. Prepare the entry to record the additional shares issued.

E 5-6 **Separating Cost into Major Conceptual Elements** Potasha Inc. acquired 100% of Sulpha Inc.'s outstanding common stock at a cost of $1,000,000. Sulpha's net assets have a *book value* of $600,000 and a *current value* of $880,000 as of the acquisition date.

Required Separate the cost of the investment into its major conceptual elements as of the acquisition date.

E 5-7 **Separating Cost into Major Conceptual Elements** Pomona Inc. acquired 100% of the outstanding common stock of Sonora Inc., a manufacturing company with extensive manufacturing facilities, at a cost of $2,000,000. Sonora's net assets have a *book value* of $1,800,000 and a *current value* of $2,100,000 as of the acquisition date.

Required Separate the cost of the investment into its major conceptual elements as of the acquisition date.

E 5-8 **Separating Cost into Components of the Major Conceptual Elements** Penn Inc. acquired all of Senn Inc.'s outstanding common stock for $800,000 cash. (Assume that there were no direct costs or contingent consideration.) Information about Senn as of the acquisition date is as follows:

	Book Value	Current Value
Cash	$ 50,000	$ 50,000
Accounts receivable, net	100,000	100,000
Inventory	200,000	210,000
Land	300,000	420,000
Buildings and equipment	670,000	680,000
Accumulated depreciation	(120,000)	
Total Assets	$1,200,000	$1,460,000
Payables and accruals	$ 100,000	$ 100,000
Long-term debt	600,000	625,000
Total Liabilities	$ 700,000	$ 725,000
Common stock	$ 50,000	
Additional paid-in capital	300,000	
Retained earnings	150,000	
Total Stockholders' Equity	$ 500,000	735,000
Total Liabilities and Equity	$1,200,000	$1,460,000

Required

1. Separate the cost of the investment into the individual components of the major conceptual elements as of the acquisition date.
2. Explain why the *current value* of the long-term debt is *higher* than its *book value.*

Problems

P 5-1 **Analyzing Cost** Perusal Inc. acquired 100% of Scanner Inc.'s outstanding *common stock* for $1,500,000 cash. Information with respect to Scanner as of the acquisition date is as follows:

	Book Value	Current Value
Cash	$ 55,000	$ 55,000
Accounts receivable, net	180,000	180,000
Notes receivable	100,000	60,000
Inventory	300,000	330,000
Land	500,000	600,000
Buildings and equipment	600,000[a]	750,000
Patent	45,000	105,000
Goodwill	120,000	See note.
Total Assets	$1,900,000	
Payables and accruals	$ 300,000	$ 300,000
Long-term debt (10% bonds)	700,000	650,000
Total Liabilities	$1,000,000	
Common stock	$ 100,000	
Additional paid-in capital	500,000	
Retained earnings	300,000	
Total Stockholders' Equity	$ 900,000	
Total Liabilities and Equity	$1,900,000	

[a] Net of accumulated depreciation of $123,000.

Note: The $120,000 of goodwill arose from Scanner's acquisition two years ago of the assets of a local competitor.

Required

1. For other than existing goodwill, what procedures and guidelines are used to determine current values of assets acquired and liabilities assumed? (Refer to paragraphs 37 and 38 of *FAS 141.*)
2. As to the 10% bonds payable, is the *current rate* of interest *more or less than* 10%? Will future interest expense be at a rate *more or less than* 10%?
3. Separate the investment cost into the individual components of the major conceptual elements.
4. Prepare all consolidation entries as of the acquisition date.

P 5-2 **Analyzing Cost** Pladd Inc. acquired 100% of Stripes Inc.'s outstanding *common stock* for $310,000 cash. Information about Stripes as of the acquisition date is as follows:

	Book Value	Current Value
Cash	$ 20,000	$ 20,000
Accounts receivable, net	40,000	40,000
Inventory	200,000	140,000
Land	90,000	300,000
Buildings, net	130,000[a]	180,000
Equipment, net	100,000[b]	120,000
Total Assets	$ 580,000	$800,000
Payables and accruals	$ 100,000	$100,000
Long-term debt	280,000	280,000
Total Liabilities	$ 380,000	$380,000
Common stock	$ 30,000	
Additional paid-in capital	270,000	
Accumulated deficit	(100,000)	
Total Stockholders' Equity	$ 200,000	420,000
Total Liabilities and Equity	$ 580,000	$800,000

[a] Net of accumulated depreciation of $55,000.

[b] Net of accumulated depreciation of $44,000.

Required

1. Separate the investment cost into the components of the major conceptual elements.
2. Prepare all consolidation entries as of the acquisition date.

P 5-3 **Analyzing Cost** Plugg Inc. acquired 100% of Sparks Inc.'s outstanding common stock for $160,000 cash. Information about Sparks, which leases its manufacturing facilities and which is in poor financial condition as of the acquisition date, is as follows:

	Book Value	Current Value
Cash	$ 20,000	$ 20,000
Accounts receivable, net	390,000	390,000
Inventory	300,000	270,000
Equipment, net	100,000[a]	60,000
Total Assets	$ 810,000	$740,000
Payables and accruals	$ 450,000	$450,000
Long-term debt	50,000	50,000
Total Liabilities	$ 500,000	$500,000
Common stock	$ 220,000	
Additional paid-in capital	340,000	
Accumulated deficit	(250,000)	
Total Stockholders' Equity	$ 310,000	240,000
Total Liabilities and Equity	$ 810,000	$740,000

[a] Net of accumulated depreciation of $77,000.

Required

1. Separate the investment cost into the components of the major conceptual elements.
2. Prepare all consolidation entries as of the acquisition date.

P 5-4* **Consolidation Worksheet** Pya Inc., which is a calendar-year–reporting company, acquired 100% of Sya Inc.'s outstanding common stock at a cost of $325,000 on 12/31/05. The analysis of Pya's investment account by the individual components of the major conceptual elements as of the acquisition date is as follows:

*The financial statement information presented for problems accompanied by asterisks is also provided on Model 5 (filename: MODEL05) at the **http://pahler.swlearning.com** website, allowing the problem to be worked on the computer.

Book value element:	
Common stock	$100,000
Retained earnings	90,000
Under- or (over)valuation of net assets element:	
Inventory	(5,000)
Land	30,000
Equipment	50,000
Covenant-not-to-compete	40,000
Goodwill element	20,000
Cost	$325,000

Each company's financial statements for the year ended 12/31/05 immediately *after* the acquisition are as follows:

	Pya Inc.	Sya Inc.
Income Statement (2005)		
Sales	$ 900,000	$ 500,000
Cost of sales	(500,000)	(250,000)
Expenses	(260,000)	(202,000)
Net Income	$ 140,000	$ 48,000
Balance Sheet (as of 12/31/05)		
Cash	$ 45,000	$ 20,000
Accounts receivable, net	75,000	70,000
Inventory	105,000	80,000
Investment in Sya (total cost)	325,000	
Land	100,000	70,000
Buildings and equipment	250,000	204,000
Accumulated depreciation	(150,000)	(44,000)
Total Assets	$ 750,000	$ 400,000
Payables and accruals	$ 80,000	$ 60,000
Long-term debt	20,000	150,000
Common stock	300,000	100,000
Retained earnings	350,000	90,000
Total Liabilities and Equity	$ 750,000	$ 400,000
Dividends declared in 2005	$ 80,000	$ 10,000

Required

1. Prepare all consolidation entries as of 12/31/05. (First split the Investment account into the book value element and the excess cost elements.)
2. Prepare a consolidation worksheet as of 12/31/05.

P 5-5* 

Consolidation Worksheet Poz Inc., which is a calendar-year–reporting company, acquired 100% of Soz Inc.'s outstanding common stock at a cost of $210,000 on 12/31/05. The analysis of Poz's Investment account by the individual components of the major conceptual elements as of the acquisition date is as follows:

Book value element:	
Common stock	$ 5,000
Additional paid-in capital	95,000
Retained earnings	160,000
Under- or (over)valuation of net assets element:	
Inventory	(20,000)
Land	30,000
Building	(100,000)
Long-term debt	40,000
Cost	$ 210,000

Each company's financial statements for the year ended 12/31/05 immediately after the acquisition are as follows:

	Poz	Soz
Income Statement (2005)		
Sales	$ 950,000	$ 800,000
Cost of sales	(500,000)	(600,000)
Expenses	(320,000)	(250,000)
Net Income	$ 130,000	$ (50,000)
Balance Sheet (as of 12/31/05)		
Cash	$ 5,000	$ 10,000
Accounts receivable, net	65,000	40,000
Inventory	140,000	150,000
Investment in Soz (total cost)	210,000	
Land	190,000	100,000
Buildings and equipment	500,000	305,000
Accumulated depreciation	(440,000)	(55,000)
Total Assets	$ 670,000	$ 550,000
Payables and accruals	$ 60,000	$ 15,000
Long-term debt	10,000	275,000
Common stock	20,000	5,000
Additional paid-in capital	380,000	95,000
Retained earnings	200,000	160,000
Total Liabilities and Equity	$ 670,000	$ 550,000
Dividends declared during 2005	$ 75,000	-0-

Required

1. Prepare all consolidation entries as of 12/31/05. (First split the Investment account into the book value element and the excess cost elements.)
2. Prepare a consolidation worksheet as of 12/31/05.

P 5-6* 

Analyzing Cost and Consolidation Worksheet Pud Inc. acquired 100% of Sud Inc.'s outstanding common stock for $900,000 cash on 1/1/05. Pud also incurred $55,000 of costs in connection with the acquisition. Of this amount, $15,000 was a finder's fee, $12,000 an allocation of overhead from the mergers and acquisition department, and $8,000 an allocated portion of the president's salary (the president had devoted approximately 20% of her time during 2004 to the merger). The remaining $20,000 was for legal and accounting fees and travel costs.

Financial data for each company immediately *before* the acquisition are as follows:

	Pud Inc.	Sud Inc.	
	Book Value	Book Value	Current Value
Cash	$ 1,345,000	$ 100,000	$ 100,000
Accounts receivable, net	900,000	140,000	140,000
Notes receivable		80,000	60,000
Inventory	1,100,000	310,000	340,000
Land	500,000	250,000	410,000
Buildings and equipment	4,500,000	800,000	620,000
Accumulated depreciation	(1,400,000)	(300,000)	
Patent, net	200,000	40,000	100,000
Goodwill, net of amortization		80,000	
Deferred acquisition costs	55,000		
Total Assets	$ 7,200,000	$1,500,000	$1,770,000
Payables and accruals	$ 1,800,000	$ 250,000	$ 250,000
Long-term debt	4,000,000	600,000	670,000
Common stock	600,000	150,000	
Retained earnings	800,000	500,000	
Total Liabilities and Equity	$ 7,200,000	$1,500,000	

If Sud's sales for 2006 exceed $850,000, Pud must pay an additional $60,000 cash to Sud's stockholders. Management is optimistic that this sales level can be attained.

Required

1. Analyze the investment account by the components of the major conceptual elements as of 1/1/05.
2. Prepare the consolidation entries as of 1/1/05.

3. Prepare a consolidation worksheet as of 1/1/05.

P 5-7 **Step Acquisition: No Significant Influence** Penco acquired two blocks of Senco, a *family-owned* company. Related information is as follows:

			Information Relating to Investee		
Percentage Acquired	Date Block Was Required	Pomco's Cost	Common Stock	Retained Earnings	Undervaluation of Net Assets
10%	1/1/06	$ 100,000	$400,000	$300,000	$ 80,000
90%	12/31/08	1,260,000	400,000	640,000	110,000
100%					

Additional information:

1. Senco's only under- or (over)valued asset or liability at 1/1/06 and 12/31/08 was land.
2. Senco declared cash dividends on its common stock of $90,000 in 2006, 2007, and 2008.
3. Penco was *not* able to exert *significant influence* after acquiring the first block of stock.
4. No impairment of value adjustment was made to Penco's Investment account in 2006, 2007, or 2008.
5. Penco has decided to use the *parent company concept.*

Required 1. Prepare an analysis of the Investment account through the date control was achieved.
2. Prepare all consolidation entries at 12/31/08.

P 5-8 **Step Acquisition: Significant Influence** Pomco acquired blocks of Somco's outstanding common stock over a two-year period. Related information is as follows:

			Information Relating to Investee		
Percentage Acquired	Date Block Was Required	Pomco's Cost	Common Stock	Retained Earnings	Undervaluation of Net Assets—Patent
20%	1/1/05.	$ 40,000	$100,000	$ 25,000	$50,000
20%	1/1/06.	56,000	100,000	55,000	40,000
60%	12/31/06	208,000	100,000	120,000	35,000
100%					

Additional information:

1. Somco's only under- or (over)valued asset or liability at each acquisition date was a patent.
2. Somco declared cash dividends on common stock of $15,000 in both 2005 and 2006.
3. The undervalued patent has a remaining life of five years at 1/1/05.
4. Pomco *was* able to *exert significant influence* after acquiring the first block of stock.
5. Pomco has decided to use the *parent company concept.*

Required 1. Prepare an analysis of the Investment account through the date control was achieved.
2. Prepare all consolidation entries at 12/31/06.

THINKING CRITICALLY

Cases

C 5-1 **Manner of Reporting "Cost in Excess of Net Assets"** Hyde Company's consolidated balance sheet has the following described asset:

Excess of cost over related net assets of businesses acquired $75,000,000

Required

1. Is the title of the asset informative?
2. What does the asset represent?

C 5-2 **Assigning Excess of Cost over Book Value** Ponda Inc., a highly diversified company, acquired 100% of the outstanding common stock of three companies during the current year. In each case, Ponda's cost was $500,000 in excess of the $4,000,000 book value of the net assets. The reason Ponda paid *more than* the *book value* of the net assets of each company is stated below:

1. **Acquisition of Ironex Inc.** Ironex mines iron ore from land it owns. Ponda acquired Ironex to ensure a continual supply of iron ore for its steel-making operation.
2. **Acquisition of Memco Inc.** Memco manufactures high-quality memory chips for computers. Few companies can manufacture high-quality chips of this type. Ponda acquired Memco to ensure a continual supply of high-quality memory chips for its computer manufacturing operation.
3. **Acquisition of Farmco Inc.** Farmco manufactures farm machinery and earns a return on investment that is average for its industry. On this basis, Farmco was *not* worth acquiring. Ponda believes, however, that it can bring about substantial efficiencies by integrating Farmco's operations with those of another subsidiary, which also manufactures farm machinery. The combined results are expected to increase substantially the overall return on investment of each previously separate operation.

Required For each of these acquisitions, determine how you would classify Ponda's cost in excess of book value and how you would account for it in future period consolidated statements.

C 5-3 **Theory: Bargain Purchase Element** Pinkle Inc. recently acquired 100% of Sinkle Inc.'s assets at an amount *below* their current value. The controller has listed the following ways to account for the bargain purchase element:

1. Credit it to income in the year of the acquisition, possibly classified as an *extraordinary item*.
2. Amortize it to income over the two-year period needed to turn the acquired operation into a profit-making operation.
3. Allocate it to the acquired assets based on relative current values, thereby lowering the recorded values of these items.
4. Credit it to *contributed capital*.

Required Evaluate the theoretical soundness of each alternative regardless of the requirements of *FAS 141*.

C 5-4 **Acquiring R&D in Process** Plado Inc. recently acquired Slado Inc. in a purchase business combination. The acquisition's cost was allocated based on an independent appraisal. Of the $50 million acquisition cost, $18 million was allocated to Research & Development in Process.

Required How would you report the $18 million in the consolidated balance sheet at the acquisition date? In subsequent period consolidated statements?

C 5-5 **Recording a Liability Before Its Time?** Palto Inc. and Salto Inc. recently combined in a purchase business combination. Goodwill of $10,000,000 was initially calculated residually. To integrate the two operations, certain facilities of both entities will be closed. Consequently, some of the employees will be terminated. The controller has proposed that the estimated severance pay of $4,000,000 ($1,000,000 pertaining to Palto's employees and $3,000,000 pertaining to Salto's employees) be reflected as an undervalued liability of Salto in assigning Palto's cost to Salto's assets and liabilities.

Required

1. How will treating the $4,000,000 as an undervalued liability at the acquisition date impact goodwill?
2. Does a financial reporting benefit result from this proposal?
3. Is this proposed treatment theoretically correct?

C 5-6 **Valuing "Cost in Excess of Net Assets" in Subsequent Years** Payto Inc. acquired the business of Sayto Inc. on 1/1/06 at a cost of $800,000 in excess of the *current value* of Sayto's net assets. Sayto's operations had been *unprofitable* for the two years preceding the business combination and thus did *not* possess superior earning power. Payto paid the $800,000 so that it could readily establish itself in this high-risk industry. Payto expects Sayto's operations to report profits within three years. The cost in excess of current value was assigned to goodwill.

Required

1. Assume that at 12/31/08, Sayto's operations are still unprofitable. Management is uncertain whether Sayto's operations will ever be profitable. What are the implications of this situation?
2. What if Sayto were only marginally profitable for 2008 (Payto earning only 6% return on its investment), a situation expected to continue?

Financial Analysis Problems

FAP 5-1 **Evaluating Future Results under the Purchase Method in a Business Combination with a Troubled Savings and Loan** You are the auditor for Pyramid Savings and Loan Association, which recently acquired 100% of the outstanding common stock of Sham Savings and Loan Association. Sham had incurred *losses* for approximately two years prior to the combination as a result of paying a higher interest rate to its depositors than it was earning on its loans. Federal regulators arranged the combination to prevent Sham's liquidation because it had exhausted its net worth. Selected data for Sham as of the 1/1/06 combination date are as follows:

	Book Value	Current Value
Assets	$300,000,000[a]	$260,000,000
Liabilities	300,000,000	300,000,000
Common stock	12,000,000	
Accumulated deficit	(12,000,000)	

[a] Includes real estate loans of $270 million.

The *current value* of the assets is *lower than* the *book value* because the current lending rate on home mortgages is roughly 14%, whereas the yield on its loans (which have an average remaining life of 10 years) is only 10%. Accordingly, a $40 million *over*valuation component exists and will be amortized to interest income to report a 14% yield on the loan portfolio's $230 million *current value* instead of reporting a 10% yield on the portfolio's $270 million *book value*. Pyramid did *not* have to pay any consideration—it merely took title to all of Sham's outstanding common stock. Management intends to amortize goodwill over 20 years (which you are to **assume is GAAP** for the purpose of this problem). For simplicity, assume that the debtors on the notes will make 10 annual payments of $43,941,000 at the end of each of the next 10 years.

Required

1. Analyze the Investment account at the acquisition date.
2. Prepare all consolidation entries as of the acquisition date. (Assume that *non-push-down accounting* was used.)
3. For Years 1–10 (in total) and for Years 11–20 (in total), show in T accounts the effect on income of amortization's made from the parent's Investment account.
4. Evaluate the soundness of the results that are reported under the *purchase method* at the acquisition date and for future periods.
5. What, if anything, should be done differently to better reflect the economics of the situation?
6. Using Excel, prepare an amortization table for the $40 million *over*valuation (use 13.911%—*not* 14%).

7. *Optional (Chapter 6 material)*: Prepare the parent's amortization entries at 12/31/06 assuming that the amortization pertaining to the $40 million overvaluation component is $5 million for 2006.

FAP 5-2 Time to Write Down Goodwill: Pick a Number On 1/1/06, Pong Inc. acquired 100% of Spinner Inc.'s outstanding common stock. Spinner's net assets (excluding goodwill) had a current value of $4,000,000.

Pong estimated that Spinner would have $700,000 of average annual earnings for the foreseeable future, a 17.5% return on the $4,000,000 of its net assets at current value. For this industry, a 15% return on equity was considered normal. Accordingly, the expected superior earnings were $100,000 (2.5% × $4,000,000). Pong agreed to pay for five years of expected superior earnings, discounted to its *present value*. In choosing a discount rate, a minimum of 10% was established, inasmuch as this was deemed appropriate for a relatively risk-free investment. Pong added to the 10% minimum an extra 10% for the additional risk associated with this industry. Thus, a 20% discount rate was used in arriving at the present value of the goodwill to be paid for, the calculation of which follows:

Expected superior earnings.	$100,000
Present value factor for an annuity of 5 years at 20%	2.9906
Goodwill calculated.	$299,060

Accordingly, the *purchase price* was $4,300,000. This is $4,000,000 for the *current value* of the net assets and $300,000 (rounded) for the goodwill.

For 2005 and 2006, Spinner reported annual earnings of approximately $650,000 (approximately $50,000 *below* initial expectations). The shortfall was attributable partly to overly optimistic projections and partly to new product innovations introduced by competitors. Management does *not* expect Spinner's future annual earnings to increase beyond $650,000. Pong is amortizing the goodwill over a five-year life.

Required How much should the unamortized goodwill be written down to at 12/31/07 (two years later)?

FAP 5-3 Time to Sell the Family-Owned Business and Retire: Seller Beware! Ponzi Equities is a publicly owned company with approximately five million common shares outstanding, which are traded (thinly) on the over-the-counter market. During its 15 years of existence, Ponzi issued common stock to acquire all of the outstanding common stock of approximately 20 companies, all of which were small, financially strong, family-owned businesses in which the owner(s) was (were) planning to retire. All of the combinations were structured to obtain purchase accounting.

Required

1. What major item must be addressed in applying the provisions of *FAS 141* in which common stock is given as consideration?
2. If you were the owner of such a company, what would you do differently if Ponzi offered you *common stock* as consideration instead of *cash*?

chapter

6

The Purchase Method: Postacquisition Periods and Partial Ownerships

The way you win is a measure of your talent. The way you lose is a measure of your character.
BILL WATTENBURG

LEARNING OBJECTIVES

To Understand

- The way to achieve the purchase method accounting results in postacquisition periods—*100%-ownership* situations.
- The conceptual difference between the *parent company concept* and the *economic unit concept* in revaluing assets.
- The way to apply the purchase method at the acquisition date—*non-100%-ownership* situations.
- The way to achieve purchase method accounting results in postacquisition periods—*non-100%-ownership* situations.

TOPIC OUTLINE

(this appendix appears on pages 229–230 of the text)

CHAPTER OVERVIEW

The first part of this chapter continues the discussion that we began in Chapter 5 by examining the application of the purchase methods for periods *after* the acquisition date for *100%-owned* subsidiaries. Next, we discuss goodwill impairment testing procedures.

We then discuss applying the purchase method to situations in which only *partial ownership* of the target company is obtained. We address an additional conceptual issue unique to partial ownership situations. In addition to discussing and illustrating *existing GAAP* for partial ownership situations, we also discuss and illustrate **in Appendix 6A** the FASB's 1995 *proposed new rules* for partial ownership situations—namely, the **full goodwill method under the economic unit concept.**

For both of these topics, we show the preparation of consolidated statements. For postacquisition periods, we present illustrations for the *equity method*.

A: POSTACQUISITION PERIODS—100% OWNERSHIPS

I. ACCOUNTING FOR THE PARENT'S INVESTMENT

The Equity Method

Accounting for the Book Value Element

Recall that the procedures for applying the equity method to a *created* subsidiary were discussed in Chapter 2. The identical procedures are used for an *acquired* subsidiary to account for the *book value element* of the parent's cost (the various elements of the parent's cost having been discussed in Chapter 5).

We now continue with the purchase acquisition example discussed on pages 152–158 in Chapter 5. We further assume that Subbco Company reported (1) earnings of $24,000 for 2006 and $32,000 for 2007 and (2) dividends declared of $4,000 for 2006 and $12,000 for 2007. Under the equity method, Parrco Company makes the following *general ledger* entries:

	2006		2007	
Investment in Subsidiary	24,000		32,000	
Equity in Net Income (of Subbco) .		24,000		32,000
Dividend Receivable	4,000		12,000	
Investment in Subsidiary		4,000		12,000

The analysis of the book value element of the parent's cost is updated as shown in Illustration 6-1.

Review Points for Illustration 6-1. Note the following:

1. **Procedures.** No special procedures were needed merely because Parrco *acquired* rather than *created* the subsidiary.
2. **The basic *elimination* entry.** The basic elimination entry at each year-end will be obtained from this analysis—the same analysis used for a *created* subsidiary.
3. **Liquidating dividends.** In this example, the *postacquisition dividends* (totaling $16,000) did *not* exceed the ***postacquisition earnings*** (totaling $56,000). If the postacquisition dividends had exceeded the postacquisition earnings, the subsidiary would be paying dividends out of the

ILLUSTRATION 6-1 UPDATING THE BOOK VALUE ELEMENT OF THE CONCEPTUAL ANALYSIS

	Parent's Investment Account— Book Value	=	BOOK VALUE ELEMENT Subsidiary's Equity Accounts Common Stock	+	Retained Earnings
Balances, 1/1/06	$ 60,000		$10,000		$ 50,000
+ Equity in net income	24,000				24,000
– Dividends declared	(4,000)				(4,000)
Balances, 12/31/06	$ 80,000		$10,000		$ 70,000
+ Equity in net income	32,000				32,000
– Dividends declared	(12,000)				(12,000)
Balances, 12/31/07	$100,000		$10,000		$ 90,000

$50,000 of retained earnings existing at the acquisition date and thus liquidating part of the parent's initial investment cost. Such dividends are called **liquidating dividends. Under the *equity method*, liquidating dividends are treated the same as *non*liquidating dividends.**

Accounting for the Excess Cost Elements

Under the *equity method*, the parent's cost in excess of book value is accounted for as though these were separate general ledger accounts. Accordingly, amounts pertaining to land are *not* amortized to income, but amounts pertaining to depreciable or amortizable assets *are* amortized to income. This amortization can be recorded in the parent's general ledger under the *equity method*. Continuing with the Chapter 5 acquisition example shown in Illustration 5-5 (on page 158), the cost in excess of book value elements would be updated for 2006 and 2007 as shown in Illustration 6-2.

The parent's *general ledger* amortization entries for 2006 and 2007 (based on the amounts calculated in Illustration 6-2) are as follows:

	2006		2007	
Equity in Net Income (of Subbco)	8,000		4,000	
Investment in Subsidiary		8,000		4,000

ILLUSTRATION 6-2 UPDATING THE COST IN EXCESS OF BOOK VALUE ELEMENTS OF THE CONCEPTUAL ANALYSIS

	Parent's Investment Account— Excess Cost	=	UNDER- OR (OVER)VALUATION OF NET ASSETS ELEMENT Inventory	+	Land	+	Equipment	+	GOODWILL ELEMENT[a]
Remaining Life			(3 months)		(Indefinite)		(4 years)		(Indefinite)
Balances, 1/1/06	$40,000		$ 4,000		$8,000		$16,000		$12,000
– Amortization—2006	(8,000)		(4,000)				(4,000)		
Balances, 12/31/06	$32,000		$ -0-		$8,000		$12,000		$12,000
– Amortization—2007	(4,000)						(4,000)		
Balances, 12/31/07	$28,000		$ -0-		$8,000		$ 8,000		$12,000

[a] We assume that no goodwill impairment writedown was made during these two years.

The advantages to recording this amortization in the general ledger are as follows:

1. **Provides a better means to keep records.** The alternative is to make these entries on the worksheet (as under the *cost method*).[1] General ledger entries provide a more efficient means to keep records than do consolidation worksheet entries.
2. **Retains the built-in checking feature.** The built-in checking features discussed in Chapter 2 (consolidated net income and retained earnings equaling the parent's net income and retained earnings) are retained.

Charging the Amortization to the Equity in Net Income Account

Note that under the *equity method*, the parent's amortization of cost in excess of book value is charged *directly* to the Equity in Net Income of Subsidiary account—**it is improper to charge the parent's expense accounts because the amortization relates solely to the parent's investment in the subsidiary, not to any of the parent's separate operations.** Charging this amortization to the Equity in Net Income of Subsidiary account reveals the true earnings of the subsidiary—**using the *new basis of accounting* that results from the purchase transaction.** This may be depicted as follows for the example we have been using:

	Equity in Net Income (of Subsidiary)			
	2006		2007	
	Dr.	Cr.	Dr.	Cr.
Subsidiary's **reported earnings** using basis applicable to previous owners		$24,000		$32,000
Parent's amortization of cost in excess of book value	8,000		4,000	
Subsidiary's **true earnings** using new basis applicable to new owner (the parent)		$16,000		$28,000

Under the *non*-push-down basis of accounting, no revaluation to *current values* is made in the subsidiary's *general ledger*. Accordingly, the financial statement amounts reported by the subsidiary reflect the *old basis* of accounting. From the parent's perspective, such amounts are wholly irrelevant. Under the push-down basis of accounting (discussed briefly in Chapter 5 and in detail in Chapter 7), adjustments *are* made in the subsidiary's general ledger to revalue the subsidiary's assets and liabilities to their *current values* as of the acquisition date. If Subbco had applied push-down accounting, the amortization relating to the undervalued assets ($8,000 for 2006 and $4,000 for 2007) would have been recorded on Subbco's books. As a result, Subbco reported net income for 2006 and 2007 would have been $16,000 and $28,000, respectively.

CHECK POINTS

On 4/1/06, Pax Inc. acquired 100% of Sax Inc.'s outstanding common stock for cash of $500,000. For 2006, Sax had net income of $20,000 each quarter. Also for 2006, Sax declared and paid cash dividends of $12,000 for each of the first *three* quarters and $40,000 for the *fourth* quarter. Amortization of cost in excess of book value for 2006 is $10,000.

What is the *carrying value* of Pax's investment in Sax at 12/31/06 under the *equity method*?

a. $486,000
b. $494,000
c. $496,000
d. $504,000
e. $546,000

Answer: a

---

[1] This alternative is called the "simplified" equity method.

Assume the same information as in the previous Check Point. What amount appears in Pax's 2006 income statement if Pax accounts for its investment in Sax under the *equity method*?

a. $(6,000)
b. $4,000
c. $46,000
d. $50,000
e. $70,000

Answer: d

Reclassifying the Amortization in Consolidation

Charging the amortization recorded by the parent to the Equity in Net Income of Subsidiary account adds a minor extra step to the consolidation effort. An additional entry must be made to *reclassify* this amortization to the appropriate income statement accounts it would have been charged to had Subbco (1) adjusted its assets and liabilities to their *current values* and (2) used the *new basis* of accounting in computing depreciation and amortization.

Because the Equity in Net Income of Subsidiary account was *debited* on Parrco's books for the amortization, the reclassification is effected by (1) *crediting* the Equity in Net Income of Subsidiary account and (2) *debiting* the various appropriate expense accounts. This entry does *not* affect consolidated net income because it takes place entirely within the income statement section of the worksheet.[2]

The following table shows the accounts to which various amortizations would be reclassified:

Amortization Pertaining to	Appropriate Income Statement Account
Inventory	Cost of Sales
Buildings and equipment	Cost of Sales, Marketing Expenses, and Administration Expenses (as appropriate)[a]
Patents	Cost of Sales
Long-term debt	Interest Expense
Notes receivable	Interest Income
Intangibles—limited useful lives	Cost of Sales, Marketing Expenses, and Administrative Expenses (as appropriate)

[a] Amortization pertaining to manufacturing assets would be charged solely to Cost of Sales.

For ease of reference, we call the entry made to effect this reclassification the *Amortized Excess Cost Reclassification Entry*. An example of this entry for a parent having $30,000 of amortization relating to (1) an *under*valued building, (2) a noncompetition agreement (marketing-related), (3) an *over*valued note payable, (4) an *over*valued patent, and (5) an *over*valued note receivable is as follows:

WORKSHEET ENTRY ONLY

	Debit	Credit
Cost of Sales (for the **undervalued** building)	22,000	
Expenses (for the covenant-not-to-compete)	7,000	
Interest Expense (for the **overvalued** note payable)	8,000	
Cost of Sales (for the **overvalued** patent)		3,000
Interest Income (for the **overvalued** note receivable)		4,000
Equity in Net Income (of subsidiary)		30,000

Note that **the debits and credits depend on whether an item is under- or overvalued.** In this case, a $30,000 *debit* amount was reclassified, which is the usual case when an economy has been inflationary. Situations could exist, however, in which a *credit* amount is reclassified.

[2] Recall from intermediate accounting that (1) in an *adjusting* entry, both the income statement and the balance sheet are adjusted and (2) in a *reclassification* entry, the debit and credit are both posted to the same financial statement; thus net income does not change.

II. CONSOLIDATION WORKSHEETS: *POSTACQUISITION PERIODS*

We now continue with the example we have been using. The consolidation entries at the end of 2006 and 2007 are as follows:

1. **The basic *elimination* entry** (amounts are from Illustration 6-1):

WORKSHEET ENTRY ONLY

	Consolidation Date			
	December 31, 2006		December 31, 2007	
Common Stock	10,000		10,000	
Retained Earnings, 1/1/06 and 1/1/07	50,000		70,000	
Equity in Net Income (of Subbco)	24,000		32,000	
Dividends Declared		4,000		12,000
Investment in Subsidiary		80,000		100,000

2. **The *unamortized* excess cost *reclassification* entry** (for BS) (amounts are from Illustration 6-2):

WORKSHEET ENTRY ONLY

	Consolidation Date			
	December 31, 2006		December 31, 2007	
Land	8,000		8,000	
Equipment	16,000		16,000	
Goodwill	12,000		12,000	
Accumulated Depreciation		4,000		8,000
Investment in Subsidiary		32,000		28,000

3. **The *amortized* excess cost *reclassification* entry** (for IS) (amounts are from Illustration 6-2):

WORKSHEET ENTRY ONLY

	Consolidation Date			
	December 31, 2006		December 31, 2007	
Cost of Sales	8,000		4,000	
Equity in Net Income (of Subbco)		8,000		4,000

Note: For simplicity, we arbitrarily assumed that *all* of the equipment amortization should be classified as part of Cost of Sales. The amortization relating to the inventory obviously belongs in Cost of Sales.

4. **The accumulated depreciation *elimination* entry** (same amounts as used in Illustration 5-5 [on page 158] at the acquisition date):

WORKSHEET ENTRY ONLY

	Consolidation Date			
	December 31, 2006		December 31, 2007	
Accumulated Depreciation	56,000		56,000	
Buildings and Equipment		56,000		56,000

These consolidation entries are used in preparing the consolidation worksheets shown in Illustrations 6-3 and 6-4 on pages 188 and 189.

Mid-Year Acquisitions

The preceding examples used an acquisition date as of the *beginning* of the parent's reporting year (January 1, 2006). Most business combinations occur at various times during a year. **Regardless of**

ILLUSTRATION 6-3 *EQUITY* METHOD: *FIRST* YEAR SUBSEQUENT TO THE ACQUISITION DATE—100% OWNERSHIP

Parrco Company and Subbco Company
Consolidation Worksheet as of December 31, 2006

	PARRCO COMPANY	SUBBCO COMPANY	CONSOLIDATION ENTRIES DR.			CONSOLIDATION ENTRIES CR.	CONSOLIDATED
Income Statement (2006)							
Sales	600,000	234,000					834,000
Cost of sales	(360,000)	(110,000)	8,000	3			(478,000)
Expenses	(190,000)	(100,000)					(290,000)
Equity in net income (of Subbco)	16,000[a]		24,000	1	3	8,000	–0–
Net Income	66,000	24,000	32,000			8,000	66,000
Statement of Retained Earnings							
Balances, 1/1/06	100,000	50,000	50,000	1			100,000
+ Net income	66,000	24,000	32,000			8,000	66,000
– Dividends declared	(51,000)	(4,000)			1	4,000	(51,000)
Balances, 12/31/06	115,000	70,000	82,000			12,000	115,000
Balance Sheet							
Cash	25,000	16,000					41,000
Accounts receivable, net	75,000	37,000					112,000
Inventory	110,000	55,000					165,000
Investment in Subsidiary:							
Book value element	80,000				1	80,000	–0–
Excess cost elements	32,000				2	32,000	–0–
Land	220,000	32,000	8,000	2			260,000
Buildings and equipment	500,000	200,000	16,000	2	4	56,000	660,000
Accumulated depreciation	(320,000)	(70,000)	56,000	4	2	4,000	(338,000)
Goodwill			12,000	2			12,000
Total Assets	722,000	270,000	92,000			172,000	912,000
Liabilities	407,000	190,000					597,000
Parrco Company:							
Common stock ($1 par)	10,000						10,000
Add'l Paid-in Capital	190,000						190,000
Retained earnings	115,000						115,000
Subbco Company:							
Common stock (no par)		10,000	10,000	1			–0–
Retained earnings		70,000	82,000			12,000	–0–
Total Liabilities and Equity	722,000	270,000	92,000			12,000	912,000
Proof of debit and credit postings			184,000			184,000	

[a] Subbco's $24,000 of reported net income less $8,000 of amortization of cost in excess of book value.

Explanation of entries:

1 The basic *elimination* entry.
2 The *unamortized* excess cost *reclassification* entry (for **BS**).
3 The *amortized* excess *reclassification* cost entry (for **IS**).
4 The accumulated depreciation *elimination* entry.

the acquisition date, only the *postacquisition income statement* of the subsidiary is consolidated. For example, assume that the acquisition date is April 1, 2006, and that Subbco Company had the following income statement amounts for 2006:

	Jan. 1–Mar. 31	April 1–Dec. 31	Total
Revenues	$ 64,000	$170,000	$ 234,000
Cost of sales	(23,000)	(87,000)	(110,000)
Expenses	(34,000)	(66,000)	(100,000)
Net Income	$ 7,000	$ 17,000	$ 24,000
Relevance of above amounts:	**Disregard**	**Use**	**Disregard**

Accordingly, the parent would apply the *equity method* of accounting to the $17,000 of earnings occurring *after* the acquisition date, and only the income statement amounts for this period

ILLUSTRATION 6-4 *EQUITY* METHOD: *SECOND* YEAR SUBSEQUENT TO THE ACQUISITION DATE—100% OWNERSHIP

Parrco Company and Subbco Company
Consolidation Worksheet as of December 31, 2007

	PARRCO COMPANY	SUBBCO COMPANY	CONSOLIDATION ENTRIES DR.			CR.	CONSOLIDATED
Income Statement (2007)							
Sales	710,000	282,000					992,000
Cost of sales	(390,000)	(130,000)	4,000	3			(524,000)
Expenses	(210,000)	(120,000)					(330,000)
Equity in net income (of Subbco). . .	28,000[a]		32,000	1	3	4,000	-0-
Net Income.	138,000	32,000	36,000			4,000	138,000
Statement of Retained Earnings							
Balances, 1/1/07.	115,000	70,000	70,000	1			115,000
+ Net income	138,000	32,000	36,000			4,000	138,000
– Dividends declared	(85,000)	(12,000)			1	12,000	(85,000)
Balances, 12/31/07	168,000	90,000	106,000			16,000	168,000
Balance Sheet							
Cash	26,000	31,000					57,000
Accounts receivable, net.	84,000	51,000					135,000
Inventory	140,000	82,000					222,000
Investment in Subsidiary:							
Book value element	100,000				1	100,000	-0-
Excess cost elements	28,000				2	28,000	-0-
Land	220,000	32,000	8,000	2			260,000
Buildings and equipment	500,000	200,000	16,000	2	4	56,000	660,000
Accumulated depreciation	(360,000)	(86,000)	56,000	4	2	8,000	(398,000)
Goodwill.			12,000	2			12,000
Total Assets	738,000	310,000	92,000			192,000	948,000
Liabilities	370,000	210,000					580,000
Parrco Company:							
Common stock ($1 par).	10,000						10,000
Add'l Paid-in Capital.	190,000						190,000
Retained earnings	168,000						168,000
Subbco Company:							
Common stock (no par).		10,000	10,000	1			-0-
Retained earnings		90,000	106,000			16,000	-0-
Total Liabilities and Equity	738,000	310,000	116,000			16,000	948,000
Proof of debit and credit postings			208,000			208,000	

[a] $32,000 of income recorded under the equity method, net of $4,000 of amortization of cost in excess of book value.

Explanation of entries:

1 The basic *elimination* entry.
2 The *unamortized* excess cost *reclassification* entry (for **BS**).
3 The *amortized* excess cost *reclassification* entry (for **IS**).
4 The accumulated depreciation *elimination* entry.

would be consolidated. As a practical matter, however, it is also acceptable to (1) consolidate the entire year and (2) report an artificial debit in the income statement called **preacquisition earnings** to negate the nonreportable net income earned *prior to* the acquisition date.

CHECK POINT

Which of the following choices is an *incorrect* completion of the sentence? Consolidated financial statement amounts are always the same regardless of whether

a. The acquisition is of common stock or assets.
b. The *equity method* or the *cost method* is used.

c. The *non*-push-down basis of accounting or the push-down basis of accounting is used.
d. The "purchase" acquisition occurs at the beginning of the parent's reporting year or later in the year.

Answer: d

Amortization Relating to Over- or Undervalued Receivables and Payables

On page 186, we briefly explained how the amortizations pertaining to an overvalued note receivable and an overvalued note payable are reclassified in consolidation. To understand over- and undervalued receivables and payables more fully, assume that, at the acquisition date of January 1, 2006, Subbco had (1) a 12% $100,000 note *receivable* that was *under*valued by $3,470 (as a result of the current interest rate being 10%) and (2) a 12% $75,000 bond *payable* that was *under*valued by $2,600 (as a result of the *current interest rate* being 10%).

For simplicity, also assume that (1) the parent's total cost in excess of book value at the acquisition date was $870 and (2) the entire total excess cost of $870 was assigned solely to these two *under*valued accounts. Thus $3,470 was assigned to the 12% note receivable (Subbco's equity is *under*stated by this much), and $2,600 was assigned to the 12% bond payable (Subbco's equity is overstated by this much) [$3,470 – $2,600 = $870].

Illustration 6-5 shows (1) an analysis of the 12% $100,000 note receivable and the 12% $75,000 bond payable for the two years subsequent to the acquisition date, (2) an analysis of Parrco Company's excess cost for the two years subsequent to the acquisition date, (3) Parrco's general ledger entry for 2006, and (4) the consolidation entries relating to these accounts at December 31, 2006.

Illustration 6-6 on page 192 shows a consolidation worksheet at December 31, 2006, assuming that the only over- or undervalued accounts of Subbco Company as of the acquisition date are the *under*valued 12% note receivable and the 12% *under*valued bond payable.

Demonstration Problem 1: 100%-Owned Subsidiary

On 4/1/06, Poda Inc. acquired 100% of Soda Inc.'s outstanding common stock at a cost of $540,000 cash. Soda's capital accounts at the acquisition date follow:

Common stock	$ 90,000
Retained earnings	310,000

Soda's only assets and liabilities that were over- or undervalued at the acquisition date were (1) patents on a manufacturing process (*over*valued by $40,000 [10-year remaining life]) and (2) land (*under*valued by $120,000). For 2006, Soda had the following earnings and dividends:

	First Quarter	Remainder of Year	Total[a]
Net income	$30,000	$70,000	$100,000
Dividends declared	20,000	60,000	80,000

[a] All dividends were paid in the same quarter in which they were declared.

Required

1. Prepare the entry to record the acquisition.
2. Prepare the entries Poda would make for the year ended 12/31/06 under the *equity method*.
3. Prepare an analysis of the Investment account as of the acquisition date, and update it through 12/31/06.
4. Prepare all consolidation entries at 12/31/06.

ILLUSTRATION 6-5 PARENT'S AMORTIZATION RELATING TO SUBSIDIARY'S UNDERVALUED 12% NOTE RECEIVABLE AND UNDERVALUED 12% BOND PAYABLE

	12% Note Receivable			12% Bond Payable		
Date	Face Value	Under-Valuation	Reportable Value	Face Value	Under-Valuation	Reportable Value
Jan. 1, 2006	$100,000	$ 3,470	$103,470	$75,000	$ 2,600	$77,600
Amortization		(1,650)	(1,650)		(1,240)	(1,240)
Dec. 31, 2006	$100,000	$ 1,820	$101,820	$75,000	$ 1,360	$76,360
Amortization		(1,820)	(1,820)		(1,360)	(1,360)
Dec. 31, 2007	$100,000	$ -0-	$100,000	$75,000	$ -0-	$75,000

	2006 Interest Income		2006 Interest Expense	
Contractual interest	$12,000	(12%)	$ 9,000	(12%)
Parrco Company's amortization	(1,650)		(1,240)	
Reportable interest	$10,350	(10% of $103,470)	$ 7,760	(10% of $77,600)

	Parent's Investment Account—Excess Cost	=	Under- or (Over) Valuation of Net Assets Element: 12% Note Receivable	+	12% Bond Payable
Jan. 1, 2006	$ 870		$ 3,470		$(2,600)
Amortization	(410)		(1,650)		1,240
Dec. 31, 2006	$ 460		$ 1,820		$(1,360)
Amortization	(460)		(1,820)		1,360
Dec. 31, 2007	$ -0-		$ -0-		$ -0-

Parrco Company's *general ledger* amortization entry for 2006:

Equity in Net Income ($1,650 – $1,240)	410	
Investment in Subsidiary		410

Parrco Company's *consolidation* entries at December 31, 2006:

WORKSHEET ENTRY ONLY

Note Receivable	1,820	
Bond Payable		1,360
Investment in Subsidiary—Excess Cost		460

WORKSHEET ENTRY ONLY

Interest Income	1,650	
Interest Expense		1,240
Equity in Net Income		410

Solution to Demonstration Problem 1

1. Investment in Subsidiary	540,000	
Cash		540,000
To record the acquisition.		
2. Investment in Subsidiary	70,000	
Equity in Net Income (of subsidiary)		70,000
To record share of subsidiary's earnings from 4/1/06 to 12/31/06.		
Dividends Receivable (when declared)	60,000	
Investment in Subsidiary		60,000
To record dividends from subsidiary for period 4/1/06 to 12/31/06.		

ILLUSTRATION 6-6 *EQUITY* METHOD: *FIRST* YEAR SUBSEQUENT TO THE ACQUISITION DATE—SUBSIDIARY HAS *UNDER*VALUED RECEIVABLE AND *UNDER*VALUED PAYABLE

Parrco Company and Subbco Company
Consolidation Worksheet as of December 31, 2006

	PARRCO COMPANY	SUBBCO COMPANY	CONSOLIDATION ENTRIES DR.			CR.	CONSOLIDATED
Income Statement (2006)							
Sales	600,000	234,000					834,000
Cost of sales	(360,000)	(110,000)					(478,000)
Expenses	(190,000)	(100,000)					(290,000)
Interest income		12,000	1,650	3			10,350
Interest expense		(9,000)			3	1,240	(7,760)
Equity in net income ($27,000 – $410)	26,590		27,000	1	3	410	-0-
Net Income	76,590	27,000	28,650			1,650	76,590
Statement of Retained Earnings							
Balances, 1/1/06	100,000	50,000	50,000	1			100,000
+ Net Income	76,590	27,000	28,650			1,650	76,590
– Dividends declared	(51,000)	(4,000)			1	4,000	(51,000)
Balances, 12/31/06	125,590	73,000	78,650			5,650	125,590
Balance Sheet							
Note receivable, 12% **[undervalued]**		100,000	1,820	2			101,820
Investment in Subsidiary:							
Book value element	83,000				1	83,000	-0-
Excess cost elements	460				2	460	-0-
Other assets	649,130	173,000					822,130
Total assets	732,590	273,000	1,820			83,460	923,950
Liabilities—nonbond	407,000	115,000					522,000
Bond payable, 12% **[undervalued]**		75,000			2	1,360	76,360
Parrco Company:							
Common stock ($1 par)	10,000						10,000
Add'l paid-in capital	190,000						190,000
Retained earnings	125,590						125,590
Subbco Company:							
Common stock (no par)		10,000	10,000	1			-0-
Retained earnings		73,000	78,650			5,650	-0-
Total Liabilities & Equity	732,590	273,000	88,650			7,010	923,950
Proof of debit and credit postings			***90,470***			***90,470***	

Explanation of entries:

1 The basic *elimination* entry.
2 The *unamortized* excess cost *reclassification* entry (for **BS**).
3 The *amortized* excess cost amortization *reclassification* entry (for **IS**).

Investment in Subsidiary	3,000	
Equity in Net Income (of subsidiary)		3,000
To amortize cost in excess of [*below* for the patent] book value.		

3. Analysis of Investment account:

	Parent's Investment Account—Book Value	=	BOOK VALUE ELEMENT — Subsidiary's Equity Accounts: Common Stock	+	Retained Earnings
Balances, 4/1/06	$400,000		$90,000		$310,000
+ Net income	70,000				70,000
– Dividends	(60,000)				(60,000)
Balances, 12/31/06	$410,000		$90,000		$320,000

	Parent's Investment Account Excess Cost	=	UNDER- OR (OVER)VALUATION OF NET ASSETS ELEMENT: Land	+	Patent	+	GOODWILL ELEMENT
Balances, 4/1/06	$140,000		$120,000		$(40,000)		$60,000
– Amortization	3,000				3,000[a]		
Balances, 12/31/06	$143,000		$120,000		$(37,000)		$60,000
Investment carrying value at 12/31/06 (in total)	$553,000						

[a] $40,000 × 1/10 × 3/4 yr. = $3,000.

4. The basic *elimination* entry:

Common Stock	90,000	
Retained Earnings, 4/1/06	310,000	
Equity in Net Income (of subsidiary)	70,000	
Dividends Declared		60,000
Investment in Subsidiary		410,000

The *unamortized* excess cost *reclassification* entry (for **BS**):

Land	120,000	
Goodwill	60,000	
Patent		37,000
Investment in Subsidiary		143,000

The *amortized* excess cost *reclassification* entry (for **IS**):

Equity in Net Income (of subsidiary)	3,000	
Cost of Sales		3,000

III. Assessing Goodwill for Possible Impairment of Value

Recall from Chapter 5 that goodwill that is bought and paid for in a business combination (1) is determined *residually* and (2) must be subsequently evaluated *annually* (or more often if certain events occur) for possible *impairment of value.*

Often when goodwill is bought and paid for in a business combination, the acquired entity's subsequent operating results are far lower than that anticipated when the entity was acquired. In retrospect, managements often find that (1) they "overpaid" for goodwill, (2) the goodwill has diminished in value, and (3) the goodwill should be written down or written off entirely. Later, we describe two relatively recent goodwill writedowns, which resulted in the largest quarterly loss and annual loss reported by any U.S. company.

Recent Historical Focus (1970–2001): *Recoverability*

From 1970 to 2001, goodwill had to be amortized to earnings over no more than 40 years. Accordingly, the focus of goodwill as a reported asset was on assessing the *recoverability* of the unamortized balance—which is *not* the same as assessing whether an *impairment of value* had occurred.

During this period, goodwill writedowns were generally *not* made if the goodwill was being *recovered.* If the acquired entity was at least *breaking even*, the goodwill reported in its balance sheet was being *recovered*. That is, the ***goodwill was being converted back into cash*** each year to the extent of that year's goodwill amortization. If the acquired entity was reporting *losses*, however, the goodwill charge to earnings was *not* being *fully* recovered (*partial* recovery of $1 million would occur if the amortization charge was $3 million and the net loss was $2 million)—goodwill writedowns were commonly made in these situations.

The conceptual problem that existed during these years was that goodwill could be impaired (a loss of value occurred) but no writedown would be made because the goodwill was considered *recoverable*. Remember that an acquired business's postacquisition earnings could be far lower than that expected at the acquisition date (for a multitude of reasons, such as a change in market conditions or an inability to successfully integrate operations as originally planned) and ***recoverability* of goodwill would occur as long as the acquired business was at least *breaking even*.**

Unfortunately during these years, far too many instances occurred in which goodwill was carried on the books long after it had greatly diminished in value as a result of either (1) poor (but still profitable) operating results or (2) *unrealized* expected synergies.

The New Focus (2001 Onward): *Impairment of Value*

When the FASB decided in June 2001 to *not* require amortization of goodwill, the issue of whether the current period amortization charge was being recovered became nonexistent. Accordingly, the entire focus became whether goodwill had diminished in value. Thus the focus shifted from solely on *recoverability* to solely on proper *valuation*. FASB *Statement No. 142*, "Goodwill and Other Intangibles" sets forth the manner of assessing whether an impairment of value has occurred. (A two-step impairment test is required, which we illustrate shortly.)

Reporting Goodwill Impairment Losses

Goodwill impairment losses are (1) recognized in the *income statement* and (2) ***reported as a separate line item before*** the subtotal "*Income from Continuing Operations*." See the Case in Point for two recent, huge reported goodwill impairment losses.

CASE IN POINT

Goodwill Impairment of Value Write-Down—Big Time (World Record)

In 2001, JDS Uniphase Corp. (the world's largest manufacturer of components for fiber-optic telecommunications equipment, having total revenues of $3.2 billion for its fiscal year ended June 30, 2001) reported a ***goodwill impairment write-down of $45 billion.*** The loss for the third and fourth *quarters* (the quarters in which the goodwill write-downs occurred) were $42 billion and $12 billion, respectively; the *annual* loss was more than $50 billion.

The goodwill had resulted primarily from several acquisitions made ***over the previous two years*** (when JDS's stock was soaring) using common stock as the consideration given. JDS stated that the write-down was necessary because of the deep, industry-wide slump (more like a collapse) in the telecom market and JDS's own sinking stock price (which declined from $110 to $5 in approximately one year).

In 2002, media titan AOL Time Warner, Inc. reported a **$99 billion goodwill impairment write-down** (from $130 billion to $31 billion)—$130 billion of goodwill resulted from the merger of AOL and Time Warner in 2001.

Testing Goodwill for Impairment at the Appropriate *Reporting Unit Level*

FAS 142 requires goodwill to be tested for impairment at an appropriate level—called the **reporting unit.** Thus depending on the situation, goodwill could be tested for impairment at any of several levels. Examples of reporting unit levels follow:

1. **The *Subsidiary* Level (appropriate when the acquired business is to be a stand-alone unit).** Assume that (1) the *acquiring entity* is solely a *computer manufacturer*, (2) the *acquired business* is a *refrigerator manufacturer*, (3) no synergism is expected to occur because the two operations

will *not* be integrated, and (4) the acquirer purchased *common stock* (creating a *parent-subsidiary* relationship). Therefore, ***the subsidiary is the reporting unit.*** (If the acquirer had purchased *assets* instead of *common stock*, the *new division* would be the reporting unit.)

2. **The Consolidated Level (appropriate when the acquired business is fully integrated into the parent's existing operations).**[3] Assume that (1) the *acquiring entity* is solely a *computer manufacturer* (for businesses), (2) the *acquired entity* also is a *computer manufacturer* (for businesses), (3) synergism is expected to occur because the two operations will be integrated, which is expected to produce efficiencies and substantial cost-savings, and (4) the acquirer purchased common stock (creating a *parent-subsidiary* relationship). Thus the acquired business will be fully absorbed into the acquirer. Because of the integration of operations, ***the parent and the subsidiary consolidated are the reporting unit.*** (Integration usually is easier to accomplish if an acquired *subsidiary* is liquidated into a *division* shortly after the acquisition date using the *statutory merger* procedure discussed in Chapter 4.)
3. **The Partial-Consolidated Level (appropriate when the acquired business is fully integrated into the operations of one or more of the parent's existing subsidiaries).** Assume that (1) the *acquiring entity* is a holding company that has five subsidiaries in completely unrelated lines of business, (2) one of those subsidiaries is a *grocery store chain*, (3) the *acquired entity* also is a grocery store chain, and (4) synergism is expected to occur because the acquired business's operations will be integrated with the operations of the parent's existing grocery store chain subsidiary, which is expected to produce efficiencies and substantial cost-savings. Thus the acquired business will be fully absorbed into a portion of the acquirer. Because of the manner of integration of operations, ***the two grocery store chain subsidiaries consolidated are the reporting unit.***

The preceding examples are relatively simple common sense determinations of the reporting unit. *FAS 142* has a more formal set of rules for determining reporting units, which we briefly discuss next.

Formally Determining Reporting Units—Must Be Consistent With *FAS 131*

Depending on the situation, a *reporting unit* is either (1) an **operating segment** (as that term is defined in paragraph 10 of FASB *Statement No. 131*, "Disclosures about Segments of an Enterprise and Related Information" (discussed in Chapter 12) or (2) one level *below* an operating segment (referred to as a ***component of an operating segment***). In general, an operating segment is a portion of an enterprise that (1) earns revenues and incurs expenses, (2) has its operating results

ETHICS

Would You Fudge the Numbers?

The company president has instructed you to inflate the current year's earnings by roughly 20%.

Questions

1. What would you do?
2. What are the potential consequences of (a) following these instructions and (b) not following these instructions?
3. What if the president had asked you to overstate profits by only 2% to enable the company to report a small increase in net income from the prior year?
4. How many of Enron's accountants have either been indicted by the federal government or pleaded guilty to falsifying financial statement reports?

[3] A special problem occurs in this situation if the subsidiary issues separate company financial statements (such as to one of its lenders). The impairment test must be performed at both the *consolidated level* and the *subsidiary level*. The impairment loss determined at the *subsidiary level* is recognized at the *subsidiary level*. If the impairment loss at the *subsidiary level* is more than the impairment loss at the *consolidated level*, however, the incremental impairment loss is deferred in consolidation (on the consolidation worksheet) and thus *not* recognized at the *consolidated level*.

regularly reviewed by the enterprise's ***chief operating decision maker*** (for assessing performance and allocating assets), and (3) has discrete financial information available.

Components of a Segment

A *component* of an operating segment is a *reporting unit* if (1) the component constitutes a business, (2) ***segment management*** assesses performance at the *component level,* (3) *discrete financial information* is available and used regularly by ***segment management*** to review the components operating results, and (4) its ***economic characteristics differ from other components in that operating segment.*** If the first *three* conditions are satisfied but *not* the *fourth* condition, the *component* is combined with the components that *do* have *similar economic characteristics*. Accordingly, those *combined components* are a *reporting unit*. Thus an operating segment with *three* components could have (1) *three* reporting units (if all *three* components ***differed*** from each other), (2) *two* reporting units (if *two* of the three components were ***similar***), and (3) *one* reporting unit (if all *three* components were ***similar***).

The Presumption of Synergism in Certain Situations

Note that because of the *economic characteristics* rule, the two grocery store chains in the earlier example (example 3 on page 195) are the *reporting unit* if they have similar economic characteristics (which they most likely would)—regardless of whether (1) their operations are integrated, (2) they share valuable marketing information, or (3) they share valuable managerial practices and information. Thus the *economic characteristics* rule essentially presumes synergism *always* exists for all of an operating segment's components that have *similar economic characteristics.*

No Arbitrary Assignment of Goodwill Allowed

FAS 142 requires a "reasonable and supportable" approach in assigning goodwill to reporting units—thus using either "free choice" or an arbitrary method is *not* permitted.

In practice, determining reporting units is proving to be one of the more complex aspects of *FAS 142*. Accordingly, it is likely that the FASB (or the Emerging Issues Task Force [EITF]) will publish guidance in some form (such as an implementation guide), as it has done with other complex pronouncements.

Assignment of the Acquired Business's Assets and Liabilities and the Goodwill Paid for by the Acquirer

For the purpose of testing goodwill for impairment, both the acquired business's assets and liabilities and the goodwill paid for by the acquirer must be *assigned* to one or more **reporting units** at the acquisition date. Doing so enables goodwill to be tested for impairment at the ***reporting unit level.***

The Two-Step Impairment Test

Because an observable marketplace for goodwill does *not* exist, the goodwill's *implied fair value* is determined *residually* by using a two-step test. The two-step impairment test is as follows:

1. **Step One—Determining if an Indication of Impairment Exists.** The reporting unit's *fair value* is determined using estimation techniques (such as calculating the present value of probability weighted estimated future cash flows). Both *recognized* and ***unrecognized intangible assets*** are included in determining the reporting unit's fair value. If the reporting unit's *fair value* is below the unit's *carrying value*, an indication of impairment exists.[4] Therefore, step two is performed. Otherwise, stop—an indication of impairment does *not* exist.
2. **Step Two—Measuring the Impairment Loss.** The reporting unit's *fair value* (including recognized and *unrecognized* intangible assets) is allocated on a "memo" basis to the reporting unit's

[4] Assets and liabilities that entities often account for at the corporate level (such as those for income taxes, pensions, and environmental cleanup) must be assigned to a reporting unit if (1) they pertain to the reporting unit's operations and (2) they will be considered in determining the reporting unit's fair value.

assets and liabilities ***as though the reporting entity had just been acquired in a business combination***—this is a *pro forma* exercise. The implied fair value of goodwill is determined *residually* (just as it was at the acquisition date). If the goodwill's *implied fair value* is less than the goodwill's *carrying value*, the deficiency is the impairment loss to be charged to earnings.

Comprehensive Illustration

Acquired Subsidiary Is the Reporting Unit—Assigned 100% of Goodwill

Illustration 6-7 shows an application of the impairment test at a postacquisition date for an *acquired subsidiary* that is the reporting unit to which all goodwill was assigned at the acquisition date.

CHECK POINT

At a goodwill impairment testing date, a reporting unit's *fair value* (including *unrecognized* intangible assets of $55,000) is $2,000,000 ($400,000 *below* the unit's *carrying value*). If goodwill's *carrying value* is $500,000 and *implied fair value* is $350,000, what is the impairment loss to be recognized?

a. $95,000
b. $150,000
c. $205,000
d. $400,000
e. $455,000

Answer: b ($500,000 – $350,000)

When to Test Goodwill for Impairment

As stated earlier, goodwill must be tested for impairment *annually* (and between annual dates in certain situations, as discussed shortly). The annual test must be at the same time each year. (*Different* reporting units, however, may be tested for impairment at different times.)

ILLUSTRATION 6-7 IMPAIRMENT TEST AT A POSTACQUISITION DATE

STEP ONE—Determining if an Indication of Impairment Exists

	SITUATION			
	1	2	3	4
	(amounts in millions)			
Reporting Unit's:				
Carrying value (including goodwill of $20)	$100	$100	$100	$100
Fair value (including both *recognized **and** unrecognized intangible assets*)	85	85	85	110
Excess Carrying Value	$ 15	$ 15	$ 15	None
Is Step Two Required?	YES	YES	YES	NO

STEP TWO—Measuring the Impairment Loss

	1	2	3
Reporting Unit's:			
Fair value (from Step 1)	$ 85	$ 85	$ 85
Fair value other than goodwill	80	85	60
Goodwill's Implied Fair Value (residual)	$ 5	$ -0-	$ 25
Goodwill's Carrying Value	$ 20	$ 20	$ 20
Goodwill Impairment Loss (charge to earnings)	$ 15	$ 20	$ -0-

Carryforward of Prior Year Fair Value Determinations

The detailed determination of a reporting unit's fair value may be carried forward from one year to the next if *all* of the following criteria are met:

1. **No Significant Change in Composition.** The reporting unit's assets and liabilities have *not* changed significantly from the most recent fair value determination date. (Examples of possible significant changes are (1) an acquisition of a business that becomes part of the reporting unit and (2) a reorganization of the entity's segment reporting structure.)
2. **Previous Existence of a Substantial Cushion.** A substantial excess of *fair value* over *carrying value* existed at the most recent fair value determination date.
3. **No Subsequent Adverse Change in Events and Circumstances.** No change in events or circumstances has occurred since the most recent fair value determination date that would indicate a likelihood that the reporting unit's current *carrying value* is above its *fair value.*

Testing for Impairment Between Annual Tests—Triggering Events

If events have occurred or circumstances have changed since the last annual test such that it is "more-likely-than-not" that the reporting unit's current *carrying value* is above the unit's *fair value*, the impairment test is required between the annual test dates. Examples of such "triggering events" or circumstances are (1) a loss of key personnel, (2) unanticipated competition, (3) it is "more-likely-than-not" (a greater than 50% chance) that the reporting unit (or a significant portion thereof) will be disposed of (sold, spun off, abandoned), (4) an adverse action or assessment by a regulator, and (5) a significant adverse change in the business climate or legal factors.

Hollow and Dubious Assets

In light of the staggering goodwill writedowns that have occurred shortly after the business combination, it seems that the FASB should give serious consideration to requiring the use of a special category in the asset section of the balance sheet called "Hollow and Dubious Assets." The distinguishing characteristics of items that would be reported in this category are that they (1) cannot be used to pay creditors, (2) cannot be sold separately, (3) cannot be used as collateral to borrow money against, and (4) are highly evaporable. The more notable items that would be reportable in this category are (1) goodwill, (2) prior-service costs relating to pension plans, (3) debt issuance costs, and (4) deferred stock option compensation costs.

B: Partial Ownerships—Conceptual Issues

IV. The Purchase Method: Conceptual Issues (*Parent Company Concept* versus *Economic Unit Concept*)

Partial or *Full* Revaluation of the Subsidiary's Assets and Liabilities

When a partially owned subsidiary has under- or overvalued assets or liabilities at the acquisition date, to what extent should these items be revalued to their *current values*? Two schools of thought exist: ***partial*** **revaluation** and ***full*** **revaluation**.

Partial Revaluation (Allowed under *Current* GAAP)

Under *partial revaluation*, undervalued items are revalued only to the extent of the parent's ownership interest. For example, assets that are undervalued by $28,000 are revalued upward by only $21,000 if the parent's ownership percentage was 75%. Partial revaluation occurs under the *parent company concept* [one of the two concepts that fit under full *consolidation*] (discussed in Chapter 3). This reporting result also occurs under *proportionate consolidation* (also discussed in Chapter 3). We demonstrate partial revaluation later using the *parent company concept*.

Full Revaluation (Allowed under *Current* GAAP—*Except* for Goodwill[5])

Under *full revaluation*, undervalued items are revalued to 100% of current values. In comparison with the *partial revaluation* method example in which assets undervalued by $28,000 are revalued upward by only $21,000, an additional $7,000 of valuation is reported in the asset section of the consolidated balance sheet. On the other side of the balance sheet, an additional $7,000 is reflected for the noncontrolling interest.

The $7,000 of additional valuation results in additional amortization charges in future consolidated income statements. A corresponding reduction in the amount of consolidated net income is allocated, however, to the noncontrolling interest shareholders. Thus the amount of consolidated net income allocated to the controlling interest (the parent's shareholders) is *not* affected.

Full revaluation occurs under the *economic unit concept* (discussed in Chapter 3). We demonstrate this manner of valuation in Appendix 6A.

Determining the Amount to Report for Goodwill

When part of the parent's purchase price includes an amount for goodwill, the issue arises as to whether goodwill should be reported at (1) this cost-based amount or (2) its amount *implicit* in the transaction.

The Concept of *Implicit* Goodwill

To illustrate the concept of implicit goodwill, assume that an acquiring company was willing to pay $12,000 for goodwill in acquiring 100% of the common stock. If the acquiring company acquired only a 75% ownership interest, however, it should have been willing to pay only $9,000 for goodwill (75% of $12,000). Accordingly, if the acquiring company paid $9,000 for goodwill in acquiring a 75% ownership interest, the goodwill *implicit* in the transaction must be $12,000. Thus $3,000 of additional goodwill is presumed to exist.

The *Purchased Goodwill Way* versus the *Full Goodwill Way*

Under both the *parent company concept* and one form of the *economic unit concept*, only $9,000 of goodwill is reported. Under the "pure" form of the *economic unit concept*, an additional $3,000 of goodwill is reported in the consolidated balance sheet. Accordingly, an additional $3,000 is also reported on the other side of the balance sheet for the *noncontrolling interest*. As in the case of undervalued assets, this additional goodwill results in additional amortization expense in future consolidated income statements. A corresponding reduction in the amount of consolidated net income is allocated, however, to the *noncontrolling shareholders*. Therefore, the amount of consolidated net income allocated to the *controlling interest* (the parent's shareholders) is *not* affected.

The FASB's Current Thinking Regarding Possible Changes to *Consolidation Procedures*

In its 1995 consolidation policy and procedures exposure draft, the FASB proposed to allow use of only the *economic unit concept* in its "nonpure" form (thus prohibiting the *parent company*

[5] See the FASB's 1992 Discussion Memorandum or *Consolidation Policy and Procedures*, p. 35.

concept). In its May 1996 deliberations, the FASB modified this proposal to allow only the "pure" form of the *economic unit concept*.

Later in 1996, however, the FASB decided to (1) focus solely on *consolidation policy* for the near term and (2) consider reassessing whether to pursue the *consolidation procedures* area only *after* a consensus is reached on *consolidation policy*. Thus *consolidation procedures* is currently on hold. Consequently, changes to current practice (which allows *both* the *parent company concept* and the "nonpure" form of the *economic unit concept*) are *not* expected in the near term.

C: PARTIAL OWNERSHIPS—*PARENT COMPANY CONCEPT* (PCC) PROCEDURES

V. THE PURCHASE METHOD USING PCC: ANALYZING COST

Separating the Parent's Cost into the Major Conceptual Elements

Knowing the factors that enter into how much the acquiring company is willing to pay in partial ownership situations, we separate the parent's cost into its major conceptual elements using the following procedures:

1. **The book value element.** Multiply the book value of the subsidiary's stockholders' equity by the parent's ownership percentage.
2. **The undervaluation of net assets element.** Multiply the total amount of the undervaluation of the subsidiary's net assets by the parent's ownership percentage.
3. **The goodwill element.** Add the amounts determined in procedures 1 and 2 to arrive at the parent's interest in the current value of the subsidiary's net assets. Subtract this total from the parent's cost to obtain goodwill (a residually determined amount).

In the illustrations in Chapter 5, we assumed that Parrco Company acquired 100% of the outstanding common stock of Subbco Company at a cost of $100,000, which was $40,000 in excess of the book value of the subsidiary's net assets. The $40,000 excess payment was identified as undervalued assets ($28,000) and goodwill ($12,000). Assume instead that Parrco purchased only 75% of the outstanding common stock for $75,000 (75% of $100,000). The separation of the parent's cost into its major conceptual elements is shown as follows:

Parent's Cost	=	Book Value Element (75% of $60,000)	+	Undervaluation of Net Assets Element (75% of $28,000)	+	Goodwill Element (Residual)
$75,000		$45,000		$21,000		$9,000

As was done in Chapter 5, once the cost of the parent's investment has been broken down in this manner, the future consolidation procedures can be simplified by splitting the parent's cost into the parent's share of the *book value element* and the parent's *excess cost elements*:

Investment in Subbco Company:	
Book value element	$45,000
Excess cost elements ($21,000 + $9,000)	30,000

Separating the Undervaluation of Net Assets Element into Its Components

We separate the undervaluation of net assets element into its components by multiplying the appropriate ownership percentages by the amount that each asset is undervalued. In Illustration 5–4, the $28,000 undervaluation was attributed to Inventory, Land, and Equipment accounts. This $28,000 is separated into its components as follows:

Asset	Undervaluation	Parent's Interest in Undervaluation (75%)	Noncontrolling Interest in Undervaluation (25%)
Inventory	$ 4,000	$ 3,000	$1,000
Land	8,000	6,000	2,000
Building	16,000	12,000	4,000
	$28,000	$21,000	$7,000

As shown in Chapter 5, the individual components within each category will be tracked outside the general ledger in supporting schedules, which are used to prepare consolidation entries. For the preceding situation, the supporting schedules at the acquisition date are as follows:

				BOOK VALUE ELEMENT		
				Subsidiary's Equity Accounts		
Noncontrolling Interest (25%)	+	Parent's Investment Account—Book Value	=	Common Stock	+	Retained Earnings
$15,000		$45,000		$10,000		$50,000

		UNDERVALUATION OF NET ASSETS ELEMENT						
Parent's Investment Account—Excess Cost	=	Inventory	+	Land	+	Equipment	+	GOODWILL ELEMENT
$30,000		$3,000		$6,000		$12,000		$9,000

The excess cost entry obtained with this procedure (which would be used only if *non*-push-down accounting were used) revalues the subsidiary's assets upward to the extent of 75% of their undervaluation and reports Goodwill in the consolidated statements at the amount of goodwill paid for by the parent.

VI. CONSOLIDATION WORKSHEETS USING PCC: *AT DATE OF ACQUISITION*

For this example, the consolidation entries as of the acquisition date, taken from these supporting schedules to the parent's Investment account, are as follows:

1. The basic *elimination* entry:

WORKSHEET ENTRY ONLY

Common Stock	10,000	
Retained Earnings	50,000	
Investment in Subsidiary		45,000
NCI in Net Assets		15,000

2. The *unamortized* excess cost *reclassification* entry (for BS):

WORKSHEET ENTRY ONLY

Inventory	3,000	
Land	6,000	
Equipment	12,000	
Goodwill	9,000	
Investment in Subsidiary		30,000

3. The accumulated depreciation *elimination* entry:

WORKSHEET ENTRY ONLY

Accumulated Depreciation	56,000	
Equipment		56,000

Even though only 75% of the common stock was acquired, the entire $56,000 balance in the Accumulated Depreciation account at the acquisition date is eliminated for practical reasons even though doing so is inconsistent with the *partial revaluation method*.

These consolidation entries are used in Illustration 6-8 to prepare a consolidation worksheet as of January 1, 2006 (the acquisition date), for Parrco Company and Subbco Company.

ILLUSTRATION 6-8 AT THE ACQUISITION DATE—75% OWNERSHIP (PCC)

Parrco Company and Subbco Company
Consolidation Worksheet as of January 1, 2006

	PARRCO COMPANY	75%-OWNED SUBBCO COMPANY	CONSOLIDATION ENTRIES DR.			CR.	CONSOLIDATED
Balance Sheet							
Cash	43,000	15,000					58,000
Accounts receivable	52,000	27,000					79,000
Inventory	90,000	42,000	3,000	2			135,000
Investment in Subsidiary:							
Book value element	45,000				1	45,000	-0-
Excess cost elements	30,000				2	30,000	-0-
Land	220,000	32,000	6,000	2			258,000
Buildings and equipment	500,000	200,000	12,000	2	3	56,000	656,000
Accumulated depreciation	(280,000)	(56,000)	56,000	3			(280,000)
Goodwill			9,000	2			9,000
Total Assets	700,000	260,000	86,000			131,000	915,000
Liabilities	400,000	200,000					600,000
NCI in net assets					1	15,000	15,000
Parrco Company:							
Common stock	10,000						10,000
Add'l Paid-In Capital	190,000						190,000
Retained earnings	100,000						100,000
Subbco Company:							
Common stock		10,000	10,000	1			-0-
Retained earnings		50,000	50,000	1			-0-
Total Liabilities and Equity	700,000	260,000	60,000			15,000	915,000
Proof of debit and credit postings			146,000			146,000	

Explanation of entries:
1 The *basic elimination* entry.
2 The *unamortized* excess *cost reclassification* entry (for **BS**).
3 The accumulated *depreciation* entry.

CHECK POINT

Pantu Inc. acquired 60% of Santu Inc.'s outstanding common stock for $156,000 cash. The *book value* of Santu's net assets is $200,000. Santu's only over- or undervalued asset or liability is land that has a *book value* of $100,000 and a *current value* of $150,000. Under the *parent company concept*, at what amounts are the land, the noncontrolling interest, and goodwill reported in the consolidated balance sheet?

	Land	Goodwill	Noncontrolling Interest
a.	$130,000	$6,000	$80,000
b.	$130,000	$10,000	$100,000
c.	$130,000	$44,000	$104,000
d.	$150,000	$6,000	$80,000
e.	$150,000	$10,000	$100,000
f.	$150,000	$44,000	$104,000
g.	$150,000	$6,000	$100,000
h.	$150,000	$6,000	$104,000
i.	$150,000	$10,000	$104,000

Answer: a

VII. CONSOLIDATION WORKSHEETS USING PCC: *POSTACQUISITION PERIODS*

The Equity Method

Updating the Supporting Schedules to the Investment Account

Assume that Subbco had the following earnings and dividends for the two years subsequent to the acquisition date:

	2006	2007
Net income	$24,000	$32,000
Dividends	4,000	12,000

Also assume the following amortizations pertaining to the undervalued assets and goodwill:

	2006	2007
Excess cost amortizations	6,000	3,000

Under the *equity method*, Parrco makes the following *general ledger* entries (the amounts in the first two entries are at 75% of Subbco's reported amounts):

	2006		2007	
Investment in Subsidiary	18,000		24,000	
Equity in Net Income		18,000		24,000
To record equity in Subbco's earnings.				
Dividend Receivable	3,000		9,000	
Investment in Subsidiary		3,000		9,000
To record dividend from Subbco.				
Equity in Net Income (of Subbco)	6,000		3,000	
Investment in Subsidiary		6,000		3,000
To record amortization of excess cost.				

Illustrations 6-9 and 6-10 show the updated supporting schedules to the Investment account for the two years following the acquisition date, using the preceding information. These illustrations also show the related consolidation entries required at the end of 2006 and 2007.

Illustrations 6-11 and 6-12 show the related consolidation worksheets at the end of 2006 and 2007.

CHECK POINT

How are dividends paid to noncontrolling shareholders reported in the consolidated statements?

a. They reduce the amount reported as "noncontrolling interest in net income of subsidiary" in the consolidated income statement.

b. They reduce the amount reported as "noncontrolling interest in net assets of subsidiary" in the consolidated balance sheet.

c. They are included in the dividends declared line in the consolidated statement of retained earnings.

d. They are combined with expenses in the consolidated income statement.

e. None of the above.

Answer: b

ILLUSTRATION 6-9 UPDATING THE BOOK VALUE ELEMENT OF THE INVESTMENT ACCOUNT—75%-OWNED

				BOOK VALUE ELEMENT		
				SUBSIDIARY'S EQUITY ACCOUNTS		
	NONCONTROLLING INTEREST (25%)	PARENT'S INVESTMENT ACCOUNT—BOOK VALUE	=	COMMON STOCK	+	RETAINED EARNINGS
Balances, 1/1/06	$15,000	$45,000		$10,000		$50,000
+ Equity in net income:						
To parent (75%)		18,000				18,000
To NCI (25%)	6,000					6,000
– Dividends:						
To parent (75%)		(3,000)				(3,000)
To NCI (25%)	(1,000)					(1,000)
Balances, 12/31/06	$20,000	$60,000		$10,000		$70,000
+ Equity in net income:						
To parent (75%)		24,000				24,000
To NCI (25%)	8,000					8,000
– Dividends:						
To parent (75%)		(9,000)				(9,000)
To NCI (25%)	(3,000)					(3,000)
Balances, 12/31/07	$25,000	$75,000		$10,000		$90,000

The Basic *Elimination* Entry (using the amounts in the preceding analysis)

WORKSHEET ENTRY ONLY

	CONSOLIDATION DATE			
	DECEMBER 31, 2006		DECEMBER 31, 2007	
Common Stock	10,000		10,000	
Retained Earnings, 1/1/06 and 1/1/07	50,000		70,000	
Equity in Net Income	18,000		24,000	
NCI in Net Income	6,000		8,000	
Dividends Declared		4,000		12,000
Investment in Subsidiary		60,000		75,000
NCI in Net Assets		20,000		25,000

ILLUSTRATION 6-10 UPDATING THE EXCESS COST ELEMENTS OF THE INVESTMENT ACCOUNT: 75%-OWNED SUBSIDIARY

	PARENT'S INVESTMENT ACCOUNT—EXCESS COST	=	UNDERVALUATION OF NET ASSETS ELEMENT: INVENTORY	+	LAND	+	EQUIPMENT: COST	EQUIPMENT: ACCUM. DEPR.	+	GOODWILL ELEMENT
Remaining Life			**(3 mo.)**		**n/a**		**(4 yrs.)**			**(Indefinite)**
Balances, 1/1/06	$30,000		$ 3,000		$6,000		$12,000			$9,000
– Amortization for 2006	(6,000)		(3,000)					$(3,000)		
Balances, 12/31/06	$24,000		$ -0-		$6,000		$12,000	$(3,000)		$9,000
– Amortization for 2007	(3,000)							(3,000)		
Balances, 12/31/07	$21,000		$ -0-		$6,000		$12,000	$(6,000)		$9,000

The *Unamortized* Excess Cost *Reclassification* Entry (for BS)

WORKSHEET ENTRY ONLY

	CONSOLIDATION DATE: DECEMBER 31, 2006		DECEMBER 31, 2007	
Land	6,000		6,000	
Equipment	12,000		12,000	
Goodwill	9,000		9,000	
Accumulated Depreciation		3,000		6,000
Investment in Subsidiary		24,000		21,000

The *Amortized* Excess Cost *Reclassification* Entry (for IS)

WORKSHEET ENTRY ONLY

	DECEMBER 31, 2006		DECEMBER 31, 2007	
Cost of Sales	6,000		3,000	
Equity in Net Income (of Subbco)		6,000		3,000

Review Points for Illustrations 6-11 and 6-12. Note the following:

1. The basic elimination entry was obtained from the updated analysis of the book value element as is usually done.
2. From Parrco's perspective—but not from that of the noncontrolling interest shareholders—**the amounts reported in Subbco's financial statements are wholly irrelevant amounts.** Under the non-push-down basis of accounting, such amounts do *not* reflect the *new basis of accounting* that occurs as a result of accounting for the acquisition as a *purchase*. Accordingly, when Parrco records its 75% share of Subbco's reported net income, it has recorded income based on the *old basis of accounting*. By also recording amortization of cost in excess of book value, Parrco's investment income is adjusted from the *old basis of accounting* to the *new basis of accounting*.

Demonstration Problem 2: *Partially Owned* Subsidiary—*Parent Company Concept* Procedures

On 5/1/06, Parr Inc. acquired 60% of Subb Inc.'s outstanding common stock at a cash cost of $273,000. Subb's capital accounts at the acquisition date were

Common stock	$ 10,000
Retained earnings	240,000

All of Subb's assets and liabilities had current values equal to book values as of the acquisition date, except copyrights, which had a *current value* of $90,000 and a *book value* of $20,000. The copyrights had a remaining life of 14 years.

ILLUSTRATION 6-11 THE *EQUITY* METHOD: *FIRST* YEAR SUBSEQUENT TO THE ACQUISITION DATE—75% OWNERSHIP (PCC)

Parrco Company and Subbco Company
Consolidation Worksheet as of December 31, 2006

	PARRCO COMPANY	75%-OWNED SUBBCO COMPANY	CONSOLIDATION ENTRIES DR.			CR.	CONSOLIDATED
Income Statement (2006)							
Sales	600,000	234,000					834,000
Cost of sales	(360,000)	(110,000)	6,000	3			(476,000)
Expenses	(190,000)	(100,000)					(290,000)
Equity in net income (of Subbco)	12,000[a]		18,000	1	3	6,000	-0-
Net Income	62,000	24,000	24,000			6,000	68,000
NCI in net income			6,000	1			(6,000)
CI in net income			30,000			6,000	62,000
Statement of Retained Earnings							
Balances, 1/1/06	100,000	50,000	50,000	1			100,000
+ Net income	62,000	24,000	30,000			6,000	62,000
– Dividends declared	(51,000)	(4,000)			1	4,000	(51,000)
Balances, 12/31/06	111,000	70,000	80,000			10,000	111,000
Balance Sheet							
Cash	49,000	16,000					65,000
Accounts receivable	75,000	37,000					112,000
Inventory	110,000	55,000					165,000
Investment in Subsidiary:							
Book value element	60,000				1	60,000	-0-
Excess cost elements	24,000				2	24,000	-0-
Land	220,000	32,000	6,000	2			258,000
Buildings and equipment	500,000	200,000	12,000	2	4	56,000	656,000
Accumulated depreciation	(320,000)	(70,000)	56,000	4	2	3,000	(337,000)
Goodwill			9,000	2			9,000
Total Assets	718,000	270,000	83,000			143,000	928,000
Liabilities	407,000	190,000					597,000
NCI in net assets					1	20,000	20,000
Parrco Company:							
Common stock	10,000						10,000
Add'l paid-in capital	190,000						190,000
Retained earnings	111,000						111,000
Subbco Company:							
Common stock (no par)		10,000	10,000	1			-0-
Retained earnings		70,000	80,000			10,000	-0-
Total Liabilities and Equity	718,000	270,000	90,000			30,000	928,000
Proof of debit and credit postings			173,000			173,000	

[a] $18,000 share of Subbco's reported net income, net of $6,000 of excess cost amortization = $12,000.

Explanation of entries:

1 The *basic elimination* entry.
2 The *unamortized* excess cost *reclassification* entry (for **BS**).
3 The *amortized* excess cost *reclassification* entry (for **IS**).
4 The *accumulated depreciation elimination* entry.

For 2006, Subb had the following earnings and dividends:

	Jan. 1– April 30, 2006	May 1– Dec. 31, 2006	Total[a]
Net income	$25,000	$55,000	$80,000
Dividends declared	15,000	60,000	75,000

[a] All dividends were paid in the same quarter in which they were declared.

ILLUSTRATION 6-12 THE *EQUITY* METHOD: *SECOND* YEAR SUBSEQUENT TO THE ACQUISITION DATE—75% OWNERSHIP (PCC)

Parrco Company and Subbco Company
Consolidation Worksheet as of December 31, 2007

	PARRCO COMPANY	75%-OWNED SUBBCO COMPANY	CONSOLIDATION ENTRIES DR.			CONSOLIDATION ENTRIES CR.	CONSOLIDATED
Income Statement (2007)							
Sales	710,000	282,000					992,000
Cost of sales	(390,000)	(130,000)	3,000	3			(523,000)
Expenses	(210,000)	(120,000)					(330,000)
Equity in net income (of Subbco)	21,000[a]		24,000	1	3	3,000	-0-
Net Income	131,000	32,000	27,000			3,000	139,000
NCI in net income			8,000	1			(8,000)
CI in net income			35,000			3,000	131,000
Statement of Retained Earnings							
Balances, 1/1/07	111,000	70,000	70,000	1			111,000
+ Net income	131,000	32,000	35,000			3,000	131,000
– Dividends declared	(85,000)	(12,000)			1	12,000	(85,000)
Balances, 12/31/07	157,000	90,000	105,000			15,000	157,000
Balance Sheet							
Cash	47,000	31,000					78,000
Accounts receivable	84,000	51,000					135,000
Inventory	140,000	82,000					222,000
Investment in Subsidiary:							
Book value element	75,000				1	75,000	-0-
Excess cost elements	21,000				2	21,000	-0-
Land	220,000	32,000	6,000	2			258,000
Buildings and equipment	500,000	200,000	12,000	2	4	56,000	656,000
Accumulated depreciation	(360,000)	(86,000)	56,000	4	2	6,000	(396,000)
Goodwill			9,000	2			9,000
Total Assets	727,000	310,000	83,000			158,000	962,000
Liabilities	370,000	210,000					580,000
NCI in net assets					1	25,000	25,000
Parrco Company:							
Common stock	10,000						10,000
Add'l paid-in capital	190,000						190,000
Retained earnings	157,000						157,000
Subbco Company:							
Common stock (no par)		10,000	10,000	1			-0-
Retained earnings		90,000	105,000			15,000	-0-
Total Liabilities and Equity	727,000	310,000	115,000			40,000	962,000
Proof of debit and credit postings			198,000			198,000	

[a] $24,000 share of Subbco's reported net income, net of $3,000 of excess cost amortization = $21,000.

Explanation of entries:

1 The *basic elimination* entry.
2 The *unamortized* excess cost *reclassification* entry (for **BS**).
3 The *amortized* excess cost *reclassification* entry (for **IS**).
4 The *accumulated depreciation elimination* entry.

Required

1. Prepare the entry to record the acquisition.
2. Prepare the entries Parr would make for the year ended 12/31/06 under the *equity method*.
3. Prepare an analysis of the Investment account as of the acquisition date and update it through 12/31/06.
4. Prepare all consolidation entries at 12/31/06.

Solution to Demonstration Problem 2

1. Investment in Subsidiary	273,000	
Cash		273,000
2. Investment in Subsidiary	33,000	
Equity in Net Income		33,000
To record share of earnings of subsidiary from 5/1/06 to 12/31/06 ($55,000 × 60%).		
Dividends Receivable (when declared)	36,000	
Investment in Subsidiary		36,000
To record dividends from subsidiary from 5/1/06 to 12/31/06 ($60,000 × 60%).		
Equity in Net Income	2,000	
Investment in Subsidiary		2,000
To amortize cost in excess of book value ($2,000 for copyrights).		

3. Analysis of Investment account:

	Noncontrolling Interest (40%)	+	Parent's Investment Account— Book Value	=	BOOK VALUE ELEMENT: Subsidiary's Equity Accounts: Common Stock	+	Retained Earnings
Balances, 5/1/06			$150,000		$ 6,000		$144,000
+ NCI amounts	$100,000				4,000		96,000
Balances, 5/1/06	$100,000		$150,000		$10,000		$240,000
+ Net income:							
To Parr (60%)			33,000				33,000
To NCI (40%).	22,000						22,000
– Dividends:							
To Parr (60%)			(36,000)				(36,000)
To NCI (40%).	(24,000)						(24,000)
Balances, 12/31/06. . . .	$ 98,000		$147,000		$10,000		$235,000

	Parent's Investment Account— Excess Cost	=	UNDER- OR (OVER)VALUATION OF NET ASSETS ELEMENT	+ Copyrights	+	GOODWILL ELEMENT
Balances, 5/1/06.	$123,000			$42,000		$81,000
Amortizations	(2,000)			(2,000)[a]		
Balances, 12/31/06	$121,000			$40,000		$81,000
Investment carrying value at 12/31/06 (in total) $147,000 + $121,000	$268,000					

[a] $42,000 × 1/14 × 2/3 yr. = $2,000.

4. The basic *elimination* entry:

Common Stock	10,000	
Retained Earnings, 5/1/06	240,000	
Equity in Net Income	33,000	
NCI in Net Income	22,000	
Dividends Declared		60,000
NCI in Net Assets		98,000
Investment in Subsidiary		147,000

The *unamortized* excess cost *reclassification* entry (for **BS**):

Copyrights	40,000	
Goodwill	81,000	
Investment in Subsidiary		121,000

The *amortized* excess cost *reclassification* entry (for **IS**):

Cost of Sales	2,000	
Equity in Net Income		2,000

CHECK POINT

Plumex Inc. acquired 75% of Soarex Inc.'s outstanding common stock on 4/1/06. For 2006, Soarex reported $80,000 of net income, all of which it earned evenly throughout the year. In 2006, Plumex recorded $3,000 of amortization of cost in excess of *book value.* Plumex's share of Soarex's true earnings (from Plumex's perspective) are

a. $60,000.
b. $56,000.
c. $45,000.
d. $42,000.
e. $41,000.

Answer: d

END-OF-CHAPTER REVIEW

Summary of Key Points

1. **Only postacquisition** income statements can be consolidated.
2. **Amortization** of the parent's **cost in excess of book value** is recorded in the **general ledger** under the **equity method.**
3. When **non-push-down accounting** is used, the subsidiary's reported amounts are **irrelevant** because they are based on the subsidiary's **old basis of accounting**—not the parent's **new basis of accounting.**
4. Goodwill must be tested for impairment **annually** (or more often if "triggering events" occur) using a **lower of *cost* or *estimated fair value.***
5. Goodwill impairment losses are recognized in the *income statement* and reported as a **separate line item** *before* the subtotal "*Income from Continuing Operations.*"
6. **For goodwill impairment testing purposes,** goodwill (*along with the acquired entity's assets and liabilities*) must be **assigned** to one or more *reporting units* at the acquisition date.
7. A *reporting unit* is either **an *operating segment*** (as defined in *FAS 131*) **or a *component* thereof.**
8. In determining *reporting units,* components of an operating segment (*having discrete financial information that is reviewed by management*) must be *combined* if they have **similar economic characteristics.**
9. If the reporting unit's **carrying value** exceeds the unit's **estimated fair value** (*determined in Step 1 of the impairment test*), goodwill may be impaired. In such cases, Step 2 of the impairment test is performed.
10. In Step 2 of the impairment test, goodwill's ***implied*** **fair value**—determined **residually** as if the reporting unit had been acquired on that testing date (**a pro forma exercise**)—is compared with goodwill's **carrying value.**

11. Under the **parent company concept**, a partially owned subsidiary's assets and liabilities are revalued to their current values **only to the extent that the undervaluation is bought and paid for** (likewise for goodwill).

12. Under the **economic unit concept**, a partially owned subsidiary's assets and liabilities are **revalued to their full current values**. Goodwill can be reported either at its full value or at the parent's purchased amount.

Glossary of New Terms

Liquidating dividend Dividends declared by a subsidiary that are in excess of its earnings subsequent to the acquisition date.

Postacquisition earnings Earnings of a subsidiary that occur subsequent to the acquisition date.

Operating segment A portion of an enterprise that (1) earns revenues and incurs expenses, (2) has its operating results regularly reviewed by the enterprise's chief operating decision maker, and (3) has discrete financial information available.

Reporting unit The level of reporting at which goodwill is to be tested for impairment of value. A reporting unit is an *operating segment* (or one level below an operating segment).

ASSIGNMENT MATERIAL

Review Questions

1. How are an acquired business's *preacquisition* earnings treated under the purchase method?
2. What is a *liquidating dividend*?
3. How are *liquidating dividends* treated under the *equity* method?
4. How is amortization of cost in excess of book value treated under the *equity* method?
5. Under what circumstances are an *acquired* subsidiary's financial statements relevant amounts from the *parent's* perspective?
6. When must goodwill be tested for impairment?
7. What is a "*reporting unit*" as it pertains to goodwill impairment testing?
8. How is a *reporting unit's* fair value determined?
9. At what level is goodwill tested for impairment?
10. How is goodwill's *implied* fair value determined?
11. How is a goodwill impairment writedown reported?
12. To what extent are a partially owned *acquired* subsidiary's assets and liabilities revalued to current values under the *parent company concept*? Under the *economic unit concept*?
13. How is goodwill determined under the *parent company concept*? Under the *economic unit concept*?
14. In an acquisition of less than 100% of the voting shares, how is goodwill calculated?
15. In a *step acquisition* in which a noncontrolling interest exists, to what extent are the subsidiary's assets and liabilities reported at their current values in the consolidated statement prepared at the date control was obtained?

Exercises for 100%-Owned Subsidiaries

E 6-1 **Recording Parent's Entries under the Equity Method** For 2006, a 100%-owned subsidiary reported net income of $90,000 and declared dividends of $40,000. Amortization of cost in excess of book value, as calculated by the parent, was $12,000.

Required Prepare the parent's general ledger entries under the *equity method.*

E 6-2 **Calculating Consolidated and Parent Company Amounts** On 9/30/06, Port Inc. acquired all of Shipp Inc.'s outstanding common stock for cash. Both companies have calendar year-ends. Data for each company pertaining to its *own separate operations* follows:

	Port	Shipp
Net Income:		
9 months ended 9/30/06	$700,000	$280,000
3 months ended 12/31/06	200,000[a]	120,000
	$900,000	$400,000
Dividends Declared:		
9 months ended 9/30/06	$150,000	$ 75,000
3 months ended 12/31/06	50,000	25,000
	$200,000	$100,000
Amortization of cost in excess of book value	$8,000	

[a] Excludes any amounts relating to Shipp.

Required

1. Determine the consolidated net income for 2006.
2. Determine the consolidated dividends declared for 2006.
3. Determine the investment income recorded in the parent's separate income statement for 2006 under the *equity method.*

E 6-3 **Applying the Equity Method: Consolidation Entries** On 1/1/06, Pele Inc. acquired 100% of Soccerex Inc.'s outstanding common stock at a cost of $400,000. The analysis of Pele's investment in Soccerex by the individual components of the major conceptual elements *as of* the acquisition date follows:

		Remaining Life
Book value element:		
Common stock	$100,000	
Retained earnings	60,000	
Under- or (over)valuation of net assets element:		
Inventory	5,000	3 months
Land	105,000	Indefinite
Building	90,000	15 years
Goodwill element	40,000	Indefinite
Cost	$400,000	

Soccerex declared the following net income (loss) and dividends for 2006 and 2007:

	Net Income (Loss)	Dividends Declared (and Paid)
2006	$ 35,000	$5,000
2007	(10,000)	5,000

Required

1. Assuming that the parent company uses the *equity method* of accounting, prepare the journal entries it would make for 2006 and 2007 for its investment in the subsidiary.
2. Prepare an analysis of the Investment account by the components of the major conceptual elements as of the acquisition date, and update it for the entries developed in requirement 1.
3. Prepare all consolidation entries as of 12/31/06 and 12/31/07.

E 6-4 **Applying the Equity Method: Consolidation Entries** Pitt Inc. acquired 100% of Sitters Inc.'s outstanding common stock at a cost of $310,000 on 1/1/06. The analysis of the investment by the components of the major conceptual elements *as of* the acquisition date (after appropriate allocation of the bargain purchase element) follows:

		Remaining Life
Book value element:		
Common stock	$250,000	
Retained earnings	100,000	
Under- or (over)valuation of net assets element:		
Inventory	5,000	3 months
Land	30,000	Indefinite
Building	(75,000)	25 years
Cost	$310,000	

Sitters declared the following net income (loss) and dividends for 2006 and 2007:

	Net Income (Loss)	Dividends Declared (and Paid)
2006	$(15,000)	$1,000
2007	30,000	5,000

Required

1. Assuming that Pitt uses the *equity method* of accounting, prepare the journal entries it would make for 2006 and 2007 with respect to its investment in the subsidiary.
2. Prepare an analysis of the Investment account by the individual components of the major conceptual elements *as of* the acquisition date and update it for the entries developed in requirement 1.
3. Prepare all consolidation entries as of 12/31/06 and 12/31/07.

E 6-5 **Testing Goodwill for Impairment** At a postacquisition impairment evaluation date, the following information exists for an *acquired* subsidiary that is a *reporting unit:*

	Book Value	Fair Value
Tangible net assets	$500,000	$520,000
Recognized intangible assets	200,000	250,000
Goodwill	290,000	
Unrecognized intangible assets (two internally developed patents)		100,000
	$990,000	

The reporting unit's estimated fair value (determined by discounting estimated future cash inflows) is $900,000.

Required

1. What is the *implied* fair value of goodwill?
2. What is the impairment loss to be recognized, if any?
3. Prepare the appropriate adjusting entry, if necessary. (Assume that the parent (a) had acquired *common stock* and (b) uses *non-push-down accounting.*)
4. If an impairment evaluation is performed one year later and goodwill's *implied* fair value is $300,000 at that date, what adjusting entry would be made?
5. Repeat requirements 1, 2, and 3, but assume that ***the reporting unit's fair value is $1,000,000.***

Exercises for *Partially Owned* Subsidiaries

E 6-6 **Calculating Consolidated Net Income** Pushco Inc. owns 75% of Shovex Inc.'s outstanding common stock. The 2006 net income from each company's own separate operations, exclusive of earnings and amortization recorded under the *equity method,* follows:

Pushco	$1,000,000
Shovex	600,000

During 2006, Pushco amortized from its Investment account $30,000 of cost in excess of book value.

Required

1. Determine the amount of consolidated net income accruing to the controlling interest.
2. Determine the amount of consolidated net income accruing to the noncontrolling interest.

E 6-7 **Calculating Consolidated Net Income** Potter Inc. owns 90% of Stane Inc.'s outstanding common stock and 80% of Steele Inc.'s outstanding common stock. The 2006 net income from each company's *own separate operations,* exclusive of earnings recorded under the *equity method* and amortization of cost over book value of net assets, follows:

Potter	$1,000,000
Stane	300,000
Steele	100,000

Amortization of cost over book value of net assets on a full-year basis is $27,000 and $8,000 for Stane and Steele, respectively.

Required

1. Calculate (a) the noncontrolling interest in each subsidiary's net income and (b) the controlling interest in the consolidated net income for 2006, assuming that the subsidiaries were owned during the *entire* year.
2. Calculate (a) the noncontrolling interest in each subsidiary's net income and (b) the controlling interest in the consolidated net income for 2006, assuming that Stane was acquired on 5/1/06 and Steele was acquired on 7/1/06. (Assume that earnings occurred evenly throughout the year.)

E 6-8 **Calculating Consolidated Net Income** On 1/1/06, Palmer Inc. acquired 75% of Snead Inc.'s outstanding common stock at an amount equal to 75% of Snead's net assets at carrying value. Each company's 2006 income statement, exclusive of earnings recorded under the *equity method,* follows:

	Palmer	Snead
Sales	$ 800,000	$ 200,000
Cost of sales	(400,000)	(100,000)
Expenses	(150,000)	(40,000)
Net Income	$ 250,000	$ 60,000

Balance sheet amounts for each company at 12/31/06 are purposely *not* furnished; therefore, a formal consolidation worksheet cannot be prepared. The consolidated amounts still can be determined, however, if you understand the main concept of the chapter.

Required

1. Determine the consolidated income statement amounts.
2. Determine the consolidated income statement amounts assuming that Palmer had excess cost and amortized from its Investment account (under the *equity method*) $3,000 of cost that pertains to intangible assets *other than* goodwill.

E 6-9 **Calculating Consolidated and Parent Company Amounts** On 4/30/06, Pal Inc. acquired 75% of Salle Inc.'s outstanding common stock for cash. Both companies have calendar year-ends. Data for each company pertaining to its *own separate operations* follow:

	Pal	Salle
Net Income:		
4 months ended 4/30/06	$350,000	$100,000
8 months ended 12/31/06	450,000[a]	200,000
	$800,000	$300,000
Dividends Declared:		
4 months ended 4/30/06	$140,000	$ 40,000
8 months ended 12/31/06	280,000	80,000
	$420,000	$120,000
Amortization of cost in excess of book value recorded by Pal for 2006	$ 24,000	

[a] Excludes any amounts relating to Salle.

Required

1. Determine the consolidated net income for 2006 that accrues to the controlling interest.
2. Determine the consolidated dividends declared for 2006.

3. Determine the investment income recorded in the parent's separate income statement for 2006 under the *equity method.*

E 6-10 **Separating Parent's Cost into Components** On 5/1/06, Pana Inc. acquired 60% of Sonic Inc.'s outstanding common stock at a cost of $219,000. Sonic's capital account balances at that date are as follows:

Common stock	$ 50,000
Additional paid-in capital	550,000
Accumulated deficit	(200,000)

Each of Sonic's assets and liabilities has a *current value* equal to its *book value*, except for the following items:

	Book Value	Current Value
Leasehold improvements	$ 95,000	$ 60,000
Deferred charges	40,000	-0-
Note receivable	75,000	85,000
12% bonds payable	100,000	120,000

Required Analyze the Investment account as of the acquisition date. Include the noncontrolling interest.

E 6-11 **Separating Parent's Cost into Components** On 1/1/06, Prima Inc. acquired 70% of Seconde Inc.'s outstanding common stock at a cost of $203,000. Seconde's capital account balances at 12/31/05 are as follows:

Common stock	$100,000
Additional paid-in capital	50,000
Retained earnings	60,000
	$210,000

Each of Seconde's assets and liabilities has a *current value* equal to its *book value*, except for the following items:

	Book Value	Current Value
Land	$170,000	$240,000
Goodwill	50,000	-0-
10% bonds payable	160,000	140,000

Required Analyze the Investment account as of the acquisition date. Include the noncontrolling interest.

E 6-12 **Determining Subsidiary's Equity from Consolidated Data** Popp Inc. acquired 70% of Soda Inc.'s outstanding common stock. Popp's separate balance sheet immediately *after the acquisition* and the consolidated balance sheet (under the *parent company concept*) follow:

	Popp	Consolidated
Current assets	$101,000	$163,000
Investment in Soda (cost)	105,000	—
Goodwill	—	7,000
Fixed assets (net)	270,000	370,000
Total Assets	$476,000	$540,000
Current liabilities	$ 15,000	$ 46,000
Noncontrolling interest	—	33,000
Capital stock	350,000	350,000
Retained earnings	111,000	111,000
Total Liabilities and Equity	$476,000	$540,000

Of the excess payment for the investment in Soda, $21,000 was attributed to undervaluation of its fixed assets; the balance was attributed to goodwill. Soda's no par Common Stock account had a $50,000 balance at the acquisition date.

Required

1. Calculate the total stockholders' equity of the subsidiary when it was acquired.
2. Prepare a conceptual analysis of the Investment account at the acquisition date.

Problems for *100%-Owned* Subsidiaries

P 6-1* 

Consolidation Worksheet (Continuation of Problem 5-4) Pya Inc., a calendar-year reporting company, acquired 100% of Sya Inc.'s outstanding common stock at a cost of $325,000 on 12/31/05. The analysis of the parent's Investment account as of the acquisition date follows:

		Remaining Life
Book value element:		
Common stock	$100,000	
Retained earnings	90,000	
Under- or (over)valuation of net assets element:		
Inventory	(5,000)	2 months
Land	30,000	Indefinite
Equipment	50,000	10 years
Covenant-not-to-compete	40,000	4 years
Goodwill element	20,000	
Cost	$325,000	

Each company's financial statements for the year ended 12/31/06 follow:

	Pya	Sya
Income Statement (2006)		
Sales	$ 950,000	$ 600,000
Cost of sales	(520,000)	(300,000)
Expenses	(370,000)	(240,000)
Equity in net income (of Sya)	50,000	
Dividend income		
Net Income	$ 110,000	$ 60,000
Balance Sheet (as of 12/31/06)		
Cash	$ 75,000	$ 25,000
Accounts receivable, net	95,000	60,000
Inventory	115,000	120,000
Investment in Sya	340,000	
Land	100,000	70,000
Buildings and equipment	250,000	224,000
Accumulated depreciation	(210,000)	(59,000)
Total Assets	$ 765,000	$ 440,000
Payables and accruals	$ 65,000	$ 75,000
Long-term debt	20,000	150,000
Common stock	300,000	100,000
Retained earnings	380,000	115,000
Total Liabilities and Equity	$ 765,000	$ 440,000
Dividends declared during 2006	$ 80,000	$ 35,000

Required

1. Update the analyses of the Investment account through 12/31/06.
2. Prepare all consolidation entries as of 12/31/06.
3. Prepare a consolidation worksheet at 12/31/06. (The parent's retained earnings as of 1/1/06 were $350,000.)

P 6-2* 

Consolidation Worksheet (Continuation of Problem 5-5) Poz Inc., a calendar-year reporting company, acquired 100% of Soz Inc.'s outstanding common stock at a cost of $210,000 on 12/31/05. The analysis of Poz's Investment account as of the acquisition date follows:

*The financial statement information presented for problems accompanied by asterisks is also provided on Model 6 (filename: MODEL06) at the **http://pahler.swlearning.com** website, allowing the problem to be worked on the computer.

		Remaining Life
Book value element:		
Common stock	$ 5,000	
Additional paid-in capital	95,000	
Retained earnings	160,000	
Under- or (over)valuation of net assets element:		
Inventory	(20,000)	6 months
Land	30,000	Indefinite
Building	(100,000)	20 years
Long-term debt	40,000	4 years
Cost	$ 210,000	

Each company's financial statements for the year ended 12/31/06 follow:

	Poz	Soz
Income Statement (2006)		
Sales	$ 910,000	$ 820,000
Cost of sales	(510,000)	(505,000)
Expenses	(310,000)	(245,000)
Equity in net income (of Soz)	85,000	
Net Income (Loss)	$ 175,000	$ 70,000
Balance Sheet (as of 12/31/06)		
Cash	$ 40,000	$ 20,000
Accounts receivable, net	115,000	80,000
Inventory	90,000	120,000
Investment in Soz	240,000	
Land	190,000	100,000
Buildings and equipment	500,000	305,000
Accumulated depreciation	(460,000)	(85,000)
Total Assets	$ 715,000	$ 540,000
Payables and accruals	$ 75,000	$ 25,000
Long-term debt	10,000	230,000
Common stock	20,000	5,000
Additional paid-in capital	380,000	95,000
Retained earnings	230,000	185,000
Total Liabilities and Equity	$ 715,000	$ 540,000
Dividends declared during 2006	$ 135,000	$ 45,000

Required

1. Update the analyses of the Investment account through 12/31/06.
2. Prepare all consolidation entries as of 12/31/06.
3. Prepare a consolidation worksheet at 12/31/06. (The parent's retained earnings as of 1/1/06 were $200,000.)

P 6-3* 

COMPREHENSIVE: Recording the Acquisition; Analyzing the Investment Account; Applying the Equity Method; Consolidation Worksheet On 1/1/06, Pina Inc. acquired 100% of Sina Inc.'s outstanding common stock by issuing 6,000 shares of $10 par value common stock (which was trading at $20 per share on that date). In addition, Pina incurred direct costs of $95,000 relating to the acquisition, $25,000 of which was for registering the shares issued with the SEC. (All these direct costs were charged to the Investment account.) The balances in the subsidiary's capital accounts as of the acquisition date follow:

Common stock	$100,000
Retained earnings	102,000
	$202,000

All of the subsidiary's assets and liabilities have a *current value* equal to their *book value*, except for the following:

	Book Value	Current Value	Remaining Life
Land held for development	$600,000	$710,000	Indefinite
Deferred charges	42,000	-0-	3 years
Long-term debt, 10%	200,000	230,000	6 years

Additional Information

1. Sina is a real estate development company that owns several parcels of land. None of the land owned was developed during 2006. One parcel acquired eight years ago was sold, however, in its undeveloped stage. This was the only sale for 2006.
2. Pina is privately owned, and it chose to use *non*-push-down accounting.
3. The only entry Pina made in its books relating to the subsidiary was at the acquisition date.
4. Sina's buildings and equipment were fully depreciated at the acquisition date.

Each company's financial statements for the year ended 12/31/06 follow:

	Pina	Sina
Income Statement (2006)		
Sales	$ 950,000	$ 330,000
Cost of sales	(520,000)	(200,000)
Expenses	(204,000)	(45,000)
Net Income	$ 226,000	$ 85,000
Balance Sheet (as of 12/31/06)		
Cash	$ 28,000	$ 22,000
Accounts receivable, net	70,000	
Notes receivable		50,000
Inventory	130,000	
Investment in Sina	215,000	
Land	88,000	
Buildings and equipment	700,000	5,000
Accumulated depreciation	(600,000)	(5,000)
Land held for development		400,000
Deferred charges		28,000
Total Assets	$ 631,000	$ 500,000
Payables and accruals	$ 26,000	$ 13,000
Dividends payable		35,000
Long-term debt		200,000
Common stock	10,000	100,000
Additional paid-in capital	155,000	
Retained earnings	440,000	152,000
Total Liabilities and Equity	$ 631,000	$ 500,000
Dividends declared during 2006	$ 100,000	$ 35,000

Required

1. Analyze the Investment account by the components of the major conceptual elements as of the acquisition date. Make any appropriate adjusting entries.
2. Update the analysis of the Investment account to reflect activity under the *equity method* through 12/31/06.
3. Prepare the consolidation entries as of 12/31/06.
4. Adjust Pina's financial statements as shown above to reflect the *equity method*, and then prepare a consolidation worksheet at 12/31/06.

P 6-4*

COMPREHENSIVE CHALLENGER: Converting to the Equity Method from the Cost Method Two Years After the Acquisition Date; Consolidation Worksheet Pali Inc. acquired all of Sali Inc.'s outstanding common stock for $820,000 cash on 1/1/05. Pali also incurred $47,000 of direct costs in connection with the acquisition. Selected information on Sali as of the acquisition date follows:

	Book Value	Current Value	Remaining Life
Inventory	$ 303,000	$ 310,000	4 months
Buildings and equipment	1,400,000[a]	1,490,000	15 years
Patent	20,000	60,000	5 years
Goodwill	60,000	-0-	Indefinite
10% bonds payable	1,200,000	1,000,000	10 years

[a] Net of $300,000 of accumulated depreciation.

Additional Information

1. Pali is privately owned and chose to use *non*-push-down accounting.
2. Pali has used the *cost method* since the acquisition date and has decided to change to the *equity method* to account for its investment in the subsidiary.

Each company's financial statements for the year ended 12/31/06 (two years after the acquisition date) follow:

	Pali	Sali
Income Statement (2006)		
Sales	$ 8,500,000	$ 980,000
Cost of sales	(4,500,000)	(530,000)
Expenses	(3,640,000)	(310,000)
Dividend income	50,000	
Net Income	$ 410,000	$ 140,000
Balance Sheet (as of 12/31/06)		
Cash	$ 458,000	$ 98,000
Accounts receivable, net	750,000	190,000
Inventory	820,000	380,000
Investment in Sali	867,000	
Land	760,000	240,000
Buildings and equipment	6,260,000	1,720,000
Accumulated depreciation	(2,465,000)	(480,000)
Patent	100,000	12,000
Goodwill		60,000
Total Assets	$ 7,550,000	$2,220,000
Payables and accruals	$ 1,600,000	$ 370,000
Long-term debt	3,000,000	1,200,000
Common stock	2,000,000	250,000
Retained earnings	950,000	400,000
Total Liabilities and Equity	$ 7,550,000	$2,220,000
Dividends declared during 2006	$ 100,000	$ 50,000
Dividends declared during 2005	80,000	40,000
Reported net income for 2005	200,000	90,000

Required

1. Analyze the Investment account by the components of the major conceptual elements as of the acquisition date.
2. Update the analysis of the Investment account to reflect activity under the *equity method* of accounting through 12/31/06 (a two-year period).
3. Prepare the journal entry(ies) to convert to the *equity method* from the *cost method*.
4. Prepare the consolidation entries as of 12/31/06.
5. Adjust the parent's financial statements to reflect the *equity method*, and then prepare a consolidation worksheet at 12/31/06.
6. Would the parent's outside auditors have to mention the change to the *equity method* in their audit report?

P 6-5* **COMPREHENSIVE: Recording the Acquisition and Selecting Relevant Data; Consolidation Worksheet** On 7/1/06, PBM Inc. acquired 100% of SOS Inc.'s outstanding common stock by is-

suing 6,000 shares of its $10 par value common stock (which was trading at $70 per share on that date). In addition, PBM incurred direct costs of $90,000 relating to the acquisition, $40,000 of which was to register the shares issued with the SEC. Selected relevant data follow:

	June 30, 2006		
	Book Value	Current Value	Remaining Life
SOS			
Inventory	$ 66,000	$ 70,000	3 months
Buildings and equipment	310,000[a]	382,000	12 years
Goodwill	20,000	-0-	5 years
Long-term debt	400,000	384,000	8 years
Common stock	200,000		
Retained earnings	138,000		
PBM			
Common stock	100,000		
Additional paid-in capital	500,000		
Retained earnings	800,000		

[a] Net of $140,000 accumulated depreciation.

Additional Information

1. Assume that any goodwill arising from the combination has a 10-year life from the acquisition date of 7/1/06.
2. The *non*-push-down basis of accounting was selected.
3. The *equity method* of accounting is to be used.
4. For 2006, SOS had the following earnings and dividends:

	Jan. 1– June 30, 2006	July 1– Dec. 31, 2006	Total
Sales	$ 400,000	$ 500,000	$ 900,000
Cost of sales	(220,000)	(260,000)	(480,000)
Expenses	(130,000)	(180,000)	(310,000)
Net Income	$ 50,000	$ 60,000	$ 110,000
Dividends declared and paid	$ 15,000	$ 20,000	$ 35,000

5. During 2006, PBM declared and paid $75,000 of dividends each quarter. Also, PBM reported a net income of $200,000 for the six months ended 6/30/06.

Required

1. Prepare the entry to record the business combination on 7/1/06.
2. Complete PBM's and SOS's financial statements that follow:

	PBM	SOS
Income Statement (2006)		
Sales	$ 2,600,000	
Cost of sales	(1,300,000)	
Expenses	(800,000)	
______________		
Net Income		
Statement of Retained Earnings		
Balances, beginning	$ 750,000	
+ Net Income		
– Dividends declared	(300,000)	
Balances, 12/31/06		

(continued)

	PBM	SOS
Balance Sheet (as of 12/31/06)		
Current assets	$ 700,000	$ 398,000
Land	943,000	202,000
Buildings and equipment	2,200,000	450,000
Accumulated depreciation	(330,000)	(170,000)
Investment in SOS		
Goodwill		20,000
______________		
Total Assets		$ 900,000
Payables and accruals	$ 433,000	$ 122,000
Long-term debt	1,600,000	400,000
PBM:		
Common stock		
Additional paid-in capital		
Retained earnings		
SOS:		
Common stock		200,000
Retained earnings		178,000
Total Liabilities and Equity		$ 900,000

3. Prepare an analysis of the Investment account updated through 12/31/06.
4. Prepare the consolidation entries at 12/31/06.
5. Prepare a consolidation worksheet at 12/31/06.

Problems for Partially Owned Subsidiaries

P 6-6*

Consolidation Worksheet as of the Acquisition Date On 12/31/05, Pya Inc., a calendar-year reporting company, acquired 80% of Sya Inc.'s outstanding common stock at a cost of $260,000. Selected information on Sya *as of* the acquisition date follows:

	Book Value	Current Value	Remaining Life
Inventory	$80,000	$ 75,000	2 months
Land	70,000	100,000	Indefinite
Equipment	40,000	90,000	10 years
Covenant-not-to-compete	-0-	40,000[a]	4 years

[a] This amount was assigned by Pya.

Each company's financial statements for the year ended 12/31/05, immediately after the acquisition date, follow:

	Pya	Sya
Income Statement (2005)		
Sales	$ 900,000	$ 500,000
Cost of sales	(500,000)	(250,000)
Expenses	(260,000)	(202,000)
Net Income	$ 140,000	$ 48,000
Balance Sheet (as of 12/31/05)		
Cash	$ 110,000	$ 20,000
Accounts receivable, net	75,000	70,000
Inventory	105,000	80,000
Investment in Sya	260,000	
Land	100,000	70,000
Buildings and equipment	250,000	204,000
Accumulated depreciation	(150,000)	(44,000)
Total Assets	$ 750,000	$ 400,000
Payables and accruals	$ 80,000	$ 60,000
Long-term debt	20,000	150,000
Common stock	300,000	100,000
Retained earnings	350,000	90,000
Total Liabilities and Equity	$ 750,000	$ 400,000
Dividends declared during 2005	$ 80,000	$ 10,000

Required

1. Prepare an analysis of the Investment account by the components of the major conceptual elements as of 12/31/05. (First separate the Investment account into the book value element and the excess cost elements.)
2. Prepare the consolidation entries required as of 12/31/05.
3. Prepare a consolidation worksheet at 12/31/05.
4. What amount of income does Pya report to its stockholders for the year 2005?

P 6-7* 

Consolidation Worksheet Subsequent to the Acquisition Date (Continuation of Problem 6-6) As described in Problem 6-6, Pya Inc. acquired 80% of Sya Inc. for $260,000 on 12/31/05. The financial statements as of 12/31/06, one year *after* the acquisition date, follow:

	Pya	Sya
Income Statement (2006)		
Sales	$ 950,000	$ 600,000
Cost of sales	(520,000)	(300,000)
Expenses	(370,000)	(240,000)
Equity in net income	40,000	
Net Income	$ 100,000	$ 60,000
Balance Sheet (as of 12/31/06)		
Cash	$ 133,000	$ 25,000
Accounts receivable, net	95,000	60,000
Inventory	115,000	120,000
Investment in Sya	272,000	
Land	100,000	70,000
Buildings and equipment	250,000	224,000
Accumulated depreciation	(210,000)	(59,000)
Total Assets	$ 755,000	$ 440,000
Payables and accruals	$ 65,000	$ 75,000
Long-term debt	20,000	150,000
Common stock	300,000	100,000
Retained earnings	370,000	115,000
Total Liabilities and Equity	$ 755,000	$ 440,000
Dividends declared during 2006	$ 80,000	$ 35,000

Required

1. Update the analysis of the Investment account through 12/31/06.
2. Prepare the consolidation entries at 12/31/06.
3. Prepare a consolidation worksheet at 12/31/06. (The parent's retained earnings at 12/31/05 were $350,000.)

P 6-8* 

Consolidation Worksheet as of the Acquisition Date Poz Inc., a calendar-year reporting company, acquired 80% of Soz Inc.'s outstanding common stock at a cost of $168,000 on 12/31/05. Selected information on Soz *as of* the acquisition date follows:

	Book Value	Current Value	Remaining Life
Inventory	$150,000	$130,000	6 months
Land	100,000	130,000	Indefinite
Building	410,000	310,000	20 years
Long-term debt	275,000	235,000	4 years

Each company's financial statements for the year ended 12/31/05, *immediately after* the acquisition date, follow:

	Poz	Soz
Income Statement (2005)		
Sales	$ 950,000	$ 800,000
Cost of sales	(500,000)	(600,000)
Expenses	(320,000)	(250,000)
Net Income (Loss)	$ 130,000	$ (50,000)

(continued)

	Poz	Soz
Balance Sheet (as of 12/31/05)		
Cash	$ 47,000	$ 10,000
Accounts receivable, net	65,000	40,000
Inventory	140,000	150,000
Investment in Soz	168,000	
Land	190,000	100,000
Buildings and equipment	500,000	305,000
Accumulated depreciation	(440,000)	(55,000)
Total Assets	$ 670,000	$ 550,000
Payables and accruals	$ 60,000	$ 15,000
Long-term debt	10,000	275,000
Common stock	20,000	5,000
Additional paid-in capital	380,000	95,000
Retained earnings	200,000	160,000
Total Liabilities and Equity	$ 670,000	$ 550,000
Dividends declared during 2005	$ 75,000	–0–

Required

1. Prepare an analysis of the Investment account by the components of the major conceptual elements as of 12/31/05. (First separate the Investment account into the *book value element* and the *excess cost elements*.)
2. Prepare the consolidation entries at 12/31/05.
3. Prepare a consolidation worksheet at 12/31/05.
4. What amount of income does the parent company report to its stockholders for 2005?

P 6-9* **Consolidation Worksheet Subsequent to the Acquisition Date (Continuation of Problem 6-8)** As described in Problem 6-8, Poz acquired 80% of Soz for $168,000 on 12/31/05. The financial statements as of 12/31/06, one year after the acquisition date, follow:

	Poz	Soz
Income Statement (2006)		
Sales	$ 910,000	$ 820,000
Cost of sales	(510,000)	(505,000)
Expenses	(310,000)	(245,000)
Equity in net income (of Soz)	68,000	
Net Income (Loss)	$ 158,000	$ 70,000
Balance Sheet (as of 12/31/06)		
Cash	$ 73,000	$ 20,000
Accounts receivable, net	115,000	80,000
Inventory	90,000	120,000
Investment in Soz	200,000	
Land	190,000	100,000
Buildings and equipment	500,000	305,000
Accumulated depreciation	(460,000)	(85,000)
Total Assets	$ 708,000	$ 540,000
Payables and accruals	$ 75,000	$ 25,000
Long-term debt	10,000	230,000
Common stock	20,000	5,000
Additional paid-in capital	380,000	95,000
Retained earnings	223,000	185,000
Total Liabilities and Equity	$ 708,000	$ 540,000
Dividends declared during 2006	$ 135,000	$ –0–

Required

1. Update the analysis of the Investment account through 12/31/06.
2. Prepare the consolidation entries at 12/31/06.
3. Prepare a consolidation worksheet at 12/31/06. (Poz's retained earnings at 12/31/05 were $200,000.)

P 6-10* **COMPREHENSIVE: Analyzing the Investment; Applying the Equity Method; Consolidation Worksheet** PDQ Inc. acquired 60% of SAS Inc.'s outstanding common stock for cash of $503,000

on 1/1/06. PDQ also incurred $25,000 of direct out-of-pocket costs in connection with the acquisition. Information with respect to SAS as of the acquisition date follows:

	Book Value	Current Value	Remaining Life
Cash	$ 74,000	$ 74,000	
Accounts receivable, net	266,000	266,000	
Inventory	280,000	260,000	6 months
Land	780,000	780,000	Indefinite
Buildings and equipment	900,000	675,000	15 years
Accumulated depreciation	(300,000)		
Patent	40,000	165,000	5 years
Goodwill	60,000		Indefinite
Total Assets	$2,100,000	$2,220,000	
Payables and accruals	$ 380,000	$ 380,000	
Long-term debt	1,200,000	1,040,000	4 years
Common stock	200,000	800,000	
Retained earnings	320,000		
Total Liabilities and Equity	$2,100,000	$2,220,000	

PDQ intends to use the *equity method* to account for its investment. The only entry it has made to the Investment account since the acquisition date, however, is to reflect the receipt of its share of $55,000 of dividends that SAS declared and paid during 2006.

Each company's financial statements for the year ended 12/31/06, one year *after* the acquisition date, follow:

	PDQ	SAS
Income Statement (2006)		
Sales	$ 9,000,000	$ 870,000
Cost of sales	(5,000,000)	(470,000)
Expenses	(2,800,000)	(190,000)
Net Income	$ 1,200,000	$ 210,000
Balance Sheet (as of 12/31/06)		
Cash	$ 665,000	$ 138,000
Accounts receivable, net	840,000	270,000
Inventory	1,200,000	560,000
Investment in SAS	495,000	
Land	1,000,000	780,000
Buildings and equipment	4,800,000	1,050,000
Accumulated depreciation	(1,700,000)	(390,000)
Patent	300,000	32,000
Goodwill		60,000
Total Assets	$ 7,600,000	$2,500,000
Payables and accruals	$ 1,100,000	$ 625,000
Long-term debt	2,600,000	1,200,000
Common stock	2,000,000	200,000
Retained earnings	1,900,000	475,000
Total Liabilities and Equity	$ 7,600,000	$2,500,000
Dividends declared during 2006	$ 900,000	$ 55,000

Required

1. Analyze the Investment account as of the acquisition date.
2. Update the analyses of the Investment account to reflect activity under the *equity method* through 12/31/06.
3. Adjust the parent's statements as of 12/31/06 to reflect the equity method of accounting.
4. Prepare the consolidation entries at 12/31/06.
5. Prepare a consolidation worksheet at 12/31/06.

P 6-11 REVIEW (Chapters 5 and 6): Analyzing the Investment; Applying the Equity Method; Computing Noncontrolling Interest and Consolidated Retained Earnings On 1/1/06, Puttnam Inc. made the following investments:

1. It acquired 75% of Shaft Inc.'s outstanding common stock for $14 cash per share. Shaft's stockholders' equity on 1/1/06 consisted of the following:

Common stock, $10 par value	$100,000
Retained earnings	20,000

2. It acquired 60% of Tee Inc.'s outstanding common stock for $40 cash per share. Tee's stockholders' equity on 1/1/06 consisted of the following:

Common stock, $20 par value	$60,000
Paid-in capital in excess of par value	10,000
Retained earnings	50,000

The current values of each subsidiary's net assets equal their book values except for a parcel of land Shaft owned that has a current value of $40,000 *less* than its book value. At the time of these acquisitions, Puttnam expected both companies to have superior earnings for the next 15 years. Puttnam has accounted for these investments using the *cost method*. An analysis of each company's retained earnings for 2006 follows:

	Puttnam	Shaft	Tee
Balances, 1/1/06	$ 300,000	$ 20,000	$ 50,000
+ Net income (loss)	193,000	36,000	(15,000)
– Cash dividends declared and paid	(110,000)	(28,000)	(10,000)
Balances, 12/31/06	$ 383,000	$ 28,000	$ 25,000

Required

1. Under the *equity method*, what entries should have been made on the parent's books during 2006 to record the following:
   a. Investments in subsidiaries.
   b. Parent's share of subsidiary income or loss.
   c. Subsidiary dividends received.
   d. Amortization of cost in excess of (under) book value, if any.
2. Compute the amount of the noncontrolling interest in each subsidiary's stockholders' equity at 12/31/06 using each's *book values*.
3. What were the earnings from *the parent's own operations* for 2006, excluding accounts relating to the parent's ownership in these subsidiaries?
4. What amount should be reported as consolidated retained earnings as of 12/31/06?

P 6-12* **COMPREHENSIVE: Recording the Acquisition; Selecting Relevant Data; Consolidation Worksheet** On 7/1/06, in a business combination that did *not* qualify as a pooling of interests, Pepsi Inc. acquired 80% of Sprite Inc.'s outstanding common stock by issuing 8,000 shares of its $5 par value common stock (which was trading at $65 per share on that date). In addition, Pepsi incurred *direct costs* of $92,000 relating to the acquisition, $60,000 of which was for registering the shares issued with the SEC. Selected relevant data follow:

	June 30, 2006		
	Book Value	Current Value	Remaining Life
Sprite			
Inventory	$110,000	$120,000	2 months
Buildings and equipment	700,000[a]	770,000	14 years
Patents	90,000	60,000	3 years
Long-term debt	500,000	475,000	1 year
Common stock	300,000		
Retained earnings	225,000		
Pepsi			
Common stock	$500,000		
Additional paid-in capital	500,000		
Retained earnings	367,000		

[a] Net of $200,000 of accumulated depreciation.

Additional Information

1. Assume that any goodwill arising from the combination has a three-year life.
2. The *equity method* of accounting is to be used.
3. For 2006, Sprite had the following earnings and dividends:

	Jan. 1– June 30, 2006	July 1– Dec. 31, 2006	Total
Sales	$ 600,000	$ 800,000	$1,400,000
Cost of sales	(320,000)	(430,000)	(750,000)
Expenses	(240,000)	(310,000)	(550,000)
Net Income	$ 40,000	$ 60,000	$ 100,000
Dividends declared	$ 25,000	$ 35,000[a]	$ 70,000
Dividends paid	25,000	-0-	25,000

[a] This dividend was paid 1/5/07.

4. During 2006, Pepsi declared and paid $80,000 of dividends each quarter. Also, Pepsi reported a net income of $200,000 for the six months ended 6/30/06.

Required

1. Prepare the entry to record the business combination on 7/1/06.
2. Complete Pepsi's and Sprite's financial statements that follow for consolidation purposes:

	Pepsi	Sprite
Income Statement (2006)		
Sales	$ 2,200,000	
Cost of sales	(1,100,000)	
Expenses	(600,000)	
Net Income		
Statement of Retained Earnings		
Balances, beginning		
+ Net income		
– Dividends declared		
Balances, 12/31/06		
Balance Sheet (as of 12/31/06)		
Current assets	$ 1,356,000	$ 475,000
Investment in Sprite		
Land	700,000	200,000
Buildings and equipment	3,000,000	900,000
Accumulated depreciation	(600,000)	(250,000)
Patents	-0-	75,000
________		
Total Assets		$1,400,000
Accounts payable	$ 913,000	$ 350,000
Long-term debt	2,100,000	500,000
________		
________		
________		
Common stock		300,000
Additional paid-in capital		
Retained earnings		250,000
Total Liabilities and Equity		$1,400,000

3. Prepare an analysis of the Investment account updated through 12/31/06.
4. Prepare the consolidation entries at 12/31/06.
5. Prepare a consolidation worksheet at 12/31/06.

P 6-13 Step Acquisition: Significant Influence; 90% Ownership Obtained Use the information in Problem 5-8 but assume that on 12/31/06 Pomco acquired only 50% of Somco's outstanding common stock for $180,000 (instead of 60% for $208,000), thus obtaining a 90% ownership interest (instead of a 100% ownership interest).

Required

1. Analyze the Investment account through the date control was achieved. Be sure to include the noncontrolling interest.
2. Prepare all consolidation entries at 12/31/06.

P 6-14 **Step Acquisition: Significant Influence; 75% Ownership Obtained; Mid-Year Acquisition—Postacquisition Period** On 1/1/06, Plazco Inc. acquired 30% of Slazco Inc.'s outstanding common stock at a cost of $380,000. At that time, Slazco's capital accounts were as follows:

Common stock	$ 600,000
Retained earnings	400,000
	$1,000,000

On 4/1/06, Plazco acquired 45% of Slazco's outstanding common stock at a cost of $501,000. Earnings and dividend information for Slazco for 2006 are as follows:

	First Quarter	Remaining Quarters	Full Year
Net income	$70,000	$240,000	$310,000
Dividends declared	50,000	140,000	190,000

Assume also that *none* of Slazco's assets or liabilities is over- or undervalued at either block acquisition date.

Required

1. Analyze the Investment account through the date control was achieved (4/1/06). Include the noncontrolling interest.
2. Prepare all consolidation entries at 4/1/06.
3. Update the Investment account analysis through 12/31/06.
4. Prepare all consolidation entries at 12/31/06.
5. If Plazco chose to consolidate Slazco's income statement for *all* of 2006—instead of only the nine-month period from 4/1/06 through 12/31/06—what *two* acceptable manners of presentation could it use?

THINKING CRITICALLY

Case

C 6-1 **Actual Practice Case: Subsequently Found Unrecorded Liability** On 6/30/06, Primex Inc. acquired 100% of Sumex Inc.'s outstanding common stock for consideration of $300 million. Of this purchase price, $50 million was assigned to undervalued assets and $70 million to goodwill. In September 2006, Primex discovered that Sumex's liabilities at the acquisition date were understated by $40 million.

Required

1. Does Primex have legal recourse to Sumex's previous owners? Why or why not?
2. How should the $40 million be accounted for if Primex does *not* have recourse to Sumex's previous owners?

Financial Analysis Problems

FAP 6-1 **Calculating Parent's Annual Return on Investment: 100% Ownership** On 1/1/06, Pynco Inc. acquired 100% of Synco Inc.'s outstanding common stock for $1,000,000 cash. For 2006, Synco reported net income of $150,000. On 12/31/06, Synco declared and paid a $100,000 cash dividend to Pynco. During 2006, Pynco (which uses the *equity method*) amortized $30,000 of cost in excess of *book value*.

Required

1. Calculate Pynco's annual return on investment (AROI) for 2006.
2. Calculate Pynco's AROI for 2006 assuming that the dividend was declared and paid on 1/3/06—not 12/31/06.

FAP 6-2 **Calculating Parent's Annual Return on Investment: 75% Ownership** Certain accounts of PBM Inc. and its 75%-owned subsidiary, SOS Inc. (acquired in a purchase business combination in 2005), for the year ended 12/31/06 follow:

	PBM	SOS
Sales	$ 900,000	$150,000
Costs and expenses	(500,000)	(70,000)
Net Income	$ 400,000	$ 80,000
Dividends Declared in 2006:		
Declared and paid on 1/2/06		$100,000
Declared and paid on 12/30/06		100,000
Investment in SOS Inc., balance at 1/1/06	$ 325,000	

PBM uses the *equity method* but has *not* made any entries on its books in 2006 pertaining to the subsidiary's 2006 earnings. SOS reported $20,000 of net income for each quarter of 2006. For 2006, amortization of cost in excess of book value has not yet been recorded in PBM's general ledger; the unrecorded amount is $10,000. Thus PBM is using *non*-push-down accounting.

Calculate the annual return on PBM's investment (AROI) in SOS for 2006.

FAP 6-3 **Evaluating the Profitability of the Parent's Investment** PTA Inc. acquired 80% of Scoole Inc.'s outstanding common stock on 1/1/04 for $400,000 cash. Selected financial information follows:

	PTA	Scoole	
Year	Amortization of Cost in Excess of Book Value	Reported Net Income (Loss)	Dividends Declared
2004	$20,000	$150,000	
2005	20,000	275,000	$125,000
2006	20,000	100,000	200,000
2007	10,000	(75,000)	–0–

Additional Information

1. The decision to acquire Scoole was based on cash flow projections, which showed an estimated internal rate of return of approximately 30%.
2. Of the $400,000 purchase price, $150,000 was assigned to goodwill having a 15-year life, $20,000 to land, and $30,000 to depreciable assets having a remaining life of three years. (Scoole had a book value of $250,000 on 1/1/04.) **Contrary to *FAS 142*, you are to assume that GAAP requires goodwill to be amortized.**
3. PTA chose to use (a) *non*-push-down accounting and (b) the *equity method*.
4. Scoole's reported net income or loss amounts occurred evenly throughout the year.
5. Scoole declared and paid its dividends on December 20 of each year.
6. In early 2007, Scoole's major competitor announced a startling patented improvement to its main product, placing Scoole at a major competitive disadvantage.
7. On 12/31/07, PTA (in light of its assessment that Scoole would be only marginally profitable in the future because of the competitor's improvement) sold its entire interest in Scoole for $288,640 cash. Just prior to this sale, the market price of Scoole's common stock was approximately 7% below the book value of Scoole's common stock.

8. PTA had net income of $500,000 in 2007 from its own separate operations, excluding any amounts relating to Scoole's operations.

Required

1. Prepare a T-account analysis of the Investment in Subsidiary account over the life of the investment.
2. Prepare PTA's entry to record the sale of Scoole.
3. What amounts should be reported in PTA's 2007 income statement relating to Scoole?
4. Calculate the annual return on PTA's investment (AROI) for each year.
5. Is it correct to use the *beginning-of-year* investment balance or the *average* investment balance for the year in the denominator in requirement 4? Why?
6. Repeat requirement 4 for 2005 under each of the following changed assumptions concerning the $125,000 of dividends declared in 2005:

Assumption	Date Declared and Paid
A	1/1/05
B	7/1/05

7. Calculate the internal rate of return (IRR) over the life of the investment. State your answer to the nearest whole percent, for example, 15%.
   Spreadsheet Integration: You may easily obtain this answer using the IRR function available in EXCEL. You merely need to set up a cash flow table and *then* program the IRR function.
8. Repeat requirement 7 under each of the following changed assumptions concerning the $125,000 of dividends declared in 2005:

Assumption	Date Declared	Date Paid
A	12/20/05	1/3/06
B	1/1/05	1/5/05
C	6/25/05	7/1/05

9. Prepare a T-account analysis of the Investment account by year over the life of the investment using (a) the dividend information provided and (b) the net income amounts assumed under the IRR method. (Use the percentage you calculated in requirement 7 to calculate each year's assumed net income.)
10. Compare the AROI calculations in requirement 4 with the IRR calculation in requirement 7. Which is best suited for evaluating the profitability on this investment? Why?
11. If Scoole had been sold on 1/3/08 (instead of 12/31/07), would PTA's AROI for 2007 be any different? Why or why not?

Appendix 6A

Partial Ownerships—Economic Unit Concept (EUC) Procedures

In this appendix, we illustrate the procedures under the "pure" form of the *economic unit concept*. Thus amounts *are* imputed to the NCI for goodwill that implicitly exists. Recall that (1) the FASB tentatively decided in 1996 (in deliberations subsequent to the issuance of its 1995 exposure draft on consolidation policy and procedures) to require this method exclusively (thus prohibiting the *parent company concept*) and (2) the FASB's *consolidation procedures* portion of its consolidations project is currently on hold—**thus the FASB may or may *not* address *consolidation procedures* in the near future.**

I. THE PURCHASE METHOD: ANALYZING COST

Separating the Parent's Cost into the Major Conceptual Elements

Knowing the factors that enter into how much the acquiring company is willing to pay in partial ownership situations, we separate the parent's cost into its major conceptual elements using the following procedures:

1. **The book value element.** Multiply the book value of the subsidiary's stockholders' equity by the parent's ownership percentage.
2. **The undervaluation of net assets element.** Multiply the total amount of the undervaluation of the subsidiary's net assets by the parent's ownership percentage.
3. **The goodwill element.** Add the amounts determined in procedures 1 and 2 to arrive at the parent's interest in the current value of the subsidiary's net assets. Subtract this total from the parent's cost to obtain goodwill (a residually determined amount).

Once these procedures are completed, we can include the noncontrolling interest in the conceptual analysis. In the illustrations in Chapter 5, we assumed that P Company acquired 100% of the outstanding common stock of S Company at a cost of $100,000, which was $40,000 in excess of the book value of the subsidiary's net assets. The $40,000 excess payment was identified as undervalued assets ($28,000) and goodwill ($12,000).

Assume instead that P Company purchased only 75% of the outstanding common stock for $75,000 (75% of $100,000). The separation of the parent's cost into its major conceptual elements and the inclusion of amounts for the noncontrolling interest are shown as follows:

Noncontrolling Interest (25%)	+	Parent's Cost	=	Book Value Element (100% of $60,000)	+	Underevaluation of Net Assets Element (100% of $28,000)	+	Goodwill Element (Residual)
		$75,000		$45,000 (75%)		$21,000 (75%)		$ 9,000
$25,000				15,000 (25%)		7,000 (25%)		3,000
$25,000		$75,000		$60,000		$28,000		$12,000

As was done in Chapter 5, once the cost of the parent's investment has been broken down in this manner, the future consolidation procedures can be simplified by splitting the parent's cost into the parent's share of the *book value element* and the parent's *excess cost elements*:

Investment in S Company:	
Book value element	$45,000
Excess cost elements ($21,000 + $9,000)	30,000

Separating the Undervaluation of Net Assets Element into Its Components

We separate the undervaluation of net assets element into its components by multiplying the appropriate ownership percentages by the amount that each asset is undervalued. In Illustration 5-4, the $28,000 undervaluation was attributed to Inventory, Land, and Equipment accounts. This $28,000 is separated into its components as follows:

Asset	Undervaluation	Parent's Interest in Undervaluation (75%)	Noncontrolling Interest in Undervaluation (25%)
Inventory	$ 4,000	$ 3,000	$1,000
Land	8,000	6,000	2,000
Building	16,000	12,000	4,000
	$28,000	$21,000	$7,000

As shown in Chapter 5, the individual components within each category will be tracked *outside* the general ledger in supporting schedules, which are used to prepare consolidation entries. For the preceding situation, the supporting schedules at the acquisition date are as follows:

				BOOK VALUE ELEMENT		
				Subsidiary's Equity Accounts		
Noncontrolling Interest (25%)	+	Parent's Investment Account—Book Value	=	Common Stock	+	Retained Earnings
$15,000		$45,000		$10,000		$50,000

				UNDERVALUATION OF NET ASSETS ELEMENT						
Noncontrolling Interest (25%)	+	Parent's Investment Account—Excess Cost	=	Inventory	+	Land	+	Equipment	+	GOODWILL ELEMENT
		$30,000		$3,000		$6,000		$12,000		$ 9,000
$10,000				1,000		2,000		4,000		3,000
$10,000		$30,000		$4,000		$8,000		$16,000		$12,000

The excess cost entry obtained with this procedure (which would be used only if *non-push-down* accounting were used) revalues the subsidiary's assets to 100% of their current values and reports Goodwill in the consolidated statements at the amount of goodwill implicit in the transaction.

CHECK POINT

Pantu Inc. acquired 60% of Santu Inc.'s outstanding common stock for $156,000 cash. The *book value* of Santu's net assets is $200,000. Santu's only over- or undervalued asset or liability is land that has a *book value* of $100,000 and a *current value* of $150,000. Under the *economic unit concept*, at what amounts are the land, the noncontrolling interest, and goodwill reported in the consolidated balance sheet?

	Land	Goodwill	Noncontrolling Interest
a.	$130,000	$6,000	$80,000
b.	$130,000	$10,000	$100,000
c.	$130,000	$44,000	$104,000

d.	$150,000	$6,000	$80,000
e.	$150,000	$10,000	$100,000
f.	$150,000	$44,000	$104,000
g.	$150,000	$6,000	$100,000
h.	$150,000	$6,000	$104,000
i.	$150,000	$10,000	$104,000

Answer: i

II. CONSOLIDATION WORKSHEET USING EUC: *AT DATE OF ACQUISITION*

For this example, the consolidation entries as of the acquisition date, taken from these supporting schedules to the parent's Investment account, are as follows:

1. The basic *elimination* entry:

WORKSHEET ENTRY ONLY

Common Stock	10,000	
Retained Earnings	50,000	
Investment in Subsidiary		45,000
NCI in Net Assets		15,000

2. The unamortized excess cost *reclassification* entry:

WORKSHEET ENTRY ONLY

Inventory	4,000	
Land	8,000	
Equipment	16,000	
Goodwill	12,000	
Investment in Subsidiary		30,000
NCI in Net Assets		10,000

3. The accumulated depreciation *elimination* entry:

WORKSHEET ENTRY ONLY

Accumulated Depreciation	56,000	
Equipment		56,000

Even though only 75% of the common stock was acquired, the entire $56,000 balance in the Accumulated Depreciation account at the acquisition date is eliminated because doing so is consistent with the *full revaluation method* used.

These consolidation entries are used in Illustration 6A-1 to prepare a consolidation worksheet as of January 1, 2006 (the acquisition date), for Parrco Company and Subbco Company.

ILLUSTRATION 6A-1 AT THE ACQUISITION DATE—75% OWNERSHIP (EUC)

Parrco Company and Subbco Company
Consolidation Worksheet as of December 31, 2006

	PARRCO COMPANY	75%-OWNED SUBBCO COMPANY	CONSOLIDATION ENTRIES DR.			CR.	CONSOLIDATED
Balance Sheet							
Cash	43,000	15,000					58,000
Accounts receivable	52,000	27,000					79,000
Inventory	90,000	42,000	4,000	2			136,000
Investment in S Company:							
Book value element	45,000				1	45,000	-0-
Excess cost elements	30,000				2	30,000	-0-
Land	220,000	32,000	8,000	2			260,000
Buildings and equipment	500,000	200,000	16,000	2	3	56,000	660,000
Accumulated depreciation	(280,000)	(56,000)	56,000	3			(280,000)
Goodwill			12,000	2			12,000
Total Assets	700,000	260,000	96,000			131,000	925,000
Liabilities	400,000	200,000					600,000
NCI in net assets					1	15,000	25,000
					2	10,000	
Parrco Company:							
Common stock ($1 par)	10,000						10,000
Add'l paid-in capital	190,000						190,000
Retained earnings	100,000						100,000
Subbco Company:							
Common stock (no par)		10,000	10,000	1			-0-
Retained earnings		50,000	50,000	1			-0-
Total Liabilities and Equity	700,000	260,000	60,000			25,000	925,000
Proof of debit and credit postings			156,000			156,000	

Explanation of entries:

1 The *basic elimination* entry.
2 The *unamortized excess cost reclassification* entry (for **BS**).
3 The *accumulated depreciation elimination* entry.

III. CONSOLIDATION WORKSHEETS USING EUC: *POSTACQUISITION PERIODS*

The Equity Method

Updating the Supporting Schedules to the Investment Account

Assume that Subbco Company had the following earnings and dividends for the two years subsequent to the acquisition date:

	2006	2007
Net income	$24,000	$32,000
Dividends	4,000	12,000

Also assume the following amortizations pertaining to the undervalued assets and goodwill:

	2006	2007
Excess cost amortizations—Parent	6,000	3,000
Excess cost amortizations—NCI	2,000	1,000

Under the *equity method*, Parrco makes the following *general ledger* entries (the amounts in the first two entries are at 75% of Subbco's reported amounts):

	2006		2007	
Investment in Subsidiary	18,000		24,000	
Equity in Net Income		18,000		24,000
To record equity in Subbco's earnings.				
Dividend Receivable	3,000		9,000	
Investment in Subsidiary		3,000		9,000
To record dividend from Subbco.				
Equity in Net Income (of Subbco)	6,000		3,000	
Investment in Subsidiary		6,000		3,000
To record amortization of excess cost.				

Illustrations 6A-2 and 6A-3 show the updated supporting schedules to the Investment account for the two years following the acquisition date, using the preceding information. These illustrations also show the related consolidation entries required at the end of 2006 and 2007.

ILLUSTRATION 6A-2 UPDATING THE BOOK VALUE ELEMENT OF THE INVESTMENT ACCOUNT—75%-OWNED

					BOOK VALUE ELEMENT		
					SUBSIDIARY'S EQUITY ACCOUNTS		
	NONCONTROLLING INTEREST (25%)	+	PARENT'S INVESTMENT ACCOUNT	=	COMMON STOCK	+	RETAINED EARNINGS
Balances, 1/1/06	$15,000		$45,000		$10,000		$50,000
+ Equity in net income:							
To parent (75%)			18,000				18,000
To NCI (25%)	6,000						6,000
– Dividends:							
To parent (75%)			(3,000)				(3,000)
To NCI (25%)	(1,000)						(1,000)
Balances, 12/31/06.	$20,000		$60,000		$10,000		$70,000
+ Equity in net income:							
To parent (75%)			24,000				24,000
To NCI (25%)	8,000						8,000
– Dividends:							
To parent (75%)			(9,000)				(9,000)
To NCI (25%)	(3,000)						(3,000)
Balances, 12/31/07.	$25,000		$75,000		$10,000		$90,000

The Basic *Elimination* Entry (using the amounts in the preceding analysis)

WORKSHEET ENTRY ONLY

	CONSOLIDATION DATE			
	DECEMBER 31, 2006		DECEMBER 31, 2007	
Common Stock	10,000		10,000	
Retained Earnings, 1/1/06 and 1/1/07	50,000		70,000	
Equity in Net Income	18,000		24,000	
NCI in Net Income	6,000		8,000	
Dividends Declared		4,000		12,000
Investment in Subsidiary		60,000		75,000
NCI in Net Assets		20,000		25,000

ILLUSTRATION 6A-3 UPDATING THE EXCESS COST ELEMENTS OF THE INVESTMENT ACCOUNT: 75%-OWNED SUBSIDIARY

	Noncontrolling Interest (25%)	+	Parent's Investment Account— Excess Cost	=	Undervaluation of Net Assets Element: Inventory	+	Land	+	Equipment: Cost	+	Equipment: Accum. Depr.	+	Goodwill Element
Remaining Life					**(3 mo.)**		**n/a**		**(4 yrs.)**				**n/a**
Balances, 1/1/06:													
Parent's amounts. . .			$30,000		$ 3,000		$6,000		$12,000				$ 9,000
NCI amounts	$10,000				1,000		2,000		4,000				3,000
Subtotal	$10,000		$30,000		$ 4,000		$8,000		$16,000				$12,000
Amortizations:													
Parent's share.			(6,000)		(3,000)						$(3,000)		
NCI share.	(2,000)[a]				(1,000)						(1,000)		
Balances, 12/31/06 . .	$ 8,000		$24,000		$ -0-		$8,000		$16,000		$(4,000)		$12,000
Amortizations													
Parent's share.			(3,000)								(3,000)		
NCI share.	(1,000)[a]										(1,000)		
Balances, 12/31/07 . .	$ 7,000		$21,000		$ -0-		$8,000		$16,000		$(8,000)		$12,000

[a] No general ledger entry concerning the amortization relating to the noncontrolling interest is ever made in the parent's books. A consolidation entry (following), however, is made to reflect this amortization in the consolidated income statement.

Consolidation Entries (using the amounts in the preceding analysis)

		Consolidation Date: December 31, 2006		December 31, 2007	
WORKSHEET ENTRY ONLY	**The *Unamortized* Excess Cost *Reclassification* Entry**				
	Land	8,000		8,000	
	Equipment	16,000		16,000	
	Goodwill.	12,000		12,000	
	Accumulated Depreciation.		4,000		8,000
	Investment in Subsidiary		24,000		21,000
	NCI in Net Assets		8,000		7,000
WORKSHEET ENTRY ONLY	**The *Amortized* Excess Cost *Reclassification* Entry**				
	Cost of Sales.	6,000		3,000	
	Equity in Net Income (of Subbco)		6,000		3,000
WORKSHEET ENTRY ONLY	**The NCI Additional Amortization Entry**				
	Cost of Sales.	2,000		1,000	
	NCI in Net Income.		2,000		1,000

Illustrations 6A-4 and 6A-5 show the related consolidation worksheets at the end of 2006 and 2007.

Review Points for Illustrations 6A-4 and 6A-5. Note the following:

1. The basic elimination entry was obtained from the updated analysis of the *book value element* as is usually done.
2. Entry (4) in Illustrations 6A-4 and 6A-5 is new and is necessary because of the additional values attributable to the noncontrolling interest. These entries have no effect on the *parent's net income* or the *consolidated net income* because the additional amounts reported for Cost of Sales ($2,000 for 2006 and $1,000 for 2007) are exactly offset by the lower amounts reported for the noncontrolling interest in Subbco's net income.

ILLUSTRATION 6A-4 THE *EQUITY* METHOD: *FIRST* YEAR SUBSEQUENT TO THE ACQUISITION DATE—75% OWNERSHIP

Parrco Company and Subbco Company
Consolidation Worksheet as of December 31, 2006

	PARRCO COMPANY	75%-OWNED SUBBCO COMPANY	CONSOLIDATION ENTRIES DR.			CONSOLIDATION ENTRIES CR.	CONSOLIDATED
Income Statement (2006)							
Sales	600,000	234,000					834,000
Cost of sales	(360,000)	(110,000)	6,000	3			(478,000)
			2,000	4			
Expenses	(190,000)	(100,000)					(290,000)
Equity in net income (of S Co.)	12,000[a]		18,000	1	3	6,000	-0-
Net Income	62,000	24,000	26,000			6,000	66,000
NCI in net income			6,000	1	4	2,000	(4,000)
CI in net income			32,000			8,000	62,000
Statement of Retained Earnings							
Balances, 1/1/06	100,000	50,000	50,000	1			100,000
+ Net income	62,000	24,000	32,000			8,000	62,000
– Dividends declared	(51,000)	(4,000)			1	4,000	(51,000)
Balances, 12/31/06	111,000	70,000	82,000			12,000	111,000
Balance Sheet							
Cash	49,000	16,000					65,000
Accounts receivable	75,000	37,000					112,000
Inventory	110,000	55,000					165,000
Investment in S Company:							
Book value element	60,000				1	60,000	-0-
Excess cost elements	24,000				2	24,000	-0-
Land	220,000	32,000	8,000	2			260,000
Buildings and equipment	500,000	200,000	16,000	2	5	56,000	660,000
Accumulated depreciation	(320,000)	(70,000)	56,000	5	2	4,000	(338,000)
Goodwill			12,000	2			12,000
Total Assets	718,000	270,000	92,000			144,000	936,000
Liabilities	407,000	190,000					597,000
NCI in net assets					1	20,000	28,000
					2	8,000	
Parrco Company:							
Common stock ($1 par)	10,000						10,000
Add'l paid-in capital	190,000						190,000
Retained earnings	111,000						111,000
Subbco Company:							
Common stock (no par)		10,000	10,000	1			-0-
Retained earnings		70,000	82,000			12,000	-0-
Total Liabilities and Equity	718,000	270,000	92,000			40,000	936,000
Proof of debit and credit postings			184,000			184,000	

[a] $18,000 share of S Company's reported net income, net of $6,000 of excess cost amortization = $12,000.

Explanation of entries:

1 The *basic elimination* entry.
2 The *unamortized* excess cost *reclassification* entry (for **BS**).
3 The *amortized* excess cost *reclassification* entry (for **IS**).
4 The NCI additional amortization entry.
5 The accumulated depreciation *elimination* entry.

ILLUSTRATION 6A-5 THE *EQUITY* METHOD: *SECOND* YEAR SUBSEQUENT TO THE ACQUISITION DATE—75% OWNERSHIP

Parrco Company and Subbco Company
Consolidation Worksheet as of December 31, 2007

	PARRCO COMPANY	75%-OWNED SUBBCO COMPANY	CONSOLIDATION ENTRIES DR.			CR.	CONSOLIDATED
Income Statement (2007)							
Sales	710,000	282,000					992,000
Cost of sales	(390,000)	(130,000)	3,000	3			(524,000)
			1,000	4			
Expenses	(210,000)	(120,000)					(330,000)
Equity in net income (of S Co.)	21,000[a]		24,000	1	3	3,000	-0-
Net Income	131,000	32,000	28,000			3,000	138,000
NCI in net income			8,000	1	4	1,000	(7,000)
CI in net income			36,000			4,000	131,000
Statement of Retained Earnings							
Balances, 1/1/07	111,000	70,000	70,000	1			111,000
+ Net income	131,000	32,000	36,000			4,000	131,000
– Dividends declared	(85,000)	(12,000)			1	12,000	(85,000)
Balances, 12/31/07	157,000	90,000	106,000			16,000	157,000
Balance Sheet							
Cash	47,000	31,000					78,000
Accounts receivable	84,000	51,000					135,000
Inventory	140,000	82,000					222,000
Investment in S Company:							
Book value element	75,000				1	75,000	-0-
Excess cost elements	21,000				2	21,000	-0-
Land	220,000	32,000	8,000	2			260,000
Buildings and equipment	500,000	200,000	16,000	2	5	56,000	660,000
Accumulated depreciation	(360,000)	(86,000)	56,000	5	2	8,000	(398,000)
Goodwill			12,000	2			12,000
Total Assets	727,000	310,000	92,000			160,000	969,000
Liabilities	370,000	210,000					580,000
NCI in net assets					1	25,000	32,000
					2	7,000	
Parrco Company:							
Common stock ($1 par)	10,000						10,000
Add'l paid-in capital	190,000						190,000
Retained earnings	157,000						157,000
Subbco Company:							
Common stock (no par)		10,000	10,000	1			-0-
Retained earnings		90,000	106,000			16,000	-0-
Total Liabilities and Equity	727,000	310,000	116,000			48,000	969,000
Proof of debit and credit postings			208,000			208,000	

[a] $24,000 share of S Company's reported net income, net of $3,000 of excess cost amortization = $21,000.

Explanation of entries:

1 The *basic elimination* entry.
2 The *unamortized* excess cost *reclassification* entry (for **BS**).
3 The *amortized* excess cost *reclassification* entry (for **IS**).
4 The NCI additional amortization entry.
5 The accumulated depreciation entry *elimination*.

3. Illustration 6A-4 shows that $4,000 of the consolidated net income accrues to the noncontrolling interest for 2006. The proof of this amount follows:

	2006
Subbco Company's reported net income (**old basis**)	$24,000
Less—Amortization of undervalued assets and goodwill	
Parrco Company's portion	(6,000)
Noncontrolling interest portion	(2,000)
Subbco Company's Adjusted Net Income (**new basis**)	$16,000
Noncontrolling interest ownership percentage	25%
Noncontrolling Interest in Net Income	$ 4,000

4. From *Parrco's* perspective—but *not* from that of the *noncontrolling interest shareholders*—**the amounts reported in Subbco's financial statements are wholly irrelevant amounts.** Under the *non*-push-down basis of accounting, such amounts do *not* reflect the *new basis of accounting* that occurs as a result of accounting for the acquisition as a *purchase* (as opposed to a *pooling of interest*). Accordingly, when Parrco records its 75% share of Subbco's reported net income, it has recorded income based on the *old basis of accounting*. By also recording amortization of cost in excess of book value, Parrco's investment income is adjusted from the *old basis of accounting* to the *new basis of accounting*.

EXERCISES FOR APPENDIX 6A

E 6A-1 **Comparison of the Parent Company Concept and the Economic Unit Concept for Treatment of Tangible Assets** On January 1, 2004, Placido Company acquired 60% of the outstanding common stock of Scotto Company for $2,400,000. All cost in excess of Placido's share of net assets at carrying value is entirely attributable to a parcel of land owned by Scotto. Scotto acquired this land many years ago for $50,000; its current value is $1,050,000. (The book value of Scotto's net assets is $3,000,000.)

Required

1. Under the parent company concept, at what amount would the land be reported in the consolidated balance sheet?
2. Under the economic unit concept, at what amount would the land be reported in the consolidated balance sheet?
3. Compare the results in requirement 1 with those in requirement 2. What is the effect on the stockholders' equity section and the noncontrolling interest in the subsidiary's net assets as reported in the consolidated balance sheet?

E 6A-2 **Comparison of the Parent Company Concept and the Economic Unit Concept for Treatment of Goodwill** Poem Company acquired 70% of the outstanding common stock of Sonnet Company on January 1, 2003, for $4,200,000. The cost in excess of its share of book value is entirely attributable to Sonnet's expected superior earnings ability. (The book value of Sonnet's net assets is $5,000,000.)

Required

1. Under the parent company concept, at what amount would goodwill be reported in the consolidated balance sheet?
2. Under the economic unit concept, at what amount would the goodwill be reported in the consolidated balance sheet?
3. Compare the results in requirement 1 with those in requirement 2. What is the effect on the stockholders' equity section and the noncontrolling interest in the net assets of the subsidiary as reported in the consolidated balance sheet?

E 6A-3 **Comparison of the Parent Company Concept and the Economic Unit Concept for Treatment of Tangible Assets and Goodwill** Pocahontas Company purchased 80% of the outstanding common stock of Smith Company for $6,400,000. All of Smith's assets and liabilities have book values equal to current values, except that land has a book value of $400,000 and a current value of $700,000. (The book value of Smith's net assets is $7,500,000.)

Required

1. Under the parent company concept, at what amount would the land and goodwill be reported in the consolidated balance sheet?
2. Under the economic unit concept, at what amount would the land and goodwill be reported in the consolidated balance sheet?
3. Compare the results in requirements 1 with those in requirement 2. What is the effect on the stockholders' equity section and the noncontrolling interest in the net assets of the subsidiary as reported in the consolidated balance sheet?

chapter

7

New Basis of Accounting

New opinions are always suspected, and usually opposed, without any reason but because they are not already common.
JOHN LOCKE, 1690

LEARNING OBJECTIVES

To Understand

- The different types of situations in which a new basis of accounting might be appropriate.
- The various factors that can arise when deciding whether a new basis of accounting is appropriate in stock purchase transactions.
- The way to reflect a new basis of accounting using the push-down basis of accounting.
- The historical development of leveraged buyouts, how they work, and the critical accounting issue.

TOPIC OUTLINE

I. Recognizing a New Basis of Accounting for Stock Purchase Transactions Resulting in the Purchase of a Majority Residual Interest
II. The Push-Down Basis of Accounting
III. Leveraged Buyouts

CHAPTER OVERVIEW

One phase of the FASB's current project on consolidations and related matters addresses the subject of when, if ever, an entity should recognize a "new basis of accounting (or accountability)." In other words, which transactions or other events should cause a change to be made in the basis of accounting of *all* or *most* of a company's assets and liabilities from *historical cost* to *current fair value*?[1]

The FASB's 1991 *Discussion Memorandum*, "New Basis Accounting," identified four general areas in which a new basis of accounting might be appropriate. Even though we deal with only one of these areas in this chapter, we now list all four areas so that you can appreciate the many areas in which new basis accounting is an issue:

1. **Stock purchase transactions involving a change in majority ownership.** For business combinations in which *common stock* is acquired, this is the *push-down accounting* issue discussed briefly in Chapter 5, which we discuss in detail in this chapter. This issue also applies to *leveraged buyouts*, which we also discuss in this chapter.
2. **Significant borrowing transactions not involving a change in majority ownership.** This is a situation in which a lender lends a company amounts that are far greater than the company's recorded *book values* justify. In other words, the *carrying values* of the company's assets and liabilities have lost their practical significance to financial statement users.
3. **Reorganizations in bankruptcy, quasi-reorganizations, unleveraged recapitalizations, and spin-offs of subsidiaries.** In Chapter 23, we discuss *reorganizations* in bankruptcy, when a company is given a fresh start in business. Similar to category 1, a change in majority ownership usually occurs in a bankruptcy reorganization because the creditors usually become the owners of the company as a result of being issued substantial quantities of common stock in exchange for forgiveness of debt granted.
4. **Formation of and sales of interests in corporate joint ventures.** The issue here is whether the assets and liabilities contributed to a joint venture should be valued using the *existing basis* or a *new basis* reflecting the negotiated values agreed to by the joint venturers.

I. Recognizing a New Basis of Accounting for Stock Purchase Transactions Resulting in the Purchase of a Majority Residual Interest

Many different kinds of stock purchase transactions resulting in the purchase of a majority residual interest in an entity can occur. The new basis of accounting issue can be raised in all of them. Some examples follow. For ease of reference, we refer to the target company as Entity T:

1. **Cash purchase of 100% of Entity T's outstanding common stock by a corporate entity.** This is the easiest area of all to address. To date, the FASB has tentatively decided to require a new basis of accounting when **another entity** purchases the voting stock for cash.[2] Accordingly, if Entity T (now a *subsidiary*) were to issue its *separate* financial statements to users other than its *parent* (such as lenders), the financial statements would be on the new basis of accounting.

[1] For convenience, the current accounting model is commonly described as the *historical cost* model, even though it uses ***ten* measurement bases** (historical cost, historical proceeds, current cost, fair value, net realizable value, net settlement value, face amount (for cash), the equity method, the lower of cost or market, and present (or discounted) value of future cash flows.

[2] *Financial Accounting Series,* Status Report No. 238, December 31, 1992, p. 3.

2. **Cash purchase of 51% of Entity T's outstanding common stock by a corporate entity.** This situation raises the question of **whether a 100% change in ownership** (or a high percentage) should be required to reflect a new basis of accounting in Entity T's financial statements furnished to users other than its *parent*. Without such a requirement, a new basis of accounting could be implemented only *partially*, such as to the extent of 51% of the difference between *book values* and *current values*.
3. **Purchase of 100% of Entity T's outstanding common stock by a corporate entity using nonmonetary consideration.** This situation raises the question of **whether the type of consideration** is a relevant factor in determining whether a new basis of accounting is appropriate.
4. **Cash purchase of 100% of Entity T's outstanding common stock by a single individual.** This situation raises the question of **whether the "corporate veil" can be pierced** to establish a new basis of accounting. If not, the single individual would first have to **create a legal entity to be used as a vehicle** for acquiring the common stock of Entity T. By doing so, this barrier to using a new basis of accounting would be removed. Entity T could subsequently be liquidated into the newly created legal entity, however, achieving the same result as if the new legal entity had never been created. Is form needed to create substance?[3]
5. **Cash purchase of 100% of Entity T's common stock by many individual stockholders in market trading activity.** This situation differs from the previous situation in that the trading activity **did not produce a majority owner** of Entity T. To date, the FASB has tentatively decided that a new basis of accounting should be prohibited in these situations.[4]

Many more situations are possible. We listed only some of the more common situations to give an idea of the various factors that can arise. In the discussion that follows concerning the push-down basis of accounting, we deal only with situations 1 and 2.

II. The Push-Down Basis of Accounting

Under the push-down basis of accounting, the subsidiary does the following as of the acquisition date:

1. Adjusts its assets and liabilities to their *current values* and records goodwill, if there is any. This makes its adjusted net assets equal the parent company's Investment in Subsidiary account.
2. Eliminates the balance(s) in its Accumulated Depreciation account(s). This recognizes that a new basis of accounting has been established for its fixed assets.
3. Closes its Retained Earnings account balance to Additional Paid-in Capital.
4. Uses this new basis of accounting in its separate financial statements. Retained earnings should be dated.

The Rationale for Using the Push-Down Basis of Accounting

The rationale for having the subsidiary adjust its assets and liabilities to their current values as of the acquisition date rests on an argument of *substance* over *form*. Advocates of push-down accounting contend that **the relevant factor is the acquisition itself, not the form of consummating the acquisition.** In their view, whether the parent company acquires assets or common stock is irrelevant. Recall that when assets are acquired, the individual assets and liabilities are revalued to their current values when they are recorded in the acquiring company's general ledger (or in the *division's* general ledger if *decentralized* accounting is used). Because the acquisition itself is the relevant factor, a new basis of accounting has been established for the assets and liabilities. Common

[3] Later we discuss leveraged buyouts. In those situations, the FASB's Emerging Issues Task Force required that a new legal entity be created to effect the acquisition so that a new basis of accounting could be implemented.

[4] *Financial Accounting Series*, Status Report No. 238, p. 3.

stock's being acquired, instead of assets, should *not* prevent this new basis of accounting from being reflected at the subsidiary level. Furthermore, in most cases **the parent controls the form of the ownership.** That is, **it has the legal power to *liquidate* the subsidiary into a *division*.** The fact that the parent chooses to maintain the acquired business as a separate legal entity should not have a bearing on whether a new cost basis should be established at the subsidiary level.

Check Point

The rationale for the *push-down* basis of accounting is

a. The parent effectively acquires assets instead of common stock.
b. The consolidated statements are the same whether assets or common stock is acquired.
c. The parent controls the form of the organization of the acquired business.
d. It is easier to account for assets on *one* set of books than on *two* sets of books.

Answer: c

The SEC Leads the Way

Push-down accounting did not gain significant acceptance or use until 1983 when the Securities and Exchange Commission (SEC) issued *Staff Accounting Bulletin No. 54*. **This bulletin requires push-down accounting in the *separate* financial statements of a subsidiary acquired in a purchase transaction.** (Exceptions to this policy are discussed later.)

The SEC was convinced about the soundness of its position and concerned by the potentially misleading results from the many subsidiaries that had recently issued common stock based on *historical cost-based* financial statements using *non*-push-down accounting. The result of this practice was that these subsidiaries did *not* report their true cost of doing business and thus overstated their earnings. The SEC concluded that the time for *substance* over *form* had come.

General Motors Tests the Waters

Perhaps to test the SEC's conviction, General Motors Corp. argued before the commission that it should *not* have to apply push-down accounting to its 1985 $5 billion acquisition of all of Hughes Aircraft Co. (in which there was $4 billion of *cost* in excess of *book value*). The SEC stood its ground.

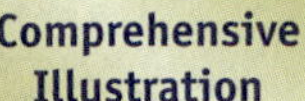

Most Commonly Encountered Situation

Acquisition of Common Stock Where

> Assets Are *Under*valued
> Goodwill Exists

To illustrate the entries that are made under the push-down basis of accounting and the elimination entry made in preparing consolidated statements as of the acquisition date, we use the same information from Chapter 5 to illustrate the non-push-down basis of accounting (page 152), in which the assets of the acquired business were *under*valued and the purchase price included an amount for goodwill (the most commonly encountered situation). Recall that Parrco Company acquired *all* of the outstanding common stock of Subbco Company on January 1, 2006, by paying $100,000 cash. For convenience, we repeat the rest of the assumed information used earlier:

1. Total cost. $100,000
2. *Current value* of net assets. 88,000
3. *Book value* of net assets 60,000
4. The *current values* of Subbco's assets and liabilities are assumed to equal their *book values*, except for the following assets:

	Book Value	Current Value	Undervaluation
Inventory	$ 42,000	$ 46,000	$ 4,000
Land	32,000	40,000	8,000
Buildings and equipment	144,000[a]	160,000	16,000
			$28,000

[a] Net of $56,000 accumulated depreciation.

5. Goodwill of $12,000 ($100,000 – $88,000) exists.

Additionally, Subbco's Retained Earnings balance at the acquisition date is $50,000. The *subsidiary* makes the following entries *as of the acquisition date.*

1. To *adjust* assets to their *current values* and record goodwill:

Inventory	4,000	
Land	8,000	
Equipment	16,000	
Goodwill	12,000	
Revaluation Capital		40,000

2. To *eliminate* the balance in the Accumulated Depreciation account:

Accumulated Depreciation	56,000	
Buildings and Equipment		56,000

3. To *eliminate* the balance in the Retained Earnings account:

Retained Earnings	50,000	
Additional Paid-in Capital		50,000

CHECK POINT

In applying the *push-down* basis of accounting, which of the following accounts is used when reflecting the increase in valuation of undervalued fixed assets?

a. Accumulated Depreciation.
b. Additional Paid-in Capital.
c. Retained Earnings.
d. Revaluation Capital.

Answer: d

Illustration 7-1 is a worksheet that shows the effect of these entries *at the acquisition date.*

Review Points for Illustration 7-1. Note the following:

1. The equity accounts of the subsidiary, which totaled $60,000 *before* adjustment to the new basis of accounting, now total $100,000, the amount that *equals* the *parent's* cost.
2. A conceptual analysis of the parent's Investment in Subsidiary account shows that only the *book value* element exists:

		BOOK VALUE ELEMENT						
Total Cost	=	Common Stock	+	Additional Paid-in Capital	+	Retained Earnings	+	Revaluation Capital
$100,000		$10,000		$50,000		$-0-		$40,000

ILLUSTRATION 7-1 WORKSHEET TO REFLECT THE PUSH-DOWN BASIS OF ACCOUNTING

Subbco Company
Worksheet as of January 1, 2006

	OLD BASIS	ADJUSTING ENTRIES DR.			CR.	NEW BASIS
Balance Sheet						
Cash	15,000					15,000
Accounts receivable	27,000					27,000
Inventory	42,000	4,000	1			46,000
Land	32,000	8,000	1			40,000
Buildings and equipment	200,000	16,000	1	2	56,000	160,000
Accumulated depreciation	(56,000)	56,000	2			-0-
Goodwill		12,000	1			12,000
	260,000	96,000			56,000	300,000
Liabilities	200,000					200,000
Common stock	10,000					10,000
Additional paid-in capital				3	50,000	50,000
Retained earnings	50,000	50,000	3			-0-
Revaluation capital				1	40,000	40,000
	260,000	50,000			90,000	300,000
Proof of debit and credit postings		*146,000*			*146,000*	

Explanation of entries:

1 To *adjust* assets to their current fair values and record goodwill paid for by the parent.
2 To *eliminate* the balance in the Accumulated Depreciation account.
3 To eliminate the balance in the Retained Earnings account.

Note: It is logical to expect these adjustments to be recorded in Subbco's *general ledger.* However, this is *not* absolutely necessary. Subbco has the alternative *not* to adjust its general ledger but to prepare a worksheet such as this one at each date that it prepares financial statements to issue to its external financial statement users other than its parent.

3. The consolidated amounts will be identical regardless of whether the push-down basis of accounting or the *non*-push-down basis of accounting is used.
4. The only difference between the push-down basis and the *non*-push-down basis is that the push-down basis accomplishes in the *subsidiary's general ledger* what the *non*-push-down basis accomplishes on the *consolidation worksheet.*
5. The push-down basis of accounting is the more logical method because it makes little sense to account for a given asset on *two* sets of books.
6. The push-down versus non-push-down accounting issue is a debate between *relevancy* and *historical cost.*

CHECK POINT

In applying the *push-down* basis of accounting, which of the following accounts is *not* brought to a zero balance?

a. Additional Paid-in Capital.
b. Retained Earnings.
c. Accumulated Depreciation.
d. Revaluation Capital.

Answers: a, d

Consolidation Worksheet at Date of Acquisition

Illustration 7-2 shows a consolidation worksheet at the date of acquisition—***after* the subsidiary has applied push-down accounting.**

ILLUSTRATION 7-2 CONSOLIDATION WORKSHEET AT DATE OF ACQUISITION *AFTER* THE SUBSIDIARY HAS APPLIED PUSH-DOWN ACCOUNTING

Parrco Company and Subbco Company
Consolidation Worksheet as of January 1, 2006

	PARRCO COMPANY	SUBBCO COMPANY	CONSOLIDATION ENTRIES DR.			CR.	CONSOLIDATED
Balance Sheet							
Cash	18,000	15,000					33,000
Accounts receivable, net	52,000	27,000					79,000
Inventory	90,000	46,000					136,000
Investment in subsidiary	100,000				1	100,000	-0-
Land	220,000	40,000					260,000
Buildings and equipment	500,000	160,000					660,000
Accumulated depreciation	(280,000)	-0-					(280,000)
Goodwill		12,000					12,000
Total Assets	700,000	300,000				100,000	900,000
Liabilities	400,000	200,000					600,000
Parrco Company							
Common stock ($1 par)	10,000						10,000
Add'l paid-in capital	190,000						190,000
Retained earnings	100,000						100,000
Subbco Company							
Common stock (no par)		10,000	10,000	1			-0-
Additional paid-in capital		50,000	50,000	1			-0-
Revaluation capital		40,000	40,000	1			-0-
Retained earnings		-0-					-0-
Total Liabilities and Equity	700,000	300,000	100,000				900,000
Proof of debit and credit postings			*100,000*			*100,000*	

Explanation of entry:

1 The basic *elimination* entry.

Review Points for Illustration 7-2. Note the following:

1. The consolidation effort is minimal relative to the effort involved for the comparable consolidation worksheet under *non*-push-down accounting shown in Illustration 5-5 (page 158).
2. The consolidation entry is identical to that for a *created* subsidiary (except for the added Revaluation Capital account).

Consolidation Worksheet Subsequent to Date of Acquisition

The minimal consolidation effort shown in Illustration 7-2 carries through to consolidations performed at all later dates. **Again, the entries are nearly identical to those for *created* subsidiaries.** For example, the consolidation entries at the end of 2006 are as follows (using assumed earnings and dividend amounts):

WORKSHEET ENTRY ONLY

	December 31, 2006 Equity Method		Cost Method	
1 The basic *elimination* entry:				
Common Stock	10,000		10,000	
Additional Paid-in Capital	50,000		50,000	
Revaluation Capital	40,000		40,000	
Equity in Net Income (of subsidiary)	33,000			
Retained Earnings, 1/1/06	-0-			
Dividends Declared		8,000		
Investment in Subsidiary		125,000		100,000

WORKSHEET ENTRY ONLY

	December 31, 2006			
	Equity Method		Cost Method	
2 The intercompany dividend *elimination* entry:				
Dividend Income (from subsidiary)			8,000	
Dividends Declared				8,000

Allowable Exceptions to Push-Down Accounting

Despite its hard line on the matter, the SEC does *not* require the use of push-down accounting when the parent does *not* control the "form of ownership" in its subsidiary. When a subsidiary has *preferred stock* outstanding, *public debt* outstanding, or a substantial noncontrolling interest (the parent owns *less than* 100% of the subsidiary's outstanding common stock), the parent is presumed to be unable to control the form of its ownership in the acquired business. In other words, it probably could not legally liquidate the subsidiary into a division if it desired. In such cases, *SEC Staff Accounting Bulletin No. 54* does *not* require the push-down basis of accounting to be used.

In the absence of *preferred stock* or *public debt* outstanding, the SEC staff uses the following guidelines to determine when a firm should use push-down accounting:

Parent's Ownership Percentage	Guidelines
90% or more	Substantially owned. Push-down accounting is required.
80–89%	Push-down accounting is encouraged but not required.
Below 80%	Push-down accounting may *not* be appropriate.

When a subsidiary is partially owned and push-down accounting is applied, it is done in the same manner illustrated earlier.

Pushing Down Certain Parent Company Debt

In *Staff Accounting Bulletin No. 73* (issued in 1987), the SEC staff imposed the pushing down of certain debt of the parent company (including related interest expense and debt issuance costs) to the separate financial statements of a subsidiary when the subsidiary's financial statements are included in a registration statement for (1) a public offering of its stock or debt under the Securities Act of 1933 or (2) trading under the Securities and Exchange Act of 1934. (For a discussion of these acts, see Chapter 18.) The parent company debt to be pushed down is that debt incurred in connection with or otherwise related to the acquisition of the common stock of a company in a *purchase transaction*. The debt should be "pushed down" to the *separate* financial statements of the *subsidiary* if (1) the *subsidiary* is to assume the debt of the *parent*, either presently or in a planned transaction in the future; (2) the proceeds of a debt or equity offering of the *subsidiary* will be used to retire all or a part of the parent's debt; or (3) the *subsidiary* guarantees or pledges its assets as collateral for the *parent's* debt.

III. LEVERAGED BUYOUTS

A **leveraged buyout** (LBO) is the acquisition of a target company's assets or common stock in which the acquirer uses an extremely high percentage of debt and thus a very low percentage of equity—typically 10%, but sometimes as low as 1% of the purchase price—to pay for the acquisition. The acquirer uses the target company's assets as collateral to secure the loans. Thus the target company's debt structure is refinanced simultaneously with the acquisition, **making an LBO nothing more than a combination of an acquisition and a refinancing.**

Historical Development

Pioneered in the 1960s, LBOs became immensely popular and widespread in the early 1980s when large conglomerates began their drive to divest marginal subsidiaries. Because of the recession and resultant depressed stock market from 1980 to 1982, numerous subsidiaries were purchased at bargain prices. As the technique grew in popularity, it also began to be used widely in acquiring *privately* and *publicly* owned companies.

In the early days of LBOs, the ideal LBO candidate was in a recession-resistant industry and had abundant hard assets. Currently, however, investors place substantial emphasis on projected cash flows.

Since 1981, more than 1,700 companies have gone private in LBO transactions (the approximate number of companies listed on the New York Stock Exchange), including RJR Nabisco in 1988, the tenth largest company in the country based on stock market valuation. The LBO phenomenon of the 1980s restructured companies, reshaped management's way of thinking, and challenged the status quo of the professionally managed public corporation. In 2000, there were 38 LBOs in the U.S. valued at $1 billion or less.

The Motivation Behind Leveraged Buyouts

The phenomenal surge in the use of LBOs resulted primarily from recognizing and eliminating the inherent conflicts of interest that exist between *stockholders* and *management* in *publicly* owned companies. In a *public* company, management typically must devote an enormous amount of time to managing the market price of its stock. Recall that if the price of the stock falls to a depressed level in relation to the value of the firm, the company can quickly become a takeover candidate. If the company becomes the object of a takeover attempt, management is forced to spend still less time running the business while it concentrates on fighting the takeover attempt. Accordingly, a short-term focus on quarterly profits takes hold. When given a choice between acting in the best interest of the business and doing what will look good to the public, management all too often chooses the latter. Underlying all of this is the natural conflict of interest between the *stockholders* (whose desire is wealth maximization) and *management* (who wish to keep their jobs). These divergent interests become more pronounced when managers have very little of their own personal wealth invested in the companies they run. A contributing factor is the corporate culture, which fosters incentives to build empires. Managements of mature companies that generate more than sufficient cash flow from operations are reluctant to distribute excess cash to stockholders. Instead, in far too many instances, they use cash to expand the company (often by diversification) beyond the size that maximizes shareholders' wealth. (The oil industry is the prime example of this; according to *Fortune* magazine, it made seven of the worst large acquisitions of the 1970s.) Thus managements go through the motions of acting as though their own money were at stake. Being accountable to a largely anonymous group of stockholders, management is accountable more in theory than in practice and ends up doing what it pleases with the corporation's assets.

The LBO's Solution: Aligning the Interests

In the typical LBO transaction, the buyer is a group of investors including management of the target company. In most cases, this investment group forms a corporation that acquires the target company's assets or common stock. Because management is included in the investment group, LBOs are sometimes referred to as *management buyouts*. Participating managers are required to invest a substantial portion of their own money, which results in their having as much as a 50% equity position. Thus these managers are given an enormous incentive to manage effectively. And because they answer to only a handful of co-owners—who want exactly what the managers want—nearly perfect alignment of interests is formed, which makes a tremendous difference that is hard to overstate.

LBO–Generated Debt as Disciplinarian

By saddling the acquired business with a mountain of debt, the investment group creates management's early fear of disaster, causing management to focus its attention and forcing it to be more aggressive in making tough decisions. In most cases, virtually all of the cash flow from operations is needed to service the debt. Consequently, a discipline is imposed on management that denies it the opportunity to overexpand the existing business or diversify into new businesses by acquiring other companies. With a rededicated management, the expectation is that (1) the business's operations will substantially improve, (2) the huge debt load will be paid down reasonably fast, and (3) the business (which may have been acquired at 4–10 times earnings) may be taken public in a few years at 20–30 times earnings or sold to another company.

Nevertheless, LBOs are often criticized on the grounds that (1) financial institutions make excessively risky loans to companies effecting takeovers and (2) the large cash flow required to service the debt may deprive a company of cash needed to stay competitive (such as that needed for research and development or reinvestment in fixed assets). Later we discuss some LBOs that encountered financial difficulty.

Other Changes That Affect Cash Flows

The annual direct costs of *public* ownership generally range between $100,000 and $900,000, depending on the size of the company (excluding management time). Taking the company *private* eliminates this cost. Because the purchase of the target company is a *taxable* transaction, the target company's assets are revalued to their current values (based on the purchase price). This allows greater depreciation charges for *tax-reporting* purposes. The combination of increased depreciation expense and increased interest expense often results in the target company *not* having to pay income taxes for several years.

Some Spectacular Results of LBOs

For most leveraged buyouts, the yearly returns on equity have been in the 50%–120% range. The most spectacular LBO success story of all is the $1 million equity investment made in 1981 in Gibson Greetings, Inc. (owners of the Garfield the Cat cartoon character). The investors, who were leveraged to the amount of $79 million, later sold their equity interest for $290 million, a phenomenal return on their investment.

Another extremely successful LBO occurred in 1981 when 21 franchisees of ***Krispy Kreme*** donuts staged a leveraged buyout from Beatrice Foods which had (1) acquired Krispy Kreme in 1976 and (2) made significant recipe changes to cut costs and improve profit margins (which resulted in declining revenues until the LBO). Since the LBO, Krispy Kreme has evolved into a doughnut-dispensing phenomenon that has become quite profitable (primarily because of resurrecting the original recipe). However, a few LBOs have gone into bankruptcy or troubled debt restructurings. LBOs leave little room for error, but the rewards for managements—if they are successful—are sensational.

Leveraged Buyout Transactions Are Not Business Combinations

Recall that business combinations occur only when two *existing* companies—**both of which have operations**—combine. In the typical LBO transaction, however, only the target company has an operating business. Accordingly, LBO transactions are *not* business combinations. Thus, FASB *Statement No. 141*, "Business Combinations," does *not* apply.

Forming a New Corporation to Effect the LBO Transaction

In most LBO transactions, however, the new ownership group forms a new corporation (which we call Newco for ease of reference) to acquire the outstanding common stock of the target company (which we call Oldco). Even though Newco's acquisition of Oldco's outstanding common shares is a stock acquisition as in a business combination, such acquisitions are still *not* the combining of **two existing operating businesses** to be accounted for under *FAS 141*. Nonetheless, the issue of whether or not a **buyout** has occurred—which is at the heart of accounting for business combinations—is also the key issue for LBOs. Only if a buyout has occurred can a new basis of accounting be established for Oldco's assets and liabilities. Of course, a buyout *cannot* occur without a change in control. Before discussing the buyout/change-in-control issue in more detail, the rationale for forming Newco to acquire Oldco's outstanding common stock is explained.

The Rationale for Forming Newco

After the LBO transaction is consummated, the two companies are usually merged; thus Oldco ceases its corporate existence. The reason for forming Newco to acquire Oldco's outstanding common stock pertains to the general practice of **not allowing personal transactions to pierce the corporate veil.** In other words, a new basis of accounting is *not* allowed on a corporation's books as a result of personal transactions between the corporation's stockholders. For example, the purchase of Oldco's outstanding common shares directly from Oldco's shareholders by an investor or by Oldco's management is a personal transaction. By forming Newco for the purpose of effecting the acquisition of Oldco's outstanding common shares, this objection is overcome. However, creating and using Newco solely for this purpose is mere *form* over *substance.* A more valid reason for forming Newco is that **it facilitates the process of effecting the transaction.** For example, if Oldco's management and the new outside investor each are to have a 50% ownership interest, this result usually can be more easily accomplished using a new entity rather than having each party buy a specific number of outstanding Oldco shares from the existing Oldco shareholders.

The Key Issue: Has a Change in Control Occurred?

Recall that for business combinations, we did *not* consider the transaction to be a business combination until a change in control of the target company's outstanding common shares had occurred. Then we dealt with how to apply the **purchase method** (which results in a *new basis* of accounting being established in the consolidated statements for the target company's assets and liabilities).

Accordingly, a change in control was necessary before the purchase method—and the resulting *new basis* of accounting—could be used. Likewise in LBOs, a change in control must occur before a *new basis* of accounting can be used.

Using a New Basis Partially and the Old Basis Partially

Recall further that *FAS 141* requires that business combinations *must* be recorded using the purchase method (establishing a *new basis* of accounting)—**regardless of the type of consideration given.** In contrast, however, LBO transactions can be recorded partially using the *new basis* of accounting and partially using the *old basis* of accounting. Compared with business combinations, this is substantively the equivalent of using a "part purchase/part *non*purchase method" (for example, using (1) the purchase method [change in basis occurs] for the ownership interest acquired using cash as consideration and (2) the nonpurchase method [no change in basis occurs] for the ownership interest acquired using the acquirer's common stock as consideration).[5] Later we explain the rationale and procedures for this manner of recording.

The Additional Complexity of Determining Whether a Change in Control Has Occurred in a Leveraged Buyout

Unlike most business combinations, in which determining whether a change in control has occurred is quite simple, determining whether an LBO transaction results in a change in control can be more involved, depending on the terms of the LBO. The additional complexity usually occurs when some or all of Oldco's shareholders become partial owners of Newco, whose ownership interest is usually called the **continuing ownership interest.** In such cases, it can be difficult sometimes to assess the extent of control that the new controlling shareholder group (collectively referred to as the **control group**) will have after the consummation—even if it has a majority voting interest in Newco at the consummation date. For example, dilutive or convertible securities issued to the continuing ownership interest could allow the former Oldco shareholders to regain control. Likewise, if the terms of nonvoting securities substantially limit the new voting shareholder group's

[5] Under the now superseded *Accounting Principles Board Opinion No. 16*, the "pooling of interests" method existed as well as the purchase method. Under the pooling of interests method, no change in basis occurred. Thus what we call "part purchase/part *non*purchase" used to be referred to as "part purchase/part pooling" before *APBO 16* was superseded by *FAS 141* in 2001.

ability to implement major operating and financial policies (such as acquiring and selling assets and refinancing debt), a change in control has *not* occurred.

The key point is that **the change in control must be genuine, substantive, and nontemporary.** Only if such a change in ownership has occurred can the new basis of accounting be used—either fully or partially. Accordingly, items **other than a change in the voting equity** must be evaluated. In the absence of these other factors, we now indicate the events that constitute a change in control of the voting equity.

What Constitutes a Change in Control of the Voting Equity?

The rules for leveraged buyouts are set forth in *Issue No. 88–16*, "Basis in Leveraged Buyout Transactions," issued by the FASB's Emerging Issues Task Force. (The role of the task force is discussed in more detail in Chapter 22.) *EITF 88-16* stipulates that any one of the following events constitutes a change in control of the voting equity:

1. **New investors.** A single investor (or a group of investors) having no equity interest in Oldco obtains unilateral control of more than 50% of Newco's voting equity. For instance, an independent investor having no equity interest in Oldco obtains a 51% voting interest in Newco.
2. **Oldco's management.** A single member of Oldco's management (or management as a group) having no control of Oldco obtains unilateral control of *more than* 50% of Newco's voting equity. For example, management owning 5% of Oldco obtains a 51% voting interest in Newco.
3. **Certain Oldco nonmanagement shareholders.** A single nonmanagement shareholder of Oldco having no control of Oldco obtains unilateral control of *more than* 50% of Newco's voting equity interest. For example, an Oldco nonmanagement shareholder owning 10% of Oldco obtains a 51% equity ownership in Newco.
4. **Combinations of 1, 2, and 3.** Combinations of the three preceding events also constitute a change in the voting equity interest. For example, a new investor having no control over Oldco could obtain a 40% voting interest in Newco, and Oldco management, having *no* control over Oldco, could *increase* its ownership interest from 5% in Oldco to 40% in Newco. The *new investor* and *management* **together** now have control.

In Illustration 7-3, we present a graphic depiction of two hypothetical LBO changes in control and the resulting "control group" for each situation.

ILLUSTRATION 7-3 DEPICTION OF CHANGES OF CONTROL AND THE RESULTING CONTROL GROUP

SITUATION 1

Owners	Nonmanagement *Not* Continuing	+	Nonmanagement Continuing	+	Management	+	New Investors	=	Total
Before the LBO.	0%		90%		10%		n/a		100%
After the LBO.	0%		45%		10%		45%		100%
Control group's ownership percentage.					55% (Management + New Investors)				

SITUATION 2

Owners	Nonmanagement *Not* Continuing	+	Nonmanagement Continuing	+	Management	+	New Investors	=	Total
Before the LBO.	70%		20%		10%		n/a		100%
After the LBO.	0%		25%		30%		45%		100%
Control group's ownership percentage					100% (Continuing + Management + New Investors)				

What If No Change in Control Occurs?

If no genuine, substantive, and nontemporary change in control occurs, the cash given to Oldco's shareholders that exceeds the book value of Oldco's equity is accounted for as a charge to Newco's equity—a **recapitalization**—rather than a transaction that qualifies for a new basis of accounting. In such cases, Newco usually has a *negative* stockholders' equity at the consummation date and for many years thereafter. This often is considered undesirable for reporting to lenders.

Using a New Basis of Accounting Prevents Reporting Negative Stockholders' Equity

In LBOs, the new owners usually desire to have the assets of the acquired business revalued *upward* to reflect the new higher basis of accounting. Using the new basis of accounting usually prevents reporting a *negative* stockholders' equity at the consummation date. Accordingly, **structuring the transaction to achieve the new basis of accounting to the maximum extent possible is usually of major importance.**

Accounting for a Change in Control

We now discuss how to account for a change in control, first for the simplest situation, in which *none* of Oldco's shareholders become owners of Newco, and then for the more involved situations, in which they *do* become its owners.

No Continuing Ownership Situations

When *none* of Oldco's shareholders (including management shareholders) continue as owners of Newco, the assets and liabilities of Oldco are adjusted to their current values based on the value of the consideration given (usually cash) to the Oldco shareholders. Thus the new basis of accounting is used entirely. The procedures to assign the investment cost to the individual assets and liabilities parallel the procedures discussed in Chapter 5 for purchase accounting for business combinations. Note that if Oldco had been a *publicly* owned company, it has now become a *privately* owned company (owned 100% by Newco).

Continuing Ownership Situations

When *some* of Oldco's shareholders (some of which may be management) become owners of Newco, the issue is determining Newco's cost basis of the Oldco shares acquired in exchange for Newco shares. The amount assigned impacts whether Oldco's assets and liabilities are valued *fully* at the new basis of accounting or only *partially* at the new basis of accounting. When the basis of the Oldco common stock (the book value of these shares) is assigned as the cost of the Oldco shares acquired in exchange for the Newco shares, it is said that there is **carryover of predecessor basis.** This results in Oldco's assets and liabilities being partially valued on the *new basis* of accounting and partially on the *old basis* of accounting. On the other hand, if the amount assigned to the cost of the Oldco shares acquired in exchange for Newco shares is based on the value of the Newco shares issued (as determined by referring to the cash consideration given to acquire the remaining shares of Oldco), the *new basis* of accounting is used in its entirety.

Continuing ownership situations are best discussed as to whether the continuing ownership percentage **increases** or **decreases**, inasmuch as the *EITF 88-16* rules differ for each situation.

The Bulls and the Bears

In practice, Oldco shareholders whose continuing ownership percentage **increases** are called **bulls.** Thus these individuals are **buying out some or all of the remaining ownership interest.** Oldco shareholders whose continuing ownership percentage **decreases** are called **bears.** Thus these individuals are **selling out to a large extent** but still maintain a small ownership in the business. For both bears and bulls, the issue is whether Newco should (1) maintain book value for the ownership interest they keep or (2) use a new basis of accounting.

The Continuing Ownership Percentage *Increases*

This result usually occurs only for Oldco's management that owns a *low* percentage of Oldco common stock. For example, Oldco's management owning 10% of Oldco's common stock could become a 50% owner in Newco.

Comprehensive Illustration

The Continuing Ownership Percentage Increases

Assume the following information:

1. Management having 10% ownership in Oldco exchanges these shares for a 50% ownership interest in Newco.
2. A new investor makes a $100,000 cash investment in Newco in exchange for a 50% ownership interest in Newco.
3. Management's basis in Oldco is assumed to be equal to its 10% share of Oldco's book value of $500,000.
4. Oldco's net assets have a *current value* of $800,000.
5. Newco borrowed $800,000 from a financial institution, a loan that is secured by Oldco's assets.
6. Newco paid $900,000 cash to the nonmanagement shareholders of Oldco, who own 90% of Oldco.

The amount by which Oldco's net assets can be revalued *upward* to reflect a new basis of accounting is $270,000, as calculated in Illustration 7-4. As a practical matter, *EITF 88-16* does *not* allow carryover of predecessor basis treatment if the continuing ownership percentage in Newco does *not* exceed 5%—this results in only the use of the new basis of accounting.

To illustrate how the amounts in Illustration 7-4 are used in presenting a consolidated balance sheet at the buyout date, assume the following information:

1. Both Oldco and Newco have *no par* common stock.
2. Oldco has the following equity account balances at the buyout date:

Common stock	$ 75,000
Retained earnings	425,000
Total Stockholders' Equity	$500,000

3. For simplicity, the entire $300,000 *under*valuation of Oldco's net assets is attributable solely to land.

ILLUSTRATION 7-4 LEVERAGED BUYOUT: THE CONTINUING OWNERSHIP PERCENTAGE *INCREASES*

Percent of Oldco Acquired	Cost	=	Book Value Element	+	Undervaluation of Net Assets Element	+	Goodwill Element
90%	$900,000		$450,000		$270,000[a]		$180,000
10%	50,000[b]		50,000				
100%	$950,000		$500,000		$270,000		$180,000

[a] 90% of $300,000 of undervaluation equals $270,000.

[b] 10% of Oldco's $500,000 book value equals $50,000. This is the "carryover of predecessor basis."

Note: The alternative to using the *old basis* for the 10% interest acquired by Newco is to impute a value for the shares issued to management in exchange for their 10% interest in Oldco. The imputed amount is $100,000 using the following logic: If cash of $900,000 is paid to acquire 90% of the Oldco shares, cash of $1,000,000 is needed to acquire 100% of the Oldco shares. Accordingly, $100,000 must be the value of the Newco shares issued to acquire the 10% interest in Oldco.

A consolidation worksheet at the buyout date is shown in Illustration 7-5.

Review Points for Illustration 7-5. Note the following:

1. The amount of consolidated retained earnings is zero. Thus the clock has been reset to zero for retained earnings. This holds true even if Oldco is dissolved and merged into Newco.
2. The land has been revalued upward only 90% of its total undervaluation of $300,000.
3. Goodwill is reported only to the extent that it has been bought and paid for. No amounts are imputed for goodwill for the continuing ownership percentage.
4. If the new basis of accounting were used *entirely*, an additional $50,000 is assigned to the cost of acquiring the 10% ownership interest in Oldco ($100,000 instead of $50,000). Consequently, an additional $30,000 is reported for land (10% of $300,000 of undervaluation)—an *imputed* amount. Also an additional $20,000 is reported for goodwill—an *imputed* amount.

Continuing Ownership Situations—The Continuing Ownership Percentage *Decreases*

In many LBOs, Oldco's existing nonmanagement owners do not sell their entire interest in Oldco for cash (as was assumed in Illustration 7-4). Instead, they receive as consideration both cash and Newco common stock. For example, a sole owner of Oldco could receive $1,600,000 cash and a 20% equity interest in Newco in exchange for 100% of Oldco's outstanding common stock. In such situations, logic dictates that the same approach shown in Illustration 7-4 be used. Using such

ILLUSTRATION 7-5 CONSOLIDATION WORKSHEET AT DATE OF BUYOUT: THE CONTINUING OWNERSHIP PERCENTAGE *INCREASES*

Newco and Subsidiary (Oldco)
Consolidation Worksheet (Balance Sheet Only) at Date of Buyout

	NEWCO	OLDCO	CONSOLIDATION ENTRIES DR.			CR.	CONSOLIDATED
Balance Sheet							
Cash		90,000					90,000
Accounts receivable		310,000					310,000
Inventory		470,000					470,000
Investment in Oldco:							
Book value element	500,000				1	500,000	-0-
Excess cost element	450,000				2	450,000	-0-
Land		120,000	270,000	2			390,000
Buildings and equipment		980,000			3	330,000	650,000
Accumulated depreciation		(330,000)	330,000	3			-0-
Goodwill			180,000	2			180,000
	950,000	1,640,000	780,000			1,280,000	2,090,000
Payables and accruals		440,000					440,000
Long-term debt	800,000	700,000					1,500,000
Newco:							
Common stock, no par	150,000						150,000
Retained earnings	-0-						-0-
Oldco:							
Common stock, no par		75,000	75,000	1			-0-
Retained earnings		425,000	425,000	1			-0-
	950,000	1,640,000	500,000				2,090,000
Proof of debit and credit postings			1,280,000			1,280,000	

Explanation of entries:

1 The basic *elimination* entry.
2 The excess cost *reclassification* entry.
3 The accumulated depreciation *elimination* entry.

an approach results in revaluing Oldco's net assets to the extent that they would be revalued if Newco had merely acquired 80% of Oldco's outstanding common stock for cash (leaving a 20% noncontrolling interest). This is the general approach of *EITF 88-16*.

As a practical matter, however, *EITF 88-16* does *not* require carryover of the predecessor basis if the nonmanagement Oldco shareholders' continuing ownership interest in Newco is *below 20%* and certain similar tests (a 20% capital-at-risk test and a 20% residual-interest test), which are complex and beyond the scope of this chapter, are satisfied. Accordingly, the *new basis* of accounting is used in its *entirety* even though a 100% cash buyout has *not* occurred. The rationale here is that with such a low level of continuing ownership/investment, the former owners would *not* have any control and possibly *not* any significant influence. Therefore, it is best to account for the entire transaction using a single basis of accounting.

CHECK POINTS

In a *leveraged buyout* transaction in which the continuing ownership by the nonmanagement shareholders of Oldco in Newco decreases from 100% to 30%, what is the rationale for carrying forward the predecessor basis of accounting for the 30% interest?

a. A change of control has not occurred.
b. A buyout has *not* occurred.
c. The continuing ownership interest is not part of management.
d. Control by the 70% group is likely to be temporary.
e. None of the above.

Answer: e

Oldco has 10,000 common shares outstanding and total stockholders' equity of $500,000. Joe and Betty Munee, who founded Oldco six years ago with a cash investment of $50,000, own all shares. The Munees surrendered all 10,000 shares in exchange for $420,000 cash and 30,000 shares of Newco common stock. Newco was formed by a new investor to acquire the Oldco common stock outstanding. The new investor invested $100,000 in Newco in exchange for 70,000 shares of Newco common stock. What amount should be assigned to the Investment in Oldco account on Newco's books for the 10,000 shares of Oldco common stock acquired?

a. $420,000
b. $500,000
c. $570,000
d. $600,000

Answer: c ($420,000 + $150,000)

END-OF-CHAPTER REVIEW

Summary of Key Points

1. The **new basis of accounting** issue is only one of five phases of the FASB's project on **consolidations and related matters.**
2. The **new basis of accounting** issue arises in four general areas, one of which is **stock purchase transactions involving a change in ownership.**
3. In applying the **push-down basis of accounting,** the subsidiary adjusts the general ledger carrying values of its assets and liabilities to their **current values.** This is required only for reporting to financial statement users other than the parent.
4. In applying the **push-down basis of accounting,** the subsidiary's Retained Earnings account is brought to a zero balance.

5. After applying the **push-down basis of accounting,** the net assets of a 100% owned subsidiary, as adjusted, equal the balance in the parent's Investment in Subsidiary account.

6. A **leveraged buyout** is a combination of an **acquisition** and a **refinancing.**

7. The primary attraction of a **leveraged buyout** is the **alignment of interest** of *management* and *owners.*

8. To establish a **new basis of accounting** for the target company's assets and liabilities in a leveraged buyout, there must be (1) a **genuine, substantive, and non-temporary change in ownership** and (2) a **buyout** (cash or debt securities given as consideration).

9. In an LBO, that portion of the ownership interest in the target company that is acquired **in exchange for common stock** of the new company formed to acquire the common stock of the target company is valued at the basis (usually the *book value*) of the shares **surrendered.**

10. **Carryover of predecessor basis** is *not* required if the continuing ownership interest is (1) *below 5%* for **bulls** and (2) *less than 20%* for **bears** (providing two additional tests are satisfied).

Glossary of New Terms

Bears Shareholders of the target company of a leveraged buyout whose continuing ownership has *decreased* (the group being mostly bought out).

Bulls Shareholders of the target company of a leveraged buyout whose continuing ownership has *increased* (usually the case for the target company's management).

Carryover of predecessor basis In leveraged buyouts, the use of the basis of accounting that exists for the target company's common stock in valuing any common stock issued to the target company's shareholders in exchange for *some* of their common stock holdings.

Continuing ownership interest In leveraged buyouts, that portion of the target company's ownership that is *not* bought out for cash (or debt securities) but is exchanged for common stock of the acquiring company.

Control group A group of shareholders who have obtained control over an entity (can include *prior owners* who did *not* previously have control).

Assignment Material

Review Questions

1. What are the four general areas to which a new basis of accounting could be applied?

2. What does the *push-down basis of accounting* mean?

3. What is the rationale for using the push-down basis of accounting?

4. Which new account is created in implementing the push-down basis of accounting when the target company's assets are *under*valued?

5. Which general ledger accounts are brought to a zero balance in implementing the push-down basis of accounting?

6. To which entities does *Staff Accounting Bulletin No. 54* apply?

7. What are the two major differences between a purchase business combination and a leveraged buyout?

8. In leveraged buyouts, what two things occur *simultaneously*?

9. How do leveraged buyouts solve the conflict of interest that exists between stockholders and management?

10. Are leveraged buyouts business combinations? Why or why not?

11. What is the difference between a change in control and a buyout?
12. What reasons exist for forming a *new* corporation to effect a leveraged buyout?
13. Even though *more than* 50% of a target company's common stock may be acquired in an LBO, what additional factors must be considered to determine whether a change in control is genuine, substantive, and nontemporary?
14. What are four ways in which a *change of control* could occur in a leveraged buyout?
15. How is a leveraged buyout transaction accounted for if *no* change in control occurs?
16. In an LBO, when can the new basis of accounting be used in its entirety even though a 100% cash buyout has not occurred?

Exercises

E 7-1 **Push-Down Applied to Exercise 5-8** Use the information provided in Exercise 5-8 (pages 172–173).

Required

1. Prepare the entries the subsidiary makes under the push-down basis of accounting.
2. Prepare the basic elimination entry as of the acquisition date.

Problems

P 7-1 to P 7-6* **Push-Down Applied to Problems 5-1 to 5-6: At the Acquisition Date** Use the following requirements to implement push-down accounting for Problems 5-1 to 5-6 (pages 173–177).

Required under Push-down Accounting

1. Prepare the general ledger entries the subsidiary makes under the push-down basis of accounting.
2. Prepare the basic elimination entry as of the acquisition date.
3. For Problems 5-4, 5-5, and 5-6, also prepare a consolidation worksheet *after* having applied push-down accounting.

P 7-7* **Push-Down Applied to Problem 6-1: One Year *After* the Acquisition Date** Use the following requirements for working Problem 6-1 (page 215) under push-down accounting.

Required

1. Adjust the parent and subsidiary column amounts to reflect (1) the push-down accounting adjustments you determined for Problem 7-4 and (2) the related amortization for 2006.
2. Prepare all consolidation entries as of 12/31/06.
3. Prepare a consolidation worksheet at 12/31/06.

P 7-8 **LBO: Continuing Ownership *Increases*** Oldco is a publicly owned company having 10,000 shares of common stock outstanding. In November 2006, Oldco's upper management, which owns 500 common shares (5%) of Oldco, approached an independent investment firm concerning a leveraged buyout of Oldco. The investment company has strong relationships with lending institutions. In December 2006, a new corporation (Newco) was formed as a holding company to acquire *all* of Oldco's outstanding common stock. Newco issued 200 shares of common stock as follows:

1. 100 shares to the investment firm for $25,000 cash.
2. 100 shares to Oldco's upper management in exchange for the 500 shares of Oldco common stock it held.

---

*The financial statement information presented for problems accompanied by asterisks is also provided on Model 7 (filename: MODEL07) at the **http://pahler.swlearning.com** website, allowing the problem to be worked on the computer.

In December 2006, Newco borrowed $450,000 from a lending institution, a loan secured by Oldco's assets. On 12/31/06, Newco acquired Oldco's remaining 9,500 outstanding common shares by paying cash of $475,000 ($50 per share). Information concerning Oldco at 12/31/06 follows:

	Book Value	Current Value
Assets	$600,000	$850,000
Liabilities	$400,000	$400,000
Stockholders' equity	200,000	450,000
	$600,000	$850,000

Assume that management's basis (collectively as individuals) totals $7,000. In solving this problem, it may be helpful to use the following format:

Cost = Book Value of Net Assets + Undervaluation of Net Assets + Goodwill

Required

1. At what amount should the 100 shares of Newco common stock issued to upper management be recorded?
   a. At their personal basis of $7,000.
   b. At 5% of the book value of $200,000.
   c. At the imputed fair market value of their 5% interest ($475,000 = 95%; thus 5% = $25,000).
2. Determine the extent to which Oldco's assets are revalued *upward*.
3. Determine the amount of goodwill to be reported.
4. Would your answers to requirements 2 and 3 be different if the transaction had been structured as follows: Oldco (a) borrowed $450,000 from the lending institution, (b) issued 500 shares of its common stock to the investment firm for $25,000 cash, and (c) acquired the 9,500 shares of its outstanding common stock held by the outside investors for $475,000 cash through a self-tender offer?

P 7-9 **LBO: Continuing Ownership *Decreases*** Oldco is a privately owned company having 1,000 shares of common stock outstanding, 100% of which is owned by Ralph and Ruth Richy, the founders of the company. The Richys retired several years ago and are no longer active in the management of the business. In November 2006, upper management proposed a leveraged buyout to the Richys. The Richys agreed to this, and management approached an independent investment firm that has strong relationships with lending institutions. In December 2006, a new corporation (Newco) was formed as a holding company to acquire *all* of the outstanding common stock of Oldco. Newco borrowed $350,000 from a lending institution, a loan secured by Oldco's assets. On 12/31/06, Newco issued 1,000 shares of common stock as follows:

1. 350 shares to the investment firm for $35,000 cash.
2. 350 shares to upper management for $35,000 cash.
3. 300 shares to the Richys for $30,000 cash.

Also on that date, Newco paid the Richys $450,000 cash for the entire 1,000 shares of Oldco common stock they held.

Information concerning Oldco at 12/31/06 follows:

	Book Value	Current Value
Assets	$500,000	$800,000
Liabilities	$300,000	$300,000
Stockholders' equity	200,000	500,000
	$500,000	$800,000

Required

1. Prepare a conceptual analysis of the Investment in Oldco account by the major conceptual elements (showing the extent to which Oldco's assets would be revalued *upward* in consolidation and the amount to be reported for goodwill in consolidation).

2. Would your answer to requirement 1 be different if the transaction had been structured as follows: (a) Oldco borrowed $350,000 from the financial institution, (b) Oldco paid the Richys a special dividend of $350,000 cash, (c) the *investment firm* acquired 350 shares of Oldco common stock directly from the Richys for $35,000 cash, and (d) *upper management* acquired 350 shares of Oldco common stock directly from the Richys for $35,000 cash?
3. Would your answer to requirement 1 be different if the Richys had been issued only 100 shares of Newco common stock (with the remaining 900 shares having been issued to *upper management* and the *investment firm* for $90,000 in cash)?

THINKING CRITICALLY

Case

C 7-1 **Push-Down: Evaluation of Applicability** Press Inc. acquired 100% of the outstanding common stock of Serch Inc. by issuing a new class of common stock (Class B) valued at $700 million. The terms of the issuance call for dividends to be based on Serch's audited net income using its historical cost basis. Serch remains a separate legal entity under the terms of the acquisition and continues to use its own auditors.

For the year following the acquisition, assume that Serch expected the following:

1. To have net income of $100 million.
2. To pay cash dividends of $80 million to the Class B stockholders.
3. To have net income of only $60 million if push-down accounting is used.

Required

1. Evaluate whether the push-down basis of accounting makes sense in this situation.
2. If push-down accounting were used, could the dividends still be based on the earnings excluding the additional depreciation and amortization of $40 million resulting from push-down accounting?

Financial Analysis Problems

FAP 7-1 **Push-Down: To Whom Does It Really Matter?** Pert, Inc.'s 100%-owned subsidiary, Savy, Inc., is considering raising capital from the public by issuing bonds, preferred stock, or common stock. Pert acquired Savy (a 20-year-old company) one year ago at a cost of $500 million. At that time, Savy's net assets had a *book value* of $300 million and a *current value* of $460 million.

Required

1. What purpose would be served by furnishing to prospective providers of capital financial statements on the push-down basis instead of on the *non*-push-down basis?
2. Would any particular category of capital provider be more interested than the others in having financial statements on the push-down basis? Why or why not?
3. If at the acquisition date, Savy had $50 million of bonds payable (maturing in 5 years), would financial statements on the push-down basis be useful to the bondholders? Why or why not?
4. Assume that (1) Savy defaults on its minimum debt to capital ratio requirement of the bond issue described in requirement 3 (using the *non*-push-down basis) and (2) Savy's financial statements on the push-down basis of accounting do *not* result in a violation. Is Savy no longer in violation legally?

FAP 7-2 **LBO: Evaluating a Change in Ownership** An outside investor formed Newco Inc. as a vehicle for acquiring all of the outstanding common stock of Oldco Inc. The new investor invested $50,000 cash in Newco in exchange for 7,000 shares of Newco common stock. Newco issued 3,000 shares of its common stock in exchange for *all* of the outstanding common stock of Oldco.

Required

1. Has a change in ownership occurred?
2. Has a buyout occurred?
3. What is the substance of this transaction?

FAP 7-3 **LBO: Evaluating a Change in Ownership** A new investor and the management of Oldco Inc. form Newco Inc. as a vehicle for acquiring all of the outstanding common stock of Oldco Inc., which is owned solely by the Moola family. The new investor and Oldco's management each invested $50,000 cash in exchange for 450 shares of Newco common stock. Newco borrowed $1,500,000 from a financial institution. The Moola family was given $1,600,000 cash and 100 shares of Newco common stock in exchange for *all* of its Oldco common stock holdings.

Required

1. How does this transaction differ from the acquisition of 90% of Oldco's common stock by an established operating company that pays $1,600,000 cash?
2. How is the preceding transaction accounted for differently from the transaction described in requirement 1?
3. What rationale exists for the different accounting treatment?

FAP 7-4 **Sale of a Subsidiary in a Leveraged Buyout** On 6/30/06, Pylox sold its 100% interest in its subsidiary, Sylox Company, to Newco. Sylox had been reported as a separate reportable industry segment prior to the sale. Newco was recently formed by the top management of Sylox and a group of wealthy outside investors. The transaction is a leveraged buyout (LBO). The carrying value of Pylox's investment in Sylox at the sale date was $7,000,000. Newco paid Sylox $10,000,000 cash (virtually all borrowed from a financial institution). The sales agreement provided that Pylox *guarantee* payment of $2,000,000 of the Newco debt. Furthermore, if Newco's cash flow falls *below* certain levels, Pylox is obligated to purchase $500,000 of preferred stock of Newco.

Required Determine how Pylox should report its $3,000,000 gain.

part three

Consolidated Financial Statements: Intercompany Transactions

chapter

8

Introduction to Intercompany Transactions

Our lives change in two ways: through the people we meet and the books we read.
HARVEY MACKAY

LEARNING OBJECTIVES

To Understand

- The operational importance of intercompany transactions.
- The nature and variety of intercompany transactions.
- The tax and consolidated statement ramifications of using unsupportable (unfair) transfer prices.
- The basic conceptual reporting issue for intercompany transactions.
- Basic procedures for simplifying the consolidation effort.
- The undoing of intercompany transactions in consolidation.
- The distinction between transfers that do and do *not* involve unrealized intercompany profit.

TOPIC OUTLINE

CHAPTER OVERVIEW

Recall from Chapter 1 that when a parent and a subsidiary have transactions with each other, such transactions are (1) called **intercompany transactions,**[1] (2) viewed as **internal transactions** from a consolidated perspective, and (3) eliminated (undone on a worksheet) in preparing consolidated statements. Recall also that the consolidated statements can reflect only transactions between the consolidated entity and outside parties—the **external transactions.** As a result, the consolidated statements are presented as though the intercompany transactions had *never* occurred.

This chapter discusses intercompany transactions as to (1) their importance operationally, (2) the many different types that can occur, (3) the importance of using supportable (fair) transfer prices, (4) the distinction between (a) no unrealized intercompany profit situations (no significant conceptual reporting issues exist) and (b) unrealized intercompany profit situations (significant conceptual reporting issues do exist), and (5) the general process of eliminating them (along with any related unrealized intercompany profit).

Using Only *100%-Owned* Subsidiaries

In discussing the concept of unrealized intercompany profit, we address only the most basic conceptual issues by assuming that the subsidiary is 100% owned. Additional issues that arise when a subsidiary is *not* 100% owned are discussed in Chapters 9 and 10, which deal with types of intercompany transactions that are more difficult to undo in consolidation.

The same conceptual issues that exist for intercompany transactions (*parent-subsidiary* relationships) also exist for **intracompany transactions** (*home office-branch* relationships). We discuss the intricacies of handling intracompany transactions for *home office-branch* relationships in the Appendix to Chapter 9.

Using Only *Created* Subsidiaries

All intercompany transaction examples in this chapter (and in Chapters 9 and 10) **assume that the parent *created* (incorporated) the subsidiary rather than *acquired* it in a business combination.** This assumption follows the typical situation found in practice. Accordingly, the additional complexity of dealing with cost in excess of book value is avoided, enabling the sole focus to be on how to *undo* the intercompany transactions in consolidation.

I. OPERATIONAL IMPORTANCE OF INTERCOMPANY TRANSACTIONS

Intercompany transactions between a parent company and its subsidiaries are often critical to the mission of these entities.

High Volume of International Intercompany Transactions

Internationally, nearly 40% of world trade constitutes intercompany and intracompany transactions. Accordingly, many companies have high volumes of such transactions that must be undone for consolidated reporting purposes.

[1] When a home office and branch have transactions with each other, such transactions are called **intracompany transactions.**

CASE IN POINT

General Motors is highly integrated vertically, producing about 65% of the value of its vehicles internally, which results in a relatively high volume of internal inventory transfers among its many locations. These percentages are much lower than those of Ford and Chrysler (30%) and of most large Japanese firms, which prefer outside suppliers that are subject to the discipline of free markets.*

* The downside of having a highly vertically integrated operation with a just-in-time inventory system is that a strike at one critical parts factory can have far-reaching shut-down consequences, as happened in 1996 for General Motors when employees at two of its Ohio brake plants went on strike. This caused GM to shut down almost immediately 26 North American assembly plants, idling 178,000 workers.

Proper Assessment of a Subsidiary's Performance

It is often *not* possible to meaningfully evaluate a subsidiary's operating performance using financial analysis, unless certain types of intercompany transactions are made. This fact is so important that when a subsidiary of a publicly owned parent company issues separate financial statements for capital-raising purposes, the Securities and Exchange Commission (SEC) mandates that expenses incurred at the parent level that benefit a subsidiary be "pushed down" and reported in the subsidiary's financial statements to give potential investors a fairer picture of the subsidiary's profitability.[2] Thus certain types of intercompany transactions must be recorded—even if the parent prefers *not* to record them.

We now discuss the nature and variety of intercompany transactions that can occur.

II. Nature and Variety of Intercompany Transactions

First we discuss the unique nature of intercompany transactions.

All Intercompany Transactions Are Related-Party Transactions

Related-party transactions are transactions an entity has with its (1) management and nonmanagement employees, (2) directors, (3) stockholders, and (4) affiliates. An **affiliate** is an entity that, directly or indirectly, through one or more intermediate entities (1) **controls another entity,** (2) **is controlled by another entity,** or (3) **is one of two or more entities under common control** (for instance, Lynn Inc. and Barr Inc. are both owned 100% by Lynn Barr, an individual). Thus *not* all *related-party* transactions are *intercompany* transactions, but all *intercompany* transactions are *related-party* transactions.

Intercompany transactions are eliminated in consolidation **because they are internal transactions from a consolidated perspective**—*not* because they are related-party transactions. The other types of related-party transactions (for example, the purchase or sale of land from or to company officers, directors, and stockholders) are *not* eliminated in reporting to stockholders but merely require disclosure.

We now discuss the various types of intercompany transactions that can occur.

Type 1—Dividend Payments

For many parent companies, the importance of regularly obtaining cash from their subsidiaries via dividends *cannot* be overstated, especially for parent companies that are **holding companies** (which

[2] Likewise, the SEC requires certain debt of the parent company to be pushed down and reported in the subsidiary's balance sheet (for example, debt that is secured by the subsidiary's assets).

are quite prevalent in both the banking and savings and loan industries). Recall that a holding company has no operations of its own but only the investments in its subsidiaries. Such parent companies often reduce or suspend their own dividend payouts if they *cannot* obtain dividends from their subsidiaries. And for some holding companies, the parent's ability to meet operating expenses depends almost entirely on regularly receiving dividends from the subsidiary.

Not being able to have access to a subsidiary's cash for paying (1) dividends to the parent and (2) liabilities owed the parent (such as that for royalties, inventory purchases, and overhead charges) is commonly referred to as having a **blocked funds** problem.

Strategies for Foreign Subsidiaries to Get Around the Blocked Funds Problem

Many foreign governments impose cash transfer restrictions on foreign-owned local subsidiaries. Accordingly, many parent companies that have such a blocked funds problem often find it necessary to enter into creative contractual agreements (involving loans, asset swaps, or the sale of the local currency of the subsidiary [often at a discount]) with other companies that need to acquire currency of that foreign country. The result is that the parent companies are effectively able to either (1) repatriate a subsidiary's earnings (and thus minimize the investment at risk) or (2) receive payment for monies legally owed them.[3]

Attempts by Financial Institution Subsidiaries to Get Around the Blocked Funds Problem

During the savings and loan crisis of the 1980s, some parent companies created novel accounting schemes (the courts found some to be illegal) to get around regulatory dividend restrictions. As a result, financial institution regulators now closely monitor all transactions between parents and subsidiaries to determine whether any cash transfers from a subsidiary to a parent (such as those for intercompany management fee charges) are either (1) dividend payments in disguise (for subsidiaries having retained earnings) or (2) improper transfers (for subsidiaries *not* having any retained earnings).

Furthermore, these regulators now not only impose dividend restrictions when necessary but also simultaneously prohibit *all* intercompany transactions unless prior regulatory approval has been obtained.

Recall from Chapter 2 the ways that dividends are negated in consolidation in (1) the *basic elimination entry* when the parent uses the *equity method* and (2) the *intercompany dividend elimination entry* when the parent uses the *cost method*. Accordingly, we do *not* show these procedures again here.

Type 2—Loans

Subsidiaries often do *not* have local banking relationships because treasury functions are usually centralized at the parent's headquarters for efficiency and economic reasons. This practice also allows the parent to monitor closely the cash positions of its subsidiaries, which obtain needed cash from the parent in the form of loans. Practice varies widely as to charging interest on loans to subsidiaries (manipulating income is a motive sometimes).

Type 3—Reimbursements for Directly Traceable Costs

Often a parent arranges and pays for a specific external service that is to be performed for a subsidiary. For example, a parent's outside legal counsel may handle a matter relating to the subsidiary's operations, such as a lawsuit. In paying for such services, the parent debits Intercompany

[3] Perhaps the most widely known example of a company's having a foreign subsidiary with a blocked funds problem was that of Disney, when it was operating in Japan after World War II. Disney began amassing royalty receivables from showing Mickey Mouse and Donald Duck films in Japan. Disney arranged for U.S. companies that wanted to invest in Japan (which companies needed to purchase yen to do so) to buy Disney's blocked royalty receivables. (The money became known as "Disney yen.")

Receivable and credits Cash. The parent then requests reimbursement from the subsidiary, which debits Legal Expenses and credits Intercompany Payable (and eventually cash).

Under the SEC's *Staff Accounting Bulletin No. 55* (hereafter *SAB*), "Corporate-level Expenses That Benefit Subsidiaries" (applicable when a subsidiary issues separate financial statements), expenses incurred at the parent level that clearly pertain to a subsidiary must be reported in the subsidiary's income statement.

Note that reimbursements pertain to costs that are **directly traceable** to a subsidiary. Such costs are quite different from **allocations**, which by definition are (1) *not* directly traceable, and (2) always transferred at cost without a market price component. Allocations will be discussed shortly.

Unfortunately, the existence of a parent-subsidiary relationship creates the opportunity for expenses to be improperly charged to a subsidiary intentionally, as discussed in the following Case in Point.

CASE IN POINT

In 1997, the federal government investigated Columbia/HCA Healthcare Corporation's Medicare reimbursement billing practices. One confidential informant alleged that officials at Columbia's headquarters in Nashville inappropriately transferred an $800,000 expense to Gulf Coast Hospital in Florida, where it was recorded as a Gulf Coast construction expense, thereby *inflating* reimbursement from Medicare.

Type 4—Corporate Headquarters Services and Expense Allocations

Parents usually charge their subsidiaries for general corporate services and expenses that benefit the subsidiaries, such as centralized research and development services, central computer services, legal and accounting services, and advertising expenses. Procedurally, such charges can be handled in two ways, usually depending on whether the service is from a *profit center* or a *cost center*:

1. **A billing arrangement from a *profit center*.** The parent bills the subsidiary using an invoice. As a result, the parent (1) debits Intercompany Receivable and (2) credits a descriptive revenue account. The subsidiary (1) debits a descriptive expense account and (2) credits Intercompany Payable.
2. **An allocation arrangement from a *cost center*.** The parent allocates amounts to the subsidiary. The parent (1) debits Intercompany Receivable and (2) credits Overhead Allocation to Subsidiary (a contra account to its general and administrative expenses). The subsidiary (1) debits Overhead Allocation from Parent (part of its general and administrative expenses) and (2) credits Intercompany Payable.

Allocation Methods

Corporate-level *common expenses* can be allocated to a subsidiary on either (1) an *incremental basis* or (2) a *proportional basis* (such as sales, number of employees, payroll costs, or some other arbitrary manner). Dramatically different results usually occur between the two methods. The SEC's *SAB No. 55* requires (1) allocation of common expenses to subsidiaries, (2) disclosure in a subsidiary's financial statement notes of the method of allocation, and (3) an assertion by management that the allocation method used is reasonable.

Allocations can have far-reaching consequences, as shown in the Case in Point on the following page.

A thorough understanding of intercompany charges and allocations is necessary in analyzing the profitability of a subsidiary and its relative contribution (as you will more fully appreciate after working FAP 8-1).

CASE IN POINT

Recall from Chapter 1 that in the movie industry, a separate subsidiary is used for each movie. Many authors and movie stars, being naive about accounting practices, once negotiated to receive a percentage of a movie's net income. In practice, after corporate allocations had been made for distribution, advertising, and overhead, many of these individuals were often dismayed at being told that the movie's net income was minuscule or a loss, even though the movie did quite well at the box office. Frequently, lawsuits resulted (often successful) in which claims were made that the manner of allocation (1) was inappropriate (because the allocated amounts did *not* closely reflect the actual expenses) and (2) served only to deprive claimants of profits otherwise due them. (Among the big-name recent movies that lost money under this accounting system are the huge box-office hits *Forrest Gump* and *Batman*.)

Consequently, a major shift has occurred in recent years by such individuals to negotiate instead for a percentage of the *gross revenues*—an amount that *cannot* be reduced by arbitrary allocations. (The article "Where's the Profit?" in the January 1997 issue of *Management Accounting* discusses this practice in depth.)

Allocations for Income Tax Reporting

Under **Section 482** of the Internal Revenue Code, the Internal Revenue Service may adjust the deductions of related companies if necessary to reflect an "arm's-length" price on transactions between them. Thus U.S. parent companies are required to allocate a portion of their development and administration costs to foreign subsidiaries that benefit from those costs. The effect of such allocations is to report to the IRS more taxable income on the parent's tax return.

CASE IN POINT

In 1994, the Internal Revenue Service assessed Seagate Technology (the world's largest independent maker of disk drives) $68 million for taxes, interest, and penalties for underpaying taxes for 1988 through 1990. The IRS contended that Seagate held down its U.S. profits—and U.S. taxes—by incurring development and administrative costs here that actually benefited its subsidiary in Singapore (which pays no corporate income taxes because of *tax concessions* granted by the government).

Type 5—Income Tax Expense Allocations

When a parent company and a domestic subsidiary file a consolidated federal income tax return (discussed in Appendix 3B), it is common practice to have an income tax–sharing agreement, whereby a portion of the consolidated tax expense is allocated to the subsidiary. Such allocations serve two purposes:

1. To justify cash transfers from the subsidiary to the parent so that the parent has sufficient cash to make the required tax payment for the consolidated group.
2. To have each entity within the consolidated group bear a reasonable portion of the company-wide income tax expense.

The second objective is particularly important when one of the entities within the consolidated group issues its own separate financial statements, such as to a lender who can look only to the assets of that subsidiary for repayment or for operating performance evaluation.

A reporting issue—from the subsidiary's perspective—is whether the allocated income tax expense should be determined using (1) **a formula-driven allocation method** or (2) **a pro forma separate return method** (as though the subsidiary had filed a separate return on a "stand-alone basis"). Both methods are found in practice.

Requirements of *FAS 109*

Statement of Financial Accounting Standard No. 109, "Accounting for Income Taxes," requires (1) the use of an allocation method consistent with the broad principles of *FAS 109* (the *pro forma separate return method* complies[4]) and (2) the following disclosures by the consolidated entity:

a. The aggregate amount of current and deferred tax expense for each statement of earnings presented and the amount of any tax-related balances due to or from affiliates as of the date of each statement of financial position presented.
b. The principal provisions of the method by which the consolidated amount of current and deferred tax expenses is allocated to members of the group and the nature and effect of any changes in that method (and in determining related balances to or from affiliates) during the years for which the disclosures in (a) above are presented.[5]

Requirements of the SEC

In *SAB No. 55*, the SEC staff expresses a preference for the pro forma separate return method. The SEC staff requires companies that do *not* comply with this "preference" to include in the notes a *pro forma income statement* reflecting tax expense calculated on a *separate return basis.*

Requirements of Federal Financial Institution Regulators

These regulators require the use of the pro forma separate return method in both (1) the monthly "call" reports submitted to the regulators and (2) any separate financial statements issued.

Type 6—Intangibles

Parent companies often transfer to subsidiaries patents, trademarks, the use of expertise, or other intangibles. For financial reporting purposes, the transfer prices charged can be (1) set (imposed) by the parent or (2) negotiated between the two entities. Transferring the "rights to" an item is a *sale*; transferring the "right to use" an item is *granting a license.* License income can be either (1) a one-time payment or (2) royalty payments over time based on subsequent use or sales.

Type 7—Inventory Transfers

Sales of inventory are most common in vertically integrated operations in which a customer-supplier relationship exists. Because the *selling* and *buying* entities are legally separate, the transfer prices usually approximate outside market prices (a necessary condition for meaningful performance evaluation). Consequently, the *selling entity* usually reports a gross profit on the sale.

Intercompany inventory sales are classified as (1) **downstream sales** (parent sells to subsidiary), (2) **upstream sales** (subsidiary sells to parent), and (3) **lateral sales** (subsidiary sells to a sister subsidiary). Inventory transfers at other than cost are discussed in Chapter 9.

Type 8—Fixed Asset Transfers

Far less common than inventory transfers are transfers of land, buildings, and equipment. Such transfers occur most often when one entity has surplus fixed assets or one entity is an equipment manufacturer. Fixed asset transfers are discussed in Chapter 10.

Type 9—Investment in a Subsidiary's Bonds

Infrequently, an entity within a consolidated group purchases bonds of another entity within the group. Intercompany bond holdings are discussed in Chapter 11.

---

[4] See paragraphs 40(a), (b), and (c) of *FAS 109* for example of *in*consistent tax allocation methods.

[5] *FAS 109*, "Accounting for Income Taxes" (Norwalk: Financial Accounting Standards Board, 1992), par. 49.

CHECK POINT

In consolidation, which of the following intercompany transactions need *not* be undone?

a. Long-term intercompany borrowings.
b. Intercompany royalty income and expense.
c. Intercompany dividend income (when the parent uses the cost method).
d. Intercompany land transfers involving a gain or loss.
e. None of the above.

Answer: e

Increased Inherent Risk for Covering Up Fraud

When a parent-subsidiary relationship exists, the potential to cover up losses by shifting one entity's losses to the other entity is possible; thus an element of inherent risk exists. Several spectacular frauds have been perpetrated over many years by shifting account balances from one entity to another using intercompany transactions.

CASES IN POINT

United American Bank

With its eight subsidiaries, United American, the largest bank in Tennessee at the time, was able to shift tens of millions of dollars of illegal loans from one entity to another entity, always one step ahead of the federal examiners who followed the practice of never examining all nine entities simultaneously. The fraud was uncovered as a result of an anonymous phone call to the regulators, who then descended on all nine entities at once with more than 150 examiners (at which time the bank's outside auditors were completing their examination).

Very shortly thereafter, the outside auditors (one of the so-called Big 8 accounting firms at that time) issued an unqualified "clean" audit report on the bank's consolidated statements. Three weeks later, the federal examiners declared the bank and its subsidiaries insolvent and proceeded to liquidate them.

ESM Government Securities, Inc.

This 100%-owned subsidiary of ESM Group, Inc. was able to shift massive securities' trading losses ($10 million initially and $200 million eventually) and embezzlement losses by employees ($100 million) to another unaudited sister subsidiary over several years by using thousands of intercompany transactions.

ESM's eventual collapse shook the international financial markets and triggered a banking crisis in Ohio. (The governor imposed a "banking holiday," the first in the United States since the Great Depression.) Banks and municipalities, ESM's major customers, lost hundreds of millions of dollars.

III. IMPORTANCE OF USING SUPPORTABLE (FAIR) TRANSFER PRICES

In this section, we discuss, in general, the pricing of transfer transactions between a parent and a subsidiary that result in one of the entities recording revenues, namely (1) sales of inventory (intercompany sales), (2) sales of fixed assets (intercompany gain on fixed asset sale), (3) billings for services (intercompany services income), (4) licensing arrangements (intercompany license fee income, a one-time revenue, or royalty income, revenue reported over time as the buying entity manufactures or sells a unit made using the licensed technology), (5) leases (intercompany lease income), and (6) loans (intercompany interest income). Thus this section does *not* apply to allocations of costs.

The prices used in these transactions (called *transfer prices*) are either (1) set by the parent company or (2) negotiated between the entities. Determining transfer prices to achieve goal congruence is a topic usually addressed in a separate chapter of cost accounting textbooks. In this text, we are concerned only with consolidated financial reporting implications that may arise.

Transfer Prices Affect Legal Entity-Level Profitability—*Not* Consolidated Before Tax Profitability under GAAP

When an asset is sold within a consolidated group of entities at other than its carrying value, the transfer price becomes the new basis of accounting for the item transferred. For example, if a parent's inventory costing $6,000 is sold to a subsidiary for $10,000, the subsidiary's inventory accounting basis is $10,000, *not* $6,000. Accordingly, the more the selling entity charges, the lower the gross profit that the buying entity will eventually report when it resells the inventory. (Likewise, this holds true for prices charged for services, licenses, royalties, leases, and interest.)

Thus the transfer prices directly impact the profitability of each entity. Consequently, the potential exists to manipulate the profit reported by each entity if it would serve a useful purpose (as it often does for tax planning). Illustration 8-1 shows how the gross profit of each entity is affected by different transfer prices.

In reviewing Illustration 8-1, note that it is *not* possible to manipulate the total profit from a consolidated perspective, regardless of the intercompany transfer price used in an *internal* transaction.

Because all intercompany transactions are eliminated in consolidation (as if they had *never* occurred), the transfer prices used appear, at first glance, to be irrelevant from a consolidated perspective. This is *not* always true. To understand why, we first need to address the importance of fair transfer pricing for income tax–reporting purposes—something that is of enormous concern to the taxing authorities in a global economy.

Tax Consequences of *Unsupportable* Transfer Prices

The intercompany transfer prices used are extremely important for income tax-reporting purposes because they determine the amount of income taxes paid domestically versus overseas. Thus

ILLUSTRATION 8-1 SHOWING THE IMPACT OF DIFFERENT TRANSFER PRICES

Intercompany Inventory Transfer Price of $10,000

	U.S. PARENT		FOREIGN SUBSIDIARY		TOTAL
Sales Price	$10,000		$ 14,000		
Cost (the entity's cost basis)	(6,000)		(10,000)		
Gross Profit Reported	$ 4,000	+	$ 4,000	=	$8,000

Intercompany Inventory Transfer Price of $13,000

	U.S. PARENT		FOREIGN SUBSIDIARY		TOTAL
Sales Price	$13,000		$ 14,000		
Cost (the entity's cost basis)	(6,000)		(13,000)		
Gross Profit Reported	$ 7,000	+	$ 1,000	=	$8,000

Calculation of Consolidated Gross Profit

Sales Price to outside third party—as reported on the **foreign subsidiary's books**	$14,000
Cost to the consolidated entity—as reported on the **parent's books**	(6,000)
Consolidated Gross Profit	$ 8,000

national governments may be pitted against each other in efforts to collect taxes. (For transfers within the United States, state governments are pitted against each other.)

The Arm's-Length Rule

Transactions between a parent and its child are *not* **"arm's-length" transactions** in a family. Likewise, transactions between a parent company and its subsidiaries are *not* arm's-length transactions—even if the transfer prices *equal* prices charged to *third parties*. Under Section 482 of the Internal Revenue Code, the pricing for related-party transactions must be at **arm's-length**, which means that **a company must charge a related party the same price it would charge an unrelated party.** The arm's-length standard applies to all intercompany inventory transfers, including (1) inventory transfers from domestic parent companies to foreign subsidiaries or branches (**"outbound" transfers**) and (2) inventory transfers from foreign companies to their U.S. subsidiaries or branches (**"inbound" transfers**). **The arm's-length standard also applies to (1) services provided, (2) fixed asset sales, (3) transfers of technology, patents, trademarks, and other intangible assets, and (4) interest rates on loans.**

The huge growth of international trade in the last 60 years, especially in the last 25 years, has made transfer pricing a hot topic for taxing authorities and the U.S. Congress, as discussed in the Business Perspective on transfer pricing.

Recent IRS Efforts to Prevent Transfer Pricing Abuses

For years, the IRS was frustrated by the lack of cooperation by foreign companies having transactions with subsidiaries or branches in the United States. Armed with reports of widespread use of artificially high inbound transfer prices by foreign firms to evade U.S. income taxes, the Internal Revenue Service in 1990 was able to get Congress to grant it broad new enforcement powers to deal with the transfer pricing issue:

1. A new **20% nondeductible penalty** may be imposed if transfer pricing adjustments during a year exceed the lesser of (a) $5 million or (b) 10% of the taxpayer's gross receipts. This penalty increases to 40% if the IRS adjustments exceed $20 million.
2. U.S. subsidiaries and branches of foreign firms engaged in transactions with related companies outside the U.S. **must be able to produce detailed records of the transactions with their foreign parents/home offices that document the basis for their transfer prices.** The transfer pricing records must be kept in the U.S. offices or, if located abroad, produced within 60 days of an IRS request.
3. Failure to comply triggers a **"doomsday"** penalty, whereby **the IRS can make its own determination of what the proper transfer prices should be.**

CASE IN POINT

Just How Aggressive Are Foreign Companies in Setting Transfer Prices with Their U.S. Units?

In 1995 congressional investigators reported that large foreign-owned corporations are becoming more successful at avoiding taxes on their U.S. operations. Of the foreign-owned U.S. subsidiaries that had $100 million or more in total assets in 1991, 73% (715 of 980 firms) paid no U.S. income taxes despite having sales of $359 billion (an amount that continually increases each year). In comparison, 62% (297 of 479 firms) of such firms paid no U.S. federal taxes for 1987.

The Multistate Tax Commission, an organization of state tax authorities, estimated that transfer pricing abuse costs the federal government $10 billion to $15 billion a year.

How Prevalent Are Tax Disputes Involving Transfer Pricing?

Tax disputes concerning transfer pricing are becoming quite prevalent.

CASE IN POINT

Survey of Prevalence of Transfer Pricing Disputes

In a recent survey of 210 U.S. multinational companies concerning transfer pricing for tax-reporting purposes, Ernst & Young found the following:

Firms that have had a transfer pricing dispute with the tax authorities	83%
Firms that are currently engaged in a transfer pricing dispute	49%
Transfer pricing disputes that involve management and administrative fees charged to subsidiaries	93%

Note: The contested areas involving the most money by far are royalties and transfers of finished goods.

E & Y also found that 85% of global tax and finance directors consider transfer pricing to be **their most important international tax issue**.

California's Worldwide Combined Reporting Method

Most countries use the *arm's-length method* of taxation and support its use through various treaties between the United States and other countries. In contrast, California uses a *worldwide combined reporting method* (also referred to as the *unitary tax method*) that considers affiliated corporations that share common management and support services **as one single corporate unit.** (Six other states also use this approach, but California is the most aggressive.) It then applies a three-factor—employees, revenues, and properties—apportionment percentage to the worldwide income of all affiliated corporations within the unit and subjects the resulting portion to state tax. Thus if 20% of the unit's employees are in California, 22% of the unit's revenues occur in California, and 33% of the unit's properties are located in California, 25% (20% + 22% + 33% = 75%; 75%/3 = 25%) of the unit's total income is taxed in California. Under this method, transfer prices are irrelevant.

Both domestic and foreign-based multinationals are required to use this method. In 1994, the United States Supreme Court, in a suit brought by Barclays Bank Ltd. of the United Kingdom, upheld the constitutionality of this method of taxation, ending two decades of controversy.[6]

Consolidation Consequences of Unsupportable Transfer Prices under Non-Unitary Taxation Systems

Even though all intercompany transactions are eliminated in consolidation, the use of unsupportable transfer prices may have important consequences on the consolidated financial statements. If taxing authorities find that the transfer prices are *not* supportable and the courts uphold their claims, consolidated income taxes payable will have been understated, and consolidated net income and consolidated retained earnings both will have been *over*stated. Furthermore, the company exposes itself to potential lawsuits from investors who relied on such financial statements and suffered losses (the investors could assert that the company issued *false* and *misleading* financial statements).

CHECK POINT

Which of the following is true?

a. The IRS transfer pricing rules apply only to outbound transfers (exports), not to inbound transfers (imports).

b. A company trying to minimize consolidated income taxes is inclined to set artificially *low* transfer prices for inventory transfers to countries having a *higher* income tax rate than that of the United States.

c. Other things not considered, the IRS is *more* inclined to audit intercompany transfers *from* a foreign country having a *higher* income tax rate than the U.S. income tax rate versus the opposite situation.

---

[6] California's tax method was formulated decades ago to prevent movie companies from shifting profits to another state or country with a *lower* tax rate.

d. The IRS can assess a nondeductible 40% penalty for transfer pricing adjustments that exceed $10 million for a taxable year.
e. None of the above.

Answer: e

Business Perspective

Transfer Pricing: The Corporate Shell Game

For taxpayers battling their 1040 forms and legislators peering into the black hole of the federal budget deficit, there's good news: the Internal Revenue Service, armed with fresh troops and new legal tools, is setting out to mine a mother lode of $25 billion in unpaid taxes. But there's also a catch: nobody expects much more than a trickle of new revenue to come from it.

The mother lode is unpaid business taxes, largely from foreign corporations doing business in the United States. In effect, like street-corner artists hiding peas under walnut shells, such companies play games with their profits. By manipulating the prices charged among their own subsidiaries, the multinationals can concentrate profits in countries with low corporate rates and thus get away with a smaller total tax bite. The bottom line is that most foreign corporations operating in the United States pay little or no tax to Washington.

Tax Loss

All told, the Treasury's loss is enormous. At hearings last summer before the House Oversight Subcommittee, chairman J. J. Pickle of Texas said he had heard estimates ranging up to $30 billion. IRS Commissioner Fred T. Goldberg, Jr., said that was "on the high side," but conceded that the agency should be doing better. Michigan tax experts James Wheeler and Richard Weber calculate that foreign-based multinationals dodge $20 billion in U.S. taxes every year. And that's not considering U.S.–based companies, many of which also find ways to tuck away profits in tax havens. They usually do it on a smaller scale, since it's harder for them to dodge the IRS.

The corporate shell game has been going on for at least 30 years, ever since multinational operations became a significant factor in the corporate world, and there have been periodic attempts to crack down. The latest was prompted last summer, when the IRS published a table showing that foreign-based companies sold $543 billion worth of goods and services in the United States in 1986, but claimed to have net losses of $1.5 billion on that trade. That year was an aberration; before and since, overseas companies in the United States have actually reported net profits, albeit tiny ones. But the 1986 "loss" was riveting. "That tore it," says Ronald Pearlman, former chief of staff of the congressional Joint Tax Committee, now practicing law at Covington & Burling. Congress voted a stiff new 20% fine and gave the IRS broader power to subpoena records from parent companies overseas. The tax agency also got to expand its overworked international staff and dangle a small salary premium to recruit talent.

Abuses in pricing across borders—"transfer pricing," in corporate jargon—are illegal, if they can be proved. Corporations dealing with their own subsidiaries are required to set prices at "arm's length," just as they would for unrelated customers. And there's no question that abuses can be enormous. In its biggest known victory, the IRS made its case that Japan's Toyota had been systematically overcharging its U.S. subsidiary for years on most of the cars, trucks, and parts sold in the United States. What would have been profits from the United States had wafted back to Japan. Toyota denied improprieties but agreed to a reported $1 billion settlement, paid in part with tax rebates from the government of Japan.

But such triumphs are rare, and the hurdles are mountainous. For one thing, small armies of accountants are needed to sift through corporate records in several countries, even if access is granted—by no means a sure thing. In one case, an agent who requested a specific document was sent 40 boxes of papers without an index. Trained economists must rule in each case whether costs were realistically allocated. And since real-world cases are

(continued)

Business Perspective, continued

usually far more subtle than simple illustrative anecdotes, there is room for years of legal maneuvering over disputed facts, accounting practices, and business judgments.

Some abuses are blatant. One foreign manufacturer, for instance, sold TV sets to its U.S. subsidiary for $250 each, but charged an unrelated company just $150. Most cases are nowhere near as clear. What if the set sold outside has a slight change in the casing? Which subsidiary gets charged for shipping and insurance? In one current case, the IRS says Japan's Yamaha forced Yamaha Motor Corp., U.S.A., to overstock motorcycles and all-terrain vehicles in the early '80s, and then made the subsidiary pay for discounts and promotions to unload the excess inventory. The result, says the tax agency, was that Yamaha Motor U.S.A. paid only $5,272 in corporate tax to Washington over four years. Proper accounting would have shown a profit of $500 million and taxes of $127 million, the agency says. But Yamaha argues that the IRS case ignores the colossal reality of the 1982 recession, which caught the company just as unprepared as its U.S. competitors. The U.S. Tax Court is mulling the case.

American-based multinationals have also been accused of squirreling profits away. Tax agents find it easier to monitor their books, since they're all in this country and follow SEC standards; as Wheeler explains it, "It's the difference between examining the head and several arms of an octopus, rather than just one tentacle." Even so, he thinks the U.S. multinationals could easily account for an additional $5 billion in lost taxes on profits dubiously allocated to tax havens. Wheeler and Richard Weber say they've found one case that is suggestive: Westinghouse Electric managed to book 27% of its 1986 domestic profit in Puerto Rico, where its final sales are tiny. To spur the Puerto Rican economy, Washington has set the corporate-tax rate there at zero. (Westinghouse says the accounting is proper, since its "highest-profit products are made in Puerto Rico.")

The IRS professes to be delighted with its new powers and loaded for bear. "We've been outmanned and outgunned in the past," says Steven Lainoff, chief IRS lawyer for international enforcement. "Now we've got the tools and people to really attack the problem." But that is at least questionable. The new fine, for instance, stipulates a 20% penalty for any company whose transfer pricing results in underpayment of $10 million or more in taxes. Experts call that a crude weapon that may well fail to stand up in court; even the IRS initially objected to it. And in testing their new subpoena powers in foreign countries, IRS agents will be under the scrutiny of tax people there, who stand to lose any taxes that Uncle Sam succeeds in claiming. The prospects for litigation are wearying.

When it comes to litigation, the IRS may also find little comfort in its expanded international staff (up to 700 from 550) or its big-city salary premiums of 8% over government standards. The agency is now eight years behind in merely auditing multinationals; corporate officials who make a decision may well be dead or transferred when the tax people finally show up to question it. And in competing for legal and accounting talent, the IRS is still severely outmatched. Senior partners in private tax practice routinely get $500,000 to $1 million a year. Goldberg recalls ruefully that when he took office as IRS commissioner in 1989, his new salary of $80,000 was just what his former firm was paying newly fledged lawyers fresh out of school.

Bad Record

All told, it's not surprising that when the IRS does bring a case, it frequently loses. Thomas Field of Tax Analysts says the agency typically settles for just 10 cents on the dollar of its initial claims against foreigners, and the IRS doesn't dispute that. At one major multinational firm, the head of taxes says he tries to do the right thing. "But there's no way the IRS is going to find chinks in our armor," he says. "We're just too smart and way too well prepared."

If the new reforms don't bear fruit, Pickle and Senate Finance Committee chairman Lloyd Bentsen say they are ready to propose something else. Ideally, that might be a whole new approach to international taxes, one that ignores the details of transactions and focuses on allocating shares of the total profit. Most U.S. states have similar laws, essentially basing corporate taxes on what percentage of a company's employees, sales, and assets are located in the state. In the long run, reforming international taxes along those lines may be inevitable. But any such attempt would be formidably complicated; few major foreign countries would welcome an overhaul of the entire structure, which in effect would require unanimous consent. For the foreseeable future, the corporate shell game goes on.

Source: Larry Martz with Rich Thomas, "The Corporate Shell Game," *Newsweek*, April 19, 1991, pp. 48–49. From *Newsweek*, April 19, 1991

ETHICS

Corporate Loyalty—Does It Require Questionable Practices?

Your boss, the president of a parent company, has asked you, the company controller, to devise a tax-sharing arrangement that would effectively get around the dividend restriction imposed on your financial institution subsidiary. (The solutions manual discusses the role of such an accountant in a real-world case.)

Questions

1. What would you do?
2. Should you seek approval of this arrangement from the financial regulators?
3. What might be the consequences to you if you implement this arrangement without the regulators' knowledge?

IV. The Basic Conceptual Issue: Should Intercompany Transactions Be Eliminated?

Although five major conceptual issues exist regarding intercompany transactions, none of them is highly controversial (as was the case for goodwill and pooling of interests). In this chapter, we discuss only the first and most basic conceptual issue of all: Should intercompany transactions be eliminated?

If intercompany transactions are *not* eliminated, management has virtually unlimited opportunity to influence or manipulate the consolidated sales and earnings, thus violating the criterion of reliability in the Financial Accounting Standards Board's *Statement of Financial Accounting Concepts No. 2*, "Qualitative Characteristics of Accounting Information." Thus the consolidated statements would include transactions and balances outstanding that are of no value to users of the statements. The criterion of relevance, as discussed in *SFAC No. 2*, is also not met.

GAAP Requirements

The existing accounting consolidation rules require the elimination of (1) *all* intercompany transactions and balances and (2) *all* profits and losses on transactions between affiliates of a consolidated group. The concept applied for this purpose is *gross profit* or *loss*.

The potential for profit and revenue manipulation alone is a sound reason for eliminating intercompany transactions in consolidation. Even if the internal transactions were made at prices equaling or closely approximating what an *outside party* would charge, however, the intercompany transactions must still be eliminated (nullified for consolidated reporting purposes) because they are *internal* transactions. Ultimately, **the reason for elimination is not just that profit could be manipulated by management in setting prices. More importantly intercompany transactions are *not* external transactions. Intercompany transactions are considered bona fide and reportable only from a separate legal company perspective;** even then, adjustments may be needed to the separate company statements to defer the reporting of unrealized intercompany profit.

Intercompany transfers conveniently fall into two broad categories: those that *do* and *do not* involve *unrealized intercompany profit*. Before addressing each of these categories, we show some basic procedures for minimizing the effort involved in preparing consolidated statements.

Check Point

Which of the following is the correct reason for eliminating intercompany transactions in consolidation?

a. Intercompany transactions are related-party transactions.
b. Consolidated statements are based on the assumption that they represent the financial position and operating results of a single business enterprise.

c. It is often impractical and in many cases impossible to determine whether the transfer prices approximate prices that could have been obtained with outside independent parties.
d. The parent company could manipulate the intercompany transfer prices in a manner that is not equitable to the subsidiary.

Answer: b

V. Minimizing the Consolidation Effort: Basic Procedures

Several procedures can greatly simplify the consolidation effort.

Using Separate Intercompany Accounts

Intercompany transactions are normally recorded in *separate general ledger accounts* to make the consolidation process easier. The income statements usually have several intercompany accounts, as shown shortly in Illustration 8-2. For the balance sheets, however, most intercompany transactions can be dealt with using *only one* account on each entity's books, Intercompany Receivable/Payable, the balance of which can change back and forth between *debit* or *credit* positions.

Reconciling All Intercompany Accounts

Before the consolidation process begins, all intercompany accounts that are to have *reciprocal* balances (both in the income statement and the balance sheet) must be reconciled and adjusted, if necessary, to bring them into agreement. Only by being in agreement will they completely eliminate (offset) each other in consolidation. (Recall that *no* consolidation elimination entry is ever posted to the general ledger.)

Illustration 8-2 summarizes accounts for which reciprocal balances *do* or *do not* exist.

Check Points

Which of the following accounts would *not* require reconciliation or adjustment to a reciprocal balance *prior* to beginning the consolidation process?

a. Intercompany Long-Term Debt.
b. Intercompany Interest Expense.
c. Intercompany Sales.
d. Intercompany Management Fee Expense.

Answer: c

Which of the following accounts require reconciliation or adjustment to a reciprocal balance *prior* to beginning the consolidation process?

a. Long-Term Intercompany Receivables.
b. Intercompany Sales.
c. Intercompany Cost of Sales.
d. Intercompany Dividend Income—when the parent uses the cost method.

Answer: a

Elimination by Rearrangement

Companies often minimize the number of elimination entries required in consolidation by arranging the individual intercompany accounts on the consolidation worksheet so that elimination

ILLUSTRATION 8-2 SUMMARY OF ACCOUNTS FOR WHICH RECIPROCAL BALANCES DO OR DO *NOT* EXIST

Accounts for which Reciprocal Balances Exist on the Other Entity's Books

DEBIT BALANCE	CREDIT BALANCE
Income Statement	
Intercompany interest expense	Intercompany interest income
Intercompany management fee expense	Intercompany management fee income
Intercompany lease expense	Intercompany lease revenue
Intercompany royalty fee expense	Intercompany royalty fee income
Intercompany overhead allocation *in*	Intercompany overhead allocation *out* (a *contra* expense account)
Balance Sheet	
Intercompany receivable	Intercompany payable
Intercompany note receivable	Intercompany note payable
Investment in a subsidiary that was **created** by the parent—*equity method* used	Common stock, additional-paid in capital, and retained earnings—**in total**

Accounts for Which Reciprocal Balances Do *Not* Exist on the Other Entity's Books

Intercompany sales[a]
Intercompany cost of sales
Intercompany gain on equipment transfer
Intercompany dividend income[b]

[a] This assumes that the buying entity uses a **perpetual inventory system** in which the inventory account is debited at the time of purchase. Under a **periodic inventory system**, however, the buying entity uses the Intercompany Purchases account, which has a reciprocal balance to the Intercompany Sales account.

[b] This account is used only when the *cost method* is used to account for the parent's investment. Although a 100%-owned subsidiary will have a *debit* balance in its Dividends Declared account equal to the *credit* balance in the parent's Dividend Income account, these accounts are normally not viewed as being reciprocal accounts because they do *not* exist in the *same* financial statement.

entries do not have to be made there. It is necessary only to show in parentheses the intercompany accounts of one of the entities in the corresponding section of the worksheet. For example, by putting the subsidiary's Intercompany Loan Payable amount in parentheses on the *same* line as the parent's Intercompany Loan Receivable in the asset section of the balance sheet, the balances add across to zero in the Consolidated column, as shown:

	Parrco Company	Subbco Company	Consolidation Entries Dr.	Consolidation Entries Cr.	Consolidated
Intercompany interest income (expense)	1,000	(1,000)			-0-
Intercompany overhead allocation (out) in..........	(33,000)	33,000			-0-
Intercompany receivable (payable)................	10,000	(10,000)			-0-

CHECK POINT

Elimination by rearrangement is *not* possible for

a. Intercompany interest charges.
b. Intercompany receivables and payables.
c. Intercompany inventory transfers.
d. Intercompany management charges.

Answer: c

VI. INTERCOMPANY TRANSFERS *NOT* INVOLVING UNREALIZED INTERCOMPANY PROFIT

This category of intercompany transfers has no substantive, conceptual, consolidated reporting issues because the consolidated net income *always* equals the sum of the parent's and subsidiary's net incomes from their own *separate* operations (in 100% ownership situations).

Even if the consolidation entries for this category of internal transfers were omitted, the consolidated net income would be the *same*. The only impact would be *over*reporting both consolidated revenues and consolidated expenses by the identical amount.

In this category of transfers, an intercompany revenue and an intercompany cost/expense are *simultaneously* reported—**for the identical amount in the same accounting period.** Some examples are (1) corporate services and management charges, (2) interest on loans, (3) operating leases, (4) royalty payments based on units sold, and (5) intercompany inventory transfers at cost.

To show how the consolidated reporting results would include meaningless amounts if intercompany revenues/expenses and intercompany receivable/ payable accounts were *not* eliminated, we use an intercompany loan transaction as an example. Assume that on January 1, 2006, Parrco Company made a $100,000 three-year loan bearing interest at 8% to its subsidiary, Subbco Company. If *no* elimination entries are made in consolidation at December 31, 2006 (the assumed reporting year-end), the following amounts are reported in the consolidated statements:

	Consolidated—If Intercompany Transactions Were *Not* Eliminated
Income Statement	
Intercompany interest income	$ 8,000
Intercompany interest expense	(8,000)
Balance Sheet	
Intercompany note receivable	$ 100,000
Intercompany note payable	(100,000)

Reporting these offsetting amounts clearly serves no useful purpose to users of consolidated statements.

The intercompany revenue and expense accounts used in this category are easily eliminated in consolidation as shown in the following four examples for the first four items listed above—situations in which the revenue is reported on the *transferor's* books and the expense is recorded on the *transferee's* books:

WORKSHEET ENTRY ONLY

INTERCOMPANY MANAGEMENT CHARGES

Intercompany Management Fee Income	XXX	
Intercompany Management Fee Expense		XXX

WORKSHEET ENTRY ONLY

INTERCOMPANY LOANS

Intercompany Interest Income	XXX	
Intercompany Interest Expense		XXX

WORKSHEET ENTRY ONLY

INTERCOMPANY OPERATING LEASES

Intercompany Lease Income	XXX	
Intercompany Lease Expense		XXX

WORKSHEET ENTRY ONLY

INTERCOMPANY ROYALTIES

Intercompany Royalty Income	XXX	
Intercompany Royalty Expense		XXX

Such intercompany accounts readily lend themselves to be even more easily dealt with in consolidation using the *elimination by rearrangement* technique discussed earlier.

Intercompany Inventory Transfers at Cost

For inventory transfers at cost, the offsetting Intercompany Revenue and Intercompany Cost of Sales accounts are reported on the *same* set of books (of the *selling* entity). Regardless, the consolidation effort is as simple as shown in the preceding examples. (Elimination by rearrangement is *not* possible, however, when the revenue and expense are recorded on the *same* set of books.) The consolidation entry is as follows:

WORKSHEET ENTRY ONLY

INTERCOMPANY INVENTORY TRANSFER AT COST

Intercompany Sales	XXX	
Intercompany Cost of Sales		XXX

Importance of Fully Understanding Transfers at Cost

Inventory transfers at cost deserve special attention here so that you are well prepared for dealing with transfers *at other than cost*, which are discussed in Chapter 9. Accordingly, assume that Parco sold inventory costing $40,000 to its 100%-owned subsidiary, Subbco, in 2006 for $40,000 (no intercompany markup). Assume also that by year-end Subbco had resold all of this inventory for $90,000. If *no* elimination entry is made in consolidation at December 31, 2006, the following amounts are reported in the 2006 consolidated income statement:

	Consolidated—If Intercompany Transactions Were *Not* Eliminated
Sales	$ 90,000
Cost of sales	(40,000)
Intercompany sales	40,000
Intercompany cost of sales	(40,000)
Gross Profit	$ 50,000

From a consolidated perspective, the only useful amounts are the $90,000 of sales to *outside third parties* and the related consolidated entity's $40,000 cost of sales pertaining to that sale. The fact that the inventory had been transferred between companies within the consolidated group prior to the sale to the third party is irrelevant. Reporting total sales of $130,000 and total cost of sales of $80,000 would be misleading; clearly, double counting is taking place. Note also that if intercompany sales were *not* eliminated in consolidation, management would be able to influence the amounts reported for *total sales* and *total cost of sales* by merely transferring inventory repetitively between the entities within the consolidated group.

VII. Intercompany Transfers Involving Unrealized Intercompany Profit

When a perfect offsetting of intercompany revenues and intercompany costs/expenses does *not* occur in the income statement in the *same* accounting period, the transferee entity has reported some or all of the initially recorded debit amount as an asset. Consequently, profit would be reported in consolidation if the transaction were *not* eliminated. For example, assume the following:

1. Parrco sold a parcel of land to its 100%-owned subsidiary, Subbco, in 2006.
2. Parrco's cost was $50,000.
3. The intercompany transfer price was $60,000, which was fully paid by the end of 2006.

Showing only the amounts created as a result of this intercompany transaction, the financial statements of each entity at the end of 2006 are as follows:

	Parrco	Subbco
Income Statement		
Intercompany gain on land sale	$10,000	
Balance Sheet		
Land		$60,000
Retained earnings	10,000	

If *no* consolidation entry is made to *undo* this intercompany transaction, consolidated net income is $10,000. The consolidated entity *cannot* report profit as a result of an *internal* transaction. Thus this $10,000 is viewed as being an *unrealized intercompany gain* from a consolidated perspective. The consolidation entry to *undo* the intercompany transaction is as follows:

WORKSHEET ENTRY ONLY

	December 31, 2006	
Intercompany Gain on Land Sale	10,000	
Land		10,000

Upon posting, the worksheet appears as shown in Illustration 8-3 (we show only the amounts that resulted from this intercompany transaction).

Review Points for Illustration 8-3. Note the following:

1. Either the *cost method* or the *equity method* can be assumed because we do not show either a Dividend Income account or an Equity in Net Income account.
2. Regardless of which method is used, the *parent's* net income will be $10,000 *higher* than the *consolidated* net income. In Chapter 9, we show how an adjustment can be made to the *par-*

ILLUSTRATION 8-3 UNREALIZED INTERCOMPANY GAIN DEFERRED AT THE END OF 2006

Parrco Company and Subbco Company
Partial Consolidation Worksheet as of December 31, 2006

	PARRCO	*100%-OWNED* SUBBCO	CONSOLIDATION ENTRIES DR.			CR.	CONSOLIDATED
Income Statement (2006)							
Intercompany gain on land sale	10,000		10,000	1			-0-
Net Income	10,000		10,000				-0-
Statement of Retained Earnings							
Balances, 1/1/06							
+ Net Income	10,000		10,000				-0-
- Dividends declared							
Balances, 12/31/06	10,000		10,000				-0-
Balance Sheet							
Land		60,000 (*new* basis)			1	10,000	50,000 (*old* basis)
Retained earnings	10,000		10,000				-0-

ent's books under the *equity method* of accounting (**Module 1** procedures discussed in depth in Chapter 9) so that the *parent's* net income and the *consolidated* net income are the *same*, which preserves the self-checking feature discussed in Chapter 2 for the *equity method*.

3. The procedures shown, however, are the **Module 2** procedures discussed in depth in Chapter 9.

Issuing Parent-Company-Only Statements

If Parrco were to issue its own separate statements in addition to consolidated statements, it would *not* make sense for it to report a *higher* profit in its *unconsolidated* income statement than it could in its *consolidated* income statement. Accordingly, Parrco makes an adjusting entry so that its net income *equals* the consolidated net income. The exact entry depends on whether the *equity method* or *cost method* is used. As a challenge, we leave you to see whether you can create these entries using the information in Case 8-3.

Consolidation Entries in Later Periods

If Subbco still owned the land at the end of 2007, the following consolidation entry would be made:

WORKSHEET ENTRY ONLY

	December 31, 2007	
Retained Earnings (beginning of year)	10,000	
Land		10,000

If Subbco sold the land in 2008, however, the previously deferred intercompany gain of $10,000 would be realized and reportable in the 2008 consolidated income statement. The following consolidation entry would be made:

WORKSHEET ENTRY ONLY

	December 31, 2008	
Retained Earnings (beginning of year)	10,000	
Gain on Land Sale		10,000

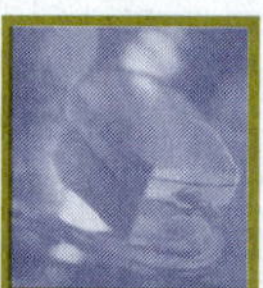

CHECK POINT

Which of the following is true?

a. Elimination by rearrangement is mandatory under GAAP.
b. Intercompany inventory transfers *at cost* need *not* be eliminated.
c. The concept of unrealized intercompany profit applies only to transfers of tangible assets.
d. Downstream intercompany inventory transfers *at cost* must be eliminated, even if the subsidiary has resold the inventory in the same year.

Answer: d

A More Typical Situation Concerning Unrealized Profit

Assume that Parrco Company charged Subbco Company $40,000 for technical advice concerning Subbco's manufacturing process—***an inventoriable cost on Subbco's books that is relieved into cost of sales as sales occur.*** Illustration 8-4 shows the applicable accounts and the adjustments required to these accounts in consolidation under three different situations. In Illustration 8-5, Illustration 8-4 is revised to reflect Subbco's Sales account and the related cost of sales account at 100%.

These entries are explained more fully in later chapters. Our purpose here is to introduce you to the general idea of *holding back* the reporting of intercompany profit until realization occurs at a later date as a result of a transaction with an outside third party.

ILLUSTRATION 8-4 INTERCOMPANY MANAGEMENT FEE CHARGES—THREE DIFFERENT SITUATIONS

Parrco Company and Subbco Company
Partial Consolidation Worksheet as of December 31, 2006

	PARRCO COMPANY	SUBBCO COMPANY	CONSOLIDATION ENTRIES DR.			CR.	CONSOLIDATED
Situation I: 100% of Intercompany Management Fee Income *Realized* at Year-End							
Income Statement (2006):							
Cost of Sales		(40,000)			1	40,000	-0-
Intercompany management fee income	40,000		40,000	1			-0-
Balance Sheet (12/31/06):							
Inventory—Intercompany		-0-					-0-
Situation II: 100% of Intercompany Management Fee Income *Unrealized* at Year-End							
Income Statement (2006):							
Cost of Sales		-0-					-0-
Intercompany management fee	40,000		40,000	1			-0-
Balance Sheet (12/31/06):							
Inventory—Intercompany		40,000			1	40,000	-0-
Situation III: 20% of Intercompany Management Fee Income Unrealized at Year-End ($8,000 of unrealized intercompany profit exists)							
Income Statement (2006):							
Cost of Sales		(32,000)			1	32,000	-0-
Intercompany management fee income	40,000		40,000	1			-0-
Balance Sheet (12/31/06):							
Inventory—Intercompany		8,000			1	8,000	-0-

Explanation of entry:

1 To eliminate the intercompany management fee income and change the Cost of Sales and Inventory accounts (as applicable) back to the selling entity's cost basis (the **"old basis"** of accounting).

ETHICS

Relatives on the Payroll—A Family Matter?

You are the outside (and presumably independent) auditor for a parent and its subsidiary. The parent is a publicly owned holding company that is thinly traded on one of the major stock exchanges. The subsidiary is a financial institution that submits its audited financial statements to the federal financial regulators.

The parent's president has numerous relatives on the parent's payroll, all at seemingly excessive salaries. For instance, the president's son became a real estate vice-president at an annual salary of $1,000,000 at the beginning of the current year; his prior real estate experience consisted solely of being a residential real estate salesperson for six months. As you best can determine, these relatives are employees in name only because they often are absent from work.

Questions

1. What appears to be the substance of this situation? What is the most likely reason that these salaries are on the parent's books instead of the subsidiary's books?
2. What should you do, if anything?

ILLUSTRATION 8-5 ILLUSTRATION 8-4 REVISED TO REFLECT SUBBCO'S SALES AND RELATED COST OF SALES

Parrco Company and Subbco Company
Partial Consolidation Worksheet as of December 31, 2006

	PARRCO COMPANY	SUBBCO COMPANY	CONSOLIDATION ENTRIES				CONSOLIDATED
			DR.			CR.	
Situation I: 100% of Intercompany Management Fee Income *Realized* at Year-End							
Income Statement (2006):							
Sales		500,000					500,000
Cost of Sales		(340,000)			1	40,000	(300,000)
Intercompany management fee income	40,000		40,000	1			–0–
Balance Sheet (12/31/06):							
Inventory—Intercompany		–0–					–0–
Situation II: 100% of Intercompany Management Fee Income *Unrealized* at Year-End							
Income Statement (2006):							
Sales		–0–					–0–
Cost of sales		–0–					–0–
Intercompany management fee income	40,000		40,000	1			–0–
Balance Sheet (12/31/06):							
Inventory—Intercompany		340,000			1	40,000	300,000
Situation III: 20% of Intercompany Management Fee Income Unrealized at Year-End ($8,000 of unrealized intercompany profit exists)							
Income Statement (2006):							
Sales		400,000					400,000
Cost of sales		(272,000)			1	32,000	(240,000)
Intercompany management fee income	40,000		40,000	1			–0–
Balance Sheet (12/31/06):							
Inventory—Intercompany		68,000			1	8,000	60,000

Explanation of entry:

1 To eliminate the intercompany management fee income and change the Cost of Sales and Inventory accounts (as applicable) back to the selling entity's cost basis (the **"old basis"** of accounting).

END-OF-CHAPTER REVIEW

Summary of Key Points

1. **Intercompany transactions** can be extremely important operationally.
2. All intercompany transactions are **related-party** transactions; none are arm's-length transactions even if the transfer prices are equal to the prices charged to third parties.
3. A wide variety of intercompany transactions can occur.
4. Intercompany transfer prices must be **supportable to the taxing authorities.** If *not* supportable, the income tax amounts reported in the consolidated statements may be understated.

5. Intercompany accounts that are to have a **reciprocal balance** must be in agreement prior to consolidation.

6. **All** intercompany transactions are **undone in consolidation** as if they had *never* occurred because they are **internal transactions** from a consolidated perspective, regardless of whether unrealized intercompany profit exists.

7. **All** *unrealized* intercompany profit must be eliminated in consolidation.

Glossary of New Terms

Affiliate An entity that, directly or indirectly, through one or more intermediate entities (1) controls another entity, (2) is controlled by another entity, or (3) is one of two or more entities under common control.

Arm's-length transaction Transactions that take place between completely independent parties.

Blocked funds The inability of a parent to obtain cash from its subsidiary to pay (1) dividends or (2) liabilities owed the parent.

Downstream sale The sale of an asset from a *parent* to one of its *subsidiaries*.

Inbound transfer The sale of an asset by a *foreign* unit to a *domestic* unit.

Lateral sale The sale of an asset by a subsidiary to another subsidiary of a common parent.

Outbound transfer The sale of an asset by a *domestic* unit to a *foreign* unit.

Related-party transactions Transactions an entity has with its (1) management and nonmanagement employees, (2) directors, (3) stockholders, and (4) affiliates.

Section 482 An important section of the Internal Revenue Code that deals with (1) setting transfer prices between related entities and (2) IRS penalties if transfer prices are found to be *un*supportable.

Upstream sale The sale of an asset from a *subsidiary* to its *parent*.

ASSIGNMENT MATERIAL

Review Questions

1. What accounts for *intercompany transactions* constituting such a high volume of domestic and international transactions?
2. How do *intercompany* transactions differ from *intracompany* transactions?
3. What are 10 examples of possible *intercompany transactions*?
4. How do *upstream* transfers and *downstream* transfers differ?
5. What benefit results from recording intercompany transactions in *separately identifiable accounts*?
6. Are intercompany transactions eliminated in consolidation because they are *related-party transactions* or because they are *internal transactions*, or both?
7. How must transfer prices for *related-party transactions* be set for U.S. income tax–reporting purposes?
8. How do *inbound* and *outbound* transactions differ?
9. Why is *transfer pricing* a hot topic for taxing authorities?
10. What is Section 482?
11. What are the *IRS penalties* for transfer pricing adjustments?
12. What are the consequences to the consolidated financial statements of using *unsupportable transfer prices*?
13. What is the *primary justification* for eliminating intercompany transactions under current GAAP?

14. What is *elimination by rearrangement*? Is it required or optional?

15. Would a downstream inventory transfer at cost have to be eliminated if the subsidiary sold the inventory in the year of the transfer? Why or why not?

Exercises

E 8-1 **Consolidation Entries: Intercompany Loan & Interest** Ply Inc. owns 100% of Stry Inc.'s common stock. On 11/1/06, Ply lent $100,000 to Stry. The loan is to be repaid on 1/30/07 along with $3,000 of interest. All aspects of the intercompany transaction were properly recorded by each company in its separate books.

Required 1. What amounts should be reported in each company's separate 2006 income statement and 12/31/06 balance sheet (asset and liability sections only)? Use the following format:

			Consolidation Entries		
Account	**Ply Inc.**	**Stry Inc.**	**Dr.**	**Cr.**	**Consolidated**

2. Prepare and post to your format the consolidation entries as of 12/31/06, relating only to these accounts.

E 8-2 **Consolidation Entries: Intercompany Computer Charges** Plo Inc. owns 100% of Stro Inc.'s common stock. Plo billed Stro $6,000 per quarter for computer services. The fourth quarter billing was unpaid at year-end. All aspects of the intercompany transaction were properly recorded by each company in its separate books.

Required 1. What amounts should be reported in each company's separate 2006 income statement and 12/31/06 balance sheet (asset and liability sections only)? Use the following format:

			Consolidation Entries		
Account	**Plo Inc.**	**Stro Inc.**	**Dr.**	**Cr.**	**Consolidated**

2. Prepare and post to your format the consolidation entries as of 12/31/06, relating only to these accounts.

E 8-3 **Consolidation Entries: Intercompany Operating Lease** Prin Inc. owns 100% of Strin Inc.'s common stock. On 1/1/06, Strin leased manufacturing equipment from Prin under an operating lease requiring payments of $3,000 per month. Cash payments of $30,000 were made in 2006. All aspects of the intercompany transactions were properly recorded by each company in its separate books. (Prin bought the equipment for $110,000 on 1/1/06 and is using *straight-line* depreciation and a *5-year* life.)

Required 1. Determine the amounts that should be reported in each company's separate 2006 income statement and 12/31/06 balance sheet (asset and liability sections only).
2. Prepare the consolidation entries as of 12/31/06, relating only to these accounts. Use the following format in working both requirements:

			Consolidation Entries		
Account	**Prin Inc.**	**Strin Inc.**	**Dr.**	**Cr.**	**Consolidated**

E 8-4 **Consolidation Entries: Inventory Transfer at Cost** In 2006, Parma Inc. sold inventory costing $40,000 to its 100%-owned subsidiary, Sarma Inc., for $40,000.

Required Prepare the consolidation entry at the end of 2006, 2007, and 2008 relating to this intercompany inventory transfer under each of the following assumptions:
1. Sarma resold all of the inventory in 2008 for $60,000.
2. Sarma resold all of the inventory in 2006 for $60,000.
3. In 2006 Sarma sold 75% of the inventory for $45,000 and the remaining 25% in 2008 for $15,000.

E 8-5 **Reconciling Intercompany Accounts** The following entries are reflected in the intercompany accounts of a parent and its subsidiary for June 2006:

Parent's Intercompany Receivable/Payable

Date	Description	Debit	Credit	Date	Description
6/1	Balance	$50,000			
6/4	Inventory sale	17,000	10,000	6/3	Remittance
			2,000	6/7	Collection of subsidiary's customer receivable
6/15	Advertising allocation at 40% of $15,000 incurred	6,000			
6/29	Inventory sale	14,000			
6/30	G & A allocation	7,000			
6/30	Balance	$82,000			

Subsidiary's Intercompany Receivable/Payable

Date	Description	Debit	Credit	Date	Description
			$50,000	6/1	Balance
6/2	Remittance	10,000	17,000	6/9	Inventory purchase
			600	6/17	Advertising allocation
6/28	Return of defective inventory	5,000[a]			
			$52,600	6/30	Balance

[a] The parent's cost of inventory sold to the subsidiary is always 60% of the transfer price.

Required

1. Prepare a schedule to reconcile the intercompany accounts.
2. Prepare the adjusting entries to bring the accounts into balance.

E 8-6 **Tax Effects of Different Transfer Prices** During 2006, Perling Inc. sold inventory costing $100,000 to its 100%-owned British subsidiary, Sterling Inc., for $200,000. Sterling resold all of this inventory locally in 2006 for 300,000 pounds. For simplicity, assume that during 2006 one pound equalled one U.S. dollar.

Required

1. Calculate worldwide income tax in dollars. Assume a U.S. income tax rate of 40% and a British income tax rate of 50%.
2. Repeat requirement 1 using a transfer price of $250,000.

Problems

P 8-1 **Recording a Variety of Intercompany Transactions** During 2006, Parr Inc. had the following transactions with Subb Inc., its 100%-owned subsidiary:

1. Parr lent Subb $50,000 on a noninterest-bearing basis.
2. Parr charged Subb management fees of $36,000.
3. On 5/1/06, Parr shipped to Subb inventory costing $128,000 at a billing price of $160,000. Of this inventory, Subb resold $145,000 worth for $220,000 by the end of 2006.
4. Subb declared dividends of $25,000.
5. Subb paid cash dividends of $20,000. The remaining $5,000 was paid on 1/4/07.
6. Parr charged Subb $15,000 for legal expenses incurred solely on behalf of Subb (a directly traceable cost).
7. On 12/10/06, Parr shipped to Subb inventory costing $24,000 at a billing price of $30,000. Subb received this inventory on 1/2/07.
8. On 12/31/06, Parr allocated 10% of its 2006 general and administrative expenses of $440,000 to Subb.

Required

1. Prepare T-account analyses of the intercompany receivable and payable accounts for 2006.
2. Determine the amounts for the following accounts pertaining to the intercompany inventory transactions:

Account	Parr Inc.	Subb Inc.
Income Statement (2006):		
Sales.		
Cost of sales		
Intercompany sales		
Intercompany cost of sales.		
Balance Sheet (as of 12/31/06):		
Intercompany acquired inventory		

3. For the 5/1/06 intercompany inventory shipment, how much intercompany profit exists at year-end on the $15,000 portion that Subb still has on hand?

P 8-2 Consolidation Entries: Intercompany Patent License Fee Pota Inc. owns 100% of Sota Inc.'s common stock. In 2006 Pota licensed to Sota the right to use a manufacturing patent developed by Pota, the costs of which were expensed as research and development on Pota's books.

For each inventory item that Sota *manufactures,* Sota pays a $10 royalty fee to Pota. During 2006, Sota manufactured 12,000 units (reporting this number to Pota) using the patented process, of which 10,000 units had been *sold* by the end of 2006. On Sota's books, the royalty fee is properly reportable as an inventoriable cost. In 2006, Sota made cash royalty payments of $77,000 to Pota.

Required

1. How much of the royalty fee charges remain in Sota's inventory at 12/31/06?
2. What amounts would be reported in each company's separate 2006 income statement and 12/31/06 balance sheet (asset and liability sections only)? Use the following format:

			Consolidation Entries		
Account	**Pota Inc.**	**Sota Inc.**	**Dr.**	**Cr.**	**Consolidated**

3. Prepare and post to your format the consolidation entries as of 12/31/06, relating only to these accounts.

P 8-3* Consolidation Worksheet: Intercompany Software Use Charges Comparative financial statements for Puda Inc. and its 100%-owned subsidiary, Suda Inc., are as follows:

	Puda Inc.		
	Cost Method[a]	**Equity Method[b]**	**Suda Inc.**
Income Statement (2006)			
Sales.	$ 400,000	$ 400,000	$ 225,000
Cost of sales.	(220,000)	(220,000)	(120,000)
Expenses	(140,000)	(140,000)	(80,000)
Dividend income (from Suda)	20,000		
Equity in net income (of Suda)		25,000	
Intercompany license fee income.	10,000	10,000	
Net Income.	$ 70,000	$ 75,000	$ 25,000
Statement of Retained Earnings			
Balances, 1/1/06	$ 75,000	$ 130,000	$ 55,000
+ Net income	70,000	75,000	25,000
– Dividends declared	(40,000)	(40,000)	(20,000)
Balances, 12/31/06.	$ 105,000	$ 165,000	$ 60,000

(continued)

*The financial statement information presented for problems accompanied by asterisks is also provided on Model 8 (filename: MODEL08) at the **http://pahler.swlearning.com** website, allowing the problem to be worked on the computer.

	Puda Inc.		
	Cost Method[a]	Equity Method[b]	Suda Inc.
Balance Sheet (as of 12/31/06)			
Cash	$ 45,000	$ 45,000	$ 11,000
Accounts receivable	80,000	80,000	64,000
Inventory	90,000	90,000	85,000
Investment in subsidiary	65,000	125,000	
Property and equipment	370,000	370,000	180,000
Accumulated depreciation	(160,000)	(160,000)	(40,000)
	$ 490,000	$ 550,000	$ 300,000
Payables and accruals	$ 135,000	$ 135,000	$ 85,000
Long-term debt	150,000	150,000	90,000
Common stock	100,000	100,000	65,000
Retained earnings	105,000	165,000	60,000
	$ 490,000	$ 550,000	$ 300,000

[a] Use this column for working under the *cost method.*

[b] Use this column for working under the *equity method.*

Additional Information

1. On 1/2/06, Puda acquired a manufacturing software package costing $100,000, which cost it capitalized into a fixed asset account for amortization (over five years) to a manufacturing overhead account. Thus the amortization expense is an inventoriable cost on Puda's books.
2. On 1/3/06, Puda made this software available to Suda for use in its manufacturing process at an annual fee of $10,000. On this date, Suda paid $10,000 to Puda and *debited* Deferred Charges. By year-end, the $10,000 had been written off to a manufacturing overhead account. Thus the intercompany software charge is an inventoriable cost on Suda's books.
3. During 2006, Puda *manufactured* 500 units and *sold* 400 units; Suda *manufactured* 300 units and *sold* 210 units.
4. In applying the *equity method* of accounting, the accountant recorded 100% of the subsidiary's reported net income of $25,000.

Required *Equity Method*

1. How much of the royalty fee charges remains in Suda's inventory at 12/31/06?
2. Prepare all consolidation entries as of 12/31/06.
3. Prepare a consolidation worksheet at 12/31/06.

Cost Method

4. Prepare all consolidation entries as of 12/31/06.
5. Prepare a consolidation worksheet at 12/31/06.

THINKING CRITICALLY

Case

C 8-1 **Auditing a Subsidiary's Intercompany Receivable** You are the audit senior (in charge of the field work) for a parent's 100%-owned subsidiary that is a financial institution and issues its separate financial statements to regulatory authorities. The subsidiary has a very large intercompany receivable (30% of total assets and 500% of stockholders' equity) from its parent company. The balance in this account increased from $10 million to $300 million in the past three years. The parent is audited by a different auditing firm.

Required 1. What specific audit procedures would you perform in auditing this receivable?

2. If you believe that substantially more audit work is necessary than the audit partner does, how would you resolve such an impasse?

C 8-2 **Suspicious Upstream Cash Transfers** You are the outside (and presumably independent) auditor for a parent and its subsidiary. The parent is a publicly owned holding company that historically has paid for its executive payroll and other expenses using cash dividends received from the subsidiary. The subsidiary is a financial institution, which regulatory authorities prohibited at the beginning of the year from paying dividends until it becomes stronger financially. During the audit, you came across several cash payments from the subsidiary to the parent for management services. You suspect that these payments are dividends in disguise.

Required If all intercompany transactions are eliminated in consolidation as if they had *never* occurred for consolidation reporting, should these payments concern you as you issue your audit report on the consolidated statements? If so, why?

C 8-3 **Making Parent-Company-Only Statements Articulate** During 2006, Pero Inc. recorded $10,000 of intercompany royalty income. As of 12/31/06, its 100%-owned subsidiary, Sero Inc., which treats the intercompany royalty charge as an inventoriable cost, had charged $9,000 of the royalty cost to cost of sales. The remaining $1,000 remains in inventory.

Additional Information

1. The parent created Sero on 1/1/06, making a $400,000 cash investment.
2. During 2006, Sero reported net income of $80,000 and declared (and paid) $30,000 in cash dividends.
3. Pero issues both consolidated statements and parent-company-only statements.

Required
1. If Pero uses the *equity method,* what adjusting entry does it record to present its parent-company-only statements?
2. Repeat requirement 1, assuming that Pero uses the *cost method.*

C 8-4 **Accounting Theory: Substance of Over- and Underallocating Taxes** Assume that Poxco and Soxco, Poxco's 100%-owned subsidiary, file a consolidated income tax return. Poxco allocates income tax expense to Soxco using a method that is inconsistent with FASB *Statement of Financial Accounting Standard No. 109,* "Accounting for Income Taxes."

Required
1. How should an *over*allocation of income taxes be reported by each entity?
2. How should an *under*allocation of income taxes be reported by each entity?

Financial Analysis Problems

FAP 8-1 **Assessing a Newly Created Subsidiary's Performance** Data for Pola Inc., which operates a large retail store, for the *year* ended 12/31/05 (its tenth year of business) follow:

Operating income	$ 160,000
Interest expense	(40,000)
Income before Income Taxes	120,000
Income tax expense @ 40%	(48,000)
Net Income	$ 72,000
Current liabilities (beginning, average, and ending balances)	200,000
Long-term debt, 10% (beginning, average, and ending balances)	400,000
Stockholders' equity (beginning, average, and ending balances)	400,000[a]
Total Liabilities and Equity	$1,000,000
Revenues	$1,600,000

[a] At the end of 2005, Pola declared and paid dividends equal to its net income for 2005. Pola had no other capital transactions in 2005.

During 2005, Pola took steps to open a new store, which opened for business on 1/1/06. Data for the new store's ***quarter*** ended 3/31/06 follow:

Liabilities (beginning, average, and ending balances)	$200,000
Revenues	400,000
Income for the quarter (***after*** allocations), as reported to Pola	48,000

Additional Information

1. **Financing.** To finance the new store, on 1/1/06, Pola (a) issued 10,000 shares of its common stock, thus raising $200,000 and (b) borrowed $800,000 at 12% interest, due in five years. This debt is recorded on Pola's books.

2. **Form of organization.** To legally insulate the new store, Pola (a) created a 100%-owned subsidiary, Sola Inc., and (b) invested the $1,000,000 of capital in Sola.

3. **Use of proceeds.** Sola used the $1,000,000 to acquire fixed assets ($700,000), acquire inventory ($250,000), and provide working capital ($50,000) for the new store. Sola's fixed assets are pledged as collateral on the $800,000, 12% loan.

4. **Inventory purchases.** Pola's purchasing department buys inventory for Sola. All inventory shipments to Sola were billed to Sola at Pola's cost.

5. **Fixed assets.** Sola's store has the same square footage of retail space as Pola. For each location, the land and building are owned. Pola's fixed assets have a *fair value* of $200,000 more than their *book value* of $450,000.

6. **Annual audit cost.** For 2005, the annual audit by the company's outside auditors cost $20,000. For 2006, the cost of the audit will be approximately $24,000. The $4,000 increase is entirely attributable to having the new location. Pola's interim reporting policy is to spread its audit cost over the four quarters. Accordingly, Pola expensed $6,000 on its books for the first quarter of 2006, of which $1,000 was allocated to Sola.

7. **Corporate charges.** The only other expenses recorded on Pola's books that were charged or allocated to Sola were for insurance ($16,000) and advertising ($7,000). The insurance expense (an *incremental* cost) was directly traceable to Sola. On a standalone basis, Sola's insurance would cost $21,000 (thus a $5,000 reduction because this is for a *second* location). The advertising allocation was a *proration* based on square footage of retailing space for the two locations.

8. **Sola's expenses.** Expenses incurred directly at the subsidiary level, such as employee salaries, payroll taxes, and utilities, were expensed on Sola's books.

9. **Depreciation.** Both entities use the double-declining-balance method.

10. **Income taxes.** All income taxes are recorded on Pola's books. Pola and Sola will file a *consolidated* income tax return.

Required

1. **ROE and BEP for Pola.** Make a return on equity (ROE) calculation and a basic earning power (BEP) calculation (operating income/total assets) for Pola for 2005 to be used as a standard in evaluating Sola's profitability. For the ROE calculation, use the beginning-of-year balance in the denominator for simplicity (rather than an average balance).
2. **ROE and BEP for Sola.** Make the same two calculations for Sola for the first quarter of 2006. *One* of the objectives here is to enable Pola to evaluate its investment in Sola from the perspective of an investor in the same manner that stockholders evaluate a company's performance from their unique perspective. (From Pola's perspective, the ROE calculation for Sola is the same as the annual return on investment [AROI] calculation discussed in Chapter 2.)
3. **ROTC.** In annually evaluating the profitability of companies, analysts use a return on "total" capital calculation (as done by both *Forbes* and *Business Week*) in addition to the ROE calculation. Total capital includes long-term debt and preferred stock (as well as common stock). Make this calculation for Pola and Sola.

4. **ROA.** Make a return on asset (ROA) calculation for both entities. Is this calculation of any value? Why or why not?
5. **Manner of handling the new debt.** Can you think of two other ways in which the $800,000 bank borrowing and cash transfer to Sola could have been recorded or handled? Does it matter whether the debt is recorded on the parent's or the subsidiary's books?
6. **Evaluation.** Using the percentages calculated for requirements 1 and 2, evaluate the new store relative to the old store. Can you think of other items that should be considered in making this comparison? Was opening the new store worthwhile? To which store manager would you give a cash bonus?
7. **Separate statements.** If Sola were to issue separate financial statements for whatever reason, what reporting issues would arise? What special disclosures would be needed?

chapter

9

Intercompany Inventory Transfers

Some see things as they are and say why. I dream things that never were and say why not.
ROBERT F. KENNEDY

LEARNING OBJECTIVES

To Understand

> The way to calculate unrealized intercompany profit.
> The way to procedurally defer unrealized intercompany profit.
> The way to procedurally recognize previously deferred unrealized profit.
> The way to share unrealized profit with a noncontrolling interest.

TOPIC OUTLINE

Appendices can be found at
http://www.pahler.swlearning.com

CHAPTER OVERVIEW

Inventory transfers at other than cost, fixed asset transfers at other than cost (Chapter 10), and bond investments (Chapter 10) require procedures that are more involved than those shown in Chapter 8. This chapter discusses the added complexity that results from the intercompany profit or loss reported by the selling entity on inventory transfers—something that changes the basis of accounting for the inventory at the individual entity level. This chapter shows how to change in consolidation from the **buying entity's *new basis*** of accounting back to the **selling entity's *old basis*** of accounting.

Three equally acceptable detailed deferral procedures can be used to achieve the desired consolidated reporting results of not reporting this intercompany profit or loss. The *first* procedure is shown in Module 1 (The Complete Equity Method). The *second* procedure is shown in Module 2 (The Partial Equity Method). The *third* procedure is a slight variation of the deferral procedure used for inventory transfers between a *home office* and a *branch*, which is shown in Appendix 9A.

We present two self-contained independent modules; each stands on its own when read in conjunction with the nonmodule textual matter. When time does *not* permit, only one of the modules may be assigned. As might be expected, each of the deferral procedures presented has its own merits. The order in which the two modules are presented is arbitrary and completely irrelevant. The two modules are as follows:

MODULE 1: The Complete Equity Method (deferral occurs in the *general ledger*)
MODULE 2: The Partial Equity Method (deferral occurs on the *consolidation worksheet*)

When a subsidiary is only *partially owned,* conceptual issues arise as to whether any unrealized intercompany profit deferred in consolidation should be shared with the noncontrolling interests. We discuss these and other conceptual issues.

I. CONCEPTUAL ISSUES

Conceptual Issue 1: Should Intercompany Transactions Be Eliminated?

Recall that we addressed this issue in Chapter 8. We do so here, as well, in discussing inventory transfers at *other than* cost.

Accordingly, assume that Parrco Company sold inventory costing $40,000 to its 100%-owned subsidiary, Subbco Company, in 2006 for $70,000 (a $30,000 intercompany markup). Also assume that by year-end, Subbco had resold *all* of the inventory for $90,000. Thus Parrco has $30,000 of gross profit, and Subbco has $20,000. If *no* elimination entry is made in consolidation at December 31, 2006, the following amounts are reported in the consolidated income statement:

	Consolidated If Intercompany Transactions Were *Not* Eliminated
Sales	$ 90,000
Cost of sales (**new basis**)	(70,000)
Intercompany sales	70,000
Intercompany cost of sales (**old basis**)	(40,000)
Gross Profit	$ 50,000

The only useful reported amounts are the $90,000 of sales to *outside third parties* and the related consolidated entity's $40,000 cost of sales pertaining to those sales. To achieve this meaningful reporting result, the *two* intercompany accounts must be eliminated, and a *downward* adjustment of $30,000 to the cost of sales account must be made.

Note that as long as the *entire* intercompany-acquired inventory is resold in the *same* accounting period in which the intercompany transfer occurs, the reportable gross profit for consolidated reporting is *always* $50,000—regardless of whether the intercompany transfer price is *more* or *less* than $70,000.

An even more compelling reason for eliminating intercompany inventory transfers at other than cost can be seen if the intercompany-acquired inventory is still *on hand* at year-end. In this case, the following amounts are reported in the consolidated statement if *no* elimination entry is made:

	Consolidated If Intercompany Transactions Were *Not* Eliminated
Income Statement	
Intercompany sales	$ 70,000
Intercompany cost of sales (**old basis**)	(40,000)
Gross Profit	$ 30,000
Balance Sheet	
Inventory	$ 70,000
Retained earnings	30,000

In this case, management is able to report profits merely by transferring inventory *within* the consolidated group. This is clearly an **artificial profit from a consolidated perspective**, and the intercompany profit must be deferred and *not* recognized until the subsidiary resells the inventory. Accordingly, the $30,000 of intercompany profit is unrealized, and realization does *not* occur until sale to an *outside third party*. At that time, the entire gross profit—some of which belongs to the parent and some to the subsidiary—is reported.

Thus **from a consolidated perspective**, (1) the sale of inventory among entities within a consolidated group is considered merely the physical movement of inventory from one location to another (similar to the movement of inventory from one branch to another branch) and (2) a bona fide transaction does *not* occur—regardless of the reasonableness of the transfer price. Only **from a separate company perspective** is the transaction considered bona fide.

CHECK POINT

When consolidating, elimination entries are needed for all

a. Intercompany inventory sales.
b. Intercompany inventory sales at other than cost.
c. Intercompany inventory sales at cost.
d. Intercompany inventory sales, unless the inventory has been resold to an outside third party.

Answer: a

The Changing Back to the Old Basis of Accounting Objective

As is evident from the preceding two scenarios, undoing an intercompany inventory transfer in consolidation has two results. **The first result** is eliminating the Intercompany Sales and Intercompany Cost of Sales accounts in the income statement. **The second result**—which is peculiar to transfers at other than cost—is changing two account balances **from the *buying* entity's *new basis* back to the *selling* entity's *old basis*.** These two accounts are (1) Inventory (the remaining portion on hand) and (2) Cost of Sales (the portion that the buying entity has resold). Later we show how to calculate the amounts needed to make these adjustments.

Conceptual Issue 2: Should Intercompany Gross Profit, Operating Profit, or Profit Before Income Taxes Be Eliminated?

Recall from Chapter 8 that when inventory and fixed assets are transferred from one entity to another within a consolidated group, the amount of profit to be eliminated in consolidation is the ***selling* entity's gross profit**. In selecting *gross profit* as the amount to be eliminated, other measures of profit—such as *operating profit* and *profit before income taxes*—were rejected *to prevent the effect of capitalizing the selling entity's marketing, administrative, and borrowing expenses*. Such expenses are *period costs* on a *separate company* basis, and there is no justification for treating them otherwise on a *consolidated basis*.

Conceptual Issue 3: Should Income Taxes Provided on Gross Profit Eliminated in Consolidation Also Be Eliminated?

The accounting rules for preparing consolidated statements require elimination of any income taxes that have been provided ***on gross profit deferred in consolidation***. For simplicity, however, we assume in our illustrations for Chapters 9 and 10 that this year-end elimination entry *has already been recorded in the parent's or the subsidiary's general ledger*. Thus a separate entry dealing with the tax effects of gross profit deferred in consolidation is *not* required on the consolidation worksheet.

Conceptual Issue 4: Should Intercompany Profit on Downstream Sales to Partially Owned Subsidiaries Be Considered Realized to the Extent of the Noncontrolling Interest?

Assume that a *parent* company has **downstream** inventory sales to its 70%-owned *subsidiary* and that the *subsidiary* has on hand at year-end $60,000 of intercompany-acquired inventory, which cost the *parent* company $40,000. Thus the total intercompany gross profit is $20,000. Two schools of thought exist regarding the amount of gross profit to be deferred in consolidation.

1. **Complete elimination.** Under this approach, *all* of the $20,000 of intercompany profit is considered unrealized and is deferred.
2. **Fractional elimination.** By following this approach, $6,000 ($20,000 × 30%) is considered realized due to the 30% noncontrolling interest ownership in the subsidiary. Accordingly, only $14,000 is deferred in consolidation.

GAAP Requirements

The accounting rules for preparing consolidated statements require the *first* alternative, *complete elimination*, because it is consistent with the underlying assumption that the consolidated statements represent the financial position and operating results of a single economic unit.

Conceptual Issue 5: When a Partially Owned Subsidiary Has *Upstream* Sales, Should the Intercompany Profit Accruing to the Noncontrolling Interest Be Deferred in Consolidation?

Assume that an 80%-owned *subsidiary* has **upstream** inventory sales to its *parent* company and the *parent* has on hand at year-end $15,000 of intercompany acquired inventory, which cost the *subsidiary* $10,000. Thus the total intercompany gross profit is $5,000, of which $4,000 accrues to the *parent company*, and $1,000 accrues to the *noncontrolling interest*. Again, two schools of thought exist regarding the amount of gross profit to be deferred in consolidation.

1. **Complete elimination.** This approach eliminates the *entire* $5,000 of gross profit on the grounds that to do otherwise would be inconsistent with the underlying purpose of consolidated statements, which is to report activities as though a single entity exists. As a result, the consolidated net income that accrues to the *controlling interest* is reduced by $4,000, and the *noncontrolling interest* is reduced by $1,000.
2. **Fractional elimination.** This approach eliminates only the portion of the gross profit that accrues to the *parent*. It does *not* eliminate the portion of the gross profit that accrues to the *noncontrolling interest* on the grounds that profit has been realized from the viewpoint of the noncontrolling interest shareholders. To whom the subsidiary sells as far as the subsidiary's noncontrolling shareholders are concerned is irrelevant. As a result, the consolidated net income that accrues to the *controlling interest* is reduced by $4,000. The *noncontrolling* interest is *not* reduced by $1,000.

GAAP Requirements

The accounting rules for preparing consolidated statements require the first alternative, *complete elimination*. Thus the *entire* $5,000 is deferred. Furthermore, the elimination of the intercompany profit or loss is to be allocated *proportionately* between the *controlling interest* and the *noncontrolling interests*.

In Module 2 of this chapter, the sharing of the unrealized intercompany profit (on *upstream* transfers) with the noncontrolling interest requires a unique and separate consolidation worksheet entry. In Module 1, however, a separate consolidation worksheet entry is *not* needed because the entire amount of the unrealized intercompany profit is deferred in the *subsidiary's* general ledger. Consequently, the amounts developed in the basic elimination entry for the noncontrolling interest, namely, the *NCI in Net Income* and the *NCI in Net Assets*, are calculated using lower subsidiary net income and subsidiary retained earnings amounts, respectively, than under Module 2. Thus Module 1 is simpler than Module 2 in consolidation when unrealized intercompany profit on *upstream* transfers exists.

When the *noncontrolling interest* ownership percentage is quite *low* and the dollar amounts are immaterial, however, companies that use Module 2 procedures—*in the interest of expediency*—usually do *not* make the separate consolidation worksheet entry to share the deferral of unrealized intercompany profit with the noncontrolling interest. Thus the full amount of the unrealized intercompany profit reduces the *controlling interest* in the combined earnings of both companies.

CHECK POINT

Under current GAAP, unrealized intercompany profit is eliminated to the extent

a. Of 100% regardless of the parent's ownership interest.
b. Of the parent's ownership interest in the subsidiary.
c. Of the noncontrolling interest in the subsidiary.
d. That the inventory has been resold to a third party.

Answer: a

ETHICS

Can You Take It With You?

As a controller, you designed a comprehensive consolidation software model that you use at work. You are in the midst of changing employers.

Question

Can you take a copy of this software package with you for use at your new employer inasmuch as you created it?

II. PROCEDURES FOR CALCULATING UNREALIZED INTERCOMPANY PROFIT

The first step for inventory transfers at *above* the *selling entity's* cost is to determine how much of the intercompany-acquired inventory remains on hand at the consolidation date. The amount of the markup pertaining to this inventory is then calculated. This profit is then deferred until the *acquiring entity* resells the inventory to a third-party customer.

Recording the Intercompany Sale and Partial Resale

Assume that in 2006 Parrco Company sold inventory costing $60,000 to Subbco Company for $100,000 and that Subbco reports $20,000 of this inventory in its balance sheet at December 31, 2006. Thus Subbco has charged to Cost of Sales $80,000 of the $100,000 of inventory acquired from Parrco. Each company records the following **general ledger entries:**

	Parent's Books		Subsidiary's Books	
Parrco Company				
Intercompany Receivables.	100,000			
Intercompany Sales		100,000		
Intercompany Cost of Sales.	60,000			
Inventory.		60,000		
Subbco Company				
Inventory.			100,000	
Intercompany Payable				100,000

Note: This transfer establishes a **new basis** of accounting for the inventory from Subbco's perspective—but *not* from a consolidated perspective.

Cost of Sales			80,000	
Inventory				80,000

Accordingly, the financial statements of each company at December 31, 2006, appear as follows:

	Parrco Company	Subbco Company
Income Statement		
Cost of sales (**new basis**).		$(80,000)
Intercompany sales	$100,000	
Intercompany cost of sales (**old basis**)	(60,000)	
Balance Sheet		
Inventory—intercompany-acquired (**new basis**)		20,000

It is now necessary to calculate how much intercompany profit is associated with the $20,000 of *ending* inventory, the *unrealized* portion of Parrco's $40,000 of gross profit.

Calculating the Unrealized Intercompany Profit

Usually a formal analysis, such as the following one, is prepared to show how much of the total intercompany gross profit is associated with the (1) inventory *on hand* at year-end (remains within the consolidated group) and (2) inventory that has been *resold* to an outside third party (has left the consolidated group). Also shown is the activity in the subsidiary's Inventory and Cost of Sales accounts as a result of this intercompany inventory transfer.

	Total (given)	Resold	On Hand
Intercompany sales (**new basis**)	**$100,000**	$ 80,000	**$20,000** (given)
Intercompany cost of sales @ 60% (**old basis**).	**(60,000)**	(48,000)	(12,000)
Gross Profit	**$ 40,000**	$ 32,000	$ 8,000
		(Realized)	**(Unrealized)**

Gross profit percentage as a percentage of the:

Transfer price ($40,000/$100,000)	40%
Parent's cost ($40,000/$60,000).	66 ⅔%

Subsidiary's General Ledger Accounts—New Basis
(amounts are from the top line of the preceding analysis)

INTERCOMPANY ACQUIRED INVENTORY

	Debit	Credit
(**new basis**)	(1) $100,000	
		80,000 (2)
(**new basis**)	(1) $ 20,000	

COST OF SALES

	Debit	Credit
	(2) $80,000	
(**new basis**)	$80,000	

(1) To record purchase of inventory from the parent.
(2) To relieve inventory into Cost of Sales as a result of sales to outside third parties.

The *first* line of the analysis, intercompany sales, shows what portion of Subbco's total intercompany purchases for the year (1) have been charged to its Cost of Sales account and (2) reside in its Inventory account at year-end. This separation is made by subtracting the $20,000 of intercompany inventory purchases on hand at year-end (determined by using either a physical count or perpetual records) from the $100,000 of total intercompany sales for the year to arrive at the $80,000 charged to the Cost of Sales account.

The *second* line of the analysis, intercompany cost of sales, shows the amounts that would have been reported (*pro forma* in nature) for the *buying entity's* (1) Cost of Sales and (2) Inventory (at year-end) had the intercompany transfer been at the *selling entity's* cost (*no* change in basis situation). The percentage of inventory resold (80%) and the percentage of inventory still on hand (20%), determined by using the amounts on the *first* line, are applied to the *total* intercompany cost of sales ($60,000) to determine the amounts in the Resold and On Hand columns.

Gross profit, the difference between the *first* and *second* lines, is the amount by which the Cost of Sales account and the Inventory account are *over*stated as to the consolidated entity because the inventory transfer was made *above* cost. Following the preceding analysis, this elimination entry is prepared:

WORKSHEET ENTRY ONLY

Intercompany Sales	100,000	
Intercompany Cost of Sales		60,000
Cost of Sales		32,000
Intercompany Profit *Deferral* (for Module 1)		8,000
or		
Inventory (for Module 2)		8,000

The postings for the first two lines *undo* the reporting of the intercompany sale. The $32,000 *credit* posting to Cost of Sales results in changing this account balance from the *new basis* of accounting back to the *old basis* of accounting. Under Module 2, the $8,000 *credit* posting to Inventory also changes this account balance from the *new basis* of accounting (as reflected in the *buying entity's* books) back to the *old basis* of accounting (as previously reflected in the *selling entity*'s books). Under Module 1, the necessary $8,000 *credit* posting to Inventory is made in a separate elimination entry, as explained in Module 1. Under Module 1, the $8,000 *credit* posting to Intercompany Profit *Deferral* eliminates the $8,000 *debit* balance in this account, which previously would have been established in the parent's *general ledger* in connection with establishing an Intercompany Profit *Deferred* account *credit* balance of $8,000 (something done only in Module 1).

CHECK POINT

In 2006, Pak Inc. sold inventory costing $240,000 to its 100%-owned subsidiary, Sak Inc., for $360,000. In consolidation at 12/31/06, the Inventory account was credited for $15,000. In Sak's balance sheet at 12/31/06, what is the reported amount of intercompany-acquired inventory?

a. $15,000
b. $30,000
c. $45,000
d. $90,000

Answer: c

Prior Year-End Unrealized Profit

The analysis of unrealized profit at each year-end encompasses only *current year* intercompany inventory transfers. If unrealized intercompany profit existed at the end of the *prior year*, it is handled separately outside the *current year* analysis. Assume that (1) $11,000 of unrealized intercompany profit existed at the end of the *prior year*, (2) the subsidiary resold all of that inventory in the *current year* for $50,000, and (3) the intercompany transfer price on that inventory was $30,000. Accordingly, the following amounts would have appeared in the **right hand column of last year's unrealized profit analysis:** $30,000 (line 1, Intercompany Sales), $19,000 (line 2 Intercompany Cost of Sales), and $11,000 (line 3, the gross profit line).

CHECK POINTS

In 2006, Pyle Inc. sold inventory costing $90,000 to its 100%-owned subsidiary for $150,000. At 12/31/06, the subsidiary reported $30,000 of intercompany-acquired inventory in its balance sheet. The unrealized profit at 12/31/06 is

a. $12,000
b. $18,000
c. $30,000
d. $60,000

Answer: a

Use the preceding information. Consolidation at 12/31/06 requires which of the following postings?

a. Debit Intercompany Cost of Sales.
b. Credit Cost of Sales.
c. Credit Intercompany Sales.
d. Debit Sales.
e. Credit Sales.

Answer: b

Answer the preceding question for 2007—*not* 2006—assuming that the inventory was resold in 2007.

Answer: b

The earlier discussed example, involving $100,000 of intercompany sales, is used in *each* of the *two* following modules.

III. PROCEDURES FOR DEFERRING UNREALIZED INTERCOMPANY PROFIT

Module 1 Overview

In a complete application of the *equity method* of accounting in 100%-ownership situations, a *general ledger adjusting entry* is made for the unrealized intercompany profit so that the *parent's* net income and its retained earnings are the *same* as *consolidated* net income and *consolidated* retained earnings, respectively. Consequently, this highly desirable built-in checking feature of the *equity method* (discussed in Chapters 2 and 6) is *not* lost.

For *downstream* sales, the general ledger adjustment is made directly to the *parent's* books. For *upstream* sales, however, the adjustment is made directly to the *subsidiary's* books—this results in recording lower income on the *parent's* books when the parent applies the *equity method* of accounting and thus a lower carrying value for the parent's Investment. Because the deferral *is* recorded in *one* of the general ledgers, *no* deferral effect need take place in consolidation.

Harmony of *APB Opinion No. 18* and the Consolidation Rules

When a parent company uses the *equity method* of accounting in its parent-company-only (PCO) statements, the requirements of *APB Opinion No. 18*, "The Equity Method of Accounting for Investments in Common Stock," must be met. For parent-subsidiary relationships, *APBO 18* requires that *all* unrealized intercompany profit be deferred until realized in a transaction with a third party (even when a *non*controlling interest exists). The accounting rules for preparing consolidated statements require the same treatment.

Similarity to Installment Method Deferral of Profit Procedures

In this module, we use *two* special income statement accounts and *one* special balance sheet account to shift the recognition of unrealized profit between periods. Except for adding the word "intercompany" to the account description, these three accounts are identical to accounts used in reporting sales accounted for under the *installment method.* Recall from *intermediate accounting* that for an installment sale totaling $90,000 for which the sales price is collected evenly over three years at $30,000 per year, the following accounts and amounts (assuming a manufacturing cost of $75,000) are reported each year (the special accounts are shown in bold):

	2006	2007	2008
Income Statement			
Installment sales	$ 90,000		
Cost of sales	(75,000)		
Gross Profit	$ 15,000		
Profit deferral	**(10,000)**		
Profit recognition		**$ 5,000**	**$5,000**
Balance Sheet (at year end)			
Installment receivables	$ 60,000	$30,000	-0-
Profit deferred	**(10,000)**	**(5,000)**	**-0-**

Section 1: *Downstream* Transfers *Above* Cost

Parent's General Ledger Entry to Defer Unrealized Profit

To convey the rationale for making a general ledger adjustment on the parent's books for downstream sales, we use the following assumed information:

1. Parrco Company *created* Subbco Company on December 31, 2006, with a $100,000 cash investment.

2. Subbco's only transaction during 2006 was to purchase $100,000 of inventory from Parrco on December 31, 2006, with full payment made on this date.
3. Parrco's cost was $60,000.
4. Subbco did *not* resell any of the $100,000 of inventory. Thus Subbco's only asset at year-end is $100,000 of inventory.

If Parrco were to issue PCO statements, it could *not* report there the $40,000 of intercompany profit on the inventory transfer but would have to defer that amount. Accordingly, assume that Parrco makes the following **general ledger adjusting entry** to defer recognizing the $40,000 of intercompany profit for PCO reporting purposes:

Intercompany Profit *Deferral* (a *special purpose* income statement account **that is closed at year end along with the other income statement accounts**)	40,000	
Intercompany Profit *Deferred* (a **contra account** to the Investment in Subsidiary account		40,000

After posting this general ledger entry, the applicable accounts of the two entities at December 31, 2006, appear as follows:

	Parrco Company	Subbco Company
Income Statement		
Intercompany sales	$100,000	
Intercompany cost of sales (**old basis**)	(60,000)	
Intercompany profit *deferral*	(40,000)[a]	
Net Income	$ -0-	
Balance Sheet		
Cash	$100,000	$ -0-
Inventory—intercompany-acquired (**new basis**)		100,000
Investment in subsidiary	100,000	
Intercompany profit *deferred*	(40,000)	
Common stock		100,000
Retained earnings	-0-	-0-

[a] This account balance is **closed to Retained earnings** along with the other income statement accounts.

Visualizing the Investment Account's True Balance

From Parrco's perspective, it truly has *not* invested $100,000 in Subbco. Parrco truly has invested only $60,000, its *cost basis* in the inventory it transferred to Subbco (Subbco's only asset). A different way to look at it is that Parrco is in the *same* position it would have been if instead it had (1) initially invested only $60,000 in Subbco and (2) immediately sold the inventory to Subbco for $60,000 (a transfer at *cost*). In such a scenario, Parrco thus would have a $60,000 balance in its Investment account, and Subbco would have total equity of $60,000 (rather than $100,000). Note that if Subbco were to *resell* the inventory for only $60,000 (the *parent's* cost), it would report a $40,000 loss. Thus its equity would *decrease* from $100,000 to $60,000—the balance in the parent's investment account, net of the $40,000 balance in the Intercompany Profit *Deferred* account.

Debiting the Intercompany Profit *Deferral* Account

By debiting this account, which generically is a *contra profit* account, the parent reports *none* of the intercompany profit in its PCO statements, which is appropriate. It *can* report (1) the intercompany sale of $100,000 and (2) the intercompany cost of sale of $60,000—these are valid transactions from a PCO perspective. However, Parrco *cannot* merely report the $40,000 of intercompany profit. By using the Intercompany Profit *Deferral* account, the parent's income statement clearly portrays (1) the intercompany transaction itself and (2) the fact that *no* profit is being reported on this intercompany transaction because it is intercompany generated (negating the need for any discussion in the notes to the PCO statements). In consolidation, the Intercompany Profit

Deferral account *debit* balance is eliminated by a *credit* posting that is part of the worksheet entry shown earlier on page 298.

A Possible Alternative Account to Debit

An alternative to debiting the Intercompany Profit Deferral account is to debit the Equity in Net Income of Subsidiary account for $40,000. This debit accomplishes the same result of *not* allowing Parrco to report any of the $40,000 of intercompany profit. The rationale for this alternative is that (1) the $40,000 of intercompany profit arises because of the relationship that exists between the two entities, and (2) things that relate to this relationship should be reported as part of the parent's investment income. Debiting Equity in Net Income of Subsidiary is the theoretically correct manner of applying the complete equity method. We find this alternative to be *less* appealing than the earlier approach because the PCO income statement portrayal is *not* as self-explanatory as when the Intercompany Profit Deferral account is used. Besides, it can be confusing to report a loss for its investment income when Subbco did *not* report a $40,000 net loss for 2006—it had only the two transactions with Parrco. Accordingly, the procedure we use is but a slight variation of the theoretically correct manner of applying the complete equity method—but the same substantive results are achieved.

Parent's General Ledger Entry to Subsequently Recognize the Previously Deferred Unrealized Profit

If Subbco eventually sells the $100,000 of intercompany-acquired inventory in 2007, Parrco no longer need defer the $40,000 of previously deferred intercompany profit. Accordingly, Parrco makes the following **general ledger adjusting entry**:

Intercompany Profit ***Deferred*** (a balance sheet account)	40,000	
Intercompany Profit ***Recognition*** (a special purpose income statement account **that is closed at year end with the other income statement accounts**)		40,000

Comprehensive Illustration

Preparing Consolidated Statements

> The Complete Equity Method
> *Downstream* Transfers *Above* Cost

We now use the example discussed on pages 297–298 in which (1) Parrco sold inventory costing $60,000 to Subbco (100% owned) for $100,000 in 2006, (2) Subbco reports $20,000 of the $100,000 of intercompany acquired inventory on its balance sheet at December 31, 2006, and (3) the results of the analysis of the total intercompany profit of $40,000 are that $32,000 relates to inventory Subbco has *resold* and $8,000 relates to inventory *on hand* at year-end. To defer recognition of the $8,000 of unrealized intercompany profit, Parrco makes the following **year-end *general ledger* adjusting entry** at December 31, 2006:

Intercompany Profit ***Deferral*** (a special purpose income statement account)	8,000	
Intercompany Profit ***Deferred*** (balance sheet)		8,000

Illustration 9-1 shows how Parrco's analysis of its investment account is updated for 2006 and 2007 using assumed net income and dividend declared amounts. For simplicity, we assume that (1) Subbco resold the $20,000 of intercompany-acquired inventory on hand at December 31, 2006, in 2007 and (2) *no* downstream inventory transfers occurred in 2007. Accordingly, Parrco makes the following **year-end *general ledger* adjusting entry** at December 31, 2007, to recognize the previously deferred $8,000 of intercompany profit:

Intercompany Profit ***Deferred*** (balance sheet)	8,000	
Intercompany Profit ***Recognition*** (a *special purpose* income statement account)		8,000

The Intercompany Profit Recognition account is **closed to Retained Earnings** along with the other income statement accounts.

Illustration 9-1 also shows the elimination entries made in consolidation at December 31, 2006 and 2007.

ILLUSTRATION 9-1

THE COMPLETE EQUITY METHOD *DOWNSTREAM* TRANSFERS *ABOVE* COST: 100% OWNERSHIP—UPDATED ANALYSIS OF THE INVESTMENT ACCOUNT AND CONSOLIDATION ENTRIES FOR *DEFERRAL* YEAR AND *RECOGNITION* YEAR

	PARENT'S INVESTMENT ACCOUNT	=	SUBSIDIARY'S EQUITY ACCOUNTS: COMMON STOCK	+	SUBSIDIARY'S EQUITY ACCOUNTS: RETAINED EARNINGS
Balances, 12/31/05	$ 60,000		$60,000		$ -0-
+ Equity in net income	24,000				24,000
– Dividends	(4,000)				(4,000)
Balance, 12/31/06	$ 80,000		$60,000		$20,000
+ Equity in net income	32,000				32,000
– Dividends	(12,000)				(12,000)
Balances, 12/31/07	$100,000		$60,000		$40,000

The Basic *Elimination* Entry (obtained from the amounts in the above analysis)

WORKSHEET ENTRY ONLY

	CONSOLIDATION DATE: DECEMBER 31, 2006		CONSOLIDATION DATE: DECEMBER 31, 2007	
Common Stock	60,000		60,000	
Retained Earnings, 1/1/06 and 1/1/07	-0-		20,000	
Equity in Net Income (of Subbco)	24,000		32,000	
Dividends Declared		4,000		12,000
Investment in Subsidiary		80,000		100,000

The COS Change in Basis *Elimination* Entry

WORKSHEET ENTRY ONLY

	CONSOLIDATION DATE: DECEMBER 31, 2006		CONSOLIDATION DATE: DECEMBER 31, 2007	
Intercompany Sales	100,000			
Intercompany Cost of Sales		60,000		
Cost of Sales		32,000		
Intercompany Profit ***Deferral***		8,000		

The Inventory Change in Basis *Elimination* Entry

WORKSHEET ENTRY ONLY

	CONSOLIDATION DATE: DECEMBER 31, 2006		CONSOLIDATION DATE: DECEMBER 31, 2007	
Intercompany Profit ***Deferred***	8,000			
Inventory (intercompany-acquired)		8,000		

The COS Change in Basis *Elimination* Entry—Prior Year Intercompany Sales

WORKSHEET ENTRY ONLY

	CONSOLIDATION DATE: DECEMBER 31, 2006		CONSOLIDATION DATE: DECEMBER 31, 2007	
Intercompany Profit ***Recognition***			8,000	
Cost of Sales				8,000

Note: This last entry, although considered an *elimination* entry, serves merely to reclassify the *credit* balance in Intercompany Profit Recognition to Cost of Sales, thereby adjusting that account's balance *downward* from the *new basis* of accounting to the *old basis* of accounting.

Illustrations 9-2 and 9-3 show consolidation worksheets for the years ended December 31, 2006 and 2007.

Dealing with Multiple-Year Transfers

Transfers usually occur each year for a typical consolidation involving intercompany inventory transfers. Accordingly, consolidation entries are required both (1) to *reclassify* to cost of sales the

ILLUSTRATION 9-2 THE COMPLETE EQUITY METHOD *DOWNSTREAM* TRANSFERS *ABOVE* COST: 100% OWNERSHIP—YEAR OF *DEFERRAL*

Parrco Company and Subbco Company
Consolidation Worksheet as of December 31, 2006

	PARRCO COMPANY	100%-OWNED SUBBCO COMPANY	CONSOLIDATION ENTRIES DR.			CONSOLIDATION ENTRIES CR.	CONSOLIDATED
Income Statement (2006)							
Sales	500,000	234,000					734,000
Cost of sales	(300,000)	(110,000)[a]			2	32,000	(378,000)
Expenses	(190,000)	(100,000)					(290,000)
Intercompany Accounts							
Equity in net income (of Subbco)	24,000		24,000	1			-0-
Intercompany sales	100,000		100,000	2			-0-
Intercompany cost of sales	(60,000)				2	60,000	-0-
Intercompany profit ***deferral***	(8,000)				2	8,000	-0-
Net Income	66,000	24,000	124,000			100,000	66,000
Statement of Retained Earnings							
Balances, 1/1/06	100,000	-0-					100,000
+ Net income	66,000	24,000	►124,000			100,000◄	66,000
– Dividends declared	(51,000)	(4,000)			1	4,000	(51,000)
Balances, 12/31/06	115,000	20,000	124,000			104,000	115,000
Balance Sheet							
Cash	65,000	11,000					76,000
Accounts receivable, net	75,000	37,000					112,000
Inventory:							
From vendors	110,000	35,000					145,000
Intercompany		20,000[b]			3	8,000	12,000
Investment in subsidiary	80,000				1	80,000	-0-
Intercompany profit ***deferred***	(8,000)		8,000	3			-0-
Land	220,000	30,000					250,000
Buildings and equipment	500,000	150,000					650,000
Accumulated depreciation	(320,000)	(13,000)					(333,000)
Total Assets	722,000	270,000	8,000			88,000	912,000
Liabilities	407,000	190,000					597,000
Common stock ($1 par)	10,000						10,000
Add'l paid-in capital	190,000						190,000
Common stock (no par)		60,000	60,000	1			-0-
Retained earnings	115,000	20,000	►124,000			104,000◄	115,000
Total Liabilities and Equity	722,000	270,000	184,00			104,000	912,000
Proof of debit and credit postings			*192,000*			*192,000*	

[a] Includes $32,000 of intercompany profit.

[b] Includes $8,000 of intercompany profit.

Explanation of entries:

1 The basic *elimination* entry.
2 The COS change in basis *elimination* entry.
3 The inventory change in basis *elimination* entry.

ILLUSTRATION 9-3 THE COMPLETE EQUITY METHOD *DOWNSTREAM* TRANSFERS *ABOVE* COST: 100% OWNERSHIP—YEAR OF *RECOGNITION*

Parrco Company and Subbco Company
Consolidation Worksheet as of December 31, 2007

	PARRCO COMPANY	100%-OWNED SUBBCO COMPANY	CONSOLIDATION ENTRIES DR.			CR.	CONSOLIDATED
Income Statement (2007)							
Sales	710,000	282,000					992,000
Cost of sales	(390,000)	(130,000)[a]			2	8,000	(512,000)
Expenses	(210,000)	(120,000)					(330,000)
Intercompany Accounts							
Equity in net income (of Subbco)	32,000		32,000	1			-0-
Intercompany profit ***recognition***	8,000		8,000	2			-0-
Net Income	150,000	32,000[b]	40,000			8,000	150,000
Statement of Retained Earnings							
Balances, 1/1/07	115,000	20,000	20,000	1			115,000
+ Net income	150,000	32,000	40,000			8,000	150,000
– Dividends declared	(85,000)	(12,000)			1	12,000	(85,000)
Balances, 12/31/07	180,000	40,000	60,000			20,000	180,000
Balance Sheet							
Cash	66,000	31,000					97,000
Accounts receivable, net	84,000	43,000					127,000
Inventory:							
From vendors	140,000	82,000					222,000
Intercompany		-0-					-0-
Investment in subsidiary	100,000				1	100,000	-0-
Land	220,000	30,000					250,000
Buildings and equipment	500,000	150,000					650,000
Accumulated depreciation	(360,000)	(26,000)					(386,000)
Total Assets	750,000	310,000				100,000	960,000
Liabilities	370,000	210,000					580,000
Common stock ($1 par)	10,000						10,000
Add'l paid-in capital	190,000						190,000
Common stock (no par)		60,000	60,000	1			-0-
Retained earnings	180,000	40,000	60,000			20,000	180,000
Total Liabilities and Equity	750,000	310,000	120,000			20,000	960,000
Proof of debit and credit postings			*120,000*			*120,000*	

[a] Includes $8,000 of intercompany profit.

[b] It is a coincidence that this amount is the same as the credit posting in entry 2 in Illustration 9-2.

Explanation of entries:

1 The basic *elimination* entry.
2 The COS change in basis *elimination* entry—prior year intercompany sales.

recognized profit on the *beginning* intercompany-acquired inventory and (2) to *eliminate* the *current year* intercompany transfers. In this regard, keeping these two entries **separate** is far simpler than attempting to handle them as a single, combined consolidation entry.

Some of the *beginning* inventory may be physically part of the *ending* inventory. The consolidation effort is simplified, however, if we assume that (1) *all* of the *beginning* inventory has been sold, and (2) *all* of the *ending* inventory came from the *current year* intercompany inventory transfers. So long as the gross profit rates are the same (or very similar) from year to year, the assumption is a safe one.

CHECK POINTS

(Module 1 only) In 2006, Palex sold inventory *above* cost to Salex, its 100%-owned subsidiary. At 12/31/06, $7,000 of unrealized intercompany profit exists. Which of the following entries is made in Palex's ***general ledger*** at 12/31/06?

	Intercompany Profit *Deferral*	Intercompany Profit *Deferred*	Inventory
a.	Debit for $7,000	Credit for $7,000	No entry
b.	Credit for $7,000	Debit for $7,000	No entry
c.	Credit for $7,000	No entry	Debit for $7,000
d.	No entry	Credit for $7,000	Debit for $7,000
e.	No entry	Debit for $7,000	Credit for $7,000

Answer: a

(Module 1 only) Use the preceding information. Which of the *debits* and *credits* are made **in consolidation** at 12/31/06?

	Intercompany Profit *Deferral*	Intercompany Profit *Deferred*	Inventory
a.	Debit for $7,000	Credit for $7,000	No entry
b.	Credit for $7,000	Debit for $7,000	Credit for $7,000
c.	Credit for $7,000	No entry	Debit for $7,000
d.	No entry	Credit for $7,000	Debit for $7,000
e.	No entry	Debit for $7,000	Credit for $7,000

Answer: b

(Module 1 only) In 2006, Pynco sold inventory *above* cost to Synco, its 100%-owned subsidiary. At 12/31/06, $9,000 of unrealized intercompany profit exists. In 2007, Synco resold this inventory for $14,000. Which of the following entries is made in Pynco **general ledger** in 2007 (not 2006)?

	Intercompany Profit *Deferral*	Intercompany Profit *Deferred*	Intercompany Profit *Recognition*
a.	Debit for $9,000	Credit for $9,000	No entry
b.	Credit for $9,000	Debit for $9,000	No entry
c.	Credit for $9,000	No entry	Debit for $9,000
d.	No entry	Credit for $9,000	Debit for $9,000
e.	No entry	Debit for $9,000	Credit for $9,000

Answer: e

(Module 1 only) Use the preceding information. Which of the entries is made **in consolidation** at 12/31/07 (not 12/31/06)?

	Intercompany Profit *Deferral*	Cost of Sales	Intercompany Profit *Recognition*
a.	Debit for $9,000	Credit for $9,000	No entry
b.	Credit for $9,000	Debit for $9,000	No entry
c.	Credit for $9,000	No entry	Debit for $9,000
d.	No entry	Credit for $9,000	Debit for $9,000
e.	No entry	Debit for $9,000	Credit for $9,000

Answer: d

SECTION 2: *UPSTREAM* TRANSFERS *ABOVE* COST

When an intercompany inventory transfer is *upstream* from a *partially owned* subsidiary, recall that *all* of the intercompany profit associated with inventory still on hand is deferred but that the deferral is ***shared* with the noncontrolling interests.**

Subsidiary's General Ledger Entry to Defer Unrealized Profit

The simplest way to readily develop the entries for consolidation when unrealized intercompany profit exists as a result of an *upstream* transfer is to have Subbco record a general ledger adjusting entry to defer the *total* unrealized profit. By doing so, the total unrealized intercompany profit is **automatically shared** between the *controlling interest* and the *noncontrolling interest*. (Thus if Subbco is 75% owned, Parrco records $6,000 [75% × $8,000] *less* income under the *equity method* of accounting.) Accordingly, to defer recognition of the $8,000 of unrealized intercompany profit, Subbco makes the following year-end ***general ledger* adjusting entry:**

Intercompany Profit *Deferral* (income statement)	8,000	
Intercompany Profit *Deferred* (a balance sheet account)		8,000

Both of these intercompany-transaction-related accounts are eliminated in consolidation. The Intercompany Profit *Deferral* entry is eliminated using the same elimination entry shown for the *downstream* sale situation. The Intercompany Profit *Deferred* account is eliminated by a *separate* consolidation entry that *reclassifies* the *credit* balance in this account to the intercompany-acquired inventory line in the balance sheet. The result is to *reduce* the $20,000 carrying value of the intercompany-acquired inventory from $20,000 to $12,000, thereby changing the basis of accounting from Parrco's *new basis* back to Subbco's *old basis*.

Recall that when Parrco made its general ledger adjusting entry for unrealized profit in the downstream sale situation, the Intercompany Profit *Deferred* account was *credited*. In this situation, the use of the Intercompany Profit *Deferred* account allows the consolidation process to be performed as efficiently as possible and equally as well.

Subsidiary's General Ledger Entry to Subsequently Recognize the Previously Deferred Unrealized Profit

If Parrco resells the $20,000 of intercompany-acquired inventory in 2007, Subbco no longer need defer the $8,000 of intercompany profit. Accordingly, Subbco makes the following ***general ledger* adjusting entry:**

Intercompany Profit *Deferred*	8,000	
Intercompany Profit *Recognition* (income statement)		8,000

In consolidation, the Intercompany Profit *Recognized* account is eliminated using the *same* entry shown previously in the *downstream* transfer situation, where the $8,000 credit balance is reclassified to Cost of Sales to achieve the *old basis* of accounting.

Subsidiary's Reporting to Its Noncontrolling Interest Shareholders

Under current reporting standards, Subbco *need not* defer any of its intercompany profit in reporting to the *noncontrolling interest*. As for the noncontrolling interest, such intercompany profit has been realized. Accordingly, to report to the noncontrolling interest, Subbco makes a "financial statement adjusting entry" (on a worksheet) to reverse the intercompany profit *deferral* entry.

The consolidation effort is greatly simplified if Subbco maintains its general ledger for reporting to Parrco rather than to the noncontrolling interest. If Subbco's general ledger were kept the opposite way, Parrco would have to make a financial statement adjusting entry to Subbco's financial statements prior to the start of the consolidation process. Some companies have hundreds of subsidiaries and large numbers of intercompany inventory transfers. Making such an entry for *each subsidiary* puts a substantial burden on the *parent's* accounting department. Thus it is far more efficient to have *subsidiaries* maintain their general ledgers for reporting to the *parent*.

Alternative Manner of Recording the Deferral in the General Ledger

An alternative manner of effecting the deferral is to have Parrco record $6,000 *less* income than it otherwise would record in applying the *equity method* of accounting. We find this alternative less appealing because it is more involved procedurally in dealing with partially owned subsidiaries. Accordingly, we do *not* present it.

Comprehensive Illustration

Preparing Consolidated Statements

> The Complete Equity Method
> *Upstream* Transfers *Above* Cost from 75%-Owned Subsidiary

We now use the example presented in the *downstream* transfer except that we have converted the situation into an *upstream* transfer. For convenience, we repeat Subbco's ***general ledger* adjusting entry** at December 31, 2006, to defer recognition of the $8,000 of unrealized intercompany profit:

Intercompany Profit *Deferral* (income statement)	8,000	
Intercompany Profit *Deferred* (balance sheet)		8,000

Illustration 9-4 shows how Parrco's analysis of its Investment account is updated for 2006 and 2007. Illustration 9-4 also shows the entries made in consolidation at December 31, 2006 and 2007. For brevity, we use the abbreviation NCI for noncontrolling interest in (1) the analysis, (2) the basic elimination entry, and (3) the consolidation worksheets.

Illustrations 9-5 and 9-6 show consolidation worksheets for the years ended December 31, 2006 and 2007.

Also for convenience we repeat Subbco's ***general ledger* adjusting entry** at December 31, 2007, to recognize the previously deferred $8,000 of unrealized intercompany profit:

Intercompany Profit *Deferred* (balance sheet)	8,000	
Intercompany Profit *Recognition* (income statement)		8,000

CHECK POINT

(Module 1 only) In 2006, Syne Inc., a 100%-owned subsidiary of Pyne Inc., sold Pyne inventory costing $98,000 for $140,000. At 12/31/06 Pyne reported $30,000 of this inventory on its balance sheet. For 2006, Syne reported net income of $100,000. Under the procedures shown in the chapter, what is the balance in Pyne's Equity in Net Income of Subsidiary account for 2006?

a. $60,000
b. $70,000
c. $79,000
d. $91,000
e. $100,000

Answer: e

ILLUSTRATION 9-4

THE COMPLETE EQUITY METHOD *UPSTREAM* TRANSFERS *ABOVE* COST: 75% OWNERSHIP—UPDATED ANALYSIS OF THE INVESTMENT ACCOUNT AND CONSOLIDATION ENTRIES FOR *DEFERRAL* YEAR AND *RECOGNITION* YEAR

	NONCONTROLLING INTEREST (25%)	+	PARENT'S INVESTMENT ACCOUNT	=	SUBSIDIARY'S EQUITY ACCOUNTS: COMMON STOCK	+	SUBSIDIARY'S EQUITY ACCOUNTS: RETAINED EARNINGS
Balances, 12/31/05	$15,000		$45,000		$60,000		$ -0-
+ Equity in net income:							
To parent (75%)			12,000				12,000
To NCI[a] (25%)	4,000						4,000
– Dividends:							
To parent (75%)			(3,000)				(3,000)
To NCI (25%)	(1,000)						(1,000)
Balances, 12/31/06	$18,000		$54,000		$60,000		$12,000
+ Equity in net income:							
To parent (75%)			30,000				30,000
To NCI (25%)	10,000						10,000
– Dividends:							
To parent (75%)			(9,000)				(9,000)
To NCI (25%)	(3,000)						(3,000)
Balances, 12/31/07	$25,000		$75,000		$60,000		$40,000

[a] NCI is the abbreviation for *noncontrolling interest.*

The Basic *Elimination* Entry (obtained from the amounts in the above analysis)

WORKSHEET ENTRY ONLY

	CONSOLIDATION DATE: DECEMBER 31, 2006		CONSOLIDATION DATE: DECEMBER 31, 2007	
Common Stock	60,000		60,000	
Retained Earnings, 1/1/06 and 1/1/07	-0-		12,000	
Equity in Net Income (of Subbco)	12,000		30,000	
NCI in Net income	4,000		10,000	
Dividends Declared		4,000		12,000
Investment in Subsidiary		54,000		75,000
NCI in Net Assets		18,000		25,000

The COS Change in Basis *Elimination* Entry

WORKSHEET ENTRY ONLY

	CONSOLIDATION DATE: DECEMBER 31, 2006		CONSOLIDATION DATE: DECEMBER 31, 2007	
Intercompany Sales	100,000			
Intercompany Cost of Sales		60,000		
Cost of Sales		32,000		
Intercompany Profit ***Deferral***		8,000		

The Inventory Change in Basis *Elimination* Entry

WORKSHEET ENTRY ONLY

	CONSOLIDATION DATE: DECEMBER 31, 2006		CONSOLIDATION DATE: DECEMBER 31, 2007	
Intercompany Profit ***Deferred***	8,000			
Inventory (intercompany-acquired)		8,000		

The COS Change in Basis *Elimination* Entry—Prior Year Intercompany Sales

WORKSHEET ENTRY ONLY

	CONSOLIDATION DATE: DECEMBER 31, 2006		CONSOLIDATION DATE: DECEMBER 31, 2007	
Intercompany Profit ***Recognition***			8,000	
Cost of Sales				8,000

ILLUSTRATION 9-5 THE COMPLETE EQUITY METHOD *UPSTREAM* TRANSFERS *ABOVE* COST: 75% OWNERSHIP—YEAR OF *DEFERRAL*

Parrco Company and Subbco Company
Consolidation Worksheet as of December 31, 2006

	PARRCO COMPANY	75%-OWNED SUBBCO COMPANY	CONSOLIDATION ENTRIES DR.			CR.	CONSOLIDATED
Income Statement (2006)							
Sales	600,000	134,000					734,000
Cost of sales	(360,000)[a]	(50,000)			2	32,000	(378,000)
Expenses	(190,000)	(100,000)					(290,000)
Intercompany Accounts							
Equity in net income (of Subbco)	12,000[b]		12,000	1			-0-
Intercompany sales		100,000	100,000	2			-0-
Intercompany cost of sales		(60,000)			2	60,000	-0-
Intercompany profit ***deferral***		(8,000)			2	8,000	-0-
Net Income	62,000	16,000	112,000			100,000	66,000
NCI in net income			4,000	1			(4,000)
CI in net income			116,000			100,000	62,000
Statement of Retained Earnings							
Balances, 1/1/06	100,000	-0-					100,000
+ Net income	62,000	16,000	116,000			100,000	62,000
– Dividends declared	(51,000)	(4,000)			1	4,000	(51,000)
Balances, 12/31/06	111,000	12,000	116,000			104,000	111,000
Balance Sheet							
Cash	79,000	11,000					90,000
Accounts receivable, net	75,000	37,000					112,000
Inventory:							
From vendors	90,000	55,000					145,000
Intercompany	20,000[c]				3	8,000	12,000
Intercompany profit ***deferred***		(8,000)	8,000	3			-0-
Investment in subsidiary	54,000				1	54,000	-0-
Land	220,000	30,000					250,000
Buildings and equipment	500,000	150,000					650,000
Accumulated depreciation	(320,000)	(13,000)					(333,000)
Total Assets	718,000	262,000	8,000			62,000	926,000
Liabilities	407,000	190,000					597,000
NCI in net assets					1	18,000	18,000
Common stock ($1 par)	10,000						10,000
Add'l paid-in capital	190,000						190,000
Common stock (no par)		60,000	60,000	1			-0-
Retained earnings	111,000	12,000	116,000			104,000	111,000
Total Liabilities and Equity	718,000	262,000	176,000			122,000	926,000
Proof of debit and credit postings			184,000			184,000	

[a] Includes $32,000 of intercompany profit.

[b] 75% of Subbco's reported net income of $16,000.

[c] Includes $8,000 of intercompany profit.

Explanation of entries:

1 The basic *elimination* entry.
2 The COS change in basis *elimination* entry.
3 The inventory change in basis *elimination* entry.

CHECK POINTS

In 2007, Pell Inc. resold for $70,000 inventory that it had acquired from its 100%-owned subsidiary in 2006 for $50,000. The subsidiary's cost was $36,000. Consolidation at 12/31/07 requires which of the following postings?

ILLUSTRATION 9-6 THE COMPLETE EQUITY METHOD *UPSTREAM* TRANSFERS *ABOVE* COST: 75% OWNERSHIP—YEAR OF *RECOGNITION*

Parrco Company and Subbco Company
Consolidation Worksheet as of December 31, 2007

	PARRCO COMPANY	75%-OWNED SUBBCO COMPANY	CONSOLIDATION ENTRIES DR.			CR.	CONSOLIDATED
Income Statement (2007)							
Sales	710,000	282,000					992,000
Cost of sales	(390,000)	(130,000)			2	8,000	(512,000)
Expenses	(210,000)[a]	(120,000)					(330,000)
Intercompany Accounts							
Equity in net income (of Subbco)	30,000[b]		30,000	1			-0-
Intercompany profit ***recognition***		8,000	8,000	2			-0-
Net Income	140,000	40,000	38,000			8,000	150,000
NCI in net income			10,000	1			(10,000)
CI in net income			48,000			8,000	140,000
Statement of Retained Earnings							
Balances, 1/1/07	111,000	12,000	12,000	1			111,000[c]
+ Net income	140,000	40,000	48,000			8,000	140,000
– Dividends declared	(85,000)	(12,000)			1	12,000	(85,000)
Balances, 12/31/07	166,000	40,000	60,000			20,000	166,000
Balance Sheet							
Cash	77,000	31,000					108,000
Accounts receivable, net	84,000	43,000					127,000
Inventory:							
From vendors	140,000	82,000					222,000
Intercompany	-0-	-0-					-0-
Investment in subsidiary	75,000				1	75,000	-0-
Land	220,000	30,000					250,000
Buildings and equipment	500,000	150,000					650,000
Accumulated depreciation	(360,000)	(26,000)					(386,000)
Total Assets	736,000	310,000				75,000	971,000
Liabilities	370,000	210,000					580,000
NCI in net assets					1	25,000	25,000
Common stock ($1 par)	10,000						10,000
Add'l paid-in capital	190,000						190,000
Common stock (no par)		60,000	60,000	1			-0-
Retained earnings	166,000	40,000	60,000			20,000	166,000
Total Liabilities and Equity	736,000	310,000	120,000			45,000	971,000
Proof of debit and credit postings			120,000			120,000	

[a] Includes $8,000 of intercompany profit.

[b] 75% of Subbco's reported net income of $40,000.

[c] Agrees with ending balance at 12/31/06 in Illustration 9-5.

Explanation of entries:

1 The basic *elimination* entry.

2 The COS change in basis *elimination* entry.

a. Credit Intercompany Cost of Sales.
b. Debit Intercompany Sales.
c. Debit Cost of Sales.
d. Credit Inventory.
e. Credit Cost of Sales.

Answer: e

At the end of 2007, Pexa Inc. reports in its balance sheet $80,000 for inventory acquired in 2006 from its 100%-owned subsidiary. The subsidiary's cost was $60,000. Consolidation at 12/31/07 requires which of the following postings?

a. Credit Cost of Sales.
b. Debit Intercompany Sales.
c. Credit Retained Earnings.
d. Credit Inventory.

Answer: d

Module 2 Overview

Under the partial equity method, the deferral of unrealized intercompany profit is accomplished entirely on the consolidation worksheet. Accordingly, in 100%-ownership situations, the *parent*'s net income and retained earnings do *not* agree with the *consolidated* net income and *consolidated* retained earnings, respectively. Thus the built-in checking feature characteristic of the equity method in going from the *Parent* column to the *Consolidated* column discussed in Chapters 2 and 3 *no longer* exists.

Section 1: *Downstream* Transfers *Above* Cost

Comprehensive Illustration

Preparing Consolidated Statements

> The Partial Equity Method
> *Downstream* Transfers *Above* Cost

We now use the example discussed on pages 297–298 in which (1) Parrco Company sold inventory costing $60,000 to Subbco Company (100% owned) for $100,000 in 2006, (2) Subbco reports $20,000 of the $100,000 of intercompany-acquired inventory on its balance sheet at December 31, 2007, and (3) the results of the analysis of the total intercompany profit of $40,000 are that $32,000 relates to inventory Subbco has resold, and $8,000 relates to inventory on hand at year-end.

Illustration 9-7 shows how Parrco's analysis of its Investment account is updated for 2006 and 2007 using assumed net income and dividend declared amounts. For simplicity, we assume that (1) Subbco resold the $20,000 of intercompany-acquired inventory on hand at December 31, 2006, during 2007 and (2) *no* downstream inventory transfers occurred during 2007. Illustration 9-7 also shows entries made in consolidation at December 31, 2006 and 2007.

Illustrations 9-8 and 9-9 show consolidation worksheets for the years ended December 31, 2006 and 2007.

Review Points for Illustrations 9-8 and 9-9. Note the following:

1. In Illustration 9-8, consolidated net income and consolidated retained earnings are both $8,000 *lower* than the comparable amounts in the parent's column.
2. In Illustration 9-9, consolidated net income is $8,000 *higher* than the parent's net income. Consolidated retained earnings is *identical* to the parent's retained earnings, however, because at the end of 2006, no unrealized intercompany profit exists to be deferred.
3. The $8,000 debit posting to *beginning* Retained Earnings in Illustration 9-9 results in the 2007 *beginning* consolidated Retained Earnings amount being $115,000—the *ending* 2006 consolidated Retained Earnings amount in Illustration 9-8.
4. If Parrco were to issue PCO statements in addition to consolidated statements in 2006, its net income of $74,000 first would have to be adjusted *downward* by $8,000. It would *not* make sense for a parent company that has intercompany transactions to report a *higher* profit by *not* consolidating a subsidiary. Accordingly, Parrco makes the following "financial statement adjusting entry" (as opposed to a *general ledger* adjusting entry) to its PCO statements:

Intercompany Profit *Deferral* (an income statement account).	8,000	
Intercompany Profit *Deferred* (a balance sheet account)		8,000
To defer the recognition of unrealized intercompany profit.		

ILLUSTRATION 9-7 THE PARTIAL EQUITY METHOD *DOWNSTREAM* TRANSFERS *ABOVE* COST: 100% OWNERSHIP—UPDATED ANALYSIS OF THE INVESTMENT ACCOUNT AND CONSOLIDATION ENTRIES FOR *DEFERRAL* YEAR AND *RECOGNITION* YEAR

	PARENT'S INVESTMENT ACCOUNT	=	SUBSIDIARY'S EQUITY ACCOUNTS COMMON STOCK	+	RETAINED EARNINGS
Balances, 12/31/05	$ 60,000		$60,000		$ -0-
+ Equity in net income	24,000				24,000
− Dividends	(4,000)				(4,000)
Balance, 12/31/06	$ 80,000		$60,000		$20,000
+ Equity in net income	32,000				32,000
− Dividends	(12,000)				(12,000)
Balances, 12/31/07	$100,000		$60,000		$40,000

The Basic *Elimination* Entry (obtained from the amounts in the preceding analysis)

WORKSHEET ENTRY ONLY

	CONSOLIDATION DATE DECEMBER 31, 2006		DECEMBER 31, 2007	
Common Stock	60,000		60,000	
Retained Earnings, 1/1/06 and 1/1/07	-0-		20,000	
Equity in Net Income (of Subbco)	24,000		32,000	
Dividends Declared		4,000		12,000
Investment in Subsidiary		80,000		100,000

The Inventory/COS Change in Basis *Elimination* Entry

WORKSHEET ENTRY ONLY

	CONSOLIDATION DATE DECEMBER 31, 2006		DECEMBER 31, 2007	
Intercompany Sales	100,000			
Intercompany Cost of Sales		60,000		
Cost of Sales		32,000		
Inventory		8,000		

The COS Change in Basis *Elimination* Entry—Prior Year Intercompany Sales

WORKSHEET ENTRY ONLY

	CONSOLIDATION DATE DECEMBER 31, 2006		DECEMBER 31, 2007	
Retained Earnings, 1/1/07			8,000	
Cost of Sales				8,000[a]

[a] If instead the inventory were still on hand at this date, Inventory, *not* Cost of Sales, is *credited*.

Dealing with Multiple-Year Transfers

Transfers usually occur each year for a typical consolidation involving intercompany inventory transfers. Accordingly, consolidation entries are required both (1) to recognize the profit on the *beginning* intercompany-acquired inventory and (2) to eliminate the *current year* intercompany transfers. In this regard, keeping these two entries **separate** is far simpler than attempting to handle them as a single, combined consolidation entry.

Some of the beginning inventory may be physically part of the ending inventory. The consolidation effort is simplified, however, if we assume that (1) *all* of the *beginning* inventory has been sold, and (2) *all* of the *ending* inventory came from the *current year* intercompany inventory transfers. So long as the gross profit rates are the same (or very similar) from year to year, the assumption is a safe one.

ILLUSTRATION 9-8 THE PARTIAL EQUITY METHOD *DOWNSTREAM* TRANSFERS *ABOVE* COST: 100% OWNERSHIP—YEAR OF *DEFERRAL*

Parrco Company and Subbco Company
Consolidation Worksheet as of December 31, 2006

	PARRCO COMPANY	100%-OWNED SUBBCO COMPANY	CONSOLIDATION ENTRIES DR.			CONSOLIDATION ENTRIES CR.	CONSOLIDATED
Income Statement (2006)							
Sales	500,000	234,000					734,000
Cost of sales	(300,000)	(110,000)[a]			2	32,000	(378,000)
Expenses	(190,000)	(100,000)					(290,000)
Intercompany Accounts							
Equity in net income (of Subbco)	24,000		24,000	1			-0-
Intercompany sales	100,000		100,000	2			-0-
Intercompany cost of sales	(60,000)				2	60,000	-0-
Net Income	74,000	24,000	124,000			92,000	66,000
Statement of Retained Earnings							
Balances, 1/1/06	100,000	-0-					100,000
+ Net income	74,000	24,000	124,000			92,000	66,000
– Dividends declared	(51,000)	(4,000)			1	4,000	(51,000)
Balances, 12/31/06	123,000	20,000	124,000			96,000	115,000
Balance Sheet							
Cash	65,000	11,000					76,000
Accounts receivable, net	75,000	37,000					112,000
Inventory:							
From vendors	110,000	35,000					145,000
Intercompany		20,000[b]			2	8,000	12,000
Investment in subsidiary	80,000				1	80,000	-0-
Land	220,000	30,000					250,000
Buildings and equipment	500,000	150,000					650,000
Accumulated depreciation	(320,000)	(13,000)					(333,000)
Total Assets	730,000	270,000				88,000	912,000
Liabilities	407,000	190,000					597,000
Common stock ($1 par)	10,000						10,000
Add'l paid-in capital	190,000						190,000
Common stock (no par)		60,000	60,000	1			-0-
Retained earnings	123,000	20,000	124,000			96,000	115,000
Total Liabilities and Equity	730,000	270,000	184,000			96,000	912,000
Proof of debit and credit postings			184,000			184,000	

[a] Includes $32,000 of intercompany profit.

[b] Includes $8,000 of intercompany profit.

Explanation of entries:

1 The basic *elimination* entry.

2 Inventory/COS change in basis *elimination* entry.

SECTION 2: *UPSTREAM* TRANSFERS *ABOVE* COST

In discussing *upstream* transfers, we use the same example discussed in the previous section regarding *downstream* transfers, in which $8,000 of unrealized intercompany profit existed at the end of 2006. We assume here, however, that the $100,000 of intercompany sales for 2006 is *upstream* from Subbco Company, a 75%-owned subsidiary of Parrco Company.

ILLUSTRATION 9-9 THE PARTIAL EQUITY METHOD *DOWNSTREAM* TRANSFERS *ABOVE* COST: 100% OWNERSHIP—YEAR OF *RECOGNITION*

Parrco Company and Subbco Company
Consolidation Worksheet as of December 31, 2007

	PARRCO COMPANY	100%-OWNED SUBBCO COMPANY	CONSOLIDATION ENTRIES DR.			CR.	CONSOLIDATED
Income Statement (2007)							
Sales	710,000	282,000					992,000
Cost of sales	(390,000)	(130,000)[a]			2	8,000	(512,000)
Expenses	(210,000)	(120,000)					(330,000)
Intercompany Accounts							
Equity in net income (of Subbco)	32,000		32,000	1			-0-
Net Income	142,000	32,000	32,000			8,000	150,000
Statement of Retained Earnings			8,000	2			
Balances, 1/1/07	123,000	20,000	20,000	1			115,000[b]
+ Net income	142,000	32,000	32,000			8,000	150,000
– Dividends declared	(85,000)	(12,000)			1	12,000	(85,000)
Balances, 12/31/07	180,000	40,000	60,000			20,000	180,000
Balance Sheet							
Cash	66,000	31,000					97,000
Accounts receivable, net	84,000	43,000					127,000
Inventory:							
From vendors	140,000	82,000					222,000
Intercompany		-0-					-0-
Investment in subsidiary	100,000				1	100,000	-0-
Land	220,000	30,000					250,000
Buildings and equipment	500,000	150,000					650,000
Accumulated depreciation	(360,000)	(26,000)					(386,000)
Total Assets	750,000	310,000				100,000	960,000
Liabilities	370,000	210,000					580,000
Common stock ($1 par)	10,000						10,000
Add'l paid-in capital	190,000						190,000
Common stock (no par)		60,000	60,000	1			-0-
Retained earnings	180,000	40,000	60,000			20,000	180,000
Total Liabilities and Equity	750,000	310,000	120,000			20,000	960,000
Proof of debit and credit postings			*120,000*			*120,000*	

[a] Includes $8,000 of intercompany profit.

[b] Agrees with ending balance at 12/31/06 in Illustration 9-8.

Explanation of entries:

1 The basic *elimination* entry.

2 The COS change in basis *elimination* entry—prior year intercompany sales.

Comprehensive Illustration

Preparing Consolidated Statements

> The Partial Equity Method
> *Upstream* Transfers *Above* Cost

Illustration 9-10 shows how Parrco's conceptual analysis of its Investment account is updated for 2006 and 2007. Illustration 9-10 also shows the entries made in consolidation at December 31, 2006 and 2007.

Illustrations 9-11 and 9-12 show consolidation worksheets for the years ended December 31, 2006 and 2007.

ILLUSTRATION 9-10

THE PARTIAL EQUITY METHOD *UPSTREAM* TRANSFERS *ABOVE* COST: 75% OWNERSHIP—UPDATED ANALYSIS OF THE INVESTMENT ACCOUNT AND CONSOLIDATION ENTRIES FOR *DEFERRAL* YEAR AND *RECOGNITION* YEAR

	NONCONTROLLING INTEREST (25%)	+	PARENT'S INVESTMENT ACCOUNT	=	SUBSIDIARY'S EQUITY ACCOUNTS: COMMON STOCK	+	SUBSIDIARY'S EQUITY ACCOUNTS: RETAINED EARNINGS
Balances, 12/31/05	$15,000		$45,000		$60,000		$ -0-
+ Equity in net income:							
To parent (75%)			18,000				18,000
To NCI[a] (25%)	6,000						6,000
– Dividends:							
To parent (75%)			(3,000)				(3,000)
To NCI (25%)	(1,000)						(1,000)
Balances, 12/31/06	$20,000		$60,000		$60,000		$20,000
+ Equity in net income:							
To parent (75%)			24,000				24,000
To NCI (25%)	8,000						8,000
– Dividends:							
To parent (75%)			(9,000)				(9,000)
To NCI (25%)	(3,000)						(3,000)
Balances, 12/31/07	$25,000		$75,000		$60,000		$40,000

[a] NCI is the abbreviation for *noncontrolling interest.*

The Basic *Elimination* Entry (obtained from the amounts in the above analysis)

WORKSHEET ENTRY ONLY

	CONSOLIDATION DATE: DECEMBER 31, 2006		DECEMBER 31, 2007	
Common Stock	60,000		60,000	
Retained Earnings, 1/1/06 and 1/1/07	-0-		20,000	
Equity in Net Income (of Subbco)	18,000		24,000	
NCI in Net Income	6,000		8,000	
Dividends Declared		4,000		12,000
Investment in Subsidiary		60,000		75,000
NCI in Net Assets		20,000		25,000

The Inventory/COS Change in Basis *Elimination* Entry

WORKSHEET ENTRY ONLY

	CONSOLIDATION DATE: DECEMBER 31, 2006		DECEMBER 31, 2007	
Intercompany Sales	100,000			
Intercompany Cost of Sales		60,000		
Cost of Sales		32,000		
Inventory		8,000		

The Sharing of Deferred Profit *Elimination* Entry (25% of $8,000 of unrealized profit)

WORKSHEET ENTRY ONLY

	CONSOLIDATION DATE: DECEMBER 31, 2006		DECEMBER 31, 2007	
NCI in Net Assets	2,000			
NCI in Net Income		2,000		

The COS Change in Basis *Elimination* Entry—Prior Year Intercompany Sales

WORKSHEET ENTRY ONLY

	CONSOLIDATION DATE: DECEMBER 31, 2006		DECEMBER 31, 2007	
NCI in Net Income (25% of $8,000)			2,000	
Retained Earnings. 1/1/07 (75% of $8,000)			6,000	
Cost of Sales				8,000[b]

[b] If instead the inventory were still on hand at this date, Inventory—*not* Cost of Sales—would be *credited.*

ILLUSTRATION 9-11 THE PARTIAL EQUITY METHOD *UPSTREAM* TRANSFERS *ABOVE* COST: 75% OWNERSHIP—YEAR OF *DEFERRAL*

Parrco Company and Subbco Company
Consolidation Worksheet as of December 31, 2006

	PARRCO COMPANY	75%-OWNED SUBBCO COMPANY	CONSOLIDATION ENTRIES DR.			CONSOLIDATION ENTRIES CR.	CONSOLIDATED
Income Statement (2006)							
Sales	600,000	134,000					734,000
Cost of sales	(360,000)[a]	(50,000)			2	32,000	(378,000)
Expenses	(190,000)	(100,000)					(290,000)
Intercompany Accounts							
Equity in net income (of Subbco)	18,000[b]		18,000	1			-0-
Intercompany sales		100,000	100,000	2			-0-
Intercompany cost of sales		(60,000)			2	60,000	-0-
Net Income	68,000	24,000	118,000			92,000	66,000
NCI in net income			6,000	1	3	2,000	(4,000)[c]
CI in net income			124,000			94,000	62,000
Statement of Retained Earnings							
Balances, 1/1/06	100,000	-0-					100,000
+ Net income	68,000	24,000	124,000			94,000	62,000
– Dividends declared	(51,000)	(4,000)			1	4,000	(51,000)
Balances, 12/31/06	117,000	20,000	124,000			98,000	111,000
Balance Sheet							
Cash	79,000	11,000					90,000
Accounts receivable, net	75,000	37,000					112,000
Inventory:							
From vendors	90,000	55,000					145,000
Intercompany	20,000[d]				2	8,000	12,000
Investment in subsidiary	60,000				1	60,000	-0-
Land	220,000	30,000					250,000
Buildings and equipment	500,000	150,000					650,000
Accumulated depreciation	(320,000)	(13,000)					(333,000)
Total Assets	724,000	270,000				68,000	926,000
Liabilities	407,000	190,000					597,000
NCI in net assets			2,000	3	1	20,000	18,000
Common stock ($1 par)	10,000						10,000
Add'l paid-in capital	190,000						190,000
Common stock (no par)		60,000	60,000	1			-0-
Retained earnings	117,000	20,000	124,000			98,000	111,000
Total Liabilities and Equity	724,000	270,000	186,000			118,000	926,000
Proof of debit and credit postings			186,000			186,000	

[a] Includes $32,000 of intercompany profit.

[b] 75% share of Subbco's reported net income of $24,000.

[c] Proof: Subbco's reported net income of $24,000 – $8,000 of unrealized profit at 12/31/06 = $16,000; $16,000 × 25% = $4,000.

[d] Includes $8,000 of intercompany profit.

Explanation of entries:

1 The basic *elimination* entry.
2 The inventory/COS change in basis *elimination* entry.
3 The sharing of deferred profit *elimination* entry.

Review Points for Illustrations 9-11 and 9-12. Note the following:

1. In Illustration 9-11, the $62,000 of consolidated net income that accrues to the *controlling interest* is $6,000 (75% × $8,000) *lower* than the $68,000 of net income reported by the *parent*.

ILLUSTRATION 9-12 THE PARTIAL EQUITY METHOD *UPSTREAM* TRANSFERS *ABOVE* COST: 75% OWNERSHIP—YEAR OF *RECOGNITION*

Parrco Company and Subbco Company
Consolidation Worksheet as of December 31, 2007

	PARRCO COMPANY	75%-OWNED SUBBCO COMPANY	CONSOLIDATION ENTRIES DR.			CR.	CONSOLIDATED
Income Statement (2007)							
Sales	710,000	282,000					992,000
Cost of sales	(390,000)[a]	(130,000)			2	8,000	(512,000)
Expenses	(210,000)	(120,000)					(330,000)
Intercompany Accounts							
Equity in net income (of Subbco)	24,000[b]		24,000	1			-0-
Net Income	134,000	32,000	24,000			8,000	150,000
NCI in net income			2,000 8,000	2 1			(10,000)[c]
CI in net income			34,000			8,000	140,000
Statement of Retained Earnings			6,000	2			
Balances, 1/1/07	117,000	20,000	20,000	1			111,000[d]
+ Net income	134,000	32,000	34,000			8,000	140,000
– Dividends declared	(85,000)	(12,000)			1	12,000	(85,000)
Balances, 12/31/07	166,000	40,000	60,000			20,000	166,000
Balance Sheet							
Cash	77,000	31,000					108,000
Accounts receivable, net	84,000	43,000					127,000
Inventory:							
From vendors	140,000	82,000					222,000
Intercompany	-0-						-0-
Investment in Subbco	75,000				1	75,000	-0-
Land	220,000	30,000					250,000
Buildings and equipment	500,000	150,000					650,000
Accumulated depreciation	(360,000)	(26,000)					(386,000)
Total Assets	736,000	310,000				75,000	971,000
Liabilities	370,000	210,000					580,000
NCI in net assets					1	25,000	25,000
Common stock ($1 par)	10,000						10,000
Add'l paid-in capital	190,000						190,000
Common stock (no par)		60,000	60,000	1			-0-
Retained earnings	166,000	40,000	60,000			20,000	166,000
Total Liabilities and Equity	736,000	310,000	120,000			45,000	971,000
Proof of debit and credit postings			*120,000*			*120,000*	

[a] Includes $8,000 of intercompany profit.

[b] 75% of Subbco's reported net income of $32,000.

[c] Proof: Subbco's reported net income of $32,000 + $8,000 of profit realized in 2007 = $40,000; $40,000 × 25% = $10,000.

[d] Agrees with ***ending*** balance at 12/31/06 in Illustration 9-11.

Explanation of entries:

1 The basic *elimination* entry.
2 The COS change in basis *elimination* entry—prior year intercompany sales.

2. In Illustration 9-12, the $140,000 of *consolidated* net income that accrues to the controlling interest is $6,000 *higher* than the *parent's* $134,000 of net income. *Consolidated* retained earnings is *identical*, however, to the *parent's* retained earnings because at the end of 2007, no unrealized intercompany profit exists to be deferred.

IV. MISCELLANEOUS AREAS

Transportation Costs

Probably because of their immateriality, the accounting consolidation rules do *not* specifically address the consolidation treatment of transportation costs incurred in moving inventory among entities of a consolidated group. Because normal transportation costs are inventoriable costs, there is no sound reason to treat them otherwise in consolidated statements.

When the *buying entity* incurs the transportation costs and treats them as inventoriable costs, the elimination of all of the selling entity's gross profit makes the transportation costs part of inventory on a *consolidated basis*. (Thus no special procedures or elimination entries relating to these costs are needed in consolidation.) When the *selling entity* incurs the transportation costs—which it records as marketing costs—the elimination of gross profit results, however, in expensing these costs on a *consolidated basis*. Accordingly, in consolidation, an additional entry must be made in these latter cases to (1) eliminate the transportation costs reported as marketing expenses and (2) charge these costs to inventory.

For the sake of simplicity, the illustrations pertaining to inventory transfers assumed that the transportation costs were *in*significant. Such costs are therefore treated as period costs for a separate company and on a consolidated basis.

Lower-of-Cost-or-Market Adjustments

Occasionally, the *buying entity* makes a market write-down on intercompany-acquired inventory (using its *own cost basis* when comparing to market). For consolidated reporting, the appropriate valuation is the lower of the *selling entity*'s cost (the *old basis*) or the market value—*not* the *buying entity*'s cost basis (the *new basis*).

Transfers at Below Cost

When transfers occur at *below* cost, the procedures are symmetrically the reverse so long as the unsold year-end inventory's market value equals or exceeds the *selling entity's* cost. If this is *not* the case, however, the inventory is reported in the consolidated statements at market value—an amount *lower* than the *selling entity's* cost.

CHECK POINTS

During 2006, Pya Inc. sold inventory costing $500,000 to Sya Inc., its 100%-owned subsidiary, at the *same* mark-up percentage as sales to third parties. As of 12/31/06, Sya had resold 80% of this inventory. Information regarding *total sales* for both entities follows:

	Pya Inc.	Sya Inc.
Sales	$ 2,000,000	$1,400,000
Cost of sales	(1,250,000)	(700,000)
Gross Profit	$ 750,000	$ 700,000

What is the reportable *consolidated sales* amount for 2006?

a. $2,320,000
b. $2,600,000
c. $2,900,000
d. $3,400,000

Answer: b

Use the preceding information. What is the reportable *consolidated cost of sales* for 2006?
a. $1,210,000
b. $1,300,000
c. $1,710,000
d. $1,950,000

Answer: a. ($1,250,000 – $500,000 = $750,000; $750,000 + $700,000 – $240,000 markup = $1,210,000)

END-OF-CHAPTER REVIEW

Summary of Key Points

1. In deferring unrealized intercompany profit, **gross profit** is the concept of profit used. (**Income taxes** provided on such gross profit must also be deferred for consolidated reporting purposes.)
2. The existence of a **noncontrolling interest** does *not* affect the amount of gross profit to be deferred.
3. For **upstream intercompany sales** from a partially owned subsidiary, the gross profit being deferred is **shared with the noncontrolling interest.**
4. Unrealized intercompany profit *cannot* be reported in parent-company-only statements.

Glossary of New Terms

Complete elimination Eliminating *all* of the intercompany profit associated with an asset regardless of the existence of a noncontrolling interest.

Fractional elimination Eliminating *less than* 100% of the intercompany profit associated with an asset because of the existence of a noncontrolling interest.

ASSIGNMENT MATERIAL

Review Questions

1. For intercompany transfers *at a markup*, what concept of profit is used for consolidation elimination purposes?
2. What does current GAAP require as to *income taxes provided on intercompany profits*?
3. Under current GAAP, can intercompany profit on downstream sales to a partially owned subsidiary be realized *to the extent of the noncontrolling interest*?
4. How does *complete elimination* differ from *fractional elimination*?
5. When can *intercompany profit* on intercompany inventory transfers be reported for *consolidated* reporting purposes?
6. Why are intercompany inventory transfers usually recorded at amounts *in excess of cost*?
7. Does the GAAP requirement to defer 100% of the intercompany profit associated with intercompany-acquired inventory fit under the *economic unit concept* or the *parent company concept*?

Exercises

E 9-1 **Unrealized Profit Determination** A parent and its subsidiary had intercompany inventory transactions in 2006 as follows:

	Total	Resold	On Hand
Intercompany sales	$ 240,000		$36,000
Intercompany cost of sales	(180,000)	______	______
Gross Profit	$ 60,000	______	______

Required 1. Complete the analysis.
2. Prepare the inventory transfer elimination entry required in consolidation at the end of 2006.

E 9-2 **Unrealized Profit Determination** In 2006, a parent and its 100%-owned subsidiary had intercompany inventory transactions. The following account balances pertain to this inventory transfer:

Account	Plax Inc.	Strax Inc.
Income Statement (2006)		
Sales	$ 650,000	
Cost of sales	(300,000)	
Intercompany sales		$ 500,000
Intercompany cost of sales		(350,000)
Balance Sheet (12/31/06)		
Intercompany-acquired inventory	$ 200,000	

Required 1. What is the unrealized intercompany profit at year-end?
2. What amounts should be reported in the Consolidated column?

E 9-3 **Reverse Analysis** In consolidation at the end of 2006, Cost of Sales was *credited* for $60,000 as a result of a posting from the inventory/COS change in basis elimination entry. During 2006 the *subsidiary* sold 60% of the inventory it had acquired from the *parent* in 2006. The *parent's* markup was 25% of *its cost.*

Required Prepare an analysis of intercompany transfers for 2006 (use the format shown in the chapter).

E 9-4 **Reverse Analysis** In consolidation at the end of 2006, Intercompany-Acquired Inventory was *credited* for $25,000 to change from the *new basis* of accounting to the *old basis* of accounting. During 2006, the *subsidiary* charged its Cost of Sales $400,000 as a result of having sold intercompany-acquired inventory. The *parent's* markup was 20% of the *transfer price.*

Required Prepare an analysis of intercompany transfers for 2006 (use the format shown in the chapter).

E 9-5 **Realized Profit Calculation—Two Years of *Downstream* Transfers** In 2007, Soxa Inc., a 100%-owned subsidiary of Poxa Inc., resold for $90,000 inventory it had purchased in 2006 for $70,000 from Poxa. Poxa's cost was $40,000. Also in 2006, Poxa sold inventory costing $250,000 to Soxa for $400,000. At the end of 2007, Soxa reported $72,000 of this 2007 intercompany-acquired inventory in its balance sheet, the remaining 2007 intercompany-acquired inventory having been resold for $500,000.

Required 1. How much intercompany profit was realized in 2007?
2. *For Module 1 only:* Prepare the *general ledger adjusting entry(ies)* pertaining to unrealized intercompany profit at the end of 2007.

E 9-6 **Realized Profit Calculation—Two Years of *Upstream* Transfers** In 2007, Perl Inc. resold for $85,000 inventory it had purchased in 2006 for $60,000 from Serl Inc., its 60%-owned subsidiary. Serl's cost was $40,000. Also in 2007, Perl purchased for $600,000 inventory costing Serl $450,000. At the end of 2007, Perl reported $100,000 of this 2007 intercompany-acquired inventory in its balance sheet, the remaining 2007 intercompany-acquired inventory having been resold for $475,000.

Required 1. How much intercompany profit was realized in 2007?

2. *For Module 1 only*: Prepare the *general ledger adjusting entry(ies)* pertaining to unrealized intercompany profit at the end of 2007.

E 9-7 **Calculating Consolidated Sales and Cost of Sales** During 2006, Pyra Inc. sold inventory costing $150,000 to Syra Inc., its 100%-owned subsidiary, at the same mark-up percentage as sales to third parties. As of 12/31/06, Syra had resold 90% of this inventory. Information regarding *total sales* for both entities follows:

	Pyra Inc.	Syra Inc.
Sales	$1,200,000	$ 900,000
Cost of sales	(720,000)	(600,000)
Gross Profit	$ 480,000	$ 300,000

Required 1. What is the reportable consolidated *sales* amount for 2006?
2. What is the reportable consolidated *cost of sales* amount for 2006?

E 9-8 **Calculating Consolidated Sales and Cost of Sales** During 2006, Sora Inc., an 80%-owned subsidiary, sold inventory costing $420,000 to Pora Inc., its parent, at the same mark-up percentage as sales to third parties. As of 12/31/06, Pora reported $90,000 in its balance sheet for intercompany-acquired inventory. Information regarding *total sales* for both entities follows:

	Pora Inc.	Sora Inc.
Sales	$ 4,000,000	$1,100,000
Cost of sales	(1,400,000)	(770,000)
Gross Profit	$ 2,600,000	$ 330,000

Required 1. What is the reportable consolidated *sales* amount for 2006?
2. What is the reportable consolidated *cost of sales* amount for 2006?

E 9-9 **Multiple-Year Elimination Entries—*Downstream* Sales** In 2006, Pobe Inc. sold inventory costing $50,000 to its 75%-owned subsidiary, Sobe Inc., for $70,000. Sobe resold a portion of this inventory for $65,000 in 2006. At the end of 2006, Sobe's balance sheet showed $21,000 of intercompany-acquired inventory on hand. Sobe resold this remaining inventory in 2008 for $28,000.

Required 1. Prepare the *general ledger adjusting entry* required for 2006, 2007, and 2008, if necessary, under the complete equity method. **Omit this requirement if you are using Module 2.**
2. Prepare the consolidation elimination entry(ies) at the end of 2006, 2007, and 2008 relating to these intercompany inventory sales.
3. At what amount is the inventory reported in the consolidated statements at the end of 2006 and 2007?

E 9-10 **Calculating the NCI Deduction—*Downstream* Transfers** In 2006, Pebb Inc. sold inventory costing $200,000 to its 90%-owned subsidiary, Sebb Inc., for $250,000. At the end of 2006, Sebb reported $30,000 of this inventory in its balance sheet. Sebb also reported net income of $100,000 for 2006.

Required Calculate the *non*controlling interest deduction to be reported in the 2006 consolidated income statement.

E 9-11 **Calculating the NCI Deduction—*Upstream* Transfers** In 2006, Sote Inc., an 80%-owned subsidiary of Pote Inc., sold inventory costing $300,000 to Pote for $400,000. Pote resold $340,000 of this inventory in 2006 for $510,000. Sote also reported net income of $200,000 for 2006, disregarding any unrealized intercompany profit at the end of 2006.

Required Calculate the *non*controlling interest deduction to be reported in the 2006 consolidated income statement.

E 9-12 **Multiple-Year Elimination Entries—*Upstream* Sales** In 2006, Pota Inc. acquired inventory from Sota Inc., its 75%-owned subsidiary, for $100,000. Sota's cost was $80,000: Pota resold a portion of this inventory in 2006 for $90,000. At 12/31/06, Pota's balance sheet showed $40,000 of intercompany-acquired inventory on hand. Pota resold this remaining inventory in 2008 for $52,000.

Required

1. Prepare the *general ledger adjusting entry(ies)* required for 2006, 2007, and 2008, if necessary, under the complete equity method. **Omit this requirement if you are using Module 2.**
2. Prepare the consolidation elimination entry(ies) at the end of 2006, 2007, and 2008 relating to these intercompany inventory sales.
3. At what amount is the inventory reported in the consolidated statements at the end of 2006 and 2007?

E 9-13 **Issuing PCO Statements** Selected items from the financial statements of Poly Inc. and Soly Inc., a 70%-owned subsidiary of Poly, at 12/31/06, are as follows:

	Poly Inc.	Soly Inc.
Income Statement		
Sales		$ 280,000
Cost of sales		(125,000)
Intercompany sales	$150,000	
Intercompany cost of sales	(90,000)	
Net income		100,000
Statement of Retained Earnings		
Dividends declared		-0-
Balance Sheet		
Inventory—intercompany acquired		25,000
Investment in subsidiary, 1/1/06	500,000	

Required

1. Calculate the unrealized intercompany profit at the end of 2006.
2. If the parent issued PCO statements in addition to consolidated statements, what amounts would appear in the PCO statements as a result of (1) the intercompany inventory transfers, (2) Soly's operations, and (3) Poly's investment in Soly?
3. Repeat requirement 2, but assume that the transfers are *upstream.*

E 9-14 **Lower-of-Cost-or-Market Adjustment** In 2006, Pondo Inc. sold inventory costing $60,000 to its subsidiary for $70,000. At the end of 2006, the subsidiary recorded a lower-of- cost-or-market adjustment relating to this inventory, 60% of which had been sold during 2006.

Required Determine the amount at which the inventory should be reported in consolidation, assuming that the adjustment was

1. $3,000.
2. $6,000.

Problems

P 9-1* **Consolidation Worksheet: *Downstream* Transfers—100% Ownership** In 2005, Peta Inc. created a 100%-owned subsidiary, Seta Inc. In 2006, intercompany inventory transfers occurred for the first time. Comparative financial statements are as follows:

*The financial statement information presented for problems accompanied by asterisks is also provided on Model 9 (filename: MODEL09) at the **http://pahler.swlearning.com** website, allowing the problem to be worked on the computer. **On rows 42–64, prepare (1) an analysis and (2) your elimination entries other than the basic elimination entry** in the space provided.

	Peta Inc.	Seta Inc.
Income Statement (2006)		
Sales	$ 200,000	$120,000
Cost of sales	(114,000)	(56,000)
Expenses	(84,000)	(48,000)
Intercompany Accounts		
Equity in net income (of Seta)	16,000	
Intercompany sales	70,000	
Intercompany cost of sales	(40,000)	
Net Income	$ 48,000	$ 16,000
Balance Sheet (as of 12/31/06)		
Inventory:		
From vendors	$ 55,000	
Intercompany		$ 14,000
Investment in subsidiary	100,000	
Other assets	345,000	286,000
Total Assets	$ 500,000	$300,000
Liabilities	$ 170,000	$200,000
Common stock	130,000	10,000
Retained earnings	200,000	90,000
Total Liabilities and Equity	$ 500,000	$300,000
Dividends declared—2006	$ 22,000	$ 11,000

Required

1. Determine the unrealized profit at year-end by preparing an analysis. (*For Module 1 only:* Also make the necessary year-end *general ledger adjusting entry* [for unrealized profit] required for this module. Adjust the statements accordingly.)
2. Prepare *all* consolidation entries as of 12/31/06.
3. Prepare a consolidation worksheet at 12/31/06.
4. Is the subsidiary a *manufacturer* or a *distributor*?
5. What is the **total** recognizable profit on the intercompany-acquired inventory that was *resold* by Seta?

P 9-2* **Consolidation Worksheet: *Upstream* Transfers—90% Ownership** In 2005, Pino Inc. created a 90%-owned subsidiary, Sino Inc. In 2006, intercompany inventory transfers occurred for the first time. Comparative financial statements are as follows:

	Pino Inc.	Sino Inc.
Income Statement (2006)		
Sales	$ 630,000	$ 90,000
Cost of sales	(475,000)	(25,000)
Expenses	(95,000)	(45,000)
Intercompany Accounts		
Equity in net income (of Sino)	63,000	
Intercompany sales		250,000
Intercompany cost of sales		(200,000)
Net Income	$ 123,000	$ 70,000
Balance Sheet (as of 12/31/06)		
Inventory:		
From vendors	$ 65,000	$ 90,000
Intercompany	50,000	
Investment in subsidiary	198,000	
Other assets	487,000	310,000
Total Assets	$ 800,000	$ 400,000
Liabilities	$ 255,000	$ 180,000
Common stock	300,000	120,000
Retained earnings	245,000	100,000
Total Liabilities and Equity	$ 800,000	$ 400,000
Dividends declared—2006	$ 80,000	$ 30,000

Required

1. Determine the unrealized profit at year-end by preparing an analysis. (*For Module 1 only:* Also make the necessary year-end *general ledger adjusting entry(ies)* [for unrealized profit] required for this module. Adjust both sets of statements accordingly.)
2. Prepare ***all*** consolidation entries as of 12/31/06.
3. Prepare a consolidation worksheet at 12/31/06.

P 9-3 **Consolidation Entries: 100% Ownership—*Downstream* Transfers; Other Intercompany Transactions** On 1/1/06, Pom Inc. created a 100%-owned subsidiary, Som Inc., with a $25,000 common stock investment.

Additional Information

1. During 2006, Pom sold inventory to Som at a profit. The markup percentage was 40% of the transfer price. At 12/31/06, Som had on hand intercompany-acquired inventory that had cost Pom $18,000. Downstream sales for 2006 totaled $160,000. Of this amount, Som had paid Pom $130,000 by year-end.
2. On 12/30/06, Pom allocated $4,000 of previously recorded advertising expense to Som, which received the allocation notice on 1/4/07.
3. During 2006, Pom charged Som $5,000 for management services, of which $3,000 had been paid by year-end.
4. On 12/29/06, Som declared a cash dividend of $10,000. The dividend was paid on 1/3/07.
5. Som reported retained earnings of $22,000 in its 12/31/06 balance sheet.
6. No other intercompany transactions occurred during 2006.

Required Prepare ***all*** consolidation entries at the end of 2006.

P 9-4* **Consolidation Worksheet: *Downstream* Multiple-Year Transfers—100% Ownership** Comparative financial statements of Puma Inc. and its 100%-owned subsidiary, Suma Inc. (created five years ago), are as follows:

	Puma Inc.	Suma Inc.
Income Statement (2006)		
Sales	$ 500,000	$210,000
Cost of sales	(290,000)	(99,000)
Expenses	(205,000)	(71,000)
Intercompany Accounts		
Dividend income		
Equity in net income (of Suma)	40,000	
Intercompany sales	100,000	
Intercompany cost of sales	(60,000)	
Net Income	$ 85,000	$ 40,000
Statement of Retained Earnings (2006)		
Balances, 1/1/06	$ 190,000	$ 50,000
+ Net income	85,000	40,000
– Dividends declared	(25,000)	(20,000)
Balances, as of 12/31/06	$ 250,000	$ 70,000
Balance Sheet (as of 12/31/06)		
Inventory:		
From vendor	$ 200,000	
Intercompany		$ 25,000
Investment in subsidiary	150,000	
Other assets	500,000	225,000
Total Assets	$ 850,000	$250,000
Liabilities	$ 300,000	$100,000
Common stock	300,000	80,000
Retained earnings	250,000	70,000
Total Liabilities and Equity	$ 850,000	$250,000

Additional Information

1. At 12/31/05 (the preceding year-end), Suma had on hand inventory it had acquired in 2005 from Puma at a cost of $24,000. Puma's cost was $20,000. Suma resold all of this inventory in 2006 for $33,000.

2. *No* general ledger entries were made at the end of 2005 or 2006 to defer unrealized intercompany profit.

Required

1. Determine the unrealized profit at year-end by preparing an analysis. (*For Module 1 only:* Also make the necessary (1) *beginning-of-year* correcting entry [a *debit* to *beginning* retained earnings and a *credit* to intercompany profit *recognition*] and (2) *end-of-year general ledger* adjusting entry to reflect the deferral of profit on Puma's books. Adjust the statements accordingly.)
2. Prepare all consolidation entries as of 12/31/06.
3. Prepare a consolidation worksheet at 12/31/06.
4. Is the subsidiary a *manufacturer* or a *distributor*?

P 9-5* **Consolidation Worksheet: *Upstream* Multiple-Year Transfers—80% Ownership** Comparative financial statements of Pebb Inc. and its 80%-owned subsidiary, Sebb Inc. (created five years ago), are as follows:

	Pebb Inc.	Sebb Inc.
Income Statement (2006)		
Sales	$ 600,000	$ 85,000
Cost of sales	(350,000)	(50,000)
Expenses	(150,000)	(40,000)
Intercompany Accounts		
Equity in net income (of Sebb)	20,000	
Intercompany sales		90,000
Intercompany cost of sales		(60,000)
Net income	$ 120,000	$ 25,000
Statement of Retained Earnings (2006)		
Balances, 1/1/06	$ 150,000	$ 55,000
+ Net income	120,000	25,000
− Dividends declared	(50,000)	(10,000)
Balances, 12/31/06	$ 220,000	$ 70,000
Balance Sheet (12/31/06)		
Inventory from vendors	$ 150,000	$ 50,000
Intercompany	15,000	
Investment in subsidiary	140,000	
Other assets	363,000	180,000
Total Assets	$ 668,000	$230,000
Liabilities	$ 298,000	$ 55,000
Common stock	150,000	105,000
Retained earnings	220,000	70,000
Total Liabilities and Equity	$ 668,000	$230,000

Additional Information

1. At 12/31/05 (the preceding year-end), Pebb had on hand inventory it had acquired in 2005 from Sebb at a cost of $25,000. Sebb's cost was $10,000. Pebb resold all of this inventory in 2006 for $44,000.

2. No general ledger entries were made at the end of 2005 or 2006 to defer unrealized intercompany profit.

Required

1. Determine the unrealized profit at year-end by preparing an analysis. (*For Module 1 only:* Also make the necessary (1) *beginning*-of-year correcting entry and (2) *end*-of-year *general ledger* adjusting entry to reflect the deferral of profit on Sebb's books. Adjust both sets of statements accordingly.)

2. Prepare all consolidation entries as of 12/31/06.
3. Prepare a consolidation worksheet at 12/31/06.

P 9-6 **Consolidation Entries: 100% Ownership—Two Years of *Downstream* Transfers; Other Intercompany Transactions; LCM Adjustment** On 1/1/06, Pano Inc. created a 100%-owned subsidiary, Sano Inc., with a $40,000 common stock investment.

Additional Information

1. During *2006,* Pano sold inventory costing $63,000 to Sano at a *transfer price* of $90,000; Sano fully paid Pano in 2006 for this purchase. At 12/31/06 Sano reported intercompany-acquired inventory of $20,000 in its balance sheet. In 2007, *all* of this inventory was resold for $15,000.
2. During *2007,* Pano sold inventory to Sano for $200,000, of which Sano had paid Pano $170,000 by year-end. The markup percentage was 33 1/3% of Pano's cost. At 12/31/07, Sano had on hand intercompany-acquired inventory that had cost Pano $24,000. Sano made a $3,000 lower-of-cost-or-market adjustment at the end of 2007 on this inventory.
3. On 12/31/07, Pano allocated $12,000 of previously recorded insurance expenses to Sano, which received the allocation notice on 1/1/08.
4. During 2006, Pano charged Sano $33,000 for technical services relating to research and development work, of which Sano paid $22,000 by year-end.
5. On 12/31/07, Sano declared a cash dividend of $20,000; it was paid on 1/4/08. In 2006, Sano declared and paid cash dividends of $15,000 (60% of its 2006 net income).
6. Sano reported retained earnings of $44,000 in its 12/31/07 balance sheet.
7. No other intercompany transactions occurred during 2007 or 2006.

Required

1. Prepare a T-account analysis of Sano's retained earnings account for 2006 and 2007.
2. Prepare an unrealized profit analysis for the inventory transfers for 2006 and 2007.
3. Prepare ***all*** consolidation entries at the end of 2007.

P 9-7 **Spreadsheet Automation of the Unrealized Profit Analysis and the Inventory Transfer Elimination Entry** Before working this assignment, you should first have worked Problems 9-1, 9-2, 9-4, or 9-5 using MODEL09 of the software package that accompanies the text. Next perform the following steps for automating the inventory transfer elimination entry on the spreadsheet.

Required

1. In the unrealized profit analysis (begins on row 26) program formulas to automatically insert from either the *Parent* column or the *Subsidiary* column of the worksheet amounts for (a) intercompany sales, (b) intercompany cost of sales, and (c) intercompany inventory on hand. To allow this analysis to accommodate the possibility of intercompany inventory transfers being either *downstream* or *upstream,* you must program a logic formula (using the = *IF* function of EXCEL) for inserting amounts from either (1) the parent's column or (2) the subsidiary's column, as appropriate.
2. In the analysis, program formulas to automatically insert the remaining three missing amounts.
3. *Below* the analysis in the required consolidation entry section that is derived from this analysis, program formulas to bring forward the appropriate amounts from the analysis.
4. In the Debit and Credit columns of the consolidation worksheet, program formulas to bring forward the amounts that are in the elimination entry you prepared in the preceding instruction.

THINKING CRITICALLY

Cases

C 9-1 **If Better Off Economically, Why Not Report It?** In late 2006, Pia Inc. sold inventory costing $60,000 to its 60%-owned subsidiary, Sia Inc., for $100,000 with payment being made on delivery. As of 12/31/06, Sia had *not* resold any of this inventory.

Required

1. Does the fact that Pia was paid in full have any significance as to whether $40,000 or only $24,000 (60% of $40,000) should be deferred for consolidated reporting purposes? Why or why not?
2. Have Pia's stockholders benefited economically to the extent of $16,000 (40% × $40,000)? Why or why not?
3. If the FASB were to change GAAP so that this $16,000 could be recognized in 2006 for reporting to Pia's stockholders, can you think of any accompanying provisions that should be stipulated to maintain financial reporting integrity?

C 9-2 ***Sole* versus *Shared* Control: Does It Really Matter? (Research Assignment)** Alpha Inc. and Beta Inc. are *co-owners* (50% owners) of a joint venture, Ventura Inc., created in early 2006 to build and market a newly conceived product. Neither company has control of the joint venture; all important decisions require the agreement of *both* investor entities.

Alpha sells a key inventory component to the joint venture at a markup, the transfer price having been negotiated with and approved by Beta. During 2006, Ventura (with Beta's formal approval) purchased $1,000,000 of this component from Alpha. (Ventura paid Alpha $1,000,000 cash.) Alpha's cost was $600,000. As of 12/31/06, Ventura had *not* shipped any of its newly conceived product.

Required

1. Because this is a *shared control* situation instead of a *sole control* situation, can Alpha report either 100% or at least 50% of the $400,000 intercompany profit for 2006?
2. In your library, or using the FASB's financial accounting research system (FARS) if available in your school's computer center (normally stored on a file-server computer), find the AICPA's *Accounting Interpretations of APB Opinion No. 18*, "The Equity Method of Accounting for Investments in Common Stock," issued in February 1972. Does it allow any profit recognition in this situation?
3. Assume that (1) Ventura *resells* the Alpha-acquired inventory for only $600,000 and (2) Ventura is *dissolved*. How much cash would Alpha and Beta receive in liquidation if (a) each had initially invested $500,000 cash and (b) Ventura reported a $400,000 *loss* from inception through the liquidation date?

Personal Situations: Interpersonal Skills

PS 9-1 **Interpersonal Skills: Looking Back?** Work environments vary greatly.

Required No matter where you will have worked in life, which one thing—usually above all other things—will (1) you always remember about where you worked and (2) your co-workers always remember about you?

chapter

10

Intercompany Fixed Asset Transfers and Bond Holdings

It's easy to have principles when you're rich. The important thing is to have principles when you're poor.

RAY KROC (FOUNDER OF McDONALD'S)

LEARNING OBJECTIVES

To Understand

- The concept of changing, in consolidation, from the *new basis* of accounting to the *old basis* of accounting.
- The additional complexities associated with intercompany *fixed asset* transfers in relation to intercompany *inventory* transfers.
- The procedures to defer recognition of unrealized intercompany gains or losses on fixed asset transfers.
- Why gains and losses occur as a result of intercompany bond purchases.
- The way to calculate such gains and losses.
- The way to report such gains and losses in the consolidated statements.

TOPIC OUTLINE

A: INTERCOMPANY FIXED ASSET TRANSFERS

I. Summary of GAAP Regarding Intercompany Transactions (discussed in Chapters 8 and 9)

II. Changing from the *New Basis* of Accounting to the *Old Basis* of Accounting in Consolidation

III. The Additional Complexities of *Fixed Asset* Transfers in Relation to *Inventory* Transfers

IV. Procedures for Deferring Unrealized Intercompany Gains and Losses

MODULE 1: The Complete Equity Method

MODULE 2: The Partial Equity Method

B: INTERCOMPANY BOND HOLDINGS

V. The Constructive Retirement of the Bonds

VI. Calculating the Gain or Loss on Debt Extinguishment

VII. *Simplified* Procedures: Premiums and Discounts Eliminated in the General Ledgers at the Bond Purchase Date

A. Intercompany Fixed Asset Transfers

SECTION OVERVIEW

This chapter discusses how to change from the *new* to the *old* basis of accounting when fixed assets have been transferred at a gain or loss among entities of a consolidated group. By changing the basis of accounting in consolidation, the intercompany *gain or loss*[1] is eliminated for consolidated reporting purposes—as intercompany *profit or loss* on *inventory* transfers is eliminated (see Chapter 9).

Frequency and Types of Depreciable Fixed Asset Transfers

In practice, intercompany *fixed asset* transfers occur much *less* frequently than intercompany *inventory* transfers. Furthermore, intercompany transfers of **nondepreciable** fixed assets occur much *less* frequently than intercompany transfers of **depreciable** fixed assets.

In the *typical* depreciable fixed asset transfer, the selling entity *sells* a **partially depreciated fixed asset** that it has been using in its operations (occurs usually in *horizontally* integrated companies). Less frequently encountered are *hybrid* inventory/fixed asset transfers whereby the selling entity *sells* **inventory** to the buying entity, which then *capitalizes* the equipment as a fixed asset (occurs usually in *conglomerates*). Sometimes one entity also *leases* equipment to another entity with the **lessor** using **sales-type** treatment and the **lessee** using **capital lease** treatment. We discuss only the *first* mentioned typical depreciable fixed asset transfer because the principles involved can be applied readily to these other situations.

Detailed Deferral Procedures Shown in Modules

As was the case with inventory transfers in Chapter 9, detailed deferral procedures are presented in separate modules with each module being self-contained and independent, and standing on its own when read in conjunction with the general material that precedes Module 1. The following are the two modules presented:

MODULE 1: **The Complete Equity Method** (deferral occurs *in the general ledger*)
MODULE 2: **The Partial Equity Method** (deferral occurs *on the worksheet*)

I. Summary of GAAP Regarding Intercompany Transactions (Discussed in Chapters 8 and 9)

Recall from Chapters 8 and 9 the following GAAP requirements for preparing consolidated financial statements:

1. *All* **intercompany transactions** must be eliminated in consolidation to present the financial position and results of operations *as if* **the two separate legal entities were a single legal entity having a branch.**
2. For intercompany profit or gain associated with assets on hand at a reporting date, **the *entire* intercompany profit or gain must be eliminated.**

[1] *Historical Note*: During the Great Depression, many parent companies had entities within the consolidated group sell fixed assets to one another to report profits in an attempt to maintain or increase the price of the parent's common stock. At that time, such intercompany gains were *not* required to be deferred for consolidated reporting purposes.

3. The concept of intercompany profit or gain to be eliminated is **gross profit**. For fixed assets, this means the selling entity's **gain (or loss)** on the intercompany sale of a fixed asset (*transfer price-carrying value* at the transfer date).
4. Any **income taxes (benefit)** recorded on such profits or gains (or losses) must also be deferred in consolidation. As in Chapter 9, we assume in our illustrations for simplicity that the elimination of the tax effects has already been recorded in the parent's or subsidiary's general ledger.
5. For ***upstream* transfers from partially owned subsidiaries**, the deferral of unrealized intercompany profit or gain **is shared with the *non*controlling interest**. Accordingly, intercompany gains or losses on fixed asset transfers require the same type of elimination treatment as for intercompany profits or losses on inventory transfers.

II. CHANGING FROM THE *NEW BASIS* OF ACCOUNTING TO THE *OLD BASIS* OF ACCOUNTING IN CONSOLIDATION

Recall from Chapter 9 that when inventory was transferred within a consolidated entity at a transfer price above or below the selling entity's carrying value, the selling (transfer) price became the buying entity's cost, which became **a *new basis* of accounting** for the inventory on the buying entity's books. Also recall that for intercompany-acquired inventory still on hand at a consolidated reporting date, the intercompany profit elimination treatment resulted in reporting the inventory in consolidation at the selling entity's carrying value (usually acquisition cost) at the transfer date—**the *old basis* of accounting**.

Thus this elimination treatment achieved consolidated reporting results *as though* the transfer instead had been made at the *selling entity's carrying value* of the inventory rather than at a higher (or lower) amount. These same consolidated reporting results must be achieved for intercompany fixed asset transfers.

Major Point: All Intercompany Transfers. The carrying value for any asset—**whether it be inventory, fixed assets, patents, copyrights, capitalized software, or some other asset**—of any company within a consolidated group *cannot* change for consolidated reporting purposes merely because the asset has been moved to a different location within the consolidated group.

Determining Amounts Based on the Old Basis versus Amounts Based on the New Basis

Having a Gain or Loss on the Sale Changes the Basis of Accounting

The selling entity's intercompany gain or loss is calculated in the same manner as the sale of a fixed asset to an outside third party by comparing (1) the **sales price** (the proceeds) with (2) the **carrying value** of the asset (**acquisition cost** minus any **accumulated depreciation**) at the transfer date. For example, used equipment costing $40,000 and having accumulated depreciation of $25,000 at the transfer date has a **carrying value** of $15,000. If the intercompany sales price is $18,000, the selling entity reports a $3,000 intercompany gain ($18,000 – $15,000). The $18,000 amount becomes **the new cost basis** to the *buying entity*, which it uses for calculating depreciation on its books. Accordingly, selling the fixed asset at $3,000 *more than* the $15,000 carrying value increases the asset's basis of accounting by $3,000, allowing the buying entity to have $3,000 of **incremental cost basis** that will be depreciated in future periods.

Changing to the *Old Basis* of Accounting in the Balance Sheet

The objective in consolidation is to report amounts based on **the *old cost basis***. Thus the *historical cost* of the equipment must be reported at $40,000, *not* $18,000. Likewise, *accumulated de-*

preciation must be reported at the sum of (1) the $25,000 of accumulated depreciation at the transfer date and (2) any depreciation recorded after the transfer date based on the $15,000 carrying value at the transfer date—*not* on the $18,000 *new cost basis*.

Changing to the *Old Basis* of Accounting in the Income Statement

Depreciation expense reported on consolidated income statements for periods *after* the transfer date must be based on the $15,000 carrying value at the transfer date—*not* on the $18,000 new cost basis. Thus if the buying entity were to use a three-year life and record $6,000 of annual depreciation expense ($18,000 ÷ 3 years), a $1,000 adjustment is needed in consolidation to report annual depreciation expense of only $5,000 ($15,000 ÷ 3 years). Note that the **incremental depreciation expense** on the buying entity's books is solely attributable to the equipment's sale at a $3,000 gain.

Using an Intercompany Gain or Loss Account Instead of Intercompany Sales and Intercompany Cost of Sales Accounts

Another difference between intercompany *inventory* transfers and intercompany *fixed asset* transfers involves the income statement accounts used to record the transfers. Instead of using an Intercompany Sales account and a related Intercompany Cost of Sales account, as it does for *inventory* transfers, the *selling entity* uses the lone Intercompany Gain (or Loss) account when it transfers fixed assets. This actually constitutes a slight simplification: Only one income statement account instead of two need be eliminated in the year of the transfer.

III. THE ADDITIONAL COMPLEXITIES OF *FIXED ASSET* TRANSFERS IN RELATION TO *INVENTORY* TRANSFERS

In comparison to the consolidation procedures for intercompany inventory transfers, the consolidation procedures pertaining to intercompany transfers of **nondepreciable** fixed assets are substantively the same, but the consolidation procedures pertaining to **depreciable** fixed assets are more involved.

Nondepreciable Fixed Asset Transfers

Because land is ***not*** depreciated, the entire unrealized intercompany gain or loss from a consolidated perspective is always associated with the cost of land as reported on the *buying entity's* books. Accordingly, the consolidation procedures merely result in adjusting the Land account upward or downward to reflect the *old basis* of accounting—as was done for intercompany-acquired inventory still on hand.

Subsequent Disposal of the Land

From a consolidated perspective, the subsequent sale of the land to an *outside third party* is no different from reselling intercompany-acquired inventory to an outside third party. For intercompany inventory transfers at a profit, recall that (1) the buying entity's subsequent sale of that inventory to an outside third party caused the buying entity's Cost of Sales account to be *overstated* from a consolidated perspective and (2) the overstatement was eliminated in consolidation. Likewise, for the sale of intercompany-acquired land to an outside third party **at *more than* the buying entity's cost basis**, (1) the buying entity's **reported Gain on Sale of Land** account is also *understated* from a consolidated perspective to the extent that the selling entity records an **intercompany gain** when the intercompany transfer occurred at an earlier date,[2] and (2) this *understatement* must also be eliminated in consolidation.

For a sale of intercompany-acquired land to an outside third party **at *less than* the buying entity's cost,** (1) the buying entity's reported Loss on Sale of Land account is *overstated* from a consolidated perspective to the extent of an intercompany gain on the earlier transfer, and (2) this *overstatement* must be eliminated in consolidation.

Concluding Point

Thus whether a nondepreciable asset continues to be held or is subsequently sold to an outside third party, the consolidation procedures for dealing with intercompany transfers of nondepreciable fixed assets are virtually identical to those used for intercompany inventory transfers.

Depreciable Fixed Asset Transfers

Because intercompany-acquired depreciable fixed assets are depreciated, any initially recorded **unrealized** intercompany gain (or loss) becomes lower and lower as time goes by—**from a consolidated perspective**—eventually becoming zero when the asset becomes fully depreciated. This occurs for depreciable fixed assets because (1) such assets are used to generate sales to outside third parties, and (2) as long as such sales occur, a portion of them is effectively a recovery of the cost of depreciable fixed assets. In other words, a portion of the depreciable fixed asset—equal to the annual depreciation charge—is converted into cash each year. Thus **partial realization** of the buying entity's cost of the intercompany-acquired fixed asset occurs each year **as though a portion of the intercompany-acquired fixed assets were sold directly to outside third parties each year.**

This gradual reduction of the unrealized intercompany gain or loss over time slightly complicates the consolidation procedures because of the additional steps involved in comparing (1) the *new basis* of accounting amounts and (2) the ***old basis*** of accounting amounts. The difference in the amounts for the two bases reveals the amounts needed at each consolidation date to change to the old basis of accounting.

A Different Way to Visualize the Result of the Consolidation Procedures

The consolidation procedures for **intercompany gain** situations achieve the same result that would occur if the intercompany gain had been deferred and then amortized to income in a manner that exactly **offsets (cancels out) the future incremental depreciation expense** that occurs each year because **the buying entity's new cost basis *exceeded* the selling entity's carrying value** at the transfer date. For **intercompany loss** situations, the consolidation procedures achieve the same result that would occur if the intercompany loss had been deferred and then amortized to income in a manner that exactly **makes up the future depreciation expense shortage** that occurs each year because **the buying entity's new cost basis is *below* the selling entity's carrying value** at the transfer date.

[2] The terms *buying entity* and *selling entity* are used in the context of the intercompany transaction—*not* in the context of the transaction with the *outside third party*.

IV. PROCEDURES FOR DEFERRING UNREALIZED INTERCOMPANY GAINS AND LOSSES

Module 1 Overview

Recall from Chapter 9 that under the **complete equity method**, the parent defers its share of any unrealized intercompany profit (gain in this chapter) in its general ledger by using an **Intercompany Gain Deferred account** (a **balance sheet** account), the balance therein being reversed later when realization—from a consolidated perspective—occurs. In this chapter, the reversal occurs either (1) in a single year for nondepreciable fixed assets (as was the case for reselling inventory to an outside third party) or (2) in increments for depreciable fixed assets over the ***new* assigned remaining life** (the *original* remaining life becomes irrelevant).

As for recording general ledger adjusting entries for unrealized intercompany **profit or gains**, recall that (1) for **downstream transfers** the *parent* adjusts the Intercompany Gain Deferred account (a **contra asset** balance sheet account), and (2) for **upstream transfers** the *subsidiary* adjusts the Intercompany Gain Deferred account.

SECTION 1: TRANSFERS OF NONDEPRECIABLE ASSETS

Downstream Land Transfers: *Gain* Situations

For the following example, assume that Parrco Company sells land costing $20,000 to its 100%-owned subsidiary, Subbco Company, for $30,000 on January 1, 2005.

Consolidation at January 1, 2005

If consolidation occurs as of January 1, 2005—the transfer date—Parrco makes the following **general ledger adjusting entry**:

Intercompany Gain *Deferral* (income statement)	10,000	
Intercompany Gain *Deferred* (balance sheet)		10,000

Accordingly, *in consolidation* at the transfer date, the following two entries are made:

WORKSHEET ENTRY ONLY

Intercompany Gain (income statement)	10,000	
Intercompany Gain *Deferral* (income statement)		10,000
Intercompany Gain *Deferred* (balance sheet)	10,000	
Land		10,000

The preceding worksheet entries are made at any other consolidation date in 2005, assuming that Subbco still owns the land at that (those) consolidation date(s).

Subsequent Year Treatment of Unrealized Gain

Land *Not* Resold at the End of 2006

If Subbco still owns the land at December 31, 2006, the only entry needed in consolidation is to debit the Intercompany Gain Deferred account and credit the land account for $10,000 (to bring Subbco's $30,000 carrying value down to Parrco's $20,000 cost, as was done in 2005).

Land Resold by the End of 2007

If Subbco sells the land in 2007 for $32,000, it then reports a $2,000 gain ($32,000 – $30,000). The previously deferred intercompany gain of $10,000 has now been realized, however, making the reportable gain for consolidated reporting purposes $12,000 ($32,000 – $20,000). Parrco makes the following **general ledger adjusting entry:**

Intercompany Gain *Deferred* (balance sheet)	10,000	
Intercompany Gain *Recognition*		10,000

Consequently, the following entry is made in consolidation:

WORKSHEET ENTRY ONLY

Intercompany Gain *Recognition* (income statement)	10,000	
Gain on Sale of Land		10,000
To report the gain based on the *old basis* of accounting ($32,000 – $20,000) instead of the *new basis* of accounting ($32,000 – $30,000).		

Downstream Land Transfers: *Loss* Situations

When an entity transfers land **at *below* its carrying value**, it must defer the intercompany loss. The principle is the same as that for a transfer above its carrying value, but the debits and credits are reversed.

Upstream Land Transfers

The procedures for an **upstream** land transfer parallel those shown in Chapter 9 for upstream inventory transfers. Recall that in those situations, the subsidiary deferred the unrealized intercompany profit (gain in this chapter) in its general ledger using an Intercompany Gain *Deferred* (a balance sheet account). Upstream transfers are discussed in the last half of Section 2 that follows.

Section 2: Transfers of Depreciable Assets

Downstream Equipment Transfers: *Gain* Situations

Assume that the following downstream equipment transfer occurred between Parrco Company and Subbco Company, its 100%-owned subsidiary created several years ago:

	Parrco Company	Subbco Company
Sales price of equipment sold to Subbco on January 1, 2005		$18,000
Carrying value on Parrco's books:		
Cost (*4-year* assigned life)	$ 40,000	
Accumulated depreciation (2 1/2 years)	(25,000)	15,000
Gain recorded by Parrco		$ 3,000
New remaining life assigned **(an *increase* of 1 1/2 yrs.)**		3 years

Note: For simplicity, we later assume that an administrative department of Subbco uses the equipment. Thus the *acquiring entity's* depreciation expense on this equipment is included in its *administrative expenses—not* its *cost of sales*.

General Ledger Adjusting Entries

Parrco makes the following **general ledger adjusting entries** as a result of transferring the asset at a $3,000 gain (which results in Subbco's recording $1,000 of incremental depreciation expense each year):

December 31, 2005 (the year of the transfer):

Intercompany Gain *Deferral*	2,000	
Intercompany Gain *Deferred*		2,000
To defer the intercompany gain unrealized at year-end (total gain of \$3,000 – \$1,000 realized in 2005).		

December 31, 2006, and December 31, 2007:

Intercompany Gain *Deferred*	1,000	
Intercompany Gain *Recognition*		1,000
To recognize that portion of the intercompany gain realized during the year.		

Illustration 10-1 shows (1) an analysis of Parrco's Investment in Subsidiary account using assumed amounts for Subbco's earnings, dividends, and equity account balances and (2) the basic elimination entry at 12/31/05 and 12/31/06.

The consolidation entries to change to the *old basis* of accounting at any consolidation date are obtained by comparing (1) the existing account balances in each entity's books at that particular consolidation date—**new basis amounts**—with (2) the balances (**pro forma**) that should be reported in consolidation—***old basis* amounts**. Illustration 10-2 shows such a comparison.

Illustration 10-3 shows a consolidation worksheet at December 31, 2005.

CHECK POINTS

On 4/1/05, Pole Inc. sold equipment costing \$105,000 and 20% depreciated (straight line and a five-year life) to its 80%-owned subsidiary, Sole Inc., for \$96,000. Sole assigned a remaining life

ILLUSTRATION 10-1 ANALYSIS OF THE INVESTMENT ACCOUNT

	Parent's Investment Account	=	Subsidiary's Equity Accounts: Common Stock	+	Subsidiary's Equity Accounts: Retained Earnings
Balances, 1/1/05.	\$100,000		\$60,000		\$ 40,000
+ Equity in net income	24,000				24,000
– Dividends	(4,000)				(4,000)
Balances, 12/31/05	120,000		\$60,000		\$ 60,000
+ Equity in net income	32,000				32,000
– Dividends	(12,000)				(12,000)
Balances, 12/31/06	140,000		\$60,000		\$ 80,000
+ Equity in net income	25,000				25,000
– Dividends	(15,000)				(15,000)
Balances, 12/31/07	\$150,000		\$60,000		\$ 90,000

The Basic *Elimination* Entry
(obtained from the amounts in the above analysis)

WORKSHEET ENTRY ONLY

	Consolidation Date: December 31, 2005		Consolidation Date: December 31, 2006	
Common Stock	60,000		60,000	
Retained Earnings, 1/1/05 and 1/1/06	40,000		60,000	
Equity in Net Income (of Subbco)	24,000		32,000	
Dividends Declared		4,000		12,000
Investment in Subsidiary		120,000		140,000

ILLUSTRATION 10-2 BASIS OF ACCOUNTING ANALYSIS: *DOWNSTREAM* EQUIPMENT TRANSFER: *GAIN* SITUATION (100% OWNERSHIP)

ANALYSIS AT THE END OF 2005

	ACTUAL BALANCES (*NEW BASIS*) PARRCO	SUBBCO	REPORTABLE BALANCES (*OLD BASIS*)	DIFFERENCES (TO BE POSTED AS A DR. [CR.])
Income Statement (2005)				
Depreciation expense		$ (6,000)	$ (5,000)	$ (1,000)
Intercompany gain	$ 3,000		-0-	3,000
Intercompany gain *deferral*	(2,000)		-0-	(2,000)
Balance Sheet (as of 12/31/05)				
Cost		$18,000	$ 40,000	$ 22,000
Accumulated depreciation		(6,000)	(30,000)[a]	(24,000)
Intercompany gain deferred	$(2,000)		-0-	2,000

[a] Accumulated depreciation of $25,000 at the *transfer date* plus $5,000 of depreciation ($15,000 ÷ 3 years) for 2005.

Consolidation Entries at December 31, 2005

WORKSHEET ENTRY ONLY

(1) The depreciation expense change in basis *elimination* entry—P/L:		
Intercompany Gain	3,000	
Intercompany Gain *Deferral*		2,000
Depreciation Expense		1,000
(2) The equipment change in basis *elimination* entry—B/S:		
Equipment	22,000	
Intercompany Gain *Deferred* (a balance sheet account)	2,000	
Accumulated Depreciation		24,000

ANALYSIS AT THE END OF 2006

	ACTUAL BALANCES (*NEW BASIS*) PARRCO	SUBBCO	REPORTABLE BALANCES (*OLD BASIS*)	DIFFERENCES (TO BE POSTED AS A DR. [CR.])
Income Statement (2006)				
Depreciation expense		$ (6,000)	$ (5,000)	$ (1,000)
Intercompany gain *recognition*	$ 1,000		-0-	1,000
Balance Sheet (as of 12/31/06)				
Cost		$ 18,000	$ 40,000	$ 22,000
Accumulated depreciation		(12,000)	(35,000)[a]	(23,000)
Intercompany gain *deferred*	$(1,000)		-0-	1,000

[a] Accumulated depreciation of $25,000 at the *transfer date* plus $5,000 of depreciation ($15,000 ÷ 3 years) for 2005 and $5,000 for 2006.

Consolidation Entries at December 31, 2006

WORKSHEET ENTRY ONLY

(1) The depreciation expense change in basis *elimination* entry—P/L:		
Intercompany Gain *Recognition*	1,000	
Depreciation Expense		1,000
(2) The equipment change in basis *elimination* entry—B/S:		
Equipment	22,000	
Intercompany Gain *Deferred* (balance sheet)	1,000	
Accumulated Depreciation		23,000

of six years (*straight line*). What are the *cost* and *accumulated depreciation*, respectively, of this equipment in the 12/31/06 (*not* 05) consolidated balance sheet?

a. $96,000 and $28,000
b. $96,000 and $42,000
c. $105,000 and $45,500
d. $105,000 and $49,000
e. $105,000 and $57,750

Answer: c ($21,000 + $14,000 + $10,500 [3/4 yr.] = $45,500)

ILLUSTRATION 10-3 THE COMPLETE EQUITY METHOD *DOWNSTREAM* EQUIPMENT TRANSFER: GAIN SITUATION (100% OWNERSHIP): YEAR OF TRANSFER

Parrco Company and Subbco Company
Consolidation Worksheet as of December 31, 2005

	PARRCO COMPANY	100%-OWNED SUBBCO COMPANY	CONSOLIDATION ENTRIES DR.			CR.	CONSOLIDATED
Income Statement (2005)							
Sales	597,000	234,000					831,000
Cost of sales	(360,000)	(110,000)					(470,000)
Expenses	(190,000)	(100,000)			2	1,000	(289,000)
Intercompany Accounts							
Equity in net income (of Subbco)	24,000		24,000	1			-0-
Intercompany gain	3,000		3,000	2			-0-
Intercompany gain ***deferral***	(2,000)				2	2,000	-0-
Net income	72,000	24,000	27,000			3,000	72,000
Statement of Retained Earnings							
Balances, 1/1/05	140,000	40,000	40,000	1			140,000
+ Net income	72,000	24,000	27,000			3,000	72,000
– Dividends declared	(51,000)	(4,000)			1	4,000	(51,000)
Balances, 12/31/05	161,000	60,000	67,000			7,000	161,000
Balance Sheet							
Cash	65,000	51,000					116,000
Accounts receivable	75,000	37,000					112,000
Inventory	110,000	55,000					165,000
Investment in subsidiary	120,000				1	120,000	-0-
Intercompany gain ***deferred***	(2,000)		2,000	3			-0-
Land	220,000	30,000					250,000
Buildings and equipment	500,000	150,000	22,000	3			672,000
Accumulated depreciation	(320,000)	(13,000)			3	24,000	(357,000)
Total Assets	768,000	310,000	24,000			144,000	958,000
Payables and accruals	157,000	70,000					227,000
Long-Term debt	250,000	120,000					370,000
Common stock ($1 par value)	10,000						10,000
Add'l paid-in capital	190,000						190,000
Common stock (no par)		60,000	60,000	1			-0-
Retained earnings	161,000	60,000	67,000			7,000	161,000
Total Liabilities and Equity	768,000	310,000	127,000			7,000	958,000
Proof of debit and credit postings			151,000			151,000	

Explanation of entries:

1 The basic *elimination* entry.
2 The depreciation expense change in basis *elimination* entry—P/L.
3 The equipment change in basis *elimination* entry—B/S.

Assume the previous information. What is the intercompany gain or loss to defer at 12/31/06 (*not* 05)?

a. $12,000
b. $8,500
c. $8,400
d. $6,800
e. $6,750

Answer: b, gain ($12,000 – $2,000 – $1,500 [3/4 yr.] = $8,500)

Upstream Equipment Transfers: *Gain* Situations

We now use the facts in the previous example except that we assume that (1) Subbco Company is a 75%-owned created subsidiary, and (2) the equipment transfer is *upstream*.

General Ledger Adjusting Entries

Subbco makes the following **general ledger adjusting entries** for 2005, 2006, and 2007 in connection with the intercompany gain:

December 31, 2005 (the year of the transfer):

Intercompany Gain *Deferral*	2,000	
Intercompany Gain *Deferred* (a balance sheet account).		2,000
To defer the intercompany gain unrealized at year-end (total gain of $3,000 – $1,000 realized in 2005).		

December 31, 2006, and December 31, 2007:

Intercompany Gain *Deferred*	1,000	
Intercompany Gain *Recognition*		1,000
To recognize that portion of the intercompany gain realized during the year.		

Illustration 10-4 shows (1) the consolidation entries required at the end of 2005 and 2006 and (2) the basis of accounting analyses for these dates. (No special adjustments are required to the noncontrolling interest because the amounts are properly established in the basic elimination entry.) Because of the similarities of the consolidation entries for *upstream* and *downstream* transfers, we do ***not*** present a consolidation worksheet for either 2005 or 2006.

CHECK POINT

On 1/1/05, Soot Inc., a 60%-owned subsidiary of Poot Inc., sold equipment having a cost of $500,000 and accumulated depreciation of $200,000 to Poot for $240,000. Soot had been using a five-year life. Poot estimated that the equipment would last four years. Each entity uses *straight-line depreciation.* On 1/4/06, Poot sold the equipment to an outside third party for $250,000. What is the gain or loss to be reported in the 2005 consolidated income statement?

a. $10,000
b. $15,000
c. $25,000
d. $70,000
e. $(35,000)

Answer: c, gain ($250,000 – $225,000 = $25,000)

ILLUSTRATION 10-4 BASIS OF ACCOUNTING ANALYSIS: *UPSTREAM* EQUIPMENT TRANSFER: *GAIN* SITUATION (75% OWNERSHIP)

ANALYSIS AT THE END OF 2005

	ACTUAL BALANCES (*NEW BASIS*) PARRCO	ACTUAL BALANCES (*NEW BASIS*) SUBBCO	REPORTABLE BALANCES (*OLD BASIS*)	DIFFERENCES (TO BE POSTED AS A DR. [CR.])
Income Statement (2005)				
Depreciation expense	$(6,000)		$ (5,000)	$ (1,000)
Intercompany gain		$ 3,000	-0-	3,000
Intercompany gain *deferral*		(2,000)	-0-	(2,000)
Balance Sheet (as of 12/31/05)				
Cost	$18,000		$ 40,000	$ 22,000
Accumulated depreciation	(6,000)		(30,000)[a]	(24,000)
Intercompany gain deferred		$(2,000)	-0-	2,000

[a] Accumulated depreciation of $25,000 at the *transfer date* plus $5,000 of depreciation ($15,000 ÷ 3 years) for 2005.

Consolidation Entries at December 31, 2005

WORKSHEET ENTRY ONLY

(1) The depreciation expense change in basis *elimination* entry—P/L:		
Intercompany Gain	3,000	
Intercompany Gain *Deferral*		2,000
Depreciation Expense		1,000
(2) The equipment change in basis *elimination* entry—B/S:		
Equipment	22,000	
Intercompany Gain *Deferred* (a balance sheet account)	2,000	
Accumulated Depreciation		24,000

ANALYSIS AT THE END OF 2006

	ACTUAL BALANCES (*NEW BASIS*) PARRCO	ACTUAL BALANCES (*NEW BASIS*) SUBBCO	REPORTABLE BALANCES (*OLD BASIS*)	DIFFERENCES (TO BE POSTED AS A DR. [CR.])
Income Statement (2006)				
Depreciation expense	$ (6,000)		$ (5,000)	$ (1,000)
Intercompany gain *recognition*		$ 1,000	-0-	1,000
Balance Sheet (as of 12/31/06)				
Cost	$ 18,000		$ 40,000	$ 22,000
Accumulated depreciation	(12,000)		(35,000)[a]	(23,000)
Intercompany gain deferred		$(1,000)	-0-	1,000

[a] Accumulated depreciation of $25,000 at the *transfer date* plus $5,000 of depreciation ($15,000 ÷ 3 years) for 2005 and $5,000 for 2006.

Consolidation Entries at December 31, 2006

WORKSHEET ENTRY ONLY

(1) The depreciation expense change in basis *elimination* entry—P/L:		
Intercompany Gain *Recognition*	1,000	
Depreciation Expense		1,000
(2) The equipment change in basis *elimination* entry—B/S:		
Equipment	22,000	
Intercompany Gain *Deferred* (balance sheet)	1,000	
Accumulated Depreciation		23,000

Module 2 Overview

Recall from Chapter 9 that under the partial equity method, the deferral of any unrealized intercompany profit (gain in this chapter) is accomplished *entirely on the consolidation worksheet.* As a result, in 100%-ownership situations the consolidated net income and consolidated retained earnings are *less than* the parent's net income and retained earnings respectively.

SECTION 1: TRANSFERS OF NONDEPRECIABLE ASSETS

Downstream Land Transfers: *Gain* Situations

When land is transferred at above its carrying value, the selling entity records a gain. In preparing consolidated statements, the gain is not reportable and must be deferred until the acquiring entity resells the land. For example, assume that Parrco Company sold land costing $20,000 to its 100%-owned subsidiary, Subbco Company, for $30,000 on January 1, 2005.

Consolidation at January 1, 2005

If consolidation occurs as of January 1, 2005—the transfer date—the following **entry is made in consolidation:**

WORKSHEET ENTRY ONLY

Intercompany Gain	10,000	
Land		10,000
To change to the *old basis* of accounting.		

The preceding worksheet entry is made at any other consolidation date in 2005, assuming that Subbco still owns the land at that (these) consolidation date(s).

Note that if Parrco were to issue **parent-company-only statements**, it first would make the following "financial statement adjusting entry" (as opposed to a *general ledger adjusting entry*) to its PCO statements:

Intercompany Gain	10,000	
Intercompany Gain *Deferred* (a balance sheet account).		10,000

Subsequent Year Treatment of Unrealized Gain

Land *Not* Resold at the End of 2006

If Subbco still owns the land at December 31, 2006, the following entry is made in consolidation at that date:

WORKSHEET ENTRY ONLY

Retained Earnings, 1/1/06	10,000	
Land		10,000
To change to the *old basis* of accounting.		

Land Resold by the End of 2007

If Subbco subsequently sells the land in 2007 for $32,000, it then reports a $2,000 gain ($32,000 – $30,000). The reportable gain in the consolidated income statement is $12,000 ($32,000 –

$20,000), however, because the previously deferred $10,000 intercompany gain has now been realized. Accordingly, the following entry is required in consolidation at the end of 2007:

WORKSHEET ENTRY ONLY

Retained Earnings, 1/1/07	10,000	
Gain on Sale of Land		10,000
To report the gain based on the *old basis* of accounting ($32,000 – $20,000) instead of the *new basis* of accounting ($32,000 – $30,000).		

Downstream Land Transfers: *Loss* Situations

When land is transferred **at *below* its carrying value**, the intercompany loss must be deferred. The principle is the same as that for a transfer above its carrying value, but the debits and credits are *reversed*.

Upstream Land Transfers

When the land transfer is **upstream**, the procedures parallel those shown in Chapter 9 for upstream inventory transfers. Upstream transfers are discussed and illustrated in the last half of Section 2 that follows.

Section 2: Transfers of Depreciable Assets

Downstream Equipment Transfers: *Gain* Situations

Assume that the following *downstream* equipment transfer occurred between Parrco Company and Subbco Company, the 100%-owned subsidiary of Parrco created several years ago:

	Parrco	Subbco
Sales price of equipment sold to Subbco on January 1, 2005		$18,000
Carrying value on Parrco's books		
Cost (*4-year* assigned life)	$ 40,000	
Accumulated depreciation (2 1/2 years)	(25,000)	15,000
Gain recorded by Parrco		$ 3,000
New remaining life assigned (**an *increase* of 1 1/2 yrs.**)		3 years

Note: For simplicity, we later assume that an administrative department of Subbco uses the equipment. Thus the acquiring entity's depreciation expense on this equipment is included in its *administrative expenses*—*not* its *cost of sales*.

The consolidation entry to change to the *old basis* of accounting at any consolidation date can be obtained by comparing (1) the existing account balances in each entity's books at that particular consolidation date—**new basis amounts**—with (2) the balances (**pro forma**) that should be reported in consolidation—**old basis amounts.** Illustration 10-5 shows such a comparison using the preceding facts as well as the required entry to change to the *old basis* of accounting in consolidation at December 31, 2005 and 2006.

Illustration 10-6 shows a consolidation worksheet at December 31, 2005 (the transfer year).

Upstream Equipment Transfers: *Gain* Situations

When a depreciable asset transfer is *upstream*, the consolidation entries are the same as those previously shown for a *downstream* transfer. When the subsidiary is *partially owned*, however, an additional entry is needed to share the deferral of the unrealized gain with the *non*controlling interest.

We now use the facts for the previous example except that we assume that (1) Subbco Company is a 75%-owned subsidiary, and (2) the equipment transfer is *upstream*. Illustrations 10-7 and

ILLUSTRATION 10-5 BASIS OF ACCOUNTING ANALYSIS: *DOWNSTREAM* EQUIPMENT TRANSFER: *GAIN* SITUATION (100% OWNERSHIP)

ANALYSIS AT THE END OF 2005

	ACTUAL BALANCES (*NEW BASIS*) PARRCO	SUBBCO	REPORTABLE BALANCES (*OLD BASIS*)	DIFFERENCES (TO BE POSTED AS A DR. [CR.])
Income Statement (2005)				
Depreciation expense		$ (6,000)	$ (5,000)	$ (1,000)
Intercompany gain	$3,000		-0-	3,000
Balance Sheet (as of 12/31/05)				
Cost		$18,000	$ 40,000	$ 22,000
Accumulated depreciation		(6,000)	(30,000)[a]	(24,000)

[a] Accumulated depreciation of $25,000 at the *transfer date* plus $5,000 of depreciation ($15,000 ÷ 3 years) for 2005.

Consolidation Entries at December 31, 2005

WORKSHEET ENTRY ONLY

(1) The equipment change in basis *elimination* entry:

Intercompany Gain	3,000	
Equipment	22,000	
Depreciation Expense		1,000
Accumulated Depreciation		24,000

Note: The desired effect on retained earnings at 12/31/05 occurs as a result of carrying forward amounts from the net income line in the income statement.

ANALYSIS AT THE END OF 2006

	ACTUAL BALANCES (*NEW BASIS*) PARRCO	SUBBCO	REPORTABLE BALANCES (*OLD BASIS*)	DIFFERENCES (TO BE POSTED AS A DR. [CR.])
Income Statement (2006)				
Depreciation expense		$ (6,000)	$ (5,000)	$ (1,000)
Balance Sheet (as of 12/31/06)				
Cost		$ 18,000	$ 40,000	$ 22,000
Accumulated depreciation		(12,000)	(35,000)[a]	(23,000)
Retained earnings, 1/1/06	$2,000[b]		-0-	2,000

[a] Accumulated depreciation of $25,000 at the *transfer date* plus $5,000 of depreciation ($15,000 ÷ 3 years) for 2005 and $5,000 for 2006.

[b] Intercompany gain of $3,000 – $1,000 of incremental depreciation expense recorded on Subbco's books in 2005 that flows through to Parrco's books as a result of applying the *equity method* of accounting.

Consolidation Entries at December 31, 2006

WORKSHEET ENTRY ONLY

(1) The equipment change in basis *elimination* entry:

Retained earnings, 1/1/06	2,000	
Equipment	22,000	
Depreciation Expense		1,000
Accumulated Depreciation		23,000

10-8 show (1) the consolidation entries required at the end of 2005 and 2006, respectively (including the adjustments required to the *non*controlling interest to share the deferral), and (2) the basis of accounting analyses for these dates that were used to develop the entry to change to the old basis of accounting.

Illustration 10-9 shows a consolidation worksheet for 2005.

ILLUSTRATION 10-6 THE PARTIAL EQUITY METHOD *DOWNSTREAM* EQUIPMENT TRANSFER: GAIN SITUATION (100% OWNERSHIP): YEAR OF TRANSFER

Parrco Company and Subbco Company
Consolidation Worksheet as of December 31, 2005

	PARRCO COMPANY	*100%-OWNED* SUBBCO COMPANY	CONSOLIDATION ENTRIES DR.			CR.	CONSOLIDATED
Income Statement (2005)							
Sales	597,000	234,000					831,000
Cost of sales	(360,000)	(110,000)					(470,000)
Expenses	(190,000)	(100,000)			2	1,000	(289,000)
Intercompany Accounts							
Equity in net income (of Subbco)	24,000		24,000	1			-0-
Intercompany gain	3,000		3,000	2			-0-
Net income	74,000	24,000	27,000			1,000	72,000
Statement of Retained Earnings							
Balances, 1/1/05	(140,000)	40,000	40,000	1			(140,000)
+ Net income	74,000	24,000	27,000			1,000	72,000
– Dividends declared	(51,000)	(4,000)			1	4,000	(51,000)
Balances, 12/31/05	163,000	60,000	67,000			5,000	161,000
Balance Sheet							
Cash	65,000	51,000					116,000
Accounts receivable	75,000	37,000					112,000
Inventory	110,000	55,000					165,000
Investment in subsidiary	120,000				1	120,000	-0-
Land	220,000	30,000					250,000
Buildings and equipment	500,000	150,000	22,000	2			672,000
Accumulated depreciation	(320,000)	(13,000)			2	24,000	(357,000)
Total Assets	770,000	310,000	22,000			144,000	958,000
Payables and accruals	157,000	70,000					227,000
Long-Term debt	250,000	120,000					370,000
Common stock ($1 par)	10,000						10,000
Add'l paid-in capital	190,000						190,000
Common stock (no par)		60,000	60,000	1			-0-
Retained earnings	163,000	60,000	67,000			5,000	161,000
Total Liabilities and Equity	770,000	310,000	127,000			5,000	958,000
Proof of debit and credit postings			*149,000*			*149,000*	

Explanation of entries:

1 The basic *elimination* entry.

2 The equipment change in basis *elimination* entry.

ILLUSTRATION 10-7

BASIS OF ACCOUNTING ANALYSIS: *UPSTREAM* EQUIPMENT TRANSFER—*GAIN* SITUATION (75% OWNERSHIP); YEAR OF TRANSFER

	ANALYSIS AT THE END OF 2005			
	ACTUAL BALANCES (*NEW BASIS*)		REPORTABLE BALANCES (*OLD BASIS*)	DIFFERENCES (TO BE POSTED AS A DR. [CR.])
	PARRCO	SUBBCO		
Income Statement (2005)				
Depreciation expense	$ (6,000)		$ (5,000)	$ (1,000)
Intercompany gain		$3,000	-0-	3,000
Balance Sheet (as of 12/31/05)				
Cost	$18,000		$ 40,000	$ 22,000
Accumulated depreciation	(6,000)		(30,000)[a]	(24,000)

[a] Accumulated depreciation of $25,000 at the *transfer date* plus $5,000 of depreciation ($15,000 ÷ 3 years) for 2005.

Consolidation Entries at December 31, 2005

WORKSHEET ENTRY ONLY

	Dr.	Cr.
(1) The equipment change in basis *elimination* entry:		
Intercompany Gain	3,000	
Equipment	22,000	
Depreciation Expense		1,000
Accumulated Depreciation		24,000
(2) The sharing of the deferral *elimination* entry:		
NCI in Net Assets	500	
NCI in Net Income		500
(25% of $2,000 of unrealized intercompany gain at 12/31/05)		

Note: The desired effect on retained earnings at 12/31/05 occurs as a result of carrying forward amounts from the net income line in the income statement.

ILLUSTRATION 10-8

BASIS OF ACCOUNTING ANALYSIS: *UPSTREAM* EQUIPMENT TRANSFER—*GAIN* SITUATION (75% OWNERSHIP); YEAR AFTER YEAR OF TRANSFER

	ANALYSIS AT THE END OF 2006			
	ACTUAL BALANCES (*NEW BASIS*)		REPORTABLE BALANCES (*OLD BASIS*)	DIFFERENCES (TO BE POSTED AS A DR. [CR.])
	PARRCO	SUBBCO		
Income Statement (2006)				
Depreciation expense	$ (6,000)		$ (5,000)	$ (1,000)
Balance Sheet (as of 12/31/06)				
Cost	$ 18,000		$ 40,000	$ 22,000
Accumulated depreciation	(12,000)		(35,000)[a]	(23,000)
Retained Earnings 1/1/06	2,000[b]		-0-	2,000

[a] Accumulated depreciation of $25,000 at the *transfer date* plus $5,000 of depreciation ($15,000 ÷ 3 years) for 2005 and $5,000 for 2006.

[b] Intercompany gain of $3,000 – $1,000 of incremental depreciation expense in 2005—the $3,000 gain flows through to Parrco's books as a result of applying the *equity method* of accounting.

Consolidation Entries at December 31, 2006

WORKSHEET ENTRY ONLY

	Dr.	Cr.
(1) The equipment change in basis *elimination* entry:		
Retained Earnings 1/1/06	2,000	
Equipment	22,000	
Depreciation Expense		1,000
Accumulated Depreciation		23,000
(2) The sharing of the deferral *elimination* entry:		
NCI in Net Income (25% of $1,000 intercompany gain realized in 2006)	250	
NCI in Net Assets (25% of $1,000 intercompany gain unrealized at 12/31/06)	250	
Retained Earnings, 1/1/06 (25% of $2,000 intercompany gain unrealized at 1/1/06)		500

ILLUSTRATION 10-9 THE PARTIAL EQUITY METHOD *UPSTREAM* EQUIPMENT TRANSFER: *GAIN* SITUATION (75% OWNERSHIP): YEAR OF TRANSFER

Parrco Company and Subbco Company
Consolidation Worksheet as of December 31, 2005

	PARRCO COMPANY	*75%-OWNED* SUBBCO COMPANY	CONSOLIDATION ENTRIES DR.			CR.	CONSOLIDATED
Income Statement (2005)							
Sales	600,000	231,000					831,000
Cost of sales	(360,000)	(110,000)					(470,000)
Expenses	(190,000)	(100,000)			2	1,000	(289,000)
Intercompany Accounts							
Equity in net income (of Subbco)	18,000		18,000	1			-0-
Intercompany gain		3,000	3,000	2			-0-
Net income	68,000	24,000	21,000			1,000	72,000
NCI in net income			6,000	2	3	500	(5,500)[a]
CI in net income			27,000			1,500	66,500
Statement of Retained Earnings							
Balances, 1/1/05	130,000	40,000	40,000	1			130,000
+ Net income	68,000	24,000	27,000			1,500	66,500
– Dividends declared	(51,000)	(4,000)			1	4,000	(51,000)
Balances, 12/31/05	147,000	60,000	67,000			5,500	145,500
Balance Sheet							
Cash	79,000	51,000					130,000
Accounts receivable	75,000	37,000					112,000
Inventory	110,000	55,000					165,000
Investment in subsidiary	90,000				1	90,000	-0-
Land	220,000	30,000					250,000
Buildings and equipment	500,000	150,000	22,000	2			672,000
Accumulated depreciation	(320,000)	(13,000)			2	24,000	(357,000)
Total Assets	754,000	310,000	22,000			114,000	972,000
Payables and accruals	157,000	70,000					227,000
Long-Term debt	250,000	120,000					370,000
NCI in net assets			500	3	1	30,000	29,500
Common stock ($1 par)	10,000						10,000
Add'l paid-in capital	190,000						190,000
Common stock (no par)		60,000	60,000	1			-0-
Retained earnings	147,000	60,000	67,000	1		5,500	145,500
Total Liabilities and Equity	754,000	310,000	127,500			35,500	972,000
Proof of debit and credit postings			*149,500*			*149,500*	

[a] Proof: Subsidiary's reported net income of $24,000 – $2,000 of unrealized gain at 12/31/05 = $22,000; $22,000 × 25% = $5,500.

Explanation of entries:

1 The basic *elimination* entry.
2 The equipment change in basis *elimination* entry.
3 The sharing of the unrealized gain *elimination* entry.

ETHICS

Let's Try a Squeeze Play!

Your client owns 90% of the outstanding common stock of a company to which it sells inventory at a markup. From the date the subsidiary was acquired four years ago, the noncontrolling interest shareholders have stubbornly refused to sell their shares to the parent. During the current year audit, you noticed that the intercompany transfer prices increased by 25% from previous years, which greatly decreased the profitability of the subsidiary. The controller's explanation was that the transfer prices are negotiated and are what they are. Also during the current year, the ***parent*** ordered the *subsidiary* to stop paying dividends, which in the past approximated its net income.

Question

Is it ethical to increase the transfer prices and change the dividend policy to pressure the noncontrolling interest shareholders to sell their shares to the parent?

B. Intercompany Bond Holdings

SECTION OVERVIEW

Recall from Chapter 8 that preparing consolidated statements involves (1) eliminating *all* amounts reported as a result of intercompany transactions (unsettled balances, intercompany revenues/gains, and intercompany expenses/losses) in consolidation and (2) *not* reporting any intercompany profit, gain, or loss until it has been realized as a result of transactions with *outside third parties.* These rules also apply to intercompany bond purchases. The situation is that of *recognizing* an immediate gain or loss in consolidation, however, *not* of *deferring* a gain or loss until a later year(s).

Intercompany bond holdings can arise in *two* ways:

1. ***Direct*** **transactions with another member of the consolidated group.** For example, a subsidiary issuing bonds could sell some or all of the bond issue directly to its parent.
2. ***Indirect*** **transactions with another member of the consolidated group.** For example, a parent could acquire in the open market some or all of a subsidiary's already issued and outstanding bonds. The result (in this example) is as if either (1) the *parent* acquired the bonds directly from the *subsidiary* or (2) the *subsidiary* reacquired its bonds in the open market and then sold them directly to the *parent.*

Why Do Indirect Bond Transactions Occur?

Recall from intermediate accounting that companies often extinguish bond indebtedness before the maturity date when (1) interest rates have *declined* significantly since the issuance date and new bonds can be issued at a *lower* interest rate or (2) excess cash has accumulated beyond foreseeable needs.

More opportunity to extinguish debt exists for a consolidated group of companies than for a single company. The entity within the consolidated group that issued the bonds—**the issuing entity**—may not have the cash available to retire the bonds, or issuing new bonds to retire the old ones may be impractical. However, another entity within the consolidated group that has available cash or the ability to issue debt—**the acquiring entity**—can purchase some or all of the outstanding bonds in the open market. Although it is not unusual for a *parent* to purchase a *subsidiary's* bonds, a *subsidiary* purchases a *parent's* bonds only if its parent directs it to do so.

No Need to Distinguish between Direct and Indirect Transactions

Because the result of an **indirect** bond transaction is the same as having had a **direct** bond transaction, no distinction need be made between the two in preparing consolidated statements. In consolidation, both types of transactions require elimination of amounts reported resulting from the intercompany bond purchase. Specifically, the Investment in Bonds account on the acquiring entity's books must be offset (on the consolidation worksheet) against the Bonds Payable account on the issuing entity's books—**substantively, this is the same as eliminating an intercompany receivable and an intercompany payable in consolidation.** From the intercompany bond purchase date until the bonds are legally retired by the issuing company, the Intercompany Interest *Income* account reported by the *acquiring* entity must be offset (on the worksheet) against the Intercompany Interest *Expense* account reported by the *issuing* entity.

The Complicating Factor: Premiums and Discounts

If all bonds were issued at face value and all intercompany bond purchases were at face value, this chapter would end here. Under such a scenario, the consolidation entries described above would be readily determinable because the reported amount for each account would have the same absolute dollar balance as its offsetting account on the other entity's books. Furthermore, no gain or loss on extinguishment of debt would ever be reported.

If bond premiums and discounts exist, however, the consolidation process is somewhat involved because these items result in a gain or loss on extinguishment of debt to be reported from a *consolidated* perspective—**as though the issuing entity had redeemed and retired the bonds.** In later periods, steps are needed to *undo* the reporting of the amortizations of these premiums and discounts, which are amortized to income in each company's general ledger. Otherwise, income or loss is *double reported, once* as a gain or loss on extinguishment of debt and *once* again as amortization adjustments are made to intercompany interest *income* and intercompany interest *expense*.

V. The Constructive Retirement of the Bonds

The result of an intercompany bond purchase is that no amounts are owed to any party *outside* the consolidated group of entities with respect to those bonds. Therefore, the purchase by one entity within the consolidated group of any or all of the outstanding bonds of another group member constitutes the **constructive retirement** of the bonds purchased. Thus from a consolidated perspective, the bonds have been **extinguished**—even though the bonds are still legally outstanding from the issuing entity's perspective.

Recall from intermediate accounting that when an entity extinguishes its debt, it has a reportable gain or loss whenever the **amount paid to extinguish the debt** differs from the debt's **carrying value** (the face amount plus any unamortized premium or minus any unamortized discount).

For constructive retirement of debt occurring among an affiliated group of companies, a gain or loss—often referred to as an **imputed** *gain or loss*—also occurs when the **acquiring entity's purchase price** differs from the **issuing entity's carrying value.** This imputed gain or loss must be reported in the consolidated income statement when the intercompany bond purchase occurs.

VI. Calculating the Gain or Loss on Debt Extinguishment

The amount of the *imputed* gain or loss on the extinguishment of debt reported in the period in which the affiliate's bonds are purchased is determined by comparing **the acquisition cost with the applicable percentage of the carrying value of the bonds payable as of the bond purchase date.**

For example, assume that (1) Parrco Company acquired in the open market 40% of the $500,000 of outstanding 10% bonds of its 100%-owned subsidiary, Subbco Company, for $197,000 on January 1, 2006, (2) the assumed maturity date of the bonds is December 31, 2008 (three years later), and (3) interest is payable on July 1 and January 1 (thus *none* of the purchase cost relates to *interest*). The gain or loss is calculated at that date as follows:

	Face Amount		Unamortized Premium (*Subbco*)		Unamortized Discount (*Parrco*)		Carrying Value
Bonds payable	$500,000	+	$30,000			=	$530,000
Percent acquired	40%		40%				40%
Amount deemed retired	$200,000	+	$12,000			=	$212,000
Investment in bonds	200,000			+	$(3,000)	=	197,000
Unrecorded Gain on Debt Extinguishment			$12,000	+	$ 3,000	=	$ 15,000

The gain is attributable to both (1) the applicable percentage (40%) of the **unamortized premium** on Subbco's books and (2) *all* of the **discount** on Parrco's books. At the bond purchase date, Subbco makes the following **general ledger reclassification entry** to reflect the fact that Parrco now holds a portion of the bonds:

Bonds Payable	200,000	
Bond Premium	12,000	
Intercompany Bonds Payable		200,000
Intercompany Bond Premium		12,000

CHECK POINT

A parent acquired in the open market 30% of its 100%-owned subsidiary's outstanding 10% bonds for $310,000. The bonds have a *face value* of $1,000,000 and a *carrying value* of $1,020,000 on the acquisition date. What is the gain or loss to be reported in the consolidated statements in the bond acquisition year?

a. A gain of $4,000.
b. A loss of $4,000.
c. A loss of $10,000.
d. A gain of $6,000.

Answer: b

Premiums and Discounts: A Gain or Loss?

If the *issuing* entity has a *premium* and the *acquiring* entity has a *discount* (as in the preceding example), a *gain* on debt extinguishments *always* results. If the *issuing* entity has a *discount* and the *acquiring* entity has a *premium*, a *loss* on debt extinguishment *always* results. When each entity has a discount or a premium, the net effect is a gain or a loss, depending on which entity has the greater discount or premium. In all of these situations, the correct procedures for preparing consolidated statements can be determined through careful application of the principles discussed and illustrated in this chapter.

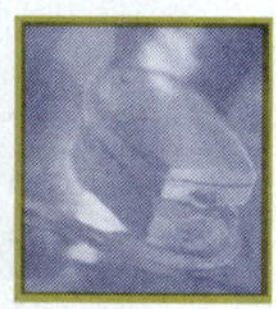

CHECK POINT

When *both* the parent and the subsidiary have *premiums*, what result is reported in consolidation in the year of an intercompany bond purchase?

a. Always a *gain*.
b. Always a *loss*.
c. A *loss* only if the applicable share of the unamortized premium exceeds the acquirer's premium.
d. A *gain* only if the applicable share of the unamortized premium exceeds the acquirer's premium.

Answer: d

Purchase *between* Interest Payment Dates

In the preceding example, we assumed for simplicity that the bond purchase occurred *on an interest payment date*. When an affiliate's bonds are acquired *between interest dates*, the only other item to account for is the additional amount paid by the acquiring entity for interest from the last interest payment date to the purchase date. This additional amount is charged to interest receivable at the purchase date. The procedures to determine and account for the gains and losses do *not* change.

Reissuance of Intercompany Bond Holdings

Infrequently, an acquiring entity sells some or all of the intercompany bonds to an outside party instead of holding them until their maturity date. In these cases, the bonds that the acquiring entity sells are considered to be *reissued* from a consolidated viewpoint. Any difference between the *face value* of the bonds and the *proceeds* (excluding amounts for interest) is treated in consolidation in the same manner as a premium or discount on the *issuance* of bonds.

Determining the Noncontrolling Interest Share of the Gain or Loss

When the subsidiary is *partially* owned and has a discount or premium, a minor conceptual issue arises as to how much of the gain or loss to allocate to the noncontrolling interest in the consolidated statements. Three possibilities exist:

1. **The *parent company* method.** Under this approach, no portion of the *subsidiary's* premium or discount is allocated to the noncontrolling interest. The rationale is that the gain or loss is entirely a result of the *parent's* decision to purchase the bonds.
2. **The *issuing company* method.** Under this approach, the entire gain or loss is assumed to be that of the issuing entity inasmuch as the acquiring entity is deemed to be merely the *issuing* entity's agent. Accordingly, amounts are allocated to the noncontrolling interest only if the *subsidiary* is the issuing entity. In such cases, the noncontrolling interest also shares in that portion of the gain resulting from the *parent's* discount or premium.
3. **The *face value* method.** Under this approach, the noncontrolling interest is allocated only its share of the gain or loss resulting from the *subsidiary's* premium or discount.

Which Method Is Correct?

In our opinion, only the *face value method* is valid. Only this method reflects the reality of the legal boundary lines that exist between the *parent* and the *subsidiary*. The proof would be in a liquidation of the *subsidiary*. After selling its assets and paying off creditors, the amount distributed to the noncontrolling interest shareholders would be their share of the *book equity*—which would *exclude* amounts relating to the gain or loss resulting from the *parent's* discount or premium. In dealing with noncontrolling interest situations in each of the modules, we use only the face value approach. (Current GAAP does *not* specify which method(s) should be used—only that the *full* gain or loss be recognized *immediately*.)

VII. *SIMPLIFIED* PROCEDURES: PREMIUMS AND DISCOUNTS ELIMINATED IN THE GENERAL LEDGERS AT THE BOND PURCHASE DATE

The *simplest* manner of dealing with premiums and discounts is to eliminate those that give rise to the imputed gain or loss. Using the preceding example, the following **general ledger adjusting entries** are made on the bond acquisition date:

	Parrco Company		Subbco Company	
Subsidiary's Entry				
Intercompany Bond Premium.			12,000	
Gain on Debt Extinguishment				12,000
Parent's Entry				
Investment in Subsidiary's Bonds.	3,000			
Gain on Debt Extinguishment (of Subsidiary's Bonds).		3,000		

Under the *equity method* of accounting, Parrco Company records $12,000 in its Equity in Net Income (of Subsidiary) account. Accordingly, Parrco's separate income statement reports $15,000 of income, which equals the gain on debt extinguishment reported in consolidation.

The Rationale for Making the General Ledger Entries

The rationale for eliminating the *discount* on Parrco's books and the intercompany *premium* on Subbco's books is that (1) the parent has three ways (discussed below) in which to substantively retire a portion of the subsidiary's outstanding bonds, and (2) **the accounting should reflect the *substance* of the end result—*not* the *form* of the particular alternative selected to achieve that result.** Under all three methods, the final result is that the *subsidiary* owes the *parent—not* an outside third party—an amount equal to the *face value* of the bonds ($200,000 in this example). The three methods are the following:

1. Parrco's *acquires* $200,000 of Subbco's bonds in the open market (as explained earlier).
2. Parrco *lends* Subbco $200,000 so that Subbco can acquire some of its bonds in the open market.
3. Parrco *acquires* $200,000 of Subbco's bonds in the open market and then, immediately thereafter, Parrco *formally exchanges* $200,000 checks with Subbco. That is, Parrco advances $200,000 to Subbco (a *loan*) with the stipulation that Subbco retire the $200,000 face value of bonds that Parrco now holds. (Using this procedure, Parrco *formally* records a $3,000 gain on the debt extinguishment, and Subbco *formally* records a $12,000 gain.)

Entries Required in Consolidation

After the general ledger entries to eliminate the intercompany premium and discount (shown earlier) are recorded, Parrco's Investment in Bonds of Subbco account has a $200,000 balance. Likewise, Subbco's Intercompany Bonds Payable account has a $200,000 balance. As a result, neither entity needs to show amortization in its general ledger in *subsequent* periods. At each future year-end consolidation date (preceding the actual retirement of the bonds), the following two entries are made in consolidation:

WORKSHEET ENTRY ONLY

Intercompany Bonds Payable	200,000	
Investment in Bonds of Subsidiary.		200,000

WORKSHEET ENTRY ONLY

Intercompany Interest Income	20,000	
Investment Interest Expense.		20,000

Comprehensive Illustration

Preparing Consolidated Statements

> Simplified Reporting: Premium and Discount Eliminated in General Ledgers
> At End of Bond Acquisition Year: 100%-Owned Subsidiary

Illustration 10-10 presents a consolidation worksheet as of December 31, 2006.

Partially Owned Subsidiaries

Even when a subsidiary is *partially* owned, the procedures are the same as those for 100%-owned subsidiaries.

The Way the Subsidiary Reports to the Noncontrolling Interest Shareholders

If the subsidiary is *partially* owned, the income or loss it records as a result of eliminating its intercompany premium or discount is *not* realized insofar as the noncontrolling interest shareholders are

ILLUSTRATION 10-10 SIMPLIFIED PROCEDURES PREMIUM AND DISCOUNT ELIMINATED IN GENERAL LEDGERS: CONSOLIDATION AT END OF BOND ACQUISITION YEAR–100%-OWNED SUBSIDIARY

Parrco Company and Subbco Company
Consolidation Worksheet as of December 31, 2006

	PARRCO COMPANY	100%-OWNED SUBBCO COMPANY	CONSOLIDATION ENTRIES DR.			CR.	CONSOLIDATED
Income Statement (2006)							
Sales	680,000	280,000					960,000
Cost of sales	(380,000)	(120,000)					(500,000)
Expenses	(270,000)	(108,000)					(378,000)
Gain on debt extinguishment	3,000	12,000					15,000
Intercompany Accounts							
Equity in net income (of Subbco)	44,000		44,000	1			-0-
Intercompany interest income	20,000		20,000	2			-0-
Intercompany interest expense		(20,000)			2	20,000	-0-
Net income	97,000	44,000	64,000			20,000	97,000
Statement of Retained Earnings							
Balances, 1/1/06	158,000	76,000	76,000	1			158,000
+ Net income	97,000	44,000	→ 64,000			20,000 ←	97,000
– Dividends declared	(51,000)	(24,000)			1	24,000	(51,000)
Balances, 12/31/06	204,000	96,000	140,000			44,000	204,000
Balance Sheet							
Intercompany interest receivable/payable	10,000	(10,000)					-0-
Investment in Subsidiary:							
Common stock	156,000				1	156,000	-0-
Bonds	200,000				3	200,000	-0-
Other assets	201,000	710,000					911,000
Total Assets	567,000	700,000				356,000	911,000
Payables and accruals	113,000	32,000					145,000
Bonds payable		300,000					300,000
Bond premium		12,000[a]					12,000
Intercompany bond payable		200,000	200,000	3			-0-
Common stock ($1 par)	10,000						10,000
Add'l paid-in capital	240,000						240,000
Common stock (no par)		60,000	60,000	1			-0-
Retained earnings	204,000	96,000	→ 140,000			44,000 ←	204,000
Total Liabilities and Equity	567,000	700,000	400,000			44,000	911,000
Proof of debit and credit postings			*400,000*			*400,000*	

[a] $18,000 at 1/1/06 – $6,000 of amortization in 2006.

Explanation of entries:

1 The basic *elimination* entry.
2 The intercompany bond interest *elimination* entry.
3 The intercompany bond holding *elimination* entry.

concerned. Accordingly, in reporting to them, the subsidiary makes a "financial statement adjusting entry" (as opposed to a *general ledger* adjusting entry) to reflect the intercompany premium or discount in its balance sheet—as though it had *not* been eliminated in the general ledger. Although keeping the general ledger for reporting to the *parent* (rather than to the *noncontrolling interest shareholders*) slightly complicates the subsidiary's process of reporting to the noncontrolling interest, the *consolidation process* is streamlined—**a much greater benefit.**

CHECK POINTS

On 4/1/05, Plow Inc. acquired in the open market 40% of the outstanding 10% bonds of Seed Inc., its 80%-owned subsidiary, for $408,000. The bonds have a face value of $1,000,000, a carrying value of $940,000 on 4/1/05, and a maturity date of 3/31/07. For 2005, Plow reported $100,000 of income—excluding any interest income or loss pertaining to its bond investment and excluding any of Seed's earnings. Also for 2005, Seed reported net income of $50,000—*after* reported interest expense of $130,000 on the bond issue. Each entity uses *straight-line amortization.*

What is the reportable gain or loss on debt extinguishment?
a. A loss of $32,000.
b. A loss of $16,000.
c. A loss of $8,000.
d. A gain of $16,000.

Answer: a ($408,000 – $376,000)

What is Plow's intercompany interest *income* in its separate income statement for 2005?
a. $40,000.
b. $30,000.
c. $27,000.
d. $22,000.

Answer: c ($30,000 – $3,000)

What is Seed's intercompany interest *expense* for 2005?
a. $42,000.
b. $39,000.
c. $30,000.
d. $21,000.

Answer: b ($30,000 + $9,000)

What is the consolidated net income for 2005?
a. $170,000.
b. $158,000.
c. $150,000.
d. $128,000.

Answer: c ($167,000 + $50,000 – $82,000 DR. + $15,000 CR.)

What is the reportable amount for NCI in Net Income for 2005?
a. $5,200.
b. $7,000.
c. $8,200.
d. $10,000.

Answer: b ($50,000 – $15,000 = $35,000 × 20% = $7,000)

End-of-Chapter Review

Summary of Key Points: Fixed Asset Transfers

1. The transfer of any asset within a consolidated group **never** changes the **basis of accounting** for the asset **from a consolidated perspective.**
2. The result of consolidation entries pertaining to intercompany fixed asset transfers is to change from **the *new basis* of accounting** to **the *old basis* of accounting.**
3. In making calculations for changing to the *new basis* of accounting in consolidation for intercompany depreciable fixed asset transfers, the **new remaining life** assigned to the asset must be used.
4. Regarding intercompany depreciable fixed asset transfers at a gain or loss, the asset's subsequent depreciation effectively results in **realization** of the intercompany gain or loss as time goes by.

Summary of Key Points: Bond Holdings

1. The acquisition of an affiliated entity's outstanding bonds is accounted for in consolidation as a retirement of those bonds, even though they are *not actually* retired.
2. A gain or loss on early extinguishment of debt is reported in the period in which the affiliate's bonds are *acquired*—but only to the extent of the intercompany portion acquired.
3. The gain or loss is the difference *between* the *acquisition cost* (excluding amounts paid for interest) and the intercompany portion of the *carrying value* of the bonds.

Glossary of New Terms

Carrying value Historical cost minus any accumulated depreciation.
Constructive retirement Substantive retirement of a bond issue rather than legal retirement.
Pro forma A presentation on an "as-if" basis.

Assignment Material

Review Questions

Fixed Asset Transfers

1. For which assets transferred within a consolidated group can an intercompany gain or loss be recognized for *consolidated reporting purposes* at the transfer date?
2. Do intercompany fixed asset transfers fall under the IRS *transfer pricing rules*?
3. What causes the *basis of accounting* for a fixed asset to change in an intercompany sale?
4. What is the effect of the *consolidation entries* relating to intercompany fixed asset transfers?
5. What is the distinction between the *historical cost,* the *book value,* and the *carrying value* of a depreciable fixed asset?
6. How is an *intercompany gain or loss* calculated for a depreciable fixed asset transfer?
7. For intercompany transfers of depreciable fixed assets at a gain or loss, how and when does *realization* of intercompany gains and losses occur?
8. Regarding an intercompany depreciable fixed asset transfer, must the buying entity continue to use the selling entity's *remaining depreciable life* of the asset at the transfer date? Why or why not?

9. What is the relevance of the *old remaining life* to intercompany depreciable fixed asset transfers from a consolidated perspective? Of the new assigned life?

10. Is it necessary for intercompany depreciable fixed asset transfers to use the selling entity's *remaining life* of the asset to reflect the *old basis of accounting* in consolidation?

11. What does a *debit* to depreciation expense in a consolidation entry signify?

12. If the selling entity has a loss on an intercompany depreciable fixed asset transfer, will there be *incremental depreciation* or a *depreciation shortage* to handle in consolidation?

Bond Holdings

13. From a *consolidated* viewpoint, what is the substance of an intercompany bond purchase?

14. How is the gain or loss on debt extinguishment determined?

15. Are gains and losses on debt extinguishment extraordinary items?

16. Does a gain or loss result when (a) each entity has a *premium,* (b) each entity has a *discount*, and (c) one entity has a *discount* and the other a *premium*?

17. To which entity should the gain or loss on debt extinguishment be assigned?

Exercises

E 10-1 **Consolidation Entries: Land Transfer—*Downstream*** On 3/31/05, Pasto Inc. sold land costing $40,000 to its 100%-owned subsidiary, Sasto Inc., for $100,000.

Required

1. Prepare the consolidation entry(ies) as of 12/31/05 and 06. (*For Module 1 only*: First prepare any necessary *general ledger* adjusting entry at these dates.)
2. Prepare the consolidation entry at 12/31/07, assuming that Sasto sold the land in 2007 for $120,000. (*For Module 1 only*: First prepare the *general ledger* adjusting entry at this date.)

E 10-2 **Consolidation Entries: Land Transfer—*Upstream*** On 6/30/05, Pilt Inc. purchased land from Silt Inc., its 80%-owned subsidiary, for $80,000. Silt's cost was $50,000.

Required

1. Prepare the consolidation entry(ies) as of 12/31/05 and 06. (*For Module 1 only*: First prepare any necessary *general ledger* adjusting entry at these dates.)
2. Prepare the consolidation entry(ies) at 12/31/07, assuming that Pilt sold the land in 2007 for $85,000. (*For Module 1 only*: First prepare the *general ledger* adjusting entry at this date.)

E 10-3 **Calculating Consolidated Amounts: Land and Building Transfer—*Upstream*** Sya Inc., a 100%-owned subsidiary of Pya Inc., manufactures and installs air conditioning systems. Sya's sales are normally to third parties, but during 2004, Pya contracted with Sya to install an air conditioning system in its new corporate headquarters. Sya charged Pya $750,000 for the system and a $125,000 installation fee. Sya's manufacturing cost was $500,000, and its installation costs were $75,000. Installation was completed on 1/2/05, at which time the billings were rendered. Pya assigned a *25-year life* to the system.

Required

1. What amounts pertaining to the air conditioning system should be reported in the consolidated statements at 12/31/05? Insert your amounts in Pya's column in the following table.
2. Without making formal consolidation or other entries, what debit and credit postings should be made to the following accounts in consolidation at 12/31/05?

	Pya Inc.	Sya Inc.
Income Statement		
Intercompany sales		$ 750,000
Intercompany cost of sales		(500,000)
Intercompany installation fee income		125,000
Intercompany installation fee expense		(75,000)
Depreciation expense	$ ______	

	Pya Inc.	Sya Inc.
Balance Sheet		
Building.	$ ______	
Accumulated depreciation.	______	

E 10-4 **Calculating Consolidated Amounts: Equipment Transfer—*Downstream*** On 1/1/05 Pacto Inc. sold equipment to its 100%-owned subsidiary, Sacto Inc., for $800,000. The equipment cost Pacto $1,000,000; accumulated depreciation at the time of the sale was $400,000. Pacto has depreciated the equipment over *10 years* using the *straight-line method* and no salvage value.

Required Determine the amounts at which the cost and accumulated depreciation should be reported in the consolidated balance sheet at 12/31/05 under each of the following assumptions:

1. Sacto does *not* revise the estimated remaining life.
2. Sacto assigns an estimated remaining life of 8 years.

E 10-5 **Reverse Analysis: Equipment Transfer—*Downstream*** In preparing consolidated statements for the year ended 12/31/05, a *debit* was made to Depreciation Expense for $2,000. This entry was necessary because of a downstream equipment transfer made on 7/3/05 between Pyna Inc. and its 100%-owned subsidiary, Syna Inc. This $2,000 entry was an adjustment to the $5,500 of depreciation expense on this equipment that Syna reported for 2005. On 7/3/05 the equipment was 62.5% depreciated and had a *3-year* remaining life. Syna estimated that the equipment would last *5 years*.

Required

1. Calculate the intercompany gain or loss on the transfer.
2. Calculate Pyna's historical cost and carrying value at the transfer date.

E 10-6 **Reverse Analysis: Equipment Transfer—*Downstream*** In preparing consolidated statements for the year ended 12/31/05, a *credit* was made to Depreciation Expense for $3,000. This entry was necessary because of a downstream equipment transfer made on 4/1/05 between Pyre Inc. and its 100%-owned subsidiary, Syre Inc. This $3,000 entry was an adjustment to the $18,000 of depreciation expense that Syre reported on this equipment for 2005. On 4/1/05 the equipment was 20% depreciated and had an *8-year* remaining life. Syre estimated that the equipment would last only *4 years*.

Required

1. Calculate the intercompany gain or loss on the transfer.
2. Calculate Pyre's historical cost and carrying value at the transfer date.

E 10-7 **Consolidation Entry: Land and Building Transfer—*Upstream* (100% ownership)** On 7/1/05, Sill Inc., a 100%-owned subsidiary, sold a warehouse facility for $129,000 cash to Pane Inc., its parent, recording a $30,000 gain on the sale. Sill's historical cost for the land and building were $33,000 and $176,000, respectively.

Pane, which allocated $43,000 of the purchase price to the land and $86,000 to the building, uses straight-line depreciation and assigned a *5-year* remaining life to the building.

Required Prepare the consolidation entry required at 12/31/05 relating to this sale. (*For Module 1 only*: First make the necessary *general ledger* adjusting entry at this date.)

E 10-8 **Consolidation Entry: Continuation of Exercise 10-7** Assume the information provided in Exercise 10-7.

Required Prepare the consolidation entry required at 12/31/06 (one year later) relating to this sale. (*For Module 1 only*: First make the necessary *general ledger* adjusting entry at this date.)

E 10-9 **Gain/Loss Calculation** Parr Inc. owns 100% of the outstanding common stock of Subb Inc. On 4/1/05, Parr acquired in the open market 25% of Subb's outstanding 10%, 10-year debentures ($4,000,000 face amount) at a cost of $1,015,000. The bonds were issued at a *premium* of

$320,000. They mature on 6/30/09 and pay interest semiannually on 6/30 and 12/31. Each entity uses *straight-line amortization.*

Required What is the gain or loss on debt extinguishment to be reported in consolidation for 2005?

E 10-10 **Gain/Loss Calculation; Bond Consolidation Entry** Pell Inc. owns 100% of the outstanding common stock of Sull Inc. On 1/1/05, Pell acquired in the open market 40% of Sull's outstanding 10% bonds at a cost of $430,000. On 1/1/05, the *carrying value* of all of the bonds ($1,000,000 *face amount*) was $1,040,000. Their maturity date is 12/31/08.

Required
1. What is the gain or loss on debt extinguishment to be reported in consolidation for 2005?
2. Prepare the bond-related consolidation entry at 1/1/05.

E 10-11 **Gain/Loss Calculation; Bond Consolidation Entry (75% ownership)** Pidd Inc. owns 75% of the outstanding common stock of Sidd Inc. On 1/1/05, Pidd acquired in the open market 20% of Sidd's outstanding 10% bonds at a cost of $160,000. On 1/1/05, the *carrying value* of all of the bonds ($1,000,000 *face amount*) was $1,020,000. Their maturity date is 12/31/08.

Required
1. What is the gain or loss on debt extinguishment to be reported in consolidation for 2005?
2. Prepare the bond-related consolidation entry at 1/1/05.

E 10-12 **Gain/Loss Calculation; Bond Consolidation Entries at Year-End** Poll Inc. owns 100% of the outstanding common stock of Soll Inc. On 1/1/05, Poll acquired in the open market 30% of Soll's outstanding 10% bonds at a cost of $340,000. On 1/1/05, the *carrying value* of all of the bonds ($1,000,000 *face amount*) was $1,035,000. Their maturity date is 12/31/09. Each entity uses straight-line amortization.

Required
1. What is the gain or loss on debt extinguishment to be reported in consolidation for 2005?
2. Prepare the bond-related consolidation entries at 12/31/05. (*For Module 1 only*: First prepare the appropriate *general ledger* adjusting entries at 12/31/05.)

Problems

P 10-1 **Reverse Analysis and Consolidation Entry: Equipment Transfer—*Upstream* (100% ownership)** On 1/1/05 Sax Inc., a 100%-owned subsidiary of Pax Inc., sold Pax office equipment to which Pax assigned a 6-year life. If Sax had *not* sold the equipment, it would have reported this equipment in its 12/31/05 balance sheet at $70,000 for *cost* and $44,000 for *accumulated depreciation.* Also if Sax had *not* sold this equipment, it would have reported *depreciation expense* of $4,000 on it for all of 2005. The equipment's carrying value on Pax's books at 12/31/05 was $60,000.

Required
1. Calculate the intercompany transfer price.
2. Calculate the intercompany gain or loss on the transfer.
3. Calculate Pax's depreciation expense on this equipment for 2005.
4. Prepare the consolidation entry at the end of 2005 relating to this transfer.

P 10-2* **Consolidation Worksheet: Year of Equipment Transfer—*Downstream* (100% ownership)** On 1/2/05, Pato Inc. sold equipment to its 100%-owned subsidiary, Sato Inc. Information relating to the sale follows:

Sales price		$35,000
Cost	$ 50,000	
Less—Accumulated depreciation (6 years)	(30,000)	20,000
Gain		$15,000
Original life used by parent		10 years
Remaining life assigned by Sato		5 years

*The financial statement information presented for problems accompanied by asterisks is also provided on Model 10 (filename: MODEL10) at the **http://pahler.swlearning.com** website, allowing the problem to be worked on the computer.

Comparative condensed financial statements follow:

	Pato Inc.	Sato Inc.
Income Statement (2005)		
Sales	$ 440,000	$150,000
Cost of sales	(230,000)	(80,000)
Expenses	(75,000)	(40,000)
Intercompany Accounts		
Equity in net income (of Sato)	30,000	
Intercompany gain	15,000	
Net Income	$ 180,000	$ 30,000
Balance Sheet (as of 12/31/05)		
Investment in subsidiary	$ 80,000	
Buildings and equipment	250,000	$ 75,000
Accumulated depreciation	(100,000)	(24,000)
Other assets	620,000	59,000
Total Assets	$ 850,000	$110,000
Liabilities	$ 110,000	$ 30,000
Common stock	300,000	45,000
Retained earnings	440,000	35,000
Total Liabilities and Equity	$ 850,000	$110,000
Dividends declared	$ 80,000	$ 20,000

Required

1. Determine the unrealized gain at year-end. (*For Module 1 only*: Also make the necessary year-end *g/l* adjusting entry for the unrealized gain required for this module; adjust the statements accordingly.) Prepare an analysis of the investment account for 2005.
2. Prepare *all* consolidation entries as of 12/31/05.
3. Prepare a consolidation worksheet at 12/31/05.

P 10-3*  **Consolidation Worksheet: Year of Equipment Transfer—*Upstream* (75% ownership)** Several years ago, Pak Inc. created a 75%-owned subsidiary, Shipp Inc. The public acquired the remaining 25% ownership interest on the creation date. On 1/3/05, Shipp sold equipment to Pak. Information related to the sale follows:

Sales price		$22,000
Cost	$ 25,000	
Less—Accumulated depreciation	(15,000)	10,000
Gain		$12,000
Original life used by subsidiary		5 years
Remaining life assigned by Pak		3 years

Comparative condensed financial statements follow:

	Pak Inc.	Shipp Inc.
Income Statement (2005)		
Sales	$ 520,000	$168,000
Cost of sales	(210,000)	(80,000)
Expenses	(93,000)	(40,000)
Intercompany Accounts		
Equity in net income (of Shipp)	45,000	
Intercompany gain		12,000
Net Income	$ 262,000	$ 60,000
Balance Sheet (as of 12/31/05)		
Investment in subsidiary	$ 135,000	
Buildings and equipment	130,000	$ 44,000
Accumulated depreciation	(40,000)	(14,000)
Other assets	275,000	165,000
Total Assets	$ 500,000	$195,000
Liabilities	$ 75,000	$ 15,000
Common stock	200,000	100,000
Retained earnings	225,000	80,000
Total Liabilities and Equity	$ 500,000	$195,000
Dividends declared	$ 135,000	$ 20,000

Required

1. Determine the unrealized gain at year-end. (*For Module 1 only*: Also make the necessary year-end *g/l* adjusting entry for the unrealized gain required for this module; adjust the statements accordingly.) Prepare an analysis of the investment account for 2005.
2. Prepare *all* consolidation entries as of 12/31/05.
3. Prepare a consolidation worksheet at 12/31/05.

P 10-4 **Reverse Analysis and Consolidation Entries (Two Years): Equipment Transfer—*Downstream* (100% ownership)** On 6/30/05, Pine Inc. sold its minicomputer to Syne Inc., its 100%-owned subsidiary, which assigned the computer a *3-year life*. If Pine had not sold the computer, it would have reported the computer in the 12/31/05 balance sheet at $720,000 for *cost* and $480,000 for *accumulated depreciation*. If Pine had *not* sold the computer, it also would have reported *depreciation expense* of $60,000 for all of 2005 on the computer. The computer's *carrying value* on Syne's books at 12/31/05 was $125,000.

Required

1. Calculate the intercompany transfer price.
2. Calculate the intercompany gain or loss on the transfer.
3. Calculate Syne's depreciation expense on this equipment for 2005.
4. Prepare the consolidation entries at the end of 2005 and 2006 relating to this transfer.

P 10-5* **Consolidation Worksheet: Year After Year of Equipment Transfer—*Upstream* (75% ownership)** Comparative condensed financial statements of Pert Inc. and its 75%-owned subsidiary, Savy Inc., follow:

	Pert Inc.	Savy Inc.
Income Statement (2006)		
Sales	$ 240,000	$156,000
Cost of sales	(120,000)	(80,000)
Expenses	(70,000)	(40,000)
Intercompany Accounts		
Equity in net income (of Savy)	27,000	
Net Income	$ 77,000	$ 36,000
Statement of Retained Earnings (2006)		
Beginning of year	$ 100,000	$ 44,000
+ Net income	77,000	36,000
- Dividends declared	(45,000)	(16,000)
End of year	$ 132,000	$ 64,000
Balance Sheet (as of 12/31/06)		
Investment in subsidiary	$ 123,000	
Buildings and equipment	300,000	$140,000
Accumulated depreciation	(90,000)	(50,000)
Other assets	290,000	210,000
Total Assets	$ 623,000	$300,000
Liabilities	$ 291,000	$136,000
Common stock	200,000	100,000
Retained earnings	132,000	64,000
Total Liabilities and Equity	$ 623,000	$300,000

On 1/4/05 (the previous year), Savy sold equipment to Pert. Information related to this sale follows:

Sales price		$31,000
Cost	$ 25,000	
Less—Accumulated depreciation	(10,000)	15,000
Gain		$16,000
Original life used by subsidiary		5 years
Remaining life assigned by parent		4 years

Neither entity made any *general ledger adjustment* for unrealized intercompany gain at the end of 2005 or 2006. (Pert created Savy 5 years ago, at which time 25% of the ownership was sold to the public.)

Required

1. Calculate the unrealized intercompany gain at the end of 2006. (*For Module 1 only*: Make the necessary year-end *g/l* adjusting entry for the unrealized gain required for this module; adjust the statements accordingly.) Prepare an analysis of the investment account for 2006.
2. Prepare *all* consolidation entries as of 12/31/06.
3. Prepare a consolidation worksheet at 12/31/06.

P 10-6*

Mini-Comprehensive—Purchased Subsidiary Consolidation Worksheet: Year of Equipment Transfer—*Upstream* (80% ownership) On 1/1/05, Puta Inc. purchased 80% of Suta Inc.'s outstanding common stock for $184,000 cash. At that date, Suta had (1) a book value of $175,000 ($100,000 common stock + $75,000 retained earnings) and (2) land that was undervalued by $10,000. On 1/3/05, Suta sold equipment to Puta. Information related to the sale follows:

Sales price		$ 18,000
Cost	$ 98,000	
Less—Accumulated depreciation	(56,000)	42,000
Loss		$(24,000)
Original life used by subsidiary		7 years
Remaining life assigned by Puta		6 years

Comparative condensed financial statements follow:

	Puta Inc.	Suta Inc.
Income Statement (2005)		
Sales	$ 625,000	$ 299,000
Cost of sales	(210,000)	(140,000)
Expenses	(180,000)	(70,000)
Intercompany Accounts		
Equity in net income (of Suta)	40,000	
Intercompany loss		(24,000)
Net Income	$ 275,000	$ 65,000
Balance Sheet (as of 12/31/05)		
Investment in subsidiary	$ 188,000	
Buildings and equipment	390,000	$ 180,000
Accumulated depreciation	(80,000)	(120,000)[a]
Other assets	202,000	215,000
Total Assets	$ 700,000	$ 275,000
Liabilities	$ 280,000	$ 80,000
Common stock	200,000	100,000
Retained earnings	220,000	95,000
Total Liabilities and Equity	$ 700,000	$ 275,000
Dividends declared	$ 150,000	$ 45,000

[a] The balance was $110,000 at the acquisition date.

Neither entity made any general ledger adjustment for unrealized intercompany loss at the end of 2005.

Required

1. Determine the unrealized loss at the end of 2005. (*For Module 1 only*: Also make the necessary year-end adjusting entry for the unrealized loss required for this module; adjust the statements accordingly.) Prepare an analysis of the Investment account for 2005.
2. Prepare *all* consolidation entries as of 12/31/05.
3. Prepare a consolidation worksheet at 12/31/05.

P 10-7*

COMPREHENSIVE—ACQUIRED SUBSIDIARY Consolidation Worksheet: Year After Year of Equipment Transfer—*Upstream* (60% ownership); Multiple Year Inventory Transfers—*Downstream* On 1/1/05, Park Inc. acquired 60% of the outstanding common stock of Stall Inc. for $153,000 cash. Park incurred an additional $12,000 of direct costs. At the time, Stall's common stock had a *book value* of $34 per share. Stall's land was *undervalued* by $50,000, and its 5% long-term debt (due 12/31/08) had a *current value* of $40,000 less than its *book value*.

On 1/3/06, Stall sold office equipment to Park. Information related to this sale follows:

Sales price		$27,000
Cost	$ 44,000	
Less—Accumulated depreciation	(32,000)	12,000
Gain		$15,000
Original life used by subsidiary		4 years
Remaining life assigned by Park		3 years

Comparative financial statements are as follows:

	Park Inc.	Stall Inc.
Income Statement (2006)		
Sales	$ 600,000	$ 395,000
Cost of sales	(360,000)	(200,000)
Expenses	(226,000)	(119,000)
Intercompany Accounts		
Equity in net income (of Stall)	24,000	
Intercompany sales	50,000	
Intercompany cost of sales	(30,000)	
Intercompany mgt. fee income	36,000	
Intercompany mgt. fee expense		(36,000)
Intercompany gain		15,000
Net Income	$ 94,000	$ 55,000
Balance Sheet (as of 12/31/06)		
Inventory:		
From vendors	$ 214,000	$ 85,000
Intercompany		5,000
Investment in subsidiary	168,000	
Land	126,000	45,000
Buildings and equipment	255,000	140,000
Accumulated depreciation	(150,000)	(55,000)[a]
Other assets	207,000	90,000
Total Assets	$ 820,000	$ 310,000
Current liabilities	$ 103,000	$ 63,500
Long-term debt	220,000	62,000
Common stock, $10 par value	250,000	
Common stock, $20 par value		100,000
Retained earnings	247,000	105,000
Less—Treasury stock (at cost) (500 shares)		(20,500)[b]
Total Liabilities and Equity	$ 820,000	$ 310,000
Dividends declared:[c]		
2005	30,000	10,000
2006	41,000	35,000

[a] The balance was $40,000 at the acquisition date.

[b] The treasury stock was purchased at a very favorable price on 12/31/06.

[c] Assume that all dividends were declared on 12/10 and paid 10 days later.

Additional Information

1. Stall's 12/31/05 inventory included $17,000 of inventory acquired from Park in 2005. Park's cost was $14,000. Stall resold this inventory for $23,000 in 2006.
2. Neither entity made any *general ledger adjustment* for unrealized intercompany gain and profit at the end of 2005 and 2006.
3. In applying the *equity method* of accounting for 2006, Park recorded $33,000 (60% of $55,000).
4. Because of an overpayment, Park owed Stall $11,000 at the end of 2006.

Required

1. Calculate the unrealized gain on the equipment transfer at the end of 2006 and prepare a matrix analysis to determine the unrealized profit on the *current year* inventory transfers. (*For Module 1 only*: Also make the necessary year-end adjusting entry(ies) for the unrealized gain

and profit; adjust the statements accordingly. Prepare an updated analysis of the investment account from inception through the end of 2006.)
2. Prepare *all* consolidation entries as of 12/31/06.
3. Prepare a consolidation worksheet at 12/31/06.

P 10-8 **Bond-Related Consolidation Entries** The partially completed income statements of Place Inc. and its 100%-owned created subsidiary, Show Inc., for the year ended 12/31/06 are as follows:

	2006	
	Place Inc.	**Show Inc.**
Sales	$ 7,000,000	$ 3,000,000
Cost of sales	(4,000,000)	(1,600,000)
Expenses (noninterest)	(1,500,000)	(1,000,000)
Interest expense	-0-	
Gain on debt extinguishment		
Intercompany Accounts		
Equity in net income (of Show)		
Dividend income (from Show)		
Intercompany interest income		
Intercompany interest expense		
Net Income	$	$

Additional information

1. On 1/1/06, Place acquired 40% of Show's outstanding 10% bonds ($1,000,000 face amount) at 90. Show had initially issued these 10-year bonds on 1/1/04 at 105.
2. Neither entity had any other investments or indebtedness that would give rise to interest *income* or interest *expense*.
3. Each entity uses *straight-line amortization*.
4. Show declared cash dividends of $200,000 in 2006.

Required
1. Fill in the blanks in the preceding income statements.
2. Prepare the bond-related consolidation entries at 12/31/06.

P 10-9 **Bond-Related Consolidation Entries: Multiple Years** Stak Inc. is a 100%-owned created subsidiary of Ptak Inc. On 1/1/03, Stak issued $10,000,000 of 5-year, 10% bonds at 98 (maturity date is 1/1/08). On 1/1/05 (2 years later), Ptak acquired in the open market 30% of these bonds at 102. Each entity uses *straight-line amortization*.

Required
1. Calculate the gain or loss on debt extinguishment to be reported for 2005.
2. Prepare the bond-related consolidation entries at 12/31/05, 06, and 07.

P 10-10 **Bond-Related Consolidation Entries: Multiple Years (90% ownership)** Sala Inc. is a 90%-owned created subsidiary of Pala Inc. On 1/1/03, Sala issued $10,000,000 of 5-year, 10% bonds at 95 (maturity date is 1/1/08). On 1/1/05 (2 years later), Pala acquired in the open market 30% of these bonds at 101. Each entity uses *straight-line amortization*.

Required
1. Calculate the gain or loss on debt extinguishment to be reported for 2005.
2. Prepare the bond-related consolidation entries at 12/31/05, 06, and 07.

THINKING CRITICALLY

Cases

C 10-1 **Maybe It Is and Maybe It Isn't** Kelly says that depreciation is part of the *accrual basis* of accounting. Lynn says it is not.

Required

1. Prepare a written solution that need be no more than one page long.
2. Is a fixed asset expensed when a company uses the *cash basis* of accounting? What about for tax purposes?

C 10-2 **Purchasing Bonds Merely to Report a Gain?** For the first nine months of 2006, Purdy Company is experiencing lower earnings than forecasted. Management is searching for ways to increase earnings during the remainder of the year. The controller has suggested that Purdy issue $1,000,000 of bonds and use the proceeds to acquire its subsidiary's outstanding 15-year, 10% bonds ($1,000,000 face value), which are currently selling at 90. Those bonds were issued at a *premium* of $75,000 five years ago; thus a $150,000 gain can be reported in 2006. Purdy's borrowing rate would be 12%.

Required Evaluate the validity and merits of the controller's idea.

part four

Consolidated Financial Statements: Other Topics

IV

chapter

11

Changes in a Parent's Ownership Interest, Cash Flow Statement, and EPS

Our characters are the result of our conduct.
ARISTOTLE

LEARNING OBJECTIVES

To Understand

- The *three* ways in which the parent's ownership level in a subsidiary can change.
- The reasons a parent may gain or lose *economically* when its ownership level changes.
- The way to calculate a parent's *economic* gain or loss upon a change in ownership.
- The way to initially report these *economic* gains and losses.
- The way to prepare a consolidated statement of cash flows.
- The way to calculate consolidated earnings per share.

TOPIC OUTLINE

I. The Acquisition of a Noncontrolling Interest
II. Parent's Partial Disposal of Its Investment
III. Subsidiary's Issuance of Additional Common Stock
IV. Other Changes in the Subsidiary's Capital Accounts
V. Consolidated Statement of Cash Flows
VI. Consolidated Earnings Per Share
APPENDIX 11A: Subsidiary with Preferred Stock Outstanding
APPENDIX 11B: Indirect and Reciprocal Holdings

Appendices can be found at http://www.pahler.swlearning.com

CHAPTER OVERVIEW

For brevity, we hereafter often use the abbreviation "NCI" for noncontrolling interest.

A parent's ownership interest in a subsidiary can change as a result of (1) a parent's or a subsidiary's acquisition of some or all of the NCI, (2) a parent's sale of a portion of its investment (thereby *increasing* the NCI), and (3) a subsidiary's issuance of additional common stock to outside parties (thereby *increasing* the NCI).

This chapter discusses the way to (1) calculate the appropriate change to be made to the parent's Investment account for these ownership changes and (2) calculate and report the parent's resulting economic gain or loss that occurs in virtually all ownership changes.

For simplicity, we assume in all illustrations that (1) the parent uses the *equity method* of accounting for its investment in the subsidiary and that (2) the Investment account has been properly applied (updated) under the *equity method* of accounting to the change in the ownership date. This procedure is necessary so that the proper adjustment can be made to the Investment account for the ownership change.

Basis of Coverage

Our discussion is based on current GAAP—*not* the Financial Accounting Standards Board's proposed *consolidation procedures* GAAP set forth in its 1995 exposure draft. Recall from Chapter 1 that (1) the FASB is currently focusing only on *consolidation policies* for the near term and (2) if a consensus is reached on *consolidation policies*, the FASB will reassess whether to pursue the *consolidation procedures* area. Thus for now, the *consolidation procedures* area is on hold.

Accordingly, our coverage is based on the consolidation procedures set forth in (1) *Accounting Research Bulletin No. 51*, "Consolidated Financial Statements," and (2) FASB *Statement No. 141*, "Business Combinations."

I. THE ACQUISITION OF A NONCONTROLLING INTEREST

Regardless of whether the *parent* or the *subsidiary* acquires some or all of the NCI, *FAS 141* permits only the use of the *purchase method*.

Parent Acquires the Noncontrolling Interest

A parent's acquisition of **any or all** of the NCI is merely a **block acquisition.** Accordingly, the cost of the block of stock acquired must be separated into its components in the same manner that the initial investment cost of an acquired partially owned subsidiary is separated into its components (illustrated in Chapter 6). Thus the *parent's* acquisition of any or all of the NCI presents no new accounting issues.

CHECK POINT

When a *parent* acquires some or all of the noncontrolling interest in a subsidiary, it must use which of the following?

a. Economic unit concept.
b. Parent company concept.
c. Purchase method.
d. Cost method.

Answer: c

Subsidiary Acquires the Noncontrolling Interest

A subsidiary's acquisition of **any or all** of the NCI is also a **block acquisition from a consolidated viewpoint.** Thus the consolidated statements must still reflect the use of the purchase method. To achieve this result, a reclassification within the parent's conceptual analysis of its Investment in Subsidiary account is made (shown shortly) as a result of the subsidiary's purchase of such shares.

Subsidiary's General Ledger Entry

The subsidiary's *general ledger entry* is the same as that made by any entity that acquires and retires its outstanding shares—that is, debit the capital accounts and credit the Cash account.

Parent's Reclassification Entry

The parent does *not* make any *general ledger entry* to adjust the total carrying value of its Investment account as a result of the contraction of the subsidiary's equity—regardless of the price paid by the subsidiary to acquire the NCI. If the subsidiary pays *more* or *less* than the book value per share, however, the parent's total dollar interest in the subsidiary's net assets at their book value *decreases* or *increases*, respectively. Accordingly, the parent's Investment account must be adjusted to reflect that the parent's interest in the subsidiary's net assets at book value has changed. The two possible situations are as follows:

1. **Subsidiary pays *more than* book value.** Because the parent's total dollar interest *decreases*, the book value element must be *decreased*, and the under- or overvaluation of net assets element or the goodwill element or both must be *increased* by an offsetting amount.
2. **Subsidiary pays *less than* book value.** Because the parent's total dollar interest *increases*, the book value element must be *increased*, and the under- or overvaluation of net assets element or the goodwill element or both must be *decreased* by an offsetting amount.

Because these adjustments do *not* change the total carrying value of the investment, they are essentially a *reclassification* of amounts from one component to another.

Comprehensive Illustration

Subsidiary Acquires 100% of the NCI at *Above* Book Value (75%-Owned *Acquired* Subsidiary)

Assume the following information in which the parent acquired *all* of the NCI at more than the book value per share:

	Percent	Shares
Parent's ownership in a created subsidiary:		
Before the acquisition of the NCI.	75	7,500
After the acquisition of the NCI.	100	10,000
Subsidiary's equity accounts immediately *before* the acquisition of the NCI:		
Common stock		$ 60,000
Retained earnings		140,000
		$200,000
Book value per share ($200,000/10,000 shares)		$20
Subsidiary's purchase price to acquire *all* 2,500 outstanding shares held by the NCI.		$80,000

Subsidiary's assumed *general ledger* entry:

Common Stock (25% of $60,000)	15,000	
Retained Earnings (residual).	65,000	
Cash		80,000

This information is used in Section I of Illustration 11-1 to calculate the *decrease* in the parent's interest in the subsidiary's net assets. Section II of Illustration 11-1 shows the required changes to the parent's analysis of its Investment account. (The procedure is the same when the parent's interest in the subsidiary's net assets *increases*.)

ILLUSTRATION 11-1 SUBSIDIARY'S ACQUISITION OF 100% OF THE NCI AT AMOUNT IN EXCESS OF BOOK VALUE (75%-OWNED ACQUIRED SUBSIDIARY)

I. Calculation of *Decrease* in Parent's Interest in Subsidiary's Net Assets

	SUBSIDIARY'S EQUITY ACCOUNTS	BOOK VALUE PER SHARE	PARENT'S INTEREST PERCENT	PARENT'S INTEREST AMOUNT	NONCONTROLLING INTEREST PERCENT	NONCONTROLLING INTEREST AMOUNT
Before acquisition of *all* of the NCI:						
Common stock.	$ 60,000		75	$ 45,000	25	$ 15,000
Retained earnings	140,000		75	105,000	25	35,000
	$200,000	$20		$150,000		$ 50,000
After acquisition of *all* the NCI:						
Common stock.	$ 45,000		100	$ 45,000		
Retained earnings	75,000	$16	100	75,000		
	$120,000			$120,000		
Decrease in equity.	$ (80,000)			$ (30,000)		$(50,000)

II. Parent's Adjustment to Its Investment Account

Analysis of the Investment Account—Book Value Element

	NONCONTROLLING INTEREST (DECREASES FROM 25% TO 0%)	+	PARENT'S INVESTMENT ACCOUNT—BOOK VALUE	=	BOOK VALUE ELEMENT — SUBSIDIARY'S EQUITY ACCOUNTS: COMMON STOCK	+	RETAINED EARNINGS
Balances immediately *before* acquiring the NCI	$ 50,000		$150,000		$ 60,000		$140,000
– Adjustment	(50,000)		(30,000)		(15,000)		(65,000)
Balances immediately *after* acquiring the NCI.	$ -0-		$120,000		$ 45,000		$ 75,000

Analysis of the Investment Account—Excess Cost Elements

	PARENT'S INVESTMENT ACCOUNT—EXCESS COST	=	UNDERVALUATION OF NET ASSETS ELEMENT: LAND	+	GOODWILL ELEMENT
Balances immediately *before* acquiring the NCI.	$ 70,000		$40,000		$30,000
+ Adjustment	30,000[a]				30,000[b]
Balances immediately *after* acquiring the NCI	$100,000		$40,000		$60,000

[a] This amount is the $30,000 excess payment—it equals the total dilution of the parent's interest in the subsidiary's net assets at book value.

[b] For simplicity, we assume the entire $30,000 was assignable to goodwill.

Review Points for Illustration 11-1. Note the following:

1. The NCI shareholders received an additional $30,000 in excess of their ownership interest in the subsidiary's net assets at book value.
2. The subsidiary's $30,000 excess payment to the NCI shareholders dilutes the parent's interest in the subsidiary's net assets by $30,000.
3. The *subsidiary's* $30,000 excess payment must be treated as an addition to the *parent's* cost in excess of book value. If instead, the *parent* had paid $80,000 to acquire the NCI, the parent would have added $30,000 to its excess cost elements when accounting for the acquisition as a *block acquisition.* Thus from a *consolidated viewpoint,* it is irrelevant that the *subsidiary* acquired the NCI rather than the *parent.*

4. The $30,000 adjustment to the excess cost elements prevents the *parent* from reporting a loss on the acquisition of the NCI relating to the dilution of the *parent's* interest in the *subsidiary's* net assets at book value.
5. The effect on the consolidated statements is as if the following entry had been made from a *consolidated viewpoint*:

NCI in Net Assets of Subsidiary	50,000	
Goodwill	30,000	
Cash		80,000

CHECK POINT

When a *subsidiary* acquires the noncontrolling interest at *less than* the book value of the noncontrolling interest, which of the following takes place or occurs?

a. A currently reportable gain under the *parent company concept.*
b. A change in the carrying value of the Investment in Subsidiary account.
c. An adjustment to the Additional Paid-in Capital account under the *parent company concept.*
d. Accretion to the parent's ownership interest in the net assets of the subsidiary at book value.

Answer: d

Subsidiary Acquires *Part* of the Noncontrolling Interest

When the subsidiary acquires only a portion of the NCI at *more* or *less* than *book value* per share, both the parent's **and the *remaining* NCI shareholders'** total dollar interests in the subsidiary's net assets at book value *decrease* or *increase*, respectively. Only the *parent's* decrease or increase results in a decrease or an increase, respectively, to its excess cost elements.

To illustrate, assume that the subsidiary (1) acquired only 1,000 (40%) of the NCI shares for $32,000 cash (instead of acquiring *all* 2,500 NCI shares for $80,000 cash) and (2) made the following *general ledger* entry (all amounts are at 40% of the amounts for the earlier illustration):

Common Stock (10% of $60,000)	6,000	
Retained Earnings (residual)	26,000	
Cash		32,000

The excess payment is $12,000 (instead of $30,000). (The $32,000 payment minus $20,000 of *book value* accruing to these 1,000 shares equals $12,000.) In this case, the remaining shareholders (7,500 shares being held by the parent and 1,500 shares being held by the remaining NCI shareholders) share the $12,000 of dilution in relation to their respective holdings (a 5:1 ratio), as shown as follows:

	Remaining Ownership		Dollar Share
	Shares	Percentage	of Dilution
Parent's holdings	7,500	83.33%	$(10,000)
Remaining NCI holdings	1,500	16.67	(2,000)
Total	9,000	100.00%	$(12,000)

This information is used in Section I of Illustration 11-2 to calculate the *decrease* in the parent's interest in the subsidiary's net assets. Section II of Illustration 11-2 shows the required changes to the parent's analyses of its Investment account.

CHECK POINT

On 5/1/06 Saxco, a 60%-owned subsidiary of Paxco, acquired 25,000 shares of its 100,000 outstanding common shares at a cost of $300,000. Prior to this purchase, Saxco's net assets had a total

ILLUSTRATION 11-2 SUBSIDIARY'S ACQUISITION OF 40% OF THE NCI AT AMOUNT IN EXCESS OF BOOK VALUE (75%-OWNED ACQUIRED SUBSIDIARY)

I. Calculation of *Decrease* in Parent's Interest in Subsidiary's Net Assets

	SUBSIDIARY'S EQUITY ACCOUNTS	BOOK VALUE PER SHARE	PARENT'S INTEREST PERCENT	PARENT'S INTEREST AMOUNT	NONCONTROLLING INTEREST PERCENT	NONCONTROLLING INTEREST AMOUNT
Before acquisition of *40%* of the NCI:						
Common stock.	$ 60,000		75	$ 45,000	25	$ 15,000
Retained earnings	140,000		75	105,000	25	35,000
	$200,000	$20		$150,000		$ 50,000
After acquisition of *40%* of the NCI:						
Common stock.	$ 54,000		83 1/3	$ 45,000	16 2/3	$ 9,000
Retained earnings	114,000	$16	83 1/3	95,000	16 2/3	19,000
	$168,000			$140,000		$ 28,000
Decrease in equity.	$ (32,000)			$ (10,000)		$(22,000)[a]

[a] Of this amount, $20,000 is the payment for the book value of the net assets (10% × $200,000). The remaining $2,000 is the dilution suffered by the remaining NCI shareholders.

II. Parent's Adjustment to Its Investment Account

Analysis of the Investment Account—Book Value Element

	NONCONTROLLING INTEREST (DECREASES FROM 25% TO 16 2/3%)	+	PARENT'S INVESTMENT ACCOUNT—BOOK VALUE	=	BOOK VALUE ELEMENT — SUBSIDIARY'S EQUITY ACCOUNTS: COMMON STOCK	+	RETAINED EARNINGS
Balances immediately *before* acquiring the NCI	$ 50,000		$150,000		$60,000		$140,000
– Adjustment	(22,000)		(10,000)		(6,000)		(26,000)
Balances immediately *after* acquiring the NCI.	$ 28,000		$140,000		$54,000		$114,000

Analysis of the Investment Account—Excess Cost Elements

	PARENT'S INVESTMENT ACCOUNT—EXCESS COST	=	UNDERVALUATION OF NET ASSETS ELEMENT: LAND	+	GOODWILL ELEMENT
Balances immediately *before* acquiring the NCI.	$70,000		$40,000		$30,000
+ Adjustment	10,000[a]				10,000[b]
Balances immediately *after* acquiring the NCI	$80,000		$40,000		$40,000

[a] This amount is 83 1/3% the $12,000 excess payment—it equals the total dilution of the parent's interest in the subsidiary's net assets at book value.

[b] For simplicity, we assume the entire $10,000 was assignable to goodwill.

book value of $1,500,000. As a result of this purchase, Paxco would report which of the following in its 2006 income statement under the *parent company concept*?

a. –0–

b. Gain of $60,000.

c. Loss of $60,000.

d. Gain of $75,000.

e. Loss of $75,000.

Answer: a

II. PARENT'S PARTIAL DISPOSAL OF ITS INVESTMENT

A parent can dispose of part of its investment in a subsidiary for many reasons (such as to raise much-needed cash for other operations of the entity). In the 1990s, many partial disposals were a prelude to the eventual disposal of the entire ownership interest. See the Case in Point.

CASE IN POINT

In 1998, General Motors made its Delphi Automotive Systems parts-making subsidiary (which had 1997 revenues of approximately $30 billion) fully independent. The first step in this transaction was the partial disposal of 15%–20% of its holdings in an initial public offering in 1999.

The accounting issue for partial disposals is that of determining how to calculate and report the gain or loss on the disposal. Under *ARB 51*, the gain or loss is reported currently in earnings (the treatment under the *parent company concept*). To determine the gain or loss, however, involves determining the amount of the reduction to the parent's Investment account. This amount is compared with the proceeds from the sale to determine the reportable gain or loss. The two categories of partial disposal are as follows:

1. **Shares acquired in a single acquisition.** When all the shares owned were acquired at one time, the investment account is reduced using the *average cost* of the shares owned.
2. **Shares acquired in block acquisitions.** When the shares owned were acquired at more than one time, three methods of reducing the Investment account are available:
   a. The average cost method.
   b. The specific identification method (*allowed for federal income tax-reporting purposes*).
   c. The first-in, first-out method (*allowed for federal income tax-reporting purposes*).

Our preference is the **average cost method** because the other two methods introduce an artificial element. For example, the gain or loss reported under the **specific identification method** could be partially determined by the particular block of stock selected for sale; whereas under the **first-in, first-out method,** we use an assumed flow concept initially intended for inventory pricing. Furthermore, the manner of acquiring the shares is irrelevant to the accounting for the disposal of shares—the issue is the amount of the total ownership interest that is disposed of. This percentage answer should also apply to the carrying value of the cost of the investment.

Regardless of the method selected to reduce the Investment account, the Investment account must be adjusted in accordance with the *equity method* of accounting up to the date of sale.

Comprehensive Illustration

Partial Disposal Using the *Average Cost* Method

Assume the following information:

	Percent	Shares
Parent's ownership in subsidiary:		
Before the partial disposal	75%	7,500
After the partial disposal	60%	6,000
Decrease in ownership	15%	1,500
Percentage Decrease in Shares Owned	20%	
Proceeds from sale of the 1,500 shares on July 1, 2006	$ 53,000	
Subsidiary's equity accounts immediately *before* the partial disposal on 7/1/06:		
Common stock	$ 60,000	
Retained earnings	160,000	
Total Equity	$220,000	

Number of shares outstanding	10,000
Book value per share ($220,000/10,000 shares)	$22
Book value of shares sold ($1,500 shares × $22)	$ 33,000

Subsidiary's Income and Dividends for 2006:	
Net Income—	
January 1, 2006–June 30, 2006	$ 40,000
July 1, 2006–December 31, 2006	45,000
Total	$ 85,000
Dividends—	
Per Quarter	$ 10,000

Illustration 11-3 shows the manner of updating the parent's analyses of its Investment account.

ILLUSTRATION 11-3 PARTIAL DISPOSAL OF INVESTMENT—UPDATING THE ANALYSES OF THE INVESTMENT ACCOUNT

Splitting the Investment Account on January 1, 2006

Total Cost	$ 220,000
Less—75% share of subsidiary's $200,000 book value	(150,000)
Excess Cost	$ 70,000

Analysis of the Investment Account—Book Value Element

	NONCONTROLLING INTEREST 25% + 15% = 40%	+	PARENT'S INVESTMENT ACCOUNT—	=	SUBSIDIARY'S EQUITY ACCOUNTS COMMON STOCK	+	RETAINED EARNINGS
Balances, January 1, 2006	$ 50,000		$ 150,000		$ 60,000		$ 140,000
+ Equity in net income for first six months:							
To CI (75% × $40,000)			30,000				30,000
To NCI (25% × $40,000)	10,000						10,000
- Dividends:							
To CI (75% × $20,000)			(15,000)				(15,000)
To NCI (25% × $20,000)	(5,000)						(5,000)
Balances, June 30, 2006	**$55,000**		**$165,000**		**$60,000**		**$160,000**
- 20% Disposal, July 1, 2006 (at $22 per share book value)	**33,000**		**(33,000)**				
Subtotal	$ 88,000		$ 132,000		$ 60,000		$ 160,000
+ Equity in net income:							
To CI (60% × $45,000)			27,000				27,000
To NCI (40% × $45,000)	18,000						18,000
- Dividends:							
To CI (60% × $20,000)			(12,000)				(12,000)
To NCI (40% × $20,000)	(8,000)						(8,000)
Balances, December 31, 2006	$ 98,000		$ 147,000		$ 60,000		$ 185,000

Analysis of the Investment Account—Excess Cost Elements

	PARENT'S INVESTMENT ACCOUNT— EXCESS COST	=	UNDERVALUATION OF NET ASSETS ELEMENT LAND	+	GOODWILL ELEMENT
Balances, January 1, 2006	$ 70,000		$ 40,000		$ 30,000
- Amortization—1/2 yr.	-0-				-0-
Balances, June 30, 2006	**$ 70,000**		**$40,000**		**$30,000**
- 20% Disposal, July 1, 2006	**(14,000)**		**(8,000)**		**(6,000)**
Subtotal	$ 56,000		$ 32,000		$ 24,000
- Amortization—1/2 yr.	-0-				-0-
Balances, December 31, 2006	$ 56,000		$ 32,000		$ 24,000

Review Points for Illustration 11-3. Note the following:

1. The reportable gain on the disposal of the shares sold is determined as follows:

Proceeds from sale	$ 53,000
Average cost of shares sold ($33,000 book value + $14,000 excess cost)	(47,000)
Gain	$ 6,000

2. The parent makes the following **general ledger** entry:

Cash	53,000	
Investment in Subsidiary ($33,000 + $14,000)		47,000
Gain on *Partial* Disposal (of Subbco)		6,000

3. The December 31, 2006 consolidation entries are as follows:

WORKSHEET ENTRY ONLY

Common Stock	60,000	
Retained Earnings, January 1, 2006	140,000	
Equity in Net Income ($30,000 + $27,000)	57,000	
NCI in Net Income ($10,000 + $18,000)	28,000	
Dividends Declared		40,000
Investment in Subsidiary		147,000
NCI in Net Assets		98,000

WORKSHEET ENTRY ONLY

Land	32,000	
Goodwill	24,000	
Investment in Subsidiary		56,000

Illustration 11-4 shows a consolidation worksheet for the year ended December 31, 2006, prepared using the preceding entries.

Check Point

When a parent *sells* a portion of its common stock holdings in a subsidiary, which of the following must be applied at the date of the disposal in relieving the Investment account?

a. The specific identification method.
b. The parent company concept.
c. The economic unit concept.
d. SEC *Staff Acct. Bulletin No. 51.*

Answer: b

III. Subsidiary's Issuance of Additional Common Stock

Rather than disposing of a portion of its stock holdings in a subsidiary to raise capital for the consolidated group, a parent may direct the subsidiary to issue additional common stock to the public.

ILLUSTRATION 11-4 PARENT'S PARTIAL DISPOSAL OF INVESTMENT IN SUBSIDIARY

Parrco Company and Subbco Company
Consolidation Worksheet as of December 31, 2006

	PARRCO COMPANY	60%-OWNED SUBBCO COMPANY	CONSOLIDATION ENTRIES DR.			CR.	CONSOLIDATED
Income Statement (2006)							
Sales	619,000	350,000					969,000
Cost of sales	(301,000)	(160,000)					(461,000)
Expenses	(263,000)	(105,000)					(368,000)
Gain on *partial* disposal (of Subbco)	6,000						6,000
Equity in net income (of Subbco)	57,000		57,000	1			-0-
Net income	118,000	85,000	57,000				146,000
NCI in net income			28,000	1			(28,000)
CI in net income			85,000				118,000
Statement of Retained Earnings							
Balances, 1/1/06	180,000	140,000	140,000	1			180,000
+ Net income	118,000	85,000	85,000				118,000
– Dividends declared	(50,000)	(40,000)			1	40,000	(50,000)
Balances, 12/31/06	248,000	185,000	225,000			40,000	248,000
Balance Sheet							
Investment in Subsidiary:							
Book value element	147,000				1	147,000	-0-
Excess cost elements	56,000				2	56,000	-0-
Land	220,000	30,000	32,000	2			282,000
Goodwill			24,000	2			24,000
Other assets	305,000	370,000					675,000
Total Assets	728,000	400,000	56,000			203,000	981,000
Liabilities	280,000	155,000					435,000
NCI in net assets					1	98,000	98,000
Common stock ($1 par)	10,000						10,000
Add'l paid-in capital	190,000						190,000
Common stock (no par)		60,000	60,000	1			-0-
Retained earnings	248,000	185,000	225,000			40,000	248,000
Total Liabilities and Equity	728,000	400,000	285,000			138,000	981,000
Proof of debit and credit postings			*241,000*			*241,000*	

Explanation of entries:

1 The basic *elimination* entry.
2 The *unamortized* excess cost *reclassification* entry (for **BS**).
3 The *amortized* excess cost *reclassification* entry (for **IS**).

If the shares issued to the public are sold *below* the *book value* per share of the subsidiary's common stock as of the issuance date, the parent's total dollar interest in the subsidiary's net assets at book value is diluted; thus it *decreases*. On the other hand, when the subsidiary issues shares *above* the *book value* of its common stock as of the issuance date, the parent's total dollar interest in the subsidiary's net assets at book value *increases*. This may be understood best by realizing that if the subsidiary were liquidated at no gain or loss in the liquidation process, the parent would receive either more or less than it would receive if the subsidiary had *not* issued the additional shares.

Accountants agree that an increase or a decrease occurs in the parent's interest in the subsidiary's net assets at book value of the investment. Accountants differ on the treatment of the offsetting credit or debit. *ARB 51* does *not* explicitly address this situation. The two alternative accounting treatments that exist are as follows:

1. **Parent company concept.** Record it as a gain or loss in the parent's income statement. (The gain or loss is **not eliminated in consolidation.**)

2. **Economic unit concept.** Record it as an adjustment to the parent's Additional Paid-in Capital account. (This treatment carries through to the consolidated balance sheet.)

Rationale of the Economic Unit Concept (EUC) Treatment

Recall from Chapter 6 that under the *EUC*, a new reporting entity with two classes of common shareholders results from the consolidation process. Under *EUC*, the subsidiary's issuance of additional common stock is viewed as a **capital-raising transaction for the consolidated group** because capital-raising transactions do *not* cause either a gain or a loss on a *consolidated basis*. Recall from intermediate accounting that *APB Opinion No. 9*, "Reporting the Results of Operations" (paragraph 28), requires that gains or losses from transactions in a company's own stock are to be excluded from the income statement. Accordingly, increases and decreases in the parent's interest in the subsidiary's book value are handled as follows:

1. **Increases.** Treat as capital contributions from the NCI shareholders ***to* the parent.**
2. **Decreases.** Treat as capital contributions ***from* the parent** to the NCI shareholders.

Rationale of the Parent Company Concept (PCC) Treatment

Recall from Chapter 6 that under the *PCC*, the parent is viewed as the reporting entity in the consolidated statement. Under *PCC*, the parent is viewed as either gaining or losing as a result of the subsidiary's issuance of additional common stock. Gains and losses are reported in the income statement. Accordingly, this type of gain or loss also should be reflected in the income statement. In regard to the requirements of *APBO 9*, the argument can be made that this is *not* a transaction in one's own stock—it is a transaction involving the investment in the subsidiary's stock; thus *APBO 9* is *not* applicable. The advocates of this approach also contend that substantively the sale of a subsidiary's shares by the parent (pursuant to a partial disposal)—whereby a gain or loss is recognized in the income statement—is no different from the issuance of additional common shares by a subsidiary.

The AICPA's Position

In 1980, the Accounting Standards Executive Committee of the American Institute of Certified Public Accountants (AICPA) prepared an issues paper, "Accounting in Consolidation for Issuances of a Subsidiary's Stock." This paper's advisory conclusions are that such gains or losses should be recognized in the consolidated income statement. The position taken here seems to be that such transactions are *not* "transactions in one's own stock." Thus *APBO 9* is *not* applicable.

The Securities and Exchange Commission's Position

In 1983, the staff of the Securities and Exchange Commission (SEC) issued *Staff Accounting Bulletin No. 51*, "Accounting for Sales of Stock by a Subsidiary," which expresses its views concerning a subsidiary's issuance of additional common stock. According to the SEC staff, companies **may** (an optional reporting treatment) recognize gains or losses resulting from these transactions when the subsidiary's sale of shares is *not* a part of a corporate reorganization contemplated or planned by the parent company. (The SEC had previously required, without benefit of any ruling or publication, that such transactions be recognized in the consolidated statements as capital transactions [the *economic unit concept*]). This change in position resulted from the SEC's acceptance of the advisory conclusions in the AICPA's 1980 issues paper. The SEC staff considers this paper to be appropriate interim guidance in the matter until the FASB addresses this issue as a part of its consolidations project (discussed in Chapter 1). Under *SAB 51*, companies electing income statement treatment must (1) report the gain or loss as **a separate item in the consolidated income statement** (regardless of size), (2) clearly **designate the gain or loss as nonoperating,** and (3) include an appropriate description of the transaction in the financial statement notes.[1]

---

[1] In 1989, the staff of the SEC expanded its views on this subject in Staff Accounting Bulletin No. 84; the additional guidance therein is beyond the scope of this text.

Comprehensive Illustration

Subsidiary's Issuance of Additional Shares at *Below* Book Value (75%-Owned *Created* Subsidiary)

The journal entry in the following illustration reflects the accounting treatment prescribed in the AICPA's 1980 issues paper. Assume the following information:

	Percent	Shares
Parent's ownership in subsidiary:		
Before subsidiary issues additional shares	75%	7,500
After subsidiary issues additional shares	60%	7,500
Noncontrolling interest ownership in subsidiary:		
Before subsidiary issues additional shares	25%	2,500
After subsidiary issues additional shares	40%	5,000
Proceeds from issuance of 2,500 additional shares of the subsidiary's no-par common stock at $18 per share.	$45,000	

This information is used in Section I of Illustration 11-5 to calculate the deemed economic *loss* to the parent. (The procedure is the same as that which occurs when a deemed economic *gain* exists.) The entry to record the loss on the *parent's* books is as follows:

Loss Resulting from Dilution of Interest in Subsidiary's Net Assets.	3,000	
Investment in Subsidiary		3,000

This loss is *not* eliminated in consolidation. The analysis of the Investment account would be adjusted as shown in Section II of Illustration 11-5.

CHECK POINT

On 6/1/06 Satco, a 90%-owned subsidiary of Patco, issued 20,000 shares of its $1 par value common stock to the public for $200,000. Satco had 100,000 outstanding shares with a total book value of $1,300,000 just prior to this issuance. Which amount does Patco report in its 2006 income statement under the *parent company concept*?

a. –0–
b. Loss of $45,000.
c. Gain of $45,000.
d. Loss of $50,000.
e. Gain of $50,000.

Answer: b

IV. OTHER CHANGES IN THE SUBSIDIARY'S CAPITAL ACCOUNTS

Stock Dividends

A subsidiary's stock dividend has no effect on the parent's books or in consolidation. The subsidiary has merely reshuffled amounts within its equity accounts by reducing the Retained Earnings account and increasing the Common Stock and Additional Paid-in Capital accounts in accordance with procedures discussed in intermediate accounting texts. Although no entry is required to adjust the carrying value of the Investment in Subsidiary account, the parent must adjust these accounts because they exist within the expanded analysis of their Investment account by components. Assume the following information:

	Subsidiary's Books	
	Common Stock	Retained Earnings
Balances immediately *before* stock dividend	$60,000	$140,000
Capitalization of retained earnings as a result of stock dividend	30,000	(30,000)
Balances immediately *after* stock dividend	$90,000	$110,000

The balances in the expanded analysis of the Investment account by individual components are adjusted accordingly.

The reclassification within the parent's expanded analysis of the Investment account by components is necessary so that the posting of the basic elimination entry used to prepare consolidated financial statements properly eliminates the subsidiary's equity accounts.

If the capitalization of retained earnings exceeds the total retained earnings as of the acquisition date, an interesting problem results. Under the *equity method* of accounting, the parent has included amounts in its Retained Earnings account that it *cannot* obtain from the subsidiary as a result of the capitalization. If this restriction on dividend availability is material, it should be disclosed in the consolidated statements.

ILLUSTRATION 11-5 SUBSIDIARY'S ISSUANCE OF ADDITIONAL COMMON STOCK AT *BELOW* BOOK VALUE (75%-OWNED CREATED SUBSIDIARY)

I. Calculation of *Decrease* (Dilution) in Parent's Interest in Net Assets of Subsidiary

	SUBSIDIARY'S EQUITY ACCOUNTS	BOOK VALUE PER SHARE	PARENT'S INTEREST		NONCONTROLLING INTEREST	
			PERCENT	AMOUNT	PERCENT	AMOUNT
Before issuance of additional shares:						
Common stock	$ 60,000		75	$ 45,000	25	$ 15,000
Retained earnings	140,000		75	105,000	25	35,000
	$200,000	$20.00		$150,000		$ 50,000
After issuance of additional shares:						
Common stock	$105,000[a]		60	$ 63,000	40	$ 42,000
Retained earnings	140,000		60	84,000	40	56,000
	$245,000	$19.60		$147,000		$ 98,000
Difference	$ 45,000	$ .40		$ (3,000)		$ 48,000
Proceeds from issuance	(45,000)	$18.00				(45,000)
Parent's dilution/NCI accretion[b]	-0-	($.40 × 7,500 shares)		$ (3,000)		$ 3,000

[a] For simplicity, we assume that the subsidiary's common stock is no-par. Thus the $45,000 of proceeds has been *credited* to the Common Stock account.

[b] The *dilution* suffered by the *parent* is offset by the *accretion* to the *noncontrolling interest*.

II. Parent's Adjustment to Its Investment Account

	NONCONTROLLING INTEREST (*INCREASES* FROM 25% TO 40%)	+	PARENT'S INVESTMENT ACCOUNT— BOOK VALUE	=	BOOK VALUE ELEMENT SUBSIDIARY'S EQUITY ACCOUNTS COMMON STOCK	+	RETAINED EARNINGS
Balances *before* issuance of additional shares	$50,000		$150,000		$ 60,000		$140,000
+ Issuance of additional shares	45,000				45,000		
Subtotal	$95,000		$150,000		$105,000		$140,000
– Adjustment for parent's dilution/ NCI accretion	3,000		(3,000)				
Balances *after* issuance of additional shares	$98,000		$147,000		$105,000		$140,000

Stock Splits

As with stock dividends, when a stock split occurs, the parent is *not* required to make an entry on its books to adjust the carrying value of its investment in the subsidiary. The parent does *not* make any reclassifications within the analysis of the Investment account by individual components, however, because no changes were made to the subsidiary's capital accounts at the time of the stock split. The parent company makes only a *memorandum notation* of the stock split.

Changes from Par Value to *No*-Par and Vice Versa

When a subsidiary changes the par value of its common stock to *no*-par or vice versa, it makes changes on its books in the Common Stock and Additional Paid-in Capital accounts. As a result, the parent makes an adjustment within the expanded analysis of the Investment account. The carrying value of the investment itself does *not* change.

Appropriation of Retained Earnings

Inasmuch as the amount of an *acquired* subsidiary's retained earnings existing as of the acquisition date is eliminated in consolidation, any appropriation of retained earnings by the subsidiary that does *not* exceed the total amount of retained earnings existing as of the acquisition date (including any amount that accrues to the noncontrolling interests) has no effect on the parent's books or the consolidated statements. When appropriations of retained earnings exceed this amount, however, the restriction on dividend availability must be disclosed in the consolidated statements if it is material.

V. CONSOLIDATED STATEMENT OF CASH FLOWS

When a consolidated balance sheet and income statements are presented, a consolidated statement of cash flows also must be presented.

The Two Possible Worksheet Approaches

Two worksheet approaches can be used to prepare a consolidated statement of cash flows: (1) analyzing the changes in the consolidated balance sheets and (2) combining the separate company cash flow statements. Regardless of which approach they take, parent companies usually require each subsidiary to submit a statement of cash flows to facilitate the preparation of the consolidated statement. Thus information is provided for each company within the consolidated group as to property additions, retirements, depreciation expense, borrowings, and repayments—items commonly presented separately in a statement of cash flows.

Approach 1: Analyzing the Changes in the Consolidated Balance

A parent can use its consolidated balance sheets for the beginning and end of the year to prepare a statement of cash flows. The change in each individual account balance for the year is analyzed in terms of sources and uses of cash (the approach illustrated in intermediate accounting texts). When transactions for intercompany inventory, fixed assets, or bonds have occurred, this method is much quicker because these intercompany transactions have been eliminated in preparing the consolidated balance sheet and income statement. Thus these intercompany transactions are not dealt with again in preparing the consolidated statement of cash flows, as they must be under the approach of combining the separate statements.

Approach 2: Combining the Separate Statements

A multicolumn worksheet can be used to consolidate the separate company statements of cash flows. The columnar headings for the worksheet follow:

P Company	S Company	Eliminations Dr.	Eliminations Cr.	Consolidated

This approach is practical when no intercompany inventory, fixed asset, or bond transactions have occurred. Consolidation entries are needed only to (1) eliminate the parent's Equity in Net Income account (to prevent double counting), (2) eliminate intercompany dividends, and (3) reflect the noncontrolling interest in the subsidiary's net income as an item that did not require the use of cash. Dividends paid to the noncontrolling interest shareholders constitute a use of cash, and they are shown as such in the consolidated statement of cash flows, along with dividends paid to the parent's stockholders.

Comprehensive Illustration

Consolidated Statement of Cash Flows

Illustration 11-6 shows a consolidating statement of cash flows worksheet using the approach of combining the separate statements for a 75%-owned subsidiary. Illustration 11-6 is relatively straightforward. Additional complexities arise when (1) the subsidiary was acquired (instead of created) and accounted for using the purchase method of accounting (discussed in Chapters 4–6), (2) the subsidiary has preferred stock outstanding, and (3) the parent's ownership percentage changes during the year. These additional complexities are beyond our purpose here, which is to merely acquaint you with the basics of this statement.

VI. Consolidated Earnings per Share

Fundamentally, consolidated earnings per share (EPS) is simply consolidated net income (income accruing to the benefit of the parent's shareholders) divided by the average number of the **parent's** common shares outstanding (adjusted for the parent's potentially dilutive securities, if any). In the example that follows, we use only a *diluted* EPS calculation, thus ignoring for now that FASB *Statement No. 128*, "Earnings per Share," requires both a *basic* EPS calculation and a *diluted* EPS calculation.

Subsidiary Has No Potentially Dilutive Securities Outstanding

Most subsidiaries do *not* have outstanding potentially dilutive securities such as stock options, warrants, convertible bonds, and convertible preferred stocks. Consequently, making the parent's *diluted* EPS calculation on a consolidated basis is simple.

The *consolidated* net income, say $700,000, is merely divided by the denominator, say 1,000,000 shares, that the parent would use in computing its *diluted* EPS for its separate *parent-company-only statements*. Consolidated *diluted* EPS in this example therefore is $0.70 ($700,000/1,000,000 shares). (The subsidiary's outstanding shares are completely ignored in making this calculation because they are deemed *not* to be outstanding from a *consolidated* perspective.)

Subsidiary Has Potentially Dilutive Securities Outstanding

If a subsidiary has dilutive securities outstanding, however, the consolidated net income amount ($700,000 in our example) *cannot* be used as the numerator in the *diluted* EPS calculation. Instead, the consolidated net income amount first must be reduced to the extent that the parent's ownership interest in the subsidiary's net income is potentially dilutive. This reduction is made only for computing consolidated *diluted* EPS—**no reduction is made to the consolidated net income amount**

ILLUSTRATION 11-6 CONSOLIDATED STATEMENT OF CASH FLOWS WORKSHEET: CREATED SUBSIDIARY—75%-OWNED

P Company and S Company
Consolidation Statement of Cash Flows
For the Year Ended December 31, 2006

	P COMPANY	S COMPANY	CONSOLIDATION ENTRIES DR.			CONSOLIDATION ENTRIES CR.	CONSOLIDATED
Cash Flows from Operating Activities:							
Net income	134,000	32,000	24,000 8,000	1 3			134,000
Charges (credits) *not* affecting cash:							
Depreciation expense	40,000	13,000					53,000
Equity in reported net income of subsidiary	(24,000)				1	24,000	-0-
Net change in receivables, inventory, and payables	(36,000)	(13,000)					(49,000)
NCI in net income of S Company					3	8,000	8,000
Net Cash Flow from Operating Activities	114,000	32,000	32,000	1		32,000	146,000
Cash Flows from Investing Activities							
Dividends received from S Company	9,000		9,000	2			-0-
Net Cash Flow from Investing Activities	9,000		9,000				-0-
Cash Flows from Financing Activities:							
Decrease in long-term debt	(40,000)						(40,000)
Dividends paid	(85,000)	(12,000)			2	9,000	(88,000)
Net Cash Flow from Financing Activities	(125,000)	(12,000)				9,000	(128,000)
Net Increase (Decrease) in Cash	(2,000)	20,000	41,000			41,000	18,000

Explanation of entries

1 To eliminate parent's Equity in Net Income of Subsidiary account.
2 To eliminate the intercompany dividend.
3 To eliminate the NCI share of S Company's net income and show the NCI deduction (that is present in the consolidated income statement) as a charge that did require the use of cash.

Source: The amounts were either obtained or developed from Illustration 3-4 and Illustration 2-13, as revised to reflect only a 75% ownership interest instead of 100%.

($700,000 in our example) reported in the consolidated income statement. Continuing with our example, assume that S Company

1. Is a 100%-owned subsidiary of P Company.
2. Reported $200,000 of net income for 2006 (which is included in determining the *consolidated* net income amount, $700,000 in our example).
3. Had 20,000 shares of common stock outstanding during all of 2006 (all owned by P Company).
4. Has granted stock options to its employees and, as a result, 5,000 additional shares (determined by using the treasury stock method) would be used in S Company's denominator in S Company's separate company EPS calculation. Thus 25,000 shares would be used in S Company's EPS denominator—*not* 20,000 shares.

Because of the potential dilution of P Company's ownership interest, P Company *cannot* use all $200,000 of S Company's net income in making the consolidated EPS calculation. Instead, only $160,000 of S Company's net income (20,000/25,000 × $200,000) can be included in the numerator in computing consolidated *diluted* EPS for 2006. Thus consolidated net income—for *diluted*

EPS purposes only—is only $660,000 ($700,000 – $40,000 of earnings that accrues to the stock option holders). Consolidated *diluted* EPS therefore is $0.66, *not* $0.70.

A Ratio for All Potential Dilution Situations

The ratio that was used to determine how much of S Company's earnings effectively accrues to the parent and can be included in the numerator for consolidated *diluted* EPS purposes (20,000/25,000) can be expressed generically as follows:

$$\frac{\text{Number of Shares in Subsidiary's } \textit{Diluted} \text{ EPS Denominator That Are Owned by or Accrue to the Parent}}{\text{Total Number of Shares in Subsidiary's } \textit{Diluted} \text{ EPS Denominator}}$$

This ratio approach for determining the parent's numerator in the calculation of consolidated EPS can be used for both *basic* EPS and *diluted* EPS (the percentages obtained from each of the ratios usually differ slightly). Furthermore, this ratio approach can be used for all types of a subsidiary's potentially dilutive securities.

End-of-Chapter Review

Summary of Key Points

1. The **acquisition** of any or all of a subsidiary's **common stock noncontrolling interest** is treated as an acquisition of a block of stock for which **purchase accounting** must be used. This holds true whether the *parent* or the *subsidiary* acquires the shares.
2. When the **subsidiary** acquires noncontrolling interest shares **at above or below book value**, the decrease or increase in the parent's interest in the book value of the subsidiary's net assets is treated as an **adjustment to cost in excess of book value** (with appropriate assignment to the individual components required).
3. For the **partial disposal** of a parent's interest in a subsidiary, the **average cost method** is the soundest method of determining the cost to be removed from the Investment account.
4. Any **gain or loss or partial disposal** is reported currently in the **income statement.**
5. The **sale of additional common stock** to the public by a subsidiary at *below* book value results in a dilution of the parent's interest in the subsidiary's net assets at book value. (The opposite occurs when sold at above book value.) Under the **parent company concept**, the loss resulting from this dilution (or the gain when accretion occurs) is reported currently in the income statement. The SEC permits this treatment (in addition to the alternative of debiting or crediting the Additional Paid-in Capital account, which is economic unit concept treatment).

Assignment Material

Review Questions

1. When some or all of a noncontrolling interest is acquired, is the *purchase method* of accounting used?
2. Does the accounting method for the acquisition of some or all of a noncontrolling interest depend on whether the *parent* or the *subsidiary* acquires the noncontrolling interest?
3. When a *subsidiary* has acquired some or all of its outstanding noncontrolling interest at an amount *in excess of* book value, has the *parent's* interest in the subsidiary's net assets increased or decreased?

4. When a parent's interest in a subsidiary was acquired in blocks, and a portion of such holdings is *sold*, what method is used to reduce the Investment account?
5. Concerning Question 4, which methods are acceptable for federal income tax-reporting purposes?
6. When a parent disposes of a portion of its common stock holdings in a subsidiary, why must the *equity method* of accounting be applied up to the date of sale?
7. In which situations does a *parent* "lose" when a *subsidiary* issues additional common shares to the public?
8. Does a *parent* make a general ledger entry when a *subsidiary* declares a stock dividend?
9. Does a *parent* make a general ledger entry when a *subsidiary* effects a stock split?

Exercises

E 11-1 **Parent's Acquisition of NCI** Prost Inc. owns 80% of the outstanding common stock of Skol Inc. A *combined* analysis of the parent's Investment account by components of the major conceptual elements at 1/1/06 follows:

Book value element (at 80%):	
Common stocks, $10 par value	$ 80,000
Retained earnings	96,000
Undervaluation of net assets element (at 80%):	
Land	8,000
Goodwill element (residual)	56,000
Parent's cost	$240,000

On 1/2/06, Prost acquired 15% of Skol's outstanding common stock from its noncontrolling interest shareholders for $50,000 cash. All of Skol's assets and liabilities have a *current value* equal to their *book value* at 1/2/06 except land, which is worth $60,000 in excess of its book value.

Required Prepare and update separate analyses of the parent's Investment account to reflect this acquisition.

E 11-2 **Subsidiary's Acquisition of NCI** Pyn Inc. owns 75% of the outstanding common stock of Syn Inc. On 1/1/06, Syn acquired 10% of its stock from its noncontrolling interest shareholders for $220,000 cash. These shares were immediately retired (the Common Stock account was charged $10,000, the Additional Paid-in Capital account was charged $90,000, and the Retained Earnings account was charged $120,000). The subsidiary's capital accounts immediately *before* the acquisition are as follows:

Common stock, $1 par value	$ 100,000
Additional paid-in capital	900,000
Retained earnings	600,000
	$1,600,000

Required

1. Prepare and update the analyses of the Investment account. Assume that Pyn had excess cost of $40,000 (all goodwill) on 12/31/05.
2. Prepare the parent's adjusting entry.

E 11-3 **Stock Dividend by Subsidiary** On 4/1/06, Sem Inc., Pem Inc.'s 75%-owned subsidiary, declared a 10% common stock dividend on its 10,000 outstanding shares of $20 par value common stock. Sem recorded the following entry:

Retained Earnings	160,000	
Common Stock		20,000
Additional Paid-in Capital		140,000

Required Determine the appropriate changes that the parent company should make to its analyses of the Investment account.

E 11-4 **Stock Split by Subsidiary** On 1/1/06, Sila Inc., Pila Inc.'s 60%-owned subsidiary, split its $10 par value common stock 4 for 1. At the time of the stock split, Sila's capital accounts were as follows:

Common stock	$ 100,000
Additional paid-in capital	900,000
Retained earnings	400,000
	$1,400,000

Required Determine the appropriate changes that the parent company should make to its analyses of the Investment account.

E 11-5 **EPS: 75%-Owned Subsidiary with Warrants** Powe Inc. owns 75% of Sowe Inc.'s outstanding common stock. Income and securities data for each company for 2006 follow:

	Powe Inc.	Sowe Inc.
Income from own operations	$500,000	$100,000
Average number of common shares outstanding	200,000	20,000
Common equivalent shares:		
Warrants—		
Average number of warrants outstanding during 2006		15,000
Shares assumed repurchased under the treasury stock method		10,000

Required
1. What is the consolidated *diluted* EPS?
2. Repeat requirement 1, assuming that the parent owns 20% of the warrants.
3. What is the consolidated net income?

E 11-6 **EPS: 100%-Owned Subsidiary with Convertible Preferred Stock** Pram Inc. owns 100% of Stam Inc.'s outstanding common stock. Income and securities data for each company for 2006 follow:

	Pram Inc.	Stam Inc.
Income from own operations	$1,000,000	$500,000
Average number of common shares outstanding	100,000	75,000
Common equivalent shares:		
Convertible preferred stock—		
Shares outstanding during 2006		5,000
Dividends per share (cumulative)		$10
Number of common shares obtainable on conversion		25,000

Required
1. What is the consolidated *diluted* earnings per share?
2. Repeat requirement 1, assuming that the parent owns 40% of the preferred stock.
3. What is the consolidated net income?

Problems

P 11-1 **Parent's Acquisition of NCI Interest** On 1/1/06, Pree Inc. acquired *all* of the noncontrolling interest shares of its 90%-owned subsidiary, Spree Inc., by issuing 10,000 shares of its $5 par value common stock. Pree's common stock had a fair market value of $17 per share on 1/1/06. Spree's capital accounts on 12/31/05 were as follows:

Common stock	$1,000,000
Retained earnings	400,000
	$1,400,000

All of Spree's assets and liabilities have a *current value* equal to their *book value* at 1/1/06 except for its building, which is worth $70,000 in excess of book value.

Required Prepare the parent's entry to record this acquisition and update the analyses of the Investment account.

P 11-2 **Subsidiary's Acquisition of NCI** Pebit Inc. owns 60% of the outstanding common stock of Scredit Inc. On 1/1/06, Scredit acquired 20% of its outstanding common stock from its noncontrolling interest shareholders for $360,000 cash. (These shares were immediately retired by debiting the

Common Stock account for $20,000, Additional Paid-in Capital account for $80,000, and Retained Earnings account for $260,000.) An analysis of Pebit's Investment account (Pebit uses the *equity method*) updated through 12/31/05 follows:

Book value element (*at 60%*):	
Common stock, $10 par value	$ 60,000
Additional paid-in capital	240,000
Retained earnings	420,000
Undervaluation of net assets element:	
Land (60% of $100,000)	60,000
Goodwill element	48,000
Total carrying value at 12/31/05	$828,000

The *current value* of all of Scredit's assets and liabilities is equal to their *book value* on 1/1/06, except for land, which has a *current value* $100,000 over its *book value*.

Required

1. Calculate the decrease in the parent's interest in the subsidiary's net assets.
2. Prepare and update *separate* analyses of the Investment account.
3. Prepare the parent's adjusting entry, if needed.

P 11-3 **Parent's Acquisition of NCI (Problem 11-2 Revised)** Assume the information provided in Problem 11-2 except that the *parent* acquired 20% of the subsidiary's outstanding common stock from the noncontrolling interest shareholders for $360,000 cash.

Required

1. Prepare and update *separate* analyses of the Investment account.
2. Prepare the parent's adjusting entry, if needed.
3. Explain why the parent's cost in excess of book value increased by a greater amount in this case than in Problem 11-2.

P 11-4 **Parent's Partial Disposal of Its Investment** On 10/1/06, Pyre Inc. sold 25% of its common stock holdings in its 80%-owned subsidiary, Syre Inc., for $500,000 cash. All of Syre's shares were acquired on 1/1/03 in a business combination. An analysis of the Investment account (Pyre uses the *equity method*) updated through 10/1/06 follows:

Book value element (*at 80%*):	
Common stock (100,000 shares outstanding)	$240,000
Retained earnings	400,000
Undervaluation of net assets element (*at 80%*):	
Land	160,000
Patent (2 1/4 yr. remaining life)	24,000
Goodwill element	8,000
Total carrying value at 9/30/06	$832,000

During 2006, Syre (1) reported net income of $85,000 ($25,000 earned in the fourth quarter) and (2) declared *quarterly* dividends of $10,000.

Required

1. Prepare and update the parent's *separate* analyses of the Investment account for this disposal.
2. Prepare the entry to record the partial disposal by the parent.

P 11-5 **Parent's Partial Disposal of Its Investment** On 7/1/06 Proe Inc. sold 3,000 of the 9,000 Soe Inc.'s common shares it held for $170,000 cash. The 9,000 common shares, a 90% interest, were acquired on 1/1/04 in a business combination accounted for as a *purchase*. An analysis of the Investment account (Proe uses the *equity method*) by components as of 12/31/05 follows:

Book value element (*at 90%*):	
Common stock	$ 90,000
Retained earnings	135,000
Undervaluation of net assets element (*at 90%*):	
Land	75,000
Bonds Payable (9-year remaining life)	54,000
Goodwill element	30,000
Total carrying value at 12/31/05	$384,000

During 2006, Soe had the following:

	Net Income	Dividends Declared
1/1/06–6/30/06	$50,000	$10,000
7/1/06–12/31/06	30,000	10,000

Required 1. Prepare and update the parent's *separate* analyses of the Investment account through 12/31/06.
2. Prepare the entry to record the parent's sale of the 3,000 shares.

P 11-6 **Subsidiary's Issuance of Additional Common Shares** On 7/1/06, Saver Inc., a 90%-owned subsidiary of Paver Inc., issued 20,000 shares of its common stock to the public for $1,200,000. The balances in Saver's equity accounts *immediately prior* to the issuance follow:

Common stock, $10 par value	$1,000,000
Additional paid-in-capital	4,000,000
Retained earnings	2,500,000
	$7,500,000

Required 1. Determine the gain or loss that the parent incurs as a result of the issuance.
2. How should the gain or loss be reported?

P 11-7 **Subsidiary's Issuance of Additional Common Shares** On 4/1/06, Sweep Inc., an 80%-owned subsidiary of Prush Inc., issued 10,000 shares of its common stock to the public for $360,000. The balances in Sweep's equity accounts *immediately prior* to the issuance follow:

Common stock, $1 par value	$ 50,000
Additional paid-in capital	250,000
Retained earnings	1,200,000
	$1,500,000

Required 1. Determine the gain or loss that the parent incurs as a result of the issuance.
2. How should the gain or loss be reported?

P 11-8* **Comprehensive Purchase Business Combination and Consolidation Worksheet: Parent's Partial Disposal and Inventory Transfers—Equity Method** On 1/1/04, Penn Inc. acquired 80% of Scribe Inc.'s outstanding common stock by paying $400,000 cash to William Braun, the company's sole stockholder. In addition, Penn acquired a patent from Braun for $40,000 cash. Penn charged the entire $440,000 to the Investment in Scribe Inc. Common Stock account.

Additional Information

1. The *book value* of Scribe's common stock on the acquisition date was $500,000. The book values of the individual assets and liabilities equaled their current values.
2. The patent had a remaining legal life of 4 years as of 1/3/04. No amortization has been recorded since the acquisition date.
3. During 2005, Scribe sold Penn for $130,000 merchandise that included a markup of 50% over Scribe's cost. At 12/31/05, $45,000 of this merchandise remained in Penn's inventory. In February 2006 Penn sold this merchandise at an $8,000 profit.
4. On 7/1/06, Penn *reduced* its investment in Scribe to 75% of Scribe's outstanding common stock by selling shares to an unaffiliated company for $60,000, a profit of $16,000. Penn *credited* the proceeds to its Investment account.
5. In November 2006, Penn sold merchandise to Scribe for the first time. Penn's cost for this merchandise was $80,000, and Penn made the sale at 120% of its cost. Scribe's 12/31/06 inventory contained $24,000 of the merchandise that Scribe purchased from Penn.

*The financial statement information presented for problems accompanied by asterisks is also provided on Model 11 (filename: MODEL11) at the **http://pahler.swlearning.com** website, allowing the problem to be worked on the computer.

6. On 12/31/06, Scribe's $40,000 payment was in transit to Penn. Accounts receivable and accounts payable include intercompany receivables and payables. (Scribe still owes Penn $25,000.)
7. In December 2006, Scribe declared and paid cash dividends of $100,000 to its stockholders.
8. Scribe had $140,000 of net income for the six months ended 6/30/06 and $160,000 of net income for the six months ended 12/31/06.
9. At no time in 2004–2006 did Penn make any adjustment to its Investment account or its financial statements for any *unrealized* intercompany profit.
10. The financial statements of each company for the year ended 12/31/06 follow:

	Penn Inc.	Scribe Inc.
Income Statement (2006)		
Sales	$ 4,000,000	$ 1,700,000
Cost of sales	(3,000,000)	(1,000,000)
Expenses	(382,000)	(400,000)
Equity in net income of subsidiary	232,000	
Dividend income	75,000	
Net Income	$ 925,000	$ 300,000
Balance Sheet (12/31/06)		
Cash	$ 306,000	$ 80,000
Accounts receivable, net	170,000	255,000
Inventory	179,000	355,000
Fixed assets, net	830,000	290,000
Investment in Scribe Inc.	804,000	
Total Assets	$ 2,289,000	$ 980,000
Liabilities	$ 384,000	$ 40,000
Common stock	1,200,000	300,000
Retained earnings	705,000	640,000
Total Liabilities & Equity	$ 2,289,000	$ 980,000
Dividends declared	$ 170,000	$ 100,000

Required

1. Prepare an analysis of the Investment account from 1/3/04 to 12/31/06 as it should have been maintained. (Pay particular attention to the requirements of the specific module from Chapter 9 that you are using to work this problem.)
2. Prepare the appropriate adjusting entries required at 12/31/06.
3. Adjust the financial statements for the entries developed in requirement 2. Modify the financial statements to reflect the use of intercompany accounts.
4. Prepare the consolidation entries at 12/31/06.
5. Prepare a consolidation worksheet at 12/31/06. (Parent and subsidiary columns should reflect the adjustments in requirement 3.)

P 11-9 Consolidated Statement of Cash Flows The 2006 separate-company statements of cash flows for Pac Inc. and its 90%-owned *created* subsidiary, Sac Inc., follow:

	Statement of Cash Flows (2006)	
	Pac	Sac
Cash Flows from Operating Activities:		
Net income	$127,000	$ 30,000
Charges (credits) not affecting cash:		
Depreciation expense	14,000	6,000
Patent amortization	4,000	
Equity in reported net income of subsidiary	(27,000)	
Net increase in receivables, inventory, and payables	(11,000)	(5,000)
Net Cash Flow from Operating Activities	$107,000	$ 31,000

(continued)

	Statement of Cash Flows (2006)	
	Pac	Sac
Cash Flows from Investing Activities:		
Purchase of equipment	$(71,000)	$(19,000)
Dividends received from Sac	9,000	
Net Cash Flow from Investing Activities	$(62,000)	$(19,000)
Cash Flows from Financing Activities:		
Sale of common stock	$ 50,000	
Sale of preferred stock	40,000	
Sale of bonds at par		$ 20,000
Retirement of debt	(30,000)	(15,000)
Dividends on common stock	(60,000)	(10,000)
Dividends on preferred stock	(2,000)	
Net Cash Flow from Financing Activities	$ (2,000)	$ (5,000)
Net Increase (Decrease) in Cash	$ 43,000	$ 7,000

Required Prepare a consolidated statement of cash flows using the approach of combining the separate statements.

THINKING CRITICALLY

Cases

C 11-1 **Statutory Merger: Rights of NCI** Several years ago, Paso Inc. acquired 80% of Sol Inc.'s outstanding common stock. Paso now decides to merge with Sol. Under state law, the merger requires approval of only two-thirds of Sol's shareholders. Paso votes its 80% of Sol's stock in favor of the merger, which provides that each of Sol's noncontrolling interest stockholders receive one share of Paso's stock in exchange for three shares of Sol's. Your examination of Paso's financial statements after the merger reveals that some of these stockholders voted against it. You are concerned that Paso properly disclose in its financial statements the liability, if any, to these stockholders.

Required

1. What are the rights of Sol's stockholders who opposed the merger?
2. What steps must noncontrolling interest stockholders ordinarily take to protect their rights in these circumstances?

C 11-2 **Theory: Parent's Partial Disposal of Its Investment** Polex Inc. sold a portion of its common stock holdings in one of its subsidiaries at a gain of $80,000. The controller is considering the following options:

1. Crediting this gain to the Investment account to reduce the $240,000 balance of goodwill.
2. Reporting the gain as an extraordinary item because this is the first such disposal.
3. Reporting the gain as a partial disposal of a segment under the special reporting provisions of *APBO 30* for disposals of segments because neither the parent nor its other subsidiaries are in the same line of business.

Required Evaluate the theoretical merits of these three options.

C 11-3 **Theory: Subsidiary's Issuance of Additional Common Stock** Sona Inc. is a partially owned subsidiary of Pona Inc. In 2008 Sona issued additional shares of its common stock to the public at an amount *below* book value. Pona is considering the following options in consolidation:

1. Computing the noncontrolling interest of these new shareholders based on the amounts they paid for their interest plus their share of earnings minus their share of dividends since the date the additional shares were issued.

2. Computing total noncontrolling interest by multiplying the total noncontrolling interest ownership percentage by the subsidiary's net assets at *book value*.

3. Treating the dollar effect of the parent's decrease in interest in the subsidiary's net assets as additional cost in excess of *book value*.

4. Treating the dollar effect of the parent's decrease in interest in the subsidiary's net assets as a loss in the current period.

Required Evaluate the theoretical merits of each option.

Financial Analysis Problem

FAP 11-1 **Whether to Sell Some of Parent's Holdings or Have Subsidiary Issue Additional Shares** Pewter Inc. owns 8,000 common shares of Silverado Inc.'s outstanding common stock. Silverado has 10,000 common shares outstanding on 6/30/06, the book value of which is $50 per share. On this date, the carrying value of Pewter's investment in Silverado is $400,000. At this time, Pewter's management realizes that Pewter's earnings for calendar 2006 will be *below* budgeted amounts. To report higher profits for 2006, management is considering either (1) selling 2,000 shares of its holdings in Silverado at $70 per share or (2) having the subsidiary sell 2,000 additional shares to the public at $70 per share. Pewter is also experiencing a slight cash flow problem. Assume that it *is* acceptable practice to recognize such gains in the *current income statement*.

Required

1. Calculate the gain that Pewter would report under both alternatives.
2. What are the advantages and disadvantages of each alternative?

chapter 12

Reporting Segment and Related Information

Nothing is particularly hard if you divide it into small jobs [or into "segments" if you are performing financial analysis].
HENRY FORD

LEARNING OBJECTIVES

To Understand

> The *reason* for reporting segment information.
> The way to identify an entity's *operating* segments.
> The types of *segment* information to be disclosed in both *annual* and *interim period* financial statements.
> The purpose and criteria for *aggregating* certain segments.
> The *quantitative tests* used to determine *reportable* operating segments.
> The types of *entity-wide* information to be disclosed.

TOPIC OUTLINE

I. Applicability of FASB *Statement No. 131*
INTERNATIONAL PERSPECTIVE: *International Segment Reporting Standards*
II. Basis of Segmentation
III. Identifying Operating Segments
IV. Required Segment Disclosures—*Annual* Reporting
V. Allowed Aggregation of Similar Operating Segments
VI. Quantitative Thresholds for Determining *Reportable* Operating Segments
VII. Required *Entity-Wide* Disclosures
VIII. Required *Segment* Disclosures—*Interim Period* Reporting
IX. Comprehensive Illustration

CHAPTER OVERVIEW

Chapters 1–11 discussed consolidated financial statements, which are useful in evaluating an enterprise's *overall* economic performance and *overall* financial condition. Trends and ratios prepared therefrom by investors and financial analysts are routinely used to assess future prospects. For entities operating in **different industries** or **geographic areas**, however, assessment becomes more difficult because of different (1) opportunities for growth, (2) returns on investments, and (3) risks (*see Chapter 13 for the unique risks associated with investing abroad*).

Because of the substantial product diversification and foreign investment that occurred after World War II, a need arose for supplementing the consolidated statements with **financial and descriptive information concerning the various segments in which an entity operates.** It is indeed no understatement that financial analysts consider it absolutely critical to have *useful* and *timely* segment information.

Segment reporting requirements are set forth in *FAS 131*, "Disclosures about Segments of an Enterprise and Related Information" (issued in 1997). *FAS 131* uses a "management" approach as a basis for segmentation. *FAS 131* superseded *FAS 14* (issued in 1976), which used both (1) an *industry* approach and (2) a *geographic* approach. *FAS 14* was heavily criticized by financial analysts for:

1. Having an imprecise definition of industry segment, which allowed companies to define industry segments too broadly and thereby report on too few industry segments.
2. Not providing enough useful information about segments.
3. Resulting in descriptive inconsistencies between segment information presented in the notes to the financial statements and information presented in other parts of the annual report (such as the business review section and the president's letter).
4. Not requiring disclosure of segment information in *interim period* financial reports.

Consequently, the FASB reexamined the segment reporting issue (1993–1997) and addressed these concerns in *FAS 131*. See the International Perspective for a comparison of *FAS 131* with the international segment reporting standard.

FAS 131's disclosure requirements are extensive for companies obliged to comply (much more *quantitative* segment information must be disclosed than was required under *FAS 14*). These disclosures fit into three broad categories:

1. Products and services (*quantitative* and *descriptive*).
2. Geographic areas (*quantitative*).
3. Major customers (*quantitative*).

International Perspective

International Segment Reporting Standards

International Accounting Standard 14, "Reporting Financial Information by Segment" (as revised in 1997 by the London-based International Accounting Standards Committee), takes a different approach to segment reporting from that in *FAS 131* issued by the FASB. Without going into the details of *IAS 14*, the key differences are as follows:

ITEM	*FAS 131*	*IAS 14*
1. Approach	Management	Products and services having similar risks and rewards
2. Basic segment unit	Operating segment	Business segment *and* geographic segment (the approach under superseded *FAS 14*)
3. Vertical integrated operations	Segment disclosure *may* be necessary	Segment disclosure is *not* required
4. Nature of accounting information	GAAP and nonGAAP	GAAP based—as used in consolidated financial statements
5. Interim reporting	Required	*Not* required

CHECK POINT

FAS 131 does *not* require disclosure of information about

a. Major customers.
b. Major suppliers.
c. Operating segments.
d. Assets of foreign operating segments.
e. Foreign sales.

Answer: b

I. APPLICABILITY OF FASB *STATEMENT NO. 131*

Publicly Held *Business* Enterprises Only

FAS 131 applies only to **publicly held *business* entities,** which are defined as those entities that have **any one** of the following attributes:

> They have *equity* or *debt* securities that are traded in a *public* market.
> They must file financial statements with the Securities and Exchange Commission.
> They provide financial statements for the purpose of issuing any class of securities in a *public* market.

Thus *FAS 131* does *not* apply to (1) *not-for-profit organizations* or (2) to *nonpublic* entities.

Interim Period Reporting

FAS 131 amended *APB Opinion 28*, "Interim Financial Reporting" (discussed in Chapter 21), to require including selected information about operating segments in interim period financial reports to shareholders. These requirements are presented later.

Financial Statements Presented in Another Enterprise's Financial Report

FAS 131's requirements do *not* apply to the following listed entities if their *"separate company"* financial statements are (1) *consolidated or combined* in a complete set of financial statements, and (2) both the *separate company* statements and the *consolidated or combined* statements **are included in the *same* financial report:**

1. Parent companies.
2. Subsidiaries.
3. Joint ventures.
4. Investees accounted for by the *equity method*.

If these entities are *public* entities and issue *separate* financial statements, however, *FAS 131*'s requirements apply to those statements.

II. BASIS OF SEGMENTATION

Possible Bases of Segmentation

Conceptually, segment information could be required to be presented in one or more ways, for example:

> By *products and services* (*not* used in *FAS 131*—was used in *FAS 14*).
> By *geographic area* (*not* used in *FAS 131*—was used in *FAS 14*).
> By *legal entity* (*not* used in *FAS 131*).
> By *type of customer* (*not* used in *FAS 131*).
> By **the internal organization of the segments** (*subsidiaries*, *divisions*, *departments*, or *other internal units*) **for reporting to management for decision making** (used in *FAS 131*). This approach is called the "management" approach.

Thus *FAS 131* requires a *single basis of segmentation*—the *management* approach. Note that under this approach, neither *industry* information nor *geographic* information is specifically required. Therefore, enterprises that manage segments on an *industry basis* will report operating segments on an *industry basis*. In contrast, enterprises that manage by *geographic areas* will report operating segments based on *geographic areas*. See the Case in Point below for an example.

CASE IN POINT

Wal-Mart's Segment Disclosures

Under FAS 14, Wal-Mart disclosed no segment information because it operated in one industry segment: ***mass merchandising stores.*** Under *FAS 131*, however, Wal-Mart now reports *three* segments: (1) ***Wal-Mart Stores*** (its U.S. discount stores), (2) "***Sam's Clubs,***" (its U.S. warehouse membership-club stores), and (3) ***International*** (all of its international operations).

The manner of identifying segments and determining which of an entity's segments require disclosure of segment information is summarized as follows:

1. Identify the operating segments—**those components for which separate financial information is (a) produced internally and (b) regularly used by the *chief operating decision maker*** (hereafter referred to as the **CODM**[1]) **to make decisions about operating matters** (allocating resources and assessing performance).
2. Apply *FAS 131*'s *aggregation criteria* and *quantitative thresholds* (discussed later) to determine which operating segments to report on separately.

Merits and Characteristics of the Management Approach

The management approach has several major advantages:

1. **Taking the same "view" as management.** It allows *external* financial statement users to view operations "through the eyes of management."
2. **Lessening subjectivity in determining segments.** The experience with *FAS 14* proved that the term *industry* is too subjective. Basing segments on an enterprise's actual internal structure should be *less* subjective.
3. **Achieving consistency in published information.** It results in the use of consistent descriptions in (a) the various financial and nonfinancial sections of the annual report and (b) various other published information.
4. **Minimizing cost and work.** Accounting policies and procedures used to produce the segment information are the *same* as those used in preparing reports for the CODM. Thus entities are not required to use a separate FASB-imposed uniform and arbitrary measure of segment profitability (which measure could differ significantly from that used internally) solely for segment reporting purposes (in contrast, *FAS 14* did impose a uniform measure of profitability).
   GAAP Point: Even if *nonGAAP* methods are used *internally* to measure either a segment's assets or its profitability (examples are *excluding* depreciation expense or *capitalizing* research and development costs), **those nonGAAP measured amounts are also disclosed for *external* segment reporting purposes.** (*Requiring disclosure of nonGAAP information is a "first" for the FASB.*)

[1] The term *CODM* identifies a *function*—it can be either (a) *one individual* or (b) a *group of executives*.

III. IDENTIFYING OPERATING SEGMENTS

The components of an enterprise that management uses for *reporting and decision making* are called *operating segments*. Such components:

1. Engage in activities with *external parties* (and possibly *other segments*) from which they may (a) **earn revenues** *and* (b) **incur expenses.**
2. Have their operating results regularly *reviewed* by the CODM for the purpose of managing the segment (*allocating resources* and *assessing performance*).
3. Have **discrete financial information** available.

Defining an Operating Segment

Examples of What *Could Be* an Operating Segment

An **operating segment** could be (1) a *start-up operation* that has yet to report any revenues or (2) a component of a *vertically integrated operation*—**providing these operations are managed that way.** Thus two components of a vertically integrated operation (such as one in which tin cans are manufactured for use in the food-canning division) could be reported as either *one* segment or *two* segments—*all depending on how they are managed.* Consequently, two competing companies that both have identical vertically integrated operations would report segment information quite differently if they manage their operations differently.

CHECK POINT

A component of a *vertically integrated business*

a. Can be both an *operating* segment and a *reportable* operating segment.
b. *Can* be an *operating* segment but can *never* be a *reportable* operating segment.
c. Can *never* be an *operating* segment and can *never* be a *reportable* operating segment.
d. Can *never* be an *operating* segment but *can* be a *reportable* operating segment.

Answer: a

Examples of What *Would NOT Be* an Operating Segment

Not every distinctive activity or operation of an entity is necessarily (1) an operating segment or (2) part of an operating segment. The following items would *not* be operating segments:

1. A *corporate headquarters* or a *functional department* that earns *no* revenues (or only *incidental* revenues).
2. An entity's *pension plan*—even though the plan is "funded" (the typical case), whereby the pension plan assets (made up of employer contributions and earnings on those invested contributions) are (a) accounted for in a separate accounting entity *and* (b) managed independently.
3. An entity's *other postemployment benefit plans*—even though the plan is "unfunded" (the typical case) and cash to pay for the benefits is (a) set aside as a *restricted asset* in the balance sheet *and* (b) invested and managed separately.

CHECK POINT

A component of an enterprise has revenues and is *not* a start-up operation. To qualify as an *operating* segment, the component

a. Must have the *majority* of its revenues from *external customers.*
b. Need *not* have *any* revenues from *external customers.*
c. Must have *at least some* revenues from *external customers.*

d. Must have no *inter*segment revenues.
e. Must have no *intra*segment revenues.

Answer: b

IV. REQUIRED *SEGMENT* DISCLOSURES—ANNUAL REPORTING

For *annual* reporting purposes (*interim period* reporting is discussed later), an entity must disclose the following three types of information about its *reportable* operating segments:

Type 1—General information (descriptive).
Type 2—Specified financial amounts (quantitative).
Type 3—Reconciliations of the *specified financial amounts* to *consolidated* amounts.

Type 1—General Information (Descriptive) Disclosures

These disclosures consist of (1) the **factors used to identify the entity's reportable segments,** including the basis of organization (such as (a) *products and services*, (b) *geographic areas*, (c) *regulatory environments*, or (d) a *combination of factors*), and (2) the **types of products and services** from which each reportable segment derives its revenues.

Type 2—Specified Financial Amounts (SFA) Disclosures

For each reportable segment, these disclosures consist of (1) **a measure of profit or loss,** (2) **a measure of total assets** (but *not liabilities*), and (3) **financial amounts for *certain accounts*—*if they are included in the measure of segment profit or loss*.** These *certain accounts* are:

> External revenues (to *external* customers).
> *Inter*segment revenues.
> Interest revenue and interest expense—**to be reported *separately*.**
Allowable Exception: These items may be reported **net** if (1) a *majority* of the segment's revenues are from interest (as occurs for *financial services* segments), and (2) the CODM relies primarily on *net interest revenue* to manage the segment. If reported net, disclosure of that fact is required.
> Depreciation, amortization, and depletion expense.
> Significant *noncash* items other than depreciation, amortization, and depletion expense.
> Unusual items (the "first cousin" to extraordinary items).
> Equity in net income of equity method investees (typically 20–50% ownership levels).
> Income tax expense or benefit.
> Extraordinary items.

CHECK POINT

Which item need *not* be disclosed for each *reportable* operating segment—*if the item* **is included** *in the measure of operating profit or loss used for managing the segment*?
a. Interest income.
b. Unusual items.
c. Research and development expenses.
d. Depreciation expense.
e. Intersegment revenues.
f. Interest expense.

Answer: c

Reporting *segment cash flows* is *not* required because an indication of both an operating segment's cash-generating ability and cash requirements may be gathered from the required *profitability-* and *asset-*related disclosures.

We now present several key points regarding the "specified financial amount" (**SFA**) disclosures.

SFA Point 1—No Imposed Uniform Definition of Segment Operating Profit or Loss

FAS 131 does *not* define segment operating profit or loss (as did *FAS 14*). **Thus any measure of performance may be displayed**—*as long as that measure of performance is used by the CODM in managing the segment.*

SFA Point 2—*Inter*segment versus *Intra*segment

In dealing with segment reporting, the term *intercompany* is not relevant. The relevant terms are:

1. *Inter*segment (sales between *segments*).
2. *Intra*segment (sales between *components of a vertically integrated operation deemed to be a* ***single*** *operating segment*).

In presenting operating segment information:

1. *Inter*segment sales must be disclosed separately *only if* they are included in the measure of profitability used by the CODM.
2. *Intra*segment sales need *not* be disclosed.

SFA Point 3—Setting Transfer Prices

FAS 131 did *not* establish a basis for setting prices for sales or transfers either *between* or *within* segments. Thus transfer prices established by management are used. (Recall from Chapter 8 that transfer pricing is most often an issue within *vertically* integrated operations rather than between *non*vertically integrated segments.)

SFA Point 4—Allocating Costs

A segment's expenses—as used in its measure of operations—*may include* both:

1. *Directly traceable* costs.
2. *Allocated common* costs (costs that benefit two or more segments).

Note that the word "may" means that allocating *common costs* to segments is *permissive—not mandatory*. Costs that *are* allocated, however, must be allocated on a reasonable basis.

A segment's expenses *may exclude* costs that entities often choose to account for at the *consolidated* level and thus *not* allocate to segments (pension costs, for example). Such costs *need not* be allocated to segments for *FAS 131* purposes.

SFA Point 5—Allowing Asymmetrical Allocations

Asymmetrical allocations *are permitted* in determining a segment's (1) measure of *profitability* and (2) measure of *total assets*. Thus *depreciation expense* could be allocated to a segment but the related *fixed assets* could *not*.

SFA Point 6—Basic Rule of Measurement

Each segment item amount reported must be the measure reported to the CODM for managing the segment. **Eliminations and adjustments made in consolidation** (such as the *deferral of unrealized* *intercompany profit*) are allocated to a segment *only if* they are included in the *measure of profit and loss* used by the CODM.

SFA Point 7—Use of Multiple Measures

If more than one measure of a segment's *profitability* and *assets* is used by the CODM, the measure selected for segment reporting must be the measure most consistent with those used in measuring those items in the entity's *consolidated financial statements*.

SFA Point 8—Additional Asset-Related Disclosures

If the following items are included in the measure of segment assets, disclosure is required of:

1. The amount of investment in *equity method investees*.
2. The total expenditures for *additions* to long-lived assets.

SFA Point 9—No Need to Disclose Segment Liabilities

Disclosure of segment liabilities is *not* required because the value of information about segment liabilities in assessing segment performance is deemed limited, partly because in many cases, liabilities are (a) *incurred centrally* and (b) *not* allocated to segments.

SFA Point 10—No Need to Disclose Segment Research and Development Costs

Disclosure of segment research and development costs is *not* required because (1) doing so could result in competitive harm by providing competitors with early insight into strategic plans, and (2) such costs are often (a) *incurred centrally* and (b) *not* allocated to segments.

SFA Point 11—Measurement-Related Descriptive Disclosures

Regarding measurement of a reportable segment's *profit or loss* and *assets,* disclosure is required, as a minimum, of:

1. The basis of accounting for *inter*segment transactions.
2. The nature of differences reported on the specified reconciliations for *profit or loss* and for *assets* (discussed shortly) to arrive at the corresponding consolidated amounts, if *not* apparent thereon.
3. The nature and effect of any *changes from prior periods* in the measurement methods used to determine a reported segment's *profit or loss*.
4. The nature and effect of any *asymmetrical allocations* to segments.

Type 3—Reconciliations of the *Specified* Financial Amounts to *Consolidated* Amounts

For the specified financial amounts disclosed for *reportable* segments, reconciliations must be presented of all of the following:

1. **Total revenues** (of all *reportable* segments) to **consolidated revenues.**
2. **Total profit or loss** (of all *reportable* segments) to **consolidated pretax income** (income *before* (a) *extraordinary items*, (b) *discontinued operations*, and (c) the *cumulative effect of changes in accounting principles*).
   Allowed Alternative: An entity that allocates *income taxes* and *extraordinary items* to its segments, however, may instead choose to reconcile to the *corresponding* consolidated amount.
3. **Total assets** (of all *reportable* segments) to **consolidated assets.**
4. **Other significant items** of information either *required* to be disclosed or *voluntarily* disclosed (for all *reportable* segments) to the *corresponding* consolidated amounts.

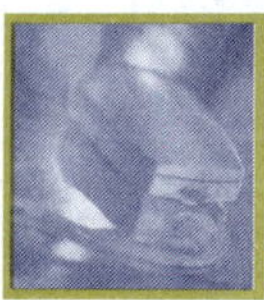

CHECK POINT

For *reportable* operating segments, which of the following items need *not* be both *disclosed* and *reconciled* to the corresponding *consolidated* amount.

a. Segment assets.
b. Segment profit or loss.
c. Segment revenues.
d. Segment liabilities.
e. None of the above.

Answer: d

V. ALLOWED AGGREGATION OF SIMILAR OPERATING SEGMENTS

Separate disclosures are required about each *identified* operating segment, subject to *FAS 131*'s (1) *aggregation criteria* and (2) *quantitative thresholds*.

In certain circumstances, two or more *identified* operating segments may be combined and treated as a *single* operating segment. Aggregation may be possible at two levels:

Level l: *Before* Performing the Quantitative Thresholds Tests
Level 2: *After* Performing the Quantitative Thresholds Tests

Level 1 aggregation is performed immediately *after* all *operating* segments have been identified—it involves combining some of these *operating segments*. (The next step is to determine which of the segments [combined and uncombined] are *reportable* segments.)

Level 2 aggregation is performed immediately *after* all *reportable* operating segments have been determined—it involves combining some of these *reportable* operating segments.

We first discuss Level 1 aggregation. Level 2 aggregation is discussed after we discuss the quantitative thresholds tests.

Why Aggregation Is Desirable

Aggregation of *certain* operating segments is desirable when information unlikely to be very useful would otherwise be disclosed. For example, an entity could have 25 home-improvement stores that individually meet the definition of an operating segment but are all essentially the same. Clearly, it is more sensible to report the 25 stores as a *single* operating segment rather than as 25 *separate* operating segments.

The rationale for aggregation is that segments having *similar economic characteristics* would be expected to have *similar long-term financial performance* (such as similar long-term average gross margins).

When Aggregation Is Permitted

Aggregation is *permitted*—but *not* required—if two or more operating segments (1) **have similar economic characteristics** *and* (2) **are similar in all of the following areas:**

- The nature of their *products and services*.
- The nature of the *production processes*.
- The type of *class of customers*.
- The *distribution methods* for products or services.
- If applicable, the *nature of any regulatory environment*, such as banking, insurance, or public utilities.

CHECK POINT

Aggregation of two operating segments would probably be *least likely* for which of the following sets of segments?

a. *Radial* tires segment and *nonradial* tires segment.
b. *Ice cream* stores segment and *yogurt* stores segment.
c. *Soft-drink* beverages segment and *wine* segment.
d. *Synthetic* fibers segment and *natural* fibers segment.
e. *Organic* grains segment and *nonorganic* grains segment.
f. *Men's* shoes segment and *women's* shoes segment.

Answer: c

VI. QUANTITATIVE THRESHOLDS FOR DETERMINING *REPORTABLE* OPERATING SEGMENTS

Ensuring That Information about All Significant Segments Is Disclosed—The Three 10% Tests

A **reportable operating segment** is that which meets *any one* of the following three 10% or more quantitative thresholds; it must be reported *separately*:

1. **Revenues.** Its reported revenues are **10% or more** of the **combined revenues of *all* operating segments** (*not* of *consolidated* revenues).
   Revenues Defined: Under *FAS 131*, "revenues" generally refers to the amount reported as revenues in the *consolidated* income statement. Thus revenues *may or may not* include (a) interest income, (b) lease income, (c) royalty income, and (d) other types of inflows—it all depends on how entities report these items. In practice, most entities report *interest income* as part of "Other Income and Expense"—*not* as *revenues*. Entities (or segments) that provide *financial services*, however, usually report their *interest income* as *revenues*—for many of these units, interest income is their *only* source of revenues. (For all assignment material, assume that these types of inflows are *not* reported as revenues *unless* a segment is identified as a *financial services* segment.)
   Segment revenues would *always* include *inter*segment sales—but **never** *intra*segment sales.

CHECK POINTS

Which of the following items is *not* included in *total revenues* in performing the revenues 10% quantitative test?

a. *Intra*segment sales.
b. *Inter*segment sales.
c. *Inter*segment interest income.
d. Interest income.
e. None of the above.

Answer: a

Total revenues as used in the revenues 10% quantitative test would always *exclude* which of the following?

a. Lease income.
b. Interest income.

c. Royalty and licensing income.
d. Product sales.
e. Fees received for services.
f. None of the above.

Answer: f

2. **Profit or loss.** The *absolute amount* of its reported profit or loss is **10% or more** of the *greater* of:
   A. The combined reported *profit* of all operating segments reporting a profit (**winners combined**) or
   B. The combined reported *loss* of all operating segments reporting a loss (**losers combined**).
3. **Assets.** Its reported assets are **10% or more** of the **combined assets of *all* operating segments** (*not* of *consolidated* assets).

CHECK POINT

Which item *is* used in one of the three 10% quantitative thresholds tests used to determine *reportable* operating segments?

a. Consolidated revenues.
b. Consolidated assets.
c. Consolidated pretax income.
d. *Combined* reported profit (or loss) of all operating segments.
e. *Combined* segment revenues.

Answer: e

Illustration of the Three Tests

In Illustration 12-1, we present (1) assumed data for an entity having six segments and (2) calculations of the three 10% quantitative thresholds tests.

Review Points for Illustration 12-1. Note the following:

1. As would be expected for most entities, a majority of the six segments satisfied at least two or three of the quantitative tests. Recall that **only one of the three quantitative tests need be satisfied**, however, for a segment to qualify as a *reportable* segment.
2. Because Segments 3 and 4 do *not* satisfy *any* of the three tests, they would be lumped and reported in the "All Other" category of the segment data schedules.
3. The *75% test* (discussed and illustrated shortly), however, might require that one of these two *apparently nonreportable segments* be reported separately after all.
4. We made certain arbitrary assumptions as to the items included in the measure of segment profitability. Recall that (a) the segment's measure of profit used by the CODM for decision making must be used in the profitability test, and (b) the measures of profitability can differ widely from entity to entity. Major common items that managements may *arbitrarily* **include** or **exclude** are as follows:

Nonintercompany Items	**Intercompany Items**
Interest income	Intersegment interest income[a]
Interest expense	Intersegment interest expense
Goodwill amortization expense	Inter*company* interest expense (on loans from headquarters)
Unusual items	Intersegment sales[a]
Income tax expense (benefit)	Unrealized intersegment profit
Extraordinary items	Expense allocations from corporate headquarters
Cumulative effect of accounting changes	

[a] If this item is *excluded* from a reportable segment's *measure of profitability*, the revenues disclosed for that segment are *less than* the segment's revenues included in the total revenues amount used in the revenues test.

ILLUSTRATION 12-1 SEGMENT DATA AND TESTS USED TO DETERMINE REPORTABLE SEGMENTS

Reported Segment Data (in millions)

SEGMENT NUMBER:	1 SOFTWARE	2 FOOTWARE	3 BICYCLES	4 MUSIC	5 AUTOS	6 FINANCING	TOTALS
Revenues:							
Sales—External	$ 850	$ 610	$ 170	$ 70	$ 880		$ 2,580
Sales—Intersegment	100						100
Interest income:							
External	n/a	n/a	n/a	n/a	n/a	$ 220	220
Intersegment	n/a	n/a	n/a	n/a	n/a	50	50
Total Revenues	**$950**	**$610**	**$170**	**$ 70**	**$880**	**$270**	**$2,950**
Costs & Expenses:							
Cost of sales	$ 210	$ 470	$ 90	$ 40	$ 430		$ 1,240
Marketing, G&A, & R&D	270	90	45	25	170	60	660
Interest expense:							
External	80	60	15	35	150	80	420
Intersegment					50		50
Corporate headquarters		20					20
Unusual items (all losses)	70	40					110
Total Costs & Expenses	**$630**	**$680**	**$150**	**$100**	**$800**	**$140**	**$2,500**
Measure of Profitability:							
Segment profit or loss	**$320**	**$ (70)**	**$ 20**	**$ (30)**	**$ 80**	**$130**	**$ 450**
Assets:							
Intercompany receivables						$ 200	$ 200
All other assets	$ 240	$ 580	$ 310	$ 180	$ 930	770	3,010
Total Segment Assets	**$240**	**$580**	**$310**	**$180**	**$930**	**$970**	**$3,210**

Quantitative Thresholds Tests Used to Determine *Reportable* Segments

	1	2	3	4	5	6	TOTALS
Test 1—Revenues:							
Total revenues	$ 950	$ 610	$ 170	$ 70	$ 880	$ 270	$ 2,950
Threshold percentage							10%
Threshold Amount							**$ 295**
Reportable Segment	**YES**	**YES**	**NO**	**NO**	**YES**	**NO**	
Test 2—Profitability:							
Segments reporting profits	$ 320		$ 20		$ 80	$ 130	$ 550
Segments reporting losses		$ 70		$ 30			$ 100
Select **LARGER** (*as an absolute value*) of combined profits or combined losses							$ 550
Threshold percentage							10%
Threshold amount							**$ 55**
Reportable Segment	**YES**	**YES**	**NO**	**NO**	**YES**	**YES**	
Test 3—Assets:							
Total assets	$ 240	$ 580	$ 310	$ 180	$ 930	$ 970	$ 3,210
Threshold percentage							10%
Threshold amount							**$ 321**
Reportable Segment	**NO**	**YES**	**NO**	**NO**	**YES**	**YES**	
Cumulative Result—All 3 Tests	**YES**	**YES**	**NO**	**NO**	**YES**	**YES**	

5. For simplicity, we did *not* use any business units that were *vertically integrated businesses*. Such business units require special consideration when one or more of their components are deemed a *single* operating segment. We illustrate this situation later in Illustration 12-2.

CHECK POINT

Which item *must* be used in determining a reportable segment's measure of reported profit or loss?

a. Income taxes.
b. Unusual items.
c. Extraordinary items.
d. Interest income.
e. Interest expense.
f. None of the above.

Answer: f

The 75% Test (An Overall Test)

Regardless of the number of reportable segments resulting from applying the three 10% tests, **enough individual segments must be used so that at least 75% of the combined revenues from sales to *external* customers of *all* operating segments is shown by *reportable* segments.** To illustrate how the 75% test is applied, we use the data and test results shown in Illustration 12-1 (amounts in millions):

Operating Segment	External Revenues	+	Intersegment Revenues	=	Total Segment Revenues	Reportable Segments—All Three Tests
1	$ 850		$100		$ 950	**1**
2	610				610	**2**
3	170				170	
4	70				70	
5	880				880	**5**
6	220		50		270	**6**
	$2,800		$150		$2,950	
	75%					
75% Threshold	$2,100					
1	$ 850					
2	610					
5	880					
6	220					
Attained	$2,560 > **$2,100 (75% Threshold *Is* Satisfied)**					

Because the 75% threshold is satisfied, Segments 3 and 4 would be lumped together and shown in the "All Other" category.

Illustration of the Revenues Test When a Vertically Integrated Business Exists

Illustration 12-2 shows how to apply the revenues test for an enterprise assumed to have *three* identified operating segments—one of which is a **vertically integrated business** having *two* components deemed a *single* operating segment. In these situations, the **intra**segment revenues must be *eliminated* when arriving at total segment revenues used in the revenues test.

Allowed Aggregation of Certain *Nonreportable* Operating Segments (Level 2 Aggregation)

Two or more operating segments that do *not* qualify as *reportable* operating segments based on any of the three 10% tests *may* be combined to produce a *reportable* operating segment—but *only if* **they share *a majority of* the aggregation criteria** discussed earlier.

ILLUSTRATION 12-2 REVENUES TEST FOR DETERMINING *REPORTABLE* OPERATING SEGMENTS—*ONE* SEGMENT IS A VERTICALLY INTEGRATED BUSINESS (AMOUNTS IN MILLIONS)

Major Assumption: The *aluminum coil manufacturing* operation is *not* managed separately from the *aluminum can manufacturing* operation. Thus these two operations are reported as a *single* operating segment.

	Aluminum Coil and Can Manufacturing	Soft Drink Beverages	Financial Services	Total Revenues
Sales of aluminum *coils*:				
To external customers	$ 4,400			$ 4,400
To can manufacturing division (an **intra**segment sale)	1,500[a]			1,500
Sales of aluminum *cans*:				
To external customers	2,300			2,300
To soft-drink division (an **inter**segment sale)	1,700			1,700
Sales of soft drinks		$5,700		5,700
Interest income—external	n/a[b]	n/a[b]	$900	900
Interest income—**inter**segment	n/a[b]	n/a[b]	-0-	-0-
Subtotal	$ 9,900	$5,700	$900	$16,500
Less—**Intra**segment sales	(1,500)			(1,500)
Total Revenues, as defined for the revenues test (**external** customers and **intersegment** revenues)	$ 8,400	$5,700	$900	$15,000
Threshold percentage				10%
Threshold amount				$ 1,500
Reportable Industry Segments:	YES	YES	NO	

Note: Because the company has only *three* operating segments and *two* of the segments qualify as *reportable* operating segments, the financial services segment must also be shown separately. It need not be identified, however—it can be labeled as an *other segment*.

[a] Note that it seems incongruous to have *intra*segment sales recorded if the aluminum coil-producing component and the can-manufacturing component are managed as a *single* segment. That is, when an entity uses billing procedures to report revenues between two components, it implies that the two components *are* managed *separately* because the usual reason for having the billings procedure is to make possible the evaluation of each component as a *separate* profit center.

[b] No amount is shown here because it is assumed that this segment reports interest income as part of "Other Income and Expense"—*not* as revenues.

CHECK POINT

For segment reporting purposes, *aggregation* of *reportable* operating segments is allowed **only if** they satisfy

	A Majority of the Aggregation Criteria	*All* of the Aggregation Criteria
a.	Yes	Yes
b.	No	No
c.	Yes	No
d.	No	Yes

Answer: c

The "Ten Is Enough" Guideline

Situations may exist in which a substantial number of segments must be presented to comply with the 75% test. *FAS 131* does *not* have a precise limit on the number of segments for which information may be reported. For practical reasons, however, *FAS 131* states that **ten may be a practical limit** so that the segment information does *not* become overly detailed.

CHECK POINTS

Disregarding the "ten is enough" guideline, *aggregation* of *operating* segments *after* performing the three quantitative tests is allowed for:

	Reportable Segments	*Non*reportable Segments
a.	Yes	Yes
b.	No	No
c.	Yes	No
d.	No	Yes

Answer: d

Answer Question 11 but do *not* disregard the "ten is enough" guideline.

Answer: a

Changes in Reportable Segments and Organizational Structure

Previously Reportable Segment No Longer Reportable

A segment that was a reportable segment in the *previous* period may *not* be identified as a reportable segment in the *current* period. If management judges that segment to be **of continuing significance**, however, the segment is **deemed a reportable segment** in the *current* period.

Newly Reportable Segments

When a segment becomes reportable for the first time, **the prior-period data presented for comparative purposes must be *restated* to include the newly reportable segment** (even though that segment did *not* qualify as a reportable segment in the prior period)—**unless it is impractical to do so.** *Impractical* means that (1) the information is *not* available, *and* (2) the estimated cost to prepare it is excessive.

Change in Organizational Structure

If a change in an entity's *internal organization* causes a change in the composition of its *reportable segments*, the corresponding information for earlier periods must be restated—**unless it is impractical to do so.** Disclosure of this change and whether the prior-period information has been restated is required.

VII. REQUIRED *ENTITY-WIDE* DISCLOSURES

The disclosures discussed in this section—products and services, geographic areas, and major customers—apply to all public entities subject to *FAS 131*—**including those that have *only one* reportable operating segment.**

An entity's business activities could be organized such that (1) *one* segment may encompass a broad range of essentially *different* products and services, or (2) *different* segments may provide essentially the *same* products and services. Similarly (1) *one* segment may include operations in *several* geographic areas, or (2) *more than one* segment may operate in the *same* geographic area. Consequently, the disclosures described in this section are made *only if* the information is not already presented in the disclosures about *reportable* operating segments.

Products and Services

Entities must report revenues derived from each product and service (or group of similar products and services) in transactions with *external customers*. If doing so is impractical, however, that fact must be disclosed. Reported amounts must be based on information used to produce the entity's *general-purpose financial statements*.

Geographic Areas

Entities must report the following geographic information, *unless* it is impractical to do so:

1. **Revenues from *external* customers** attributed to:
   - A. The entity's *country of domicile*.
   - B. *Foreign countries* **in the aggregate**, with separate disclosures of (a) external revenues attributed to **an individual foreign country** that are material and (b) the basis for attributing external revenues to that country.
2. **Long-lived assets** (excluding (a) financial instruments, (b) deferred tax assets, and (c) certain noncurrent assets of *insurance and financial institutions*) located in:
   - A. The entity's country of domicile.
   - B. Foreign countries **in the aggregate** in which the entity holds assets, with separate disclosure of material assets in **an individual foreign country**.

Disclosures about geographic areas must be based on financial information used to produce the general-purpose financial statements. If it is impractical to furnish the geographic information, however, that fact must be disclosed.

Major Customers

Entities must report the extent of their reliance on major customers. Disclosure is required if *more than* 10% of an entity's revenues is derived from transactions with one customer. The disclosure must include (1) the total amount of revenues from each such customer and (2) the segment earning the revenue. (The identity of a major customer and the revenues that each segment derives from that customer *need not* be disclosed.) Each of the following is considered *a single customer*:

- A group of entities known to be *under common control*.
- The *federal* government.
- A *state* government.
- A *local* government, such as a county or municipality.
- A *foreign* government.

VIII. REQUIRED *SEGMENT* DISCLOSURES—*INTERIM PERIOD* REPORTING

When reporting *interim period* financial information in condensed financial statements, entities must disclose the following information:

1. Any change in the *basis of segmentation* from the last *annual* report.
2. For each *reportable segment*:
   - External revenues (to third parties).
   - *Inter*segment revenues.
   - A measure of *profit or loss*.

> A measure of *total assets*—but *only if* a material change has occurred from the amount disclosed in the last annual report.
> Any change in the *basis of measurement* of segment *profit or loss* from the last *annual* report.

3. A reconciliation of the total profit or loss of the reportable segments to the entity's *consolidated pretax income* (income *before* (a) extraordinary items, (b) discontinued operations, and (c) the cumulative effect of changes in accounting principles). Significant reconciling items must be separately identified and described.

IX. Comprehensive Illustration

This comprehensive illustration shows the types of information required by *FAS 131*. The *descriptive disclosures* are followed by the *quantitative disclosures*.

Description of the Types of Products from which Each Reportable Segment Derives Its Revenues

Parco has three reportable segments (*computers*, *chemicals*, and *organic farming*) and two nonreportable segments (*grocery store chain* and *office supply chain*). The *computers* segment manufactures computers for sale to end-users and retailers. The *chemicals* segment produces chemicals that are sold to industrial firms through distributors. The *organic farming* segment produces organic food that is sold to food processors and distributors.

Measurement of Segment Profit or Loss and Segment Assets

Each segment's accounting policies are the same as those described in the summary of significant accounting policies. Parco evaluates performance based on **profit or loss from operations before income taxes—*not* including foreign currency translation gains and losses** (which occur in translating financial statements of its foreign subsidiaries into U.S. dollars).

Parco accounts for intersegment sales and transfers *as though the sales or transfers were to unrelated third parties*, that is, at current market prices.

Factors Management Used to Identify Reportable Segments

Parco's *reportable* segments are business units that offer different products and services. They are managed separately because each business unit requires different technology and marketing strategies.

Major Customers

Revenues from one customer of Parco's computer segment totaled approximately $600 million of the company's consolidated revenues.

Illustrative Quantitative Disclosures

The quantitative disclosures are set forth in Exhibits A, B, and C. These exhibits assume that:

1. *Inter*segment revenues *are* included in the measure of profitability used by the CODM of each segment.

Exhibit A
Parco and Subsidiaries
Information About the Company's Operating Segments
(amounts in millions)

	COMPUTERS	+	CHEMICALS	+	ORGANIC FARMING	+	ALL OTHER	=	TOTALS
Revenues:									
Sales—External	$2,800		$2,000		$1,300		$ 200[a]		$ 6,300
Sales—**Inter**segment	100								100
Total Segment Revenues	$2,900		$2,000		$1,300		$ 200		$ 6,400
Less—**Inter**segment sales									(100)
***Consolidated* Revenues**									**$ 6,300**
Profitability:									
Segment profit or loss	$ 400		$ 850		$ 600		$ (50)		$ 1,800
– Unrealized intersegment profit									(40)
+ Income—Equity method investees									144
Unallocated amounts:									
– Corporate *headquarters* expenses									(300)
– Corporate *interest* expense									(60)
– Goodwill amortization expense									(400)
= ***Consolidated* Pretax Income**									**$ 1,144**
Assets:									
Segment assets	$2,000		$7,000		$3,000		$1,000		$ 13,000
+ Corporate headquarters assets									1,500
– Elimination of receivables from corporate headquarters									(400)
+ Investments in *equity method* investees									600
+ Goodwill *not* allocated to segments									2,300
= *Consolidated* Assets									**$17,000**
Capital expenditures	$ 220		$ 440		$ 660		$ 80		$ 1,400
Other significant P/L items: (*included* in measure of profit or loss):									
Interest *income*—External	$ 30		$ 70		$ 90		$ 10		$ 200
Interest *income*—**Inter**segment	11								11
Interest *expense*—External	(80)		(189)		(300)		(20)		(589)
Interest *expense*—**Inter**segment			(11)						(11)
Depreciation & amortization	(140)		(210)		(390)		(70)		(810)
Income—Equity method investees	55								55
Lawsuit settlement	(111)								(111)
Other significant noncash items:									
Impairment of value loss			(777)						(777)
Currency speculation gain					333				333

[a] These revenues are from a paint store chain and an office supply chain. (Both of these segments have always been *nonreportable* segments.)

2. Unrealized profit on *inter*segment sales is *not* allocated to segments in determining the measure of profitability used by the CODM of each segment.
3. **Inter**segment interest *income* and **inter**segment interest *expense are* included in the measure of profitability used by the CODM of each segment.
4. There were no (a) *extraordinary items*, (b) *changes in accounting principles*, or (c) *discontinued operations* during the year.

For segment *revenues*, *profitability*, and *assets* (shown in Exhibit A), we present the reconciliations of *segment* amounts to *consolidated* amounts in the *same* schedule as that segment information. An equally acceptable presentation is to use a *separate* schedule to display the reconciliations.

Exhibit B
Parco and Subsidiaries
Reconciliation of *Other Significant Items* to Consolidated Amounts
(amounts in millions)

	SEGMENT TOTALS	+	ADJUSTMENTS	=	CONSOLIDATED TOTALS
Income Statement Items:[a]					
Interest *income*—External	$ 200				$ 200
Interest *income*—**Inter**segment	11		(11)		-0-
Interest *expense*—External	(589)		(60)		(649)
Interest expense—**Inter**segment	(11)		11		-0-
Depreciation & amortization	(810)		(88)		(898)
Income—Equity method investees	55		144[c]		199
Lawsuit settlement (*unusual item*)	(111)				(111)
Other significant noncash items:					
Impairment of value *loss* (fixed asset write-down)	(777)				(777)
Currency speculation *gain* (unrealized)	333				333
Balance Sheet Related Items:[b]					
Investments in equity method investees (20–50% ownerships)	222		600[c]		822
Capital expenditures	1,400		505[d]		1,905

[a] These items are *included* in the *measure of* ***profitability*** used by the chief operating decision makers in managing the segments.

[b] These items are *included* in the *measure of* ***assets*** used by the chief operating decision makers in managing the segments.

[c] This amount pertains to several 20–50% ownership investments (made at the corporate headquarters level) in companies that manufacture home-gym equipment.

[d] This amount is for costs incurred for the corporate headquarters building, which is *not* included in the segment data.

Exhibit C
Parco and Subsidiaries
Geographic Information
(amounts in millions)

	REVENUES[a] (EXTERNAL)	LONG-LIVED ASSETS[b]
United States	$3,900	$3,100
Japan	800	1,200
United Kingdom	700	1,800
Mexico	600	1,000
Other foreign countries	500	600
Total	$6,500	$7,700

[a] Revenues are attributed to countries based on the location of customers.

[b] Excluding financial instruments and deferred tax assets.

END-OF-CHAPTER REVIEW

Summary of Key Points

1. *FAS 131* applies to *annual* and *interim*-period financial statements of *public* entities.

2. *FAS 131* uses a single basis of segmentation—the "management" approach, which means that identifiable operating segments are determined based on an entity's internal decision-making structure.

3. Refer to Illustration 12-3 for a summary diagram showing the process of determining *reportable* operating segments.

4. *Segment disclosures* consist of (1) *general descriptive information* (listed in summary point 5), (2) *specified financial amounts* for (a) segment *profit or loss*, (b) segment *assets*, (c) *certain*

ILLUSTRATION 12-3 SUMMARY DIAGRAM FOR DETERMINING REPORTABLE SEGMENTS

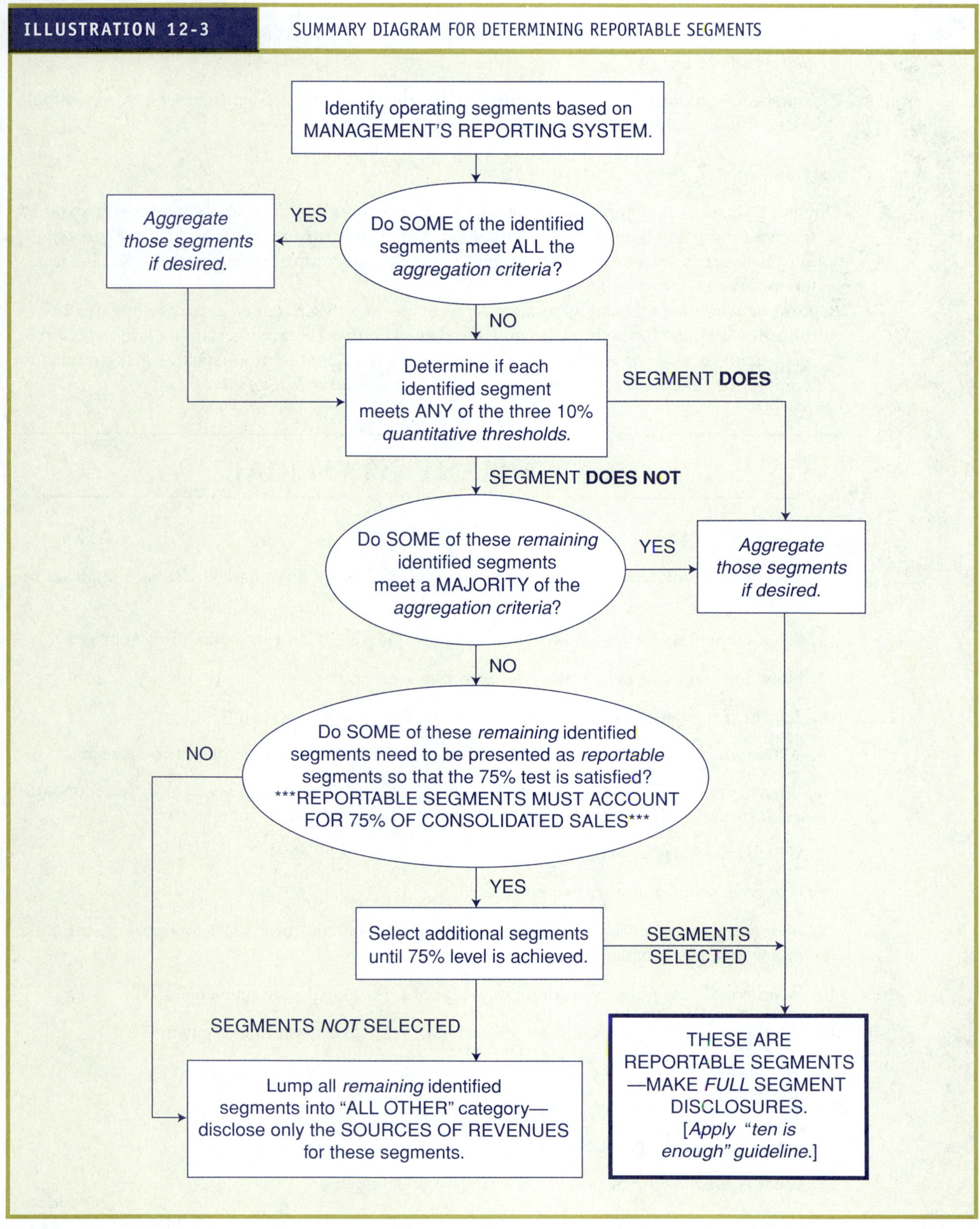

accounts (external sales, intersegment sales, and several other specified accounts), and (d) the basis of measurement for both segment profit or loss and segment assets, and (3) *reconciliations* of *segment* amounts to *consolidated* amounts.

5. The *general descriptive information* disclosures consist of (a) factors used in identifying *reportable* operating segments (including the basis of organization) and (b) each segment's types of *products and services.*
6. *Entity-wide disclosures* apply to *all* entities subject to *FAS 131*—including entities having a *single* reportable segment.
7. *Entity-wide disclosures* consist of information about (a) *products and services*, (b) *geographic areas*, and (c) *major customers.*

Glossary of New Terms

Operating segment A component of an entity that (1) engages in business activities with external parties (and possibly other segments) from which it may *earn revenues* and *incur expenses*, (2) has its operating results *regularly reviewed* by a chief operating decision maker, and (3) has *discrete financial information available.*

***Reportable* operating segment** Operating segments for which separate *quantitative* and *descriptive* information must be disclosed because the segment either (1) meets certain *quantitative thresholds* (*with* or *without* aggregation) or (2) meets a special condition (such as being needed to comply with the 75% test or is a segment having *continuing significance*).

Assignment Material

Review Questions

1. Why are *consolidated statements* alone considered insufficient and inadequate financial reports?
2. What is the *basis of segmentation* required by *FAS 131*? Can you explain this approach?
3. How does *FAS 131* define the term *operating segment*?
4. To which entities does *FAS 131* apply and to which does it *not* apply?
5. What two basic *quantitative disclosures* are required for *reportable* operating segments?
6. What *certain account amounts* must be disclosed for a *reportable* segment if those amounts *are included* in the measure of the profit or loss used to manage the segment?
7. What is the purpose of *aggregating* certain operating segments?
8. Is *aggregation* mandatory or permissive?
9. Is *aggregation* performed *before* or *after* performing the three 10% or more *quantitative thresholds* tests? Explain.
10. What conditions must exist for *aggregation* of *certain* operating segments?
11. What conditions must exist for *aggregation* of *reportable* operating segments?
12. Which three items do the 10% or more *quantitative thresholds* tests involve?
13. What is the *purpose* of the *75% test*?
14. How does one *apply* the *75% test*?
15. What is the *purpose* of the *"ten is enough"* guideline?
16. How are *non*reportable operating segments dealt with in reporting segment information?

17. What three items required to be reported for *operating segments* must be reconciled to the *corresponding consolidated* amounts?

18. What three types of information are reported for *entity-wide* disclosures?

19. Does *FAS 131* apply to *interim period* financial statements?

Exercises

E 12-1 **Determining *Reportable* Segments—Revenues Test** Payco has the following revenues *(stated in millions)* for its identified operating segments:

Operating Segments	Sales to Unaffiliated Customers	+	Intersegment Sales	=	Total Revenues
1	$ 170				$ 170
2	160				160
3	120				120
4	300		$ 50		350
5	110				110
6	140				140
7	200		250		450
	$1,200		$300		$1,500

Required

1. Determine the reportable segments based on the revenues test.
2. Assuming that the other two 10% tests (based on segment *profitability* and segment *assets*) do *not* result in any additional reportable segments, perform the 75% test.

E 12-2 **Determining *Reportable* Segments—Profitability Test** Punco has six operating segments, which have the following profits or losses:

Operating Segment	Operating Profit (Loss)
1	$ 700,000
2	5,200,000
3	(400,000)
4	(1,800,000)
5	800,000
6	3,100,000
	$ 7,600,000

Required Determine the *reportable* segments based on the profit or loss test.

E 12-3 **Determining *Reportable* Segments—Revenues Test Involving Vertically Integrated Operations** Patco has the following revenues (*stated in millions*) for its identified operating segments:

	Sales to Unaffiliated Customers	+	*Inter*segment Sales	+	*Intra*segment Sales	=	Total Revenues
Segment 1:							
Company A	$ 500						$ 500
Segment 2:							
Company B	300				$ 720		1,020
Company C	1,100						1,100
Segment 3:							
Company D	1,000						1,000
Company E	800		$600				1,400
Segment 4:							
Company F	700						700
Segment 5:							
Company G					880		880
Company H	2,000		200				2,200
	$6,400		$800		$1,600		$8,800

Required

1. Determine the *reportable* segments based on the revenues test.
2. Assuming that the other two 10% tests (based on segment *profitability* and segment *assets*) do *not* result in any additional *reportable* segments, perform the 75% test.
3. Prepare a schedule that (a) presents *segment* revenue information and (b) reconciles those revenues to *consolidated* revenues.

E 12-4 Presenting and Reconciling Segment Information—Unrealized Intercompany Profit Dubbler operates in only two industries, both of which qualify as *reportable* operating segments. Applicable data (stated in millions) follow:

Segment A:	
Sales to unaffiliated customers	$2,500
*Inter*segment sales	400
*Intra*segment sales	650
Segment profit (*before* **all** intercompany eliminations and income taxes)	900
Unrealized *inter*segment gross profit at 12/31/**05**	60
Unrealized *intra*segment gross profit at 12/31/**05**	100
Unrealized *inter*segment gross profit at 12/31/**04**	20
Unrealized *intra*segment gross profit at 12/31/**04**	-0-
Segment B:	
Sales to unaffiliated customers	$1,600
Segment profit (*before* income taxes)	200
Corporate headquarters items:	
General administrative expenses	210
Interest expense	50

The measure of profitability used by the chief operating decision maker for each operating segment:

A. Does *not* include adjustments for any unrealized *inter*segment profit.

B. *Does* include adjustments for any unrealized *intra*segment profit.

Required Prepare a schedule that (1) presents segment information for revenues and profitability and (2) reconciles that segment information to the required consolidated amounts. (Assume a 40% income tax rate and *no* changes in accounting principles.)

E 12-5 Allocating Common Costs to Segments Data for Palloco's identified operating segments for 2006 follow:

Segment	Sales	Traceable Operating Expenses
1	$1,000,000	$ 600,000
2	800,000	500,000
3	600,000	350,000
	$2,400,000	$1,450,000

Additional 2006 expenses—*not* included above—are as follows:

Indirect operating expenses	$360,000
Corporate headquarters general expenses	240,000

Palloco allocates only indirect operating expenses—to its segments for *internal reporting* purposes based on the ratio of a segment's sales to total sales of *all* segments.

Required Using only the information provided, what is Segment 3's 2006 measure of profit for *external reporting* purposes?

Problems

P 12-1 Identifying *Operating* Segments; Determining *Reportable* Segments—Revenues Test Pyco's identified operating segments are based on geographic areas. Revenues of these segments (*stated in millions*) follow:

Operating Segments	Sales to Unaffiliated Customers	+	Intersegment Sales	=	Total Revenues
Africa	$ 200				$ 200
Asia	700		$100		800
Australia	300				300
Europe	500		200		700
Middle East	500				500
United States	1,200		300		1,500
	$3,400		$600		$4,000

The African segment produces titanium (mining). The Asian and Australian segments manufacture radios. The remaining segments produce soap operas for television.

Required

1. What is the *minimum* and the *maximum* number of operating segments for which segment information could be disclosed?
2. Assuming the maximum number of operating segments, determine the *reportable* operating segments based on the *revenues* test.
3. Assuming that the other two 10% tests (based on segment *profitability* and segment *assets*) do *not* result in any additional reportable segments, perform the 75% test.

P 12-2 **Determining Reportable Segments: All Quantitative Tests** Payco has the following revenues *(stated in millions)* for its identified operating segments:

Operating Segment	Total Segment Revenues	Segment Operating Profit or (Loss)	Segment Assets
1	$ 30	$(10)	$ 75
2	210	100	400
3	80	(40)	125
4	190	20	100
5	170	(60)	250
6	70	10	100
7	250	110	450
	$1,000	$130	$1,500

The only intersegment revenues were $60 million from Segment 5 to Segment 4.

Required

1. Which operating segments are *reportable* operating segments?
2. Perform the 75% test.

P 12-3 **Determining Reportable Segments: All Quantitative Tests** Selected data (in millions) for Plazco's identified operating segments follow:

Segment Number	1	2	3	4	5	Total
Sales:						
External		$500	$ 700	$ 5,000	$ 600	$ 6,800
Intersegment		50		650		700
Interest income:						
External	800		200	500		1,500
Intersegment			50	150	300	500
Total Inflows	$ 800	$550	$ 950	$ 6,300	$ 900	$ 9,500
Profit or (loss)	**$ 150**	**$(70)**	**$(310)**	**$2,510**	**$220**	**$2,500**
Assets:						
Intersegment receivables	$ 200			$ 1,000	$ 100	$ 1,300
Fixed assets	100	$600	$ 500	3,500	200	4,900
All other assets	1,200	300	200	1,500	300	3,500
Total Assets	$1,500	$900	$ 700	$ 6,000	$ 600	$ 9,700

Required

1. Perform the *three* quantitative thresholds tests. (Only Segment 1 provides *financial services.*)
2. Determine if the 75% test's quantitative threshold is satisfied.

P 12-4 Presenting and Reconciling Segment Information—Unrealized Intercompany Profit Selected data (*in millions*) for Partex's domestic and foreign operations for 2006 follow:

	Segment Revenues		Segment Profit or Loss	Segment Assets	
	Intercompany	External		Long-Lived[a]	Non-Long-Lived
United States					
Company A.		$2,800	$ 200	$ 800	$1,100
Company B.	$500	20	240	450	160
Company C.		1,400	150	700	1,040
Mexico					
Company M.	150		30	380	320
Singapore					
Company S.		100	(40)	100	125
United Kingdom					
Company U.	60	610	(110)	410	190
Venezuela					
Company V.		70	(50)	110	115
	$710	$5,000	$ 420	$2,950	$3,050

[a] The only company having *financial instruments* and *deferred tax assets* is Company A ($200).

Additional Information

1. Assume that (a) Companies A and B constitute a vertically integrated business (*auto parts*) and are managed as a *single* operating segment, (b) Companies C and M constitute a vertically integrated business (*electronics*) but are managed *separately*, (c) Company U is in the *copier* business, (d) Company S is in the *computer* business, and (e) Company V is in the *real estate* business.
2. Only Companies S and V do *not* satisfy *any* of the three quantitative thresholds tests used to determine reportable segments.
3. All intercompany sales are at prices that approximate outside market prices. Assume a 40% gross profit margin on *all* intercompany sales.
4. The *measure of profitability* used by the chief operating decision maker for each operating segment:
   A. Does *not include* adjustments for any unrealized *inter*segment profit.
   B. *Does include* adjustments for any unrealized *intra*segment profit.
   C. *Excludes* both *extraordinary items* and *income tax expense* (assume that Partex has a 40% income tax rate).
   D. *Includes* unusual items.
5. At 12/31/06, Companies A and C each had 10% of their 2006 *intercompany* inventory purchases on hand.
6. Company U's intercompany sales (copiers) were to Company A. Company A took delivery of these copiers on 12/28/06 and capitalized them as fixed assets.
7. During 2006, Company C had both a $55 million *extraordinary* loss and a $33 million *unusual* loss. *No* changes in accounting principles occurred in 2006.
8. Data as to the corporate headquarters office follow:

	(millions)
Corporate *general* expenses	$ 66
Corporate *interest* expense	44
Corporate assets	222

Required Prepare a schedule that (1) presents the required segment information for revenues, profitability, and assets and (2) reconciles that segment information to the appropriate consolidated amounts.

P 12-5 **Presenting Entity-Wide Disclosures—Geographic Areas (Continuation of Problem 12-4)** Use the information provided in Problem 12-4.

Required Prepare a schedule that presents the required geographic areas disclosures of the entity-wide information disclosure requirements.

P 12-6 **Creating a Spreadsheet Model That Automatically Performs the Tests Used to Determine *Reportable* Segments** The performance of the thresholds tests used to determine *reportable* segments can be automated using a spreadsheet model.

Required Prepare a spreadsheet model that (1) enables you to input financial data about each of an entity's operating segments, (2) performs the *three* threshold tests, (3) performs the 75% test, and (4) displays which segments are *reportable* segments. Your model should be designed to accommodate entities having ten identified operating segments. *Hint:* Use *IF* logical formulas (EXCEL command: **insert function logical if** [or start by using the f_x button—the paste function—on the standard toolbar]).

Make the *first* portion of your model data *input fields* (for revenues, profitability, and assets). Make the *last* portion a *recap* of the results of the thresholds tests.

THINKING CRITICALLY

Cases

C 12-1 **Identifying *Operating* Segments—Possible Indicators?** Pilco has a *100%-owned* manufacturing *subsidiary*, Silco. Pilco and Silco constitute a *vertically integrated industry*. Silco sells *all* of its inventory to Pilco, which sells *all* of its inventory to external (third) parties.

Required Evaluate the following items as to whether they might serve to indicate whether *two* operating segments exist or *one* operating segment exists:

A. *Subsidiary* versus *branch/division* form of organization.
B. *Domestic* operation versus *foreign* operation for Silco.
C. *Wholly owned* subsidiary versus *partially owned* subsidiary.

C 12-2 **The 75% Test—An Intuitive Look** The results of the 75% test may cause one or more additional operating segments to become a *reportable* segment.

Required What segment facts make it likely that additional segments will have to be selected as a result of applying the 75% test in the following situations?

1. When *no* substantial *inter*segment revenues exist.
2. When substantial *inter*segment revenues *do* exist.

part five

Foreign Transactions and Foreign Operations

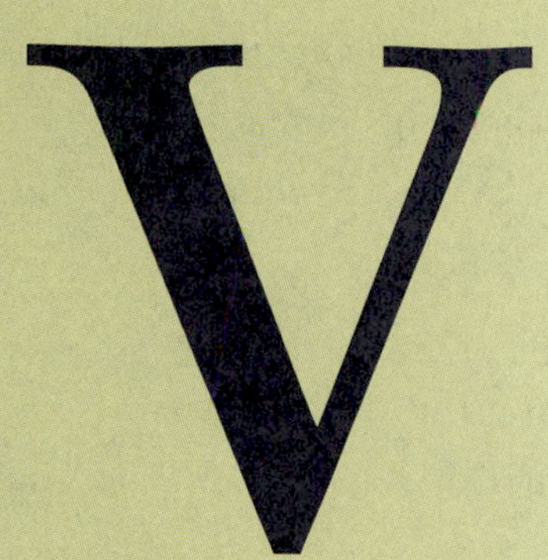

chapter

13

International Accounting Standards and Translating Foreign Currency Transactions

There is no subtler no surer means of overturning the existing basis of society than to debauch the currency.
JOHN MAYNARD KEYNES

LEARNING OBJECTIVES

To Understand

- The diversity of accounting standards that exist around the world.
- The efforts being made to *internationalize* accounting standards.
- The currency exchange rate system.
- The foreign exchange market.
- The exposures that exist under the floating exchange rate system.
- The way to account for foreign currency importing and exporting transactions.
- The causes of exchange rate changes.

TOPIC OUTLINE

INTERNATIONAL PERSPECTIVE: *The Globalization of Business*
ETHICAL PERSPECTIVE: *A Way to Avoid Environmental Cleanup Costs*
I. The Diversity of Worldwide Accounting Standards
II. Efforts to Internationalize Accounting Standards
INTERNATIONAL PERSPECTIVE: *Accounting's Global Rule Book*
III. Currency Exchange Rates
IV. The Foreign Exchange Market
V. Translating Importing and Exporting Transactions
VI. Differential Rates of Inflation: The Major Long-Term Cause of Exchange Rate Changes
APPENDIX 13A: Going International

Appendices can be found at http://www.pahler.swlearning.com

CHAPTER OVERVIEW

When a U.S. company decides to sell its products and services in a foreign country, it will first (1) compare the various alternatives available to accomplish that objective (*exporting* from the United States versus *manufacturing overseas*, using a foreign *subsidiary* or a foreign *branch*) and (2) weigh the risks and rewards associated with each alternative. In Appendix 13A to this chapter, we discuss these alternatives, risks, and rewards because they provide useful background material with which accountants should have a basic familiarity in this day and age of globalization of business. The significance of the globalization of business is succinctly described in the International Perspective that follows.

International Perspective

The Globalization of Business

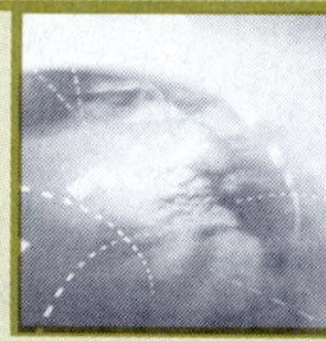

Business no longer knows national boundaries. Capital and human resources can go to work anywhere on the Earth and do a job. . . . If the world operates as one big market, you compete with every person who is capable of doing the same work—and there are a lot of them. And they are hungry! . . .

Accept that no matter where you go to work, you are not an employee—you are a business with one employee, you.

Source: Andy Grove, Chief Executive Officer, Intel Corporation. Commencement address at the Haas School of Business, University of California, Berkeley, May 1994.

We begin this chapter by discussing (1) the diversity of accounting standards that exist around the world and (2) efforts currently being made to internationalize accounting standards (so as to achieve a "world GAAP").

Next we lay the theoretical groundwork for dealing with currency exchange rate changes—including causes of exchange rate changes. We then discuss and illustrate how to translate foreign currency transactions into U.S. dollars. **Foreign currency transactions** require settlement (payment or receipt) in a foreign currency, such as an importing or exporting transaction requiring settlement in British pounds. (When foreign transactions require settlement in U.S. dollars, no accounting issues exist.)

In Chapter 14, we discuss the ways that companies can use certain types of financial instruments (generically referred to as derivatives) to manage their exposure to adverse changes in exchange rates—an area that has become an integral part of managing international operations in the last 25 years.

In Chapters 15, and 16, we discuss and illustrate how to translate the financial statements of foreign subsidiaries (formally called *foreign currency financial statements*) into U.S. dollars. In Chapter 15, we also address special problems associated with intercompany transactions between a domestic company and its foreign subsidiary.

The Governing FASB Pronouncement

FASB *Statement No. 52*, "Foreign Currency Translation," sets forth the accounting principles and procedures for translating (1) foreign currency transactions and (2) foreign currency financial statements. The issues involved in the translation of foreign currency transactions (this chapter's topic) are *not* controversial. The issues pertaining to (1) the manner of accounting for foreign currency derivatives (Chapter 14) and (2) the translation of foreign currency financial statements (Chapters 15 and 16), however, are highly controversial.

The Foreign Corrupt Practices Act of 1977 (FCPA)

Pervading all aspects of doing business in foreign countries is the Foreign Corrupt Practices Act (FCPA). This act, which is administered by the Securities and Exchange Commission (SEC) and the

Justice Department, **prohibits U.S. firms from offering funds (bribes) to foreign officials in an effort to obtain or retain business.** The FCPA also essentially forbids *indirect* payment methods; thus funds may *not* be offered if the firm has reason to believe that any part of them will be used to pay bribes.

An amendment to the FCPA allows small payments to lower-level foreign officials performing routine and lawful duties; however, the amendment does *not* clearly specify who or how much can be paid.

In contrast, bribes are *legal* and *tax deductible* to one degree or another in Austria, Belgium, Canada, Denmark, France, Germany, Greece, Ireland, Luxembourg, the Netherlands, New Zealand, Spain, and Switzerland. The U.S. State Department estimated that this unlevel playing field caused U.S. companies to lose nearly $50 billion in foreign contracts in 1998.

The U.S. Leads the Way

The FCPA, passed in 1977 after a series of bribery scandals involving American multinationals, was derided for years as naive and moralistic by many foreign officials and business executives, particularly continental Europeans. In recent years, however, many officials in many foreign governments have moved closer to the American view because of (1) popular outrage over corruption scandals abroad and (2) mounting evidence that **corruption undermines economic development in poor countries.**

A Giant Step Forward in 1997

In 1997, official representatives of the 29 richest nations on earth and five other nations signed a binding agreement outlawing bribery of foreign public officials. This agreement capped 20 years of U.S. pressure, seven years of discussions, and two years of nose-to-nose negotiations. Under the agreement, the representatives will propose laws to their parliaments that impose strict penalties for bribery and require tight accounting procedures to make it harder to hide illegal payments. This watershed accord is designed to ensure that price and quality—not greased palms—will determine who gains and loses in markets abroad.

I. The Diversity of Worldwide Accounting Standards

Each foreign unit of a domestic company (1) keeps its books and records in its *own* local currency and (2) uses the accounting principles of the country in which it is located—*not* U.S. generally accepted accounting principles (GAAP). For both internal and external reporting purposes, however, the U.S. parent or home office needs statements *in dollars* for these foreign units. Furthermore, the statements in dollars must be presented in accordance with *U.S. GAAP—not foreign GAAP*.

Obviously, it does *not* make sense to either (1) add together financial statement amounts in *dollars* and *foreign currencies* or (2) report worldwide operations using one set of accounting principles for *domestic* operations and a variety of accounting principles for *foreign* operations.

Accordingly, it is first necessary to *restate* the foreign currency statements to U.S. GAAP (done on a worksheet). These *restated* foreign currency statements are then *translated* into dollars, using appropriate currency exchange rates (also done on a worksheet). Thus **we *restate* and then *translate*—*not*** translate and then restate.[1]

In Chapter 15, we show the worksheet procedures used to restate foreign currency statements to U.S. GAAP. In this chapter, we discuss briefly the substantial diversity of accounting systems and practices that exist around the world. Thus you can more fully appreciate that it is often a monumental task to restate foreign currency statements to U.S. GAAP—a task that is usually far more time-consuming than translating foreign currency statements into dollars (which usually can be readily done using international accounting software packages and templates).

[1] Some accountants (but very few), however, believe that the process should be *translate* and then *restate*.

Differing Reporting Systems

Different accounting standards and systems have evolved throughout the world for many reasons, which are discussed in substantially more detail in international accounting texts.[2] Most countries use one of the following reporting systems.[3]

The British-American-Dutch System

Providing full and accurate financial information to *investors* is the orientation of this system, which is used by Australia, Canada, India, the Netherlands, the United Kingdom, and the United States.

The Continental System

Providing *creditor protection*, using business conservatism, and minimizing income taxes are the orientation of this system, in which *creditors* (usually banks) are viewed as the *primary* financial statement users. Accounting standards are usually written into the statutes, and major differences often do *not* exist between *financial reporting* and *tax reporting*. The accounting standards are *highly* conservative, greatly *minimizing* income taxes. Furthermore, managements are given wide discretion in many areas, and relevant information is not always provided to shareholders. Most of the European countries and Japan use this system.

A significant competitive advantage of this system compared with the British-American-Dutch system is that firms are *not* burdened with the substantial administrative costs of complying with two distinctly separate reporting systems. (Note that deferred income taxes *cannot* be an issue if the *same* reporting system is used for both *financial reporting* and *tax reporting*.)

The South American System

This system is basically the continental system with the addition of *price-level accounting* (making periodic adjustments for inflation). It is used by most of the countries in South America, the majority of which have had severe inflation for decades. For instance, Brazil has had annual inflation exceeding 200% in the past decade (the high being 2,567% in 1993); since 1960, its prices have multiplied a staggering 22 billion times.[4]

Selected Widespread Differences between U.S. GAAP and Foreign GAAP

Certain of the major widespread differences between *U.S. GAAP* and *foreign GAAP* are as follows:

1. **LIFO inventory costing.** Although widely used in the United States, this method has limited acceptance in other countries for both financial and tax reporting.
2. **Goodwill.** Although capitalization is mandatory and is required in the United States, virtually all other countries (1) allow it to be expensed or charged to equity at the business combination date or (2) require it to be amortized over a short period (five years in most cases) if capitalized.

Selected Individual Country-by-Country GAAP Differences

We show a variation from U.S. GAAP for each of the following selected countries.

---

[2] For an in-depth discussion of the different accounting systems and standards used overseas, see Zafar Iqbal, *International Accounting: A Global Perspective* (South-Western College Publishing, 2000).

[3] The reporting system for the countries formerly included in the Communist bloc is presently evolving from a rigid system in which financial statements were furnished only to government planners to a more open reporting system.

[4] "Why Does Brazil Face Such Woes? Some See a Basic Ethical Lapse," *The Wall Street Journal*, January 4, 1994, p. A1.

Australia

> All cost in excess of an acquired business's net assets at book value is usually deemed to be goodwill. Goodwill may be classified as a deduction from capital or charged to capital.

Brazil

> A provision for "maintenance of working capital" may be recorded to remove from profit the effect of inflation on current assets, long-term assets (other than fixed assets that are indexed for inflation for both financial and tax reporting purposes), and liabilities.

France

> No specific accounting standards exist for troubled debt restructurings. In practice, gains and losses on restructurings are recorded in income at the time of the restructuring.

Italy

> No standards exist as to leases. In practice, all leases are recorded as *operating* leases.

Japan

> Research and development costs may be deferred over a maximum of five years.

Mexico

> Most industrial and retail firms are allowed to write up their fixed assets annually to current appraised value (as opposed to using inflation indices).

Switzerland

> Machinery and equipment may be largely expensed at the time of purchase.

United Kingdom

> Investments below 20% ownership must be carried at cost.

An In-Depth Look at Germany's GAAP

To show how the GAAP of one country can differ greatly from U.S. GAAP, we use Germany, for which approximately 50 entries are often needed to restate German financial statements to U.S. GAAP. Germany's GAAP is possibly the most conservative and loose of any of the major industrialized countries. The use of arbitrary reserves for the purpose of smoothing earnings is rampant.

> **Translation of foreign currency statements.** No specific translation method is specified; however, strict consistency is required.

> **Foreign currency transactions.** Anticipated FX losses on FX receivables and payables as a result of *forecasted* adverse exchange rate changes can be expensed currently.

> **Inventory.** Inventory may be valued at amounts *lower than* that produced by applying the lower-of-cost-or-market rule (occurs when management believes that *future* price declines will occur). LIFO is acceptable but *only if* it matches the physical flow of the inventory.

> **Goodwill.** Goodwill can be written off against stockholders' equity at the business combination date.

> **Pensions.** Actuarial gains and losses must be recognized currently as adjustments of pension expense rather than spread over a number of years.

> **Long-term contracts.** Both the *percentage of completion method* and the *completed contract method* are allowed, but in practice the *percentage of completion method* is rarely used.

> **Contingent liabilities.** Contingent liabilities are recorded if a loss is reasonable and *possible* (not *probable* as in the United States).

> **Accruals and expenses.** Because the books are usually kept in a manner consistent with tax law, expenses *not* allowed for tax purposes are usually *not* recorded.

> **Allowances for uncollectibles and warranties.** Because these items are deductible for income tax purposes, firms may arbitrarily accrue the *maximum* amounts allowed under the tax code so that income taxes are *minimized.*

> **Prior period adjustments.** Errors discovered that pertain to a *prior year* must be reported in the *current year* income statement.

II. Efforts to Internationalize Accounting Standards

The lack of worldwide uniform accounting principles and practices is unfortunate because it (1) impedes comparability, (2) is costly and inefficient for companies having foreign operations, (3) hinders the ability of firms to raise capital in foreign markets, (4) hinders the ability of firms to list their securities on foreign stock exchanges, and (5) for U.S. firms, often places them at a competitive disadvantage to many European firms when U.S. and European firms compete against each other in proposed business combinations.

The International Accounting Standards *Committee* (1973–2000)

To promote the development of a "world GAAP," the International Accounting Standards Committee (IASC) [based in London] was formed in 1973. It eventually reached a membership of 103 countries (representing 106 professional accounting bodies). The IASC issued 41 international accounting standards, many of which were revised over the years. When a standard is revised, the same *originally assigned number* is retained (the opposite of the FASB's pronouncement numbering system in which the *old number* is discontinued and a *new number* is assigned).

Filling the Final Void

In 1999, the IASC issued *IAS 39*, "Financial Instruments: Recognition and Measurement," which filled the "biggest void" existing in accounting standards in virtually every one of the 103 member countries of the IASC. *IAS 39* formally completed the set of core financial accounting standards presented to the International Organization of Securities Commissions (IOSCO) for approval (discussed later). Thus the international standards are now very comprehensive.

Structural-Related Criticisms Lead to Changes

The IASC had the following structural deficiencies: (1) its committee was bloated (16 voting members), (2) no criteria existed for the educational or professional backgrounds of its committee members, and (3) its committee members (all part-time) served voluntarily and worked for various corporations and organizations—raising questions regarding their *independence* and *objectivity*. In response to these perceived deficiencies, the IASC was restructured in 2001 and renamed as the *International Accounting Standards Board* (IASB).

The International Accounting Standards *Board* (2001 to Present)

The IASB has a 14-member board of directors (12 are full-time). The full-time board members are paid and, more importantly, are prohibited from holding other jobs.

Starting Off by Walking into a Buzz Saw

The IASB's first project (announced in August 2001) was accounting for stock options—a highly controversial topic, especially in the United States. Thus the IASB effectively began by walking into a buzz saw. In February 2004, the IASB issued a standard that requires companies to (1) determine the fair value of stock options granted to employees and (2) report that amount as compensation expense in arriving at earnings. The issuance of this standard placed substantial pressure on the FASB and SEC to conform U.S. stock option accounting rules to this international standard.

The Historical Shortcomings of the IASC/IASB Standards

Because IASC rules required 11 votes of the 14 voting committee members before the issuance of a standard, it was usually necessary to provide *two* alternatives to get the 11 votes. From the U.S. perspective, such standards are *not* much as standards go. From an international perspective, however, they are better than having *three* alternatives, so this represents a step forward in achieving the ultimate goal. Unfortunately, almost any company can state in its annual report (as many do) that it is complying with international accounting standards—such a statement does *not* have much significance.

The Impact of International Standards on Standards Setting in *Individual Countries*

The establishment of international standards has had (1) *substantial* impact in many foreign countries and (2) *minimal* impact in the United States.

The Impact on Standards Setting in *Foreign Countries*

For many foreign countries, the international standards have served as an incentive to upgrade their standards, and some countries have done so. Other foreign countries, primarily third-world developing countries, use the international standards rather than incur the cost of maintaining their own private or government standard-setting bodies. China, for example, requires its many joint ventures to report using the international standards.

The Impact on Standards Setting in the *United States*

With a few exceptions, one of the two alternatives generally allowed for each international standard has usually coincided with the U.S. standard. Thus the FASB never had to be greatly concerned about U.S. standards *not* complying with international standards. The *major* exception pertains to inventory. *IAS 2* requires that when the LIFO inventory method is used, disclosures must be made of the benchmark treatment amount, which is FIFO—a financial statement disclosure prohibited by the U.S.'s Internal Revenue Service when LIFO is used for *income tax reporting*.

The Impact of International Standards on *Capital Markets*

Stock exchanges in several countries—but *not* in the United States—allow foreign companies to list their securities on the exchange if they furnish financial information using the *international standards* in lieu of *local standards*.

Consequently, U.S. stock exchanges have pressured the Securities and Exchange Commission (SEC) to do likewise. To date, the SEC has *not* bowed to this pressure. For a foreign company to list on a U.S. stock exchange, the SEC presently requires that the company furnish financial statements that (1) *comply* with U.S. GAAP or (2) are *reconciled* to U.S. GAAP.

Efforts to Reduce the Alternatives Allowed Under the International Standards

Major efforts have been and are still being made to reduce the alternatives allowed in most of the international standards.

The Efforts of the Early 1990s

In 1993, the IASC completed an ambitious project begun in 1989 that was aimed at improving comparability and reducing the number of allowable alternatives in 12 of its standards. The major alternatives that the ISAC hoped to eliminate were (1) the LIFO inventory method (in *IAS 2*), (2) deferring of research and development costs (in *IAS 9*), (3) the pooling of interests method (in *IAS 22*), and (4) charging goodwill directly to stockholders' equity at the combination date (in *IAS 22*).

Although the IASC revised 10 of its standards, it took only a small step forward. Some of the revised standards merely resulted in labeling one of the alternatives as a preferable treatment—called the *benchmark treatment*—with the second alternative labeled as the *allowed alternative treatment*. Of the four major proposed changes, only the alternative of charging goodwill to stockholders' equity at the business combination date was eliminated.

The IASB's "Improvement Project" (begun in 2002)

In 2002, the IASB commenced a major project (called the "Improvements Project") to upgrade its international accounting standards (14 of which were heavily criticized). By 2004, the IASB had changed 17 of the 34 standards it had inherited (in addition to issuing seven new [additional] standards).

The Short-Term Convergence Projects of the IASB and the FASB (begun in 2002)

In 2002, the IASB and the FASB issued a *memorandum of understanding*, which formalized their commitment to the convergence of U.S. and international accounting standards. Shortly after this event, the IASB and the FASB both added a joint "short-term convergence project" to their active agendas. Thus both Boards are using their best efforts to propose changes to U.S. and international accounting standards that reflect common solutions to certain specifically identified differences. The scope of this project is limited to those differences in which convergence around a high-quality solution appears achievable in the short term. The IASB and the FASB have identified 18 differences to be addressed.

As a result of these projects, both boards have issued several exposure drafts to eliminate differences (the FASB issuing five exposure drafts in late 2003). The most notable of the FASB exposure drafts pertains to *changes in accounting principles* and *error corrections*, which would require accounting changes to be reported *retroactively* (thus eliminating the "cumulative effect" approach currently required).

The IASB's Comprehensive Income Project

Both the IASB and the FASB have projects designed to improve the existing format of the income statement. The IASB proposal is innovative and unique in that it calls for a format that parallels the reporting categories used in the statement of cash flows (operating, investing, and financing). To view this robust statement format, go to the IASB's web page at **http://iasb.org** and follow these steps. First, click on ***Current Issues*** (at the top). Second, click on ***IASB Activities*** (on the left). Third, select ***Active Projects***. Fourth, scroll down and click on ***Reporting Comprehensive Income***. Fifth, click on ***Adobe Acrobat***. The proposed income statement is in Appendix 1 (page 6).

The European Union's Plan for 2005

In 2003, the European Union (consisting of 15 European countries, to be expanded to 25 countries in 2004) voted to require their member countries to use the IASB's international accounting standards beginning January 1, 2005. Consequently, 7,000 public listed companies in these member states must prepare their financial statements according to international accounting standards.

International Accounting Reports Available from the FASB

In 1999, the *FASB* has published the report *The IASC—U.S. Comparison Project: A Report on the Similarities and Differences between IASC Standards and U.S. GAAP*. Detailed information about this report (and information on how to order the report) is available at the following FASB website: **http://accounting.rutgers.edu/raw/fasb/IASC/iascpg2d.htm**.

Furthermore, the FASB Report, *International Accounting Standard Setting: A Vision for the Future*, is available for downloading at the following FASB website: **http://accounting.rutgers.edu/raw/fasb/IASC/visionpg.html.**

World GAAP—Will It Be Attained?

The goal of having all businesses use a strong world GAAP is not only one of reaching agreement on what standards should exist but also of persuading countries to adopt the standards. This goal often seems unattainable because of the vested interests that many countries have in maintaining their own standards. For example, U.S. companies strongly opposed the proposed elimination of the LIFO inventory method because they would have had to pay sizable "catch-up" income taxes had LIFO been eliminated. Thus even though scores of companies have much to gain from international GAAP and believe it is a fine idea, they do *not* want changes made to their local GAAP.

The Capital Markets: A Driving Force

The increasing practice of companies raising capital in world markets outside their home countries (approximately $400 billion of debt and equity raised in some recent years compared with $50 billion in 1980) has given added emphasis to the desirability of having a common accounting language. This desirability is underscored by the fact that multinational companies that raise capital in world markets and list their securities on foreign stock exchanges are forced to prepare financial statements on several different bases to file in different countries, a needless waste of effort.

The IOSCO's Endorsement of IASC Standards

In 1995, IOSCO, of which the SEC is a member, and the IASC agreed on a timetable for the formal endorsement of a core set of IASC standards as an alternative to national standards. The IASC was to revise or complete 16 standards on subjects such as intangibles, financial instruments, interim reporting, segment reporting, and leasing. The IASC completed this major effort in 1999 with the issuance of *IAS 39* (mentioned earlier).

In 2000, IOSCO completed its assessment of the IASC standards and recommended that its members allow multinational issuers to use all of the standards (with reconciliation, disclosure, and interpretation taken into account when necessary) for (1) crossborder offerings of securities and (2) listings of securities on stock exchanges. See the International Perspective for more discussion of international standards.

Also in 2000, the SEC issued a concept release for the purpose of obtaining feedback from domestic and foreign parties regarding the quality of the IASC standards. To date, the SEC has *not* changed its position of *not* allowing foreign registrants to sell securities and be listed on stock exchanges in the U.S. **without a reconciliation to U.S. GAAP** (as mentioned earlier on page 424).

III. Currency Exchange Rates

Distinguishing between Conversion and Translation

Conversion

Actually exchanging one currency into another is called **conversion.** Foreign currencies may be either purchased or converted into U.S. dollars at commercial banks that have a foreign exchange department.

Translation

In contrast, **translation** (for our purposes) is the process of applying an appropriate *currency exchange rate* (such as 1 British pound = $1.50) to a foreign currency amount (such as 30,000

International Perspective

Accounting's Global Rule Book

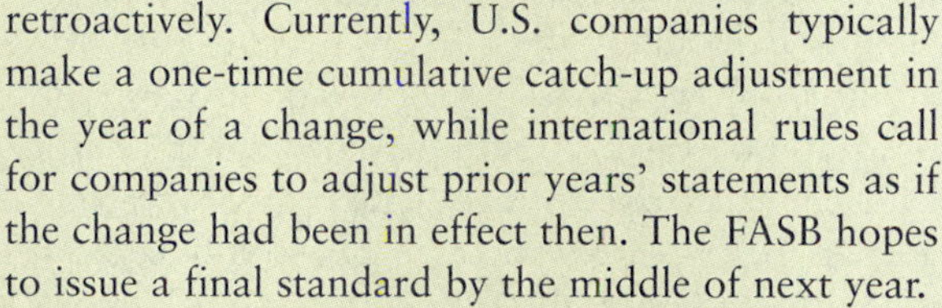

The U.S. and countries overseas can't even agree on what set of measurements to use in the kitchen. So how will they ever "harmonize" international standards on accounting?

Well, that is just what accounting rule makers are trying to do. They're stepping up efforts for a convergence of U.S. and international standards, a move that took on urgency after the Enron Corp.–led rash of accounting scandals shook investor confidence in the superiority of American standards.

The remaining huge differences will probably take years to solve—if they're even solvable.

Nevertheless, U.S. companies soon will start to feel the effect, just like international peers that already are grappling with numerous rule changes. Within the next few weeks, officials at the Financial Accounting Standards Board plan to propose changes to bring U.S. rules in line with the approach of its overseas counterpart, the International Accounting Standards Board.

It is a rare time when accounting-rule makers in the U.S. have expressly altered rules to take into account the international way of doing things—instead of expecting their overseas counterparts to conform to U.S. standards.

"Europe will be impressed that the U.S. is prepared to take the pain," says David Tweedie, IASB chairman.

Standard setters both in the U.S. and overseas envision the financial statements of a company—say, in Germany—one day being comparable with those of a U.S. rival, simplifying cross-border investment and international stock listings at exchanges in the U.S. and elsewhere.

"If we think the international approach is better or equal, we will propose moving" in that direction, says Robert Herz, the FASB's chairman. Mr. Herz anticipates resistance from corporate executives in instances where they perceive such changes would damage their companies' financial statements, adding that the board already has begun to hear from some companies with worries.

In Brussels, the seat of the European Union, a spokesman for the 15-nation European Commission trade bloc says, "Let's wait and see what they do," referring to the FASB and its proposal. He adds it is important to see that convergence "implies movement in both directions."

Among the most notable changes that the FASB proposal probably will include is a general requirement for companies to apply accounting changes retroactively. Currently, U.S. companies typically make a one-time cumulative catch-up adjustment in the year of a change, while international rules call for companies to adjust prior years' statements as if the change had been in effect then. The FASB hopes to issue a final standard by the middle of next year.

The IASB was set up with the help of the Securities and Exchange Commission and the FASB in April 2001 to develop a single set of high-quality international standards. The attitude of many in the U.S. at the time was that their standards were generally superior. The collapse of Enron in late 2001 forced U.S. regulators and standard setters to rethink the matter.

To speed up efforts, the FASB and the IASB now will meet formally twice a year. The EU has agreed to adopt the IASB's standards by 2005; as many as 91 countries in total by that date will require or allow their companies to adopt international standards. "The point isn't really about arguing over arcane accounting," says Mr. Tweedie. "This is really about growth, investment and trade."

Delivering a unified approach "will be pretty difficult," says Robert Willens, an accounting analyst at Lehman Brothers. It isn't that the differences are "insuperable," he says; the obstacles lie instead in matters of prestige. "I don't think FASB wants to sacrifice its pre-eminent position as the setter of accounting standards." The group isn't "going to be willing to compromise that much," he predicts.

The FASB, for its part, acknowledges the size of the task ahead, but says it fully supports attempts to bring together the two sets of standards. The standard-setting body also notes that support from corporate officers will be essential.

And it isn't just U.S. executives who must throw their weight behind the effort; European counterparts also face change, and resistance already has cropped up. For instance, big banks in Europe, with the French government and the European Commission by their side, have objected to the international board's proposals on the financial instruments known as derivatives. The IASB believes that derivatives should be valued at their current market

(continued)

International Perspective, continued

value, similar to the U.S. approach. European countries, under current rules, typically allow derivatives to be valued at the cost at which they were acquired. That approach is favored by the big banks there, the main users of derivatives. The banks have argued that the IASB's approach would cause unnecessary volatility in earnings.

The IASB, which has issued several proposals in this area and expects to release some final standards in December, is reluctant to compromise on a fair-value approach, in part because that could jeopardize convergence with the U.S.

Among the trickiest areas to reconcile is pension accounting. Current U.S. standards attempt to smooth short-term fluctuations in earnings by allowing companies to calculate the return on their pension-fund investments using an assumed rate, rather than the actual return on a pension fund's stocks, bonds and other assets.

The IASB's Mr. Tweedie is determined that international rules should reflect a plan's actual value, and he says the international standard likely will go even further than current U.K. rules, which require companies to give a more real-time snapshot of the value of assets than in the U.S. Given the discomfort that the U.K. standard already has caused in that country, Mr. Tweedie admits his proposals will probably "go down like a rat sandwich."

Another fundamental difference lies in re-evaluation of the value of property, plants and equipment. Overseas, it is common for countries to permit periodic re-evaluation of such assets, either up or down. The U.S. doesn't allow for such upward re-evaluations. As a result, real estate owned by American companies is often worth a lot more than is reflected in the books.

Among the next wave of projects that the boards plan to tackle: concurrent efforts to overhaul the income statement. Both boards have agreed they want to see "comprehensive income" on the income statement. Comprehensive income would include certain items that affect shareholders' equity but that aren't currently run through the income statement, such as unrealized gains and losses on certain securities. Still, there are differences between the two boards. The IASB, for instance, wants to remove net income from the income statement, while the FASB hasn't yet reached a conclusion of the matter.

Other planned projects: addressing differences in accounting for acquisitions of companies and creating a conceptual model for when revenue is booked.

Source: Cassell Bryan-Low, "Accounting's Global Rule Book," *The Wall Street Journal*, November 28, 2003, p. C-1.

pounds) so that an amount can be expressed in U.S. dollars (30,000 pounds × $1.50 = $45,000). Hereafter, we use the £ symbol for the British pound in our examples.

Methods of Expressing Exchange Rates

The ratio of the number of units of one currency needed to acquire one unit of another currency constitutes the exchange rate between the two currencies. The exchange rate may be expressed either directly or indirectly:

1. **The direct exchange rate.** The number of units of the *domestic* currency needed to acquire one unit of the *foreign* currency is the **direct** exchange rate (for example, £1 = $1.50). Accordingly, to determine the U.S. dollar equivalent of an amount stated in a foreign currency, **the foreign currency amount is *multiplied* by the *direct* exchange rate** (for example, £30,000 × $1.50 = $45,000).
2. **The indirect exchange rate.** The number of units of the *foreign* currency needed to acquire one unit of the *domestic* currency is the **indirect** exchange rate (for example, $1 = £.667). Accordingly, to determine the U.S. dollar equivalent of an amount stated in a foreign currency, **the foreign currency amount is divided by the *indirect* exchange rate** (for example, £30,000 ÷ .667 = $45,000).

Finding the *Direct* Exchange Rate from the *Indirect* Exchange Rate and Vice Versa

The *indirect* exchange rate can always be obtained from the *direct* exchange rate and vice versa. For example, if the *direct* exchange rate for the British pound is £1 = $1.50, dividing each side of the equation by $1.50 produces the *indirect* exchange rate of £.667 = $1. Likewise, if the *indirect* exchange rate is $1 = £.667, dividing each side of the equation by .667 produces the *direct* exchange rate of $1.50 = £1.

Which Exchange Rate to Use?

Banks and daily newspapers in the United States quote exchange rates both *directly* and *indirectly*. Translation of amounts stated in foreign currencies is usually performed using *direct* quotations. For this reason and because it is easier to deal with, we use the *direct* exchange rate in all examples and illustrations in this chapter and in the remaining four foreign currency chapters.

Selected Currencies and Symbols

The following are the currencies and symbols of a number of foreign countries:

Country	Currency	Symbol	Country	Currency	Symbol
Australia	Dollar	$A	Korea	Won	W
Argentina	Peso	Arg$	Mexico	Peso	Mex$
Canada	Dollar	Can$	Netherlands	Euro	€
China	Renminbi/Yuan	Y	Russia	Ruble	rub
Egypt	Pound	LE	Saudi Arabia	Riyal	SRls
France	Euro	€	Singapore	Dollar	S$
Germany	Euro	€	Spain	Euro	€
Hong Kong	Dollar	HK$	Sweden	Krona[a]	SKr
Ireland	Euro	€	Switzerland	Franc	SFr
Italy	Euro	€	Taiwan	Dollar	NT$
Israel	New shekel	NIS	United Kingdom	Pounda	£
Japan	Yen	¥	Vietnam	Dong	D

[a] This currency is expected to become fixed to the euro after 2002.

Note: The European Union's single currency is the euro, and its symbol is €.

The European Union's Euro

On January 1, 1999, the European Commission (EC), the executive body of the 15-country European Union (EU), launched its new monetary unit, the euro, as the single currency for most of Europe. Only 12 of the EU member countries are participating, but the EC hopes that its three remaining EU countries (Denmark, Sweden, and the United Kingdom) eventually will become euro countries, along with Cyprus and five Eastern European countries that are currently negotiating for entrance into the EU.

The currency union is technically the final phase of the EU's economic and monetary union (EMU), which has been following a course that began in 1992, when the Maastricht treaty on monetary union was signed. EMU is part of a political initiative whose roots lie in the debris of World War II. The goal of the EMU is to ensure lasting peace by integrating markets and economies as the first steps toward what some see as eventual political union. With an expected 21-country membership, encompassing a population close to 450 million, the EU would become the world's largest market.

Spot and Forward Exchange Rates

Exchange rates at which currencies could be *converted* immediately (for settlement in 2 days) are termed **spot rates.** Exchange rates also exist for transactions whereby conversion could be made at some stipulated date (normally up to 12 months) in the future. These rates are called **forward** or **future rates;** they are discussed in Chapter 14.

The Exchange Rate System: *Floating* versus *Fixed* Exchange Rates

From 1944 to 1974 (in the interest of promoting economic stability), the dollar was tied to gold, and most currencies were tied to the dollar. As a result, **fixed** or **official** exchange rates existed. When fixed rates no longer reflected economic conditions, governments were forced to make large changes in their fixed exchange rates (as the U.S. government did in 1973 when it announced a 10% downward adjustment). Such adjustments were called **devaluations** (the typical case) and **revaluations**, depending on the direction of the adjustment.

Although devaluations of certain currencies were often expected, it was impossible to determine exactly when they would occur or the amount of the devaluation. This major drawback and the fact that the fixed rate system could *not* deal with rapid inflation made the fixed rate system unsustainable. Accordingly, in 1974, the dollar was taken off the gold standard (that is, it was no longer backed by gold reserves), and most currencies that had not already been allowed to "float" were allowed to do so. As a result, **changing international economic conditions are reflected in the currency exchange rates on a daily basis for most major currencies.**

Under this **"floating" exchange rate system**, currency exchange rates are a function of market conditions (the forces of supply and demand), which in turn are a function of changing economic and political conditions, such as (1) the level of the internal inflation rate, (2) the level of interest rates (usually a function of the inflation rate), (3) the level of the federal spending deficit (or surplus), (4) the level of the trade (balance of payments) deficit or surplus, and (5) the imminence of various civil disorders and wars. Exchange rates determined by market conditions are commonly referred to as either **floating** or **free** rates.

Certain Exceptions to the Use of Floating Rates

Even for countries whose currencies float, however, not all exchanges of foreign currency may take place at market exchange rates. Many countries require that "official" exchange rates be used for (1) certain types of *inflows* of capital (such as investment in plant and equipment) and (2) certain types of *outflows* of capital (such as dividend payments to a foreign parent company). Typically, *official exchange rates* for *inflows* of foreign capital are *more* favorable than market rates, and *outflows* of capital are *less* favorable than market rates.

Consequences of a Floating Exchange Rate System to U.S. Exporters and Importers

When U.S. exporters and importers grant or use credit, respectively, and agree to receive payment or make payment in a foreign currency, respectively, they have **foreign currency exposure.** An entity has foreign currency exposure when it could incur a loss as a result of an adverse change in the exchange rate. A U.S. *exporter* that has a foreign currency *receivable* has an **exposed asset**, that is, an asset exposed to the risk that the exchange rate could change adversely (and thus *lose* value and create a *loss*). A U.S. *importer* that has a foreign currency *payable* has an **exposed liability**, that is, a liability exposed to the risk that the exchange rate could change adversely (and thus *gain* in value and create a *loss*).

Strengthening versus Weakening Currencies

A change in a floating exchange rate is appropriately referred to as a *strengthening or weakening of one currency in relation to another currency.*

Strengthening Currencies

A foreign currency that is **strengthening in value in relation to the dollar becomes *more* expensive to purchase** because more dollars are needed to obtain a unit of that foreign currency. Accordingly, the *direct* exchange rate *increases*. A *weakening* of the dollar has the same effect on the direct rate as does the *strengthening* of the foreign currency.

Weakening Currencies

A foreign currency that is **weakening in value in relation to the dollar becomes *less* expensive to purchase** because fewer dollars are needed to obtain a unit of it. Accordingly, the *direct* exchange rate *decreases*. A *strengthening* of the dollar has the same effect on the direct exchange rate as does the *weakening* of the foreign currency.

A graphic depiction of the effects of strengthening and weakening is shown in the following table:

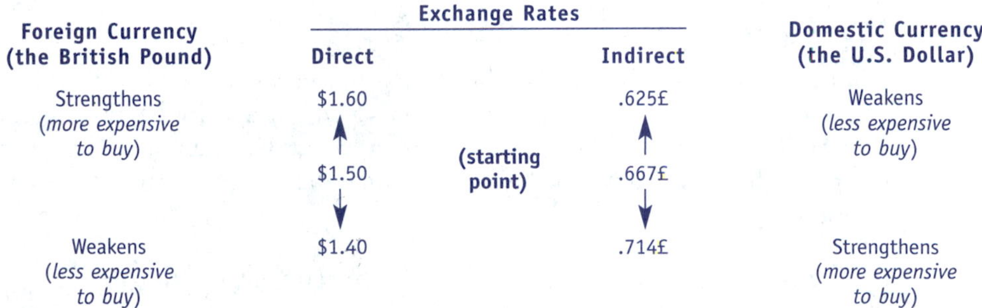

Refer to Illustration 13-1 for a summary of the effect of exchange rate changes.

Government Interventions in the Floating Exchange Rate System

Even under the floating exchange rate system, however, governments often intervene (on an unannounced basis) in the foreign currency markets by buying and selling currencies to stabilize exchange rates or bolster a currency to maintain the desired exchange rate. For this reason, the floating exchange rate system is sometimes called a "*dirty float*."

CASE IN POINT

In 1992, the Bank of England lost $7 billion in a single afternoon trying to maintain the value of its currency.

IV. THE FOREIGN EXCHANGE MARKET

It's an Over-the-Counter Market

Earlier we stated that a company can buy and sell foreign currencies at commercial banks that have foreign exchange departments. Several hundred banks worldwide maintain foreign exchange departments. The collective buying and selling of foreign currencies at these many dispersed locations compose what is referred to as the **foreign exchange market** (hereafter the **FX market**). Consequently, the FX market is an "over-the-counter market"—the conceptual opposite to an organized exchange (such as the New York Stock Exchange where traders gather in one physical location to quote stock prices and execute trades).

ILLUSTRATION 13-1 SUMMARY OF EFFECT OF EXCHANGE RATE CHANGES

I. From the Perspective of the *Foreign Currency*

		REPORTING RESULT FOR A U.S. COMPANY THAT HAS AN	
CHANGE IN FOREIGN CURRENCY	DIRECT RATE	FX RECEIVABLE	FX PAYABLE
Strengthens (*increases* in value)	Goes *up*	*Increases* in value [a **GAIN**]	*Increases* in value [a **LOSS**]
Weakens (*decreases* in value)	Goes *down*	*Decreases* in value [a **LOSS**]	*Decreases* in value [a **GAIN**]

II. From the Perspective of the *U.S. Dollar*

		REPORTING RESULT FOR A U.S. COMPANY THAT HAS AN	
CHANGE IN U.S. DOLLAR	DIRECT RATE	FX RECEIVABLE	FX PAYABLE
Weakens (*decreases* in value)	Goes *up*	*Increases* in value [a **GAIN**]	*Increases* in value [a **LOSS**]
Strengthens (*increases* in value)	Goes *down*	*Decreases* in value [a **LOSS**]	*Decreases* in value [a **GAIN**]

A Huge 24-Hour Market

Because these banks are spread throughout the world and because their business hours overlap, it is possible to buy or sell currencies 24 hours a day. The major FX trading centers are London, New York, Tokyo, Zurich, Singapore, and Hong Kong, which account for about 80% of the FX trading. The daily volume of the FX market (approximately $1.5 trillion per day) makes it the world's largest market.

Who Are the Players in the FX Market?

In general, the players in the FX market include (1) importers that have agreed to pay for goods in the currency of their vendors, (2) exporters that have agreed to receive payment in the currency of their customers, (3) portfolio managers of funds that invest in foreign stocks and bonds, (4) central banks of governments that intervene (usually unsuccessfully) to influence market prices, (5) tourists, and (6) commercial banks.[5]

The Importance of Interbank Trading

The commercial banks, whose currency traders make the FX market, continually trade currencies among themselves in interbank trading, an activity that is an integral part of making the FX market. So integral is interbank trading to "making the market" that roughly 85% of the trading that occurs in the FX market is interbank trading, while less than 15% is commercial business. The interbank trading activity keeps the market liquid and keeps prices announced by the various FX traders from diverging greatly from one another.

What Does *Making the Market* Mean?

The FX traders of the commercial banks "make the market" because they create it by (1) quoting bid and asked prices and (2) executing trades at those prices for orders placed. Thus they make possible the immediate execution of orders from buyers and sellers of currencies because, as market makers, they are willing to take the other side of the transaction themselves. The FX traders, as a group, make a profit because they provide a basic service to the external participants in the market: the importers, exporters, fund portfolio managers, and tourists. As a group, the FX traders also make a profit if a government central bank intervenes in the marketplace and loses money trying to support the price of a currency. Because of interbank trading, the FX traders compete against each other and try to profit from their interbank trading.

ETHICS

Exporting Products Banned in the U.S.

Tough federal environmental rules and health concerns have largely eliminated lead from gasoline in the U.S. (gasoline emissions being the greatest single contributor to the buildup of lead in humans according to the EPA). U.S. laws, however, do *not* bar U.S. companies from exporting leaded gasoline and lead additives. Annual U.S. exports of lead additives are near 125 million pounds. The World Health Organization has warned that chronic exposure to even low levels of lead can reduce birth weight, impair mental development and hearing, lower IQ, and seriously affect a child's ability to learn.

Questions

1. Is the exporting of lead an ethical issue or a legal issue?
2. Would you accept a job from a company that exported lead additives to Latin America, Asia, and Africa (areas that currently do *not* require unleaded gasoline)?

---

[5] Also part of the FX market in a peripheral manner are *FX brokers*, which are commercial firms that earn their profit by matching commercial buyers and sellers. Thus these FX brokers (a small part of the FX market) compete with the FX departments of the commercial banks.

V. TRANSLATING IMPORTING AND EXPORTING TRANSACTIONS

The currency in which a transaction is to be settled must be stipulated in each foreign transaction. Whether a foreign transaction is to be settled in a foreign currency or in U.S. dollars is negotiated at the inception of each foreign transaction.[6]

Measured versus *Denominated*

When a transaction is to be settled by the receipt or payment of a fixed amount of a specified currency, the receivable or payable, respectively, is said to be *denominated* in that currency. When a transaction is to be settled by the receipt or payment of a fixed amount of currency other than the U.S. dollar, from the perspective of a U.S. reporting entity, the receivable or payable is *denominated* in a foreign currency. A party to a transaction *measures* and records the transaction in the currency of the country in which that party is located. Thus one of the parties has a transaction that is *measured* and *denominated* in its *own* currency, and the other party has a transaction that is measured in its own currency but *denominated* in a *different* currency. The following examples illustrate this distinction:

1. A U.S. importer purchases goods on credit from a Swiss exporter, with payment to be made in a specified number of Swiss francs. The domestic importer *measures and records* the transaction in dollars, and the Swiss exporter *measures and records* the transaction in Swiss francs. The domestic importer's liability is *denominated* in a foreign currency, the Swiss franc. The Swiss exporter's receivable is *denominated* in Swiss francs. (If the terms of the transaction called for payment to be made in dollars, the transaction would be measured and denominated in dollars, from the perspective of the importer.)
2. A Swiss subsidiary of a U.S. company purchases goods on credit from another Swiss company, with payment to be made in a specified number of Swiss francs. The Swiss subsidiary *measures* the asset acquired and the liability incurred in Swiss francs. The Swiss subsidiary's liability is *not* denominated in a foreign currency because the liability is *denominated* in Swiss francs. From the perspective of the U.S. parent, however, the Swiss subsidiary's liability is *denominated* in a foreign currency because the liability is *not* payable in dollars.
3. A Swiss subsidiary of a U.S. company purchases goods on credit from an Italian company, with the payment to be made in European euros. The Swiss subsidiary *measures* the asset acquired and liability incurred in Swiss francs. The Swiss subsidiary's liability is *denominated* in a foreign currency. From the perspective of the U.S. parent, the Swiss subsidiary's liability is *denominated* in a foreign currency because the liability is *not* payable in dollars.

Foreign *Currency* Transactions versus Foreign Transactions

For each international transaction, both parties have a *foreign transaction*. Because payment is usually specified in only one currency, however, only one of the parties can more specifically refer to the transaction as a **foreign currency transaction**. Thus all foreign currency transactions are foreign transactions, but *not* all foreign transactions can be called foreign *currency* transactions.

Differentiating Accounts Requiring Settlement in Foreign Currency

In discussing accounts requiring settlement in a foreign currency, it is convenient to differentiate these accounts in some manner. Accordingly, in discussions *not* involving a specific example or

[6] No precise numbers are available as to the percentage of U.S. world trade that requires settlement in foreign currencies versus U.S. dollars. Furthermore, inquiries to foreign exchange traders reveal that no general rule can be given, such as the majority of U.S. exports are denominated in dollars and the majority of U.S. imports are denominated in foreign currencies. The reasons that transactions are denominated in *dollars* versus a *foreign currency* are numerous and may be found in international finance texts.

illustration, we use the designation "FX" (foreign exchange) preceding the amount, such as FX Accounts Payable and FX Accounts Receivable. When dealing with a specific foreign currency as in an illustration, however, we use the symbol for that currency, such as £ for the British pound, instead of FX.

Understanding the Relevant Dates

When a U.S. company makes or receives payment in dollars, no special accounting procedures are necessary because no accounting issues exist. When the U.S. company pays or receives in the foreign currency, however, two accounting issues arise. Before discussing these issues, we must define the following four dates that may be involved in a foreign currency transaction:

1. **The order (or commitment) date.** On this date, the purchase or sales order is issued. If noncancellable, a contract effectively has been entered into.
2. **The transaction date.** On this date, the transaction is initially recorded on the books, for example, recording a sale or a purchase of inventory.
3. **The intervening financial reporting dates.** Such dates occur between the transaction date and the settlement date. A transaction recorded on November 20, 2005, and settled on January 10, 2006, has two intervening financial reporting dates, assuming that monthly financial statements are prepared. Such dates exist only for transactions in which credit terms are granted and used.
4. **The settlement date.** On this date, payment is made. The customary payment practice for foreign transactions is to make an international **bank wire transfer.** In a bank wire transfer, the paying party authorizes its bank to subtract the amount being paid from its checking account. The paying party's bank then telexes the receiving party's bank to add to the receiving party's bank account the identical amount, as translated into the receiving party's currency using the spot rate. **Thus, no currency physically changes hands or physically moves into or out of a country in a bank wire transfer.** (Instead of the domestic importer and the foreign vendor having a payable and a receivable, respectively, the two banks now have a payable and a receivable with each other, for which they will settle with each other.)

Conceptual Issues

In foreign currency transactions, the first accounting issue pertains to how the transaction should be recorded in dollars at the *transaction date.* Accountants generally agree that the transaction should be recorded at the transaction date using the exchange rate in effect at that date. For an *importing* transaction, therefore, the *acquired asset* is initially recorded at the dollar amount needed to purchase the amount of foreign currency that would settle the transaction at the *transaction date.* For an *exporting* transaction, the *export sale* is recorded at the dollar amount that would be received from converting the foreign currency into dollars if full payment were made at the *transaction date.*

If credit terms are *not* granted, no other accounting issues exist.[7] If credit terms *are* granted and used, the following additional accounting issues arise:

1. **Whether to make adjustments at *intervening financial reporting dates.*** If the exchange rate used to record the transaction at the transaction date has changed between the *transaction date* and an *intervening financial reporting date*, should the receivable or payable pertaining to the unsettled portion of the transaction be adjusted to reflect the current rate at such *intervening financial reporting date*?
2. **How to report exchange rate change adjustments.** If the transaction is settled at an amount different from that at which it was initially recorded, how should the difference be recorded?

[7] When credit is *not* granted and cash is not paid in advance (via a bank wire transfer), payment is usually made using either a *letter of credit* (using a bank) or a *draft* (also referred to as a *bill of exchange*), which is an alternative to a letter of credit. Credit is usually given cautiously in foreign transactions because collection efforts in foreign countries can be extremely costly, time consuming, and frustrating.

With respect to the *first* issue, most accountants agree that any unsettled portion of the transaction represented by a payable or receivable should be adjusted at intervening financial reporting dates to reflect the exchange rate in effect at those dates. It makes sense to carry the receivable or payable at the amount of dollars that would be received or paid, respectively, if the transaction were settled on that date. (**This is essentially *current-value* accounting—the most relevant of all reporting bases.**) There are two viewpoints concerning the *second* issue:

1. Under the **one-transaction perspective,** all aspects of the transaction are viewed as part of a *single transaction.* A company's commitment to pay or receive foreign currency is considered a necessary and inseparable part of the transaction to purchase or sell goods, respectively. The amount initially recorded at the *transaction date* is considered an estimate until the final settlement. As a result, **the initially recorded cost of goods acquired or revenue is subsequently adjusted** for any difference between the amount recorded at the *transaction date* and the amount at which the transaction is ultimately settled.
2. Under the **two-transaction perspective,** the commitment to pay or receive foreign currency is considered a *separate transaction* from the purchase or sale of goods. The decision to grant or use credit is considered a decision separate from that of purchasing or selling goods. As a result, any difference between the amount initially recorded at the *transaction date* and the amount at which the transaction is ultimately settled is considered a foreign currency transaction gain or loss—**no adjustment is made to the initially recorded cost of goods acquired or revenues recorded pertaining to goods sold,** as the case may be.

From either perspective, the risk in a foreign currency transaction from potential adverse exchange rate changes can be eliminated by (1) *not* granting or using credit or (2) using a technique called *hedging* (discussed in Chapter 14).

FASB Adopts the Two-Transaction Perspective

The Financial Accounting Standards Board rejected the *one-transaction* perspective in *FAS 52* (as it did in *FAS 8*) on the grounds that the consequences of the risks associated with foreign currency transactions should be accounted for separately from the purchase or sale of goods. Thus the requirements of *FAS 52* reflect the *two-transaction perspective*, and a domestic importer or exporter would account for such transactions as follows:

1. At the *transaction date*, measure and record in dollars each asset, liability, revenue, expense, gain, or loss arising from the transaction using the *current exchange rate* (the rate that could be used to settle the transaction at that date).
2. At each *intervening financial reporting date*, adjust the recorded balances of any foreign currency receivable or payable to reflect the current exchange rate (the rate at which the receivable or payable could be settled at that date).
3. Report **in the income statement** a *foreign currency transaction gain or loss* resulting from (1) adjustments made at any intervening *financial reporting* dates and (2) any adjustments from settling the transaction at an amount different from that recorded at the latest *intervening financial reporting date* (or the *transaction date* when there are no *intervening financial reporting dates*).

These various dates are shown graphically in Illustration 13-2.

In summary, **the cost or the revenue arising from a transaction should be determined only once: when the transaction is initially recorded.** The fact that credit terms are granted should *not* result in a later adjustment to the asset or service acquired, or to the revenue initially recorded, if the exchange rate changes between the transaction date and the settlement date. Any higher or lower amount than that initially recorded represents a gain or loss that could have been avoided had the transaction been fully paid for when it occurred. Thus any higher or lower amount to be received or paid involves a decision to grant or exercise credit, which should be charged or credited to income in the period in which the exchange rate changes.

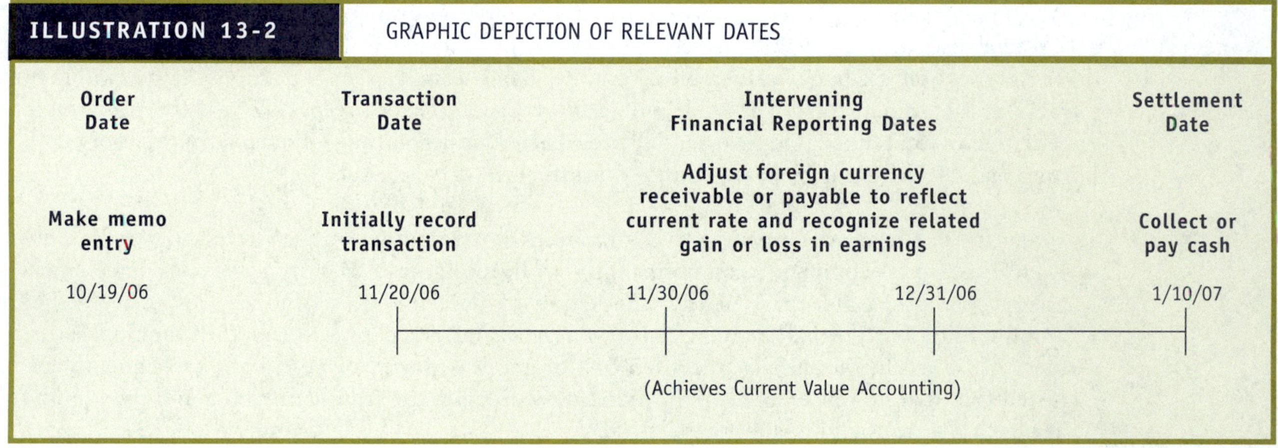

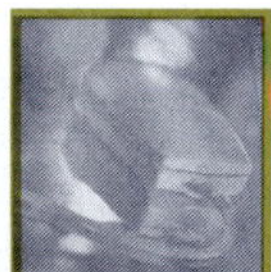

Check Point

A domestic *exporter* sold inventory to a foreign company on credit, with the transaction denominated in the foreign currency. Between the transaction date and the settlement date, the U.S. dollar strengthened. There was no intervening financial reporting date. The exporter should account for the change in the exchange rate as

a. A decrease to the initially recorded sales amount.
b. An increase to the initially recorded sales amount.
c. A gain or loss recognized currently in the income statement.
d. A gain or loss to be deferred.

Answer: c

Comprehensive Illustration

Importing and Exporting Transactions

Assume that a domestic company has the following importing and exporting transactions with suppliers and customers in Great Britain:

1. On December 11, 2006, inventory was acquired from Vendor A for 100,000 pounds. Payment is due in pounds on January 10, 2007.
2. Inventory is sold to Customer X for 200,000 pounds on December 21, 2006. Payment is due in pounds on January 20, 2007.

Illustration 13-3 shows these transactions as initially recorded and as adjusted at the intervening financial reporting date (December 31, 2006). Payments are made as required. The direct exchange rates (spot rates) for the applicable dates in December 2006 and January 2007 (when the pound was strengthening) are as follows:

December 11, 2006	December 21, 2006	December 31, 2006	January 10, 2007	January 20, 2007
$1.50	$1.52	$1.55	$1.59	$1.60

Review Points for Illustration 13-3. Note the following:

1. **Netting.** For 2006, a net FX *gain* of $1,000 ($6,000 *gain* on the receivable – $5,000 *loss* on the payable) is reported in the income statement. For 2007, the year in which settlement occurred, a net FX *gain* of $6,000 ($10,000 *gain* on the receivable – $4,000 *loss* on the payable) is reported **in the income statement.**
2. **Apportioning the transaction's exchange gains and losses.** The total gain on the *exporting* transaction is $16,000 (cash of $320,000 received minus the initially recorded sales amount of

ILLUSTRATION 13-3 RECORDING FOREIGN CURRENCY TRANSACTIONS

Entries Related to Vendor A

DECEMBER 11, 2006

Inventory (or Purchases)	$150,000	
£ Accounts Payable		$150,000

To record purchase of inventory. (£100,000 × $1.50 = $150,000)

DECEMBER 31, 2006

FX Loss	$5,000	
£ Accounts Payable		$5,000

To adjust foreign currency payable to the current spot rate.
($1.55 – $1.50 = $.05) ($.05 × £100,000 = $5,000)

JANUARY 10, 2007

FX Loss	$4,000	
£ Accounts Payable		$4,000

To adjust foreign currency payable to the current spot rate.
($1.59 – $1.55 = $.04) ($.04 × £100,000 = $4,000)

£ Accounts Payable	$159,000	
Cash		$159,000

To record payment to vendor via a bank wire transfer.

Shortcut approach at settlement date. Companies often take a shortcut approach of *not* adjusting the FX Accounts Payable account at the settlement date. Thus the following lone entry can be made at the settlement date (rather than the two entries shown for 1/10/07):

£ Accounts Payable	$155,000	
FX Loss	$4,000	
Cash		$159,000

Entries Related to Customer X

DECEMBER 21, 2006

£ Accounts Receivable	$304,000	
Sales		$304,000

To record sale. (£200,000 × $1.52 = $304,000)

DECEMBER 31, 2006

£ Accounts Receivable	$6,000	
FX Gain		$6,000

To adjust foreign currency receivable to the current spot rate.
($1.55 – $1.52 = $.03) ($.03 × £200,000 = $6,000)

JANUARY 20, 2007

£ Accounts Receivable	$10,000	
FX Gain		$10,000

To adjust foreign currency receivable to the current spot rate.
($1.60 – $1.55 = $.05) ($.05 × £200,000 = $10,000)

Cash	$320,000	
£ Accounts Receivable		$320,000

To record collection from customer **via a bank wire transfer.**
(£200,000 × $1.60 = $320,000)

Shortcut approach at settlement date. Companies often take a shortcut approach of *not* adjusting the FX Accounts Receivable account at the settlement date. Thus the following lone entry can be made at the settlement date (rather than the two entries shown for 1/20/07):

Cash	$320,000	
£ Accounts Receivable		$310,000
FX Gain		$10,000

$304,000). However, the financial reporting requirements cause the company to recognize $6,000 in 2006 and $10,000 in 2007. Likewise, the total loss on the *importing* transaction was $9,000 ($159,000 cash paid – the initially recorded purchase amount of $150,000), of which $5,000 was recognized in 2006 and $4,000 was recognized in 2007.

3. **Unrealized nature.** FX gains and losses recognized in the income statement at intervening financial reporting dates (thus, on unsettled accounts) are **unrealized**—a fact deemed irrelevant by the FASB. The FASB concluded that recognizing unrealized gains and losses in the period in which they occur would better serve financial statement users even though reversals might occur in subsequent periods. This is the only area of *FAS 52* in which unrealized gains and losses can be recognized in the income statement.[8]
4. **One-sidedness exposure.** When one of the parties to a foreign transaction incurs an FX gain or loss, the other party does *not* incur an opposite, offsetting FX loss or gain because that other party does *not* transact in a foreign currency. Accordingly, foreign currency transaction gains and losses are one sided.
5. **Tax treatment.** FX *gains* are taxable **when realized**, that is, at the settlement date—the point when the transaction is considered "closed" for tax-reporting purposes. Likewise, FX *losses* are tax deductible when realized (at the settlement date). Thus *temporary differences* between *financial reporting* and *tax reporting* will exist at *intervening financial reporting dates* for unrealized gains and losses recognized for financial reporting purposes. Consequently, deferred tax liabilities and deferred tax assets must be recognized.

In Illustration 13-3, in which the direct exchange *increased*, the domestic *importer* had a *loss*, but the domestic *exporter* had a *gain*. Thus these parties had different concerns and desires as to the future direction of the direct exchange rate. These conflicting concerns and desires of domestic importers and exporters are summarized in Illustration 13-4.

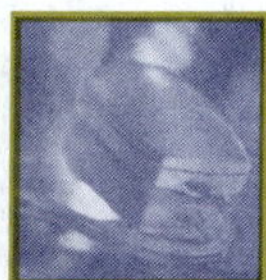

CHECK POINTS

On 12/10/06, a domestic *importer* purchased inventory on credit from a foreign vendor, with payment to be made in the foreign currency. The direct exchange rate was $.80 on 12/10/06, and $.83 on 12/31/06, (the importer's year-end). On 1/5/07 (the settlement date), the direct exchange rate was $.79. At 12/31/06, the importer should report

a. An increase to the amount initially recorded for inventory.
b. A decrease to the amount initially recorded for inventory.
c. A gain or loss to be deferred.
d. A gain in its 2006 income statement.
e. A loss in its 2006 income statement.

Answer: e

ILLUSTRATION 13-4 CONFLICTING CONCERNS AND DESIRES OF DOMESTIC IMPORTERS AND EXPORTERS

	Account Exposed	Nature of Concern	Desires
Domestic importers	FX Accounts Payable	Direct rate increases[a]	Direct rate decreases[b]
Domestic exporters	FX Accounts Receivable	Direct rate decreases[b]	Direct rate increases[a]

[a] Caused by foreign currency strengthening and U.S. dollar weakening.
[b] Caused by foreign currency weakening and U.S. dollar strengthening.

[8] Recall from intermediate accounting that under FASB *Statement No. 115*, "Accounting for Certain Investments in Debt and Equity Securities," debt and equity securities that have a *readily determinable fair value* are also valued on a current value basis and have their unrealized gains and losses reported either in the income statement (for "trading" securities) or in *other comprehensive income* (for "available-for-sale" securities).

On 11/11/06, a domestic *exporter* sold inventory on credit to a Japanese customer for 980,000 yen (the billing currency is yen). On this date, the yen was quoted at 100 to the dollar. On 12/31/06 (the exporter's year-end), the yen was quoted at 98 to the dollar. At 12/31/06, the exporter should report

a. An increase to the initially recorded sales amount.
b. A decrease to the initially recorded sales amount.
c. A gain or loss to be deferred.
d. A gain in its 2006 income statement.
e. A loss in its 2006 income statement.

Answer: d

VI. Differential Rates of Inflation: The Major Long-Term Cause of Exchange Rate Changes

Many economists (as well as the popular press as represented by *The Wall Street Journal*)[9] recognize the **purchasing power parity (PPP) theory** as the best explanation of major changes in exchange rates over long periods. Moreover, financial executives of most multinational corporations understand PPP.

Under PPP (which follows from the "law of one price"), the differential rate of inflation between two countries can be expected to result over the long term in an equal but opposite change in the exchange rate between the two currencies. For example, assume that on January 1, 2006, the direct exchange rate between the U.S. dollar and the British pound is £1 equals $1. Also assume that on this date, a bushel of wheat can be purchased in Great Britain for £1 and in the United States for $1. Thus British citizens will pay the same (one) price (£1) for a bushel of wheat, regardless of whether the wheat is purchased in Great Britain or in the United States.

For 2006, assume an inflation rate of 100% in Great Britain and zero in the United States. Accordingly, at December 31, 2006, a bushel of wheat in Great Britain should cost £2. If the exchange rate does *not* change in 2006, a British citizen will be able to purchase wheat at two prices: £2 if purchased in Great Britain and £1 if purchased in the United States (which would be convertible into $1). Then disregarding the effects of transportation costs, tariffs, taxes, and so on, British citizens will most likely purchase the wheat in the United States, thereby saving £1 per bushel. This shift in purchasing will create more demand for U.S. dollars, however, and will cause the value of the dollar to rise against the pound. Under the theory, the exchange rate by December 31, 2004, will adjust so that there is only one price to British citizens; £1 will become equal to $0.50. **Because pounds can be spent only in Great Britain, U.S. farmers effectively will demand 2£ per bushel of wheat so that they will have enough pounds to buy something of comparable value that is produced in Great Britain.**

Studies have shown that (1) in the short term, factors other than differential rates of inflation may have greater influence in determining exchange rates[10] and (2) in the long term, the effects of the other factors tend to reverse or cancel out, and eventually exchange rates closely approximate the results expected under PPP. An important question arises: How long is "in the long term"? A recent study found "that purchasing power parity holds in the long run for each of the [16] currencies studied and that the typical half-life of shock to parity is approximately three

[9] "Dollar Turmoil" (editorial), *The Wall Street Journal*, May 23, 1989, p. A22.

[10] For many South American countries that have highly inflationary economies, however, inflation (more than 1,000% annually for some countries) is the primary short-term cause of the continual weakening of their currencies. (Inflation became so high in Argentina a few years ago that it became necessary to pay employees at noon and at the end of each day.)

years."[11] An application of PPP theory for the British pound for the 15 years ended December 31, 1995, is shown in Illustration 13-5. A more extensive discussion of PPP theory may be found in textbooks on international finance.

Review Points for Illustration 13-5. Note the following:

1. With Great Britain continually experiencing higher inflation than the United States, the spot rate should trend downward under PPP theory; this trend has occurred as expected.
2. At December 31, 1995, the actual spot rate was relatively close to the expected rates under PPP theory.
3. The absolute average year-end percentage deviation from results expected under PPP theory is 22%, which is not so unreasonably high as to suggest that PPP theory is not valid.

ILLUSTRATION 13-5 AN APPLICATION OF PPP THEORY TO THE BRITISH POUND FOR THE FIFTEEN YEARS ENDED DECEMBER 31, 1995

	Annual Inflation				Actual Rate Over (Under) Expected Rate	
Date	U.S.	U.K.	Actual Direct Exchange Rate	Expected Direct Exchange Rate under PPP Theory	Amount	Percent
1-1-81			$2.40			
1981	9.6%	11.5%				
12-31-81			1.92	$2.35	$ (.43)	(18)%
1982	6.5	7.7				
12-31-82			1.62	2.33	(.71)	(30)%
1983	3.8	5.3				
12-31-83			1.45	2.30	(.85)	(37)%
1984	3.8	4.6				
12-31-84			1.16	2.27	(1.11)	(49)%
1985	3.0	5.7				
12-31-85			1.45	2.22	(.77)	(35)%
1986	2.6	3.5				
12-31-86			1.48	2.20	(.72)	(33)%
1987	3.1	5.0				
12-31-87			1.89	2.16	(.27)	(12)%
1988	3.3	6.5				
12-31-88			1.80	2.10	(.30)	(14)%
1989	4.1	6.9				
12-31-89			1.61	2.04	(.43)	(21)%
1990	4.1	6.8				
12-31-90			1.93	1.99	(.06)	(3)%
1991	4.0	6.2				
12-31-91			1.86	1.95	(.09)	(5)%
1992	2.9	4.0				
12-31-92			1.51	1.93	(.42)	(22)%
1993	2.7	4.2				
12-31-93			1.48	1.90	(.42)	(22)%
1994	2.7	3.7				
12-31-94			1.56	1.88	(.32)	(17)%
1995	2.5	3.4				
12-31-95			1.54	1.86	(.32)	(17)%
Cum.	58.7%	85.0%	Average annual deviation		$ (.47)	(22)%

[11] Francis X. Diebold, Steven Husted, and Mark Rush, "Real Exchange Rates under the Gold Standard," *Journal of Political Economy* 99, no. 6 (1991): 1253–1271. This is a study of 16 exchange rates covering more than a century. For each of the 16 exchange rates, it was found that purchasing power parity theory holds in the long term. Other studies also support PPP. For example, see Gayton's study and Treuherz's study, which are both cited in Appendix E to the FASB's 1973 discussion memorandum that preceded *FAS 8*. Other studies are cited in Professor Thomas W. Hall's 1983 article, "Inflation and Rates of Exchange: Support for *FAS 52*," in the summer 1983 issue of the *Journal of Accounting, Auditing & Finance*.

Comprehensive Illustration

Analyzing an Exchange Rate Change Using PPP: Both Countries Have Inflation, and Noninflationary Factors Exist

How to analyze and explain a change in the exchange rate for a more realistic situation in which (1) the United States has 5% inflation, (2) a foreign country has 10% inflation, and (3) noninflationary factors exist is shown in Illustration 13-6.

Review Points for Illustration 13-6. Note the following:

1. *Foreign* inflation drives the direct exchange rate *down*.
2. *Domestic* inflation drives the direct exchange rate *up*.
3. The relationship of the U.S. price index before and after inflation (1.00:1.05 above) is the relationship that exists between the actual exchange rate prior to inflation and the expected exchange rate under PPP ($2.20:$2.31 above). For foreign countries, this relationship is inverse, not direct.

ILLUSTRATION 13-6 ANALYZING AN EXCHANGE RATE CHANGE USING PPP—BOTH COUNTRIES HAVE INFLATION AND NONINFLATIONARY FACTORS EXIST

	Direct Exchange Rate
I. HANDLING *FOREIGN* INFLATION FIRST APPROACH:	
Actual rate, 1/1/06	$2.20
Less: *Decrease* expected because of the foreign country's 10% inflation rate ($2.20/110% = $2.00; $2.20 − $2.00 = $.20)	(.20)
Subtotal	$2.00
Plus: *Increase* expected because of the U.S. 5% inflation rate ($2.00 × 5%)	.10
Expected end-of-year rate (under PPP)	$2.10
Plus or minus: Noninflationary factors (forced)	(.03)[a]
Actual rate, 12/31/06	$2.07
II. HANDLING DOMESTIC INFLATION FIRST APPROACH:	
Actual rate, 1/1/06	$2.20
Plus: *Increase* expected because of U.S. 5% inflation rate ($2.20 × 5%)	.11
Subtotal	$2.31
Less: *Decrease* expected because of the foreign country's 10% inflation rate ($2.31/110% = $2.10; $2.31 − $2.10 = $.21)	(.21)
Expected end-of-year rate (under PPP)	$2.10
Plus or minus: Noninflationary factors (forced)	(.03)[a]
Actual rate, 12/31/06	$2.07

III. FORMULA APPROACH:

$$\text{Beginning Rate} \times \frac{1 + \text{Domestic Inflation Rate}}{1 + \text{Foreign Inflation Rate}} = \text{Expected Ending Rate}$$

For the above example, the formula calculation is as follows:

$$\$2.20 \times \frac{1.05}{1.10} = \$2.10$$

[a] In international finance texts, this difference is called **the "real" change in the exchange rate**, even though it may be of a temporary delayed nature (a lag under PPP). The $.10 decrease ($2.20 − $2.10) attributable to inflation effects (both domestic and foreign) is called **the "nominal" (in name only) change.**

END-OF-CHAPTER REVIEW

Summary of Key Points

1. The Foreign Corrupt Practices Act of 1977 prohibits U.S. firms from offering funds (bribes) to foreign officials in an effort to *obtain* or *retain* business.
2. The significant inefficiencies and barriers that result from the substantial diversity of accounting standards that exist worldwide have led to major efforts to develop international accounting standards ("world GAAP").
3. The *International Accounting Standards Board* is the current organization in charge of issuing international accounting standards.
4. Compliance with international accounting standards (which are *less* rigorous than U.S. accounting standards) is voluntary.
5. The ultimate objective is to develop a superior "world GAAP" that will be accepted and used by all countries.
6. A **floating exchange rate system** is currently used; thus exchange rates are determined daily by the forces of **supply and demand.**
7. **Inflation** is the major long-run cause of exchange rate changes, as explained by the **purchasing power parity theory.**
8. **Foreign inflation** causes the direct exchange rate to **go down. Domestic inflation** causes the direct exchange rate to **go up.**
9. In an international transaction, the party that must make or receive payment in other than its own local currency has a **foreign transaction** that will result in a **foreign currency transaction.** (The other party has only a foreign transaction.)
10. **Foreign currency transaction exposure** effectively begins when a commitment is established as a result of issuing a purchase order or receiving a sales order.
11. The FASB adopted the **two-transaction perspective** for importing and exporting transactions; thus the decision to grant credit or to take advantage of credit **is accounted for separately from the accounting for the item to be received or delivered.**
12. The critical dates for accounting purposes under *FAS 52* are (1) the commitment date, (2) the transaction date, (3) any **intervening financial reporting dates,** and (4) the settlement date.
13. **Between the transaction date and the settlement date,** an FX receivable and an FX payable are *exposed* because they gain or lose value as the exchange rate changes.
14. FX receivables and FX payables are always adjusted at intervening financial reporting dates to the spot rate—**thus achieving current-value accounting,** the best of all reporting bases.
15. Adjustments to FX receivables and FX payables at intervening financial reporting dates result in **unrealized FX gains or losses** that are to be **reported currently in the income statement.**

Glossary of New Terms

Bank wire transfer A procedure to settle FX receivables and payables by using a bank to electronically make settlement, negating the need to physically handle foreign currencies.

Conversion The physical change of one currency for another currency.

Exchange gain or loss A gain or loss on a foreign currency payable or receivable that arises because of a change in the exchange rate that occurs between the *transaction* date and the *settlement date.*

Exposed asset A recorded asset that is exposed to the risk that the exchange rate could change adversely.

Exposed liability A recorded liability that is exposed to the risk that the exchange rate could change adversely.

Foreign currency exposure The risk that an entity could incur a loss as a result of an adverse change in the exchange rate.

Foreign currency transactions Transactions whose terms require settlement in a *foreign* currency.

Foreign exchange market (FX market) An over-the-counter market comprising hundreds of currency traders of commercial banks who buy and sell currencies at prices they quote. These FX traders "make the market."

Forward rate (future rate) A rate quoted for future delivery of currencies to be exchanged (usually up to one year).

Purchasing power parity theory An explanation of why exchange rates change over long periods of time, the cause being the differential rate of inflation between two countries.

Settlement date The date at which a receivable is collected or a payable is paid.

Spot rate The exchange rate for immediate delivery of currencies to be exchanged.

Transaction date The date at which a transaction (such as the purchase or sale of inventory or services) is recordable in accounting records in accordance with GAAP.

Translation Expressing in U.S. dollars amounts denominated in a foreign currency.

Assignment Material

Review Questions

1. What is the name of the organization that issues international accounting standards? Where is this organization located? What was its predecessor organization?
2. What are the expected advantages of all countries complying with international GAAP?
3. Are existing international standards of a *higher* or *lower* quality than U.S. accounting standards?
4. How many international standards have been issued to date?
5. Are the financial statements of foreign registrants who use international accounting standards accepted by the Securities and Exchange Commission? Why or why not?
6. How do fluctuations in the exchange rates impact *domestic exporters*?
7. What is the difference between *conversion* and *translation*?
8. What is the *direct* quotation rate? The *indirect* quotation rate?
9. What are *floating* or *free* exchange rates?
10. What are *fixed* or *official* exchange rates?
11. What is meant when a currency is said to be *strengthening*? When a currency is *weakening*?
12. What is *purchasing power parity theory*?
13. Is purchasing power parity theory a *cause* of exchange rate changes?
14. What effect does *foreign* inflation have on exchange rates? What effect does *domestic* inflation have on exchange rates?
15. What does *denominated* mean?
16. What is the distinction between a *foreign transaction* and *foreign currency transaction*?
17. What four dates can exist in an importing or exporting foreign currency transaction?
18. Summarize the *two-transaction* perspective.
19. Summarize the *one-transaction* perspective.

20. How do *bank wire transfers* work? Does currency physically move between countries?

21. What are the concerns and desires of a domestic *exporter*? What are they for a domestic *importer*?

Exercises

E 13-1 **Expressing Exchange Rates** On 1/1/06, 100,000 Mex$ could be converted into $40,000. On 12/31/06, 100,000 Mex$ could be converted into $50,000.

Required
1. Express the relationship between the two currencies at each date directly and indirectly.
2. Did the peso strengthen or weaken during 2006? Did the dollar strengthen or weaken during 2006?

E 13-2 **Identifying Foreign Currency Exposure** Comcoe has many importing and exporting transactions that require settlement in foreign currency (often referred to as *local currency units* or LCUs). Credit terms are granted and used.

Required
1. Should Comcoe be concerned about whether the direct exchange rate will go up or down?
2. Indicate in the following table what the foreign currency exposure concern should be:

		Whether the Dollar Will		Whether the LCU Will	
Transaction	Billing Currency	Strengthen	Weaken	Strengthen	Weaken
Importing	Dollar	______	______	______	______
Importing	LCU	______	______	______	______
Exporting	Dollar	______	______	______	______
Exporting	LCU	______	______	______	______

E 13-3 **Determining Reportable Amounts on Exporting Transaction** On 9/9/06, Sella Inc. accepted a noncancellable merchandise sales order from an Australian firm. The contract price was 100,000 $A. The merchandise was delivered on 12/14/06. The invoice was dated 12/11/06, the shipping date (FOB shipping point). Full payment was received on 1/22/07. The spot direct exchange rates for the Australian dollar on the respective dates are as follows:

September 9, 2006	December 11, 2006	December 14, 2006	December 31, 2006	January 22, 2007
$.75	$.78	$.77	$.73	$.725

Required
1. What is the reportable sales amount in the 2006 income statement?
2. What is the reportable FX gain or loss amount in the 2006 income statement?
3. What is the reported value of the receivable from the customer at 12/31/06?

E 13-4 **Determining Reportable Amounts on Importing Transaction** On 9/3/06, Bycora placed a noncancellable purchase order with a Swedish company for a custom-built machine. The contract price was 1,000,000 SKr. The machine was delivered on 12/23/06. The invoice was dated 11/13/06, the shipping date (FOB shipping point). The vendor was paid on 1/7/07. The spot direct exchange rates for krona on the respective dates are as follows:

September 3, 2006	November 13, 2006	December 23, 2006	December 31, 2006	January 7, 2007
$.20	$.21	$.22	$.23	$.24

Required
1. What amount is the capitalizable cost of the equipment?
2. What is the reportable FX gain or loss amount in Bycora's 2006 income statement?
3. What is the reported value of the payable to the vendor at 12/31/06?

Problems

P 13-1 **Importing and Exporting Transactions** During July 2006, Portex had the following transactions with foreign businesses:

Date	Nature of Transaction	Billing Currency	Exchange Rate (Direct)
Vendor A			
July 1, 2006	Imported merchandise costing 100,000 pesos from Mexico City wholesaler	Pesos	$.70
July 10, 2006	Paid 40% of amount owed.		.71
July 31, 2006	Paid remaining amount owed		.66
Customer A			
July 15, 2006	Sold merchandise for 50,000 euros to French wholesaler	Euros	$.80
July 20, 2006	Received 20% payment		.75
July 30, 2006	Received remaining amount owed.		.76

Required Prepare journal entries for these transactions.

P 13-2 **Importing and Exporting Transactions** During June and July 2006, Quartex (which reports on a calendar-year basis and issues quarterly financial statements) had the following transactions with foreign businesses:

Date	Nature of Transaction	Billing Currency	Exchange Rate (Direct)
Vendor A			
June 15, 2006	Imported merchandise costing 100,000 Canadian dollars from Canadian manufacturer.	Canadian dollars	$.80
July 15, 2006	Paid entire amount owed.		.77
Customer A			
June 20, 2006	Sold merchandise for 200,000 Singapore dollars to Singapore retailer	Singapore dollars	$.650
July 10, 2006	Received full payment.		.640

On 6/30/06, the spot exchange rate for Canadian dollars was $0.79 and for Singapore dollars was $.643.

Required Prepare journal entries for these transactions. (Be sure to prepare journal entries at 6/30/06 when necessary.)

P 13-3 **Accounting for a Travel Allowance** On 12/26/06, the vice-president of marketing of Travcor was given a $6,000 travel advance for a 10-day trip to the United Kingdom. On that date, the vice-president converted the $6,000 into 12,000 pounds. During this 10-day trip, the pound steadily weakened against the dollar. The exchange rate at 12/31/06 was 1 pound equals $0.48. On 1/5/07, the vice-president returned and submitted to the company cashier 1,100 pounds and receipts for 10,900 pounds that he had spent. On this date, the exchange rate was 1 pound equals $0.42. Of the 10,900 pounds spent during the trip, 5,700 had been spent by 12/31/06.

Required Prepare all entries required at 12/31/06 and 1/5/07 in connection with this travel advance.

P 13-4 **Analyzing an Exchange Rate Change** Information concerning the United States and Mexico for 2006 follows:

Direct exchange rate on 1/1/06	$.600
Direct exchange rate on 12/31/06	$.540
U.S. 2006 inflation rate.	5%
Mexico's 2006 inflation rate	20%

Required

1. Calculate the expected exchange rate at 12/31/06 under the purchasing power parity theory.
2. Calculate the *nominal* change in the exchange rate for 2006.
3. Calculate the *real* change in the exchange rate for 2006.

THINKING CRITICALLY

Cases

C 13-1 **Whose GAAP to Use** In January 2006, Paylox's Spanish subsidiary paid 100,000 euros for a patent having a remaining life of *5 years*. Under Spanish GAAP, the amount paid must be expensed (which the subsidiary did). For simplicity, assume that 1 euro equalled $1 *throughout* 2006.

Required What amounts do you think should be reported in the consolidated financial statements for the year ended 12/31/06?

C 13-2 **Do Economic Gains and Losses Occur on Purchase Orders Outstanding?** On 10/4/06, Conrex placed a noncancellable inventory purchase order with a French vendor. On 1/11/07, Conrex received the inventory. On 2/22/07, Conrex paid the vendor the full contractual price of 100,000 euros. The spot direct exchange rates for the euro follow:

October 4, 2006	December 31, 2006	January 11, 2007	February 22, 2007
$.20	$.23	$.24	$.26

Required

1. What arguments can you make for and against requiring Conrex to record a $3,000 loss at 12/31/06?
2. In your judgment, did Conrex have a $3,000 economic loss in 2006?
3. Assume for the dates given that Conrex had also received a noncancellable sales order from a French customer. In your judgment, did Conrex have a $3,000 economic gain in 2006?

C 13-3 **Just How Many Ways Are There to Describe Gains and Losses?** Financial accountants characterize gains and losses as *realized* and *unrealized*. Tax accountants use the terms *capital* and *ordinary*. Economists use the terms *real* and *nominal*. Business executives often downplay certain losses by saying that they are only "paper losses."

Required

1. What is the distinction between each of these categories?
2. Would financial reporting be improved if *real* and *nominal* were used instead of *realized* and *unrealized*? Why or why not?

Financial Analysis Problem

FAP 13-1 **Determining the Impact of Inflation on Equity** Consider the population to be composed of the following eight groups:

Group A owns land worth $105,000.
Group B owns land worth $105,000.
Group C owns cash of $105,000.
Group D owns nothing.
Group E owns cash of $100,000.
Group F owns cash of $5,000.
Group G owns cash of $105,000 but owes $105,000.
Group H owns nothing but owes $105,000.

On 1/1/06, the following events and transactions occurred:

1. Group C deposited its $105,000 into Lincoln Savings & Loan, which has no equity capital. (The savings account is fully insured by the federal government.)
2. Lincoln S&L lent the $105,000 to Group D at 5% interest. The note is due in one year.
3. Group D purchased the land from Group B for $105,000 cash.

On 1/2/06 (one day later), the following events and transactions took place:

4. Inflation of 5% occurred; everything (real estate, commodities, services) now costs 5% more.
5. Because of inflation, the current lending rate is now 10% instead of 5%. Accordingly, Lincoln's $105,000 note receivable fell in value to $100,000.

On 1/3/06 (another day later), the following events and transactions occurred:

6. The government declared Lincoln insolvent (on a current value basis) and sold the $105,000 note receivable to Group E for $100,000.
7. For simplicity, assume that the government imposed a special savings and loan bailout tax of $5,000 on Group F and deposited the taxes collected in Lincoln. The government then distributed $105,000 cash to Group C in full liquidation of its government insured deposit.

On 1/4/06 (another day later), the government announced that it expected no future inflation. Accordingly, the lending rate returned to 5%. **Prices did *not* return to their previous level**, however; they stabilized at the higher level attained on 1/2/06.

Required

1. Determine the ***economic* gain or loss** for each group at the end of 1/4/06. At the beginning of your solution, include a summary matrix as follows (with amounts inserted in the appropriate columns):

	Asset Held during Inflationary Period	Gained	Lost	Broke Even
Group A				
Group B				
Group C				
Group D				
Group E				
Group F				
Group G				
Group H				

2. Explain why each group gained, lost, or broke even economically.
3. Which group did Group F subsidize?
4. Assume that Group A sold its land on 1/5/06 for $110,250. Assume an applicable income tax rate of 40%. Would your answer to requirement 1 change for Group A? If so, in which way or by how much?
5. How many ways can you think of to label a gain?
6. Are financial statements of U.S. companies adjusted for inflation in any way? Explain either how or why not.
7. In general, who are the *winners*, if any, when inflation occurs?
8. Can the effects of inflation be characterized as a "zero sum game" (the extent of the economic *losses* incurred by the *losers* is exactly offset by the economic *gains* of the *winners*)?

chapter

14

Using Derivatives to Manage Foreign Currency Exposures

There are two times in one's life when one should not speculate: when one can't afford it and when one can.
MARK TWAIN

LEARNING OBJECTIVES

To Understand

> The types of foreign exchange (FX) exposures that exist.

> The way companies protect against FX exposures.

> The fundamentals of using FX option contracts.

> The fundamentals of using FX forward exchange contracts.

> The accounting treatment prescribed for gains and losses on transactions entered into to protect against FX exposures.

> The nature and risks of derivative financial instruments.

TOPIC OUTLINE

I. Types of Foreign Exchange (FX) Exposures
II. The Technique of Hedging
III. The Four Cornerstone Decisions of *FAS 133*
IV. FX Option Contracts
V. FX Forward Exchange Contracts: Basics
VI. FX Forward Exchange Contracts: Premiums and Discounts
VII. Speculating in Foreign Currency
VIII. Hedging Firm Foreign-Currency-Denominated Commitments (*Fair Value* Hedges)
IX. Hedging Forecasted Transactions (*Cash Flow* Hedges)
X. Derivative Financial Instruments: A General Discussion
INTERNATIONAL PERSPECTIVE: *Foreign Accounting Standards for Derivatives*
XI. Disclosures Required for FX Derivatives

CHAPTER OVERVIEW

We begin this chapter by showing the many different kinds of foreign exchange (FX) exposures that can exist. Next we describe the technique of hedging, which companies use to protect against FX exposures. We then discuss in detail the two types of derivative financial instruments (foreign currency *option* contracts and foreign currency *forward exchange* contracts) that are commonly used to hedge FX exposures. After that, we discuss the accounting treatments for hedging gains and losses that occur in hedging the various types of FX exposures.

We then discuss in general the widespread use, nature, and risks of derivative financial instruments to (1) protect against various kinds of exposures and (2) improve returns. This leads into a discussion of disclosures required for all types of derivative financial instruments.

The Governing Pronouncements

The accounting standards for FX derivative financial instruments are set forth in *FAS 133*, "Accounting for Derivative Instruments and Hedging Activities" (which the FASB (a) issued in 1998 after seven years of research and deliberations; (b) amended in 2000 with the issuance of FASB *Statement No. 138*, "Accounting for Certain Derivatives and Certain Hedging Activities"; and (c) amended again in 2003 with the issuance of *FASB Statement No. 149*, "Amendment of Statement 133 on Derivative Instruments and Hedging Activities"). Disclosures to be made for *all* financial instruments (including derivatives) are prescribed by *FAS 107*, "Disclosures about Fair Value of Financial Instruments." These pronouncements as they pertain to FX derivatives are discussed later.

FAS 149 sets forth rules as to which category is to be used in the *statement of cash flows* for reporting cash flows from derivative contracts (it all depends on the particular situation).

I. TYPES OF FOREIGN EXCHANGE (FX) EXPOSURES

Companies having foreign currency transactions and foreign operations are subject to the risk that exchange rates can change adversely, causing losses, *lower* revenues, or *increased* costs. Because of the high potential for such adverse effects under the highly volatile exchange rate movements that occur under the current floating exchange rate system, managing foreign exchange (FX) exposures to minimize or prevent possible FX losses has increasingly become a high-level objective for most companies having international operations.

Many companies have (1) hired FX specialists, (2) invested in technology (computers, commercially available foreign currency software programs, and internally developed foreign currency modeling programs), and (3) built small trading rooms that resemble the FX trading rooms of banks and Wall Street investment firms. In turn, this desire to protect against exchange rate change losses has led to an increase in the number of available financial instruments to accomplish this objective.

Companies can manage any or all of the following types of FX exposures:

1. **Asset and liability positions.**
   a. **A parent's exposed individual assets and liabilities.** Such positions result from transactions recorded but *not* yet settled. Examples are (1) *receivables* and *payables* on *exporting* and *importing* transactions, respectively, and (2) *notes receivable* and *notes payable* on *lending* and *borrowing* transactions, respectively.
   b. **A foreign subsidiary's net *asset* position.** This is the subsidiary's *total assets* minus its *total liabilities* (which equals the parent's investment balance if the subsidiary was *created* and the parent uses the *equity method* of accounting).
   c. **A foreign subsidiary's net *monetary* position.** This is a foreign subsidiary's *monetary assets* minus its *monetary liabilities*. Monetary items are cash and accounts contractually obligated to be settled in cash.
2. **Firm commitments.** Examples are (1) noncancelable purchase orders placed or noncancelable sales orders received for which delivery has *not* yet occurred, (2) future interest expense that will be paid on loan contracts, and (3) future lease payments on operating leases.

3. **Forecasted transactions.**
   a. **Budgeted exposures.** Examples are (1) a U.S. company's budgeted export revenues or budgeted import purchases, (2) a foreign subsidiary's budgeted revenues (or a percentage of such revenues as a surrogate for budgeted net income), (3) a foreign subsidiary's budgeted net income or budgeted dividend remittances, and (4) outstanding bids.
   b. **Strategic or competitive exposures.** This is the potential for **loss of** future transactions—as opposed to the potential for **loss on** transactions. Examples are as follows:
      (1) **Export sales.** Export sales may be lost to foreign competitors if the dollar *strengthens* because foreign customers would find that U.S. products were now *more* expensive.
      (2) **Domestic sales.** Domestic sales may decline if the dollar *strengthens* because domestic customers would find that foreign products were now *less* expensive.

Companies have different policies for managing the various possible FX exposures. For example, many companies protect exposed assets and liabilities resulting from exporting and importing transactions, respectively, in all cases—this is a board of directors' policy for many companies. Other companies, however, have a policy to protect such exposed assets and liabilities only if management expects the exchange rate to change adversely to a significant extent, which is a "view" aiming at profit enhancement.

We discuss in this chapter how to protect against most of these exposures. In Chapter 15, we discuss how to protect a foreign subsidiary's net *asset* position (item 1[b]). In Chapter 16, we discuss how to protect a foreign subsidiary's net *monetary* position (item 1[c]).

Speculating versus Managing Exposure

In addition, companies can speculate on the direction of future exchange rates for the sole purpose of making profits. For example, Du Pont expects its FX trading department to operate as a profit center. Many companies prohibit speculation, however, thus limiting their activities to protecting against exchange rate change losses on their FX exposures. For example, Ford Motor Company states in its annual report that "company policy specifically prohibits the use of derivatives for speculative purposes." Speculating is discussed briefly later in the chapter.

II. THE TECHNIQUE OF HEDGING

FX exposures are commonly managed by a technique called *hedging*. By hedging, a company can avoid a loss that may otherwise arise. The idea is to have a counterbalancing gain on the financial instrument used to achieve the hedge if a loss occurs on the item being hedged. As identified earlier, the various FX exposures that can be hedged range from an existing FX receivable or FX payable to an anticipated future revenues stream. A specific FX exposure being hedged is commonly called the **hedged item**. The financial instrument used to achieve the hedge is commonly called the **hedging instrument**.

Types of Hedging Instruments

The two most common types of hedging instruments used to hedge FX exposures are (1) **foreign currency option contracts**[1] (hereafter *FX options*) and (2) **foreign currency forward exchange contracts** (hereafter *FX forwards*)[2].

---

[1] **Foreign Currency Swaps.** Another type of financial instrument that can be used to hedge foreign currency transactions expected to occur in the future is a foreign currency swap. In swaps, the two parties agree to swap future streams of foreign currency cash flows over a specified period. Although swaps are essentially a series of forward-based contracts, they are much more involved than FX forwards because of interest rate considerations. The use of swaps has become widespread for longer-term risk management in recent years; however, FX forwards are much more widely used, and they represent the essential components of swaps.

[2] **Foreign Currency Futures.** A financial instrument that is somewhat similar to an FX forward is a *foreign currency future*. These are contracts *standardized* as to amounts and duration; in contrast, *FX forwards* are *customized* as to amounts and duration. Foreign currency futures are used very infrequently by commercial companies for hedging purposes but are used extensively by (1) banking institutions (to hedge their net position) and (2) speculators. A full discussion may be found in international finance texts.

FX Options

An FX option has **"one-sided exposure"** because only the option holder pays for the potential of a *favorable* outcome and the other party (the option writer) receives payment to run the risk of an *unfavorable* outcome. Consequently, only the *downside risk* on the hedged item is counterbalanced. Stated differently, any *loss* on the *hedged item* can be offset by a *gain* on the *hedging transaction*. A *gain* on the *hedged transaction*, however, *cannot* be offset by a *loss* on the *hedging transaction* because the option holder will let the option expire and thus *not* incur a loss on the *hedging transaction*.

FX Forwards

An FX forward has **"two-sided exposure"** because each party potentially has a *favorable* or *unfavorable* outcome, depending on which direction the currency exchange rate moves. Consequently, both the *downside risk* and the *upside potential* on the hedged item are counterbalanced. Stated differently, a loss or gain on the *hedged item* will be offset by a gain or loss, respectively, on the *hedging transaction*. FX forward hedges, if perfectly matched long (receivable) and short (payable), eliminate risk and return from FX positions.

Because FX options are much simpler to explain than FX forwards, we discuss them first.

Reporting the Value of Hedging Instruments in the Balance Sheet

As illustrated later, hedging instruments are valued during the contract period, and this value is reported on the balance sheet. General ledger accounts, such as FX Contract Value—Option and FX Contract Value—Forward, net, are used. These accounts *can* accommodate being in either a *receivable* or *payable* position. Thus when these accounts appear in a company's asset and liability sections of its balance sheet, they convey that entity's *favorable* or *unfavorable* position, respectively, in the contract.

The Basic Accounting Issue Involving Hedging

The basic accounting issue for hedging is determining whether the gain or loss on the *hedging instrument* can be reported in earnings in the same period in which the loss or gain on the *hedged item* occurs. Two possibilities exist to achieve concurrent recognition:

1. ***Immediate* recognition.** Recognize both currently in earnings (in which case they most likely would be netted against each other for display purposes instead of showing both the *gain* and the *loss*).
2. ***Delayed* recognition.** Defer recognition of both until they both can be recognized in earnings later at the same time.

III. THE FOUR CORNERSTONE DECISIONS OF *FAS 133*

FAS 133 is based on the following four cornerstone decisions made by the FASB:

Cornerstone Decision 1: Derivatives are contracts that create rights and obligations that meet the definitions of *assets* and *liabilities* (thus these *rights* and *obligations* are reported in the balance sheet—*not* in an "off-balance-sheet" manner).

Cornerstone Decision 2: Fair value is the only relevant measure for reporting of derivatives (thus derivatives are reported in the balance sheet at their fair values—**whether or not they hedge an item**).

Cornerstone Decision 3: Only items that are *assets* or *liabilities* are reportable as such on the balance sheet (thus *losses* on derivatives *cannot* be deferred and reported as *assets*; likewise, *gains* on derivatives *cannot* be deferred and reported as *liabilities*).

Cornerstone Decision 4: Gains and losses on derivatives must be reported in earnings currently—except in certain specified situations in which the gains and losses must be initially reported in other comprehensive income. Furthermore, in certain specified situations in which the gain or loss on the *hedging transaction* must be reported in earnings currently, the normal accounting for the hedged item must be altered so that the offsetting loss or gain on the *hedged item* is also reported currently in earnings. The accounting treatment for both types of these certain specified situations comprises what is collectively referred to as "hedge accounting," which is discussed next.

Distinguishing between "Hedging" and "Hedge Accounting"

The word "hedging" is a broad and general term. In contrast, *FAS 133* uses the term "hedge accounting" as a special accounting treatment that alters the normal accounting for either (1) the gain or loss on the *hedging transaction* (involving the use of a derivative) or (2) the *hedged item*. The purpose of allowing hedge accounting is to prevent the reporting in earnings in different periods of the counterbalancing changes in (1) either the fair values or expected cash flows of a *hedged item* and (2) the fair value of the *hedging transaction*.

Accordingly, **hedge accounting** is defined as **a special accounting treatment that achieves concurrent recognition *(in earnings)* on either (1) an *immediate basis* or (2) a *delayed basis,* of counterbalancing gains and losses on both the *hedging transaction* and the related *hedged item*.**

FAS 133's Four Categories of Hedges

Under *FAS 133*, all hedging transaction gains and losses must be accounted for in one of four specified manners. Each of the four manners of accounting is categorized as a type of hedging transaction. Thus four categories of hedging transactions exist.

In general, the accounting for a hedging transaction gain or loss depends on (1) the intended use of the derivative and (2) the resulting designation (discussed more fully shortly). Thus, in general, hedging transactions of a certain type can only be accounted for using the accounting specified for that type of hedge. As a result of *FAS 138* (which amended *FAS 133* in 2000), however, certain foreign exchange hedging transactions may be classified as any of the first three of the four types of hedges (presented shortly).

Accordingly, all hedging transactions must fall into one of the following four categories (each category having its own unique manner of accounting):

1. **"Undesignated" hedges (hedge accounting does *not* apply).** These hedges are *not* designated as being one of the other three types of hedges because (1) they do *not* qualify as such or (2) they qualify as such but may *also* be treated as *undesignated hedges* (as allowed by *FAS 138*). Hedges of FX receivables on *exporting* transactions and FX payables on *importing* transactions may be classified as (1) *undesignated hedges*, (2) *fair value hedges*, or (3) *cash flow hedges* (as a result of *FAS 138*).

   Because hedge accounting does *not* apply, **FX gains or losses on hedging transactions classified as an *undesignated hedge* are always reported currently in earnings.** (This category could also be labeled as "hedges *not* requiring hedge accounting" or as "nonhedge accounting hedges.")

   For these types of hedges, the hedging gain or loss reported currently in earnings is automatically offset by the recognized loss or gain on the hedged item that is also reported currently in earnings. Thus no special treatment need be set forth in *FAS 133* to obtain offsetting concurrent recognition (as is required for the other three categories of hedges). The manner of accounting for *undesignated hedges* is discussed in Sections IV through VI of this chapter.

2. **Fair value hedges (hedge accounting applies).** Hedges of *unrecognized* firm commitments denominated in a foreign currency (such as *purchase orders* issued to foreign vendors and *sales orders* from foreign customers) fall into this category. **FX gains or losses on hedges of these firm commitments are always reported currently in earnings.** The special hedge accounting treatment here, however, is that of recognizing in earnings currently the gain or loss on the item being bought or sold, even though the item has *not* yet been received or shipped, respectively. Such hedges are discussed in Section VIII of this chapter.
3. **Cash flow hedges (hedge accounting applies).** Hedges of forecasted foreign transactions (such as budgeted foreign sales for which no sales order commitments have been received) fall into this category. **FX gains or losses on these hedging transactions are always reported initially in Other Comprehensive Income—*not* in earnings.** This special treatment is an application of hedge accounting. Such hedges are discussed in Section IX of this chapter.
4. **Net Investment hedges (hedge accounting applies).** This category pertains to hedges of a net investment in a foreign operation. **FX gains or losses on these hedging transactions are always reported initially in Other Comprehensive Income—*not* in earnings.** This special treatment is an application of hedge accounting. Such hedges are discussed in Chapter 15.

The Choice Between Using Three Hedging Contracts or One Hedging Contract on a *Forecasted* Transaction

Assume the following information for a company that desires to hedge from the beginning of the year to the expected settlement date of a *forecasted* transaction:

1. On January 1, 2006, Paxco forecasted that (a) it would have export sales of 100,000£ on October 31, 2006, and (b) a noncancellable sales order for these sales would be received July 1, 2006.
2. On July 1, 2006 (*six* months later), Paxco received a noncancellable sales order for 100,000£, with Paxco to deliver the inventory on October 31, 2006.
3. On October 31, 2006 (*four* months later), Paxco delivered the inventory to the British customer.
4. On January 30, 2007 (*three* months later), the British customer remitted 100,000£ to Paxco in full settlement.

Paxco can enter into either (1) *three* separate hedging contracts (one for the first *six* months—the ***uncommitted period***, one for the following *four* months—the ***firmly committed period***, and one for the remaining *three* months—the ***exposed liability period***, or (2) *one* hedging contract for the entire thirteen months. If Paxco enters into *three* separate hedging contracts, the *first* contract is accounted for as a ***cash flow hedge***, the *second* contract as a ***fair value hedge***, and the *third* contract as an ***undesignated hedge***. If instead Paxco enters into only *one* hedging contract covering the thirteen months, it accounts for the hedging contract as (1) a ***cash flow hedge*** for *six* months, (2) a ***fair value hedge*** for *four* months, and (3) an ***undesignated hedge*** for the remaining *three* months.

The Manner of Determining Fair Value of a Derivative

FAS 133 stipulates that the guidance in *FAS 107* shall apply in determining the fair value of derivatives. This guidance is as follows:

1. **Quoted market prices.** If available, quotes are the *best evidence* of fair value. (The FX trading department of banks would be the logical place to obtain a quote of an FX option.)
2. **Quoted market price of a derivative with similar characteristics.** If quoted prices are *not* available, this manner of determining fair value may be used.
3. **Valuation techniques.** Such techniques include (1) determining the present value of estimated future cash flows using an appropriate discount rate (as discussed more fully later, this technique must be used for FX forwards), (2) option pricing models, and (3) matrix pricing models.

For simplicity in later illustrations of FX options, we provide assumed fair values at financial reporting dates.

IV. FX Option Contracts

The use of FX options has increased dramatically since 1983, the year the Philadelphia Stock Exchange began offering exchange-traded FX options. In an FX option, one party has **the right to buy or sell a specific quantity of currency at a specified rate** (the **exercise** or **strike** price) during a specified future period.[3] Consequently, the other party is **obligated to deliver** or **take delivery** of the currency if the FX option is exercised.

By definition, options (in general) need *not* be exercised, enabling the purchaser to "walk away" (and thereby lose only the amount paid to purchase the option). Thus there is **only the possibility of a gain** as a result of subsequent changes in the spot rate—*not* both a gain or a loss.

Option Terminology

Types and Parties

An option to buy is a **call**. An option to sell is a **put**. The party having the contractual right to buy or sell is the **holder** of the option. From the perspective of the *holder*, the option contract is referred to as a **purchased option**. The party that grants the holder this contractual right is the **writer** of the option. From the perspective of the *writer*, the option contract is referred to as a **written option**. (A corporation that has granted an employee a stock option has *written* a *call* option; the employee is the *holder* of the call option.) Each party has conflicting desires concerning the future movement of the exchange rate for the currency involved. See Illustration 14-1 for a summary comparison of *put* and *call* options.

Fees

Because the writer assumes the responsibility of incurring a potential loss, the writer charges a fee, called a **premium** (typically ranging from 1.5% to 7% of the spot price). Thus the premium is the price paid to acquire the option. *FX options* are usually substantially more expensive than *FX forwards* (discussed later).

ILLUSTRATION 14-1 SUMMARY COMPARISON OF *PUT* AND *CALL* OPTIONS

	***Put* Option**	***Call* Option**[b]
Selling rate.	**FIXED** Price (the *exercise* price)	Variable Price (the *spot* rate)
Buying rate	Variable Price (the *spot* rate)	**FIXED** Price (the *exercise* price)
Gain occurs for the **option holder** when the spot rate[a]	Decreases (*below* the exercise price)	Increases (*above* the exercise price)
Used to hedge	FX *Receivables*	FX *Payables*

[a] However, the gain is measured by the change in the option's *fair value*—not the change in the *spot rate*.

[b] An employee that has a stock option has a *call* option.

[3] This is an *American* option; options that can be exercised only at the expiration date are called *European* options.

When to Exercise versus Walk Away

When the relationship between the *exercise price* and the *spot price* is **favorable to the holder**—in reverse position for *puts* than for *calls*—the FX option is said to be **"in the money"** because the holder would exercise the FX option and have a realized gain. On the other hand, when the relationship between the *exercise price* and the *spot price* is **unfavorable to the holder**, the FX option is said to be **"out of the money,"** in which case the holder would *not* exercise the option. When the exercise price and the spot price are the *same*, the FX option is said to be **"at the money."** These situations are shown in Illustration 14-2.

The *exercise price* need *not* be the same as the *spot price* at the inception of the option period. During the option period, the holder can sell the FX option in the open market at its market value, suggesting that the FX option should *always* be valued at its market value.

Accounting for FX Option Premiums—A "Split Accounting" Issue

Time Value Element

If at the inception of the FX option, the option is either **out of the money** (the spot price being either *below* the exercise price for a *call* option or *above* the exercise price for a *put* option) or **at the money** (the spot price equaling the exercise price), the entire premium is called the **time value.** **The time value is analogous to a prepaid insurance premium** that could be amortized to income over the life of the option period using a systematic and rational method (such as straight-line). The **time value** of an option is a function of (1) the length of the option period (which increases as the duration becomes longer), (2) the interest rate opportunity, and (3) the volatility of the underlying item. The determination of the time value is beyond the scope of this text.

Intrinsic Value Element

On the other hand, if at the inception of the FX option, the option is **in the money** (the spot price being either *above* the exercise price for a *call* option or *below* the exercise price for a *put* option), the option holder will have paid a higher premium—the incremental amount equaling the difference between the spot price and the exercise price—to be placed in this favorable position. This incremental premium paid is called the FX option's **intrinsic value.** Because the intrinsic value may be viewed as being conceptually different from the time value, it theoretically can be accounted for separately from the time value. Carving out the *time value element* and reporting its gain or loss separately from the manner of reporting the *intrinsic value element*'s gain or loss is referred to as **split accounting.**

Split Accounting Is Permitted in Certain Situations

As stated earlier, *FAS 133* requires *all* derivatives to be valued at their *fair values* (at *each* financial reporting date). Thus both the *time value element* and the *intrinsic value element* are valued at fair value. *FAS 133* does *not* require separate disclosure of either the *time value* element's fair value or the *intrinsic value* element's fair value. In practice, the fair value of FX options most always are

ILLUSTRATION 14-2 FX OPTION SITUATIONS

	Call FX Option		*Put* FX Option	
	Exercise Price (buying price)	Spot Price (selling price)	Exercise Price (selling price)	Spot Price (buying price)
In the money	$ .98	$1.00	$1.02	$1.00
At the money	1.00	1.00	1.00	1.00
Out of the money	1.02	1.00	.98	1.00

determinable in total—*not* by trying to determine the fair value of each FX option's two elements and then summing together those two elements. Accordingly, the need to determine the breakdown of the total fair value occurs only if split accounting is used.

For *"undesignated" hedges*, the FX gains and losses on both the *time value element* and the *intrinsic value element* must be reported the *same* way—in earnings currently. For both *fair value hedges* and *cash flow hedges*, however, *FAS 133* allows these elements to be reported either the same way or differently—all depending on how the entity assesses hedge effectiveness (discussed later).

Reporting an FX Option At Its *Fair Value*

At the inception date, a purchased FX option is valued at the amount of the premium paid—which amount is the *fair value* of the option on that date. (Premiums are *always* paid at the inception of the option.)

At each financial reporting date subsequent to the inception date, the FX option must be adjusted to its current fair value.

Hedging an Exposed *Liability* Position

A company that has a liability in a foreign currency is said to have an **exposed liability**. The domestic importer in Illustration 13-3 agreed to pay Vendor A £100,000 on January 10, 2007, for inventory purchased. Thus the domestic importer has an exposed liability. To avoid the risk of an exchange rate *increase* during the period from the *transaction date* (December 11, 2006) to the *settlement date* (January 10, 2007), the domestic company could enter into a 30-day *call* FX option on December 11, 2006. Thus the domestic company can effectively determine now, rather than on January 10, 2007, how many dollars it needs to obtain £100,000.

Settling Up at the Expiration Date upon Exercise

If the FX option is *in the money* at the end of the contract period, the FX option will be exercised. Accordingly, the bank must *make* delivery, and the FX option holder must *take* delivery of foreign currency. The FX option holder can *take* delivery either physically or by instructing the bank to deliver the currency to its overseas vendor via a bank wire transfer. In a **bank wire transfer**, which is the customary practice, the domestic importer's bank would (1) *charge* (debit) the *domestic importer's* bank account (in dollars) at the strike price and (2) instruct an overseas branch (via telex) to *credit* the *overseas vendor's* bank account (in foreign currency), thereby extinguishing the liability to the foreign vendor (as reflected in the FX Accounts Payable account). All illustrations assume the use of bank wire transfers.[4]

Comprehensive Illustration

Hedging an Exposed Liability

Illustration 14-3 shows the entries that would be made under a 30-day call FX option costing $1,500 (*paid at inception*) entered into to protect the domestic company's exposed liability of £100,000. For comparative purposes, we also show the entries relating to Vendor A (as shown in Illustration 13-3 on page 437). The direct exchange rates and the option's assumed fair values for the applicable dates in December 2006 and January 2007 (when the pound was *strengthening*) are as follows:

	December 11, 2006 (inception date)		December 31, 2006 (a financial reporting date)		January 10, 2007 (expiration date)
Spot rate	$1.50		$1.55		$1.59
Exercise price	$1.50				
Fair value	$1,500		$5,700		$9,000
Change in fair value		$4,200		$3,300	
Elements existing	TV		TV & IV		IV
Elements recorded as asset	TV		TV & IV		IV

[4] If, however, the company were to physically take delivery of the foreign currency from the FX trader, a *debit* to a £ Cash account would be made. Later when the foreign currency is physically delivered to the vendor, the £ Cash account is *credited*, and the £ Accounts Payable account is debited.

ILLUSTRATION 14-3 HEDGING AN EXPOSED *LIABILITY* POSITION: CALL FX OPTION JOURNAL ENTRIES

Transaction with Vendor (same as in Illustration 13-3)			*Hedging Transaction*		
DECEMBER 11, 2006 (THE TRANSACTION DATE AND THE INCEPTION OF THE 30-DAY *CALL* FX OPTION PERIOD)					
Inventory.	$150,000		*FX Contract Value—Option*	*$1,500*	
£ Accounts Payable		$150,000	*Cash*		*$1,500*
To record the inventory purchase. (£100,000 × $1.50 = $150,000)			*To record the cost of the call option acquired.*		
DECEMBER 31, 2006 (AN INTERVENING FINANCIAL REPORTING DATE)					
FX Loss	$5,000		*FX Contract Value—Option*	*$4,200*	
£ Accounts Payable		$5,000	*FX Gain*		*$4,200*
To adjust the pound payable to the current *spot rate*. ($1.55 − $1.50 = $.05) ($.05 × £100,000 = $5,000)			*To adjust the option's carrying value to fair value.* ($5,700 − $1,500 = $4,200)		
JANUARY 10, 2007 (THE SETTLEMENT DATE)					
FX Loss	$4,000		*FX Contract Value—Option*	*$3,300*	
£ Accounts Payable		$4,000	*FX Gain*		*$3,300*
To adjust the pound payable to the current *spot rate*. ($1.59 − $1.55 = $.04) ($.04 × £100,000 = $4,000)			*To adjust the option's carrying value to fair value.* ($9,000 − $5,700 = $3,300)		
£ Accounts Payable	$159,000				
FX Contract Value—Option		$9,000			
Cash		$150,000			
To exercise the option and pay vendor **via a bank wire transfer.** (The bank charges the company's checking account $150,000 [**the strike price of $1.50 × £100,000**].)					

FX Contract Value—Option

Date	Debit	Credit
12/11/06	$1,500	
	4,200	
12/31/06	$5,700[a]	
	3,300	
1/10/07	$9,000[b]	

[a] Reported as an asset on the importer's 12/31/06 balance sheet.

[b] This is the option's *intrinsic value* at this date (the *time value* is zero).

Review Points for Illustration 14-3. Note the following:

1. **Independence of transactions.** Although the hedging transaction achieves the desired mirror effect of what occurs on the hedged item, the FX option is a transaction independent of the company's transaction with Vendor A. Accordingly, the accounting entries for each transaction are prepared without regard to the other transaction. Thus the entries for the importing transaction with Vendor A are the same whether or not the company entered into the hedging transaction.
2. **Composition of the FX option's gain.** The $7,500 FX gain consists of:

Intrinsic value gain (increase in *spot rate* of $.09 × £100,000)	$ 9,000
Time value loss (the premium paid)	(1,500)
Net Gain.	$ 7,500

   By adjusting the FX option to its fair value (in total), the result is to simultaneously (1) *recognize* as an asset the *increase* in the *intrinsic value* and (2) *derecognize* as an asset the *decrease* in the *time value*.
3. **Total offset—except for the premium.** During the 30-day period of the FX option, the pound strengthened from $1.50 to $1.59. Without the FX option, the $9,000 additional amount

payable to Vendor A would *not* have been offset by the $9,000 intrinsic value gain on the FX option.

4. **Amounts reported in the income statement.** No compelling reason exists to display the $5,000 loss and the $4,200 gain for 2006 separately in the income statement. Accordingly, a net loss of $800 would be reported.
5. **A perfect hedge.** This hedge is called a *"perfect" hedge* because (1) the amount of currency in the FX option (£100,000) equals the amount of foreign currency owed the vendor and (2) the expiration date of the FX option coincided (by design) with the settlement date on the importing transaction. If the amount of currency on the hedging transaction *exceeded* the amount of currency owed the vendor, such excess would be treated as a speculation (discussed later). A difference in the expiration and settlement dates presents no accounting issues for this exposure category.
6. **Result if the exchange rate had *decreased*.** If instead of increasing from $1.50 to $1.59 the spot exchange rate had decreased to $1.41, the company would have had (1) a $9,000 gain on its importing transaction and (2) no gain on its FX option because the FX option would *not* have been exercised. The *premium*, however, would be charged to income over the life of the option period.

Hedging an Exposed *Asset* Position

A company that has a receivable in a foreign currency is said to have an **exposed asset.** An **exposed asset** most often results from an exporting transaction in which payment is to be received in the foreign currency. In these situations, the domestic exporter would buy a *put* FX option to hedge its exposed asset position. The accounting for a put FX option is identical to that shown in Illustration 14-3. Thus the FX option holder (1) charges the cost of the FX option (the time value element) to the FX Contract Value—Option account and (2) subsequently adjusts the FX Contract Value—Option account to its fair value. If the option holder exercises the FX option (occurs only if it is *in the money*), the option holder must now *deliver* foreign currency (that it does *not* have on hand) to the bank. Customarily, this is done when payment is received from the customer via a bank wire transfer.

Bank Wire Transfer Procedures

The foreign customer's payment to the domestic exporter using a bank wire transfer is deemed as having made delivery of the foreign currency to the domestic exporter's bank. Procedurally, the foreign customer instructs its bank to transfer by wire the appropriate amount of foreign currency, say £200,000, to the U.S. domestic exporter's bank account. That foreign bank would then (1) *charge* the *foreign customer's* checking account £200,000 and (2) telex the domestic exporter's U.S. bank with instructions to *credit* the *domestic exporter's* bank account for the *spot rate* dollar equivalent of the £200,000. Because of the put FX option, however, the bank will *credit* the domestic exporter's account at the *strike price.*

ETHICS

Would You Reveal Your Speculation Loss to Your Boss?

You are in charge of managing Dymex's foreign currency exposures. You recently entered into unauthorized speculation transactions and lost $1,000,000.

Questions

1. Would you reveal this loss to your boss, or would you try to "recover" this loss through additional speculations? (The instructor's manual discusses a real-world situation in which the employee took the wrong course of action.)
2. What are the ramifications of this $1,000,000 loss to Dymex as to (a) recovery on their fidelity policy and (b) tax deductibility of the $1,000,000 loss?
3. What legal action could Dymex take against you?

V. FX Forward Exchange Contracts: Basics

An *FX forward* is an agreement to buy or sell a foreign currency at (1) **a specified future date** (usually within 12 months) and (2) **a specified exchange rate.** This rate is called the *forward rate*, and it usually is slightly *above* or *below* the spot rate for reasons explained more fully later. For now, it is important to realize that one component of this difference is the amount to compensate the FX trader (a bank) for assuming the risk that the exchange rate could change adversely.[5] **Thus eliminating FX exposure involves a cost whether FX forwards or FX options are used.**

FX forwards are widely used because they generally are far less expensive than other types of financial instruments that could be used to transfer FX exposure risk to an FX trader. The FX trader's exposure risk can then be "laid off" (shifted) to other customers, which lowers the FX trader's required commissions.

"Locking Into" a Price

By entering into an FX forward, the company "locks into" a price to be paid or received for the foreign currency to be exchanged. Thus a company determines *now* the number of dollars that it (1) needs to acquire foreign currency to settle in the future a FX payable with a foreign vendor or (2) will receive in the future in settlement of an FX receivable from a foreign customer.

Availability of Forward Markets

Active FX forward markets exist only for the major trading currencies (European euro, Japanese yen, British pound, Canadian dollar, Swiss franc). FX forward markets for other less-developed countries are either limited or nonexistent, with the result that either (1) credit terms may not be as generous or (2) companies take other steps, when possible, to protect their foreign currency exposures. (Some of these other steps are listed later in the chapter.)

The Customizable Nature of Forward Exchange Contracts

Newspapers commonly provide daily quotations of FX forward exchange rates for 30-, 90-, and 180-day periods, erroneously implying that FX forwards are available only for these periods. A unique feature of FX forwards, however, is that they can be customized as to both the amount of currency and the time period. Thus a company can obtain, for example, a 44-day FX forward to buy or sell £55,555.

The Requirement to *Take* or *Make* Delivery

Unlike FX options, in which the option holder can choose *not* to exercise the FX option and thus walk away from the contract, **FX forwards require execution by each party at the expiration date of the contract.** In virtually all cases, **execution occurs simultaneously.** (For compensation, however, FX forwards can be undone prior to execution, as discussed shortly.)

Buying Forward

When the FX forward involves *buying* a foreign currency (commonly referred to as *buying forward*), **the buyer must *take* delivery from the dealer**—either physically or by designating where the foreign currency should be deposited (such as in a foreign vendor's bank account for a bank wire transfer in settlement of an inventory-importing transaction).

---

[5] Technically, forward exchange contracts can be viewed as bilateral market price risk insurance agreements because each party is both *insurer* and *insured* but for opposite directions of price change.

Selling Forward

When the FX forward involves *selling* a foreign currency (commonly referred to as *selling forward*), **the seller must *make* delivery to the dealer**—either physically or by having a third party deposit the foreign currency in an overseas bank (as is done for a bank wire transfer in settlement of an inventory-exporting transaction).

The Executory Nature of Forward Exchange Contracts

FX forwards are executory contracts for which no general ledger entries need be recorded on the books at the time they are entered into. This executory nature becomes more evident when considering the fact that FX traders will generally allow their customers to undo FX forwards prior to their execution, providing that the customer pays for transaction costs and, from the bank's perspective, any adverse change in the spot rate.

Substantively, the company has merely **issued a purchase order to acquire (or accepted a sales order to sell) a foreign currency** (a commodity). Recall that the issuance of inventory purchase orders and the receipt of inventory sales orders are also executory in nature and are *not* recorded on the books until fulfillment of the orders—that is, **until one of the parties has performed** its half of the transaction by shipping the inventory. Thus assets and liabilities are *not* created when an FX forward is entered into. For this reason, in practice, companies do *not* make any general ledger entries at the inception of a FX forward.[6] They track the FX forwards they have outstanding, however, on a memorandum basis just as they track their sales order backlogs on a memorandum basis.

For pedagogical purposes only, however, it is useful to show entries being made in the general ledger at the inception of the FX forward—a **"gross"** or **"broad"** manner of accounting—to best convey the concept of counterbalancing. Accordingly, we do so for the first FX forward hedging illustration. Later FX forward hedging illustrations (and all solutions to the assignment material) reflect the customary practice of *not* making entries at the inception of the FX forward—a **"net position" manner of accounting.**

Calculating an FX Forward's Fair Value and Changes Thereto

Calculating Fair Value

FAS 133 requires that the fair value of an FX forward be calculated by (1) discounting estimated future cash flows and (2) basing estimated future cash flows on the change in the *forward* rate—*not* the change in the *spot* rate—from the contract inception date. The FASB's rationale is that the valuation of an FX forward should consider that:

1. Currencies will be exchanged at a future date.
2. Relative interest rates determine the difference between spot and forward rates.
3. The time value of money affects valuation.

The only valuation method that considers these three items is the net present value method. Thus the FASB concluded that the net present value method is the only valuation method that is consistent with the definition of fair value in *FAS 133*.

Calculating Gain or Loss

Obviously, the change in an FX forward's fair value during a period constitutes the reportable FX gain or loss for that period. More specifically, however, an FX forward's gain or loss for a report-

---

[6] Paragraph 4.23 (p. 63) of FASB *Discussion Memorandum*, "Recognition and Measurement of Financial Instruments" (1991), states that "in present practice, forward contracts with no consideration paid at inception by either party are generally not recognized."

The illustrative journal entries presented in paragraph A58 of *Exposure Draft E48*, "Financial Instruments" (January 1994), issued by the International Accounting Standards Committee show the customary practice of *not* recording the obligations of each party as assets and liabilities at the inception of the forward contract.

ing period is composed of (1) the change in the estimated future cash flows during that period as determined by using the ***change in the forward rate*** and (2) the adjustment for the effect of discounting to reflect the time value of money until settlement.

Discussion Assuming That the Spot Rate *Equals* the Forward Rate

Accounting for the difference between the spot rate and the forward rate slightly complicates the accounting for FX forwards. Accordingly, for simplicity, we assume that the forward rate and the spot rate are identical at the inception of the contract. Later we address accounting for the difference. Doing so allows for the entire focus to be on the concept of counterbalancing.

Hedging Exposed Liabilities

The domestic importer in Illustration 13-3 agreed to pay Vendor A £100,000 on January 10, 2007, for inventory purchased. Thus the domestic importer has an exposed liability. To avoid the risk of an exchange rate *increase* during the period from the transaction date (December 11, 2006) to the settlement date (January 10, 2007), the domestic company could enter into a 30-day FX forward on December 11, 2006, agreeing to purchase £100,000 on January 10, 2007, at the currently existing forward exchange rate. Consequently, the domestic company determines *now*, rather than on January 10, 2007, how many dollars it needs to obtain £100,000 to settle its FX accounts payable balance. Thus the domestic importer is "buying forward." (A domestic exporter "sells forward" to hedge an exposed asset [an FX accounts receivable] as discussed later.)

The contractual obligations under an FX forward in which a domestic importer buys forward are as follows:

1. **Contractual obligation *to* the FX trader.** The domestic importer is obligated to pay the FX trader the agreed upon price (as determined by the forward rate) at the expiration date of the contract. Thus this obligation is a *fixed amount*—regardless of what may happen to the spot rate during the period of the contract. As stated earlier, the result is that the domestic importer has locked into the number of dollars needed to discharge its FX accounts payable to its foreign vendor.
2. **Contractual obligation *of* the FX trader.** The trader is obligated to deliver the agreed upon amount of foreign currency to the domestic importer at the expiration date of the contract. Thus the value of the foreign currency to be received from the FX trader may fluctuate during the period of the contract as a result of changes in the exchange rate. The fluctuating nature of the value of this obligation (a future asset of the domestic company) is what creates the counterbalancing to the domestic importer's FX Accounts Payable account that also fluctuates in value as a result of changes in the spot rate.

Assuming that the *spot rate* and the 30-day *forward rate* are both $1.50 for the British pound at the inception of the forward contract, a journal entry to record the obligations at the inception of an FX forward for the purchase of £100,000 for delivery in 30 days is as follows:

£ Due *from* FX trader **(a variable amount)**	$150,000[a]	
$ Due *to* FX trader **(a fixed amount)**		$150,000[b]
To record the future obligations under the forward exchange contract.		

[a] (£100,000 × $1.50 spot rate)

[b] (£100,000 × $1.50 forward rate)

Use of "Due to" and "Due From" Accounts

To readily distinguish these two accounts from accounts used to record importing and exporting transactions (FX Accounts Payable and FX Accounts Receivable), we use *due to* and *due from* terminology exclusively for FX forwards. Furthermore, to differentiate between these two accounts (one requiring settlement in U.S. dollars and the other in a foreign currency), we use the account

$ Due to FX Trader for the fixed obligation to the FX trader and the account **£ Due from FX Trader** for the value of the foreign currency to be received from the FX trader.

Reporting the FX Forward at Its *Fair Value*

When an entry *is* made to record the contractual obligations at the inception of an FX forward and when the *spot rate* and *forward rate* are the same at the inception of the contract (which we are assuming is the case for now), it is merely necessary at each subsequent financial reporting date to (1) adjust the fixed obligation amount to the *forward rate* existing at that financial reporting date and (2) make an adjustment to that amount for the effect of discounting.

The sum of these adjustments is an **unrealized** FX gain or loss, which largely offsets the unrealized FX loss or gain, respectively, on the domestic importer's exposed liability to the foreign vendor. Such adjustments may be viewed as adjustments to the FX forward's **intrinsic value.** (A **time value** element also exists, but that relates to accounting for the difference between the *spot rate* and the *forward rate*, which is discussed much later.)

For simplicity, we do *not* deal with discounting in the initial FX forward illustrations that we present shortly.

Settling Up at the Expiration Date

At the end of the contract period, the $ Due to FX Trader account is extinguished by the payment of cash (dollars) to the dealer, and the £ Due from FX Trader account is extinguished by *taking* delivery of the foreign currency from the foreign currency dealer. In a **bank wire transfer**, which is the customary practice, the FX trader (the domestic importer's bank) (1) *charges* (debits) the *domestic importer's* bank account (in dollars) for the fixed obligation amount due the FX trader and (2) then instructs an overseas branch (via telex) to *credit* the *overseas vendor's* bank account (in foreign currency), thereby extinguishing the liability to the foreign vendor (as reflected in the FX Accounts Payable account). All illustrations assume the use of bank wire transfers.[7]

Comprehensive Illustration

Hedging an Exposed *Liability*

Illustration 14-4 shows the entries that would be made under an FX forward entered into to protect the exposed liability of the £100,000 inventory purchase transaction with Vendor A. For simplicity, we ignored the effects of discounting (which would be minimal). For comparative purposes, we also show the entries relating to Vendor A, as shown earlier in Illustration 14-3. The direct exchange rates for the applicable dates in December 2006 and January 2007 (when the pound was strengthening) are as follows:

	December 11, 2006 (inception date)		December 31, 2006 (a financial reporting date)		January 10, 2007 (expiration date)
Spot rate	$1.50		$1.55		$1.59
Forward rate (*buying forward*)	1.50[a] [b]		1.55[c]		1.59
Change in rates		$.05	+	$.04	= $ .09
Elements existing			IV		IV
Element recorded as asset *or* liability			IV		IV

[a] Recall that the *forward rate* generally differs from the *spot rate* but that, for simplicity, we are temporarily assuming that they are identical to focus on the concept of achieving an offsetting gain in the event of a loss on the vendor transaction. Furthermore, as one moves closer to the expiration date, the difference between the *spot rate* and the *forward rate* for the remaining period of the contract becomes smaller and smaller so that **at the expiration date, the *forward rate* will have converged with the *spot rate*.**

[b] Box signifies a locked-in rate.

[c] The "market" forward rate for delivery on January 10, 2007 (10 days from now).

[7] If, however, the company were to physically take delivery of the foreign currency from the FX trader, a *debit* to the £ Cash account would be made. Later when the foreign currency is physically delivered to the vendor, the £ Cash account is *credited*, and the £ Accounts Payable account is *debited*.

ILLUSTRATION 14-4 HEDGING AN EXPOSED *LIABILITY*: FX FORWARD—*GROSS* OR *BROAD* ACCOUNTING JOURNAL ENTRIES

Transaction with Vendor (same as in Illustration 13-3)			*Hedging Transaction*		
DECEMBER 11, 2006 (THE TRANSACTION DATE AND THE INCEPTION OF THE FX FORWARD)					
Inventory	$150,000		*£ Due from FX Trader*	*$150,000*[a]	
£ Accounts Payable		$150,000	*$ Due to FX Trader*		*$150,000*[b]
To record inventory purchase. (£100,000 × $1.50 = $150,000)			*To record obligations under forward contract.* [a]*(£100,000 × $1.50 spot rate)* [b]*(£100,000 × $1.50 forward rate);* ***box signifies a fixed amount.***		
DECEMBER 31, 2006 (AN INTERVENING FINANCIAL REPORTING DATE)					
FX Loss	$5,000		*£ Due from FX Trader*	*$5,000*	
£ Accounts Payable		$5,000	*FX Gain*		*$5,000*
To adjust the pound payable to the current *spot rate.* ($1.55 – $1.50 = $.05) ($.05 × £100,000 = $5,000)			*To adjust the pound receivable to the current forward rate.* ($1.55 – $1.50 = $.05) ($.05 × £100,000 = $5,000)		
JANUARY 10, 2007 (THE SETTLEMENT DATE)					
FX Loss	$4,000		*£ Due from FX Trader*	*$4,000*	
£ Accounts Payable		$4,000	*FX Gain*		*$4,000*
To adjust the pound payable to the current *spot rate.* ($1.59 – $1.55 = $.04) ($.04 × £100,000 = $4,000)			*To adjust the pound receivable to the current forward rate.* ($1.59 – $1.55 = $.04) ($.04 × £100,000 = $4,000)		
£ Accounts Payable	$159,000		*$ Due to FX Trader*	*$150,000*	
Cash		$159,000	*Cash*	*9,000*	
To record payment to vendor **via a bank wire transfer.**			*£ Due from FX Trader*		*$159,000*
			To settle up with the FX Trader.		

Note: Procedurally, the FX trader (a bank) *charges* the company's checking account at the *forward rate*, which is the net amount of $150,000 ($159,000 – $9,000). Thus only a single amount appears on the company's bank statement.

SHORTCUT APPROACH AT THE JANUARY 10, 2007 SETTLEMENT DATE (NOT MAKING A SEPARATE ADJUSTMENT TO REFLECT THE CURRENT SPOT RATE)

FX Loss	$4,000		*Cash*	*$9,000*	
£ Accounts Payable	$155,000		*$ Due to FX Trader*	*$150,000*	
Cash		$159,000	*£ Due from FX Trader*		*$155,000*
			FX Gain		*$4,000*

Review Points for Illustration 14-4. Note the following:

1. **Independence of transactions.** Although the hedging transaction achieves the desired mirror effect of what occurs on the hedged item, the FX forward is a separate transaction from the company's transaction with Vendor A. Accordingly, the accounting entries for each transaction are prepared without regard to the other transaction. Thus the entries for the importing transaction with Vendor A are the same whether or not the company entered into the hedging transaction.
2. **Total break even.** During the 30-day period of the contract, the pound strengthened from $1.50 to $1.59. Without the FX forward, the $9,000 additional amount payable to Vendor A would *not* have been offset by the $9,000 FX gain on the FX forward.
3. **Amounts reported in the income statement.** No compelling reason exists to display the $5,000 loss and the $5,000 gain for 2006 separately in the income statement. Accordingly, they would be netted against each other.

4. **A perfect hedge.** This hedge is called a *"perfect" hedge* because (1) the amount of currency in the FX forward contract (£100,000) equals the amount of foreign currency owed the vendor and (2) the expiration date of the forward exchange contract coincided (by design) with the settlement date of the importing transaction. If the amount of currency on the hedging transaction *exceeded* the amount of currency owed the vendor, such excess would be treated as a speculation (discussed later). A difference in the expiration and settlement dates presents no accounting issues for this category of exposure.
5. ***Selling* forward instead of *buying* forward by mistake.** If management had unintentionally and mistakenly *sold forward* instead of *bought forward,* the company would have had two $9,000 losses because the FX forward would have been in the *same* direction as the exposed liability—*not* the *opposite* direction. Thus there would have been no counterbalancing or offsetting to the exposed liability—an additional future £ liability would have been created instead of an offsetting future £ asset.
6. **Result if the exchange rate had *decreased*.** If instead of increasing from $1.50 to $1.59 the spot exchange rate had decreased to $1.41, the company would have had (1) a $9,000 FX *gain* on its importing transaction and (2) a $9,000 FX *loss* on its FX forward. Perfect hedging results in a riskless position, but it also results in a profitless, winless outcome, with uncertainty existing only in execution by the counterparty (credit risk).
7. **Potential default by the domestic company.** If the domestic company *cannot* pay the foreign vendor at the contract expiration date and does *not* obtain a contract extension, the domestic importer must sell £100,000 to its bank as a means of fulfilling its U.S. dollar obligation under the FX forward. Procedurally at the January 10, 2007 expiration date, the bank (1) *charges* the *domestic importer's* account $150,000 for the purchase of the £100,000 (the forward rate of $1.50 × £100,000 = $150,000), (2) retains possession of the British pounds (the equivalent of the domestic importer making delivery to the dealer on the sale of the £100,000 to the dealer), and (3) *credits* the *importer's account* at the current selling price of $159,000 (the *spot rate* of $1.59 × £100,000).
8. **Readily determining whether a gain or loss occurred between any two dates.** To determine if a gain or loss occurred during any two dates, always view (1) the *forward rate* at the inception date as the ***buying rate*** (when *buying* forward, as in this illustration) or the ***selling rate*** (if *selling* forward) and (2) all *subsequent* forward rates as the *opposite rate* (in this illustration the ***selling rate***). Because the forward rate at inception is fixed, merely ask: **"Did the *opposite rate* move favorably or unfavorably?"** An increase in the ***selling rate*** is *favorable*, whereas an *increase* in the ***buying rate*** is *unfavorable*.

Reporting Receivables and Payables under Forward Contracts at Net Amounts

Because the legal *right of setoff*[8] (which arose as a practical way to eliminate unnecessary transactions between parties holding mutual debts) usually exists in FX forwards, it is customary practice to report in the balance sheet the company's net position in the contract (the fair value of the contract) rather than reporting each party's obligations.[9] Using Illustration 14-4, the net amount that would be reported in the balance sheet at December 31, 2006, is calculated as shown in the following table.

---

[8] A 1913 Supreme Court decision stated that setoff removes "the absurdity of making A pay B when B owes A." *Studley v. Boylston National Bank of Boston*, 229 U.S. 523, 57 L.Ed. 1313, 33 S.Ct. 806 (1913). (The right of setoff may *not* be available in some situations, such as when the counterparty is in a foreign country that does *not* recognize this right.)

[9] FASB *Interpretation No. 39*, "Offsetting of Amounts Related to Certain Contracts," clarifies when offsetting is allowed. For an individual contract, reporting the net position in the contract is always allowed. When multiple contracts exist, a net receivable position on *one* contract may or may not be offset against a net payable position on a *different* contract as explained next.

Multiple Contracts with the Same FX Trader. When multiple contracts exist with the *same* FX trader, a net receivable position on one contract *can* be offset against a net payable position on another contract *only* if a master netting arrangement exists. Under a **master netting arrangement,** a default on any one contract enables all of the separate contracts to be treated as one contract. This treatment entitles the other party to terminate the entire arrangement and to demand the net settlement of all of the individual contracts.

Multiple Contracts with Different FX Traders. When multiple contracts exist with *different* traders, offsetting is *not* permitted.

	Dr. (Cr.)
£ Due *from* FX trader	$ 155,000
$ Due *to* FX trader	(150,000)
Net Position (a receivable)	$ 5,000

The $5,000 net amount is the fair value of the contract.

Net Position Accounting for Forward Contracts

In Illustration 14-4, the journal entry amounts recorded at the inception of the contract reflected the contractual obligations of both parties—a *gross* or *broad* manner of recording. Although this approach has value for instructional purposes, it is *not* used in practice. Instead, companies make no journal entry at the inception of the contract. At each subsequent reporting date, **adjustments are made to reflect any change in the *forward rate*.**

Consequently, these procedures result in reflecting in the general ledger only the net position with the FX trader. This manner of accounting is shown in Illustration 14-5.[10] Again for simplicity, we assume that the forward rate and spot rate are *identical* at the inception of the contract. Also for simplicity, we do *not* deal with discounting at this point.

Hedging an Exposed *Asset*

A company that has a receivable in a foreign currency has an **exposed *asset*.** The accounting for this situation is symmetrical to that shown for exposed *liabilities*. An exposed *asset* most often results from an exporting transaction in which payment is to be received in the foreign currency. In these situations, the domestic exporter agrees to ***sell* a specified number of foreign currency units at a specified future date** to the FX trader. Because the domestic company is *selling* foreign currency under the FX forward, the **amount in dollars that it will receive from the FX trader is fixed.** Thus the domestic exporter "locks into" the number of dollars it will *receive* from its foreign customer.

Counterbalancing

In exchange for this fixed amount of dollars, the domestic company will deliver foreign currency to the FX trader. Disregarding the exporting transaction, the domestic company would have to buy the foreign currency from the FX trader so that it could deliver the currency to the FX trader to fulfill its obligation under the FX forward. This obligation (a future liability of the domestic company) creates the counterbalancing position to the domestic exporter's FX Accounts Receivable account balance with the exporter's foreign customer. Consequently, any change in the *spot rate* produces an FX gain or loss on the FX forward, which offsets the FX loss or gain, respectively, on the domestic exporter's FX Accounts Receivable.

Settling Up at the Expiration Date

Assume that a domestic exporter (1) has a £200,000 receivable from a foreign customer, (2) *sells* forward £200,000 at the *forward rate* of $1.52 on December 21, 2006, when the *spot rate* (direct) was $1.52, and (3) receives payment from the customer via a bank wire transfer on January 20, 2007, when the *spot rate* is $1.60. The use of bank wire transfer procedures is considered as the domestic exporter having made delivery to the FX trader. The procedure is for the foreign customer to instruct its bank to wire transfer £200,000 to the U.S. domestic exporter bank account. That foreign bank then (1) *charges* the *foreign customer's* checking account for £200,000 and (2) telexes the domestic exporter's U.S. bank with instructions to *credit* the *domestic exporter's* bank account for the dollar equivalent of £200,000 at the *spot rate* of $1.60 (the amount is $320,000). Because

[10] **Net Position Accounting.** This manner of accounting for forward exchange contracts is consistent with industry practice. Inquiries to audit partners of international Big Four accounting firms also confirm that companies account for forward exchange contracts in this manner—no general ledger entry is made on the books at the inception of the forward contract to reflect the obligations of each of the parties. Instead, the prevailing practice is to record a memorandum entry, which serves to track FX forwards (executory contracts) that are outstanding.

ILLUSTRATION 14-5 HEDGING AN EXPOSED *LIABILITY*: FX FORWARD—*NET POSITION* ACCOUNTING JOURNAL ENTRIES

Transaction with Vendor (same as in Illustration 13-3 and 14-4)			*Hedging Transaction*		
DECEMBER 11, 2006 (THE TRANSACTION DATE AND THE INCEPTION OF THE 30-DAY FX FORWARD)					
Inventory.	$150,000		Memorandum entry only.		
£ Accounts Payable		$150,000			
To record the inventory purchase. (£100,000 × $1.50 = $150,000)					
DECEMBER 31, 2006 (AN INTERVENING FINANCIAL REPORTING DATE)					
FX Loss	$5,000		*FX Contract Value—Forward,* ***net***	*$5,000*	
£ Accounts Payable		$5,000	*FX Gain*		*$5,000*
To adjust the pound payable to the current spot rate. ($1.55 – $1.50 = $.05) ($.05 × £100,000 = $5,000)			*To mark to market the net position with the FX Trader (change in forward rate of $.05 × £100,000 = $5,000).*		
JANUARY 10, 2007 (THE SETTLEMENT DATE)					
FX Loss	$4,000		*FX Contract Value—Forward,* ***net***	*$4,000*	
£ Accounts Payable		$4,000	*FX Gain*		*$4,000*
To adjust the pound payable to the current spot rate. ($1.59 – $1.55 = $.04) ($.04 × £100,000 = $4,000)			*To mark to market the net position with the FX Trader (change in forward rate of $.04 × £100,000 = $4,000).*		
£ Accounts Payable	$159,000				
Cash		$150,000			
FX Contract Value—Forward . . .		$9,000			
To record payment to vendor **via a bank wire transfer.** (The bank *charges* the company's checking account $150,000 [**the forward rate of $1.50 × £100,000**].)					

FX Contract Value—Forward, Net

Date	Debit	Credit
12/11/06	$ -0-	
	5,000	
12/31/06	$5,000[a]	
	4,000	
1/10/07	$9,000	

[a] Reported as an asset on the importer's 12/31/06 balance sheet.

of the FX forward, however, the bank *credits* the *domestic exporter's* account at the *forward rate* of $1.52 (the amount is $304,000). Thus the FX trader records a $16,000 gain on the difference.

Illustration 14-6 shows the entries for hedging an exposed asset using the exporting transaction shown for Customer X in Illustration 13-3. For comparative purposes, we also show the entries relating to Customer X, as shown in Illustration 13-3. The direct exchange rates at the applicable dates are repeated below for convenience:

	December 21, 2006 (inception date)		December 31, 2006 (a financial reporting date)		January 10, 2007 (expiration date)
Spot rate	$1.52		$1.55		$1.60
Forward rate (***selling forward***)	1.52[a] [b]		1.55[a]		1.60
Change in rates		$.03	+	$.05	= $ .08
Elements existing			IV		IV
Element recorded as asset *or* liability			IV		IV

[a] Assumed to be equal to the spot rate.
[b] Box signifies a locked-in rate.

ILLUSTRATION 14-6 HEDGING AN EXPOSED ASSET: FX FORWARD—NET POSITION ACCOUNTING JOURNAL ENTRIES

Transaction with Customer (same as in Illustration 13-3)			*Hedging Transaction*		
DECEMBER 11, 2006 (THE TRANSACTION DATE AND THE INCEPTION OF THE 30-DAY FX FORWARD)					
£ Accounts Receivable	$304,000		Memorandum entry only.		
Sales		$304,000			
To record sale. (£200,000 × $1.52 = $304,000)					
DECEMBER 31, 2006 (AN INTERVENING FINANCIAL REPORTING DATE)					
£ Accounts Receivable	$6,000		*FX Loss*	*$6,000*	
FX Gain		$6,000	*FX Contract Value—Forward,* ***net***		*$6,000*
To adjust the pound receivable to the current spot rate. ($1.55 − $1.52 = $.03) ($.03 × £200,000 = $6,000)			*To mark to market the net position with the FX Trader (change in the forward rate of $.03 × £200,000 = $6,000).*		
JANUARY 20, 2007 (THE SETTLEMENT DATE)					
£ Accounts Receivable	$10,000		*FX Loss*	*$10,000*	
FX Gain		$10,000	*FX Contract Value—Forward,* ***net***		*$10,000*
To adjust the pound receivable to the current spot rate. ($1.60 − $1.55 = $.05) ($.05 × £200,000 = $10,000)			*To mark to market the net position with the FX Trader* (change in the forward rate of $.05 × £200,000 = $10,000).		
Cash	$304,000				
FX Contract Value—Forward, ***net***	$16,000				
£ Accounts Receivable		$320,000			
To record payment from customer **via a bank wire transfer.** (The bank *credits* the company's checking account $304,000 [**the** ***forward rate*** **of $1.52 × £200,000**].)					

FX Contract Value—Forward, Net

Debit	Credit	Date
	$ -0-	12/11/06
	6,000	
	$ 6,000[a]	12/31/06
	10,000	
	$16,000	1/20/07

[a] Reported as a liability on the importer's 12/31/06 balance sheet.

Review Points for Illustration 14-6. Note the following:

1. **Total offset.** The FX gains on the exporting transaction are exactly offset by FX losses on the hedging transaction.
2. **Potential default by the foreign customer.** If the foreign customer does *not* pay the domestic exporter by the contract expiration date and does *not* obtain a contract extension, the domestic exporter must purchase £200,000 from its bank so that it has £200,000 to deliver to its bank in fulfillment of its obligation under the FX forward. Procedurally at the January 20, 2007, expiration date, the bank (1) *charges* the *domestic exporter's* account $320,000 for the purchase of the £200,000 (the current *spot rate* of $1.60 × £200,000 = $320,000), (2) retains possession of the British pounds (the equivalent of the domestic exporter making delivery to the dealer on the contract), and (3) *credits* the exporter's account at the fixed selling price of $304,000 (the *forward rate* of $1.52 × £200,000).
3. **Result if the exchange rate had** ***decreased.*** If instead of *increasing* from $1.52 to $1.60 the spot rate had *decreased* to $1.44, the company would have had (1) a $16,000 FX *loss* on its exporting transaction and (2) a $16,000 FX *gain* on its FX forward.

Comparing Forward Exchange Contracts to *Options*

Because either a gain or loss can occur on an FX forward, FX forwards differ considerably from FX options, in which only a gain can occur for the FX option's holder. For this reason, FX options are preferred when the occurrence of the transaction is uncertain.

The "Two-Options" View

The "holder" and "issuer" (or "writer") categories are generally *not* used in the context of FX forwards as they are in the context of FX options. Under the "two-options" view, however, the substance of an FX forward is viewed as being an arrangement in which each party effectively has written an option to the other. Thus each party is considered both a writer *and* a holder (a *call* being *written* in one currency and a *put* being *held* in the other currency). One of the options will always be executed because one of the parties will always be in a favorable position (in the money) while the other party will be in an unfavorable position (out of the money).[11]

CHECK POINT

A domestic *exporter* that enters into an FX forward to hedge an *FX receivable* must do the following:

a. Defer any hedging FX gain or loss until the *settlement date*.
b. Initially record—at the spot rate—a *receivable* from the FX trader.
c. Initially record—at the contractually fixed amount to be paid—a *liability* to the FX trader.
d. Continuously carry—at the *forward rate*—an *FX receivable* from the FX trader.
e. Reflect adjustments to its FX position based on the change in the *forward rate*.
f. Reflect adjustments to its FX position based on the change in the *spot rate*.

Answer: e

VI. FX FORWARD EXCHANGE CONTRACTS: PREMIUMS AND DISCOUNTS

Earlier we stated that the *forward rate* usually differs slightly from the *spot rate* and that one component of this difference is the fee or commission that the FX trader charges for assuming the risk that the exchange rate could change adversely. Before discussing how the FX trader's commission is embedded into the forward rate, we discuss the other component—a time value of money element—that usually accounts for the major portion of the difference.

The Primary Reason That the *Spot Rate* and *Forward Rate* Usually Differ: The Interest Rate Parity System

The difference between the *spot rate* and the *forward rate* that usually exists is primarily attributable to the difference in interest rates obtainable on the two currencies in the international money market for the duration of the contract.

[11] Such a situation would *not* occur, however, in rare instances in which the *spot rate* at the end of the contract period coincidentally equals the *forward rate* at the inception of the contract; no sound reason would exist for the parties to exchange currencies in such circumstances.

Foreign Interest Rate Is *Higher* Than the U.S. Interest Rate

When the interest rate obtainable on the foreign currency is *higher* than the interest rate obtainable on the U.S. dollar, the *forward* rate is *lower* than the *spot rate*, and the foreign currency is said to be **selling at a *discount* on the forward market.**

Foreign Interest Rate Is *Lower* than the U.S. Interest Rate

On the other hand, when the interest rate obtainable on the foreign currency is *lower* than the interest rate obtainable on the U.S. dollar, the *forward rate* is *higher* than the *spot rate*, and the foreign currency is said to be **selling at a *premium* on the forward market.**

For example, assume that (1) the interest rate obtainable in the U.S. is 6%, (2) the interest rate obtainable in Great Britain is 11%, (3) the spot rate is $2.00, and (4) a U.S. treasurer has $200,000 available for a 1-year money market investment. The 1-year forward rate for selling pounds would have to be $1.9099 (a discount to the spot rate) to offset the additional $10,000 of interest earned in Great Britain. The FX traders use the following formula: ($2.00 spot rate × 1.06/1.11 = $1.9099). The interest rates obtainable at any point in time must be the same in parity or capital floods to one country or the other.

Thus an interest rate parity system exists, which in effect prevents the transfer of money between international money markets merely to obtain a higher interest rate relatively risk free through the use of an FX forward (otherwise, it would be the equivalent of having a money machine).

The FX Trader's Commission

The FX trader earns its commission for assuming the risk of an adverse exchange rate change by adjusting the *forward rate* that is calculated to offset the effect of the interest rate differentials between the two countries. For example, assume that the 30-day *forward rate* for the British pound is $1.51 as determined by adjusting the *spot rate* of $1.50 for the lower interest rate in the United Kingdom. To earn a commission, the FX trader provides *bid* (what the FX trader is willing to *buy* at) and *ask* quotes (what the FX trader is willing to *sell* at) slightly different from this $1.51. For example, the FX trader's **bid quote to *buy* pounds forward** might be $1.505 (for when the *customer* is *selling* forward) and the trader's **ask quote to *sell* pounds forward** might be $1.515 (for when the *customer* is *buying* forward). The $.01 spread is for the FX trader's profit. Thus a commission of $.005 each way is embedded in the *forward rate.*

Calculating the Total Premium or Discount

The difference between the *spot rate* and the *forward rate* multiplied by the units of foreign currency to be received or delivered under the contract equals the total amount of the premium or discount on the FX forward. For example, assume that the 30-day *forward rate* for the domestic importer in Illustrations 14-4 and 14-5 is $1.515 (instead of equaling the $1.50 *spot rate*). Thus the domestic importer must pay an additional $1,500 (£100,000 × $.015) to the FX trader at the expiration date. The $1,500 is a premium since the domestic importer is buying at *more than* the *spot rate.*

Determining Whether Premiums or Discounts Exist and Whether They Eventually Result in Debits or Credits to Equity

The *Importer's* Situation: *Buying* a Foreign Currency to Hedge an Existing Exposed Liability

When one buys an asset (whether it be a foreign currency or a personal car) at **more** than its current value, the asset is bought at a **premium.** Buying an asset at a premium impacts stockholders' equity *negatively*; thus the accounting for the premium should result in a **debit** balance that eventually is charged to equity. Buying an asset at **less** than its current value is buying at a **discount,** which would ultimately impact stockholders' equity *favorably*; thus the accounting for the buying discount results in a **credit** balance that eventually is credited to equity.

The *Exporter's* Situation: *Selling* a Foreign Currency to Hedge an Existing Exposed Asset

When one sells an asset at more or less than its current value, the debits and credits are reversed because selling at **more** than the current value is a *favorable* event and selling at **less** than the current value is an *unfavorable* event.

In Illustration 14-7, we summarize the occurrence of premiums and discounts and when a debit or credit balance for the premium or discount results on FX forwards.

CHECK POINT

A U.S. firm that enters into an FX forward to *sell* euros when the *spot rate* is $1.15 and the *forward rate* is $1.14 has:

a. A *premium* that will eventually result in a *gain.*
b. A *premium* that will eventually result in a *loss.*
c. A *discount* that will eventually result in a *gain.*
d. A *discount* that will eventually result in a *loss.*

Answer: d

Should Earnings Be Adjusted Immediately for Premiums and Discounts?

An entity's purchase or sale forward at more or less than the *spot rate* raises the question of whether the entity has theoretically suffered an immediate economic loss or obtained an immediate economic gain, as the case may be, at the inception of the FX forward. The answer is *no.* We give the reasons for a situation in which an entity *buys forward* at *more* than the spot rate.

ILLUSTRATION 14-7 WHEN PREMIUMS AND DISCOUNTS OCCUR ON FX FORWARDS USED TO HEDGE IMPORTING AND EXPORTING TRANSACTIONS

Buying or Selling Foreign Currency Forward	Direct Rate: Spot Rate[b]	Direct Rate: Forward Rate	Result[a]: Premium	Result[a]: Discount
Importer (exposed payable):				
Buying[c]	$1.50	$1.52[d]	x(Debit)	
Buying[c]	1.50	1.48		x(Credit)
Exporter (exposed receivable):				
Selling[e]	1.50	1.52	x(Credit)	
Selling[e]	1.50	1.48		x(Debit)

[a] *Debits* eventually *reduce* stockholders' equity; *credits* eventually *increase* stockholders' equity.

[b] The spot rate is the point of reference.

[c] In the trading vernacular, entering into a contract to ***buy*** **a currency on the forward market is called being *long* in that currency.**

[d] The entries for this situation are shown later in Illustration 14-8.

[e] In the trading vernacular, entering into a contract to ***sell*** **a currency (that one does *not* currently own) on the forward market is called being *short* in that currency.**

1. **The FX forward has a value in the market place.** Thus minutes after the contract is entered into, the buyer could sell the FX forward in the market place for roughly the amount of the premium.
2. **The FX forward can be undone.** Banks usually allow FX forwards to be undone for an amount equal to the sum of (1) closing costs, (2) that portion of the premium that has expired based on the passage of time, and (3) any loss the bank has incurred as a result of an adverse change in the spot rate. Thus minutes after the contract is entered into, the buyer could undo the FX forward and pay but a fraction of the premium.

The Nature of the *Time Value* Element

Premiums and discounts are often viewed as the **cost of obtaining the hedge,** which is analogous to an insurance premium that should be accounted for solely based on the passage of time. Thus **premiums and discounts are generally viewed as a *time value* element** (because they generally lose value as a result of the passage of time) of FX forwards (the other element being the *intrinsic value* element, which we discussed earlier).

Accruing onto the Books—Not *Amortizing* What Is Already on the Books

For FX forwards, no cash payment is made for premiums and discounts on FX forwards at the contract inception—unlike what occurs for FX option premiums. Instead, FX forward premiums and discounts (because they are much *lower* than FX option premiums) are dealt with at the contract expiration date (for practical reasons) when each of the two parties executes in cash. And because no journal entry is recorded for the FX forward in the general ledger at the contract inception (to record the contractual obligations of each party), FX forward premiums and discounts (the *time value* element) must be *accrued* onto the balance sheet over the life of the contract (rather than effectively being amortized off the balance sheet over the life of the contract, as is the case with FX options).

Calculating the Time Value Element and the Intrinsic Value Element Separately

To illustrate these calculations, assume the following information for an entity that *bought forward* £100,000 on December 11, 2006:

	December 11, 2006 (inception date)		December 31, 2006 (a financial reporting date)		January 10, 2007 (expiration date)
Spot rate	$1.50		$1.55		$1.59
Forward rate (***buying* forward**)	1.52[a]		1.56		1.59[b]
Premium	.02		.01		n/a
Change in the:					
Spot rate		$.05	+	$.04	= $ .09
Forward rate		.04	+	.03	= .07
Premium.		.01	+	.01	= .02
Element existing.	**TV**		**TV & IV**		**IV**
Element recorded as asset *or* liability			**TV & IV**		**TV & IV**

[a] Note that a $2,000 premium exists (£100,000 × $.02). (The box signifies a locked-in rate.)

[b] Recall that the *forward rate* converges to the *spot rate* at the contract expiration date.

The following two ways exist to calculate the FX forward's fair value at December 31, 2006 (each produces the *same* total fair value):

1. **The combined approach.** Under this approach, the change in the *forward rate* is used. Accordingly, the FX forward's contract fair value is determined by continuously valuing the FX forward (on a net basis) using the change in the *forward rate* from the contract inception *date* to the *financial reporting date*. Consequently, **the FX forward's contract value is adjusted simultaneously**

for both the *time value* element and the *intrinsic value* element. Accordingly, the FX forward's fair value at December 31, 2006, is determined as follows:

FX Contract Value—Forward, net (a net *receivable* position):

($.04 change in the *forward rate* [from $1.52 to $1.56] × £100,000	$4,000[a]

[a] This technique works because, as explained shortly, the *forward rate* (1) moves in tandem with the *spot rate* and (2) converges to the *spot rate* at the contract expiration date.

2. **The individual elements approach.** Under this approach, the change in the *spot rate* is used for the *intrinsic value element*, and the change in the premium or discount is used for the *time value element*, as shown here:

FX Contract Value—Forward, net (a net *receivable* position):

Intrinsic value element ($.05 *change* in the *spot rate* [$1.55 – $1.50] × £100,000)—by itself an asset	$ 5,000
Time value element ($.01 *decrease* in the initial premium [$.02 – $.01] × £100,000)—by itself, a liability	(1,000)
	$ 4,000

Split versus Nonsplit Accounting—Whether to Report the Changes to the *Time Value Element* Separately from the Changes to the *Intrinsic Value Element*

The issue is whether to report the FX gains and losses resulting from the changes in these elements the same way or differently. Recall that the same issue exists for FX options. In comparison with FX options, however, this issue is far less important because premiums and discounts on FX forwards are much *lower*.

For *"undesignated" hedges*, the FX gains and losses on each element must be reported the *same* way—in earnings currently. For both *fair value hedges* and *cash flow hedges* however, *FAS 133* allows FX gains and losses on each element to be reported either the same way or differently—depending on how the entity assesses hedge effectiveness (discussed later).

Discounting Required

As discussed earlier, *FAS 133* also requires that the fair value of an FX forward (the *net* contractual amount) be discounted to its present value. Thus if the present value of the $4,000 in the preceding example were $3,990, the FX gain or loss to be recognized for the period would be $3,990—*not* $4,000. For simplicity, we assume that the effects of discounting are insignificant in all remaining illustrations—thus we ignore discounting.

Comprehensive Illustration

Hedging an Exposed *Liability*—Nonsplit Accounting for Premium

Illustration 14-8 is a recast of Illustration 14-5 assuming that the *forward rate* and the *spot rate* do differ at the contract inception date. The direct exchange rates along with other assumed information follow:

	December 11, 2006 (inception date)		December 31, 2006 (a financial reporting date)			January 10, 2007 (expiration date)
Spot rate	$1.50		$1.55			$1.59
Forward rate (***buying* forward**)	1.52[a]		1.56			1.59[b]
Premium	.02		.01			n/a
Change in the:						
Spot rate		$.05	+	$.04	=	$ .09
Forward rate		.04	+	.03	=	.07
Premium............		.01	+	.01	=	.02
Element existing..........	**TV**		**TV & IV**			**IV**
Element recorded as asset *or* liability			**TV & IV**			**TV & IV**

[a] Note that a $2,000 premium exists (£100,000 × $.02). (The box signifies a locked-in rate.)

[b] Recall that the *forward rate* converges to the *spot rate* at the contract expiration date.

ILLUSTRATION 14-8 HEDGING AN EXPOSED *LIABILITY*: FX FORWARD—*NET POSITION*
ACCOUNTING JOURNAL ENTRIES—NONSPLIT ACCOUNTING FOR PREMIUM

Transaction with Vendor (same as in Illustration 13-3 and 14-5)			*Hedging Transaction*		
DECEMBER 11, 2006 (THE TRANSACTION DATE AND THE INCEPTION OF THE 30-DAY FX FORWARD)					
Inventory....................	$150,000		Memorandum entry only.		
Accounts Payable		$150,000			
To record inventory purchase. (£100,000 × $1.50 = $150,000)					
DECEMBER 31, 2006 (AN INTERVENING FINANCIAL REPORTING DATE)					
FX Loss	$5,000		*FX Contract Value—Forward,* ***net***	*$4,000*	
Accounts Payable		$5,000	*FX Gain*		*$4,000*
To adjust the pound payable to the current *spot rate.* ($1.55 – $1.50 = $.05) ($.05 × £100,000 = $5,000)			*To mark to market the net position with the FX Trader* (change in *forward rate* of $.04 × £100,000 = $4,000).		
JANUARY 10, 2007 (THE SETTLEMENT DATE)					
FX Loss	$4,000		*FX Contract Value—Forward,* ***net***	*$3,000*	
Accounts Payable		$4,000	*FX Gain*		*$3,000*
To adjust the pound payable to the current *spot rate.* ($1.59 – $1.55 = $.04) ($.04 × £100,000 = $4,000)			*To mark to market the net position with the FX Trader* (change in *forward rate* of $.03 × £100,000 = $3,000).		

Transaction with Vendor		
Accounts Payable	$159,000	
Cash		$152,000
FX Contract Value—Forward ...		$7,000
To record payment to vendor **via a bank wire transfer.** (The bank *charges* the company's checking account $152,000 [**the forward rate of $1.52 × £100,000**].)		

FX Contract Value—Forward, (net)

12/11/06	$ -0-	
	4,000	
12/31/06	$4,000[a]	
	3,000	
1/10/07	$7,000	

[a] Reported as an asset on the importer's 12/31/06 balance sheet.

Review Points for Illustration 14-8. Note the following:

1. Because of the existence of the $2,000 premium, the FX gains on the FX forward ($7,000 cumulative) do *not* completely offset the FX losses on the importing transactions ($9,000 cumulative) during each reporting period. The difference between the two occurs because of the $2,000 premium.
2. In many instances, the effects of discounting are immaterial. Thus, in the interest of practicality, discounting can be ignored in those instances.

The Relationship between the Forward Rate and the Future Spot Rate

Current expectations of future events influence both the spot rate and the forward rate. Both rates move in tandem with the difference between them based on interest rate differentials. Because interest rates reflect expectations about inflation rates, the forward rates effectively forecast future spot rates based on differential rates of expected inflation—**the expected nominal change in the exchange rate.**

Because noninflationary factors have such a major day-to-day (short-term) impact on exchange rates, however, future spot rates rarely coincide with the forward rates—**the difference being the**

real change in the exchange rate. If this were not so and instead an extremely high correlation existed between forward rates and future spot rates, little justification for hedging would exist. For example, the spot and 180-day forward rates for the British pound in March 1992 were near $1.80 and $1.75 respectively. Shortly after the European currency crisis of September 1992 occurred, the spot rate was about $1.50—nearly 15% below the 180-day forward rate in March 1992. FX traders having bought pounds 180 days forward in March 1992 lost heavily (they also had huge gains on contracts in which they sold pounds 180 days forward). A fuller discussion of forward rates, expected future spot rates, and interest parity may be found in international finance texts. The basics presented here cannot be observed in FX quotes empirically without allowing for other economic variables.

CHECK POINT

On 12/10/06, Hegex entered into a 90-day FX forward involving 1,000,000 euros in anticipation that the euro would *weaken.* The following direct exchange rates are assumed:

	December 10, 2006	December 31, 2006	March 10, 2007
Spot rate	$1.20	$1.18	$1.21
Forward rate	1.16	1.17	1.21

The amount of the hedging FX gain or loss to be reported **in earnings** in 2006 and 2007, assuming that the FX forward hedges an *FX receivable* arising from an *exporting* transaction, is:

a. a $10,000 gain.
b. a $10,000 loss.
c. a $20,000 gain.
d. a $20,000 loss.
e. a $30,000 gain.
f. a $30,000 loss.
g. a $40,000 gain.
h. a $40,000 loss.
i. a $50,000 gain.
j. a $50,000 loss.
k. $-0-.
l. None of the above.

Answers: b, h

VII. SPECULATING IN FOREIGN CURRENCY

Speculating occurs when a company attempts to make a gain from an expected change in the spot rate without regard to any particular area of FX exposure. Thus there is no intent to create a counterbalancing position to obtain a hedge. To gain from an expected change in the exchange rate, one merely hopes to buy *low* and sell *high.*

Speculating is risky as evident from the following Case in Point.

CASE IN POINT

In 1998, the giant hedge fund Tiger Management lost $2 billion *speculating* on the future direction of the Japanese yen.

Assume that the Swiss franc has a current spot rate of $.50 and a 180-day forward rate of $.53. If managers expected the Swiss franc to rise higher than the $.53 forward rate in the next six months and wanted to make a gain if the spot rate rose as they expected, they would *buy* Swiss francs forward (at $.53) now and hope that they could sell them in the open market in 180 days at *more* than $.53. On the other hand, if managers expected the Swiss franc to fall, then they would *sell* Swiss francs forward (at $.53) now and hope that they could buy them in the open market in 180 days at *less* than $.53.

Accounting Treatment

Under *FAS 133*, any gains or losses on such speculative FX forwards are recognized currently in *earnings* as they arise.

Comprehensive Illustration

Speculating in Foreign Currency

Assume that a domestic company takes the view on November 1, 2006, that the Swiss franc (SFr) will strengthen within 100 days. Accordingly, it *buys* forward 1,000,000 SFr at the 100-day forward rate of $.510. Illustration 14-9 shows the entries that would be made for this contract assuming the following direct exchange rates:

	November 1, 2006 (inception date)		December 31, 2006 (a financial reporting date)			February 9, 2007 (expiration date)
Spot rate	$.500		$.550			$.570
Forward rate (***buying* forward**)	.510		.553			.570
Premium	.010		.003			n/a
Change in the:						
Spot rate		$.050	+	$.020	=	$.070
Forward rate		.043	+	.017	=	.060
Premium.		.007	+	.003	=	.01
Elements existing	**TV**		**TV & IV**			**IV**
Element recorded as asset *or* liability			**TV & IV**			**TV & IV**

ILLUSTRATION 14-9 SPECULATING IN FOREIGN CURRENCY: NET POSITION ACCOUNTING JOURNAL ENTRIES

NOVEMBER 1, 2006
(THE INCEPTION OF THE 100-DAY FX FORWARD)

No general ledger entries are made.

DECEMBER 31, 2006
(AN INTERVENING FINANCIAL REPORTING DATE)

FX Contract Value—Forward, **net** (a receivable)	$43,000	
FX Gain.		$43,000

To mark to market the net position with the FX dealer (using the change in the forward rate).
($.553 – $.510 = $.043)
($.043 × 1,000,000 SFr = $43,000)

FEBRUARY 9, 2007
(THE EXPIRATION DATE OF THE FX FORWARD)

FX Contract Value—Forward, **net** (a receivable)	$17,000	
FX Gain.		$17,000

To mark to market the net position with the FX trader (using the change in the forward rate).
($.570 – $.553 = $.017)
($.017 × 1,000,000 SFr = $17,000)

Cash.	$60,000	
FX Contract Value—Forward, **net**.		$60,000

To settle up with the FX trader.
($.57 ending spot rate – $.51 initial forward rate = $.06)
($.06 × 1,000,000 SFr = $60,000)

To settle up, the speculator now sells to the FX trader at the $.570 spot rate the 1,000,000 SFr it purchased from the FX trader at the forward rate of $.510. The FX trader (a bank) credits the speculator's account for the $60,000 net amount.

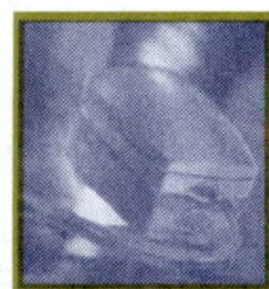

CHECK POINT

On 12/10/06, Hegex entered into a 90-day FX forward involving 1,000,000 euros in anticipation that the euro would weaken. The following *direct* exchange rates are assumed:

	December 10, 2006	December 31, 2006	March 10, 2007
Spot rate	$1.20	$1.18	$1.21
Forward rate	1.16	1.17	1.21

The amount of the hedging FX gain or loss to be reported **in earnings** in 2006 and 2007, assuming that the FX forward is for *speculating*, is:

a. a $10,000 gain.
b. a $10,000 loss.
c. a $20,000 gain.
d. a $20,000 loss.
e. a $30,000 gain.
f. a $30,000 loss.
g. a $40,000 gain.
h. a $40,000 loss.
i. a $50,000 gain.
j. a $50,000 loss.
k. $-0-
l. None of the above.

Answers: b, h

VIII. HEDGING FIRM FOREIGN-CURRENCY-DENOMINATED COMMITMENTS (*FAIR VALUE* HEDGES)

Hedging transactions can be entered into *before* the transaction date (the date an FX receivable or FX liability is recorded), a period that is called the *anticipatory transaction period.*

Firm Commitment to *Purchase*

When a domestic importer expects to issue a *purchase order* requiring payment in a foreign vendor's currency, the domestic company's FX exposure begins when the expectation arises—*not* when a liability is recorded later at the transaction date upon receipt of the inventory. The *anticipatory transaction period* may be separated into as many as three distinct periods, as shown in Illustration 14-10.

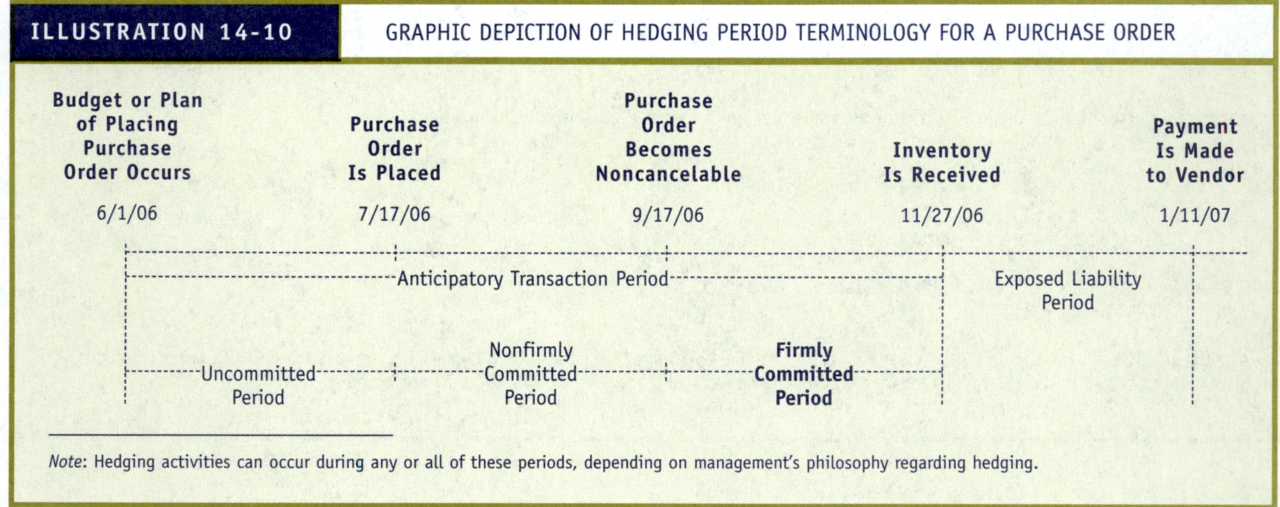

Note: Hedging activities can occur during any or all of these periods, depending on management's philosophy regarding hedging.

We discuss in this section only the accounting for hedges that occur during the *firmly committed* portion of the *anticipatory transaction period.* During the *firmly committed period*, one or more intervening financial reporting dates may occur, raising the issue of whether and how to report hedging gains and losses that occur during this period. Illustration 14-11 (an extension of that portion of Illustration 14-10 that concerns us here) shows the accounting to be followed for hedging FX gains and losses that occur during the *firmly committed period.*

Accounting During the Firmly Committed Period—"The Fair Value Hedging Model"

FAS 133 uses the term "fair value hedge" to signify hedging transactions in which (1) hedging gains and losses on the *derivative* are to be recognized in earnings currently and (2) gains and losses on the *hedged item* are also to be recognized in earnings currently. Thus concurrent recognition in earnings occurs. (Recall that the FX hedging gain or loss *cannot* be deferred and reported as a liability or an asset, respectively, because such items do *not* satisfy the definitions of liabilities and assets, respectively.)

Items that may be designated as *hedged items* in fair value hedges are (1) *unrecognized* firm commitments and (2) *recognized* assets and liabilities that are either (a) *not* accounted for on a fair value basis (such as inventory) or (b) accounted for on a fair value basis but with the market adjustment required to be initially reported in Other Comprehensive Income (such as is required for available-for-sale securities under *FAS 115*). Accordingly, **the derivative hedges the exposure to potential adverse changes in the *fair value* of the hedged item.** In this chapter, we discuss only fair value hedges of *unrecognized* firm foreign-currency-denominated commitments.

Accounting for Hedges of Unrecognized Firm Foreign-Currency-Denominated Commitments

Under the fair value hedge accounting model, the following accounting treatment occurs during the commitment period for the unrecognized firm purchase or sales commitment:

1. An FX commitment liability or FX commitment asset is recognized in the balance sheet based on the change in the exchange rate (either forward or spot as explained later).
2. The offsetting debit or credit is an FX loss or gain that is recognized currently in earnings.

Thus concurrent recognition of FX gains and FX losses occurs **in earnings** during the firmly committed period (such as a $9,000 *FX loss* on the *firm commitment* and a $9,000 *FX gain* on the

ILLUSTRATION 14-11 GRAPHIC DEPICTION OF RELEVANT DATES: FIRMLY COMMITTED PURCHASE

Purchase Order Becomes Noncancelable	Intervening Financial Reporting Date: If Hedged, Recognize in Earnings	Transaction Date: Record Transaction	Intervening Financial Reporting Date: Adjust FX Payable	Settlement Date: Pay Vendor
9/17/06	9/30/06	11/27/06	12/31/06	1/11/07

Firmly Committed Period (9/17/06 – 11/27/06) | Exposed Liability Period (11/27/06 – 1/11/07)

FX Exposure Period (9/17/06 – 1/11/07)

Must Recognize Hedging FX Gain or Loss in Earnings | **Must** Recognize Hedging FX Gain or Loss in Earnings

Must Recognize FX Commitment Gain or Loss in Earnings | **Must** Recognize FX Payable Gain or Loss in Earnings

derivative *hedging transaction*). This manner of accounting for the commitment during the commitment period is the "special hedge accounting" that exists under the fair value hedge accounting model.

Before discussing (1) the FASB's rationale for recognizing assets and liabilities on unrecognized firm commitments and (2) qualifying conditions for using the fair value hedging model, we present an illustration of a firm purchase commitment.

Comprehensive Illustration

Hedging a Firm Foreign-Currency-Denominated Purchase Commitment

Assume that a domestic company with a calendar year-end entered into the following two transactions on October 2, 2006:

1. It ordered equipment built to its specifications from a French manufacturer. The purchase price is 1,000,000 euros. Delivery is to be in 120 days (January 30, 2007), and the payment is due then (thus the *transaction date* and the *settlement date* on the purchase are to coincide).
2. It entered into an FX forward with an FX trader to *buy* 1,000,000 euros on January 30, 2007, at the *forward rate* of $1.23.
3. The *manner of assessing hedge effectiveness*—**which must be determined and documented at the *inception* of the hedge**—is to compare (1) the total change in the FX forward's *fair value* with (2) the change in the *fair value* of the FX commitment using the change in the *forward rate.* (As shown later, no hedge *ineffectiveness* occurs in such situations.)

Illustration 14-12 shows these transactions as accounted for assuming (1) an intervening financial reporting date of December 31, 2006, and (2) delivery and payments are made as required on January 30, 2007. The direct exchange rates for the euro and other assumed information follows:

	October 2, 2006 (inception date)		December 31, 2006 (financial reporting date)			January 30, 2007 (expiration date)
Spot rate	$1.20		$1.25			$1.30
Forward rate (***buying* forward**)	1.23		1.26			1.30
Premium	.03		.01			n/a
Change in the:						
Spot rate		$.05	+	$.05	=	$ .10
Forward rate		.03	+	.04	=	.07
Premium.		.02	+	.01	=	.03
Elements existing	**TV**		**TV & IV**			**IV**
Element recorded as asset *or* liability			**TV & IV**			**TV & IV**

Review Points for Illustration 14-12. Note the following:

1. The rationale for capitalizing the equipment's cost at $1,230,000 is that the company effectively locked itself into paying at the *forward rate* of $1.23 rather than having to pay at the $1.30 *spot rate* on January 30, 2007.
2. **Measuring hedge effectiveness.** Because the change in the commitment's fair value was based on the change in the *forward rate* (the same assessment method used on the FX forward) and because the currency quantities were identical on both the FX forward and the FX commitment, exactly offsetting FX gains and losses were reported in each period. Thus no hedge ineffectiveness occurred.
3. **Limiting factors in adjusting the FX commitment.** The adjustment to the FX commitment is limited to the *lower of* (1) the FX forward's gain or loss ($70,000 gain in this case) or (2) the amount produced using the documented manner of determining the change in the FX commitment's fair value (a $70,000 loss in this case).
   ***Under*hedged:** If the FX forward had been for only 800,000 euros rather than 1,000,000 euros, however, the FX forward's cumulative gain would have been only $56,000 (80% of $70,000). Thus the cumulative adjustment to the FX commitment would be only $56,000—*not* $70,000.

ILLUSTRATION 14-12 HEDGING A FIRM FOREIGN-CURRENCY-DENOMINATED PURCHASE COMMITMENT USING AN FX FORWARD; NET POSITION ACCOUNTING JOURNAL ENTRIES

Transaction with Vendor			*Hedging Transaction*		

OCTOBER 2, 2006
(THE DATE OF ISSUING THE EQUIPMENT PURCHASE ORDER AND ENTERING INTO THE 120-DAY FX FORWARD)

No G/L entries are made—only memorandum entries to reflect current position:
1. Purchase Commitment—***Short***: 1,000,000 euros
2. FX Forward Contract—***Long***: 1,000,000 euros (*bought* forward)

DECEMBER 31, 2006
(AN INTERVENING *FINANCIAL REPORTING DATE*)

Transaction with Vendor	Dr.	Cr.	Hedging Transaction	Dr.	Cr.
FX Loss—Firm Commitment	$30,000		*FX Contract Value—Forward,* ***net***	*$30,000*	
FX Firm Commitment (a liability)		$30,000	*FX Gain*		*$30,000*
To recognize *loss* on firm commitment **in earnings** (based on change in the fair value using the change in the *forward rate*).			*To recognize gain on FX forward* ***in earnings*** (change in *forward rate* of $.03 × 1,000,000 euros = $30,000).		

JANUARY 30, 2007
(THE *TRANSACTION DATE,* WHICH COINCIDES WITH THE *SETTLEMENT DATE,* AND THE FX FORWARD'S *EXPIRATION DATE*)

Transaction with Vendor	Dr.	Cr.	Hedging Transaction	Dr.	Cr.
FX Loss—Firm Commitment	$40,000		*FX Contract Value—Forward,* ***net***	*$40,000*	
FX Firm Commitment (a liability)		$40,000	*FX Gain*		*$40,000*
To recognize loss on firm commitment **in earnings** (based on change in the fair value using the change in the *forward rate*).			*To recognize gain on FX forward* ***in earnings*** (change in *forward rate* of $.04 × 1,000,000 euros = $40,000).		
Equipment	$1,230,000		*Cash*	$70,000	
FX Firm Commitment	$70,000		*FX Contract Value—Forward,* ***net***		$70,000
Cash (at *spot rate*)		$1,300,000	*To settle FX forward.*		
To record equipment purchase. . . . . . pay vendor, and extinguish FX commitment (note that $70,000 of the $1,300,000 paid to the vendor was expensed). (1,000,000 euros × $1.30 *spot rate*)					

Alternate Short-cut (combined) Entry:

Account	Dr.	Cr.
Equipment	$1,230,000	
FX Commitment	70,000	
FX Contract Value—Forward, net.		$70,000
Cash ($1,300,000 – $70,000).		$1,230,000

Key Point: The result of the *vendor transaction* and the *hedging transaction* ***together is as if*** the *importing transaction* had been denominated in $1,230,000 **dollars** initially (which would have negated the need to enter into the hedging transaction).

Earnings

	Debit	Credit	
2006:	$30,000	$30,000	
		$ -0-	12/31/06
2007:	40,000	40,000	
		$ -0-	1/30/07

FX Contract Value—Forward, (net)

	Debit	Credit
10/2/06	$ -0-	
	30,000	
12/31/06	$30,000[a]	
	40,000	
1/30/07	$70,000	

[a] Reported as an asset on the importer's 12/31/06 balance sheet.

***Over*hedged:** If the FX forward had been for 1,200,000 euros rather than 1,000,000 euros, the FX forward's cumulative gain would have been $84,000 (120% of $70,000). But the cumulative adjustment to the FX commitment would be limited to only $70,000—*not* $84,000. The excess $14,000 FX gain is the **ineffective portion of the hedge** (no corresponding offsetting change in value occurred on the FX commitment).

4. **FX forward's *intrinsic value change* versus its *time value change*.** Conceptually, by the settlement date, the FX forward's fair value was adjusted both (1) *upward* by $100,000 for the increase in its *intrinsic value* (1,000,000 euros × $0.10 *increase* in the *spot rate*) and (2) *downward* by $30,000 for the *decrease* in its *time value* ($.03 excess of *forward rate* over *spot rate* at inception × 1,000,000 euros = $30,000 premium).

   By using the change in the *forward rate* to adjust the FX forward, both the *intrinsic value element* and the *time value element* are automatically adjusted for their respective changes in fair value.

5. **Alternate method of assessing hedge effectiveness—excluding the *time value element*.** *FAS 133* permits (but does *not* require) an entity to *exclude* all or part of a derivative's *time value element* in assessing hedge effectiveness. **Thus *split accounting* (accounting for the *time value element* in a separate manner from the *intrinsic value element*) is permitted.**

If hedge effectiveness were assessed by *excluding* the *time value element*, the presumed change in fair value on the FX commitment would be based on the change in the *spot rate*—*not* the change in the *forward rate*. Thus one compares (1) only the FX forward's intrinsic value change (**attributable to the change in the *spot rate***)—[$100,000 in our illustration]) with (2) the change in the FX commitment's *fair value* **using the change in the *spot rate*** (also $100,000). Accordingly, a cumulative $100,000 FX loss on the FX commitment would be reported—*not* a $70,000 FX loss. Thus the equipment would be capitalized at $1,200,000 ($1,300,000 – the $100,000 FX loss on the FX commitment [based on the $.10 change in the *spot rate*]).

CHECK POINT

A domestic *importer* enters into an FX forward to hedge a foreign firm commitment in euros. Which of the following is correct?

a. Any hedging FX gain or loss up to the *transaction date* for the item being bought must be deferred and treated as an adjustment to the cost of the item being bought.
b. The euros to be received from the FX trader are to be initially recorded at the *fixed contractual amount*.
c. The euros to be received from the FX trader are to be continuously carried at the *forward rate*.
d. The hedging FX gain or loss will offset the loss or gain on the purchase order contract with the foreign vendor.

Answer: d

Commitment to Sell

Parallel accounting procedures are used when (1) the domestic company has entered into a firm commitment to *sell* goods to a foreign customer in the future, with payment to be received in the customer's currency, and (2) the domestic company *sells forward* to hedge its FX exposure.

The FASB's Rationale for Hedge Accounting Treatment for Firm Commitments

Firm Commitment Defined

FAS 133 defines a firm commitment as follows:

> An agreement with an unrelated party, binding on both parties and usually legally enforceable, with the following characteristics:
> a. The agreement specifies all significant terms, including the quantity to be exchanged, the fixed price, and the timing of the transaction. The fixed price may be expressed as a specified

amount of an entity's functional currency or of a foreign currency. It may also be expressed as a specified interest rate or specified yield.

b. The agreement includes a disincentive for nonperformance that is sufficiently large to make performance probable.[12]

Key Features of Firm Commitments

Firm commitments have (1) specific terms (that is, the quantity, the fixed price, and the timing), (2) certainty, and (3) enforceability. These features create exposures that are similar to exposures that exist for financial assets and financial liabilities that (1) have fixed terms and (2) are denominated in a foreign currency.

Because of these similarities, *FAS 133* requires during the commitment period (1) recognition in the balance sheet of a liability or an asset on the commitment itself and (2) recognition in earnings of the offsetting FX gain or loss. Note that this treatment parallels the accounting for FX gains and losses on FX receivables and FX payables arising from *exporting* and *importing* transactions.

Qualifying Conditions for Fair Value Hedges

For a hedge of a firm commitment to qualify as a fair value hedge under *FAS 133*, the following criteria must be met:

1. Formal documentation of the hedging relationship (between the derivative and the hedged item) must exist at the inception of the hedge. This documentation includes:
   a. The objective of the hedge and the strategy for accomplishing the objective.
   b. The nature of the risk being hedged.
   c. The derivative hedging instrument and the hedged item.
   d. For a hedge of a firm commitment, a reasonable method for recognizing in earnings the hedged firm commitment.
   e. How the entity will assess hedge effectiveness.
2. An expectation must exist that the derivative hedging instrument will be highly effective at achieving offset for the designated risk exposure.
3. A methodology must exist to periodically assess effectiveness and measure ineffectiveness.
4. Certain requirements must be met for an item to be eligible for designation as a *hedged item.*

Regarding item 3, an FX forward clearly would be effective if (1) the FX forward is in the *same* currency as the hedged item and (2) the gain or loss on the hedging transaction is **in the *opposite* direction** to the loss or gain on the hedged item.

A further discussion of these qualifying conditions is beyond the scope of this text.

CHECK POINT

On 12/10/06, Hegex entered into a 90-day FX forward involving 1,000,000 euros in anticipation that the euro would weaken. The following *direct* exchange rates are assumed:

	December 10, 2006	December 31, 2006	March 10, 2007
Spot rate	$1.20	$1.18	$1.21
Forward rate	1.16	1.17	1.21

The amount of the hedging FX gain or loss to be reported **in earnings** in 2006 and 2007, assuming that the FX forward hedges and FX receivable arising from a *foreign firm commitment* involving the sale of special equipment to be shipped on 3/10/07, is:

a. a $10,000 gain.
b. a $10,000 loss.
c. a $20,000 gain.
d. a $20,000 loss.

[12] *Statement of Financial Accounting Standards No. 133*, "Accounting for Derivative Instruments and Hedging Activities" (Norwalk, Conn.: Financial Accounting Standards Board, 1998), Appendix F.

e. a $30,000 gain.
f. a $30,000 loss.
g. a $40,000 gain.
h. a $40,000 loss.
i. a $50,000 gain.
j. a $50,000 loss.
k. $-0-.
l. None of the above.

Answers: b, h

IX. HEDGING FORECASTED TRANSACTIONS (*CASH FLOW* HEDGES)

The collapse of the Bretton Woods fixed exchange rate system in 1971 and the subsequent high volatility of exchange rate fluctuations that continuously occur under the floating exchange rate system have led to (1) the decision by numerous multinational companies to hedge many or *all* of their FX exposures and (2) an explosive growth in innovative derivatives for hedging purposes.

Consequently, hedging activities are no longer confined to hedging (1) existing balance sheet exposures (FX receivables and FX payables) and (2) firmly committed transactions. Companies also now commonly hedge their forecasted (nonfirmly committed) transactions, such as (1) budgeted U.S. export sales and (2) foreign-currency-denominated budgeted sales of their foreign subsidiaries.

The "Cash Flow Hedging Model"

FAS 133 uses the term "cash flow hedge" to signify hedging transactions in which a derivative **hedges the exposure to potential adverse *cash flow* changes on (1) a forecasted transaction or (2) a *recognized* asset or liability** (such as interest to be collected or paid on *variable rate* loans).

Recall that in cash flow hedges, the following occurs in periods before the adverse effect on the hedged item is recognized in earnings:

1. Hedging gains and losses are *initially* recognized in Other Comprehensive Income and *later* reclassified to earnings.
2. No offsetting loss or gain adjustment is made in the financial statements on the hedged item.

Achieving Concurrent Recognition in Earnings Later

Thus this delayed recognition achieves concurrent recognition in earnings at a later date of (1) the hedging gain or loss and (2) the offsetting change in revenues or expenses relating to the hedged item. This delayed earnings recognition of the hedging gain or loss constitutes the special hedge accounting under the cash flow hedge accounting model.

In this chapter, we discuss only cash flow hedges of forecasted transactions.

Comparison of Forecasted Transactions with Firmly Committed Transactions

In contrast to firmly committed transactions (which have *fixed terms* and *certainty*), forecasted transactions have (1) *no fixed terms* and (2) *no certainty of occurring*. Consequently, in addition to having potential future cash flow variability because of possible changes in currency exchange rates (the major risk that exists for firmly committed transactions), forecasted transactions also have potential future cash flow variability because of (1) possible *changes in prices* (a forecasted transaction will occur at prevailing market prices when it occurs) and (2) possible *nonoccurrence*. Thus a much greater cash flow variability exposure exists for *forecasted transactions* than for *firmly committed transactions*.

Before discussing (1) the FASB's rationale for allowing delayed earnings recognition of hedging gains or losses on forecasted transactions and (2) qualifying conditions for using the cash flow hedging model, we present the following illustration.

Comprehensive Illustration

Hedging a Domestic Company's Forecasted (Nonfirm) Importing Purchase Using an FX Forward (a *Cash Flow* Hedge)

To illustrate this type of hedge and the allowable hedge accounting treatment, we use the same information provided earlier for Illustration 14-12 involving the hedge of the firmly committed foreign-currency-denominated purchase commitment, except that we assume the equipment is *forecasted* to be purchased rather than *committed* to be purchased. The following applicable information relating to that illustration was modified as necessary:

1. The forecasted purchase from the French vendor is 1,000,000 euros. Delivery is forecasted to be in 120 days (January 30, 2007), and the payment is forecasted to be made then (thus the *transaction date* and the *settlement date* on the forecasted purchase are forecasted to coincide).
2. The importer entered into an FX forward with an FX trader to *buy* 1,000,000 euros on January 30, 2007, at the *forward rate* of $1.23.
3. The *manner of assessing hedge effectiveness*—**which must be determined and documented at the *inception* of the hedge**—is to compare (1) the **total change** in the FX forward's *fair value* (determined using the change in the *forward rate*) with (2) the change in the *expected cash flows* relating to the forecasted purchase using the change in the *forward rate.*

Illustration 14-13 shows these transactions as accounted for assuming (1) an intervening financial reporting date of December 31, 2006, and (2) delivery and payments are made on January 30, 2007, the forecasted delivery date. The direct exchange rates for the euro and other assumed information follows:

	October 2, 2006 (inception date)		December 31, 2006 (a financial reporting date)			January 30, 2007 (expiration date)
Spot rate	$1.20		$1.25			$1.30
Forward rate (***buying* rate**)	1.23		1.26			1.30
Premium	.03		.01			n/a
Change in the:						
Spot rate		$.05	+	$.05	=	$ .10
Forward rate		.03	+	.04	=	.07
Premium		.02	+	.01	=	.03
Elements existing	TV		TV & IV			IV
Element recorded as asset *or* liability			TV & IV			TV & IV

Review Points for Illustration 14-13. Note the following:

1. If delayed recognition were *not* permitted, the $30,000 FX gain at December 31, 2006, would be reported currently in earnings.
2. **Overhedges and ineffectiveness.** When an overhedge exists, the FX gain or loss relating to the ineffective portion of the hedge is recorded in earnings currently—*not* on a delayed basis.
3. **Discontinuance: Forecasted transaction becomes *improbable.*** If a cash flow hedge is discontinued because it later becomes probable that the original forecasted transaction will *not* occur, the net FX gain or loss in OCI must be immediately reclassified into earnings.
4. **Discontinuance: *Forecasted transaction* becomes a *firm commitment.*** If a forecasted transaction later becomes a firm commitment, forecasted transaction accounting is discontinued prospectively (the qualifying condition for the *cash flow hedge* treatment is no longer met). Thus the net FX gain or loss remains in accumulated Other Comprehensive Income (OCI) until it otherwise would have been reclassified into earnings. (In these cases, the derivative can be *redesignated* as a *fair value hedge*).
5. **Discontinuance: Other reasons.** The accounting treatment described in review point 4 also applies if:
   a. The derivative expires or is sold, terminated, or exercised.
   b. The entity removes the designation of the cash flow hedge.
6. **Alternate method of assessing hedge effectiveness—exclude the *time value element.*** As stated earlier, *FAS 133* permits (but does *not* require) an entity to *exclude* all or part of a derivative's *time value element* in assessing hedge effectiveness. Accordingly, if hedge effectiveness were assessed

ILLUSTRATION 14-13 HEDGING A FORECASTED PURCHASE FROM A FOREIGN VENDOR USING AN FX FORWARD; NET POSITION ACCOUNTING JOURNAL ENTRIES

Note: OCI = Other Comprehensive Income

Transaction with Vendor			*Hedging Transaction*		
OCTOBER 2, 2006 (THE DATE OF DETERMINING THAT THE PURCHASE IS PROBABLE AND ENTERING INTO THE 120-DAY FX FORWARD)					
No g/l entries are made—only memorandum entries to reflect current position: 1. Forecasted Purchase—***Short***: 1,000,000 euros 2. FX Forward Contract—***Long***: 1,000,000 euros (*bought* forward)					
DECEMBER 31, 2006 (AN INTERVENING *FINANCIAL REPORTING DATE*)					
No corresponding entry.			*FX Contract Value—Forward,* ***net***	*$30,000*	
			OCI—FX Gain		*$30,000*
			To recognize gain on FX forward ***in OCI*** (change in *forward rate* of $.03 × 1,000,000 euros = $30,000).		
JANUARY 30, 2007 (THE *TRANSACTION DATE*, WHICH COINCIDES WITH THE *SETTLEMENT DATE*, AND THE FX FORWARD'S *EXPIRATION DATE*)					
No corresponding entry.			*FX Contract Value—Forward,* ***net***	*$40,000*	
			OCI—FX Gain		*$40,000*
			To recognize gain on FX forward ***in OCI*** (change in *forward rate* of $.04 × 1,000,000 euros = $40,000).		
Equipment	$1,300,000		Cash	$70,000	
Cash		$1,300,000	*FX Contract Value—Forward*		$70,000
To record equipment purchase (1,000,000 euros × $1.30 spot rate).			*To settle FX forward,* ***net***.		

Other Comprehensive Income

	$ -0-	10/2/06
	30,000	
	$30,000	12/31/06
	40,000	
	$70,000	1/30/07

FX Contract Value—Forward (net)

10/2/06	$ -0-	
	30,000	
12/31/06	$30,000[a]	
	40,000	
1/30/07	$70,000	

The $70,000 balance in OCI is reclassified into earnings **as the equipment is depreciated.**

[a] Reported as an asset on the importer's 12/31/06 balance sheet.

by comparing (1) the change in the FX forward's *fair value* **attributable to the change in the** ***spot rate*** ($100,000 in our example) with (2) the change in the forecasted *cash flows* of the forecasted purchase using the change in the *spot rate* (also $100,000), $100,000 (the increase in the FX forward's *intrinsic value*) would be credited to Other Comprehensive Income by the FX forward's expiration date, and $30,000 (the decrease in the FX forward's *time value*) would be charged to earnings. Thus *split accounting* may be used in cash flow hedges as well as in fair value hedges.

Criteria for Using the Cash Flow Hedge Accounting Model

To use the *FAS 133* cash flow hedge accounting model, *each* of the following conditions must be satisfied:

1. At the inception of the hedge, formal documentation must be made of (1) the hedging relationship and (2) the entity's risk management objective and strategy for undertaking the hedge (includes the manner of assessing hedge effectiveness, among other things).

2. The forecasted transaction must be specifically identified as either (1) a single transaction or (2) a group of individual transactions that share the same risk exposure for which they are designated as being hedged.
3. The occurrence of the forecasted transaction must be probable (same meaning as in *FAS 5*, "Accounting for Contingencies," which describes "probable" as "likely to occur"). [Probability is supported by observable facts and attendant circumstances (such as the frequency of similar past transactions)—it is *not* based solely on management's intent.]
4. The forecasted transaction must:
   a. Be a "transaction" (an external event involving the transfer of something of value between two or more entities). [Thus an internal cost allocation, such as forecasted depreciation expense, is *not* a hedgeable item because it is *not* a transaction.]
   b. Be with a party *external* to the *reporting entity*. [This condition is *not* applicable to hedges of foreign currency forecasted transactions.]
   c. Present an exposure to variations in cash flows for the hedged risk that could affect reported earnings. [Thus forecasted intercompany dividends are *not* hedgeable items because dividends do *not* affect consolidated earnings.]
5. Entities must have:
   a. An expectation (both at inception of the hedge and on an ongoing basis) that the derivative hedging instrument will be highly effective at achieving offset for the designated risk exposure.
   b. A methodology to periodically assess effectiveness and measure effectiveness.

Commentary on the Cash Flow Hedging Model

The treatment of hedging gains and losses on forecasted transactions was the most troublesome and contentious issue during the deliberations leading to the issuance of *FAS 133*. The cash flow model is a conceptual compromise that is an accommodation to managements because it allows them to much better achieve their projected earnings forecasts (some would say *"to better manage their earnings"*).

CHECK POINT

On 12/10/06, Hegex entered into a 90-day FX forward involving 1,000,000 euros in anticipation that the euro would weaken. The following *direct* exchange rates are assumed:

	December 10, 2006	December 31, 2006	March 10, 2007
Spot rate	$1.20	$1.18	$1.21
Forward rate	1.16	1.17	1.21

The amount of the hedging FX gain or loss to be reported **in earnings** in 2006 and 2007, assuming that the FX forward hedges certain *foreign export sales*, is:

a. a $10,000 gain.
b. a $10,000 loss.
c. a $20,000 gain.
d. a $20,000 loss.
e. a $30,000 gain.
f. a $30,000 loss.
g. a $40,000 gain.
h. a $40,000 loss.
i. a $50,000 gain.
j. a $50,000 loss.
k. $ –0–.
l. None of the above.

Answers: k, j

X. DERIVATIVE FINANCIAL INSTRUMENTS: A GENERAL DISCUSSION

Financial instruments are defined to include (1) cash, (2) evidence of an ownership interest in an entity (such as stock certificates), and (3) contracts that contain rights and obligations to exchange cash or other financial instruments (an example is stock options held by employees).[13] In recent years, an explosive increase in the use of a special class of financial instruments (commonly referred to as *derivatives*) has occurred. Derivatives are used as financial tools to better manage business risks and returns.

A **derivative** is an executory (to be executed later) contract between two parties in which the eventual resulting cash flows that take place between the two parties depend on the change in some other measure of value. Thus a derivative "derives" its value from another measure of value, which may be any one or a combination of the following items:

1. **Financial instruments** (such as common stocks, corporate bonds, and government bonds). An employee who owns a stock option owns a derivative because the stock option's value depends entirely on the value of the company's common stock relative to the stock option's exercise price.
2. **Commodities** (such as corn, cotton, gold, or oil). Likewise, an investor holding an option or a future to buy 1,000 bushels of corn at a $3 per bushel for the next 180 days owns a derivative.
3. **Indexes** Indexes (such as the Dow Jones index or the Standard and Poor's index for common stocks) measure changes in specific markets and represent the values of portfolios of financial instruments and commodities.
4. **Rates** (such as currency exchange rates and interest rates). Rate changes reflect value variations in specific markets (such as currencies or Treasury bonds).

Valuing Derivatives in the Balance Sheet

Derivatives are recognized in the balance sheet at each financial reporting date at their fair value. The valuation technique involves determining the net cash flows that are to take place between the two parties by referring to **the change in the underlying financial instrument, commodity, index, or rate.** The result is to report a receivable position for one party and a payable position for the other party. The same types of general ledger accounts (Contract Value—Option and Contract Value—Forward, net) used and shown earlier for FX forwards and FX options are used to convey each entity's favorable or unfavorable position, respectively, in the derivative.

The FASB's definition of a derivative instrument is a financial instrument or other contract with *all three* of the following characteristics:

1. It has (1) one or more **underlyings** and (2) one or more **notional amounts** [sometimes other names are used; for example, the notional amount is called a face amount in some contracts] or payment provisions or both. Those terms determine the amount of the settlement or settlements, and, in some cases, whether or not a settlement is required.
2. It requires no initial net investment or an initial net investment that is smaller than would be required for other types of contracts that would be expected to have a similar response to changes in market factors.
3. Its terms require or permit net settlement, it can be settled net by a means outside the contract, or it provides for delivery of an asset that puts the recipient in a position not substantially different from net settlement.[14]

More than 1,200 types of derivative products have been created (mostly by investment bankers), a high number of which involve the use of computer programs. Our focus in this chapter has been on derivatives that (1) derive their value from changes in currency exchange rates and (2) are used to manage FX exposures. The AICPA has identified more than 75 derivatives that can be used for hedging exposures, many of which can be used to hedge FX exposures. Almost all of them, however, are variations of FX options and FX forwards.[15]

---

[13] The formal definition is in *Statement of Financial Accounting Standards No. 133*, "Accounting for Derivative Instruments and Hedging Activities," Appendix F.

[14] *Statement of Financial Accounting Standards No. 133*, "Accounting for Derivative Financial Instruments and Hedging Activities," para. 6.

[15] Some examples of these other types of derivatives are futures, swaps, synthetic forwards, range forwards, participating forwards, options to exchange currencies, deep-in-the-money purchased options, and options purchased and written as a unit.

Unique Contractual Elements of Derivatives

Unlike traditional financial instruments, such as stocks and bonds, derivatives generally have the following unique elements:

> Neither party initially performs because the eventual dollar amount of the performance is a function of subsequent value *changes*—not the static value of the assets or economic measures that serve as the base.
> No principal cash payments are made at the inception of the contract. No notional balances or other executory fixed amounts are initially recorded as receivables or payables in the balance sheet. Consequently, derivatives are often characterized as being "off-balance-sheet agreements" (even though receivables and payables are recognized later and continuously adjusted throughout the contractual period).
> Cash payments are made during or at the end of the contract.
> If one party has a *favorable* outcome (which results in a favorable position), the other party (the counterparty) has an *unfavorable* outcome (which results in an unfavorable position)—a zero-sum game. For most derivatives considered independently, favorable and unfavorable outcomes are characterized as gains and losses, respectively.

Unique Characteristics of Derivatives

Derivatives usually have most of the following unique characteristics:

> Their market value can change quickly.
> Their market value (other than option-based derivatives, as explained shortly) can alternate quickly between a positive value (receivable position) and a negative value (payable position).
> The potential future gains and losses can be huge in relation to the recognized carrying amounts (usually fair values) reported in the balance sheet for the receivable or payable position that currently is reported for the derivative. Thus the reported amounts usually do *not* convey a prudent picture of an entity's latent exposure to market risk.

A Zero-Sum Game

The financial press has widely reported numerous examples of entities that have incurred large derivative-related losses in the 1990s from exposed positions subject to latent risk games. Examples include:

1. **Orange County (California)**, $1.7 billion loss: Bet on the direction of interest rates.
2. **Metallgesellschaft AG**, $1.3 billion loss: Used a flawed hedging strategy subject to timing imbalances.
3. **Barings PLC (investment bank)**, $1.3 billion loss: Bet on the direction of the Japanese Nikkei stock index using futures contracts in unauthorized trades by one of its foreign currency traders (resulted in the company's collapse).
4. **Piper Jaffrey**, $700 million loss: Entered into interest rate derivative contracts with mutual funds.
5. **Procter and Gamble Corporation**, $157 million loss: Entered into unfavorable interest rate swaps (sued the investment banker that advised it to use derivatives, claiming it did not understand the risks involved in what it thought was hedging but effectively was speculating).

Because of their "what one party gains, the other party loses" nature, derivatives are examples of a *zero-sum game*. Thus the financial press instead could have written about the spectacular gains obtained using derivatives from the perspective of the counterparty(ies) to this list of five derivative-based losses. The winners (who were also potential losers) on the other side were probably more numerous or prudent or were parties to hedges.

It's *Not* the Derivatives—It's the *People* Using Them

These five huge losses cited here did *not* occur merely because derivatives were used. They were the result of (1) using flawed investment or risk management strategies, (2) management's willingness to take excessive risks, (3) individuals' purposely circumventing internal controls so that they could execute transactions and take risks in excess of authorized limits, and (4) management's failure to fully understand or control the risks. These spectacular derivative-related losses have awakened many to the potential risks associated with using derivatives.

Types of Derivatives

Derivatives can generally be categorized into one of the following two categories:

1. **Option-based derivatives** (examples are option contracts, interest rate caps, and interest rate floors). For this category, only *one* party can potentially have a *favorable* outcome for which it pays a premium at inception; the other party can potentially have only an *unfavorable* outcome for which it is paid the premium at inception.
2. **Forward-based derivatives** (examples are forwards, futures, and swaps). For this category, *either* party (but not both simultaneously) can potentially have a *favorable* outcome, and *either* party (but not both simultaneously) can have an *unfavorable* outcome.

International Perspective

Foreign Accounting Standards for Derivatives

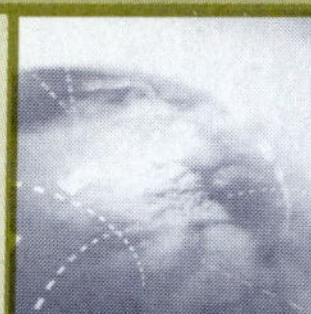

In 1999 (after 10 years of study), the International Accounting Standards Committee (discussed in Chapter 13 and superseded by the International Accounting Standards Board in 2001) issued *International Accounting Standard 39*, "Financial Instruments: Recognition and Measurement." *IAS 39* requires that all financial assets and liabilities—including derivatives—be recognized on the balance sheet. *IAS 39* (except for some compromises) is comparable to *FAS 133*. Thus it substantially increases the use of *fair value* in accounting for financial instruments for countries required to (or electing to) comply with international accounting standards.

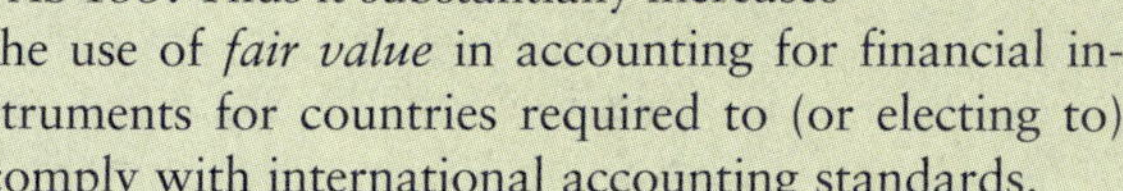

Types of Risks

Credit Risk: A Concern of the Party in the Receivable Position

The possibility of incurring a loss as a result of the counterparty's inability to fulfill financial obligations under the contract is called **credit risk**. Credit risk exists for only the party in the *receivable* position, and it is limited to the carrying value of the derivative. Credit risk can be volatile because it varies with the market value of the derivative. Credit risk is generally not a major concern, however, unless the receivable position becomes quite large as a result of spectacular gains so that the spectacular losses incurred by the counterparty cause it financial problems. Dealers lay off and balance their positions so that their commercial customers are the usual source of credit risk to the dealers.

U.S. international banks that have foreign currency transactions with Japanese banks currently have a major credit risk concern because (1) scores of Japanese banks are in considerable financial difficulty as a result of having nearly $500 billion of nonperforming loans for which (2) some of them may collapse and be unable to fulfill their obligations to the U.S. banks.

Liquidity Risk: The Concern of the Party in the Payable Position

The other side of the coin of credit risk is **liquidity risk**, which is the risk that the party in the *payable* position may not be able to fulfill its obligation because it lacks liquid assets. Thus credit risk and liquidity risk concern the same issue: whether payment can be made when due. Incurring large losses on a derivative can cause liquidity problems, particularly when offset by unrealized gains on assets, which cannot be sold without disrupting operations.

Market Risk: A Concern of Both Parties

The risk of incurring losses as a result of future adverse changes in the market value of the derivative is **market risk**. Such losses could lower or reduce to zero one party's receivable position and, in a forward-based derivative, create a payable position for that same party. Thus market risk encompasses both (1) "*balance-sheet risk*," which is **the risk of incurring a loss on a *recorded* asset** and (2) "*off-balance-sheet risk*," which is **the risk of incurring losses above and beyond an asset or liability's recorded value**. For most derivatives, a party to a contract that can go into a payable position is exposed to incurring unlimited losses. To illustrate, assume that Party A is in a $300,000 receivable position in a derivative contract and that Party B (the counterparty) is thus in a $300,000 payable position.

1. **Option-based derivatives.** In an option-based derivative (recall that only *one* party can have an *unfavorable* outcome), Party A's market risk consists entirely of *balance-sheet risk*, and the risk is limited to $300,000 (the Party's receivable). In contrast, Party B's market risk consists entirely of *off-balance-sheet risk*, and the risk is unlimited because **the potential loss is *not* limited to the recorded amount of a particular asset or liability**. (Note that Party A also has *credit risk*, and Party B also has *liquidity risk*.)
2. **Forward-based derivatives.** In a forward-based derivative (recall that *either* party can have an *unfavorable* outcome), Party A's market risk consists of both *balance-sheet risk* and *off-balance sheet risk*, and the risk is thus unlimited because the value of the Party's derivative (a $300,000 receivable position) can become negative (a payable). In contrast, Party B's market risk consists entirely of *off-balance-sheet risk*, and the risk is thus unlimited because the Party's $300,000 payable position can become larger.

Thus *market risk* problems can lead to *credit risk* and *liquidity risk* problems so *market risk* is the major concern of derivative holders. Many believe that latent *market risk* should be quantified and disclosed in notes to the financial statements. One such way is to give the hypothetical effects of several possible changes in market prices in conjunction with the likelihood of such movements occurring. Value or earnings at risk are latent risks that should be distinguished from realized or unrealized gains or losses.

In this chapter, we discussed and illustrated the use of both an option-based derivative (FX options) and a forward-based derivative (FX forwards). Discussions and illustrations of how to account for other types of derivatives can be found in various professional publications, international finance texts, and specialized books.[16]

XI. DISCLOSURES REQUIRED FOR FX DERIVATIVES

As stated previously, the use of financial hedging instruments to manage FX exposures has become enormous as a result of the globalization of business. For instance, the contractual value of Ford Motor Company's FX derivatives (forwards, options, and swaps) outstanding at the end of 2003 was $24 billion.

FAS 133's Disclosure Requirements

FAS 133 requires extensive qualitative disclosures (hedging objectives, hedging strategies, risks hedged, and risk management policy). In addition, extensive specific detailed FX gain and loss information must be disclosed for (1) *fair value hedges*, (2) *cash flow hedges*, and (3) *net investment hedges*. And finally, for *cash flow hedges*, an entity is required to display the FX gain or loss as a separate account within other comprehensive income (along with an account analysis for the period).

SEC Disclosure Requirements

The Securities and Exchange Commission requires extensive *qualitative* and *quantitative* disclosures for derivatives (Regulation S-K, Item 305). The *quantitative* disclosures go far beyond the requirements of *FAS 107*.

[16] Examples are *The Handbook of Derivatives & Synthetics* published by Probus Publishing Company (Chicago) and *Statements on Management Accounting (Statement Number 4M)*, "Practices and Techniques: Understanding Financial Instruments," published by the Institute of Management Accountants.

END-OF-CHAPTER REVIEW

Summary of Key Points

1. **FX exposures** are managed by **hedging**—a technique of deploying financial instruments (primarily FX forwards and FX options) so that a **counterbalancing** gain occurs on the financial instrument in the event of a loss on the hedged item.
2. Refer to Illustration 14-14 for a summary of hedging procedures and hedging terminology.
3. Derivatives are contracts that **create rights and obligations** that meet the definitions of assets and liabilities.
4. Derivatives are valued at their **fair value** at each financial reporting date. The amounts reported for these contract values are substantively **receivables and payables.**
5. For FX derivatives, fair value is based on (1) **quoted prices,** (2) **quoted prices for similar derivatives,** or (3) **present value valuation methods.**
6. For FX forwards, the **change in fair value** is calculated using the **change in the *forward rate*.** Discounting to present value is also required.
7. **Split versus nonsplit accounting**—accounting for changes in the *time value element* separately from changes in the *intrinsic value element*—is *not* an issue for **"undesignated" hedges** because no special hedge accounting is used. ("Accounting" encompasses both (1) **how to value** and (2) **how to report the *change* in value.**)
8. For both FX options and FX forwards, either **split accounting** or **nonsplit accounting** may be used in determining hedge effectiveness of (1) fair value hedges, (2) cash flow hedges, and (3) net investment hedges.
9. Refer to Illustration 14-15 for a summary of accounting for FX gains and losses on derivatives in the various hedging situations.
10. **Derivatives** are a special type of financial instrument (contracts) that (a) **derive their value from changes in another financial instrument, a commodity, an index, or a rate** and (b) are **used to manage risks** or improve returns.
11. Derivatives are **option based** (one-sided in nature) or **forward based** (two-sided in nature).
12. **Credit risk** is the risk of not being able to collect a derivative's *receivable* position.
13. **Market risk** is the potential for incurring losses as a result of adverse changes in the fair value of the derivative.

Glossary of New Terms

Anticipatory transactions Transactions expected to occur in the future; they may or may *not* be under contract.

ILLUSTRATION 14-14 SUMMARY OF HEDGING PROCEDURES AND HEDGING TERMINOLOGY

Inventory Transaction		To Hedge Inventory Transaction	Position Terminology Used in Hedging Contracts	
Type	**Purpose**		**FX Options**	**FX Forwards**
Importing	To buy inventory	Buy FX	"Call"	"Long"
Exporting	To sell inventory	Sell FX	"Put"	"Short"

ILLUSTRATION 14-15 SUMMARY OF ACCOUNTING FOR FX GAINS AND LOSSES ON DERIVATIVES

Purpose of the FX Derivative	Type of Hedge	Hedge Accounting Applies	Accounting Treatment	Accounting Result
To hedge an FX receivable or FX payable.	"Undesignated" Hedge	NO	Recognize in earnings currently. (Same treatment for FX gain or loss on hedged item.)	Concurrent recognition in earnings **currently.**
To hedge a firm commitment.	Fair Value Hedge[a]	YES	Recognize in earnings currently. (Same treatment for FX gain or loss on hedged item.)	Concurrent recognition in earnings **currently.**
To hedge a forecasted foreign transaction.	Cash Flow Hedge[a]	YES	Recognize in Other Comprehensive Income. Remove and recognize in earnings on the date the forecasted transaction actually impacts earnings.	Concurrent recognition in earnings on a ***delayed basis.***
To hedge an investment in a subsidiary.	Net Investment Hedge[a]	YES	Recognize in Other Comprehensive Income. Remove and recognize in earnings upon disposal of the investment.	Concurrent recognition on a ***delayed basis.***
To speculate.	N/A	NO	Recognize in earnings currently.	Recognition in earnings **currently.**
To hedge against loss of market share if the U.S. dollar strengthens.	Other (strategic hedges[b])	NO	Recognize in earnings currently.	Recognition in earnings **currently.**

[a] This term is used and defined in *FAS 133*.

[b] In these hedges, an entity is concerned that a forecasted transaction will *not* occur—*not* that the forecasted transaction *will* occur at an *unfavorable* future price or future rate. (In general, it will be quite difficult for such hedges to qualify as cash flow hedges.)

Cash flow hedge A type of hedging transaction under *FAS 133* in which hedging gains and losses on the derivative are (1) *initially* recognized in Other Comprehensive Income and (2) *later* recognized in earnings. The derivative hedges the exposure to potential adverse **changes in the future *cash flows*** of (1) a forecasted transaction (such as forecasted exporting sales denominated in a foreign currency) or (2) a *recognized* asset and liability (such as interest to be collected or paid on *variable rate* loans. [Only item (1) is covered in this chapter.])

Credit risk The possibility of *not* collecting a receivable position in a derivative.

Derivative The term used to refer to a wide array of financial products whose value depends on changes in (1) a financial instrument (such as stocks and bonds), (2) a commodity, (3) an index representing values of groups of such instruments or assets, or (4) a rate (such as currency exchange rates and interest rates). (The most commonly used derivatives are options, forwards, futures, and swaps.)

Discount (on FX forward) The amount at which a currency is contractually bought or sold (at the *forward rate*) *below* its current value (at the *spot rate*).

Effectiveness The extent to which an FX loss or gain on a hedged item is offset by a hedging FX gain or loss. Under *FAS 133*, the *time value element* may be *excluded* in assessing hedge effectiveness.

Fair value hedge A type of hedging transaction under *FAS 133* in which **current earnings recognition occurs** for both (1) hedging gains and losses on the *derivative* and (2) losses and gains on the *hedged item* (resulting from **changes in its *fair value***). Hedgeable items are (1) *unrecognized* firm commitments, (2) *recognized* assets and liabilities that are *not* accounted for on a fair value basis (such as inventory and *fixed rate* loans), and (3) certain other assets and liabilities. [Only item (1) is covered in this chapter.]

Financial instruments Cash, evidence of an ownership interest in an entity, and contracts that involve rights and obligation to exchange cash or other financial instruments.

Firm commitments Anticipated future transactions that are under contract or have such a severe penalty that nonperformance is remote.

Forecasted transactions Expected future transactions that are *not* under contract or do *not* have severe potential penalties for nonperformance.

Foreign currency forward contract See FX forward.

Foreign currency option contract See FX option.

FX forward A contractual agreement to exchange currencies of different countries at a specified future date at a specified rate (the *forward rate*).

FX forward rate A rate quoted for future delivery of currencies to be exchanged (usually up to one year).

FX option A contractual agreement giving the holder the right to buy or sell a given amount of currency at a specified price for a period of time or at a point in time.

Hedge accounting An accounting treatment in which the gain or loss on the hedging instrument and the loss or gain on the hedged item are given concurrent recognition or concurrent deferral.

Intrinsic value (in the context of *options*) The value of an option that is "in the money" as represented by the favorable difference between the *spot rate* and the *exercise* (strike) *price.*

Liquidity risk The possibility that the party in the payable position may *not* be able to fulfill its obligation because it lacks liquidity.

Market risk The possibility of incurring losses as a result of adverse changes in the fair value of a derivative.

Master netting arrangement A contractual arrangement used by traders in which a default on any one contract enables all of the separate contracts with the same party to be treated as one contract. This arrangement entitles either party to terminate the entire arrangement and to demand the net settlement of all of the individual contracts.

Net investment hedge A type of hedging transaction under *FAS 133* in which FX hedging gains and losses on the hedge of an investment in a *foreign* subsidiary are (1) initially recognized in Other Comprehensive Income (along with the offsetting FX translation loss or gain) and (2) later recognized in earnings upon disposal of the investment. (See Chapter 18 for further discussion and illustration.)

Premium (on FX forward) The amount at which a currency is contractually bought or sold (at the *forward rate*) *above* its current value (at the *spot rate*).

Purchased option An option contract viewed from the perspective of the *option holder* who acquires a right from the other party as a result of paying a fee (called a *premium*); as a result, the option holder *can* have a *gain* on the contract but *cannot* incur a *loss*.

Split accounting Accounting—*as a time value element*—for (1) premiums and discounts on forwards and (2) premiums on options separately from changes in the *intrinsic value element.*

Time value (in the context of options) That portion of an option's value that is *not* attributable to the contract's intrinsic value.

Underlying A specified foreign exchange rate, interest rate, security price, commodity price, or other variable. An underlying may be a price or rate of an asset or liability but is *not* the *asset* or *liability* itself.

"Undesignated" hedge A hedge that does *not* qualify as a *fair value hedge,* a *cash flow hedge*, or a *net investment hedge*. FX gains and losses on this type of hedge are recognized in earnings currently (because the offsetting FX loss or gain is also recognized in earnings currently under the separate accounting standards applicable to the hedged item).

Written option An option contract viewed from the perspective of the *writer* of the option who has granted a right to the other party for a fee (called a *premium*); as a result, the writer *can* incur a *loss* on the contract but *cannot* have a *gain*.

Assignment Material

Review Questions

1. What is the definition of *hedging*?
2. What are the four *FASB cornerstone decisions* upon which *FAS 133* is based?
3. What is the definition of *hedge accounting*?
4. What four *categories of hedges* are given in the chapter? Explain the differences between them.
5. For your answer to Question 3, to which categories does *hedge accounting* apply?
6. What is the *FAS 107 guidance* for determining the *fair value* of *derivatives*?
7. What is the difference between a *put* option and a *call* option?
8. What is the difference between a *written* option and a *purchased* option?
9. Can a nonbank entity lose money on an *option*?
10. To hedge an exposed asset, should a call or put option be acquired? For an exposed liability?
11. What is *split accounting*?
12. In an *FX forward*, which party is the *issuer*, and who is the *holder*?
13. What is the *forward rate*? Why does it differ from the *spot rate*?
14. When does a *premium* exist on an FX forward? A *discount*?
15. How does one fulfill an FX forward?
16. How are the *obligations* under FX forwards reported in the balance sheet?
17. What is the distinction between *hedging* and *speculating*?
18. How are FX forwards valued?
19. What is a hedge of a *firm foreign-currency-denominated commitment*?
20. What conditions must be met to qualify a forward exchange contract as the hedge of a *firm foreign-currency-denominated commitment*?
21. How do *FX options* differ from *FX forwards*?
22. What is meant when it is said that an *FX forward* is substantively *two* options?
23. What is *split accounting* as it applies to *FX forwards*?
24. Can hedges of *forecasted transactions* be given *hedge accounting* treatment? Give examples.
25. Can a domestic company hedge the *forecasted net income* of a foreign subsidiary?
26. What are *competitive* or *strategic hedges*? Give examples.
27. Can *competitive* or *strategic hedges* be given hedge accounting treatment?
28. What does the term *financial instruments* mean?
29. What does the term *derivative* mean?
30. What are four types of items from which derivatives can derive their value?
31. What are some of the unique *contractual elements* of derivatives?
32. What are some of the unique *characteristics* of derivatives?

33. How do *option-based* derivatives differ from *forward-based* derivatives?

34. What types of risks exist for derivatives?

35. What is *credit* risk? What is *market* risk?

Exercises

E 14-1 **Options: Distinguishing between Hedging and Speculating** Determine whether the following option contracts are *hedging transactions* or *speculating transactions* (assume that the domestic company has transaction exposure in each case):

Domestic Importer or Exporter	Anticipates	Type of Option Contract
1. Exporter	U.S. dollar weakening	Call
2. Importer	U.S. dollar weakening	Call
3. Exporter	Peso weakening	Put
4. Importer	Euro strengthening	Call
5. Exporter	Yen strengthening	Call
6. Importer	Euro weakening	Put
7. Exporter	No expectation	Put
8. Importer	No expectation	Call

E 14-2 ***Forwards:* Calculating the Expected Forward Rate** On 1/1/06, Cashco desires to invest $1,000,000 cash in a one-year CD at the highest possible interest rate. The interest rate obtainable in the U.S. is 7%. In Great Britain, the interest rate obtainable is 10%. The direct exchange rate on 1/1/06 is $.50.

Required

1. What is the expected *forward rate* for a one-year FX forward under the interest rate parity system?
2. Would the pound be selling at a *premium* or a *discount* on the forward market?

E 14-3 ***Forwards:* Identifying When to Use for Hedging** Hedglex has importing and exporting transactions, and it uses forward exchange contracts to hedge its exposure (but never to speculate), depending on management's assessment of whether the exchange rate will move favorably or unfavorably. Hedglex must determine whether it should contract to *buy* or *sell* a foreign currency in each of the following situations:

	Future Expectation				
Area of Foreign Currency Exposure	Direct Rate or Currency	Direction	Buy	Sell	Neither
1. Exporting	Direct rate	Up	______	______	______
	Direct rate	Down	______	______	______
	U.S. dollar	Strengthen	______	______	______
	U.S. dollar	Weaken	______	______	______
	Foreign	Strengthen	______	______	______
	Foreign	Weaken	______	______	______
2. Importing	Direct rate	Up	______	______	______
	Direct rate	Down	______	______	______
	U.S. dollar	Strengthen	______	______	______
	U.S. dollar	Weaken	______	______	______
	Foreign	Strengthen	______	______	______
	Foreign	Weaken	______	______	______

Required Place an X in the appropriate Buy, Sell, or Neither column of the table.

E 14-4 ***Forwards:* Distinguishing between Hedging and Speculating** Determine whether the following FX forwards are *hedging transactions* or *speculating transactions* (assume that the domestic company has transaction exposure in each case):

Domestic Importer or Exporter	Anticipates	Buys or Sells in Forward Market
1. Exporter	U.S. dollar weakening	Buys
2. Importer	U.S. dollar weakening	Buys
3. Exporter	Peso weakening	Sells
4. Importer	Euro strengthening	Buys
5. Exporter	Yen strengthening	Buys
6. Importer	Euro weakening	Sells
7. Exporter	No expectation	Sells
8. Importer	No expectation	Buys

E 14-5 ***Forwards:* Matching Accounts with Transactions—"Gross" or "Broad" Accounting** For each of the following accounts, identify the transaction(s) that would involve their use. For hedging purposes, assume that (1) FX forwards—*not* FX options—are used and (2) the obligations of each party under the FX forward *are* reflected in the general ledger.

	Nature of Transaction			
	Importing	Exporting	Importing Hedge	Exporting Hedge
1. FX Accounts Receivable	______	______	______	______
2. FX Accounts Payable	______	______	______	______
3. Dollars due *from* FX Trader	______	______	______	______
4. Dollars due *to* FX Trader	______	______	______	______
5. FX due *to* FX Trader	______	______	______	______
6. FX due *from* FX Trader	______	______	______	______

E 14-6 ***Forwards:* Determining Accounting Treatment of Transactions**

Transaction	Premium or Discount Can Exist	Foreign Currency Transaction Gains and Losses Are to Be Recognized Currently	
		in Earnings	in OCI
1. Importing and exporting transactions (nonhedged)	______	______	______
2. Hedge of a recorded but unsettled foreign currency transaction	______	______	______
3. Hedge of a firm foreign-currency-denominated commitment	______	______	______
4. Speculation in foreign currency	______	______	______
5. Hedge of a forecasted transaction	______	______	______

Required For each of these transactions, place an X in the applicable column(s). For hedging purposes, assume that FX *forwards—not* FX *options*—are used.

Problems

P 14-1 ***Options:* Hedging an Exposed *Liability*** On 11/1/06, Callex took delivery from a French firm of inventory costing 100,000 euros. Payment is due on 1/30/07. Concurrently, Callex paid $900 cash to acquire a 90-day "at-the-money" *call* option for 100,000 European euros.

Additional Information

	11/1/06	12/31/06	1/30/07
Spot rate (euro)	$1.20	$1.22	$1.23
Strike price	1.20	1.20	1.20
Fair value of ***call*** option.	$900	$2,200	$3,000

Required Prepare all journal entries for these transactions at *each* of the three dates assuming that all payments were made on 1/30/07.

P 14-2 ***Options:* Hedging an Exposed *Asset*** On 12/16/06, Puttex delivered inventory to a Danish firm. Payment of 1,000,000 Danish krones is due on 2/14/07. Concurrently, Puttex paid $4,000 cash to acquire a 60-day "at-the-money" *put* option for 1,000,000 Danish krones.

Additional Information

	12/16/06	12/31/06	2/14/07
Spot rate (krone)	$.16	$.15	$.147
Strike price	.16	.16	.16
Fair value of ***put*** option	$4,000	$13,300	$13,000

Required Prepare all journal entries for these transactions at *each* of the three dates assuming that all payments were made on 2/14/07.

P 14-3 ***Options:* Hedging an Exposed *Liability*** On 12/1/06, Optix Company paid $3,000 cash to purchase a 90-day **"at-the-money"** call option for 500,000 European euros. The option's purpose is to protect an exposed liability of 500,000 euros relating to an inventory purchase received on 12/1/06 and to be paid for on 3/1/07.

Additional Information

	12/1/06	12/31/06	3/1/07
Spot rate (euro)	$1.20	$1.28	$1.27
Strike price	1.20	1.20	1.20
Fair value of ***call*** option	$3,000	$42,000	$35,000

Required Prepare all journal entries for these transactions at *each* of the three dates assuming that all payments were made on 3/1/07.

P 14-4 ***Forwards:* Hedging an Exposed *Liability*—No Premium or Discount** On 10/17/06, Balco took delivery from an Italian firm of inventory costing 10,000 European euros. Payment is due on 1/15/07. Concurrently, Balco entered into an FX forward to *buy* 10,000 European euros on 1/15/07.

Additional Information

	10/17/06	12/31/06	1/15/07
Spot rate (euro)	$1.30	$1.42	$1.40
Forward rate (euro)	1.30	1.42	1.40

Required

1. Prepare all journal entries for these transactions at *each* of the three dates assuming all payments were made on 1/15/07. (Include the *time value element* in assessing hedge effectiveness.) Ignore the effect of discounting.
2. What accounts and amounts are presented in the asset and liability sections of the 12/31/06 balance sheet? (Assume that *all* of the acquired inventory is still on hand.)

P 14-5 ***Forwards:* Hedging an Exposed *Liability*—Problem 14-4 With Premium Added** On 10/17/06, Balco took delivery from an Italian firm of inventory costing 10,000 European euros. Payment is due on 1/15/07. Concurrently, Balco entered into an FX forward to *buy* 10,000 European euros on 1/15/07.

Additional Information

	10/17/06	12/31/06	1/15/07
Spot rate (euro)	$1.30	$1.42	$1.40
Forward rate (euro)	1.36	1.43	1.40

Required

1. Prepare all journal entries for these transactions at *each* of the three dates assuming that all payments were made on 1/15/07. (Include the *time value element* in assessing hedge effectiveness.) Ignore the effect of discounting.

2. What accounts and amounts are presented in the asset and liability sections of the 12/31/06 balance sheet? (Assume that *all* of the acquired inventory is still on hand.)

P 14-6 ***Forwards:* Hedging an Exposed *Asset*** On 4/4/06, Cannex delivered to a Canadian firm inventory it sold for Can$100,000. Payment is due to be received on 8/2/06. Concurrently, Cannex entered into an FX forward to *sell* Can$100,000 on 8/2/06.

Additional Information

	4/4/06	6/30/06	8/2/06
Spot rate (Canadian $)	$.80	$.84	$.82
Forward rate (Canadian $)	.77	.83	$.82

Required

1. Prepare all entries for these transactions at *each* of the three dates assuming that all payments were made on 8/2/06. (Include the *time value element* in assessing hedge effectiveness.) Ignore the effect of discounting.
2. What accounts and amounts are presented in the asset and liability sections of the 6/30/06 balance sheet?

P 14-7 ***Forwards:* Hedging a Firm *Purchase* Commitment** On 10/2/06, Skeeco ordered a custom-built aerial tram from a Swiss firm. The purchase order is *noncancelable*. The purchase price is SFr 1,000,000 with delivery and payment to be on 3/31/07. Concurrently, Skeeco entered into a FX forward to *buy* SFr 1,000,000 on 3/31/07. On 3/31/07, the tram was delivered.

Additional Information

	10/2/06	12/31/06	3/31/07
Spot rate (SFr)	$.50	$.56	$.57
Forward rate (SFr)	.53	.58	.57

Required

1. Prepare all entries for these transactions at *each* of the three dates assuming that all payments were made on 3/31/07. (Include the *time value element* in assessing hedge effectiveness.) Ignore the effect of discounting.
2. What accounts and amounts are presented in the asset and liability sections of the 12/31/06 balance sheet?

P 14-8 ***Forwards:* Hedging a Firm *Sales* Commitment** On 10/12/06, Wingex obtained a noncancelable sales order from a Maltese firm for a custom-made marble statue of a falcon. The contract price was Lm 100,000. Concurrently, Wingex entered into an FX forward to *sell* Lm 100,000 in 100 days at the *forward rate* of $3.15. The statue was delivered on 12/11/06.

Additional Information

	10/12/06	12/11/06	12/31/06	1/20/07
Spot rate (Lm)	$3.20	$3.00	$3.09	$2.97
Forward rate (Lm)	3.15	2.98	3.08	2.97

Required

1. Prepare all entries for these transactions at *each* of the *four* dates assuming that all payments were made on 1/20/07. (Include the *time value element* in assessing hedge effectiveness.) Ignore the effects of discounting.
2. Prepare a partial balance sheet at 12/31/06.
3. Prepare a partial income statement for 2006.

P 14-9 ***Forwards:* Speculating** On 11/1/06, Riskco concluded that the European euro would *weaken* during the next six months. In hopes of reporting a gain, Riskco entered into an FX forward on 11/1/06 to *sell* 1,000,000 euros on 4/30/07 at the *forward rate*.

Additional Information

	11/1/06	12/31/06	4/30/07
Spot rate (euro)	$1.190	$1.180	$1.210
Forward rate (euro)	1.199	1.187	1.210

Required Prepare all journal entries at *each* of the three dates. (Ignore discounting.)

P 14-10 ***Options:* Hedging Forecasted *Sales*** On 1/1/06, Sellex paid $16,000 cash to acquire a *put* FX option for 1,000,000 European euros, with an expiration date of 12/31/06. The option hedges 2006's forecasted *exporting* sales of 1,000,000 euros.

Additional Information

	1/1/06	6/30/06	12/31/06
Spot rate (euro)	$1.20	$1.12	$1.15
Strike price	1.19	1.19	1.19
Fair value of ***put*** option at 6/30/06		$81,000	

Required

1. Calculate the option's *time value* and *intrinsic value* at inception.
2. Prepare all journal entries required at *each* of the three dates under each of the following three assumptions concerning Sellex's total export sales for 2006 (include the *time value element* in assessing hedge effectiveness):
   a. Zero export sales for 2006.
   b. Export sales of 1,000,000 euros—all occurred in 12/06.
   c. Export sales of 1,000,000 euros—60% of which occurred in the *first* six months.

P 14-11 ***Options:* Hedging Forecasted *Purchases*** On 1/1/06, Buyco paid $17,000 cash to acquire a *call* FX option for 1,000,000 European euros, with an expiration date of 12/31/06. The option hedges 2006's forecasted *importing* purchases of 1,000,000 euros. At 6/30/06, import purchases totaled 750,000 euros, of which 600,000 euros had been resold to U.S. customers.

Additional Information

	1/1/06	6/30/06	12/31/06
Spot rate (euro)	$1.15	$1.18	$1.17
Strike price	1.14	1.14	1.14
Fair value of ***call*** option at 6/30/06		$44,000	

Required

1. Calculate the option's *time value* and *intrinsic value* at inception. (Include the *time value element* in assessing hedge effectiveness.)
2. Prepare all journal entries required at *each* of the three dates.

THINKING CRITICALLY

Cases

C 14-1 **To Hedge or Not to Hedge Exposed Assets** A domestic exporter having FX receivables denominated in British pounds expects the British pound to strengthen.

Required Should the exporter's treasury department hedge the FX receivables?

C 14-2 **To Speculate or Not to Speculate** A domestic importer has FX payables denominated in euros, all of which are hedged with FX forwards as called for by company operating policies. The importer is virtually certain that the euro will strengthen.

Required Should the importer's treasury department speculate in addition to hedging?

C 14-3 ***Forwards:* To Offset or Not to Offset** At 12/31/06, Hedgem Inc.'s net position in an FX forward that hedges an FX receivable (resulting from an exporting transaction with a French customer) is a $90,000 liability to a FX trader.

Also at this date, Hedgem is in a net asset position (a $70,000 receivable) on an FX forward that hedges an FX payable (resulting from an importing transaction with a Japanese vendor) with an FX trader.

Required Should these amounts be presented separately or offset in the 12/31/06 balance sheet? Why or why not?

C 14-4 ***Forwards:* Is Selling Forward at a Premium an Immediate Economic Gain?** On 4/1/06, simultaneously with the recording of a £100,000 receivable from a British customer, Hedgco Inc. entered into a 60-day FX forward to hedge this exposed receivable. The relevant exchange rates follow:

	April 1, 2006	May 31, 2006
Spot rate	$1.50	$1.53
Forward rate	1.51	1.53

Required What arguments can you make for and against immediately recognizing the $1,000 premium on 4/1/06 as an asset and as income? If not on 4/1/06, when?

C 14-5 **Evaluating the Propriety of Deferring Hedging Gains and Losses on Forecasted Transactions** In Illustration 14-13, a $30,000 gain is reported (in OCI) at 12/31/06.

Required
1. What is the rationale for deferring the gain?
2. How does the deferred gain classification fit under the accounting model of Assets = Liabilities + Stockholders' Equity?
3. Would your answers to requirements 1 and 2 differ if the company were deferring a $30,000 loss in OCI rather than a $30,000 gain.

C 14-6 **Strategic Hedge—But How Much?** On 12/31/06, Quandree concluded that the Swiss franc will weaken approximately 20% for 2007. Quandree expects to lose (1) 20% of its domestic sales and (2) 20% of its export sales to Switzerland because its products are *more* expensive to domestic customers and Swiss customers. Accordingly, Quandree has decided to hedge this exposure so that it reports the same gross profit for 2006.

The direct *spot rate* at 12/31/06 is $.25; this rate was also the *average rate* for 2006. Quandree had the following sales and costs for 2006:

	Domestic Sales	Export Sales to Switzerland
Sales	$ 2,000,000	$ 400,000
Cost of sales	(1,500,000)	(300,000)
Gross Profit	$ 500,000	$ 100,000

Required
1. What types of FX options and FX forwards should be used to hedge this exposure?
2. What amount of currency should Quandree hedge because the forecasted export sales for 2007 (forecasted at 20% lower than 2006's actual export sales) will result in fewer dollars?
3. What amount of currency should Quandree hedge to make up for lost dollar gross profits because of lost sales?

Financial Analysis Problems

FAP 14-1 **We Hedged But Lost Money Anyway?** In the second quarter for the three months ended March 31, 1995, Apple Computer stated:

> Included in the Company's pretax results for the quarter were realized and unrealized losses on certain foreign currency hedging activities. As a result of these losses, interest and other income (expense), net for the quarter totaled ($50) million in expense, compared with ($7) million in expense in the year ago period.

> Apple generates a significant portion of its revenues from international sales and therefore has an ongoing need to exchange foreign currencies for dollars. The Company **attributed** [emphasis added] its foreign currency related expenses to recent dramatic declines in the value of the dollar relative to other currencies, and the impact of that decline on its outstanding foreign exchange contracts undertaken for hedging purposes. As part of its normal business practices, Apple, like many international companies, hedges its identified, and a portion of its anticipated, foreign currency flows against the risk of fluctuations in exchange rates against the U.S. dollar. This hedging is done through the purchase and sale of forward currency contracts and currency options.
>
> As a result of the decline in the value of the dollar, the value of the Company's net foreign currency forward and option contracts declined significantly, and the overall cost of hedging increased. The majority of the foreign exchange related expenses included in other income and expense, net for the second quarter is due to the unrealized marked-to-market valuation of sold currency options which Apple typically employs as part of its practice to hedge future anticipated revenues. Although the Company cannot predict movements in currency exchange rates [who can?], or their effect on its overall competitive position (and the situation is very complex), the Company believes that in general, it benefits more by a weaker dollar than by a stronger dollar.

During a press conference, Apple executives emphasized that (1) the $50 million is mostly a "paper loss" right now, (2) the majority of the $50 million is from unrealized valuations of unclosed currency options in the quarter, and (3) if the dollar gets stronger (against the Japanese yen and the German mark), the unrealized loss goes away.

Required

1. How could Apple have lost $50 million if it were hedging?
2. What was Apple really doing? Be specific as to the exact type of option contracts that Apple entered into.
3. What does Apple mean when it says that most of the $50 million is only a paper loss?
4. What other information does Apple's statement that the loss could reverse reveal to you?

FAP 14-2 **Accounting for the Hedge of a Forecasted Transaction** Expecto Inc. has a calendar year-end. For each of the eight years ended 12/31/08, a major customer in England placed a noncancelable sales order (£1,000,000) in June (with Expecto shipping the inventory the following month). A similar noncancelable sales order is expected to be placed in June 2009.

On 1/2/09, Expecto's foreign currency exchange management department concluded that the British pound would decrease in value from the current direct exchange rate of $1.50 (£1 = $1.50) to $1.40 by 6/30/09.

Thus, instead of the 2009 sale occurring when the exchange rate is $1.50, it is expected to occur when the exchange rate is closer to $1.40.

Accordingly, on 1/2/09, management entered into an FX option with a foreign currency dealer to sell £1,000,000 at the current direct exchange rate of $1.50. The cost of the option was $10,000—something that need not be dealt with in this problem. The option expires on 6/30/09. Thus if the direct exchange rate is *below* $1.50 on 6/30/09, Expecto will exercise the FX option. Because it will *not* have received any pounds from its British customer by 6/30/09, Expecto will have to buy £1,000,000 in the open market on that date to be able to deliver £1,000,000 to the foreign currency dealer under the FX option.

Assume that on 6/30/09, the direct exchange rate (spot) was $1.43 and Expecto exercised the option. Consequently, it has a gain (gross) of $70,000 on the FX option (£1,000,000 pounds × $.07), less the $10,000 cost of the option, resulting in a net gain of $60,000. For simplicity, also assume the following:

1. On 3/31/09, the direct exchange rate was $1.45.
2. On 6/27/09, the British customer placed a £1,000,000 order that Expecto will fill in July 2009.

Assume that Expecto could have accomplished its hedging objective using an FX forward instead of an FX option.

Disregarding current GAAP, several theoretical ways to account for the hedging gain (using either an option contract or a forward contract) at the end of the first and second quarters are as follows:

1. Report as **Deferred Income—classified *among* liabilities** until either realization occurs or the expected inventory sale occurs.
2. Report as **Deferred Income—classified *between* liabilities and equity** until either realization occurs or the expected inventory sale occurs.
3. Report **as a direct adjustment to equity**—bypassing the income statement until realization occurs or the expected inventory sale occurs.
4. Report in a **Statement of Comprehensive Income—classified as part of Other Changes in Stockholders' Equity until realization occurs** (this statement is illustrated in Chapter 15 on page 524).
5. Report in the income statement—**classified as part of Sales.**
6. Report in the income statement—**classified as part of Other Income.**

Required

1. What (a) underlying rationale, (b) theoretical and practical merits, and (c) theoretical and practical shortcomings exist for each method?
2. Which method do you think is the correct method (regardless of current GAAP)? Why?

chapter

15

Translating Foreign Currency Statements: The Current Rate Method

When you can measure what you are speaking about and express it in numbers, you know something about it; but when you cannot express it in numbers, your knowledge is of a meager and unsatisfactory kind.
LORD KELVIN, 1891

LEARNING OBJECTIVES

To Understand

> The way to *restate* foreign currency statements to U.S. GAAP.
> The translation issue of *which* exchange rate(s) to use.
> The procedures for applying the current rate method of translation.
> The way to account for a hedge of a foreign unit's net asset position.
> The translation issue of *how* to report the effect of exchange rate changes.
> The way to report the effect of an exchange rate change in comprehensive income.

TOPIC OUTLINE

Appendices can be found at http://www.pahler.swlearning.com

CHAPTER OVERVIEW

The translation of foreign currency financial statements into U.S. dollars is one of the most complex and controversial of all accounting issues. The complexity exists because currency exchange rates change daily under the floating exchange rate system for both *inflationary* and *non-inflationary* reasons. Unlike foreign currency importing and exporting transactions in which nearly unanimous agreement exists regarding how to report exchange rate changes, substantial diversity of opinion exists as to (1) *which* exchange rates to use and (2) whether the favorable or unfavorable effects of exchange rate changes should be reported currently in the income statement.

The Accounting Issues

Five accounting issues must be addressed for a foreign operation of a domestic company.

1. How should the use of foreign accounting practices that differ from U.S. GAAP be handled?
2. Which translation *method* should be used to translate the financial statements of foreign units into U.S. dollars?
3. Should the effect of exchange rate changes be reported currently in the income statement?
4. What additional risks must be considered in reporting earnings from foreign operations? Is consolidation appropriate?
5. Should the extent of a company's foreign operations be disclosed as supplementary information?

We begin this chapter by discussing the way to *restate* foreign currency financial statements to U.S. GAAP. We then discuss the *first* of the two major conceptual issues pertaining to translating foreign currency statements into dollars: *which* exchange rates to use. In this chapter, we discuss the *current rate method* of translation, which is by far the predominant of the two translation methods allowed under U.S. GAAP. The other allowable method, the *temporal method,* is discussed in Chapter 16. Next we discuss the *second* major conceptual issue pertaining to translating foreign currency statements into dollars: *how* to report the effect of a change in the exchange rate. Finally, we discuss *hedging transactions* used to negate the effect of adverse changes in the exchange rate.

The Governing Pronouncements

Translation and Reporting

FASB *Statement No. 52*, "Foreign Currency Translation," was issued in 1981 after three years of intensive research and extensive participation by professionals in industry, public accounting, higher education, and finance. The cornerstone of *FAS 52* is the *functional currency concept*, which is used to determine which of the two translation methods to use for each particular foreign operation.

So that you can better understand and apply this concept, we discuss it in detail in the latter part of Chapter 16—*after* you have become technically proficient with the two allowable translation methods. Furthermore, because of the highly conceptual and controversial nature of the *functional currency concept*, we do not examine its validity until Chapter 20. Delaying this examination enables you to understand more readily the analysis presented. This examination is essential for assessing whether (1) the translated reporting results under GAAP reflect the economics of what has transpired and (2) these numbers should be used for managerial decision making.

Additional Risks and the Appropriateness of Consolidation

Recall that the additional risks associated with foreign operations were listed in Appendix 13A. Recall also that (1) the appropriateness of consolidating foreign subsidiaries was addressed in Chapter 1 and (2) the consolidation of foreign subsidiaries *is* mandatory unless control is lacking, in which case consolidation is prohibited.

Supplemental Disclosures

The issue of presenting in financial statements the supplemental information pertaining to the extent of a company's foreign operations is addressed in FASB *Statement No. 131*, "Disclosures about Segments of an Enterprise and Related Information." This pronouncement was discussed in detail in Chapter 12, which covers segment reporting.

I. METHODOLOGY FOR RESTATING TO U.S. GAAP

As discussed in Chapter 13 (page 420) it is necessary (and often a major task) to *restate* foreign currency statements to U.S. GAAP ***before translating*** the foreign currency amounts into dollars. Adjusting a foreign unit's financial statements to U.S. GAAP is the equivalent of making *correcting entries*, a subject covered in intermediate accounting. A simple approach to developing the necessary restatement entries is to (1) compare actual balances ("what was done") with desired balances under U.S. GAAP ("what we wish had been done") and (2) use a step-by-step ("with and without") approach in determining the deferred income tax effects. An example of this methodology is shown in Illustration 15-1.

ILLUSTRATION 15-1 MANNER OF DEVELOPING RESTATEMENT TO U.S. GAAP ENTRIES

I. Assumed Facts:

1. On 1/1/03, a foreign subsidiary acquired a copyright for 100,000 LCU (local currency units).
2. The foreign subsidiary expensed this cost in accordance with its local GAAP and local income tax laws, even though the copyright's remaining legal life was 10 years.
3. The foreign subsidiary's income tax rate is 40%.
4. A worksheet restatement entry is required at 12/31/06.

II. Comparison of Actual Balances to Desired Balances:

	LOCAL CURRENCY UNITS		
	FOREIGN GAAP (*WHAT WAS DONE*)	U.S. GAAP (*WHAT WE WISH HAD BEEN DONE*)	REPORTING DIFFERENCES
Balance Sheet—12/31/06:			
Copyright	-0-	70,000	70,000
Retained earnings, 1/1/06	(100,000)	(20,000)	80,000
Income Statement—2006:			
Copyright expense	-0-	(10,000)	(10,000)

III. Worksheet Restatement Entry at 12/31/06:

	WITHOUT PROVIDING DEFERRED INCOME TAXES (STEP 1)		*WITH* PROVIDING DEFERRED INCOME TAXES (STEP 2)	
Copyright	70,000		70,000	
Copyright Expense	10,000		10,000	
Retained Earnings, 1/1/06		80,000		48,000[a]
Deferred Income Tax Expense				4,000[b]
Deferred Income Taxes Payable				28,000[c]

[a] Reporting difference at 12/31/05 of 80,000 LCU x 60% = 48,000.

[b] Reporting difference for 2006 of 10,000 LCU x 40% = 4,000.

[c] Reporting difference at 12/31/06 of 70,000 LCU x 40% = 28,000

Note: The net effect on retained earnings at 12/31/06 is 42,000 (48,000 + 4,000 – 10,000 = 42,000). This 42,000 is 60% of the copyright's $70,000 year-end reporting difference.

II. Translation Conceptual Issue 1: Which Exchange Rates to Use

The process of translating foreign currency financial statements into dollars is merely a mechanical process once the exchange rate for each account has been determined. For many decades, however, a raging controversy has existed over the following *two* conceptual issues:

1. Which exchange rates should be used for many of the accounts.
2. Whether to report the effect of a change in the exchange rate *currently* in ***earnings*** (discussed later).

The *first* conceptual issue centers around determining the appropriate exchange rates for translating individual assets and liabilities. The translation of the stockholders' equity accounts is *not* part of the issue because the total translated stockholders' equity is a forced residual amount that is the difference between the *total translated assets* and the *total translated liabilities*. Once the appropriate exchange rates have been determined for the assets and liabilities, consistency and logic dictate the appropriate exchange rates for translating the income statement accounts.

Criteria Used for Determining Appropriate Exchange Rates

Accountants have used the following criteria in determining the appropriate exchange rates to use:

1. Does the exchange rate selected for a specific account result in a **meaningful dollar amount**?
2. Does the exchange rate selected for a specific account **change the basis of accounting in translation**? For example, is the historical cost basis for a fixed asset in the foreign currency retained when translation is made into U.S. dollars?
3. When a change in the exchange rate has occurred, do the translated results **reflect the true economic impact of the change**?

Although these criteria seem simple enough, substantial controversy exists in practice because accountants often answer these questions differently for many accounts. Furthermore, the criteria are *not* always compatible. For instance, in dealing with fixed assets, satisfying the *second* criterion can prevent satisfying the *third* criterion.

Making Generalizations as to the Economic Effects of Exchange Rate Changes

In dealing with the *third* criterion, it would be convenient to have some *broad generalizations*, such as (1) a *decrease* in the direct exchange rate is always an adverse economic event, which should always result in reporting an *unfavorable* effect on stockholders' equity, or (2) an *increase* in the direct exchange rate is always a *favorable* economic event, which should always result in reporting a *favorable* effect on stockholders' equity. It is *not* possible to make such broad generalizations, however, because the economic effect of an exchange rate change depends on the following three items:

1. **The *causes* of the exchange rate change**—For instance, foreign inflation, domestic inflation, and noninflationary factors.
2. **The nature of the foreign unit's assets**—For instance, the extent to which the assets are monetary versus nonmonetary.
3. **The extent of *debt financing* relative to *equity financing*.**

For **specific situations**, though, **situational generalizations** can be made. For example, when the direct exchange rate *decreases* (for whatever reason), the economic effect of holding in foreign countries *monetary assets* that are financed by *equity* is always an *adverse* economic event, which should always result in reporting an *unfavorable* effect on stockholders' equity. As you develop an understanding of this material, you will be able to make *situational generalizations*.

Illustration 15-2 shows the economic effect of certain exchange rate changes when a subsidiary holds certain types of assets under different financing assumptions.

Monetary and Nonmonetary Account Classifications

Assets and liabilities may be conveniently grouped into **monetary accounts** and **nonmonetary accounts** (the same classification scheme used in constant-dollar accounting to adjust for inflation). Monetary items include **cash and accounts that are obligated to be settled in cash**, such as:

Assets	Liabilities
Accounts receivable	Accounts payable
Long-term receivables	Long-term debt
Deferred income tax receivables	Deferred income tax payables
Intercompany receivables	Intercompany payables
Investments in bonds	Accrued liabilities

All other asset and liability accounts—such as Inventory, Fixed Assets, Intangible Assets—are *nonmonetary items*. Equity accounts and income statement accounts are neither *monetary* nor *nonmonetary* items. This classification scheme is useful in determining the appropriate translation exchange rate to use for each asset and liability.

The *Current Rate* versus the *Historical Rate*

Which exchange rate to use for a given asset or liability requires choosing between (1) the exchange rate existing at the balance sheet date—the *current rate* (the spot rate)—and (2) the exchange rate existing when the balance in the account arose—the *historical rate.*

Translating *Monetary* Accounts

For cash, no controversy exists whatsoever. Accountants *agree* that the *current rate* should be used because this produces a *current value* amount in dollars, the only sensible amount to report. All three criteria listed earlier are satisfied. For each remaining *monetary item*, accountants almost unanimously agree that only the *current rate* makes sense because it also results in a largely *current value* amount in dollars, which again is the only sensible amount to report.[1]

Translating *Nonmonetary* Accounts—The Highly Controversial Area

Accountants strongly *disagree* on the appropriate exchange rates to use to translate *nonmonetary* accounts. Because of this disagreement, several translation approaches exist.

ILLUSTRATION 15-2 HOW DIFFERENT ASSET COMPOSITIONS AND FINANCING STRUCTURES RESULT IN REPORTING DIFFERENT ECONOMIC RESULTS

	Nature of Subsidiary's Assets	Type of Financing	***Economic Effect* on Subsidiary's Stockholders' Equity of an *Exchange Rate Change Caused By*[a]**	
			Foreign Inflation	**U.S. Inflation**
I.	All Cash	All Equity	Unfavorable	Favorable
II.	All Cash	All Foreign Debt	No effect	No effect
III.	All Land	All Equity	No effect	Favorable
IV.	All Land	All Foreign Debt	Favorable	No effect

[a] Recall from Chapter 13 that *foreign inflation* causes the direct exchange rate to *decrease*, and *U.S. inflation* causes the direct exchange rate to *increase*.
Note: We suggest you read the remainder of the chapter *before* trying to intuitively understand why the above reporting results occur.

[1] Prior to the issuance in 1975 of *FAS 8* (the predecessor of *FAS 52*), it was acceptable practice to use *historical exchange rates* for *long-term receivables* and *long-term payables*, a practice that began to lose support in 1956 when Professor Samuel Hepworth (University of Michigan) published a convincing article advocating using the *current exchange rate*.

The Three General Translation Approaches

Three translation approaches have been developed over the years, only *two* of which are allowed by *FAS 52:* The **foreign currency unit of measure approach** and the **U.S. dollar unit of measure approach.** We discuss and illustrate the *first* approach in this chapter and the *second* approach in Chapter 16. In Appendix 16B, the *third* translation approach, a **current value approach using purchasing power parity theory,** is discussed and illustrated. We use this third approach to (1) reveal the characteristics (*strengths* and *weaknesses*) of the two allowable translation approaches and (2) evaluate whether the *functional currency concept* set forth in *FAS 52* is valid.

In illustrating the *foreign currency unit of measure approach* in this chapter, we *initially* call the effect of the exchange rate change an **economic gain or loss from exchange rate change.** Furthermore, we show this effect as a separate item in equity, which coincidentally happens to be the required treatment under *FAS 52* for this approach. Accordingly, a discussion of the other major controversial issue of *how to report the effect of exchange rate changes* can be and is delayed until later in the chapter.

III. THE FOREIGN CURRENCY UNIT OF MEASURE APPROACH (THE *CURRENT RATE METHOD* OF TRANSLATION)

The Rationale

Under this approach, a foreign operation is viewed as a separate business unit whose only factual financial statements are those prepared in its foreign currency. From this premise, it is reasoned that **the item-to-item relationships that exist in the foreign currency statements (such as profitability ratios, liquidity ratios, and specific asset to total asset percentages) must be maintained in translation.** The only way to maintain these relationships is to use a **single exchange rate for all assets and liabilities.** Thus by using a single exchange rate, the translated financial statements in U.S. dollars retain a **"foreign currency feel"** to them.

Managerially, the U.S. parent, in looking at the *translated financial statements*, is able to view the foreign operation using the same perspective as that of the local management in the foreign country, which uses the *foreign currency statements*. Thus it is said that even though the amounts are *expressed* in U.S. dollars, the **unit of measure** is the foreign currency.

The *Current Rate Method* of Translation

Although numerous translation methods have been developed to express foreign currency statements in U.S. dollars, only the **current rate method** achieves the result of retaining the foreign currency as the unit of measure. **For the balance sheet, the current rate is defined as the rate existing at the balance sheet date**—all assets and liabilities are translated at this rate. **For the income statement, the current rate is defined as the exchange rate existing when an item was recognized in earnings**; there are conceivably 365 current rates in dealing with the income statement (*averages* are used to simplify matters).

The Focus: The Net Asset Position

Under the *current rate method*, all assets and liabilities are effectively valued (1) *higher* as a result of a direct rate *increase* and (2) *lower* as a result of a direct rate *decrease*. Because the liabilities offset a portion of the assets—thus constituting what is called a *natural hedge*—it is the subsidiary's assets that are *not* offset by liabilities (the net assets) that are exposed. Thus the effect of the exchange rate change can readily be determined by multiplying the foreign unit's **average net asset position** (average total assets – average total liabilities) by the change in the exchange rate.

Viewed from the *parent's perspective,* the foreign unit's *net asset position* is really the *parent's investment* in the subsidiary.[2] Thus, in substance, the parent's *Investment account balance* is effectively exposed to the risk of exchange rate changes. As shown later, a parent using the *equity method* adjusts its Investment account upward or downward for exchange rate changes (as is done for an FX Accounts Receivable account on the parent's books).

Reported Effects of Exchange Rate Changes

When the foreign unit is in a *net asset position,* an *increase* in the *direct* exchange rate causes a *favorable* result to be reported (a presumed economic gain from the exchange rate change). A *decrease* in the *direct* exchange rate causes an *unfavorable* result to be reported (a presumed economic loss from the exchange rate change). These effects are summarized in Illustration 15-3.

Key Observations as to the Current Rate Method

This approach makes no distinction as to the *nature* of the assets and liabilities (*monetary* versus *nonmonetary*) or their *longevity* (*current* versus *noncurrent*). **Nor is any attempt made to understand why the change in the exchange rate occurred.** Any distortions that exist in the *foreign currency statements* (such as fixed assets being substantially undervalued because of inflation) are perpetuated and carried over to the *translated financial statements.* Thus the status quo is preserved.

CHECK POINT

Under the *foreign currency unit of measure approach,* the focus is on which of the following?

a. Net current position.
b. Net asset position.
c. Net monetary position.
d. Net exposed position.

Answer: b

ILLUSTRATION 15-3 THE FOREIGN CURRENCY UNIT OF MEASURE APPROACH: REPORTING EFFECTS OF EXCHANGE RATE CHANGES

Translation Method Used	Possible Relevant Financial Positions	*Increase*[a] (Foreign Currency Has *Strengthened* or Dollar Has *Weakened*)	*Decrease*[b] (Foreign Currency Has *Weakened* or Dollar Has *Strengthened*)
Current rate	Net asset (assets exceed liabilities)[c]	Favorable	Unfavorable
Current rate	Net liability (liabilities exceed assets)[d]	Unfavorable	Favorable

[a] In all situations, the effect is *favorable* on the assets and *unfavorable* on the liabilities.

[b] In all situations, the effect is *unfavorable* on the assets and *favorable* on the liabilities.

[c] From the parent's perspective, the subsidiary's *net asset position* constitutes the *parent's investment.*

[d] From the parent's perspective, the parent has an investment that has been written down to *zero* (and a *liability* to the subsidiary if obligated to the subsidiary in some manner).

[2] The infrequent case in which a foreign unit is in a **net liability position** (total liabilities exceeding total assets) would be considered a *negative investment* position from the parent's perspective only if the parent is obligated to make an additional investment (usually because of having guaranteed the subsidiary's debt). In such cases, the parent reports a *liability* on its books (as discussed in Chapter 2).

Introductory Illustration

Translation Using the Current Rate Method

Assume that in late 2004, a U.S. company created a 100%-owned subsidiary in Mexico, making a $1,000,000 cash equity investment at that time when the direct exchange rate was $.50. For simplicity, assume that this direct exchange rate did *not* fluctuate through December 31, 2004. The subsidiary's first sales were on January 1, 2005.

Additional assumptions are that (1) no dividends were declared or paid in 2005; (2) fixed asset additions of 200,000 pesos (equal to 2004's depreciation expense) occurred on January 3, 2005, when the exchange rate was $.50; (3) Mexico had 25% inflation for 2005; (4) the United States had 10% inflation for 2005; and (5) the direct exchange rates were $.50 at December 31, 2004, $.44 at December 31, 2005, and $.47 for 2005 as an average.

The subsidiary's balance sheets at the end of 2004 and 2005 and its 2005 income statement are shown in Illustration 15-4.

The *current rate method* of translation for the year ended 2005 is shown in Illustration 15-5.

Is the Translated Amount for Fixed Assets Historical Cost?

The most difficult result to understand under the foreign currency unit of measure approach is whether the amount expressed in U.S. dollars for fixed assets should be considered *historical cost* or some form of *current value*. Unlike *domestic* fixed assets, *foreign* fixed assets are reported at different amounts at each financial reporting date under the *current rate method* because of exchange rate changes (*as if* they were marketable securities being accounted for at *market prices*). Advocates of this approach contend that the amounts in U.S. dollars *do* constitute *historical cost* **using the foreign currency as the unit of measure.** Critics of this approach contend that this is merely an abandonment of *historical cost*. Other critics contend that it produces amounts that are difficult to interpret and *not* meaningful. In our opinion, the amounts are meaningful—**but only to the extent that the local currency statements are meaningful.** If fixed assets are undervalued by 25% because of inflation, which causes total assets to be undervalued by 15%, this same percentage level of distortion is reflected in the translated statements. Thus consistency is maintained with the way U.S. domestic assets are valued (no adjustment for inflation). Perhaps the best way to look

ILLUSTRATION 15-4 FOREIGN CURRENCY FINANCIAL STATEMENTS

	Pesos	
	December 31, 2004	**December 31, 2005**
Balance Sheets:		
Monetary assets	2,200,000	2,500,000
Inventory	1,000,000	1,250,000
Fixed assets, net	4,800,000	4,800,000[a]
Total Assets	8,000,000	8,550,000
Monetary liabilities	6,000,000	6,250,000
Common stock	2,000,000[b]	2,000,000
Retained earnings	-0-	300,000
Total Liabilities and Equity	8,000,000	8,550,000
Net Asset Position	**2,000,000**	**2,300,000**
Income Statements (2005):		
Revenues		5,300,000
Cost of sales		(4,300,000)
Depreciation		(200,000)
Expenses		(500,000)
Net Income		300,000

[a] Because of the 25% inflation in Mexico during 2005, these assets are undervalued 25%.

[b] This amount is the peso equivalent of the $1,000,000 cash investment made by the parent when it *created* the subsidiary in late 2004 ($1,000,000/$.50 = 2,000,000 pesos).

ILLUSTRATION 15-5 THE CURRENT RATE METHOD FOR THE YEAR ENDED DECEMBER 31, 2005

	Pesos	Exchange Code	Exchange Rate	U.S. Dollars
Income Statement (2005):				
Revenues	5,300,000	A	$.47	$ 2,491,000
Cost of sales	(4,300,000)	A	$.47	(2,021,000)
Depreciation	(200,000)	A	$.47	(94,000)
Expenses	(500,000)	A	$.47	(235,000)
Net Income	300,000			$ 141,000
Balance Sheet (12/31/05):				
Monetary assets	2,500,000	C	$.44	$ 1,100,000
Inventory	1,250,000	C	$.44	550,000
Fixed assets, net	4,800,000	C	$.44	2,112,000
Total Assets	8,550,000			$ 3,762,000
Monetary liabilities	6,250,000	C	$.44	$ 2,750,000
Common stock	2,000,000	H	$.50	$ 1,000,000
Retained earnings	300,000	(Per *above*)		141,000
Economic loss from exchange rate change		(See *below*)		(129,000)
Total Equity	2,300,000			$ 1,012,000
Total Liabilities and Equity	8,550,000			$ 3,762,000

Calculation of Economic Loss from Exchange Rate Change:

Net asset (stockholders' equity) position at 1/1/05 of 2,000,000 pesos × $.06 *decrease* in the *direct* exchange rate equals	$ (120,000)
Net income of 300,000 pesos × $.03 difference between the *average rate* and the *year-end rate* ($.47 – $.44) equals	(9,000)
Total Economic Loss from Exchange Rate Change	$ (129,000)

Key Review Points:

1. **Note how ratios and relationships *are* maintained *after* translation:**

	Pesos	U.S. Dollars
Debt-to-equity ratio	2.71:1	2.71:1
Gross profit margin ratio	19%	19%
Net income to sales ratio	6%	6%
Fixed assets to total assets percent	56%	56%
Undervaluation of fixed assets	25%	25%

2. **Note the *increase* in the stockholder's equity:**

Ending stockholder's equity (per above)	$1,012,000
Less—*Beginning* stockholder's equity (parent's initial capital investment per Illustration 15-4)	1,000,000
Increase in Stockholder's Equity	$1,012,000

Code: A = *Average* rate; C = *Current* rate; H = *Historical* rate.

at it is to say that the translated amounts are *historical cost amounts* that have been adjusted for exchange rate changes—adjustments that are made to *monetary assets* as well.

The Disappearing Plant Problem

Many countries (primarily in South America) currently have highly inflationary economies (sometimes exceeding 2,000% annually for some countries). The use of the **foreign currency unit of measure approach** (current rate method) can quickly result in reporting meaningless fixed asset amounts in these situations. To illustrate, consider the following example of a manufacturing plant in Argentina that cost 10,000,000 pesos when it was purchased on December 31, 1974, using $2,000,000 of the parent's money:

	Amount (pesos)	December 31, 1974 Rate	December 31, 1974 Amount	December 31, 2004 Rate	December 31, 2004 Amount
Plant	10,000,000	$.20	$2,000,000	$.00000001	$.10

Clearly, the application of the December 31, 2004, *current exchange rate* to the *historical cost* in pesos produces an amount that bears no relationship to *current value* or a reasonable *historical cost* amount. The use of the *current rate* would produce a meaningful amount only if it were applied to the *inflation-adjusted historical cost* in pesos. This procedure, however, would depart from *historical cost* in the foreign currency. Even though the $.10 is the *historical cost* using the *foreign currency as the unit of measure*, it obviously makes no sense to use this method when foreign inflation has caused the *direct* exchange rate to *decrease* so severely. Unfortunately, the problem exists for all foreign countries because they all have inflation. The problem is just more readily evident in *highly* inflationary economies. Even in relatively *low* inflationary economies, the reporting results can lose meaning fairly quickly. This inability to deal with the effects of foreign inflation is the Achilles' heel of this translation method.

We now provide a more comprehensive illustration of the *current rate method* that shows (1) the use of the **Cumulative Translation Adjustment** account, which is a sub-account of the **Accumulated Other Comprehensive Income** (AOCI) equity account discussed in Section VI; (2) *beginning* balances for the Retained Earnings account and the Cumulative Translation Adjustment account; (3) the translation treatment for a cash dividend payment to the parent; and (4) *all* of the individual asset and liability accounts.

In addition, we discuss (1) certain pretranslation procedures, (2) the finer points of this method, and (3) certain post-translation procedures. This comprehensive illustration is for 2006, the year following the year in Illustration 15-5.

Basic Procedures *Before* Translation

Certain fundamental procedures must be performed *before* the financial statements of foreign subsidiaries (and branches) may be translated into dollars.

Restatement to U.S. GAAP

Operations conducted in a foreign country must be accounted for using that country's accounting principles. When foreign currency financial statements use accounting principles that differ from U.S. generally accepted accounting principles, appropriate restatement adjustments must be made to those statements *before* translation so that they conform to U.S. generally accepted accounting principles. These restatement adjustments, which are **made on a worksheet**, are *never* posted to the *general ledger* of the foreign accounting entity. The restatement adjustments are necessary regardless of (1) the organizational form through which foreign operations are conducted and (2) whether or not the foreign operation's statements are consolidated (if a subsidiary) or combined (if a division or a branch) with the financial statements of the domestic accounting entity.

Similarly, when a domestic company has a 20% to 50% interest in a foreign operation, which must be accounted for under the *equity method* of accounting if significant influence exists, the investee's foreign statements must be adjusted to conform to U.S. generally accepted accounting principles before translation into dollars. The *equity method* is then applied *after* the translation process in accordance with *FAS 52*.

Adjustments to Receivables and Payables

A foreign operation's receivables or payables in *other than* its local currency must be adjusted to reflect the current rate between the local currency (of the foreign country) and the currency in which the receivable or payable is stated. Recall that the way to make and account for such adjustments was discussed in Chapter 13. In the illustration of the translation process in this section, we assume that any such adjustments have already been made.

Reconciliation of Inter- or Intracompany Receivable and Payable Accounts

Inventory and cash are commonly transferred between *domestic* and *foreign* operations. Such transactions are usually recorded in *separate* Inter- or Intracompany Receivable and Payable accounts by each accounting entity. Such accounts must be reconciled to each other *before* translation to ensure that no clerical errors or unrecorded in-transit items exist. Only by performing this reconciliation will these accounts completely offset each other after translation.

Furthermore, when the inter- or intracompany account is to be settled in *dollars* (rather than in the foreign unit's *local currency*), the *foreign unit's* accounts must be adjusted as described in the preceding section. If settlement is to be made in the foreign unit's *local currency*, the *domestic operation* must adjust its books. Such adjustments are illustrated later in the chapter where the fine points of intercompany transactions with foreign subsidiaries are discussed.

Exchange Rates Used in Translation

Current Exchange Rate

Recall that *FAS 52* has a dual definition of the current exchange rate. For the *balance sheet*, this is the **exchange rate existing at the balance sheet date.** For the *income statement*, this is the **exchange rate in effect when an item is recognized in the income statement.**

Average Exchange Rates

Because it is impractical to translate the various income statement items at the numerous exchange rates that could apply throughout a period, *FAS 52* allows firms to calculate and use *average* exchange rates (either *simple* or *weighted*, as appropriate) for each period.

Multiple (Official) Exchange Rates

In addition to the floating rates, many countries declare one or more official rates for certain types of currency conversions. For example, to discourage the repatriation of dividends to a foreign parent company, a country would use a rate whereby the parent company would receive a *lower* amount of its own currency than it otherwise would receive had the free rate been used. When such multiple rates exist, the *current exchange rate* is the rate **that could be used for dividend remittances.**

Specific Translation Procedures

Balance Sheet Accounts

The following procedures translate the individual balance sheet accounts:

1. *All* **assets and liabilities** are translated at the exchange rate existing at the balance sheet date.
2. **Common stock and additional paid-in capital** are translated at *historical exchange rates* (to isolate the effect of the change in the exchange rate for the current period).
3. **Beginning retained earnings** is the dollar balance in the Retained Earnings account at the end of the *prior period*.
4. Dividend payments, if any, are translated using the exchange rate in effect at the time of the declaration.

CHECK POINT

Which exchange rates should be used in expressing the following accounts in dollars under the *current rate* method?

	Additional Paid-in Capital	Deferred Income Taxes Payable
a.	Current	Historical
b.	Historical	Current
c.	Historical	Historical
d.	Current	Current

Answer: b

Revenue, Cost of Goods Sold, and Expense Accounts

All revenues, costs of sales, and expenses (as well as gains and losses) are translated using exchange rates that were in effect when these items were **recognized** in the income statement. Thus exchange rates **in effect during the current period**—*current exchange rates*—are used. (The following two paragraphs explain how this process can be simplified.) For income statement account balances that come *directly from the balance sheet* (Cost of Sales, Depreciation Expense, and Amortization Expenses), the result is to use an **"exit date" rate** (as opposed to the rate when the item "entered" the balance sheet [an **"entry date"** rate]).

The Use of *Average* Exchange Rates

When translating income statement accounts, *average* exchange rates may be used provided that approximately the same results can be obtained from translating each individual transaction into dollars using the exchange rate that was in effect when the transaction was recognized. If the item being translated occurred *evenly* throughout the period (month, quarter, or year), a *simple average* is sufficient. Otherwise, a *weighted average* is necessary. (Most publicly owned companies achieve a *weighted average* result by multiplying each individual month's amount by each month's *average* exchange rate.) *Average* exchange rates must be calculated using the *direct* exchange rates that existed during the period; *indirect* exchange rates would *not* give the proper translated amounts.

The Substitution Technique

A simplifying technique commonly used to translate income statement accounts that arise from activity with the parent or home office is to **substitute the amount in the *domestic company's* account for the *subsidiary's* or *branch's* account.** For example, the Intercompany Interest *Expense* account on the *foreign subsidiary's* books would be translated at the amount recorded in the Intercompany Interest *Income* account on the *parent company's* books. Likewise, the Intercompany *Sales* account on the *foreign subsidiary's* books would be translated at the amount recorded in the Intercompany *Purchases* account on the *parent's* books. This procedure automatically translates these items at the rates in effect on each transaction date, thus negating the need to use *average rates*.

For *downstream sales* to foreign *marketing* units (no manufacturing-related costs would be incurred by these units) that have resold *all* the intercompany-acquired inventory, this technique *cannot* be used to translate the foreign unit's Cost of Sales amount because it would result in a Cost of Sales amount based on exchange prices in existence when the inventory was *acquired* by the foreign unit rather than when the foreign unit *sold* the inventory. The latter is required under the translation process.

In most cases, inter- or intracompany *revenue and expense* accounts *need not* be reconciled *before* doing the substitution. By reconciling the Inter- or Intracompany *Receivable and Payable* accounts *before* this substitution is made (as discussed on page 511), any clerical errors or unrecorded in-transit items affecting these income statement accounts would have been detected.

CHECK POINT

Which exchange rates should be used in expressing the following accounts in dollars under the *current rate* method?

	Cost of Sales	Depreciation Expense
a.	Current	Historical
b.	Historical	Current
c.	Historical	Historical
d.	Current	Current

Answer: d

Translation Using the Current Rate Method

Assume the following information for this 100%-owned subsidiary located in Mexico:

1. **Conformity with U.S. GAAP:** The financial statements in pesos already have been adjusted to conform with U.S. GAAP.

2. **Intercompany Receivable and Payable accounts:** The parent company and the subsidiary have no intercompany transactions (other than dividends declared by the subsidiary). Accordingly, no Intercompany Receivable and Payable accounts exist, and no adjustments must be made at the balance sheet date prior to the translation process relating to changes in the exchange rate.
3. **Exchange rates:** The *direct* exchange rate at December 31, 2005, was $.44. The peso *weakened* or the dollar *strengthened* during 2006 such that the *direct* exchange rate at December 31, 2006, was $.40. The *average rate* for 2006 was $.42.
4. **Common stock:** The subsidiary was created in late 2005 when the direct exchange rate was $.50. No additional capital stock changes have occurred since then.
5. **Retained earnings—*beginning* of year:** The translated amount of retained earnings at the end of the prior year was $141,000 (the balance at December 31, 2005, was shown in Illustration 15-5 on page 510).
6. **Dividends declared:** The subsidiary declared and paid a cash dividend of 100,000 pesos on November 11, 2006, when the *direct* exchange rate was $.41.
7. **Sales, costs, and expenses:** All sales, costs, and expenses occurred *evenly* throughout 2006.
8. **Cumulative translation adjustment—*beginning* of year:** The amount of the cumulative *translation adjustment* at the end of the prior year was a *debit* balance of $129,000 (as shown in Illustration 15-5).
9. **Current year translation adjustment:** The *current year* translation adjustment is a *debit* of $100,000. The manner of calculating this amount is shown in a supporting schedule to this illustration.
10. At January 1, 2006, the subsidiary's assets exceeded its liabilities by 2,300,000 pesos (as shown in Illustration 15-5).

Illustration 15-6 uses the preceding information to translate the foreign subsidiary's financial statements into dollars. The calculation of the current year translation adjustment is shown in supporting Illustration 15-7.

Parent's Procedures *After* Translation

Under the *equity method* of accounting, the parent company makes the following entries:

Investment in Subsidiary	189,000	
Equity in Net Income of Subsidiary		189,000
To record equity in net income.		
Other Comprehensive Income (OCI)—Translation Adjustment.	100,000[a]	
Investment in Subsidiary		100,000
To record effect of change in exchange rate.		

Note: These entries *always* maintain the *book value element* of the Investment account balance at the difference between the subsidiary's assets and liabilities.

[a] This balance is closed to the Accumulated Other Comprehensive Income (AOCI) account.

The analysis of the parent's Investment account is updated in 2006 as follows:

	Parent's Investment Account	=	Subsidiary's Equity Accounts: Common Stock	+	Retained Earnings	+	AOCI—Cumulative Translation Adjustments
Balances, 1/1/06	$1,012,000[a]		$1,000,000		$ 141,000		$(129,000)
Equity in net income	189,000				189,000		
Dividends declared	(41,000)				(41,000)		
Translation adjustment	(100,000)						(100,000)
Balances, 12/31/06	$1,060,000[a]		$1,000,000		$ 289,000		$(229,000)

[a] No *cost in excess of book value* exists because the subsidiary was *created* by the parent company.

ILLUSTRATION 15-6 TRANSLATION WORKSHEET: THE CURRENT RATE METHOD—FOR THE YEAR ENDED DECEMBER 31, 2006

		Foreign Currency Pesos	Exchange Code	Exchange Rate	U.S. Dollars
	Income Statement (2006):				
	Sales	6,000,000	A	$.42	$ 2,520,000
	Cost of sales	(4,600,000)	A	$.42	(1,932,000)
	Depreciation expense	(200,000)	A	$.42	(84,000)
	Operating expenses	(600,000)	A	$.42	(252,000)
	Income before Taxes	600,000			$ 252,000
	Income tax expense at 25%	(150,000)	A	$.42	(63,000)
	Net Income	450,000			$ 189,000
	Statement of Retained Earnings:				
	Balance, 1/1/06	300,000			$ 141,000
	+ Net income	450,000	(Per above)		189,000
	– Dividends	(100,000)	H	$.41	(41,000)
	Balance, 12/31/06	650,000			$ 289,000
	Balance Sheet (12/31/06):				
	Cash	400,000	C	$.40	$ 160,000
	Accounts receivable, net	1,600,000	C	$.40	640,000
Beginning Net Assets 2,300,000 pesos	Inventory	1,500,000	C	$.40	600,000
	Land	1,000,000	C	$.40	400,000
	Buildings and equipment	4,000,000	C	$.40	1,600,000
	Accumulated depreciation	(400,000)	C	$.40	(160,000)
	Total Assets	8,100,000			$ 3,240,000
	Payables and accruals	1,950,000	C	$.40	$ 780,000
	Long-term debt	3,500,000	C	$.40	1,400,000
	Total Liabilities	5,450,000			$ 2,180,000
	Common stock	2,000,000	H	$.50	$ 1,000,000
	Retained earnings	650,000	(Per above)		289,000
	AOCI—Cumulative translation adjustment:				
	Prior years				(129,000)
	Current year		(Per Illus. 15-7)		**(100,000)**
Ending Net Assets 2,650,000 pesos	Total Equity	2,650,000			$ 1,060,000
	Total Liabilities and Equity	8,100,000			$ 3,240,000

Code:
C = *Current* rate existing at the balance sheet date.
A = *Average* rate, as given in the introduction to this illustration.
H = *Historical* rate.

Key Review Points:

1. When the *direct* exchange rate *decreases*, a foreign subsidiary's profits are translated into *fewer* dollars. The dollar effect of the decrease is not shown on a *separate line item* in the income statement, however, because the effect is reported instead by reporting *lower* amounts for the *individual income statement accounts.*
2. Security analysts would like to know, however, the amount of the dollar effect of the *direct* exchange rate *decrease*. Some managements calculate this amount for *internal* purposes.

The basic elimination entry to consolidate the subsidiary at December 31, 2006, is developed from the preceding analysis and is as follows:

WORKSHEET ENTRY ONLY

	Dr.	Cr.
Common Stock	1,000,000	
Retained Earnings, 1/1/06	141,000	
Equity in Net Income of Subsidiary	189,000	
Dividends Declared		41,000
AOCI—Cumulative Translation Adjustment		229,000
Investment in Subsidiary		1,060,000

ILLUSTRATION 15-7 CALCULATION OF CURRENT YEAR TRANSLATION ADJUSTMENT: SUPPORTING SCHEDULE TO ILLUSTRATION 15-6

Method I: Analysis of the Net Asset Position

	PESOS	*DECREASE IN* DIRECT EXCHANGE RATE	*INCREASE* (DECREASE IN DOLLARS)
Net Assets at 1/1/06:			
Portion that lost \$.04 of valuation (\$.44 – \$.40):	**2,200,000**	\$(.04)	\$ (88,000)
Portion (assumed used to pay the dividend) that lost \$.03 of valuation (\$.44 – \$.41):	**100,000**[a]	(.03)	(3,000)
	2,300,000		\$ (91,000)
– **Dividend declared**.	(100,000)		
+ Increase in net assets from earnings—a loss of \$.02 of valuation (\$.42 *average rate* – \$.40 *year-end rate*).	**450,000**	(.02)	(9,000)
Net Assets at 12/31/06.	**2,650,000**		\$(100,000)

[a] A "flow" assumption must be made. By making a **FIFO assumption** that the 100,000 pesos dividend was paid out of *beginning* retained earnings (part of *beginning* net assets), it can be assumed that (1) 2,200,000 pesos of the *beginning* net assets existed for the entire year (losing \$.04 of valuation) and (2) the remaining 100,000 pesos of *beginning* net assets existed only through the dividend declaration date (11/1/06) (losing only \$.03 of valuation). (Under a **LIFO assumption**, the comparable U.S. dollar amounts are \$(92,000), \$(9,000), and \$1,000.)

Method II: Residual Force Out

1.		Translated assets	\$3,240,000
2.	Less	Translated liabilities	2,180,000
3.	Equals	Total stockholders' equity	\$1,060,000
4.	Less	Translated common stock and additional paid-in capital accounts	1,000,000
5.	Equals	Total retained earnings and the cumulative translation adjustment	\$ 60,000
6.	Less	*Ending* retained earnings.	289,000
7.	Equals	The cumulative translation adjustment	\$ (229,000)
8.	Less	The cumulative translation adjustment at the *beginning* of the year (a known amount from the prior year).	(129,000)
9.	Equals	The Current Period Translation Adjustment	\$ (100,000)

Comparative Note: In practice, most companies perform their translations using templates on electronic spreadsheet software. The templates are designed so that the current period translation adjustment is *forced out*.

The equity accounts on the consolidation worksheet appear as follows:

	Parrco	Subbco	Consolidation Entries Dr.			Cr.	Consolidated
Parrco Company							
Common stock.	2,000,000[a]						2,000,000
Retained earnings	1,334,000[a]						1,334,000
AOCI—Cumulative translation adjustment	(229,000)						(229,000)
Subbco Company							
Common stock.		1,000,000	1,000,000	1			–0–
Retained earnings		289,000	330,000[b]			41,000[b]	–0–
AOCI—Cumulative translation adjustment		(229,000)			1	229,000	–0–

1 This posting comes from the basic elimination entry.

[a] Assumed amount.

[b] Carried forward from the statement of retained earnings.

The OCI and AOCI accounts are discussed in detail in Section VI.

Translating a Statement of Cash Flows

Foreign units that are consolidated will also have their translated statement of cash flows consolidated. We purposely do *not* illustrate this statement because that would take away the opportunity to learn how to deal with the unique aspects of this statement. Information for preparing this statement is presented in many of the problems in the chapter.

Income Tax Consequences of Exchange Rate Changes

The income tax consequences of exchange rate changes are discussed in Appendix 15A.

Disposition of Translation Adjustments

The translation adjustments reported as a separate component of stockholders' equity are removed from that component (along with any income taxes) and reported in the income statement as part of the gain or loss on (1) complete or substantially complete liquidation or (2) sale of the investment. To illustrate, assume that on January 2, 2007, the parent company *sold* all of its common stock holdings in the subsidiary for $1,090,000 cash ($30,000 more than the $1,060,000 carrying value of its investment at December 31, 2006, as shown in the analysis of the Investment account).

The entry to record the sale and remove the $229,000 *debit* balance in the AOCI-Cumulative Translation Adjustment account follows:[3]

Cash	1,090,000	
Loss on Sale of Subsidiary	199,000	
Investment in Subsidiary		1,060,000
AOCI—Cumulative Translation Adjustment		229,000

A company that has foreign operations in more than one country must, of course, maintain a separate translation component of AOCI for each such foreign operation that has translation adjustments.

Intercompany Transactions with Foreign Units

Certain procedures must be followed when a parent has intercompany transactions with a foreign unit.

Adjustments to Intercompany Receivables and Payables

When intercompany receivables and payables exist, the entity that makes or receives payment in the foreign currency (that is, in other than its own currency) must adjust its intercompany receivable or payable to reflect the current (spot) exchange rate at the financial reporting date. Otherwise, these accounts will *not* agree in dollars and will *not* be eliminated in consolidation. These accounts are adjusted using the identical procedures shown in Chapter 13 for FX receivables and FX payables arising from *exporting* and *importing transactions*, respectively. The treatment of the offsetting FX gain or loss, however, depends on whether the account is expected to be settled in the foreseeable future:

1. **Expected to be settled in the foreseeable future.** In these cases, the FX gain or loss is recognized currently in ***earnings***.
2. ***Not*** **expected to be settled in the foreseeable future.** A parent's Long-Term Intercompany Receivable account is, in substance, an *addition* to the Investment account. Likewise, a parent's Long-Term Intercompany Payable account is, in substance, a *reduction* of the investment. When

[3] *FAS Interpretation 37* requires such treatment on a *pro rata basis* when only *part* of the ownership in a foreign operation is sold.

such receivables and payables are denominated in a foreign currency and settlement is *not* planned or anticipated in the foreseeable future, *FAS 52* requires that FX gains and losses from adjusting these accounts be treated as translation adjustments. Thus they are **charged or credited to the OCI—Translation Adjustment account rather than reported currently in earnings.** This provision ensures that the *entire* effect of an exchange rate change on the parent's *true* investment in a foreign unit is reported in the same way.

Intercompany Dividend Receivable

When a subsidiary declares a dividend, the parent uses the exchange rate existing at the *dividend declaration date* to record its dividend receivable. Any changes in the exchange rate between the *declaration date* and the *remittance date* result in an FX gain or loss that is recognized currently in the income statement. Which entity incurs the FX gain or loss depends on the currency in which the dividend is denominated. (Such FX gains and losses can be avoided, of course, if dividends are remitted at their *declaration date*.)

CHECK POINT

A *long-term* intercompany receivable from a parent's Japanese subsidiary (denominated in yen) is *not* expected to be settled in the foreseeable future. During 2006, the direct exchange rate increased. The parent uses the *current rate* method. At year-end, the parent should do which of the following?

a. Adjust the receivable and *debit* an income statement account.
b. Adjust the receivable and *credit* an income statement account.
c. Adjust the receivable and *debit* the OCI—Translation Adjustment account.
d. Adjust the receivable and *credit* the OCI—Translation Adjustment account.

Answer: d

Unrealized Intercompany Profit to Be Deferred in Consolidation

Recall from Chapter 8 that all intercompany transactions are eliminated in consolidation. In preparing the analysis for determining the amount of unrealized intercompany profit to be deferred, **the exchange rate at the *transfer date*—*not*** the exchange rate at the *financial reporting date*—is used. This procedure is required even though any remaining intercompany-acquired inventory (or fixed asset) is translated in the balance sheet at the *current rate*, which usually differs from the rate that existed at the *transfer date*.

To do otherwise produces nonsensical results in relation to the physical proportion of the inventory *resold* versus that *still on hand*. Stated differently, if the subsidiary's records show that 20% of the intercompany-acquired inventory is still on hand, 20% of the parent's gross profit must be deferred; using the current (spot) rate at the balance sheet date in preparing the analysis instead produces a percentage *other than* 20%.

CHECK POINT

During 2006, a parent sold inventory costing $70,000 to its British subsidiary for $100,000. At 12/31/06, the subsidiary reported in its balance sheet £40,000 of this inventory. At the transfer date, the direct exchange rate was $.50. At 12/31/06, the direct exchange rate was $.40. How much intercompany profit must be deferred at 12/31/06?

a. $6,000
b. $4,800
c. $12,000
d. $18,000

Answer: a

Special Disclosures Required Regarding the AOCI—Cumulative Translation Adjustment Account

For the AOCI—Cumulative Translation Adjustment account, an analysis must be presented (either in notes, in a separate statement, or as part of a statement of changes in stockholders' equity) of the following items:

1. The *beginning* and *ending* balance of the account.
2. The aggregate adjustment for the period to the account resulting from (a) translation adjustments, (b) adjustments to long-term intercompany receivables and payables, and (c) FX gains and losses arising from hedges of the net asset position (discussed shortly).
3. The amount of income taxes for the period charged or credited to the account as a result of the current period translation adjustment.
4. The amounts transferred from the account and recognized in earnings as a result of the *sale* or complete or substantially complete *liquidation* of the investment in the foreign subsidiary.

Maintaining Relationships Is a Critical Element of Interpersonal Skills—But Is It the Critical Factor in Determining How to Translate Financial Statements?

Recall that the *foreign currency unit of measure approach* results in maintaining in translation the relationships that exist in the foreign currency. These are fair questions to ask:

1. Is maintaining the relationships important? To whom? Why?
2. Are foreign managers evaluated using local currency statements or dollar statements?
3. If dollar statements are used to evaluate foreign managers, do firms use for this evaluation the results produced under the current rate method or the results produced under one of the other methods (discussed in the following two chapters)?
4. Do the results reflect the true economic consequences of an exchange rate change?

We deal with these questions in Appendix 16B.

ETHICS

Can You Tell the Truth about Former Accountants?

You are an accounting supervisor at Oldco Inc. The accounting supervisor at Newco Inc. has called you in reference to an accountant whom Newco is considering for employment. The accountant was terminated from Oldco several months ago for embezzling small amounts of money.

Questions

1. What can you say to the accounting supervisor at Newco?
2. If Newco hires the accountant who then embezzles large sums of money, does Newco have any legal recourse against Oldco if Oldco concealed the accountant's embezzlement while in its employment?

IV. HEDGING A FOREIGN SUBSIDIARY'S *NET ASSET POSITION*

Recall that (1) a subsidiary's *net asset position* (total assets – total liabilities) is what is exposed to the effect of exchange rate changes and (2) a subsidiary's *net asset position* is effectively the equivalent of the *parent's Investment account* from the parent's perspective. Thus hedging the subsidiary's *net asset position* accomplishes the same result as though the *parent* hedged its *Investment account balance* (which fluctuates in value merely as a result of exchange rate changes).

When the parent uses the *current rate method* of translation and hedges a foreign unit's *net asset position*, the FX gain or loss on the hedging transaction (net of the related tax effects) must be reported in **Other Comprehensive Income (OCI)**. As with the FX translation adjustment, the FX hedging gain or loss is closed to the **Accumulated Other Comprehensive Income (AOCI)** equity account—*not* to the Retained Earnings account. (More about OCI and AOCI in Section VI.) This requirement allows the hedging of FX gain or loss to offset partially or fully the FX translation adjustment for the year. For the hedging FX gain or loss to be treated in this manner, the transaction must be (1) designated as a hedge of the net asset position and (2) effective. These are the hedge criteria of *FAS 52*. (Unlike hedges of other foreign currency exposures, *net investment hedges* [briefly discussed in Chapter 17] are *not* subject to any of the extensive hedge criteria of FASB *Statement No. 133*, "Accounting for Derivative Instruments and Hedging Activities." Instead, they are subject only to the criteria in paragraph 20 of *FAS 52*, which criteria were *not* changed by *FAS 133*.)

Comprehensive Illustration

Hedging a *Net Asset Position* When the Parent Uses the Current Rate Method

Assume that on December 31, 2005, the parent of the 100%-owned Mexican subsidiary used in the earlier example expected the Mexican peso to *weaken* by the end of 2006. Accordingly, the parent contracted with an FX trader on December 31, 2005, to *sell* 2,300,000 pesos (the subsidiary's *net asset position* at that date) in 365 days at the forward rate of $.435. Illustration 15-8 shows this special accounting treatment for this hedging transaction. (For simplicity, we do *not* deal with interim quarterly reporting dates.) The following *direct* exchange rates are assumed:

	December 31, 2005 (the inception date)	December 31, 2006 (the expiration date and financial reporting date)
Spot rate	$.440	$.400
Forward rate (***selling* forward**).	.435	.400
Discount.	.005	n/a

Review Points for Illustration 15-8. Note the following:

1. **The net change in the AOCI—CTA account.** Recall that a $100,000 *unfavorable* translation adjustment occurred for 2006 in Illustration 15-6. Accordingly, the activity in the AOCI—CTA account for 2006 is as follows:

Accumulated Other Comprehensive Income—Cumulative Translation Adjustment

	Debit	Credit	
Balance, 1/1/06 (per Illustration 15-6)	$129,000		
Translation adjustment for 2006	100,000		
		80,500	Hedging gain
Balance, 12/31/06	$148,500		

Obviously, the hedge was effective.

2. **Realized versus unrealized.** The $80,500 gain on the FX forward is a *cash* gain, and thus it has been **realized.** The adverse translation adjustment of $100,000, however, is **unrealized.** Furthermore, it will reverse itself in later periods if the direct exchange rate *increases* by $.04.
3. **What if the *spot* exchange rate had *increased from* $.44 to $.48?** If the *spot rate* had *increased* by $.04 instead of *decreasing* by $.04, the company would have incurred a $103,500 loss on its FX forward ($.48 – $.435 = $.045; $.045 × 2,300,000 pesos = $103,500), which would have been mostly offset by a $100,000 *favorable* translation adjustment. The *favorable* translation adjustment will reverse itself in later periods if the *spot* rate *decreases* by $.04. The $103,500 loss on the FX forward, however, is a *cash* loss that will *not* reverse itself in later periods.

ILLUSTRATION 15-8 HEDGING THE SUBSIDIARY'S NET ASSET POSITION: NET POSITION ACCOUNTING

December 31, 2005
(the date the 365-day FX forward was entered into)

No general ledger entries are made—only memorandum entries are made.

December 31, 2006

FX Contract Value—Forward, **net**	$80,500	
OCI—Translation Adjustment		$80,500
To mark to market the net position with the FX trader ($.435 - $.40 = $.035 [change in the **forward rate**]) ($.035 × 2,300,000 pesos = $80,500).		
Cash	$80,500	
FX Contract Value—Forward, **net**		$80,500
To settle up with the FX trader. The FX trader (a) **Credits** the company's bank account $1,000,500 (2,300,000 pesos × $.435 [the contracted **forward rate**]). (b) **Debits** the company's bank account $920,000 (2,300,000 pesos × .40 [the spot rate]) because the company has to buy 2,300,000 pesos at the **spot rate** of $.40 on 12/31/06 to make delivery to the FX trader on the FX forward ($1,000,500 - $920,000 = $80,500).		

Thus hedging a *net asset position* presents a dilemma that does *not* exist when *hedging FX receivables* and *FX payables* because **these balances are settled at the expiration of the FX forward and they *cease* to exist.** In contrast, the *net asset position* **continues to exist.**

What Are the Economic Consequences of Hedging Exposed Positions of Foreign Units as a Result of *FAS 52 Not* Allowing Translation Adjustments to Be Charged or Credited Directly to Earnings?

Prior to *FAS 52*'s issuance in 1981, it was necessary to charge or credit translation adjustments directly to ***earnings*** in *all* cases. Also, substantial volatility occurred in the income statement. To eliminate potential income statement volatility, managements often hedged a foreign unit's exposed position. Some studies have shown that since the issuance of *FAS 52*, managements that now use the *current rate method* (a method *not* allowed prior to the issuance of *FAS 52*) have *decreased*—but *not* eliminated altogether—their hedging of the exposed position of their foreign units. As one unidentified executive put it (in one such study), "There's less need to play around [to hedge a foreign unit's exposed position] under *FAS 52* because the P&L [***earnings***] isn't getting hammered."[4]

Whether to Hedge the *Net Asset Position*, the *Net Monetary Position*, or *Projected Cash Flows*

Differing views exist as to what the true FX exposure is for a foreign unit. Some companies using the *current rate method* hedge the *net asset position* with the objective of canceling out some or all of the translation adjustment. Other companies using the *current rate method* view their true economic exposure as being either (1) the **net *monetary* position** (the difference between *monetary assets* and *monetary liabilities*) or (2) the **projected cash flows** (usually from dividends).[5] Accordingly,

[4] Business International Corporation, *BIMR Handbook on Global Treasury Management* (New York: Business International Corporation, 1984), p. 68.

[5] International finance texts, however, define the true *economic exposure* as **the extent to which the value of the firm—as measured by the *present value* of its expected *cash flows*—will change when exchange rates change.**

these companies may choose to hedge one of these items. (Hedging a *net monetary position* is explained in Chapter 16 in the discussion of the *temporal method* in which the focus is on the *net monetary position* rather than the *net asset position*.) Possibly for competitive reasons, disclosures in virtually all annual reports of multinational companies are presently too general and vague to determine either the extent or the exact exposure being hedged of foreign units. Which exposure to hedge is (1) discussed more fully in international finance texts and (2) usually a high-level finance decision.

V. TRANSLATION CONCEPTUAL ISSUE 2: *HOW* TO REPORT THE EFFECT OF AN EXCHANGE RATE CHANGE

We now discuss the controversial issue of how the effect of an exchange rate change should be theoretically reported (even though *FAS 52*, as amended by *FAS 130*, requires translation adjustments arising under the *current rate method* to be reported in ***Other Comprehensive Income***).

Criteria Used as a Frame of Reference

Accountants use the following criteria to evaluate how to report the effects of exchange rate changes:

1. Do the reported effects relate to *day-to-day operations*?
2. Do the reported effects impact *cash flows*?
3. Are the reported effects *realized* or *unrealized* in nature?

Some Readily Apparent Manners of Reporting

The effects of exchange rate changes can be reported in many ways, the most readily apparent being the following:

1. **Report as a *deferred* gain or loss in the balance sheet** and then amortize to income in some rational manner to minimize the volatility that otherwise would occur in the income statement. This method was the general practice prior to the issuance of *FAS 8* in 1975 (the predecessor to *FAS 52*). Under *SFAS Concepts Statement 6*, "Elements of Financial Statements" (paragraphs 35 and 25), however, such gains are *not* liabilities (probable future sacrifices of economic benefits), and such losses are *not* assets (probable future economic benefits).
2. **Report currently in earnings** (in accordance with the "all-inclusive" income statement concept). This method was the required treatment under *FAS 8* (1975 to 1981). *FAS 52* requires this treatment if the *temporal method* of translation is used (as discussed in Chapter 19).
3. **Report as a direct adjustment to equity—bypassing *earnings* until *disposition* or *liquidation* of the investment.** *FAS 52*, as initially issued, requires this treatment if the *current rate method* is used. In 1997, however, *FAS 52* was amended (by *FAS 130*, which we discuss shortly) such that this treatment is no longer current GAAP.
4. **Report in *Other Comprehensive Income*** (OCI)**—bypassing *earnings* until *disposition* or *liquidation* of the investment.** This treatment is current GAAP.

The fact that the rule makers have tried four different approaches attests to the diversity of opinion that exists.

The *FAS 8* Experience

What may have driven the FASB to its current position was the disastrous experience with *FAS 8* (whereby only the *temporal method* was allowed), which by fate was issued in 1975 shortly after the relatively new floating exchange rate system began in 1971. *FAS 8* had two problems. *First*, it usually reported exchange gains or losses when the events indicated that no economic gain or loss had occurred and vice versa. *Second*, it required such exchange gains or losses to be reported currently in the income statement, which greatly increased the volatility of earnings. As an example of the volatility, consider the experience of ITT under *FAS 8* for the first three quarters of 1981 in comparison to the prior year amounts:

	Exchange Gains or Losses	
	Included	**Excluded**
First quarter	(45)%	—
Second quarter	109%	(29)%
Third quarter	(119)%	2%
Full nine months	(53)%	(8)%

The volatility problem *cannot* be overemphasized. In financial reporting, it is well known that companies try to "manage their earnings" to report smooth quarter-to-quarter and year-to-year earnings gains that security analysts treasure. Few things are more upsetting to chief executives than accounting rules that result in reporting wildly fluctuating amounts over which they have absolutely *no* control and which they *cannot* predict. Such reporting experiences resulted in the quick reconsideration of *FAS 8*. In the process that led to *FAS 52*, the business community strongly opposed reporting the effects of exchange rate changes in earnings.

VI. Reporting the Effect of Exchange Rate Changes in *Other Comprehensive Income*

Recall from intermediate accounting that FASB *Statement No. 130*, "Reporting Comprehensive Income" (issued in 1997), requires that certain items—one of which is the effects of exchange rate changes under the *current rate method*—be reported in **"other comprehensive income"** rather than as items in determining *net income*. Recall also that

1. *Comprehensive income* is the sum of (1) *net income* and (2) *other comprehensive income*.
2. *Comprehensive income* is the change in an entity's equity for the period—exclusive of transactions (investments and distributions) with owners.
3. An amount showing an entity's *comprehensive income* for the period must be displayed in one of the following three formats:
   a. At the *bottom* of the income statement (the "one-statement" format).
   b. In a *separate* statement of comprehensive income (the "two-statement" format). (The first line in the statement begins with *net income*.)
   c. In the statement of changes in stockholders' equity.

To best show how these certain items are initially reported in **other comprehensive income** and later reclassified into *earnings* when required, we do the following:

1. We present the **one-statement format** in Illustration 15-9 (which also shows *below* the income statement the equity accounts as they would appear in the consolidated balance sheet at 12/31/06).
2. We incorporate into Illustration 15-9 the translation adjustments shown in Illustrations 15-5 ($129,000 *unfavorable* for 2005) and 15-6 ($100,000 **unfavorable** for 2006) for the **Mexican** subsidiary (the cumulative translation adjustment at 12/31/06 is $229,000 *unfavorable* inasmuch as this subsidiary has been in existence only two years).
3. We assume in Illustration 15-9 that (1) the parent had a *French* foreign subsidiary that it sold on 1/2/06 and (2) the cumulative translation adjustment at 12/31/05 for this subsidiary was $60,000 *unfavorable*.

ILLUSTRATION 15-9 STATEMENT OF INCOME AND COMPREHENSIVE INCOME FORMAT A: ONE-STATEMENT APPROACH

Enterprise Consolidated Statement of Income and Comprehensive Income
For the Year Ended December 31, 2006

Revenues		$ 9,870,000
Costs and expenses		(9,610,000)
Gain on Sale of *French* subsidiary (**net of unfavorable cumulative translation adjustment of $60,000 at date of sale**)		35,000
Income *before* Extraordinary Item		$ 295,000
Extraordinary loss, net of tax		(50,000)
Net Income		**$ 245,000**
Other Comprehensive Income:[a]		
Foreign currency translation adjustments:		
Translation adjustments arising during the period (on *Mexican* subsidiary)	$(100,000)	
Less: Reclassification adjustment for translation adjustments included in net income (on *French* subsidiary)	60,000	(40,000)
Unrealized gains on *available-for-sale* securities (*none* were sold in 2006)		22,000[b]
Minimum pension liability adjustment		(12,000)[c]
Other Comprehensive Income		**$ (30,000)**
Comprehensive Income		**$ 215,000**

Equity Section of Consolidated Balance Sheet at 12/31/06

Stockholders' Equity:[d]		
Common stock		$ 2,000,000
Retained earnings		1,334,000
***Accumulated* other comprehensive income:**		
Cumulative Translation adjustments (*FAS 52*)	$(229,000)	
Unrealized gains on *available-for-sale* securities (*FAS 115*)	115,000	
Minimum pension liability adjustment (*FAS 87*)	(87,000)	
Unrealized gain on hedge of a forecasted transaction [a cash flow hedge] (*FAS 133*)	133,000	(68,000)
Total Stockholders' Equity		$ 3,266,000

[a] Other comprehensive income items are *always* presented net of tax. For simplicity, we assume that *none* of these items has income tax effects.

[b] If any of these securities had been sold in 2006, it would have been necessary to show a reclassification adjustment.

[c] This illustrates the *required* net display for this item.

[d] The first *three* account balances are from the worksheet shown on page 516. The last *three* account balances are assumed amounts. (The balances of the accounts that comprise *accumulated other comprehensive income* can also be presented in either (1) a statement of changes in stockholders' equity or (2) notes to the financial statements rather than being displayed in the statement of financial position.)

END-OF-CHAPTER REVIEW

Summary of Key Points

1. Foreign currency financial statements must be **restated** to U.S. GAAP **before translation.**
2. The **economic effect of an exchange rate change** on a foreign unit depends on (a) the *causes* of the exchange rate change, (b) the *nature* of the foreign unit's assets (monetary versus nonmonetary), and (c) the extent of *debt financing* relative to *equity financing.*
3. **Monetary items** are cash and accounts that are **obligated** to be settled in cash.
4. In translating the balance sheet, the **current rate** is defined as the spot exchange rate existing *at* the balance sheet date, whereas the **historical rate** is the exchange rate existing when the balance in the account *arose.*
5. Under the **foreign currency unit of measure approach,** the foreign currency relationships are maintained in translation, the **current rate method** is used, and the financial position focus is on the **subsidiary's net asset position** (*total assets – total liabilities*).

6. The **effect of an exchange rate change** under the current rate method is (a) called a **translation adjustment** and (b) charged or credited **to *Other Comprehensive Income*.**

7. FX gains or losses from adjusting intercompany receivable and payable balances **expected to be settled in the foreseeable future** are reported currently in ***earnings***. If the parent uses the *current rate method,* FX gains and losses from adjusting **long-term** receivables and payables that are ***not* expected to be settled in the foreseeable future** are charged or credited **to *Other Comprehensive Income.***

8. When **intercompany-acquired inventory exists** at a financial reporting date, the amount of any unrealized intercompany profit to be deferred is the gross profit recorded **on that inventory at the transfer date** (requires using the exchange rate *at the transfer date* to calculate that gross profit).

9. If the parent uses the *current rate method*, FX gains and losses arising from **hedging a net asset position** are charged or credited **to *Other Comprehensive Income*.**

Glossary of New Terms

Current rate method The only translation method that achieves a *foreign currency unit of measure* in translation.

Current value approach using PPP A translation approach in which *nonmonetary assets* are adjusted for inflation *before* translation at the current rate. See Appendix 16B.

Foreign currency unit of measure approach A way to translate foreign currency financial statements that *maintains the financial relationships* in the foreign currency (accomplished by using a *single* exchange rate for *all* assets and liabilities).

Monetary accounts Cash and all asset and liability accounts that are obligated to be settled in cash.

Net asset position Having *assets* in excess of *liabilities*.

Net liability position Having *liabilities* in excess of *assets*.

Net monetary position The difference between *monetary assets* and *monetary liabilities* (discussed in Chapter 16).

Nonmonetary accounts All asset and liability accounts that are *not* monetary accounts.

Statement of comprehensive income A financial statement in which the bottom line reports the change in stockholders' equity *excluding* transactions with owners.

Translation adjustments The name given to the effects of exchange rate changes reported under the *current rate method*.

Unit of measure The currency that serves as a perspective from which a foreign unit's financial statements are measured when expressing amounts in U.S. dollars.

U.S. dollar unit of measurement approach A manner of translating foreign currency financial statements that changes the unit of measure to the U.S. dollar (financial relationships *are* changed).

ASSIGNMENT MATERIAL

Review Questions

1. *Restate* and then *translate* or *translate* and then *restate*—which is correct?

2. What is the general procedure for *restating* foreign GAAP to U.S. GAAP?

3. What is meant by the term *monetary accounts*?

4. As to foreign units, is a *decrease* in the direct exchange rate a favorable or unfavorable economic event? Is an *increase* favorable or unfavorable?

5. What is meant by the *current exchange rate*? What is meant by the *historical exchange rate*?

6. What is the *foreign currency unit of measure approach*? Summarize it.

7. What is the *financial position focus* under the *foreign currency unit of measure approach*?
8. Is the translated amount for fixed assets historical cost under the *foreign currency unit of measure approach*?
9. What is the major shortcoming of the *current rate method*?
10. What is the effect of an exchange rate change called when the *current rate method* is used?
11. When the *current rate method* is used, how is the effect of an exchange rate change reported under *FAS 52*?
12. If the *current rate method* were used, how is the effect of an exchange rate change reported in a *statement of comprehensive income*?
13. What are the *basic procedures* required before the translation process begins?
14. What eventually happens to accumulated translation adjustments?
15. How are exchange rate change adjustments relating to a parent's *long-term* receivables and payables reported? Why?
16. How are exchange rate change adjustments relating to a parent's intercompany *dividend* receivable reported?
17. Which exchange rate is used to calculate the amount of *unrealized* intercompany profit?
18. How are FX gains and losses on hedging a *net asset position* treated?

Exercises

E 15-1 **Restating to U.S. GAAP for Deferred Taxes** A foreign subsidiary of a U.S. parent does *not* record deferred income taxes because this does *not* follow *local* GAAP. The subsidiary's income tax rate is 30%. The following temporary differences relating to the use of accelerated depreciation for income tax-reporting purposes exist:

	Cumulative Excess Depreciation Claimed for Tax Reporting
At 12/31/05	200,000 Local currency unit (LCU)
At 12/31/06	240,000 LCU

Required Prepare the worksheet adjusting entry necessary to restate to U.S. GAAP at 12/31/06.

E 15-2 **Restating to U.S. GAAP for Foreign Inflation Adjustment** To comply with local GAAP, a foreign subsidiary adjusts its fixed assets for inflation every 10 years. Inflation adjustments for depreciable fixed assets are depreciable for income tax–reporting purposes. The foreign country's income tax rate is 40%. The first such adjustment for the subsidiary occurred 1/1/02. *Separate* general ledger accounts are used for these adjustments. The balances in these *separate* general ledger accounts at 12/31/06 (except for one account) follow:

	Debit	Credit
Land—revaluation	500,000	
Building—revaluation	800,000	
Accumulated depreciation—revaluation		200,000
Depreciation expense—revaluation	40,000	

Required
1. What account did the subsidiary credit when it wrote up its fixed assets for inflation? You must determine this before you can proceed.
2. Prepare the worksheet adjusting entry necessary to restate to U.S. GAAP at 12/31/06.
3. If U.S. GAAP—but *not* the U.S. tax code—allowed fixed assets to be written up in value based on the annual inflation rate, what entry would the *parent* make to revalue its land upward by $300,000? (First try to determine what entry the parent would make if it had been donated land having a *current value* of $300,000 by a city for the purpose of building a factory that would provide jobs for local citizens.) **Hint:** *Three* accounts are involved in *both* situations.

E 15-3 **Calculating the Effect of an Exchange Rate Change** Pondox has a foreign subsidiary in a country in which the direct exchange rate *decreased* from $.25 to $.20 during 2006. The average balances of the individual assets and liabilities during 2006 follow:

	Local Currency Units
Cash	80,000
Accounts receivable	220,000
Inventory	275,000
Fixed assets, net	425,000
Total Assets	1,000,000
Accounts payable and accruals	325,000
Current portion of long-term debt	25,000
Intercompany payable	100,000
Long-term debt	300,000
Deferred income taxes payable	50,000
Total Liabilities	800,000

Assume that the carrying value of the parent's Investment account on 1/1/06 was $50,000 for this 100%-owned subsidiary that was created in late 2005 when the direct exchange rate was $.25.

Required Determine the effect of the exchange rate change for 2006 under the *current rate method*.

E 15-4 **Calculating the Effect of an Exchange Rate Change** Kobb Inc. has a 100%-owned foreign subsidiary. The average balances of the subsidiary's assets and liabilities during 2006 follow:

	Local Currency Units
Monetary assets	4,000,000
Nonmonetary assets	6,000,000
Total Assets	10,000,000
Liabilities (all monetary)	9,000,000
Stockholders' equity	1,000,000
Total Liabilities and Equity	10,000,000

The *direct* exchange rate *decreased* steadily during 2006 from $.40 at 1/1/06 to $.30 at 12/31/06.

Required Determine the effect of the change in the exchange rate for 2006 under the *current rate method*.

E 15-5 **Selecting Proper Exchange Rates: Balance Sheet Accounts** The following accounts exist in a foreign subsidiary's books:

1. Allowance for Doubtful Accounts.
2. Inventory (carried at *cost*).
3. Inventory (carried at *market*, which is *below* cost).
4. Inventory (carried at *market*, which *exceeds* cost).
5. Marketable Equity Securities (carried at *market* [readily determinable], which *exceeds* historical cost).
6. Marketable Bonds (*expected* to be held to maturity).
7. Marketable Bonds (*not* expected to be held to maturity).
8. Patents.
9. Equipment.
10. Accumulated Depreciation.
11. Intercompany Payable.
12. Long-Term Debt.

13. Income Taxes Payable.
14. Deferred Income Taxes Payable.
15. Common Stock.
16. Additional Paid-in Capital.
17. Retained Earnings.
18. Revaluation Capital (from inflation adjustments).

Required Determine whether the *historical* exchange rate, the *current* exchange rate, an *average* exchange rate, or some other procedure should be used to translate these accounts.

E 15-6 **Selecting Proper Exchange Rates: Income Statement Accounts** The following accounts exist in a foreign subsidiary's books:

1. Revenues.
2. Intercompany Sales to Parent Company.
3. Purchases.
4. Intercompany Purchases from Parent Company.
5. Cost of Sales.
6. Marketing Expenses.
7. Depreciation Expense.
8. Income Tax Expense.
9. Goodwill Amortization Expense.
10. Loss on Abandonment of Fixed Assets.
11. Gain on Sale of Equipment.
12. Intercompany Interest Expense.
13. Depreciation Expense (incremental amount resulting from adjusting assets for inflation).
14. Inventory Loss from Flood Damage.

Required Determine whether the *historical* exchange rate, the *current* exchange rate, an *average* exchange rate, or some other procedure should be used to translate these accounts.

E 15-7 **Forcing Out the CTA** Following are certain items (accounts or account totals) that have been translated into dollars at or for the year ended 12/31/06:

Total assets	$200,000
Total liabilities	110,000
Common stock	20,000
Revenues	80,000
Expenses	50,000
Amounts reported **in dollars** at the end of the prior year (12/31/05)	
Retained earnings	$ 12,000
AOCI—Cumulative translation adjustment (credit)	15,000

The subsidiary did *not* declare any dividends in 2006.

Required Use the "forcing out" process to determine the following items:
1. Ending balance for the Retained Earnings account at 12/31/06.
2. Current period effect of the change in the exchange rate.

E 15-8 **Adjusting Intercompany Accounts** Pond Inc. created a foreign subsidiary on 12/3/06. The parent lent the subsidiary $90,000 at that time when the direct exchange rate between the dollar and the LCU was $.10. The subsidiary immediately converted the $90,000 into LCUs and used the entire amount to purchase land on 12/3/06. At 12/31/06, the year-end of the parent and the subsidiary, the direct exchange rate was $.09.

Required

1. Make the appropriate adjustments at 12/31/06, assuming that the loan is denominated in *LCUs*.
2. Make the appropriate adjustments at 12/31/06, assuming that the loan is denominated in *dollars*.
3. Express in dollars the effect of the adjustments made in requirement 2. (Show the calculations for the two ways to determine this amount.)

E 15-9 **Accounting for Intercompany Dividend** For the year ended 12/31/06, a 100%-owned foreign subsidiary had net income of 60,000,000 LCU, which was appropriately translated into $5,900,000. On 7/25/06, when the exchange rate was 10 LCU to $1, the subsidiary declared a dividend of 27,000,000 LCU. The dividend represented the subsidiary's net income for the six months ended 6/30/06, during which time the weighted average of the exchange rate was 11 LCU to $1. The dividend was paid on 8/3/06 when the exchange rate was 9 LCU to $1. The exchange rate existing at 12/31/06 was 8.5 LCU to $1. The parent uses the *equity* method of accounting for the foreign subsidiary.

Required

1. Prepare the parent company's entry to record the dividend receivable.
2. Prepare the entry related to the receipt of the dividend on 8/3/06.

E 15-10 **How to Record a General Price-Level Change** Subbco is a 100%-owned foreign subsidiary. *Foreign* financial reporting GAAP permits annual price-level adjustments to land for inflation.

Additional Information

1. On 1/1/06, Subbco acquired land for 1,000,000 LCU.
2. Foreign inflation for 2006 was 10%.
3. The foreign government (which has a 25% income tax rate) will allow the land's *tax basis* to be restated upward by 8% for 2006—*not* 10%.
4. Subbco's functional currency is its *local currency.*

Required

1. What entry(ies) should you have Subbco make to reflect the 2006 price-level adjustment?
2. Record the related deferred tax adjustment required under *FAS 109* (assume that it is proper to record deferred income taxes for this situation).
3. What entry(ies) would Subbco make if the land were sold for 1,100,000 on 1/2/07?

Problems

P 15-1 **Restating to U.S. GAAP for Patent Life Difference** On 1/1/05, a foreign subsidiary of a U.S. parent company acquired a patent for 150,000 LCU. The foreign country's GAAP requires amortization over no more than 5 years. Accordingly, the subsidiary uses a 5-year life even though the patent has a remaining legal life of 15 years. The foreign subsidiary's income tax rate is 40%.

Required Prepare the worksheet adjusting entry necessary at 12/31/06 to *restate* the foreign subsidiary's financial statements to U.S. GAAP.

P 15-2* **Translation Worksheet** The financial statements of Lee & Willinger Inc., a foreign subsidiary domiciled in France, for the year ended 12/31/06 follow:

* The financial statement information presented for problems accompanied by asterisks is also provided on MODEL 15 (filename: MODEL15) at the **http://pahler.swlearning.com** Web site, allowing the problem to be worked on the computer.

		Euros
Income Statement (2006)		
Sales		10,000,000
Cost of sales		
Beginning inventory	1,500,000	
Purchases	6,000,000	
	7,500,000	
Less—*Ending* inventory	(2,000,000)	(5,500,000)
Depreciation expense (total)		(300,000)
Operating and interest expenses		(3,200,000)
Income before Income Taxes		1,000,000
Income tax expense		(400,000)
Net Income		600,000
Balance Sheet (12/31/06)		
Cash		300,000
Accounts receivable, net		1,000,000
Inventory		2,000,000
Land		1,000,000
Buildings and equipment		5,200,000
Accumulated depreciation		(500,000)
Total Assets		9,000,000
Payables and accruals		2,500,000
Income taxes payable		200,000
Long-term debt		2,800,000
Total Liabilities		5,500,000
Common stock		1,500,000
Retained earnings		2,000,000
Total Equity		3,500,000
Total Liabilities and Equity		9,000,000

Additional Information

1. **Conformity with U.S. GAAP.** Assume that the financial statements in euros have been adjusted to conform with U.S. GAAP.
2. **Exchange rates** (direct):

Current rate at 12/31/05	$.15
Average rate for 2006	12
Current rate at 12/31/06	10

3. **Inventory.** The *ending* inventory is valued at the lower of cost or market in euros; however, no write-down to market was necessary on the subsidiary's books. Assume that the inventory at 12/31/06 was acquired when the exchange rate was $.11. Inventory at 12/31/05 was acquired when the exchange rate was $.16.
4. **Property, plant, and equipment.** All were acquired in *prior years* when the exchange rate was $.16, *except* equipment costing 200,000 euros, which was acquired in early 2006 when the exchange rate was $.14. (Depreciation of 50,000 euros was recorded on this equipment for 2006.)
5. **Sales, purchases, and operating expenses.** All occurred evenly throughout the year.
6. **Common stock.** The subsidiary was *created* on 12/31/04 when the direct exchange rate was $.16. No additional capital transactions have occurred since that time.
7. **Dividends.** The subsidiary did *not* declare any dividends in 2004 or 2005.
8. **Information for statement of cash flows.** The *beginning-of-year* cash balance was 600,000 euros. Cash collections from customers (9,700,000 euros), cash payments to suppliers and employees (9,100,000 euros), and cash payments to lenders for interest (400,000 euros) were made evenly throughout the year. A cash payment for income taxes (300,000 euros) was made on 5/30/06 when the direct exchange rate was $.13. The only cash flows pertaining to *investing activities* were for the purchase of equipment in early 2006 (200,000 euros) when the direct ex-

change rate was $.14. No dividends were paid during 2006. Nor were there any other financing activities during 2006.

Required

1. Calculate the translation adjustment for 2006 using the analysis of the *net asset approach*. Approximately how much of this amount is the result of *lowering* the value of (a) assets and (b) liabilities?
2. Translate the financial statements into dollars assuming the following:
   a. Retained earnings at 12/31/05 (per the translated financial statements) were $217,000.
   b. The cumulative translation adjustment at 12/31/05 was $(22,000).
3. Prepare the parent's entry or entries at 12/31/06 relating to the *equity method* of accounting.
4. Prepare a T-account analysis of the parent's Investment account since the subsidiary's creation.
5. Prepare an updated analysis of the Investment account for the year ended 12/31/06.
6. Prepare the general ledger entry that would be made if the subsidiary were sold for $400,000 cash on 1/3/07.
7. Qualitatively assess whether the subsidiary had a *good* year or a *bad* year. Do you think the parent's price-earnings ratio is based on *net income* or *comprehensive income*?
8. If you were in charge of paying bonuses to both the *parent's* CEO and the *subsidiary's* CEO, on what income amount would you base the bonus to each CEO?
9. Assume that you are the parent's CEO. If the parent broke even on its *own separate operations* for 2006 and pays dividends *only if* there is current period income, how much of a dividend do you think the parent *could* declare for 2006 and *should* declare for 2006?
10. **Optional** (check with your instructor): Prepare a translated statement of cash flows for 2006 using the *direct* method.

P 15-3* **Translation Worksheet** The financial statements of Tipperary Inc., a foreign subsidiary domiciled in Ireland, for the year ended 12/31/06 follow:

		Euros
Income Statement (2006)		
Sales		4,000,000
Cost of sales		
Beginning inventory	800,000	
Purchases	3,200,000	
	4,000,000	
Less—*Ending* inventory	(900,000)	(3,100,000)
Depreciation expense (in total)		(50,000)
Operating and interest expenses		(450,000)
Income before Income Taxes		400,000
Income tax expense @ 25%		(100,000)
Net Income		300,000
Balance Sheet (as of 12/31/06)		
Cash		200,000
Accounts receivable		500,000
Allowance for doubtful accounts		(50,000)
Inventory (FIFO)		900,000
Land		300,000
Buildings and equipment		1,100,000
Accumulated depreciation		(250,000)
Total Assets		2,700,000
Payables and accruals		700,000
Accrued income taxes payable		100,000
Intercompany payable (to parent)		500,000
Long-term debt		600,000
Total Liabilities		1,900,000
Common stock		100,000
Retained earnings		700,000
Total Equity		800,000
Total Liabilities and Equity		2,700,000

Additional Information

1. **Conformity with U.S. GAAP.** Assume that the financial statements in punts are in accordance with U.S. GAAP; thus no adjustments are required.

2. **Exchange rates** (direct):

Current rate at 12/31/05	$1.25
Average rate for 2006	1.40
Current rate at 12/31/06	1.50

3. **Inventory.** The *ending* inventory is valued at the lower of cost or market in punts; however, no write-down to market was necessary on the subsidiary's books. Assume that the inventory at 12/31/06 was acquired evenly during the last quarter of 2006 (which had an *average* exchange rate of $1.45).

   The *beginning* inventory was all acquired when the exchange rate was $1.20, and no market adjustment in punts was necessary.

4. **Fixed assets.** The land, buildings, and equipment were acquired in early 2005 when the exchange rate was $1.60, except for some office equipment costing 100,000 euros that was acquired in early 2006 when the exchange rate was $1.30. (Depreciation of 10,000 euros was recorded on this equipment for 2006.)

5. **Sales and operating expenses.** Assume that they occurred *evenly* throughout the year.

6. **Purchases.** Assume that purchases occurred *evenly* throughout the year.

7. **Intercompany payable.** The intercompany payable is denominated in euros.

8. **Common stock.** The subsidiary was *created* on 12/31/04 when the direct exchange rate was $1.60. No additional capital transactions have occurred since then.

9. **Dividends.** Dividends of 200,000 euros were declared and paid in 2006 when the direct exchange rate was $1.45. No dividends were declared in 2005.

10. **Information for statement of cash flows.** The *beginning-of-year* cash balance was 250,000 euros. Cash collections from customers (4,100,000 euros), cash payments to suppliers and employees (3,300,000 euros), and cash payments to lenders for interest (90,000 euros) were made evenly throughout the year. A cash payment for income taxes (60,000 euros) was made on 4/1/06 when the direct exchange rate was $1.30. The only cash flow pertaining to *investing activities* was for the purchase of equipment in early 2006 when the direct exchange rate was $1.30. The only activity in the long-term debt account during the year was a principal repayment (400,000 euros) on 6/3/06 when the direct exchange rate was $1.35. The cash dividend (200,000 euros) was paid on 11/1/06 when the *direct* exchange rate was $1.45.

Required

1. Calculate the translation adjustment for 2006 using the *analysis of net assets approach*. Approximately how much of this amount is the result of lowering the value of (a) assets and (b) liabilities?
2. Translate the financial statements into dollars assuming the following:
   a. From the dollar financial statements, retained earnings at 12/31/05 were $840,000.
   b. The cumulative translation adjustment at 12/31/05 was $(125,000).
3. Prepare the parent's entry or entries at 12/31/06 under the *equity method* of accounting.
4. Prepare a T-account analysis of the parent's Investment account since the subsidiary's creation.
5. Prepare an updated analysis of the Investment account for the year ended 12/31/06.
6. Prepare the general ledger entry that would be made if the subsidiary were sold for $1,240,000 on 1/3/07.
7. If you were in charge of paying bonuses to both the *parent's* CEO and the *subsidiary's* CEO, on what income amount would you base the bonus to each CEO?
8. Assume that you are the parent's CEO. If the parent broke even on its *own separate operations* for 2006 and pays dividends *only if* there is current period income, how much of a dividend do you think the parent *could* declare for 2006 and *should* declare for 2006?

9. **Optional** (check with your instructor): Prepare a translated statement of cash flows for 2006 using the *direct method.*

P 15-4 **Adjusting Intercompany Accounts and Calculating Unrealized Intercompany Profit** The following are certain accounts of PBX and its 100%-owned foreign subsidiary SBX for the year ended 12/31/06.

	PBX (in dollars)	SBX (in pounds)
Intercompany sales	$ 500,000	
Intercompany cost of sales	(300,000)	
Intercompany receivable	500,000	
Intercompany payable		250,000 pounds
Inventory		
Vendor acquired		700,000 pounds
Intercompany acquired		50,000 pounds
Direct Exchange Rates for 2006		
December 31, 2005	$2.40	
December 31, 2006	1.20	
Average rate for 2006	1.80	
Exchange rate at time of intercompany sale	2.00	

Additional Information

1. SBX's intercompany payable is denominated in pounds.
2. At year-end, SBX still owes PBX the entire amount relating to this inventory purchase (of 100 widgets).
3. No adjustment has been made at year-end because of the change in the exchange rate.

Required

1. Make the necessary adjustment at 12/31/06 to the appropriate Intercompany Receivable or Intercompany Payable account balance.
2. What adjusting entry would be made if the intercompany payable were denominated in dollars?
3. Complete the following analysis:

	Total	Sold	On Hand
Intercompany sales	$ 500,000		
Intercompany cost of sales	(300,000)	_______	_______
Gross Profit	$ 200,000	_______	_______

4. What is the translated amount for inventory in the 12/31/06 balance sheet under the *current rate method*?
5. Prepare the universal intercompany elimination entry or entries (discussed in Chapter 9) required in consolidation at 12/31/06 relating to the preceding intercompany transaction.
6. Repeat requirement 3 assuming that the $1.20 direct exchange rate *at year-end* is to be used in determining the inventory on hand at year-end in dollars.
7. Repeat requirement 3 assuming the following:
   a. The 12/31/06 direct exchange rate is $.10.
   b. This exchange rate is to be used in determining the inventory on hand at year-end in dollars.
8. Note that the amount of gross profit deferred at year-end using a year-end exchange rate (as in requirements 6 and 7) can differ significantly from the amount deferred using the exchange rate prescribed by *FAS 52*. Which exchange rate makes the most sense to use? Why?
9. How many widgets does SBX still have on hand?

P 15-5 **Determining the Net Effect of Adjustments to Intercompany Account** Pyox created Syox, a German subsidiary, on 12/1/06. On that date, Pyox made a $360,000 noninterestbearing loan to Syox. Syox immediately converted the $360,000 into marks and used all of them to purchase land. For simplicity, assume that Syox was so thinly capitalized that we can ignore the capital accounts. The direct exchange rate was $.40 at 12/1/06 and $0.45 at 12/31/06. The loan is denominated in marks.

Required

1. Make the appropriate adjusting entry at 12/31/06 relating to the intercompany loan.
2. Translate the subsidiary's 12/31/06 balance sheet into dollars using the current rate method.
3. What is the net effect of the change in the exchange rate as reported in the equity section of the consolidated balance sheet at the end of 2006?
4. Is the effect on the parent's equity calculated in requirement 3 the result of the adjustment to the intercompany account?

P 15-6* 

Comprehensive: Translation Worksheet, Consolidation Worksheet, and Intercompany Transactions The financial statements of Piper Inc. and its 100%-owned British subsidiary, Swan Inc., for the year ended 12/31/06 follow:

	Piper (dollars)	Swan (pounds)
Income Statement (2006)		
Sales	$ 7,000,000	£1,500,000
Cost of sales	(4,000,000)	(800,000)
Depreciation expense	(86,000)	(30,000)
Expenses	(1,900,000)	(470,000)
Intercompany Accounts		
Intercompany sales	465,000	
Intercompany cost of sales	(279,000)	
Net Income	$ 1,200,000	£ 200,000
Balance Sheet (as of 12/31/06)		
Cash	$ 569,000	£ 50,000
Accounts receivable	800,000	300,000
Intercompany receivable	472,000	
Inventory Vendor acquired	700,000	400,000
Intercompany acquired		100,000
Investment in Swan	359,000	
Land	200,000	150,000
Buildings and equipment	1,000,000	500,000
Accumulated depreciation	(300,000)	(100,000)
Total Assets	$ 3,800,000	£1,400,000
Accounts payable	$ 700,000	£ 160,000
Accrued liabilities	500,000	40,000
Intercompany payable		300,000
Long-term debt	1,500,000	500,000
Total Liabilities	$ 2,700,000	£1,000,000
Common stock	$ 500,000	£ 60,000
Retained earnings	609,000	340,000
Cumulative translation adjustment	(9,000)	
Total Equity	$ 1,100,000	£ 400,000
Total Liabilities and Equity	$ 3,800,000	£1,400,000
Dividends declared	$ 900,000	£ 100,000

Additional Information

1. **Conformity with U.S. GAAP.** Assume that the financial statements of the subsidiary are in accordance with U.S. GAAP.
2. **Exchange rates** (direct):

Current rate at 12/31/05	$1.70
Average rate for 2006	1.60
Current rate at 12/31/06	1.50

3. **Inventory.** The *ending* inventory was acquired during the last quarter of 2006 when the average exchange rate was $1.55. (No intercompany-acquired inventory was on hand at the *beginning* of 2006.)

4. **Fixed assets.** The fixed assets were acquired when the subsidiary was created in 2003, at which time the exchange rate was $1.75.

5. **Sales and operating expenses.** These occurred *evenly* throughout the year.

6. **Intercompany accounts.** All intercompany transactions are denominated in *pounds*. No adjustment has been made at year-end because of changes in the exchange rate during the year. The activity in the intercompany accounts for 2006 follows:

Subsidiary's Intercompany Payable (in Pounds)

Date	Debit	Credit	Date
		£ 60,000	Bal., 1/1/06
6/30/06	60,000[a]		
		300,000[b]	11/20/06
		100,000[c]	12/20/06
12/30/06	100,000[d]		
		£300,000	Bal., 12/31/06

Parent's Intercompany Receivable (in Dollars)

Date	Debit	Credit	Date
Bal., 1/1/06	$102,000		
		96,000[a]	7/1/06
11/15/06	465,000[b]		
12/20/06	151,000[c]		
		150,000[d]	12/30/06
Bal. 12/31/06	$472,000		

[a] Cash payment to parent when direct rate was $1.60.

[b] Downstream inventory transfer.

[c] Dividend declaration.

[d] Dividend payment.

7. **Common stock.** *No* common stock transactions have occurred since the *creation* of the subsidiary by the parent in 2003 when the direct exchange rate was $1.75.

8. **Retained earnings.** From the dollar financial statements, the subsidiary's Retained Earnings account at 12/31/05 was $414,000.

9. **Cumulative translation adjustment.** The cumulative translation adjustment at 12/31/05 was $(9,000).

10. **Dividends.** The subsidiary declared its 2006 dividends on 12/20/06 (when the direct exchange rate was $1.51) and paid the dividend on 12/30/06 (when the direct exchange rate was $1.50). (Intercompany dividends are recorded in the Intercompany Payable and Intercompany Receivable accounts and were properly recorded by *both* entities.)

11. **Income taxes.** For simplicity, ignore income tax considerations.

12. **Equity method of accounting.** The parent uses the *equity method* of accounting but has yet to record the earnings of the subsidiary for 2006. No adjustment has been made to the parent's books for *unrealized* intercompany profit.

13. **Information for statement of cash flows.** The *beginning-of-year* cash balance was £250,000. Cash collections from customers (£1,400,000), cash payments to suppliers and employees (£1,410,000), and cash payments to lenders for interest (£40,000) were made evenly throughout the year. A cash payment for income taxes (£50,000) was made on 4/15/06 when the direct exchange rate was $1.64. There were no cash flows pertaining to *investing activities* nor was there activity in the long-term debt account during the year. A short-term borrowing (£200,000) was made on 4/1/06 when the direct exchange rate was $1.65. This borrowing was repaid on 11/15/06 when the *direct* exchange rate was $1.45. The cash dividend (£100,000) was paid on 12/30/06 when the *direct* exchange rate was $1.50.

Required

1. Calculate the translation adjustment for 2006 using the *analysis of net assets approach*. Approximately how much of this amount is the result of *lowering* the value of (1) assets and (2) liabilities?
2. Translate the subsidiary's financial statements into dollars.
3. Prepare the appropriate adjusting entry to bring the Intercompany Receivable and Intercompany Payable accounts into agreement.
4. Prepare an analysis showing the intercompany profit that is *unrealized* at year-end.
5. Prepare the entries the parent would record under the *equity method* of accounting.

6. Prepare an analysis of the Investment account as of 12/31/05, and update it through 12/31/06. (*Hint:* The components at 12/31/05 total $510,000.)
7. Prepare all consolidation entries needed at 12/31/06 to consolidate the subsidiary's financial statements properly.
8. Prepare a consolidation worksheet.
9. **Optional** (check with your instructor): Prepare a translated statement of cash flows for 2006 using the direct method. Why does the amount calculated for the translation adjustment in requirement 1 differ from the $78,000 amount that is supposed to appear in the translated statement of cash flows?

P 15-7 **Hedging a *Net Asset Position*** Pemco uses the *current rate method* of translation for its 100%-owned foreign subsidiary, Semco (created in 2005). For 2006, Semco's net income was 100,000 LCU, which translated into $33,000. (Earnings occurred evenly throughout the year and were remitted to Pemco monthly.) An *unfavorable* translation adjustment of $64,000 resulted for 2006. At 12/31/05, the Accumulative Other Comprehensive Income—Cumulative Translation Adjustment account had a *credit* balance of $18,000.

On 12/31/05, in expectation that the LCU would *weaken* throughout 2006, management entered into a one-year *forward exchange contract* to *sell* 600,000 LCU (Semco's net asset position at 12/31/05) on 12/31/06 at the forward rate of $.40. (No hedging was done in 2005.) The following direct exchange rates are assumed:

	December 31, 2005 (inception date)	June 30, 2006 (a financial reporting date)	December 31, 2006 (expiration date)
Spot rate.	$.42	$.37	$.30
Forward rate (***selling* rate**).	$.40	$.36	$.30

Required

1. Prepare the journal entries pertaining to the forward exchange contract.
2. Was the hedge effective?

P 15-8 **Cumulative Translation Adjustments: What Also Must Be Considered in Reporting These Amounts?** On 12/4/05, Paxel Inc. created Saxel Inc., a 100%-owned Russian subsidiary (making a $600,000 cash investment at that time). Shortly thereafter, Paxel's management reversed course and decided to shut down Saxel. Saxel, which had *not* spent any of the money invested by Paxel, remitted all of its money (1,000,000 rubles) to Paxel on January 5, 2006. The direct exchange rates for the ruble follow:

	December 4, 2005	December 31, 2005	January 5, 2006
Spot rate.	$.60	$.61	$.64

Required In the financial statements that Paxel issues to its stockholders, what accounts and amounts should appear in (1) the 2005 and 2006 income statements, (2) the 12/31/05 consolidated balance sheet, and (3) the parent's 1/5/06 balance sheet? Use the *current rate method*.

THINKING CRITICALLY

Cases

C 15-1 **Determining How to Report the Effect of an Exchange Rate Change** On 1/1/06, Plattco invested $110,000 cash in its newly created foreign subsidiary, Slattco. During 2006, Slattco's only asset was cash of 100,000 pesos. During 2006, the *direct* exchange rate *decreased* from $1.10 to $1.00 solely because of *foreign* inflation.

Required

1. What result would be reported under *FAS 52* under the *current rate method*? Does this manner of reporting reflect the economics of what occurred in 2006?

2. Would your answers to requirement 1 change if Slattco's only asset during 2006 was *land*?
3. Would your answers to requirement 1 change if the *direct* exchange rate *increased* from $1.10 at 1/1/06 to $1.21 at 12/31/06 solely because of *domestic* (U.S.) inflation of 10%?

C 15-2 **Determining How to Report the Effect of an Exchange Rate Change** A foreign subsidiary has only cash as an asset and no liabilities. During 2006, the direct exchange rate changed 10%.

Required

1. Disregarding *FAS 52*'s requirements, what is the most meaningful way to report the effect of the exchange rate change? Use the criteria listed in the chapter for conceptual issue 2, and consider the possible different causes of the exchange rate change in arriving at your answer.
2. Repeat requirement 1, but assume that the subsidiary's only asset is land.

C 15-3 **Evaluating Translated Amounts** A foreign subsidiary has the following balance sheet at year-end:

	LCUs
Cash	100,000
5% Note receivable	200,000
Land	500,000
	800,000

Additional Information

1. The land has a *current value* of 750,000 LCUs.
2. The note receivable has a current value of 150,000 LCUs as a result of the *current interest rate* being substantially higher than the 5% *fixed interest rate.*
3. The *spot* exchange rate at year-end is $1.00.
4. The land was acquired when the *direct* exchange rate was $1.40.

Required Determine whether the translated amounts under the *current rate method* are meaningful.

C 15-4 **Evaluating Reporting Results** On 11/10/06, a domestic company transferred inventory costing $150,000 to its 100%-owned foreign subsidiary at cost. At 12/31/06, the subsidiary had all of this inventory on hand. The *direct* exchange rates were $1.50 at 11/10/06 and $1.60 at 12/31/06.

Required Economically, at what amount should the inventory be valued in the 12/31/06 consolidated balance sheet?

C 15-5 **Determining How to Report the Effect of an Exchange Rate Change** Kalla Inc. has a 100%-owned foreign subsidiary. Annual inflation in the foreign country is generally about 5%. Consequently, the subsidiary's local lender, a bank, charges the subsidiary an additional 5% interest above and beyond the 4% that it otherwise would charge on its 1,000,000 LCU loan to the subsidiary. This loan is the sole financing for a manufacturing plant. During 2006, the *direct* exchange rate *decreased* from $1.05 to $1.00 as a result of inflation in the foreign country.

Required

1. Disregarding the requirements of *FAS 52*, what is the most appropriate manner of reporting the economics of this situation?
2. Would your answer to requirement 1 change if the lender indexed the debt for inflation and instead charged a lower interest rate?
3. Under the *current rate method*, what would be reported?

C 15-6 **Issuing Partially Price-Level-Adjusted Statements: How Is It Routinely Done and Concealed?** Some foreign countries, such as Brazil and Italy, allow companies to adjust periodically their fixed assets for inflation. In the United States, one side of the balance sheet is effectively adjusted for inflation for the large majority of companies. This is *not* evident, however, from the financial statements and disclosures made.

Required How is one side of the balance sheet effectively adjusted for inflation in the United States?

C 15-7 **Determining Just How Many Equity Accounts There Are** Some accountants favor using fewer than the twelve equity accounts that currently can be used.

Required Try to identify the existing *twelve* equity accounts. Can you think of any new ones that you have *not* been exposed to in your accounting courses?

C 15-8 **Hedging Net Asset Exposures: What Is There to Lose?** On 12/31/05, Parrex hedged its Swedish subsidiary's 500,000 krone net asset position (using a one-year forward exchange contract) because it thought the krone would *weaken* during 2006. The *forward rate* was $.19. During 2006, the direct *spot* exchange rate *increased* from $.20 to $.24. Disregard the change in net assets from 2006's operations in responding to the requirements.

Required

1. What is the translation adjustment for 2006 under the *current rate method*?
2. What is the change in the cumulative translation adjustment account for 2006?
3. Evaluate economically the outcome of Parrex's actions in light of the krone *strengthening* instead of *weakening*.

Financial Analysis Problem

FAP 15-1 **Calculating Parent's AROI: Subsidiary Disposed of After Three Years** PDX created a 100%-owned foreign subsidiary (SDX) on 1/1/04, with a capital investment of $400,000 when the *direct* exchange rate was $.50. Selected data for SDX follow:

	Net Income		Dividends Declared		Current Year Translation Adjustment	Direct Exchange Rate at Year-End
Year	LCU	Dollars	LCU	Dollars		
2004	200,000	$100,000	-0-	$ -0-	$ -0-	$.50
2005	200,000	90,000	200,000	80,000	(110,000)	.40
2006	200,000	70,000	200,000	80,000	(90,000)	.30

Additional Information

1. SDX declared and paid its 2005 dividend at the *end* of 2005 and its 2006 dividend at the *beginning* of 2006.

2. On 12/31/06, PDX sold its entire interest in SDX to a group of local investors for cash of 1,120,000 LCU.

3. SDX's reported net income each year was earned evenly throughout the year.

4. PDX used the *current rate method* of translation.

Required

1. Prepare a T-account analysis of PDX's Investment in Subsidiary account for 2004 through 2006.
2. Calculate PDX's annual return on investment (AROI) for 2004, 2005, and 2006 using SDX's reported net income—*without* the current period translation adjustment included in the numerator.
3. Repeat requirement 2, but *with* the current period translation adjustment included in the numerator.
4. Which manner of calculation—requirement 2 or 3—is consistent with *FAS 52*?
5. Calculate an average AROI for the three years first using the percentages in requirement 2 and then the percentages in requirement 3. Which average reflects the economic reality of what occurred?
6. Explain whether it is correct to use the *beginning-of-year* investment balance or the *average* investment balance for the year in the denominator in requirements 2 and 3.

7. Calculate the internal rate of return (IRR) over the life of the investment. (You may readily obtain this answer using the IRR function available in EXCEL or LOTUS 1-2-3 by merely setting up a cash flow table and then programming the IRR function with the cursor in the cell in which you want your answer to appear.)
8. Explain why the IRR in requirement 7 differs from the AROI calculations in requirements 2, 3, and 5. Which should be used in evaluating the profitability of SDX?

chapter

16

Translating Foreign Currency Statements: The Temporal Method & the Functional Currency Concept

The first panacea for a mismanaged nation is inflation of the currency; the second is war. Both bring a temporary prosperity; both bring a permanent ruin.

ERNEST HEMINGWAY

LEARNING OBJECTIVES

To Understand

> **The procedures for applying the *temporal method* of translation.**
>
> **The way to hedge a foreign operation's exposed monetary position.**
>
> **The objectives of translation under *FAS 52*.**
>
> **The *functional currency concept* and its underlying rationale.**
>
> **When and how to record U.S. income taxes on earnings of foreign subsidiaries.**

TOPIC OUTLINE

I. The U.S. Dollar Unit of Measure Approach (The *Temporal Method*)

II. Hedging a Net Monetary Position

III. The Objectives of Translation under *FAS 52*

IV. The Functional Currency Concept

V. Changes in the Functional Currency

VI. Concluding Comments

INTERNATIONAL PERSPECTIVE: *Worldwide Translation Practices*

APPENDIX 16A: U.S. Taxation of Foreign Subsidiary Earnings

APPENDIX 16B: Evaluating the Validity of the Functional Currency Concept

Appendices can be found at
http://www.pahler.swlearning.com

CHAPTER OVERVIEW

In this chapter, we first discuss and illustrate the other translation approach allowed under FASB *Statement No. 52*: The **U.S. dollar unit of measure**, which is implemented using the *temporal method* of translation. Next we discuss hedging a foreign operation's exposed *monetary* position. After that, we review the objectives of translation under *FAS 52*. Finally, we explain the *functional currency concept*, which is the underlying foundation conceived to support the use of (1) the *current rate method* of translation in certain situations and (2) the *temporal method* of translation in all other situations.

The validity of the *functional currency concept* is addressed in Appendix 16B. That discussion reveals the characteristics (*strengths* and *weaknesses*) of the *current rate method* and the *temporal method* under the existing floating exchange rate system.

I. THE U.S. DOLLAR UNIT OF MEASURE APPROACH (THE *TEMPORAL METHOD*)

The Rationale

Under the U.S. dollar unit of measure approach, no consideration is given to trying to preserve the relationships that exist in the foreign currency statements. Instead, **the objective is to translate the nonmonetary assets** (with one exception mentioned later) **at rates that produce the equivalent number of dollars that would have been needed to acquire the nonmonetary assets when they were purchased.** Thus it is said that the *nonmonetary assets* are not only expressed in U.S. dollars but also are "remeasured" in the process (**to the dollars that would have been needed to acquire them**). Only *historical rates* achieve these results. In the income statement, depreciation and amortization expenses are likewise translated at historical rates.

By using historical rates for nonmonetary items and the current rate for monetary items, the item-to-item relationships that exist in the foreign currency statements are ***not*** maintained in translation—**an entirely different set of relationships is produced.** Thus the translated financial statements in U.S. dollars **do *not* have a "foreign currency feel" to them.** Managerially, the U.S. parent, in looking at the translated financial statements, views the foreign operation using a different perspective from that of the local management in the foreign country that uses the foreign currency statements.

Some claim that this remeasuring is tantamount to simulating what the cost of a foreign plant would have been had it been located in the United States. Some claim that it results in treating foreign operations as though all of the transactions had occurred in U.S. dollars. Others disagree with these views and believe that it merely results in expressing in U.S. dollars the cost of a foreign plant.[1]

Translation Methods for Achieving a U.S. Dollar Unit of Measure

Three translation methods exist for achieving a U.S. dollar unit of measure: the **temporal method,** the **monetary-nonmonetary method**, and the **current-noncurrent method.**

1. **The temporal method.** Under this method, **the measurement basis of an asset or liability determines the exchange rate used in translating that asset or liability.** Accordingly, different exchange rates are used for different measurement bases (for example, *historical exchange rates* for fixed assets and the *current exchange rate* for receivables). Consequently, a foreign currency

[1] *FAS 52*, pp. 20–21.

measurement is changed into a dollar measurement **without changing the basis.** Thus the accounting principles are *not* changed (even though the unit of measure has been changed to the dollar). The temporal method can accommodate any measurement basis (*historical cost*, *current replacement price*, or *current market price*). This highly flexible method developed in 1968 by Leonard Lorenson attracted such wide support that it was adopted in 1975 in *FAS 8* (superseded by *FAS 52* in 1981), which allowed only this method of translation.

2. **The monetary-nonmonetary method.** Under this method, **monetary assets are translated using the *current rate*, and nonmonetary assets are translated using historical rates.** This is merely a classification scheme. The results of the *temporal method* and the *monetary-nonmonetary method* coincide except for the translation of (1) inventories carried at market (below cost) and (2) certain debt and equity securities having readily determinable fair values and classified as either "trading securities" or "available-for-sale" securities (under *FAS 115*, "Accounting for Certain Investments in Debt and Equity Securities"). Thus inventory valued at market (below cost) is translated using (1) the *current rate* under the *temporal method* and (2) the *historical rate* under the *monetary-nonmonetary method*. Consequently, the *temporal method* accommodates current market valuation of nonmonetary assets; the *monetary-nonmonetary method* does *not* because the measurement basis is *not* maintained in translation.
3. **The current-noncurrent method.** Under this method, **current assets and current liabilities are translated using the *current rate*, and noncurrent assets and noncurrent liabilities are translated using *historical rates*.** This is also merely a classification scheme. This method was general practice from the early 1930s until 1975 when *FAS 8* was issued.[2]

For simplicity, in discussing the U.S. dollar unit of measure approach hereafter, we refer only to the *temporal method* because it is the soundest of the three translation methods that achieve a U.S. dollar unit of measure.

CHECK POINT

Which of the following is a translation method that does *not* fit under the U.S. dollar unit of measure approach?

a. Current rate method
b. Monetary-nonmonetary method
c. Current-noncurrent method
d. Temporal method

Answer: a

The Focus: The Net Monetary Position

Under the *temporal method*, the composition of the individual assets and liabilities is critical in determining whether a *favorable* or *unfavorable* result is reported as a consequence of an exchange rate change. An excess of *monetary assets* over *monetary liabilities* is referred to as a **net monetary asset position**; an excess of *monetary liabilities* over *monetary assets* is referred to as a **net monetary liability position.**

CHECK POINT

Under the U.S. dollar unit of measure approach, the focus is on which of the following?

a. Net monetary asset position
b. Net monetary liability position

---

[2] The death knell for this method was sounded with Hepworth's historic turning point article in 1956 that advocated translating *noncurrent receivables* and *noncurrent payables* based on their *nature* (which would result in using the *current rate*)—*not* on their *classification*.

c. Net exposed asset position
d. Net exposed liability position
e. Net monetary position

Answer: e

Reported Effects of Exchange Rate Changes

If a foreign unit is in a net monetary *asset* position, an increase in the direct exchange rate causes a *favorable* result to be reported (an economic gain from the exchange rate change); however, if it is in a net monetary *liability* position, it reports an *unfavorable* result (an economic loss from the exchange rate change). On the other hand, if a foreign unit is in a net monetary *asset* position, a *decrease* in the direct exchange rate causes an *unfavorable* result to be reported; however, if it is in a net monetary *liability* position, a *favorable* result is reported. These reporting results are summarized in Illustration 16-1.

Key Observations of the Temporal Method

This approach considers only the **monetary assets** (with the two exceptions discussed earlier) and **monetary liabilities** to be exposed to the economic consequences of exchange rate changes—*not* the foreign unit's *net assets* (total assets – total liabilities). As was true for the *current rate method* (discussed in Chapter 15), no attempt is made to understand **why a change in the exchange rate occurred.** Because *historical exchange rates* are used for *nonmonetary assets*—**effectively freezing the values of these items in dollars**—any distortions that exist in the foreign currency statements resulting from nonmonetary assets being *undervalued* because of inflation are negated in translation. (This result is discussed fully in Appendix 16B.)

CHECK POINT

When the direct exchange rate *decreases* during the year, and a *favorable* effect for this change in the exchange rate is reported in the income statement, the foreign unit had to be in which position?

a. Net asset
b. Net current
c. Net monetary
d. Net monetary asset
e. Net monetary liability

Answer: e

ILLUSTRATION 16-1 THE U.S. DOLLAR UNIT OF MEASURE APPROACH: REPORTING EFFECTS OF EXCHANGE RATE CHANGES

Translation Method Used	Possible Relevant Financial Positions	Increase[a] (*foreign currency has strengthened or dollar has weakened*)	Decrease[b] (*foreign currency has weakened or dollar has strengthened*)
Temporal	Net monetary assets	Favorable	Unfavorable
Temporal	Net monetary liability	Unfavorable	Favorable

[a] In all situations, the effect is *favorable* on the assets and *unfavorable* on the liabilities.

[b] In all situations, the effect is *unfavorable* on the assets and *favorable* on the liabilities.

Introductory Illustration

Translation Using the Temporal Method

For convenience, we repeat the factual data given in Chapter 15 for illustrating the two translation approaches allowed by *FAS 52*.

Assume that in late 2004, a U.S. company created a 100%-owned subsidiary in Mexico when the direct exchange rate was $.50, making a $1,000,000 cash equity investment at that time. For simplicity, assume that this direct exchange rate did *not* fluctuate through December 31, 2004. The subsidiary's first sales were on January 1, 2005.

Additional assumptions are that (1) *no* dividends were declared or paid in 2005; (2) fixed asset additions of 200,000 pesos (Mex$) (equal to 2005's depreciation expense) occurred on January 3, 2005, when the exchange rate was $.50; (3) Mexico had 25% inflation for 2005; (4) the United States had 10% inflation for 2005; and (5) the *direct* exchange rates were $.50 at December 31, 2004, $.44 at December 31, 2005, and $.47 for 2005 as an average.

The subsidiary's balance sheets at the end of 2004 and 2005 and the 2005 income statement are shown in Illustration 16-2.

The *temporal method* of translation is shown in Illustration 16-3.

We now provide a more comprehensive illustration of the *temporal method* that shows (1) the use of the *Remeasurement Gain or Loss* account, which is the name assigned to the *income statement* account to which the effect of a change in the exchange rate change is charged or credited under this translation method (pursuant to *FAS 52*), (2) a *beginning* balance for the Retained Earnings account, (3) the treatment for a *cash dividend* payment to the parent, and (4) *all* of the individual asset and liability accounts. (As explained later, *FAS 52* refers to translation under the *temporal method* as the *remeasurement process*.)

ILLUSTRATION 16-2 FOREIGN CURRENCY FINANCIAL STATEMENTS

	Pesos	
	12/31/04	12/31/05
Balance Sheets		
Monetary assets	2,200,000	2,500,000
Inventory	1,000,000	1,250,000
Fixed assets, net	4,800,000	4,800,000[a]
Total Assets	8,000,000	8,550,000
Monetary liabilities	6,000,000	6,250,000
Common stock	2,000,000[b]	2,000,000
Retained earnings	-0-	300,000
Total Liabilities and Equity	8,000,000	8,550,000
Net Monetary Liability Position		
At 12/31/04 (6,000,000 - 2,200,000)	**3,800,000**	
At 12/31/05 (6,250,000 - 2,500,000)		**3,750,000**
Average for 2005		3,875,000[c]
Income Statements (2005)		
Revenues		5,300,000
Cost of sales		(4,300,000)
Depreciation		(200,000)
Expenses		(500,000)
Net Income		300,000

[a] Because of the 25% inflation in Mexico during 2005, these assets are *undervalued* 25%.

[b] This amount is the peso equivalent of the $1,000,000 cash investment made by the parent when it created the subsidiary in late 2004 ($1,000,000/$.50 = Mex$ 2,000,000).

[c] Mex$ 3,800,000 + Mex$ 200,000 for the equipment acquired on 1/3/05 = Mex$ 4,000,000; (Mex$ 4,000,000 + Mex$ 3,750,000)/2 = Mex$ 3,875,000.

ILLUSTRATION 16-3 TRANSLATION WORKSHEET: THE TEMPORAL METHOD FOR THE YEAR ENDED DECEMBER 31, 2005

	Pesos	Exchange Code	Exchange Rate	U.S. Dollars
Income Statement (2005):				
Revenues	5,300,000	A	$.47	$ 2,491,000
Cost of sales	(4,300,000)	H	$.483[a]	(2,078,000)
Depreciation	(200,000)	H	$.50	(100,000)
Expenses	(500,000)	A	$.47	(235,000)
Net Income	300,000			$ 77,500
Balance Sheet (12/31/05):				
Monetary assets	2,500,000	C	$.44	$ 1,100,000
Inventory	1,250,000	H	$.448[a]	560,000
Fixed assets, net	4,800,000	H	$.50	2,400,000
Total Assets	8,550,000			$ 4,060,000
Monetary liabilities	6,250,000	C	$.44	$ 2,750,000
Common stock	2,000,000	H	$.50	$ 1,000,000
Retained earnings	300,000	(Per above)		77,500
Economic *gain* from exchange rate change		(See below)		232,500
Total Equity	2,300,000			$ 1,310,000
Total Liabilities and Equity	8,550,000			$ 4,060,000

Calculation of Economic Gain from Exchange Rate Change

Average *net monetary liability* position of Mex$ 3,875,000 × $.06 *decrease* in the exchange rate .... $ 232,500

Note: Because the nonmonetary assets are translated at historical rates (effectively being held constant), an economic gain or loss is reported only on the *monetary accounts*. In this case, the exchange rate *decreased* by $.06. Thus a valuation *loss* occurs on *monetary assets*; a valuation *gain* occurs on *monetary liabilities*. Monetary *liabilities* exceeded *monetary assets*, thus a net ***gain***.

Key Review Points

1. Note how ratios and relationships are *not* maintained *after* translation:

	Pesos	U.S. Dollars
Debt-to-equity ratio	2.71:1	2.10:1
Gross profit margin ratio	19%	17%
Net income to sales ratio	6%	3%
Fixed assets to total assets percent	56%	59%
Undervaluation of fixed assets	25%	10%

2. Note the *increase* in the stockholder's equity:

Ending stockholder's equity (per above)	$1,310,000
Less—*Beginning* stockholder's equity (parent's initial capital investment per Illustration 16-2)	1,000,000
Increase in Stockholder's Equity	$ 310,000

Code: A = Average rate; C = Current rate; H = Historical rate.

[a] This is an *average* historical rate.

In addition, we discuss (1) certain pretranslation procedures, (2) the finer points of this method, and (3) certain post-translation procedures. This comprehensive illustration is for 2006, the year following the year in Illustration 16-3.

Basic Procedures *Before* Translation

The same basic pretranslation procedures discussed in Chapter 15 (restating to U.S. GAAP, adjusting FX Receivable and Payable accounts to the spot rate, and reconciling intercompany account balances) must be performed *prior to* translation.

Specific Translation Procedures

Balance Sheet Accounts

FAS 52 identifies the specific balance sheet accounts that must be translated at the *historical exchange rate*—the exchange rate existing **when the item *entered* the balance sheet.** All other accounts are translated at the *current exchange rate* (the *spot rate* at the balance sheet date). The balance sheet accounts for which *historical exchange rates* are to be used are listed in Illustration 16-4. It is *not* necessary to memorize this list. An easier way to readily determine the exchange rate to use for translating each asset or liability is to use the *monetary-nonmonetary* distinction, which works for all accounts other than those related to (1) marketable securities and (2) inventory valued at market (below cost).

Income Statement Accounts

FAS 52 identifies the specific income statement accounts that must be translated at the *historical exchange rate*—the exchange rate existing **when the item *entered* the balance sheet.** Thus consistency occurs between the balance sheet and the income statement for related accounts (such as depreciation expense and equipment). All other accounts are translated at the *current exchange rate*—**the *spot rate* when the item *entered* the income statement.** The income statement accounts for which historical exchange rates are to be used are also listed in Illustration 16-4.

ILLUSTRATION 16-4 ACCOUNTS TRANSLATED (REMEASURED) USING HISTORICAL EXCHANGE RATES

Assets

- Marketable securities carried at cost:[a]
  - Equity securities
  - Debt securities *not* intended to be held until maturity
- Inventories carried at cost
- Prepaid expenses, such as insurance, advertising, and rent
- Property, plant, and equipment
- Accumulated depreciation on property, plant, and equipment
- Patents, trademarks, licenses, and formulas
- Goodwill
- Deferred charges and credits
- Other intangible assets

Liabilities

- Deferred income (unearned revenue)

Equity

- Common stock
- Additional paid-in capital
- Preferred stock carried at issuance price

Revenues, Costs, and Expenses (examples of accounts related to nonmonetary items)

- Cost of sales[b]
- Depreciation of property, plant, and equipment
- Amortization of intangible items, such as goodwill, patents, licenses, and so on
- Amortization of deferred charges or credits

---

[a] Those *not* carried at fair value pursuant to the requirements of *FAS 115*, "Accounting for Certain Investments in Debit and Equity Securities," because they do *not* have a "readily determinable fair market value."

[b] No *single* historical exchange rate is used because historical rates are applied to *beginning* inventory, purchases, and *ending* inventory.

Note: The Retained Earnings account is *not* listed because it represents a "forced out" amount—*not* because the current exchange rate is used.

Note: Under *FAS 109*, "Accounting for Income Taxes," deferred income taxes reported in the balance sheet are *not* deferred charges or deferred credits; they are receivables and payables. Accordingly, they are translated using the *current exchange rate*.

Source: Based on *FAS 52*, par. 48.

CHECK POINT

Which exchange rates should be used in expressing cost of sales in dollars for a foreign subsidiary under each of the following methods?

	Current Rate Method	Temporal Method
a.	Current	Current
b.	Historical	Historical
c.	Current	Historical
d.	Historical	Current

Answer: c

Comprehensive Illustration

Translation Using the Temporal Method

Assume the following information for this 100%-owned subsidiary located in Mexico (much of which is identical to the information used for the comparable comprehensive illustration using the *current rate method* presented in Chapter 15).

1. **Conformity with U.S. GAAP.** The financial statements in pesos have already been adjusted to conform with U.S. GAAP.
2. **Intercompany Receivable and Intercompany Payable accounts.** The parent and subsidiary *do* have intercompany transactions (other than dividends declared by the subsidiary), a condition that often leads to the use of the *temporal method* (as explained later). All necessary adjustments to reflect the spot rate at year-end have already been made to the Intercompany Receivable and Intercompany Payable accounts. (These accounts are included with other accounts on the worksheet.)
3. **Exchange rates.** The *direct* exchange rates were $.44 at December 31, 2005, $.40 at December 31, 2006, and $.42 for 2006 as an average.
4. **Inventory.** The 2006 *beginning* inventory was translated (remeasured) at $560,000 in the December 31, 2005, balance sheet (as shown in Illustration 16-3, which shows an *average* historical exchange rate of $.448). The 2006 *ending* inventory cost was *below* market in pesos; thus no adjustments in pesos for valuation purposes were needed. The 2006 *ending* inventory was acquired when the exchange rates were as follows:

Pesos	Rate	Dollars
200,000	$.42	$ 84,000
500,000	.41	205,000
800,000	.40	320,000
1,500,000	$.406[a]	$609,000

[a] This is the average rate ($609,000 ÷ Mex$ 1,500,000).

5. **Fixed assets.** All fixed assets were *acquired* in prior years when the direct exchange rate was $.50. No fixed assets were *retired* during 2006.
6. **Common stock.** The subsidiary was formed in late 2004 when the direct exchange rate was $.50. No additional capital stock changes have occurred since then.
7. **Retained earnings—beginning of year.** The translated retained earnings amount at the end of the prior year was $310,000 (the 2005 *increase* in equity shown in Illustration 16-3).
8. **Dividends declared.** The subsidiary declared and paid a cash dividend of 100,000 Mex$ on November 11, 2006, when the *direct* exchange rate was $.41.
9. **Sales, purchases, and expenses.** All sales, purchases, and expenses occurred evenly throughout 2006.
10. **Certain monetary information.** At the beginning of 2006, the subsidiary had *monetary assets* of Mex$ 2,500,000 and *monetary liabilities* of Mex$ 6,250,000 (the amounts shown at December 31, 2005, in Illustration 16-3). During 2006, cash disbursements in payment of liabilities totaled Mex$ 6,400,000 (excluding the Mex$ 100,000 cash dividend payment).

Illustration 16-5 uses this information to translate the foreign subsidiary's financial statements into dollars. The calculation of the remeasurement gain is shown in supporting Illustration 16-6.

Review Points for Illustration 16-5. Note the following:

1. **Applying the equity method.** The *equity method* of accounting is applied to the subsidiary's net income of $260,000 as follows:

Investment in Subsidiary	260,000	
Equity in Net Income (of subsidiary)		260,000

ILLUSTRATION 16-5 TRANSLATION WORKSHEET: THE TEMPORAL METHOD FOR THE YEAR ENDED DECEMBER 31, 2006

	Foreign Currency (Pesos)	Exchange Code	Exchange Rate	U.S. Dollars
Income Statement (2006):				
Sales	6,000,000	A	$.42	$ 2,520,000
Cost of sales:				
Beginning inventory	(1,250,000)	H	$.448	(560,000)
+ Purchases	(4,850,000)	A	$.42	(2,037,000)
= Goods available for sale	(6,100,000)			$(2,597,000)
– Ending inventory	1,500,000	H	$.406	609,000
= Cost of sales	(4,600,000)			$(1,988,000)
Depreciation expense	(200,000)	H	$.50	(100,000)
Operating expenses	(600,000)	A	$.42	(252,000)
Income before Taxes	600,000			$ 180,000
Income tax expense @ 25%	(150,000)	A	$.42	(63,000)
Subtotal	450,000			$ 117,000
Remeasurement gain		(Per Illus. 16-6)		**143,000**
Net Income	450,000			$ 260,000
Statement of Retained Earnings				
Balance, 1/1/06	300,000	(Given)		$ 310,000
+ Net income	450,000	(Per above)		260,000
– Dividends	(100,000)	H	$.41	(41,000)
Balance, 12/31/06	650,000			$ 529,000
Balance Sheet (as of 12/31/06)				
Cash	400,000	C	$.40	$ 160,000
Accounts receivable, net	1,600,000	C	$.40	640,000
Inventory	1,500,000	H	$.406	609,000
Land	1,000,000	H	$.50	500,000
Buildings and equipment	4,000,000	H	$.50	2,000,000
Accumulated depreciation	(400,000)	H	$.50	(200,000)
Total Assets	8,100,000			$ 3,709,000
Payables and accruals	1,950,000	C	$.40	$ 780,000
Long-term debt	3,500,000	C	$.40	1,400,000
Total Liabilities	5,450,000			$ 2,180,000
Common stock	2,000,000	H	$.50	$ 1,000,000
Retained earnings	650,000	(Per above)		529,000
Total Equity	2,650,000			$ 1,529,000
Total Liabilities and Equity	8,100,000			$ 3,709,000

Code:

C = Current rate existing at the balance sheet date.

A = Average rate, as given in the introduction to this illustration.

H = Historical rate.

ILLUSTRATION 16-6 CALCULATION OF THE TRANSACTION GAIN FROM REMEASUREMENT: SUPPORTING SCHEDULE TO ILLUSTRATION 16-5

Method I: Analysis of Monetary Assets and Liabilities for 2006

	PESOS		
	MONETARY ASSETS	MONETARY LIABILITIES	NET MONETARY LIABILITY POSITION
Monetary items, 1/1/06 (per Illustration 16-3 on p. 545)	2,500,000	6,250,000	3,750,000
Sales	6,000,000		(6,000,000)
Purchases		4,850,000	4,850,000
Operating expenses (excluding depreciation expense)		600,000	600,000
Income tax expense		150,000	150,000
Payment of liabilities	(6,400,000)	(6,400,000)	
Dividend payment (cash)	(100,000)		100,000
Monetary Items, 12/31/06	2,000,000	5,450,000	3,450,000

Calculating the Transaction Gain from Remeasurement Using the Preceding Analysis of the Monetary Accounts

	U.S. DOLLARS		
	LOSS OF VALUATION		
	MONETARY ASSETS (A LOSS)	MONETARY LIABILITIES (A GAIN)	TRANSACTION GAIN (LOSS) FROM REMEASUREMENT
Monetary assets at 1/1/06 (Mex$ 100,000 assumed used for the dividend shown separately)			
Mex$ 2,400,000 × $.04 ($.44 – $.40)[a]	$ (96,000)		$ (96,000)
Mex$ 100,000 × $.03 ($.44 – $.41)[b]	(3,000)		(3,000)
Monetary liabilities at 1/1/06			
Mex$ 6,250,000 × $.04 ($.44 – $.40)[a]		$250,000	250,000
Sales (Mex$ 6,000,000 × $.02 [$.42 – $.40][c])	(120,000)		(120,000)
Purchases (Mex$ 4,850,000 × $.02 [$.42 – $.40][c])		97,000	97,000
Operating expenses (Mex$ 600,000 × $.02 [$.42 – $.40][c])		12,000	12,000
Income tax expense (Mex$ 150,000 × $.02 [$.42 – $.40][c])		3,000	3,000
	$(219,000)	$362,000	$ 143,000

[a] *Beginning*-of-Year Rate – *End*-of-Year Rate.

[b] *Beginning*-of-Year Rate – Rate at Dividend Declaration Date.

[c] Average Rate – *End*-of-Year Rate.

Method II: Residual Force Out

1.		Remeasured assets	$ 3,709,000
2.	Less	Remeasured liabilities	2,180,000
3.	Equals	**Total Stockholders' Equity**	**$1,529,000**
4.	Less	Remeasured common stock and additional paid-in capital	1,000,000
5.	Equals	**Total Retained Earnings**	**$ 529,000**
6.	Less	*Beginning* retained earnings in dollars as reported in the prior period's remeasured financial statements reduced for any dividends declared ($310,000 – $41,000)	269,000
7.	Equals	**Current Period Net Income**	**$ 260,000**
8.	Less	Remeasured revenues and expenses (as shown in Illustration 16-5)	117,000
9.	Equals	**The Current Period Foreign Currency Translation Gain from Remeasurement**	**$ 143,000**

Recall that the $143,000 remeasurement gain *is* included in determining net income.

2. **Managing the monetary position.** The $143,000 remeasurement gain would *not* have resulted if the company had kept *monetary assets* and *monetary liabilities* at approximately the same level during 2006. Doing this merely to *minimize* remeasurement gains and losses, however, counteracts the long-standing practice of *minimizing* the risks associated with foreign operations by

financing them with foreign borrowings (payable in the foreign currency of the foreign unit) to the *maximum* extent possible. Obviously, firms must carefully weigh these conflicting objectives. Later we discuss other ways to *minimize* remeasurement gains and losses.

3. **Realization review procedures for nonmonetary assets.** Because of the use of *historical exchange rates* for *nonmonetary assets*, the results under the *temporal method* create a special problem that does *not* arise with the *current rate method*. Namely, *nonmonetary assets* translated (remeasured) at *historical rates* are *not* necessarily realizable in dollars—even though no realizability problem exists in the foreign currency. **This problem arises only when (1) the *direct* exchange rate has *decreased* and (2) the *decrease* is for reasons *other than* inflation in the foreign country.**

Accordingly, a lower-of-cost-or-market test is required **in dollars** for inventory (using identical procedures shown in intermediate accounting texts) and fixed assets, with adjustments made to the dollar amounts in the translation worksheet prior to consolidation. In Illustration 16-5, if the *nonmonetary assets cannot* be sold for *more than* their *book value* of Mex$ 6,100,000, their net realizable value *in dollars* is only $2,440,000 (Mex$ 6,100,000 × $.40). This $2,440,000 is $469,000 *below* the $2,909,000 amount shown in dollars ($609,000 + $500,000 + $2,000,000 – $200,000 = $2,909,000). An adjustment of this magnitude would be *more than* the $143,000 remeasurement gain (which by itself would be illusory if such a lower-of-cost-or-market adjustment were necessary).

4. **Comparison to Illustration 15-6 (the *current rate method*).** Total assets and total equity are both *higher* by $469,000 in Illustration 16-5 than in Illustration 15-6 (on page 515) in which the *current rate method* was used. This difference is the result of using *historical exchange rates* for inventory (a $9,000 difference) and fixed assets (a $460,000 difference) rather than the rate existing at the balance sheet date (the current rate). Thus these two methods can often produce dramatically different reporting results.
5. **What if the exchange rate had increased? *If the direct exchange rate had* increased** rather than *decreased* during 2006, a remeasurement *loss* would have resulted (the loss from revaluing *monetary liabilities* higher would have been more than the gain from revaluing *monetary assets* higher). The loss would be imaginary, however, if the *nonmonetary assets* could be sold for *at least* their *book values*. If so, their realizable value in dollars would be much *higher* than the amounts reported in dollars under the *temporal method*. Unfortunately, no upward mark-to-market provision exists for revaluing inventory and fixed assets upward in dollars to obtain an offsetting effect (as is possible when the *direct* exchange *decreases*). Accordingly, the reporting of a current period remeasurement loss would be offset in later periods, as the *nonmonetary assets* are realized (transformed into *monetary assets*).

Special Disclosures Concerning Remeasurement Gains and Losses

The total of all **remeasurement gains and losses**, along with any FX gains and losses that are to be reported in the income statement (such as those resulting from importing and exporting transactions), must be **disclosed as a net amount** either in the income statement or in notes to the financial statements. Remeasurement gains and losses are *not* considered *extraordinary items*, no matter how material they might be.

CHECK POINT

The effect of a change in the exchange rate should be reported as a charge or credit to which of the following?

	Under the U.S. Dollar Unit of Measure Approach	**Under the Foreign Currency Unit of Measure Approach**
a.	The income statement	The income statement
b.	Other Comprehensive Income	The income statement

c. The income statement	Other Comprehensive Income
d. Other Comprehensive Income	Other Comprehensive Income

Answer: c

II. HEDGING A NET MONETARY POSITION

When the *temporal method* of translation is used, a company that desires to negate the potential negative effect of an adverse change in the exchange rate (that will be reported in ***earnings***) must hedge the **net monetary position** (whether it be a net monetary *asset* position or a net monetary *liability* position).

One of the criticisms leveled at the *temporal method* of translation when *FAS 8* required it to be used for *all* foreign operations was that it caused firms to focus their attention on hedging the net *monetary* position—even when they believed that (1) the net *asset* position was their true economic exposure, or (2) the net *asset* position was *not* at risk and thus did *not* need to be hedged. Because the *temporal method* is still permitted, firms using it may be influenced by *FAS 52* to focus their hedging on the net *monetary* position.

Hedging a net monetary *asset* position presents no dilemma. In contrast, hedging an exposed monetary *liability* position does present one. The following discussion assumes the use of forward exchange contracts (FX forwards).

Hedging an Exposed Net Monetary *Asset* Position

In this situation, the entity treats the net monetary *asset* position the same way it would an FX Accounts Receivable. Its concern is that the *direct* exchange will *decrease*; thus it *sells forward*. If the *direct* exchange rate does *decrease*, the *gain* on the FX forward (an actual cash gain) offsets the remeasurement *loss* from translation, which is unquestionably **a true economic loss because the net monetary assets are liquid.** If instead the *direct* exchange rate *increases*, the *loss* on the FX forward (an *actual* cash loss) is offset by the remeasurement *gain* from translation, which again is unquestionably a true economic gain because **the net monetary assets are liquid.** Thus the results of hedging a net monetary *asset* position reflect the economic consequences of the change in the exchange rate.

Hedging an Exposed Net Monetary *Liability* Position: Direct Exchange Rate *Increases*

In this situation, the entity treats the net monetary *liability* position the same way it would an FX Accounts Payable. Its concern is that the *direct* exchange rate will *increase;* thus it *buys forward.* If the *direct* exchange rate does *increase*, the *gain* on the FX forward (an *actual* cash gain) offsets the remeasurement *loss* from translation. The remeasurement loss, however, may *not* be a true economic loss because the nonmonetary assets being financed with the net monetary liability position may have gained in value and be worth more than their translated dollar amounts as a result of the increase in the direct exchange rate. Furthermore, the remeasurement loss will reverse itself in later periods if the *direct* exchange rate *decreases*. This scenario is ideal.

Hedging an Exposed Net Monetary *Liability* Position: Direct Exchange Rate *Decreases*

In this situation, if the direct exchange rate *decreases*, the *loss* on the FX forward (an *actual* cash loss) is offset by the remeasurement *gain* from translation. The remeasurement gain, however, may not be a true economic gain because the nonmonetary *assets* being financed by the net monetary liability position may have lost value and be worth *less than* their translated dollar amounts as a result of the *decrease* in the direct exchange rate. Furthermore, the remeasurement gain will reverse itself in later periods if the direct exchange rate *increases*. The loss on the FX forward, however, is an *actual* cash loss that will *not* reverse itself in later periods. This scenario points out the dilemma that exists in hedging a net monetary liability position because the direct exchange rate could *decrease* (resulting in a cash loss) rather than *increase* (resulting in a cash *gain*).

ETHICS

Should "Corporate Welfare" Be Reported as Income?

Many newspaper columnists use the term *corporate welfare* to characterize the tax breaks that corporations receive under various provisions of the Internal Revenue Code. Under current financial reporting standards, such tax savings are reported in the income statement as a reduction of income tax expense.

Questions

1. Is it ethical to report as income the positive effect that can result from such legislative provisions?
2. What might be a better and more informative way of reporting this effect?

III. The Objectives of Translation Under *FAS 52*

FAS 52 states that the objectives of translation are to

a. Provide information that is generally compatible with the expected economic effects of a rate change on an enterprise's cash flows and equity.
b. Reflect in consolidated statements the financial results and relationships of the individual consolidated entities as measured in their *functional currencies* in conformity with U.S. generally accepted accounting principles.[3]

The First Objective

Note that this objective does *not* use unequivocal wording, such as "provide information that reports the **true economic effect** of an exchange rate change." Instead, it uses the words "provide information that is **generally compatible** with the expected economic effects of a rate change." This raises such questions as this: If the *true economic effect* of an exchange rate change is $800,000 *favorable*, is the reporting of a $500,000 *favorable* result using one translation method generally compatible enough? Certainly, reporting a $300,000 *unfavorable* effect using the other translation method generally would *not* be compatible.

The looseness of this objective apparently is an acknowledgment that the translation methods required in *FAS 52* are incapable of reflecting the true economic effect of an exchange rate change—**probably because of the constraints of having to maintain historical cost in translating nonmonetary assets.** Reflecting the true economic effect of an exchange rate change is shown in Appendix 16B.

The Second Objective

Concerning *nonmonetary* accounts, this objective effectively requires the use of translation methods that produce dollar amounts that can be considered historical cost to conform with U.S. GAAP. This raises a critical question: Can the general compatibility goal of the first objective be attained using translation methods that are presumed to preserve the historical cost basis of accounting? In other words, are these objectives compatible?

In less abstract terms, are these two objectives the equivalent of having the objective of valuing a building at its near *market value* (based on economic conditions) using the *straight-line* or

[3] *FAS 52* "Foreign Currency Translation" (Stamford: Financial Accounting Standards Board, 1981), par. 4.

double declining-depreciation methods? (Such a result would occur only by coincidence.) Appendix 16B addresses these questions. For now, it is important to understand that *FAS 52* makes a major presumption that the two translation methods that it allows (1) preserve historical cost for nonmonetary assets and (2) achieve results that are generally compatible with the economic effects of exchange rate changes.

IV. The Functional Currency Concept

FAS 52 presumes that foreign operations may be conducted in one or more economic and currency environments. The primary economic environment must be determined for each separate foreign operation; however, *FAS 52* does *not* specifically define the economic environment concept. Each foreign country has its own economic environment composed of taxation policies, currency controls, government policies toward intervention in the international currency markets, economic stability, and inflation. The primary economic environment concept, however, pertains to the manner in which the foreign unit conducts its operations—**the currency it primarily uses to generate and expend cash**. This concept presumes that each foreign operation has a primary currency.

The currency of the primary economic environment is then designated as that foreign unit's functional currency. The FASB has developed some economic factors that are to be considered *individually* and *collectively* in determining the functional currency for each foreign operation of an enterprise. A list of these factors appears in Illustration 16-7. The functional currency determined for each foreign operation is the basis for the method of translation into dollars. If the *foreign currency* is the functional currency, the foreign unit of measure is required (implemented using the *current rate method*). If the *U.S. dollar* is the functional currency, the U.S. dollar unit of measure is required (implemented using the *temporal method*).

Check Points

A subsidiary's functional currency is the *local* currency, which has *not* experienced significant inflation. Which exchange rate should be used in expressing the following accounts in dollars?

	Depreciation Expense	**Plant and Equipment**
a.	Current	Current
b.	Historical	Historical
c.	Current	Historical
d.	Historical	Current

Answer: a

Assume the same information from above, except that the functional currency is the dollar.

Answer: b

The Two Different Types of Foreign Operations

In reviewing Illustration 16-7, realize that *FAS 52* presumes that each foreign operation fits into one of two categories.

Category 1: Relatively Autonomous Foreign Units

These foreign units primarily generate and expend the local currency of the country in which they are located. One example is a French subsidiary that (1) pays its employees and vendors in francs, (2) sells its products for francs in France, (3) has its debt denominated in francs, and (4) has no intercompany inventory purchases or sales with the domestic parent. Thus the subsidiary is relatively **independent and self-contained**. Obviously, the *French franc* is the functional currency.

ILLUSTRATION 16-7 ECONOMIC FACTORS TO BE CONSIDERED IN DETERMINING THE FUNCTIONAL CURRENCY

Type of Factor	Factors Pointing to a Foreign Functional Currency	Factors Pointing to a Dollar Functional Currency
Cash flows	Cash flows related to the foreign entity's individual assets and liabilities are primarily in the foreign currency and do not directly impact the parent company's cash flows.	Cash flows related to the foreign entity's individual assets and liabilities directly impact the parent's cash flows on a current basis and are readily available for remittance to the parent company.
Sales prices	Sales prices for the foreign entity's products are not primarily responsive on a short-term basis to changes in exchange rates but are determined more by local competition or local government regulation.	Sales prices for the foreign entity's products are primarily responsive on a short-term basis to changes in exchange rates: for example, sales prices are determined more by worldwide competition or by international prices.
Sales market	An active local sales market exists for the foreign entity's products, although significant amounts of exports might also be available.	The sales market is mostly in the parent's country, or sales contracts are denominated in the parent's currency.
Cost and expenses	Labor, materials, and other cost for the foreign entity's products or services are primarily local costs, even though imports from other countries might also be available.	Labor, materials, and other costs for the foreign entity's products or services, on a continuing basis, are primarily costs for components obtained from the country in which the parent company is located.
Financing	Financing is primarily denominated in foreign currency, and funds generated by the foreign entity's operations are sufficient to service existing and normally expected debt obligations.	Financing is primarily from the parent or other dollar-denominated obligations, or funds generated by the foreign entity's operations are not sufficient to service existing and normally expected debt obligations without the infusion of additional funds from the parent company. Infusion of additional funds from the parent company for expansion is not a factor, provided that funds generated by the foreign entity's expanded operations are expected to be sufficient to service that additional financing.
Intercompany transactions and arrangements	There is a low volume of intercompany transactions, and an extensive interrelationship does not exist between the operations of the foreign entity and the parent company. However, the foreign entity's operations may rely on the parent's or affiliates' competitive advantages such as patents and trademarks.	There is a high volume of intercompany transactions, and an extensive interrelationship exists between the operations of the foreign entity and the parent company. Additionally, the parent's currency generally would be the functional currency if the foreign entity is a device or shell corporation for holding investments, obligations, intangible assets, and so on, that could readily be carried on the parent's or an affiliate's books.

Source: Adapted from *Statement of Financial Accounting Standards, No. 52*, "Foreign Currency Translation" (Stamford: Financial Accounting Standards Board, 1981), Appendix A, par. 42.

Category 2: Relatively *Non*autonomous Foreign Units

These units primarily generate and expend U.S. dollars. One example is an assembly plant on the Mexican side of the Rio Grande that (1) purchases parts from the U.S. parent (paying in dollars), (2) pays its employees in dollars, (3) sells the processed product back to the U.S. parent (billing in dollars), and (4) has its debt denominated in dollars. Thus the operation is viewed as **an extension of the parent's operations**—not a relatively self-contained and independent operation. In these cases, the *dollar* is the functional currency.

No Arbitrary Selection Allowed

The determination of the functional currency is to be based on the economic facts—it *cannot* be an arbitrary selection. Because significant differences in reported net income can occur as a result of choosing the foreign currency or the dollar as the functional currency, the intent is to prevent managements from arbitrarily choosing one of the two translation methods. When the economic factors listed in Illustration 16-7 do *not* clearly indicate the functional currency, management must weigh the individual economic factors and use its judgment, considering the stated objectives of translation.

What Occurs in Practice

In practice, determining the functional currency is largely a management call; in effect, managements may choose the translation method they desire. This might explain why the six largest U.S. oil companies are split evenly as to the functional currencies of most of their foreign units.[4] Otherwise, one must conclude that three of them conduct foreign operations quite differently from the other three. Considering that these companies are in the same industry and several operate in the same foreign countries, the fact that they have different functional currencies raises serious questions as to whether they conduct their operations that differently. Some rigorous studies are needed to determine just how much differently competing companies conduct foreign operations in common countries; the FASB has *not* commissioned any such studies.[5] The potential for abuse and arbitrary selection of translation methods is quite high. Beyond the *FAS 52* indicators, the large public accounting firms have developed additional indicators, some of which are rather novel and could well serve a client that desires a certain translation method. For instance, one that puts emphasis on repatriating earnings instead of on currencies used in generating earnings is found in PricewaterhouseCoopers' foreign currency booklet, which states:

> Accordingly, it would seem that a foreign operation's policy of converting its available funds into dollars for current or near-term distribution to the parent may be one of the most significant indicators suggesting a dollar functional currency.[6]

CHECK POINT

Which of the following methods should be used for expressing in dollars the financial statements of a foreign operation that is relatively *self-contained* and *independent* of the parent's operations?

a. The current rate method
b. The monetary-nonmonetary method
c. The temporal method
d. The current-noncurrent method

Answer: a

Highly Inflationary Economies: Functional Currency Concept to Be Disregarded (Reporting Results Under the *Current Rate Method* Are *Not* Meaningful)

An exception to the approach of determining the functional currency from the economic factors specified in *FAS 52* is made for operations in highly inflationary economies. *FAS 52* defines a highly inflationary economy as **"one that has cumulative inflation of approximately 100 percent or more over a three-year period."**[7] In these cases, the *dollar* is used as the functional currency. The purpose of the exception is to deal with the "disappearing plant" problem discussed in Chapter 15. Recall that applying the *current exchange rate* to *historical cost* amounts in foreign currency financial statements can produce meaningless dollar amounts for fixed assets in such economies. The problem is the foreign currency's lack of stability, which makes it completely unsuitable for use as a functional currency.

In the exposure draft that preceded *FAS 52*, the FASB proposed restating the historical cost amounts for inflation *prior to* translation (and then allowing the use of the *current rate method*).

---

[4] See "Plenty of Opportunity to Fool Around," *Forbes*, June 2, 1986, p. 139.

[5] In 1986, the FASB published a research report, *Determining the Functional Currencies under Statement 52*, by Thomas G. Evans and Timothy Doupnik. However, this was a more general study based on questionnaires received from 180 firms having 543 foreign units. The responses to the questionnaires by the managements indicated that they determine their functional currencies "consistent with the guidelines presented in Appendix A of Statement 52." As the report's authors pointed out, these responses could *not* be independently verified, nor was there any interaction with the respondents. Thus it was *not* a rigorous analytical study along the lines suggested here.

[6] Price Waterhouse, *Foreign Currency Translation—Understanding and Applying SFAS 52* (New York: 1981), p. 14.

[7] *FAS 52*, par. 11.

The proposal was dropped, however, because of (1) conceptual objections to mixing *historical cost* with *inflation-adjusted amounts* and (2) the inadequacy of published indices for several countries. As a practical alternative, which is an acknowledged conceptual compromise, the FASB designated the *dollar* as the functional currency in highly inflationary economies (whereby the *historical cost amounts* are translated at *historical exchange rates*). The results are more reasonable dollar amounts for the fixed assets of these foreign operations. Numerous countries, primarily in South America, have cumulative inflation rates near or exceeding 100% over three-year periods. Although 100% may seem high, an annual inflation rate of only 26% results in 100% inflation cumulatively over a three-year period.

The Judgment Factor in Highly Inflationary Economies

The use of 100% is arbitrary, but the use of the modifier "approximately" in the pronouncement allows management some latitude in judgment. Thus a cumulative inflation rate of 90%, for example, could be sufficient grounds for using the *dollar* as the functional currency, whereas a foreign unit operating with a cumulative inflation rate of 110% could still use the *foreign currency* as the functional currency. We must also consider management's latitude when the economic facts do *not* clearly indicate the functional currency. In such a case and when the cumulative inflation rate is *high* but *below* 100%, management may lean toward using the *dollar* as the functional currency.

CHECK POINT

A subsidiary located in a foreign country having a *highly inflationary economy* should use which of the following methods in expressing the financial statements in dollars?

a. The current rate method
b. The temporal method
c. The monetary-nonmonetary method
d. The functional currency method

Answer: b

Distinguishing *Translation* from *Remeasurement*

For simplicity, we have referred to the process of applying exchange rates to a foreign operation's financial statements to arrive at dollar amounts as *translation*. Historically, this has been the definition of the term. The use of the functional currency concept, however, has resulted in a narrower definition of the term in *FAS 52*.

Translation: Going from the Functional Currency (a Foreign Currency) to the Reporting Currency (the Dollar)

In *FAS 52*, **translation** refers to the process of **expressing functional currency amounts in the reporting currency**. Accordingly, the term is restricted to situations in which the *foreign currency* is the functional currency. Recall that when the *foreign currency* is the functional currency, the *current rate method* is required, and it merely *expresses* the foreign currency financial statements in dollars—it does *not* "remeasure" the *nonmonetary accounts* to obtain their dollar equivalents at the time the transactions were recorded.

Remeasurement: Going from a Nonfunctional Currency (a Foreign Currency) to the Functional (and Reporting) Currency (the Dollar)

In *FAS 52*, **remeasurement** is the process of expressing nonfunctional currency amounts in the functional (and reporting) currency. Accordingly, the term almost always refers to situations in which the *foreign currency* is *not* the functional currency, but the U.S. dollar is.

Foreign operations normally maintain their books and prepare their financial statements in the currency of the country in which they are located—regardless of whether the dollar is their functional currency. Recall that when the *dollar* is the functional currency, *historical exchange rates* are used so that the ***nonmonetary assets* are remeasured into the dollar equivalent of the transactions at the time of the purchase.** Thus the remeasurement process in *FAS 52* refers to the remeasuring that takes place in expressing amounts in the functional currency. Note that when the dollar is the functional currency, translation (as narrowly defined in the preceding paragraph) is *not* necessary because the functional currency is also the reporting currency.

Illustration 16-8 graphically depicts the *FAS 52* distinction between *translation* and *remeasurement*.

Remeasurement and Translation Situations

Infrequently, a foreign operation's functional currency is a foreign currency that is different from the currency it uses to maintain its books and prepare its financial statements. An example would be a Swiss operation that keeps its books in Swiss francs (most likely because of tax laws) but uses the French euro as its functional currency. In such a case, the Swiss financial statements must be "remeasured" and expressed in French euros. Then, the French euro financial statements must be "translated" into dollars. Thus, a *two-step process* is required to obtain amounts in dollars. Most foreign operations require only a *one-step process*, however—either the *translation process or* the *remeasurement process*.

V. CHANGES IN THE FUNCTIONAL CURRENCY

The Foreign Economy *Becomes* Highly Inflationary

If a foreign country's economy becomes a highly inflationary economy for purposes of *FAS 52* (as happened for Mexico in 1997), a change in the functional currency *to* the U.S. dollar is accounted for as follows (pursuant to paragraph 46 of *FAS 52*):

1. The cumulative translation adjustment for *prior periods* is *not* removed from the Accumulated Other Comprehensive Income equity account.

ILLUSTRATION 16-8 DISTINGUISHING TRANSLATION FROM REMEASUREMENT

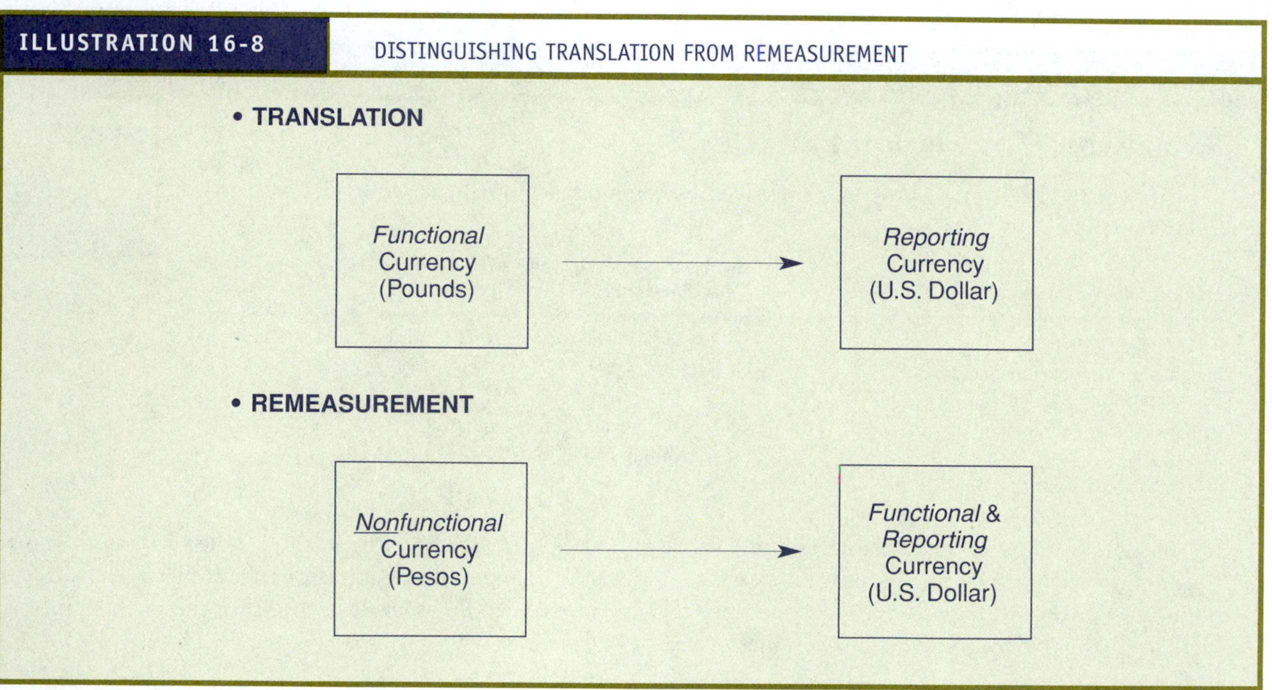

2. The translated amount for *nonmonetary assets* at the end of the *prior period* becomes the financial reporting accounting basis for those assets in the *period of the change* and in *subsequent periods*.

The Foreign Economy *Ceases* Being Highly Inflationary

Occasionally, a change occurs in which (1) a highly inflationary foreign economy *ceases* to be highly inflationary and (2) except for inflation considerations, the subsidiary's functional currency would have been the *local currency*. Paragraph 46 of *FAS 52* does *not* apply to these situations. Instead, Emerging Issues Task Force Issue No. 92–4 applies. The prescribed manner of accounting is somewhat complex and beyond the scope of this text.

VI. Concluding Comments

Even though corporations have expressed hardly any dissatisfaction with *FAS 52* (unlike *FAS 8*, and possibly only because income statement volatility is largely eliminated), it is unfortunate that more of those who studied and voted on this issue did not agree, suggesting that the solution that most closely reflects economic reality was *not* found.

Proponents of the functional currency concept contend that the economic exposure differs for *autonomous* foreign units versus *nonautonomous* foreign units and that the functional currency is intended to deal with these differences.

In Appendix 16B, we present the *current value approach using PPP*. This approach revolves around the **causes of exchange rate changes**—*not* whether the foreign unit uses a *foreign currency* or the *U.S. dollar* in conducting its operations. Under this approach, **the economic exposure for all foreign units is competition** (the same risk that domestic operations face). Thus the *autonomous* versus *nonautonomous* distinction made in *FAS 52* is deemed artificial, irrelevant, and misguided.

Also in Appendix 16B, the financial reporting results under the *current value approach using PPP* are compared with the financial reporting results under both the *current rate method* and the *temporal method*. Accordingly, you will be able to evaluate whether (1) the functional currency concept in *FAS 52* is theoretically sound, (2) management should use the *FAS 52* financial reporting results for internal decision-making purposes, and (3) stockholders should rely on *FAS 52* financial reporting results.

A summary of worldwide translation practices is shown in the International Perspective.

International Perspective

Worldwide Translation Practices

A review of the translation practices employed by the most significant 50 countries reveals the following:

Translation Methods	Number or Percentage of Countries Using This Particular Translation Method
Current rate method	Nearly 50% (including almost all of Western Europe and Japan)
Temporal method or its monetary-nonmonetary method equivalent	Nearly 50%
Current-noncurrent method	Very few (no major countries)
Both the current rate method and the temporal method	Three (United States, United Kingdom, Canada)

In 1983, the International Accounting Standards Committee (discussed in Chapter 13) issued *International Accounting Standard No. 21*, "Accounting for the Effects of Changes in Foreign Exchange Rates." This pronouncement (revised slightly in 1993) mirrors *FAS 52* in that it allows the use of either the *current rate method* or the *temporal method*, depending on the circumstances.

END-OF-CHAPTER REVIEW

Summary of Key Points

1. Under the **U.S. dollar unit of measure approach,** the foreign currency relationships are **not** maintained in translation (a new set of relationships is produced), the **temporal method of translation** is used, and the financial position focus is on the **net monetary (asset or liability) position.**
2. *FAS 52* is built on the **functional currency concept,** which presumes that the currency in which a foreign unit **primarily generates and expends cash** reflects whether the foreign unit is relatively *autonomous* or *nonautonomous*.
3. **Autonomous** foreign units have the **foreign currency** as the functional currency—their financial statements are translated using the **current rate method.**
4. **Nonautonomous** foreign units have the **U.S. dollar** as the functional currency—their financial statements are translated using the **temporal method.**
5. Illustration 16-9 contains a summary of accounting for the translation of foreign currency financial statements once the functional currency has been determined.
6. Illustration 16-10 compares the various translation methodologies.

Glossary of New Terms

Current-noncurrent method One of three translation methods that achieves a U.S. dollar unit of measure. An asset or liability's classification as to current or noncurrent determines the exchange rate to use.

ILLUSTRATION 16-9 SUMMARY OF ACCOUNTING FOR THE TRANSLATION OF FOREIGN CURRENCY FINANCIAL STATEMENTS

	Functional Currency	
	Foreign Currency	**U.S. Dollar**
Approach/unit of measure to be used	Foreign Currency	U.S. Dollar
Translation method to be used	Current rate	Temporal
Exchange rates to be used for:		
Assets and liabilities	Current rate[a]	Combination of current[a] and historical rates
Income statement accounts	Current rate[b]	Combination of current[b] and historical rates
Treatment to be accorded the effect of a change in the exchange rate	Direct charge or credit to ***Other Comprehensive Income*** (pending liquidation or disposal of the investment)	Immediate recognition in ***earnings***
Terms used in *FAS 52* to describe:		
The translation process	Translation	Remeasurement
The effect of a change in the exchange rate	Translation adjustment	Foreign currency transaction gain or loss from remeasurement
Deemed functional currency for operations in highly inflationary economies		U.S. Dollar

[a] *Current rate* here means the exchange rate existing ***at* the balance sheet date.**

[b] *Current rate* here means the exchange rate existing **when the items were *recognized* in the income statement.**

ILLUSTRATION 16-10 SUMMARY COMPARISON OF TRANSLATION RATES USED

	Current Rate Method *Chapter 15*	Temporal Method *Chapter 16*	PPP Current Value Approach *Appendix 16B*
Income Statement:			
Sales	A	A	A
Cost of Sales:			
Beginning inventory	*(not translated)*	P	*(not translated)*
+ Purchases	*(not translated)*	A	*(not translated)*
= Goods Available for Sale	*(not translated)*	*(a subtotal)*	*(not translated)*
− Ending inventory	*(not translated)*	H	*(not translated)*
= Cost of Sales	A	*(a subtotal)*	A
Depreciation expense	A	H	A
Operating expenses	A	A	A
Income tax expense	A	A	A
Statement of Retained Earnings:			
Beginning Balance	P	P	P
+ Net Income	(per P/L)	(per P/L)	(per P/L)
− Dividends declared	D	D	D
Ending Balance	*(a subtotal)*	*(a subtotal)*	*(a subtotal)*
Balance Sheet:			
Assets			
Cash	C	C	C
Accounts receivable	C	C	C
Inventory	C	H	C
Land	C	H	F
Buildings and equipment	C	H	F
Accumulated depreciation	C	H	F
Liabilities			
Accounts payable and accruals	C	C	C
Long-term debt	C	C	C
Equity Accounts			
Common stock	H	H	H
Retained earnings	*(a subtotal)*	*(a subtotal)*	*(a subtotal)*
Cumulative translation adjustment:			
Prior years	P	P	P
Current year	(forced out)	(forced out)	(forced out)

Code:

A = AVERAGE RATE: But only if it produces results close to those produced using the current rate when the item was ***recognized in earnings***—otherwise use the current rate.

C = CURRENT RATE: The spot rate at the balance sheet date for assets and liabilities; the spot rate when the item was ***recognized in earnings*** for income statement accounts.

D = DIVIDEND DECLARATION DATE RATE

F = Adjusted for foreign inflation ***before*** translation at the current rate.

H = HISTORICAL RATE: The date when the item (or related item) ***entered*** the balance sheet.

P = PRIOR YEAR END AMOUNT

Monetary-nonmonetary method One of three translation methods that achieves a U.S. dollar unit of measure (an asset or liability classification as to monetary or nonmonetary determines the exchange rate to use).

Net monetary asset position Having monetary *assets* in excess of monetary *liabilities*.

Net monetary liability position Having monetary *liabilities* in excess of monetary *assets*.

Remeasurement The process of going from a *nonfunctional currency* (a foreign currency) to the *functional* (and reporting) *currency* (the dollar).

Remeasurement gains and losses The name given to the effects of exchange rate changes reported under the temporal method (formally called foreign currency transaction gains and losses in *FAS 52*).

Temporal method One of three translation methods that achieves a U.S. dollar unit of measure (an asset or liability basis of valuation determines the exchange rate to use).

Translation (distinguished from remeasurement) The process of going from the *functional currency* (a foreign currency) to the *reporting currency* (the dollar).

U.S. dollar unit of measure approach A manner of translating foreign currency financial statements that changes the unit of measure to the U.S. dollar (changes financial relationships).

Assignment Material

Review Questions

1. What is the *U.S. dollar unit of measure approach*? Summarize it.
2. What translation methods achieve a *U.S. dollar unit of measure approach*?
3. What is the theory underlying the *temporal method*?
4. What is the financial focus of the *U.S. dollar unit of measure approach*?
5. When the *temporal method* is used, how is the effect of the exchange rate change reported under *FAS 52*?
6. When the *temporal method* is used, what is the effect of the exchange rate change called under *FAS 52*?
7. What are six balance sheet accounts for which *historical exchange rates* are used under the *temporal method*?
8. What are five income statement accounts for which *historical exchange rates* are used under the *temporal method*?
9. When is it necessary to address *realization* of a foreign unit's *nonmonetary* assets in dollars?
10. What dilemma exists in considering whether to hedge a net monetary liability position?
11. On what critical assumption is *FAS 52* constructed?
12. Are the two *FAS 52 objectives of translation* incompatible? Why or why not?
13. What purpose does the *functional currency concept* serve?
14. Is the *functional currency concept* necessary to use *multiple units of measure*?
15. What are the *factors* used to determine the functional currency?
16. What *two categories* of foreign operations are presumed to exist under the functional currency concept?
17. When the *economic factors* set forth in *FAS 52* do not clearly indicate the functional currency, which currency must be used?
18. How are *highly inflationary economies* dealt with in *FAS 52*?
19. What is the definition of a *highly inflationary economy*?
20. What is the difference between *translation* and *remeasurement*?
21. How are the effects of exchange rate changes treated in *remeasurement* situations?
22. What two essential elements are necessary for achieving meaningful translated reporting results?
23. How is the *true economic effect* of an exchange rate change determined?

Exercises

E 16-1 **Determining the Financial Position from the Effect and Direction of Exchange Rate Changes** Information for the overseas subsidiaries of Hubb Inc. for 2006 follows:

Country	Translation Method	Direction of Direct Exchange Rate in 2006	Effect of Change in Exchange Rate
Brazil	Temporal	Decreased	Favorable
Mexico	Temporal	Decreased	Unfavorable
Sweden	Current rate	Increased	Favorable
Belgium	Current rate	Increased	Unfavorable
Ireland	Current rate	Decreased	Unfavorable
Spain	Current rate	Decreased	Favorable
Saudi Arabia	Temporal	Increased	Favorable
Japan	Temporal	Increased	Unfavorable

Required Determine the appropriate financial position that each of these foreign operations was in during the year for the listed effect to have resulted.

E 16-2 **Calculating the Effect of an Exchange Rate Change** Pondox has a foreign subsidiary in a country in which the *direct* exchange rate *decreased* from $.25 to $.20 during 2006. The average balances of the individual assets and liabilities during 2006 follow:

	Units of Foreign Currency
Cash	80,000
Accounts receivable	220,000
Inventory	275,000
Fixed assets, net	425,000
Total Assets	1,000,000
Accounts payable and accruals	325,000
Current portion of long-term debt	25,000
Intercompany payable	100,000
Long-term debt	300,000
Deferred income taxes payable	50,000
Total Liabilities	800,000

Assume that the carrying value of the parent's Investment account on 1/1/06 was $50,000 for this 100%-owned subsidiary that was created in late 2005 when the *direct* exchange rate was $.25.

Required

1. Determine the effect of the exchange rate change for 2006 under the *temporal method.*
2. Repeat requirement 1 using the *current rate method.*

E 16-3 **Calculating the Effect of an Exchange Rate Change** Kobb Inc. has a 100%-owned foreign subsidiary. The average balances of the subsidiary's assets and liabilities during 2006 follow:

	LCU
Monetary assets	4,000,000
Nonmonetary assets	6,000,000
Total Assets	10,000,000
Liabilities (all monetary)	9,000,000
Stockholders' equity	1,000,000
Total Liabilities and Equity	10,000,000

The *direct* exchange rate *decreased* steadily during 2006 from $.40 at 1/1/06 to $.30 at 12/31/06.

Required

1. Determine the effect of the change in the exchange rate for 2006 under the temporal method.
2. Repeat requirement 1 using the *current rate method.*
3. Which reporting result best reflects economic reality?

E 16-4 **Selecting Proper Exchange Rates: Balance Sheet Accounts** The following accounts exist in a foreign subsidiary's books:

1. Allowance for Doubtful Accounts.
2. Inventory (carried at *cost*).
3. Inventory (carried at *market*, which is *below* cost).
4. Inventory (carried at *market*, which *exceeds* cost).
5. Marketable Equity Securities (carried at *market*, which *exceeds* historical cost).
6. Marketable Bonds (*expected* to be held to maturity).
7. Marketable Bonds (*not* expected to be held to maturity).
8. Patents.
9. Equipment.
10. Accumulated Depreciation.
11. Intercompany Payable.
12. Long-Term Debt.
13. Income Taxes Payable.
14. Deferred Income Taxes Payable.
15. Common Stock.
16. Additional Paid-in Capital.
17. Retained Earnings.
18. Revaluation Capital (from inflation adjustments).

Required Determine whether the *historical exchange rate*, the *current exchange rate*, an *average exchange rate*, or some other procedure should be used to translate these accounts under the *temporal method*.

E 16-5 **Selecting Proper Exchange Rates: Income Statement Accounts** The following accounts exist in a foreign subsidiary's books:

1. Revenues.
2. Intercompany Sales to Parent Company.
3. Purchases.
4. Intercompany Purchases from Parent Company.
5. Cost of Sales.
6. Marketing Expenses.
7. Depreciation Expense.
8. Income Tax Expense.
9. Goodwill Amortization Expense.
10. Loss on Abandonment of Fixed Assets.
11. Gain on Sale of Equipment.
12. Intercompany Interest Expense.

13. Depreciation Expense (incremental amount resulting from adjusting assets for inflation).

14. Inventory Loss from Flood Damage.

Required Determine whether the *historical exchange rate*, the *current exchange rate*, an *average exchange rate*, or some other procedure should be used to translate these accounts under the *temporal method*.

E 16-6 **Translating Depreciation Expense** Kona Inc. owns a foreign subsidiary with 3,600,000 local currency units (LCU) of property, plant, and equipment before accumulated depreciation at 12/31/06. Of this amount, 2,400,000 LCU were acquired in 2004 when the exchange rate was 5 LCU to $1; 1,200,000 LCU were acquired in 2005 when the exchange rate was 8 LCU to $1.

The exchange rate in effect at 12/31/06 was 10 LCU to $1. The average of exchange rates that were in effect during 2006 was 12 LCU to $1. Assume that the property, plant, and equipment are depreciated using the *straight-line method* over a 10-year period with *no* salvage value.

Required
1. Are these exchange rates given the *direct* rates or the *indirect* rates?
2. Determine the dollar amount of depreciation expense for 2006 assuming that the foreign operation's functional currency is the
   a. LCU.
   b. Dollar.

E 16-7 **Translating a Gain on a Fixed Asset Disposal** A Mexican subsidiary sold equipment acquired in prior years costing Mex$ 6,000,000 on 4/1/05 for Mex$ 2,500,000 when the exchange rate was $.008. (The exchange rate existing when the equipment was purchased several years ago was $.05.) A Mex$ 1,000,000 gain relating to this disposal is recorded in the general ledger.

The exchange rate at 12/31/05 is Mex$ 200 to $1; however, the average relationship for 2005 was Mex$ 150 to $1.

Required Determine the amount of the gain in dollars assuming the following:
1. The peso is the functional currency.
2. The dollar is the functional currency.

E 16-8 **Translating and Performing a Lower-of-Cost-or-Market Test in Dollars for Inventory** The following selected information is provided in connection with the translation of a Mexican subsidiary's 12/31/06 financial statements. The 12/31/06 inventory was acquired when the following exchange rates existed:

Pesos	Direct Rate
1,000,000	$.009
3,000,000	.008
7,000,000	.007
10,000,000	.006
15,000,000	.005
36,000,000	

The *replacement cost* of the inventory is Mex$ 38,000,000, the net realizable value is Mex$ 60,000,000, and the *net realizable value* less a normal profit margin is Mex$ 40,000,000.

The exchange rate at 12/31/06 is Mex$ 200 to $1; however, the average relationship for 2006 was Mex$ 150 to $1.

Required Perform a lower-of-cost-or-market test in dollars assuming the following:
1. The *peso* is the functional currency.
2. The *dollar* is the functional currency.

E 16-9 **Determining When to Hedge Balance Sheet Exposure** Ponder Inc. often enters into forward exchange contracts to hedge its exposure on its foreign operations. Ponder must determine whether it should contract to *buy* or *sell* a foreign currency in each of the following situations:

Area of Foreign Currency Exposure	Future Expectation: Direct Rate or Currency	Future Expectation: Direction	Buy	Sell	Neither
1. Net investment in a foreign subsidiary	U.S. dollar	Strengthen	______	______	______
	U.S. dollar	Weaken	______	______	______
	Foreign	Strengthen	______	______	______
	Foreign	Weaken	______	______	______
2. Net monetary asset position of a foreign subsidiary	U.S. dollar	Strengthen	______	______	______
	U.S. dollar	Weaken	______	______	______
	Foreign	Strengthen	______	______	______
	Foreign	Weaken	______	______	______
3. Net monetary liability position of a foreign subsidiary	U.S. dollar	Strengthen	______	______	______
	U.S. dollar	Weaken	______	______	______
	Foreign	Strengthen	______	______	______
	Foreign	Weaken	______	______	______

Required Put an X in the appropriate column in the table.

Problems

P 16-1 **Comparing Reporting Results** On 12/3/05 Pella created a 100%-owned real estate development subsidiary, Sella, in France. Pella paid $2,500,000 cash for common stock of Sella on this date. Also on this date, Sella converted the $2,500,000 into 5,000,000 euros. It immediately acquired land for 4,000,000 euros and left the remaining 1,000,000 euros in a checking account for all of 2006 (earning no interest). Sella had no expenses in 2006. The exchange rate at 12/31/06 is 1 euro equals $.40. France had 25% inflation during 2006, which caused the 2006 exchange rate decrease.

Required

1. Translate Sella's balance sheet at 12/31/06 under the *current rate method.*
2. Translate Sella's balance sheet at 12/31/06 under the temporal method.
3. Calculate the parent's increase or decrease in cash for 2006 if the subsidiary were liquidated at 12/31/06 (with the land being sold at its current value of 5,000,000 euros). Compare this reporting result to the results in requirements 1 and 2. Comment accordingly.

P 16-2* **Translation (Remeasurement) Worksheet** Assume the information provided in Problem 15-2 (pages 529–531).

Required

1. Calculate the remeasurement gain or loss for 2006 by analyzing the monetary items. (Assume that at the *beginning* of 2006, the subsidiary had *monetary assets* of 1,300,000 euros and *monetary liabilities* of 5,700,000 euros. Also assume that cash disbursed in payment of liabilities during 2006 was 9,800,000 euros [*excluding* the 200,000 euros paid for the equipment purchase in early 2006 when the direct exchange rate was $.14]).
2. Remeasure the financial statements into dollars, assuming the following:
   a. The *dollar* is the functional currency.
   b. From the dollar financial statements, the retained earnings amount at 12/31/05 was $268,000.
3. Prepare the parent company's entry or entries at 12/31/06 relating to the *equity method* of accounting.
4. Prepare a T-account analysis of the parent's Investment account since the creation of the subsidiary.
5. Qualitatively assess whether the subsidiary had a good year or a bad year, considering whether its nonmonetary assets are realizable in dollars.
6. Prepare the general ledger entry that would be made if the subsidiary were sold for $400,000 cash on 1/3/07.
7. **Optional** (check with your instructor): Prepare a translated statement of cash flows for 2006 using the direct method.

---

* The financial information presented for problems accompanied by asterisks is also provided on Model 16 (filename: MODEL16) at the **http://pahler.swlearning.com** website, allowing the problem to be worked on the computer.

P 16-3* **Translation (Remeasurement) Worksheet** Assume the information provided in Problem 15-3 (pages 531–533).

Required

1. Calculate the remeasurement gain or loss for 2006 by analyzing the monetary items. (Assume that at the *beginning* of 2006, the subsidiary had *monetary assets* of 800,000 euros and *monetary liabilities* of 2,000,000 euros. Also assume that cash disbursed in payment of liabilities during 2006 was 3,850,000 euros.)
2. Remeasure the financial statements into dollars assuming the following:
   a. The dollar is the functional currency.
   b. From the dollar financial statements, the retained earnings amount at 12/31/05 was $1,060,000.
3. Prepare the parent company's entry or entries at 12/31/06 under the *equity method* of accounting.
4. Prepare a T-account analysis of the parent's Investment account from inception of the subsidiary.
5. Evaluate whether the subsidiary is likely to have a realizability problem in dollars for its nonmonetary assets.
6. Prepare the general ledger entry that would be made if the subsidiary were sold for $1,240,000 cash on 1/3/07.
7. **Optional** (check with your instructor): Prepare a translated statement of cash flows for 2006 using the direct method.

P 16-4 **Translating a Statement of Cash Flows** Use the information provided in Illustrations 16-5 and 16-6. In addition, assume that cash receipts from collections on accounts receivable totaled Mex$ 6,200,000 during 2006. Also assume that cash receipts and cash disbursements (*other than* the cash dividend paid to the parent) occurred evenly throughout the year. There were no borrowings or repayments of debt in 2006—only debt interest payments totaling Mex$ 300,000.

Required

1. Calculate the subsidiary's 1/1/06 balances in pesos for its Cash account and its Accounts Receivable account. (See if you can find the *two* ways to determine the cash balance.)
2. Prepare a translated statement of cash flows for 2006 using the *direct* method. (*Hint*: Think about what amount would appear in the translated statement of cash flows if [a] the subsidiary's only asset or liability during all of 2006 was a noninterest-bearing checking account having a balance of Mex$ 400,000 throughout the year and [b] the subsidiary had no revenues or expenses for 2006.)
3. Assuming that the average balance of the subsidiary's assets for 2006 was Mex$ 8,000,000, calculate the approximate loss of valuation on the *total* assets for 2006 under the *current rate method*. To what amount in the translated statement of cash flows does this amount relate? Explain the relationship.

P 16-5 **Hedging Net Asset and Net Monetary Positions** Puntex's foreign subsidiary had the following average account balances for 2006 expressed in its local currency (LCU):

Monetary assets	400,000	Monetary liabilities	300,000
Nonmonetary assets	400,000	Stockholders' equity	500,000

Net income for 2006 was 100,000 LCU earned evenly throughout the year and remitted to the parent monthly. During 2006, the LCU weakened 25%, the *direct* (spot) rate going from $.40 to $.30. Various assumptions for different situations follow:

Situation	Functional Currency	Item Hedged
A	LCU	Net investment
B	LCU	Net monetary asset position
C	U.S. dollar	Net investment
D	U.S. dollar	Net monetary asset position
E	U.S. dollar	Net monetary liability position (For situation E, assume that average monetary liabilities were 500,000 LCU and average stockholders' equity was 300,000 LCU.)

For situations A, B, C, and D, assume that management expected the LCU to weaken during 2006 and hedged the item indicated using forward exchange contracts entered into on 1/1/06 and terminated 12/31/06. For situation E, assume that management expected the LCU to strengthen during 2006 and hedged accordingly. (For simplicity, assume that the forward rate on 1/1/06 for a one-year *forward exchange contract* was $.40.)

Required For each situation, determine the following and indicate how the amounts should be reported for 2006:

1. The hedging gain or loss.
2. The translation adjustment or the gain or loss from the remeasurement process, as appropriate.

P 16-6 **Highly Inflationary Economy: Recording a General Price-Level Change** Subbco is a 100%-owned foreign subsidiary located in a country that wishes to prepare financial statements that are (a) restated for general price-level changes and (b) in accordance with U.S. GAAP (except for price-level adjustments). Assume that

1. Subbco has just completed its first year of operations (2006).
2. On 1/1/06, Subbco acquired land at a cost of 100,000 LCU.
3. The inflation rate for 2006 was 50%.
4. The foreign government, which has a 25% corporate income tax rate, will allow the tax basis of fixed assets to be restated by 40% for 2006.

Required

1. What entry(ies) should be made on the foreign subsidiary's books to restate for general price-level changes?
2. Record the related deferred tax adjustment required under *FAS 109*, "Accounting for Income Taxes." Assume that it is proper GAAP to record *deferred* taxes relating to this item for this particular subsidiary.
3. What entry(ies) would be made if the land were sold for 150,000 LCU on 1/2/07?

THINKING CRITICALLY

Cases

C 16-1 **Analyzing an Annual Report Disclosure** In its 1995 annual report, Ford Motor Company stated that the remeasurement gains reported in the 1995 income statement from operations in highly inflationary economies were mostly offset by higher cost of sales that resulted from the use of *historical exchange rates* for inventories sold during 1995.

Assume that (1) the *direct* exchange rate *decreased* in 1995 for the countries in which these operations were located and (2) each foreign operation's total assets were composed of 20% monetary items, 30% inventory, and 50% fixed assets.

Required

1. For this to occur, what had to be the financial position of these foreign units?
2. What was the percentage of debt to total assets for these operations?

C 16-2 **Crediting the Remeasurement Gain to Interest Expense: Why Would They Do That?** Some companies having foreign subsidiaries in *highly inflationary economies* report their foreign currency transaction gains from remeasurement as a *reduction* of interest expense.

Required What justification might exist for this treatment?

C 16-3 **Evaluating One of the FASB Objectives of Translation** *FAS 52* states that translation should accomplish the objective of providing "information that is generally compatible with the expected economic effects of a rate change on an enterprise's cash flows and equity." For simplicity, assume that the foreign unit's *monetary assets* equal its *monetary liabilities* and that its *fixed assets* are financed entirely by *equity*.

Required

1. If the direct exchange rate *decreases* solely because of *foreign* inflation.
2. If the direct exchange rate *increases* solely because of *domestic* inflation.
3. If the direct exchange rate *decreases* solely because of *noninflationary* factors.

Determine whether the current rate method accomplishes the preceding objective.

C 16-4 **Determining the Functional Currency** Handy Company manufactures soap domestically and in a foreign country, which has low labor costs. The foreign operation (conducted through a wholly owned subsidiary) purchases all of its raw materials from the parent company, which can obtain volume discounts because of its size. (Were it not for the volume discount, the foreign subsidiary would purchase the raw materials directly from suppliers.) The foreign subsidiary's purchases from the parent company are denominated in dollars.

All of the subsidiary's sales are in the subsidiary's local currency, the mun, and all employees are paid in muns. The parent company has established that the subsidiary's dividend policy is to convert available funds into dollars as quickly as possible each month for current or near-term distribution to the parent.

Required Determine whether the functional currency is the dollar or the mun.

C 16-5 **Translating Land When No Functional Currency Exists** Puzzlex Inc. formed a foreign manufacturing subsidiary in 2001. In 2008 an earthquake destroyed the subsidiary's manufacturing facility. Because the subsidiary had become marginally profitable in recent years, the parent decided not to rebuild the manufacturing plant. The parent decided to maintain the subsidiary as a passive investment, however, with the subsidiary having land as the only asset because the location was highly desirable and the opportunity for significant appreciation in the near future existed. All liabilities were paid off with the insurance proceeds. Until the earthquake, the subsidiary's functional currency had been the local currency.

Required

1. Should the balance in the AOCI—Cumulative Translation Adjustment account be taken into income?
2. How should the land be translated in future periods?
3. How would you translate the land in future periods if the land had been purchased outright as a passive investment in 2008?

Financial Analysis Problems

FAP 16-1 **Evaluating the Impact of the 1997–98 Asian Currency Crisis** Seagate Technology, Inc., the world's largest disk drive maker, manufactures nearly all of its disk drives in seven Southeast Asian countries. More than 75% of Seagate's disk drives go into computers and servers that are sold in markets *other than* Japan and Asia. Most components are paid for in U.S. dollars.

The currencies of nearly all of these countries weakened between 50% and 80% between 7/1/97 and 6/30/98.

Required Assess the financial impact of this currency crisis.

FAP 16-2 **Evaluating the Impact of a Weakening Dollar** Zell Inc. is a domestic company that established a manufacturing subsidiary in Belgium in 2001. In establishing this foreign operation, Zell minimized the number of dollars taken out of the United States by financing the subsidiary's manufacturing plant through a loan obtained from a Belgian financial institution. This loan is being repaid over 25 years. As a result, the subsidiary is thinly capitalized.

During 2006 the dollar weakened approximately 20% against the euro, as concerns arose over the sizable U.S. foreign trade deficit, the federal spending deficit, and the inability to control inflation. (The euro held steady against the other major currencies of the world.) In *euros,* the subsidiary had a *profit* for the current year comparable to that of the prior year. In *dollars,* the subsidiary had a *loss* for the current year, compared with a *profit* for the prior year.

Required

1. Considering the following, how is it possible to report a loss on the foreign operation for the current year?
   a. The parent minimized its dollars at risk by financing the foreign plant with local borrowings.
   b. The operation was run as efficiently this year as in the prior year.
2. Is this an *economic loss* or a *paper loss*? Explain your answer.
3. Is there any way the loss could have been avoided?

FAP 16-3 **Evaluating the Impact of a Weakening Foreign Currency** Assume that you are the controller of a domestic company that established operations in Mexico two years ago. These foreign operations are conducted through a Mexican subsidiary. The subsidiary has three operational manufacturing plants, all of which cost approximately the same amount and were financed as follows:

1. The first plant was financed entirely from the parent's *capital stock investment* in the subsidiary.
2. The second plant was financed entirely from a *long-term loan from a local Mexican bank,* none of which has been repaid.
3. The third plant was financed entirely from an interest-bearing, *long-term loan from the parent,* none of which has been repaid. (The loan is payable in dollars.)

During the month preceding the annual shareholders' meeting, the Mexican peso declined approximately 30% in value. You are sure a question will arise at the shareholders' meeting concerning the financial consequences of this decline.

Required

1. Without regard to using a particular translation method, prepare a brief summary of the impact of the decline in the value of the peso on the company's foreign operations.
2. Indicate the effect of the exchange rate change that will be reported for the current year for each of the plants under the *current rate* method.
3. Repeat requirement 2 using the *temporal* method.

part six

Miscellaneous Corporate Reporting Topics

VI

chapter

17

Interim Period Reporting

Time has no divisions to mark its passage; there is never a thunderstorm or blare of trumpets to announce the beginning of a new month or year. Even when a new century begins, it is only we mortals who ring bells and fire off pistols.

THOMAS MANN

LEARNING OBJECTIVES

To Understand

- **The importance of the quarterly reporting process.**
- **The conceptual issues peculiar to interim period reporting.**
- **The requirements of the various professional pronouncements, particularly the latitude that exists in several areas.**
- **The role of certified public accountants in the interim period reporting process.**
- **The high potential for arbitrarily shifting profits between interim periods, often called *managing the earnings*.**

TOPIC OUTLINE

CHAPTER OVERVIEW

Applicability

Users of financial data need continuous, timely information about the performance of an enterprise to make investment or credit-related decisions. Although it has the benefit of an independent audit, an annual report is inadequate by itself in meeting these needs. Accordingly, the reporting of quarterly financial data has become a basic part of the corporate reporting process. *Quarterly* periods are sufficiently short to reveal business turning points, which may be obscured in *annual* reports. For companies that have significant seasonal variations in their operations, quarterly financial reports may give investors a better understanding of the nature of the business.

No official accounting pronouncement of the FASB or of any of its predecessor organizations requires quarterly financial reporting. The New York Stock Exchange and the American Stock Exchange, however, require their listed companies to furnish interim quarterly operating results to their stockholders. Companies not subject to these stock exchange listing requirements usually furnish such reports voluntarily. In fact, many privately owned companies furnish financial information to their stockholders as often as monthly.

Requirements of the Securities and Exchange Commission

Publicly owned companies that are subject to the continuous reporting requirements of the Securities and Exchange Commission (SEC) must file with it interim period financial statements on Form 10-Q. This form must be filed for each of the first three quarters of each fiscal year within 35 days after the end of each such quarter.[1] Furthermore, the SEC requires specified quarterly financial data pertaining to operations for the latest two years to be presented in the annual report sent to stockholders and in the annual financial statements that must be filed with the SEC on Form 10-K.[2] (Forms 10-Q and 10-K are discussed in detail in Chapter 18.) Such disclosures inform investors of the pattern of corporate activities throughout the year.

See the International Perspective for (1) foreign interim period reporting intervals used and (2) SEC reporting requirements for foreign issuers whose securities are traded in the United States.

Official Accounting Pronouncements

The first and still current pronouncement specifically dealing with interim reports is *APB Opinion 28*, "Interim Financial Reporting," issued in 1973. This pronouncement has been amended by FASB *Statement 3*, "Reporting Accounting Changes in Interim Financial Statements," and interpreted by FASB *Interpretation 18*, "Accounting for Income Taxes in Interim Periods." Also, slight amendments were made to the pronouncement by FASB *Statement 109*, "Accounting for Income Taxes." *APBO 28* is divided into two major parts:

1. Part I does *not* require interim financial reports to be issued but sets accounting standards to be used in preparing them.
2. Part II sets minimum disclosures to be included in interim financial reports issued by publicly owned companies.

Interim period financial statements filed with the SEC on Form 10-Q must be prepared in accordance with the provisions of *APBO 28* and any amendments. We discuss these items shortly.

---

[1] Companies whose securities are listed on a stock exchange and companies meeting certain size tests whose securities are traded in the over-the-counter market are subject to the continuous reporting requirements of the SEC.

[2] Proxy and Information Statement Rule 14a-3(b)(3): Form 10-K, Item 8 and Regulation S-K, Item 302(a) (Washington, D.C.: Securities and Exchange Commission).

International Perspective

Foreign Interim Period Reporting Practices

For foreign countries that have interim period reporting requirements, the frequency of reporting is **semiannually.**

SEC Rules Applicable to Foreign Issuers Whose Securities Are Traded in the United States

SEC Accommodation #1. Foreign companies whose securities are traded in the United States need file only *semiannual* reports—not *quarterly* reports—with the Securities and Exchange Commission (on SEC *Form 6-K*, a form applicable only to *foreign* issuers). Thus these companies *need not* file interim period reports more frequently in the *United States* than they do in their *home countries.* (Such reports, however, must either (1) conform to U.S. GAAP or (2) contain a schedule that reconciles foreign GAAP net income to U.S. GAAP net income.)

SEC Accommodation #2. The information to be included on SEC Form 6-K *need not* be any more extensive than what the issuer is required to furnish in the issuer's *home country.* (In almost all cases, those requirements are *less stringent* than those of U.S. GAAP.)

Commentary. Granting concessions to foreign companies has its pros and cons. The main argument against concessions is that it is unfair to hold domestic companies to reporting standards *higher* than those used by foreign companies. Doing so implies that U.S. investors need *more* protection from *domestic* companies than they do from *foreign* companies. Thus domestic companies can argue that the U.S. reporting standards should be *lowered.*

I. The Impact of Technology on the Quarterly Reporting Process

Electronic Delivery to Shareholders

In general, publicly owned companies have traditionally mailed hard copy quarterly reports to their shareholders. Many companies (Apple Computer, Inc., and Intel Corporation, for example) have discontinued this practice, however, to save money and enable their shareholders to obtain the information more quickly by using the Internet to view and download the information electronically (typically using Netscape Navigator, Microsoft Internet Explorer, or one of the computerized information services, such as America Online). For most companies that make their quarterly reports available in this fashion, investors who desire a hard copy quarterly report must write for one each quarter.

Electronic Delivery to SEC

As explained in Chapter 18, the SEC requires companies subject to its continuous reporting requirements to file their *quarterly* and *annual* reports with the SEC electronically (using EDGAR).

Speeding the Delivery and Filing Dates

The use of e-mail and electronic commerce has enabled most companies to greatly speed up their quarterly closing process, enabling them to (1) make the quarterly reports available earlier, (2) save money, and (3) concentrate more quickly on the new quarter. (See the Case in Point.)

CASE IN POINT

In 2001, Cisco Systems (which does nearly 75% of its business using electronic commerce) became the first major company to develop a highly sophisticated reporting system that enables it to close its books **each and every day.** (Numerous other companies can do so in *several days*, enabling them to file their quarterly 10-Q reports within 10 days of the quarter-end.)

In 1999, Microsoft's finance team stated that it can close its books in four days (down from two weeks five years earlier). By 2003, Microsoft had nearly achieved a "continuous close"—where information is accurate and current every day of the month.

II. CONCEPTUAL ISSUES

The fundamental conceptual issue concerning interim period financial statements (whether *complete* or *condensed*) is whether or not they should be prepared in accordance with the same accounting principles and practices used to prepare annual financial statements. **This issue pertains almost solely to the recognition of costs and expenses** because accountants generally agree that for interim period reporting purposes, no sensible alternatives exist to the long-established practice of recognizing revenue when it is earned. The following examples of costs and expenses illustrate the problems associated with their treatment for interim period reporting purposes:

1. **Major advertising expenditures.** Suppose that a major advertising campaign is launched early in the year. For *interim* reporting purposes, should the cost be deferred as an asset and amortized throughout the year, even though no portion of advertising costs can be deferred and reported as an asset at the end of the *annual* reporting period?
2. **Seasonal repairs.** Suppose that a company historically makes major *annual* repairs late in the year. Accruing liabilities for future repair costs (other than warranty-related costs) is not proper at the end of an annual reporting period. Is it proper, therefore, to spread total estimated repairs throughout the year by accruing such costs in *interim* periods prior to their incurrence?
3. **Depreciation and rent.** In most cases, depreciation and rent expenses are computed for *annual* reporting purposes based on the *passage of time*. Should a year's depreciation and rent expense associated with nonmanufacturing activities be assigned to *interim* periods for interim reporting purposes on this same basis, or should some other basis (such as sales) be used?
4. **Social security taxes.** The employer pays social security taxes only during a *portion* of the year for employees who have incomes higher than the maximum amount on which employer's social security taxes must be paid. Should the employer's social security taxes for these employees be charged to expense over the *entire* year, using deferrals?
5. **Year-end bonuses.** Should year-end bonuses be anticipated and accrued for *interim* period reporting purposes?

Three schools of thought concerning the approach used in interim reporting exist: the *discrete view*, the *integral view*, and the *combination discrete-integral view*.

The Discrete View

Under the **discrete view**, an *interim period* is a **discrete, self-contained segment of history**, as is an *annual period*; therefore, an *interim period* must stand on its own. From this perspective, the results of operations for each *interim* period are determined employing the same accounting principles and practices used to prepare *annual* reports. No special deferral or accrual practices are used for interim reporting purposes unless they can be used for annual reporting purposes. As a result, the components of assets, liabilities, revenues, expenses, and earnings are defined for *interim reporting* purposes the same way they are for *annual reporting* purposes. Under the discrete view, **the**

function of accounting is to record transactions and events as they occur. Thus the period of time for which results of operations are determined should *not* influence how such transactions and events are reported.

This approach is unacceptable to most accountants because it does *not* allow *accruals*, *deferrals*, and *estimations* at *interim* dates for *annual* items.

The Integral View

Under the **integral view**, an *interim period* is an **integral part of an *annual period*.** From this perspective, the expected relationship between revenues and expenses for the *annual period* should be reflected in the *interim periods* so that reasonably constant operating profit margins can be reported throughout the year. Under this "pure form" of the integral view, ***annual expenses* are estimated and assigned to *interim periods* in proportion to revenues recognized.** Consequently, special deferral and accrual practices are used for *interim reporting* purposes that may *not* be used for *annual reporting* purposes. As a result, the components of assets, liabilities, revenues, expenses, and earnings are defined differently for *interim reporting* purposes than for *annual reporting* purposes. The costs of unforeseen events and certain other nonoperating items—such as *settlement of litigation*, *discontinued operations*, and *asset disposals*—are recorded in the interim period in which they occur.

This approach is also unacceptable to most accountants because of the artificial assumption that each dollar of revenue attracts the same rate of operating profit margin. Such an assumption is no more appropriate for periods within a year than it is over a company's entire life cycle.

The Combination Discrete-Integral View

Between the extremes of the *discrete view* and the pure form of the *integral view* are various **combination discrete-integral approaches.** Under these approaches, the *integral view* is used for some costs, and the *discrete view* is used for the remaining costs. All methods of deciding which costs are treated with integral techniques and which are treated under the discrete view are arbitrary. The remainder of this chapter discusses *APBO 28*, which prescribes a combination discrete-integral approach.

Check Point

Under the *discrete view*

a. An interim period *cannot* stand on its own.
b. The period of time for which results of operations are being determined influences how such transactions and events are reported.
c. Accounting procedures that result in reasonably constant operating profit margins throughout the year are used.
d. Events and transactions are recorded as they occur.

Answer: d

III. Current Reporting Standards: The Requirements of *APBO 28*

Revenues

Revenue from products sold or services rendered should be recognized as earned during an interim period on the same basis as followed for the full year.[3]

[3] *Opinions of the Accounting Principles Board*, No. 28, "Interim Financial Reporting" (New York: American Institute of Certified Public Accountants, 1973), par. 11.

This provision, which requires that each interim period be viewed as an annual period, produces the following results:

1. Companies that have *seasonal revenues* must report such revenues in the interim period in which they are earned as opposed to *allocating* them over the full year.
2. When receipts at an interim date *precede* the earning process, the revenues are deferred until the interim period in which the product is delivered or the service is rendered.
3. Companies using the percentage-of-completion method for long-term construction-type contracts must recognize revenues in *interim periods* using the same procedures that are used at the end of the *annual period*.

Costs Associated with Revenues (Product Costs)

> Those costs and expenses that are associated directly with or allocated to the products sold or to the services rendered for annual reporting purposes (including for example, material costs, wages and salaries and related fringe benefits, manufacturing overhead, and warranties) should be similarly treated for interim reporting purposes. . . . Companies should generally use the same inventory pricing methods and make provisions for write-downs to market at interim dates on the same basis used at annual inventory dates.[4]

Although this provision appears to treat each *interim period* as though it were an annual period, the following four specified exceptions allow each *interim period* to be viewed **as part of** an *annual period*:

1. Estimated gross profit rates may be used to determine the cost of goods sold during *interim periods*. This procedure is merely a practical modification because complete physical inventories are usually not taken at *interim dates*. See the Case in Point.

CASE IN POINT

In 2000, the federal government began an investigation of **possible criminal fraud** in connection with Rite Aid Corp.'s past accounting practices. Rite Aid, the nation's No. 3 drugstore chain, was shaken in 2000 as a result of having to restate downward by $500 million its earnings for 1997–1999. Investigators also are looking into whether Rite Aid pumped up earnings in unaudited *quarterly statements* by **using overly aggressive estimates of gross margins** in costing out inventory (a process that can be easily abused).

2. Liquidation at an *interim date* of LIFO base-period inventories that the company expects to replace by the end of the *annual period* does not affect interim results; that is, cost of goods sold for the *interim reporting period* should include the expected cost of replacing the liquidated LIFO base.
3. Declines in market price at interim dates that will probably be recovered by the end of the *annual period* (temporary declines) **"need not"** be recognized at the interim date. If inventory losses from market declines are recognized at an *interim date*, any subsequent recoveries should be recognized as *gains* in those periods but only to the extent of previously recognized *losses*.
4. For companies using standard cost accounting systems, purchase price variances or *volume* or *capacity* variances of costs that are inventoriable **"should ordinarily"** be deferred at *interim reporting dates*, providing that such variances are (1) **planned** and (2) **expected to be absorbed by the end of the *annual period*.**

With respect to the *third* exception, assume that a company has on hand at the *beginning* of the year 15,000 units of a particular inventory item, each of which is valued at its historical FIFO cost of $20. For simplicity, we assume that no additional purchases of this item are made during

[4] *APBO 28*, pars. 13–14.

the year. Assumed sales for each quarter and replacement costs (assumed to be market) at the end of each quarter are as follows:

Quarter	Units Sold during Quarter	Replacement Cost at End of Quarter
1	1,000	$16 (*not* considered a temporary decline)
2	2,000	$14 (considered a temporary decline)
3	3,000	$17
4	4,000	$21

Illustration 17-1 shows the adjustments that would be made to the Inventory account for this item during the year for market changes.

In reviewing Illustration 17-1, note that *no* market adjustment was made at the end of the *second quarter*. The market decline during that quarter was considered a temporary decline that was reasonably expected to disappear by the end of the *annual period*.

Note also that the use of the language "need not" in the pronouncement (rather than the mandatory term "should") **permits** companies to recognize temporary market declines in the interim period in which they occur **if they choose to do so.** Thus alternative treatments for temporary market declines are sanctioned.

With respect to the *fourth* exception dealing with companies using standard cost accounting systems, the use of "should ordinarily" in the pronouncement (rather than an unqualified "should") permits alternative treatments for purchase price and volume variances **that are planned and expected to be absorbed by year-end.** In summary, *APBO 28* allows substantial leeway for dealing with certain aspects of inventory costing and manufacturing cost variances in interim reports.

CHECK POINT

Under *APBO 28*

a. *Temporary declines* in inventory market prices are to be recognized at interim reporting dates.
b. Inventory price declines at interim dates that are considered *not* to be temporary need not be recognized at the interim date.
c. Physical inventories must be taken at the end of each interim quarter.
d. Temporary and *non*temporary declines in inventory market prices are to be recognized at interim reporting dates.
e. None of the above.

Answer: e

ILLUSTRATION 17-1 ANALYSIS OF THE INVENTORY ACCOUNT FOR THE YEAR

	Units					Amount
Balance, January 1	**15,000**	×	**$20**		=	**$300,000**
First-quarter sales	(1,000)	×	$ 20		=	(20,000)
						$ 280,000
First-quarter market adjustment	14,000	×	$ (4)	[$20 – $16]	=	(56,000)
Balance, March 31	**14,000**	×	**$16**		=	**$224,000**
Second-quarter sales	(2,000)	×	$ 16		=	(32,000)
Balance, June 30	**12,000**	×	**$16**		=	**$192,000**
Third-quarter sales	(3,000)	×	$ 16		=	(48,000)
						$ 144,000
Third-quarter market adjustment	9,000	×	$ 1	[$17 – $16]	=	9,000
Balance, September 30	**9,000**	×	**$17**		=	**$153,000**
Fourth-quarter sales	(4,000)	×	$ 17		=	(68,000)
						$ 85,000
Fourth-quarter market adjustment	5,000	×	$ 3	[$20 – $17]	=	15,000
Balance, December 31	**5,000**	×	**$20**		=	**$100,000**

All Other Costs and Expenses

The Accounting Principles Board (APB) developed the following standards for all costs and expenses other than product costs:

> **a.** Costs and expenses other than product costs should be charged to interim periods as incurred, or be allocated among interim periods based on an estimate of time expired, benefit received, or activity associated with the periods. Procedures adopted for assigning specific cost and expense items to an interim period should be consistent with the bases followed by the company in reporting results of operations at annual reporting dates. However, when a specific cost or expense item charged to expense for annual reporting purposes benefits more than one interim period, the cost or expense item may be allocated to those interim periods.
> **b.** Some costs and expenses incurred in an interim period, however, cannot be readily identified with the activities or benefits of other interim periods and should be charged to the interim period in which incurred. Disclosure should be made as to the nature and amount of such costs unless items of a comparable nature are included in both the current interim period and in the corresponding interim period of the preceding year.
> **c.** Arbitrary assignment of the amount of such costs to an interim period should not be made.
> **d.** Gains and losses that arise in any interim period similar to those that would not be deferred at year-end should not be deferred to later interim periods within the same fiscal year.[5]

These standards do the following:

1. They prohibit "normalizing" or "spreading" expenditures over a fiscal year on a revenue basis as under a *pure integral approach*.
2. They require that most expenditures be treated as though each *interim period* were an *annual reporting* period.
3. They permit certain expenditures that clearly benefit *more than one interim period* to be allocated among the *interim periods* benefited. Note that this treatment is **permissive, not mandatory**. Some examples of expenditures that may qualify for **allocation among interim periods** are major annual repairs, costs of periodic advertising campaigns, social security taxes, and charitable contributions.

In addition to the preceding standards, estimation procedures must be used at *interim dates* for items that historically have resulted in year-end adjustments (usually charges to income) or that can be reasonably approximated at *interim dates*. Examples are allowances for uncollectible accounts, inventory shrinkage, quantity discounts, and accruals for discretionary year-end bonuses. The purpose is to prevent the reporting of material fourth-quarter adjustments that cast a shadow on the reliability of prior interim reports and undermine the integrity of the *interim period* reporting process.

CHECK POINT

Under *APBO 28*, if annual major repairs made in the *first quarter* and paid for in the *second quarter* clearly benefit the entire year, they

a. Must be expensed in the first quarter.
b. Must be expensed in the second quarter.
c. Must be expensed in each of the four quarters using allocation procedures.
d. May be expensed in the first quarter or allocated over the four quarters.

Answer: d

Seasonal Revenues, Costs, and Expenses

Many businesses—such as amusement parks, professional sports teams, farming corporations, department stores, and toy manufacturers—receive all or a major portion of their revenues in one or two interim periods. As a result, these companies report wide fluctuations in revenues and

---

[5] *APBO 28*, par. 15.

profitability in their interim reports. Such companies must disclose the seasonal nature of their activities to avoid misleading inferences about revenues and profitability for the entire year. Furthermore, these companies should consider providing supplemental financial information for the 12-month periods ended at the interim date for the current and prior years.

Income Tax Provisions

The basic provision for the computation of income taxes for interim periods is as follows:

> At the end of each interim period the company should make its best estimate of the effective tax rate expected to be applicable for the full fiscal year. The rate so determined should be used in providing for income taxes on a current year-to-date basis. The effective tax rate should reflect anticipated investment tax credits, foreign tax rates, percentage depletion, capital gains rates, and other available tax planning alternatives.[6]

The following points concerning this provision should be understood:

1. Each *interim period* is not a separate taxable period.
2. If the estimated tax rate for the year changes as the year proceeds, the effect of the change is included in the appropriate *interim period* as a **change in estimate.** No retroactive restatement of *prior interim periods* is made. The provision for income taxes for the *third quarter* of a company's fiscal year, for example, is the result of applying the expected tax rate to *year-to-date earnings* and subtracting the combined provisions reported for the *first* and *second* quarters.

The basic provision as stated here is supplemented for the tax effects of unusual or extraordinary items as follows:

> However, in arriving at this effective tax rate no effect should be included for the tax related to significant unusual or extraordinary items that will be separately reported or reported net of their related tax effect in reports for the interim period or for the fiscal year.[7]

Illustration 17-2 shows how to calculate the income tax expense for the first interim quarter and *subsequent* interim quarters using assumed estimates of the effective *annual* income tax rate at the end of each *interim* quarter.[8]

Illustration 17-3 then shows how to calculate the estimated effective *annual* income tax rate at the end of the *first* interim quarter.

More Complex Situations

For simplicity, the facts assumed in Illustrations 17-2 and 17-3 did *not* involve any complexities. Computing interim period income taxes is more involved when one or more of the following elements is present:

1. Unusual items reported separately.
2. Extraordinary items reported net of related tax effects.
3. Losses in one or more interim periods.
4. Prior year operating loss carryforwards available.
5. Discontinued operations.
6. Changes in accounting principles.
7. Effects of new tax legislation.

---

[6] *APBO 28*, par. 19.

[7] *APBO 28*, par. 19.

[8] *FAS 109* has made estimating the *annual* effective tax rate more difficult (than under its predecessor) because it uses the *liability method* (instead of the "with-and-without" method). Under the *liability method*, companies must (1) project the deferred tax effects of expected year-end temporary differences and (2) take into consideration the tax effect of a valuation allowance expected to be necessary at the end of the year for deferred tax assets related to originating deductible temporary differences and carryforwards. Thus the estimated *annual* effective tax rate is calculated by dividing the sum of (1) the **estimated current taxes payable** and (2) the **change in the deferred taxes accounts** (deferred tax *asset*, deferred tax *liability*, and *valuation allowance*) by the estimated ordinary pretax income for the year. For simplicity, we assumed in Illustration 17-3 that *no* originating temporary differences were expected at year-end.

ILLUSTRATION 17-2 CALCULATION OF INTERIM INCOME TAX EXPENSE

	First Quarter	Second Quarter	Third Quarter
Estimated **annual** pretax earnings made at the end of each quarter	$600,000	$700,000	$750,000
Estimated **annual** income tax rates calculated at the end of each quarter	36%[a]	34%	37%
Actual **cumulative** pretax earnings at the end of each quarter	$100,000	$300,000	$650,000
Income tax rate to be used at the end of each quarter	36%	34%	37%
Cumulative income tax expense to be reported at the end of each quarter	$ 36,000	$102,000	$240,500
Income tax expense to be reported			
For the first quarter	$ 36,000		
For the second quarter ($102,000 – $36,000)		$66,000	
For the third quarter ($240,500 – $102,000)			$138,500
Actual **quarterly** pretax earnings	$100,000	$200,000	$350,000
Effective income tax rate for each quarter	36%[a]	33%[b]	39.6%[c]

[a] The calculation of this **estimated annual** income tax rate is shown in Illustration 17-3.

[b] $66,000/$200,000 = 33%. Note that 34% of $200,000 is $68,000. The $2,000 difference between this amount and the $66,000 amount calculated here is the 2% decrease in the estimated annual income tax rate multiplied by the first-quarter pretax earnings of $100,000. Thus the $66,000 amount is net of this $2,000 downward correction (a "catch-up" adjustment) of the first quarter's previously reported income tax expense of $36,000. Accordingly, **no retroactive restatement** was made to the first quarter's previously reported income tax expense of $36,000.

[c] $138,500/$350,000 = 39.6%. Note that 37% of $350,000 is $129,500. The $9,000 difference between this amount and the $138,500 amount calculated above is the 3% increase in the estimated annual income tax rate multiplied by the first- and second-quarter combined pretax earnings of $300,000. Thus the $138,500 amount includes a $9,000 upward correction (a "catch-up" adjustment) of the first- and second-quarter previously reported combined income tax expense of $102,000. Accordingly, **no retroactive restatement** was made to the first- and second-quarter previously reported income tax expense of $36,000 and $66,000, respectively.

FASB *Interpretation No. 18*, "Accounting for Income Taxes in Interim Periods," clarifies the application of *APBO 28* with respect to accounting for income taxes. This interpretation, containing more than 20 detailed examples spread over more than 40 pages, shows how to compute income taxes involving these more complex areas, which, except for a brief discussion of seasonal businesses, are beyond the scope of this chapter.

Seasonal Businesses Having Losses During Early Interim Periods

Frequently, a seasonal business has a loss during an early *interim period*, but management expects the *annual* results to be profitable. In these cases, the tax effects of losses arising in the early portion of a fiscal year are recognized only when the **tax benefits** are expected to be realized. A historical pattern of losses in ***early** interim periods* offset by profits in ***later** interim periods* normally constitutes sufficient evidence that realization is *more likely than not* (the *FAS 109* criterion for reporting a deferred tax asset), unless other facts indicate that the historical pattern will *not* repeat.

Illustration 17-4 shows the income tax expense or benefit reported in each *interim reporting period* for an enterprise engaged in a *seasonal business* that shows a loss for the first *interim reporting period*. We assume that the enterprise anticipates being profitable for the entire year and that this expectation proves to be correct. For simplicity, we also assume that (1) the estimated effective *annual* tax rate is 40%, (2) this rate does *not* change during the year, and (3) no unusual or extraordinary items are present.

Disposal of a Segment of a Business and Extraordinary, Unusual, Infrequently Occurring, and Contingent Items

The effects of the disposal of a business segment and extraordinary, unusual, and infrequently occurring items are reported in the period in which they occur. If the effects are material in relation to the operating results of the *interim period*, they are reported separately.

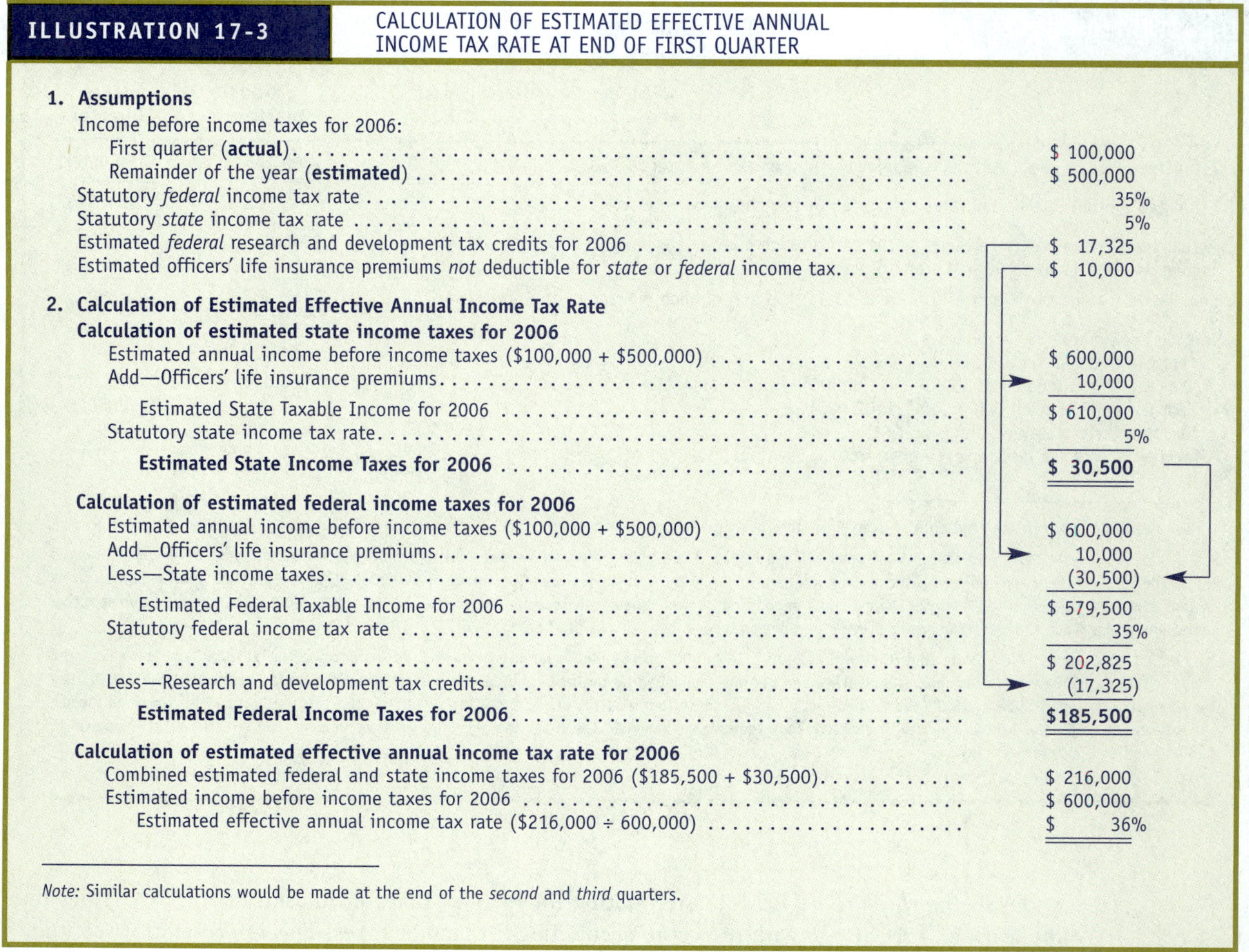

ILLUSTRATION 17-3 CALCULATION OF ESTIMATED EFFECTIVE ANNUAL INCOME TAX RATE AT END OF FIRST QUARTER

1. Assumptions	
Income before income taxes for 2006:	
First quarter (**actual**)	$ 100,000
Remainder of the year (**estimated**)	$ 500,000
Statutory *federal* income tax rate	35%
Statutory *state* income tax rate	5%
Estimated *federal* research and development tax credits for 2006	$ 17,325
Estimated officers' life insurance premiums *not* deductible for *state* or *federal* income tax	$ 10,000
2. Calculation of Estimated Effective Annual Income Tax Rate	
Calculation of estimated state income taxes for 2006	
Estimated annual income before income taxes ($100,000 + $500,000)	$ 600,000
Add—Officers' life insurance premiums	10,000
Estimated State Taxable Income for 2006	$ 610,000
Statutory state income tax rate	5%
Estimated State Income Taxes for 2006	**$ 30,500**
Calculation of estimated federal income taxes for 2006	
Estimated annual income before income taxes ($100,000 + $500,000)	$ 600,000
Add—Officers' life insurance premiums	10,000
Less—State income taxes	(30,500)
Estimated Federal Taxable Income for 2006	$ 579,500
Statutory federal income tax rate	35%
	$ 202,825
Less—Research and development tax credits	(17,325)
Estimated Federal Income Taxes for 2006	**$185,500**
Calculation of estimated effective annual income tax rate for 2006	
Combined estimated federal and state income taxes for 2006 ($185,500 + $30,500)	$ 216,000
Estimated income before income taxes for 2006	$ 600,000
Estimated effective annual income tax rate ($216,000 ÷ 600,000)	$ 36%

Note: Similar calculations would be made at the end of the *second* and *third* quarters.

The basic thrust of *APBO 28* concerning contingencies is a *discrete approach*; that is, disclosures are made in *interim reports* in the same manner that they are made in *annual reports*, except that the significance of a contingency should be judged in relation to annual financial statements. FASB *Statement No. 5*, "Accounting for Contingencies," was issued after *APBO 28*. The application of *FAS 5* provisions to interim periods as though each *interim period* were an *annual period* is consistent with the basic thrust of *APBO 28* in this area. Thus the **probable** and **reasonably estimable** criteria of *FAS 5* are used to determine the *interim period* in which a loss contingency should be accrued.

ILLUSTRATION 17-4 INCOME TAX EXPENSE OR BENEFIT TO BE REPORTED FOR A SEASONAL BUSINESS (IN THOUSANDS OF DOLLARS)

	Reporting Quarter				Fiscal
	1	2	3	4	Year
Income (loss) before income taxes	$(200)	$100	$150	$ 950	$1,000
Income tax benefit (expense) @ 40%	80	(40)	(60)	(380)	(400)
Net Income (loss)	$(120)	$ 60	$ 90	$ 570	$ 600

CHECK POINT

Under *APBO 28*

a. Revenues may be artificially smoothed over the four quarters, providing that full disclosure is made of the procedures used.
b. Unplanned capacity variances arising at an interim date should not be deferred at interim reporting dates.
c. Certain expenditures (other than product costs) that clearly benefit *more than* one interim period are required to be allocated among interim periods benefited.
d. Extraordinary items must be prorated over the current and remaining interim periods.

Answer: b

Accounting Changes and Error Corrections

Interim financial reports must disclose any **changes in accounting principles or practices.** In December 2003, the FASB issued a proposed new standard for reporting *accounting changes* and *error corrections.* This proposed standard emanated from the FASB's current short-term convergence project, which involves studying areas of U.S. GAAP that could be improved by converging with the GAAP of the International Accounting Standards Board (as discussed in detail in Chapter 13).

Under the proposed standard (which would amend *APBO 28* and supersede *FAS 3*), the cumulative effect of a new accounting principle on periods prior to those presented must be reflected in (1) the reported carrying amounts of assets and liabilities as of the beginning of the first period presented and (2) the opening balance of retained earnings for that period. Accordingly, all changes in an accounting principle made in any *interim period* must be reported by ***retrospective application*** (application of a new accounting principle to all prior accounting periods as if the new principle had *always* been used). Thus previously issued interim financial statements (of the *current year* or of *prior years* that are presented for comparative purposes) must be revised to reflect the use of the new accounting principle. *Consequently, the cumulative effect is no longer calculated as of the beginning of the current year and reported in the current year's income statement.*

Changes in accounting estimates must be accounted for in (1) the period of change if the change affects that period only or (2) the period of change and future periods if the change affects both.

Errors found in previously issued *interim reports* must be reported as prior-period adjustments, just as previously issued *annual financial statements* must be restated for such items.

Disclosures of Summarized Interim Financial Data by Publicly Owned Companies

According to *APBO 28*, the following minimum disclosures must be furnished to stockholders in interim reports (including fourth-quarter reports):

a. Sales or gross revenues, provision for income taxes, extraordinary items (including related income tax effects), cumulative effect of a change in accounting principles or practices, net income and comprehensive income.
b. Basic and diluted earnings per share data for each period presented. . . .
c. Seasonal revenue, costs or expenses.
d. Significant changes in estimates or provisions for income taxes.
e. Disposal of a component of an entity and extraordinary, unusual or infrequently occurring items.
f. Contingent items.
g. Changes in accounting principles or estimates.
h. Significant changes in financial position.
i. The following information about reportable operating segments determined according to the provisions of *FAS 131*, "Disclosures about Segments of an Enterprise and Related

Information," including provisions related to restatement of segment information in previously issued financial statements:
(1) Revenues from external customers
(2) Intersegment revenues
(3) A measure of segment profit or loss
(4) Total assets for which there has been a material change from the amount disclosed in the last annual report
(5) A description of differences from the last annual report in the basis of segmentation or in the measurement of segment profit or loss
(6) A reconciliation of the total of the reportable segments' measure of profit or loss to the enterprise's consolidated income before income taxes, extraordinary items, discontinued operations, and the cumulative effect of changes in accounting principles. . . .[9]

Most publicly owned companies exceed these requirements by furnishing either a *condensed* or a *complete* income statement. These income statements (condensed or complete) are usually presented in comparative form. For reports other than the first quarter report, quarterly data and **year-to-date** amounts are usually presented. Many companies also furnish complete or condensed balance sheets (usually in comparative form) in their interim reports. In addition to financial data, these interim reports usually contain a narrative discussion of interim period highlights.

Many publicly traded companies do *not* issue a separate report covering *fourth-quarter results.* Such companies often disclose *fourth-quarter results* (as outlined in paragraph 30 of *APBO 28*) in the *annual report.* If the results of the *fourth quarter* are *not* furnished in a *separate report* or in the *annual report*, a company must disclose the following items recognized in the *fourth quarter* in a note to the *annual* financial statements:

1. Disposals of components of an entity.
2. Extraordinary items.
3. Unusual or infrequently occurring items.
4. The aggregate effect of year-end adjustments that are material to the results of the *fourth quarter.*

In addition, the effects of accounting changes made during the fourth quarter are disclosed in a note to the annual financial statements in the absence of a separate fourth-quarter report or other disclosure in the annual report.

A Comparison of the Requirements of *APBO 28* and of SEC Form 10-Q

The disclosure requirements of SEC Form 10-Q are more extensive than those of *APBO 28*. Form 10-Q requires that the following condensed financial statements be included in interim reports filed with the SEC:

1. **Balance sheets.** Balance sheets are presented for (1) the end of *the most recent fiscal quarter* and (2) the end of the *preceding fiscal year.*
2. **Income statements.** Income statements are presented for (1) *the most recent fiscal quarter*, (2) the period between *the end of the last fiscal year* and *the end of the most recent fiscal quarter* (year-to-date amounts in *second-* and *third-quarter reports*), and (3) the corresponding periods of the preceding fiscal year. An amount for **comprehensive income** must be reported.
3. **Statements of cash flows.** Statements of cash flows are presented for (1) the period between the end of *the last fiscal year* and the end of *the most recent fiscal quarter* and (2) the corresponding period of the preceding fiscal year.

[9] *APBO 28*, par. 30, as amended by *FAS 131*, "Disclosures about Segments of an Enterprise and Related Information," *FAS 130*, "Reporting Comprehensive Income," and *FAS 128*, "Earnings Per Share."

As stated earlier, financial statements included in Form 10-Q reports are prepared in accordance with *APBO 28* provisions and any amendments to the opinion that may be adopted by the FASB. Disclosures must be complete enough so that none of the information presented is misleading. Furthermore, management must provide an analysis of the quarterly results of operations. Information required in Form 10-Q may be omitted from that form if such information is contained in a quarterly report to the stockholders and a copy of that quarterly report is filed with Form 10-Q.

ETHICS

Booking Sales Before Their Normal Time?

Near the end of Fudgco's *third quarter*, it became evident that *actual sales* for the quarter would be significantly below the budgeted sales. Accordingly, Fudgco offered discounts and extended payment terms (no payments necessary for 120 days) to many of its distributors to induce them to take delivery in the *third quarter*. As a result, Fudgco was able to meet its *third-quarter* sales budget.

Question
Is this practice ethical? Should this practice be disclosed to stockholders in the *third quarter's interim report*?

IV. INVOLVEMENT OF CERTIFIED PUBLIC ACCOUNTANTS IN INTERIM PERIOD REPORTING

Audited interim period financial reports are virtually nonexistent. For many years prior to 1975, common deficiencies in unaudited reports included a preponderance of unusual charges and, less often, credits to income late in the year and corrections to previously issued interim period financial data. In recognition of such significant, continuing deficiencies and abuses in the interim reporting process, the SEC took steps in 1975 to improve the quality of interim period financial reports by effectively forcing the accounting profession to accept auditor involvement in the interim reporting process. At that time, most members of the profession did not want to be associated with interim period financial reports on anything less than a *complete audit basis*, fearing potential lawsuits in the event that interim period financial report data proved to be false or misleading. The SEC obtained auditor involvement in quite an interesting way. First, it passed a rule requiring that *quarterly* financial data appear in a note to the *annual* financial statements included in the annual 10-K report filed with the SEC. This requirement caused auditors to be "associated" with these data by virtue of reporting on the financial statements in which the note was included. This occurred even though the SEC allowed the note to be labeled "unaudited" and the auditors had not audited the data in the note.

Second, the SEC passed a rule informing auditors that the SEC presumed that auditors applied "appropriate professional standards and procedures with respect to the data in the note." Thus auditors had to perform some form of "review" of the data included in this note. Furthermore, the SEC indicated that unless the American Institute of Certified Public Accountants (AICPA) developed professional standards and procedures in connection with reviewing the data in this note, the SEC would do so. The AICPA chose to develop them and issued review standards in 1979. The current review standards (several revisions have been made since 1979) are contained in *Statement on Auditing Standards No. 100*, "Interim Financial Information."[10] Because this pronouncement

[10] *Statement on Auditing Standards No. 100*, "Interim Financial Information" (New York: American Institute of Certified Public Accountants, 2002).

is the subject of an auditing course, it is not discussed in detail here. Briefly, auditors must perform certain procedures that are **substantially less than an audit**.

Auditors are *not* specifically required to perform these review procedures as part of the *interim reporting process during the year*. Thus the review can be made *at year-end*. The SEC took these steps, however, in the belief that companies would have the reviews made as part of the *interim reporting process* for the following reasons:

1. The likelihood of having to revise *quarterly* data when the *annual* statements are published should *decrease*.
2. The likelihood of discovering needed adjustments on a timely basis should increase so that unusual charges and credits are less frequent in the last month of the year.
3. The added expertise of professional accountants increases the quality of the interim reporting process.[11]

To encourage auditors to be more involved in the interim reporting process, the SEC adopted a rule in 1979 that exempts *interim financial reports* from a federal securities law provision automatically making certified public accountants liable for a client's false and misleading financial statements unless such accountants can prove that they were diligent. (Certified public accountants are *not* exempted, however, from the section of the federal securities law that deals with fraud.) Even before the adoption of this rule, the opposition of auditors to involvement in the interim reporting process had, for the most part, dissipated.

Most auditors of publicly held companies now encourage their clients to have the review performed as part of the interim reporting process rather than at *year-end*. In 1999, the then "Big 5" accounting firms agreed to perform financial audits only for companies that allow them to review their financial statements every quarter. **In 2000, the SEC adopted rules requiring registrants to obtain reviews of interim financial information by their independent auditors *prior to filing of their quarterly reports on Form 10-Q*** (or Form 10-QSB if a qualifying small business).

In 1980, the SEC revised its reporting requirements so that (1) quarterly financial data may be presented *outside* of the notes to the annual financial statements and (2) auditors must follow the AICPA's review standards and procedures regardless of the placement of the quarterly financial data.[12]

The Importance of Furnishing Accurate Quarterly Reports

The ramifications of not issuing truthful quarterly reports can be costly and embarrassing. Frequently, shareholders sue companies (often successfully) for allegedly issuing false and misleading quarterly reports. (See the Case in Point.)

CASE IN POINT

In 1993, Oracle Corporation (a leading software company that competes with Microsoft Inc.) agreed to settle charges brought by the Securities and Exchange Commission that Oracle had inflated its *quarterly revenues* and *earnings* in 1990 and 1991 by double-billing customers, failing to deduct product returns, and using other accounting irregularities.

The overstatements were as much as 150% of *actual* net income and earnings per share. Oracle paid a $100,000 fine but did *not* admit or deny that it had violated SEC quarterly reporting rules. Earlier, Oracle had restated its quarterly reports for the periods in question.

In 1994, Oracle paid $24 million to settle civil lawsuits filed by shareholders who had similar complaints about the accounting practices.

---

[11] *Accounting Series Release No. 177* (Washington, D.C.: Securities and Exchange Commission, 1975).

[12] *Regulation S-K*, Item 302(a)(1) and (4) (Washington, D.C.: Securities and Exchange Commission, 1980).

End-of-Chapter Review

Summary of Key Points

1. Interim reporting raises the fundamental issue of whether *interim period* financial statements should be prepared using the *same* accounting principles and practices used in preparing *annual financial statements.*
2. Under the **discrete view**, each *interim period* must stand on its own without regard to the fact that it is part of an *annual reporting period.*
3. Under the **integral view**, the fact that an *interim period* is part of an *annual reporting period* is a basis for assigning the total estimated annual costs and expenses to *interim periods* based on revenues to report reasonably constant operating margins.
4. *APBO 28* adopted a **combination discrete-integral approach.**
5. **Revenues, extraordinary items,** gains or losses from the disposal of a segment, unusual items, and infrequently occurring items are treated under the *discrete view.*
6. For **costs associated with revenue** (product costs), the *discrete view* is used—four specified exceptions to this rule produce *integral* results.
7. The *discrete view* must be used for **all other costs and expenses** unless an item meets specified standards for integral treatment. If the standards *are* met, the company may use *integral techniques.*
8. For **income taxes,** the *integral view* is prescribed.
9. *Segment information* must be disclosed.

Glossary of New Terms

Discrete view A manner of measuring interim period earnings by viewing each interim period as *an independent period* that must stand on its own.

Integral view A manner of measuring interim period earnings by viewing each *interim period* as an integral part of an *annual reporting period.* Under this view, each *interim period* should bear part of the *annual expenses* that are incurred in generating revenues for the entire year.

Combination discrete-integral view A manner of measuring *interim period* earnings by accepting the *integral view* for certain costs and expenses and using the *discrete view* for all other costs and expenses.

Assignment Material

Review Questions

1. Do the principles and practices that apply to interim reporting apply only to *publicly owned* companies?
2. What is the fundamental issue pertaining to interim reporting?
3. Are the issues associated with interim reporting primarily related to *revenues* or to *costs and expenses?*
4. What are the *three* schools of thought that exist concerning the approach to interim reporting?
5. Under which approach must each interim period stand on its own?
6. Does *APBO 28* impose *integral techniques* for costs and expenses *not* associated with revenue? Explain.

7. What factors could cause the estimated annual income tax rate to change from quarter to quarter?

8. If *fourth-quarter results* are *not* furnished in a separate report or in the annual report, which items recognized in the fourth quarter must be disclosed in a note to the *annual financial statements*?

Exercises

E 17-1 **Inventory Loss from Market Decline** A $420,000 inventory loss from market declines occurred in April 2006. At that time, the market decline was not considered temporary. Of this loss, $100,000 was recovered in the fourth quarter ended 12/31/06.

Required How should this loss be reflected in the quarterly income statements for 2006?

E 17-2 **Annual Major Repairs and Property Taxes** On 1/1/06, Luca Company paid property taxes of $40,000 on its plant for calendar year 2006. In March 2006, Luca made its annual-type major repairs to its machinery amounting to $120,000. These repairs benefit the entire calendar-year operations.

Required How should these expenditures be reflected in the quarterly income statements for 2006?

E 17-3 **Year-End Bonuses** In January 2006, Gelt Company estimated that its 2006 year-end bonuses to executives would be $240,000. The actual amount paid for 2005 year-end bonuses was $224,000. The 2006 estimate is subject to year-end adjustment.

Required What amount of expense, if any, should be reflected in the quarterly income statement for the three months ended 3/31/06?

E 17-4 **Percentage-of-Completion Method on Long-Term Contracts** For annual reporting purposes, Candu Company appropriately accounts for revenues from long-term construction contracts under the percentage-of-completion method. In December 2005, for budgeting purposes, Candu estimated that these revenues would be $1,600,000 for 2006. As a result of favorable business conditions in October 2006, Candu recognized revenues of $2,000,000 for the year ended 12/31/06. If the percentage-of-completion method had been used for the quarterly income statements on the same basis as followed for the year-end income statement, revenues would have been as follows:

Three months ended 3/31/06	$ 300,000
Three months ended 6/30/06	400,000
Three months ended 9/30/06	200,000
Three months ended 12/31/06	1,100,000
Total	$2,000,000

Required What amount of revenues from long-term construction contracts should be reflected in the quarterly income statement for the three months ended 12/31/06?

E 17-5 **Severance Pay** During the *second quarter* of its current reporting year, Shears Company announced that it would trim its workforce by 7% as a result of below-normal demand for its products. Employees being laid off are given three to six weeks' severance pay, depending on their length of employment.

Required Assuming that the severance pay was paid in the second quarter, how should it be accounted for in the quarterly reports for the current year?

Problems

P 17-1 **Incentive Compensation Plan for Sales Personnel** Pavlov Inc. uses an incentive system for its sales personnel whereby each salesperson receives

1. A base salary of $1,000 per month.
2. A commission of 2% of the individual salesperson's sales.
3. A bonus of 10% on the individual salesperson's annual sales in excess of $1,200,000. (This bonus is paid in the *first quarter* of the year following the year on which the bonus is based.)

The company's sales do *not* occur in a seasonal pattern. Sales generated by certain sales personnel for the *first* and *second quarters* of 2006 are as follows:

	First Quarter	Second Quarter	Cumulative
Ace	$ 400,000	$ 370,000	$ 770,000
Bridges	360,000	210,000	570,000
Cardell	260,000	380,000	640,000
Decker	280,000	290,000	570,000
Total	$1,300,000	$1,250,000	$2,550,000

Payments made during the first quarter of 2006 for bonuses based on total 2005 sales are as follows:

Ace	$24,000
Decker	3,000

Required Determine the compensation expense to be reported for the *first* and *second* quarters of 2006 using two different approaches for the bonuses.

P 17-2 Income Taxes: Calculating Interim Expense Reviso Inc. had the *following pretax income* for the first two reporting quarters of 2006:

First quarter	$500,000
Second quarter	700,000

Reviso's actual *annual* effective income tax rate for 2005 was 40%. For budgeting purposes, Reviso estimated that the effective *annual* income tax rate for 2006 would also be 40%. Near the end of the *second quarter*, Reviso changed its estimated effective *annual* income tax rate for 2006 to 35%. Reviso issues its quarterly reports within 45 days of the end of the quarter.

Required Determine the income tax expense to be reported for the first and second quarters of 2006.

P 17-3 Income Taxes: Calculating Estimated Annual Rate and Interim Expense Antax has developed the following data for 2006 at the end of its first reporting quarter:

Income *before* income taxes:	
First quarter (actual)	$200,000
Remainder of year (estimated)	$800,000
Statutory federal income tax rate	40%
Statutory *state* income tax rate	10%
Estimated *federal* research and development tax credits	$44,600
Officers' life insurance premiums *not* deductible for state or federal purposes	$10,000
Excess of *accelerated depreciation* over *straight-line depreciation* for state and federal purposes	$50,000

Required
1. Calculate the estimated effective annual income tax rate at the end of the *first quarter*.
2. Calculate the income tax provision for the *first quarter*.
3. Calculate the estimated effective annual income tax rate at the end of the *second quarter* assuming that
   a. Income before income taxes for the *second quarter* was $400,000.
   b. The estimated income before income taxes for the *third* and *fourth quarters* is $500,000 in total.
4. Calculate the income tax provision for the *second quarter*.

Thinking Critically

Cases

C 17-1 **Thinking of Ways to "Manage Earnings"** The president of Manipulex has instructed you, the controller, to report quarterly profits within 2% of budgeted profits.

Required

1. See how many ways you can think of to shift profits between quarters or arbitrarily report profits.
2. If you were the company's outside auditor performing a quarterly review and you became aware of such practices, would you require disclosure of these practices in the quarterly financial report?

C 17-2 **Treatment of Annual Furnace Relining Costs** Harthco was formed in 2004 to produce steel. Production commenced in October 2005, and sales began in November 2005. The company expects to close down its furnaces each September to reline them, which takes about a month. Members of the controller's staff disagree on how the costs of relining the furnaces should be reported. The following approaches are advocated:

1. Expense the costs in the period in which they are incurred.
2. Expense the costs over the company's calendar reporting year.
3. Expense the costs over a period from September to August of the following year.

Required Evaluate the theoretical soundness of these proposed treatments, and comment on their conformity with the provisions of *APBO 28*.

C 17-3 **Treatment of Accounting and Legal Fees** Callex reports on a calendar year-end basis. The accounting firm that performs the annual year-end audit renders approximately one-third of its audit-related services in the fourth quarter of each calendar year and approximately two-thirds of its audit-related services in the first quarter of each calendar year. The accounting firm renders an interim billing in the fourth quarter for services performed during that quarter.

The legal firm that assists the company in preparing its annual 10-K report, which must be filed with the SEC within 90 days after year-end, renders all of its 10-K-related services in the first calendar quarter of each year. The legal firm renders its billing sometime in the second quarter.

Required Determine how these accounting and legal fees should be reported in the quarterly financial statements.

C 17-4 **Material Year-End Physical Inventory Adjustment** Pilferex uses a periodic inventory system and takes an annual physical inventory at year-end. Historically, the company's adjustments from book value to physical inventory have been insignificant. Current year sales and production increased substantially over the prior year, and a material book to physical inventory adjustment (a shortage) occurred. Management has not determined the cause of the physical inventory adjustment.

The market price of the company's common stock rose during the year due to the favorable sales and earnings pattern reported for the first three quarters. The market price declined sharply when the company announced that the annual earnings would be below estimated amounts as a result of the large physical inventory adjustment.

Required

1. How should the physical inventory adjustment be reported?
2. What are the possible consequences of large *fourth-quarter* adjustments?

C 17-5 **Revising Previously Issued Quarterly Results** Fudgco, Inc. announced results for its fourth quarter prior to the completion of its annual audit. (The company assumed that its outside auditors would *not* have any proposed adjustments.) Shortly after the auditors completed their work, however, Fudgco announced a restatement of third- and fourth-quarter results because (1) recorded sales included shipments that had occurred after the end of those quarters and (2) previously recorded sales did *not* have sufficient documentation. Reported results (in millions of dollars) follow:

	Initially Reported	Restated	Decrease	
			Amount	Percent
Sales	$337	$312	$(25)	(7)
Net income	37	30	(7)	(20)

After this announcement, the price of the company's common stock immediately fell 6 points, a 20% decline.

Required

1. What are the ramifications of restating results for these quarters?
2. If the auditors reviewed quarterly information at the end of each quarter, why did they *not* discover this problem at the end of the third quarter?

C 17-6 **Treatment of Unresolved Item** During its *second quarter*, Newtex entered into a new type of transaction, which will result in the immediate reporting of substantial income. The company believes that its proposed accounting treatment is in accordance with GAAP. Its outside auditors have been noncommittal, however, as to whether the company's interpretation of the applicable FASB accounting standard is proper. At the end of the *second quarter*, the auditors indicate that they need more time to study the issue and do research. (Assume that the auditors review quarterly results *at year-end*.)

Required

1. Should the company record the transaction and report the income in the second quarter? State the reasons for your position.
2. What steps might the outside auditors take in doing research?
3. What other steps should the auditors consider?

Financial Analysis Problems

FAP 17-1 **Identifying Weaknesses in an Interim Report and Evaluating Treatment of Selected Items** Budgco, which is listed on the American Stock Exchange, budgeted activities for 2006 as follows:

	Amount	Units
Sales, net	$ 6,000,000	1,000,000
Cost of sales	(3,600,000)	1,000,000
Gross Margin	$ 2,400,000	
Selling, general, and administrative expenses	(1,400,000)	
Operating Income	$ 1,000,000	
Nonoperating revenue and expenses	-0-	
Income before Income Taxes	$ 1,000,000	
Estimated income taxes (current and deferred)	(400,000)	
Net Income	$ 600,000	
Earnings per share of common stock	$6.00	

Budgco has operated profitably for many years and has experienced a seasonal pattern of sales volume and production similar to those forecasted for 2006. Sales volume is expected to follow a quarterly pattern of 10%, 20%, 35%, and 35%, respectively, because of the seasonality of the industry. Because of production and storage capacity limitations, production is expected to follow a pattern of 20%, 25%, 30%, and 25% per quarter, respectively.

At the conclusion of the first quarter of 2006, the controller prepared and issued the following interim report for public release:

	Amount	Units
Sales, net	$ 600,000	100,000
Cost of sales	(360,000)	100,000
Gross Margin	$ 240,000	
Selling, general, and administrative expenses	(260,000)	
Operating Loss	$ (20,000)	
Loss from warehouse fire	(140,000)	
Loss before Income Taxes	$(160,000)	
Estimated income taxes	-0-	
Net Loss	$(160,000)	
Loss per share of common stock	$(1.60)	

The following additional information is available for the first quarter just completed but was not included in the information released to the public:

1. Budgco uses a *standard costing system*, in which standards are set annually at currently attainable levels. At the end of the first quarter, a $50,000 *underapplied* fixed factory overhead (volume variance) was treated as an asset at the end of the quarter. Production during the quarter was 200,000 units, of which 100,000 units were sold.
2. The selling, general, and administrative expenses were budgeted on the basis of $800,000 *fixed expenses* for the year plus $0.50 *variable expenses* per unit of sales. (A $10,000 *unfavorable* variance was incurred in the *first quarter*.)
3. Assume that the warehouse fire loss met the conditions of an extraordinary loss. The warehouse had an undepreciated cost of $320,000; $180,000 was recovered from insurance on the warehouse. No other gains or losses are anticipated this year from similar events or transactions, nor has the company had any similar losses in preceding years; thus the full loss is deductible as an *ordinary loss* for income tax purposes.
4. The effective annual income tax rate, for federal and state taxes combined, is expected to average 40% of earnings before income taxes during 2006. No differences exist between pretax accounting earnings and taxable income.
5. Earnings per share was computed on the basis of 100,000 shares of capital stock outstanding. Budgco has only one class of stock issued, no long-term debt outstanding, and no stock option plan.

Required

1. Without reference to the specific situation described, what standards of disclosure exist for interim financial data (published interim financial reports) for publicly traded companies? Explain.
2. Identify the form and content weaknesses of the interim report without reference to the additional information.
3. Indicate for interim reporting purposes the preferable treatment for each of the five items of additional information, and explain why that treatment is preferable.

FAP 17-2 **Analyzing Propriety of "Bill and Hold" Sales** To meet its second-quarter budgeted sales, Parco's management enticed many of its customers to enter into **noncancelable** sales agreements in June 2005 whereby:

1. Customers agree to buy inventory **without taking delivery**.
2. Parco agrees to warehouse the inventory for free **until the earlier of**:
   a. October 1, 2005, or
   b. The date the customer instructs Parco to deliver the inventory.
3. Customers are to be billed in June 2005.
4. Customers have 90 days *after the delivery date* to pay Parco.

5. Customers receive a 10% price discount under this arrangement if payment is made on time.
6. Returns are permitted only for *defective products*; any *returned* product is to be *replaced* with a replacement product—no cash refunds.

As a result of entering into these sales agreements, Parco was able to substantially increase its sales for the second quarter of 2005 and thus meet its *second-quarter* budgeted sales.

Required Can Parco properly report these sales in its second quarter of 2005?

chapter

18

Securities and Exchange Commission Reporting

One's judgment cannot be better than the information on which it is based. Given the truth, one may still go wrong when one has the chance to be right. But given no news, or presented only with distorted or incomplete data, with ignorant, sloppy or biased reporting, with propaganda and deliberate falsehoods, you destroy one's whole reasoning process.

ARTHUR HAYS SULZBERGER

LEARNING OBJECTIVES

To Understand

- The SEC's purpose and organization structure.
- The SEC's role in relation to the FASB.
- The SEC's *enforcement* powers.
- The various types of promulgations issued by the SEC to carry out its duties.
- The nature of the Securities Act of 1933 and the Securities Exchange Act of 1934.
- The nature of *Regulation S-X,* which has special significance to accountants.

TOPIC OUTLINE

I. The Purpose of the SEC
II. The Organization Structure of the SEC
III. The Role of the SEC in Relation to the FASB
IV. The SEC's Enforcement Powers
V. SEC Promulgations
VI. The Integrated Disclosure System (IDS)
VII. The Securities Act of 1933
VIII. The Securities Exchange Act of 1934
IX. The Small Business Integrated Disclosure System
X. Regulation of Foreign Securities Traded in the United States
XI. *International* Offerings and *Global* Offerings by U.S. Companies
XII. *Regulation S-X*: A Closer Look

CHAPTER OVERVIEW

This chapter discusses the manner by which the Securities and Exchange Commission (SEC) regulates (1) the *sale* of corporate securities to the public, (2) the *trading* of securities of *publicly owned* companies (***approximately 30,000 companies***), and (3) the financial reporting process of all *publicly owned* companies and the *larger privately owned* companies.

Companies subject to this federal regulatory process must have an extensive understanding of a host of statutory laws as well as SEC regulations, releases, interpretations, bulletins, and forms. Usually, they obtain expert legal counsel.

We also discuss the SEC's statutory powers to (1) establish GAAP, (2) enforce SEC rules and decisions on companies, (3) take various disciplinary actions against auditors of publicly owned companies, and (4) recommend that the Justice Department begin a criminal investigation into the conduct of publicly owned companies, their officers, or their auditors.

The SEC's Web site is **http://www.sec.gov**. Throughout this chapter, we cite many more specific SEC URLs for accessing certain SEC pronouncements and documents.

I. THE PURPOSE OF THE SEC

Historical Background

The nature of securities is such that their purchase and sale can create substantial opportunities for *misrepresentation*, *manipulation*, and other *fraudulent acts*. In reaction to a rapidly increasing number of flagrant abuses in this area, all but one state enacted some form of legislation between 1911 and 1933 to regulate the purchase and sale of corporate securities. Commonly referred to as the **blue sky laws**, these laws vary widely among the states. In addition, because these laws apply only to *intrastate transactions*, they have proved to be ineffective from an overall standpoint of protecting the public. The stock market crash of 1929, testimonial to the inadequacy of this type of regulation, was preceded by (1) the issuance of billions of dollars of securities during the preceding decade that proved to be worthless, (2) the excessive use of credit to purchase stocks on margin, (3) the extensive manipulation of stock prices by various means, (4) the extensive use of *inside information* by officers and directors for purposes of self-enrichment, and (5) lax standards governing the solicitation of votes from shareholders whereby managements were often able to perpetuate themselves in power. The magnitude of the inadequate financial reporting and questionable ethical standards that led to this financial collapse substantially undermined the integrity of the capital markets and thus raised serious questions concerning the survival of our system of free capital markets.

To restore investor confidence and reestablish integrity in the capital markets, Congress passed the Securities Act of 1933 (the 1933 Act) and the Securities Exchange Act of 1934 (the 1934 Act). These two acts do not replace the intrastate regulation provided by the blue sky laws but merely supplement them. **The 1933 Act applies to the *initial distribution* of securities to the public.** The purpose of this act, as expressed in its preamble, is

> to provide full and fair disclosure of the character of securities sold in interstate and foreign commerce and through the mails, and to prevent frauds in the sale thereof.

This required disclosure is accomplished by "registering" securities with the SEC before they may be offered to the public. The registration procedure involves filing specified financial and nonfinancial information with the SEC for examination.

The 1934 Act applies to the subsequent trading **in outstanding securities that are listed on organized stock exchanges and in the over-the-counter markets.** The purpose of this act, as expressed in its preamble, is

> to provide for the regulation of securities exchanges and of over-the-counter markets operating in interstate and foreign commerce and through the mails to prevent inequitable and unfair practices on such exchanges and markets.

Companies that come under the provisions of the 1934 Act must file with the SEC periodic reports of specified financial and *nonfinancial* information. In addition, certain practices are prohibited.

Because each act constitutes a major piece of legislation, we cannot discuss each in great detail in one chapter. Accordingly, this chapter provides a general familiarity with selected portions of each act and the means to comply with the financial reporting requirements established by the SEC.

The Functions of the SEC

Before discussing the two acts, we must examine the functions and organizational structure of the Securities and Exchange Commission. Created in 1934 to administer the 1933 Act and the 1934 Act, the SEC is a quasi-judicial agency of the U.S. government. Since its creation, the SEC's responsibilities have broadened so that it now administers and enforces the following additional acts (or sections thereof):

1. **The Public Utility Holding Company Act of 1935**, which requires geographic integration of operations and simplification of unduly cumbersome and complex capital structures of public utility holding companies. Because these objectives were accomplished many years ago through the registration process, current efforts are directed toward maintaining the status quo.
2. **The Trust Indenture Act of 1939**, which requires the use of a trust indenture that meets certain requirements for debt securities offered to the public to protect the rights of investors in such securities. Although a separate act, it is substantively an amendment to the 1933 Act.
3. **The Investment Company Act of 1940**, which regulates investment companies, that is, companies engaged primarily in the business of investing, reinvesting, owning, holding, or trading in securities. Mutual funds are the most visible investment companies. Regulation is effected through the registration process.
4. **The Investment Advisers Act of 1940**, which regulates the conduct of investment advisors similarly to the manner in which the 1934 Act regulates the conduct of brokers and dealers. Regulation is effected through the registration process.
5. **The Foreign Corrupt Practices Act of 1977 (FCPA)**, which prohibits U.S. firms from offering funds (bribes) to foreign officials in an effort to obtain or retain business. The FCPA also essentially forbids indirect payment methods in that funds may not be offered if the firm has reason to believe that any part of these funds will be used to pay bribes. Although an amendment to the FCPA allows small payments to be made to lower-level foreign officials performing routine and lawful duties, the amendment does not clearly specify who or how much can be paid. (In 1995, the SEC requested IBM Corporation to furnish information on its Argentine operations because of a massive bribery scandal involving several high-level government officials.)
6. **The Insider Trading Sanctions Act of 1984 and the Insider Trading and Securities Fraud Enforcement Act of 1988**, which substantially increased (1) *monetary penalties* for those who profit by trading securities using inside information—**the penalty is now the higher of $1 million or three times the profit gained or loss avoided** (rather than merely the profit gained or loss avoided)—and (2) *criminal penalties* for securities fraud, market manipulation, and other violations—**individuals can now be fined up to $1 million and receive prison sentences of up to 10 years.**
7. **The Private Securities Litigation Reform Act of 1995.** This law's purpose is to curtail frivolous lawsuits. Later, we discuss the illegal acts section and auditors' responsibility to disclose illegal acts to the SEC.
8. **The Sarbanes-Oxley Act of 2002.** This comprehensive and sweeping legislation dealing with the accuracy of financial reporting was passed in response to the massive accounting frauds perpetrated by Enron Corporation and WorldCom that came to light in 2001 and 2002. (These two companies were the largest Chapter 11 bankruptcy filings ever.) The effects of this far-reaching act consist of (1) the establishment of independent oversight of external auditors (done through the Public Companies Accounting Oversight Board [PCAOB]), (2) the imposition of major constraints on external auditors (as to their non-audit consulting activities) to ensure that they remain independent, (3) the imposition of certain constraints on corporate managements, and (4)

the imposition of internal control and ethics requirements on corporate managements. As a result of this act, many companies have created "corporate-governance" websites, which provide extensive information dealing with items required under the act. This act is discussed extensively in auditing textbooks.

The Relationship of the Federal Securities Laws to the State Securities Laws

Dual Compliance Is Necessary

The *federal* government and each state government have separate autonomous securities laws and regulations. Compliance with the laws and rules of one does not constitute compliance with the laws and regulations of the other. An entity selling securities must comply with *federal* securities laws as well as with the laws of each *state* in which it intends to offer its securities. In addition, the fact that a particular offering may be exempt from certain provisions of the *federal* securities laws does not necessarily mean that it is exempt from the notice and filing requirements of *state* laws.

Disclosure Regulation versus Merit Regulation

In certain states, the law permits a state official to judge the merits of an offering. In these "**merit regulation**" states, even though a company complies with the registration or filing procedures, the state may prohibit the offering because the state official does not consider it to be "fair, just, and equitable" for purchase by citizens of that state. Consequently, an issuer of securities must be careful to make sure there is compliance with all the appropriate state requirements as well as with the federal securities laws.[1]

In enforcing the 1933 Act, the SEC has no authority to evaluate the quality of securities offered or to pass judgment on the merits of each offering. Rather, the "**disclosure regulation**" approach permits a company to offer its securities for sale if it has disclosed sufficient and accurate information about the business it conducts or proposes to conduct. In this respect, the SEC requires the following disclaimer be prominently shown on the cover page of each prospectus or offering circular given to potential investors:

> These securities have not been approved or disapproved by the Securities and Exchange Commission nor has the Commission passed upon the accuracy or adequacy of this prospectus. Any representation to the contrary is a criminal offense.

II. The Organization Structure of the SEC

The SEC is composed of five members appointed by the president of the United States, with the advice and consent of the Senate, for a five-year term, with one term expiring each year. No more than three members may be of the same political party. An extensive professional staff—primarily comprising *lawyers*, *accountants*, *economists*, and *financial analysts*—has been organized into numerous separate offices and divisions. We list the more important ones:

Offices

Administrative Law Judges
Filings and Information Services
Chief Accountant
Inspector General
Compliance Inspections and Examinations
Public Affairs, Policy Evaluation and Research

Economic Analysis
Executive Director
General Counsel

Information Technology
Secretary

[1] We know of one case in which the State of New York would *not* allow an issuer to sell its securities in New York *unless* the issuer's president made full restitution to the creditors of a former New York company that (1) the president had owned and (2) had gone bankrupt 15 years earlier.

Divisions	
Corporation Finance	Investment Management
Enforcement	Market Regulation

Each office and each division is responsible to the commissioners and carries out their orders and legal responsibilities. In addition to this bureaucracy located in Washington, D.C., five regional offices and six district offices are located in major cities throughout the country. The roles of the Office of Chief Accountant and the Division of Corporation Finance are pertinent to this chapter.

The Division of Corporation Finance

The Division of Corporation Finance reviews the registration statements and reports that registrants file with the SEC. The review determines (1) that all required financial statements and supporting schedules have been included and (2) that such financial statements apparently have been prepared in accordance with GAAP as well as the rules, regulations, and policies issued by the SEC. Because the SEC does *not* perform audits of registrants' financial statements, it *cannot* absolutely determine whether they have been prepared in accordance with GAAP. For this it relies on the reports of registrants' outside certified public accountants (discussed later in the chapter).

The Chief Accountant

The Chief Accountant is the commission's chief accounting officer for all accounting and auditing matters in connection with the administration of the various acts. The Chief Accountant advises the commission of accounting problems and recommends courses of action. For example, in 1986 the Chief Accountant proposed that the full cost method used by oil- and gas-producing companies be abolished. Following an outcry by 2 cabinet members and 10 senators from oil- and gas-producing states, the SEC's commissioners voted to abandon the proposal. Thus **the power to establish accounting standards** (discussed in detail in the following section) **resides with the SEC's commissioners**—*not* with the Chief Accountant. Administratively, the Chief Accountant drafts rules and regulations governing the form and content of the financial statements that must be filed with the commission under the various acts.

CHECK POINT

With which body does the statutory authority to establish GAAP reside?

a. The SEC commissioners
b. The Chief Accountant of the SEC
c. The Division of Corporation Finance
d. The FASB
e. The SEC staff

Answer: a

ETHICS

Should the SEC Discipline Audit *Managers* as Well as Audit *Partners*?

Assume that you are the audit manager of a publicly owned company that is aggressively trying to report income for the current year. You are near the conclusion of the fieldwork and have major unresolved differences with the chief financial officer regarding what is acceptable GAAP.

On returning from an out-of-town audit engagement, the audit partner informs you that (1) all differences have been resolved as a result of compromises worked out with the client and (2) the client has released its financial statements.

Questions

1. What would you do?
2. What arguments can be made for and against the SEC disciplining an audit *manager* in addition to an audit *partner*?
3. What do you think the SEC does in practice?

III. The Role of the SEC in Relation to the FASB

The Statutory Authority of the SEC

Under the 1933 Act and the 1934 Act, the SEC has the power to do the following:

1. Adopt, amend, and rescind rules and regulations as necessary to carry out the provisions of these acts.
2. Prescribe the form or forms on which required information is filed with the SEC.
3. Prescribe the accounting methods to be followed in the financial statements filed with the SEC.
4. Prescribe the items or details to be shown in the financial statements filed with the SEC.

In relation to item 3, the SEC has the **statutory authority** (given to it by Congress) **to prescribe accounting standards** for companies falling under its jurisdiction. Recognizing the expertise and substantial resources of the public accounting profession, however, the SEC has usually looked to the accounting profession's standard-setting bodies to establish and improve accounting and reporting standards. When the Financial Accounting Standards Board (FASB) was established in 1973, for example, the SEC specifically announced that

> principles, standards and practices promulgated by the FASB in its Statements and Interpretations will be considered by the Commission as having substantial authoritative support and those contrary to such FASB promulgations will be considered to have no such support.[2]

The alternative of having the SEC establish GAAP is alarming to many because it is feared that our Washington legislators would either pass legislation or bring pressure on the SEC to lower accounting standards in return for PAC money.

The policy of looking to the *private sector* to establish and improve standards, however, is by no means an abdication of the commission's responsibilities or authority. When the SEC has concluded that such bodies were moving *too slowly* or in the *wrong direction*, it has *not* hesitated to take one of the following courses of action:

1. Establish its own additional financial reporting requirements (calling for additional disclosures).
2. Impose a moratorium on accounting practices.
3. Overrule a pronouncement of the FASB.

Concerning items 1 and 2, in most instances the SEC has later rescinded its own action as a result of the passage of new or revised accounting standards or disclosure requirements by the profession's standard-setting bodies. The following two paragraphs present examples of the most recent major actions of the SEC along these lines.

Examples of Additional Disclosures Required

We present three examples:

1. **Segment reporting.** The SEC imposed line-of-business disclosure requirements long before the 1976 issuance of FASB *Statement No. 14*, "Financial Reporting for Segments of a Business Enterprise." Shortly after this statement was issued, the SEC modified its previous line-of-business disclosure requirements to conform in most respects to the requirements of *FAS 14*. (In 1998, the SEC repeated this process again as a result of the FASB issuing FASB *Statement No. 131*,

[2] *Accounting Series Release No. 150*, "Statement of Policy on the Establishment and Improvement of Accounting Principles and Standards" (Washington, D.C.: Securities and Exchange Commission, 1973). In April 1982, *Accounting Series Release No. 150* was codified in *SEC Financial Reporting Release No. 1*, Section 101.

"Disclosures about Segments of an Enterprise and Related Information," in 1997, which superseded *FAS 14*.)

2. **Price-level accounting.** In 1976, because of concerns about relatively high inflation (at the time) making the historical-cost-based financial statements nonmeaningful, the SEC required certain large companies to disclose replacement cost data (*Accounting Series Release No. 190*). After FASB *Statement No. 33*, "Financial Reporting and Changing Prices," was issued in 1979, the SEC rescinded its requirements in this area. (In 1986, FASB *Statement No. 89*, "Financial Reporting and Changing Prices," superseded *FAS 33* and made *voluntary* the supplementary disclosure of current cost/constant purchasing power information. Virtually no companies *voluntarily* disclose this information, however.)
3. **Derivative financial instruments.** In 1997, the SEC amended its rules to expand greatly the existing disclosure requirements for derivative financial instruments. Of major importance is the requirement to disclose quantitative information about market risk exposures—something *not* then required by GAAP and *not* even required in FASB *Statement No. 133*, "Accounting for Derivative Instruments and Hedging Activities," which was issued in 1998. Thus the SEC's rules in this area (contained in Regulations S-X, S-K, and S-B and in Form 20-F, which are discussed later) constitute major (and quite involved) disclosures well above and beyond current GAAP.

Examples of Prohibiting Accounting Practices

In 1974, the SEC imposed a moratorium on the capitalization of interest (*Accounting Series Release No. 163*). It had noted with concern an increase in the number of companies changing their accounting methods to a policy of capitalizing interest cost. Because no authoritative statement on this subject existed at that time (except for two specific industries), this action stopped a developing trend until the FASB could deal with the issue. In 1979, after the FASB issued FASB *Statement No. 34*, "Capitalization of Interest Cost," the SEC rescinded its moratorium.

In another action, the SEC moved in 1983 to halt the spread of a controversial accounting method that more than a dozen computer software companies were using to increase their earnings. The SEC had noticed a trend in the industry toward capitalization without adequate criteria—the accounting standards and related interpretation that existed then were somewhat fuzzy. Therefore, the SEC imposed a moratorium on the capitalization of software development costs for companies that had *not* publicly disclosed the practice of capitalizing those costs prior to April 14, 1983 (*Financial Reporting Release No. 12*). In 1985, after the FASB issued *Statement No. 86*, "Accounting for the Costs of Computer Software to Be Sold, Leased, or Otherwise Marketed," the SEC rescinded its moratorium.

The SEC has *not* deemed it necessary to issue a moratorium since 1984, the year that the FASB created the Emerging Issues Task Force (discussed shortly).

Overruling the FASB

Only once has the SEC overruled a pronouncement of the FASB. This ruling occurred in 1978 when the SEC rejected the standards set forth in FASB *Statement No. 19*, "Financial Accounting and Reporting by Oil and Gas Producing Companies." The SEC favored developing a new system of "reserve recognition accounting" (RRA). The conflict between the requirements of *FAS 19* and those of the SEC (as set forth in *Accounting Series Release No. 253*) resulted in an untenable situation. *Privately owned* companies were subject to *FAS 19*, and *publicly owned* companies were subject to *ASR No. 253*. Lack of comparability resulted. Accordingly, the FASB voluntarily (and to be practical) issued *FAS 25*, which suspended the effective dates of most requirements in *FAS 19*. In 1981, the SEC abandoned its efforts to develop RRA and announced that it would support FASB's efforts to develop disclosure requirements for oil and gas producers. In 1982, the FASB issued *Statement No. 69*, "Disclosures about Oil and Gas Producing Activities," which amended *FAS 19* and *25*. Shortly thereafter, the SEC amended its disclosure requirements for oil and gas producers to require compliance with the provisions of *FAS 69*.

Current Working Relationship

The Securities and Exchange Commission and the FASB now try to maintain a close working relationship to prevent any future conflicts. The full FASB *board* meets *annually* or *biennially* with all of the commissioners to exchange information on the status of projects and plans and to discuss other matters of mutual interest. The FASB *staff* meets *quarterly* in Washington with the SEC staff. Members of the Chief Accountant's staff are responsible for keeping track of the development of specific FASB technical projects. SEC staff members participate in advisory task force meetings on those projects and frequently observe FASB meetings. When the SEC has proposed changes to its rules and regulations, the FASB has occasionally expressed its views on such proposals. In summary, **both organizations strive for a climate of *mutual cooperation* and *no surprises*.**

The SEC's Push for Market Value Accounting

The SEC was the driving force behind the issuance of (1) FASB *Statement No. 107*, "Disclosures about Fair Value of Financial Instruments" (1991), which requires companies to disclose in notes the fair values of their financial instruments, (2) FASB *Statement No. 115*, "Accounting for Certain Investments in Debt and Equity Securities" (1993), which requires companies to account for certain debt and equity investments at their *fair value*, and (3) FASB *Statement No. 133*, "Accounting for Derivative Instruments and Hedging Activities" (1998), which requires companies to (a) recognize *all* derivatives as either *assets* or *liabilities* in the statement of financial position and (b) measure those instruments at fair value—something that banks, bank regulators, the secretary of the treasury, the chairman of the FDIC, and the chairman of the Federal Reserve System strongly opposed.

SEC Involvement in the FASB's Emerging Issues Task Force

The Chief Accountant is a participant in the FASB's Emerging Issues Task Force (EITF) that conducts an open 1-2 day meeting every other month (at the FASB's offices in Norwalk, Connecticut) to discuss emerging issues on a timely basis. (For example, *EITF Issue 00-2*, "Accounting for Web Site Development Costs," requires the expensing of most types of costs other than those to actually create the site's functionalities and features.) The consensus views of the EITF constitute generally accepted accounting principles for public and nonpublic companies. Thus the SEC has a very active and direct role in establishing GAAP.[3]

The Open Door Policy

The SEC encourages registrants to bring *novel accounting treatments* and new types of accounting transactions to its attention for immediate resolution *before* reporting the accounting effects to stockholders. Unfortunately, many registrants do *not* avail themselves of this opportunity (possibly fearing that the answer will be ***no***). Instead, they try to slip liberal accounting practices and interpretations past the SEC—hoping that it will *not* notice these practices when making its reviews—and placing themselves in the position of having enforcement actions brought against them.

CHECK POINT

Which of the following is the SEC not empowered to do?

a. Require additional disclosures
b. Prohibit accounting practices
c. Overrule the FASB
d. Establish GAAP
e. Rescind FASB pronouncements

Answer: e

---

[3] In 1992, the consensus views of the EITF officially became part of GAAP as a result of being added to category c of the GAAP hierarchy applicable to nongovernmental entities. This GAAP hierarchy is set forth in *Statement on Auditing Standards No. 69*, "The Meaning of Present Fairly in Conformity with Generally Accepted Accounting Principles" (issued by the AICPA's Auditing Standards Board in 1992). (EITF issue summaries and opinions are available through the FASB publication, *EITF Abstracts*, in either a looseleaf or an annual softbound format.)

IV. The SEC's Enforcement Powers

Enforcement Actions against Registrants

In its efforts to prevent violations of the federal securities laws, the SEC has several enforcement weapons at its disposal.

1. **Instituting administrative proceedings with the SEC's Office of Administrative Law Judges.** Under this course of action, which is generally used **for less egregious violations**, the Enforcement Division notifies the entity that the Enforcement Staff intends to recommend to the SEC commissioners (who must approve initiation of all enforcement actions) that an enforcement action be brought against the entity. The entity usually is given 14 days to respond and submit an offer of settlement (which usually includes willingness to accept a *cease and desist order* to refrain from violating the securities laws in the future).

   The Enforcement Division's recommendations and the entity's response are then sent to the SEC commissioners. If the commissioners approve the Enforcement Division's recommendation, the Enforcement Division begins administrative proceedings (also commonly referred to as *cease and desist proceedings*) by filing a complaint with the SEC's Office of Administrative Law Judges.

   An administrative law judge then holds a hearing with Enforcement Division lawyers and the entity's legal counsel to determine whether a cease and desist order should be issued. (If the issues are complex, the hearing essentially becomes a trial that can last several weeks.) A *cease and desist order* against an individual may (1) require the disgorgement of ill-gotten gains and (2) result in a suspension (for up to one year) or a bar (for longer than one year) from practicing before the commission. (If barred, the person must reapply to the SEC to practice before it again.)

   If the administrative law judge issues a *cease and desist order*, the entity can appeal the decision to the SEC commissioners. If the commissioners uphold the order, the entity can appeal the decision to a federal district court.

   The advantage to this course of action is that it usually is swifter, more efficient, and more flexible than the alternative of seeking a federal district court injunction.
2. **Obtaining an injunction in a federal district court.** Under this course of action, which is usually used **for egregious violations**, the SEC files a complaint with the district court seeking a court order that (1) enjoins the defendant **from future violations of specified sections of the federal securities laws**, (2) may impose **monetary penalties**, (3) may require **disgorgement of unlawful gains**, or (4) **bars or suspends a person(s) from serving as an officer(s) or director(s) of a public company**. (Bars and suspensions are usually sought only when a defendant has engaged in fraudulent conduct while serving in a corporate or other fiduciary capacity.) A future violation of a judge's order (the SEC monitors) can result in court-ordered civil penalties for being in contempt of court. (*The SEC files roughly 100 civil lawsuits a year.*)

   Consenting. When an entity chooses *not* to litigate the SEC action in court (as usually occurs), the entity consents to a court order, usually without admitting or denying liability, and the court enters an order based on the consent. (See the accompanying Case in Point.) In these cases, the SEC actions can have other major consequences to the entity because its shareholders usually sue it to recover related losses that they suffered. The monetary amounts recovered are often astronomical compared with any court-imposed penalties.
3. **Suspending stock trading for a 10-day period.** Under this course of action, the SEC—**without the permission of either a federal district court judge or an SEC administrative law judge**—can suspend trading in an entity's stock for 10 days. (In 1978, the Supreme Court outlawed the SEC's practice of stringing together 10-day suspensions to keep a stock from trading for months at a time, a practice the Court called "flagrantly abusive.") In these cases, a district court injunction is usually sought as well.

CASE IN POINT

The SEC versus America Online, Inc.: Accounting and Auditing Enforcement Release No. 1257 (5/15/00)

The SEC filed a complaint in civil court seeking injunctive relief and civil penalties alleging that America Online Inc. (AOL) committed violations of Sections 13(a), 13(b)(2)(A) of the Exchange Act and Rules 13a-1 and 13a-13 thereunder. The commission's complaint alleged that AOL improperly deferred *direct marketing acquisition costs* in 1995 and 1996 by erroneously applying the AICPA's *Statement of Position 93-7*, which contains a limited exception to the general rule under GAAP that all advertising costs be expensed as incurred.

AOL consented to the entry of a permanent injunction prohibiting future violations of the named sections of the Exchange Act and to the entry of an order imposing civil penalties pursuant to Section 21(d) of the Exchange Act in the amount of $3,500,000, without admitting or denying the commission's allegations. In 1997, AOL announced that it was writing off $385 million of previously deferred direct marketing acquisition costs (which wiped out all previously reported earnings to date).

Actively Questioning Accounting Practices

The SEC does *not* hesitate to question the accounting and reporting practices of the financial statements filed with it, regardless of whether a registrant's *outside* auditors concur with the registrant's accounting treatment. The SEC pays great attention to ensuring that *substance* prevails over *form*. Countless instances have occurred in which the SEC has cast aside a registrant's literal interpretation of generally accepted accounting principles that the SEC deemed superficial and unreflective of the economics. Some of the more notable and recent such actions are as follows:

1. In 2003, MCI (formerly known as WorldCom) agreed to pay a $1.5 billion fine (the largest the SEC has ever imposed) to settle charges that it inflated profits by at least $9 billion in the biggest accounting scandal in U.S. history.
2. In 2002, Xerox Corp. agreed to pay a record (at that time) $10 million civil penalty and restate its earnings for four years to settle SEC charges that it engaged in fraudulent accounting practices.
3. In 2002, Siebel Systems agreed to settle charges that it had violated SEC Regulation FD (discussed later), which prohibits companies from selectively disclosing information to favored Wall Street analysts *before* releasing the news to ordinary investors. (This was the first litigation brought by the SEC to enforce Regulation FD).
4. Sony Corp. agreed to pay $1 million in 1998 to settle a complaint filed by the SEC that the Japanese entertainment company did *not* properly disclose hundreds of millions of dollars in merger-related losses at Sony Pictures Entertainment Inc., its movie division.
5. 3Com had to reduce by $157 million the size of a merger-related restructuring charge that was taken after its 1997 acquisition of U.S. Robotics. The SEC has taken similar actions against several high-technology companies. The SEC's concern is that companies that set up reserves that are too high will (1) cause investors to ignore the initial large "one-time" charge to income and (2) leave the company in a position to later report higher profits than it otherwise would have reported (by reversing the unneeded portion of the reserve—a liability).
6. America Online (AOL) had to change to more conservative accounting practices in 1997 for both marketing acquisition costs and certain revenues, substantially reducing its income. The SEC presumably targeted AOL because (1) it is the industry leader and (2) the SEC wants to use AOL to set the industry standard.
7. BankAmerica Corp. had to reclassify as an extraordinary item a $30.8 million gain from a debt-equity exchange that it previously had reported as part of operating income.
8. Aetna Life & Casualty Co. was prohibited from giving tax effects to an operating loss carryforward.

9. Alexander and Alexander Services Inc. had to report as an extraordinary loss the unanticipated $40 million it had proposed to add to goodwill and amortize over 40 years. The registrant had purchased a target company and, shortly after the consummation, discovered that the acquired company's liabilities had been understated by $40 million.
10. Several financial institutions were ordered in the 1980s to reduce their goodwill amortization lives from 40 years to 25 years or less because of SEC's perception that artificial income was being reported in the use of 40 years for goodwill and a much shorter life for loan discounts (the amortization of which increased income). (Partly as a result of SEC pressure, the FASB subsequently addressed the issue in *Statement No. 72*, "Accounting for Certain Acquisitions of Banking or Thrift Institutions," with similar conclusions.)
11. Several companies that had formed "nonsubsidiary subsidiaries" (discussed in Chapter 3) to avoid recognition of expenses or losses in their statements during the early years of the affiliates' operations were ordered to consolidate such companies.

Concerned that the use of abusive accounting gimmicks had become too widespread, the SEC began an intensive initiative in 1998 to ensure that managements are managing the business—not the earnings. The issues of greatest concern to the SEC were:

1. Write-off of in-process research and development in a purchase business combination (discussed in Chapter 5).
2. Revenue recognition policies involving "market channel stuffing."
3. Unsupportable restructuring charges and loss accruals (ostensibly established for the purpose of reversing the accruals in later periods and thus increasing earnings in those periods).
4. Other overnight "nonrecurring" charges such as write-downs of fixed assets and goodwill that could have been prevented if more conservative depreciation and amortization lives had been used.
5. Intentional immaterial misapplications of GAAP.

These efforts resulted in the issuance of SEC *Staff Accounting Bulletins 99*, *100*, and *101*, which had a substantial impact on the financial reporting practices of public companies—especially their revenue recognition practices. (Staff Accounting Bulletins are discussed in detail later.)

In recent years, the SEC has investigated and filed more than 100 accounting-related enforcement cases per year. Overall, the SEC is given high marks and has won the reputation as a tough police officer of corporate conduct. (SEC Enforcement releases can be found at **http://www.sec.gov/divisions/enforce.shtml**.)

Disciplinary Actions against Auditors

If the SEC finds that a registrant's certified public accountants are not qualified, lack integrity, have engaged in unethical or improper professional conduct, or have willfully violated or aided and abetted the violation of any provision of the federal securities laws or rules thereunder, the SEC is empowered to take the following steps:

1. Bar the auditor(s) from (1) practicing before the SEC either permanently or for a specified period of time or (2) accepting new *publicly owned* companies as clients for a stipulated period of time. In 2003, the SEC barred for life the PricewaterhouseCoopers engagement partner on the Tyco International audit for reckless conduct. (Tyco's officers were indicted as part of the alleged Tyco criminal enterprise, in which hundreds of millions of dollars were allegedly looted from the company.)

   In 2004, the SEC (1) ruled that Big Four accounting firm Ernst & Young had engaged in "improper professional conduct" in connection with its audit of PeopleSoft Inc., by having entered into a joint marketing agreement with PeopleSoft (*business dealings with* audit clients *are prohibited under auditing independence rules*), (2) suspended E&Y from accepting new publicly traded companies as audit clients for six months, and (3) ordered E&Y to pay $1.7 million (the amount of their audit fees) as restitution.
2. Censure the auditor(s).

3. Require the auditor(s) to submit to a peer review.
4. Recommend criminal proceedings against the auditor(s) (as the SEC did in the well-publicized Continental Vending case and the National Student Marketing case of the early 1970s in which partners of two large accounting firms were convicted and sent to prison).

In recent years, the SEC has brought about 25 professional misconduct cases a year against auditing firms. See the Case in Point.

CASE IN POINT

The SEC versus Andersen, LLP in the Matter of Waste Management, Inc. Accounting and Auditing Enforcement Release No. 1405 (6/19/01)

In 2001, in one of the first fraud cases ever filed against a Big Five accounting firm, the SEC fined Andersen LLP and three partners more than $7 million in settlement of a civil lawsuit in which the SEC alleged that Andersen issued false and misleading audit reports that inflated Waste Management's earnings by roughly $1 billion for the years 1992 to 1996. In addition, the SEC censured the three Waste Management audit partners plus Andersen's regional audit director. As part of the censure, the four audit partners were barred from doing accounting work for *public companies* for a period of one to five years.

Waste Management and Andersen agreed to pay $220 million to settle *shareholder litigation* in the matter. (In 1998, Waste Management took a $3.5 billion charge to earnings and admitted that it had *overstated* its pretax earnings $1.43 billion in 1992 to 1996—the largest restatement in SEC history [up until 2001].)

The S&L Crisis: Government Action against S&L Outside Auditors

Because Congress created the Resolution Trust Corporation (RTC) to deal with the S&L crisis of the late 1980s, the SEC had no role in bringing enforcement actions against auditors of S&Ls that issued false and misleading financial statements. The RTC, as a surrogate for the SEC, however, exacted more than $1 billion in settlements (in total) from most of the Big Five international accounting firms regarding their role (grossly incompetent auditing that, in the minds of some, often bordered on collusion with management) in auditing dozens of S&Ls that committed massive frauds. (To the surprise of some in light of the publicity regarding the well below par manner of conducting these audits, the RTC brought no criminal charges against any of these S&L auditors as it brought against many of the S&L managements.)

CHECK POINT

Which of the following actions can the SEC not take against auditors?

a. Censure the auditors
b. Require the auditors to submit to a peer review
c. Institute criminal proceedings
d. Bar the auditors from practicing before the SEC either temporarily or permanently
e. Require the auditors to take continuing education courses

Answer: c

V. SEC PROMULGATIONS

To carry out its responsibilities, the SEC issues various rules, regulations (a group of rules), releases, and staff accounting bulletins, and prescribes certain forms that companies must use in filing registration statements and reports. The 1933 Act and the 1934 Act have their own regulations, rules, releases, and forms. In addition, certain regulations and releases apply to both the 1933 Act and the 1934 Act. The Staff Accounting Bulletins also apply to both acts. An understanding of all these items is essential to comply with the registration and reporting requirements of these acts.

The General Rules and Regulations, Forms, and Releases

General Rules and Regulations

The Securities Act of 1933 is divided into 26 *sections*, and the Securities Exchange Act of 1934 is divided into 35 sections (***sections constitute the statutory law***). The SEC has adopted ***rules*** pertaining to the 1933 Act, which are assigned three-digit numbers starting with 100. The rules are grouped into various categories, most of which are designated ***regulations***. For example, Rules 400-494 make up *Regulation* C, which deals with the mechanics of registering securities with the SEC.

The SEC's *rules* and *regulations* pertaining to the 1934 Act are assigned numbers that correspond to the section of the act to which they relate. The major sections are referred to as *regulations*, and the detailed rules within each regulation are *rules*. For example, Section 10(b) of the act is called Regulation 10B, and the individual rules within that section are referred to as Rule 10b-1 through Rule 10b-17.

Forms

The **forms** are enumerations of the form and content of the information included in registration statements and reports. (***They are not blank forms to be filled out***, as the Internal Revenue Service and other taxing authorities use the term.) Each act has its own forms. (The meaning of "form" here differs from when accountants refer to the "form and content" of particular financial statements.)

Releases

Releases are announcements pertaining to the various rules, regulations, and forms. Releases are numbered sequentially as issued. To date, approximately 8,000 releases have been issued under the 1933 Act and approximately 45,000 under the 1934 Act. A release is formally designated as follows: Securities Act of 1933, Release No. 5307. A release is informally referred to simply as Release 33-5307, for example, under the 1933 Act, and Release 34-9310, for example, under the 1934 Act. Some SEC releases under the 1934 Act also apply under the 1933 Act. In these cases, a release is assigned a number under the 1933 Act and a different number under the 1934 Act. Except for Interpretative Releases, they are subject to the Administrative Procedures Act and must be exposed for public comment before becoming effective. The primary matters to which these releases pertain are as follows:

1. **Proposals to amend or adopt new rules and forms.** Changes are often necessary to keep up with the times. In some instances, better ways of disclosure are found. For example, to improve the readability of information provided to investors, the SEC issued Release 33-5164, which proposed certain amendments to Rules 425A and 425 of the Securities Act of 1933.

   Interested companies and certified public accountants usually make comments and suggestions to the SEC. The final adopted amendment or new rule or form probably reflects many of these comments and suggestions. Sometimes a proposed item is not adopted for various reasons.
2. **Adoption of amendments or new rules and forms.** To continue with the preceding example, the proposals contained in Release 33-5164 were revised to reflect the comments and suggestions that the SEC considered significant and were subsequently adopted in Release 33-5278.

Regulation S-K, *Regulation S-X*, *Regulation S-T*, *Regulation FD*, and *Regulation G*

All nonfinancial disclosure requirements are contained in *Regulation S-K*. All financial disclosure requirements are contained in *Regulation S-X*. Each form under the 1933 Act and the 1934 Act specifies the disclosures contained in *Regulations S-K* and *S-X* that are to be made for that form.

Regulation S-K (*Nonfinancial* Statement Disclosure Requirements)

The major disclosure requirements contained in *Regulation S-K* deal with (1) a description of the company's *business*, (2) a description of the company's *properties*, (3) a description of the company's *legal proceedings*, (4) *selected financial data for the last five years* (including sales, income from continuing operations, cash dividends per common share, total assets, and long-term obligations), (5) *supplementary financial information* (quarterly financial data and information on the effects of changing prices), (6) information about the company's *directors and management* (including management remuneration), and (7) management's discussion and analysis (commonly referred to as the MDA) of financial condition and results of operations.

Regulation S-X (*Financial* Statement Disclosure Requirements)

Regulation S-X, which accountants deal with most often, not only lists the **specific financial statements** that must be filed under all acts administered by the SEC but also details the **form and content of such financial statements.** The term *financial statements* as used in this regulation includes (1) all notes to the financial statements and (2) all related financial statement supporting schedules. The financial statements filed under *Regulation S-X* are (1) audited balance sheets as of the end of the two most recent fiscal years and (2) audited statements of income and cash flows for the three fiscal years preceding the date of the most recent audited balance sheet being filed. (Variations from these requirements are permitted for certain specified filings.) In addition, the regulation contains requirements for filing interim financial statements. (*Regulation S-X* is discussed in more detail later in the chapter.)

Regulation S-T: Electronic Data Gathering and Retrieval System (EDGAR)

The SEC has designed an electronic database (named EDGAR) to keep track of financial documents filed with it by publicly traded companies. All 15,000 of the nation's public corporations and investment firms are required to file their reports electronically. *Regulation S-T* set forth the rules prescribing requirements for filing electronically and the procedures for making such filings.

In addition to serving the SEC's internal needs, EDGAR is expected to increase efficiency and fairness in the securities markets by allowing a means for quick public distribution of corporate information. EDGAR can be accessed using the Internet. It is also the centerpiece of the SEC's home page on the World Wide Web, (**http://www.sec.gov**). The page offers to investors a wide range of SEC information formerly available only from dispersed sources—**including recently *proposed* and *adopted* rules and bulletins.**

Regulation FD: Fair Disclosure

This regulation prohibits U.S. companies from disseminating important information to securities analysts, institutional investors, and others before releasing it to the general public. (Answers to inquiries about this regulation may be found at **http://www.sec.gov/interps/telephone/phonesupplement4.htm**.)

Regulation G: (Designed to End Abuses of non-GAAP Earnings Disclosures)

In 2003, the SEC issued *Regulation G*, **"Conditions for Use of Non-GAAP Financial Measures,"** which restricts the release of non-GAAP financial measurements in earnings reports. In the two years prior to the issuance of *Regulation G*, a rapidly increasing number of companies had started disclosing pro forma earnings amounts, which generally put the most positive spin on financial results. In many instances, these pro forma disclosures (such as *"pro forma earnings," "income before one-time charges," and "operating cash flow"*) were misleading. (Many astute investors and analysts had begun referring to such disclosures as EBBS, "everything but bad stuff.")

Regulation G covers all public disclosures, defines non-GAAP financial measures ***("any numerical measure of historical or future financial performance, financial position, or cash flows that excludes amounts that would be included in analogous GAAP measures")***, and creates standards for their disclosures. For any public disclosure of a non-GAAP measure, companies must present the most directly comparable GAAP based measure, along with reconciliation between the two figures. Furthermore, such disclosures may not omit any material fact that would otherwise cause the disclosure to be misleading.

Financial Reporting Releases (and the "Codification of Financial Reporting Policies")

The Financial Reporting Releases (FRRs), numbered sequentially (60 to date), contain the SEC's views and *interpretative guidance* on financial reporting matters. Prior to 1982, such views and interpretative guidance (as well as enforcement matters) were contained in the now discontinued *Accounting Series Releases* (of which 307 had been issued).

Financial Reporting Release No. 1 is the codification of the earlier releases that had continuing relevance to financial reporting. This codification (officially called the "*Codification of Financial Reporting Policies*" [CFRP]) is updated periodically to include selected new FRRs (thus not all new FRRs are codified). The codification is *not* intended to supplant the rules of *Regulations S-K* and *S-X* and is to be used only as a *supplement* to those regulations. Furthermore, the items in the codification do *not* affect the *Staff Accounting Bulletins* (discussed shortly). This codification (with its topical index) makes thousands of pages of material available in a concise and much more accessible format. The FRRs can be generally categorized as pertaining to the following major areas:

1. **Adoption of amendment or revision of *Regulation S-X*.** Many FRRs include financial reporting requirements that go beyond the pronouncements of the FASB and its predecessor organizations. In addition to setting forth an amendment or a revision to *Regulation S-X*, such FRRs also discuss the purpose of the new reporting requirements and comments received in response to the SEC's proposed revisions to *Regulation S-X* (including the SEC's reaction to those comments). In some cases, an FRR contains exhibits and examples to assist companies in understanding and complying with the new reporting requirements of *Regulation S-X*.

   Many FRRs have been rescinded as a result of the issuance of subsequent accounting pronouncements. The SEC rescinds such requirements, however, only when it concurs with an accounting pronouncement.
2. **Interpretations pertaining to accounting matters.** These releases provide guidance on specific accounting matters.

Accounting and Auditing Enforcement Releases (AAERs)

Accounting and Auditing Enforcement Releases (AAERs) announce accounting and auditing matters related to the SEC's enforcement activities that have been finalized. Because of their nature, AAERs are *not* codified. (A separate series of releases, Litigation Releases, announces litigation actions.) The most recent ones may be found at **http://www.sec.gov/litigation.shtml.**

Staff Accounting Bulletins (SABs)

The Staff Accounting Bulletins (SABs) represent interpretations and practices followed by certain departments of the SEC that are responsible for reviewing the disclosure requirements of the federal securities laws. These bulletins do *not* constitute official rules or regulations, nor do they have the official approval of the SEC commissioners. The bulletins essentially accomplish on an *informal* basis what otherwise would be dealt with *formally* through releases. Much of the subject matter of the bulletins arises from specific questions raised by registrants. The dissemination of answers to these questions in this manner rather than solely to the company making an inquiry avoids needless repetition of inquiries pertaining to the same subject. More than 100 SABs have been issued to date. In 2003, the staff recodified by topic all bulletins issued to date in *Staff Accounting Bulletin No. 103*, (after comprehensively removing obsolete material for the first time in more than 20 years), making the SABs substantially more easy to use. (Recall from Chapter 7 *that push-down accounting* was implemented as a result of the issuance of *Staff Accounting Bulletin No. 54*.) The most recent SABs may be found at **http://www.sec.gov/interps/account.shtml.**

Two Big-Impact SABs

By far, the most far-reaching SAB has been *SAB No. 101*, ***"Revenue Recognition in Financial Statements"*** (1999), which severely curtailed the revenue recognition practices of scores of companies (that previously thought they had been complying with revenue recognition standards), forcing nearly 1,000 of them to drastically reduce their revenues and restate prior years. *SAB No. 99*, ***"Materiality in the Preparation or Audit of Financial Statements"*** (1999) resulted in virtually all public accounting firms using a much lower threshold in evaluating material misstatements. These SABs were issued in response to the perceived practice of excessive earnings manipulation, something the SEC waged a crusade against in the late 1990s.

Concept Releases, Interpretative Releases, and Policy Statements

Concept Releases are for the purpose of soliciting the public's views on securities issues in order to better evaluate the need for future rule making. *Interpretative Releases* provide guidance relating to topics of general interest to the business and investment communities. *Policy Statements* clarify Commission positions on certain matters.

Staff Legal Bulletins (SLBs)

Staff Legal Bulletins are issued by the Divisions of Corporation Finance, Market Regulation, and Investment Management. They represent *interpretations* and *policies* followed by the staff of these divisions regarding (1) various aspects of the federal securities laws and (2) SEC regulations. Because they represent the view of the staff, they are *not* legally binding.

Manual of Publicly Available Telephone Interpretations

The Division of Corporation Finance makes available on the SEC webpage a downloadable manual of publicly available telephone interpretations that are intended to be helpful to the persons making the inquiries—they are *not* binding due to their highly informal nature (**http://www.sec.gov/interps/telephone.shtml**).

CHECK POINT

Where can one find interpretations and practices followed by certain departments of the SEC that are responsible for reviewing the disclosure requirements of the federal securities law?

a. *Regulation S-K*
b. *Regulation S-X*
c. Financial Reporting Releases
d. Staff Accounting Bulletins
e. Accounting and Auditing Enforcement Releases
f. SEC releases

Answer: d

VI. THE INTEGRATED DISCLOSURE SYSTEM (IDS)

Before discussing the 1933 Act and 1934 Act in detail, we discuss how the two acts are designed purposely to interact with each other to provide each class of investor equal protection while minimizing the time, cost, and effort of providing information to investors. The SEC calls this system of interaction between the two acts its **"integrated disclosure system."**

Requiring Identical Disclosures under Both Acts

Investors purchasing securities in the primary market—that is, *directly* from the company (regulated by the 1933 Act)—and investors purchasing securities in the secondary market—that is, on stock exchanges or in the over-the-counter market (regulated by the 1934 Act)—are each provided the **identical disclosures** in the documents required to be furnished to investors and to the SEC. Thus each group of investors receives exactly the same information for investment decision purposes (equal protection).

Incorporation by Reference

Information required to be disclosed under the 1933 Act filings may be omitted from those filings if the same information is already available in the periodic reports required under the 1934 Act. The issuing company need only make a reference in the 1933 Act document to the 1934 Act periodic reports that contain the information. This is known as **"incorporation by reference."**

VII. The Securities Act of 1933

Registration

The Securities Act of 1933 prohibits sales of, or offers to sell, securities to the public (in interstate commerce or through the use of the mails) by an **issuer** or an underwriter unless the securities have been registered with the SEC. Certain exemptions to this prohibition are discussed later in the chapter. A **security** is defined broadly as

> any note, stock, treasury stock, bond, debenture, evidence of indebtedness, certificate of interest or participation in any profit-sharing agreement, . . . transferable share, investment contract, voting trust certificate . . . or in general any interest or instrument commonly known as a security. . . .

To avoid having a technical loophole in the law, the prohibition also applies to underwriters. An **underwriter** is defined as

> any person who has purchased from an issuer with a view to, or offers or sells for an issuer in connection with, the distribution of any security, or participates [directly or indirectly] . . . in any such undertaking. . . .

It is important at this point to understand that registration under the 1933 Act refers only to the **actual quantity of securities being registered,** not to the registration of an **entire class of securities.** This is just the opposite of the 1934 Act, which is discussed in detail later in the chapter.

The Essence of Registration

Registration of a security offering under the 1933 Act begins with the filing of specified financial and nonfinancial information with the SEC using the appropriate form. The appropriate SEC form in a particular case is a legal determination. All specified financial and nonfinancial information submitted as set forth in the appropriate form is called a **registration statement.** The SEC examines the registration statement and almost always issues a **letter of comments** (commonly referred to as a **deficiency letter**). The registrant must respond to this letter of comments to the SEC's satisfaction before it may sell the securities to the public. Responding to a letter of comments usually involves a combination of direct written responses to the SEC in a letter, revision of certain information in the registration statement, and addition of information to the statement. The revised registration statement, called an **amended registration statement,** is filed with the SEC for reexamination. When the SEC is satisfied that the items in its letter of comments have been appropriately addressed, it permits the amended registration statement to become "effective," and the securities being offered are deemed registered under the 1933 Act and may be sold to the public.

Prospectuses

Prospective investors in a security being registered with the SEC under the 1933 Act must be furnished a **prospectus**. The registration statement is divided into two basic parts:

> Part I: Information required to be included in the prospectus.
> Part II: Information *not* required to be included in the prospectus.

Part I is the major part of the registration statement. It includes all required financial statements and related notes (according to the provisions of *Regulation S-X*), as well as reports by the registrant's auditors on financial statements that must have been audited. Part I also includes, among other things, such *nonfinancial* information as an extensive description of the registrant's business (including risk factors associated with the purchase of the securities offered) and properties, an explanation of how the proceeds are to be used, a description of any current legal proceedings, the names of the registrant's directors and officers (including their backgrounds), and the amount of their remuneration. The financial and *nonfinancial* disclosures included in the prospectus should provide potential investors with an adequate basis for deciding whether to invest in the securities offered. Preliminary prospectuses, which may be distributed to potential investors before the effective date, are commonly referred to as red herrings because certain information on the cover is printed in red ink.

Part II of the registration statement lists all exhibits filed with the registration statement and includes specified financial statement supporting schedules and other miscellaneous information *not* deemed necessary for distribution to potential investors.

Writing in Plain English

Concerned that prospectuses were starting to contain too much "legalese," the SEC adopted a rule in 1998 that requires companies to make certain sections of prospectuses more readable for the general public. The thrust of the rule is to require the use of (1) the active voice rather than the passive voice, (2) shorter sentences, and (3) everyday language—*not* legal jargon. Here is one of the SEC's "before and after" examples:

> **Before:** The proxies solicited hereby for the Heartland Meeting may be revoked, subject to the procedures described herein, at any time up to and including the date of the Heartland Meeting.
>
> **After:** You may revoke your proxy at any time up to and including the day of the meeting by following the directions on page 18.

Regulation C

Regulation C deals with the mechanics of registering securities under the 1933 Act. A company's legal counsel usually assumes responsibility for ensuring that the registration statement complies with *Regulation C*.

Exemptions from Registration

Certain types of securities and securities transactions, which have no practical need for registration or for which the benefits of registration are too remote, are exempt from the registration requirements of the 1933 Act. The major categories of exemptions are listed here.

1. **The intrastate offering exemption** [Section 3(a)(11) of the 1933 Act]. This *statutory exemption* is intended to facilitate the local financing of local business operations. To qualify, the security must be offered and sold only to the residents of the state in which the corporate issuer is incorporated and doing business. No fixed limits exist on (1) the size of the offering or (2) the number of purchasers.
2. **The nonpublic (private) offering exemption** [Section 4(2) of the 1933 Act]. This *statutory exemption* applies to offerings made to so-called sophisticated investors, those who have access to information about the company and are able to fend for themselves. Examples of **private offerings** are (1) bank loans; (2) private placements of securities with such institutions as venture

capital firms, insurance companies, and pension funds; (3) offerings to individuals directly managing the business; and (4) offerings for the promotion of a business venture by a few closely related persons. To qualify, each buyer must (1) have sufficient knowledge and experience in financial and business matters so that he or she is capable of evaluating the risks and merits of the investment or is able to bear the economic risk of the investment, (2) have access to the type of information normally provided in a prospectus, and (3) agree not to resell or distribute the securities for a specified number of years.

Substance versus form. If the investor were to turn around and immediately sell the securities purchased, the sale is considered a distribution of securities to the public because the investor is acting as a conduit for sale to the public on behalf of the issuer—that is, *as an underwriter*. In such cases, the resale of the security to the public must be registered. Because of these restrictions on the buyer, the securities are referred to as **restricted securities**.

Rule 144. Rule 144 sets the conditions that must be satisfied to resell restricted securities to the public *other than through registration*. This rule emphasizes that (1) the investor must have paid for and held the security for a reasonable period of time (a minimum of one to four years, depending on the category of issuer) and (2) adequate current public information with respect to the issuer of the securities must be available. Even if the holding period has been satisfied, the securities can only be sold in small increments over a three-year period.

Rule 144A. Under Rule 144A, neither a *holding period limitation* nor a *quantity that may be sold limitation* is imposed for restricted securities that are resold to *qualified institutional buyers* (QIBs), such as banks, pension funds, and insurance companies. The rationale is that such buyers presumably have enough business savvy to "fend for themselves." Certain quantitative tests must be met, however, for an institution to be a QIB.

3. **The small offering *(Regulation A)* exemption.** [Rules] 251-263. This *statutory authorized exemption* is a conditional exemption for security offerings that involve relatively small dollar amounts. To qualify, the offering, together with other exempt offerings within a one-year period, cannot exceed $5,000,000. Although *Regulation A* is technically an exemption from the registration requirements of the 1933 Act, it is often referred to as a *short form* of registration because (1) an **offering circular** (similar in content to a *prospectus*) must be given to each purchaser, (2) the securities are freely tradable in an aftermarket, and (3) an offering statement (consisting of a notification, an offering circular, and exhibits) must be filed with the closest SEC regional office.

   Advantages. The major advantages of *Regulation* A offerings, as opposed to full registration on Form S-1, are that (1) the required financial statement disclosures are less extensive, (2) the issuer does not become subject to the continuous reporting requirements of the 1934 Act (discussed later) unless assets exceed $5 million and the number of shareholders exceeds 500, and (3) three offering circular formats are permitted, one of which is a relatively simple question-and-answer document.

4. **The limited offering *(Regulation D)* exemption** [Rules 501-506]. *Regulation D* embodies three types of *statutory authorized exemptions* in which the number of parties to be offered securities is limited. The detailed requirements and restrictions (involving whether investors are "accredited," "nonaccredited," or "sophisticated") of each type are beyond the scope of this text. Compared to the *Regulation A* exemption, the *Regulation D* exemption is generally much less time consuming and costly to prepare.
5. **The bank and savings and loan offering exemption.** This statutory exemption exists because these entities are regulated by other federal or state agencies.
6. **The governmental offering exemption.** This *statutory exemption* covers the federal, state, and local governments. It exists as a matter of public policy—not because investors never need protection from governmental units that issue securities. Some state and local governments do issue securities to the public without adequate disclosure. (Later, we discuss an SEC enforcement action brought against Orange County in California.)

Who Decides Whether a Securities Offering or Transaction Is Exempt?

Whether a security offering or transaction is exempt from registration under the 1933 Act is strictly a legal and factual determination and outside the expertise of accountants. Accordingly, an entity's legal counsel usually makes this determination. If all conditions of the exemption are not met, purchasers may seek to have their purchase price refunded. (As stated earlier, a determination is also necessary to decide whether the offering is exempt from state laws.)

Antifraud Provisions Still Apply

Regardless that a security offering qualifies as being exempt from the registration requirements of the 1933 Act, the sale of these securities is subject to the antifraud provisions of the federal securities laws. This means that issuers are responsible for false or misleading statements (whether written or oral), which may be redressed through private or government legal action, including criminal sanctions. (See the Case in Point.)

CASE IN POINT

In 1996, the SEC brought enforcement actions against Orange County (California) and certain of its officials because of material misstatements and omissions of fact regarding more than $2 billion of municipal securities the county sold to investors in 1993 and 1994 in 11 offerings. Many of these offerings were made for the purpose of investing in derivatives. Orange County lost $1.7 billion on its investments in derivatives in 1994.

The county either misrepresented or did *not* disclose (1) information that brought into question the county's ability to repay its securities, (2) information concerning investment strategies, and (3) other material matters.

The county and individuals charged consented to the entry of an Order that makes findings and orders them to cease and desist from committing or causing any violation or future violation of the antifraud provisions of the federal securities laws.

CHECK POINT

The Securities Act of 1933, in general, exempts certain stock offerings from full registration. Which of the following is *not* exempt from full registration?

a. Private offerings
b. *Regulation A* offerings
c. Strictly intrastate issues
d. Securities of governmental units
e. Securities registered using Form S-1

Answer: e

Forms Used in Registration

The Securities and Exchange Commission has devised numerous forms to deal with the diverse companies (and their maturity) seeking to offer securities to the public. Although the general contents of a registration statement have already been described, each form has its own detailed table of contents and related instructions. (Recall that the financial statement requirements for these forms are set forth in *Regulation S-X*.) Two categories of forms are used under the 1933 Act: general forms and special forms.

General Forms

The SEC has three *general forms*: S-1, S-2, and S-3. These three forms are set up on a tier system based on the issuer's following in the stock market. Although all three forms basically require the same information to be furnished to potential investors, **the method of furnishing that information varies.** Form S-1, the most widely used of the forms, is required when one of the special forms is *not* authorized or prescribed, or when a company eligible to use Form S-2 or S-3 chooses to use companies that are already registered under the 1934 Act but have been filing reports with the SEC for less than 36 months. All financial and nonfinancial disclosures must be included in the prospectus. The detailed table of contents to Form S-1 appears in Illustration 18-1.

ILLUSTRATION 18-1 TABLE OF CONTENTS OF FORM S-1

The following is the table of contents from Form S-1, the most widely used of the SEC's forms. It is reprinted here to provide a more complete look at what is called for in a registration statement.

I. Information Required in Prospectus

Item

1. Forepart of the registration statement and outside front cover page of prospectus
2. Inside front and outside back cover page of prospectus
3. Summary information, risk factors, and ratio of earnings to fixed charges
4. Use of proceeds
5. Determination of offering price
6. Dilution
7. Selling security holders
8. Plan of distribution
9. Description of securities being registered
10. Interest of named experts and counsel
11. Information with respect to the registrant.[a] This item represents the bulk of the registration statement and consists of the following categories of information (those that are generally prepared by accountants are shown in bold):
    > Description of Business
    > Description of Property
    > Legal Proceedings
    > Market Price and Dividends
    > **Financial Statements and Financial Statement Schedules**
    > **Selected Financial Data**
    > **Supplementary Financial Information**
    > Management's Discussion and Analysis (MDA) of Financial Condition and Results of Operations
    > **Changes in and Disagreements with Accountants on Accounting and Financial Disclosure**
    > Directors and Executive Officers
    > Executive Compensation
    > Security Ownership of Certain Beneficial Owners and Management
    > Certain Relationships and Related [-Party] Transactions
12. Disclosure of commission position on indemnification for securities act liabilities

II. Information Not Required in Prospectus

13. Other expenses of issuance and distribution
14. Indemnification of directors and officers
15. Recent sales of unregistered securities
16. Exhibits and financial statement schedules
17. Undertakings

Signatures
Instructions as to Summary Prospectuses

---

[a] This item specifies (1) the nonfinancial disclosure requirements in *Regulation S-K* and (2) the financial statement requirements of *Regulation S-X* that are to be included.

To be eligible to use Forms S-2 and S-3, a company must have been subject to the reporting requirements of the 1934 Act for at least 36 months and must satisfy other conditions. Form S-3 is used by large companies having a wide following in the stock market; accordingly, such firms must meet an additional requirement based on annual trading volume and outstanding voting stock. The advantage to these forms is time and effort—that is, financial and nonfinancial information need not be included in the prospectus; it may simply be *incorporated by reference* to reports already filed with the SEC under the 1934 Act. Thus these forms are effectively a *simplified* Form S-1.

Special Forms

The SEC has 12 *special forms* that pertain to specific types of *transactions* or types of *entities*. Five of these forms are commonly used:

1. **Form S-4**, for registration of securities issued in connection with most business combinations and reofferings. (Substantial information may be incorporated by reference.)

2. **Form S-8**, for securities offered to employees pursuant to employee benefit plans, such as stock option plans (usually substantially shorter than Form S-1).
3. **Form S-11**, applicable to real estate investment trusts and real estate companies.
4. **Form S-15**, for securities issued in certain business combinations (involving a large company and a much smaller company). This streamlined form requires only an abbreviated prospectus.
5. **Form 4**, for disclosing "changes in beneficial ownership of securities," including stock purchases and sales, as well as the exercise of options by company *executives* and *directors*.

Legal Liability for Filing a False Registration Statement

Section 6 of the Securities Act of 1933 requires that the registration statement be signed by the following persons:

1. The principal executive officer or officers.
2. The principal financial officer.
3. The controller or principal accounting officer.
4. The majority of the board of directors or persons performing similar functions.

The 1933 Act sets forth the following civil liabilities for a false registration:

> In case any part of the registration statement, when such part became effective, contained an untrue statement of a material fact or omitted to state a material fact required to be stated therein or necessary to make the statements therein not misleading, any person acquiring such security (unless it is proved that at the time of such acquisition he knew of such untruth or omission) may . . . sue [for recovery of losses suffered]—
>
> 1. every person who signed the registration statement;
> 2. every person who was a director of . . . the issuer . . . ;
> 3. every person who, with his consent, is named in the registration statement as being or about to become a director . . . ;
> 4. every accountant, engineer, appraiser, or any person whose profession gives authority to a statement made by him, who has with his consent been named as having prepared or certified part of the registration statement, . . . with respect to the statement in such registration statement, report, or valuation, which purports to have been prepared or certified by him;
> 5. every underwriter with respect to such security [Section 11].

In addition to these *civil proceedings* whereby a purchaser may recover damages suffered, Section 24 of the 1933 Act provides for *criminal penalties* (monetary fines and imprisonment) if the untrue statement of a material fact or omission thereof was "willful."

Shareholders Often Sue if Stock Prices Fall

Countless instances have occurred in which stock prices have substantially *declined* from the offering price within 6 to 12 months of the offering. In such cases, it is common for disgruntled stockholders to file class action lawsuits alleging that unfavorable information was purposely omitted from the prospectus. Such information could include known problems in developing anticipated new products or shipping and order delays. In fact, many attorneys actively search out investors who have sustained losses on public offerings, hoping to represent them in such lawsuits, which have a high settlement potential.

Ramifications to Outside Auditors

This section of the 1933 Act has special significance to certified public accountants of companies registering securities. When securities are not registered, *gross negligence* must be proved for a company's certified public accountant to be held liable for civil damages. When a company registers securities under the 1933 Act, however, the focal point is not whether the outside auditors were grossly negligent in the performance of their duties. Instead, the issue is merely whether or not the financial statements and related notes in the registration statement **contained an untrue**

statement of a material fact or omitted a material fact. Thus, the 1933 Act imposes an additional potential liability on the certified public accountants of companies registering securities. Certain defenses are available to the outside auditors, however, under Section 11 of the 1933 Act that relate to their having made a "reasonable investigation" and having "reasonable grounds for belief."

CHECK POINT

Which of the following must a company desiring to issue common stock to the public file with the SEC?

a. Prospectus
b. Registration statement
c. Proxy statement
d. Offering circular
e. S-1 registration statement

Answer: b

VIII. THE SECURITIES EXCHANGE ACT OF 1934

The Securities Exchange Act of 1934, which deals with the trading in (exchange of) securities, has two broad purposes:

1. To require publicly held companies to disclose on a continual basis current information to holders and prospective purchasers of their securities comparable to the information that must be disclosed in a registration statement under the 1933 Act. In this respect, the 1934 Act supplements the 1933 Act, which applies only to public offerings of securities, not to subsequent *trading* in such securities.
2. To regulate the public trading markets (organized exchanges and over-the-counter markets) and the broker-dealers who operate in such markets.

Major Provisions of the 1934 Act

Unlike the 1933 Act, which is a unified piece of legislation, the 1934 Act covers a wide range of areas. Its major provisions are discussed in the following paragraphs.

Registration of Securities Exchanges

Securities exchanges (such as the New York Stock Exchange) must be registered with the SEC, which has supervisory control over them.

Registration of Securities on Securities Exchanges

Securities exchanges cannot effect transactions in any security unless that security is registered on the exchange. The registration process involves filing a registration statement on Form 10 (or another appropriate form) with the securities exchange and with the SEC. Form 10 requires information comparable to that required in Form S-1 under the 1933 Act. A security that is traded on a securities exchange is referred to as a listed security. Companies having securities registered on a securities exchange are referred to as *Section 12(b) companies.*

Registration of Over-the-Counter Securities

The over-the-counter market encompasses all securities transactions that do not take place on organized securities exchanges. The 1934 Act was amended in 1964 to require registration of securities traded in the over-the-counter market that meet certain size tests. Companies that have total assets exceeding $10 million and a class of equity security with 500 or more stockholders must register such security with the SEC by filing a registration statement (usually Form 10). Securities traded in the over-the-counter market are referred to as unlisted. Companies meeting these tests are referred to as Section 12(g) companies. Once a company meets these size tests, it is subject to all the requirements of the 1934 Act that are imposed on listed companies. **Thus an entity that has never registered the sale of securities under the 1933 Act may be subject to the 1934 Act by virtue of the entity's (1) size and (2) number of its stockholders.**

A Section 12(g) company may deregister when it has (1) less than 500 shareholders for the class of equity security and total assets of less than $10 million at the end of each of its last three fiscal years or (2) fewer than 300 shareholders.

Filing Periodic and Other Reports

Issuers of securities that must be registered under the 1934 Act must file *annual* and *quarterly* reports with the SEC containing specified financial and nonfinancial information. In addition, reports describing specified important events must be filed promptly after they occur. These periodic reports are discussed in detail shortly.

Proxy Regulations

For companies subject to the registration requirements of the 1934 Act, the SEC is authorized to prescribe regulations and rules governing the solicitation of proxies by management from shareholders regarding matters to be voted on by shareholders. A **proxy** is merely a document empowering one person to vote in place of another. Because all shareholders do not normally attend annual or special shareholders' meetings, companies typically request each shareholder to sign a proxy empowering management to vote either as the shareholder indicates or in accordance with the recommendations of management. When soliciting proxies, a **proxy statement** containing information specified by the SEC must be furnished to the stockholders. Furthermore, preliminary proxy material must be filed with the SEC for review at least 10 days before the proposed mailing date.

Antifraud and Insider Trading Provisions

Section 10 of the 1934 Act makes it unlawful for any person directly or indirectly to use deceptive or fraudulent practices or to misstate or omit any material fact in connection with the purchase or sale of a security. Criminal fines up to $100,000 can be imposed. Persons suffering losses as a result of fraud are entitled to sue for recovery of actual losses.

Corporate "insiders" are prohibited from trading in a corporation's securities using material information that has not been disseminated to the public. Inside traders can be forced to give up their profits and be fined up to the higher of $1,000,000 or three times the profit gained or loss avoided. Also, criminal fines of $1,000,000 can be imposed. An **insider** is any person who has material nonpublic information, including any officer or director or any person who obtains such information from others. In addition, under the **short-swing profit** rule in Section 16(b), any profit realized from any purchase and sale (or from any sale and purchase) of any such issuer's equity security within any period of less than six months by certain persons accrues to the issuer and is recoverable by the issuer, with certain exceptions. These certain persons are officers, directors, or any person who is the beneficial owner of more than 10% of any security that is registered under the 1934 Act. Under Section 16(a), officers, directors, and such 10% security holders must report to the SEC any changes in their beneficial ownership of registered securities. Changes in ownership are reported using either Form 3 (Initial Statement of Ownership) or Form 4 (Changes in Ownership). The form must be filed within 10 days after the end of the month in which the transaction occurs.

The definition of *officer* is *not* based on title but instead **focuses on individuals who have access to inside information** that may allow them to profit from securities transactions. Officers now include a company's CEO; president; CFO; vice presidents in charge of principal business units, divisions, or functions; other persons who perform policy-making decisions; and executive officers of parents or subsidiaries who perform policy-making functions. See the Case in Point.

CASE IN POINT

In 2002, Tyco International sued its former chief executive officer, Dennis Kozlowski, and former chief financial officer, Mark Swartz, charging the two made more than $40 million in "short-swing" stock trades.

Brokers and Dealers

The 1934 Act requires brokers and dealers to register with the SEC and to comply with regulations imposed on them. Certain trading practices are prohibited. Specific sections of the 1934 Act deal with unlawful representations, liability for misleading statements, and criminal penalties.

Forms Used in Reporting

The SEC has devised approximately 20 forms to be used by companies whose securities are registered under the 1934 Act. Because most of these forms are of a specialized nature, a complete list is not presented. By far the most commonly used forms (for domestic companies) are the following:

- Form 8-K, current reports.
- Form 10-K, annual report.
- Form 10-Q, quarterly report.

Regulation 12B of the 1934 Act sets forth the mechanics of reporting in the same manner that *Regulation C* does under the 1933 Act. Small business issuers (defined earlier) use periodic reporting forms 10-KSB and 10-QSB.

Form 8-K, Current Reports

Form 8-K provides certain information to investors on a reasonably current basis. A report on this form must be filed when any of approximately 20 events occur. Examples are:

1. Changes in control of the registrant.
2. Significant acquisitions or dispositions of assets (including business combinations).
3. Bankruptcy or receivership.
4. Changes in the registrant's outside auditors. (The disclosures here are designed to discourage "opinion shopping." We discuss this event more fully in the following section.)
5. Other events that the registrant deems important to its security holders.
6. The resignation of a director.
7. Illegal acts.
8. Earnings releases.

For most items, Form 8-K reports must be filed within 4 business days after the occurrence of the event.

Changes in Outside Auditors

Companies must report to the SEC when their auditors are fired, resign, or inform the company that they do not intend to seek reappointment for the following year. **The report must state whether the company and its auditor disagreed about accounting principles or practices, financial statement disclosures, or auditing scope or procedures.** Form 8-K elaborates on what circumstances are deemed to be disagreements. Within 10 days after the 8-K report is filed, the former auditor must submit a letter to the SEC stating whether he or she agrees or disagrees with the company's statement. Furthermore, **if the company has held discussions with its *new* auditors concern-**

ing accounting and financial reporting matters within the *two years* prior to their appointment, **the issues discussed must be reported.**

Illegal Acts

The *Private Securities Litigation Reform Act of 1995* requires auditors to report certain illegal acts to a client's board of directors if management fails to take appropriate remedial action. In turn, the board must notify the SEC that it has received such a report. If the auditor is not furnished a copy of the client's notice to the SEC **within one business day after giving the report to the board,** the auditor must provide the SEC with a copy of the report given to the board. Thus **auditors, for the first time, are placed in the position of having to be "whistle-blowers" to a federal agency.**

From the time the law took effect in 1996 through mid 2003, the SEC received only 29 reports from auditors that they uncovered likely illegal acts—none of which pertained to the numerous, major accounting scandals that occurred from 1999–2003.

Form 10-K, Annual Report

Within 60 days after the end of the fiscal year, a company must file an annual report with the SEC, using Form 10-K if no other form is prescribed. Although it must be furnished to stockholders on request, this report is in addition to the company's annual report to its stockholders. Form 10-K must include substantially all *nonfinancial statement information* set forth in *Regulation S-K* (the major items were indicated on page 607) and the *financial statement information* specified in *Regulation S-X* (described on page 607).

Form 10-K Compared with the Annual Report to Stockholders

Substantially all the information called for in the 10-K annual report also must be included in the annual report sent to the stockholders. Companies may omit information from the 10-K annual report if it is included in the annual report sent to the stockholders. A copy of the annual report sent to the stockholders must be filed with the 10-K annual report, and the 10-K annual report must indicate that the omitted information is included in the annual report sent to the stockholders. (This is known as *incorporation by reference.*)

Form 10-K Compared with a Form S-1

The bulk of the information called for in a 10-K annual report is identical to the information called for in a Form S-1 registration statement (discussed earlier).

Form 10-Q, Quarterly Report

Within 35 days of the end of each of the first three fiscal quarters of each fiscal year, a company must file a *quarterly report* with the SEC on Form 10-Q. No report is necessary for the fourth quarter. Form 10-Q calls for the interim financial statements specified in *Regulation S-X*. These financial statements, which may be condensed, are as follows:

1. An interim **balance sheet** as of the end of the most recent fiscal quarter and a balance sheet at the end of the preceding fiscal year.
2. Interim **income statements** for the most recent fiscal quarter and for the period between the end of the last fiscal year and the end of the most recent fiscal quarter (year-to-date amounts in second- and third-quarter reports) and corresponding periods of the preceding fiscal year. Entities must report a total for *comprehensive income*.
3. Statements of **cash flows** for the period between the end of the last fiscal year and the end of the most recent fiscal quarter and for the corresponding period of the preceding fiscal year.

Detailed notes to these statements are *not* required; however, disclosures must be complete enough so that the information presented is not misleading. In this respect, companies may presume that users of the interim financial information have read or have access to the audited financial statements for the preceding fiscal year. Thus disclosures deal primarily with events after the end of the most recent fiscal year. The interim financial information *need not* be audited or reviewed by an independent public accountant.

Form 10-Q also calls for a *management discussion and analysis* (MDA) of the financial condition and results of operations pursuant to the nonfinancial statement disclosure requirements of *Regulation S-K*.

Form 10-Q Compared with the Quarterly Report to Stockholders

As with the rules concerning the 10-K annual report, information called for on Form 10-Q may be omitted if such information is contained in a quarterly report to the stockholders and a copy of that report is filed with Form 10-Q.

CHECK POINT

Which form is used to report a change in auditors?

a. Form S-1
b. Form 10-K
c. Form 8-K
d. Form F-4
e. Form S-X
f. Form 10

Answer: c

Major Distinction between the 1933 Act and the 1934 Act

As stated earlier, the 1933 Act deals with **registering a *quantity* of securities** (such as 100,000 shares of common stock) and the 1934 Act deals with **registering a *class* of securities** (such as common stock, preferred stock, and debenture bonds).

Primary Offerings: To Raise Capital

To show the difference between the two acts, assume that Parrco Inc. is a *privately owned* company with 300,000 common shares outstanding as a result of shares issued to its founders, its employees (pursuant to a stock option plan), and an insurance company (as a result of a private placement). Assume also that Parrco desires to become a *publicly owned* company and, therefore, registers the sale of 100,000 new shares of its common stock with the SEC under the 1933 Act. The sale of these shares, in which the proceeds go to the company, is characterized as a **primary offering.**

The Initial Result

For any of Parrco's common stock to be publicly tradable, however, the common stock—**as a class of securities**—must also be registered under the 1934 Act. Doing so does *not* mean that all of Parrco's 400,000 common shares outstanding become immediately tradable—only the 100,000 common shares registered under the 1933 Act do so. Thus the result **at the time that an entity first becomes publicly owned is as if** the 100,000 common shares were actually registered under the 1934 Act (even though quantities of shares are *not* registered under that act).

As Time Goes By

Subsequent to the *primary offering* date, however, the remaining 300,000 common shares become tradable slowly over time pursuant to Rule 144—without having to be registered with the SEC. The purpose of not allowing these 300,000 common shares to become immediately tradable is to limit the ability of the owners of these shares to immediately dump all of their holdings on the public, which might cause a sharp drop in the price of the stock and cause the new owners to believe that they were defrauded.

Secondary Offerings: To Enable More Shares to Be Publicly Traded

The only way to enable the 300,000 common shares to become publicly tradable more quickly is to register some or all of these shares under the 1933 Act in a **secondary offering,** which process allows them to become publicly traded under the 1934 Act. In a *secondary offering*, the proceeds go to the selling shareholders—*not* to the company. Thus the company acts merely as a conduit between these shareholders and the public.

Illustration 18-2 is a summary of the example used in the preceding discussion, with a *secondary offering* of 50,000 shares included.

IX. The Small Business Integrated Disclosure System

This system is designed to assist smaller companies in obtaining easier and less-expensive access to the capital markets. For qualifying companies, the extent of the information required to be disclosed (under *Regulation S-X and S-K*) is less than that required for larger companies.

Companies having both (1) revenues of less than $25 million and (2) a *public float* (the total market value of its outstanding stock) of *less than* $25 million, qualify as **small business issuers.** The SEC estimates that more than 3,000 public entities are eligible to use this system. Tens of thousands of nonpublic entities qualify as well.

The small business IDS has its own set of dedicated forms (except that it uses the same Form 8-K for current events that larger companies use). These forms are:

1933 Act	1934 Act
Form SB-1, for the registration of securities with a total offering price of no more than $10 million in a fiscal year	**Form 10-SB**, registration
	Form 10-KSB, annual report
Form SB-2, for the registration of securities with no limit on the total offering price	**Form 10-QSB**, quarterly report
	Form 8-K, current events

Regulation S-B prescribes rules for filings by entities that qualify *as small business issuers.*

ILLUSTRATION 18-2 SHARES REGISTERED FOR SALE VERSUS SHARES TRADABLE

Shares issued to founders on 1/1/01 (**restricted securities**)	200,000
Shares issued to employees in 2003 pursuant to stock options granted in 2001 (**restricted securities**)	60,000
Shares issued to an insurance company in a private placement on 4/4/04 (**restricted securities**)	40,000
Common Shares Outstanding on 7/6/05	**300,000**
Primary offering on 7/7/05 (registered under the **1933 Act** using Form S-1)	100,000
Common Shares Outstanding on 7/7/05	**400,000**
Common shares that may be publicly traded on 7/7/05 (assuming that the common stock was registered with the SEC on 7/7/05 under the **1934 Act** using Form 10)	100,000
Secondary offering on 12/12/05 of common shares held by founders, employees, and the insurance company (registered under the **1933 Act** using Form S-1)	50,000
Common Shares That May Be Publicly Traded on 12/12/05	**150,000**[a]

[a] A small percentage of the 250,000 common shares that have not been registered under the 1933 Act become tradable on 7/7/06 (one year *after* the public offering) as allowed under Rule 144.

Note on Subsequent *Primary Offering* on 6/6/06: If on 6/6/06, the company were to have a *primary offering* for 75,000 shares, those shares would have to be registered under the 1933 Act. No registration would be necessary under the 1934 Act for these shares to publicly trade because the common stock (as a class of security) was previously registered under the 1934 Act on 7/7/05.

X. Regulation of Foreign Securities Traded in the United States

The U.S. capital market is the largest of the world's capital markets. The market capitalization of the companies listed on the New York Stock Exchange alone is approximately $5,000 billion, which about equals the market capitalization of the four largest foreign stock exchanges (Tokyo, London, Paris, and Frankfurt) combined.

Approximately 700 foreign companies have their stocks traded in the U.S. either in (1) **direct** form (less than 100 companies, most of which are Canadian) in which the U.S. investor buys the actual common shares or (2) **American Depository Receipt (ADR)** form in which the U.S. investor buys a "negotiable certificate of ownership" (using a bank as an intermediary) that serves as a *surrogate* for the actual common shares. ADRs (discussed in detail in international finance texts) are generally considered a more convenient form of ownership than the direct form.

Foreign firms desiring access to the U.S. capital market must comply with U.S. federal securities laws. The SEC's *International Series Releases* (ISRs) deal with matters specifically related to *foreign issuers* and the internationalization of the securities market. (More than 1,200 ISRs have been issued to date.)

Foreign issuers may choose to use *registration* and *continuous reporting* forms formulated for either (1) *domestic issuers* or (2) *foreign issuers*. The forms formulated for foreign issuers are summarized in Illustration 18-3.

XI. *International* Offerings and *Global* Offerings by U.S. Companies

Just as *foreign companies* desire to raise capital in the United States, U.S. companies desire to raise capital overseas. *U.S. companies* have two ways of raising capital overseas.

ILLUSTRATION 18-3 FORMS FORMULATED FOR FOREIGN ISSUERS

1933 Act

Forms	**Comments**
F-1, F-2, F-3 (*general* forms)	These forms are comparable to the S-1, S-2, S-3 *domestic* forms.
F-4 (*special* form—business combinations)	This form is comparable to the S-4 *domestic* form.

1934 Act

20-F *Annual* report	This form is comparable to the *domestic* Form 10-K.

Unique Aspects of Form 20-F

1. Form 20-F need not be filed until **six months** after year-end.
2. **A reconciliation of foreign GAAP net income to U.S. GAAP net income must be included if the financial statements are not presented in accordance with U.S. GAAP**—preparing this reconciliation can be very time consuming.

6-K *Other Periodic* reports	This form is comparable to the *domestic* form 8-K. It also is used to report *interim period results*.

Unique Aspects of Form 6-K

1. The interim reporting period is **six months**—not quarterly. (This is an accommodation to foreign issuers because they report interim period information only every six months in their home countries.)
2. Only material information that the issuer is required to make public (**pursuant to the laws of its home country** or the rules of a stock exchange) or provides to its security holders need be reported using Form 6-K.

International Offerings

An **international offering** comprises securities that are being sold in foreign countries—but not in the issuer's home country. *Regulation S* (adopted in 1990) sets forth the conditions that must exist for an international offering by a U.S. company to be deemed to have taken place entirely outside of the United States and thus not be subject to the registration requirements of the 1933 Act. (U.S. companies must, of course, comply with the securities laws of each foreign country in which they offer securities.) The following two general conditions must exist:

1. All of the offering and sale must take place in a so-called off-shore transaction in which **no offer is made to investors in the United States.**
2. No direct selling efforts may be made in the United States.

Regulation S also has certain other requirements that come into play if there is a likelihood that the securities offered abroad will ultimately flow back into the United States and thus wind up in the hands of U.S. investors.

Global Offerings

In a **global offering,** securities are offered abroad and in the issuer's home country. Thus a global offering by a U.S. company requires registration under the 1933 Act (unless the securities being sold in the United States qualify as a *private placement*).

XII. *Regulation S-X*: A Closer Look

Recall from the introduction to *Regulation S-X* on page 607 that this regulation sets forth not only the financial statements filed with the SEC under the various acts but also the "*form and content*" of those financial statements. As a result of recent revisions to modernize *Regulation S-X* and integrate the various reporting requirements of companies, the regulation also applies to annual reports to stockholders. Accordingly, the financial statements included in the Form 10-K annual report are now identical to the financial statements in annual reports to stockholders.

Because this regulation is approximately 100 pages long, a detailed discussion is beyond the scope of this book. The objective here is to provide a general familiarity with the contents of *Regulation S-X*.

Regulation S-X is composed of the following articles, each of which has its own rules:

Article	Description
1A	Application of *Regulation S-X*
2A	Qualifications and reports of accountants
3	General instructions as to financial statements
3A	Consolidated and combined financial statements
4	Rules of general application
5	Commercial and industrial companies
6	Registered investment companies
6A	Employee stock purchase, savings, and similar plans
7	Insurance companies
9	Bank holding companies
10	Interim period financial statements
11	Pro forma financial information
12	Form and content of schedules

Because Articles 6, 6A, and 7 have at most only limited application to most companies, they are *not* discussed in this chapter. The remaining articles are discussed briefly.

Article 1: Application of *Regulation S-X*

Article 1 specifies the nature of *Regulation S-X*, states the acts to which it applies, and defines the terms used in the regulation.

Article 2: Qualifications and Reports of Accountants

Article 2 discusses (1) the qualification of certified public accountants (primarily conditions necessary for their independence) and (2) specific requirements concerning the content of a certified public accountant's report on audited financial statements included in one of the designated forms filed with the SEC. In 2001, the SEC made its auditor independence more strict.

Article 3: General Instructions as to Financial Statements

Article 3 specifies the balance sheets, income statements, and statements of cash flows to be included in registration statements and reports filed with the SEC.

Article 3A: Consolidated and Combined Financial Statements

Article 3A deals with the presentation of consolidated and combined financial statements. It specifies which subsidiaries should not be consolidated and requires, in general, that all intercompany items and transactions be eliminated.

Article 4: Rules of General Application

Article 4, the rules of general application, pertains to a variety of items regarding the form, classification, and content of notes to the financial statements. Rule 4-08, "General Notes to Financial Statements," comprises most of this article. It is an extensive rule specifying certain information to be set forth in notes to the financial statements. This rule is not a duplication of FASB disclosure requirements. Instead, the requirements pertain to items *not* specifically addressed in FASB pronouncements and those of its predecessor organizations. Generally, preparing the additional disclosures called for by this article is not a major task.

Article 5: Commercial and Industrial Companies

Article 5 applies to all companies that are not required to follow Articles 6, 6A, 7, and 9. Rules 5-02 and 5-03 set forth the various line items and certain additional disclosures that should appear in the balance sheet, income statement, or related notes.

Rule 5-04 is a list and description of certain financial statement supporting schedules (commonly referred to as **schedules**) that are filed in support of the basic financial statements. The exact form and content of the schedules are specified by Article 12.

Article 9: Bank Holding Companies

This article is discussed in Chapter 2, page 58.

Article 10: Interim Period Financial Statements

Article 10 deals with the form and content of presentation of interim period financial statements (quarterly reports under the 1934 Act and interim period financial statements in registration statements filed under the 1933 Act).

Article 11: Pro Forma Financial Information

Article 11 specifies when pro forma financial statements must be presented. Such financial statements are required when business combinations have occurred or are probable.

Article 12: Form and Content of Schedules

Article 12 prescribes the form and content of the financial statement supporting schedules required by Rule 5-04 under Article 5 and certain rules in other articles. The exact columnar headings used for each schedule are specified, along with detailed instructions on how to prepare each schedule.

Check Point

In which of the following are the financial statements in filings with the SEC to be included in the material being filed?

a. The appropriate form being used
b. *Regulation S-X*
c. *Regulation S-K*
d. Staff Accounting Bulletins
e. Financial Reporting Releases

Answer: b

End-of-Chapter Review

Summary of Key Points

1. The Securities Act of 1933 and the Securities Exchange Act of 1934 protect investors from fraudulent actions and unethical practices by the promoters of securities and the managements of companies issuing securities.

2. The Securities and Exchange Commission administers the 1933 Act and the 1934 Act as well as several other acts.

3. The SEC has the **statutory authority** (granted by Congress) to establish GAAP, but to date, it has allowed the private sector to establish them. The SEC works closely with the FASB and the Emerging Issues Task Force in establishing GAAP.

4. Unlike the FASB, the SEC has **enforcement powers** that it uses as necessary to order a company to change its interpretation of GAAP. Also, the SEC is empowered to take **disciplinary actions** against auditors.

5. Companies subject to the registration and reporting requirements of these statutes must be familiar with a labyrinth of regulations, rules, releases, forms, and bulletins to comply with these statutes. For the disclosure of *nonfinancial* information, companies usually rely heavily on their legal counsel for assistance and guidance. For the disclosure of *financial* information, company accountants must be intimately familiar with the detailed requirements of *Regulation S-X*.

6. In some areas, *Regulation S-X* imposes significant additional reporting requirements beyond those required under generally accepted accounting principles.

7. See Illustration 18-4 for a summary of the various SEC rules, releases, and bulletins. See Illustration 18-5 for the differences in meaning of various terms between the SEC and Internal Revenue Service.

Glossary of New Terms

American Depository Receipt (ADR) A "negotiable certificate of ownership" (bought through a bank intermediary) that serves as a surrogate for the actual common shares owned in a foreign firm. (ADRs are generally considered a more convenient form of ownership than the direct form of ownership.)

Blue sky laws State laws dealing with the purchase and sale of securities.

Electronic data gathering, analysis, and retrieval (EDGAR) The SEC's database system whereby (1) 1933 Act and 1934 Act documents are filed electronically and (2) investors have online access to the data.

Exempt offering An offering of securities that need not be registered with the SEC because of an available statutory exemption.

ILLUSTRATION 18-4 SUMMARY OF SEC ACT-RELATED RELEASES AND REGULATIONS

Applicable *Only* to the 1933 Act

	Rules Pertaining to
Releases (33–xxxx)	Changes to SEC rules for enforcing the 1933 Act (announcements of *new, amended*, and *proposed* rules)
Regulation A	The *small* offering exemption
Regulation C	The mechanics of registering securities
Regulation D	The *limited* offering exemption
Regulation S	International offerings

Applicable *Only* to the 1934 Act

	Rules Pertaining to
Releases (34–xxxx)	Changes to SEC rules for enforcing the 1934 Act (announcements of *new, amended*, and *proposed* rules)

Applicable to *Both* the 1933 Act *and* the 1934 Act

	Rules Prescribing Requirements for Filing or Disclosure
Regulation S-B	By entities qualifying as *small business issuers*
Regulation S-K	*Nonfinancial* statement information disclosures
Regulation S-X	*Financial* statement information disclosures (form and content thereof)
Regulation T	Electronically (using EDGAR)
Regulation FD	Requires dissemination to the *public* of significant information provided to securities analysts, institutional investors, and others.
Regulation G	Conditions for use of non-GAAP financial measures

Summary of SEC Special Purpose Releases and Bulletins

Financial Reporting Releases (FRRs)	*Opinions* of the commissioners and the Chief Accountant regarding accounting and financial reporting matters
Accounting and Auditing Enforcement Releases (AAERs)	Accounting, financial reporting, and *auditing* enforcement (disciplinary) matters
Staff *Accounting* Bulletins (SABs)	*Interpretations* of GAAP and practices by the Division of Corporation Finance (some bulletins effectively establish GAAP for issues *not* explicitly addressed by GAAP)
Staff *Legal* Bulletins (SLBs)	*Views* of the Division of Corporation Finance on *legal* issues
International Series Releases (ISRs)	Matters pertaining to *foreign issuers* and the internationalization of the securities market
Litigation Releases (LRs)	Announcements of litigation actions
Concepts Releases	For seeking the financial community's views on certain matters.

F-1, 2, 3 scheme A three-tier registration system under the 1933 Act for *foreign issuers*. All three forms essentially require the same information, but the manner of disseminating the information is different under each form.

Forms Specific enumerations of the form and content of information included in registration statements and reports filed with the SEC.

Global offering The offering of securities in *foreign countries* and in the issuer's *home country*.

Incorporation by reference The process of referring readers of a 1933 Act registration statement to 1934 Act documents already containing the same information.

Integrated disclosure system (IDS) A system whereby virtually the same information about a company is required in 1933 Act and 1934 Act filings.

International offering The offering of securities in *foreign countries*—but *not* in the issuer's *home country*.

Offering circular A scaled-down version of a *prospectus* (used in *Regulation A* exempt offerings).

Primary offering The sale of new (previously unissued) securities to the public.

Private offering "Transactions by an issuer *not* involving a *public offering*."*

Prospectus The portion of a registration statement that must be furnished to prospective investors in connection with an offering of securities being registered with the SEC.

Proxy A document empowering a person to vote in place of another person.

ILLUSTRATION 18-5 TERMINOLOGY DIFFERENCES—THE INTERNAL REVENUE SERVICE VERSUS THE SEC

Different departments of the federal government have entirely different meanings of various terms.

Terminology Item	Internal Revenue Service Usage	Securities and Exchange Commission Usage
Statutes:	*Internal Revenue Code*	*Securities Act of 1933* *Securities Exchange Act of 1934*
Regulations:	**Treasury Department** *interpretations* of the Internal Revenue Code	Collections of *rules* adopted/issued by the SEC to administer various Acts passed by Congress
Rules:	*Revenue Rulings* (**IRS's National Office** interpretations that serve as broad guidance) *Revenue Procedures*	Rules adopted/issued by the SEC
Interpretations:	*Regulations, Revenue Rulings, Revenue Procedures, Private Letter Rulings and Technical Advice Memorandums,* and *Determination Letters*	*Staff Accounting Bulletins* (SABs)—issued by the **Division of Corporation Finance**—these are interpretations of Generally Accepted Accounting Principles (GAAP)
Rulings:	*Private Letter Rulings* (IRS determination letters to specific company situations)	Term is *not* formally used (answers to specific inquiries are either given by phone or informally in writing).
Forms:	Preprinted forms to be filled out	Listings of instructions for filing of specified financial and *non*financial information.
Filings:	Tax returns	Registration statements, annual and quarterly reports, and other specified information
Releases:	Term is not formally used.	Various announcements (such as of new or proposed rules)

Proxy statement A statement containing specified information furnished to stockholders in connection with the solicitation of proxies for use at an annual meeting (or special meetings) of shareholders.

Registration The process of submitting certain specified financial and nonfinancial information to the SEC for the purpose of obtaining approval to sell securities to the public.

Registration statement All of the specified financial and nonfinancial information filed with the SEC (set forth according to an appropriate form) for purposes of registering an offering of securities to the public.

Regulation A offering The *small-offering* exemption under the 1933 Act.

Regulation D offering The *limited-offering* exemption under the 1933 Act.

Restricted securities Securities acquired in an offering that was exempt from registration under the 1933 Act. Such securities may not be resold without registration—unless another exemption is available (such as those allowed under Rules 144 and 144A whereby a small percentage may be sold each year *after* a company becomes publicly owned).

S-1, 2, 3 scheme A three-tier registration system under the 1933 Act for *domestic issuers*. All three forms essentially require the same information, but the manner of disseminating the information is different under each form.

Secondary offering The sale of restricted securities (securities that were issued by means other than a *primary offering*) to the public.

Security Stocks and bonds (including *variations thereof* and derivatives therefrom). The two essential elements of a security are (1) the purchaser is led to expect a profit or return on the investment and (2) the actual profit or return to be earned is largely in the hands of the issuing company.

Short-swing profit The profit earned by an officer or director of an entity from *buying* or *selling* that entity's stock within a 6-month period—such profit is recoverable by that entity.

Small business issuer An issuing company whose sales and public float each do *not* exceed $25 million.

Underwriter "Any person who has purchased from an issuer with a view to, or offers or sells for an issuer in connection with, the distribution of any security, or participates [directly or indirectly] . . . in any such undertaking."*

ASSIGNMENT MATERIAL

Review Questions

1. How does the Securities Exchange Act of 1934 differ from the Securities Act of 1933?
2. What purpose do the SEC's Staff Accounting Bulletins serve?
3. What purpose do SEC releases serve?
4. What is the SEC's role in the formation and improvement of generally accepted accounting principles?
5. How do a registration statement and a prospectus differ?
6. What is the distinction between Form S-1 and Form 10-K?
7. What do *Regulations A* and *D* have in common?
8. What do Forms 8-K, 10-K, and 10-Q have in common?
9. How is *Regulation C* under the 1933 Act similar to *Regulation 12B* under the 1934 Act?
10. What is the distinction between *Regulation S-X* and *Regulation S-K*?
11. How do a proxy and a proxy statement differ?
12. How are financial statements prepared in accordance with *Regulation S-X* requirements different from financial statements prepared in accordance with GAAP?

Exercises

E 18-1 **The Role of the SEC in Relation to the FASB** Indicate whether each of the following statements is true or false. Discuss the reasons for your answers.

1. The pronouncements of the FASB must be *formally* approved by the SEC before they can be issued.
2. The accounting-related pronouncements of the SEC must be *formally* approved by the FASB before they are issued.
3. The SEC has given the FASB the *statutory authority* to prescribe accounting principles.
4. *Publicly owned* companies are subject to the SEC and FASB financial reporting requirements.
5. *Privately owned* companies are *not* subject to the SEC's continuous financial reporting requirements.
6. The SEC automatically rescinds a pronouncement when the FASB issues a Statement of Financial Accounting Standards involving a particular accounting issue.
7. When the SEC has noticed an emerging accounting practice in the last 15 years or so, it has usually established accounting standards in that area until the FASB can address the issue.
8. Unlike the FASB, the SEC can order a company subject to its reporting requirements to alter its financial statements.

* Securities Act of 1933.

E 18-2 **SEC Promulgations** Complete the following statements:

1. The *form and content* of financial statements included with filings with the SEC are set forth in ______________.
2. The pronouncements that announce the SEC's proposed revisions to its rules and regulations are called ______________.
3. *Nonfinancial* statement disclosure requirements are set forth in ______________.
4. An SEC regulation is merely a collection of ______________.
5. The SEC rules and regulations that pertain to the various sections of the 1933 Act and the 1934 Act are referred to as the ______________ rules and regulations.
6. The regulation that specifies the financial statements included in SEC filings is ______________.
7. The interpretations and practices followed by certain departments of the SEC are called ______________.
8. Accounting-related releases used to be announced in ______________, but now they are set forth in ______________.
9. The promulgation of the SEC that accountants deal with more than any other is ______________.
10. A list of instructions concerning what is included in a particular SEC filing is called a ______________.

E 18-3 **The 1933 and 1934 Acts: Terminology** Complete the following statements:

1. Under the 1933 Act, issuers of securities must furnish potential investors with a(n) ______________.
2. A registration statement is divided into the following two basic parts:
   a. Information ______________.
   b. Information ______________.
3. A "red herring" is a(n) ______________.
4. Stocks and bonds are ______________.
5. A person who purchases an issuer's stock with a view to distributing that stock to the public is a(n) ______________.
6. Security offerings that *need not* be registered with the SEC are considered ______________ offerings.
7. All the information filed with the SEC using an appropriate form under the 1933 Act is called a(n) ______________.
8. The Securities Act of 1933 pertains to the ______________ of securities.
9. The Securities Exchange Act of 1934 pertains to ______________ of issued securities.
10. Securities acquired by means that did not involve a public offering are called ______________.
11. A document authorizing one person to vote in place of another person is a ______________.
12. A statement furnished to stockholders in connection with soliciting their votes is called a ______________.

E 18-4 **The 1933 and 1934 Acts: Forms Used in Registrations and Filings** Indicate the SEC form applicable to each of the following items:

1. The most commonly used *annual* reporting form under the 1934 Act.
2. The most commonly used registration form under the 1933 Act.
3. The *quarterly* reporting form used under the 1934 Act.

4. The form used under the 1934 Act to report *certain transactions or events* that arise during the year.
5. The form that may be used to register *stock option plans*, providing certain other conditions are met.
6. The most commonly used registration form under the 1934 Act.
7. The three general forms used under the 1933 Act.
8. The item filed with the SEC when a *Regulation A* offering is involved.

E 18-5 **The Securities Act of 1933: The Role of the SEC and Responsibility of Outside Auditors** Select the best answer for each of the following items:

1. One of the SEC's functions is to
   a. Judge the merits of the securities being offered to the public.
   b. Ascertain the wisdom of investing in securities being offered to the public.
   c. Warrant that registration statements contain all necessary financial and nonfinancial statement information required by the investing public to evaluate the merit of the securities being offered.
   d. Warrant that the information contained in registration statements examined and approved by the SEC is true and accurate.
   e. Require that all material information be furnished to potential investors.
2. A company registers securities with the SEC under the 1933 Act. Because this event concerns its outside auditors, which of the following is correct?
   a. The SEC will defend any action brought against certified public accountants who have reported on financial statements included in a registration statement examined and approved by the SEC.
   b. Any action brought against the auditors would have to be decided on the basis of ordinary negligence versus gross negligence.
   c. The auditors could be held liable in the event of ordinary negligence as well as gross negligence.
   d. The auditors could be held liable for misleading statements in the notes to the financial statements even if negligence is not involved.
   e. None of the above.
3. One of the major purposes of the federal security statutes is to
   a. Establish the qualifications for accountants who are members of the profession.
   b. Eliminate incompetent attorneys and accountants who participate in the registration of securities offered to the public.
   c. Provide a set of uniform standards and tests for accountants, attorneys, and others who practice before the Securities and Exchange Commission.
   d. Provide sufficient information to the investing public who purchase securities in the marketplace.
   e. None of the above.
4. Under the Securities Act of 1933, subject to some exceptions and limitations, it is unlawful to use the mails or instruments of interstate commerce to sell or offer to sell a security to the public unless
   a. A surety bond sufficient to cover potential liability to investors is obtained and filed with the SEC.
   b. The offer is made through underwriters qualified to offer the securities on a nationwide basis.
   c. A registration statement that has been properly filed with the SEC has been found to be acceptable and is in effect.
   d. The SEC approves of the financial merit of the offering.
   e. None of the above.

5. A company registers securities with the SEC under the 1933 Act. As this event concerns its outside auditors, which of the following is correct?
   a. The outside auditors may disclaim any liability under the federal securities acts by an unambiguous, boldfaced disclaimer of liability on the audit report.
   b. The outside auditors must determine which SEC form the company should use in the filing.
   c. As long as the outside auditors engage exclusively in intrastate business, the federal securities laws do not apply to them.
   d. The outside auditors have primary responsibility for the nonfinancial statement portions of the registration statement as well as responsibility for the financial statement portions of the registration statement.
   e. None of the above choices is correct.

E 18-6 **The 1933 and 1934 Acts: Technical Understanding** Select the best answer for each of the following items:

1. What subjects do *Regulation A* and *Regulation D* deal with?
   a. The mechanics of registering securities under the 1933 Act.
   b. The responsibilities of outside auditors under the 1933 Act.
   c. The forms used under the 1933 Act.
   d. Allowable exemptions from registration under the 1933 Act.
   e. None of the above.
2. Concerning the relationship between the 1933 Act and the 1934 Act, which of the following is correct?
   a. Having once become subject to the reporting requirements of the 1934 Act, a company may offer securities to the public in the future *without* having to register such securities with the SEC under the 1933 Act.
   b. If a *privately owned* company having 200,000 common shares outstanding registers the sale of 50,000 *new shares* under the 1933 Act, all 250,000 common shares are deemed to be registered under the 1933 Act.
   c. A company that registers securities under the 1933 Act becomes subject to the reporting requirements of the 1934 Act.
   d. If a *privately owned* company having 500,000 common shares outstanding registers the sale of 100,000 *new shares* under the 1933 Act, only the 100,000 *new shares* may be registered under the 1934 Act.
   e. None of the above.
3. Under the 1933 Act, which of the following is the most important criterion in determining whether a private placement to a limited number of persons or a *public offering* has been made?
   a. The size of the issuing corporation.
   b. The type of security offered.
   c. The prompt resale of the securities by the purchasers.
   d. Whether the company engages exclusively in intrastate business.
   e. None of the above.
4. Which of the following is not *exempt* from registration under the 1933 Act?
   a. Securities offered through underwriters.
   b. Securities offered to a limited number of persons in a private placement.
   c. Securities offered only to residents of the state in which the company is located.
   d. Securities offered by a government unit.
   e. None of the above.
5. Concerning the 1934 Act, which of the following is *correct*?
   a. A company may be subject to the reporting requirements of the 1934 Act even though it *never* has registered securities under the 1933 Act.
   b. A company that has been subject to the reporting requirements of the 1934 Act is always subject to such requirements unless it becomes privately held again.

c. A company is no longer subject to the reporting requirements of the 1934 Act if its *total assets* are *below* $10 million at the end of its last three fiscal years.
d. A company that is no longer subject to the reporting requirements of the 1934 Act is also no longer subject to the requirements of the 1933 Act.
e. None of the above.

E 18-7 ***Regulation S-X*: True or False** Indicate whether each of the following statements is true or false.

1. *Regulation S-X* specifies the financial statements included in registration statements and reports filed with the SEC.
2. Some Financial Reporting Releases explain and illustrate certain rules in *Regulation S-X*.
3. *Regulation S-X* applies to the 1933 Act but not to the 1934 Act.
4. Some *Regulation S-X* rules permit the deletion of certain notes in financial statements otherwise required by GAAP.
5. The form and content of financial statements included in registration statements and reports filed with the SEC are set forth in *Regulation S-X*.
6. The SEC automatically amends *Regulation S-X* to comply with any new FASB pronouncements.
7. Annual reports to shareholders need not present financial statements in compliance with *Regulation S-X*.
8. In general, it is a major task to convert financial statements and the related notes (prepared in accordance with GAAP) to meet the requirements of *Regulation S-X*.
9. *Regulation S-X* is a guide for preparing financial statements included in the registration statements and reports filed with the SEC—it need not be strictly followed.
10. *Regulation S-X* does not specify which SEC form is used to prepare reports filed under the 1934 Act.
11. Certain rules in *Regulation S-X* require additional financial disclosures above and beyond disclosures normally made pursuant to GAAP.
12. Changes in *Regulation S-X* can be announced through the issuance of a Financial Reporting Release.

Problems

P 18-1 **The Securities Exchange Act of 1934: Stock Transactions by Employees** Discoverex is a manufacturing company whose securities are registered on a national securities exchange. On 5/5/05, one of the company's engineers disclosed to management that he had discovered a new product that he believed would be quite profitable to the corporation. Prescott and Trout, the corporation's *president* and *treasurer*, and members of the board of directors were quite impressed with the prospects of the new product's profitability.

Trout had such confidence in the corporation's prospects that on 5/11/05, he purchased on the open market 1,000 shares of the corporation's common stock at $10 per share. This purchase occurred before news of the new product reached the public in late February and caused a rise in the market price to $30 per share.

Prescott did *not* purchase any shares in February because she had already purchased 600 shares of the corporation's common stock on 4/1/05 for $10 per share.

On 7/7/05, because of unexpected expenses arising from a fire in her home, Prescott sold on the open market for $35 per share the 600 shares of stock she had purchased in April. Trout continues to hold his 1,000 shares.

Required

1. What questions related to the federal securities laws are suggested by these facts? Discuss.
2. What would be a reasonable corporate policy designed to have employees buy and sell stock on the same basis as *nonemployees*?

P 18-2 **The Securities Exchange Act of 1934: Public Disclosures** B&S Inc.'s sole issue of stock is traded on a national exchange. In conducting the year-end examination of the financial statements, the auditor learned that B&S's research department had perfected a manufacturing process that would have a positive material effect on future earnings. B&S did not announce the development.

When a rumor about the new process started in late January, B&S's president promptly telephoned financial papers in several states and announced that there was no substance to the rumor. A number of papers reported the president's denial of the rumor. Thereafter, B&S's stock traded in its normal narrow range. In February, relying on the information reported in the financial press, Sellinger (an outside shareholder) sold a large block of his B&S stock at the current market price.

B&S's president made a public announcement about the perfection of the new process the following June. The announcement precipitated a dramatic increase in both the price and volume of trading of B&S's stock. Neither B&S nor any person with knowledge of the process engaged in trading B&S's stock before the public announcement of the discovery.

Required What questions related to federal securities laws are suggested by these facts? Discuss.

chapter 19

Bankruptcy Reorganizations and Liquidations

Some debts are fun when you are acquiring them, but none are fun when you set about retiring them.
OGDEN NASH

LEARNING OBJECTIVES

To Understand

- The nature and purpose of the bankruptcy statutes.
- The difference between a *troubled debt restructuring* and a *bankruptcy reorganization* under Chapter 11 of the bankruptcy statutes.
- The establishment of a *new basis of accounting* in a *bankruptcy reorganization*.
- The special types of accounting reports used in *bankruptcy liquidations*.

TOPIC OUTLINE

I. Historical Perspective
II. Bankruptcy Statutes
III. *Bankruptcy Reorganization* versus *Troubled Debt Restructuring*: Advantages and Disadvantages
IV. Bankruptcy Reorganizations
V. Bankruptcy Liquidations
VI. Accounting by Trustees
VII. Concluding Comments

CHAPTER OVERVIEW

Options for Financially Distressed Companies

Any type of economic entity (including corporations, partnerships, sole proprietorships, and municipalities) can encounter financial difficulties. Business entities in financial difficulty first usually retrench and undertake cost-cutting steps to conserve cash and reduce operating losses. Such steps may include revamping the organization structure to eliminate or consolidate functions (often resulting in the termination of a substantial number of personnel), seeking wage and fringe-benefit concessions from employees, seeking relaxation of restrictive union work rules, and disposing of unprofitable segments. In addition, the entity may eventually need to (1) raise additional capital, (2) dispose of profitable segments, (3) combine with another business, (4) restructure its debt *outside* the bankruptcy courts, (5) reorganize *through* the bankruptcy courts, or (6) liquidate.

This chapter deals with corporations that select the last two options. Option 4, restructuring debt *outside* the bankruptcy courts, (discussed in *intermediate accounting textbooks*), usually consists of extending due dates, forgiving some portion of debt, and reducing the interest rate on the debt. This option gives the business a reasonable chance to continue as a viable entity and recover from the financial difficulties, thereby avoiding liquidation, at least for the time being. Although option 5, reorganization *through* the bankruptcy courts, is identical in its objective to that of option 4, it is considered less desirable even though it usually results in a substantial forgiveness of debt. Option 6, **liquidation**, consists of converting all noncash assets into cash, paying creditors to the extent possible, and ending the legal existence of the corporation. In discussing the options of restructuring debt and reorganizing *through* the bankruptcy courts, we exclude railroads and municipalities because of their special nature. We also exclude these special entities from the discussion of liquidation because *public policy* dictates that these entities *not* be liquidated.

I. Historical Perspective

An Escape Mechanism

Petitioning the courts for bankruptcy protection is primarily used as a means of settling debts for *less than* the full amount owed. In most cases, filing for bankruptcy protection means the company is broke. In other cases, however, it merely means the company *cannot* pay its bills as they become due.

As an escape mechanism, the bankruptcy process usually produces bitter feelings among creditors that are *not* paid in full. It also gives debtor companies that continue to operate significant operating advantages over nonbankrupt competitors. Some critics fault corporate bankruptcy laws for making it too easy to unload financial burdens and keep existing management in place. Others argue that the process is too limited and ignores the role large corporations play in the community.

The Early Days

Bankruptcy, which dates to A.D. 118, has evolved over the years from a punitive measure in which *debtors* could be killed or enslaved to a means of adjusting the relationship between *debtors* and *creditors*. For most of the nineteenth century, the United States did *not* have bankruptcy laws, which is why some of those who heeded Horace Greeley's call to "go West, young man" were *debtors* who literally went west for their health.

From Death Knell to Strategic Tool

Traditionally, filing for bankruptcy protection was a company's death knell. Beginning in the 1980s, however, filing for bankruptcy protection changed from being a shield used for temporary protection from creditors to being a strategic tool that companies can use to cut themselves free of their mistakes. For instance, retail companies that overexpand and become financially distressed often use bankruptcy filings against their landlords to escape from their leases at a fraction of their future lease commitments. Similarly, some companies who have violated their real estate lease terms use the threat of filing for bankruptcy protection against landlords who otherwise would seek legal redress by civil proceedings. See the Cases in Point for examples of how specific companies have used the bankruptcy statutes in recent years.

CASE IN POINT

> *PG&E Corp.* (one of California's two huge utilities) filed for bankruptcy protection in 2001 with the hope of obtaining substantial (and much-needed) utility rate increases.
> *Sizzler International* used bankruptcy protection *to get out of* long-term leases on approximately 130 of its restaurants. Likewise, *United Artists* tried in bankruptcy proceedings in 2000 to reject the long-term leases of 70 theaters it had closed.
> *LTV Corporation* used bankruptcy *to get out* of pension obligations.
> *Continental Airlines* used it *to break* labor contracts.
> Chevron*Texaco Corporation* used the bankruptcy process *to reduce* the amount a jury had ordered it to pay *Pennzoil Corporation* in an antitrust settlement.
> Many companies have used bankruptcy *to delay* tax payments.
> *Owens Corning* and *Armstrong World Industries* used it to try to help cap potential asbestos-related liabilities against them.

A Change for the Better or Worse

Even when corporate restructuring became fashionable in the early 1990s, corporate bankruptcy never shed its tainted status. But it seems as though something has changed. As recently as **1997** (*a nonrecession year*), **82** public companies with total assets of only **$17 billion** filed for Chapter 11 bankruptcy protection. In **2000**, it was **176** companies with **$94** billion of assets. For the first two-thirds of **2001** (*prior to the events of September 11, 2001*), it was approximately **150** companies with roughly **$160** billion of assets. Thus more and more large companies having financial difficulties are concluding that the *advantages* of Chapter 11 bankruptcy protection (discussed in detail later) clearly outweigh the *disadvantages*. Furthermore, the far-reaching events of September 11, 2001, appear to be both a catalyst and a cause for a more encompassing wave of restructurings.

II. BANKRUPTCY STATUTES

Bankruptcy statutes attempt to strike a balance between two deeply rooted, and sometimes conflicting, American principles: (1) **those who *can* afford to pay their debts should**, and (2) **honest but overextended borrowers deserve a fresh start—*not* debtor's prison.**

Their Purpose

Debt capital markets would be inhibited without some provisions for ensuring fair and equitable means to resolve rights and protect public interests. This is the purpose of the bankruptcy laws. Distressed companies and their creditors must decide whether it is necessary to resort to the bankruptcy process. Accordingly, we now discuss the federal bankruptcy statutes.

Their Substance

Under the bankruptcy statutes, a company or an individual is placed under the protection of the court, whereby creditors (including creditors possessing security interests, unsecured creditors, tax collectors, and public utilities) are prevented from taking other legal action (such as foreclosing on loans, filing lawsuits, repossessing or seizing assets, and placing padlocks on the doors of the company's real property). When a company's rehabilitation and future viable operations are feasible, the company's debt is restructured under the supervision and control of the court in such a manner that the debtor may be legally freed from the payment of certain past debts. When rehabilitation and recovery are *not* feasible, an orderly liquidation takes place under the supervision and control of the bankruptcy court. Approximately 1,300,000 bankruptcy filings (of which roughly 90% are by *individuals* and 10% are by *businesses*) have occurred annually—more than *double* the number 15 years ago.

The Federal Bankruptcy Code

The U.S. Constitution grants to the Congress the power to establish uniform laws throughout the United States pertaining to the subject of bankruptcies. The federal bankruptcy statutes are set forth in Title 11 of the United States Code. These laws are commonly referred to as the **Bankruptcy Code**. Federal statutes pertaining to bankruptcy prevail over state laws that conflict with federal laws.

The Bankruptcy Code is periodically amended (as it was in 1994 and 1998). Under the Bankruptcy Code, separate bankruptcy courts (adjuncts to the district courts) are required, along with special judges (commonly referred to as bankruptcy judges) who supervise and review all bankruptcy petitions and proceedings. (If a case involves broad bankruptcy issues, however, *district judges*—not the *bankruptcy judges*—decide such issues.)

The Bankruptcy Code consists of the following eight chapters (even-numbered chapters do not exist except for Chapter 12):

Chapter 1	General provisions
Chapter 3	Case administration
Chapter 5	Creditors, the debtor, and the estate
Chapter 7	**Liquidation** (*discussed in Section V of this chapter*)
Chapter 9	Adjustment of debts of a municipality
Chapter 11	**Reorganization** (*discussed in Section IV of this chapter*)
Chapter 12	Adjustment of debts of a family farmer with regular annual income
Chapter 13	Adjustment of debts of an individual with regular income

The general provisions of Chapters 1, 3, and 5 pertain to Chapters 7, 9, 11, 12, and 13 unless otherwise indicated. In this section, we discuss certain basic aspects of Chapters 1, 3, and 5. Chapters 9, 12, and 13 do *not* pertain to corporations organized to make a profit; accordingly, they are *not* discussed in this chapter. (Chapter 9 applies only to municipalities that seek relief voluntarily; their creditors *cannot* force a municipality into bankruptcy proceedings against their will.)

In the Bankruptcy Code, the subject of the bankruptcy proceedings is referred to as a **debtor**. The commencement of a bankruptcy case creates an **estate**. The estate includes all of the debtor's property no matter where located (Section 541).[1]

Applicability of the Bankruptcy Code

The Bankruptcy Code applies to individuals, partnerships, corporations (all of which are collectively referred to as *persons*), and municipalities. Insurance companies and certain financial institutions (such as banks, savings and loan associations, building and loan associations, and credit unions) are excluded because they are subject to alternative regulations. Railroads may not use the liquidation provisions of Chapter 7 and may use only the reorganization provisions of Chapter 11. Stockbrokers and commodity brokers are not eligible for the reorganization provisions of Chapter 11 and may use only the liquidation provisions of Chapter 7 (Section 109[b]).

---

[1] This reference is to the Bankruptcy Code. Hereafter, only the section number of the code is provided.

Voluntary Petitions

An eligible corporation (that is, a corporation other than an insurance company or certain financial institutions) may file a voluntary petition with the bankruptcy courts under Chapter 7 or 11 and thereby obtain the benefits available under the statutes (Section 109). Filing a voluntary petition constitutes an **order for relief**, which has the same full force and effect as if the bankruptcy court had issued an order that the debtor be granted relief under the statutes (Section 301). The court can dismiss a voluntary filing, however, if it is in the best interests of creditors (Section 707 and 112[b]).

The **voluntary petition** initiates bankruptcy proceedings; it is an official form that must be accompanied by a summary of the debtor's property (at market or current values) and debts, including supporting schedules, all on official forms. The supporting schedules for property consist of separate schedules for real property, personal property, and property not otherwise scheduled. The supporting schedules for debts consist of separate schedules for creditors with priority (a special class of creditors explained later in the book), creditors holding security, and creditors having unsecured claims without priority. Information must also include each creditor's address (if known), when the debt was incurred, and whether the debt is contingent, disputed, or subject to setoff. In addition, the petitioner must respond to a questionnaire regarding all aspects of its financial condition and operations. Although this questionnaire is called the *statement of affairs*, it should not be confused with the statement of affairs that accountants prepare regarding asset values and debts owed, which is explained later in the chapter.

Check Point

Which of the entities listed are entitled to file a *voluntary* bankruptcy petition under Chapter 7 or 11?

a. A banking corporation
b. A partnership
c. A corporation that manufactures consumer goods
d. A corporation that provides personal services
e. A municipal corporation
f. A railroad
g. An insurance corporation

Answers: b, c, d, f

Involuntary Petitions

Under Chapter 7 or 11, an eligible corporation may be forced into bankruptcy proceedings against its will by its creditors. One or more creditors may file an **involuntary petition** with the bankruptcy court. If a debtor has 12 or more creditors, at least 3 of them who have claims totaling a minimum of $10,000 more than the value of any lien on the property of the debtor securing such claims must sign the petition (Section 303[b][1]). If a company has fewer than 12 creditors, one or more creditors having such claims of at least $10,000 must sign the petition (Section 303[b][2]). These dollar amounts apply to both liquidation and reorganization cases.

For an involuntary petition filed under Chapter 7 or 11, the bankruptcy court enters an order for relief against the debtor only if either of the following conditions pertains:

1. The debtor is generally not paying its debts as they become due.
2. A custodian was appointed or took possession of the debtor's property within 120 days before the date of the filing of the petition. (This does not apply to a trustee, receiver, or agent appointed or authorized to take charge of less than the majority of the debtor's property for the purpose of enforcing a lien against such property.) (Section 303[h])

The *first test* listed is an equity *insolvency test*; that is, the debtor's assets equitably belong to the creditors to the extent of their claims. In the *second test*, the appointment of a custodian presumes that the debtor *cannot* pay its debts as they mature.

In practice, *voluntary bankruptcies* occur much more frequently than *involuntary bankruptcies*. Regardless of whether a company enters bankruptcy proceedings voluntarily or involuntarily, it should immediately obtain the assistance of an attorney who specializes in bankruptcy proceedings.

CHECK POINTS

Which of the entities listed may have an *involuntary* bankruptcy petition filed against them?

a. A banking corporation
b. A partnership
c. A corporation that manufactures consumer goods
d. A corporation that provides personal services
e. A municipal corporation
f. A railroad
g. An insurance corporation

Answers: b, c, d, f

In which of the following situations could an *involuntary* bankruptcy petition be filed?

a. The debtor has debts of at least $10,000.
b. The appropriate number of creditors required to sign the petition are owed at least $10,000.
c. The debtor has committed a fraudulent act.
d. The debtor has recently appointed a custodian.
e. The debtor has made asset transfers that constitute a preference to one or more creditors.
f. Wages are owed to employees for more than 90 days.
g. The debtor is not paying its debts as they mature.
h. The debtor has entered into discussions with its creditors to restructure its debt.
i. The debtor's net worth is negative as a result of operating losses.

Answers: a, b, d, g

Creditors with Priority

A company entering bankruptcy proceedings can have two general classes of creditor—secured and unsecured. **Secured creditors** have been pledged certain of the company's assets as security on their claims. Creditors that have no right to any of the company's specific assets are **unsecured creditors**. In addition to these two general classes of creditors, the Bankruptcy Code creates a special class of creditor termed **creditors with priority**. Nine categories of debt are given priority status. We list the major ones *in the order of their priority*, as follows:

1. **Administrative expenses, fees, and charges assessed against the estate.** Administrative expenses are the actual and necessary costs and expenses of preserving the estate after the petition has been filed. This includes trustee's fees; legal, accounting, and appraisal fees incurred in connection with the bankruptcy proceedings; filing fees paid by creditors in an involuntary bankruptcy petition; and expenses incurred in recovering assets that were concealed or fraudulently transferred.
2. **Certain postfiling "gap" claims.** This category, which exists only for *involuntary filings*, includes unsecured claims arising in the ordinary course of the debtor's business *after* the involuntary filing but *before* (1) the appointment of a trustee or (2) an order of relief is entered, whichever occurs first.
3. **Wages, salaries, and commissions.** Wages, salaries, and commissions are limited to unsecured amounts earned by an individual within 90 days before the filing date or the date of the cessation of the debtor's business, whichever occurs first, but only up to $4,000 for each individual. This category includes vacation, severance, and sick leave pay.
4. **Employee benefit plans.** This category pertains to unsecured claims for contributions to employee benefit plans arising from services rendered by employees within 180 days before the date of the filing of the petition or the date of the cessation of the debtor's business, whichever

occurs first. The claims are limited to the number of employees covered by each such plan multiplied by $4,000, minus (a) the total amount paid to such employees as items in priority 3 and (b) the total amount paid by the estate on behalf of such employees to any other employee benefit plan.

5. **Deposits by individuals.** This category includes unsecured claims of up to $900 for each such individual, arising from the deposit of money before the commencement of the case in connection with the purchase, lease, or rental of property, or the purchase of services for the personal, family, or household use of such individuals, which were not delivered or provided.
6. **Taxes.** This category includes income taxes, property taxes, withholding taxes, employer payroll taxes, excise taxes, and customs duties. Most of these taxes are limited to amounts relating to a specified period of time preceding the date of the filing, usually one or three years, depending on the item.

With regard to payment, creditors with priority are given a statutory priority over the claims of other unsecured creditors. Later in the chapter, we illustrate this priority in a liquidation through the bankruptcy courts.

CHECK POINT

Which of the following debts have priority under the Bankruptcy Code?

a. Amounts owed to secured creditors
b. In an involuntary petition, amounts owed to the creditors who signed the petition
c. Costs of administering the bankruptcy proceedings
d. Debts incurred by issuing materially false statements as to financial condition
e. All wages owed to employees that were earned within 90 days prior to filing the bankruptcy petition
f. Wages of up to $4,000 per employee, no matter when earned
g. Taxes owed to the United States or any state or subdivision thereof

Answers: c, g

III. *BANKRUPTCY REORGANIZATION* VERSUS *TROUBLED DEBT RESTRUCTURING*: ADVANTAGES AND DISADVANTAGES

Technically, debts can be restructured either (1) *through* the bankruptcy courts or (2) *outside* the bankruptcy courts. For simplicity, we use (1) the term reorganization when the bankruptcy courts *are* used and (2) the term ***troubled debt restructuring*** when the bankruptcy courts are *not* used.

Before discussing the required manner of accounting for *bankruptcy reorganizations*, we briefly discuss, in general, the advantages and disadvantages of a *bankruptcy reorganization* compared with a *troubled debt restructuring* (an *intermediate accounting* topic).

First, however, recall that the prescribed manner of accounting for *troubled debt restructurings* is set forth in FASB *Statement No. 15*, "Accounting by Debtors and Creditors for Troubled Debt Restructurings."[2] As explained later, *FAS 15* rarely applies to bankruptcy reorganizations, the accounting for which is prescribed by an AICPA Statement of Position that we discuss later.

[2] This statement was amended slightly by FASB *Statement No. 114*, "Accounting by Creditors for Impairment of a Loan," and FASB *Statement No. 121*, "Accounting for the Impairment of Long-Lived Assets and for Long-Lived Assets to Be Disposed Of."

Advantages of Restructuring *Outside* the Bankruptcy Courts versus Reorganizing under Chapter 11

One advantage of restructuring outside the bankruptcy courts is that the restructuring can be completed in far less time than a Chapter 11 reorganization, which takes a minimum of approximately 18 months. Of greater importance, however, is the desire to avoid the stigma associated with being or having been subject to bankruptcy proceedings. More uncertainty is associated with Chapter 11 reorganizations concerning the distressed company's chances of survival—many companies that file for Chapter 11 reorganizations are unable to work out a successful plan of reorganization and are liquidated instead. Thus filing for reorganization under Chapter 11 is usually considered the last resort, short of liquidation.

Needless to say, filing for a Chapter 11 reorganization has far greater consequences to the distressed company in terms of its impact on suppliers, competitors, customers, and employees than does a restructuring outside the bankruptcy courts. For example, a distressed company that is restructuring may be able to obtain some credit from suppliers; when a company reorganizes under Chapter 11, suppliers usually require payment on delivery. During restructuring, competitors tend to get sales leverage from a distressed company's problems; during a Chapter 11 reorganization, competitors have that much more ammunition. (Competitors often show customers press clippings of the distressed company's financial problems.)

When a company has filed for reorganization under Chapter 11, customers have that much *less* assurance that the company will survive—this can be critical for a distressed company that sells products requiring the company's continued existence for purposes of providing service and stocking spare parts. Employees are more likely to look for greener pastures once a company files for reorganization under Chapter 11 because of the uncertainty associated with bankruptcy proceedings. (Personnel placement firms tend to zero in on distressed companies to hire away their employees; their chances of success increase when a company files for a Chapter 11 reorganization.)

Working out a troubled debt restructuring agreement is usually a substantial and difficult undertaking, especially when major differences exist among various groups of creditors as to the sacrifices each is willing to make. A distressed company often resorts to a Chapter 11 reorganization when it is impossible to work out a troubled debt restructuring agreement with its creditors, when its lenders refuse to lend any more money, or when suppliers begin requiring payment on delivery. Although the advantages of restructuring debt outside the bankruptcy courts are considerable, there are certain advantages to filing for reorganization under Chapter 11.

The primary advantages of a Chapter 11 reorganization to a distressed company are as follows:

1. **Achieving sanctuary status.** Creditors *cannot* sue or take other steps to collect amounts owed while a debtor is under Chapter 11 protection. Thus distressed companies have some "breathing room" to develop a plan of reorganization.
2. **Freezing amounts owed for interest.** For unsecured debt, no interest accrues while the company is in Chapter 11, thus allowing the debtor to conserve substantial amounts of cash. Some companies have saved several hundred million dollars of interest while under Chapter 11 protection. Competitors of such debtors often complain (as did the competitors of Eastern Airlines and Braniff Airlines several years ago) that the debtors have an unfair advantage because of this feature.
3. **Obtaining modifications to collective bargaining agreements.** Companies usually are more effective in obtaining wage reductions or modifications to collective bargaining agreements than when they are *not* under Chapter 11 protection.
4. **Obtaining a massive reduction in debt.** Companies usually are able to obtain a massive reduction of the debtor's liabilities (forgiveness of debt) compared with the amount of debt forgiven in a restructuring *outside* of the bankruptcy courts.
5. **Enabling use of "fresh-start financial reporting."** As explained later, obtaining a massive reduction of debt usually results in debtors having to use this special manner of reporting, which has its advantages.

What Percentage Survives Chapter 11?

To file for reorganization under Chapter 11 is to flirt with extinction. Of all Chapter 11 filings (currently about 15,000 per year), only about 15% emerge as viable companies (and then usually with new top management); the remainder are transferred to Chapter 7 and *liquidated*.

IV. Bankruptcy Reorganizations

Although Chapter 11 of the Bankruptcy Code is the reorganization chapter, the statutes do not define the term reorganization. We may assume from Chapter 11's purpose and procedures, however, that the chapter intends that the term have a broad meaning. Basically, a **reorganization** encompasses the development of a plan—called a *plan of reorganization*—to alter the company's liability and/or equity structure so that the company has a reasonable chance of surviving bankruptcy proceedings and prospering on its own.

Companies that file for Chapter 11 bankruptcy protection often hire an outside public accounting firm to assist them in preparing a *feasible plan of reorganization*. In these situations, a company receiving such services sometimes sues the outside public accounting firm in connection with the perceived poor quality of services rendered. See the Case in Point.

CASE IN POINT

In one of the largest settlements involving a Big Five accounting firm, Ernst & Young, LLP agreed in 1999 to pay $185 million to settle claims that E & Y committed fraud and gave incompetent advice in the bankruptcy-court reorganization of now-defunct Merry-Go-Round Enterprises, Inc.

Most reorganization plans involve a negotiated settlement between the company and its unsecured creditors to repay debts, usually at so many cents on the dollar. Thus the company is provided with a "fresh start," a unique opportunity in business. Approximately 10% to 20% of all *business* bankruptcy filings are Chapter 11 filings (the remainder being Chapter 7 filings).

The Sequence of Events in a Chapter 11 Filing

The typical sequence of events in a Chapter 11 filing is as follows:

1. **Filing the petition.** Either a *voluntary* or an *involuntary* petition can initiate bankruptcy proceedings. The company in question may prepare a statement showing asset values and amounts that would be paid to each class of creditor in the event of liquidation. As noted earlier, accountants called this a *statement of affairs*. We illustrate the preparation of this statement later in the chapter in connection with *liquidations*.
2. **Management of the company.** The debtor company's management usually continues to control and operate the debtor's day-to-day activities. Under certain conditions, however, and for just cause (such as fraud, incompetence, or gross mismanagement of the company), and if in the best interests of creditors, the court may appoint a trustee to manage the debtor's business (Section 1104[a]). **The appointment of a trustee in a Chapter 11 filing is infrequent.** We discuss the duties of trustees later in the chapter in connection with liquidations, for which trustees are always appointed.
3. **Creditors' and equity security holders' committees.** After an order for relief has been entered, the court appoints a committee of *unsecured* creditors. (The court may also appoint additional committees of creditors, or of equity security holders if necessary, to ensure adequate representation of these groups. Such a court-appointed committee may
   a. select and authorize [with the court's approval] the employment by such committee of one or more attorneys, accountants, or other agents to represent or perform services for such committee [Section 1103(a)];
   b. consult with the trustee or debtor in possession concerning the administration of the case;

c. investigate the acts, conduct, assets, liabilities, and financial condition of the debtor, the operation of the debtor's business and the desirability of the continuance of such business, and any other matter relevant to the case or to the formulation of a plan;
d. participate in the formulation of a plan [of reorganization], advise those represented by such committee of such committee's determinations as to any plan formulated, and collect and file with the court acceptances or rejections of a plan;
e. request the appointment of a trustee or examiner . . . ; and
f. perform such other services as are in the interest of those represented [Section 1103(c)].

4. **Plan of reorganization.** Under Chapter 11 of the Code, a plan of reorganization may alter the legal, equitable, and contractual rights of any class of creditors' claims, secured or unsecured, or of equity interests. Such an alteration is known as **impairment** of a claim or an interest (Section 1124). In a common plan of reorganization, all unsecured creditors agree to accept payment at a percentage of their respective claims—for example, 25 cents on the dollar—with the remainder of the debt canceled.

   The debtor has the exclusive right to propose a plan during the 20 days after the order for relief. At the end of this period, any party of interest—such as the trustee, committee, a creditor, or an equity security holder—may file a plan, provided certain conditions are met (Section 1121). The role of the Securities and Exchange Commission (SEC) is quite limited:

   > The Securities and Exchange Commission may raise and may appear and be heard on any issue . . . but the SEC may not appeal from any judgment, order, or decree entered in the case [Section 1109].

   Fast track for small businesses. A significant new provision enacted in 1994 is the special fast-track option for debtors that (1) have debts of $2 million or less and (2) are prepared to reorganize immediately upon filing. Among other things, this treatment (1) entitles the debtor to an exclusive 100-day period for filing a plan of reorganization and (2) includes the obligation to file the plan within 160 days and the right to request that no creditors' committee be appointed.

5. **Disclosure statement.** Before acceptance of a plan of reorganization can be solicited, the debtor must furnish the plan or a summary of the plan to the various classes of creditors and equity interests, along with a written disclosure statement approved by the court as containing *adequate information* (Section 1125[b]). Adequate information is defined as "information of a kind, and in sufficient detail, as far as is reasonably practicable in light of the nature and history of the debtor and the condition of the debtor's books and records, that would enable a hypothetical reasonable investor . . . to make an informed judgment about the plan" (Section 1125[a][1]). This is obviously determined on a case-by-case basis.

6. **Acceptance of plan.** Each class of creditor and equity interest then votes to accept or reject the plan of reorganization. The requirements for approval are as follows:
   a. **Creditors' claims.** "A class of *claims* has accepted a plan if such plan has been accepted by creditors . . . that hold at least **two-thirds in amount and more than one-half in number** [emphasis added] of the allowed claims of such class . . ." (Section 1126[c]).
   b. **Equity interests.** "A class of *interests* has accepted a plan if such plan has been accepted by holders of such interests . . . that hold at least **two-thirds in amount** [emphasis added] of the allowed interests of such class . . ." (Section 1126[d]).

7. **Confirmation of the plan by the court.** After the plan of reorganization has been submitted to the court, a hearing is held. A plan must meet 13 specific requirements to be approved by the court. The overriding requirement is that the debtor must be unlikely to be liquidated or have need for further financial reorganization after the plan is confirmed. In other words, the plan of reorganization must be feasible. Another major requirement is that each class of claims or equity interests must have accepted the plan or must not be impaired under the plan. A provision in the law (referred to in House committee reports as *cram down*), however, allows the court to confirm the plan (if requested by the proponent of the plan) even if each class of claims or equity interests has not accepted it. For this to occur, the plan must not discriminate unfairly and must be fair and equitable with respect to each class of claims or equity interests that is impaired or has not accepted the plan (Section 1129).

If the court does *not* confirm the plan of reorganization, it may, on request of a party of interest and after notice and a hearing, either *dismiss* the case or convert it to a Chapter 7 case (whereby the debtor is forced out of business through liquidation). Such action depends on which course is in the best interest of creditors and the estate (Section 1112).

8. **Discharge of indebtedness.** After the court confirms the plan of reorganization, the debtor is discharged of certain indebtedness as set forth in the plan. If the debtor has committed certain acts, however, discharge of indebtedness does not occur even though a plan has been confirmed (Section 1141[d]). In general, discharge of indebtedness is not granted if (a) the debtor has not fully cooperated with the court (for example, by *not* making all properties and records available to the court's representative, failing to explain losses satisfactorily, or refusing to obey court orders) and (b) the debtor has performed certain specified acts involving the debtor's properties and records to hinder, delay, or defraud creditors (for example, concealing property, destroying records, failing to keep or preserve records, or obtaining money or property fraudulently) (Section 727[a]). A discharge is not granted if the debtor was granted a discharge in a case commenced within six years before the filing date of the petition (Section 727[a]). See the Case in Point.

CASE IN POINT

The largest bankruptcy filing to date was for WorldCom [later renamed MCI] (pre-bankruptcy assets and liabilities of $107 billion and $41 billion, respectively) in 2002. In late 2003 (just 21 months later), a federal bankruptcy judge approved WorldCom's plan of reorganization, which erased $35 billion in debt.

9. **Exceptions to discharge of indebtedness.** Certain types of indebtedness cannot be discharged under the bankruptcy statutes. These debts, which eventually must be paid if the debtor survives Chapter 11 proceedings, are as follows:
   - **a.** Taxes owed to the United States or any state, county, district, or municipality, and customs duties.
   - **b.** Debts incurred in obtaining money, property, services, an extension renewal, or refinance of credit by either:
     - (1) False pretenses, a false representation, or actual fraud, other than a statement concerning the debtor's financial condition.
     - (2) Use of a written statement that is materially false with respect to the debtor's financial condition on which the creditor reasonably relied and that the debtor made or published with intent to deceive.
   - **c.** Debts that have not been duly scheduled in time for proof and allowance because a creditor had no notice or knowledge of bankruptcy proceedings.
   - **d.** Debts for fraud or defalcation while acting in a fiduciary capacity, embezzlement, or larceny.
   - **e.** Debts related to willful and malicious injury by the debtor to another entity or to the property of another entity.
   - **f.** Fines, penalties, and forfeitures payable to and for the benefit of a governmental unit (Section 523).

CHECK POINTS

Which of the following statements is *false*?

a. In a Chapter 11 *reorganization*, management usually continues to operate the business.

b. The legal and contractual rights of any class of creditors may be altered or impaired under a plan of *reorganization*.

c. A *plan of reorganization* must be approved by the Securities and Exchange Commission.

d. A simple majority of creditors in a class of claims is required to approve a *plan of reorganization*.

e. None of the above.

Answer: c

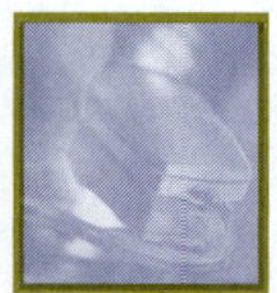

Which of the following statements is *true*?

a. A simple majority in the amount of claims in a class of creditors is required to approve the dollar amount of claims in a *plan of reorganization*.
b. The bankruptcy court usually imposes a *plan of reorganization* on the creditors.
c. The rights of secured creditors are eliminated when a company files for *reorganization* under Chapter 11.
d. In a *reorganization* under Chapter 11, the discharge provisions have no meaningful application.
e. None of the above.

Answer: e

Conceptual Issues

Bankruptcy reorganizations usually result in the creditors giving a substantial reduction of the debtor's financial obligations (required payments for principal and interest). Accordingly, a comparison of (1) the total amount owed (including unpaid interest) immediately before the restructuring, which is commonly referred to as the **carrying amount of the debt**, with (2) the **total future payments** (including amounts designated as interest) to be made pursuant to the plan of reorganization is required. If the *carrying amount of the debt* **exceeds** the *total future payments*, the debtor's liabilities must be reduced. This reduction constitutes a **forgiveness of debt.** If the debtor's *total future payments* ***exceed*** the *carrying amount of the debt*, however, the excess is reported as **interest expense** in future periods. This latter situation presents no accounting issue. The accounting issues pertain solely to forgiveness-of-debt situations and are as follows:

1. **How should any forgiveness of debt be measured?** The focus of this issue is primarily whether the new (postrestructuring) liability amount should be measured and reported at (a) the *undiscounted* total future payments to be made or (b) the *present value* of total future payments. The *difference between (a) or (b)* and the *carrying amount of the debt* is the amount of the forgiveness. Obviously, the choice between (a) and (b) affects the amount of forgiveness that is reported.
2. **How should a forgiveness of debt be classified and reported?** This issue is concerned with whether a forgiveness of debt should be considered (a) a **gain** and, therefore, reported in the **income statement** or (b) a **capital contribution** by the creditor or creditors and, therefore, credited directly to an **equity account.**

The resolution of these issues should be based on the *substance* of the restructuring rather than its *form*. Varying perceptions exist, however, as to what constitutes the substance.

Conceptual Issue 1: Calculation of Forgiveness of Debt

In some situations, the calculation of forgiveness of debt is quite simple. For example, assume that a creditor that is owed $100,000 agrees to cancel $40,000 of the debt in return for the immediate payment of the remaining $60,000. Obviously, the amount of debt forgiven is $40,000. Most situations, however, are more complex. For example, assume that (1) a creditor is owed $100,000 of principal related to a delinquent loan bearing interest at 10% (for simplicity, we assume that no interest is owed) and (2) the creditor agrees to be paid in full in *two* years **with no interest to be charged.** Two approaches have been advocated for such situations—one that **imputes interest** and one that **does *not* impute interest.** When interest is not imputed, the calculation to determine any forgiveness of debt is as follows:

Carrying amount of debt	$100,000
Total future payments	100,000
Amount of Forgiveness	$ -0-

Under this approach, the liability reported in the balance sheet *immediately after* the restructuring is $100,000, and it bears a *zero* interest rate. No interest expense is reported in either year.

When interest is *imputed* (using present value techniques), the amount of forgiveness, if any, depends on the imputed interest rate used. Assuming that the 10% *prerestructuring interest rate* is appropriate, the calculation to determine any forgiveness of debt is as follows:

Carrying amount of debt		$100,000
Total future payments	$100,000	
Present value factor (10%, 2 years)	0.82645	
Present value of total future payments		82,645
Amount of Forgiveness		$ 17,355

Under this approach, the liability reported in the balance sheet immediately after the restructuring is $82,645, and it bears interest at 10%. Interest expense of $8,264 (10% of $82,645) would be reported in Year 1, and $9,091 [10% of ($82,645 + $8,264)] would be reported in Year 2.

Rationale for *Not* Imputing Interest

Arguments for not imputing interest are as follows:

1. Debt restructurings under Chapter 11 are *not* "exchanges of debt" and, therefore, do *not* require the use of present value techniques as set forth in APB *Opinion No. 21*, "Interest on Receivables and Payables," which deals with "exchanges."
2. A creditor does not grant any forgiveness under the restructuring so long as the total future payments to be received equal or exceed the recorded investment in the receivable; that is, the ***recoverability*** of the recorded investment in the receivable is *not* affected.
3. A reduction of the debtor's financial obligations (before the restructuring) to the amount of the recorded investment in the receivable merely changes the creditor's ***future profitability*** on the loan. Thus a creditor's effective interest rate *after* the restructuring could vary from the *prerestructuring interest rate* of 10%, for example, down to zero.

Recall from the *nonimputing* example that no forgiveness of debt existed because the total future payments of $100,000 were *not* below the $100,000 carrying amount of the debt. Thus, from the creditor's perspective, the future profitability on the loan had been reduced to zero, but the *recoverability* of the recorded amount of the receivable had not been affected.

Rationale *for* Imputing Interest

Arguments for imputing interest are as follows:

1. The debtor's liability after restructuring ($82,645 in the *imputing* example) is reported on the *same basis* as the borrowings of all debtors—that is, the present value of the future cash outflows for principal and interest.
2. The debtor's *future* income statements reflect a reasonable amount of interest expense, which should enhance comparability of those statements with the debtor's *past* income statements and with *future* income statements of other companies.

An implementation issue under this approach is whether the **prerestructuring interest rate** or a **current market interest rate** should be used. Most accountants believe that the debtor's obligation after the restructuring results from a modification of an *existing* loan. Therefore, the prerestructuring rate should be used. Other accountants who view the debtor's obligation after restructuring as arising from the execution of a new lending agreement conclude that a *current market interest rate* should be used. An advantage of the *prerestructuring approach* is that the interest rate is known. However, the *current market rate approach* involves determining the interest rate at which a debtor in a precarious financial position might be able to borrow when, in fact, no lenders may be available.

Conceptual Issue 2: Reporting Forgiveness of Debt

One alternative is to report the forgiveness of debt in the income statement. In this approach, **a forgiveness of debt is a gain on restructuring**, which is **similar to a gain on extinguishment of debt.**

Under APB *Opinion No. 26*, "Early Extinguishment of Debt," gains on extinguishments of debt must be reported in the income statement either as an *ordinary* or *extraordinary item*, as appropriate. In most cases, such gains are reported as an *extraordinary item* because the criteria of *unusual* and *infrequent* are met. (In 2002, the FASB proposed amending *APBO 26* so that such gains no longer would be reported as extraordinary items.)

In a second alternative, **a forgiveness of debt may be reported as a direct addition to paid-in capital.** The arguments for this approach are as follows:

1. Because the transaction infuses capital to the debtor, in substance, the debtor has received a capital contribution from the creditor.
2. It should make no difference whether the additional capital needed to keep the debtor in business comes from stockholders or creditors.
3. A company in serious financial difficulty, which has probably reported substantial operating losses, should *not* report income on a transaction intended to assist it in eventually returning to profitable operations.

The Accounting Literature

Note that the accounting issues in *bankruptcy reorganizations* are the same as those for *troubled debt restructurings*—that is, how to calculate and report the amount of debt forgiven. After some initial confusion about the application of *FAS 15*—which does ***not*** **allow the imputing of interest**— to bankruptcy reorganizations, FASB *Technical Bulletin No. 81-6* was issued to clarify the matter. This bulletin states that *FAS 15* does *not* apply to bankruptcy reorganizations that result in a "general restatement of the debtor's liabilities" (defined earlier as a restructuring of most of the amount of a company's liabilities). Because this usually occurs in *bankruptcy reorganizations*, *FAS 15* rarely applies. Consequently, the following questions must be addressed:

> What is meaningful accounting for a reorganized company?
> What, if any, guidance is contained in promulgated accounting standards?

SOP No. 90-7 Plugs a Gaping Hole in the Accounting Literature

In 1990, the AICPA issued *Statement of Position No. 90-7*, "Financial Reporting by Entities in Reorganization under the Bankruptcy Code." *SOP 90-7* brought much-needed uniformity to an area for which widely diverse accounting practices existed. The areas of diverse practices were (1) whether the restructured liabilities should be reported at *discounted* or *undiscounted* amounts—this issue greatly determines the reported amount of debt forgiven, (2) whether the amount of debt forgiven should be reported as an *extraordinary item* (as a gain from forgiveness of debt) or credited *directly to capital* (as a capital contribution), (3) whether a deficit in retained earnings should be eliminated or carried forward, and (4) whether *assets* should be adjusted *upward* to their fair values.

Key Characteristics of Typical Chapter 11 Reorganizations

Before discussing the requirements of *SOP 90-7*, it is important to note that in the typical Chapter 11 reorganization, the following two items are present:

1. The former owners *lose control* because they receive *less than* 50% of the voting shares of the emerging entity. Thus a ***change in ownership*** occurs because the creditors effectively acquire the company as a result of now owning more than 50% of the voting shares.
2. The *fair value* of the emerging entity's assets immediately *before* the date of confirmation is less than the total of the entity's existing liabilities (including both allowed claims and postpetition liabilities). Thus a substantial forgiveness of debt—called a *discharge of indebtedness* in Chapter 11—occurs.

The Requirements of *SOP 90-7*

In Chapter 11 reorganizations, in which both of these two items are present, *SOP 90-7* requires the following:

1. The entity that emerges from Chapter 11 is deemed to be a **new entity** for which **fresh-start financial statements** should be prepared. One major feature of fresh-start reporting is that **no beginning retained earnings or deficit is reported.**
2. Comparative financial statements that straddle a confirmation date *cannot* be presented because doing so would be an inappropriate comparison of a *former entity* and a *new entity.*
3. The discharge of indebtedness should be reported as an *extraordinary item* in the predecessor entity's final statement of operations.
4. The discharge of indebtedness should be calculated using the *present values* of amounts to be paid, determined by using appropriate current interest rates.
5. All *assets* are to be restated to reflect their fair value at the date of reorganization.
6. Prior to the confirmation date, the "old entity" is to (a) report bankruptcy-related losses and expenses in a separate "reorganization items" category in its statement of operations and (b) report its liabilities in specified categories in any balance sheets issued.

Procedurally, item 5 is accomplished by (1) first determining the ***reorganization value*** of the entity—an amount that approximates what a willing buyer would pay for the assets of the emerging entity *immediately after* the restructuring (done generally by discounting expected future cash flows), (2) allocating the reorganization value to the entity's tangible and intangible assets using the purchase accounting procedures specified in FASB *Statement No. 141*, "Business Combinations," and (3) reporting any excess reorganization value (the *unallocated* amount) as goodwill, which is to be periodically evaluated for *impairment*. Determining the reorganization value often requires arm's-length negotiations or litigation between the interested parties. A summary depiction of the *SOP 90-7* requirements appears in Illustration 19-1.

Comprehensive Illustration

Typical Entries in a Chapter 11 Reorganization

Assume that Emergco Inc. has the following capitalization immediately before the confirmation of the plan of reorganization:

Prepetition liabilities subject to compromise	$ 900,000[a]
Prepetition liabilities *not* subject to compromise	$ 72,000[b]
Postpetition liabilities	$ 300,000[b]
Stockholders' equity (deficiency):	
Preferred stock ($100 par value)	$ 250,000
Common stock ($5 par value)	50,000
Additional paid-in capital	105,000
Accumulated deficit	(555,000)
	$(150,000)

[a] Includes partially secured liabilities.

[b] These liabilities would be paid in full.

The entries to reflect the plan of reorganization, using assumed amounts as appropriate, follow:

1. To record discharge of indebtedness—creditors having liabilities subject to compromise receive cash, notes, and a 93% controlling equity interest:

Liabilities Subject to Compromise	900,000	
Cash		200,000
Senior Debt (a new issue)		180,000
Subordinated Debt (a new issue)		120,000
Common Stock—new issue (93,000 shares × $1 par)		93,000
Gain on Discharge of Debt		307,000

ILLUSTRATION 19-1 SUMMARY DEPICTION OF TYPICAL CHAPTER 11 REORGANIZATION

Chapter 11 Petition Filed (3-17-05)	**Plan of Reorganization Confirmed (9-1-06)**
Old Entity →	**New Entity** →

Old Entity

1. Reports gain on discharge of debt in final statement of operations as an **extraordinary item**.
2. Classifies liabilities between:
   a. **Prepetition** liabilities **subject to compromise**—at the expected amount of the allowed claims.[a]
   b. **Prepetition** liabilities **not subject to compromise**—at the expected amount of the allowed claims.
   c. **Postpetition** liabilities.
3. Reports bankruptcy-related items in a special **reorganization items** category in its statement of operations:
   a. Loss of disposal of facilities.
   b. Professional fees relating to bankruptcy proceeding.
   c. Interest earned on cash accumulated during bankruptcy proceeding.

New Entity

1. Begins with **fresh-start** reporting.
   a. No beginning retained earnings or deficit.
   b. Assets adjusted to *fair values*.
   c. Excess of reorganization value over amounts allocated to assets is reported as *goodwill* (to be periodically evaluated thereafter for possible impairment).
   d. Liabilities adjusted to *present values* (other than Deferred Taxes).
2. *Never* presents financial statements of *old entity* for comparison purposes.

[a] Even though these liabilities (which consist of both **unsecured claims** and **undersecured claims**) most likely will be settled at amounts substantially *below* the amount of allowed claims, the full amount of the claims expected to be allowed by the court is to be reported up until the confirmation date at which time any discharge of debt is reported.

2. To record cancellation of preferred and common stock issues in exchange for new common stock issue—preferred and common stockholders receive a 7% equity interest:

Preferred Stock	250,000	
Common Stock—old issue ($5 par)	50,000	
Common Stock—new issue (7,000 shares × $1 par) . . .		7,000
Additional Paid-in Capital		293,000

Note: Although it would seem that the old stockholders should receive nothing by virtue of the fact that Chapter 11 provides creditors with the right to enforce the **absolute priority rule,** whereby equity claims can be wiped out using the allowable "cram-down" procedure, creditors normally give up this right because it is costly to pursue and they can end up worse off than if they provide some payment to old stockholders.

3. To adopt fresh-start reporting by revaluing assets to fair values:

Inventory	30,000	
Property, Plant, and Equipment.	180,000	
Goodwill (*new*)	40,000	
Goodwill (*old*)		205,000
Additional Paid-in Capital (residual amount to balance) .		45,000

4. To "restart" Retained Earnings/Accumulated Deficit account balance at zero:

Additional Paid-in Capital.	248,000	
Accumulated Deficit ($555,000 – $307,000) gain on debt discharge)		248,000

Illustration 19-2 shows (1) a Bankruptcy Reorganization Adjusting Entries Worksheet and (2) the stockholders' equity section on a fresh-start basis.

ILLUSTRATION 19-2 BANKRUPTCY REORGANIZATION ADJUSTING ENTRIES WORKSHEET

Emergco Inc.
Bankruptcy Reorganization Adjusting Entries Worksheet

	(PRE-CONFIRMATION) BOOK VALUE	ADJUSTMENTS DR.			ADJUSTMENTS CR.	(POST-CONFIRMATION) CONSOLIDATED
Assets						
Cash	$ 267,000			1	200,000	$ 67,000
Accounts receivables, net	330,000					330,000
Inventory, LIFO	80,000	30,000	3			110,000
Fixed assets, net	240,000	180,000	3			420,000
Goodwill (*old*)	205,000			3	205,000	-0-
Goodwill (*new*)		40,000	3			40,000
Total Assets	**$1,122,000**					**$967,000**
Liabilities						
Postpetition debt:						
Accounts payable	$ 300,000					$ 300,000
Prepetition debt:						
Not subject to compromise	72,000					72,000
Subject to compromise	900,000	900,000	1			-0-
Senior Debt (new)				1	180,000	180,000
Subordinated Debt (new)				1	120,000	120,000
Total Liabilities	**$1,272,000**					**$672,000**
Stockholders' Equity						
Preferred stock	$250,000	250,000	2			$ -0-
Common stock, $5 par value	50,000	50,000	2			-0-
Common stock, $1 par value				1	93,000	100,000
				2	7,000	
Additional paid-in capital	105,000	248,000	4	2	293,000	195,000
				3	45,000	
Retained earnings (deficit)	(555,000)			1	307,000	-0-
				4	248,000	
Total Equity	**$ (150,000)**					**$295,000**
Total Liabilities & Equity	**$1,122,000**					**$967,000**
Proof of Dr. & Cr. totals		*1,698,000*			*1,698,000*	

Emergco Inc.
Stockholders' Equity on Fresh-start Basis

Common stock	$100,000
Additional paid-in capital	195,000
Retained earnings	-0-
Total Stockholders' Equity	$295,000
Fresh-start book value per common share	$2.95

Companies *Not* Qualifying for *Fresh-Start Reporting*

Some companies file for Chapter 11 protection merely to seek relief from creditors with no expectation that existing stockholders will lose control, as was the case for Texaco's Chapter 11 filing in 1987. Fresh-start reporting is allowed only for companies in which a loss of control and change in ownership occur, which occur in most cases. The small percentage of companies emerging from Chapter 11 that do *not* qualify for fresh-start reporting must (1) report liabilities subject to compromise at present values of amounts to be paid using appropriate interest rates, (2) report any discharge of indebtedness as an extraordinary item, and (3) report bankruptcy-related costs and expenses in the special reorganization items category in its statement of operations.

The Role of Accountants in Bankruptcy Reorganizations

Certified public accountants are commonly employed in varying capacities in bankruptcy proceedings. Many accounting firms can generate substantial (and often lucrative) fees for their services in this area. (Bankruptcy assistance is *not* considered charity work.) The most common capacity for outside accountants is that of rendering advice and assistance on financial projections used in developing a reorganization plan. Both the distressed company and its creditors' committee commonly hire their own outside accountants. Occasionally, outside accountants are responsible for determining the quality of the distressed company's accounts receivable. If management is suspected of improper actions, bankruptcy judges may need to appoint outside accountants to investigate such charges. The creditors' committee often hires outside accountants to determine the following:

1. Has the debtor made any transfers of assets that would constitute preferences to certain creditors?
2. Has management committed any acts that would constitute fraud, deception, or bad faith?
3. Has management committed any acts that would bar it from obtaining a discharge of certain indebtedness?
4. In what condition are the company's books and records?
5. What would be obtained in liquidation? (Answering this question requires the preparation of a statement of affairs, which is discussed and illustrated later in the chapter.)

The creditors' accountants need not perform an audit of the debtor's financial statements to be of assistance in these areas; a limited special-purpose examination is usually sufficient. Obviously, the scope of any such limited examination must be worked out with the creditors' committee.

V. BANKRUPTCY LIQUIDATIONS

Large companies with common stock publicly traded on the New York Stock Exchange are seldom liquidated because they usually have adequate capital and managerial talent to deal with adverse developments. The growing trend toward diversification also works against liquidation. A large, diverse business is less apt to be affected overall by an adverse development resulting from poor management decisions in one of its industry segments. Furthermore, if management cannot deal effectively with such problems in one of its industry segments, that segment will most likely be disposed of through sale (or possibly abandonment), but the remainder of the business will continue. Consequently, liquidation is generally associated with small and moderate-size businesses. The smaller and more unseasoned a company is, the more likely it is to face liquidation.

Liquidation *Outside* the Bankruptcy Courts

In some instances, liquidation may take place outside the bankruptcy courts. In these situations, a formal **general assignment for the benefit of creditors** usually is executed, whereby the debtor's property is transferred to a designated assignee or assignees (who are often the debtor's creditors) for the purpose of converting the assets into cash and making appropriate distributions of cash to the creditors. Any assets that remain after creditors have been paid in full are returned to the debtor for ultimate distribution to its stockholders. If the proceeds from the conversion of assets into cash are insufficient to pay creditors in full, however, the creditors have no other recourse, and the stockholders receive nothing.

There are three possible advantages to liquidating outside the bankruptcy court:

1. Legal fees are usually lower.
2. The debtor can designate the assignee or assignees.
3. The conversion of assets into cash is more flexible.

Under an involuntary proceeding, a general assignment for the benefit of creditors is considered grounds for the bankruptcy court to enter an order for relief. Accordingly, to avoid liquidation through the bankruptcy court, a general assignment must be agreed to by all of the creditors for all practical purposes. If a sufficient number of qualified creditors subsequently file an *involuntary petition* of bankruptcy, the general assignment for the benefit of creditors is null and void, and the bankruptcy court then supervises and controls the liquidation of the company.

Liquidation through Bankruptcy Court

After a company has filed for liquidation under Chapter 7, one of the court's first duties is to determine whether the case should be dismissed. As we mentioned at the beginning of the chapter, filing a *voluntary petition* constitutes an order for relief. Dismissals of voluntary filings are infrequent. When the debtor does *not* dispute an involuntary petition, the court enters an order for relief against the debtor. Dismissals of uncontested involuntary filings are also infrequent. If the debtor disputes an *involuntary petition*, however, a trial must be held to determine whether the case should be dismissed or an order for relief should be entered.

The Role of the Trustee

After an order for relief has been entered, the bankruptcy court must promptly appoint an interim trustee (Section 701[a]). In an involuntary filing, the debtor may continue to operate the business from the filing date until an order for relief is entered, just as though the petition had not been filed (Section 303[f]). The court may appoint an interim trustee during this period, however, if necessary to preserve the property of the estate or to prevent loss to the estate, providing certain procedures are followed (Section 303[g]).

After an order for relief has been entered, the court must also call a meeting of the debtor's creditors (Section 341). In this meeting, the creditors first vote for a trustee and then select a creditors' committee that consults with the trustee in connection with the administration of the estate. If the creditors are unable to select a trustee, the interim trustee becomes the trustee (Section 702[d]). Trustees are usually professionals, mostly practicing lawyers, who specialize in this type of work. The following duties of trustees are set forth under Section 704:

1. Collect and reduce to money the property of the estate for which such trustee serves, and close such estate as expeditiously as is compatible with the best interests of parties in interest.
2. Be accountable for all property received.
3. Ensure that the debtor shall perform [certain] intentions [that the debtor specifies].
4. Investigate the financial affairs of the debtor.
5. If a purpose would be served, examine proofs of claims and object to the allowance of any claim that is improper.
6. If advisable, oppose the discharge of the debtor.
7. Unless the court orders otherwise, furnish such information concerning the estate and the estate's administration as is requested by a party in interest.
8. If the business of the debtor is authorized to be operated, file with the court, with the United States trustee, and with any governmental unit charged with responsibility for collection or determination of any tax arising out of such operation, periodic reports and summaries of the operation of such business, including a statement of receipts and disbursements, and such other information as the United States trustee or the court requires. (Under Section 721, "the court may authorize the trustee to operate the business of the debtor for a limited period, if such operation is in the best interest of the estate and consistent with the orderly liquidation of the estate.")
9. Make a final report and file a final account of the administration of the estate with the court and with the United States trustee.

Accounting by trustees is discussed in detail later in the chapter.

Technical Aspects of the Duties of Trustees

The following technical aspects of the trustee's duties should be noted:

1. **Employment of professionals.** With the court's approval, the trustee may employ attorneys, accountants, appraisers, auctioneers, or other professional persons to represent or assist the trustee in carrying out his or her duties (Section 327).
2. **Avoidance powers.** A trustee is authorized to void both *fraudulent and preferential transfers* made by the debtor within certain specified periods preceding the filing date. (Such transfers include giving a security interest in a property.) Creditors, therefore, may be required to return monies and/or properties recovered or may lose their security interest, or both. The section of the act dealing with preferences is intended to prevent a debtor from giving certain creditors preferential treatment over other creditors. The Bankruptcy Code sets forth the conditions that must exist for a trustee to void a property transfer to a creditor. It also sets forth certain transfers that a trustee *cannot* void (Sections 544–550).
3. **Setoffs.** With respect to mutual debts between the debtor and allowable claims of a creditor, the amount owed the debtor by the creditors is subtracted from or *offset* (thus the term **setoff**) against the amount owed to the creditor (Section 553). (There are certain technical exceptions to this rule that we need not deal with now.)

Distribution of Cash to Creditors

The sequence of payments to creditors is as follows:

1. The proceeds from the sale of assets that have been pledged to secured creditors are applied to satisfy those claims. Note that the bankruptcy proceedings do not alter the rights of the secured creditors to the assets that have been pledged to them; these rights are only temporarily suspended.
2. If the proceeds exceed the secured creditors' claims, such excess is available to pay creditors with priority and unsecured creditors.
3. If the proceeds are insufficient to satisfy the claims of the secured creditors, the secured creditors become unsecured creditors to the extent of the deficiency.
4. The proceeds from the sale of unpledged assets are used to pay creditors with priority.
5. After creditors with priority have been paid, payments are made to the unsecured creditors. Payments are always stated as a percentage of all allowed claims.
6. To the extent that any creditors are *not* paid in full, the deficiency represents a loss.

After the final payment has been made to the unsecured creditors, the corporation is a *shell corporation* without any assets or liabilities. In most instances, the corporation then ceases its legal existence. The bankruptcy court is *not* authorized to grant a formal discharge of indebtedness with respect to any unpaid claims when the debtor is other than an individual (Section 727[a][1]). According to House of Representatives Bankruptcy Committee reports, this change is intended to prevent trafficking in corporate shells and bankrupt partnerships.

Selling assets and paying proceeds to the debtor's various creditors does not always conclude a liquidation. Trustees may file suit against former directors and officers, asking for monetary damages on the grounds of gross negligence in the management of certain aspects of the business. When the sudden collapse of a company occurs shortly after its outside auditors have issued an unqualified ("clean") audit report on the company's financial statements, serious questions may be raised concerning the performance of the audit. In such situations, the auditors may be sued for alleged breach of performance.

CHECK POINTS

Which of the following statements is *true*?

a. In *involuntary* filings under Chapter 7, the case is dismissed if the debtor contests the filing.
b. In a Chapter 7 filing, the bankruptcy court usually appoints a trustee.
c. In a Chapter 7 filing, management usually continues to operate the business until the liquidation is completed.

d. The primary function of a trustee in Chapter 7 filings is to settle disputes between the debtor and the debtor's creditors.
e. None of the above.

Answer: b

Which of the following statements is *false*?
a. When a company is liquidated under Chapter 7, the bankruptcy court discharges all unpaid debts (except those specified in the bankruptcy statutes).
b. In a Chapter 7 filing, trustees have the authority to dispose of the debtor's assets.
c. Trustees are authorized to void preferential transfers made to certain creditors.
d. The concept of creditors with priority applies to both Chapter 7 and Chapter 11 filings.
e. None of the above.

Answer: a

The Role of the Accountant in Liquidations

Bankruptcy trustees often employ certified public accountants to assist them in preserving the assets of the bankrupt's estate. The extent of the accountant's services usually depends on the complexity of the estate. If the debtor's in-house accountants have *not* resigned *before* the bankruptcy petition is filed, they generally leave shortly thereafter. A certified public accountant can provide the following types of services to the bankruptcy trustee:

1. Determining what accounting books and records exist at the debtor's offices.
2. Determining the condition of the accounting records, including the filing status of all tax reports.
3. Updating the debtor's accounting records as necessary.
4. Preparing current year tax reports and informational forms.
5. Comparing creditors' claims (as filed with the court) with the debtor's books and records and with the schedule of liabilities filed with the court by the debtor.
6. Examining certain of the debtor's books and records in detail and submitting a formal report to the trustee in certain instances if fraud is suspected or known.

This list is not exhaustive; the accountant may be called on to perform any service within the realm of accounting expertise.

The Statement of Affairs

Regardless of whether liquidation takes place outside or through bankruptcy court, a special **statement of affairs** is prepared showing the company's financial condition. The statement of affairs is prepared on the basis that the company is going out of business. Because the company is *not* considered a going concern, the *historical cost basis* for carrying assets loses its significance, and the amount expected to be realized in liquidation is the relevant valuation basis.

The statement of affairs **provides information concerning how much money each class of creditors can expect to receive on liquidation of the company**, assuming that assets are converted into cash at the estimated realizable values used in preparing the statements. Thus conventional classifications, such as current assets and current liabilities, lose their significance. Instead, assets are classified as to whether they are pledged with creditors or not pledged with creditors; **liabilities are classified by category of creditor**—namely, *creditors with priority*, *secured creditors*, and *unsecured creditors*. Stockholders' equity also loses its significance because companies in the process of liquidation usually have a negative net worth. The specific categories of assets and liabilities in the statement of affairs are as follows.

Assets

1. **Assets pledged with *fully secured* creditors** are expected to realize an amount at least sufficient to satisfy the related debt.

2. **Assets pledged with *partially secured* creditors** are expected to realize an amount below the related debt.
3. **Free assets** are not pledged and are available to satisfy the claims of creditors with priority, partially secured creditors, and unsecured creditors.

Liabilities

1. **Liabilities with priority** have priority under the bankruptcy statutes (explained earlier in the chapter).
2. **Fully secured creditors** expect to be paid in full as a result of their having sufficient collateral (pledged assets) to satisfy the indebtedness.
3. **Partially secured creditors** have collateral (pledged assets), the proceeds of which are expected to be insufficient to satisfy the indebtedness.
4. **Unsecured creditors** have no collateral (pledged assets) relating to their indebtedness.

Contingent liabilities that are reasonably calculable and probable as to payment (the criteria under FASB *Statement No. 5*, "Accounting for Contingencies") are shown in the statement of affairs. Contingent liabilities that do not meet these criteria should be disclosed in a note to the statement of affairs.

Comprehensive Illustration

The Statement of Affairs

The balance sheet of Fold-Up Company, which filed a voluntary bankruptcy petition (for liquidation under Chapter 7) on September 23, 2006, is shown in Illustration 19-3. Additional information regarding realization follows:

1. **Receivables.** The notes and accounts receivable are considered to have been adequately provided for in preparing the balance sheet; thus the company expects to realize the amounts shown.
2. **Finished goods.** The finished goods can be sold for $47,000; however, the company expects to incur $4,000 of direct selling and shipping costs.
3. **Work in process.** The work in process can be completed if $3,000 of direct costs are incurred for labor. On completion, this inventory can be sold for $37,000; however, the company expects to incur $2,000 of direct selling and shipping costs.
4. **Raw materials.** The raw materials can be converted into finished goods if $7,000 of direct costs are incurred for labor. On completion, this inventory can be sold for $19,000; however, the company expects to incur $1,000 of direct selling and shipping costs.
5. **Supplies.** The supplies will be substantially consumed in the completion of the work in process and the conversion of raw materials into finished goods. The estimated realizable value of the remaining supplies after completion and conversion is $1,000.
6. **Prepayments.** The prepayments are expected to expire during the liquidation period.
7. **Land.** The land has a current market value of $90,000.
8. **Building.** The building has a current market value of $135,000.
9. **Equipment.** The equipment can be sold at auction for an estimated $35,000.
10. **Deferred charges.** Deferred charges include organization costs, issuance expenses relating to the notes payable to the insurance company, and plant rearrangement costs.
11. **Salaries and wages.** All salaries and wages were earned within the last 90 days, and no employee is owed more than $4,000.
12. **Liquidation expenses.** The company estimates that $15,000 in court and filing fees, appraisal fees, and legal and accounting fees will be incurred in connection with the liquidation. No amounts have been provided in these expenses at September 23, 2006.
13. **Accounts payable.** Accounts payable include $6,000 to the company's attorneys for legal work incurred in connection with patent research and collection efforts on certain accounts receivable that have been written off. Accounts payable also include $5,000 owed to the company's certified public accountants in connection with the December 31, 2005, audit of the company's financial statements.

A statement of affairs prepared using this information is shown in Illustration 19-4.

ILLUSTRATION 19-3 A BALANCE SHEET FOR A COMPANY IN CHAPTER 7 BANKRUPTCY PROCEEDINGS

Fold-Up Company
Balance Sheet as of September 23, 2006

ASSETS	
Current Assets	
Cash	$ 2,000
Notes receivable	5,000
Accounts receivable, net	25,000
Inventory:	
Finished goods	40,000
Work in process	30,000
Raw materials	20,000
Supplies	5,000
Prepayments	8,000
Total Current Assets	$ 135,000
Noncurrent Assets	
Land	70,000
Building, net	110,000
Equipment, net	60,000
Deferred charges	15,000
Total Assets	**$390,000**
LIABILITIES AND STOCKHOLDERS' DEFICIENCY	
Current Liabilities	
10% Notes payable to bank, secured by accounts receivable	$ 35,000
Accounts payable	246,000
Accrued liabilities:	
Interest ($2,000 to bank, $6,000 to insurance company)	8,000
Salaries and wages	7,000
Payroll taxes	2,000
Total Current Liabilities	$ 298,000
Long-Term Debt	
8% Notes payable to insurance company, secured by land and building	175,000
Total Liabilities	**$473,000**
Stockholders' Deficiency	
Common stock, no par	$ 100,000
Accumulated deficit	(183,000)
Total Stockholders' Deficiency	$ (83,000)
Total Liabilities in Excess of Stockholders' Deficiency	**$390,000**

Review Points for Illustration 19-4. Note the following:

1. The Book Value column is shown only for purposes of tying into the September 23, 2006, balance sheet, which was prepared in the conventional manner.
2. Each asset and liability is assigned to its appropriate descriptive category. The categories themselves are the key to producing the desired information—that is, how much money can the unsecured creditors expect to receive in liquidation?
3. Accrued interest payable is classified with the debt to which it relates because the pledged assets are security for both the principal and the interest.
4. Although the company has not recorded the $15,000 of estimated liquidation expenses in its general ledger at September 23, 2006, the statement of affairs should reflect this estimate so that it is as useful as possible.
5. Legal and accounting fees incurred in connection with matters not related to the bankruptcy are not considered debts with priority under the bankruptcy statutes.
6. The bank is an unsecured creditor to the extent of $12,000, the amount by which the $25,000 collateral is insufficient to satisfy its $37,000 claim.

ILLUSTRATION 19-4 A STATEMENT OF AFFAIRS FOR A COMPANY IN BANKRUPTCY PROCEEDINGS

Fold-Up Company
Statement of Affairs as of September 23, 2006

BOOK VALUE	ASSETS	ESTIMATED CURRENT VALUE	ESTIMATED AMOUNT AVAILABLE FOR UNSECURED CREDITORS	GAIN OR LOSS ON REALIZATION
	Assets Pledged with Fully Secured Creditors			
$ 70,000	Land	$ 90,000		$ 20,000
110,000	Building	135,000		25,000
		$ 225,000		
	Less—Fully secured claims (**contra—from liability side**)	(181,000)	$ 44,000	
	Assets Pledged with Partially Secured Creditors			
25,000	Accounts receivable (deducted on liability side)	$ 25,000		
	Free Assets			
2,000	Cash	$ 2,000	2,000	
5,000	Notes receivable	5,000	5,000	
	Inventory			
40,000	Finished goods	43,000[a]	43,000	3,000
30,000	Work in process	32,000[b]	32,000	2,000
20,000	Raw materials	11,000[c]	11,000	(9,000)
5,000	Supplies	1,000	1,000	(4,000)
8,000	Prepayments			(8,000)
60,000	Equipment	35,000	35,000	(25,000)
15,000	Deferred charges			(15,000)
	Estimated amount available for unsecured creditors, including creditors with priority		$ 173,000	
	Less—Liabilities with priority (**contra—from liability side**)		(24,000)	
	Estimated amount available for unsecured creditors		$ 149,000	
	Estimated deficiency to unsecured creditors (plug)		109,000	
$390,000				$ (11,000)
	Total Unsecured Debt		**$258,000**	

[a] Net of $4,000 of estimated disposal costs.
[b] Net of $3,000 of estimated labor to complete and $2,000 of disposal costs.
[c] Net of $7,000 of estimated labor to convert into finished goods and $1,000 of disposal costs.

BOOK VALUE	LIABILITIES AND STOCKHOLDERS' DEFICIENCY		AMOUNT UNCENSORED
	Liabilities with Priority		
$ -0-	Estimated liquidation expenses	$ 15,000	
7,000	Salaries and wages	7,000	
2,000	Payroll taxes	2,000	
	(deducted from amount available for unsecured creditors on asset side)	$ 24,000	
	Fully Secured Creditors		
175,000	Notes payable to insurance company	$ 175,000	
6,000	Accrued interest on notes	6,000	
	Total (deducted on asset side)	$ 181,000	
	Partially Secured Creditors		
35,000	Note payable to bank	$ 35,000	
2,000	Accrued interest on note	2,000	
		$ 37,000	
	Less—Pledged accounts receivable (**contra—from asset side**)	(25,000)	$ 12,000
	Unsecured Creditors		
246,000	Accounts payable and accruals		246,000
(83,000)	**Stockholders' deficiency**		
$390,000			
	Total Unsecured Debt		**$258,000**

7. The unsecured creditors are estimated to receive $149,000 of the $258,000 owed them. This figure is often expressed in terms of recovery per dollar owed. In this situation, it would be 58 cents on the dollar ($149,000 ÷ $258,000).

Once a liquidation has occurred, no accounting issues exist for the former company. An accountant performing services for a trustee in liquidation, however, should have a basic familiarity with the liquidation process.

VI. Accounting by Trustees

The accountability of trustees to the bankruptcy court was stated earlier in the discussion of *liquidations* under Chapter 7 of the Bankruptcy Code. The same accountability exists in *reorganizations* under Chapter 11 of the code in which a trustee is appointed to operate the debtor's business. The code sets specific requirements concerning the type of report or reports rendered to the courts by trustees only when a trustee operates the debtor's business. In most liquidation cases, normal operations cease immediately. Accordingly, we discuss accounting by trustees in *liquidations* separately from *reorganizations* (when normal operations continue).

Accounting in *Liquidation*

When normal operations immediately cease, the preparation of an operating statement for the period covering the trustee's administration of the estate is inappropriate. This holds true even when a trustee, with the court's permission, continues the operations necessary to convert work in process (and possibly raw materials) into finished goods. Such activities by themselves do not constitute normal operations; accordingly, costs incurred in this regard are treated as bankruptcy administration costs. Because the Bankruptcy Code does *not* prescribe the type of report or reports rendered by trustees when normal operations are not conducted (as was the case under the old law), each bankruptcy court establishes its own requirements. Most bankruptcy courts simply require a written explanation as to the disposition of the various assets and a statement of cash receipts and disbursements. Such a statement typically shows the following: (1) cash balances of the debtor that were turned over to the trustee at the trustee's appointment, (2) the proceeds from the conversion of noncash assets into cash, (3) cash disbursements (which are usually limited to bankruptcy administration costs), (4) the remaining cash balance available for distribution to creditors, and (5) a summary of how the remaining cash balance should be distributed to the various classes of creditors (including creditors with priority). In most cases, only one report (called the final report) is rendered. In some cases, cash is distributed to creditors on an interim basis, after an interim report proposing such a distribution is filed with and approved by the court. Some courts require the cash disbursements in summary form only; others require detail by check number, payee, and purpose of disbursement.

Most trustees find it expedient to (1) open a separate checking account for each estate they administer and (2) use the related cash receipts and disbursement records to prepare the required statement of cash receipts and disbursements. Trustees usually do not use the debtor's general ledger or any of the debtor's journals to record transactions and events. If the court or creditors desire information that relates the trustee's activity with the book balances existing when the trustee was appointed, a **statement of realization and liquidation** can be prepared. Such a statement for Fold-Up Company is shown in Illustration 19-5. The beginning balances are taken from Illustration 19-4. The activity during the assumed period that the trustee administers the estate is consistent with the estimated amounts and information provided in the data used to prepare the statement of affairs in Illustration 19-4.

In some cases, a trustee may be authorized to operate the debtor's business. This is often done when a larger amount may be realized by selling the business in its entirety rather than in piecemeal and when a larger amount may be realized by selling an active business rather than one that has been shut down. The accounting reports rendered during the time that a trustee operates the debtor's business are the same as those required in reorganizations, which are discussed in the following section.

ILLUSTRATION 19-5 A STATEMENT OF REALIZATION AND LIQUIDATION

Fold-Up Company
Statement of Realization and Liquidation
For the Period September 23, 2006 to May 18, 2007

	ASSETS		LIABILITIES				
	CASH	NONCASH	WITH PRIORITY	FULLY SECURED	PARTIALLY SECURED	UNSECURED	STOCKHOLDERS' DEFICIENCY
Book balances, September 23, 2006 (from the Book Value column in Illustration 19-4)	$ 2,000	$388,000	$ 9,000	$181,000	$ 37,000	$246,000	$ (83,000)
Cash Receipts							
Collection of note receivable and related interest	5,200	(5,000)					200
Proceeds from sale of inventory, net of $16,700 "actual" direct costs	85,800[a]	(90,000)					(4,200)
Proceeds from sale of supplies	1,100[a]	(5,000)					(3,900)
Proceeds from sale of equipment	35,400[a]	(60,000)					(24,600)
Proceeds from sale of land and building, net of $181,000 withheld by title company to pay off fully secured creditor	45,500[a]	(180,000)		(181,000)			46,500
Cash Disbursements							
Payment of bankruptcy administration costs, net of $16,700 "actual" inventory conversion and selling costs shown above	(2,000)						(2,000)
Other							
Amortization of prepaids		(8,000)					(8,000)
Write-off of deferred charges		(15,000)					(15,000)
Release of accounts receivable to partially secured creditor		(25,000)			(25,000)		
Reclassification of residual amount to unsecured status					(12,000)	12,000	
Accrual of bankruptcy administration costs			12,600				(12,600)
Book Balances, May 18, 2007	$173,000	$ -0-	$21,600	$ -0-	$ -0-	$258,000	$(106,600)
Proposed distribution	$ 173,000		$ 21,600 (100%)			$ 151,400 (58.7%)	

[a] The actual proceeds here are purposely slightly different from the "estimated" current values shown in Illustration 19-4 because it is highly unlikely that the actual proceeds would agree with the estimated proceeds in a real-world situation.

Accounting in *Reorganization*

When a trustee is appointed in a Chapter 11 reorganization, the Bankruptcy Code requires trustees to submit

> periodic reports and summaries of the operation of such business, including a statement of receipts and disbursements, and such other information as the court requires [Sections 704 and 1106].

In addition to these items, the courts usually require that a balance sheet be presented when operating statements or summaries are furnished. In most cases, trustees find it practical to use the debtor's books and records to record transactions and events. The date the trustee was appointed is usually recorded, however, so that the activity during the trustee's administration can be reported separately. Also, a distinction is usually made between (1) assets on hand and liabilities owed at the trustee's appointment and (2) assets acquired and liabilities incurred during the trustee's administration. This distinction is necessary because trustees are responsible for the acquisition and realization of new assets as opposed to only the realization of old assets and for the incurrence and liquidation of new liabilities as opposed to only the liquidation of old liabilities.

The preparation of required reports and statements presents no unusual problems when the trustee uses the debtor's books and records. In some cases, a trustee may account for some or all of the debtor's assets and operations in a new set of books. In this case, the transfer of assets to the new set of books and the accounting for subsequent operations parallel the accounting for a home office and a branch. Accordingly, the balances and activity on each set of books must be combined to the extent necessary in preparing financial reports. Traditionally, advanced accounting textbooks have included a discussion and illustration of a somewhat involved statement of realization and liquidation encompassing assets, liabilities, and operations. Current practice favors the use of the separate conventional financial statements, however, and we do not present a discussion and illustration of this single comprehensive statement.

VII. CONCLUDING COMMENTS

Most companies in serious financial difficulty never recover and must be liquidated. A company that can feasibly effect a successful recovery must show complete honesty and good faith with its creditors during this difficult period. Creditors should realize that often they can minimize their losses if a successful troubled debt restructuring can be achieved. The use of professionals in insolvency proceedings can minimize the procedural problems and help the company and its creditors to be realistic in arriving at an acceptable plan of recovery.

Not all proposed plans of reorganization succeed. Many are rejected as infeasible, with liquidation best serving the creditors' interests. Others are rejected as the result of evidence of management fraud, deception, or bad faith—again, liquidation best serves the creditors' interests. Consequently, an accountant furnishing assistance to a debtor or a creditors' committee must be skeptical, alert, and imaginative in carrying out this difficult assignment.

END-OF-CHAPTER REVIEW

Summary of Key Points

1. The accounting issues involved with all debt restructurings—both those done outside and *through* the bankruptcy courts—consist of (1) **how to calculate whether any debt has been forgiven** and (2) **how to report a forgiveness of debt.**

2. *FAS 15*—**which does *not* allow the imputing of interest** in determining the amount of debt forgiveness and which must be used for all debt restructurings that occur outside of bankruptcy court—**rarely applies** to debts restructured by means of a Chapter 11 *bankruptcy reorganization.*

3. The AICPA's *SOP 90-7*—**which *requires* the imputing of interest** in determining the amount of debt forgiveness—applies solely to *bankruptcy reorganizations.*

4. Under *SOP 90-7*, the total amount owed (the **carrying amount of the debt** is compared with the *present value* of the **total amount to be paid back** (includes interest) to determine the amount of debt forgiveness.

5. For bankruptcy reorganizations under Chapter 11, the AICPA's *SOP 90-7* specifies the manner of accounting whereby **fresh-start reporting** is implemented when the plan of reorganization is confirmed—providing a **change in ownership** has occurred and the fair value of the debtor's *assets* is less than the debtor's *liabilities.*

6. Under fresh-start reporting of *SOP 90-7*, a **new reporting entity** exists. Accordingly, no beginning retained earnings or accumulated deficit is reported. Also, **assets** are adjusted to their **fair values,** and **liabilities** are reported at their **present values.** Comparative statements with the *old entity* are *never* presented.

7. Adjusting assets to their fair values first requires determining the **reorganization value** of the company, which generally involves **discounting expected future cash flows.** An **excess of reorganization value over the amount allocated to specific tangible and intangible assets** is reported as goodwill and periodically evaluated for possible impairment thereafter.

8. The **discharge of indebtedness** in a Chapter 11 reorganization is reported as an **extraordinary item** in the **old entity's** final statement of operations. Bankruptcy-related costs and losses are presented in a special **reorganization items** category in the old entity's statement of operations.

Glossary of New Terms

Bankruptcy Code The federal bankruptcy statutes set forth in Title 11 of the United States Code.

Creditors with priority A special class of creditors created by the bankruptcy statutes. These creditors are entitled to payment before a debtor's other unsecured creditors may be paid.

Debtor Under the bankruptcy statutes, the party that is the subject of a bankruptcy proceeding.

Estate Under the bankruptcy statutes, all of a debtor's property.

Impairment The alteration of the rights of a creditor or equity holder in a bankruptcy reorganization case.

Involuntary petition A petition filed by the creditors of a company in financial distress to have the distressed company liquidated or financially reorganized under the control and supervision of the bankruptcy court.

Liquidation The process of converting a company's assets into cash, paying off creditors to the extent possible, and ceasing operations.

Reorganization The altering of a distressed company's liability and/or equity structure under Chapter 11 of the bankruptcy statutes for purposes of financially rehabilitating the company to avoid liquidation.

Setoff In a bankruptcy proceeding, offsetting amounts owed to a debtor by a creditor against amounts owed to that creditor by the debtor.

Troubled debt restructuring Granting a creditor's concession because of a debtor's financial difficulties.

Voluntary petition A petition filed with the bankruptcy court by a company in financial distress to have the company liquidated or financially reorganized under the control and supervision of the bankruptcy court.

Assignment Material

Review Questions

1. Between what two broad categories is the Bankruptcy Code divided (pertaining to business corporations)?

2. What fundamental objectives does the Bankruptcy Code accomplish?
3. Under what conditions may an involuntary petition be filed?
4. What is meant by the term *creditors with priority*?
5. What is the *order of priority* of creditors with priority?
6. In an *involuntary* bankruptcy filing, do secured creditors lose their right to their security?
7. Why do companies try to restructure their debt *outside* Chapter 11 of the Bankruptcy Code if at all possible?
8. What are the *advantages* of filing for reorganization under Chapter 11 of the Bankruptcy Code?
9. What are the general procedures for determining whether a gain on the restructuring of debt exists as set forth in *SOP 90-7*?
10. How are material gains on the restructuring of debt reported under *SOP 90-7*?
11. Does *FAS 15* apply to *bankruptcy reorganizations*?
12. What is the key difference between *SOP 90-7* and *FAS 15*?
13. What is meant by a *discharge of indebtedness* in a bankruptcy reorganization?
14. Which debts *cannot* be discharged in a bankruptcy reorganization?
15. Is a discharge of indebtedness automatic in a *liquidation* proceeding? In a *reorganization* proceeding?
16. On what basis is the *statement of affairs* prepared?
17. What are two purposes for which a *statement of affairs* may be used?
18. How does the *statement of affairs* differ from the *balance sheet*?
19. What are four classifications of liabilities that can appear in a statement of affairs?

Exercises

E 19-1 **Bankruptcy Reorganization: Settlement for Cash and Stock** New Life Company's plan of reorganization under Chapter 11 of the Bankruptcy Code calls for a cash payment of $4,000,000 and the issuance of 800,000 shares of $1 par value common stock to unsecured creditors on a pro rata basis. These *unsecured creditors* are composed of vendors (owed $8,000,000) and a bank (owed $3,500,000 principal and $500,000 interest). New Life's common stock has a value of $1.25 per share based on the reorganization value of the company.

Required Prepare the journal entry related to this settlement.

E 19-2 **Bankruptcy Reorganization: Settlement for Cash and Notes** Skiddex Company's plan of reorganization under Chapter 11 of the Bankruptcy Code calls for a cash payment of $1,500,000 and the issuance of $2,000,000 of 14% notes payable to the company's *unsecured creditors* on a pro rata basis. These unsecured creditors are composed of vendors (owed $2,300,000) and a bank (owed $3,300,000 principal and $400,000 interest). (The 14% interest rate on the notes is considered reasonable under the circumstances.) The notes are to be paid in full in three years.

Required Prepare the journal entry related to this settlement.

E 19-3 **Statement of Affairs: Calculating Expected Settlement Amounts** The statement of affairs for Defuncto Company reflects the following amounts:

	Book Value	Estimated Current Value
Assets		
Assets pledged with fully secured creditors	$150,000	$180,000
Assets pledged with partially secured creditors	80,000	60,000
Free assets	220,000	150,000
	$450,000	$390,000
Liabilities		
Liabilities with priority	$ 20,000	
Fully secured creditors	130,000	
Partially secured creditors	100,000	
Unsecured creditors	260,000	
	$510,000	

Required Compute the amount that each class of creditors can expect to receive if assets are converted into cash at their estimated current values.

Problems

P 19-1 **Bankruptcy Reorganization under Chapter 11** The following balance sheet was prepared for Newcoe Inc. immediately before its plan of reorganization under Chapter 11 was confirmed:

	Book Value (preconfirmation)	Fair Value
Cash	$ 270,000	$ 270,000
Accounts receivable, net	130,000	130,000
Inventory, LIFO	280,000	440,000
Fixed assets, net	400,000	510,000
Patents	80,000	60,000
Goodwill	40,000	–0–
	$1,200,000	$1,410,000
Postpetition liabilities:		
Accounts payable and other	$ 280,000	$ 280,000
Short-term borrowings	90,000	90,000
	$ 370,000	$ 370,000
Prepetition Liabilities *Not* Subject to Compromise	$ 60,000	$ 60,000
Prepetition Liabilities Subject to Compromise	$1,300,000	
Shareholders' deficiency:		
Preferred stock	$ 100,000	
Common stock, $1 par values	5,000	
Additional paid-in capital	215,000	
Retained earnings (deficit)	(850,000)	
	$ (530,000)	
	$1,200,000	

Details of the confirmed plan of reorganization follow:

1. Creditors having liabilities subject to compromise agree to forgive debt of $1,300,000 in exchange for
   a. A pro rata cash payment of $150,000.
   b. Senior debt of $650,000 bearing 12% interest, repayable over five years. The 12% interest rate is deemed reasonable.
   c. Eighty thousand shares of the existing common stock issue; the existing common stock issue is to have a fresh-start book value of $2.70 per share.
2. The preferred stock issue is canceled in exchange for 15,000 shares of the existing common stock issue.
3. The reorganization value of the company's assets was deemed to be $1,500,000.

Required 1. Prepare the entry to record the discharge of indebtedness.

2. Prepare the entry to record cancellation of the preferred stock.
3. Prepare the entries to adopt fresh-start reporting.
4. Prepare (1) a bankruptcy reorganization adjusting entries worksheet and (2) the stockholders' equity section on a *fresh-start basis.*

P 19-2 Bankruptcy Reorganization: Settlement with Unsecured Creditors—Use of Present Value Concepts Debtorex Corporation's plan of reorganization was confirmed by the bankruptcy court on 6/30/06. Under the plan, unsecured creditors (who are owed $850,000,000) are to receive the following:

Cash	$300,000,000
12% Unsecured notes	$300,000,000
Common stock, $1 par value	10,000,000 shares

The company's investment bankers have determined that the 12% unsecured notes will trade at a discount on issuance to yield a return of approximately 15%. These notes are to be paid off at $60,000,000 per year beginning 6/30/07 until their maturity five years from now. Interest is to be paid annually in arrears each June 30.

The company's common stock (2,000,000 shares now outstanding) traded at $1.50 per share when the company's plan of reorganization was confirmed.

Assume that *APBO 21* applies to the 12% unsecured notes. Selected present value factors follow:

	Present Value Factors	
Periods	12%	15%
1	0.89286	0.86957
2	0.79719	0.75614
3	0.71178	0.65752
4	0.63552	0.57175
5	0.56743	0.49718
Five payments (annuity)	3.60478	3.35216

Required

1. Prepare the journal entries related to the discharge of indebtedness.
2. Prepare the journal entries made for the first two years following confirmation of the plan, assuming that all required payments are made on time. (Assume that the company has a June 30 fiscal year-end.)

P 19-3* Liquidation: Preparing a Statement of Affairs As Die-Hard Corp.'s CPA, you are aware that Die-Hard Corp. is facing bankruptcy proceedings. Its balance sheet at 6/30/06 and supplementary data are as follows:

Assets	
Cash	$ 2,000
Accounts receivable, less allowance for uncollectibles	70,000
Inventory, finished goods	60,000
Inventory, raw materials	40,000
Marketable securities	20,000
Land	13,000
Buildings, net of accumulated depreciation	90,000
Machinery, net of accumulated depreciation	120,000
Goodwill	20,000
Prepaid expenses	5,000
Total Assets	$440,000

Liabilities and Equity	
Accounts payable	$ 80,000
Notes payable	135,000
Accrued wages	15,000
Mortgages payable	130,000
Common stock	100,000
Accumulated deficit	(20,000)
Total Liabilities and Equity	$440,000

* This problem may be worked on the computer using Model 19 (filename: MODEL19) at the **http://pahler.swlearning.com** website.

Additional information

1. Cash includes an expended $500 travel advance.
2. Accounts receivable of $40,000 have been pledged to bank loans of $30,000. Credit balances of $5,000 are netted in the accounts receivable total.
3. Marketable securities consist of government bonds costing $10,000 and 500 shares of Bumm Company stock. The market value of the bonds is $10,000, and the stock is $18 per share. The bonds have accrued interest due of $200. The securities are collateral for a $20,000 bank loan.
4. Appraised value of raw materials is $30,000 and of finished goods is $50,000. For an additional cost of $10,000, the raw materials would realize $70,000 as finished goods.
5. The appraised value of fixed assets is land, $25,000; buildings, $110,000; and machinery, $75,000.
6. Prepaid expenses will be exhausted during the liquidation period.
7. Accounts payable include $15,000 of withheld payroll taxes and $6,000 owed to creditors who had been reassured by Die-Hard's president that they would be paid. Unrecorded employer's payroll taxes total $500.
8. Wages payable are not subject to any limits under bankruptcy laws.
9. Mortgages payable consist of $100,000 on land and buildings and $30,000 chattel mortgages on machinery. Total unrecorded accrued interest for these mortgages amounts to $2,400.
10. Estimated legal fees and expenses connected with the liquidation are $10,000.
11. Probable judgment on a pending damage suit is $50,000.
12. You have not rendered a $5,000 invoice for last year's audit, and you estimate a $1,000 fee for liquidation work.

Required

1. Prepare a statement of affairs. (The Book Value column should reflect adjustments that properly should have been made at 6/30/06 in the normal course of business.)
2. Compute the estimated settlement per dollar of unsecured liabilities.

P 19-4* **Liquidation: Preparing a Statement of Affairs** Last-Legg Corporation is in financial difficulty because of low sales. Its stockholders and principal creditors want an estimate of the financial results of the liquidation of the assets and liabilities and the dissolution of the corporation.

Last-Legg Corporation
Postclosing Trial Balance—December 31, 2006

	DEBIT	CREDIT
Cash	$ 5,000	
Accounts receivable	82,000	
Allowance for uncollectibles		$ 3,000
Inventories	160,000	
Supplies inventory	12,000	
Investment in Hye-Flyer Company's 10% bonds (at face value)	20,000	
Accrued bond interest receivable	3,000	
Advertising	24,000	
Land	16,000	
Building	120,000	
Accumulated depreciation—Building		20,000
Machinery and equipment	184,000	
Accumulated depreciation—Machinery and equipment		32,000
Accounts payable		104,000
Notes payable—Bank		100,000
Notes payable—Officers		80,000
Wages payable		6,000
Payroll taxes payable		3,000
Mortgage payable		168,000
Mortgage interest payable		2,000
Capital stock		200,000
Accumulated deficit	117,000	
Estimated liability for product guarantees		25,000
	$743,000	$743,000

The following information has been collected for a meeting of the stockholders and principal creditors to be held on 1/10/07:

1. Cash includes a $2,000 protested check from a customer. The customer stated that funds to honor the check will be available in about two weeks.
2. Accounts receivable include accounts totaling $40,000 that are fully collectible and that have been assigned to the bank in connection with the notes payable. Included in the unassigned receivables is an uncollectible account of $1,000. The Allowance for Uncollectibles account of $3,000 now on the books will adequately provide for other doubtful accounts.
3. Purchase orders totaling $36,000 are on hand for the corporation's products. Inventory with a *book value* of $24,000 can be processed at an additional cost of $2,000 to fill these orders. The balance of the inventory, which includes obsolete materials with a book value of $4,000, can be sold for $41,000.
4. In transit at December 31 but not recorded on the books is a shipment of defective merchandise being returned by a customer. The president of the corporation authorized the return and the refund of the $1,000 purchase price after the merchandise had been inspected. Other than this return, the president knows of no other defective merchandise that would affect the Estimated Liability for Product Guarantees account. The merchandise being returned has no salvage value.
5. The supplies inventory comprises advertising literature, brochures, and other sales aids, which could not be replaced for less than $14,000.
6. The investment in 10% bonds of Hye-Flyer Company is recorded at face value (two bonds each having a $10,000 face value). They were purchased in 2004 for $8,500, and the adjustment to face value was credited to the Retained Earnings account. At 12/31/06 the bonds were quoted at 30.
7. The Advertising account represents the future benefits of a 2006 advertising campaign. The account contains 10% of certain advertising expenditures. The president stated that this figure was too conservative and that 20% would be a more realistic measure of the market that was created.
8. The land and building are in a downtown area. A $200,000 firm offer has been received for the land, which would be used as a parking lot; the building would be razed at a cost of $48,000 to the buyer. Another offer of $160,000 was received for the real estate, which the bidder stated would be used for manufacturing that would probably employ some employees of Last-Legg.
9. The highest offer received from used machinery dealers was $72,000 for all the machinery and equipment.
10. One creditor, whose account for $16,000 is included in the accounts payable, confirmed in writing that he would accept 75 cents on the dollar if the corporation paid him by January 10.
11. Wages payable are for amounts earned within the last 30 days.
12. The mortgage payable is secured by the land and building. Neither of the last two monthly principal payments of $800 was made.
13. Estimated liquidation expenses amount to $13,000.
14. For income tax purposes, the corporation has the following net operating loss carryovers (the combined federal and state tax rate is 40%): 2003, $40,000; 2004, $48,000; and 2005, $32,000.

Required

1. Prepare a *statement of affairs*. (The Book Value column should reflect adjustments that should have been made at 12/31/06 in the normal course of business.
2. Prepare a schedule that computes the estimated settlement per dollar of unsecured liabilities.

THINKING CRITICALLY

Cases

C 19-1 **Bankruptcy Reorganization: Theory** You are the controller of a company that has been attempting to work out a troubled debt restructuring at lengthy meetings with its major creditors. At the last meeting, the company's president told the creditors that if they did not agree to the restructuring plan proposed by the company, management would file for reorganization under Chapter 11 of the bankruptcy statutes.

Required

1. How would the accounting change as a result of restructuring the debt through the bankruptcy courts versus outside the bankruptcy courts?
2. What is the rationale for having different rules for restructuring debt in bankruptcy reorganizations?

part seven

Partnerships and Estates and Trusts

VII

chapter

20

Partnerships: Formation and Operation

Be nice to people on the way up. They're the same people you'll pass on the way down.
JIMMY DURANTE

LEARNING OBJECTIVES

To Understand

- The various types of partnerships that can be formed.
- The distinguishing features of partnerships.
- The way to form a partnership.
- The various ways to share partnership profits and losses.
- The financial reporting issues peculiar to partnerships.
- The fundamental income tax aspects of partnerships.

TOPIC OUTLINE

I. Types of Partnerships
II. Major Features of the Partnership Form of Business
III. Formation of a Partnership
IV. Methods to Share Profits and Losses
V. Financial Reporting Issues
APPENDIX 20A: Income Tax Aspects

Appendices can be found at http://www.pahler.swlearning.com

CHAPTER OVERVIEW

A **partnership** is an association of two or more persons who contribute money, property, or services to operate as co-owners of a business, the profits and losses of which are shared in an agreed-upon manner. The term *person* refers to *individuals*, *corporations*, and even *other partnerships*.

Partnerships that are owned by one or more partnerships or corporations usually are formed to combine managerial talent and financial resources to conduct a specific undertaking—for example, designing and developing a large shopping center. Such partnerships are commonly referred to as *joint ventures*. Regardless of whether the partners are individuals, corporations, or other partnerships, the accounting and tax issues are the same.

According to the latest Internal Revenue Service (IRS) publications, more than 1.5 million partnerships exist (nearly 16 million partners), an increase of more than 50% in the last 25 years. Of all business income tax returns filed, nearly 8% are partnership returns.

In this chapter, we discuss the formation and operation of partnerships. Changes in ownership are discussed in Chapter 21, and liquidations of partnerships are discussed in Chapter 22.

Alternatives to the Partnership Form of Organization

The alternatives to the partnership form of organization are (1) a *regular corporation* (known as a C corporation for federal tax-reporting purposes), which in some ways is the most complex form of organization; (2) a *professional corporation* (a special corporation type for *state* statutory purposes but *not* for federal tax-reporting purposes; thus they are C corporations for federal tax purposes); (3) an *S corporation* (a small business company that elects special tax status with the result that its income is taxed only at the shareholder level); and (4) a *limited liability company (LLC)*, a hybrid form of organization that (a) has a corporation's limited liability feature but is taxed as a partnership for federal purposes and (b) is generally a stronger version of a limited liability partnership, discussed shortly.

Determining the form of organization that is most appropriate for a particular entity requires an in-depth understanding of each of these alternatives, which is beyond the scope of this text. Some of the major accounting firms have prepared lengthy booklets that discuss (1) the advantages and disadvantages of these alternatives and the partnership form of organization and (2) the conditions that must be met to use these various forms of organization.[1]

I. TYPES OF PARTNERSHIPS

General Partnerships

Chapters 20–22 deal with **general partnerships**—that is, those in which each partner is personally liable to the partnership's creditors if partnership assets are insufficient to pay such creditors. Such partners are referred to as *general partners*. Two other types of partnerships exist, however: limited partnerships and limited liability partnerships.

Limited Partnerships

In a **limited partnership**, only *one* partner need be a general partner. The remaining partners can be limited partners, which means that their obligations to creditors are limited to their capital contributions. Thus their personal assets are *not* at risk. Furthermore, they play no role in the partnership management, which is the complete responsibility of the general partner.

[1] For example, see *Choosing a Business Entity in the 1990s* (Coopers and Lybrands LLP., Washington, D.C., 1994).

Limited partnerships can be used for almost any business venture. During the 1970s and 1980s, passive investors widely used such partnerships as investment vehicles for various types of ventures, such as (1) real estate (by far, the most popular investment), (2) oil and gas explorations, (3) research and development, (4) leveraged buyouts, (5) motion pictures, (6) cable television, and (7) horse breeding. Because of the much publicized staggering losses that investors had in these ventures overall, they are no longer widely used.[2]

Enron Corporation's Massive Use of Limited Partnerships

Enron Corporation had created more than 1,000 limited partnerships prior to its bankruptcy filing in late 2001. Many of these entities were special-purpose entities, or SPEs (discussed in Chapter 3), designed to keep debt off the balance sheet. Nearly 900 of these limited partnerships were created in the Bahamas (a tax-haven country) merely to shift income between years for tax-reporting purposes.

Limited Liability Partnerships (LLPs)

In **limited liability partnerships**, a partner's personal assets are *not* at risk for the negligence and wrongdoings of the other partners. Each partner is at risk, however, for (1) his or her own negligence and wrongdoing and (2) the negligence and wrongdoing of those under his or her direction and control. Of course, all partners could lose their entire partnership investment as a result of the negligence or wrongdoing (malpractice and torts) of any one partner.

In the accounting profession, many general partnerships (including all of the then Big Six accounting firms) changed to limited liability partnerships in the mid-1990s to protect their partners' personal assets.

LLPs, which debuted in the mid-1990s, came about because the accounting profession heeded the unfortunate consequences of the bankruptcy and liquidation of the then seventh-largest accounting partnership (Laventhol and Horwath—L&H) in 1991 (discussed in detail in Chapter 22), in which the 350 L&H partners lost $47 million of their *personal assets* (in addition to all of their *partnership capital* of approximately $60 million). In response, the American Institute of Certified Public Accountants (AICPA) (1) changed its rules in 1992 so that accounting firm members no longer had to be *general partnerships*—they could use whatever business form was available to them by their state governments—and (2) conducted an extensive effort to pass LLP legislation in each state. So successful were these efforts that nearly all states subsequently enacted legislation that allows LLPs. This relatively new form of organization has become quite popular.

The size of the Big Four accounting LLPs is staggering—see the accompanying Case in Point.

CASE IN POINT

Andersen's Failure

In 2002, the giant accounting firm Andersen LLP (formerly Arthur Andersen & Co. LLP), one of the then *Big Five* accounting firms, was indicted on criminal charges by the U.S. Justice Department in connection with allegedly faulty audits of Enron Corporation. Immediately after the indictment, Andersen's clients started leaving in droves. As a result, Andersen imploded and gave up its state auditing licenses several months later. Although its U.S. partners most likely have lost all of their capital investment (estimated at roughly $600 million), the personal assets (for the overwhelming majority of its partners) were insulated and thus are not at risk because Andersen was an LLP.

---

[2] In 1994, Prudential Securities Inc. reached a settlement with the Justice Department over its role in promoting the sale of limited partnerships in the 1980s. Under the terms of the settlement, Prudential (1) admitted criminal wrongdoing for the first time, (2) agreed to pay $330 million into a restitution fund for investors (in addition to the $371 million settlement it reached with state and federal regulators in 1993), and (3) agreed to be put on probation for three years. By doing so, the firm avoided a potentially crippling criminal indictment, which might have brought the firm down. Also in 1994, Paine Webber Inc. agreed to pay $303 million to settle regulators' charges that it had defrauded customers by luring them into highly risky limited partnership investments by describing them as safe investments.

CASE IN POINT

PricewaterhouseCoopers has (1) nearly 8,000 partners, (2) nearly $15 billion in annual revenues, (3) approximately 115,000 employees, and (4) approximately 800 offices in roughly 140 countries.

II. Major Features of the Partnership Form of Business

Partnerships have many unique features.

Ease of Formation

Forming a partnership is a relatively simple process. The partners merely put their agreement into writing concerning who contributes assets or services, who performs which functions in the business, and how profits and losses are shared. The written document is called the **partnership agreement.**

Thus, compared with the corporation form of business, a partnership *need not* prepare articles of incorporation, write bylaws, print stock certificates, prepare minutes of the first meeting of the board of directors, pay state incorporation fees, or register stocks.

Potential *Noncontinuity of Existence*

Historically, the possibility that the operations of a partnership could *not* continue after the death or withdrawal of a partner (with the business subsequently liquidated) was considered a major disadvantage of this form of organization. In practice, this problem occurs only for *small* partnerships. Even then, some steps can be taken to minimize the impact of the loss of a partner. For example, life insurance proceeds on the death of a partner can be used to settle with the deceased partner's estate, thus conserving the assets of the business so that the remaining partners can continue the operation. For larger partnerships, this feature usually is *not* significant. Some of the largest partnerships have more than 1,000 partners. Obviously, the loss of one or even several partners in a partnership of such size has minimal impact on the day-to-day operations of the business.

Difficulty in Disposing of Interest

An ownership interest in a partnership is a personal asset, as is the ownership of stock in a corporation. No formal established marketplace exists for the sale of a partnership interest, however, as exists for the sale of stock in a publicly owned corporation. Accordingly, a partner who wishes to sell or assign his or her partnership interest has more difficulty finding a buyer than a shareholder who wishes to sell stock in a publicly owned corporation. To make this process even more difficult, the person buying a partnership interest does *not* have the automatic right to participate in the business management—the consent of the remaining partners is necessary.

Unlimited Liability

If a partnership's assets are insufficient to pay its creditors, the creditors have recourse to the personal assets of any and all general partners of the partnership. This characteristic contrasts sharply with the corporate form of organization in which the personal assets of the shareholders are insulated from the corporation's creditors. This is undoubtedly the major disadvantage of the partnership form of organization.

Mutual Agency

The partnership is bound by each partner acting within the scope of partnership activities. Thus each partner acts as an agent for the partnership in dealing with persons outside the partnership. Furthermore, partners have a duty to conduct every transaction in full view of their partners.

Sharing Profits and Losses

Profits and losses are shared among the partners in any manner to which they agree.

Nontaxable Status

Unlike a corporation, a partnership does *not* pay income taxes. Instead, partnerships must file with the IRS information on Form 1065, which shows the partnership's taxable income and each partner's share of such income. Each partner then reports and pays taxes on his or her share of the partnership's taxable income. These procedures eliminate the undesirable "double taxation," a feature of corporations. That is, a corporation's earnings are taxed, and then its dividends are also taxed—whereas partnership income is taxed only once, at the individual partner level. Thus partnerships serve as *conduits* through which income flows to the partners.

Concluding Comments

For professionals, the partnership form of organization is simple and flexible compared with that of a professional corporation, which is generally considered complex and cumbersome. The partnership form is still common largely because it is a more effective way for partners to relate to each other.

Partnerships often begin with great enthusiasm and rosy expectations. Keeping the partnership going is much harder. In many cases, the partners must seek the help of a professional business therapist (often a psychologist) because they *cannot* work together harmoniously.

Incorporating a Partnership

Many corporations began as partnerships. Then at some point in the enterprise's existence, the advantages of incorporation outweighed the advantages of the partnership form of organization. When a partnership incorporates, its assets are transferred to the corporation, which assumes the partnership's liabilities. One technical point should be noted: The corporation's board of directors is responsible for valuing the assets transferred to the corporation. In theory, the assets can be revalued to their *current values*, which is often done. If the corporation ever decides to register its common stock with the Securities and Exchange Commission, however, the SEC will insist that assets transferred to the corporation be carried at the partnership's *historical cost*, adjusted for depreciation and amortization. In other words, no *upward* revaluation of assets on incorporation is allowed. (Presumably, a *downward* revaluation would be permitted if appropriate.)

III. Formation of a Partnership

The Revised Uniform Partnership Act [revised in 1994 and last amended in 1997]

Before discussing the partnership agreement in detail, some understanding of the laws that govern partnerships is necessary. Although each of the 50 states has laws pertaining to partnerships, virtually all states have adopted either (1) the Uniform Partnership Act UPA [1914] or (2) the Revised Uniform Partnership Act (RUPA) to govern partnerships. In this text, we consider the RUPA the governing statute.

The RUPA gives supremacy to the *partnership agreement* in almost all situations. Thus the RUPA effectively serves largely as a series of comprehensive "default rules" that govern the relations among partners in specific situations in which the partners have *not* addressed in their partnership agreement. The primary focus of the RUPA is on the small, often informal, partnerships. Medium and large partnerships almost always have a comprehensive partnership agreement that addresses many of the provisions of the RUPA. For the most part, the RUPA embodies the *entity approach* of treating the partnership as an distinct entity. The committee drafting the RUPA spent considerable effort on rules governing partnership breakups so as to provide stability for partnerships that have continuation agreements. For our purposes, the RUPA's more relevant sections pertain to the following:

1. Relations of partners to one another.
2. Relations of partners to persons dealing with the partnership.
3. *Dissociations* (withdrawal of a partner) and *dissolutions* (winding up the partnership's activities and terminating the partnership's existence).

To illustrate how the RUPA would apply to a situation in which the partnership agreement is silent and the partners are in disagreement, assume that a partner *personally* makes a payment that results in a *partnership obligation* under section 401 (c) or (d). Under the section 401 (e) of the RUPA, the payment constitutes a *loan* to the partnership that accrues interest from the date the partner made the payment. Inserting a contrary provision into the partnership agreement overrides this provision. In contrast, other sections of the RUPA *cannot* be overridden by having contrary provisions in the partnership agreement.

The RUPA is *not* so comprehensive, however, that it provides for every possible provision that otherwise could be included in a partnership agreement. For example, Section 503 discusses certain consequences of a partner's transfer of his or her partnership interest. Although a partner need *not* give the remaining partners the first opportunity to acquire the partnership interest, neither does the RUPA prevent a partnership agreement from containing a clause to the effect that if a partner desires to transfer any or all of his or her interest, the remaining partners must be given the right of first refusal.

The full text of the RUPA can be found on the web at **http://www.law.upenn.edu/bll/ulc/fnact99/1990s/upa97fa.htm**.

The Partnership Agreement

The partnership agreement is merely a written expression of what the partners have agreed to. Because state laws govern the consequences of partnership relationships, an attorney who is experienced in partnership law should prepare the partnership agreement. This is essential for the following reasons:

1. Mandatory provisions of the RUPA may be included or referred to so that the partners are aware of and somewhat familiar with partnership law.
2. Provisions that conflict with the RUPA can be avoided.
3. Optional provisions that do *not* conflict with the RUPA can be considered for possible inclusion.

A well-written partnership agreement should be a guide to the partners' relationship and any allowable variations from the RUPA to which they have agreed. It should also minimize potential disputes among the partners.

In addition to essential legal provisions, the partnership agreement should address the following:

1. **Noninvolved provisions.**
   a. The partnership's exact name and designated place of business.
   b. The partners' names and addresses.

c. The date that the partnership was formed.
d. The partnership's business purpose.
e. The partnership's duration.
f. The basis of accounting to be used (for example, the accrual basis, the cash basis, the tax basis).
g. The partnership's accounting year-end.

2. **Assets contributed.** A list of the assets contributed by each partner and their agreed-upon valuation to the partnership.
3. **Profit sharing.** The specific procedures for sharing profits and losses.
4. **Withdrawals.** The amounts that partners can periodically withdraw from the business and any conditions for withdrawals (for example, a certain amount per month or an amount up to a percentage of current period earnings).
5. **Additional capital contributions.** Provisions for making future capital infusions should the firm have financial difficulties.
6. **Rights of partners.** Provisions detailing the rights of partners (such as to accept clients, incur incidental expenses in connection with professional activities, and perform certain tasks).
7. **Avoidance of conflicts of interest.** A requirement that each partner is obligated to (a) bring all business opportunities to the partnership and (b) refrain from activities that create a conflict of interest.
8. **Designation of a managing partner or executive committee.** Provisions for designating a managing partner or an executive committee and the authority granted to such partner and committee (managing partners are commonly used in all but the smallest of firms).
9. **Tax matters.** Procedures to follow to comply with Internal Revenue Code requirements pertaining to partnerships.
10. **Notice of withdrawal.** The minimum time period for giving notice prior to withdrawing.
11. **Settling with withdrawing partners.** Provisions for settling with a partner (or a partner's estate) who withdraws from the partnership through choice, retirement, or death.
12. **Expulsion of a partner.** Causes for expulsion and manners of expelling and settling with (a) a partner who breaches the terms of the partnership agreement and (b) an unwanted partner. Larger firms usually empower executive committees to expel a partner without a vote of all the partners. The alternative to expulsion provisions is to allow the other partners to vote to dissolve the firm and then reestablish it, *minus one member*. Even so, partners forced out in this manner sometimes file troublesome civil lawsuits against the firm, which take time and money to defend (see the accompanying Case in Point).

CASE IN POINT

In 1995, KPMG Peat Marwick "dropped" 265 weak-performing partners from its 1,876 partners. The cost was $52 million in severance pay and benefits.

13. **Nonsolicitation.** Provisions that (a) either permit or prohibit a departing partner's solicitation of the partnership's clients and (b) set the compensation to be given the firm if clients are taken. *Not* having such provisions sometimes leads to civil lawsuits between the firm and the departing partner.
14. **Noncompetition.** Provisions regarding whether a departing partner can or *cannot* compete against the partnership for a specified period of time in a specified geographic area. (Prohibitions must be reasonable, or the courts will *not* enforce them.)
15. **Forfeitures.** Provisions specifying whether any termination or retirement payments shall be forfeited if a withdrawing partner violates any nonsolicitation or noncompetition provisions.

Many partnerships that (1) have a significant number of partners, (2) admit new partners annually, and (3) do business in more than one state have fashioned their partnership agreements so that they can operate in the same general manner as corporations. Thus such partnerships exhibit the *corporate* characteristics of (1) centralized management and decision making, (2) continuity of life (in substance but *not* form), and (3) an annual meeting of the owners (the partners) to vote on various matters. For additional information on partnerships, refer to *Management of an Accounting Practice*, which the AICPA publishes.

An accountant can assist persons who are in the preliminary stages of forming a partnership in the following ways:

1. By explaining the *cash basis* and *accrual basis* of accounting.
2. By explaining and illustrating the numerous alternative methods available to share profits and losses and the appropriateness of each. (A significant portion of this chapter is devoted to this subject.)
3. By discussing the tax ramifications compared with other methods of organizing the business. (This subject is discussed in Appendix 20A.)

The Partnership as an Entity

The business of the partnership should logically be accounted for separately from the personal transactions of the partners. Although partnerships are *not* separate legal entities with unlimited lives, as are corporations, their status does *not* prevent partnerships from being accounted for as separate, operating business entities.

Although partners legally must contribute additional cash or property to the partnership to satisfy creditors' claims, the liability system does *not* mean that the partnership is inseparable from the partners. It is a common banking practice for certain top officers of corporations to personally guarantee loans made to the corporation. Thus the fact that additional collateral for creditors exists is irrelevant.

Income tax laws do *not* determine sound accounting theory. They do treat partnerships as *separate **reporting** entities*, although *not* as *separate **tax-paying** entities*. Most partnerships are considered *separate **business** entities* in that they prepare monthly financial statements for internal use. Some of the large public accounting firms even publish annual reports, complete with financial statements, for their partners, employees, and other interested parties to use.

Applicability of *Generally Accepted Accounting Principles*

To study partnerships, we must make an important transition from corporate accounting (in which GAAP is almost always followed) to partnership accounting (in which GAAP need *not* be and often is *not* followed). The professional pronouncements of the AICPA and the Financial Accounting Standards Board (FASB) apply to businesses that present their financial statements in accordance with GAAP. Such businesses include (1) publicly held corporations, which must present their financial statements in accordance with GAAP; (2) nonpublicly held corporations, which usually present their financial statements in accordance with GAAP (often pursuant to requirements of loan agreements with financial institutions); and (3) partnerships and sole proprietorships that choose to present their financial statements in accordance with GAAP.

When a partnership does *not* maintain its books in accordance with GAAP, such a departure usually falls into one of the following categories:

1. ***Cash basis* instead of *accrual basis*.** The cash basis of recording receipts and expenses is often more efficient and economical than the accrual basis.
2. **Prior period adjustments.** To achieve greater equity among the partners, prior period adjustments are often made even though the items do *not* qualify as such under FASB *Statement No. 16*, "Prior Period Adjustments."
3. ***Current values* instead of *historical cost*.** When the ownership of the partnership changes, it is sometimes more expedient to reflect assets at their current values than to continue to value them at their historical cost.
4. **Recognition of goodwill.** To accommodate a partner's wishes, goodwill may be recognized on the admission or retirement of a partner, even though a business combination has *not* occurred.

Categories 3 and 4 are discussed and illustrated in Chapter 21 on changes in ownership.

Partners' Accounts

Unlike corporations, which can currently have up to *twelve* equity accounts, partnerships typically have only *two* types of equity accounts. Each partner, however, may use each of these two types of equity accounts.

Capital Accounts

Each partner has a **capital account**, created when the partner contributes assets to the partnership. The account is *increased* for subsequent capital contributions and *decreased* for withdrawals. In addition, the account is *increased* for the partner's share of earnings and *decreased* for the partner's share of losses.

Traditionally, accountants have *not* attempted to maintain a balance sheet distinction between *contributed capital* and *earnings* that have been retained in the partnership, as is customary for *corporations*. This is primarily because the partnership's earnings do *not* reflect any salary expense for the partners (they are owners, *not* employees), and therefore they must be evaluated carefully. If the corporate form of business were used rather than the *partnership* form, the *corporation's* earnings would be lower than those reported by the partnership because the services performed by the partners would be performed by salaried officers and employees of the corporation. Earnings under the *corporate* form of business would also be *lower* because of income taxes. To avoid the implication that the earnings retained in the *partnership* are comparable to the retained earnings of a *corporation*, a retained earnings account is considered inappropriate for *partnerships*. Accordingly, a *partnership's* earnings or losses are added or subtracted, respectively, to the *capital* accounts of the individual partners.

Drawing Accounts

Typically, partners do *not* wait until the end of the year to determine how much of the profits they wish to withdraw from the partnership. To meet personal living expenses, partners customarily withdraw money on a periodic basis throughout the year. Such withdrawals could be charged directly to the capital accounts of the individual partners. A special account called **Drawings** is used, however, to charge current-year withdrawals. In substance, drawing accounts are contra capital accounts. At year-end, each partner's drawing account is closed to that partner's capital account. The maximum amount partners may withdraw during the year is usually specified in the partnership agreement.

Loan Accounts

Partners may make loans to the partnership in excess of their required capital contributions. Section 401 of the RUPA provides that unless the partners agree otherwise, "a partner, who in aid of the partnership makes any payment or advance beyond the amount of capital which he agreed to contribute, shall be paid interest from the date of the payment or advance." Interest on partners' loans to the partnership is a bona fide borrowing expense of the business, is treated as interest expense in the general ledger, and enters into the determination of profit or loss.

If a partnership loans money on an interest-bearing basis to a partner, the interest is recorded as interest income in the general ledger. It also enters into the determination of the profit or loss.

Recording the Initial Capital Contributions

The following two fundamental principles are deeply rooted in partnership accounting:

1. *Non*cash assets contributed to a partnership should be valued at their *current values*.
2. Liabilities assumed by a partnership should be valued at their *current values*.

These principles **achieve equity among the partners**, an objective repeatedly stressed in partnership accounting. If these principles are *not* followed, the subsequent operations do *not* reflect the true earnings of the partnership, and certain partners are treated inequitably.

For example, assume that a partner contributed to a partnership marketable securities with a $10,000 *current market value* and a $7,000 *cost basis* to the individual partner. If the partnership later sells the marketable securities for $12,000, the recorded gain on the partnership's books is $2,000, the amount of appreciation that occurred during the period that the partnership held the asset. If the marketable securities had been valued on the partnership's books at the partner's *cost basis* of $7,000, however, the recorded gain is $5,000. This results in the other partner's sharing in an additional $3,000 of profit—the appreciation that occurred *before* the asset was contributed to the partnership. ***Current values* must be used to prevent such inequities.** The partnership agreement normally indicates the agreed-upon valuation assigned to noncash assets contributed and liabilities assumed. (Alternatively, the partnership agreement can specify that the first $3,000 of profit go to the contributor with the balance distributed in the profit and loss sharing ratio.)

The entry to record initial capital contributions for an assumed two-person partnership follows using these assumed facts:

Assets Contributed and Liabilities Assumed	Adjusted Basis[a]	Current Value
By Partner A		
Cash	$ 23,000	$ 23,000
Marketable securities	7,000	10,000
	$ 30,000	$ 33,000
By Partner B		
Cash	$ 5,000	$ 5,000
Land	15,000	20,000
Building, net.	25,000	35,000
Note payable, secured by land and building	(20,000)	(20,000)
	$ 25,000	$ 40,000

[a] Adjusted Basis means each partner's *historical cost,* as adjusted for depreciation and amortization previously *allowed* (or *allowable*) for income tax–reporting purposes.

Entry to Record Initial Contributions

Cash	28,000	
Marketable securities	10,000	
Land	20,000	
Building	35,000	
Notes payable		20,000
Capital, Partner A		33,000
Capital, Partner B		40,000

The Adjusted Basis column above is completely irrelevant for recording the initial capital contributions in the general ledger, but it is significant for income tax-reporting. Income tax aspects are discussed in the Appendix.

CHECK POINTS

Don Doss and Kim Keyes form a partnership. Doss contributes into the partnership personal equipment that he has used at home in business-related activities. He paid $10,000 for the equipment two years ago. Doss claimed $1,250 of depreciation expense each year on his personal tax return. Its *replacement cost* (and *fair market value*) is $9,000. The partners, after reviewing IRS rules, assigned the equipment a remaining life of *six* years. For *financial reporting* purposes, at what amount should the equipment be recorded in the partnership's general ledger?

a. $10,000
b. $9,000
c. $7,500
d. $6,750

Answer: b

For *income tax-reporting* purposes, at what amount should the equipment in the previous Check Point be accounted for by the partnership?

a. $10,000
b. $9,000
c. $7,500
d. $6,750

Answer: c

Repeat the second Check Point but assume that Doss had forgotten to depreciate the equipment and thus had *not* claimed any depreciation in his sole proprietorship tax returns.

Answer: c

Repeat the second Check Point but assume that Doss *had* used the equipment for *personal* (nonbusiness) purposes.

*Answer: b**

---

* Lower of cost or market rule applies.

ETHICS

An Unusual Client Billing Practice

On January 5, 2004, the *Wall Street Journal* reported that PricewaterhouseCoopers LLP (PWC) (1) had been obtaining large rebates on airline tickets used for client business and (2) did not pass along those savings to its clients (who were billed at retail ticket prices). For 2000 alone, the rebates totaled $45 million, more than half of which pertained to client-related travel.

Questions

1. Is this billing practice ethical?
2. What do you think the reaction was by PWC clients when they learned of this practice?

IV. METHODS TO SHARE PROFITS AND LOSSES

Section 401 of the RUPA specifies that profits and losses be shared equally unless the partnership agreement provides otherwise. Because the sharing of profits and losses is such an important aspect of a partnership relationship, it would be rare to find a partnership agreement that did *not* spell out the divisions of profits and losses in detail. The formula used to divide profits and losses is determined through negotiations among the partners. Whether it is fair does *not* concern the accountant.

Profits and losses can be shared in many ways. Partners should select a formula that is sensible, practical, and equitable. Most profit and loss sharing formulas include one or more of the following features or techniques:

1. Equal shares or some other agreed-upon ratio.
2. Imputed salary allowances to acknowledge time devoted to the business.
3. Imputed interest on capital investments to recognize capital invested.
4. Expense-sharing arrangements.
5. Performance criteria to recognize above- or below-average performance.

Note that the computations determining the profit and loss allocation among the partners are made on worksheets. The only journal entry that results from this process is to close the Profit and

Loss Summary account to the partners' capital accounts, using the amounts determined from the worksheet computations.

Ratios

Under the *ratio method*, each partner is allocated a percentage of the profits and losses. For example, partner A receives 60%, and partner B receives 40% of the profits and losses. These percentages are then expressed as a ratio. Thus profits and losses are shared between A and B in the ratio 3:2, respectively. If the A and B partnership had profits of $100,000, the entry to record the division of the profits is as follows:

Profit and Loss Summary	100,000	
Capital, Partner A		60,000
Capital, Partner B		40,000

An infrequently used variation of this method specifies one ratio for profits and a different ratio for losses. Because profit and loss years may alternate, it is extremely important that profit or loss for each year be determined accurately in all material respects when this variation is used.

CHECK POINT

Kelly, a partner in the Kelly and Green partnership, is entitled to 40% of the profits and losses. During 2006, Kelly contributes land to the partnership that cost her $50,000 but has a *current value* of $60,000. Also during 2006, Kelly has drawings of $80,000. The balance in Kelly's capital account was $120,000 at the *beginning* of the year and is $150,000 at the *end* of the year. What are the partnership's earnings for 2006?

a. $(75,000)
b. $(50,000)
c. $150,000
d. $125,000

Answer: d

Salary Allowances and Ratios

Sometimes certain partners devote more time to the business than do other partners. In these cases, a frequently used method for sharing profits and losses provides for salary allowances, with any residual profit or loss allocated in an agreed-upon ratio. For example, assume that partner A devotes all of her time to the business, and partner B devotes only one-third of his time to the business. The partners could agree to salary allowances in relation to the time devoted to the business—for example, $30,000 to partner A and $10,000 to partner B. All remaining profits or losses could then be divided in the agreed-upon ratio—that is, 3:2, respectively.

Using these salary allowances and a residual sharing ratio of 3:2 for partner A and partner B, respectively, the partnership divides $100,000 in profits in the following way:

		Allocated to	
	Total	**Partner A**	**Partner B**
Total profit	$100,000		
Salary allowances	(40,000)	$30,000	$10,000
Residual Profit	$ 60,000		
Allocate 3:2	(60,000)	36,000	24,000
	$ -0-	$66,000	$34,000

The general ledger entry to divide the profits follows:

Profit and Loss Summary	100,000	
Capital, Partner A		66,000
Capital, Partner B		34,000

Remember that partners are owners, *not* employees. Accordingly, it is *not* appropriate to charge a Salary Expense account and credit Accrued Salary Payable. Some partnerships do record salary allowances in this manner, however. Although *not* technically correct, it does *not* affect the final profit and loss allocations. In these cases, cash distributions that relate to salary allowances are charged to Accrued Salary Payable. Any remaining credit balance in a partner's Accrued Salary Payable account at year-end is then transferred to that partner's capital account.

In the preceding example, the total profit was higher than the total salary allowances of $40,000. What if that were *not* the case? Profit of only $25,000 is shared as follows:

		Allocated to	
	Total	**Partner A**	**Partner B**
Total profit	$ 25,000		
Salary allowances	(40,000)	$30,000	$10,000
Residual Loss	$(15,000)		
Allocate 3:2	15,000	(9,000)	(6,000)
	$ -0-	$21,000	$ 4,000

The general ledger entry to divide the profits follows:

Profit and Loss Summary	25,000	
Capital, Partner A		21,000
Capital, Partner B		4,000

Another way to handle this situation would be if the partners agreed *not* to use a residual sharing ratio in the event profits were less than the total salary allowances. In this case, the first $40,000 of profit is divided in the ratio of the salary allowances. Using the same example, a $25,000 profit is divided as follows:

		Allocated to	
	Total	**Partner A**	**Partner B**
Total profit	$(25,000)		
Salary allowances—up to $40,000 in a 3:1 ratio	(25,000)	$18,750	$6,250
	$ -0-	$18,750	$6,250

Large and moderate-sized partnerships usually function with an administrative hierarchy. Partnership positions within such a hierarchy have greater responsibilities than do positions outside the hierarchy. To compensate the partners who assume these greater responsibilities, salary allowances commonly are used; their amounts are correlated to the various levels of responsibility within the hierarchy.

Imputed Interest on Capital, Salary Allowances, and Ratios

When partners' capital investments are *not* equal, the profit-sharing formula frequently includes a feature that recognizes the larger capital investment of certain partners. Accordingly, interest is imputed on each partner's capital investment. For example, a profit and loss sharing formula could specify that interest be imputed at 10% of each partner's average capital investment. To illustrate this procedure's application, assume the following profit-sharing formula and *average* capital investments:

	Partner A	**Partner B**
Profit-sharing formula:		
Salary allowances	$30,000	$10,000
Interest on average capital balance	10%	10%
Residual profit or loss (3:2)	60%	40%
Average capital investments	$10,000	$40,000

Profits of $100,000 are divided as follows:

	Total	Allocated to Partner A	Allocated to Partner B
Total profit	$100,000		
Salary allowances	(40,000)	$30,000	$10,000
Interest on average capital investments	(5,000)	1,000	4,000
Residual Profit	$ 55,000		
Allocate 3:2	(55,000)	33,000	22,000
	$ -0-	$64,000	$36,000

The general ledger entry to divide the profits follows:

Profit and Loss Summary	100,000	
Capital, Partner A		64,000
Capital, Partner B		36,000

Remember that the partners' capital investments are just that—they are *not* loans to the partnership. Accordingly, it is *not* appropriate to charge an Interest Expense account and an Accrued Interest Payable account. Some partnerships do record imputed interest in this manner, however. This procedure is *not* technically correct, but it does *not* affect the final profit and loss allocations. In these cases, cash distributions that relate to imputed interest are charged to Accrued Interest Payable. Any remaining credit balance in a partner's Accrued Interest Payable account at year-end is then transferred to that partner's capital account.

In this example, the profit was higher than both the $40,000 total of the salary allowances and the $5,000 total of imputed interest. A profit of only $25,000 is divided as follows:

	Total	Allocated to Partner A	Allocated to Partner B
Total profit	$ 25,000		
Salary allowances	(40,000)	$ 30,000	$10,000
Interest on average capital investments	(5,000)	1,000	4,000
Residual Loss	$(20,000)		
Allocate 3:2	20,000	(12,000)	(8,000)
	$ -0-	$ 19,000	$ 6,000

The general ledger entry to divide the profits follows:

Profit and Loss Summary	25,000	
Capital, Partner A		19,000
Capital, Partner B		6,000

Order of Priority Provision

Alternatively, the partners could agree *not* to use a residual sharing ratio if profits do *not* exceed the total of the salary allowances and the imputed interest on average capital balances. In this case, the partners must agree on **the priority of the various features.** If the partnership agreement gives salary allowances priority over imputed interest on capital balances, the first $40,000 of profit is divided in the ratio of the salary allowances, and the next $5,000 is divided in the ratio of the imputed interest amounts. Using the profit-sharing formula and data from the preceding example, a profit of only $42,000 is divided as follows:

	Total	Allocated to Partner A	Allocated to Partner B
Total profit	$ 42,000		
Salary allowances	(40,000)	$30,000	$10,000
Available for Interest on Capital	$ 2,000		
Interest on average capital investment 1:4	(2,000)	400	1,600
	$ -0-	$30,400	$11,600

Note: If *interest on capital* had priority over *salary allowances*, the $42,000 profit division results in Partner A being allocated $28,750 ($1,000 for interest and $27,750 for salary) and Partner B being allocated $13,250 ($4,000 for interest and $9,250 for salary).

In these examples, interest is imputed on the *average* capital investments. Although this is apparently the most equitable method, using the *beginning* or *ending* capital investments is another option. When this imputed interest on capital feature is used, the partnership agreement should specify whether the *beginning*, *average*, or *ending* capital balances should be used. Furthermore, if the partnership agreement calls for using average or ending capital investments, it should define specifically how these are determined. Only the capital account or the capital account and the drawing account of each partner may be used. For the *average* capital balance method, the method to compute the average must be selected—that is, using daily balances, *beginning-of-month* balances, or *end-of-month* balances.

The following assumptions and capital account activities illustrate the computation of an *average* capital investment:

1. The drawing account activity is considered in arriving at the annual average capital investment.
2. An average capital investment for each month is used to arrive at the annual average capital investment.

Capital, Partner X			Drawings, Partner X		
	$50,000	1/1/05	6/30/05	$6,000	
	10,000	4/1/05	9/15/05	6,000	
	2,000	11/15/05	12/31/05	6,000	

Computation Month	Monthly Averages
January	$ 50,000
February	50,000
March	50,000
April	60,000
May	60,000
June	60,000
July	54,000
August	54,000
September	51,000
October	48,000
November	49,000
December	50,000
	$636,000
Average Capital Investment for 2005 ($636,000 ÷ 12)	$ 53,000

Capital Balances Only

Many international accounting firms allocate profits and losses solely on the basis of capital balances. In these cases, each partner must maintain a specified capital balance, which is correlated to the level of responsibility assumed in the partnership. This method not only is easy to apply but also can prevent certain inequities from occurring among partners if the partnership is liquidated. These potential inequities are discussed in Chapter 26, which deals with partnership liquidations.

Expense-Sharing Arrangements

Sometimes a small partnership operates as a confederation of sole proprietorships, in that the profit-sharing formula entitles each partner to all net billings he or she generates. Expenses are then allocated to partners on the basis of total floor space, amount of billings, or some other arbitrary method. This arrangement is common when two or more sole proprietorships form a partnership, with each partner maintaining former clients. Any net billings from clients obtained after the formation of the partnership may be assigned either to the partner responsible for obtaining the client or to a common pool to be allocated to all partners on some arbitrary basis.

Performance Methods

Many partnerships use profit and loss sharing formulas that give some weight to the specific performance of each partner to provide incentives to perform well. Some examples of the use of performance criteria are listed here:

1. **Chargeable hours.** These are the total number of hours that a partner incurred on client-related assignments. Weight may be given to hours in excess of a norm.
2. **Total billings.** The total amount billed to clients for work performed and supervised by a partner constitutes total billings. Weight may be given to billings in excess of a norm.
3. **Write-offs.** Write-offs consist of the amount of uncollectible billings. Weight may be given to a write-off percentage below a norm.
4. **Promotional and civic activities.** Time devoted to developing future business and enhancing the partnership name in the community is considered promotional and civic activity. Weight may be given to time spent in excess of a norm or to specific accomplishments resulting in new clients.
5. **Profits in excess of specified levels.** Designated partners commonly receive a certain percentage of profits in excess of a specified level of earnings.

An additional allocation of profits to a partner on the basis of performance is frequently referred to as a **bonus.** As with salary allowances and imputed interest, a bonus should *not* be charged to an expense account in the general ledger, although some partnerships improperly do this. For example, assume that the A and B partnership has a bonus provision whereby partner A is to receive 50% of partnership income in excess of $100,000, with all remaining profits and losses to be shared 60%–40%, respectively. Partnership income of $110,000 is shared as follows:

		Allocated to	
	Total	Partner A	Partner B
Total profit	$ 110,000		
Bonus (50% × $10,000)	(5,000)	$ 5,000	
Residual profit	$ 105,000		
Allocate 3:2	(105,000)	63,000	$42,000
	$ -0-	$68,000	$42,000

Many types of bonus provisions can exist. Also, the bonus feature can be applied at any level of partnership income; for example, a bonus can be based on a percentage of the remaining profits after salary allowances and imputed interest on capital have been allocated.

Subsequent Changes in Methods to Share Profits and Losses

If the partners subsequently agree to change the method to share profits and losses, equity dictates that assets be revalued to their *current values* at the time of the change. To illustrate, assume that partners A and B shared profits and losses equally but that at a later date agree to share profits and losses in a 3:2 ratio, respectively. Suppose also that the partnership holds a parcel of land carried on the books at $60,000, but with an $80,000 current value. Partner A would receive a larger share of the profit on the land (when it is *later* sold) than had the land been sold before the change in the method to share profits and losses. This is *not* equitable because the land appreciated $20,000 while the profits and losses were shared equally.

An alternative to revaluing the land to its *current value* is to stipulate in the *new* profit-sharing formula that the first $20,000 of profit on the sale of that parcel of land is to be shared in the *old* profit and loss sharing ratio. Under this method, the partnership avoids making an entry that is at variance with GAAP. This is *not* a major reason for selecting this alternative, however, if revaluing assets is more practical.

When the profit and loss sharing formula is revised, the *new* formula should contain a provision specifying that the *old* formula applies to certain types of subsequent adjustments arising out of activities that took place *before* the revision date. Examples are as follows:

1. Unrecorded liabilities existing at the revision date.
2. Settlements on lawsuits *not* provided for at the revision date, even though the liability may *not* have been probable as to payment or reasonably estimable at that time.
3. Write-offs of accounts receivable existing as of the revision date.

Regardless of the fact that some of these items do *not* qualify as *prior period adjustments* under FASB *Statement No. 16*, "Prior Period Adjustments," greater equity usually is achieved among the partners by using the *old* sharing formula. Because partnerships need *not* follow GAAP, **the *will of the partners* may prevail.**

CHECK POINTS

Partners Harry and Sally share profits and losses of their business equally after (a) annual salary allowances of $25,000 for Harry and $20,000 for Sally and (b) 10% interest is provided on *average* capital balances. During 2006, the partnership had earnings of $50,000; Harry's average capital balance was $60,000, and Sally's *average* capital balance was $90,000. How should the $50,000 of earnings be divided?

	Harry	Sally
a.	$26,000	$24,000
b.	$27,000	$23,000
c.	$25,000	$25,000
d.	$27,500	$22,500

Answer: a

Assume the same information in the preceding question and that an *order of priority* is specified whereby *salary allowances* have a higher priority than *interest on capital.*

Answer: b

V. FINANCIAL REPORTING ISSUES

Because partnerships are *not* publicly owned, their financial statements are prepared primarily for internal use. Such statements normally include all of those that a corporation prepares, except for the statement of changes in stockholders' equity, for which a statement of changes in partners' equity is substituted.

One common reason for making partnership financial statements available to outside parties is to borrow money from financial institutions. (Under the UPA, partnerships can hold debt in the partnership name rather than in the names of its individual partners.) Financial statements made available to outside parties should be converted to the accrual basis if the *cash basis* is used for book purposes. (Most partnerships use the cash basis as a matter of convenience.) Because partnership earnings are *not* comparable to what they would have been had the business been organized as a *corporation*, an indication to this effect should be made in the notes to the financial statements.

Some accountants have suggested that a partnership's income statement should reflect an *imputed* amount for salaries that would have been paid to the partners had the corporate form of business been used. Presumably, such an approach would state the "true earnings" of the partnership. In our opinion, this is a somewhat futile exercise involving substantial subjectivity. Furthermore, from a technical standpoint, consideration should also be given to (1) additional payroll taxes; (2) deductions for fringe benefits (primarily pension and profit-sharing plans), which are *not* available to partners; and (3) income taxes. It seems sufficient to state in a note that, because the partnership form of organization is used, the earnings must be evaluated carefully because, conceptually, earnings should provide for equivalent salary compensation, return on capital invested in the partnership, retirement, and payroll-type fringe benefits.

Virtually all partnerships maintain strict confidentiality of their financial statements. Financial statements issued by international public accounting partnerships to interested parties are commonly characterized as follows:

1. Conversion from the *cash basis* to the *accrual basis* of accounting.
2. No imputed amount for salaries in the income statement.
3. A note to the financial statements indicating that the firm's earnings are *not* comparable to those of a corporation.
4. Preparation of the financial statements in accordance with GAAP, with the notes to the financial statements complete as to required disclosures—for example, of accounting policies, lease commitments, and segment information.

The income statement of small partnerships commonly shows how the profit or loss is divided. The allocation can be shown immediately below net income, as follows:

A & B Partnership
Income Statement
For the Year Ended December 31, 2006

Revenues		$1,000,000
Expenses		(900,000)
Net Income		$ 100,000
Allocation of Net Income to Partners:		
	PARTNER A	PARTNER B
Salary allowances	$30,000	$10,000
Imputed interest on capital	1,000	4,000
Residual (3:2)	33,000	22,000
Total	$64,000	$36,000

Furthermore, a small partnership's statement of changes in partners' equity is often shown by partner, as follows:

A & B Partnership
Statement of Changes in Partners' Equity
For the Year Ended December 31, 2006

	PARTNER A	PARTNER B	TOTAL
Beginning capital	$ 25,000	$ 85,000	$110,000
Contributions	5,000	-0-	5,000
Drawings	(10,000)	(15,000)	(25,000)
Net income	64,000	36,000	100,000
Ending Capital	$ 84,000	$106,000	$190,000

END-OF-CHAPTER REVIEW

Summary of Key Points

1. In **general partnerships**, each partner is personally liable to the partnership's creditors if partnership assets are insufficient to pay such creditors. In **limited partnerships**, the limited partners are *not* personally liable to the partnership creditors.
2. In **limited liability partnerships**, a partner is personally liable to creditors only as a result of (a) his or her own actions and (b) the actions of those under his or her supervision and control.
3. The **partnership agreement** governs the manner of operating the partnership, including the manner of dividing profits and losses and withdrawing earnings and capital.
4. Partnerships are accounted for as separate business entities, with the primary accounting objective being **to achieve equity** among the partners.
5. Partnership accounting often deviates from GAAP to achieve equity.
6. Upon formation of a partnership, assets and liabilities contributed into the partnership are recorded at their **current values**, usually resulting in a **new basis of accounting** for financial reporting purposes. For tax purposes, no change in basis occurs.

Glossary of New Terms

Drawings A *contra* capital account used to keep track of amounts withdrawn during the year by a partner.

General partnerships Partnerships in which all the partners are personally liable to the partnership's creditors.

Limited liability partnerships (LLPs) Partnerships in which each partner is *not* personally liable to the partnership's creditors as a result of actions by other partners.

Limited partnerships Partnerships in which certain partners (called limited partners) are *not* personally liable to the partnership's creditors (there must be at least one general partner).

ASSIGNMENT MATERIAL

Review Questions

1. What is a *general partnership*?
2. How is *partnership* defined?
3. What is a *limited partnership*?
4. What is a *limited liability partnership*?
5. Why is it advisable to use an attorney's services in preparing a *partnership agreement*?
6. What is the function of the *partnership agreement*?
7. What essential items should be set forth in the *partnership agreement*?
8. Must partnerships follow GAAP? Why or why not?
9. What common features may be structured into a profit and loss sharing formula?
10. Can partners be paid *salaries*?
11. What performance criteria may be incorporated into a profit-sharing formula?
12. What is the function of the *drawings* account? Is it really necessary?
13. How are loans *from* a partner to a partnership accounted for on the partnership's books?
14. Why might it be appropriate to use the *old* profit and loss sharing formula in certain transactions instead of the new formula?
15. In what broad areas do partnerships commonly deviate from GAAP?
16. Should partnership financial statements be prepared so that partnership earnings are comparable to what they would have been had the *corporate* form of business been used? Why or why not?

Exercises

E 20-1 **Dividing the Profit or Loss: Partnership Agreement Is Silent** The partnership of Reed and Wright had earnings of $40,000 for the year. Reed devotes all of her time to the business, and Wright devotes 50% of his time to it. The average capital balance for Reed was $60,000, and Wright's was $30,000. The partnership agreement is silent regarding profit distribution.

Required

1. Prepare a schedule showing how the profit should be divided.
2. Prepare the entry to divide the profit.

E 20-2 **Dividing the Profit or Loss: Performance Features and Ratio** The partnership of Monte and Carlo has the following provisions:

1. Monte, who is primarily responsible for obtaining new clients, is to receive a 30% bonus on revenues in excess of $200,000.

2. Carlo, who is primarily responsible for administration, is to receive a 30% bonus on profits in excess of 50% of revenues, as reflected in the general ledger.

3. All remaining profits or losses are to be divided equally.

Additional Information

Revenues for the year	$280,000
Operating expenses.	120,000

Required 1. Prepare a schedule showing how the profit or loss should be divided for the year.
2. Prepare the entry to divide the profit or loss for the year.

E 20-3 **Dividing the Profit or Loss: Ratio and Salary Allowances** The partnership of Bunn and Frye shares profits and losses in a 7:3 ratio, respectively, after Frye receives a $10,000 salary allowance.

Required 1. Prepare a schedule showing how the profit or loss should be divided, assuming the profit or loss for the year is
a. $30,000.
b. $6,000.
c. $(10,000).
2. Prepare the entry to divide the profit or loss in situations a to c of requirement 1.

E 20-4 **Dividing the Profit or Loss: Ratio, Salary Allowance, and Imputed Interest on Capital** The partnership of Agee and Begee has the following provisions:

1. Agee and Begee receive salary allowances of $33,000 and $22,000, respectively.

2. Interest is imputed at 10% of the average capital investments.

3. Any remaining profit or loss is shared between Agee and Begee in a 3:2 ratio, respectively.

Additional Information

Average capital investments	
Agee	$ 60,000
Begee	120,000

Required 1. Prepare a schedule showing how the profit would be divided, assuming the partnership profit or loss is
a. $98,000.
b. $58,000.
c. $(27,000).
2. Prepare the entry to divide the profit or loss in situations a to c of requirement 1.

E 20-5 **Dividing the Profit or Loss: Ratio, Salary Allowances, and Imputed Interest on Capital—Order of Priority Specified** Assume the information provided in Exercise 20-4, except that the partnership agreement stipulates the following **order of priority** in the distribution of profits:

1. *Salary allowances* (only to the extent available).

2. *Imputed interest* on average capital investments (only to the extent available).

3. Any remaining profit in a 3:2 ratio. (No mention is made regarding *losses*.)

Required The requirements are the same as for Exercise 20-4.

E 20-6 **Recording Initial Capital Contributions** On 5/1/06, Booker and Page formed a partnership. Each contributed assets with the following agreed-upon valuations:

	Booker	Page
Cash	$80,000	$ 20,000
Machinery and equipment	50,000	60,000
Building	-0-	240,000

The building is subject to a $100,000 mortgage loan, which the partnership assumes. The partnership agreement provides that Booker and Page share profits and losses 40% and 60%, respectively.

Required

1. Prepare the journal entry to record each partner's capital contributions.
2. *Optional:* Assuming that no difference exists between the agreed-upon valuation of each asset contributed and its related adjusted basis, determine the *tax basis* of each partner on 5/1/06.

Problems

P 20-1 **Dividing Profits: Interest on Capital, Bonuses, and Salary Allowances** Horn and Sax are in a partnership. The activity in each partner's capital account for 2006 follows:

Horn				Sax			
		$20,000	1/1			$30,000	1/1
		8,000	2/12	3/23	5,000		
5/25	4,000			7/10	5,000		
		7,000	10/19	9/30	5,000		
12/10	2,000					18,000	12/5
		1,000	12/30	12/30	23,000		
		$30,000	12/31			$10,000	12/31

A drawing account is *not* used. The profit for 2006 is $200,000.

Required

Divide the profit for the year between the partners using each of the following formulas:

1. *Beginning* capital balances.
2. *Average* capital balances. (Investments and withdrawals are assumed to have been made as of the *beginning* of the month if made before the middle of the month, and assumed to have been made as of the *beginning* of the following month if made *after* the middle of the month.)
3. *Ending* capital balances.
4. Bonus to Horn equal to 20% of profit in excess of $150,000; remaining profit divided equally.
5. Salary allowances of $45,000 and $35,000 to Horn and Sax, respectively; interest on average capital balances imputed at 10%; any residual balance divided equally. (Investments and withdrawals are treated as explained in item 2.)

P 20-2 **Dividing Profits: Revision of Profit-Sharing Agreement—Prior Period Adjustments** The partnership agreement of Archer, Bowes, and Cross written in 2000 specifies that profits and losses are determined on the accrual basis and are divided as follows:

	Archer	Bowes	Cross	Total
Salary allowances	$15,000	$15,000	$5,000	$35,000
Bonuses (percentage of profits in excess of $90,000)	20%	20%		
Residual profit or loss	40%	40%	20%	

On 1/1/06, the partnership agreement was revised to provide for the sharing of profits and losses in the following manner:

	Archer	Bowes	Cross	Total
Salary allowances	$20,000	$20,000	$15,000	$55,000
Bonuses (percentage of profits in excess of $110,000)	20%	20%	10%	
Residual profit or loss	35%	35%	30%	

The partnership books show a profit of $145,000 for 2006 before the following errors were discovered:

1. Inventory at 12/31/04 was *over*stated by $7,000.
2. Inventory at 12/31/05 was *under*stated by $8,000.
3. Inventory at 12/31/06 was *under*stated by $18,000.
4. Depreciation expense for 2006 was *under*stated by $5,000.

Required

1. Divide the profit among the partners for 2006, assuming that the partnership agreement calls for any prior years' errors to be treated as *prior period adjustments*.
2. Assuming that the reported profits for 2004 and 2005 were $85,000 and $110,000, respectively, prepare the proper adjusting entry to correct the capital balances as of 1/1/06. The old profit-sharing agreement is used for these items.

P 20-3 **Combining Two Partnerships: Recording the Initial Capital Contributions** The partnerships of Altoe & Bass (A&B) and Sopra & Tennor (S&T) began business on 7/1/01; each partnership owns one retail appliance store. The two partnerships agree to combine as of 7/1/06 to form a new partnership, Four Partners Discount Stores.

Additional Information

1. **Profit and loss ratios.** The profit and loss sharing ratios for the *former* partnerships were 40% to Altoe and 60% to Bass, and 30% to Sopra and 70% to Tennor. The profit and loss sharing ratio for the *new* partnership is Altoe, 20%; Bass, 30%; Sopra, 15%; and Tennor, 35%.
2. **Capital investments.** The *opening* capital investments for the new partnership are to be in the same ratio as the profit and loss sharing ratios for the new partnership. If necessary, certain partners may have to contribute additional cash, and others may have to withdraw cash to bring the capital investments into the proper ratio.
3. **Accounts receivable.** The partners agreed to set the new partnership's allowance for bad debts at 5% of the accounts receivable contributed by A&B and 10% of the accounts receivable contributed by S&T.
4. **Inventory.** The new partnership's *opening* inventory is to be valued by the FIFO method. A&B used the FIFO method to value inventory (which approximates its current value), and S&T used the LIFO method. The LIFO inventory represents 85% of its FIFO value.
5. **Property and equipment.** The partners agree that the land's *current value* is approximately 20% *more than* the land's historical cost, as recorded on each partnership's books.

   The depreciable assets of each partnership were acquired on 7/1/01. A&B used *straight-line depreciation* and a 10-year life. S&T used *double-declining-balance depreciation* and a 10-year life. The partners agree that the *current value* of these assets is approximately 80% of their historical cost, as recorded on each partnership's books.
6. **Unrecorded liability.** After each partnership's books were closed on 6/30/06, an unrecorded merchandise purchase of $4,000 by S&T was discovered. The merchandise had been sold by 6/30/06.
7. **Accrued vacation.** The A&B accounts include a vacation pay accrual. The four partners agree that S&T should make a similar accrual for their five employees, who will receive a one-week vacation at $200 per employee per week.

The 6/30/06 postclosing trial balances of the partnerships follow:

	Altoe & Bass Trial Balance—June 30, 2006		Sopra and Tennor Trial Balance—June 30, 2006	
Cash	$ 20,000		$ 15,000	
Accounts receivable	100,000		150,000	
Allowance for doubtful accounts		$ 2,000		$ 6,000
Merchandise inventory	175,000		119,000	
Land	25,000		35,000	
Buildings and equipment	80,000		125,000	
Accumulated depreciation		24,000		61,000
Prepaid expenses	5,000		7,000	
Accounts payable		40,000		60,000
Notes payable		70,000		75,000
Accrued expenses		30,000		45,000
Altoe, capital		95,000		
Bass, capital		144,000		
Sopra, capital				65,000
Tennor, capital				139,000
Totals	$405,000	$405,000	$451,000	$451,000

Required

1. Prepare the journal entries to record the initial capital contribution after considering the effect of this information. Use separate entries for each of the combining partnerships.
2. Prepare a schedule computing the cash contributed or withdrawn by each partner to bring the initial capital account balances into the profit and loss sharing ratio.

P 20-4 Combining Three Sole Proprietorships: Dividing the Profit for the First Year of Operations Arby, Bobb, and Carlos, attorneys, agree to consolidate their individual practices as of 1/1/06. The partnership agreement includes the following features:

1. Each partner's capital contribution is the net amount of the assets and liabilities assumed by the partnership, which are as follows:

	Arby	Bobb	Carlos
Cash	$ 5,000	$ 5,000	$ 5,000
Accounts receivable	14,000	6,000	16,000
Furniture and library	4,300	2,500	6,200
	$23,300	$13,500	$27,200
Allowance for depreciation	$ 2,400	$ 1,500	$ 4,700
Accounts payable	300	1,400	700
	$ 2,700	$ 2,900	$ 5,400
Capital Contribution	$20,600	$10,600	$21,800

   Each partner guaranteed the collectibility of receivables.

2. Carlos had leased office space and was bound by the lease until 6/30/06; the monthly rental is $600. The partners agree to occupy Carlos's office space until the expiration of the lease and to pay the rent. The partners concur that the rent is too high for the space and that a fair rental value is $450 per month. The excess rent is charged to Carlos at year-end. On July 1, the partners move to new quarters with a $500 monthly rental.

3. No salaries are paid to the partners. The individual partners receive 20% of the gross fees billed to their respective clients during the first year of the partnership. After deducting operating expenses (including the excess rent), the balance of the fees is credited to the partners' capital accounts in the following ratios: Arby, 40%; Bobb, 35%; and Carlos, 25%.

   On 4/1/06, Mack is admitted to the partnership, receiving 20% of the fees from new business obtained after April 1, after deducting expenses applicable to that new business. Expenses (including the excess rent) are apportioned to the new business in the same ratio that total expenses, other than bad debt losses, bear to total gross fees.

4. The following information pertains to the partnership's 2006 activities:
   a. Fees are billed as follows:

Arby's clients	$ 44,000
Bobb's clients	24,000
Carlos's clients	22,000
New business:	
Prior to April 1	6,000
After April 1	24,000
Total	$120,000

   b. Total expenses, excluding depreciation and bad debt expenses, are $29,350, including the total amount paid for rent. Depreciation is computed at the rate of 10% on original cost. Depreciable assets purchased during 2006, on which one-half year's depreciation is taken, total $5,000.
   c. Cash charges to the partners' accounts during the year are as follows:

Arby	$5,200
Bobb	4,400
Carlos	5,800
Mack	2,500
	$17,900

   d. Of Arby's and Bobb's receivables, $1,200 and $450, respectively, proved to be uncollectible. A new client billed in March for $1,600 went bankrupt, and a settlement of 50 cents on the dollar was made.

Required

1. Determine the profit for 2006.
2. Prepare a schedule showing how the profit for 2006 is to be divided.
3. Prepare a statement of the partners' capital accounts for the year ended 12/31/06.

P 20-5* 

Converting from Cash to Accrual Basis The partnership of Arfee, Barker, and Chow engaged you to adjust its accounting records and convert them uniformly to the accrual basis in anticipation of admitting Pupp as a new partner. Some accounts are on the accrual basis, and others are on the cash basis. The partnership's books were closed at 12/31/06 by the bookkeeper, who prepared the following trial balance:

Arfee, Barker, and Chow
Trial Balance 12/31/06

	DEBIT	CREDIT
Cash	$ 10,000	
Accounts receivable	40,000	
Inventory	26,000	
Land	9,000	
Buildings	50,000	
Accumulated depreciation—Buildings		$ 2,000
Equipment	56,000	
Accumulated depreciation—Equipment		6,000
Goodwill	5,000	
Accounts payable		55,000
Allowance for future inventory losses		3,000
Arfee, capital		40,000
Barker, capital		60,000
Chow, capital		30,000
Totals	$196,000	$196,000

* The financial statement information presented for problems accompanied by asterisks is also provided on Model 20 (filename: MODEL20) at the http://pahler.swlearning.com website, allowing the problem to be worked on the computer.

The partnership was organized on 1/1/05, with no provision in the partnership agreement for the distribution of partnership profits and losses. During 2005, profits were distributed equally among the partners. The partnership agreement was amended effective 1/1/06 to provide for the following profit and loss ratio: Arfee, 50%; Barker, 30%; and Chow, 20%. The amended partnership agreement also stated that the accounting records should be maintained on the *accrual basis* and that any adjustments necessary for 2005 should be allocated according to the 2005 distribution of profits.

1. The following amounts were *not* recorded as prepayments or accruals:

	December 31	
	2006	2005
Prepaid insurance	$700	$ 650
Advances from customers	200	1,100
Accrued interest expense		450

   Customers' advances were recorded as sales in the year the cash was received.

2. In 2006, the partnership recorded a $3,000 provision for anticipated declines in inventory prices. You convinced the partners that the provision was unnecessary and should be removed from the books.

3. The partnership charged equipment purchased for $4,400 on 1/3/06 to expense. This equipment has an estimated life of 10 years. The partnership depreciates its capitalized equipment under the *double-declining-balance method* at twice the *straight-line depreciation* rate.

4. The partners want to establish an allowance for doubtful accounts at 2% of current accounts receivable and 5% of past due accounts. At 12/31/05, the partnership had $54,000 of accounts receivable, of which only $4,000 was past due. At 12/31/06, 15% of accounts receivable were past due, of which $4,000 represented sales made in 2005 that were generally considered collectible. The partnership had written off uncollectible accounts in the year the accounts became worthless, as follows:

	Accounts Written Off in	
	2006	2005
2006 accounts	$ 800	
2005 accounts	1,000	$250

5. Goodwill was recorded on the books in 2006 and credited to the partners' capital accounts in the profit and loss ratio in recognition of an increase in the value of the business resulting from improved sales volume. The partners agreed to write off the goodwill *before* admitting the new partner.

Required Prepare a worksheet showing the adjustments and the adjusted trial balance for the partnership on the accrual basis at 12/31/06. All adjustments affecting income should be made directly to partners' capital accounts. Number your adjusting entries. (Prepare formal journal entries and show supporting computations.)

P 20-6* 

Preparing Worksheets to Determine Current Trial Balance Pace & Runn is a partnership that has *not* maintained adequate accounting records because it has been unable to employ a competent bookkeeper. The company sells hardware items to the retail trade and sells wholesale to builders and contractors. As Pace & Runn's CPA, you prepare the company's financial statements as of 6/30/06.

The company's records provide the following postclosing trial balance at 12/31/05:

Pace & Runn
Postclosing Trial Balance—12/31/05

	DEBIT	CREDIT
Cash	$10,000	
Accounts receivable	8,000	
Allowance for bad debts		$ 600
Merchandise inventory	35,000	
Prepaid insurance	150	
Automobiles	7,800	
Accumulated depreciation—Automobiles		4,250
Furniture and fixtures	2,200	
Accumulated depreciation—Furniture and fixtures		650
Accounts payable		13,800
Bank loan payable (due 1/2/06)		8,000
Accrued liabilities		200
Pace, capital		17,500
Runn, capital		18,150
Totals	$63,150	$63,150

You collect the following information at 6/30/06:

1. Your analysis of cash transactions, derived from the company's bank statements and checkbook stubs, follows:

Deposits:	
Cash receipts from customers	$65,000
($40,000 of this amount represents collections on receivables including redeposited protested checks totaling $600)	
Bank loan, 1/2/06 (due 5/1/06, 5%)	7,867
Bank loan, 5/1/06 (due 9/1/06, 5%)	8,850
Sale of old automobile	20
Total Deposits	$81,737
Disbursements:	
Payments to merchandise creditors	$45,000
Payment to IRS on Runn's 2003 declaration of estimated income taxes	3,000
General expenses	7,000
Bank loan, 1/2/06	8,000
Bank loan, 5/2/06	8,000
Payment for new automobile	7,200
Protested checks	900
Pace, withdrawals	5,000
Runn, withdrawals	2,500
Total Disbursements	$86,600

2. The protested checks include customers' checks totaling $600 that were redeposited and an employee's check for $300 that was redeposited.

3. At 6/30/06, accounts receivable from customers for merchandise sales amount to $18,000 and include accounts totaling $800 placed with an attorney for collection. Correspondence with the client's attorney reveals that one of the accounts for $175 is uncollectible. Experience indicates that 1% of credit sales will prove uncollectible.

4. On 4/1/06, a new automobile was purchased. Its list price was $7,500, and $300 was allowed for the trade-in of an old automobile, even though the dealer stated that its condition was so poor that he did *not* want it. The client sold the old automobile, which cost $1,800 and was fully depreciated at 12/31/05, to an auto wrecker for $20. The old automobile was in use up to the date of its sale.

5. Depreciation is recorded by the *straight-line method* and is computed on acquisitions to the nearest full month. The estimated life for furniture and fixtures is 10 years and for automobiles is 3 years. (Salvage value is ignored in computing depreciation. No asset other than the car in item 4 was fully depreciated prior to 6/30/06.)

6. Other data as of 6/30/06 follow:

Merchandise inventory	$37,500
Prepaid insurance	80
Accrued expenses	166

7. Accounts payable to merchandise vendors total $18,750. A $750 credit memorandum was received from a merchandise vendor for returned merchandise; the company will apply the credit to July merchandise purchases. Neither the credit memorandum nor the return of the merchandise had been recorded on the books.

8. Profits and losses are divided *equally* between the partners.

Required Prepare a worksheet that provides, on the *accrual basis*, information regarding transactions for the six months ended 6/30/06, the results of the partnership operations for the period, and the financial position of the partnership at 6/30/06. (Do *not* prepare formal financial statements or formal journal entries, but show supporting computations when necessary.)

Thinking Critically

Cases

C 20-1 **Planning for Settlement in the Event of a Partner's Death** Cross and Penn are in the process of forming a partnership. Each partner desires to obtain control of the business in the event of the death of the other partner and to make settlement with the deceased partner's estate in an orderly manner with little conflict and minimal taxation.

Required How might the partners accomplish these objectives?

C 20-2 **Preparing the Partnership Agreement** Nichols and Dimer have formed a partnership. They personally prepared the partnership agreement to save legal costs, but they ask you to study the agreement for completeness when you record the initial capital contributions in the general ledger.

Required How would you respond to this request?

C 20-3 **Dividing Profits and Losses** Barr and Courtner, both lawyers, have decided to form a partnership. They have asked your advice on how the profits and losses should be divided and have provided you with the following information:

Initial capital contributions	
Barr	$20,000
Courtner	80,000
Time devoted to the business	
Barr	75%
Courtner	100%

Personal facts

Barr has an excellent reputation in the community. Substantially all new clients will come from her efforts.

Courtner is strong technically and is an excellent supervisor of staff lawyers who are expected to do most of the detailed legal research and initial preparation of legal documents.

Required How would you advise the partners to share profits and losses?

C 20-4 **Recording the Initial Capital Contributions** Hye and Lowe have agreed to form a partnership in which profits are divided equally. Hye contributes $100,000 cash, and Lowe contributes a parcel of land, which the partnership intends to subdivide into residential lots on which to build custom homes for sale. Data regarding the parcel of land follow:

Cost of land to Lowe (acquired three years ago)	$100,000
Current market value, based on most recent county property tax assessment notice	120,000
Appraised value, based on recent appraisal by independent appraiser	150,000

Hye believes that the land should be recorded on the partnership books at $120,000. Lowe believes that the land should be recorded at $100,000 so that the *tax basis* to Lowe carries over to the partnership. Neither believes that the *current appraised value* is appropriate because an objective, verifiable transaction has *not* occurred. They have asked your advice on how to record the land.

Required

1. How would you respond?
2. Assuming that the land is sold two years later for $140,000 (the land having been *over*-appraised by $10,000), would this change your answer in requirement 1?

C 20-5 **Selecting the Form of Business Organization** Sandy Seeker has invested $600,000 in a new business venture in which two, possibly three, former business associates will join him. He has purchased the patent rights to a revolutionary adhesive substance known as "sticko." He is considering the various forms of business organization he might use in establishing the business. You have been engaged to study the accounting and business problems he should consider in choosing either a *general partnership* or a *corporation*. Seeker requests specific advice on the following aspects as they relate to one of these two forms of business organization:

1. Personal liability if the venture is a disaster.
2. The borrowing capacity of the entity.
3. Requirements for operating a multistate business.
4. The recognition of the entity for income tax–reporting purposes and major income tax considerations in selecting one of these forms of business organization.

Required Discuss the legal implications of each form of organization mentioned for each specific aspect on which Seeker requests advice.

chapter

21

Partnerships: Changes in Ownership

Never tell people how to do things. Tell them what to do and they will surprise you with their ingenuity.
General George S. Patton

LEARNING OBJECTIVES

To Understand

- The way to treat partners equitably when changes in ownership occur.
- The bonus method.
- The goodwill method.
- The legal ramifications of changes in ownership.
- The tax aspects of changes in ownership.

TOPIC OUTLINE

I. *Tangible* Assets Having *Current Values* Different from *Book Values*
II. *Intangible* Element Exists: Recording Methods and Alternative Approaches
III. *Intangible* Element Exists: Specific Situations
IV. Legal Aspects of Changes in Ownership
APPENDIX 21A: Tax Aspects of Changes in Ownership

Appendices can be found at http://www.pahler.swlearning.com

CHAPTER OVERVIEW

A business conducted as a partnership usually has changes in ownership during its existence. In this chapter, we discuss the changes in ownership that do not result in the termination of the partnership's business activities. Such changes in ownership may be categorized as follows:

1. **An *increase* in the number of partners.**
   a. **Admission of a new partner.** More partners may be needed to serve clients properly, or additional capital may be required above and beyond existing partners' personal resources.
   b. **Business combinations.** Two partnerships may combine, resulting in a pooling of interests—that is, the partners of each individual partnership become partners in a larger, combined business.
2. **A *decrease* in the number of partners.**
   a. **Willful or forced withdrawal.** A partner may withdraw from a partnership to (1) engage in another line of work, (2) continue in the same line of work but as a sole proprietor, or (3) retire. In addition, a partner may be forced out of a partnership for economic reasons or for *not* having performed adequately the responsibilities entrusted to him or her.
   b. **Death or incapacity.** A partner may die or become so seriously ill that he or she *cannot* continue partnership duties.
3. **Purchase of an existing partnership interest.** A partner may decide to sell his or her partnership interest to someone *outside* the partnership.

The first two categories may generate issues of how to treat each partner equitably when (1) *tangible* assets have *current values* different from *book values* and (2) *intangible* elements exist. For simplicity, we discuss these issues separately. The third category consists entirely of personal transactions conducted outside the partnership. Because no partnership accounting issues are associated with this category, we discuss it only briefly at this point before discussing the first two categories.

Purchase (Buyout) of an Existing Partner's Interest

The purchase of an interest from one or more of a partnership's existing partners is a *personal transaction* between the incoming partner and the selling partner(s). No additional money or properties are invested in the partnership. In this respect, the transaction is similar to individuals' sale of a corporation's stock. The only entry made on the partnership's books **transfers** an amount from the *selling* partner's capital account to the *new* partner's capital account. For example, assume the following information:

1. A and B are in partnership and share profits and losses equally.
2. A and B have capital account balances of $30,000 each.
3. C purchases B's partnership interest for $37,500, making payment *directly* to B.

The entry to record the transaction on the books of the partnership follows:

Capital, Partner B	30,000	
Capital, Partner C		30,000

The purchase price paid by C is completely irrelevant to the entry recorded on the books, regardless of why C paid *more than* the book value of the partnership interest. The fact that the partnership may have undervalued tangible assets or possible superior earnings power is *not* relevant to the accounting issues. A *personal transaction* has occurred, which is independent of accounting for the business of the partnership.

Alternatively, C could purchase a portion of each existing partner's interest in the partnership. For example, assume that C purchased one-third of A's interest for $12,500 and one-third of B's interest for $12,500, making payments *directly* to A and B. The entry to record the transaction on the books follows:

Capital, Partner A	10,000	
Capital, Partner B	10,000	
Capital, Partner C		20,000

Again, the purchase of an existing partnership interest is a personal transaction between the old and the new partners.

An *Increase* or *Decrease* in the Number of Partners: Methods to Prevent Inequities

The number of partners in a partnership may *increase* or *decrease* without the purchase of an existing partner's interest. Recall that in Chapter 20 we stated that to prevent partners from being treated inequitably as a result of revisions to the profit and loss sharing formula, either the partnership assets should be revalued to their *current values* or the *new* profit and loss sharing formula should include a special provision whereby the *old* profit and loss sharing formula is used in specified instances. Because a change in ownership of a partnership produces a *new* profit and loss sharing formula, the same techniques to prevent inequities may be applied to situations of changes in ownership. In addition, we introduce a new method—the **bonus method**—that also may be used to prevent inequities.

The determination of the journal entry to reflect a change in the ownership of a partnership is to some extent an after-the-fact mechanical process using the terms and methods selected by the partners. A far more important role for the accountant when a change in ownership is contemplated involves explaining and illustrating the various methods (and their ramifications) of dealing with situations in which assets have current values different from book values and/or intangible elements exist. The accountant may even assist partners in determining the amount of any goodwill by demonstrating some of the common methods used to calculate goodwill. Remember that in these situations, the accountant is only an advisor. It is *not* his or her role to select a method to determine the amount of goodwill or to select one of the three methods available for achieving equity among the partners.

I. *Tangible* Assets Having *Current Values* Different from *Book Values*

Admission of a New Partner

In most cases, a partner is admitted into a partnership by making a capital contribution to it. In accountant and attorney partnerships, virtually all partners admitted make substantial contributions after spending years in lower levels of the business obtaining the necessary training and experience. A capital contribution creates a new partner's interest. In substance, this is similar to a corporation's issue of additional shares of its stock to new stockholders.

One of the three methods available to prevent an inequity must be applied when a new partner is admitted. Each method, although different procedurally, produces the same result. To illustrate how each method is applied to a situation in which a new partner is admitted into a partnership by making a capital contribution, assume the following facts:

1. The partnership of A and B desires to admit C.
2. A's capital account is $25,000, as is B's.
3. Profits and losses are shared equally between A and B. On admission of C, profits and losses are **shared equally** among the three partners.
4. All partnership assets have *carrying values* equal to their *current values*, except for a parcel of land worth $12,000 *more than* its book value of $100,000.

5. Because the *current value* of the existing partners' equity is $62,000 ($25,000 + $25,000 + $12,000), A and B agree to admit C into the partnership on contribution of $31,000 cash.

The *credit* to the new partner's capital account regarding the $31,000 capital contribution is determined only *after* the partners agree on one of the following three methods.

Revaluing of Assets Method

Under the **revaluing of assets method**, the parcel of land merely is written up to its *current value* using the following entry:

Land	12,000	
Capital, Partner A		6,000
Capital, Partner B		6,000

Because the *old* partners shared profits and losses *equally* until C was admitted, each of their capital accounts increases by 50% of the upward revaluation. The entry to record C's contribution follows:

Cash	31,000	
Capital, Partner C		31,000

The *revaluing of assets method* is the simplest of the three methods. Although it is *not* in accordance with GAAP, this disadvantage is usually *not* important to the partnership form of business. If the partners agree to this method, the *new* partnership agreement should specify that the new partner is to receive a one-third interest in the *new* net assets of the partnership ***after* the land has been written up by $12,000**, thus receiving a full credit to her capital account for the $31,000 capital contribution ($62,000 + $31,000 = $93,000; $93,000 × 1/3 = $31,000).

Special Profit and Loss Sharing Provision Method

Under the **special profit and loss sharing provision** approach, the land is carried at its historical cost. The new profit and loss sharing formula contains a provision, however, that (1) acknowledges that the land's *current value* is $12,000 in excess of its *book value* at the time of C's admission and (2) specifies that the old partners are entitled to share equally in the first $12,000 profit on the sale of the land. Assuming that the land is sold for a $15,000 profit several years after C's admission to the partnership, the profit on the sale is divided as follows:

	Total	Partner A	Partner B	Partner C
First $12,000	$12,000	$6,000	$6,000	
Excess over $12,000	3,000	1,000	1,000	$1,000
	$15,000	$7,000	$7,000	$1,000

The entry to record C's contribution is the same as shown for the preceding method. If the partners agree to this method, the new partnership agreement should state that the new partner is to receive a full credit to her capital account for the $31,000 capital contribution, **with *no* revaluation made to the assets of the partnership.**

The Bonus Method

Under the **bonus method,** no adjustment is made to the *carrying amount* of the land, nor is any special provision included in the new profit and loss sharing formula because the land is worth more than its book value. When the land is subsequently sold, C will receive one-third of the entire profit. From an equity viewpoint, C is *not* entitled to one-third of the first $12,000 profit; therefore, C's capital account is *reduced* at her admission by the amount that will be credited to her capital account in the event the land is sold for $12,000 in excess of its current book value.

Thus one-third of $12,000, or $4,000, of C's $31,000 initial capital contribution is *not* credited to her capital account. Instead, the $4,000 is credited to the *old* partners' capital accounts. The $4,000 is shared by partners A and B in the *old* profit and loss sharing ratio. The entry to record C's admission into the partnership is as follows:

Cash	31,000	
Capital, Partner A		2,000
Capital, Partner B		2,000
Capital, Partner C		27,000

Note that the total partnership capital is now $81,000 ($50,000 + $31,000) and that the $27,000 amount is one-third of $81,000.

Assuming that the land is sold for a $15,000 *profit* several years after C's admission to the partnership, the profit on the sale is divided as follows:

	Total	Partner A	Partner B	Partner C
Total Profit	$15,000	$5,000	$5,000	$5,000

In this situation, C initially gives up part of her capital contribution, only to recover the amount given up at a later date. The *old* partners initially receive a bonus, but on the subsequent sale of the land, they are *not* allocated all of the first $12,000 profit. In this sense, *bonus* is a misnomer because it is *not* permanent. If the partners agree to the *bonus method*, the new partnership agreement should state that the *new* partner is to receive a one-third interest in the new assets of the partnership of $81,000 ($50,000 + $31,000), **with *no* revaluation to be made to the partnership assets.**

Review Points Regarding the Three Methods. Note the following:

1. If the land subsequently is sold for $112,000 ($12,000 *more than* its $100,000 book value immediately *before* C was admitted into the partnership) the individual capital account balances are identical under each method. Thus each method ensures that partners A and B share equally in the first $12,000 of profit on the sale of the land. Furthermore, each method ensures that partners A, B, and C share equally any profit on the sale of the land *in excess of* $12,000.
2. The method chosen depends on the partners' personal whims. Often an incoming partner desires to have the full amount of his or her capital contribution credited to his or her capital account, if only for psychological reasons. The *new* partnership agreement should specify the method agreed upon by the partners.
3. If the *new* profit and loss sharing formula includes a feature providing for imputed interest on capital investments, the second method results in an inequity to the old partners because their individual capital accounts are *less than* that of the *new* partner.
4. The key to achieve the same result with each method is the assumption that the partnership assets actually are worth the agreed-upon amounts. If they are *not*, these methods do *not* always prevent inequities from occurring. We discuss this situation more fully next.

What If Agreed-Upon *Current Values* Are Erroneous?

Because the determination of the current value of assets is so subjective, the possibility exists that the land is *not* really worth $12,000 *more than* its book value. What if shortly after C's admission into the partnership, the land is sold for only $9,000 *more than* its *book value* immediately *before* C was admitted? Does each method still treat each partner equitably? The answer is no. Partner C is *not* treated equitably under the **revaluation of assets method** because she is allocated one-third of the book loss of $3,000; she effectively loses $1,000 of her initial $31,000 capital contribution. Partner C is *not* treated equitably under the **bonus method** because she does *not* recoup all of the $4,000 bonus she initially gave to the *old* partners. She recoups only $3,000 (one-third of the $9,000 book profit) and, therefore, loses $1,000 of her initial $31,000 capital contribution. Under the **special provision in the new profit and loss sharing method**, however, C *cannot* lose any of her initial capital contribution; she is best protected under this method.

The land may actually have a *current value* $12,000 more than its book value *immediately before* C is admitted into the partnership but may decline in value *afterward*. The same question must be asked: Does each method treat each partner equitably? Under the special provision in the new profit and loss sharing formula, partners A and B are treated inequitably because they share the entire loss of value that occurred *after* C's admission. From an equity standpoint, C should share in this loss of value, which she does only under the *revaluation of assets method* and the *bonus method*.

Obviously, each partner strives to select the method that best protects his or her personal interest. Often there is a conflict between an incoming partner and the old partners concerning which method to use. The ultimate resolution takes place through negotiation. In large partnerships—such as the national accounting firms—differences between current values and book values usually are ignored for the sake of simplicity. Of course, such partnerships usually do *not* have significant amounts of land and depreciable assets, which are most likely to have *current values* different from *book values*.

Business Combinations

Historically, business combinations are considered to occur only between corporations. A large number of business combinations involve partnerships, however, especially public accounting partnerships. Business combinations in the public accounting sector range from a two-person partnership combining with a sole proprietorship to a large international firm combining with another large international firm (as occurred in 1998 when Price Waterhouse, the *sixth* largest accounting firm, combined with Coopers & Lybrand, the *fourth* largest accounting firm, to form PricewaterhouseCoopers, the largest accounting firm). Technically, FASB *Statement No. 141*, "Business Combinations," sets forth GAAP to be followed—whether the combination involves *incorporated* entities or *unincorporated* entities. Most partnerships, however, often choose to ignore GAAP (as discussed in Chapter 20). Accordingly, a business combination of two or more existing partnerships may be classified as either a *purchase* (discussed in Chapters 4 and 5) or a *pooling of interests* (a method no longer permitted under *FAS 141*). Recall that in *purchase accounting*, the target company's assets and liabilities are revalued to their *fair values* at the combination date. Under *pooling of interests* accounting, however, **no revaluation to *current values* occurs.** Whether the substance of a combination is one or the other depends on whether the owners of the combining businesses continue as owners in the new, enlarged business.

One Set of Owners Does *Not* Continue

If the owners of one business do *not* continue as owners of the enlarged business, a *purchase* has occurred. Purchases do *not* increase the number of partners. Thus no change in ownership of the acquiring partnership occurs, and such transactions do not concern us here. The acquiring firm merely applies the provisions of *FAS 141* with respect to the assets acquired. The assets of the acquiring business are *not* revalued to their current values.

Both Sets of Owners Continue

If the owners of *both* businesses continue as owners of the enlarged business, the partners may deem that, in substance, a *pooling of interests* has occurred. Pooling of interests results in an increase in the number of partners; thus the issues associated with changes in ownership exist. If the assets of *either* or *both* of the combining firms have *current values* that differ from their *book values*, one of the methods to prevent inequities from occurring must be used (*revaluing the assets*, using a *special provision in the new profit and loss sharing formula*, or the *bonus method*). A strict application of *the pooling of interests* procedures does *not* permit the revaluing of assets of either combining firm. If the partners revalue the assets, however, they may do so. These three methods are procedurally the same as those used when a *new* partner is admitted, other than through a business combination.

A unique aspect of business combinations is that both entities can have (1) under- or overvalued assets and (2) goodwill. Under the *bonus method*, this situation requires that the following sequential steps be followed so that the proper set of partners receives the proper bonus:

1. For each partnership, calculate the bonus that the partnership would receive or give, assuming that the other partnership had no under- or overvalued assets or goodwill.
2. If both partnerships are to *receive* or *give* bonuses, use the *difference* between the two bonus amounts in step 1 to adjust for the bonuses. Thus the bonus that one set of partners is to receive (or give) is more than offset by the bonus to be received (or given) by the other set of partners, who receive (or give) a net bonus amount in total.
3. If one partnership is to *receive* a bonus and the other partnership is to *give* a bonus, use the *sum* of the two bonus amounts in step 1 to adjust for the bonuses.

Remember that the objective is to prevent partners from *not* sharing in what they are *not* entitled to share.

Decrease in Number of Partners

If a partnership's assets have current values different from their book values when a partner withdraws from the partnership, the partners are *not* treated equitably unless this difference in value is considered in settling with the withdrawing partner or his or her estate. In these situations, all methods of preventing an inequity are available. To illustrate how each method is applied in such a situation, we assume the following facts:

1. A, B, and C are in partnership.
2. The capital account of each partner is $25,000.
3. Carrying values of the partnership's tangible assets equal their *current values*, except for a parcel of land worth $12,000 more than its *book value*.
4. Profits and losses are shared equally.
5. C decides to withdraw from the partnership.

Revaluing of Assets Method

Under the *revaluing of assets method*, the land is merely written up to its current value using the following entry:

Land	12,000	
Capital, Partner A		4,000
Capital, Partner B		4,000
Capital, Partner C		4,000

Each partner's capital account is *increased* by one-third of the upward revaluation because the partners shared profits and losses equally until C decided to withdraw from the partnership. The entry to record C's withdrawal from the partnership is as follows:

Capital, Partner C	29,000	
Payable to Partner C		29,000

As indicated previously, this is the simplest of the three methods. The fact that it departs from GAAP may be of little concern to a partnership.

.Special Profit and Loss Sharing Provision Method

Under the *special profit and loss sharing provision method*, the land is carried at its *historical cost*. The new profit and loss sharing formula contains a provision, however, (1) acknowledging that the land's estimated *current value* is $12,000 in excess of its *current book value* and (2) specifying that the withdrawing partner is entitled to one-third of the first $12,000 profit on the sale of the land. The entry to record C's withdrawal from the partnership follows:

Capital, Partner C	25,000	
Payable to Partner C		25,000

Effectively, a contingent liability exists with respect to the amount to be paid to C upon sale of the land. This method has limited application in situations involving withdrawing partners. If different appraisals of current value of partnership assets exist, this method may be a practical alternative to the other two methods, especially if such assets are expected to be sold within a relatively short period of time. Normally, however, this method is impractical because a withdrawing partner does *not* want to wait until such assets are disposed of to obtain his or her final settlement from the partnership.

The Bonus Method

Under the *bonus method*, no adjustment is made to the carrying amount of the land, nor is any special provision included in the *new* profit and loss sharing formula because the land is worth *more than* its book value. Consequently, when the land is later sold, A and B share *all* the profit. From an equity viewpoint, A and B are *not* entitled to one-third of the first $12,000 profit; therefore, their capital accounts are reduced at C's withdrawal by the amount that represents C's share of the $12,000 of unrealized profit. Thus one-third of $12,000, or $4,000, is charged to the capital accounts of A and B in their respective profit and loss sharing ratio. A and B will recoup this bonus to C later if the land is sold for $12,000 in excess of its *current book value*. The entry to record the bonus and C's withdrawal from the partnership follows:

Capital, Partner A	2,000	
Capital, Partner B	2,000	
Capital, Partner C		4,000
To record the bonus to the *withdrawing* partner.		
Capital, Partner C	29,000	
Payable to Partner C		29,000
To record the withdrawal of Partner C.		

In this situation, A and B gave up part of their capital account balances, expecting to recover the amounts given up at a later date. Thus the bonus is *not* permanent because it will be recovered later.

Review Points Regarding the Three Methods. Note the following:

1. If the land is later sold for $112,000 ($12,000 *more than* its $100,000 *book value* immediately before C withdrew from the partnership), the settlement to C is the same under each method. Also, the capital account balances of A and B are identical under each method. Thus each method ensures that the withdrawing partner receive one-third of the first $12,000 profit on the sale of the land. Furthermore, each method ensures that C not share in any of the profit on the sale of the land in excess of $12,000.
2. The real problem is obtaining a reasonable assurance of the *current value* of partnership assets. If the agreed-upon values are *overstated*, the revaluing of the asset method and the *bonus method* results in an excess settlement to the withdrawing partner. Under the *special profit and loss sharing provision method*, however, no such excess payment is possible; thus A and B are best protected under this method. If the agreed-upon values are understated, no method protects the withdrawing partner. The remaining partners share the entire increase above the agreed-upon value.

3. If the land declined in value *after* C withdrew, C is *not* treated equitably under the special profit and loss sharing provision method because she is sharing in a loss that occurred *after* she withdrew.

In all the preceding examples, the partnership's tangible assets were *undervalued*. When tangible assets have *current values* less than their *book values*, the first method—which writes down the assets—makes the most sense. (This procedure is in accordance with GAAP.) The second choice is the *bonus method*. The use of the *special profit and loss sharing provision* method is usually impractical.

II. *INTANGIBLE* ELEMENT EXISTS: RECORDING METHODS AND ALTERNATIVE APPROACHES

We restricted our discussion in the preceding section to situations in which the *current values* of a partnership's tangible assets differ from their *book values*. In this section, we discuss situations in which either the existing partnership or an incoming partner possesses an intangible element. In discussing these situations, we assume that all partnership tangible assets have *current values* equal to their *book values*. Although this assumption is not necessarily realistic, it allows us to concentrate on the issue of accounting for this intangible element.

The discussion of intangible elements usually has wider application than the earlier discussion of tangible assets because most partnerships—other than those engaged in real estate development—do *not* have substantial investments in the types of assets that appreciate or depreciate, such as inventory, land, buildings, and equipment. The largest asset for such partnerships is usually accounts receivable.

Intangible elements are usually associated with an *existing* partnership. The most common intangible element is a partnership's *superior earnings*. Obviously, a partner's interest in such a partnership is worth *more than* its book value. Even when a partnership has only *average* earnings, a partner's interest may be worth *more than* its book value to an incoming partner merely because the organization already has clients and the potential to develop superior earnings.

An incoming partner may also possess intangible elements. For example, the incoming partner may have a successful sole proprietorship with superior earnings power. He or she may have individual potential for which the existing partners are willing to pay. This is similar to situations in which corporations pay one-time bonuses to executives to induce them to accept a position and in professional sports when a rookie may receive a one-time bonus just for signing with a particular team.

In these situations, whether the existing partnership or an incoming partner possesses the intangible element, the intangible element is referred to as goodwill. The accounting issue is how to compensate the partner or partners who created or possess the goodwill. If there is no compensation, the other partner or partners share unfairly in a portion of the partnership's future earnings.

Recording Methods

The general approach to compensating the appropriate partners parallels the approach for situations in which tangible assets have current values different from book values—that is, we may apply the same three methods that we discussed and illustrated in the preceding section of the chapter. The first method is called *recording the goodwill*, however, rather than *revaluing assets*. Other than this descriptive change, the three methods are procedurally the same.

The larger the partnership, the less likely are the partners to compute the value of goodwill. For example, in the interest of simplicity, most national public accounting firms completely ignore goodwill for all changes in ownership situations. Instead, a simpler approach is for an *incoming* partner to accept a *lower-than-normal* profit and loss sharing percentage; that percentage increases on a sliding scale over a period of years until the *incoming* partner eventually shares profits and losses equally with other partners. Such an approach has the same overall effect as the three mechanical methods of dealing with goodwill, although the exact effect on each partner is different.

Assumed Equality of Profit-Sharing Percentage and Interest in Partnership Net Assets

In examples used later involving the admission of a partner when goodwill exists, we assume that the incoming partner's agreed-upon profit and loss sharing percentage equals his or her agreed-upon ownership interest in the partnership's net assets. In practice, this is common.[1]

Alternative Approaches for Illustrating Goodwill Situations

Apart from the three methods (*recording the goodwill method*, the *bonus method*, and the *special profit and loss sharing method*), two pedagogical approaches can be used to discuss and illustrate these methods. The difference between the two pedagogical approaches is the information furnished:

The *Working-Forward* Approach. The negotiated value of goodwill is given.
The *Working-in-Reverse* Approach. The negotiated value of goodwill is *not* given.

Understanding both of these approaches enables you to understand this material both forward and backward because that is the conceptual difference between the two approaches. In each of the later examples dealing with goodwill, we present *both* approaches. Before presenting these examples, however, we briefly discuss these approaches in general.

The *Working-Forward* Approach: The Value of Goodwill *Is* Given

When a partner is admitted into a partnership, the normal process among the parties involves negotiating the following four items (the sequence of which may vary):

1. The value of the existing goodwill is agreed upon between the *old* partners and the *new* partner.
2. The capital contribution of the *incoming* partner is agreed upon.
3. The profit or loss ratio is agreed upon.
4. One of the available accounting methods designed to compensate the partner who created or possesses the goodwill is selected.

Once these items are agreed upon, each partner's capital account balance may be adjusted or recorded using the accounting method selected. After determining each partner's capital account balance, we may express each partner's interest as a percentage of the partnership's net assets (as defined to either include or exclude goodwill). Thus each partner's ownership percentage in the partnership's net assets is a *derived amount*—**not the value of the goodwill agreed upon during negotiations.**

The *Working-in-Reverse* Approach: The Value of Goodwill Is *Not* Given

Under this approach, the following information is furnished:

1. The total of the capital balances of the *old* partners.
2. The capital contributed by the *new* partner.

---

[1] If these percentages do *not* coincide, the partners are financially impacted differently (in comparison to when the percentages are the *same*) only if the agreed-upon value of goodwill does *not* materialize. Situations in which these percentages are different have *not* been tested on past disclosed CPA examinations to any significant extent.

3. The percentage interest the *new* partner receives in the partnership's net assets (the old partners have the remaining interest).
4. Whether the net assets in that percentage interest include or exclude the value of the goodwill.

Given all this information, one then determines (as though trying to solve a puzzle) which method the partners used to compensate the partner or partners who created or possess the goodwill. Under the *valuing of the goodwill* method, the value of the goodwill may then be determined and recorded on the books of the partnership. Under *the bonus method*, the amount of the bonus given to the old partners or their new partner may then be determined and recorded on the partnership's books. Thus one works in reverse—**from the given ownership percentages**—to find the value of the goodwill.[2] This approach can be reduced to a step-by-step process, as shown in Illustration 21-1.

CHECK POINT

Flutie and Harper are partners with capital balances of $90,000 and $60,000, respectively. They share profits and losses in a 2:1 ratio, respectively. Tuba is *admitted* into the partnership for a cash contribution of $50,000. Tuba receives a 20% capital interest and a 20% interest in profits and losses. What is the *implied* goodwill in the transaction? Do the *old* partners or the *new* partner possess the goodwill?

a. $10,000
b. $12,500
c. $40,000
d. $50,000

a. New partner
b. Old partners

Answers: d, b

ILLUSTRATION 21-1 THE *WORKING-IN-REVERSE* APPROACH: STEP-BY-STEP PROCESS

I. Calculating the *Negotiated* Value of Goodwill

1. *Divide* the *new* partner's tangible capital contribution by his or her ownership percentage in the net assets of the partnership (for example, $35,000 ÷ 20% = $175,000).
2. *Divide* the total recorded capital balances of the *old* partners by their total **ownership interest in the net assets** of the partnership (for example, $120,000 ÷ 80% = $150,000).
3. *Add* the numerators used in steps 1 and 2 ($35,000 + $120,000 = $155,000) to arrive at the total recorded net assets of the *new* partnership excluding goodwill.
4. *Select* the **larger** of the amounts calculated in steps 1 and 2 ($175,000). From this amount, *subtract* the total calculated in step 3 ($155,000) to obtain the *negotiated* value of goodwill ($20,000).
5. If the amount calculated in step 1 is selected, the *old partners* possess goodwill; if the amount calculated in step 2 is selected, the *new partner* possesses goodwill.

II. Calculating the Bonus (for the bonus method)

A. **Using the negotiated value of the goodwill** (calculated above): *Multiply* the goodwill amount calculated in step 4 by the **profit and loss sharing percentage(s)** of the partner(s) **not** possessing goodwill (for example, $20,000 × 20% = $4,000).
B. **Using the ownership percentage of tangible net assets** (must be given—implicit amount of goodwill is *not* given):
   1. *Multiply* the sum of the numerators in step 3 by the ownership percentage the *new* partner has in the net assets (for example, $155,000 × 20% = $31,000). (The 20% is a given.)
   2. *Compare* the amount calculated in step B1 ($31,000) to the *new* partner's *tangible* capital contribution (the same amount used in step 1 [$35,000]) to determine the bonus to be given by the *incoming* partner ($4,000 in this example) or received.

Note: If desired, the *implicit* amount of goodwill can then be calculated from the bonus amount and the profit and loss sharing percentages.

[2] An understanding of this approach is required for taking the CPA examination because most CPA examination questions regarding ownership changes can be answered using only this approach.

III. *INTANGIBLE* ELEMENT EXISTS: SPECIFIC SITUATIONS

In each of the following examples involving goodwill, we first show the *working-forward approach* and then the *working-in-reverse approach.*

Admission of a New Partner: *Existing* Partnership Possesses Goodwill

In the first illustration, the partnership possesses the goodwill. To illustrate the application of the three methods to compensate the old partners for the goodwill they have created, we assume the following information:

1. A and B are in partnership, **sharing profits equally.**
2. C is to be admitted into the partnership.
3. A, B, and C agreed that the existing partnership will generate *superior earnings* of $10,000 for one year *after* C's admission.
4. C contributes $30,000 cash to the partnership.
5. Profits and losses are to be shared among A, B, and C in a ratio of 4:3:3, respectively. (Thus the *old* partners are to receive 70% of the profits and losses, and the *new* partner is to receive 30%.)
6. A and B have capital account balances of $45,000 and $15,000, respectively (for a total of $60,000), *immediately before* admitting C.

Recording the Goodwill Method

Under the **recording the goodwill method,** C's admission into the partnership results in recording the entire amount of the agreed-upon goodwill in the partnership's books, as follows:

Goodwill	10,000	
Capital, Partner A		5,000
Capital, Partner B		5,000
To record the agreed-upon value of the goodwill, shared equally between the *old* partners using their *old* profit and loss sharing ratio.		

The entry to record C's $30,000 capital contribution follows:

Cash	30,000	
Capital, Partner C		30,000
To record C's capital contribution.		

The following points are important for understanding the preceding entries:

1. C has a 30% interest in the net assets of the partnership ($30,000 ÷ $100,000 total of the capital accounts).
2. Recording goodwill in this manner is *not* in accordance with GAAP because the goodwill did *not* result from the purchase of a business.
3. The goodwill will be amortized over a one-year period because the partnership is expected to produce *superior earnings* only for one year. Recall from Chapter 4 that under FASB *Statement No. 142* goodwill is periodically evaluated for impairment—not amortized. **Thus amortizing is a departure from GAAP.**
4. Because of the goodwill amortization in the year after C's admission, earnings will be $10,000 *lower than* they would have been if goodwill had *not* been recorded on the books.

5. Effectively, $10,000 of future profits has been capitalized into the *old* partners' capital accounts. In this respect, the partners have guaranteed that they alone will receive the first $10,000 of *future earnings* (determined without regard to the goodwill amortization expense).
6. If $10,000 of *superior earnings* results in the following year, such superior earnings completely absorb the $10,000 goodwill amortization.
7. If the *superior earnings* in the following year are *less than* $10,000, C effectively loses a portion of her initial capital contribution of $30,000. This happens because the partnership's *normal earnings* must absorb a portion of the goodwill amortization, and C *cannot* share in a portion of the *normal earnings*.

To illustrate how this method may favor the *old* partners over the *new* partner if the entire amount of the superior earnings does not materialize, assume that during the year *after* C's admission, only $8,000 of *superior earnings* materialize. These superior earnings absorb only $8,000 of goodwill amortization. The remaining $2,000 of goodwill amortization is absorbed by *normal earnings*. Thus, C does *not* share in $2,000 of normal earnings. Because C's profit and loss sharing percentage is 30%, she effectively loses $600 (30% of $2,000) of her $30,000 initial capital contribution.

Special Profit and Loss Sharing Provision Method

Under the *special profit and loss sharing provision method*, no entry is made on the partnership's books with respect to the goodwill. As under the previous method, C's capital account is credited with the full amount of her $30,000 capital contribution. It can be stated that C has a one-third interest in the partnership's net assets ($30,000 ÷ $90,000 total of the capital accounts). The *new* profit and loss sharing formula stipulates that the old partners are entitled to share (in accordance with their *old* profit and loss sharing ratio) in the first $10,000 of earnings in excess of a specified amount, which is the expected *normal earnings* for the year of C's admission into the partnership.

If the *superior earnings* of $10,000 do *not* materialize during this year, the old partners will have credited to their capital accounts only those amounts that do materialize. Of course, the *normal earnings* and any earnings above the $10,000 of *superior earnings* during the next year are shared in accordance with the *new* profit and loss sharing ratio. This method protects the *new* partner's initial capital contribution of $30,000 in the event that *superior earnings* of $10,000 do *not* materialize. Obviously, the *old* partners would prefer the previous method, under which they are assured of the first $10,000 of earnings, regardless of whether such earnings are *superior*.

The Bonus Method

Under the *bonus method*, no entry is made on the partnership books with respect to goodwill. Unlike the previous two methods, C does *not* receive full credit to her capital account for her $30,000 capital contribution because she must give a bonus to the *old* partners. The amount of the bonus to the *old* partners is C's profit and loss sharing percentage of 30% times the agreed-upon value of the $10,000 goodwill. Thus the bonus to the *old* partners is $3,000, which they share in their *old* profit and loss sharing ratio as follows:

Cash	30,000	
Capital, Partner A		1,500
Capital, Partner B		1,500
Capital, Partner C		27,000
To record C's capital contribution and to record the bonus to the *old* partners.		

The following points are important to understand this entry:

1. C has a 30% interest in the partnership's net assets ($27,000 ÷ $90,000 total of the capital accounts).
2. GAAP is followed by *not* recording goodwill on the books.

3. If superior earnings of $10,000 materialize in the year following C's admission, C shares in them ($3,000, or 30% of $10,000). Consequently, she recoups the bonus she initially gave the *old* partners.
4. The *bonus method* compensates the *old* partners currently for the portion of the *superior earnings* that will later be credited to the *new* partner's capital account. Thus if all the *superior earnings* materialize, the bonus is temporary.
5. If the *superior earnings* in the year following C's admission are *less than* $10,000, C effectively loses a portion of her initial $30,000 capital contribution. This happens because she does *not* share in the amount of *superior earnings* she expected to materialize and for which she was willing to give a bonus to the *old* partners.

To illustrate how the *bonus method* may favor the *old* partners over the *new* partner if the entire amount of *superior earnings* does *not* materialize, assume that during the year following C's admission, only $8,000 of *superior earnings* materialized. C's share of the $8,000 that did materialize is $2,400 (30% of $8,000). Because C gave a bonus of $3,000, she recouped only $2,400 of the bonus, effectively losing $600 of her initial $30,000 capital contribution.

Approach if the Value of Goodwill Is *Not* Given

Assume that the partners in their negotiations agree upon an amount for the goodwill, but that they do *not* state this amount in the *new* partnership agreement. Instead, knowing the amount of agreed-upon goodwill, they merely calculate the percentage that the *incoming* partner has in the partnership's net assets. In these situations, the accountant may determine the goodwill using the available information regarding the individual ownership percentage the *new* partner has in the partnership's net assets. We demonstrate this approach using the information in our example.

If the value of the goodwill is to be recorded on the partnership's books and the new partner has a 30% interest in the net assets (tangible and intangible) of the partnership, the goodwill implicit in the transaction can be determined as follows:

1. Divide C's $30,000 capital contribution by her 30% interest in the net assets to arrive at $100,000.
2. *Subtract* from the amount determined in step 1 the sum of the old partners' capital account balances *immediately before* C is admitted ($60,000) plus her capital contribution ($30,000). Thus the goodwill is $10,000 ($100,000 – $90,000).

Alternatively, if goodwill is *not* to be recorded on the partnership's books and the *new* partner has a 30% interest in the net assets (*tangible* assets only) of the partnership, the bonus and the related goodwill *implicit* in the transaction can be determined as follows:

1. Determine the total *tangible net assets* of the partnership *including* C's contribution ($60,000 + $30,000).
2. *Multiply* the amount determined in step 1, $90,000, by C's given ownership percentage in the partnership's net assets ($90,000 × 30% = $27,000).
3. *Subtract* the $27,000 determined in step 2 from C's $30,000 capital contribution to determine the $3,000 bonus to be given to the *old* partners.
4. *Divide* the $3,000 bonus by C's profit and loss sharing percentage of 30% to obtain the value of the goodwill *implicit* in the transactions, $10,000.

Admission of a New Partner Possessing Goodwill

Although in most situations the existing partnership has created the goodwill, an incoming partner may possess goodwill. To illustrate the three methods of compensating an incoming partner for goodwill, assume the following information:

1. A and B are in partnership, **sharing profits equally**.
2. C is to be admitted into the partnership.

3. A, B, and C agree that C is expected to generate superior earnings of $10,000 for one year following her admission.
4. C contributes $30,000 cash to the partnership.
5. Profits and losses are to be shared among A, B, and C in a ratio of 3:3:4, respectively.
6. A and B have capital account balances of $45,000 and $15,000, respectively (a total of $60,000), *immediately before* admitting C.

Recording the Goodwill Method

Under the *recording the goodwill method*, the entire amount of the agreed-upon value of the goodwill is credited to C's capital account, along with C's capital contribution of $30,000, as follows:

Goodwill	10,000	
Cash	30,000	
Capital, Partner C		40,000
To record the agreed-upon value of the goodwill and C's capital contribution.		

Compared with the situation in which the old partners created the goodwill, the roles are now reversed. The *new* partner receives the first $10,000 of *future earnings* (determined without regard to the goodwill amortization expense), even if *superior earnings* do *not* materialize. If the *superior earnings* of $10,000 do *not* materialize, the *old* partners lose the anticipated increases to their capital accounts. In this situation, C has a 40% interest in the partnership's net assets ($40,000 ÷ $100,000 total of the capital accounts).

Special Profit and Loss Sharing Provision Method

Under the special profit and loss sharing provision method, no entry is made on the partnership's books with respect to the goodwill. C receives a credit to her capital account equal to her $30,000 capital contribution. C has a one-third interest in the partnership's net assets ($30,000 ÷ $90,000 total of the capital accounts). The *new* profit and loss sharing formula stipulates that the *new* partner is entitled to receive the first $10,000 of earnings in excess of a specified amount. That amount is the expected *normal earnings* for the year after C's admission into the partnership. If *superior earnings* of $10,000 do *not* materialize during this year, C will have credited to her capital account only the amount that does materialize. In this situation, this method protects the *old* partners' capital balances that existed when C was admitted into the partnership.

The Bonus Method

Under the bonus method, no entry is made on the partnership's books with respect to goodwill. Because the *new* partner possesses the goodwill, the *old* partners give her a bonus. Its amount is the total of the *old* partners' profit and loss sharing percentage of 60% times the agreed-upon value of the goodwill, which is $10,000. Thus the bonus to the *new* partner is $6,000, recorded as follows:

Cash	30,000	
Capital, Partner A	3,000	
Capital, Partner B	3,000	
Capital, Partner C		36,000
To record C's capital contribution and to record the bonus given to her.		

C has a 40% interest in the partnership's net assets ($36,000 ÷ $90,000). Compared with the situation in which the *old* partners created the goodwill, the roles now are reversed. The *old* partners will recoup the bonus they gave to the *new* partner only if *superior earnings* of $10,000 materialize. To the extent that they are *less than* $10,000, the old partners will lose a portion of the balances that existed in their capital accounts *immediately before* C was admitted.

Approach If the Value of Goodwill Is *Not* Given

If the agreed-upon value of the goodwill is *not* available (an unusual situation), the accountant may determine this amount so long as information is available regarding the individual ownership percentage the new partner has in the partnership's net assets. We demonstrate the general approach using the information in our example.

If the value of the goodwill is to be recorded on the partnership's books and the *new* partner has a 40% interest in the net assets (tangible and intangible) of the partnership, the goodwill *implicit* in the transaction can be determined as follows:

1. *Divide* the total of the old partners' capital accounts by their total interest in the net assets ($60,000 ÷ 60%) to arrive at $100,000.
2. *Subtract* from the amount determined in step 1 the sum of the *old* partners' capital account balances *immediately before* C is admitted ($60,000) plus her $30,000 tangible capital contribution. Thus the goodwill is $10,000 ($100,000 – $90,000).

Alternatively, if goodwill is *not* to be recorded on the partnership's books and the new partner has a 40% interest in the net assets (*tangible assets only*), the bonus to be given by the *old* partners and the goodwill implicit in the transaction can be determined as follows:

1. Determine the total net assets of the partnership, including C's tangible contribution ($60,000 + $30,000).
2. *Multiply* the amount determined in step 1, $90,000, by C's given ownership percentage in the partnership's net assets ($90,000 × 40% = $36,000).
3. *Subtract* from the $36,000 amount determined in step 2 C's $30,000 *tangible* capital contribution to determine the $6,000 bonus that C receives from the *old* partners.
4. *Divide* the $6,000 bonus by the *old* partners' combined profit and loss sharing percentage of 60% to obtain the value of the goodwill *implicit* in the transaction, $10,000. (Recall the profit and loss sharing ratio of 3:3:4.)

CHECK POINTS

Horne and Picolo are partners with capital balances of $140,000 and $100,000, respectively. They share profits and losses in a 2:1 ratio, respectively. Sax is *admitted* into the partnership for a $60,000 cash contribution. Sax shares in 25% of the profits and losses and is to have a 25% capital interest. Assuming that goodwill *is* recorded, how much should be credited to Sax's capital account?

a. $60,000
b. $75,000
c. $80,000
d. $100,000

Answer: c

Use the data in the preceding Check Point, but assume that goodwill is *not* recorded. How much should be credited to Sax's capital account under the bonus method?

a. $60,000
b. $75,000
c. $80,000
d. $100,000

Answer: b

Business Combinations

When two businesses combine so that the owners of each separate business continue as owners in the enlarged business (substantively, a *pooling of interests*) and when one of the businesses possesses goodwill, we may apply the same three methods that have been illustrated in this section to compensate the partners of the business possessing the goodwill. Procedurally, these three methods are the same as in situations in which a *new* partner is admitted other than through a business combination. The mechanics become more involved, however, as the number of combining partners increases.

A Decrease in the Number of Partners

If a partnership possesses unrecorded goodwill when a partner withdraws from it, the withdrawing partner is not treated equitably unless this difference in value is considered in settling with the withdrawing partner or his or her estate. In these situations, each method to compensate the partner is available—the recording the goodwill method, the special profit and loss sharing provision method, and the bonus method. To illustrate the application of each method, assume the following facts:

1. A, B, and C are in partnership, sharing profits equally.
2. The capital accounts of A, B, and C are $40,000, $30,000, and $20,000, respectively.
3. All the partnership's *tangible assets* have *carrying values* equal to their *current values*.
4. C withdraws from the partnership.
5. The partners agree that the partnership currently has unrecorded goodwill of $15,000.

Recording the Goodwill Method

Under the recording the goodwill method, goodwill is recorded on the books and shared among the partners in their profit and loss ratio, as follows:

Goodwill	15,000	
Capital, Partner A		5,000
Capital, Partner B		5,000
Capital, Partner C		5,000
To record the agreed-upon value of goodwill existing at the time of C's withdrawal from the partnership.		

The entry to record C's withdrawal follows:

Capital, Partner C	25,000	
Payable to Partner C		25,000

An alternative to recording all the goodwill is to record only C's share of the goodwill, which is $5,000 (one-third of $15,000), as follows:

Goodwill	5,000	
Capital, Partner C		5,000

Whether all or a portion of the goodwill is recorded is irrelevant from an equity standpoint; both methods produce the same result for the withdrawing partner. As previously indicated, the goodwill method is *not* in accordance with GAAP, which the partners need not follow. If *superior earnings* of $15,000 do *not* materialize after C's withdrawal, the remaining partners, as a result of writing off the goodwill, lose a portion of their capital balances existing when C withdraws.

Special Profit and Loss Sharing Provision Method

Under the *special profit and loss sharing provision method*, goodwill is *not* recorded on the books. Instead, C's withdrawal is conditional on the *new* profit and loss sharing formula between A and B, which contains a provision that C is to share in one-third of *future earnings* in excess of a specified level for a certain time period. If past *superior earnings* have largely depended on C's efforts, the partnership may *not* be able to generate *superior earnings* after she withdraws. Accordingly, this method best protects the remaining partners in the event that *superior earnings* do *not* materialize during the stipulated period of time *after* C's withdrawal.

The Bonus Method

Under the bonus method, the old partners give the withdrawing partner a bonus. The bonus equals C's share of the agreed-upon value of the goodwill, which is one-third of $15,000, or $5,000. The bonus is shared between the *remaining partners* in their respective profit and loss sharing ratio as follows:

Capital, Partner A	2,500	
Capital, Partner B	2,500	
Capital, Partner C		5,000
To record the bonus to C on her withdrawal from the partnership.		

This method does *not* deviate from GAAP. If $15,000 of *above-normal earnings* does *not* materialize during the stipulated time period *after* C withdraws, however, the *remaining partners* do not recoup *all* of the bonus they gave her.

Spin-Off Situations

A partner may withdraw from a partnership and immediately commence business in the same line of work as a sole proprietor. In this situation, the *withdrawing partner* often requests the partnership's clients and customers that he or she personally has been serving to give their future business to the newly formed sole proprietorship. When this happens, the method selected for equitably treating the *withdrawing* partner should be accompanied by provisions that protect the *remaining partners* from any loss of clients and customers as the result of the *withdrawing partner's* forming a sole proprietorship. In other words, the remaining partners must guard against recording goodwill or paying a bonus *and* losing clients or customers to the newly formed sole proprietorship.

CHECK POINTS

Bell, Ring, and Toner are partners having capital balances of $72,000, $48,000, and $40,000, respectively. Their profit and loss sharing ratio is 5:3:2, respectively. Toner is *withdrawing* from the partnership. The partners agree that the partnership possesses $50,000 of goodwill, which is *not* to be recorded. What is the total cash payment to Toner in full settlement of his partnership interest?

a. $40,000
b. $50,000
c. $52,500
d. $53,333

Answer: b

Use the information in the preceding question. What is Bell's capital balance, assuming that all of the goodwill is recorded?

a. $72,000
b. $88,667
c. $94,500
d. $97,000

Answer: d

What is Bell's capital balance, assuming that the *bonus method* is used? Use the information in this first Check Point.

a. $65,750
b. $66,000

c. $67,000
d. $72,000

Answer: a

IV. Legal Aspects of Changes in Ownership

Although a thorough discussion of the legal aspects of a change in ownership of a partnership is properly the subject of an upper-division course on business law, a brief discussion of the major legal aspects is appropriate at this point.

Withdrawal of a Partner

Because of the embodiment of the *entity concept* in the Revised Uniform Partnership Act (RUPA), **almost all departures of a partner are treated as a *buyout* of that partner's interest by the partnership** (analogous to the acquisition of *treasury stock* by a corporate entity). Consequently, the partnership as an entity continues its existence, unaffected by the departure of that partner.

Specifically, RUPA uses (1) the *broad* term "dissociation" to refer to *all* departures of a partner and (2) the *narrow* term "dissolution" to refer to departures that will result in the termination of the partnership's existence.

Dissolution

A **dissolution** is when (1) a partnership is dissolved and (2) its business must be wound up. Thus a **dissolution commences the winding up process.** When this process is completed, the partnership's existence is *terminated*. Only in limited instances (as specified in RUPA) does the departure of a partner trigger the *dissolution* of a partnership (these situations are beyond the scope of this chapter).

Dissociation

Under RUPA, the term **dissociation** is used to denote **the change in relationship caused by a partner's ceasing to be associated in the carrying on of the business.** In the vast majority of instances, the departure of a partner results in **a *buyout* (by the partnership) of the partner's interest in the partnership**—*not* a *dissolution*. Thus the departure of a partner is always a *dissociation*, but very few *dissociations* trigger the *dissolution* of the partnership.

Responsibility for Partnership Obligations

Section 703 of the RUPA provides that "a partner's *dissociation* does *not* of itself discharge the partner's liability for a partnership obligation incurred *before* dissociation." (A creditor, however, *may* agree to release the partner from an obligation.) Also of importance is that a dissociated partner *may be* liable for partnership obligations incurred *after dissociation*, unless certain steps are taken (these detailed steps are beyond the scope of this chapter). In general, notice must be given directly to persons who *have* dealt with the partnership. For persons who have *not* dealt with the partnership, a notice usually may be given by publication in a newspaper or some other appropriate manner.

Admission of a Partner

With respect to an incoming partner, Section 306(b) of the RUPA provides that "a person admitted as a partner into an existing partnership is not personally liable for any partnership obligation incurred before the person's admission as a partner." This provision insulates the personal assets of the new partner from creditors' claims existing at his or her admission.

In practice, the *existing partners* usually insist that an *incoming partner* be jointly responsible for all such preexisting partnership debts. If the *new partner* agrees to this, Section 306(b) of the RUPA may be circumvented by including a provision to that effect in the new partnership agreement. Because of the possibility of undisclosed liabilities (actual or contingent), the *new partner* in these situations should limit his or her responsibilities to the liabilities that are set forth in a scheduled exhibit to the partnership agreement.

END-OF-CHAPTER REVIEW

Summary of Key Points

1. The **bonus method** may be applied when

$$\text{New Partnership Capital} = \text{Old Partners' Capital} + \text{New Partner's Asset Investment}$$

2. The **goodwill method** is applied when

$$\text{New Partnership Capital} > \text{Old Partners' Capital} + \text{New Partner's Asset Investment}$$

3. Both methods attempt to achieve equity among the partners; however, both methods result in an inequity to one or more partners if goodwill does *not* materialize.

Glossary of New Terms

Bonus method A method to achieve equity among partners upon a change in the number of partners when partnership assets are *undervalued* or goodwill exists. Adjustments are made within the partners' equity accounts to the extent of the *undervaluation* or the agreed-upon value of goodwill, thereby neither changing the recorded amounts of the partnership assets nor recording goodwill as an asset.

Dissociation The change in relationship caused by a partner's ceasing to be associated in the carrying on of the business. Most *dissociations* result in a buyout—*not* a *dissolution* of the partnership.

Dissolution When a partnership is dissolved and its business must be wound up. Upon completion of the wind-up process, the partnership's existence is terminated.

Goodwill method A method to achieve equity among partners upon a change in the number of partners when goodwill is deemed to exist. Goodwill is recorded on the books of the partnership with an offsetting credit made to the partner(s) who possesses or created the goodwill.

ASSIGNMENT MATERIAL

Review Questions

1. What is the *primary objective* of accounting for changes in the ownership of a partnership?
2. What *three* methods are available to achieve equity among partners when a change in ownership occurs?
3. Does each method to achieve equity always treat each partner equitably?
4. Under the *bonus method*, is the bonus temporary or permanent?

5. Is recognizing goodwill on a partner's admission into a partnership considered to be in accord with GAAP?

6. How would you describe a business combination of two partnerships that is in substance a *pooling of interests*?

7. Is a business combination that is in substance a *purchase* (as opposed to a *pooling of interests*) deemed a change in ownership with respect to the acquiring partnership?

8. How does an accountant know whether the *bonus method*, the *special profit and loss sharing provision method*, or the *recording the goodwill method* should be used to reflect a change in ownership?

9. Under the *recording the goodwill method*, what substantively has occurred?

10. Under the *bonus method*, what substantively has occurred?

11. What is the distinction between a *dissociation* and a *dissolution* when a partner withdraws?

12. When a partner withdraws from a partnership after many years and has a gain on the liquidation of his or her interest, is such gain treated as a capital gain for income tax–reporting purposes?

Exercises

E 21-1 **Admission: Calculation of Required Contribution** Partners Angel, Bird, and Crow share profits and losses 50:30:20, respectively. The 4/30/04 balance sheet is as follows:

Cash	$ 40,000
Other assets	360,000
	$400,000
Accounts payable	$100,000
Capital, Angel	74,000
Capital, Bird	130,000
Capital, Crow	96,000
	$400,000

The assets and liabilities are recorded and presented at their respective fair values. Dove is to be admitted as a new partner with a 20% capital interest and a 20% share of profits and losses in exchange for a cash contribution. No goodwill or bonus is to be recorded.

Required

1. Determine how much cash Dove should contribute.
2. Prepare the entry to record Dove's admission.

E 21-2 **Admission: Recording the Goodwill Method** Abbey and Landly are partners with capital balances of $80,000 and $40,000, and they share profits and losses in the ratio of 2:1, respectively. Deere invests $36,000 cash for a one-fifth interest in the capital and profits of the *new partnership*. The partners agree that the implied partnership goodwill is to be recorded simultaneously with the admission of Deere.

Required

1. Calculate the firm's total implied goodwill.
2. Prepare the entry or entries to record the admission of Deere.

E 21-3 **Admission: The Bonus Method** Cord and Stringer are partners who share profits and losses in the ratio of 3:2, respectively. On 8/31/06 their capital accounts are as follows:

Cord	$ 70,000
Stringer	60,000
	$130,000

On that date, they agreed to admit Twiner as a partner with a one-third interest in the capital and profits and losses, for an investment of $50,000. The new partnership will begin with a total capital of $180,000.

Required Prepare the entry or entries to record the admission of Twiner.

E 21-4 **Admission: Recording the Goodwill Method and the Bonus Method** Waters is admitted into the partnership of Dunes, Kamel, and Sanders for a $40,000 total cash investment. The capital accounts and respective percentage interests in profits and losses *immediately before* Waters' admission are as follows:

	Capital Accounts	Percentage Interests in Profits and Losses
Dunes	$ 80,000	60
Kamel	40,000	30
Sanders	20,000	10
	$140,000	100

All tangible assets and liabilities are fairly valued. Waters receives a one-fifth interest in profits and losses and a 20% interest in the new partnership's net assets.

Required

1. Prepare the entry to record Waters' admission into the partnership, assuming that goodwill *is* to be recorded.
2. Prepare the entry to record Waters' admission into the partnership, assuming that goodwill is *not* to be recorded.

E 21-5 **Admission: Determining Bonus and Goodwill from Interest in Net Assets** Ball and Batt are partners—they share profits and losses equally, and they have capital balances of $30,000 and $20,000, respectively. All *tangible assets* have *current values* equal to *book values*. Glover is admitted into the partnership.

Required Determine the entry to record Glover's admission in each of the following independent situations:

1. Glover contributes $10,000 cash for a 10% interest in the *new net assets* of the partnership of $60,000.
2. Glover contributes $10,000 cash for a 10% interest in the *new net assets* of the partnership and receives a *credit* to his capital account equal to his full cash contribution.
3. Glover contributes $10,000 cash for a one-sixth interest in the *new net assets* of the partnership of $60,000.
4. Glover purchases 10% of each existing partner's interest for a total cash payment of $10,000 to the existing partners.
5. Glover contributes $10,000 cash for a 20% interest in the *new net assets* of the partnership of $60,000.
6. Glover contributes $10,000 cash for a 20% interest in the *new net assets* of the partnership, with the old partners' capital accounts *not* to decrease.

E 21-6 **Retirement** On 6/30/06, the balance sheet for the Oakley, Pine, and Woods partnership, together with their respective profit and loss ratios, was as follows:

Assets, at cost	$180,000
Oakley, loan	$ 9,000
Capital, Oakley (20%)	42,000
Capital, Pine (20%)	39,000
Capital, Woods (60%)	90,000
	$180,000

Oakley has decided to retire from the partnership. By mutual agreement, the assets are to be adjusted to their *current value* of $216,000, and the partnership is to pay Oakley $61,200 for her partnership interest, including her loan, which is to be repaid in full.

Required

1. Prepare the required entries, assuming that goodwill *is* to be recorded on the partnership's books. (Note: Two alternative amounts may be recorded for goodwill. Prepare entries under each alternative.)
2. Prepare the entries, assuming that goodwill is *not* to be recorded on the partnership's books.

E 21-7 **Calculation of Gain on Sale of Partnership Interests** The capital accounts of the partnership of Fender, Hood, and Shields on 5/31/06 follow with their respective profit and loss ratios:

Fender	$200,000	1/2
Hood	150,000	1/3
Shields	100,000	1/6
	$450,000	

On 5/31/06, Wheeler was admitted into the partnership when she purchased for $120,000 an interest from Fender in the net assets and profits of the partnership. As a result of this transaction, Wheeler acquired a one-fifth interest in the net assets and profits of the firm. Assume that *implied* goodwill is *not* to be recorded. Fender's *tax basis* just prior to the sale was $180,000.

Required

1. What gain does Fender realize on the sale of a portion of this interest in the partnership to Wheeler?
2. Is the gain calculated in requirement 1 for book purposes, for tax purposes, or for both?
3. Prepare the entry required on the partnership's books.
4. *Optional*: What is Fender's taxable gain or loss if he retires on 6/1/06 and receives cash equal to the balance in his capital account at this date? (Assume that the partnership had no liabilities at this date.)

Problems

P 21-1 **Admission: Tangible Assets Are *Undervalued* and Goodwill Exists** Fields and Hill are in partnership—they share profits and losses in the ratio of 4:1, respectively, and they have capital balances of $22,500 each. The partnership's *tangible assets* have a *fair value* of $15,000 in excess of *book value*. Mounds is admitted into the partnership for a cash contribution of $30,000. The new profit and loss sharing formula is Fields, 56%; Hill, 14%; and Mounds, 30%. The value of the partnership's existing goodwill is agreed to be $10,000.

Required

1. Prepare the required entries, assuming that the tangible assets *are* to be revalued and the goodwill *is* to be recorded on the partnership's books.
2. Prepare the required entries, assuming that the *bonus method* is to be used with respect to the undervalued tangible assets *and* the goodwill.

P 21-2 **Retirement: Tangible Assets Are *Undervalued* and Goodwill Exists** The 4/30/06 balance sheet of the partnership of Arbee, Karle, and MacDonald follows. The partners share profits and losses in the ratio of 2:2:6, respectively.

Assets, at cost	$100,000
Arbee, loan	$ 9,000
Capital, Arbee	15,000
Capital, Karle	31,000
Capital, MacDonald	45,000
	$100,000

Arbee retires from the partnership. By mutual agreement, the assets are to be adjusted to their fair value of $130,000 at 4/30/06. Karle and MacDonald agree that the partnership will pay Arbee $37,000 cash for his partnership interest, exclusive of his loan, which is to be paid in full. No goodwill is to be recorded.

Required

1. Prepare the entry to record the revaluation of assets to their *fair value*.
2. Prepare the entry to record Arbee's retirement.
3. What is the *implicit* goodwill?

P 21-3 Business Combination: Each Partnership Has *Undervalued* Tangible Assets and Goodwill The partnership of A, B, C, and D has agreed to combine with the partnership of X and Y. The individual capital accounts and profit and loss sharing percentage of each partner follow:

	Capital Accounts	Profit and Loss Sharing Percentages	
		Now	Proposed
A.	$ 50,000	40	28
B.	35,000	30	21
C.	40,000	20	14
D.	25,000	10	7
	$150,000	100	70
X.	$ 60,000	50	15
Y.	40,000	50	15
	$100,000	100	30

A, B, C, and D's partnership has undervalued *tangible assets* of $20,000, and the X and Y partnership has undervalued *tangible assets* of $8,000. All the partners agree that (1) the partnership of A, B, C, and D possesses goodwill of $30,000 and (2) the partnership of X and Y possesses goodwill of $10,000. (Assume that the combined businesses will continue to use the general ledger of A, B, C, and D.)

Required

1. Prepare the entries required to reflect the combination, assuming that tangible assets *are* to be revalued and goodwill *is* to be recorded.
2. Prepare the entries required to reflect the combination, assuming that the *bonus method* is to be used with respect to the undervalued tangible assets *and* the goodwill.

P 21-4 Admission: Tangible Assets Are *Overvalued* and Goodwill Exists Diamond and Hart are in partnership; they have (1) capital balances of $110,000 and $75,000, respectively, and (2) a profit and loss sharing ratio of 3:2, respectively. Klubb is to be admitted with a $60,000 cash contribution. The parties agree that the partnership possesses goodwill of $65,000 and its equipment is *overvalued* by $10,000. Klubb will share in 20% of the profits and losses.

Required

1. Prepare the required entries, assuming that the equipment *is* to be written down and goodwill *is* to be recorded.
2. Prepare the required entries, assuming that the equipment is *not* to be written down and goodwill is *not* to be recorded.

P 21-5 Retirement: Tangible Assets Are *Overvalued* and Goodwill Exists Acres, Barnes, and Cowes are in partnership; they have (1) capital balances of $200,000, $60,000, and $210,000, respectively, and (2) a profit and loss sharing ratio of 4:1:5, respectively. Cowes is retiring. The parties agree that the partnership possesses goodwill of $100,000 and its equipment is *overvalued* by $20,000.

Required

1. Prepare the required entries, assuming that the equipment *is* to be written down and goodwill *is* to be recorded.
2. Prepare the required entries, assuming that the equipment is *not* to be written down and goodwill is *not* to be recorded.

P 21-6 COMPREHENSIVE: Admission of *New* Partners—Withdrawal of *Old* Partner and Division of Profits You have been engaged to prepare the 6/30/06 financial statements for the partnership of Ash, Cherry, and Douglas. You have obtained the following information from the partnership agreement, as amended, and from the accounting records.

1. Ash and Burch originally formed the partnership on 7/1/05 when
   a. Burch contributed $400,000 cash.
   b. Ash contributed land, a building, and equipment with fair market values of $110,000, $520,000, and $185,000, respectively. The land and buildings were subject to a mortgage securing an 8% per annum note (interest rate of similar notes at 7/1/05). The note is due in *quarterly payments* of $5,000 plus interest on January 1, April 1, July 1, and October 1 of each year. Ash made the 7/1/05 principal and interest payment *personally*. The partnership then assumed the obligation of the remaining $300,000 balance.
   c. The agreement further provided that Ash had contributed a certain intangible benefit to the partnership because of her many years of business activity in the area serviced by the new partnership. The assigned value of this intangible asset plus the net tangible assets she contributed gave her a 60% initial capital interest in the partnership.
   d. Ash was designated the only active partner, at an annual salary of $24,000 plus an annual bonus of 5% of net income after deducting her salary but before deducting interest on partners' capital investments (see below). Both the salary and the bonus are to be recorded as operating expenses of the partnership.
   e. Each partner is to receive a 10% return on *average* capital investment; such interest is to be an expense of the partnership.
   f. All remaining profits or losses are to be shared equally.

2. On 10/1/05, Burch sold his partnership interest and rights as of 7/1/05 to Cherry for $370,000. Ash agreed to accept Cherry as a partner if he would contribute sufficient cash to meet the 10/1/05 principal and interest payment on the mortgage note. Cherry made the payment from *personal funds*.

3. On 1/1/06, Ash and Cherry admitted a new partner, Douglas. Douglas invested $150,000 cash for a 10% capital interest based on the initial investments (tangible and intangible) at 7/1/05 of Ash and Burch, plus Douglas' capital contribution of $150,000. At 1/1/06, the *book values* of the partnership's assets and liabilities approximated their *fair values*. Douglas contributed no intangible benefit to the partnership.

   Similar to the other partners, Douglas is to receive a 10% return on his *average* capital investment. His investment also entitles him to 20% of the partnership's profits or losses as defined above. For the year ended 6/30/06, however, Douglas receives one-half his pro rata share of the profits or losses.

4. The accounting records show that on 2/1/06, the Other Miscellaneous Expenses account had been charged $3,600 for hospital expenses incurred by Ash's eight-year-old daughter, Fern.

5. All salary payments to Ash have been charged to her drawing account. On 6/1/06, Cherry made a $33,000 withdrawal. These are the only transactions recorded in the partners' drawing accounts.

6. The following is a trial balance summarizing the partnership's general ledger balances at 6/30/06. The general ledger has *not* been closed.

		Debit	Credit
	Current assets	$ 307,000	
	Fixed assets	1,285,000	
	Current liabilities		$ 104,100
	8% Mortgage note payable		285,000
	Capital, Ash		515,000
	Capital, Cherry		400,000
	Capital, Douglas		150,000
	Drawing, Ash	24,000	
	Drawing, Cherry	33,000	
	Drawing, Douglas	-0-	
Net income $194,900	Sales		946,900
	Cost of sales	695,600	
	Administrative expenses	28,000	
	Other miscellaneous expenses	11,000	
	Interest expense	17,400	
	Totals	$2,401,000	$2,401,000

Required Prepare a worksheet to adjust the net income (loss) and partners' capital accounts for the year ended 6/30/06 and to close the net income (loss) to the partners' capital accounts at 6/30/06. Supporting schedules should be in good form. Amortization of goodwill, if any, is to be over a 10-year period. (Ignore all tax considerations.) Use the following column headings and begin with balances from the books as shown:

		Partners' Capital			Other Accounts	
	Net Income (Loss)	Ash	Cherry	Douglas	Amount	
Description	(Dr.) Cr.	(Dr.) Cr.	(Dr.) Cr.	(Dr.) Cr.	Dr. (Cr.)	Name
Book balances at 6/30/05	$194,900	$515,000	$400,000	$150,000		

THINKING CRITICALLY

Cases

C 21-1 **Admission: Evaluation of the Bonus Method** Gentry and Royals are in partnership and are contemplating admitting Squires. Gentry and Royals have proposed that Squires give them a $20,000 bonus as a condition of admittance. Squires believes that this bonus is ridiculous considering that (1) all tangible assets have *fair values* equal to their *book values*, (2) all partners are to devote 100% of their time to the partnership business, (3) future profits and losses are to be shared equally, (4) Squires' capital contribution is to be 50% of the existing partnership capital of $100,000 *immediately before* admission, and (5) Squires' *tax basis* would be reduced by $20,000. Squires has asked you, as his accountant, to counsel him on this matter.

Required How would you respond to this request?

C 21-2 **Admission: Adherence to Generally Accepted Accounting Principles** Castle and Hurst are partners negotiating with Randolph regarding his admission into the partnership. They have reached agreement regarding the value of goodwill that the existing partnership possesses. The partners disagree, however, as to whether the goodwill should be recorded on the books. Castle and Hurst believe that goodwill should be recognized and recorded on the books at Randolph's admission. Randolph believes that it is improper to record goodwill because it was *not* bought and paid for. Furthermore, Randolph contends that recording goodwill is senseless because it would *not* be deductible for income tax purposes in this situation. They have asked you as the partnership's accountant to settle this disagreement.

Required How would you respond to this request?

C 21-3 **Admission: Role of the Accountant** Disnee and Walters are partners contemplating Duckett's admission as a partner. They have requested that you, the partnership's accountant, determine how this should be done.

Required How would you respond to this request? Be specific about the advice you would give them.

C 21-4 **Admission: Role of the Accountant** Berry and Knott are partners contemplating Farmer's admission into the partnership. Berry and Knott believe that the partnership possesses goodwill of $60,000, whereas Farmer believes that it possesses goodwill of only $20,000. As the partnership's accountant, you have been asked to determine the amount of goodwill that the partnership possesses.

Required How would you respond to this request?

chapter

22

Partnerships: Liquidations

Nothing endures but personal qualities.
WALT WHITMAN

LEARNING OBJECTIVES

To Understand

- The fundamental safeguard that all partnerships should use to minimize inequities in the event of a liquidation.
- The rule of *setoff*.
- The way to prepare a statement of realization and liquidation.
- The way to properly distribute cash to partners in an installment liquidation.

TOPIC OUTLINE

I. Fundamental Procedures in Liquidations
II. Lump-Sum Liquidations
III. Installment Liquidations

CHAPTER OVERVIEW

The termination of a partnership's business activities is known as **liquidation**. A partnership may be liquidated for many reasons; for example, its original agreed-upon term of existence has expired, it is marginally profitable, or it is in serious financial difficulty.

A partnership in serious financial difficulty may attempt rehabilitation either by (1) filing under Chapter 11 of the federal bankruptcy statutes or (2) restructuring its debt outside bankruptcy court. Such alternatives for partnerships, however, do *not* entail any significant special problems not already discussed for corporations in Chapter 19. Consequently, we restrict our discussion in this chapter to the liquidation process.

Even the Big Ones Can Fall

In the last 15 years, two very large accounting partnerships collapsed and went out of business. We briefly discuss each of these situations.

Laventhol & Horwath's Bankruptcy in 1990

In 1990, the then seventh-largest accounting partnership filed for bankruptcy protection and was subsequently liquidated because it had severe financial difficulties resulting from litigation and overexpansion. The unfortunate personal consequences of L&H's demise (which we list below) motivated many accounting *general* partnerships to become *limited liability* partnerships (LLPs)—all of the then *Big Six* accounting firms changed from being general partnerships to LLPs in 1994.

1. The partners lost their entire capital investment (approximately $60 million in total, which averaged $175,000 per partner).
2. The active partners and all partners who had retired in the preceding seven years were assessed $47.3 million (averaging $76,000 per partner, with some paying nearly $400,000).
3. Retired partners stopped receiving pension payments (ranged from $20,000 to $80,000 per year).
4. Several partners declared personal bankruptcy.

Arthur Andersen's Collapse in 2002

In 2002, Arthur Andersen LLP collapsed after it was indicted by the U.S. Justice Department on criminal charges of obstruction of justice (destroying evidence) in connection with its audit of Enron Corporation (Andersen's largest client). Certain particulars and the current status of Andersen follow:

1. A jury found Andersen U.S. partnership guilty of obstruction of justice.
2. Andersen was fined $500,000 but is appealing its criminal conviction.
3. Andersen still faces lawsuits by Enron's creditors and shareholders, as well as lawsuits arising from other audit engagements (such as WorldCom Inc.).
4. Andersen ceased to exist as a U.S. accounting firm in the fall of 2002 (it surrendered all of its state licenses).
5. Some of its operations were acquired by its competitors.
6. Many of its overseas partnerships split off and still operate.
7. The U.S. partnership, which once had about 26,000 employees, now effectively exists as a shell with about 250 workers.
8. The pension checks of $40,000 (annually) to approximately 5,000 retired partners, which began at age 62, have been terminated.
9. The cash distributions to partners who had retired prior to the collapse and had elected to withdraw their invested capital over a 10-year period (the majority of retired partners elect this

option) have been terminated. Partners who had retired fairly recently prior to the collapse and who had elected to withdraw all of their invested capital at the time of their withdrawal were threatened with legal action if they did not put their capital back into the firm, pending settlement of the lawsuits against the firm. (Virtually all of these retired partners put their withdrawn funds back into the firm.)

10. Andersen sits with approximately $2 billion cash (the vast majority of it having come from the sale of its operations to other firms).
11. No cash will be distributed to partners until all outstanding lawsuits are settled, which may take several more years.

Recall that LLPs were discussed in Chapter 20 and that an LLP partner is *not* subject to personal liability for any tort or malpractice liability of another partner in the partnership. In this chapter, the discussion and illustrations focus on the liquidation of *general partnerships*—not LLPs. Much of the chapter, however, applies to LLPs—only the material that discusses and illustrates partners having to make additional capital contributions because a partner is personally insolvent does *not* apply to LLPs.

"Quitting Concern" Instead of "Going Concern"

In the liquidation process, the entity is a "quitting concern"—*not* a "going concern." As explained in the bankruptcy liquidation section of Chapter 19, income statements are *not* prepared for periods in which an entity is liquidating; thus no need exists to match asset costs into the proper time period. Furthermore, all assets and liabilities become current.

The Liquidation Process in a Nutshell

The liquidation process for partnerships is in several respects identical to the liquidation process for corporations. Over a period of time, (1) the entity's noncash assets are converted to cash (the realization process), (2) creditors are paid to the extent possible, and (3) remaining funds, if any, are distributed to the owners (partners). Partnership liquidations, however, differ from corporate liquidations in the following respects:

1. Because **partners have unlimited liability**, any partner may be asked to contribute additional funds to the partnership if its assets are insufficient to satisfy creditors' claims.
2. To the extent that a partner does *not* make good a deficit balance in his or her capital account, the remaining partners must absorb that deficit balance. Absorption of a partner's deficit balance gives the absorbing partners legal recourse against him or her.

The special problems created by these two situations are discussed throughout this chapter.

Types of Liquidations

Liquidations may be categorized broadly as lump-sum liquidations and installment liquidations.

1. In *lump-sum liquidations*, no distributions are made to the partners until the realization process is completed when the full amount of the realization gain or loss is known.
2. In *installment liquidations*, distributions are made to some or all of the partners as cash becomes available. Thus cash distributions are made to partners *before* the full amount of the realization gain or loss is known.

Within each category, a variety of situations may arise concerning the ability of the partnership and the individual partners to satisfy the claims of partnership creditors. Before discussing each situation in detail, we discuss some fundamental procedures in liquidations.

I. FUNDAMENTAL PROCEDURES IN LIQUIDATIONS

Procedures for Minimizing Inequities Among Partners

Sharing of Gains and Losses

Gains and losses incurred on the realization of assets may be allocated among the partners in the manner they have agreed to in the partnership agreement. If the partnership agreement is silent with respect to sharing gains and losses during liquidation, the Revised Uniform Partnership Act (RUPA) treats such gains and losses in the same way as it does *pre*liquidation profits and losses—that is, gains and losses are allocated in accordance with the profit and loss sharing formula. Most partnerships follow the profit and loss sharing formula in distributing gains and losses incurred during liquidation. This is the most equitable manner for the following reasons:

1. The cumulative profit and loss of a partnership during its existence is the difference between total capital *contributions* and total capital *withdrawals*. Accordingly, a partnership's cumulative profit or loss during its existence should include *start-up periods*, *normal operating periods*, and *wind-down periods*.
2. Certain gains and losses recognized during the liquidation process actually may have occurred *during* normal operating periods. This is the case when (a) land or buildings have been held for several years and have appreciated in value *prior to* the liquidation and (b) certain accounts receivable should have been written off as uncollectible *before* liquidation. The use of a method other than the profit and loss sharing formula results in inequities among the partners.

If a partner's capital account is *not* sufficient to absorb his or her share of the losses incurred in liquidation, Section 807(b) of the RUPA requires that the partner must contribute additional funds to the partnership to eliminate any deficit balance in his or her capital account—regardless whether created by (1) losses incurred through *normal operations* or (2) *in the liquidation process*. If such a partner does *not* have the personal resources to eliminate this deficit, the remaining partners must absorb the capital deficit, resulting in inequities to them. A basic procedure that may minimize such potential inequities is discussed in the next section.

Advanced Planning When the Partnership Is Formed

Although every partnership commences business under the "going concern" concept, the partners' failure to acknowledge the possibility that the partnership may have to be liquidated at some time is unrealistic. It is in the interest of each partner, therefore, to take prudent steps to minimize the possibility of inequities occurring in liquidation. Inequities among partners may arise during liquidation if a deficit balance is created in a partner's capital account (as a result of losses incurred during the conversion of noncash assets into cash) and that partner *cannot* contribute capital to eliminate the deficit. The partners who do *not* have deficit balances in their capital accounts must absorb the deficit balance of the partner who does. In other words, they must absorb losses *larger than* their agreed-upon profit and loss sharing percentage.

Because a partnership has no control over its partners' personal affairs, it has no assurance that its partners will have sufficient personal funds to contribute if a deficit balance is created during liquidation. Accordingly, the partnership should be operated in a manner that *minimizes* the possibility of a deficit balance occurring. If the partnership agreement specifies that all partners' capital balances are to be maintained in the profit and loss sharing ratio, a partnership may incur losses on the conversion of noncash assets into cash up to the total equity of the partnership, without creating a deficit balance in any partner's capital account. This safeguard is so important that many partnerships (including most of the international accounting partnerships) require capital accounts to be maintained in the profit and loss sharing ratio. Furthermore, as cash is available for distribution to the partners (a situation that occurs only if losses during liquidation are less than the total partnership equity), such cash may be distributed to the partners in the profit and loss sharing ratio with complete assurance that no inequities will result. In such situations, the liquidation process is quite simple. Unfortunately, not all partnerships use such a provision. Partners in such partnerships needlessly expose themselves to potential inequities in the event of liquidation, making the liquidation process much more complex.

Although the potential for inequities occurring during liquidation cannot be completely eliminated, a partnership that requires maintaining capital accounts in the profit and loss sharing ratio has taken a big step toward minimizing any potential inequities that may arise.

Rule of *Setoff*—Partnership Loans to the Partners

When a partnership has a loan outstanding **to a partner**, the partnership receivable should be subtracted, or set off, from the partner's capital account. It is *not* equitable to assume that the receivable is uncollectible (even though the partner may *not* have sufficient personal assets to repay the loan) and thereby to allocate the loss among all the partners. The partner's capital account less the receivable represents the partner's true capital investment.

Rule of *Setoff*—Partner Loans to the Partnership

When a partner has a loan outstanding **to the partnership**, the loan may or may not rank on an equal level with other partnership liabilities as to priority—it depends on whether the partner's loan is subordinate to the other partnership liabilities. Practice varies in this respect. Under Section 807 of the RUPA, a partner's loan to the partnership ("inside debt") that is *not* subordinated ranks on an *equal level* with other partnership liabilities ("outside debt"). Primarily for simplicity, however, all subsequent illustrations and assignment material assume that any partner loans to the partnership *are* subordinated. **Thus other partnership liabilities are assumed to have priority over partner's loans to the partnership.** Accordingly, the following priority system occurs under this assumption:

1. All *outside debt* (amounts owed to *non*partners) are to be fully paid *before* any cash is distributed to any of the partners.
2. Partner's loans to the partnership are to be paid *before* payments to any partner in partial or full settlement of that partner's capital account balance.

A strict application of this order of payment, however, could result in inequities among the partners. For example, a partner with a loan to the partnership could be repaid the loan, a deficit balance could be created in his or her capital account at a later date because of losses on the realization of assets, and the partner might *not* be able to make a capital contribution to eliminate that deficit balance. The other partners would have to absorb that partner's deficit balance and thus incur a larger portion of the losses during liquidation than they originally agreed to. The legal doctrine of ***setoff***—whereby a deficit balance in a partner's capital account may be set off against any balance existing in his or her loan account—has been incorporated into accountants' procedures for determining which partners would receive cash as it becomes available. **These procedures effectively treat the loan as an *additional capital investment*.** The mechanical procedures, which are different in lump-sum liquidations and installment liquidations, are discussed and illustrated later in the chapter.

CHECK POINT

Under the *rule of setoff*, which of these is true?

a. A partnership's loan to a partner is deemed the equivalent of partnership capital.
b. A deficit in a partner's capital account may be eliminated against his or her loan account to the partnership.
c. *Partnership assets* must be set aside to pay off *personal creditors* of an insolvent partner before any cash distributions may be made to that partner.
d. Partnership creditors have first priority against partnership assets.

Answer: b

The Statement of Realization and Liquidation

Because normal operations do *not* take place during the liquidation period, traditional financial statements are *not* appropriate. Instead, the partners prefer to have a statement that provides information on the following:

1. Gains and losses on the realization of assets, including the impact of such gains and losses on the partners' capital accounts.
2. Payments that have been made to creditors and partners.
3. The noncash assets still to be converted into cash.

Accordingly, accountants have devised the **statement of realization and liquidation** to provide this information. The statement is *entirely historical*; it reflects only the *actual transactions* that have occurred during the liquidation period up to the date of the statement. If the liquidation process takes place over several months, the statement is updated periodically as noncash assets are converted into cash and payments are made to creditors, partners, or both. Other than the allocation of realization gains and losses among the partners and the exercising of the right of setoff, the statement is essentially a summary of cash *inflows* and *outflows*.

Liquidation Expenses

Certain costs incurred during the liquidation process should be treated as a reduction of the proceeds from the sale of noncash assets—for example, costs to complete inventory, sales commissions and shipping costs related to the disposal of inventory, escrow and title transfer fees associated with the sale of real property, and costs of removing equipment. Other liquidation costs should be treated as expenses. Making a reasonable estimate of these expenses at the beginning of the liquidation process and recording an estimated liability in the general ledger at that time are preferable, adjusting the liability as necessary during the liquidation process. **Recording the estimated liability at the inception of the liquidation process minimizes the possibility of making excess cash distributions to partners.** Any cash available for distribution to partners should be set aside in an amount equal to the remaining estimated liability so that it is *not* distributed to partners.

ETHICS

To Hit the Delete Key or Not to Hit the Delete Key!

One of your firm's biggest audit clients is having serious financial difficulties and has become the subject of an accounting practices investigation by the Securities and Exchange Commission. Assume that (1) you work on this audit and (2) the audit partner in charge of this engagement has instructed you to delete certain prior year audit working paper files and e-mail messages.

Questions

1. Would you follow your superior's instructions?
2. What might be the subsequent consequences of following (or not following) these instructions?

II. LUMP-SUM LIQUIDATIONS

In a **lump-sum liquidation,** all noncash assets are converted to cash, and outside creditors are paid in full before cash is distributed to the partners. Thus the full amount of the gain or loss on realization of assets is known before the partners receive any cash distributions. Lump-sum liquidations are rare or nonexistent because partners liquidate their loan and capital accounts as cash becomes available for distribution. Usually, partners have personal needs for cash, and there is no sound business reason to wait until the very last asset is converted to cash before distributing any cash to the partners. We illustrate several lump-sum liquidations for instructional purposes only.

Partnership Is Solvent and All Partners Are Personally Solvent

In the first three illustrations in this section, (1) the partnership is solvent (the fair value of its assets is sufficient to satisfy outside creditors' claims), and (2) all partners who must make capital contributions have either sufficient loans to the partnership (for exercising the right of setoff) or are personally solvent so that the capital deficit from losses incurred during the realization process is eliminated by contributions.

Comprehensive Illustration

Loss on Realization Does *Not* Create a Deficit Balance in Any Partner's Capital Account

To illustrate the preparation of the statement of realization and liquidation in a lump-sum liquidation, assume that partners A and B share profits and losses in the ratio 3:2, respectively, and the balance sheet of the partnership is as follows:

A and B Partnership
Balance Sheet—May 31, 2006

Cash.	$ 5,000	Liabilities	$20,000
Noncash assets	70,000	Loan, Partner B	3,000
		Capital:	
		Partner A.	37,000
		Partner B.	15,000
	$75,000		$75,000

Also assume that during June 2006, (1) the $70,000 noncash assets are converted into $40,000 cash, resulting in a $30,000 loss, which is distributed 60% to partner A ($18,000) and 40% to partner B ($12,000); (2) outside creditors are paid in full; and (3) the remaining cash is distributed to the partners. The statement of realization and liquidation covering the entire liquidation period is prepared as in Illustration 22-1.

Review Points for Illustration 22-1. Note the following:

1. The statement format does *not* combine the loan account of partner B with his capital account. The loan is a bona fide loan—*not* a capital investment.

ILLUSTRATION 22-1 *LUMP-SUM* LIQUIDATION: PARTNERSHIP AND ALL PARTNERS PERSONALLY *SOLVENT*

A and B Partnership
Statement of Realization and Liquidation
June 2006

	ASSETS		OUTSIDE	LOAN	PARTNERS' CAPITAL	
	CASH	NONCASH	LIABILITIES	B	A (60%)[a]	B (40%)[a]
Preliquidation Balances	$ 5,000	$ 70,000	$ 20,000	$ 3,000	$ 37,000	$ 15,000
Realization of assets and allocation of loss.	40,000	(70,000)			(18,000)	(12,000)
Subtotal.	$ 45,000	$ -0-	$ 20,000	$ 3,000	$ 19,000	$ 3,000
Cash distributions:						
Outside creditors	(20,000)		(20,000)			
Partner's loan	(3,000)			(3,000)		
Partner's capital	(22,000)				(19,000)	(3,000)
Postliquidation Balances	$ -0-		$ -0-	$ -0-	$ -0-	$ -0-

[a] Denotes profit and loss sharing percentage.

2. Cash distributions were made in accordance with the priority set forth in Section 40 of the UPA.

Comprehensive Illustration

Loss on Realization Creates a Deficit Balance in One Partner's Capital Account: *Right of Setoff* Exercised

Assume the information in the preceding illustration except that partner B's loan account is $10,000 instead of $3,000 and his capital account is $8,000 instead of $15,000. The statement of realization and liquidation is prepared as shown in Illustration 22-2.

Review Points for Illustration 22-2. Note the following:

1. The fact that partners' loans are assigned a higher priority for repayment than partnership capital accounts under Section 40 of the UPA is *not* significant if a partner with a loan account also has a deficit balance in his or her capital account—that is, the full amount of the loan is *not* paid *before* payments are made to partners in liquidation of their capital accounts.
2. The $4,000 deficit in partner B's capital account after the $30,000 realization loss on the noncash assets means that partner B must contribute $4,000 to the partnership so that he can fully absorb his share of the loss on realization.
3. Partner B did *not* contribute $4,000 to the partnership to eliminate his capital account deficit because he exercised the *right of setoff* whereby he transferred $4,000 from his loan account to his capital account.
4. Each partner received the same amount of cash in Illustrations 22-1 and 22-2. For all practical purposes, partner B's loan account is **the equivalent of an *additional capital investment* for liquidation purposes.**

Comprehensive Illustration

Loss on Realization Creates a Deficit Balance in One Partner's Capital Account: *Right of Setoff* Exercised and Additional Capital Contribution Is Required and Made

Assume the information in the preceding illustration except that the loss on the realization of the noncash assets is $50,000, *not* $30,000. This additional $20,000 loss causes partner B to have a

ILLUSTRATION 22-2 *LUMP-SUM* LIQUIDATION: PARTNERSHIP AND ALL PARTNERS PERSONALLY *SOLVENT*

A and B Partnership
Statement of Realization and Liquidation
June 2006

	ASSETS			LOAN	PARTNERS' CAPITAL	
	CASH	NONCASH	OUTSIDE LIABILITIES	B	A (60%)[a]	B (40%)[a]
Preliquidation Balances	$ 5,000	$ 70,000	$ 20,000	$10,000	$ 37,000	$ 8,000
Realization of assets and allocation of loss	40,000	(70,000)			(18,000)	(12,000)
Subtotal	$ 45,000	$ -0-	$ 20,000	$10,000	$ 19,000	$ (4,000)
Exercised right of setoff				(4,000)		4,000
Subtotal	$ 45,000		$ 20,000	$ 6,000	$ 19,000	$ -0-
Cash distributions:						
Outside creditors	(20,000)		(20,000)			
Partner's loan	(6,000)			(6,000)		
Partner's capital	(19,000)				(19,000)	
Postliquidation Balances	$ -0-		$ -0-	$ -0-	$ -0-	

[a] Denotes profit and loss sharing percentage.

capital deficit, which is *not* completely eliminated when he exercises the *right of setoff*. Assume that partner B is personally solvent and that he makes the required capital contribution to eliminate the remainder of his capital deficit. The statement of realization and liquidation is prepared as shown in Illustration 22-3.

Partnership Is Solvent and at Least One Partner Is Personally Insolvent

In the next two illustrations, at least one partner is personally insolvent and unable to make a capital contribution to eliminate his or her capital deficit. In such circumstances, the remaining partners must absorb the capital deficit of the insolvent partner in their respective profit and loss sharing ratio. If this, in turn, causes a capital deficit for an absorbing partner, that partner must make a capital contribution to eliminate the deficit. If such partner also is personally insolvent, his or her capital deficit must be absorbed by the remaining partners, using their respective profit and loss sharing ratio.

The absorption of a partner's deficit capital balance by other partners violates the UPA, in that the partner who *cannot* eliminate his or her deficit capital balance has broken the terms of the partnership agreement. The other partners have legal recourse against the personal assets of the defaulting partner. This situation raises the question of how such claims against the defaulting partner's personal assets are treated in relation to claims of that partner's personal creditors. In the next section of the chapter, we answer this question and discuss situations in which the **partnership is insolvent** and at least one partner is personally insolvent.

Comprehensive Illustration

Loss on Realization Creates a Deficit Balance in One Partner's Capital Account: *Right of Setoff* Exercised and Additional Capital Contribution Is Required but *Not* Made

Assume that partners A, B, C, and D share profits in the ratio 4:2:2:2, respectively. The partnership's balance sheet at the beginning of the liquidation process is as shown on the following page.

ILLUSTRATION 22-3 *LUMP-SUM* LIQUIDATION: PARTNERSHIP AND ALL PARTNERS PERSONALLY *SOLVENT*

A and B Partnership
Statement of Realization and Liquidation
June 2006

	ASSETS			LOAN	PARTNERS' CAPITAL	
	CASH	NONCASH	OUTSIDE LIABILITIES	B	A (60%)[a]	B (40%)[a]
Preliquidation Balances	$ 5,000	$ 70,000	$ 20,000	$ 10,000	$ 37,000	$ 8,000
Realization of assets and allocation of loss	20,000	(70,000)			(30,000)	(20,000)
Subtotal	$ 25,000	$ -0-	$ 20,000	$ 10,000	$ 7,000	$(12,000)
Right of setoff exercised				(10,000)		10,000
Subtotal	$ 25,000		$ 20,000	$ -0-	$ 7,000	$ (2,000)
Cash contribution by B	2,000					2,000
Subtotal	$ 27,000		$ 20,000		$ 7,000	$ -0-
Cash distributions:						
Outside creditors	(20,000)		(20,000)			
Partner's capital	(7,000)				(7,000)	
Postliquidation Balances	$ -0-		$ -0-		$ -0-	

[a] Denotes profit and loss sharing percentage.

A, B, C, and D Partnership
Balance Sheet—June 30, 2006

Cash	$ 10,000	Liabilities	$157,000
Noncash assets	290,000	Loan:	
		Partner B	10,000
		Partner C	5,000
		Partner D	2,000
		Capital:	
		Partner A	70,000
		Partner B	30,000
		Partner C	20,000
		Partner D	6,000
	$300,000		$300,000

Assume also that during July 2006, the noncash assets realize $210,000 cash, resulting in an $80,000 realization loss, which is shared among the partners (using the profit and loss sharing ratio 4:2:2:2) as follows: A, $32,000; B, $16,000; C, $16,000; and D, $16,000. The realization loss creates a deficit in D's capital account, which D's exercise of the *right of setoff* does *not* completely eliminate. D must make an additional $8,000 capital contribution but is unable to do so. As a result, her $8,000 capital deficit must be allocated to partners A, B, and C in their profit and loss sharing ratio of 4:2:2, respectively. Assuming that all cash was distributed in July 2006, the statement of realization and liquidation is prepared as shown in Illustration 22-4 (see page 734).

Review Points for Illustration 22-4. Note the following:

1. Because partner D was unable to eliminate the deficit balance in her capital account, the remaining partners had to bear a higher percentage of the realization loss than their individual profit and loss sharing percentages. For example, partner A suffered a total loss of $36,000 ($32,000 + $4,000). This represents 45% of the $80,000 total realization loss, which is *higher than* her stipulated profit and loss sharing percentage of 40%. Partners A, B, and C needlessly exposed themselves to this additional $8,000 loss by *not* employing the fundamental safeguard provision of maintaining capital accounts in the profit and loss sharing ratio.
2. The illustration assumes that partner D was unable to make any of the required contribution. If a partner contribution had been made, the remaining partners would have had to absorb a *smaller* deficit balance.
3. A partner with a deficit balance may indicate that he or she is unable to completely eliminate the deficit balance when it is created, but that he or she might be able to make a capital contribution at a later date (which may or may not be specified). If partner D had indicated this, the available $220,000 cash could have been distributed to the outside creditors and the remaining partners. The partnership books then could be kept open until partner D made a capital contribution or subsequently determined that she could not make a payment after all. This procedure could result in a lengthy delay in completing the partnership liquidation. There is no sound reason for keeping the partnership books open indefinitely, thereby delaying the completion of the liquidation process, merely because of partner D's uncertain financial situation. When partner D's capital account deficit was created (and *not* completely eliminated by exercising the *right of setoff*), she became liable for her deficit to the other partners. Accordingly, if partner D later makes a capital contribution, she makes the payment *directly* to the other partners. Consequently, in situations involving lump-sum liquidations in which a partner *cannot* immediately eliminate his or her capital deficit, the accountant should complete the liquidation process by transferring the capital deficit to the capital accounts of the remaining partners (using their respective profit and loss sharing ratios). The partnership books may then be closed, and the liquidation process can be completed.

Comprehensive Illustration

Loss on Realization Creates a Deficit Balance in One Partner's Capital Account; Absorption by Other Partners Creates a Deficit Balance in Another Partner's Capital Account

Assume the information in the preceding illustration except that the noncash assets are sold for only $170,000. This results in a realization loss of $120,000 rather than $80,000. The $120,000

ILLUSTRATION 22-4 *LUMP-SUM* LIQUIDATION: PARTNERSHIP AND ALL BUT ONE PARTNER PERSONALLY *SOLVENT*

A, B, C, and D Partnership
Statement of Realization and Liquidation
July 2006

	ASSETS		OUTSIDE	PARTNERS' LOANS			PARTNERS' CAPITAL			
	CASH	NONCASH	LIABILITIES	B	C	D	A (40%)[a]	B (20%)[a]	C (20%)[a]	D (20%)[a]
Preliquidation Balances, 7/1/06	$ 10,000	$ 290,000	$ 157,000	$ 10,000	$ 5,000	$ 2,000	$ 70,000	$ 30,000	$ 20,000	$ 6,000
Realization of assets and allocation of loss	210,000	(290,000)					(32,000)	(16,000)	(16,000)	(16,000)
Subtotal	$ 220,000	$ -0-	$ 157,000	$ 10,000	$ 5,000	$ 2,000	$ 38,000	$ 14,000	$ 4,000	$(10,000)
Exercise right of setoff						(2,000)				2,000
Subtotal	$ 220,000		$ 157,000	$ 10,000	$ 5,000	$ -0-	$ 38,000	$ 14,000	$ 4,000	$ (8,000)
Write-off of D's deficit							(4,000)	(2,000)	(2,000)	8,000
Subtotal	$ 220,000		$ 157,000	$ 10,000	$ 5,000		$ 34,000	$ 12,000	$ 2,000	$ -0-
Cash Distributions:										
Outside creditors	(157,000)		(157,000)							
Partners' loan	(15,000)			(10,000)	(5,000)					
Partners' capital	(48,000)						(34,000)	(12,000)	(2,000)	
Postliquidation Balances, 7/31/06	$ -0-		$ -0-	$ -0-	$ -0-		$ -0-	$ -0-	$ -0-	

[a] Denotes profit and loss sharing percentage.

realization loss is allocated among the partners (using the profit and loss sharing ratio 4:2:2:2) as follows: A, $48,000; B, $24,000; C, $24,000; and D, $24,000. In addition to the previously described consequences to partner D, the greater loss results in partner C's inability to absorb fully C's share of partner D's deficit balance. Thus, partner C has a deficit balance that he *cannot* eliminate through *setoff* or *contribution*. His capital deficit, in turn, must be allocated to partners A and B in their respective profit and loss sharing ratio of 4:2. (Partners A and B have legal recourse against the personal assets of partners C and D—such recourse is discussed in the next section.) Assuming that all cash was distributed in July 2006, the statement of realization and liquidation is prepared as shown in Illustration 22-5 (see page 736).

Partnership Is Insolvent and at Least One Partner Is Personally Solvent

In the next two illustrations, the partnership is insolvent—that is, the loss on the realization of noncash assets is higher than the total of the partners' capital (including their loan accounts). Because unlimited liability is a feature of the partnership form of organization, creditors may seek payment from *any* or *all* of the partners as individuals.

Comprehensive Illustration

Loss on Realization Creates a Deficit Balance in Certain Partners' Capital Accounts: All Partners *Are* Personally Solvent

In this situation, all partners *are* personally solvent, and those with deficit capital balances contribute funds to the partnership to eliminate their capital deficits, enabling the partnership to pay creditors in full. Using the same preliquidation balances given for Illustration 22-5, assume that the $290,000 noncash assets are sold for $130,000, resulting in a $160,000 realization loss. The realization loss is shared among the partners (using the profit and loss sharing ratio 4:2:2:2) as follows: A, $64,000; B, $32,000; C, $32,000; and D, $32,000. After exercising the *right of setoff*, partner A has a $6,000 capital balance; partner B has an $8,000 loan balance; and partners C and D have $7,000 and $24,000 capital deficits, respectively. At this point, the available $140,000 cash may be distributed to outside creditors. Assuming that partners C and D contribute funds to the partnership to eliminate their capital deficits, the $31,000 cash then may be distributed to outside creditors and partners A and B. The statement of realization and liquidation is prepared as shown in Illustration 22-6 (see page 737).

In this illustration, we assume that partners C and D made additional cash contributions to the partnership, thereby eliminating their capital deficits. Thus the partnership *could* make the remaining $17,000 payment to the outside creditors. Creditors occasionally take legal action against some or all of the partners as individuals when the creditors do *not* receive full satisfaction from the partnership. As a result, a partner personally may make payments to partnership creditors. Such payments should be reflected in the general ledger and on the statement of realization and liquidation as a reduction of partnership liabilities and an additional capital contribution by that partner. A partner's personal payments to creditors are in substance **the equivalent of a cash contribution to the partnership that the partnership then distributes to the creditors.**

Comprehensive Illustration

Loss on Realization Creates a Deficit Balance in Certain Partners' Capital Accounts: Certain Partners Are Personally Insolvent

Before illustrating in detail a situation in which a partnership is insolvent and certain of its partners are insolvent, we discuss the following legal questions raised in such circumstances:

1. If a partner is personally insolvent, to what extent may such partner's *personal creditors* obtain payments from the partnership?
2. If *partnership creditors* initiate legal proceedings against a partner who is personally insolvent, what is the legal status (priority of payment) of such claims in relation to the claims of that partner's *personal creditors*?
3. If a partner is personally insolvent and unable to eliminate the deficit balance in his or her capital account, thereby causing other partners to absorb that deficit balance (which is a breach of the partnership agreement entitling the wronged partners to legal recourse against the

ILLUSTRATION 22-5 *LUMP-SUM* LIQUIDATION: PARTNERSHIP *INSOLVENT* AND SOME PARTNERS PERSONALLY *INSOLVENT*

A, B, C, and D Partnership
Statement of Realization and Liquidation
July 2006

	ASSETS		OUTSIDE	PARTNERS' LOANS			PARTNERS' CAPITAL			
	CASH	NONCASH	LIABILITIES	B	C	D	A (40%)[a]	B (20%)[a]	C (20%)[a]	D (20%)[a]
Preliquidation Balances, 7/1/06	$ 10,000	$ 290,000	$ 157,000	$ 10,000	$ 5,000	$ 2,000	$ 70,000	$ 30,000	$ 20,000	$ 6,000
Realization of assets and allocation of loss	170,000	(290,000)					(48,000)	(24,000)	(24,000)	(24,000)
Subtotal	$ 180,000	$ -0-	$ 157,000	$ 10,000	$ 5,000	$ 2,000	$ 22,000	$ 6,000	$ (4,000)	$(18,000)
Exercise right of setoff					(4,000)	(2,000)			4,000	2,000
Subtotal	$ 180,000		$ 157,000	$ 10,000	$ 1,000	$ -0-	$ 22,000	$ 6,000	$ -0-	$(16,000)
Write-off of D's capital deficit							(8,000)	(4,000)	(4,000)	16,000
Subtotal	$ 180,000		$ 157,000	$ 10,000	$ 1,000		$ 14,000	$ 2,000	$ (4,000)	$ -0-
Exercise right of setoff					(1,000)				1,000	
Subtotal	$ 180,000		$ 157,000	$ 10,000	$ -0-		$ 14,000	$ 2,000	$ (3,000)	
Write-off of C's capital deficit							(2,000)	(1,000)	3,000	
Subtotal	$ 180,000		$ 157,000	$ 10,000			$ 12,000	$ 1,000	$ -0-	
Cash Distributions:										
Outside creditors	(157,000)		(157,000)							
Partners' loan	(10,000)			(10,000)						
Partners' capital	(13,000)						(12,000)	(1,000)		
Postliquidation Balances, 7/31/06	$ -0-		$ -0-	$ -0-			$ -0-	$ -0-		

[a] Denotes profit and loss sharing percentage.

ILLUSTRATION 22-6 *LUMP-SUM* LIQUIDATION: PARTNERSHIP *INSOLVENT* AND ALL PARTNERS PERSONALLY *SOLVENT*

A, B, C, and D Partnership
Statement of Realization and Liquidation
July 2006

	ASSETS			PARTNERS' LOANS			PARTNERS' CAPITAL			
	CASH	NONCASH	OUTSIDE LIABILITIES	B	C	D	A (40%)[a]	B (20%)[a]	C (20%)[a]	D (20%)[a]
Preliquidation Balances, 7/1/06	$ 10,000	$ 290,000	$ 157,000	$10,000	$ 5,000	$ 2,000	$ 70,000	$ 30,000	$ 20,000	$ 6,000
Realization of assets and allocation of loss	130,000	(290,000)					(64,000)	(32,000)	(32,000)	(32,000)
Subtotal	$ 140,000	$ -0-	$ 157,000	$10,000	$ 5,000	$ 2,000	$ 6,000	$ (2,000)	$(12,000)	$(26,000)
Exercise right of setoff				(2,000)	(5,000)	(2,000)		2,000	5,000	2,000
Subtotal	$ 140,000		$ 157,000	$ 8,000	$ -0-	$ -0-	$ 6,000	$ -0-	$ (7,000)	$(24,000)
Distribution to outside creditors	(140,000)		(140,000)							
Subtotal	$ -0-		$ 17,000	$ 8,000			$ 6,000		$ (7,000)	$(24,000)
Contributions by C and D	31,000								7,000	24,000
Subtotal	$ 31,000		$ 17,000	$ 8,000			$ 6,000		$ -0-	$ -0-
Cash Distributions:										
Outside creditors	(17,000)		(17,000)							
Partners' loan	(8,000)			(8,000)						
Partners' capital	(6,000)						(6,000)			
Postliquidation Balances, 7/31/06	$ -0-		$ -0-	$ -0-			$ -0-			

[a] Denotes profit and loss sharing percentage.

defaulting partner), what is the legal status of such claims in relation to the claims of that partner's *personal creditors*?

The answers to these questions are found in Section 807 of the RUPA, which **eliminated the long-standing "dual priority" requirement** in the UPA (also called **the marshalling of assets** procedure) under which (1) *partnership creditors* had first priority as to *partnership assets* and (2) *personal creditors* of an insolvent partnership had first priority as to such partner's *personal assets*. Under the RUPA, the following (which is consistent with the **federal bankruptcy statutes**) holds true:

1. *Partnership creditors* have first priority as to *partnership assets*.
2. *Partnership creditors* share **on a pro rata basis** with *personal creditors* of an insolvent partner in the distribution of such partner's *personal assets*.

Application of Section 807 of the RUPA

To illustrate the application of the RUPA assume the information in Illustration 22-6 with respect to partners' balances after (1) the realization loss of $160,000 is distributed, (2) the *right of setoff* is exercised, and (3) a $140,000 payment is made to *outside creditors*, leaving $17,000 owed to them. At this point, the partners' accounts are as follows:

Partner	Loan Balance	Capital Balance
A		$ 6,000
B	$8,000	
C		(7,000)
D		(24,000)

Assume that the personal status of each partner (exclusive of interest in or obligation to the partnership) is as follows:

Partner	Personal Assets	–	Personal Liabilities	=	Personal Net Worth (Deficit)
A	$50,000		$25,000		$ 25,000
B	4,000		15,000		(11,000)
C	16,000		6,000		10,000
D	20,000		33,000		(13,000)

1. Partner D has a capital deficit and is personally insolvent. Thus assume that none of his personal assets is readily available for contribution to the partnership. Consequently, partners A, B, and C must absorb his $24,000 capital deficit in their respective profit and loss sharing ratio, 4:2:2. Partner A's share is $12,000, partner B's is $6,000, and partner C's is $6,000.
2. Partner C had a $7,000 capital deficit, which increased to $13,000 when he absorbed his share of partner D's capital deficit. Partner C has a personal net worth of $10,000. Thus assume that he can readily contribute only $10,000 to the partnership, leaving a $3,000 deficit, which partners A and B must absorb in their respective profit and loss sharing ratio of 4:2. Partner A's share is $2,000, and partner B's share is $1,000.
3. Partner B had an $8,000 loan balance. His capital account, however, was charged with $6,000 when partner D's capital deficit was written off and $1,000 when partner C's capital deficit was written off. Thus $7,000 must be transferred from his loan account under the *right of setoff* to eliminate his capital deficit. This leaves $1,000 in his loan account, which, when distributed to him, is available to his *personal creditors* because he is personally insolvent.
4. Because partner A has the largest personal net worth, assume that *partnership creditors* took legal action against her (as opposed to proceeding against partners A, B, or C *even though the* ***partnership creditors*** *would share on a pro rata basis with these three partners'* ***personal creditors*** *in the* ***personal assets*** *of each of these partners*). The *partnership creditors* collected the $17,000 owed them from partner A personally. Partner A had a $6,000 capital balance, which was reduced by $12,000 for her share of partner D's capital deficit and $2,000 for her share of partner C's capital deficit. This gives her a capital deficit of $8,000. Her $17,000 payment to the *partnership creditors*, however, is *the equivalent of a capital contribution*. Thus, her capital account deficit is eliminated, and she now has a *positive* capital balance of $9,000.

5. This leaves the partnership with $10,000 cash, which is distributed to partner B ($1,000 in payment of his loan) and partner A ($9,000 in liquidation of her capital balance).

Illustration 22-7 summarizes the preceding sequence of events in a statement of realization and liquidation.

III. INSTALLMENT LIQUIDATIONS

In an **installment liquidation**, the conversion of noncash assets into cash occurs over a period of time. As a result, the partnership realizes more proceeds than would be possible in a quick liquidation. Because of the lengthier conversion period, cash may become available for distribution to partners long before the last noncash asset is sold. In such situations, the partners usually want cash distributed as it becomes available.

The Two Worst-Case Assumptions

If capital accounts are *not* maintained in the profit and loss sharing ratio, cash may *not* be distributed to the partners on some arbitrary basis such as the profit and loss sharing ratio, the capital balances ratio, or personal needs. Such a distribution might result in later inequities to certain partners. For example, cash may be distributed to a partner who may *not* be able to return such cash to the partnership if a deficit balance subsequently is created in his or her capital account as a result of future losses on the conversion of noncash assets into cash. Such partner's deficit balance would have to be allocated to partners who have credit balances, and those partners would have to bear a larger portion of the loss than their profit and loss sharing percentages. To prevent this potential inequity, accountants use two worst-case assumptions to determine which partners should receive available cash at any particular time. These assumptions are as follows:

1. *First* Worst-Case Assumption: **All noncash assets are assumed to be completely worthless.** Thus a hypothetical loss equal to the carrying values of noncash assets is assumed to have occurred. On a worksheet, the hypothetical loss is allocated to the partners' capital account balances existing at that time.
2. *Second* Worst-Case Assumption: **Partners with deficit positions are assumed to be personally insolvent.** If, as a result of the first worst-case assumption, a partner's capital account is in a deficit position (on the worksheet only), we assume that **such partner is *not* able to make contributions to the partnership to eliminate the hypothetical deficit.** (This assumption is made regardless of the partner's personal financial status.) Accordingly, the hypothetical deficit balance is allocated to the partners who have credit balances, using their respective profit and loss sharing ratio. If, in turn, this process creates a *hypothetical deficit balance* in another partner's capital account, this *hypothetical deficit balance* is allocated (on the worksheet only) to the remaining partners who still have credit balances. This process is repeated until only partners with credit balances remain on the worksheet. Cash may then be distributed to the partners who have *credit* balances on the worksheet.

The result of these two assumptions is that cash is distributed only to the partners who have capital balances sufficient to absorb their share of (1) the maximum potential loss on noncash assets and (2) any capital deficiencies that may result to other partners as a result of a maximum loss on noncash assets. In other words, payments may be made safely to such partners with full assurance that the money will *not* have to be returned to the partnership at some later date in the event of future realization losses.

Under this method of distributing cash to the partners, **the capital accounts are brought into the profit and loss sharing ratio**, usually only after several cash distributions have been made. Once the capital accounts have been brought into the profit and loss sharing ratio, cash distributions may be made using that ratio. The two worst-case assumptions need *not* be used for any future cash distributions because their use produces the same result as the profit and loss sharing ratio.

ILLUSTRATION 22-7 *LUMP-SUM* LIQUIDATION: PARTNERSHIP *INSOLVENT* AND SOME PARTNERS PERSONALLY *INSOLVENT*

A, B, C, and D Partnership
Statement of Realization and Liquidation
July 2006

	ASSETS			PARTNERS' LOANS			PARTNERS' CAPITAL			
	CASH	NONCASH	OUTSIDE LIABILITIES	B	C	D	A (40%)[a]	B (20%)[a]	C (20%)[a]	D (20%)[a]
Preliquidation Balances, 7/1/06	$ 10,000	$ 290,000	$ 157,000	$10,000	$ 5,000	$ 2,000	$ 70,000	$ 30,000	$ 20,000	$ 6,000
Realization of assets and allocation of loss	130,000	(290,000)					(64,000)	(32,000)	(32,000)	(32,000)
Subtotal	$ 140,000	$ -0-	$ 157,000	$10,000	$ 5,000	$ 2,000	$ 6,000	$ (2,000)	$(12,000)	$(26,000)
Exercise right of setoff				(2,000)	(5,000)	(2,000)		2,000	5,000	2,000
Subtotal	$ 140,000		$ 157,000	$ 8,000	$ -0-	$ -0-	$ 6,000	$ -0-	$ (7,000)	$(24,000)
Distribution to outside creditors	(140,000)		(140,000)							
Subtotal	$ -0-		$ 17,000	$ 8,000			$ 6,000		$ (7,000)	$(24,000)
Write-off D's capital deficit							(12,000)	$ (6,000)	(6,000)	24,000
Subtotal	$ -0-		$ 17,000	$ 8,000			$ (6,000)	$ (6,000)	$(13,000)	$ -0-
Contributions by C	10,000								10,000	
Subtotal	$ 10,000		$ 17,000	$ 8,000			$ (6,000)	$ (6,000)	$ (3,000)	
Write-off C's capital deficit							(2,000)	(1,000)	3,000	
Subtotal	$ 10,000		$ 17,000	$ 8,000			$ (8,000)	$ (7,000)	$ -0-	
Exercise right of setoff				(7,000)				7,000		
Subtotal	$ 10,000		$ 17,000	$ 1,000			$ (8,000)	$ -0-		
Contributions by A			(17,000)				17,000			
Subtotal	$ 10,000		$ -0-	$ 1,000			$ 9,000			
Cash Distributions:										
Partners' loan	(1,000)			(1,000)						
Partners' capital	(9,000)						(9,000)			
Postliquidation Balances, 7/31/06	$ -0-			$ -0-			$ -0-			

[a] Denotes profit and loss sharing percentage.

Applying the two worst-case assumptions shows that a partner's capital account (on the worksheet) is *reduced* for any loans the partnership has outstanding to the partner. Also, a partner's capital account (on the worksheet) is *increased* for any loan the *partner* may have outstanding to the *partnership*; this automatically provides for the hypothetical exercising of the *right of setoff*.

CHECK POINT

In the *installment liquidation* of a partnership, how is cash distributed to partners?

a. Equally
b. In their normal profit and loss sharing ratio
c. Using the ratio of the partners' capital balances
d. Using the *marshaling of assets* procedure
e. Based on the ability to absorb losses

Answer: e

Loss on Realization Creates a Deficit Balance in Certain Partners' Capital Accounts: One Partner Is Personally Insolvent

To illustrate how these two worst-case assumptions apply to an installment liquidation, assume the following:

1. The partnership of A, B, C, and D has the same preliquidation balances as shown in Illustration 22-7.
2. The noncash assets of $290,000 are sold as follows:

Date Sold	Book Value	Proceeds	Loss
July 3, 2006	$183,000	$168,000	$(15,000)
August 6, 2006	70,000	25,000	(45,000)
September 9, 2006	37,000	27,000	(10,000)
	$290,000	$220,000	$(70,000)

3. Cash was distributed to outside creditors and partners as it became available.
4. Partner D could contribute only $4,000 to the partnership during the liquidation proceedings. The other partners had to absorb his remaining $2,000 capital account deficit.

The statement of realization and liquidation is prepared as shown in Illustration 22-8. The cash distributions to partners were determined from the **schedule of safe payments** shown in Illustration 22-9, which is a supporting schedule to Illustration 22-8. The schedule of safe payments shows the cash distributions that may be made safely to individual partners concerning the objectives to minimize potential inequities and limit the accountant's legal exposure.

Review Points for Illustrations 22-8 and 22-9. Note the following:

1. The *statement of realization and liquidation* reflects only *the historical transactions* recorded in the *general ledger*. Although the statement covers the entire liquidation period, it was started when the liquidation process began and periodically updated as noncash assets were sold and cash distributions were made.
2. The *schedule of safe payments* to partners reflects **the assumptions made at those dates when cash was available for distribution to partners.** The purpose of the schedule is to determine which partners should receive the cash available at those dates.
3. The payments that may be made to partners, as shown on the schedule of safe payments, are *first* applied as a reduction of a partner's *loan* and then as a reduction of that partner's *capital* in the statement of realization and liquidation.
4. After the *first* cash distribution to partners on July 3, 2006, the capital accounts of partners A and B are in their respective profit and loss sharing ratio of 4:2. All *future* cash distributions to these two partners are in this 2:1 ratio.

5. After the *second* cash distribution to partners on August 6, 2006, the capital accounts of partners A, B, and C (which include partner C's *loan account* balance) are in their respective profit and loss sharing ratio of 4:2:2. All *future* cash distributions to these three partners are in this 4:2:2 ratio.
6. Obviously, the schedule of safe payments is prepared only after cash is available to distribute to partners. Thus it may be used only when the partnership is solvent.

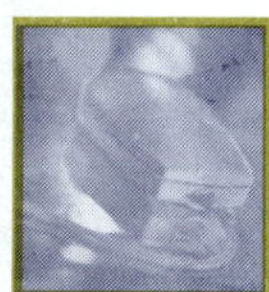

CHECK POINT

Under Section 807 of the RUPA (which deals with settlement of legal claims), which is true?

a. The capital and loan balances of the partners are combined.
b. The two worst-case assumptions are used.
c. A cash distribution plan is prepared.
d. Cash is distributed to the partner having the *highest* capital balance.
e. A distinction is made between personal liabilities and partnership liabilities.

Answer: e

The following condensed balance sheet is presented for the partnership of Acres, Farmer, and Tillman, who share profits and losses in the ratio of 3:2:1, respectively:

Cash	$ 60,000
Other assets	440,000
	$500,000
Liabilities	$200,000
Capital, Acres	30,000
Capital, Farmer	100,000
Capital, Tillman	170,000
	$500,000

The partners decided to liquidate the partnership and sell the other assets for $320,000. How should the available cash be distributed?

a. Acres, –0–; Farmer, $40,000; Tillman, $140,000
b. Acres, $60,000; Farmer, $60,000; Tillman, $60,000
c. Acres, –0–; Farmer, $45,000; Tillman, $135,000
d. Acres, –0–; Farmer, $53,333; Tillman, $127,667

Answer: a

Cash Distribution Plan

When cash is available to distribute to partners, a *schedule of safe payments* to partners must be prepared using the *two worst-case assumptions* (except for the final payment, of course). Distributing cash to partners in the sequence resulting from the use of the two worst-case assumptions brings the capital accounts into the profit and loss sharing ratio. (As determined earlier in the chapter, a partner's *loan* to the partnership is, in substance, part of that partner's *capital investment.*) Once the capital accounts are in this ratio, all future cash distributions to partners are made in the profit and loss sharing ratio.

By understanding the results of this process, we may analyze the relationship of the capital accounts at the *beginning* of liquidation to determine which partners receive cash as it becomes available. The analysis results in a **cash distribution plan.** A cash distribution plan has the advantage of informing partners at **the *beginning* of the liquidation process** when they will receive cash **in relation to the other partners.**

Understanding the methodology underlying the preparation of a cash distribution plan requires an intuitive understanding of the fact that when the capital accounts are *not* in the profit and loss

ILLUSTRATION 22-8 *INSTALLMENT* LIQUIDATION: PARTNERSHIP *INSOLVENT* AND SOME PARTNERS PERSONALLY *INSOLVENT*

A, B, C, and D Partnership
Statement of Realization and Liquidation
July 1, 2006, through September 9, 2006

	ASSETS			PARTNERS' LOANS			PARTNERS' CAPITAL			
	CASH	NONCASH	OUTSIDE LIABILITIES	B	C	D	A (40%)[a]	B (20%)[a]	C (20%)[a]	D (20%)[a]
Preliquidation Balances, 7/1/06	$ 10,000	$ 290,000	$ 157,000	$ 10,000	$ 5,000	$ 2,000	$ 70,000	$30,000	$20,000	$ 6,000
Realization of assets and allocation of loss, 7/3/06	168,000	(183,000)					(6,000)	(3,000)	(3,000)	(3,000)
Subtotal	178,000	$ 107,000	$ 157,000	$ 10,000	$ 5,000	$ 2,000	$ 64,000	$27,000	$17,000	$ 3,000
July Cash Distribution										
Outside creditors	(157,000)		(157,000)							
Partners' loan	(10,000)[b]			(10,000)[b]						
Partners' capital	(11,000)[b]						(10,667)[b]	(333)[b]		
Subtotal	$ -0-	$ 107,000	$ -0-	$ -0-	$ 5,000	$ 2,000	$ 53,333	$26,667	$17,000	$ 3,000
Realization of assets and allocation of loss, 8/6/06	25,000	(70,000)					(18,000)	(9,000)	(9,000)	(9,000)
Subtotal	$ 25,000	$ 37,000			$ 5,000	$ 2,000	$ 35,333	$17,667	$ 8,000	$(6,000)
Exercise right of setoff						(2,000)				2,000
Subtotal	$ 25,000	$ 37,000			$ 5,000	$ -0-	$ 35,333	$17,667	$ 8,000	$(4,000)
Cash contribution by D	4,000									4,000
Subtotal	$ 29,000	$ 37,000			$ 5,000		$ 35,333	$17,667	$ 8,000	$ -0-
August Cash Distribution										
Partners' loan	(3,750)[b]				(3,750)[b]					
Partners' capital	(25,250)[b]						(16,833)[b]	(8,417)[b]		
Subtotal	$ -0-	$ 37,000			$ 1,250		$ 18,500	$ 9,250	$ 8,000	
Realization of assets and allocation of losses, 9/9/06	27,000	(37,000)					(4,000)	(2,000)	(2,000)	(2,000)
Subtotal	$ 27,000	$ -0-			$ 1,250		$ 14,500	$ 7,250	$ 6,000	$(2,000)
Write-off of D's deficit							(1,000)	(500)	(500)	2,000
Subtotal	$ 27,000				$ 1,250		$ 13,500	$ 6,750	$ 5,500	$ -0-
Final Cash Distribution										
Partners' loan	(1,250)				(1,250)					
Partners' capital	(25,750)						(13,500)	(6,750)	(5,500)	
Postliquidation Balances, 9/9/06	$ -0-				$ -0-		$ -0-	$ -0-	$ -0-	

[a] Denotes profit and loss sharing percentage.
[b] See supporting schedule in Illustration 22-9.

ILLUSTRATION 22-9 SUPPORTING SCHEDULE TO ILLUSTRATION 22-8

A, B, C, and D Partnership
Schedule of Safe Payments to Partners

	PARTNER			
	A (40%)[a]	B (20%)[a]	C (20%)[a]	D (20%)[a]
Computation to Determine How Available Cash on 7/3/06 Should Be Distributed				
Capital and loan balances at cash distribution (from Illustration 22-8)				
Capital	$ 64,000	$ 27,000	$ 17,000	$ 3,000
Loan		10,000	5,000	2,000
Total	$ 64,000	$ 37,000	$ 22,000	$ 5,000
First worst-case assumption—Assume full loss on noncash assets of $107,000	(42,800)	(21,400)	(21,400)	(21,400)
Subtotal	$ 21,200	$ 15,600	$ 600	$(16,400)
Second worst-case assumption—Assume A, B, and C must absorb D's deficit	(8,200)	(4,100)	(4,100)	16,400
Subtotal	$ 13,000	$ 11,500	$ (3,500)	$ -0-
Repeat second worst-case assumption—Assume A and B must absorb C's deficit	(2,333)	(1,167)	3,500	
Cash to Be Distributed to Each Partner	$ 10,667	$ 10,333[b]	$ -0-	
Computation to Determine How Available Cash on 8/6/06 Should Be Distributed				
Capital and loan balances at cash distribution (from Illustration 22-8)				
Capital	$ 35,333	$ 17,667	$ 8,000	
Loan			5,000	
Total	$ 35,333	$ 17,667	$ 13,000	$ -0-
First worst-case assumption—Assume full loss on noncash assets of $37,000	(14,800)	(7,400)	(7,400)	(7,400)
Subtotal	$ 20,533	$ 10,267	$ 5,600	$ (7,400)
Second worst-case assumption—Assume A, B, and C must absorb D's deficit	(3,700)	(1,850)	(1,850)	7,400
Cash to be distributed by each partner	$ 16,833	$ 8,417	$ 3,750[c]	$ -0-

[a] Denotes profit and loss sharing percentage.

[b] Of this amount, $10,000 is deemed a repayment of the loan.

[c] All of this amount is deemed a repayment of the loan.

sharing ratio, one or more partners have capital balances sufficient to absorb his, her, or their share of losses that exceed the partnership's net worth, whereas one or more other partners have capital balances sufficient to absorb only his, her, or their share of losses that are *less than* the partnership's net worth. To illustrate this fact, we present the following comparative analysis:

		Partner			
	Total	**W (40%)**	**X (30%)**	**Y (20%)**	**Z (10%)**
Actual preliquidation capital and loan balances	$100,000	$48,000	$33,000	$11,000	$8,000
Hypothetical capital and loan balances in the profit and loss sharing ratio of 4:3:2:1	$100,000	$40,000	$30,000	$20,000	$10,000
Percentage relationship of actual balances to hypothetical balances		120%	110%	55%	80%

Because their actual balances *exceed* the balances that would exist if they were kept in the profit and loss sharing ratio, only partners W and X could absorb their share of losses higher than the $100,000 partnership capital. On the other hand, because their actual balances are *less than* the balances that would exist if they were kept in the profit and loss sharing ratio, partners Y and Z could absorb only their share of losses that are less than the partnership capital of $100,000.

Ranking the Partners

The percentage line of the preceding analysis ranks the partners in terms of which could absorb the largest loss to which could absorb the smallest loss. The ranking in this example is W, X, Z, and Y—that is, partner W (who has the *highest* percentage) can absorb the largest loss, and partner Y (who has the lowest percentage) can absorb the *smallest* loss. This ranking can be readily proved by calculating the exact loss needed to eliminate each partner's capital and loan balance. We divide each partner's capital and loan balance by that partner's profit and loss sharing percentage. Continuing with our example, this calculation is as follows:

	Partner			
	W	X	Y	Z
Actual preliquidation capital balances	$48,000	$33,000	$11,000	$8,000
Profit and loss sharing percentage	40%	30%	20%	10%
Loss absorption potential	$120,000	$110,000	$55,000	$80,000
Ranking	1	2	4	3

Note that a $120,000 loss eliminates the capital and loan balance of partner W (the highest-ranking partner), whereas for partner Y (the lowest-ranking partner), a loss of only $55,000 eliminates his capital and loan balance.

Ranking the partners in this manner reveals the order in which cash should be distributed to them as it becomes available. Distributing cash in this order **brings the capital balances into the profit and loss sharing ratio on a step-by-step basis,** as follows:

1. **Distribution to *highest*-ranking partner.** Distribute sufficient cash to partner W so that his capital balance is brought into the profit and loss sharing ratio with the *next highest-ranking partner* (partner X).
2. **Distribution to *two highest*-ranking partners.** Distribute sufficient cash to partners W and X in their respective profit and loss sharing ratio of 4:3 so that their capital balances are brought into the profit and loss sharing ratio with the *next highest-ranking partner* (partner Z).
3. **Distribution to *three highest*-ranking partners.** Distribute sufficient cash to partners W, X, and Z in their respective profit and loss sharing ratio of 4:3:1 so that their capital balances are brought into the profit and loss sharing ratio with the *next highest-ranking partner* (partner Y).

Only the exact amount of cash distributed at each stage in this sequence needs to be determined. The calculations are shown in Illustration 22-10.

Review Points for Illustration 22-10. Note the following:

1. The cash distribution plan is operable only *after* outside creditors have been paid *in full.*
2. The schedule reflects only the order in which cash distributions to the partners will be made *if* cash is available to distribute to the partners.
3. The sequence of distributing cash in the cash distribution plan coincides with the sequence that would result if cash were distributed using the schedule of safe payments.

ILLUSTRATION 22-10

W, X, Y, and Z Partnership
Schedule of Cash Distribution to Partners

	PARTNER			
	W	X	Y	Z
Preliquidation capital and loan balances	$48,000	$33,000	$11,000	$8,000
Ranking	1	2	4	3
Step 1: Cash to be distributed to W				
Balances, per above	$48,000	$33,000		
Balances in profit and loss ratio of 4:3 using X's actual balance as the base	44,000[a]	33,000		
	$ 4,000	$ -0-		
Step 2: Cash to be distributed to W and X				
Balances, per above	$44,000	$33,000		$8,000
Balances in profit and loss ratio of 4:3:1 using Z's actual balance as the base	32,000[b]	24,000[c]		8,000
	$12,000	$ 9,000		$ -0-
Step 3: Cash to be distributed to W, X, and Z				
Balances, per above	$32,000	$24,000	$11,000	$8,000
Balances in profit and loss ratio of 4:3:2:1 using Y's actual balance as the base	22,000	16,500	11,000	5,500
	$10,000	$ 7,500	$ -0-	$2,500

After this distribution, all capital accounts are in the profit and loss sharing ratio of 4:3:2:1. Accordingly, all future cash distributions are made in this ratio.

Summary of Cash Distribution Plan

	W	X	Y	Z
First $4,000	$ 4,000			
Next $21,000 (4:3)	12,000	$ 9,000		
Next $20,000 (4:3:1)	10,000	7,500		$2,500
Any additional amounts (4:3:2:1)	40%	30%	20%	10%

[a] $33,000 × 4/3.

[b] $8,000 × 4/1.

[c] $8,000 × 3/1.

CHECK POINT

The following condensed balance sheet is presented as of 7/1/06 for the partnership of Rane, Waters, and Wells, who share profits and losses in the ratio of 5:3:2, respectively:

Cash	$ 20,000
Other assets	380,000
	$400,000
Liabilities	$100,000
Capital, Rane	210,000
Capital, Waters	43,000
Capital, Wells	47,000
	$400,000

The partners decided to liquidate the partnership. On 7/3/06, the first cash sale of other assets with a $240,000 carrying amount realized $190,000. Safe installment payments to the partners were made on the same date. How should the available cash be distributed to the partners?

a. Rane, $55,000; Waters, $33,000; Wells, $22,000
b. Rane, $108,000; Waters, –0–; Wells, $2,000
c. Rane, $105,000; Waters, –0–; Wells, $5,000
d. Rane, $115,000; Waters, –0–; Wells, $9,000

Answer: c

END-OF-CHAPTER REVIEW

Summary of Key Points

1. Partners may greatly minimize the possibility of having to absorb another partner's deficit balance by specifying in the partnership agreement that capital balances are to be maintained in the profit and loss sharing ratio.

2. To the extent that a partner must absorb some or all of another partner's capital account deficit, the absorbing partner has **legal recourse** against the personal assets of the partner who could *not* make good the deficit balance through **setoff** or contribution.

3. In **lump-sum liquidations**, no distributions are made to the partners until the realization process is completed, when the full amount of the gain or loss on realization of the partnership assets is known. In these cases, cash is distributed to the partners who have credit balances in their capital and loan accounts.

4. In **installment liquidations**, distributions are made to some or all of the partners as cash becomes available; thus, cash is distributed to partners before the full amount of the gain or loss on realization of the partnership assets is known. In these cases, cash distributions are made to partners in such a manner that the capital and loan balances of the individual partners are brought into line with the profit and loss sharing ratio.

5. The settlement of legal claims is **no longer governed by the marshalling of assets procedure.** Under Section 807 of RUPA (which is consistent with bankruptcy rules), (1) *partnership creditors* have first priority as to *partnership assets* and (2) the claims of *partnership creditors* (in an *insolvent partnership*) rank *equally* with the claims of a partner's *personal creditors* against the partner's *personal assets*.

Glossary of New Terms

Liquidation The termination of a partnership's business activities.

Marshaling of assets A superseded legal procedure whereby a *partnership's creditors* are given first claim on *partnership assets*, and *personal creditors* of an insolvent partner are given first claim on his or her *personal assets*. (See review point 5.)

Rule of setoff The subtraction of a partner's deficit balance in his or her capital account from the balance of any loan outstanding to the partnership. Also, the subtraction of a partnership's loan to a partner from the partner's capital account.

ASSIGNMENT MATERIAL

Review Questions

1. How are *partnership* liquidations different from *corporate* liquidations?

2. What is the significance of maintaining partners' capital accounts in the profit and loss sharing ratio?

3. How is a *deficit balance* in a partner's capital account disposed of if that partner is unable to eliminate the deficit through setoff or contribution?
4. In what ratio should realization gains and losses during liquidation be shared among the partners? Why?
5. How is the *rule of setoff* applied?
6. What is the function of the *statement of realization and liquidation*?
7. In what order does the RUPA specify that cash distributions are to be made to creditors and partners during liquidation?
8. Is the order in Question 7 strictly followed in all situations? Why or why not?
9. How does the *marshaling of assets* procedure work? What procedure replaced it?
10. Under what conditions may cash be distributed to partners on the installment basis rather than in a *lump sum*?
11. When a partnership is insolvent and some partners have positive capital account balances, but other partners have deficit balances, against which partners may creditors proceed personally to obtain full payment of their claims?
12. How is a partner's personal payment to partnership creditors treated on the partnership's books?

Exercises

E 22-1 **Lump-Sum Liquidation: Solvent Partnership Having Partners' Loans—All Partners Personally Solvent** Partners Hall, Lane, and Tower share profits and losses in the ratio 3:2:1, respectively. The partners voted to liquidate the partnership when its assets, liabilities, and capital were as follows:

Cash	$ 2,000	Liabilities	$20,000
Noncash assets	78,000	Loans:	
		Hall	5,000
		Tower	10,000
		Capital:	
		Hall	20,000
		Lane	15,000
		Tower	10,000
	$80,000		$80,000

Assume that all the *noncash assets* were sold for $36,000 and that all cash was distributed to outside creditors and partners.

Required Prepare a *statement of realization and liquidation*.

E 22-2 **Lump-Sum Liquidation: Insolvent Partnership Having Loans to and from Partners—All Partners Personally Solvent** Partners Bass, Singer, and Tennor share profits and losses equally. The partners voted to liquidate the partnership when its assets, liabilities, and capital were as follows:

Cash	$ 14,000	Liabilities	$ 80,000
Note receivable from Tennor	11,000	Loans:	
Other noncash assets	120,000	Bass	4,000
		Singer	16,000
		Capital:	
		Bass	15,000
		Singer	15,000
		Tennor	15,000
	$145,000		$145,000

Additional Information

1. All the *noncash assets* of $120,000 were sold for $54,000.

2. Tennor instructed the partnership to write off the $11,000 he borrowed from the partnership because he has no liquid personal assets at this time (even though he is *personally* solvent).
3. All partners could eliminate any *deficits* in their capital accounts through *setoff* or *contribution*, or both.
4. All cash was distributed to outside creditors and partners.

Required Prepare a *statement of realization and liquidation.*

E 22-3 Lump-Sum Liquidation: Solvent Partnership Having Loans to and from Partners—Certain Partners Personally Insolvent Partners Criss, Kross, and Zigge share profits and losses in the ratio of 3:3:2, respectively. The partners voted to liquidate the partnership when its assets, liabilities, and capital were as follows:

Cash	$ 1,000	Liabilities	$34,000
Note receivable from Zigge	9,000	Loans:	
Other noncash assets	75,000	Kross	15,000
		Capital:	
		Criss	11,000
		Kross	10,000
		Zigge	15,000
	$85,000		$85,000

Additional Information

1. All the *noncash assets* of $75,000 were sold for $43,000.
2. Zigge was *personally insolvent* and unable to contribute any cash to the partnership.
3. Criss and Kross were both *personally solvent* and able to eliminate any deficits in their capital accounts through setoff or contribution.
4. All cash was distributed to outside creditors and partners.

Required Prepare a *statement of realization and liquidation.*

E 22-4 Lump-Sum Liquidation: Insolvent Partnership Having Loans from Partners—Certain Partners Personally Insolvent Partners Cattie, Deere, Fox, and O'Hare share profits and losses in the ratio of 5:2:2:1, respectively. The partners voted to liquidate the partnership when its assets and liabilities were as follows:

Cash	$ 15,000	Liabilities	$165,000
Noncash assets	235,000	Loans:	
		Deere	7,000
		Fox	5,000
		O'Hare	3,000
		Capital:	
		Cattie	40,000
		Deere	16,000
		Fox	10,000
		O'Hare	4,000
	$250,000		$250,000

Additional Information

1. All the *noncash assets* were sold for $135,000.
2. Cattie contributed $5,000 to the partnership after the noncash assets were sold. She has no additional funds beyond that needed to satisfy personal creditors.
3. All other partners were personally solvent; they made capital contributions as necessary to eliminate deficits in their capital accounts.
4. All cash was distributed to outside creditors and partners.

Required Prepare a *statement of realization and liquidation.*

E 22-5 Insolvent Partnership and Insolvent Partners: Theory Q, R, S, and T are partners sharing profits and losses equally. The partnership is insolvent and is therefore being liquidated; its status and that of each partner follow:

Partner	Partnership Capital Balance	Personal Assets (exclusive of partnership interest)	Personal Liabilities (exclusive of partnership interest)
Q	$ 15,000	$100,000	$40,000
R	10,000	30,000	60,000
S	(20,000)	80,000	5,000
T	(30,000)	1,000	28,000
	$(25,000)		

Required Select the correct response to the following:

Assuming that the RUPA applies, the partnership creditors

1. Must first seek recovery against S because she is personally solvent and has a negative capital balance.
2. Will *not* be paid in full regardless of how they proceed legally because the partnership assets are less than its liabilities.
3. Must share R's interest in the partnership on a pro rata basis with R's personal creditors.
4. Have first claim to the partnership assets before any partner's personal creditors have rights to them.

E 22-6 Installment Liquidation: Solvent Partnership Having Partner's Loan—First Cash Distribution to Partners Partners Deeds, Grant, and Trusty share profits and losses in the ratio 6:3:1, respectively. The partners voted to liquidate the partnership when its assets, liabilities, and capital were as follows:

Cash	$ 1,000	Liabilities	$35,000
Noncash assets	94,000	Loan:	
		Trusty	10,000
		Capital:	
		Deeds	30,000
		Grant	15,000
		Trusty	5,000
	$95,000		$95,000

Assume that *noncash assets* with a *book value* of $74,000 were sold for $54,000.

Required Determine how the cash available after this sale should be distributed.

E 22-7 Installment Liquidation: Solvent Partnership—First Cash Distribution to Partners Partners Springer, Sumner, and Winters share profits and losses in the ratio 5:3:2, respectively. The partners voted to liquidate the partnership when its assets, liabilities, and capital were as follows:

Cash	$ 40,000	
Other assets	210,000	
Liabilities		$ 60,000
Capital:		
Springer		48,000
Sumner		72,000
Winters		70,000
	$250,000	$250,000

The partnership will be liquidated over a long period of time. Cash is to be distributed to the partners as it becomes available. The *first* sale of *noncash assets* having a *book value* of $120,000 realized $90,000.

Required Determine how the available cash should be distributed to the partners after this first sale.

E 22-8 Installment Liquidation: Solvent Partnership with Partnership's and Partner's Loans—First Cash Distribution to Partners Partners Castle, King, and Queen share profits and losses in the ratio

4:4:2, respectively. The partners voted to liquidate the partnership when its assets, liabilities, and capital were as follows:

Cash	$ 20,000	
Note receivable from Castle	10,000	
Other assets	170,000	
Liabilities		$ 50,000
Loan from King		30,000
Capital:		
Castle		37,000
King		15,000
Queen		68,000
	$200,000	$200,000

The partnership will be liquidated over a long period of time. Cash will be distributed to the partners as it becomes available. The *first* sale of *noncash assets* having a book value of $90,000 realized $50,000.

Required Determine how the available cash should be distributed to the partners after this first sale.

Problems

P 22-1* **Lump-Sum Liquidation: Solvent Partnership Having Partner's Loan—All Partners Personally Solvent** Partners Rockne and Stone share profits in the ratio 3:2, respectively. The partners agreed to liquidate the partnership when the assets, liabilities, and capital were as follows:

Cash	$ 6,000	Liabilities	$27,000
Noncash assets	44,000	Loan:	
		Stone	6,000
		Capital:	
		Rockne	14,000
		Stone	3,000
	$50,000		$50,000

Additional Information

1. Rockne agreed to personally take certain equipment having a $5,000 *book value*. (The partners estimated its current value at $6,500.)
2. Stone agreed to personally take certain office furniture having a *book value* of $3,000. (The partners estimated its current value at $2,000.)
3. All other noncash assets were sold for $25,000.
4. Liquidation expenses of $1,000 were incurred.
5. Cash was distributed to outside creditors and partners.

Required Prepare a *statement of realization and liquidation*.

P 22-2* **Lump-Sum Liquidation: Solvent Partnership Having Partners' Loans—Certain Partners Personally Insolvent** Partners Duke, Lord, Noble, and Prince share profits and losses in the ratio 4:3:2:1, respectively. The partners agreed to liquidate the partnership when it had assets, liabilities, and capital as follows:

Cash	$ 10,000	Liabilities	$ 78,000
Noncash assets	140,000	Loans:	
		Duke	4,000
		Lord	3,000
		Capital:	
		Duke	10,000
		Lord	10,000
		Noble	30,000
		Prince	15,000
	$150,000		$150,000

* The financial statement information presented for problems accompanied by asterisks is also provided on MODEL 22 (filename: MODEL22) at the **http://pahler.swlearning.com** website, allowing the problem to be worked on the computer.

Additional Information

1. The noncash assets were sold for $90,000.
2. Duke is *personally* insolvent.
3. Lord contributed $2,000 cash to the partnership; he had no other available funds in excess of amounts needed to satisfy *personal* creditors.
4. All cash was distributed to *outside* creditors and partners.

Required Prepare a *statement of realization and liquidation.*

P 22-3*  **Lump-Sum Liquidation: Insolvent Partnership Having Partners' Loans—Certain Partners Personally Insolvent** Partners Oates, Ryley, and Wheatman share profits and losses in the ratio 3:3:2, respectively. The partners agreed to liquidate the partnership when assets, liabilities, and capital were as follows:

Cash	$ 5,000	Liabilities	$48,000
Noncash assets	85,000	Loans:	
		Oates	10,000
		Ryley	3,000
		Capital:	
		Oates	11,000
		Ryley	10,000
		Wheatman	8,000
	$90,000		$90,000

Additional Information

1. The noncash assets were sold for $29,000.
2. Outside creditors of the partnership proceeded against Wheatman and collected from her $14,000 that the partnership was unable to pay.
3. The partnership incurred liquidation expenses of $4,000, which Ryley paid *personally*.
4. Oates is *personally* insolvent.
5. Ryley and Wheatman (who are both personally solvent) make a personal settlement between themselves.

Required Prepare a *statement of realization and liquidation.*

P 22-4 **Installment Liquidation: Schedule of Safe Payments—First Cash Distribution to Partners** On 1/1/06, the partners of Allen, Brown, and Cox, who share profits and losses in the ratio of 5:3:2, respectively, decide to liquidate their partnership. The partnership trial balance at this date follows:

	Debit	Credit
Cash	$ 18,000	
Accounts receivable	66,000	
Inventory	52,000	
Machinery and equipment	249,000	
Accumulated depreciation		$ 60,000
Loan, Allen	30,000	
Accounts payable		53,000
Loan, Brown		20,000
Capital, Allen		118,000
Capital, Brown		90,000
Capital, Cox		74,000
	$415,000	$415,000

The partners plan a program of piecemeal conversion of assets to minimize liquidation losses. All available cash, less an amount retained to provide for future expenses, is to be distributed to the partners at the end of each month. The liquidation transactions for January 2006 follow:

Additional Information

1. Accounts receivable of $51,000 was collected; the balance is uncollectible.
2. The amount of $38,000 was received for the entire inventory.
3. Liquidation expenses of $2,000 were paid.
4. Outside creditors were paid $50,000 after offset of a $3,000 credit memorandum received on 1/11/06.
5. Cash of $10,000 was retained in the business at the end of the month for potential unrecorded liabilities and anticipated expenses.

Required Prepare a schedule of safe payments showing how cash was distributed to the partners as of 1/31/06.

P 22-5* **Installment Liquidation: Schedule of Safe Payments and Statement of Realization and Liquidation** Partners Barley, Flax, and Rice share profits and losses in the ratio 6:3:1, respectively. The partners decided to liquidate the partnership on 6/30/06, when its assets, liabilities, and capital were as follows:

Cash	$ 10,000	Liabilities	$ 42,000
Noncash assets	130,000	Loans:	
		Barley	4,000
		Flax	1,000
		Capital:	
		Barley	84,000
		Flax	5,000
		Rice	4,000
	$140,000		$140,000

Additional Information

1. On 7/1/06, liquidation expenses were estimated at approximately $3,000. Actual liquidation expenses totaled only $2,500—they were paid as follows:

July 31, 2006	$1,000
August 31, 2006	1,000
September 30, 2006	500
	$2,500

2. Noncash assets were sold as follows:

Date	Book Value	Proceeds
July 5, 2006	$ 30,000	$ 36,000
August 7, 2006	40,000	28,000
September 9, 2006	60,000	44,000
	$130,000	$108,000

3. Partners were able to eliminate any deficits in their capital accounts through *setoff* or *contribution* as deficit balances occurred.
4. Cash was distributed to outside creditors and partners as it was available at the end of each month.

Required Prepare a *statement of realization and liquidation*, including supporting schedules showing how cash was distributed to outside creditors and partners as it was available.

P 22-6 **Installment Liquidation: Schedule of Cash Distribution** Partners Brickley, Glass, Steele, and Woods decide to dissolve their partnership. They plan to sell the assets gradually to minimize losses. They share profits and losses as follows: Brickley, 40%; Glass, 35%; Steele, 15%; and Woods, 10%. The partnership's trial balance as of 10/1/06, the date on which liquidation begins, is shown as follows.

	Debit	Credit
Cash	$ 200	
Receivables	25,900	
Inventory, 10/1/06	42,600	
Equipment (net)	19,800	
Accounts payable		$ 3,000
Loan, Brickley		6,000
Loan, Glass		10,000
Capital, Brickley		20,000
Capital, Glass		21,500
Capital, Steele		18,000
Capital, Woods		10,000
	$88,500	$88,500

Required

1. Prepare a statement as of 10/1/06 showing how cash will be distributed among partners by installments as it becomes available.
2. On 10/31/06, $12,700 cash was available to the partners. How should it be distributed?

P 22-7 **Installment Liquidation: Schedule of Cash Distribution** Partners Arbuckle, Beltmore, and Tanner want you to assist them in winding up the affairs of their partnership. You gather the following information:

1. The 6/30/06 trial balance of the partnership is as follows:

	Debit	Credit
Cash	$ 6,000	
Accounts receivable	22,000	
Inventory	14,000	
Plant and equipment (net)	99,000	
Note receivable—Arbuckle	12,000	
Note receivable—Tanner	7,500	
Accounts payable		$ 17,000
Capital, Arbuckle		67,000
Capital, Beltmore		45,000
Capital, Tanner		31,500
	$160,500	$160,500

2. The partners share profits and losses as follows: Arbuckle, 50%; Beltmore, 30%; and Tanner, 20%.

The partners are considering a $100,000 offer for the accounts receivable inventory and for plant and equipment as of June 30. The $100,000 will be paid to the partners in installments, the number and amounts of which are to be negotiated.

Required Prepare a *cash distribution schedule* as of 6/30/06, showing how the $100,000 will be distributed as it is available.

P 22-8* **Installment Liquidation: Schedule of Cash Distribution and Statement of Realization and Liquidation** Assume the facts in Problem 22-7, except that the partners decide to liquidate their partnership instead of accepting the $100,000 offer. Cash is distributed to the partners at the end of the month.

A summary of the liquidation transactions follows:

July

1. Collected $16,500 on accounts receivable; the balance is uncollectible.
2. Received $10,000 for the entire inventory.
3. Paid $1,000 liquidation expenses.
4. Retained $8,000 cash in the business at month-end.

August

1. Paid $1,500 liquidation expenses. As part payment of his capital, Tanner accepted a piece of special equipment that he developed that had a $4,000 book value. The partners agreed that a $10,000 value should be placed on the machine for liquidation purposes.
2. Retained $2,500 cash in the business at month-end.

September

1. Received $75,000 on sale of remaining plant and equipment.
2. Paid $1,000 liquidation expenses.
3. No cash retained in the business.

Required Prepare a *statement of realization and liquidation.*

THINKING CRITICALLY

Cases

C 22-1 **Manner of Sharing Realization Losses During Liquidation** Jennings and Nelson recently formed a partnership under the following terms:

	Jennings	Nelson
Capital contributions	$80,000	$20,000
Time devoted to the business	100%	100%
Profit and loss sharing formula		
Interest rate on capital over $20,000	10%	10%
Residual profit and loss	50%	50%

You have been hired as the partnership's accountant. While closing the partnership books for the first month of operations, Jennings casually mentions to you that he believes that a "good and equitable" partnership agreement had been negotiated between himself and Nelson.

Required How would you respond to this comment?

C 22-2 **Manner of Sharing Realization Losses During Liquidation** Harper, McCord, and Stringer are attempting to form a partnership in which profits and losses are shared in the ratio 4:4:2, respectively. They *cannot* agree on terms of the partnership agreement relating to potential liquidation. Harper believes that it is a waste of time to have any provisions relating to liquidation because the prospective partners firmly believe that the business will be successful. McCord believes that in the event of liquidation, any realization losses should be shared *in the ratio of the capital balances* because this method allows each partner to absorb losses in relation to his or her capacity to do so. Stringer believes that any liquidation losses should be shared *equally* because if the business is *not* successful, it will most likely be the fault of each partner. As the accountant who will be keeping the partnership's books, you have been asked to settle this dispute.

Required How would you respond to this request?

C 22-3 **Procedures for Distributing Available Cash to Partners** The partnership of Dials and Winder is in the process of liquidation, which is expected to take several months. Dials, who is in need of cash, wants cash distributed to the partners as it is available. Winder believes that no cash should be distributed to either partner until all the assets are sold and the total realization gain or loss is known. Thus the partnership would *not* distribute cash to a partner and later request a capital contribution to absorb any capital deficits created by realization losses.

Required Evaluate the position of each partner.

C 22-4 Procedures for Distributing Available Cash to Partners The partnership of Jurnell, Ledgley, and Post is in the process of being liquidated. The trial balance immediately after the sale of a portion of the noncash assets and full payment to outside creditors is as follows:

Cash	$31,000	
Note receivable from Ledgley	13,000	
Other assets	36,000	
Loan, Jurnell		$11,000
Capital:		
Jurnell		9,000
Ledgley		21,000
Post		39,000
	$80,000	$80,000

Jurnell wants the available cash distributed to her to pay off her *loan*—she cites Section 807 of the RUPA, which states that *partners' loans* have priority over *partners' capital.* Post wants the cash distributed to him because he has the *largest* capital investment. Ledgley believes that it should be distributed *equally*, which is how profits and losses are shared.

Required

1. Evaluate the position of each partner.
2. Who should receive the $31,000 available cash?
3. Optional: If subsequent to the cash distribution of $31,000, *noncash assets* having a *book value* of $27,000 are sold for $6,000, who would receive the $6,000?

chapter

23 Estates and Trusts

The minute you read something that you can't understand, you can almost be sure it was drawn up by a lawyer.
WILL ROGERS

LEARNING OBJECTIVES

To Understand

- The way to account for a decedent's estate.
- The estate tax rules in general.
- The way to account for a trust established by a decedent.
- Why a conflict of interest exists between the *income* and *principal* beneficiaries of a trust.
- The way to determine whether a transaction relates to *principal* or *income*.

TOPIC OUTLINE

INTERNATIONAL PERSPECTIVE

I. The Role Accountants Play in Estate Planning

II. Principal versus Income

III. Accounting for Estates

IV. Accounting for Trusts

CHAPTER OVERVIEW

The ownership of property is part of our nature as humans, as the collapse of communism showed. How we handle that ownership at death is part of our culture. The rights to own property and inherit property are so deep in our culture that they are not mentioned in the U.S. Constitution—**because these rights had already been in place for seven centuries when the Constitution was written.**

Assets that are accumulated in life can be purposely disposed of (1) in life as gifts or (2) after death (pursuant to the terms of a will) as legacies (personal property) and devises (real property). This is one part of freedom—the right to hold and dispose of property.

In disposing of property, it is common to establish trusts for various reasons, which we explain later. In this regard, it is worth noting that bank trust departments and other fiduciaries manage billions of dollars of assets.

In this chapter, we discuss (1) the "charge-and-discharge" manner of accounting used by estates (which was in place for five centuries before double-entry accounting reached England), (2) the manner of accounting for trusts, and (3) the role accountants play in estate planning, which takes place before an individual dies. But first we present an International Perspective.

International Perspective

In the United States, wills are handled at the *county level* (as handled in the shires of England to this day). In other countries, however, all wills are handled in the *national capital.*

I. THE ROLE ACCOUNTANTS PLAY IN ESTATE PLANNING

Estate Planning

People commonly make plans for the orderly transfer of their property upon their death to relatives, other persons, organizations, or trusts to be set up for the benefit of relatives. Such forethought is known as **estate planning** and is accomplished under the guidance of attorneys, often working closely with accountants. The *attorney's* role centers around preparing wills and, in many cases, trust agreements (discussed in detail later in the chapter). The *accountant's* role consists of suggesting planning techniques consistent with the objective of minimizing transfer costs (federal estate taxes, state inheritance taxes, and fees and expenses). In this capacity, an accountant often determines expected transfer costs under various options. An accountant may also play an important role in advising his or her client on accounting matters pertaining to trusts that are to be established.

Accountants' participation in estate planning is usually limited to cases in which individuals are wealthy or moderately wealthy. Under current law, roughly 99.5% of all estates are exempt from estate and gift tax laws. An *accountant* participating in estate planning must have substantial expertise in estate and gift taxes—a complex area of the tax laws. A detailed discussion of these laws and the use of planning techniques to minimize transfer costs is properly the subject matter of a tax course. A brief discussion of the estate and gift tax laws is included, however, later in the chapter.

The Trust Feature of Estate Planning

Frequently, a will contains a provision for the establishment of a **trust**, whereby certain designated property of the decedent's estate is to be transferred to a **trustee** when the person dies. The trustee holds legal title to the property and administers it for the benefit of one or more other persons, who are called **beneficiaries**. Thus the trustee serves in a position of trust with respect to the beneficiaries. This is a fiduciary relationship, and the trustee is commonly referred to as a **fiduciary**. (Recall another type of fiduciary relationship discussed in Chapter 19 in connection with companies in bankruptcy proceedings.) The person creating the trust is referred to as the **trustor** (also known as the *grantor*, *donor*, *creator*, and *settlor*). The legal document creating the trust is the *trust agreement*. Trust beneficiaries are of the following two classes:

1. **Income beneficiary.** An **income beneficiary** is entitled to the income earned by the trust's assets, referred to as the *trust principal*, or *corpus*.
2. **Principal beneficiary.** A **principal beneficiary** is entitled to the *principal*, or *corpus*, of the trust, which is distributed according to the terms of the trust agreement (usually at the specified termination date of the trust). A principal beneficiary is also known as a **residuary beneficiary** or **remainderman**.

The *income* and *principal* beneficiaries may or may *not* be the same person. A common arrangement is to name one's *spouse* as the *income* beneficiary for his or her remaining life and name one's *children* as the *principal* beneficiaries. Another common arrangement is to name one's *children* as both *income* and *principal* beneficiaries, with some or all of the *income* to be used for their support and the *principal* to be distributed to them when they reach a specified age.

The Basic Accounting Problem

Regardless of whether the *income* or *principal* beneficiaries of a trust are the same person or persons, **it is necessary to account for the separate interests of each class**. Accomplishing this task is the subject of this chapter. The requirement of correct separate accounting for the interests of each class is the reason for the special theories and techniques for accounting for the administration of estates and trusts by fiduciaries. Otherwise, quite simple record-keeping procedures are adequate.

Accounting for the separate interests of each class of beneficiaries is even more difficult because a **built-in clash of interests exists between the two classes**. When the *principal* and *income* beneficiaries are *not* the same person or persons, the clash revolves around ***who* gets *what***. When the *principal* and *income* beneficiaries *are* the same person or persons, the clash concerns **the *timing* of distributions**. Frequently, disputes between these interests lead to litigation.

Although a trust may be established by a transfer of property to the trustee during the transferor's lifetime (known as an **inter vivos trust**), we deal solely with trusts that are created by a gift made in the will of a decedent (known as a **testamentary trust**). Thus we must consider the administration of a decedent's estate in connection with the establishment of a trust.

Relationship between an Estate and a Testamentary Trust

All states have enacted some form of legislation concerning the administration of trusts. State statutes pertaining to trusts are operative, in most cases, only to the extent that they do *not* conflict with the terms of a trust agreement. Forty-one states have adopted the Revised Uniform Principal and Income Act (of 1962) either in its entirety or with modifications; accordingly, we base our discussion on this act. (Seven of these forty-one states have adopted the 1997 Revised UPIA.) Under it, testamentary trusts are deemed to be created at the time of a person's death, even though the property to be placed in trust usually is *not* actually distributed to the trustee until some time after the person dies.[1] Property to be placed in trust becomes subject to the trust at the time of death; the rights of the *income* beneficiary are also established at the time of death. Therefore, the interests of the *income* beneficiary of the trust must be accounted for separately from the interests of the *principal* beneficiary of the trust **during the period of the estate administration**, as well as after the property is actually transferred to the trustee. (Some trust agreements simplify matters by specifying that the rights of the income beneficiary do *not* begin until the assets are actually transferred to the trustee.) The RUPIA can be found on the web at: **http://www.law.upenn.edu/bll/ulc/ulc_frame.htm**.

---

[1] Revised Uniform Principal and Income Act, U.L.A. Volume 7A, Section 4 (St. Paul: West Publishing Co.).

The Accounting View

For accounting purposes, we treat the estate and the trust as separate *accounting entities*. Furthermore, we conceptually view each of these separate *accounting entities* as composing ***two** accounting entities*—a "principal entity" and an "income entity." Thus, conceptually, ***four** accounting entities* exist.

The Tax View

For tax-reporting purposes, estates and trusts both are treated as *taxable entities*. They are not *legal entities*, however, in the sense that corporations are *legal entities*.

II. PRINCIPAL VERSUS INCOME

When a *testamentary* trust is established, every transaction must be analyzed to determine whether it relates to *principal* or *income*. An incorrect determination has important legal consequences to a fiduciary. If it is later determined that *income* has been *overstated* and the fiduciary *cannot* recover the amount of the overpayment from the *income beneficiary*, the fiduciary must make up the deficiency. In turn, if the error was made by the accountant or was based on the bad advice of the fiduciary's legal counsel, these persons may be professionally responsible to the fiduciary.

Manner of Analyzing Transactions

Reference to the *Trust Agreement*

In determining whether a transaction pertains to principal or income, **GAAP is *not* the point of reference.** The trustor may create his or her own definition of income. In other words, the trustor may specify the receipts that are to be *income* and the receipts that are to be *principal*. Likewise, the trustor may specify disbursements to be treated as charges against *income* and disbursements to be treated as reductions of the *principal*. Accordingly, all transactions must be analyzed as to the ***decedent's intent.***

Because the decedent is *not* available, the ***first step*** is to determine whether the decedent's *intent* is expressed in the trust agreement. Unfortunately, a common shortcoming of estate planning is that trust agreements usually do *not* explain in detail the treatment to be accorded specific types of receipts and disbursements. Many potential problems can be avoided if the decedent's personal accountant, who should have a knowledge of his or her client's properties, participates in the preparation of the trust agreement sections that pertain to accounting matters.

Reference to *State Law*

If the treatment of an item *cannot* be resolved by referring to the trust agreement, the ***second step*** is to find out what the *state law* is on the subject. Again, GAAP is *not* the point of reference. The Revised Uniform Principal and Income Act specifically addresses the principal versus income treatment of several items. Much of the impetus for revising the original Uniform Principal and Income Act (of 1931) resulted from the development of new forms of investment property, the treatment of which was not specified in state statutes. The treatment accorded many items specifically dealt with in the act produces income results that would be obtained if GAAP is applied. For numerous other items, however, the treatment produces results that are quite contrary to GAAP. For example, the act provides that the following items be treated as increases and decreases, respectively, to the trust *principal*—not the trust *income*:

1. Gains and losses on the sale of corporate securities.
2. Gains and losses on the sale of rental property.
3. Bond discounts (with certain exceptions) and bond premiums.

We present the general thrust of the act's accounting requirements later in the chapter. Section 5 of the act calls for income during the administration of an estate to be determined in the same manner that income is to be determined by a trustee in administering a trust. Thus the act applies to *estates* as well as *trusts*.

Reference to *Case Law*

If the treatment of an item is *not* covered in *state law*, the **third step** is to determine whether the courts have encountered and ruled on the same problem. If so, the answer is found in *case law*. If the answer *cannot* be found there, the fiduciary may petition the court for a determination.

The Accountant's Role in Analyzing Transactions

When the treatment to be accorded an item is *not* clearly set forth in the trust agreement or state statutes, the accountant does *not* determine whether an item pertains to *principal* or *income*. This is the function of the fiduciary, the fiduciary's legal counsel, or the courts. The accountant's role is expanded, of course, when the trust agreement specifies that income is to be determined in accordance with GAAP. Such cases, however, are the exception—*not* the rule.

CHECK POINT

In determining whether a transaction pertains to principal or income, which of the following is *not* a point of reference, unless specified?

a. Case law
b. Generally accepted accounting principles
c. State law
d. The trust agreement
e. None of the above

Answer: b

Manner of Record Keeping

Because the interests of the principal beneficiary and the income beneficiary must be accounted for separately, it is necessary to identify the assets and transactions pertaining to *principal* and those pertaining to *income*. Conceptually, we may view the assets and transactions pertaining to *principal* as belonging to *a separate accounting entity* and do likewise for the assets and transactions pertaining to *income*. Thus a *trust* may be viewed as comprising *two accounting entities*, each with a self-balancing set of books.

One method of record keeping is to physically maintain separate journals and general ledgers for *each* accounting entity. An alternate method is to use *one* set of books for *both* entities but to use separately identified columns in the journals and separately identified accounts in the general ledger for *principal* and *income*. This technique allows separate trial balances to be prepared for each accounting entity, as though two general ledgers were used. In practice, this technique is quite simple to work with, largely because cash is usually the only type of asset common to both *principal* and *income*.

Regardless of which method is used, it is *not* necessary to use one bank account for cash pertaining to *principal* and another for cash pertaining to *income*, unless the trust agreement requires it. When only one set of books is used, the separation of the total cash balance is reflected in the general ledger through a Principal Cash ledger account and an Income Cash ledger account. One set of books is generally used in practice. We illustrate this manner of record keeping later in the chapter.

Cash Basis versus *Accrual Basis*

At the *Beginning* and the *End* of the *Income* Beneficiary's Rights

In most respects, the Revised Uniform Principal and Income Act provides for the use of the *accrual basis* in determining at the time of the person's death the assets to be treated as part of the trust *principal*. The purpose, of course, is to establish a reasonably fair and practical starting point to determine income for the *income* beneficiary. Specifically, the following items are to be included as part of the trust *principal* at the time of death:

1. Amounts due but *not* paid at the time of death (Section 4[a]).
2. Prorations of amounts *not* due at the time of death that pertain to periodic payments, including rents, interest, and annuities (Section 4[b]).
3. Corporate distributions declared for which the date of record *precedes* the person's death (Section 4[e]).

The *cash basis* is specified for all other items (Section 4[c]). In a somewhat parallel manner, the act provides in most respects for the use of the *accrual basis* on termination of an income interest to effect a reasonably fair and practical cutoff of the *income beneficiary's* interest (Sections 4[d] and [e]).

Accounting Periods between the *Beginning* and the *End* of the *Income* Beneficiary's Rights

For accounting periods between the *beginning* and the *end* of the *income beneficiary's* rights, the *accrual basis* in most respects does *not* fit in with the underlying objective of the fiduciary, which is to account for the **flow of assets in and out of his or her control**. Accordingly, with one major exception, the *cash basis* is considered more appropriate for such accounting periods. The *accrual basis* offers much better measuring results, however, when determining the income of a business in which principal is invested.

At the *End* of the Estate Administration

When the income rights of the *income* beneficiary are established at the time of the person's death, the end of the estate administration is *not* relevant to the *income* and *principal* beneficiaries. Using the accrual basis is therefore unnecessary at the *end* of probate administration. Of course, if the trust agreement provides that income rights do *not* start until the *end* of the estate administration, accrual techniques are appropriate.

CHECK POINT

Under the Revised Uniform Principal and Income Act (of 1962), when are the rights of the *income beneficiary* established?

a. At the time of death of the deceased person
b. At the completion of the probate proceedings
c. At the time the property is physically transferred to the trustee
d. At the time the trust agreement is drawn up
e. None of the above

Answer: a

III. ACCOUNTING FOR ESTATES

Probate Administration

When a person dies, his or her property and liabilities (collectively referred to as the **estate**) must be administered, regardless of whether the person died with a will (referred to as having died **testate**) or without a will (referred to as having died **intestate**). Each state has laws concerning the affairs of decedents, commonly known as **probate law** or the **law of decedent estates**. A Uniform Probate Code exists, but only eighteen states have adopted it. Accordingly, uniformity among the states in this area is limited. The objectives of probate laws are to (1) discover and make effective the decedent's intent in the distribution of property, (2) gather and preserve the decedent's property, and (3) provide for an efficient and orderly system of making payments of estate debts and distributions in the course of liquidating the estate. If the decedent does *not* have a will, property is distributed according to state inheritance tax laws.

Under the probate laws, a decedent's affairs must be administered by fiduciaries who are subject to the control of the state **probate courts** (referred to in a few states as **surrogate** or **orphans' courts**). The following terms are used for estate fiduciaries:

1. An **executor** (if male) or **executrix** (if female) is named in the decedent's will as the decedent's personal representative in administering the estate and is appointed by the court to serve in that capacity.
2. An **administrator** (if male) or **administratrix** (if female) is appointed by the court when (a) a person dies intestate, (b) a person does not name anyone in his or her will, (c) the person named in the decedent's will refuses to serve as executor, or (d) the court refuses to appoint the person named in the will.

The title to a decedent's property is subject to the possession of the fiduciary and the control of the court, even though title passes at the time of death to the person or persons to whom the property is to be distributed. In short, the probate court serves as guardian of the estate. If a person dies testate, his or her will has no legal effect until it has been *probated*. **Probate** is the act by which the court determines whether the will meets the statutory requirements concerning wills. If the court so determines, it issues a certificate or decree that enables the terms of the will to be carried out. The will is said to have been *admitted to probate*. (Probate can be costly, running as high as an average of 7% of the gross estate in California.)

Basically, an estate fiduciary must (1) inventory the decedent's assets; (2) settle the claims of the decedent's creditors; (3) prepare and file the applicable income, estate, and inheritance tax returns; (4) distribute the remaining assets as gifts as the will provides; and (5) make the appropriate accountings to the court.

Gift Terminology

A gift of personal property by means of a will is called a **legacy**. The recipient of a legacy is called a **legatee**. Legacies are classified as follows:

1. A **specific legacy** is a gift of specified noncash items. For example, "my automobile to my son, Otto."
2. A **demonstrative legacy** is a gift of cash for which a particular fund or source is designated from which payment is to be made. For example, "$1,000 to my sister, Sara, out of my savings account."
3. A **general legacy** is a gift of cash for which no particular fund or source is designated from which to make payment. For example, "$2,000 to my brother, Bob."
4. A **residual legacy** is a gift of all personal property remaining *after* distribution of specific, demonstrative, and general legacies. For example, "the balance of my personal property to my wife, Wilma."

If the balance of the estate assets *after* payment of estate liabilities, taxes, and administrative expenses is insufficient to make good all the various types of legacies, the legacies are deemed to be null and inoperative in the reverse of the order listed here (referred to as the process of **abatement**).

A gift of *real property* by means of a will is called a **devise**. The recipient of a devise is called a **devisee**. Devises are classified as *specific*, *general*, or *residual*. Estate assets to be transferred to a trustee pursuant to the establishment of a testamentary trust may be any type of legacy or devise. The most common type of legacy given to a trustee is a *residual legacy*, which we illustrate later in the chapter.

Inventory of Decedent's Property

The estate fiduciary's first major task in administering the estate is to inventory the decedent's property. Each item must then be valued at its current market value for federal estate and state inheritance tax purposes (using state inheritance tax or private appraisers, as required), and the appropriate tax forms must be filed. (We discuss these in more detail in the following section.) In addition, the estate fiduciary must submit to the probate court an inventory of the decedent's property subject to probate administration. Not all items included for estate tax and state inheritance tax purposes are subject to probate administration. Many states allow real property to pass *directly to* the beneficiaries (or to the trustee, in the case of real property placed in trust), *bypassing* probate administration. Likewise, many states allow certain types of personal property—such as personal effects, clothing, household items, and a limited amount of cash—to pass directly to beneficiaries outside of probate. State probate law must be consulted to determine which items are subject to probate administration; an attorney's services are usually used for this. Although required only by some states, a separate schedule should list the items not subject to probate administration, if only for the record.

In general, the following items are subject to probate administration:

1. Cash in checking and savings accounts, in a safety deposit box, and on hand.
2. Investments in stocks and bonds.
3. Interest accrued on bonds through the date of the person's death.
4. Dividends declared on stocks prior to the person's death.
5. Investments in businesses and partnerships.
6. Life insurance proceeds that name the estate as the beneficiary.
7. Notes and accounts receivable, including interest accrued through the date of the person's death.
8. Accrued rents and royalties receivable.
9. Advances to those named in the will as beneficiaries, including interest accrued through the date of death.
10. Unpaid wages, salaries, and commissions.
11. Valuables, such as jewelry and coin collections.
12. Real estate not specifically exempted (the most common exemption is property held in joint tenancy because all rights in such property immediately pass to the surviving tenant at the time of death).

Even though other items may be included for federal estate tax and state inheritance tax purposes, the fiduciary's accountability to the probate court comprises only the items subject to probate administration. The fiduciary must take control of these items for estate preservation purposes.

Payment of Estate Liabilities

The estate's liabilities must be paid before any distributions to beneficiaries can be made. Probate laws usually require the estate fiduciary to publish promptly notices in newspapers for a certain period calling for persons having claims against the decedent to file them within a specified period of time or be barred forever. The estate fiduciary is responsible for determining the validity of claims filed. If the estate assets are insufficient to pay all liabilities, payment must be made in accordance with the priority provided for in state law. This general order of priority follows:

1. Funeral expenses.
2. Estate administration expenses.
3. Allowances to support the decedent's spouse and dependent children for a specified period of time.
4. Expenses of the deceased's last illness.
5. Wages owed to the decedent's employees.

6. Debts owed to the federal, state, or local government that have priority under federal or state law.
7. Lien claims.
8. All other debts.

Tax Matters

The estate fiduciary is responsible for preparing and filing tax returns for the decedent and the decedent's estate.

Decedent's Final Income Tax Return

A final income tax return must be filed for the decedent, covering the period from the date of the decedent's last income tax return to the date of death. Any taxes owed are paid from estate assets.

Taxation of Estate Income

An estate is a taxable entity, which comes into being at the time of the person's death. Estate income taxes must be filed annually on federal Form 1041 (U.S. Fiduciary Income Tax Return) until the estate is terminated upon discharge of the fiduciary by the probate court. The gross income of an estate is computed in the same manner as that of an individual. In addition to deductions for expenses relating to the generation of income, a deduction is allowed for net income currently distributable to beneficiaries. As a result, **the *estate* is taxed only on the remaining net income *not* currently distributable**. The ***beneficiaries*, in turn, are taxed on the *currently distributable* net income.** The tax rates that apply to estates are those that apply to trusts:

Taxable Income	Tax Rate
First $1,900	15%
$1,901–$4,500	25%
$4,501–$6,850	28%
$6,851–$9,350	33%
Over $9,350	35%

The concept of estate income for *income tax-reporting* purposes differs in many respects from the concept of estate income for *fiduciary-reporting* purposes. Accordingly, working paper adjustments to *fiduciary book income amounts* are usually necessary to determine gross income and deductions for *income tax-reporting* purposes.

State Inheritance Taxes

Most states impose an inheritance tax on the value of property to be distributed to each individual heir. This tax is based on the **right to receive or inherit** property; thus the burden of taxation falls on the *recipient* of the property. Although the taxes are paid to the state out of the estate assets, the estate fiduciary either seeks reimbursement from the individual heirs (when noncash assets are distributed) or reduces proportionately the amount to be distributed to each individual heir (when cash is distributed). The *tax rates* and *allowable exemptions* are based on the relationship of the heir to the decedent, with tax rates *increasing* and exemptions *decreasing* as the relationship becomes *more distant*. It is quite common, however, for wills to provide specifically that state inheritance taxes be paid out of the residue of the estate, so that the entire burden of taxation falls on the heirs who receive the residue.

Federal Estate Taxes

Unlike *state* inheritance taxes, the *federal* estate tax is based on the **right to give** property. The burden of taxation, therefore, falls entirely on the estate, not on each individual heir. Of course, this merely reduces the amount of the residue of the estate that otherwise would be distributed to heirs. (Some state probate codes require the *federal* estate tax to be borne by each heir, as with the *state* inheritance taxes.) Assuming a decedent has made no gifts during his or her lifetime, estate taxes are calculated in the following manner:

1. The total value, or **gross estate**, of the decedent's property is determined at the time of death or, if the estate fiduciary elects, at a date six months after death. Property sold within six months of the person's death is valued at its selling price. (Recall that the gross estate for federal estate tax purposes is usually larger than the probate estate.)
2. The taxable estate is determined by deducting the following from the gross estate determined in step 1:
   a. Liabilities of the estate.
   b. Administrative expenses, including funeral expenses, court costs, and attorney fees.
   c. Casualty and theft losses during the administration of the estate.
   d. A **marital deduction** (a term used to describe a **transfer between spouses** that is exempt from transfer taxes). The marital deduction is unlimited; thus, any amount may be used.
   e. Charitable contributions.
3. The estate tax rates are then applied to the taxable estate to arrive at the **gross estate tax**. The estate tax rates are graduated from 18% on taxable estates up to $10,000 to a maximum of 50% (phases down 1% a year from 2003 through 2007 to 45% in 2007) on taxable estates in excess of $3,000,000.
4. Certain specified tax credits—such as state death taxes (with limitations) and the ***unified transfer tax credit***—are subtracted from the gross estate tax to arrive at the **net estate tax**.

The unified transfer tax credit is ***the equivalent of an exemption***. The following table shows the *unified tax credits* and the related *exemption equivalents*:

Years	Unified Transfer Tax Credit	Exemption Equivalent
2004–05	$ 555,800	$1,500,000
2006–08	780,800	2,000,000
2009	1,540,800	3,500,000
2010 Estate tax is ***repealed***	n/a	n/a
2011 Estate tax is ***reinstated***	345,800	1,000,000

Accordingly, a single individual may transfer a taxable estate of $1,500,000 in 2005 and incur no federal estate tax.

Because a surviving spouse may take a *marital deduction* for any amount, all federal estate taxes otherwise payable can be deferred until the death of that surviving spouse. Thus the tax law treats a married couple as a *single economic unit*.

To use the unified credit fully, the *marital deduction* amount chosen generally is small enough to leave a taxable estate equal to the *exemption equivalent* of the unified transfer tax credit. (The taxable estate of this amount is then placed in a trust for the decedent's children.) For example, assume that (1) Henry Steele passed away in 2005, (2) his gross estate is $3,800,000, and (3) all deductions other than the *marital deduction* are $100,000. With a *marital deduction* amount of $2,200,000, the taxable estate is $1,500,000, resulting in a gross estate tax of $555,800. Because of the unified transfer tax credit of $555,800, however, no net estate tax is payable. The unified transfer tax credit also can be used on the death of Steele's surviving spouse (who was transferred $2,200,000). Thus the *exemption equivalent* of $1,500,000 is really $3,000,000 for a married couple.

The calculation of estate taxes is substantially more complicated when the decedent has made gifts during his or her lifetime. One of the major changes in the Tax Reform Act of 1976 was to unify the previously separate estate and gift tax rate schedules into a combined transfer tax system so that lifetime transfers and transfers at death would no longer be taxed at different rates. The unified transfer tax credit is labeled as such because it also may be applied against gift taxes due on lifetime gifts. The amount of any unused credit is then applied against the gross estate tax.

Federal Form 706 (U.S. Estate Tax Return) is used for reporting the federal taxes owed on the estate. See Illustration 23-1 for a depiction of the federal tax forms to be filed for (1) a deceased person, (2) the deceased person's estate, and (3) a trust established by the decedent.

In closing our discussion of estate taxes, we point out that (1) the estate tax (which has been in place in some form since 1916) has raised little money and is persistently unpopular, (2) Canada, Australia, and Israel have recently repealed their wealth transfer taxes, and (3) in 1982,

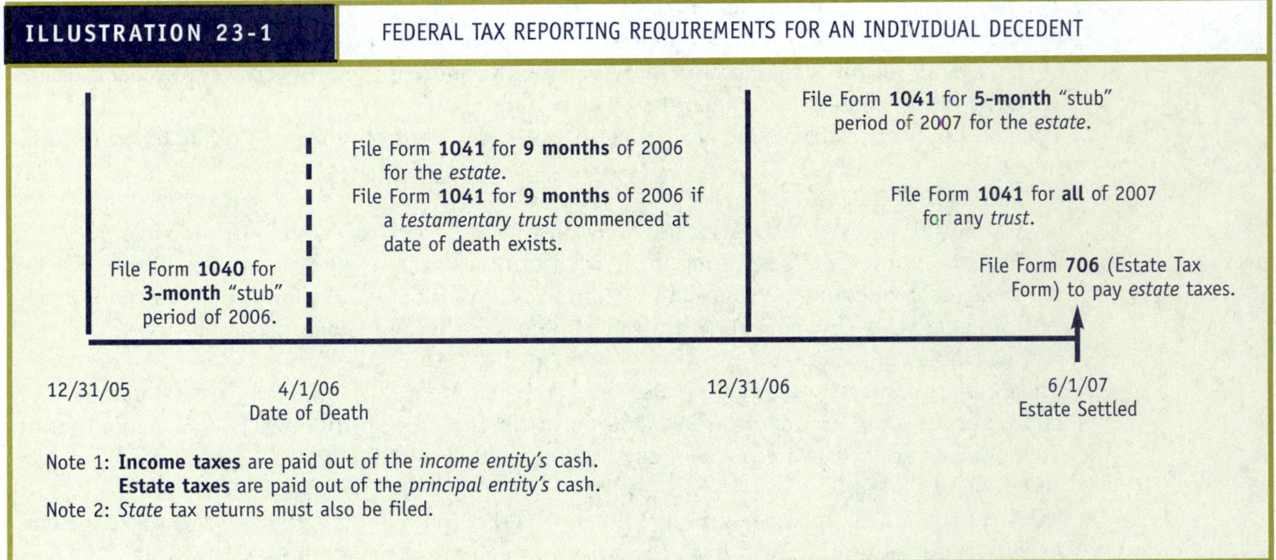
ILLUSTRATION 23-1
FEDERAL TAX REPORTING REQUIREMENTS FOR AN INDIVIDUAL DECEDENT
File Form 1040 for 3-month "stub" period of 2006.
File Form 1041 for 9 months of 2006 for the estate.
File Form 1041 for 9 months of 2006 if a testamentary trust commenced at date of death exists.
File Form 1041 for 5-month "stub" period of 2007 for the estate.
File Form 1041 for all of 2007 for any trust.
File Form 706 (Estate Tax Form) to pay estate taxes.
12/31/05
4/1/06
Date of Death
12/31/06
6/1/07
Estate Settled
Note 1: Income taxes are paid out of the income entity's cash.
Estate taxes are paid out of the principal entity's cash.
Note 2: State tax returns must also be filed.

Californians voted overwhelmingly to abolish that state's inheritance tax, which applied to fewer than one in twenty state residents.

CHECK POINT

Which of the following statements concerning tax matters is *false*?

a. Federal estate tax is based on the right to give property.
b. State inheritance taxes are based on the right to receive or inherit property.
c. The marital deduction is unlimited in amount.
d. The tax rates that apply to estate income are different from those that apply to trust income.
e. None of the above.

Answer: d

The Opening Entry

Once an inventory of the decedent's property that is subject to probate administration has been compiled, the opening entry for the *principal entity* of the estate is made. The entry consists of debits to the various assets and a *credit* to an Estate Principal account. This account is merely a balancing account that facilitates the double-entry bookkeeping system. It does *not* reflect the net worth of the estate because the decedent's liabilities are *not* recorded as part of the opening entry. Liabilities are recorded in the books when they are paid, and such payments are eventually reflected as *reductions* to the Estate Principal account. This manner of accounting reflects the fiduciary's role, which is to **administer the decedent's assets** rather than attempt to establish and account for the net worth of the estate. As expected, no opening entry pertains to the *income entity*.

Transactions Pertaining to *Principal*

Transactions pertaining to principal are recorded by debiting or crediting the appropriate asset account and crediting or debiting, respectively, an account that is descriptive of the transaction. Transactions pertaining to principal may be grouped as follows:

1. Transactions that *increase* principal:

   a. Assets subsequently discovered.
   b. Gains on disposition of principal assets.

2. **Transactions that *decrease* principal:**
   a. Losses on disposition of principal assets.
   b. Payments of debts and certain taxes.
   c. Payment of funeral expenses.
   d. Payment of administrative expenses.
   e. Distributions of gifts.
3. **Transactions that do *not* affect principal:**
   a. Dispositions of principal assets at their carrying values.
   b. Receipts of amounts to be given to legatees (which are reflected as liabilities until paid)—for example, interest on a bond.
   c. Disbursements of amounts held for legatees, as described in category (3)b.
   d. Payments of amounts chargeable to a beneficiary (which are reflected as receivables until collected).

The nonasset accounts debited or credited in categories 1 and 2 are *nominal* or *temporary* accounts that eventually are closed to the Estate Principal account. (Some finer points concerning principal transactions are discussed later in the chapter.)

Transactions Pertaining to *Income*

The accounting techniques used for the *principal entity* also are used for the *income entity*. An income asset account is debited or credited, and the other half of the entry is to an account that substantively explains the transaction. Initially, the income entity has no assets. Revenues, expenses, and distributions to income beneficiaries are closed periodically to an Estate Income account, which accumulates undistributed earnings.

A detailed discussion of the various types of income transactions and charges made against income is delayed until after the illustration of estate accounting. For simplicity, the illustration limits its income transactions to interest on savings and bond investments, cash dividends on corporate stock investments, and interest on a partnership investment.

Comprehensive Illustration

The Opening Entry and Subsequent Transactions

David Diamond died testate on March 27, 2005, with the following provisions in his will:

1. The decedent's residence and household items are left to wife, Krystal Diamond, who assumes the mortgage on the residence.
2. Cash of $150,000 is to be given to Krystal Diamond.
3. All the corporate stocks are to be given to the decedent's alma mater, Krebitsville University, for scholarships in accounting.
4. The decedent's automobile is to be given to Ruby Diamond, the decedent's sister.
5. The residual balance of the estate is to be placed in trust with the following terms:
   a. ***Trustee***: Coral Point Bank
   b. ***Income beneficiary***: Krystal Diamond, wife of the decedent, for the remainder of her natural life.
   c. ***Principal beneficiaries***: Jade and Opal Diamond, the decedent's only two children. The principal is to be distributed at the later of (1) the date of death of Krystal Diamond or (2) when both Jade and Opal Diamond reach the age of 25. (If Krystal Diamond dies before both children reach the age of 25, they succeed her as income beneficiaries until they both reach age 25.)
   d. The *accrual basis* is to be used to determine principal at the time of death.
6. State inheritance taxes are to be paid out of the residue of the estate, not by the individual heirs, except for the case of the automobile given to Ruby Diamond.
7. The decedent's personal financial advisor, Jack Cass, is named executor of the estate.

David Diamond's estate consists of the following items, each listed at its current value:

Assets Subject to Probate Administration		
Cash (including checking and savings accounts)		$ 70,000
U.S. government and corporate bonds—face value, $350,000; cost, $341,000		337,000
Corporate stocks—cost, $38,000		63,000
Life insurance (payable to the estate)		100,000
Investment in partnership of Diamond, Ring, and Stone:		
Capital account balance at date of death, net of drawings	$84,000	
Share of profits from close of preceding partnership accounting period to date of death	14,000	
Share of partnership goodwill deemed to exist at date of death (calculated according to the terms of the partnership agreement)	22,000	120,000
Accrued interest receivable on bonds		10,000
Accrued interest receivable on savings accounts		2,000
Dividends declared on corporate stocks		1,000
Automobile		7,000
Total		$ 710,000
Assets *Not* Subject to Probate Administration		
Residence and household items		240,000
Duplex rental unit (cost, $75,000) subject to secured loan of $55,000		110,000
Total Estate Assets		**$1,060,000**
Liabilities to Be Paid out of Probate Estate		
Outstanding balance on credit cards		$ 1,100
Medical expenses pertaining to illness		3,700
State and federal income taxes for the period 1/1/05 to 3/27/05		5,500
Total		$ 10,300
Liabilities Not to Be Paid out of Probate Estate		
Mortgage on residence		30,000
Mortgage on duplex rental unit		55,000
Total Estate Liabilities		**$ 95,300**

In reviewing the items making up the estate, note that we have assumed that the decedent's residence, household items, and the duplex rental unit are *not* subject to probate administration of the state probate law. Consequently, the residence and household items pass immediately to the decedent's surviving spouse *outside* probate, and the duplex rental unit passes *immediately* to the trustee *outside* of probate. None of these items is accounted for in the administration of the estate. Accounting for the depreciable assets of a trust (such as the duplex rental unit used in this illustration) is discussed and illustrated later in the chapter.

The opening entry in the estate books follows.

Principal Cash	70,000	
Investment in Bonds	337,000	
Investment in Stocks	63,000	
Life Insurance Receivable	100,000	
Investment in Partnership of Diamond, Ring, and Stone	120,000	
Accrued Interest Receivable on Bonds	10,000	
Accrued Interest Receivable on Savings Accounts	2,000	
Dividends Declared on Corporate Stocks	1,000	
Automobile	7,000	
Estate Principal		710,000

No liabilities are recorded because the accounting concerns the administration of estate assets.

Assumed transactions and related journal entries pertaining to activities completed by the executor during the administration of the estate from March 27, 2005, to June 30, 2006, are as follows:

Transaction	Entry		
1. Subsequent discovery of a checking account.	Principal Cash	700	
	Asset Subsequently Discovered		700

Transaction	Entry		
2. Receipt of life insurance proceeds.	Principal Cash	100,000	
	Life Insurance Receivable		100,000
3. Receipt of proceeds from liquidation of investment in partnership, along with interest to date of receipt.	Principal Cash	120,000	
	Income Cash	4,000	
	Investment in Partnership		120,000
	Interest Income		4,000
4. Receipt of interest on bonds.	Principal Cash	10,000	
	Income Cash	18,000	
	Accrued Bond Interest Receivable		10,000
	Interest Income		18,000
5. Receipt of interest on savings accounts.	Principal Cash	2,000	
	Income Cash	6,000	
	Accrued Interest Receivable on Savings Accounts		2,000
	Interest Income		6,000
6. Receipt of cash dividends on corporate stocks. (Receipts pertaining to dividends declared during the estate administration accrue to the legatee.)	Principal Cash	4,000	
	Accrued Dividends Receivable		1,000
	Liability to Krebitsville University		3,000
7. Payment of credit card, medical, and income tax liabilities.	Debts of Decedent	10,300	
	Principal Cash		10,300
8. Payment of funeral and administrative expenses.	Funeral and Administrative Expenses	11,000	
	Principal Cash		11,000
9. Payment of $49,300 inheritance taxes, $300 of which is to be borne by Ruby Diamond, who received the decedent's automobile.	Inheritance Taxes	49,000	
	Receivable from Legatee, Ruby Diamond	300	
	Principal Cash		49,300
10. Distribution of automobile as gift (a specific legacy) and collection of related inheritance taxes from legatee.	Principal Cash	300	
	Legacies Distributed	7,000	
	Receivable from Legatee, Ruby Diamond		300
	Automobile		7,000
11. Distribution of corporate stocks as gift (specific legacy) to Krebitsville University, along with dividend receipts pertaining to dividends declared and received during the estate administration.	Legacies Distributed	63,000	
	Liability to Krebitsville University	3,000	
	Investment in Stocks		63,000
	Principal Cash		3,000
12. Sale of a portion of the bonds to raise cash. (Current value at Diamond's death was $9,600.)	Principal Cash	9,800	
	Investment in Bonds		9,600
	Gain on Sale of Principal Asset		200
13. Distribution of cash (general legacy) to Krystal Diamond.	Legacies Distributed	150,000	
	Principal Cash		150,000
14. Payment of income taxes relating to estate income.	Estate Income Tax Expense	4,600	
	Income Cash		4,600
15. Payment of administration expenses pertaining to income.	Administration Expenses	300	
	Income Cash		300
16. Distributions to income beneficiary of trust.	Distributions to Income Beneficiary	18,000	
	Income Cash		18,000

We assume that no estate taxes are owed because of the use of the unlimited marital deduction. If estate taxes had been paid, the entry is as follows:

Estate Taxes	xxx	
Principal Cash		xxx

Comprehensive Illustration

Charge and Discharge Statements

Continuing with our illustration, the only remaining task for the estate fiduciary is to submit an accounting to the probate court with a request to distribute the residual balance of the estate to the trustee, Coral Point Bank. Trial balances for the principal entity and the income entity as of June 30, 2006, are presented in Illustration 23-2. Charge and discharge statements, which portray the activity of these entities through June 30, 2006, are shown in Illustration 23-3. The charge and discharge statements are usually accompanied by supporting schedules—such as the detail of the decedent's debts paid and the detail of legacies distributed. Because they are quite simple, such schedules are not presented.

Comprehensive Illustration

Closing Entries for the Estate

Assuming that the probate court authorizes the distribution of the residual Diamond estate assets to the trustee, the entries to record the distributions and close the estate books are as follows:

Transaction	Entry		
1. Distribution of residual estate assets of principal entity to Coral Point Bank, trustee.	Legacies Distributed	420,600	
	Principal Cash		93,200
	Investment in Bonds		327,400
2. Distribution of residual estate assets of income entity to Coral Point Bank, trustee.	Distribution to Trustee for Income Beneficiary	5,100	
	Income Cash		5,100
3. Closing of nominal accounts of principal entity into estate principal.	Asset Subsequently Discovered	700	
	Gain on Sale of Principal Asset	200	
	Estate Principal	710,000	
	Debts of Decedent		10,300
	Funeral and Administrative Expenses		11,000
	Inheritance Taxes		49,000
	Legacies Distributed		640,600
4. Closing of nominal accounts of income entity.	Interest Income	28,000	
	Estate Income Tax Expense		4,600
	Administrative Expenses		300
	Distributions to Income Beneficiary		18,000
	Distribution to Trustee for Income Beneficiary		5,100

IV. ACCOUNTING FOR TRUSTS

Accounting for trusts is identical to accounting for estates, except that a Trust Principal account is used rather than Estate Principal for the principal entity, and a Trust Income account is used rather than Estate Income for the income entity to accumulate undistributed earnings. The nature of the transactions is also different. An estate fiduciary is concerned primarily with cleaning up a decedent's affairs and properly distributing estate property. A trustee, on the other hand, is concerned primarily with prudently managing a pool of assets in accordance with the powers granted to him or her by the trust agreement. This task usually involves buying and selling trust assets. Trustees must make periodic accountings to the principal and income beneficiaries and the probate court. A charge and discharge statement similar to the one illustrated for estates is used. Upon termination of the life of the trust, the trustee distributes the assets of the trust principal to the remainderman, makes a final accounting to the court, and requests to be discharged.

ILLUSTRATION 23-2 TRIAL BALANCES—PRINCIPAL AND INCOME

Estate of David Diamond
Trial Balance—Principal
June 30, 2006

	DEBIT	CREDIT
Cash	$ 93,200	
Investments in bonds	327,400	
Estate principal		$710,000
Asset subsequently discovered		700
Gain on sale of principal asset		200
Debts of decedent	10,300	
Funeral and administrative expenses	11,000	
Inheritance taxes	49,000	
Legacies distributed	220,000	
Totals	$710,900	$710,900

Estate of David Diamond
Trial Balance—Income
June 30, 2006

	DEBIT	CREDIT
Cash	$ 5,100	
Interest income		$28,000
Estate income tax expense	4,600	
Administrative expenses	300	
Distributions to income beneficiary	18,000	
Totals	$28,000	$28,000

ILLUSTRATION 23-3 CHARGE AND DISCHARGE STATEMENTS

Estate of David Diamond
Jack Cass, Executor of the Estate
Charge and Discharge Statements
March 27, 2005–June 30, 2006

First, as to Principal:		
I *charge* myself as follows:		
Assets per inventory	$710,000	
Assets discovered	700	
Gain on asset realization	200	$ 710,900
I *credit* myself as follows:		
Debts of decedent paid	$ 10,300	
Funeral and administrative expenses paid	11,000	
Inheritance taxes paid	49,000	
Legacies distributed	220,000	(290,300)
Balance of the estate:		
Principal cash	$ 93,200	
Investment in bonds	327,400	$ 420,600
Second, as to Income:		
I *charge* myself as follows:		
Interest received on bonds	$ 18,000	
Interest received on savings accounts	6,000	
Interest received on partnership investment	4,000	$ 28,000
I *credit* myself as follows:		
Estate income taxes paid	$ 4,600	
Administrative expenses paid	300	
Distributions made to income beneficiary	18,000	(22,900)
Balance of the estate:		
Income Cash		$ 5,100

Using the illustration from the preceding section, the entries to record the receipt of the gifts from David Diamond's estate are as follows. This is the principal entity:

Principal Cash	93,200	
Investment in Bonds	327,400	
Trust Principal		420,600

This is the income entity:

Income Cash	5,100	
Trust Income		5,100

Transactions Pertaining to *Principal*

Early in the chapter, we summarized the general thrust of the accounting requirements of the Revised Uniform Principal and Income Act regarding principal transactions. Some finer points of principal transactions follow:

1. The costs of investing and reinvesting principal assets are charged against *principal.*
2. The costs of preparing property for rental or sale are charged against *principal.*
3. Taxes levied on gains or profits allocated to principal are charged against *principal.*
4. The costs incurred in maintaining or defending any action to protect the trust or trust property or ensure title to any trust property are charged against *principal.*
5. Extraordinary repairs or costs incurred in making capital improvements paid for out of *principal* may be recouped from *income* through depreciation charges.
6. Trustee's fees and costs relating to the periodic accounting to the court of jurisdiction (court costs, attorney fees, and accounting fees, for example) are shared equally between *principal* and *income.*
7. Liquidating dividends are considered to be *principal.*
8. Stock dividends go to *principal,* not *income.*

Transactions Pertaining to *Income*

As mentioned earlier, under the Revised Uniform Principal and Income Act, interest and cash dividends are considered income transactions. The act also includes the following as income: rents, loan repayment penalties, lease cancellation charges, lease renewal fees, and the net profits of any business in which principal is invested. Losses of any business in which principal is invested are charged to principal because no provision exists for loss carryforward or carryback into any other calendar or fiscal year for purposes of calculating net income. Profits and losses of such businesses are to be determined using GAAP.

Among other things, the act includes as charges against *income* the interest expense on trust liabilities (such as a mortgage on a trust rental property), property taxes, insurance premiums, ordinary repairs, depreciation expenses (including depreciation charges pertaining to extraordinary repairs), income taxes attributable to trust income, a share of trustee fees and costs relating to periodic accounting to the court, and any other ordinary expense incurred in connection with the administration, management, or preservation of trust property. (Depreciation and unusual charges are discussed in detail in the following paragraphs because of the unique manner in which journal entries are recorded.)

Depreciation

Under the act, depreciation is mandatory (at the trustee's discretion under the 1997 Revision) and results in preserving the estate principal for the principal beneficiaries. Under many state statutes, however, depreciation is provided *at the discretion of the trustee.* When depreciation is to be provided, a portion of the income entity's revenue flow must go to the principal entity. Because we view the trust as comprising two entities, the accounting entries to record depreciation produce results as if the principal entity had sent a bill to the *income entity* for the use or consumption of the depreciable asset. The entries are as follows:

	Income Entity		Principal Entity	
1. To record depreciation:				
Depreciation Expense	1,000			
Due to Principal		1,000		
Due from Income			1,000	
Accumulated Depreciation				1,000
2. To record payment:				
Due to Principal	1,000			
Income Cash		1,000		
Principal Cash			1,000	
Due from Income				1,000

Whether or not to provide depreciation should be thoroughly explored in estate planning. Depreciation charges may deprive an *income beneficiary* of income necessary to maintain the standard of living intended by the decedent. Depreciation makes no sense if the properties are *appreciating* in value, as is the case with many rental properties. If depreciation is to be provided, it should be computed based on the *current value* of the property when it becomes subject to the trust.

CHECK POINT

Under the Revised Uniform Principal and Income Act (of 1962), which of the following is *false*?

a. Gains on disposition of principal assets increase principal.
b. Costs of investing and reinvesting principal assets are to be charged against principal.
c. Depreciation is mandatory.
d. Insurance premiums on principal assets are chargeable against income.
e. None of the above.

Answer: e (c is false under the 1997 Act)

Unusual Charges against Income

The Revised Principal and Income Act states:

> If charges against income are of unusual amount, the trustee may by means of reserves or other reasonable means charge them over a reasonable period of time and withhold from distribution sufficient sums to regularize distributions. [Section 13(b)]

The provision is somewhat ambiguous and open-ended. Under the "by means of reserves" approach, the trustee must anticipate and estimate expected unusual charges *before* they are incurred. Charges are then made against income over a reasonable period of time *prior to* their incurrence, resulting in the buildup of a "reserve," or estimated liability. The cash distributable to the *income beneficiary* during these periods is limited; thus funds accumulate from which to make the expenditure when it actually arises. Under the "by other reasonable means" option, the trustee can have the *principal entity* make the expenditure when it arises but record the expenditure as a deferred charge, which is subsequently amortized against income.

The entries under each approach for an unusually large expenditure, such as painting an apartment building exterior, are as follows:

	Income Entity		Principal Entity	
1. Accumulation Method:				
a. Periodic charge.				
Estimated Painting Expense	1,000			
Estimated Future Liability		1,000	(no entry)	
b. Actual payment.				
Estimated Future Liability	5,000		(no entry)	
Income Cash		5,000		
2. Amortization Method:				
a. Actual payment.				
Painting of Building	(no entry)		5,000	
Principal Cash				5,000
b. Periodic amortization.				
Painting Expense	1,000			
Due to Principal		1,000		
Due from Income			1,000	
Painting of Building				1,000

End-of-Chapter Review

Summary of Key Points

1. The fundamental function of estate and trust fiduciaries is to administer assets under their control rather than attempt to determine the net worth of an estate or a trust. Accordingly, accounting for estates and trusts involves **accounting for assets** rather than **accounting for net worth**. As a result, special bookkeeping practices and accountability statements are used for estates and trusts that are quite unlike those found in commercial enterprises. Furthermore, the cash basis of accounting suffices in most instances.

2. Generally accepted accounting principles have virtually no application to estates and trusts. **Trust income** (including trust income during the administration of an estate) is determined according to the terms and provisions of the trust agreement. If the trust agreement is silent on the treatment to be accorded an item, **state statutes** control.

3. An accountant rendering services to a trust must recognize that his or her role is a passive one when it comes to determining the treatment to be accorded items that are not clearly set forth in the trust agreement or state statutes. Decisions on such matters should be referred to *legal counsel* or the courts. In most cases, an accountant rendering services to an estate or trust must also have expertise in *estate*, *inheritance*, and *trust* taxation.

Glossary of New Terms

Administrator/Administratrix A person appointed by the court to administer the affairs of a decedent when an executor is not appointed.

Bequest Property received from a decedent's estate pursuant to terms in the decedent's last will and testament.

Demonstrative legacy A gift of cash for which a particular fund or source is designated from which payment is to be made.

Devise A gift of real property.

Devisee The recipient of a devise.

Estate The property of a decedent.

Estate planning Making plans for the orderly transfer of one's property on death as desired, with a view toward minimizing transfer costs.

Executor/Executrix A person who is named in a will to serve as the decedent's personal representative in administering the estate and who is appointed by the court to serve in that capacity.

General legacy Gifts of cash for which no particular fund or source is designated.

Income beneficiary The party to a trust who is entitled to the income earned on trust assets.

Inter vivos trust A trust created during a person's life.

Intestate A term used to refer to a person having died without a will.

Legacy A gift of personal property.

Legatee The recipient of a legacy.

Principal beneficiary The party to a trust who is entitled to the trust principal.

Probate The act by which a probate court determines whether a decedent's will meets the statutory requirements concerning wills.

Probate court Courts in the state court system that have jurisdiction over the affairs of decedents.

Remainderman The party to a trust who is entitled to the trust principal.

Residual legacy A gift of all personal property remaining after distribution of specific, demonstrative, and general legacies.

Specific legacy A gift of specified noncash items.

Testamentary trust A trust that comes into being on a person's death, pursuant to provisions in the decedent's will.

Testate A term used to refer to a person having died with a will.

Trust An arrangement in which property is transferred to a person, called a trustee, who holds title to the property but administers it for the benefit of other parties, called the *beneficiaries*.

Trustee That party to a trust who takes title to trust property and administers the property for the benefit of others.

Trustor The party to a trust agreement who created the trust (also referred to as a *settlor*, *grantor*, *donor*, or *creator*).

ASSIGNMENT MATERIAL

Review Questions

1. What role does GAAP play in determining trust income? Explain.
2. How do we determine whether a transaction pertains to *principal* or *income*?
3. What is the nature of the relationship between a trust *income beneficiary* and a trust *principal beneficiary*?
4. What are *legacies* and *devises*?
5. Are estate liabilities recorded in the opening entry for an estate? Explain why or why not.
6. An *estate fiduciary* may have to deal with what four types of taxes?
7. Under the Revised Uniform Principal and Income Act, when do the rights of *income beneficiaries* begin?
8. When is the *accrual method* used in accounting for estates and trusts?

9. What is the function of *probate administration*?

10. What are the major tasks of an estate fiduciary?

11. What is an accountant's role with respect to distinguishing between *principal* and *income* transactions?

12. Must assets and transactions pertaining to income be accounted for in *separate* general ledgers? Explain.

Exercises

E 23-1 **Estates: True or False** Indicate whether the following statements are true or false. Explain any *false* ones.

1. An estate is a taxable entity.
2. An estate is a legal entity.
3. The probate estate is usually smaller than the estate for federal tax purposes.
4. One function of an estate fiduciary is to account for the estate in a manner that continually reflects the estate's net worth.
5. *Federal estate taxes* are effectively borne by the residual beneficiaries of the estate.
6. *State inheritance taxes* are based on the right to give away one's property.
7. The Estate Principal account reflects the net worth of the estate at a given point in time.
8. Accounting for estates revolves around the administration of the decedent's assets.
9. The probate court essentially serves as the guardian of the estate.
10. A legacy is a gift of real property.

E 23-2 **Estates: Fill-in Statements** Fill in the missing words for the following items.

1. An estate fiduciary named in a decedent's will is called a(n) ______________.
2. An estate fiduciary who is appointed by the probate court when no person is named in a decedent's will is called a(n) ______________.
3. A gift of *personal* property is called a(n) ______________.
4. A gift of *real* property is called a(n) ______________.
5. The four types of *legacies* are ______________, ______________, ______________, and ______________.
6. A person who dies *without* a will is said to have died ______________.
7. A person who dies *with* a will is said to have died ______________.
8. State laws dealing with the affairs of decedents are commonly known as ______________.
9. *Federal estate taxes* are based on the right to ______________ property.
10. *State inheritance taxes* are based on the right to ______________ property.

E 23-3 **Trusts: True or False** Indicate whether the following statements are true or false. Explain any *false* ones.

1. When the *income beneficiary* and the *principal beneficiary* are the *same* person, no built-in clash of interests exists as in trusts in which these beneficiaries are *not* the same person.
2. An *income beneficiary's* rights begin when assets are actually transferred to the trustee.
3. In trust accounting matters, the terms of the *trust agreement* prevail over GAAP.

4. When the accounting treatment of an item is *not* clearly specified in the trust agreement, reference is made to GAAP.

5. The Revised Uniform Principal and Income Act of 1962 is somewhat outdated because it is based on GAAP in effect at that time.

6. When reference must be made to state laws to distinguish *trust principal* from *trust income*, the accountant's role is to interpret those laws concerning accounting matters.

7. The Revised Uniform Principal and Income Act of 1962 specifies the use of the *accrual basis* for many items at the commencement of a trust.

8. Accounts and transactions pertaining to trust income must be accounted for in a separate ledger to prevent commingling of accounts and transactions with that of trust principal.

9. If the answer to an accounting question *cannot* be found by referring to the *trust agreement*, *state law*, or *case law*, reference is made to GAAP.

10. Trustors may specify their own definition of net income, even if this definition is contrary to state law pertaining to trust principal and income.

E 23-4 **Trusts: Fill-in Statements** Fill in the missing words for the following items.

1. The person creating a trust is commonly called the ______________.

2. Trusts established pursuant to the provisions of a will are called ______________ trusts.

3. Trusts established during a person's life are called ______________ trusts.

4. The party taking title to trust assets is called the ______________.

5. The two classes of trust beneficiaries are the ______________ beneficiaries and the ______________ beneficiaries.

6. Another term for trust principal is trust ______________.

7. The basis of accounting used in most respects when an *income beneficiary's* rights are established is the ______________ basis.

8. Depreciation is ______________ under the Revised Uniform Principal and Income Act of 1962.

9. When the accounting treatment of an item is in doubt, the *first* place to look is the ______________ ______________.

10. The ______________ basis of accounting is used during the administration of a trust but *not* at the *beginning* and *end* of an *income beneficiary's* rights.

E 23-5 **Estates: Preparing Journal Entries** Emory Feldspar died on 5/12/05 with a provision in his will to establish a testamentary trust. His estate had the following assets subject to probate administration:

	Current Value
Cash in checking and savings accounts	$ 42,000
Investment in U.S. government bonds	387,000
Coin collection	11,000
Bond interest receivable	6,500
Total	$446,500

The estate fiduciary had the following receipts and disbursements from 5/12/05 to 1/20/06:

1. Personal liabilities totaling $2,200 were paid.

2. Funeral expenses of $1,800 were paid.

3. Federal estate taxes of $37,000 were paid.

4. *State inheritance taxes* of $14,000 were paid. Of this amount, $400 is to be borne by the legatee receiving the coin collection, and $1,100 is to be borne by the legatee (Children's Hospital) that is to receive $25,000 cash.
5. Administrative expenses of $3,300 were paid.
6. A note receivable of $2,000 was discovered in September 2005.
7. The note receivable in item 6 was collected in December 2005, along with $150 interest.
8. Interest on bonds totaling $22,000 was received.
9. Bonds having a *current value* of $60,500 at Feldspar's death were sold for $58,800.
10. The coin collection was distributed to the specified legatee, who reimbursed the estate for the inheritance taxes at that time.
11. Cash of $23,900 was distributed to Children's Hospital ($25,000 specified in the will—$1,100 *state inheritance taxes*).
12. Estate income taxes of $3,800 for the period 5/12/05 to 12/31/05 were paid.
13. Cash of $10,000 was distributed to the *income beneficiary* of the trust, Pearl Feldspar.

Required
1. Prepare the *opening* and subsequent transaction journal entries for the estate.
2. Prepare *closing* journal entries as of 1/20/06.

E 23-6 **Trusts: Preparing Journal Entries** Following are the 2005 transactions of a trust that has investments in corporate bonds and an apartment house:

1. Rental receipts totaled $38,500.
2. Property taxes of $1,400 were paid.
3. Mortgage payments of $15,500 were made. Of this amount, $14,900 pertained to interest and $600 pertained to principal. (Assume that the mortgage liability is reflected as a liability in the trust general ledger only on a memorandum basis.)
4. Normal operating costs of the apartment totaling $7,300 were paid.
5. The exterior of the apartment building was painted in January 2005 for $2,100, and payment was made at that time. The apartment exterior is painted approximately every seven years. (Assume that this qualifies as an "unusual amount" because that term is used in Section 13[b] of the Revised Uniform Principal and Income Act.)
6. The annual depreciation charge on the apartment is $4,500.
7. Bond investments having a face value of $50,000 matured during the year, and they were redeemed. (These bonds had a current value of $48,800 when they became subject to the trust.)
8. Federal trust income taxes of $450 pertaining to the prior year were paid.
9. Estimated federal trust income tax payments of $1,850 for the current year were paid.
10. The $2,200 trustee's fee for the year was paid.
11. Interest receipts on bond investments totaled $14,400.
12. Cash distributions of $9,000 were made to the income beneficiary.

Required
1. Prepare the trust transaction journal entries for the year.
2. Prepare the year-end *closing entries*.

Problems

P 23-1 **Estates: Preparing Charge and Discharge Statements** The will of Elaine Ford, deceased, directed that her executor, Wayne Pilgrim, liquidate the entire estate within two years of the date of her death and pay the net proceeds and income, if any, to the Children's Town Orphanage. Ford, who never married, died 2/1/05 after a brief illness.

An inventory of the decedent's property subject to probate administration was prepared, and the fair market value of each item was determined. The preliminary inventory, before the computation of any appropriate income accruals on inventory items, follows:

	Fair Market Value
Monument Valley Bank checking account	$ 6,000
$60,000 of 8% Bootville City school bonds, payable January 1 and July 1, maturity date of 7/1/09	59,000
2,000 shares of Rider Corporation capital stock	220,000
Term life insurance, beneficiary—estate of Elaine Ford	20,000
Personal residence ($75,000) and furnishings ($15,000)	490,000

The following transactions occurred during 2005:

1. The interest on the Bootville City bonds was collected. The bonds were sold on July 1 for $59,000, and the proceeds and interest were paid to the orphanage.
2. Rider Corporation paid cash dividends of $1 per share on March 1 and December 1, as well as a 10% stock dividend on July 1. All dividends were declared 45 days before each payment date and were payable to stockholders of record as of 40 days before each payment date. On September 2, Pilgrim sold 1,000 shares at $105 per share and paid the proceeds to the orphanage.
3. Because of a depressed real estate market, the personal residence was rented furnished at $300 per month commencing April 1. The rent is paid monthly, in advance. Real estate taxes of $900 for calendar year 2005 were paid. The house and furnishings have estimated lives of 45 and 10 years, respectively. On April 30, the part-time caretaker was paid four months' wages totaling $500 for services performed and was released.
4. The Monument Valley Bank checking account was closed; the $6,000 balance was transferred to an estate bank account.
5. The term life insurance was paid on March 1 and deposited in the estate bank account.
6. The following disbursements were made:
   a. Funeral expenses, $2,000.
   b. Final illness expenses, $1,500.
   c. April 15 income tax remittance, $700.
   d. Attorney's and accountant's fees, $12,000.
7. On December 31, the balance of the undistributed income, except for $1,000, was paid to the orphanage. The balance of the cash on hand derived from the estate principal also was paid to the orphanage on December 31.

Required Prepare charge and discharge statements, separating principal and income, together with supporting schedules, on behalf of the executor for the period 2/1/05 through 12/31/05. The following supporting schedules should be included:

1. Original principal of estate.
2. Gain or Loss on Disposal of Estate Assets.
3. Funeral, Administration, and Other Expenses.
4. Debts of Decedent Paid.
5. Legacies Paid or Delivered.
6. Assets (Corpus) on Hand, 12/31/05.
7. Income Collected.
8. Expenses Chargeable to Income.
9. Distributions of Income.

P 23-2 **Estates: Preparing Charge and Discharge Statements** Ron Ho died in an accident on 5/31/05. His will, dated 2/28/01, provided that all just debts and expenses be paid and that his property be disposed of as follows:

1. Personal residence is devised to Donna Ho, widow. (Real property is *not* subject to probate administration in the state in which the deceased resided.)
2. U.S. Treasury bonds and Bubb Company stock are to be placed in trust. All income is to go to Donna Ho during her lifetime, with right of appointment on her death.
3. Happe Company mortgage notes are bequeathed to Lulu Ho Waters, daughter.
4. A bequest of $10,000 cash goes to Dave Ho, son.
5. Remainder of estate is to be divided equally between the two children.

The will further provided that during the administration period, Donna Ho was to be paid $800 a month out of estate income. Estate and inheritance taxes are to be borne by the residue. Dave Ho was named executor and trustee.

An inventory of the decedent's property was prepared. The fair market value of all items as of Ho's death was determined. The preliminary inventory, before computing any appropriate income accruals on inventory items, is as follows:

Personal residence property	$145,000
Jewelry—Diamond ring	9,600
Oahu Life Insurance Company—Term life insurance policy on life of Ron Ho; beneficiary, Donna Ho, widow	120,000
Marble Trust Company—8% savings account, Ron Ho, in trust for Lelani Waters (grandchild), interest credited January 1 and July 1; balance 5/31/05	400
Hilo National Bank—Checking account; balance 5/31/05	141,750
$200,000 U.S. Treasury bonds, 10%; interest payable March 1 and September 1, due in 2008	200,000
$10,000 Happe Company first mortgage notes, 12%, due in 2009; interest payable June 30 and December 31	9,900
800 shares Bubb Company common stock	64,000
700 shares Maui Manufacturing Company common stock	70,000

The executor opened an estate bank account, to which he transferred the decedent's checking account balance. Other deposits, through 7/1/06, follow:

Interest collected on bonds	
$200,000 U.S. Treasury	
7/1/05	$10,000
3/1/06	10,000
Dividends received on stock	
800 shares Bubb Company	
6/15/05, declared 5/7/05, payable to holders of record 5/27/05	800
9/15/05	800
12/15/05	1,200
3/15/06	800
6/15/06	800
Net proceeds of 6/19/05 sale of 700 shares of Maui Manufacturing Company	68,810
Interest collected on Happe Company first mortgage notes, 6/30/05	600

Payments were made from the estate's checking account through 7/1/06 for the following items:

Funeral expenses	$2,000
Assessments for additional 2004 federal and state income tax ($1,700) plus interests ($110) to 5/31/05	1,810
2005 income taxes of Ron Ho for the period 1/1/05 through 5/31/05 in excess of estimated taxes paid by the decedent	9,100
Federal and state fiduciary income taxes, fiscal year ended 6/30/05 ($75), and 6/30/06 ($1,400)	1,475
State inheritance taxes	28,000
Monthly payments to Donna Ho: 13 payments of $800	10,400
Attorney's and accountant's fees	25,000
Payment of interest collected on Happe Company mortgage notes that accrues to legatee	600

The executor waived his commission; however, he wanted his father's diamond ring in lieu of the $10,000 specific legacy. All parties agreed to this in writing, and the court's approval was secured. All other specific legacies were delivered by 7/15/05.

Required Prepare charge and discharge statements for principal and income, and supporting schedules to accompany the attorney's formal court accounting on behalf of the executor of the estate of Ron Ho for the period 5/31/05 through 7/1/06. The following supporting schedules should be included:

1. Original Capital of Estate.
2. Gain on Disposal of Estate Assets.
3. Loss on Disposal of Estate Assets.
4. Funeral, Administration, and Other Expenses.
5. Debts of Decedent Paid.
6. Legacies Paid or Delivered.
7. Assets (Corpus) on Hand, 7/1/06.
8. Proposed Plan of Distribution of Estate Assets.
9. Income Collected.
10. Distribution of Income.

P 23-3 **Trusts: Treatment of Disputed Items** A CPA firm has assigned you to work with the trustees of a large trust in the first annual accounting to the court. The income beneficiaries and the remaindermen cannot agree on the proper allocation of the following items on which the trust agreement is silent:

1. Costs incurred in expanding the garage facilities of an apartment house owned by the trust and held for rental income.
2. Real estate taxes on the apartment house.
3. Cost of casualty insurance premiums on the apartment house.
4. A 2-for-1 stock split of common stock held by the trust for investment.
5. Insurance proceeds received as the result of a partial destruction of an office building that the trust owned and held for rental income.
6. Costs incurred by the trust in the sale of a tract of land.
7. Costs incurred to defend title to real property held by the trust.

Required Locate a copy of the Revised Uniform Principal and Income Act in your library or on the Internet. Indicate the allocations between principal and income to be made for each item, using the act as the point of reference. Be sure to quote the applicable section of the act. (The purpose of this problem is to force you to search out items in the act, a task that is necessary in actual practice.)

P 23-4 **Trusts: Preparing Journal Entries and Charge and Discharge Statements** The postclosing combined trial balance for the principal entity and the income entity of a trust as of 12/31/05 is as follows:

	Debit	Credit
Principal cash	$ 3,500	
Income cash	800	
Investments in bonds	123,400	
Investment in E & T Corporation common stock	86,200	
Duplex rental unit	95,000	
Accumulated depreciation on duplex rental unit		$ 12,000
Trust principal		296,100
Trust income		800
Totals	$308,900	$308,900

Following are the 2006 trust transactions:

1. Rental receipts were $11,500.
2. Property taxes of $1,000 were paid.
3. Mortgage payments of $6,500 were made. Of this amount, $5,800 pertained to interest and $700 to principal. (The mortgage liability of $57,500 on the duplex at 12/31/05 is recorded in the trust general ledger on a memorandum basis.)
4. Normal operating costs of the duplex rental unit totaling $600 were paid.

5. New carpeting was installed in both units of the duplex in January 2006 at a cost of $1,800, with payment being made at that time. (New carpeting is installed approximately every 10 years.)
6. The annual depreciation charge on the duplex is $2,000. (Of the $95,000 value assigned to the duplex when it became subject to the trust, $15,000 was assigned to land, and $80,000 was assigned to the building, carpets, and drapes. The $80,000 is depreciated over 40 years.)
7. Bond investments having a face value of $25,000 matured during the year, and they were redeemed. (These bonds had a $25,500 *current value* when they became subject to the trust.)
8. Bonds having a face value of $20,000 were purchased in the open market for $19,000 on 7/1/06. The maturity date of the bonds is 6/30/09.
9. Interest receipts on bond investments totaled $9,800.
10. E & T Inc. declared a 10% stock dividend on 4/1/06. The trust held 200 shares of E & T's common stock prior to this declaration. (The *market price* of common stock increased $30 per share during 2006.)
11. Cash dividends of $3,300 on E & T's common stock were received.
12. The $1,500 trustee's fee for the year was paid.
13. Attorney's and accountant's fees for periodic judicial accounting totaling $1,200 were paid.
14. Cash distributions totaling $8,000 were made to the income beneficiary.
15. "Due to" and "due from" accounts are settled at year-end.

Required

1. Prepare the trust transaction journal entries for the year.
2. Prepare the year-end *closing entries.*
3. Prepare charge and discharge statements for the year for trust principal and trust income.

THINKING CRITICALLY

Cases

C 23-1 **Estate Planning** Your client, Jan Landers, has asked your advice on accounting matters with respect to her attorney's preparation of a testamentary trust agreement. Jan wants all her residential property holdings placed in trust for the benefit of her husband (as *income beneficiary*) and her children (as *principal beneficiaries*).

Required On what points should you advise your client? (Assume that you are located in a state that has adopted the Revised Uniform Principal and Income Act without modification.)

C 23-2 **Role of the Accountant** An attorney who is your acquaintance has suggested that you attend a meeting that may lead to some work for you. At the meeting, you are informed that (1) Ken Dall died approximately one year ago, (2) the attorney is serving as the executor of the estate, (3) the residual balance of the estate is to be placed in trust, and (4) the trustee is Barbara Dall, Ken's widow. Barbara Dall describes the nature of the trust assets as bonds, residential rental properties, and the stock of a wholly owned corporation, which continues to operate. She requests that you become the accountant for the trust and, in that capacity, do the following:

1. Maintain the books and records.
2. Make all accounting decisions.
3. Prepare the fiduciary income tax returns.
4. Prepare the annual financial statements.

Required How would you respond to this request? Elaborate on the points you should discuss with Barbara Dall.

part eight

Governmental and Nonprofit Organizations

VIII

chapter

24

Governmental Accounting: Basic Principles and the General Fund

Nobody spends somebody else's money as wisely as they spend their own.
MILTON FRIEDMAN
NOBEL PRIZE WINNER IN ECONOMICS

LEARNING OBJECTIVES

To Understand

> The standard-setting process for governmental GAAP.
> The *nature* and *diversity* of governmental activities.
> The *objectives* of governmental financial reporting.
> The two different manners of reporting required—*fund-based* statements and *government-wide* statements.
> The unique type of measurement focus (*flow of current financial resources*) and basis of accounting (*modified accrual*) used in the *fund-based* manner of reporting applicable to the majority of governmental activities.
> The enormous reporting deficiency in governmental financial reporting.
> The basic principles used in governmental financial reporting.
> The way to account for the transactions of a *General Fund*.

TOPIC OUTLINE

CHAPTER OVERVIEW

In this chapter, we first discuss the Governmental Accounting Standards Board (GASB), which establishes accounting standards for state and local governmental units and which is a sister organization of the Financial Accounting Standards Board (FASB). We then discuss (1) the nature and diversity of governmental activities, (2) the objectives of governmental financial reporting, (3) the two different kinds of flow statements that are used to present operating statements for governmental activities, and (4) other major reporting.

Last, we discuss the *General Fund* of governmental units, which is the fund that accounts for most of the operations of governmental units. All other funds, which are specialized funds, are discussed in Chapter 25. Likewise, accounting for capitalizable fixed assets and long-term liabilities—both (1) those that are reported *within* certain funds and (2) those that are reported *outside* any of the funds—are discussed in Chapter 25.

Most importantly, Chapter 25 also discusses the manner of preparing the ***government-wide financial statements***—statements that present *an overall picture of the governmental unit*.

Although entire textbooks are devoted to accounting for state and local governmental units, the coverage in this and the following chapter is sufficiently broad and deep to prepare for the governmental portion of the CPA examination.

I. THE GOVERNMENTAL ACCOUNTING STANDARDS BOARD

Its Purpose, Structure, and Location

In 1984, the Governmental Accounting Standards Board was created as an arm of the Financial Accounting Foundation (FAF) to establish state and local governmental accounting standards. Thus the FAF now oversees both the FASB and the GASB. The GASB has a seven-member board (appointed for five-year terms), with a full-time chairperson. A simple majority (four votes) is needed to issue a pronouncement (compared with a super-majority of five votes for the FASB). The GASB is located in the same Norwalk, Connecticut, headquarters as the FASB.

No Authority to Establish Standards for the Federal Government

The GASB does *not* have authority to establish financial reporting standards for the federal government. The Federal Accounting Standards Advisory Board (FASAB), which functions independently of the FAF, the FASB, and the GASB, however, proposes reporting standards to (1) the Office of Management and Budgets (OMB), (2) the General Accounting Office (GAO), and (3) the Treasury department, all of which issue their own standards.

Status of Pre-GASB Standards

Prior to GASB's creation, state and local governmental accounting standards were established by various bodies (the last one being the National Council on Governmental Accounting—NCGA—which made some major reporting improvements during its existence from 1978 to 1984). These various bodies were sponsored by the Government Finance Officers Association (GFOA), which is for the governmental sector what the American Institute of Certified Public Accountants (AICPA) is for the private sector.[1] The GFOA's web site is **http://www.gfoa.org**.

[1] Prior to1984, the GFOA was called the Municipal Finance Officers Association. In this chapter, we use its new name. The GFOA, as does the AICPA for the private sector, offers the governmental sector a wide range of (1) publications (including 85 books, periodicals, and a monthly newsletter), (2) services, and (3) software, all of which are designed to enhance and promote the professional management of governmental units.

State and local governmental accounting standards in force at the time of GASB's creation continue in force until their status is changed by a subsequent GASB pronouncement (as mandated by GASB *Statement No. 1*, "Authoritative Status of NCGA Pronouncements and AICPA Industry Audit Guide").

The Jurisdictional Arrangement for the GASB and the FASB

The current jurisdictional arrangement (effective since November 30, 1989) for the GASB and the FASB is that each board has primary responsibility for setting standards for the reporting entities within its jurisdiction. Under this arrangement, an entity subject to the jurisdiction of one board

1. **Is** *not required* to change its reporting methods as a result of a standard issued by the other board.
2. **Must** follow a pronouncement of the *other* board if required to do so by the *primary* board.
3. **May** elect to follow the pronouncements of the other board (or look to other sources for guidance) when the *primary* board has *not* addressed a specific issue. Furthermore, a governmental unit that elects to use such FASB standards must use them on an **all-or-nothing basis;** thus a governmental unit *cannot* pick and choose among those FASB standards (the ones that do *not* conflict with or contradict GASB pronouncements).

Governments have the *option* of *consistently* following compatible FASB guidance issued *after* November 30, 1989, for activities reported as (1) *business-type activities* in government-wide statements and (2) Enterprise Funds (discussed later).

The Governmental GAAP Hierarchy

Auditors of private companies and governmental units that issue *unqualified* opinions usually use wording as follows in their audit reports:

> In our opinion, the financial statements referred to above present fairly, in all material respects, the financial position of X Company or X City as of December 31, 2005, and the results of its operations and its cash flows for the year then ended, in conformity with generally accepted accounting principles [hereafter GAAP].

The Auditing Standards Board of the AICPA has issued an auditing standard that (1) requires the auditor's judgment concerning "fairness" be applied within the framework of GAAP and (2) sets forth a hierarchy of GAAP for *both* nongovernmental and governmental entities.[2] The governmental GAAP hierarchy (in which Level 1 is the highest authoritative source) is presented in Illustration 24-1.

GAAFR: "The Blue Book"

Note that in footnote d of Illustration 24-1 we mention the 2001 (7th) edition of *GAAFR*, the acronym for *Governmental Accounting, Auditing and Financial Reporting*, which the GFOA publishes. With more than 30,000 copies in print, *GAAFR* is widely used by government finance practitioners as a nonauthoritative source of practical guidance on properly applying GAAP to state and local governments. The 2001 edition (680 pages) includes updated guidance on all facets of governmental accounting and auditing, including detailed discussions and extensive examples of governmental reporting standards.[3]

---

[2] This guidance is set forth in *Statement on Auditing Standards No. 69*, "The Meaning of *Present Fairly in Conformity With Generally Accepted Accounting Principles*," issued in 1992, and in paragraphs 1.16–18 of the AICPA's audit guide, *Audits of State and Local Governmental Units*, which was issued in 1994 (the third edition).

[3] Prior to the formalization of the governmental standard-setting process through the NCGA, *GAAFR* was the authoritative source of governmental GAAP.

ILLUSTRATION 24-1 SUMMARY OF HIERARCHY OF GOVERNMENTAL GAAP

	Source			
LEVEL	GASB	FASB	AICPA	OTHER
1	Statements and Interpretations	Applicable[a] pronouncements[b]	Applicable[a] pronouncements[b]	
2	Technical Bulletins		Applicable[c] Industry Audit and Accounting Guides Applicable[c] Statements of Position	
3	Emerging Issues Task Consensus Positions (if and when a GASB EITF is formed)		Applicable[c] Practice Bulletins	
4	Implementation Guides (Questions and Answers published by the GASB staff)			Industry Practices[d]
5[e]				Other Accounting Literature[f]

[a] Applicable at this level means if designated as applying to state and local governmental entities by a GASB Statement or Interpretation.

[b] *Proprietary funds* of governmental units (which are the funds that report in the same manner as for-profit entities as explained later) are subject to private-sector authoritative guidance issued prior to 11/30/89 (through FAS 102), unless it is *inconsistent* with GASB guidance. Furthermore, proprietary funds retain the option of following pronouncements of the FASB issued subsequent to that date if (1) they do so consistently and (2) the guidance is *not* inconsistent with GASB guidance.

[c] *Applicable* at this level means those designated by the AICPA as applying to state and governmental entities and cleared by the GASB (no formal objection given to the issuance of the pronouncement).

[d] Must be widely recognized and prevalent. (The 2001 edition of GAAFR would be a useful reference at this level.)

[e] This is referred to as *Other Sources* in *SAS 69* rather than as Level 5.

[f] Includes GASB Concepts Statements, FASB and AICPA pronouncements *not* specifically made applicable to state and local governmental units, Technical Information Service Inquiries and Replies included in AICPA Technical Practice Aids, accounting textbooks, articles (such as GAAFR Review, a monthly publication by the GFOA).

The GASB's Accomplishments to Date

Since its inception in 1984, the GASB has issued two *Concepts Statements*, 45 *Statements of Governmental Accounting Standards* (hereafter we use GAS in referring to specific standards), six *Interpretations*, and three *Technical Bulletins*. The GASB statements have simplified or upgraded governmental financial reporting. The most substantial upgrade, by far, was *GAS 34* (issued in 1999).

GAS 34—A Major Milestone

GAS 34 was the result of a complete reexamination of the governmental financial reporting model that took 15 years of study. *GAS 34* mandates the issuance of both (1) *fund* financial statements (the only manner of reporting allowed prior to *GAS 34*) and (2) *government-wide* financial statements. The significance of requiring *government-wide* financial statements is that citizens and government officials—for the first time—are provided information specifically designed to inform about the governmental unit's (1) **overall financial condition,** (2) **cost of providing services,** and (3) **manner of obtaining resources** (such as through taxation, fees, grants, and borrowings) **to pay for the cost of providing those services.**

The GASB *Codification* of Governmental GAAP

In 1984, the GASB codified all existing governmental accounting and financial reporting standards, interpretations, and technical bulletins in a joint effort with the GFOA. This book, *Codification of*

Governmental Accounting and Financial Reporting Standards, is periodically updated for subsequent changes.[4]

In referring to governmental GAAP, the AICPA's governmental audit guide cites the GASB *Codification* (for example, "GASB *Cod.*, sec. xxx") rather than the various GASB and NCGA statements and interpretations in force at the time of the *Codification*. We, however, usually cite the *original* GASB pronouncement.

II. THE NATURE AND DIVERSITY OF GOVERNMENTAL ACTIVITIES

Governmental operations are unique for several reasons: (1) their absence of a profit motive, (2) their extensive legal requirements, (3) their diverse activities, and (4) their use of fund accounting.

The Absence of a Profit Motive: *What* to Measure?

The fundamental difference between the *private* sector and the *governmental* sector is that the *former* is organized and operated to make a profit for its owners while the *latter* exists to provide services to its citizens on a substantially nonprofit basis. In the *private sector*, profit measurement is possible because a causal relationship exists between expenses and revenues: costs and expenses are incurred to generate revenues. As a result, it is appropriate to compare these categories and determine profitability. The services of governmental units, however, are *not* intended to generate revenues. Thus revenues are *not* earned; they stand alone. This circumstance raises two key questions:

> Should revenues be compared with the costs of providing services?
> Is some other comparison of inflows and outflows more appropriate?

We discuss this issue in depth in Section IV, Measurement Focus: *What* Flows to Measure for Operations.

Extensive Legal Requirements

Constitutions, charters, and statutes regulate governmental units. Many legal provisions pertain to financial accounting areas. For example, certain activities or specified revenues must frequently be accounted for separately from all other operations. The uses of certain revenues may be limited. In some instances, a certain method of accounting—such as the *cash basis*—may be stipulated. We discuss the accounting ramifications of these requirements later in the chapter.

Many governmental units are required by law to follow GAAP and be audited annually by outside CPA firms or governmental audit agencies.

Diversity of Activities

Governmental activities are tremendously diverse and are classified into three broad categories:

1. **Governmental Activities.** Activities that do *not* resemble commercial activities are classified in this category. These operations provide *primary services*, and they are normally financed from tax revenues. Examples are education, public safety, the judicial system, social services, and administration.
2. **Business-Type Activities.** These activities resemble *commercial activities*. Usually financed wholly or partially from user charges, these operations may be considered *secondary services*. Examples

[4] The most recent update was effective June 30, 2003.

are utilities, public transportation, parking facilities, and recreational facilities. Business-type operations usually have the objective to earn a profit or recover a certain level of operating costs from fees charged the public for their use.

3. **Fiduciary Activities.** These activities pertain to accounting for assets held by a governmental unit as trustee or agent. The most common example is a pension fund for *current* and *former* public employees. **Key Point:** These assets and their earnings benefit parties *other than* the governmental unit or its citizens.

The Use of Fund Accounting

Because of the legal requirements pertaining to financial accounting areas and the diversity of governmental activities, the use of a single set of accounts to record and summarize all the financial transactions of a governmental unit is neither legally possible nor practical. Accordingly, the GASB *Codification* requires that governmental accounting systems be organized and operated on a *fund basis*. Under a *fund-based* accounting system, certain activities are accounted separately from all other operations. **Thus each governmental unit uses multiple general ledgers** (if 10 funds are used, 10 different general ledgers are used). The GASB *Codification* defines a **fund** as follows:

> A fund is . . . a fiscal and accounting entity with a self-balancing set of accounts recording cash and other financial resources, together with all related liabilities and residual equities or balances, and changes therein, which are segregated for the purpose of carrying on activities or attaining certain objectives in accordance with special regulations, restrictions, or limitations.[5]

Fund Balance versus *Net Assets* Terminology

The difference between a fund's assets and liabilities might be loosely thought of as the fund's "equity." This term, however, is deemed inappropriate except for *business-type activities*. The following table shows the terminology used:

Governmental **Activities**[a]	***Business-Type*** **Activities**
	Fund **Statements and**
Fund **Statements:**	***Government-Wide*** **Statements:**
Fund balance—	Net Assets (or Fund Equity)—
Reserved[b]	Invested in capital assets, net of related debt[b]
Unreserved[b]	Restricted[b]
Government-Wide **Statements:**	Unrestricted
(Same net assets categories as used for business-*type* activities)	

Note that the classifications shown above are based on ***accessibility***—not based on *source* of capital, which is used in the *private sector*.

Note: ***Fiduciary*** **activities** only have *fund-based* statements, and they use the same terminology used for business-*type activities*.

[a] For *governmental activities accounted for in Internal Service Funds* (discussed later) the individual fund statements use the terminology required for business-type activities.

[b] The nature of these accounts is explained later.

III. THE OBJECTIVES OF GOVERNMENTAL FINANCIAL REPORTING

GASB Concepts Statement No. 1, "Objectives of Financial Reporting," sets forth three overall objectives of governmental financial reporting and nine additional objectives that flow from the three overall objectives. We list the three overall objectives and selected additional ones in Illustration 24-2.

[5] *Codification of Governmental Accounting and Financial Reporting Standards* (Norwalk, CT: Governmental Accounting Standards Board, 1995), sec. 1100.102.

ILLUSTRATION 24-2 OBJECTIVES OF GOVERNMENTAL FINANCIAL REPORTING

"1. Financial reporting should assist in fulfilling a government's duty to be publicly accountable and enable users to assess that accountability (the paramount objective from which all other objectives must flow). Financial reporting should
   a. Provide information to determine whether current-year revenues were sufficient to pay for current-year services.
   b. Demonstrate whether revenues were obtained and used in accordance with the entity's legally adopted budget.

"2. Financial reporting should assist users in evaluating the operating results of the governmental entity for the year. Financial reporting should
   a. Provide information about sources and uses of financial resources.
   b. Determine whether the entity's financial position improved or deteriorated as a result of the year's operations.

"3. Financial reporting should assist users in assessing the level of services that can be provided by the governmental entity and its ability to meet its obligations as they become due."

Source: GASB Cod., sec. 100.177-179.

IV. MEASUREMENT FOCUS: *WHAT* FLOWS TO MEASURE FOR OPERATIONS

The concept of *measurement focus* pertains to presenting in an operating statement information concerning flows for a period of time (examples are (a) *cash flows*, (b) *cash and receivable* flows combined, (c) *cash*, *receivables*, *and accounts payable flows* combined, or (d) *all assets and liabilities* flows. Thus measurement focus is exclusively an *operating statement* concept of **"which assets and liabilities should be included in the flow presented in the measure for operations."**[6]

Because of the diversity of governmental activities, the reporting issue is raised as to whether (1) the *same* flows should be measured for all three types of activities or (2) *different* flows should be measured.

As a point of reference, recall that business enterprises (proprietary in nature) present an *operating statement* called an *income statement*. An *income statement* **measures the inflows and outflows that impact an entity's net assets (total assets—total liabilities) for a period of time.** Thus an income statement uses the **economic resources measurement focus.** In addition, business enterprises present a *statement of cash flows*, which has a much more limited measurement focus than that of an *income statement*. Thus business enterprises present *two* flow statements.

Business-Type Activities of Government

Some governmental activities are managed in a manner similar to those of business enterprises because the objective is to recover either all or a majority of the cost of providing services through user charges. For such activities, it is sensible to use the *economic resources measurement focus* and thus present an operating statement that shows revenues, gains, expenses (including depreciation expense), and losses. Rather than calling this operating statement an *income statement*, however, **the title "*Statement of Revenues and Expenses and Changes in Net Assets*" is deemed more appropriate in view of the fact that the intent is *not* to generate income or maximize profits as in the *private* sector.** Thus a statement of revenues and expenses for *business-type activities* answers the following questions:

1. What revenues were generated during the year?
2. What expenses were incurred during the year?

[6] The word *operations* in the private sector refers exclusively to transactions and events that impact equity. For nonproprietary- type activities of government, *operations* has (1) a broader meaning in some respects because it *includes* borrowings, repayments of debt, and expenditures for the acquisition of capital assets and (2) a narrower meaning in some respects because it *excludes* both (a) depreciation expense and (b) long-term liabilities and pension obligations not expected to be funded currently. This becomes evident as you read this section of the chapter.

3. What was the improvement or deterioration in the governmental unit's overall *economic condition* as a result of events and transactions that occurred during the year? (Stated differently, what was the *change in net assets* that resulted from operations?)

A Secondary Statement as Well

It is also sensible to present a *statement of cash flows* for *business-type activities*, as the *private sector* does. This comprehensive manner of reporting (*two* flow statements, one of which is the *economic resources measurement flow*), is required in both *fund statements* and *government-wide statements* for *business-type activities*. Consequently, negligible reporting issues exist for *business-type activities*. In contrast, reporting *governmental activities* has historically been quite controversial (as evidenced by the 15 years of study and debate involving how to report *governmental activities* that occurred prior to the issuance of *GAS 34*).

Governmental Activities of Governments

For *governmental activities*, the reporting issues are (1) whether to use the *same* measurement focus (economic resources measurement focus) as for *business-type activities* or a *different* measurement focus and (2) whether *one* or *two* flow statements are needed. The various proposed alternative flows that are possible—for the operating statement—are as follows:

1. **Flows of economic resources and claims against those resources that impact net assets** (the *economic resources measurement focus* discussed earlier). [The measurement focus in the *primary* flow statement in the *private* sector.]
2. **Flows of cash** (A very narrow measurement focus). [The measurement focus in the *secondary* flow statement in the *private* sector.]
3. **Flows of *current* financial resources** (*essentially cash and receivables*) **and claims against those items that will be *paid* in the current period or shortly thereafter** (the *current financial resources measurement focus*). [A *narrow* measurement focus that was the *exclusive* manner of reporting for governmental activities prior to *GAS 34's* issuance.] Thus it measures the impact on certain net assets (certain *current assets* – certain *current liabilities*).
4. **Flows of *total* financial resources** (*essentially cash, receivables, prepaids, and inventories*) **and claims against those items that will be** paid **in the current period or shortly thereafter** (the *total financial resources measurement focus*). [A ***slightly*** **broader** measurement focus than alternative 3.]
5. **Flows of *current* financial resources** (*essentially cash and receivables*) **and claims against those items that were** incurred **in the current period**—regardless of when paid. [A ***substantially*** **broader** measurement focus than alternatives 3 and 4.]
6. **Flows of *total* financial resources** (*essentially cash, receivables, prepaids, and inventories*) **and claims against those items that were** incurred **in the current period**—regardless of when paid. [A slightly broader measurement focus than alternative 5.]

Comparison of Alternatives 1 and 3—Expenditures Example

Assume that (1) a city having a December 31 year-end reached an injury settlement claim near year-end with an employee who had been accidentally injured earlier in the year (2005) and (2) the city agreed to pay the employee $100,000 as follows: $60,000 on December 1, 2005 (which *was* paid), and $10,000 annually for *four* years beginning on January 31, 2006. Under the ***economic resources measurement focus*** (and ignoring discounting), $100,000 of expenses are recognized in the 2005 *operating statement*, and a $40,000 liability is recognized in the *balance sheet* at December 31, 2005. In contrast, only $70,000 is recognized in the 2005 statements under the ***current financial resources measurement focus***—the $60,000 paid in 2005 plus the $10,000 expected to be paid January 31, 2006 (shortly after year-end). The remaining $30,000 is reported as an expenditure *in later periods* ($10,000 in years 2006, 2007, and 2008).

Thus under ***current financial resources measurement focus***, the *fund-based* operating statement effectively is a statement of virtually *all* the *revenues* and *some* of the *costs incurred to provide services* for the period.

Assessment of the Six Alternatives

None of the last five alternatives produces a result that would come close to the result obtained in alternative 1 (the *economic resources measurement focus*). Also, alternatives 3 and 4 generally produce results that are somewhat close to those that would be obtained using *cash flows* as the measurement focus. (Alternatives 5 and 6 do so as well but to a lesser extent.) To drive home the point that alternatives 2 through 5 are essentially nothing more than slight to moderate variations of a *cash flows statement*, you should realize that the following major types of cash flow (but *not* depreciation expense, which is *not* a cash flow) are reported in the operating statement under each of these five alternatives:

> Proceeds from borrowings.
> Repayments of debt.
> Interest payments on debt.
> Acquisitions of capital assets.
> Proceeds from the sale of capital assets.

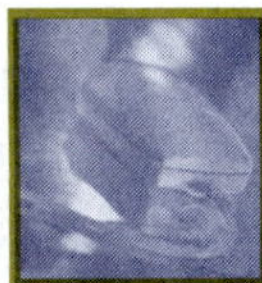

CHECK POINT

To what is the *use* of *financial resources* of a fund broadly referred?

a. Encumbrance
b. Expenditure
c. Appropriation
d. Disbursement

Answer: b

Meeting the Objectives of GASB *Concepts Statement 1*

To meet all the reporting objectives in GASB *Concepts Statement 1* (discussed earlier), *GAS 34* requires that the *operating statement* for *governmental activities* be based on (1) the *first* alternative (the flow of *economic resources*) in *government-wide statements* and (2) the *third* alternative (the flow of *current financial resources* in *fund statements*). Interestingly enough, a *cash flow* statement is *not* required as a *secondary* flow statement in the *government-wide statements*. (Requiring a *cash flow* statement as a *secondary* flow statement in the *fund statements* would serve no useful purpose because the amounts would *not* differ significantly from the *first* flow statement amounts.)

Governmental Activities: The *Government-Wide* Statement Measure of Operations

The operating statement for *governmental activities* using the *economic resources measurement focus* required in the *government-wide statements* is called a *Statement of Activities* (rather than an *income statement*, which is inappropriate terminology for governmental reporting). This statement reports revenues, **expenses** (*including* depreciation), special gains and losses, extraordinary items, contributions received, and any other items that increase or decrease net assets of the *governmental activities*. Because of the ***all-inclusive* concept** used, the "bottom line" in this statement is appropriately called **"the increase (or decrease) in net assets."**

Governmental Activities: The *Fund-Based* Statement Measure of Operations

The operating statement using the flow of *current financial resources* (alternative 3) reports only *near-term* inflows and outflows of *financial* resources. Accordingly, it answers the following questions:

1. What financial resources were **received** during the year?
2. What financial resources were **expended** during the year?
3. What increase or decrease occurred in the net financial resources that can be spent in the near future?

To facilitate reporting under this rather *narrow* measurement focus, general capital assets and general long-term liabilities (defined and discussed later and in detail in Chapter 25) are excluded from the balance sheets of the *governmental funds* used to account for *governmental activities*. They are reported instead in a *separate* general ledger called the *general Capital Assets and General Long-Term Liabilities* general ledger. **In Chapter 25, we explain how to prepare a "consolidation/conversion worksheet" in which the amounts in the various general ledgers pertaining to *governmental activities* are added together and adjusted to obtain the *governmental activities section* of the *government-wide* Statement of Net Assets.**

Governmental Activities: "Interperiod Equity"—It Can Be Assessed Only with *Government-Wide Statements*

The concept of interperiod equity (or interperiod fairness) focuses on whether financial resources *received* during the year were sufficient to cover claims *incurred* during the year. Stated from a *citizen's* perspective, it focuses on **whether *current year* citizens received services for which *future year* citizens will be required to pay.** From a broader perspective, realize that the concept of interperiod equity is also **an intergenerational equity issue.** Assessing the extent to which interperiod equity exists is possible if and only if the operating statement uses the flow of *economic resources and related claims* (used in the *government-wide statements*).

Requiring *government-wide statements* is the major accomplishment of *GAS 34*, the passage of which was necessary because of continuing major deficiencies in financial reporting that led to one crisis after another for governmental units. For example, the city of Miami in Florida had a 1996 budget collapse that was blamed on the inability to know the city's true economic condition. *GAS 34* is intended to solve this "visibility" deficiency.

Balanced Budget Laws

The interperiod equity concept is also consistent with the balanced-budget laws in 49 of the 50 states, **the intent of which is to require governments to live within their means.** Many accountants believe that the former manner of reporting (presenting only a statement that measures the flows of *current financial resources*) was merely a way for politicians to circumvent the intent of these laws.

A Remaining Major Financial Reporting Deficiency—Employee Benefit Obligations Greatly Exceed Amounts Recognized to Date in the Government-Wide Statements

The inability to assess interperiod equity problem (which was enormous before *GAS 34*'s issuance), however, has *not* been fully eliminated by *GAS 34* because an unrealistic manner of calculating *pension costs* and *other postemployment benefit costs* (primarily health care) is allowed.

Concerning pensions, the GASB codification requires that the manner of *funding* the pension benefit obligation be used to determine the pension cost to be recorded.[7] Unfortunately, much of the *retroactive benefit enhancements* that are frequently made to the plans are being funded (monies set aside in a *Pension Trust Fund)* to a significant extent during the employees' *retirement years* (rather than *totally* during their *working years* when the employees rendered their services). As a result, enormous costs are shifted to postretirement years, and massive liabilities (determined realistically) are *not* reported. Such accounting practices partly explain why many state employee pension plans are substantially underfunded (some are funded as low as 20%).

---

[7] Accounting for governmental pensions is set forth in GASB *No. 27*, "Accounting for Pensions by State and Local Governmental Employers," issued in 1994. It is patterned after *APB Opinion No. 8*, "Accounting for the Cost of Pension Plans," which was superseded by the substantially more rigorous *FAS 87*, "Employers' Accounting for Pensions."

Furthermore, no disclosure of the *pension benefit obligation* (the true obligation) need be made for comparison with the amounts set aside so as to show the amount by which the pension plan is truly underfunded.

If governmental units were required to follow the much more *demanding FASB Statement No. 87*, "Employers' Accounting for Pensions" (which (1) separates the manner of calculating *pension costs* from the *funding* of those costs and (2) requires that a liability be reported for the unfunded accumulated benefit obligation), the *government-wide statements* would report a staggering additional amount of liabilities. (One estimate is $125 billion.[8]) Consequently, *current year* citizens are now receiving substantial benefits for which they are shifting the burden of payment to *future year* citizens. Note that this problem is *both* a GAAP deficiency problem *and* a measurement focus problem.

Refer to the *Business Perspective* that follows for a discussion of the political factors causing (1) this serious interperiod equity problem and (2) serious liquidity problems for a high percentage of public pension funds.

Business Perspective

West Virginia's Pensioners Come Up Short

CHARLESTON, W. Va.—Mary Alice Johnson, a 74-year-old retired clerk-typist for the state tax department, wishes she could afford an air conditioner. But the cost would bust her budget, because she hasn't seen an increase in her $318 monthly pension check since she retired in 1988.

The irony is that if Mrs. Johnson lived across the border—in Kentucky or Virginia, for example—she wouldn't have to shuffle electric fans around her row-house to try to cool off during the steamy summer months. That's because most public pension systems in other states are well-funded and can afford to pay steady cost-of-living increases to their retirees.

But not West Virginia, which has the most underfunded pension plan in the nation. How did it manage to accomplish this during one of the greatest bull markets in U.S. history, while many public pension plans elsewhere are flush with surplus assets?

West Virginia's woes, which are shared by a handful of public pension systems around the nation, are caused in part by outdated state laws, which until 1998 prohibited their pension funds from investing in stocks. But its problems have been compounded by the exemption of public pension plans from federal rules that require managers to fund plans adequately in the first place and to invest the assets prudently.

As a result, West Virginia's state pension plans, with 41,400 retirees, have just 19.7% of the assets needed to pay accrued $4.3 billion in liabilities. Many retirees haven't seen a pension increase in 25 years. "Every chance the legislature gets, they give themselves a raise," Mrs. Johnson says. "But they don't care about retired people."

Now, West Virginia legislators are scrambling to find money to pay the looming pension bills. Lawmakers hope to float one of the largest municipal-bond offerings in U.S. history—$4 billion—in a taxpayer bailout of the system.

While acknowledging the shortcomings of public-worker pension plans in the state, West Virginia officials say the move to allow funds to buy stocks, together with the proposed bond issue, are designed to help the state overcome its pension funding problems over time.

"Our plan has never been in good shape," says Joseph Markus, who recently took a private sector job after serving as cabinet secretary in the state's Department of Administration, where he helped look into ways to address the pension issue. "Our big concern now is to make sure we're never in this situation again."

Corporate pension plans usually don't wind up in such sorry shape as some state plans because the Employee Retirement Income Security Act, a federal pension law, mandates prudent portfolio management. Erisa doesn't apply to state and municipal plans.

Century-Long Hiatus

Poor investment decisions can be one result. Skittishness about stock investments kept many public

[8] "West Virginia's Pensioners Come Up Short," *The Wall Street Journal*. June 5, 2000, p. C1.

Business Perspective, continued

pension systems on the sidelines for years. After an 1880s shipping canal deal went sour, for example, Indiana stayed out of stocks until 1998. Today, its teachers' retirement plan has only about one-third the assets needed to meet $7.7 billion in expected liabilities.

Even though West Virginia finally began allowing its state and local pension plans to start investing in stocks two years ago, 30% of local plans still haven't waded into stocks, according to a state treasurer's survey last year. The state plans are moving into stocks slowly, and the hope with the bond issue is that West Virginia can invest the proceeds in the market and generate returns substantially above the interest it will be required to pay.

Still, cash, in the form of short-term money-market investments, is the favored asset in some plans. In the northern pan-handle, the Moundsville policemen's plan had 60% of its assets in cash, while Fairmont's police plan, which is only 17% funded, had about 40% of its assets in certificates of deposit at the local bank.

In contrast, the state of Florida, which invested about three-quarters of its pension assets in stocks during the 1990s, has racked up average annual returns of roughly 14%. The assets nearly tripled to $100 billion, and the plan is now over-funded by $10 billion. Michigan's four state pension plans, thanks to 18% average annual returns for the past five years, are 100% funded, which has enabled the state to use some of the excess to pre-fund employee medical insurance premiums. Overall, most public plans have at least 75% of the funds necessary to meet future liabilities, a level many pension experts consider healthy.

A Lack of Money

But healthy isn't a word heard often in West Virginia. Poor investment performance has been compounded by the lack of money to actually invest. While federal pension law required private pension plans to put enough money into pension plans to pay future obligations, the law doesn't apply to public plans.

Consequently, critics say, state lawmakers for decades have taken a pass-the-buck attitude toward local funding mandates. "Such large sums of money are involved that states see pension plans as a way to solve budgetary problems," says Steve Willborn, a law professor at the University of Nebraska, who has been working with the National Conference of Commissioners on Uniform State Laws to persuade legislatures to adopt uniform prudent portfolio-management principles.

In Oklahoma, lawmakers contributed the actuarially required amount to the state teachers' system only five times during the past 30 years. Today, that plan is $5 billion in the hole.

In West Virginia, 40 of the state's public plans have less than half the funding they need. In some cities, pensions for police and firefighters are so underfunded that "bankruptcy is a possibility [for the cities] if this isn't addressed soon," says Jerry Simpson, the state's assistant treasurer.

Fire Department Plan

That's because there isn't enough money in the city coffers to pay the pension checks when the money in the pension plans runs out. For Huntington, the state's second-largest city with a population of about 54,000, that day could come soon: that city's fire department plan is just 2.3% funded. "This all scares the hell out of me," says Glenn White, the city's finance director.

Exacerbating the pension problem in West Virginia and elsewhere is the practice of recruiting trustees who are short on financial expertise but long on political obligations. Unlike the California Public Employees Retirement System, whose board includes the state treasurer, the state controller, and appointed officials from the financial industries, typical trustees in West Virginia city pension plans include plan members and the mayor.

That helps explain why retired firefighters in some cities get steady cost-of-living increases—even as the pension plans are running out of money—while some retired state employees haven't seen an increase since a decade or more.

Scott Wilson, a 20-year veteran of Huntington's fire department, and a trustee of its plan, sees no problem with continued pension raises for retired firefighters, even if the city can't afford it. He concedes the trustees have no investment knowledge, but bristles at suggestions that outsiders should have any influences.

"It's our fund," he says. If public workers don't get the continued pension increases they're asking for, he says, they'll sue the city.

It's this kind of no-win loop that Rep. Robert Andrews (D., N.J.), is trying to close. He has introduced a bill that would extend some federal Erisa standards to state and local pension plans, including

Business Perspective, continued

management by financial professionals rather than political appointees or plan members. Other provisions would make it tougher for local governments or politicians to fail to fund the plans or siphon off state contributions earmarked for the pension plans to pay for other things in the budget. Similar bills have been floated in years past, but either faded away or were shot down.

But in places such as West Virginia, pension reform will likely continue to be a hard sell. Few are willing to publicly suggest change. Police and firefighters "see that as a threat to their control," Mr. White says. "You might not make it home," he jokes.

Source: Jeff D. Opdyke, "West Virginia's Pensioners Come Up Short," *The Wall Street Journal*, June 5, 2000, p. C1 © 2000 by *The Wall Street Journal*. Reprinted with permission.

Illustration 24-3 summarizes the measurement focus differences between governmental-type activities and *business-type* activities.

V. Basis of Accounting: *When* to Recognize Transactions and Events

The concept of *basis of accounting* involves when to recognize a transaction or event in the financial statements. Only if recognized can a transaction or event be included in the measurement of the flow that has been selected for the *operating statement*. The possible alternative bases of accounting that could be used in government are[9]

1. **The *accrual* basis.** Recognizes revenues and expenditures/expenses when the transactions or events occurs.
2. **The *cash* basis.** Recognizes revenues when cash is *received*; recognizes expenditures/ expenses when cash is *paid*.

ILLUSTRATION 24-3 SUMMARY OF MEASUREMENT FOCUS–RELATED DIFFERENCES

	Current Financial Resources	**Economic Resources and Claims Incurred**
Information provided:	Financial resources received Financial resources spent Increase or decrease in net financial resources available for spending in the near future	Revenues generated Expenses incurred Extent of improvement in or deterioration of financial condition
Terminology used for *increases:*	Revenues Other financing *sources*	Revenues Gains
Terminology used for *decreases:*	Expenditures Other financing *uses*	Expenses Losses
Where used:	Fund-based statements for *governmental activities*	*Fund-based* statements for *business-type activities* and *fiduciary activities* *Government-wide statements* for both *governmental activities* and *business-type activities*

[9] The remaining bases of accounting that exist are (1) the *tax basis*, (2) *the price-level basis*, and (3) *regulatory accounting basis* (used by certain financial institutions in reporting to governmental regulators).

3. **The *modified accrual* basis.** Recognizes certain revenues using special revenue recognition criteria applicable to the situation.

The Modified Accrual Basis— A Special Treatment for Revenues

Recall that under the *current financial resources measurement focus*, the objective is to report in the *operating statement* **only *near-term* inflows and outflows of *current financial resources*.** Accordingly, *many* revenues and expenditures are reported in the *operating statement* in periods *later than* when the event or transaction occurred—**because the amounts were *not* expected to be *collected* or *paid* in the near future (shortly *after* year-end).** Thus some items are recognized in the *operating statement* on a delayed basis under this measurement focus.

Regardless of the measurement focus used, the customary private sector revenue *recognition criterion* of recognizing revenues at the time of shipment (or delivery) *cannot* be used. Accordingly, the *modified accrual basis* is used under which *revenue recognition* is conditioned on the **"availability"** of the financial resources.[10]

Revenues Example

Assume that (1) a city had $500,000 of property tax assessments for the year (*all of which* was expected to be collected), (2) $400,000 was collected *by year-end*, and (3) $75,000 was expected to be collected *shortly after year-end*. Under the accrual basis, reportable revenues for the year are $500,000. Under the *modified accrual basis*, however, reportable revenues for the year are only $475,000—thus "deferred revenues" of $25,000 are reported among liabilities at year-end.

For expenditures, expenditure recognition under the *modified accrual basis* is *identical* with expense recognition under the *accrual basis* (except for recognizing interest on certain government debt as discussed in Chapter 25).

CHECK POINT

Under the *modified accrual basis*, revenues are recognized in which accounting period?

a. When they are collected
b. When they are measurable
c. When they become available
d. When they become available and measurable

Answer: d

Business-type Activities and *Fiduciary Activities*: Only the *Accrual Basis* Is Allowed

At *both* the *fund-based* reporting level and the *government-wide* reporting level, *GAS 34* requires use of the *accrual basis* of accounting for *business-type activities* (along with the all-encompassing *economic resources measurement focus*). The same requirements exist for *fiduciary activities*, which report only at the *fund-based* reporting level. Both of these activities are discussed in Chapter 25.

---

[10] Several exceptions exist to the exclusive use of the *modified accrual basis* in reporting *governmental activities*. **Example 1:** When collections are delayed beyond the normal time of receipt (such as monthly sales tax collections) because of *highly unusual circumstances*, the amounts involved are still recognized as revenue in the current period, so as to *not* distort normal revenue patterns. **Example 2:** As for *not* recording liabilities in a governmental fund unless they are expected to be paid shortly after year-end, *tax refunds owed* are always reported as a governmental fund liability (resulting in a reduction of reported revenues) even though the amounts may *not* be expected to be paid shortly after year-end. **Example 3***: Interest on general long-term borrowings* is recorded as an expenditure and a liability in a *governmental fund* only *when due*. Thus the accounting for such interest in a *governmental fund* is entirely on the *cash basis*.

Governmental Activities: Both the *Accrual Basis* and the *Modified Accrual Basis* Are Required—But at *Different* Reporting Levels

At the *fund-based* reporting level, the *modified accrual basis* is required (along with the narrow *current financial resources measurement focus*, as discussed earlier). At the *government-wide* reporting level, however, the *accrual basis of accounting* (along with the broad *economic resources measurement focus*, as discussed earlier) is required. Accordingly, **all liabilities are reported in the *government-wide statements*—regardless of when they are expected to be paid.** (More about this shortly.)

Governmental Activities: The *Modified Accrual Basis*—The *Exceptions* to the *Accrual Basis* in Perspective

For items reported in the *operating statement* on a delayed basis (under the ***current financial resources measurement focus***), the cumulative unrecognized *expenditures* are enormous compared with the cumulative unrecognized *revenues*. Because of this huge disparity, the GASB decided to require the issuance of *government-wide statements* (in addition to *fund statements*), so that the big picture can be seen. Thus think of the *fund statements* for *governmental activities* as being the "small picture" (*narrow perspective*) and *government-wide statements* as the "big picture" (*overall perspective*).

Governmental Activities: A Special General Ledger Needed for *Government-Wide* Reporting

The liabilities (relating to expenditures) that are temporarily omitted from the governmental funds (under the ***current financial resources measurement focus***), however, are recorded in the period in which the liabilities are incurred *in the* ***General Capital Assets and General Long-Term Liabilities*** **(GCA-GLTL)** general ledger (GAAFR illustrates how to record the changes in these liabilities for the year as a year-end adjustment). This general ledger only contains "real" accounts (*assets* and *liabilities*)—it does *not* contain any "nominal" accounts (*revenues* and *expenses*).

Because the *GCA-GLTL g/l* is *not* a *fund*, it does *not* have cash as an asset and, therefore, *cannot* be used to record receipts and payments. Accordingly, the liabilities recorded therein are eventually transferred to a *governmental* fund general ledger when they become due—*usually years after the liabilities were incurred for most of these items*—so that the liabilities can be paid. At that time, recognition occurs in the *governmental fund* general ledger (both the *expenditure* and the *liability* are recognized). This unique manner of recordkeeping enables these liabilities to be (1) temporarily excluded from governmental fund financial statements and (2) tracked in an efficient manner that readily enables the *government-wide statements* to be prepared.

As briefly mentioned earlier, in Chapter 25 we (1) discuss the *GCA-GLTL g/l* in detail, (2) explain when and how entries are made therein, (3) illustrate how its balances are consolidated with the *fund-based* general ledger amounts to prepare *government-wide statements* (which use the *accrual basis* of accounting and the *flow of economic resources measurement basis*), and (4) explain and illustrate the adjusting entries needed to convert from the *modified accrual basis* to the *accrual basis*.

Revenue Recognition Standards

Governmental activities do *not* "earn" revenues as do business enterprises (except for interest earned on bond investments). Furthermore, business revenues result from **"exchange" transactions** (in which each party receives and gives up *equal* values). In contrast, substantially all revenues of *governmental activities* are **"*nonexchange*" transactions** (in which the government receives value *without* giving equal value from another party). Examples are sales taxes, income taxes, property taxes, and grants. Accordingly, a different revenue recognition criterion from the "when earned" criterion of the *private sector* is necessary. The objective, however, is still to try to record revenues in the period to which they relate to the extent that it is practical to do so.

To **accrue a revenue (and the related receivable), it must be "susceptible to accrual."** To be susceptible to accrual, it must be **available** and **measurable**. As discussed earlier, **available** means that a revenue source is **"collectible within the current period or soon enough thereafter to be used to pay liabilities of the current period."** Thus the timing of the collectibility of the revenue is a critical factor under the *modified accrual basis*. This "availability" criterion applies to *all* revenues.

CHECK POINT

Under the *modified accrual basis*, which of the following would be a revenue *susceptible to accrual*?

a. Income taxes
b. Business licenses
c. Sales taxes
d. Property taxes
e. Parking meter receipts
f. None of the above.

Answer: d

Specific Guidance on the "Availability" of Property Taxes

The GASB *Codification* gives specific guidance about applying the "availability" criterion for **property taxes—collection must occur within 60 days.** For revenues *other than* property taxes, some governmental units use a 60-day cutoff date. Other cutoff dates (such as 90 days) are also used.

Nonexchange Transactions

Because tax revenues are not *earned* by governments (they are compelled), it is hard to see when tax revenues (and the related assets) should be accrued. To define a sense of "accrual" that would be applicable to governments for such transactions and other kinds of nonexchange transactions, GASB *Statement No. 33*, "Accounting and Financial Reporting for Nonexchange Transactions" was issued. *GAS 33* defines when to recognize assets and revenues for *non*exchange *transactions*. It categorizes *non*exchange transactions into the following four conceptual categories:

1. ***Derived* Tax Revenues.** These items result from governmental assessments on the taxpayers' *exchange* transactions. Common examples include taxes on (a) *earnings* (such as personal and corporate income taxes) and (b) *consumption* (such as sales taxes and gasoline taxes). **Recognition Standard: *In the period in which the transactions underlying the derived tax revenue occur.*** (Report *advance receipts* as deferred revenues.)
2. ***Imposed* Nonexchange Transactions.** These items result from governmental assessments ***on other than governmental assessments on exchange transactions*** (common examples include property taxes, most fines, and forfeitures). **Recognition Standard: *For "ASSET" recognition—in the period in which the government has an enforceable legal claim to the resources or when the resources are received, whichever occurs first. For "REVENUE" recognition—in the period in which the resources are required to be used or the first period that use is permitted* (for property taxes, it is the period for which the taxes are levied).** (Report advance *receipts* as *deferred revenues* [such as a property tax overpayment that the taxpayer instructs the city to apply to the following year's tax bill] and advance *payments* as *advances* [an asset].)
3. **Government-Mandated Nonexchange Transactions.** These items typically result from a *higher* level of government giving resources to a *lower* level government—with stipulations that the resources must be used for a certain purpose(s). (Common examples are state-mandated road upgrading and federal grants for mandated drug and alcohol abuse prevention programs.) **Recognition Standard: *In the period in which ALL "eligibility requirements" (including any "time" requirements [limitations on when the resources may be used]) have been met.*** (More on eligibility requirements shortly.)

4. **Voluntary Nonexchange Transactions.** These items result from "legislative or contractual agreements" (other than "exchanges") entered into willingly by the parties. (Common examples are certain grants and entitlements and most donations, including *permanent* and *temporary* endowments.) **Recognition Standard:** ***Same as for Government-Mandated Nonexchange Transactions.***

*Non*exchange Transactions: Some Finer Points

1. ***Purpose*** **"Restrictions."** Such restrictions do *not* affect the timing of recognition *for any class of nonexchange transaction*. For recipients that have unspent resources, however, they must report the resulting net assets (or fund balances, as appropriate) as *restricted* in the statement of net assets (or balance sheet, as appropriate).
2. ***Eligibility*** **Requirements for Government-Mandated and Voluntary Exchange Transactions.** These requirements comprise one or more of the following: (1) the *required characteristics of recipients* (for example, the recipients must be *states*), (2) *time requirements* (as to the period in which the resources must be or may be spent), (3) *reimbursements* (for example, the provider offers resources on a reimbursement [expenditure-driven] basis, and the recipient has incurred allowable costs), and (4) *contingencies* [applies only to voluntary nonexchange transactions] (the provider's offer of resources is contingent upon a specified recipient action that has occurred, for example, having raised matching funds or used its own resources for the specified purpose).
3. **Shared Revenues.** Often governments share certain of their revenues with other governments (such as when a *state government* shares a portion of its sales tax revenues with *county governments*). Both the *provider government* and the *recipient government* must treat the sharing as either (1) *a voluntary nonexchange transaction* or (2) a *government-mandated nonexchange transaction*, all depending upon the specific circumstances.

   In either case, both the *provider government* and the *recipient government* recognize the transaction as soon as all eligibility requirements are met. Thus the accounting is *symmetrical* (the simultaneous recognition of both an *intergovernmental payable* and an *intergovernmental receivable* and the related *expenditures* and *revenues*, respectively).

VI. Other Major Reporting Requirements

We have grouped the remaining *major* reporting requirements of the GASB *Codification* into the following *seven* broad categories:

	Category
1	Accounting and Reporting Capabilities (GAAP, Legal Provisions, and Conflicts)
2	Fund Types
3	Financial Reporting (presented in three subcategories)
4	Capital Assets
5	Long-Term Liabilities
6	Investments and Endowments
7	Budgets and Budgetary Accounting

Category 1: Accounting and Reporting Capabilities (GAAP, Legal Provisions, and Conflicts)

The GASB *Codification* recommends the following:

> A governmental accounting system must make it possible both: (a) to present fairly and with full disclosure the funds and activities of the government in conformity with generally accepted accounting principles; and (b) to determine and demonstrate compliance with finance-related legal and contractual provisions.[11]

[11] GASB *Cod.*, sec 1100.101.

In many cases, using a separate fund for a designated activity and preparing separate financial statements for the separate fund satisfies both objectives. In some cases, a legal provision may specify the use of a practice that is *not* in accordance with GAAP—for example, requiring that a certain fund maintain its books on the *cash basis*. In these cases, the books must be maintained according to the law. For financial reporting purposes, however, the *cash basis trial balance* must be adjusted (on a worksheet) to arrive at a presentation in accordance with GAAP. Financial statements would then be prepared and reported according to GAAP. The GASB *Codification* addresses such conflicts as follows:

> Where financial statements prepared in conformity with GAAP do *not* demonstrate finance-related legal and contractual compliance, the governmental unit should present such additional schedules and narrative explanations in the comprehensive annual financial report as may be necessary to report its legal compliance responsibilities and accountabilities. In extreme cases, preparation of a separate legal-basis special report may be necessary.[12]

The long-range solution to this problem is to eliminate any legal provisions that conflict with GAAP.

Category 2: Fund Types

The GASB *Codification* recognizes and recommends the use of 11 major fund types (categorized into *three* broad areas), as follows:

Governmental Funds

1. ***General Fund***—to account for all financial resources except those required to be accounted for in another fund.
2. ***Special Revenue Funds***—to account for the proceeds of specific revenue sources (*other than* trusts for individuals, private organizations, or other governments or for major capital projects) that are legally restricted to expenditure for specified purposes.
3. ***Capital Projects Funds***—to account for financial resources to be used for the acquisition or construction of major capital facilities (*other than* those financed by proprietary funds or in trust funds for individuals, private organizations, or other governments).
4. ***Debt Service Funds***—to account for the accumulation of resources for, and the payment of, general long-term debt principal and interest.
5. ***Permanent Funds***—To account for resources that are legally restricted to the extent that only *earnings* on the resources (the *principal*) may be used for purposes that support the reporting government's programs—that is, for the benefit of the government or its citizenry. [Includes most *temporary endowments* (up to their expiration dates, at which time the money is transferred to another fund) and most *permanent endowments*.]

Proprietary Funds

6. ***Enterprise Funds***—to account for any activity for which a fee is charged to external users for goods or services. [If certain specified criteria (discussed in Chapter 25) are met, that activity *must* be accounted for in this fund.]
7. ***Internal Service Funds***—to account for activity that provides goods or services to other funds, departments, or agencies of the primary government and its component units, or to other governments, on a cost-reimbursement basis.

Fiduciary Funds

8. ***Pension (and other employee benefit) Trust Funds***—to account for resources required to be held for the members and beneficiaries of defined benefit pension plans, defined contribution plans, other postemployment benefit plans, or other employee benefit plans.

---

[12] GASB *Cod.*, sec 1200.113.

9. ***Investment Trust Funds***—to account for the external portion of investment pools reported by the sponsoring government. [Almost all state governments have these because they manage investments for their counties and cities.]
10. ***Private-Purpose Trust Funds***—to account for all other trust arrangements under which the principal and income benefit individuals, private organizations, or other governments.
11. ***Agency Funds***—to account for resources held by the reporting government in a purely custodial capacity (*assets equal liabilities*).

The number of funds used by a given governmental unit depends on legal requirements and practicality in relation to the scope of operations. The *General Fund*, which usually accounts for the largest part of a governmental unit's total operations, is discussed and illustrated later in the chapter. The remaining types of funds are discussed and illustrated in Chapter 25.

CHECK POINT

Which of the following is *not* a *fund type*?
a. Budgetary
b. Fiduciary
c. Governmental
d. Proprietary
e. None of the above

Answer: a

Category 3 (A): Financial Reporting: Reporting *Governmental Activities* in Fund-Based Statements—The Basics

Both the balance sheets and the operating statements *of governmental funds* have some unique reporting aspects at the fund-based reporting level (that do *not* exist at the *government-wide* reporting level).

The Balance Sheet

As discussed earlier, *governmental funds* use the term *fund balance* to describe the difference between a fund's assets and liabilities. If no restrictions exist on the fund balance, the Fund Balance account may be viewed as a "surplus" that is available for spending in the new fiscal year. (Newspapers often use the term surplus, however, to refer to ***the excess of revenues over expenditures for a particular period—not the accumulation from prior periods.***) In most cases, however, restrictions earmark a portion of the fund balance for a specific purpose exist. These restrictions are reflected in the Fund Balance section as reservations of the fund balance. For example, a restriction pertaining to outstanding (unfilled) purchase orders of $33,000 at year-end would be presented as follows:

Fund balance:	
Reserved for encumbrances[a]	$ 33,000
Unreserved	427,000
	$460,000

[a] Encumbrances are explained shortly.

The discussion of how to present the difference between a fund's assets and liabilities in *government-wide statements*, in *proprietary funds*, and in *fiduciary funds* is presented in Chapter 25.

The Operating Statement

Recall that for governmental activities, the **operating statement** presents the *inflows and outflows of current financial resources* (the measurement focus in these funds). Recall that although this statement is called *the statement of revenues, expenditures, and changes in fund balances*, substantively it is merely a *statement of sources and uses of current financial resources*. Note that the format of this statement (shown in Illustration 24-4) includes the *beginning* and *ending* fund balance amounts, thereby requiring all changes in the fund balance for the period to be shown. This "all-inclusive" format makes it unnecessary to present a separate *statement of changes in fund balance* (similar to a *statement of changes in stockholders' equity* for a *business enterprise*). Furthermore, the statement format is modified slightly when (1) bond proceeds are recorded in a governmental fund and (2) a governmental fund has certain types of transactions with other funds. These modifications are discussed and illustrated in the following section.

Category 3 (B): Financial Reporting: Reporting *Governmental Activities* in Fund-Based Statements—Bond Proceeds and Interfund Transactions

Bond proceeds (and other borrowings) that are recorded in *governmental funds* are *inflows* that must be classified separately from revenues and expenditures in the operating statement. (Such borrowings are part of the liabilities called "general long-term liabilities"—they are discussed in more detail shortly.)

Such proceeds are shown in a separate section of the operating statement of the recipient fund. This section is called **Other Financing Sources and Uses.** Likewise, certain *interfund transactions* are also reported in this section.

Types of *Interfund Activities*

Recall that transactions with parties outside the primary government were broadly divided into (1) *exchange* transactions (each party receives or gives *equal* or *almost equal* value) and (2) *nonexchange* transactions. Likewise, interfund activities can be divided into these same two categories. Furthermore, each category can be subdivided into two subcategories as follows:

Exchange Transactions (*reciprocal* in nature):
- Interfund Loans.
- Interfund Services Provided and Used.

***Non*exchange Transactions (*nonreciprocal* in nature):**
- Interfund Reimbursements.
- Interfund Transfers.

1. Interfund *Loans* (reciprocal in nature)

Often the *General Fund* makes a loan to another fund. **Interfund loans affect only the balance sheets** of the funds involved. The *lending* fund reports a *receivable*; the *borrowing* fund reports a *liability*. (The specific accounts are usually called "Due from (or to) Other Funds.") If some or all of the loan is *not* expected to be repaid "within a reasonable time," however, the interfund balances must be reduced by that amount—the reduction is reported as an interfund *transfer* (discussed shortly). (As shown in Chapter 25, Interfund loan balances *are* eliminated in preparing the *government-wide statements*.)

ILLUSTRATION 24-4 STATEMENT OF REVENUES, EXPENDITURES, AND CHANGES IN FUND BALANCE

Revenues (an *inflow* of resources)	$ 550,000
Expenditures (an *outflow* of resources)	(450,000)
Excess of Revenues over Expenditures	**$100,000**
Fund Balance, January 1, 2005	360,000
Fund Balance, December 31, 2005	**$460,000**

2. Interfund *Services Provided and Used* (reciprocal in nature)

Often one fund provides a service to another fund at a price approximating its *external* exchange value. An example is a city's water utility (which would be accounted for in an Enterprise Fund) that supplies water to the city. The most meaningful form of reporting for such transactions is to report (1) *expenditures* in the *recipient* fund and (2) *revenues* in the *provider* fund. The rationale is that the fund *receiving* the services would have had to charge *expenditures/expenses* if it had obtained the services from an organization *external* to the governmental unit. Furthermore, recording *revenues* in the fund *providing* the services is essential to the proper determination of that fund's operating results when such fund is a proprietary fund. The entries that would be recorded in the *General Fund* and the Municipal Water Utility Enterprise Fund for supplying water to the city are as follows:

General Fund

Expenditures	45,000	
Due to Municipal Water Utility Enterprise Fund		45,000

Municipal Water Utility Enterprise Fund

Due from *General Fund*	45,000	
Revenues		45,000

Other examples of interfund charges for services are as follows:

- Payments *in lieu of taxes* from an Enterprise Fund to the *General Fund.*
- Internal Service Fund billings for services to departments of other funds.
- Routine service charges for inspection, engineering, utility, or similar charges.
- Routine employer contributions from the *General Fund* to a *Pension Trust Fund.*

Charges for services are the only type of interfund transaction that may be recorded as *revenues*, *expenditures*, or *expenses*. (To preserve the integrity of the cost information for each function, interfund revenues and expenditures/expenses are *not* eliminated in preparing the *government-wide statements* (except for services provided and used within a single function). In contrast, *all* intercompany transactions are eliminated in preparing *consolidated statements* in the *private sector.*)

3. Interfund *Reimbursements* (*non*reciprocal in nature)

Interfund reimbursements occur when a fund that is ultimately responsible for a particular expenditure or expense repays (or agrees to repay) some other fund that *initially* paid the expenditure or expense on its behalf. Obviously, the objective is to have the expenditure or expense recorded in the fund that ultimately benefits from the outlay. (Any open "due to" and "due from" accounts *are* eliminated in preparing *government-wide statements.*)

4. Interfund *Transfers* (*non*reciprocal in nature)

Interfund transfers are flows of assets (such as cash or supplies inventories) between funds of the primary government (1) without equivalent flows of assets in return and (2) **without a repayment requirement**. The manner of presentation in the operating statements differs slightly for *governmental funds* at the *fund-based reporting level* than for *proprietary funds* as shown here:

Governmental Funds	Proprietary Funds
Revenues	Revenues
Expenditures	Expenses
Other Financing Sources and Uses:	Transfers In
Transfers In	Transfer Out
Transfers Out	

CHECK POINT

Which of the following is *not* one of the four types of *interfund transactions*?

a. All-inclusive external transactions
b. Services provided and used
c. Transfers
d. Loans

Answer: a

The difference in presentation of these two fund types is attributable to the difference in the nature of the operating statement used (*a statement that reports revenues and expenses* for the *proprietary funds* and a statement that reports *source and use of current financial resources* for *governmental funds*). The following entries assume that the *General Fund* made an interfund transfer to the Municipal Golf Course Enterprise Fund (the transfer's purpose could be either to subsidize day-to-day operations or help pay for a capital asset improvement or expansion):

General Fund

Other Financing Uses—Transfers Out	20,000	
Cash		20,000

Enterprise Fund

Cash	20,000	
Transfers In		20,000

Other examples of interfund transfers are as follows:

1. Transfers of tax revenues from a *Special Revenue Fund* to a *Debt Service Fund* or the *General Fund*.
2. Transfers from the *General Fund* to a *Capital Projects Fund* to help pay for construction costs.
3. Transfers from the *General Fund* to a *Debt Service Fund* to enable interest and principal payments to be made on general long-term debt.
4. Transfers from an *Enterprise Fund* to the *General Fund other than payments in lieu of taxes* to finance *General Fund* expenditures.

(Interfund transfers are eliminated in preparing *government-wide statements* using a two-step process.)

The Operating Statement for Governmental Funds: Modified for Reporting Bond Proceeds and Interfund Transfers

In Illustration 24-5, we present the statement of revenues, expenditures, and changes in fund balance used by governmental funds when bond proceeds have been received in such a fund and interfund transfers exist. To enhance understanding of this illustration, we used the amounts shown in Illustration 24-4 plus the following previously illustrated interfund transactions:

1. **Interfund services provided and used.** The purchase of water by the *General Fund* from the Municipal Water Utility Fund for $45,000.
2. **Interfund transfer.** The transfer of $20,000 from the *General Fund* to subsidize the day-to-day operations or expand the Municipal Golf Course Enterprise Fund.

Because the illustration is for the *General Fund*, no amount is shown on the bond proceeds line because virtually all bond proceeds of governmental funds are recorded in Capital Projects Funds.

ILLUSTRATION 24-5 STATEMENT OF REVENUES, EXPENDITURES, AND CHANGES IN FUND BALANCE—FORMAT FOR REPORTING BOND PROCEEDS AND INTERFUND TRANSFERS

General Fund Statement of Revenues, Expenditures, and Changes in Fund Balance For the Year Ended December 31, 2005

Revenues	$ 550,000
Expenditures	(495,000)[a]
Excess of Revenues over Expenditures	$ 55,000
Other financing sources and uses:	
Bond proceeds	-0-
Transfers in	-0-
Transfers out	(20,000)
Excess of Revenues and Other Financing Sources over Expenditures and Other Financing Uses	**$ 35,000**
Fund Balance, January 1, 2005	360,000
Fund Balance, December 31, 2005	**$395,000**

[a] Includes $45,000 for purchase of water from *Municipal Water Enterprise Fund* (an *interfund services* received transaction).

(Most governmental units are prohibited by law from issuing bonds to finance current operations; thus it is rare for the *General Fund* to report bond proceeds.) The *General Fund* rarely is the *recipient* fund for transfers—it usually is the *provider* fund for transfers.

Additional Items to Be Classified under the Other Financing Sources and Uses Category

When a governmental unit sells some of its General Capital Assets (discussed shortly), the proceeds are to be reported under the other financing sources and uses category. Also, when a governmental unit enters into a capital lease, the present value of the lease payments is deemed to be the equivalent of proceeds from a loan, an amount that is to be reported under the other financing sources and uses category. Accordingly, this category of the operating statement could appear as follows if all types of transactions occur:

Other Financing Sources and Uses:	
Bond proceeds	xxx
Transfers in	xxx
Transfers out	(xxx)
Proceeds from sale of general capital assets	xxx
Proceeds from capital lease	xxx

No other types of transactions are reportable under the other financing sources and uses category.

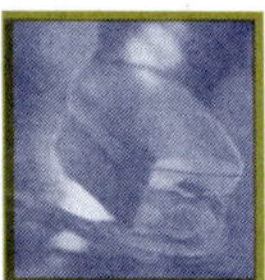

CHECK POINT

How are each of the following *interfund transactions* classified in the *operating statement* of a governmental fund at the *fund-based reporting level*?

	Under Other Financing Sources and Uses	**Revenue or Expenditure**
a.	Loans	Transfers
b.	Services	Reimbursements
c.	Reimbursements	Loans
d.	Transfers	Services

Answer: d

Category 3 (C): Financial Reporting: General-Purpose Financial Statements and the Comprehensive Annual Financial Report (CAFR)

The annual financial report for governmental units is called the comprehensive annual financial report (CAFR). The basic financial statements required in this report are as follows:

1. **Government-wide financial statements—Governmental Funds, Proprietary Funds, and Component Units (discretely presented).** These are *two* specific financial statements that **present an overview** in much the same manner as consolidated financial statements for corporations. (Recall that the *government-wide statements* use the *economic resources measurement focus* and the *accrual basis*.) The two specific financial statements are as follows:
   a. ***Statement of Net Assets*** (assets minus liabilities equals net assets format) **or *Balance Sheet*** (assets equals liabilities plus net assets format)—Governmental Funds, Proprietary Funds, and discretely presented component units.
   b. ***Statement of Activities***—Governmental Funds, Proprietary Funds, and discretely presented component units.
2. **Fund statements—Governmental Funds.** These are *two* specific financial statements that provide information on each *major* fund. Each major fund is presented in a separate column. *Non*major funds are aggregated and displayed in a single column. A total column is required so that the amounts can be reconciled to the *government-wide statements*—a reconciliation must be presented.
   a. *Balance Sheet.*
   b. *Statement of Revenues, Expenditures, and Changes in Fund Balances.*
3. **Fund statements—Proprietary Funds.** These are *three* specific financial statements that provide information on each *major* fund. Each major fund is presented in a separate column. *Non*major funds are aggregated and displayed in a single column. A total column is required—the amounts in the total column tie *directly* to the corresponding amounts in the *government-wide statements.*
   a. *Balance Sheet.*
   b. *Statement of Revenues, Expenses, and Changes in Net Assets* (or Fund Equity).
   c. *Statement of Cash Flows.*
4. **Fund statements—Fiduciary Funds and Similar Component Units.** These are *two* specific financial statements that provide information on each fund-*type* (*pension* [and other employee benefit] *trust funds, investment trust funds, private-purpose trust funds, and agency funds*). Each major fund-type is presented in a separate column. A total column is *not* used.
   a. *Statement of Fiduciary Net Assets.*
   b. *Statement of Changes in Fiduciary Net Assets.*

Illustrations of these nine statements are shown in Chapter 25 on pages 873–891. At this point, we suggest you briefly review those illustrations before proceeding. Also, certain additional financial statements (such as *combining statements* and *budgetary comparison statements*) must be presented in the "Required Supplementary Information" (RSI) section of the governmental units annual report. Such statements are discussed near the end of Chapter 25.

Component Units

A primary government's **component units** *are* reported in the *government-wide statements.* Component units are legally separate organizations; however, the primary government's elected officials are financially accountable for them. A component unit's financial data are presented in two possible manners:

1. **Discrete presentation.** The data are presented in one or more columns separate from the primary government's financial data. (State universities are component units of state governments that are typically presented in this manner.)

2. **Blended presentation.** The data are combined—called "blending"—with the data of the primary government in the *government-wide statements*. Thus the amounts are *not* shown separately. This manner of presentation is required when (1) the component unit's governing body is substantively the same as that of the primary government or (2) the component unit's activities serve or benefit entirely or almost exclusively the government. (The component unit's General Revenue Fund must be reported as a *Special Revenue Fund*, however, rather than being combined with the primary government's *General Fund*.)

   GASB *Statement No. 14*, "The Financial Reporting Entity," is the authoritative guidance for how to (1) identify component units and (2) report the financial data of such units in the financial statements of the primary reporting entity. *GAS 14* strictly limits "blending" to situations in which component units "despite being legally separate from the primary government, are so intertwined with the primary government that they are, in substance, the same as the primary government."[13]

Category 4: Capital Assets

Reporting Capital Assets

A distinction is made between (1) ***"general capital assets"*** and (2) capital assets required to be accounted for in *proprietary funds* and *fiduciary funds*. *General capital assets*, by definition, are capital assets that are *not* required to be reported in either *proprietary funds* or *fiduciary funds*. *General capital assets* are *not* accounted for in any of the *governmental funds*. They are accounted for in a special general ledger (the "General Capital Assets and General Long-Term Liabilities" general ledger [hereafter, we usually use the abbreviation *GCA-GLTL g/l*], that was mentioned earlier). Accordingly, these capital assets are *reported* only in the *government-wide* "statement of net assets" for *governmental activities*.

General capital assets are excluded from the governmental funds because such assets do *not* constitute financial resources available for spending purposes. Because one of the reporting objectives of the governmental funds is to reflect the financial resources available for spending purposes, these assets must be *excluded* from governmental funds to accomplish this objective.

Valuation of Capital Assets

Capital assets are recorded at *historical cost*. *Donated* capital assets are reported at their estimated fair value at the donation date, plus any ancillary charges.

Depreciation of Capital Assets

Capital assets (other than land and land improvements) are depreciated over their estimated useful lives unless they are either *inexhaustible* or are *infrastructure assets using the "modified approach"* (explained in Chapter 29 and under which depreciation is *not* recorded).

Depreciation is reported only in (1) *government-wide statements* (includes *governmental activities* and *business-type activities*), *(2) proprietary fund statements*, and (3) *fiduciary fund statements*.

The omission of depreciation in the *fund-based statements* for *the governmental funds* results from having a ***current financial resources measurement focus*** instead of an ***economic resources measurement focus***. Depreciation is an *outflow* of **economic resources**—the *outflow* of ***current financial resources*** occurred when the depreciable asset was acquired. Note further that depreciation is a *cost allocation* (and *not* part of either the *accrual basis* or the *modified accrual basis*). Thus to determine income (or the changes in the net assets), one needs (1) the ***economic resources measurement focus***, (2) the *accrual basis*, and (3) *cost allocations*.

---

[13] GASB *Statement of Financial Accounting Standard No. 14*, "The Financial Reporting Entity" (Norwalk, CT: Governmental Accounting Standards Board), para. 52.

Category 5: Reporting Long-Term Liabilities

A clear distinction is made between (1) **"general long-term liabilities"** and (2) long-term liabilities required to be reported in *proprietary funds* and *fiduciary funds*. *General long-term liabilities*, by definition, are long-term liabilities *not* directly related to and expected to be paid from either *proprietary funds* or *fiduciary funds*. *General long-term liabilities* are recorded in the special "General Capital Assets and General Long-Term Liabilities" general ledger. Accordingly, these liabilities are reported only in the *government-wide* Statement of Net Assets for *governmental activities*.

General long-term liabilities are the liability of the governmental unit as a whole—*not* that of any specific fund. As such, they are secured by the taxing powers of the governmental unit—*not* by the resources available in a specific fund. These liabilities are discussed in more detail in Chapter 25.

Category 6: Investments and Endowments

Investments are valued at *fair value*. Accordingly, unrealized gains and losses on investments are recognized as *investment earnings* currently (classified among revenues at both the *fund-based reporting level* and the *government-wide* reporting level).

An **endowment** is a restricted contribution in which the donor stipulates that the principal be maintained intact either *in perpetuity* or *for a specified period*. Thus only the income from the investment of the *principal* (the corpus) may be spent. ***Endowments*** received usually are recorded in a Permanent Fund (some endowments are made to *proprietary funds* [almost always an Enterprise Fund] and are recorded therein). Endowments received are reported as a separate line item (if material) in the operating statement at *both* reporting levels—**but *not* as a *revenues* item.**

Category 7: Budgets and Budgetary Accounting

Budgets

Budgets are used in the public sector for planning, controlling, and evaluating operations just as they are used in the private sector. A **budget** is merely a plan of financial operations covering a specified period of time. For all governmental, proprietary, and fiduciary funds (other than Agency Funds), the GASB *Codification* recommends that an annual budget(s) be adopted by every governmental unit.

Prepared under the direction of the governmental unit's chief executive officer, the annual budget is submitted to the legislative body for review, possible modification, and formal adoption. The significance of the budget for each of these funds is as follows:

Fund Type	Significance
Governmental funds	The statutory authorization for spending an estimated amount during the subsequent fiscal year. The authorization is referred to as an appropriation.
Proprietary funds and certain fiduciary funds	The approval of a proposed operating plan (as distinct from a statutory authorization to spend a certain amount in dollars).

A long-term budget covers a period of several years. Long-term budgets restricted to major capital additions and improvements are referred to as capital budgets.

Budgetary Accounting

Because legal limitations are imposed on certain of the funds (primarily the governmental funds) as to the amount that may be spent during a fiscal year, it is exceedingly important to monitor and control spending so that expenditures do *not* exceed this limitation. The GASB *Codification* recommends that the accounting system should provide the basis for appropriate budgetary control.

The GASB *Codification* specifies the following two areas in which **budgetary accounts** should be used to monitor and control spending: (1) recording the annual budget in the general ledger and (2) recording purchase order commitments in the general ledger, which is referred to as encumbrance accounting.

To enhance the understanding of budgetary integration in the general ledger, we use the technique, illustrated in the 2001 edition of *GAAFR*, of **printing budgetary account descriptions in all capital letters**. As a result, we can consider all budgetary accounts as a separate trial balance from the regular general ledger accounts. We also use the same account descriptions for budgetary and actual accounts used in the 2001 edition of *GAAFR*.

CHECK POINT

Authority granted by a legislative body to make *expenditures* and to incur obligations during a fiscal year is the definition of which of these?

a. Appropriation
b. Authorization
c. Encumbrance
d. Expenditure
e. None of the above

Answer: a

Recording the Annual Budget: Simplified Situation Involving No Interfund Transfers

The budgets for the *General Fund* and *Special Revenue Funds* are recorded in the applicable general ledgers. (The annual budget pertaining *to Capital Projects Funds* and *Debt Service Funds* is recorded in the general ledger only if it serves a useful purpose, determined on a case-by-case basis.) Assuming that a governmental unit expects its *General Fund* revenues to exceed its *General Fund* appropriations for the new fiscal year, the budget is recorded in the *General Fund*'s general ledger as follows:

ESTIMATED REVENUES	1,000,000	
APPROPRIATIONS		980,000
BUDGETARY FUND BALANCE		20,000
To record the legally adopted annual operating budget.		

The ESTIMATED REVENUES account is a control account. *Actual revenues* are usually recorded in individual subsidiary Revenue accounts (and in a Revenues Control account). The detail making up the ESTIMATED REVENUES account is also recorded directly in the individual subsidiary Revenue accounts at the start of the year. As a result, *estimated revenues* may be compared readily with *actual revenues* throughout the year. Although revenues *cannot* be "controlled" in the manner that *expenditures* can be controlled, a governmental unit may be able to curtail spending if it appears that *actual revenue* will *not* be reasonably close to *estimated revenues*.

Likewise, the APPROPRIATIONS account is a control account. Actual expenditures are usually recorded in individual subsidiary Expenditures accounts (and in an Expenditures Control account). The detail making up the APPROPRIATIONS account is also recorded directly in the individual subsidiary Expenditures accounts at the start of the year. As a result, expenditures to date may be readily compared with the authorized spending limitation, revealing how much more may be spent.

A governmental unit's budget for the coming fiscal year may reflect an intention to increase (as in the preceding example) or decrease the fund balance amount existing at the *beginning* of the year. Most governmental units (with the notable exception of the federal government) try to accumulate a reasonable "surplus" in the Fund Balance account in case unforeseen adverse events occur. In recording the budget in the general ledger, the difference between the *debit* to ESTIMATED REVENUES and the *credit* to APPROPRIATIONS is *credited* (as in the preceding example) or debited to BUDGETARY FUND BALANCE.

Recording the budget in the general ledger does *not* affect the year-end balance in the Fund Balance account because the budget entry is *reversed* at year-end as part of the normal closing process.

Recording the Annual Budget: Typical Situation Involving Interfund Transfers

When interfund transfers exist, up to four additional budgetary accounts may be used to record the budget. The budgetary accounts can be classified as either those that pertain to *inflows* or those that pertain to *outflows* as shown here:

Budgetary Accounts Pertaining to Estimated *Inflows* (recorded as *debits*):
ESTIMATED REVENUES
ESTIMATED TRANSFERS IN

Budgetary Accounts Pertaining to Legally Authorized *Outflows* (recorded as *credits*):
APPROPRIATIONS (a general category)
APPROPRIATIONS—TRANSFERS OUT

The budgetary account BUDGETARY FUND BALANCE is *not* listed in either of these categories because it is merely used to balance the entry recording the budget. Later in the chapter, we illustrate the use of some of these additional budgetary accounts that pertain to interfund transfers.

COMPARATIVE PRACTICE NOTE

The illustrative entries shown in the 2001 edition of *GAAFR* use (1) the account ESTIMATED OTHER FINANCING SOURCES—TRANSFERS IN and (2) the account APPROPRIATIONS: OTHER FINANCING USES—TRANSFERS OUT. The use of the additional descriptive terminology OTHER FINANCING SOURCES and OTHER FINANCING USES (the category in the operating statement under which transfers are reported) is unnecessary and cumbersome in our opinion. Inquiries to numerous cities and counties reveal that almost all governmental units bypass this additional descriptive terminology in recording their annual budgets.

CHECK POINT

Which of the following is a *budgetary account* in governmental accounting?

a. Fund balance reserved for encumbrances
b. Unreserved fund balance
c. APPROPRIATIONS
d. Estimated uncollectible property taxes
e. Expenditures

Answer: c

Encumbrance Accounting

As stated earlier, expenditures are recognized when the fund liability is incurred—usually when goods are received or services are rendered. Many expenditures involve the issuance of purchase orders, whereby goods are received or services are rendered at a later date. **Outstanding purchase orders are *commitments for future expenditures.*** To monitor and control spending properly, governmental units must keep track of the amount of each purchase order (*including* the amount of contracts entered into) in the general ledger at the time of issuance. For example, assuming that a purchase order for $50,000 is issued, the following budgetary entry is made:

ENCUMBRANCES	50,000	
BUDGETARY FUND BALANCE RESERVED FOR ENCUMBRANCES		50,000
To record encumbrances for purchase orders issued.		

The ENCUMBRANCES account may be thought of as an "expenditure-to-be" account. Likewise, the BUDGETARY FUND BALANCE RESERVED FOR ENCUMBRANCES account may be thought of as a "liability-to-be" account. At a later date, when the goods are received or services are rendered, the entry is reversed and the expenditure and liability are recorded. Assume that in the preceding example the actual cost of the goods received under the purchase was $49,000. The following entries are made:

BUDGETARY FUND BALANCE RESERVED FOR ENCUMBRANCES	50,000	
ENCUMBRANCES		50,000
To cancel encumbrances of $50,000 upon receipt of materials and rendering of services totaling $49,000.		

Expenditures	49,000	
Vouchers Payable		49,000
To record expenditures of $49,000 for goods and services that were previously encumbered for $50,000.		

Check Point

An *encumbrance* could *not* be thought of as which of the following?

a. Commitment
b. Contingent liability
c. Future expenditure
d. Eventual reduction of the fund balance
e. Liability of the period in which the encumbrance was *created*

Answer: e

Like the APPROPRIATIONS account, the ENCUMBRANCES account is a control account. Each encumbrance is usually recorded in the individual subsidiary Expenditures accounts. As a result, the remaining amount that may be legally spent at a given time is readily determined by subtracting expenditures to date and encumbrances outstanding from appropriations. (Because an Expenditures Control account is also maintained, this calculation can be done at the control level or at the detail level using the individual subsidiary accounts.)

Illustration 24-6 shows what a subsidiary ledger might look like at the departmental level. Note that the format indicates the spendable amount remaining at the end of each month. (Only two months' activities are illustrated.) If an Encumbrances column were *not* included, the department supervisor might erroneously conclude that $94,000 ($100,000 appropriations – $6,000 expenditures) was available for spending at July 31, 2005. This figure is *incorrect* because purchase orders outstanding at July 31, 2005, total $7,000. Thus, of the $94,000 *not* yet spent at July 31, 2005,

ILLUSTRATION 24-6 EXAMPLE OF A DEPARTMENT'S SUBSIDIARY LEDGER ACCOUNT

	Department No. 34			
Date	Appropriation	Expenditures	Encumbrances	Remaining Spendable Amount
July 1, 2005.	$100,000			$100,000
July 2005		$ 6,000	$ 7,000	(13,000)
July 31, 2005.	$100,000	$ 6,000	$ 7,000	$ 87,000
August 2005.		11,000	(3,000)	(8,000)
August 31, 2005	$100,000	$17,000	$ 4,000	$ 79,000

$7,000 is earmarked for the outstanding purchase orders. This leaves only $87,000 available for spending at July 31, 2005. The objective of the procedure, of course, is **to prevent spending more than has been authorized** (appropriated).

From the preceding discussion and analysis, you should realize that only the *debit* entry recording the encumbrance is used in controlling spending. The credit to the BUDGETARY FUND BALANCE RESERVED FOR ENCUMBRANCES account serves no control function other than to provide a *credit* for double-entry bookkeeping. Thus it is merely a *contra account*. The steps in the process of using financial resources may be summarized as follows:

1. **Appropriation** (legal authorization to spend by governing body).
2. **Encumbrances** (commitment to spend by issuing purchase orders or signing contracts).
3. **Expenditures** (liability incurred upon vendor or contractor performance).
4. **Disbursement** (actual payment of liability).

Budgetary Comparisons

A financial reporting requirement of the GASB *Codification* is the preparation of "budgetary comparison statements or schedules" (as appropriate) in which budgeted data are compared with actual data for the year. Under GAAP reporting, encumbrances outstanding at year-end are *not* reported in the statement of revenues, expenditures, and changes in fund balance. They would become expenditures in the following year and be reported as expenditures in that year. To present a meaningful comparison of *actual expenditures* with the *budgeted expenditures*, the budgeted expenditures must be prepared on a basis consistent with GAAP. To do this, amounts must be included in the following year's budget for **encumbrances outstanding at the current year-end. Thus it can be said that encumbrances outstanding at the end of the *current year* "lapse" but are then "rebudgeted" and "reappropriated" in the *following year*.** Without this procedure, the following year's expenditures would include amounts relating to the encumbrances outstanding at the end of the prior year, but no amount would appear in the *following year's* budget for these expenditures, resulting in a meaningless comparison.

To illustrate this comparison process, we assume the following data:

1. For 2005, a governmental unit *expects* routine expenditures of $500,000 and the purchase of a new fire truck for $30,000. Thus it budgets $530,000 for 2005 expenditures.
2. *Actual* spending occurs according to budget, except that the fire truck is received in early 2006 rather than 2005.
3. The governmental unit *expects* routine expenditures of $500,000 for 2006. It also "reappropriates" or "rebudgets" an additional $30,000 to cover the fire truck for 2006. Thus the total budget for 2006 expenditures is $530,000.
4. *Actual* spending for 2006 occurs according to budget.

The budgetary comparison is as follows:

	Budget	Actual	Variance Favorable (Unfavorable)
2005:			
Expenditures	$530,000	$500,000	$30,000
2006:			
Expenditures	530,000	530,000	–0–

CHECK POINT

At the end of 2005, a governmental unit has unfilled purchase orders. In 2006, these purchase orders are filled. In the 2006 operating statement, which of the following is reported?

a. Encumbrances
b. Expenditures

c. Neither encumbrances nor expenditures
d. Expenditures only if the items were rebudgeted for in the 2006 budget

Answer: b

VII. THE *GENERAL FUND*

Recall that (1) the *General Fund* is a governmental fund, (2) governmental funds use the modified accrual basis of accounting, and (3) the measurement focus for governmental funds is the flow of current financial resources.

Nature and Scope of Activities

The *General Fund* accounts for all revenues and expenditures of a governmental unit that are *not* accounted for in one of the special-purpose funds. Because all other funds are special-purpose funds, most activities and current operations of governmental units are financed from the *General Fund*. For instance, general government administration, public safety, judicial system, health, sanitation, welfare, and culture recreation are usually accounted for in this fund.

Normally, more types of revenues flow into this fund than into any other fund. For example, property taxes, sales taxes, income taxes, transfer taxes, licenses, permits, fines, penalties, and interest on delinquent taxes commonly flow into the *General Fund*. In addition, the *General Fund* may receive monies from other governmental units; such receipts are classified by the GASB *Codification* as follows:

> **Grant.** A contribution or gift of cash or other assets from another government to be used or expended for a specified purpose, activity, or facility.
> **Capital grant.** A contribution or gift of cash or other assets restricted by the grantor for the acquisition and/or construction of fixed (capital) assets (which would be accounted for in a Capital Projects Fund).
> **Operating grant.** Grants that are intended to finance operations or that may be used for either operations or capital outlays at the discretion of the grantee.
> **Entitlement.** The amount of payment to which a state or local government is entitled as determined by the federal government (e.g., the Director of the Office of Revenue Sharing) pursuant to an allocation formula contained in applicable statutes.
> **Shared revenue.** A revenue levied by one government but shared on a predetermined basis, often in proportion to the amount collected at the local level, with another government or class of government.[14]

Comprehensive Illustration

Comprehensive: Journal Entries and Financial Statements

The June 30, 2005, balance sheet for Funn City's *General Fund* is shown in Illustration 24-7. Before proceeding with assumed transactions for the subsequent fiscal year, the following points should be understood with regard to Illustration 24-7:

1. **Inventory.** We assume that the *consumption method* (discussed in more detail later) is used to account for the supplies inventory. Under this method, the inventory is viewed as a resource, as are cash and property tax receivables. Although the $10,000 of inventory *cannot* be "spent" in a cash sense, it can be "expended" in the sense that its eventual use (*consumption*) will result in a future charge to the expenditures account.
2. **Deferred revenues.** Of the $40,000 net amount expected to be collected for property taxes ($43,000 – $3,000), $30,000 is expected to be collected after 60 days. Accordingly, deferred revenues of $30,000 are reported at June 30, 2005.

---

[14] GASB *Cod.*, sec. G60, 501-505.

ILLUSTRATION 24-7 FUNN CITY BALANCE SHEET—GENERAL FUND JUNE 30, 2005

Assets	
Cash	$ 120,000
Property taxes receivable—delinquent	43,000
Less: Allowance for estimated uncollectible taxes—delinquent	(3,000)
Inventory	10,000
Total Assets	**$170,000**
Liabilities and Fund Balance	
Vouchers payable	$ 35,000
Deferred revenues	30,000
Fund balance:	
Unreserved	105,000
Total Liabilities and Fund Balance	**$170,000**

3. **Unreserved fund balance.** The entire fund balance of $105,000 is designated as being "unreserved." This signifies that the fund has $105,000 of financial resources available for incurring expenditures in the *following* fiscal year.
4. **Reserving a portion of the fund balance for inventory.** Theoretically, no reservation of the fund balance should be made for inventory when the *consumption method* is used. In practice, however, some governmental units do reserve a portion of the fund balance for inventory reported under the *consumption method.* If such reservation had been done at June 30, 2005 (by *debiting* Unreserved Fund Balance for $10,000 and *crediting* Fund Balance Reserved for Inventory for $10,000), the Unreserved Fund Balance account would have been $95,000 (instead of $105,000). As a result, the $95,000 would have signified the amount of liquid financial resources available for incurring expenditures in the *following* fiscal year—this would be the amount available to "spend" in the cash sense.

Assumed transactions and related journal entries for the fiscal year July 1, 2005, through June 30, 2006, are discussed in the following paragraphs.

1. Adoption of the Budget

The city council approved and adopted the budget for the year. The budget contained the following amounts:

Estimated revenues	$700,000
Authorized expenditures	660,000
Authorized transfer *out* to the *Library Debt Service Fund*	30,000
Authorized transfer out to *establish* a *Central Motor Pool Internal Service Fund*	25,000

As explained earlier, the adoption of the budget for the *General Fund* involves the use of budgetary accounts, as follows:

	Dr.	Cr.
ESTIMATED REVENUES	700,000	
BUDGETARY FUND BALANCE	15,000	
APPROPRIATIONS		660,000[a]
APPROPRIATIONS—TRANSFERS OUT		55,000
To record the legally adopted annual operating budget.		

[a] In practice, this amount is often broken down by category, such as General Government, Public Safety, Sanitation, and so forth.

2. Property Taxes

Property taxes for the period July 1, 2005, through June 30, 2006, were levied in the amount of $515,000. Of this amount, $5,000 was estimated to be uncollectible. During the year, $485,000 was collected ($41,000 of which pertained to delinquent taxes of the prior fiscal year), and $2,000 of prior year delinquent balances was written off as uncollectible.

At June 30, 2006, it was estimated that (1) a $9,000 allowance for uncollectibles was necessary and (2) $45,000 of the net amount expected to be collected would be collected after 60 days. Property taxes unpaid at the end of the fiscal year become delinquent.

As explained earlier, the accrual basis of accounting is usually appropriate for property taxes. Under the technical guidance set forth in GASB *Statement No. 33*, "Accounting and Financial Reporting for Nonexchange Transactions," property tax revenues are recognized in the period for which the property taxes are levied, even if the lien date (generally the date when the government has an enforceable claim) or the due date occurs in a different period.

In this case, the city's fiscal year coincides with the period to which the property taxes relate; accordingly, the property tax levy is appropriately recorded on the first day of the new fiscal year. In recording the property taxes, the estimated uncollectible amount is netted against the revenues, and the use of the Bad Debts Expense account is avoided. The Bad Debts Expense account would be inappropriate because the *General Fund* has expenditures, *not* expenses. At the end of the fiscal year, remaining property tax receivables and the related allowance for uncollectible accounts are transferred to accounts that designate these items as relating to delinquent taxes. Thus tax levies of the following fiscal year may be separated from the *delinquent taxes*.

(1) Property Taxes Receivable—Current	515,000	
Allowance for Uncollectibles—Current.		5,000
Deferred Revenues		510,000
To record the property tax *levy*.		
(2) Cash	485,000	
Property Taxes Receivable—Current		444,000
Property Taxes Receivable—Delinquent		41,000
To record the *collection* of property taxes.		
(3) Allowance for Uncollectibles—Delinquent	2,000	
Property Taxes Receivable—Delinquent		2,000
To *write off* accounts determined to be uncollectible.		
(4) Allowance for Uncollectibles—Delinquent	1,000	
Deferred Revenues		1,000
To *eliminate* the remaining balance in the Allowance for Uncollectibles—Delinquent account as a result of collections of $41,000 being in excess of the $40,000 net amount estimated to be collected at the end of the prior year.[a]		
(5) Deferred Revenues	4,000	
Allowance for Uncollectibles—Current.		4,000
To *increase* the allowance for uncollectibles—current at year-end from $5,000 to $9,000.		
(6) Deferred Revenues	492,000	
Revenues		492,000
To recognize revenues by *adjusting* the Deferred Revenues account at year-end to the $45,000 amount estimated to be collected *after 60 days* ($30,000 + $510,000 + $1,000 – $4,000 = $537,000 of deferred revenues; $537,000 – $45,000 = $492,000).		

[a] The *beginning of year* balance in the Allowance for Uncollectibles—Delinquent account was $3,000.

(7) Property Taxes Receivable—Delinquent	71,000	
Allowance for Uncollectibles—Current	9,000	
Property Taxes Receivable—Current		71,000
Allowance for Uncollectibles—Delinquent		9,000
To transfer the fiscal year-end balances to the delinquent accounts.		

COMPARATIVE PRACTICE NOTE

Some governmental units (1) initially credit Revenues (instead of Deferred Revenues) and (2) make an adjusting entry at year-end to debit Revenues and credit Deferred Revenues for the amount to be deferred at year-end.

3. Revenues Other Than Property Taxes

The total estimated revenues for the year include an estimated $22,000 entitlement from the federal government. We assume that these funds are used for purposes normally financed through the *General Fund.* The amount is assumed to be susceptible to accrual; the actual amount received midway through the year is $23,000. Revenues of $181,000 are collected from sales taxes, business licenses, permits, and miscellaneous sources. Because these revenues are *not* susceptible to accrual, they are accounted for on the cash basis.

(1) Entitlement Receivable	22,000	
Revenues		22,000
To record entitlement from the federal government.		
(2) Cash	23,000	
Entitlement Receivable		22,000
Revenues		1,000
To record collection of entitlement.		
(3) Cash	181,000	
Revenues		181,000
To record revenues accounted for on the cash basis.		

4. Expenditures and Encumbrances for Items Other Than Inventory

During the year, $115,000 of encumbrances on purchase orders (pertaining to other than inventory) and contracts were recorded. For $103,000 of these encumbrances, the city received billings of $102,000, which it approved for payment. Additional expenditures of $524,000 (which did *not* involve the use of purchase orders or contracts) were incurred.

(1) ENCUMBRANCES	115,000	
BUDGETARY FUND BALANCE RESERVED FOR ENCUMBRANCES		115,000
To record encumbrances on purchase orders issued.		
(2) BUDGETARY FUND BALANCE RESERVED FOR ENCUMBRANCES	103,000	
ENCUMBRANCES		103,000
To cancel encumbrances of $103,000 upon receipt of goods and services totaling $102,000.		
(3) Expenditures	102,000	
Vouchers Payable		102,000
To record expenditures of $102,000 for goods and services that were previously encumbered for $103,000.		

(4) Expenditures	524,000	
Vouchers Payable		524,000
To record expenditures for items *not* previously encumbered.		

5. Acquisition and Consumption of Inventory

During the current year, purchase orders totaling $15,000 for supplies were issued. All of these purchase orders were filled by year-end, with billings of $15,000 having been received and approved. The government uses the "consumption" method of accounting for supplies inventories whereby the Inventory account is charged upon acquisition. As the supplies are used, the Inventory account is relieved, and the Expenditures account is charged. (Note that this manner of accounting parallels the accounting for inventories for commercial enterprises.) During the year, $11,000 of supplies were consumed.

(1) ENCUMBRANCES	15,000	
BUDGETARY FUND BALANCE RESERVED FOR ENCUMBRANCES		15,000
To record encumbrances on purchase orders issued for supplies.		
(2) BUDGETARY FUND BALANCE RESERVED FOR ENCUMBRANCES	15,000	
ENCUMBRANCES		15,000
To cancel encumbrances of $15,000 upon receipt of goods totaling $15,000.		
(3) Inventory	15,000	
Vouchers Payable		15,000
To record acquisition of supplies received.		
(4) Expenditures	11,000	
Inventory		11,000
To record consumption of supplies used during the year.		

COMPARATIVE PRACTICE NOTE

Some governmental units simplify the procedures under the *consumption method* by assuming throughout the year that the supplies *received* will always approximate the supplies *used*. Accordingly, they charge the Expenditures account as the supplies are *received* instead of charging the Inventory account. At year-end, a physical count is taken, and the Inventory account is adjusted to its proper balance (the offsetting adjustment being to the Expenditures account).

If significant amounts of inventory exist at the balance sheet date, the GASB *Codification* requires such inventory to be reported in the balance sheet. This reporting automatically occurs under the consumption method. Note that under the consumption method, the acquisition of inventory is viewed merely as **the conversion of resources (from cash to inventory)—*not* the use of resources**. The GASB *Codification* also sanctions the use of the "purchases" method, which takes the opposite position and, therefore, results in charging the Expenditures account upon acquisition of inventory. The purchases method, however, is outdated and has lost much support in recent years. At the end of the chapter, we discuss the purchases method in detail and show its procedures for reporting significant amounts of inventory in the balance sheet.

6. Disbursements (Other Than Interfund)

Cash disbursements totaled $606,000.

Vouchers Payable	606,000	
Cash		606,000
To record cash disbursements other than interfund disbursements.		

7. Interfund Transactions

The city had the following interfund transactions:

A. Services Provided and Used. During the year, the city's electric utility, which is operated as an *Enterprise Fund*, rendered billings in the amount of $21,000 for electricity supplied to the *General Fund*. Of this amount, $19,000 was paid during the fiscal year. These billings are for interfund services provided. Accordingly, they are treated as *expenditures* in the *General Fund* (and as *revenues* in the *Enterprise Fund*).

(1) Expenditures	21,000	
Due to *Electric Utility Enterprise Fund*		21,000
To record as expenditures electricity acquired from the *Electric Utility Enterprise Fund.*		
(2) Due to Electric Utility Enterprise Fund	19,000	
Cash		19,000
To record payment made to *Electric Utility Enterprise Fund.*		

B. Interfund Transfers. The transfer of $30,000 to be made to the Library Debt Service Fund is recorded on the first day of the fiscal year because the amount is susceptible to being accrued.

(1) Other Financing Uses—Transfers Out	30,000	
Due to *Library Debt Service Fund*		30,000
To record transfer to be made to the *Library Debt Service Fund.*		

The following entry assumes that the payment was made in accordance with the authorized amounts.

(2) Due to *Library Debt Service Fund*	30,000	
Cash		30,000
To record payment of transfer out to the *Library Debt Service Fund.*		

The *Central Motor Pool Internal Service Fund* was established in September 2005. An interfund transfer was made from the *General Fund.*

Other Financing Uses—Transfer Out	25,000	
Cash		25,000
To record transfer out to the newly established *Central Motor Pool Internal Service Fund.*		

The *General Fund* preclosing trial balances *after* recording the preceding items are shown in Illustration 24-8.

8. Closing Entries (excluding Encumbrances)

The closing entries at June 30, 2006, are as follows:

	Dr.	Cr.
(1) APPROPRIATIONS	660,000	
APPROPRIATIONS—TRANSFERS OUT.	55,000	
ESTIMATED REVENUES		700,000
BUDGETARY FUND BALANCE		15,000
To *reverse* the entry previously made to record the legally adopted annual operating budget.		

ILLUSTRATION 24-8 FUNN CITY PRECLOSING TRIAL BALANCES—GENERAL FUND JUNE 30, 2006

	Debit	Credit
Actual (nonbudgetary) Accounts		
Cash	$129,000	
Property taxes receivable—delinquent	71,000	
Allowance for estimated uncollectibles—delinquent		$ 9,000
Inventory	14,000	
Vouchers payable		70,000
Due to Electric Utility Enterprise Fund		2,000
Deferred revenues		45,000
Unreserved fund balance		105,000
Revenues		696,000
Expenditures	658,000	
Other financing uses—Transfers out	55,000	
Totals	$927,000	$927,000
Budgetary Accounts		
ESTIMATED REVENUES	$700,000	
BUDGETARY FUND BALANCE	15,000	
APPROPRIATIONS		$660,000
APPROPRIATIONS—TRANSFERS OUT		55,000
ENCUMBRANCES	12,000	
BUDGETARY FUND BALANCE RESERVED FOR ENCUMBRANCES		12,000
Totals	$727,000	$727,000

	Dr.	Cr.
(2) Revenues	696,000	
Unreserved Fund Balance	17,000	
Expenditures		658,000
Other Financing Uses—Transfers Out		55,000
To *close* **actual** operating statement accounts.		

9. Closing Entry Relating to Encumbrances

When encumbrances are outstanding at year-end, the encumbrances budgetary accounts must be closed as follows:

BUDGETARY FUND BALANCE RESERVED FOR ENCUMBRANCES	12,000	
ENCUMBRANCES		12,000
To *close* encumbrances outstanding at year-end by *reversing* the entry that previously recorded them.		

10. Adjusting Entry to Reserve a Portion of the Fund Balance

If the governmental unit intends to honor purchase orders and commitments outstanding at year-end (the customary practice), the encumbrances outstanding must be disclosed as a reservation of the Fund Balance account (similar to an appropriation of retained earnings for a commercial corporation). This requires the following adjusting entry:

Unreserved Fund Balance	12,000	
Fund Balance Reserved for Encumbrances		12,000
To record actual fund balance reserve account to indicate the portion of the year-end fund balance segregated for expenditure upon vendor performance.		

At the start of the new year, the preceding two $12,000 journal entries would be reversed to reestablish budgetary control over encumbrances outstanding in the normal manner. These reversing entries are as follows:

(1) Fund Balance Reserved for Encumbrances	12,000	
Unreserved Fund Balance		12,000
To *reverse* appropriation of fund balance made at the end of the prior year.		
(2) ENCUMBRANCES..............................	12,000	
BUDGETARY FUND BALANCE RESERVED FOR ENCUMBRANCES......................		12,000
To *reestablish* budgetary control over encumbrances outstanding at the end of the prior year that will be honored during the current year.		

The individual financial statements for the fiscal year ended June 30, 2006, are shown in Illustrations 24-9 and 24-10.

Manner of Classifying Expenditures

The operating statement for Funn City classifies expenditures by **character** and **function**. Character refers to the fiscal period that the expenditures are presumed to benefit. Virtually all of Funn City's expenditures were presumed to benefit the current fiscal year.

Other major categories of character classification are Capital Outlay (which benefits primarily future periods) and Debt Service (which benefits the period encompassing the useful life of the related capital assets acquired or constructed with the proceeds of the borrowing).

Note that the operating statement shows a minor amount for the Capital Outlay category and no Debt Service category. In Chapter 25, which covers the other types of funds, the Capital Outlay category is also encountered in *Capital Projects Funds* (in which the amounts are usually *not* minor); the Debt Service category is encountered in Debt Service Funds.

ILLUSTRATION 24-9 FUNN CITY BALANCE SHEET—GENERAL FUND JUNE 30, 2006

Assets	
Cash.....................	$ 129,000
Property taxes receivable—Delinquent	71,000
Less: Allowance for estimated uncollectible taxes—Delinquent........	(9,000)
Inventory	14,000
Total Assets	**$205,000**
Liabilities and Fund Balance	
Vouchers payable.............	$ 70,000
Due to *Electric Utility Enterprise Fund*	2,000
Deferred revenues	45,000[a]
Total Liabilities............	**$117,000**
Fund balance:	
Reserved for encumbrances..........	$ 12,000
Unreserved	76,000
Total Fund Balance	**$ 88,000**
Total Liabilities and Fund Balance	**$205,000**

[a] This amount is that portion of the $62,000 net realizable amount of the property taxes ($71,000 – $9,000) that is *not* expected to be collected within 60 days.

ILLUSTRATION 24-10 FUNN CITY STATEMENT OF REVENUES, EXPENDITURES, AND CHANGES IN FUND BALANCE—GENERAL FUND FOR THE FISCAL YEAR ENDED JUNE 30, 2006

Classified by		Actual
	Revenues	
	Property taxes	$ 492,000
	Intergovernmental grant	23,000
Source	Sales taxes[a]	124,000
	Licenses and permits[a]	38,000
	Miscellaneous[a]	19,000
	Total Revenues	**$696,000**
	Expenditures	
Character—Current:		
Function	General government[a]	$ 101,000
	Public safety[a]	220,000
	Sanitation[a]	49,500
	Health[a]	41,500
	Welfare[a]	62,700
	Education[a]	176,300
	Subtotal	$ 651,000
Character—Capital outlay		7,000
	Total Expenditures	**$658,000**
	Excess of Revenues over Expenditures	**$ 38,000**
	Other Financing Sources (Uses)	
	Transfers out	$ (55,000)
	Total Other Financing Sources (Uses)	$ (55,000)
	Deficiency of Revenues and Other Financing Sources under Expenditures and Other Financing Uses	**$ (17,000)**
	Fund Balance (in total)—July 1, 2005	105,000[b]
	Fund Balance (in total)—June 30, 2006	**$ 88,000[b]**

Note: Some governmental units use only the Unreserved Fund Balance rather than the total Fund Balance in the changes in fund balance section of the statement. Inquiries made to the GFOA revealed that only about 10% of the governmental units use this manner of reporting. However, the GFOA does deem this manner of reporting to be GAAP.

[a] These assumed amounts were *not* given in the transactions and journal entries.

[b] This is the total fund balance (reserved and unreserved portions).

When desirable, the major functions may be subdivided into **activities** and **objects**. For example, the sanitation function could be subdivided into sewage treatment and disposal, garbage collection, garbage disposal, and street cleaning. Alternatively, the sanitation function could be subdivided into employee salaries, contracted services, materials, and supplies. These other ways to classify expenditures may be presented in the financial statements, in supporting schedules to the financial statements, or in notes to the financial statements.

CHECK POINT

In which of the following categories can *expenditures not* be classified?

a. Character
b. Function
c. Activity
d. Object
e. Source

Answer: e

Manner of Reporting Inventory under the *Purchases* Method

Recall that under the purchases method, inventory is charged to the Expenditures account upon acquisition, regardless of when actually consumed. Thus the use of resources is deemed to occur upon the acquisition—*not* the consumption. To report significant amounts of inventory in the balance sheet when the purchases method is used, the following entry is used:

Inventory of Supplies	XXX	
Fund Balance Reserved for Inventory of Supplies		XXX
To report supplies inventory in the balance sheet.		

This entry, which is made only in the balance sheet, superimposes inventory into the balance sheet—no adjustment is made to the Expenditures account. If the amount of inventory on hand changes from the preceding balance sheet date, these two accounts are adjusted accordingly. Note that the credit side of the entry is to Fund Balance Reserved for Inventory of Supplies, *not* to the Unreserved Fund Balance Account. The reason for the credit being recorded this way is that it would be improper to credit the Unreserved Fund Balance account because doing so would indicate an additional amount available for spending, when in fact the inventory has already been reported as an expenditure in the operating statement. Thus it *cannot* be "spent" twice.

END-OF-CHAPTER REVIEW

Summary of Key Points

1. The Governmental Accounting Standards Board (GASB) establishes accounting standards for state and local governments.

2. The major deficiency of governmental financial reporting is that the accounting practices allowed for pension and other postemployment benefits are not realistic and thus do *not* achieve **interperiod equity.**

3. **Fund accounting** (in which multiple sets of books are kept for the various diverse operations) are used extensively by government.

4. **Governmental Funds:** At the *fund-based reporting level,* the **modified accrual basis** is used, which, for certain liabilities that have been *incurred,* results in the recognition of expenditures in the operating statement when financial resources become **available for their liquidation** rather than **when the liability was incurred** (a delayed manner of expenditure recognition). At the *government-wide reporting level,* however, the **accrual basis** is used.

5. **Governmental Funds:** At the *fund-based reporting level,* the **operating statement** (1) **uses the *current financial resources measurement focus*** and (2) is called the **statement of revenues, expenditures, and changes in fund balance** (an all-inclusive approach)—this is *not* an *income statement.* At the *government-wide reporting level,* however, the operating statement (1) uses the ***economic resources* measurement focus** (reports *all* revenues and *all* costs incurred to provide services) and (2) is called a **statement of activities** (also an all-inclusive approach because its "bottom line" is the ***"change in net assets for the year."***).

6. **Proprietary funds** use the *accrual basis* because activities accounted for in these funds resemble commercial activities. **Fiduciary funds** (which account for assets held in a purely custodial capacity) also use the *accrual basis.*

7. The **operating statement for proprietary funds** is an *income statement equivalent.*

8. **Interfund transactions** may be categorized as (a) **loans** (shown as *receivables* and *payables* in the balance sheets), (b) **services provided and used** (shown as *revenues* in the *provider fund*

and shown as *expenditures* in the *recipient fund*), (c) **reimbursements**, and (d) **transfers** (shown as an *other financing source or use* in *governmental funds*).

9. **Budgetary accounts** are used to control spending. All budgetary accounts—none of which are "actual" accounts—are closed at year-end.
10. Unfilled purchase orders and uncompleted contracts at year-end that are intended to be honored in the following year require a **reservation of the fund balance** in the balance sheet.

Glossary of New Terms

Appropriation A legal authorization granted by a legislative body to make expenditures and to incur obligations for specific purposes. An appropriation usually is limited in amount and time it may be expended.

Budget A plan of financial operations covering a specified period of time.

Budgetary Accounts "Special accounts used to achieve budgetary integration, but *not* reported in the general-purpose external financial statements."* [ALL CAPS convention is used in this text.]

Component units "Legally separate organizations for which the elected officials of the primary government are financially accountable. In addition, component units can be other organizations for which the nature and significance of their relationship with a primary government are such that exclusion would cause the reporting entity's financial statements to be misleading or incomplete."*

***Current financial resources* measurement focus** "A measurement focus that recognizes the net effect of transactions on current financial resources by recording accruals for those revenue and expenditure transactions which have occurred by year-end that are normally expected to result in cash receipt or disbursement early enough in the following year either (a) to provide financial resources to liquidate liabilities recorded in the fund at year end or (b) to require the use of available expendable financial resources reported at year end."

***Economic resources* measurement focus** The measurement focus used in (1) the commercial model, (2) proprietary funds, and (3) fiduciary funds to measure economic resources, the claims to those economic resources and the effects of transactions, and events and circumstances that change economic resources and claims to those resources. This focus includes depreciation of capital assets, deferral of unearned revenues, and prepaid expenses, and the amortization of the resulting liabilities and assets. Under this measurement focus, all assets and liabilities are reported on the balance sheet, whether current or noncurrent. Also, the *accrual basis* of accounting is used, with the result that operating statements report expenses rather than expenditures.

Encumbrances "Commitments related to unperformed (executory) contracts for goods or services."* Used in budgeting, encumbrances are *not* GAAP expenditures or liabilities but represent the estimated amount of expenditures ultimately to result if unperformed contracts in process *are* completed.

Endowments Endowments are restricted contributions in which the donor(s) stipulates that the principal be maintained intact either *in perpetuity* or *for a specified period*. Thus only the income from the investment of the *principal* (the corpus) may be spent.

Expenditures "Decreases in net financial resources under the current financial resources measurement focus *not* properly classified as *other financing uses*."*

Financial resources "Resources that are or will become available for spending. Financial resources include cash and resources ordinarily expected to be converted to cash (e.g., receivables, investments). Financial resources also may include inventories and prepaids (because they obviate the need to expend current available financial resources)."*

Fund "A fiscal and accounting entity with a self-balancing set of accounts recording cash and other financial resources, together with all related liabilities and residual equities or balances, and changes therein, that are segregated for the purpose of carrying on specific activities or attaining certain objectives in accordance with special regulations, restrictions or limitations."*

---

* *GAAFR*, 2000 edition, Appendix F.

Fund accounting Accounting for certain activities separately from other operations.

Fund balance "The difference between assets and liabilities reported in a governmental fund."*

General capital assets Capital assets that are *not* assets of any fund, but of the government unit as a whole. These assets arise from the expenditure of financial resources of *governmental funds*.

General Fund "The fund is one of five governmental fund types and typically serves as the chief operating fund of a government. The fund is used to account for all financial resources, except those required to be accounted for in another fund."*

General long-term liabilities (GLTL) Long-term debt (including special assessment debt for which the governmental unit is obligated) expected to be repaid from governmental funds.

Interfund loans "Amounts provided between funds and blended component units of the primary government with a requirement for repayment."*

Interfund reimbursements "Repayments from the funds or blended component units of the primary government responsible for particular expenditures or expenses to the funds or blended components units of the primary government that initially paid for them."*

Interfund services provided and used "Sales and purchases of goods and services between funds and blended component units of the primary government for a price approximating their external exchange value."*

Interfund transfers "Flows of assets (such as cash or goods) between funds and blended component units of the primary government without equivalent flows of assets in return and without a requirement for repayment."*

Modified accrual basis Recognizing *revenues* when they become available and measurable. Recognizing *expenditures* when the fund liability is incurred (which may be subsequent to when the liability is incurred and recognized in the statement of net assets [or balance sheet] in the *government-wide statements*).

Other financing sources "An increase in current financial resources that is reported separately from revenues to avoid distorting revenue trends. The use of the *other financing sources* category is limited to items co-classified by GAAP."* (Currently, the allowed items are: Governmental fund general long-term debt proceeds, amounts equal to the present value of minimum lease payments arising from capital leases, proceeds from the sale of general capital assets, and interfund transfers.)

Other financing uses "A decrease in current financial resources that is reported separately from expenditures to avoid distorting expenditure trends."* (Interfund transfers out is the most common item.)

ASSIGNMENT MATERIAL

Review Questions

1. What is the difference between the Governmental Finance Officers Association (GFOA), the National Council on Governmental Reporting (NCGA), and the Governmental Accounting Standards Board (GASB)?

2. For governmental units, what is the relationship of the pronouncements of the GASB and the FASB?

3. Where does *GAAFR* (the "blue book") fit into the governmental GAAP hierarchy?

4. Must all state and local governmental units prepare their financial statements in accordance with GASB pronouncements?

5. What are some of the unique aspects of the governmental sector compared with the *private sector*?

6. For *governmental activities*, what account(s) are used to describe a fund's equity? What account(s) is(are) used for *business-type activities*?

7. What is the relationship between revenues and expenditures?
8. What is meant by *fund accounting*?
9. What is meant by *measurement focus*?
10. What are the alternative measurement focuses?
11. What *measurement focus* is used for *governmental activities*? What *measurement focus* is used for *business-type activities*?
12. What is meant by interperiod equity?
13. To what does *basis of accounting* refer?
14. What is the major reporting deficiency that currently exists for governmental units?
15. What are the *11* major types of funds?
16. Are *general capital assets* and *general long-term liabilities* accounted for in funds? Why or why *not*?
17. When is it appropriate to depreciate a governmental unit's capital assets?
18. Is the *modified accrual basis* of accounting in accordance with GAAP? Why or why *not*?
19. What is meant by *budgetary accounting*?
20. What are the two major categories of interfund activities? What are the specific types of interfund transactions within each category?
21. How are *interfund transfers* classified in the operating statement of governmental funds? In proprietary funds?
22. What is the difference between an *interfund transfer* and an *interfund service*?
23. What is the difference between an *expenditure* and an *encumbrance*?

Exercises

E 24-1 **Recording the Budget** A city's legislative body approved the budget for the coming fiscal year. The details of the budget follow:

1. Estimated revenues of $500,000.
2. Estimated expenditures of $450,000.
3. Authorized transfer of $30,000 to a *Debt Service Fund* to pay interest on bond indebtedness.
4. Estimated receipt of $15,000 from closure of *Municipal Swimming Pool Enterprise Fund.*
5. Authorized transfer of $5,000 to *Capital Projects Fund* to pay for cost overrun on construction of new civic center.
6. Estimated receipt of $50,000 subsidy from *Electric Utility Enterprise Fund* to help finance *General Fund* expenditures (this is *not* a payment in lieu of taxes).

Required Prepare the *General Fund*'s entry to record the budget.

E 24-2 **Budgetary Control** The following balances are included in the subsidiary records of Tylersville's fire department at 5/31/06:

Appropriation—Supplies	$33,000
Expenditures—Supplies	27,000
Encumbrances—Supply orders	2,000

Required Determine how much the fire department has available for additional purchases of supplies.

E 24-3 **Interfund Transactions: Preparing Journal Entries** The City of Mityville had the following interfund transactions during the year ended 12/31/05:

1. The *General Fund* received a billing of $11,000 from its city-owned *Water Fund,* which is accounted for in an *Enterprise Fund.*
2. The *General Fund* disbursed $22,000 to its *Library Debt Service Fund* so that interest could be paid to bondholders.
3. The *General Fund* disbursed $33,000 to start a central purchasing fund, which is accounted for in an *Internal Service Fund.* Repayment is *not* expected.
4. The *General Fund* disbursed $44,000 to its *Municipal Transit Fund* (accounted for in a Special Revenue Fund) as its *annual subsidy—not* to be repaid.
5. The *General Fund* disbursed $55,000 to its *Convention Center Enterprise Fund.* Repayment is to be made in three years.
6. The *General Fund* received $66,000 from its *Library Capital Projects Fund* in repayment of money the *General Fund* had advanced to the architectural firm designing the library. The *General Fund* had charged a "Due From" account when the advance was made.

Required Prepare the entries required in the *General Fund.*

E 24-4 **Revenue Recognition** The City of Potterville, which has a calendar year-end, was awarded a $300,000 federal job development grant on 12/3/05. The grant is expected to be disbursed by the federal government in May 2006. In 2005, the city levied property taxes of $800,000. At year-end, $100,000 remains uncollected, of which $75,000 is expected to be collected within 60 days. An allowance for uncollectibles of $10,000 is deemed adequate at year-end.

Required Determine the amount to be reported for revenues for 2005 for these items.

E 24-5 **Revenue Recognition** Wilbur Whoops mistakenly paid his tax bill twice for the fiscal year ended 6/30/05. He noticed this in June 2005 and contacted the governmental unit. Rather than requesting a refund, he told the governmental unit to apply the overpayment of $3,000 to his taxes for the fiscal year ended 6/30/06. The governmental unit (which had credited the Accounts Receivable account $6,000) agreed to do this.

Required Prepare the entry or entries required by the *General Fund*, if any, at 6/30/05 relating to the overpayment.

E 24-6 **Revenue Recognition** The City of Joy has the following tax assessment–related accounts at its fiscal year-end, 6/30/06:

Property taxes receivable—Delinquent	$470,000
Allowance for uncollectibles—Delinquent	(20,000)

The net amount expected to be collected at year-end is usually collected within 60 days of the fiscal year-end. At 6/30/06, however, only about $300,000 is expected to be collected within 60 days, with the remaining $150,000 expected to be collected after that time over many months. The reason for the delay is a severe recession in the city's economy. The total property tax assessment is $1,000,000. No property tax *receivables existed at 6/30/05.*

Required
1. Prepare the entry or entries required for the *General Fund* at 6/30/06, if any.
2. Determine the amount to be reported for property tax revenues for the year ended 6/30/06.

E 24-7 **Preparation of a *General Fund*'s Operating Statement from Year-End Trial Balance** The following are selected preclosing account balances of Borrowsville Township's *General Fund* at 6/30/06:

	Dr.	Cr.
Expenditures	600,000	
Transfers Out	120,000	
Annual subsidy to *Airport Enterprise Fund*	80,000	
Amount Paid to *Internal Service Printing Fund*	10,000	
Due from City *Transit Enterprise Fund*	90,000	
Due to City *Water Enterprise Fund*		20,000
Bond Proceeds Received		100,000
Revenues		650,000
Transfers In		15,000
Unreserved Fund Balance		200,000

In some cases, the bookkeeper was *not* sure which was the proper account, so she used a description of the transaction instead. Encumbrances of $25,000 are outstanding at 6/30/06, whereas there were no encumbrances outstanding at 6/30/05.

Required Prepare a statement of revenues, expenditures, and changes in fund balance for the year ended 6/30/06.

E 24-8 **Presentation of Financial Statements: Expenditures and Encumbrances** The City of Thrillsville has the following accounts in its preclosing trial balance at 6/30/06:

	Account	
Amount	Dr.	Cr.
Expenditures—Current Year	800,000	
Expenditures—Prior Year	60,000	
ENCUMBRANCES	28,000	
APPROPRIATIONS		902,000
BUDGETARY FUND BALANCE RESERVED FOR ENCUMBRANCES		28,000

The encumbrances outstanding at each year-end ($62,000 at 6/30/05) are reappropriated in the following year's budget. The city council has requested that expenditures relating to such encumbrances be kept separate in the accounting records.

Required Prepare the applicable section of a budgetary comparison statement for the year ended 6/30/06.

E 24-9 **Preparing Budgetary Comparison Statements from Selected Data** The following information is given for the City of Budgetville:

Fund Balance at 12/31/05:	
Reserved for encumbrances	$ 30,000
Unreserved	70,000
Total Fund Balance	$100,000
Budgeted items for 2006:	
Estimated revenues	$500,000
Appropriations (including $30,000 rebudgeted for encumbrances outstanding at 12/31/05)	480,000
Actual amounts for 2006:	
Revenues	503,000
Expenditures (including $29,000 relating to encumbrances outstanding at 12/31/05)	473,000
Encumbrances outstanding at 12/31/06	5,000

Required Prepare a budgetary comparison statement of revenues, expenditures, and changes in fund balance for 2006.

E 24-10 **Preparing Closing Entries** The following information is given for the City of Closeville's *General Fund*:

Budgeted items for 2006:	
Estimated revenues—External	$711,000
Appropriations (*including* $55,000 *rebudgeted* for encumbrances outstanding at 12/31/05 and **$68,000 for purchase of natural gas from *Gas Enterprise Fund***)	800,000
Transfer *from Gas Enterprise Fund*—**In lieu of taxes**	90,000
Transfer *from Gas Enterprise Fund*—***Not* in lieu of taxes**	60,000
Transfer *to Debt Service Fund*	40,000
Actual amounts for 2006:	
Revenues—External	707,000
Expenditures (*including* $54,000 relating to encumbrances outstanding at 12/31/05 and **$66,000 for purchase of natural gas from *Gas Enterprise Fund***)	808,000
Encumbrances outstanding at 12/31/06	33,000
Transfer *from Gas Enterprise Fund*—**In lieu of taxes**	90,000
Transfer *from Gas Enterprise Fund*—***Not* in lieu of taxes**	60,000
Transfer *to Debt Service Fund*	40,000

Required Prepare the closing entries for the *General Fund*.

Problems

P 24-1 ***General Fund*: Preparing Transaction and Closing Entries—Fundamentals** The City of Smileyville had the following activities pertaining to its *General Fund* for the fiscal year ended 6/30/06:

1. **Adoption of the budget.** Revenues were estimated at $1,000,000, and authorized expenditures were $950,000. (Assume that no encumbrances were outstanding at 6/30/05.)
2. **Property taxes.** Property taxes were billed in the amount of $800,000, of which $25,000 was expected to be uncollectible. Collections were $750,000. A $22,000 allowance for uncollectibles is deemed adequate at year-end. All uncollected property taxes at year-end are delinquent. All but $11,000 of the net realizable amount at year-end is expected to be collected within 60 days.
3. **Other revenues.** Cash collections of $210,000 were received from sales taxes, licenses, fees, and fines.
4. **Purchase orders.** Purchase orders totaling $300,000 were issued to vendors and contractors during the year. For $270,000 of these purchase orders and contracts, billings totaling $268,000 were received. Cash payments totaling $245,000 were made.
5. **Payroll and other operating costs.** Expenditures for payroll and other operating costs *not* requiring the use of purchase orders and contracts totaled $631,000. Cash payments of $590,000 were made on these items.

Required

1. Prepare the journal entries relating to these items.
2. Prepare the year-end closing entries, assuming that encumbrances outstanding at year-end will be honored in the following year.
3. Prepare the entry or entries that must be made on the first day of the following fiscal year.

P 24-2 ***General Fund*: Preparing Financial Statements from Preclosing Trial Balance** Following is the trial balance of Ponder City at 6/30/06, prior to adjusting and closing entries. The bookkeeper was *not* certain of the exact account to use in some cases, so he merely used an account that was most descriptive of the nature of the transaction.

Cash	$ 550,000
Taxes receivable—Current	80,000
Allowance for uncollectibles—Current	(90,000)
Inventory	20,000[a]
BUDGETARY FUND BALANCE	220,000
ESTIMATED REVENUES	920,000
ENCUMBRANCES	80,000
Expenditures	790,000
Transfer out to New Golf Course Enterprise Fund	230,000
For services provided payment to City Utility Enterprise Fund	40,000
Annual subsidy to City Transit Enterprise Fund	60,000
	$2,900,000

Vouchers payable	$ 280,000
Due to *Internal Service Fund*	30,000
APPROPRIATIONS	840,000
APPROPRIATIONS—TRANSFERS OUT	300,000
Revenues	870,000
Unreserved fund balance	300,000
Bond proceeds received	200,000
BUDGETARY FUND BALANCE RESERVED FOR ENCUMBRANCES	80,000[b]
	$2,900,000

[a] The consumption method is used.

[b] At 6/30/05 (the end of the prior year), encumbrances outstanding totaled $25,000.

Required

1. Prepare a balance sheet and an operating statement (no comparison to budget required).
2. Prepare a T-account analysis of the Unreserved Fund Balance account as it should have been posted for the year (inclusive of any year-end adjusting entries and the year-end closing entries).

P 24-3 ***General Fund*: Preparing Transaction and Closing Entries and an Operating Statement** Ledgerville had the following events and transactions for its fiscal year ended 6/30/06:

1. **Adoption of the budget.** The budget for the year was approved. It provided for (a) $620,000 of estimated revenues, (b) $565,000 of expenditures, (c) $40,000 for servicing general long-term debt (principal and interest), and (d) $30,000 to establish a central printing department that will provide services to all city departments. (The $30,000 will *not* be repaid to the *General Fund*.)
2. Items (c) and (d) above were expended in accordance with authorizations.
3. **Property taxes.** Property taxes totaling $450,000 were levied, of which $8,000 was estimated to be uncollectible. Property tax collections totaled $405,000. At year-end, the estimated allowance for uncollectibles was increased from $8,000 to $12,000. Unpaid taxes at year-end become delinquent. The net realizable amounts at 6/30/05 and 6/30/06 were expected to be collected within 60 days.
4. **Other revenues.** City income taxes, sales taxes, business licenses, and fines totaled $162,000.
5. **Equipment sale.** Some equipment accounted for in the General Fixed Assets Account Group was sold for $11,000. This transaction was *not* included in the budget.
6. **Cost overrun.** A Capital Projects Fund was short $3,000 as a result of changes to contracts issued in connection with certain street improvements being charged to certain property owners. Authorization was given during the year to transfer funds to this fund to make up the shortage. The amount was *not* budgeted and will *not* be repaid.
7. **Purchase orders.** Purchase orders and contracts totaling $280,000 were entered into. For $255,000 of this amount, invoices for goods and services totaling $254,000 were rendered. (Assume that no encumbrances were outstanding at 6/30/05.)
8. **Nonpurchase orders.** Payroll and other operating costs *not* involving the use of purchase orders and contracts totaled $282,000.
9. **Cash payments.** Cash disbursements (other than to other funds) totaled $507,000.

Required

1. Prepare the *General Fund* entries for these items.
2. Prepare the closing entries at 6/30/06, assuming that encumbrances outstanding at year-end will be honored in the following year.
3. Prepare a statement of revenues, expenditures, and changes in fund balance for the year ended 6/30/06 for the *General Fund* that compares budgeted amounts with actual amounts. (Assume that the *General Fund* had a total fund balance of $100,000 at 6/30/05.)
4. Prepare the fund balance section of the balance sheet at 6/30/06.

P 24-4 COMPREHENSIVE: Preparing Transaction and Closing Entries and a Budgetary Comparison Statement (Several Interfund Transactions) The City of Postville had the following items and transactions pertaining to its *General Fund* for the fiscal year ended 6/30/06:

1. **Adoption of the budget.** The budget for the year was as follows:

Estimated revenues	$800,000
Authorized expenditures (including $55,000 reappropriated for encumbrances outstanding at 6/30/05, which lapsed)	725,000
Authorized transfers *out* to other funds ($35,000 + $10,000)	45,000
Estimated inflow from discontinuance of *Central Motor Pool Internal Service Fund*	25,000

2. **Property taxes.** Property taxes totaling $550,000 were levied. Of this amount, $10,000 was estimated to be uncollectible. Collections during the year were $535,000, of which $12,000 pertained to property tax levies of the prior year that had been declared delinquent at the end of the prior year. All remaining property tax receivables at the *beginning* of the current year totaling $4,000 were written off as uncollectible. The net realizable amounts at 6/30/05 ($11,000) and 6/30/06 were expected to be collected within 60 days.

3. **Entitlement.** The estimated revenues for the year include a $34,000 entitlement from the federal government. During the year, $36,000 was received.

4. **Other revenues.** City income taxes, sales taxes, licenses, permits, and miscellaneous revenues totaled $222,000.

5. **Encumbrances at 7/1/05.** Encumbrances outstanding at the beginning of the year totaled $55,000. The goods and services relating to these encumbrances were received along with invoices totaling $53,000.

6. **Purchase orders.** Purchase orders and contracts totaling $370,000 were entered into during the year. For $330,000 of this amount, invoices totaling $326,000 for goods and services were rendered. Assume that the city generally allows encumbrances outstanding at year-end to lapse but *reappropriates* amounts in the following year to honor the encumbrances. Of the $326,000 amount, $76,000 was for the acquisition of supplies inventory. The city uses the *consumption method* of accounting for supplies.

7. **Nonpurchase orders.** Payroll and other items *not* involving the use of purchase orders and contracts totaled $280,000. (This amount *excludes* interfund billings.)

8. **Cash payments.** Cash disbursements (other than to other funds) totaled $740,000.

9. **Interfund transactions.** Interfund transactions consisted of the following:
   a. The *Central Motor Pool Internal Service Fund* was discontinued pursuant to authorization of the legislative body at the beginning of the year. The actual amount disbursed to the *General Fund* during the year when the fund was discontinued was $17,000.
   b. A $30,000 payment was made to the *Electric Utility Enterprise Fund* to make up its operating deficit, initially estimated to be $35,000.
   c. A payment of $10,000 made to a *Capital Projects Fund* to finance a portion of certain street improvements *equaled* the amount budgeted.
   d. The *Electric Utility Enterprise Fund* rendered billings to the city totaling $26,000 for electricity supplied to the city by the Enterprise Fund. Cash disbursements to this fund during the year in payment of such billings totaled $22,000.
   e. An $80,000 disbursement was made to the *City Center for Performing Arts Enterprise Fund*. Repayment is expected in three years.

10. **Inventory.** A physical inventory of supplies at year-end shows that the supplies inventory *decreased* during the year from $44,000 to $42,000.

Required

1. Prepare *General Fund* journal entries only for the preceding items.
2. Prepare the closing entries at 6/30/06 for the *General Fund*.

3. Prepare a statement of revenues, expenditures, and changes in fund balance for the year ended 6/30/06 that compares budgeted amounts with actual amounts. (Assume that the fund balance at the *beginning* of the year was $100,000.)
4. Prepare the fund balance section of the balance sheet at 6/30/06.

P 24-5 **COMPREHENSIVE: Preparing Transaction and Closing Entries and a Budgetary Comparison Statement** The City of Solna's *General Fund* trial balance at 12/31/05 follows:

	Dr.	Cr.
Cash	$ 62,000	
Taxes receivable—Delinquent	46,000	
Allowance for uncollectible taxes—Delinquent		$ 8,000
Stores inventory—Program operations	18,000	
Vouchers payable		28,000
Fund balance reserved for encumbrances		12,000
Unreserved fund balance		78,000
	$126,000	$126,000

Collectible delinquent taxes are expected to be collected within 60 days after the end of the year. Solna uses the consumption method to account for stores inventory. The following data pertain to 2006 *General Fund* operations:

1. **Budget adopted** (including reappropriation of 2005 items):

Revenues and Other Financing Sources	
Taxes	$220,000
Fines, forfeits, and penalties	80,000
Miscellaneous revenues	100,000
Share of bond issue proceeds	200,000
	$600,000

Expenditures and Other Financing Uses	
Program operations	$312,000
General administration	120,000
Stores—program operations	60,000
Capital outlay	80,000
Periodic transfer to *Special Revenue Fund*	20,000
	$592,000

2. **Property taxes.** Taxes were assessed at an amount that would result in revenues of $220,800, after deduction of 4% of the tax levy as uncollectible. The net realizable amounts at 12/31/05 and 12/31/06 were expected to be collected within 60 days.
3. **Orders *placed* but *not received*:**

Program operations	$176,000
General administration	80,000
Capital outlay	60,000
	$316,000

4. **Future capital outlay.** The city council designated $20,000 of the unreserved fund balance for possible future appropriation for capital outlay.
5. **Cash collections and transfer:**

Delinquent taxes	$ 38,000
Current taxes	226,000
Refund of overpayment of invoice for purchase of equipment	4,000
Fines, forfeits, and penalties	88,000
Miscellaneous revenues	90,000
Share of bond issue proceeds	200,000
Transfer of remaining fund balance of a discontinued fund	18,000
	$664,000

6. **Canceled encumbrances:**

	Estimated	Actual
Program operations	$156,000	$166,000[a]
General administration	84,000	80,000
Capital outlay	62,000	62,000
	$302,000	$308,000

[a] Includes $36,000 of stores inventory purchases.

7. **Additional vouchers:**

Program operations	$182,000
General administration	38,000
Capital outlay	18,000
Transfer to Special Revenue Fund	20,000
	$258,000

8. **Tax overpayment.** Alberta Alberts, a taxpayer, overpaid her 2006 taxes by $2,000. She applied for a $2,000 credit against her 2007 taxes. The city council granted her request.

9. **Cash payments.** Vouchers paid amounted to $580,000 (including $20,000 paid to the *Special Revenue Fund*).

10. **Inventory.** Stores inventory on 12/31/06 amounted to $12,000.

Required

1. Prepare *General Fund* journal entries only for these items.
2. Prepare any required year-end adjusting entries.
3. Prepare the closing entries at 12/31/06.
4. Prepare a balance sheet at 12/31/06.
5. Prepare a statement of revenues, expenditures, and changes in fund balance for 2006 that compares budgeted amounts with actual amounts.
6. Qualitatively evaluate the city's financial statements.

P 24-6 *General Fund:* **Reconstructing Transaction and Closing Entries; Preparing a Budgetary Comparison Statement** The following data were obtained from the general ledger for the *General Fund* of the City of Hope after the general ledger had been closed for the fiscal year ended 6/30/06:

	Balances June 30, 2005	Fiscal 2005–2006 Activity: Debit	Fiscal 2005–2006 Activity: Credit	Balances June 30, 2006
Cash	$180,000	$ 955,000	$ 880,000	$255,000
Taxes receivable	20,000	809,000	781,000	48,000
Allowance for uncollectible taxes	(4,000)	6,000	9,000	(7,000)
	$196,000			$296,000
Vouchers payable	$ 44,000	813,000	822,000	$ 53,000
Due to *Internal Service Fund*	2,000	7,000	10,000	5,000
Due to *Debt Service Fund*	10,000	60,000	100,000	50,000
Fund balance reserved for encumbrances	40,000	40,000	47,000	47,000
Unreserved fund balance	100,000	47,000	88,000	141,000
	$196,000	$2,737,000	$2,737,000	$296,000

Additional Information

1. The budget for fiscal 2005–2006 included estimated revenues of $1,000,000, appropriations of $905,000 (including $40,000 pertaining to encumbrances outstanding at 6/30/05), and $100,000 to be transferred to a debt service fund.

2. Expenditures totaled $832,000, of which $37,000 pertained to encumbrances outstanding at 6/30/05.
3. Purchase orders issued during 2005–2006 totaled $170,000.
4. The city does *not* use delinquent accounts for delinquent taxes.
5. The net realizable amount for taxes receivable at each year-end was expected to be collected within 60 days.

Required

1. Using the given data, reconstruct the original detailed journal entries that were required to record all transactions for the fiscal year ended 6/30/06, including the recording of the current year budget. *(Hint: Using T accounts will help.)*
2. Prepare the year-end closing entries from the entries you have reconstructed.
3. Prepare a budgetary comparison statement of revenues, expenditures, and changes in fund balance for the current year.

P 24-7 ***General Fund:*** **Reconstructing Transactions and Preparing Closing Entries and Preparing an Operating Statement** The following transaction summary is from the accounts of the Good Times School District *General Fund* before the books had been closed for the fiscal year ended 6/30/06:

	Post closing Balances June 30, 2005	*Pre* closing Balances June 30, 2006
Actual Accounts		
Cash	$400,000	$ 630,000
Property taxes receivable—Delinquent	150,000	180,000
Allowance for uncollectibles—Delinquent	(40,000)	(80,000)
Expenditures		2,900,000
	$510,000	$3,630,000
Vouchers payable	$ 80,000	$ 408,000
Due to other funds	210,000	62,000
Fund balance reserved for encumbrances	60,000	
Unreserved fund balance	160,000	220,000
Revenues from property taxes		2,800,000
Miscellaneous revenues		140,000
	$510,000	$3,630,000
Budgetary Accounts		
ESTIMATED REVENUES		$3,000,000
ENCUMBRANCES		91,000
		$3,091,000
APPROPRIATIONS		$2,980,000
BUDGETARY FUND BALANCE		20,000
BUDGETARY FUND BALANCE RESERVED FOR ENCUMBRANCES		91,000
		$3,091,000

Additional Information

1. The property tax levy for the year ended 6/30/06 was $2,870,000. Taxes collected during the year totaled $2,810,000, of which $100,000 pertained to delinquent balances as of 6/30/05. Of the 6/30/05 delinquent balances, $30,000 was written off as uncollectible. Unpaid taxes become delinquent at the end of the fiscal year. The net realizable amount at each year-end was expected to be collected within 60 days.
2. Encumbrances outstanding at each year-end are always honored in the following year; they are rebudgeted or reappropriated in the following year. During the current year, invoices totaling $58,000 were rendered on encumbrances outstanding at the beginning of the year. On 5/2/06, commitment documents were issued to purchase new textbooks at a cost of $91,000. Only this encumbrance is outstanding at 6/30/06. Other purchase orders issued during the year totaled $850,000, with invoices having been rendered for $847,000.

3. An analysis of the transactions in the Vouchers Payable account for the year ended 6/30/06 follows:

Balance, 6/30/05	$ 80,000
Expenditures	2,758,000
Cash disbursements	(2,430,000)
Balance, 6/30/06	$ 408,000

4. During the year, the *General Fund* was billed $142,000 for services performed on its behalf by other city funds.

Required

1. Using these data, reconstruct the original detailed journal entries required to record all transactions for the fiscal year ended 6/30/06, including the recording of the current year's budget. *(Hint: Using T accounts will help.)*
2. Prepare the closing entries at 6/30/06.
3. Prepare a statement of revenues, expenditures, and changes in fund balance for fiscal 2005–2006.

P 24-8 Challenger: Preparing Adjusting and Closing Entries; Preparing Balance Sheet and Budgetary Comparison Statement—Non*General Fund* Transactions *Improperly* Recorded in *General Fund*
The *General Fund* trial balances of the ABC School District at 6/30/06 follow:

ABC School District
General Fund Trial Balances
June 30, 2006

	DR.	CR.
Actual Accounts		
Cash	$ 60,000	
Taxes Receivable—Current Year	31,800	
Allowance for Uncollectibles—Current Year Taxes		$ 1,800
Inventory of Supplies	10,000	
Buildings	1,300,000	
Bonds Payable		500,000
Vouchers Payable		12,000
Operating Expenses:		
Administration	25,000	
Instruction	602,000	
Other	221,000	
Capital Outlays (equipment)	22,000	
Debt Service (interest)	30,000	
State Grant Revenue		300,000
Revenues from Tax Levy, Licenses, and Fines		1,008,000
Unreserved Fund Balance		480,000
Totals	$2,301,800	$2,301,800
Budgetary Accounts		
Estimated Revenues	$1,007,000	
Appropriations		$1,000,000
Budgetary Fund Balance		7,000
Totals	$1,007,000	$1,007,000

Additional Information

1. The recorded allowance for uncollectible current year taxes is considered sufficient. Unpaid taxes become delinquent at year-end. The net realizable amount for taxes receivable at each year-end was expected to be collected within 60 days.
2. During the year, the local governmental unit gave the school district 20 acres of land for a new grade school and a community playground. The unrecorded estimated value of the land donated was $50,000. In addition, a state grant of $300,000 was received, and the full amount was used to pay contracts pertaining to the construction of the grade school. Purchases of classroom and playground equipment costing $22,000 were paid from *General Funds* of the school district.

3. On 7/1/01, a 5%, 10-year serial bond issue in the amount of $1,000,000 for constructing school buildings was issued. Principal payments of $100,000 must be made each June 30, along with interest for the year. All payments required through 6/30/06 have been made. (*Serial bonds* have annual principal payments over the life of the bond issue, whereas *term bonds* are repaid in total at the maturity date.)

4. Outstanding purchase orders for operating expenses *not* recorded in the accounts at year-end follow:

Administration	$1,000
Instruction	1,400
Other	600
Total	$3,000

The school district honors encumbrances outstanding at each year-end and reappropriates amounts in the following year's budget. No encumbrances were outstanding at 6/30/05.

5. Appropriations for the year consisted of the following:

Current	
Administration	$ 25,000
Instruction	600,000
Other	222,000
Capital Outlay	23,000
Debt Service	
Principal	100,000
Interest	30,000
	$1,000,000

6. The consumption method is used for the supplies inventory ($9,000 balance at 6/30/05).

Required

1. Prepare the appropriate adjusting entry to eliminate the activities and accounts that the school district should account for in separate funds or account groups outside the *General Fund.* (It is *not* necessary to prepare the entries that would be made in these other funds or account groups to account properly for these items.) (Note: Problem 24-8 will be used in the requirement for Problem 25-9.)
2. Prepare any adjusting entries to accounts that are properly part of the *General Fund.*
3. Prepare the closing entries relating to the *General Fund.*
4. Prepare a balance sheet at 6/30/06.
5. Prepare a statement of revenues, expenditures, and changes in fund balance for the year ended 6/30/06, comparing budgeted amounts with actual amounts. (The beginning fund balance amount must be "forced" as though a correcting entry had been made at 6/30/05.)

THINKING CRITICALLY

Cases

C 24-1 **Did They Submit a Balanced Budget?** Mirage City's finance director is required to submit a balanced budget to the city council each year. For 2006, the following budget was submitted:

Estimated revenues	$1,000,000
Appropriations	960,000

In November 2005, the city concluded three days of negotiations with its employees' union. Immediately prior to these negotiations, the city's pension fund was fully funded. Thus the city had no pension obligation. The revised union contract, however, increased pension benefits for all current active employees by 2%, a retroactive increase. As a result, the city's pension obligation immediately went from zero to $3,000,000, which will be funded over the next 30 years. The 2006 budgeted appropriations include $100,000 for funding this increase in pension benefits. For simplicity, assume that the average age of the city's union employees is 50 and that all union employees retire at age 60.

Required
1. Did the city manager submit a balanced budget for 2006?
2. How does the concept of interperiod equity apply here?

C 24-2 **Modified Accrual Basis of Accounting** As an accountant for the city of Tulipville, you assist the city manager in answering questions raised at city council meetings. At one meeting, a taxpayer asks why the city uses the modified accrual basis of accounting for its *General Fund* rather than the accrual basis, which is required for public corporations in the private sector. Furthermore, the taxpayer would like to know "the magnitude of the misstatement at the end of the recently concluded fiscal year as a result of *not* using the *accrual basis.*" Assume that the city has an income tax, a sales tax, a property transfer tax, a property tax, and annual business licenses.

Required Respond to the taxpayer's questions.

C 24-3 **What Is It?** In May 2005, a city incurred $2,000 of legal fees directly traceable to the *Airport Enterprise Fund.* The legal fees were paid out of the *General Fund* and charged to the Expenditures account. In June 2005, the *Airport Enterprise Fund* sent a $2,000 check to the *General Fund.*

Required
1. How would you report these transactions in the operating statement of the *General Fund* and the *Airport Enterprise Fund*?
2. How would you classify the June 2005 transaction between the two funds?

C 24-4 **Accruing Vested Sick Leave: It Seems Too Simple** On 1/1/06, Lynn began work at Funn City at an annual salary of $52,000. City policy allows unused sick leave to be converted into a cash payment upon termination. The city does *not* have a pension plan; its employees are covered by social security.

Lynn was *not* sick on any day during 2006. If Lynn's employment at Funn City were terminated on 12/31/06 (for whatever reason), Lynn would be entitled to receive one week's salary.

Required
1. Determine the liability to be accrued at 12/31/06 relating to this compensated absence.
2. Would your answer to requirement 1 differ if Lynn were given a $100-per-week raise effective December 31, 2006?

Financial Analysis Problem

FAP 24-1 **Developing Financial Statements without Referring to the Chapter Material** The City of Twin Hills was incorporated on 1/1/05. The city had the following transactions and events during 2005:

1. **Property taxes.** Property taxes of $650,000 for calendar-year 2005 were assessed. Collections totaled $580,000. At 12/31/05, $10,000 is expected to be uncollectible.
2. **Bond issuance.** On 1/1/05, the city issued 7% general obligation bonds (face value of $1,000,000) for $1,000,000. The proceeds were used to build a city hall, which was completed on 6/30/05 and is expected to last 50 years.
3. **Bond principal payments.** The 10% bond issue is to be repaid $40,000 per year beginning 12/31/05. The 2005 year-end principal payment was made on time.
4. **Bond interest payments.** Interest is due semiannually on July 1 and January 1 with a five-day grace period. The 7/1/05 interest payment of $35,000 was made on time. The 1/1/06 interest payment of $35,000 was made on that date.
5. **Supplies inventories.** Of the $90,000 of supplies ordered, $77,000 worth were received, $65,000 of which had been paid for by year-end. The physical inventory at year-end totals $20,000.

6. **Sidewalk improvements.** The city incurred $60,000 of costs (paid for by year-end) for making sidewalk improvements.
7. **Payroll costs.** City employees were paid $300,000. At 12/31/05, $23,000 is owed but unpaid to these employees.
8. **Compensated absences—vacation.** Two of the city's employees did *not* take vacations during 2005. Unused vacation pay vests ($4,000 for these two employees).
9. **Compensated absences—sick leave.** Unused sick leave days also vest. At 12/31/05, $16,000 would be paid to the city's employees if their employment with the city were terminated.

Required

1. Determine how these transactions should be meaningfully reported (if at all) in the city's balance sheet at 12/31/05. Make this determination independently of the chapter material (which may *not* necessarily be the best manner of reporting). Accordingly, do *not* refer to the material in the chapter.
2. Prepare a balance sheet at 12/31/05. (It may be helpful to record the transactions in T accounts for the more frequently used accounts, such as Cash and Accounts/Vouchers Payable, for ease in determining the ending balances.)
3. Consider how the increase in the city's net assets for the year should be reported in an operating statement that you deem meaningful. Again, do *not* refer to the material in the chapter to determine your answer.
4. Prepare an operating statement for the year ended 12/31/05. Compare the operating statement you developed with the one used by governmental units.

FAP 24-2 **The Social Security "Trust" Fund: Real or Imaginary—Will a Consolidated Perspective Reveal the Truth?** If FAP 1-1 was *not* assigned while covering Chapter 1, it can be assigned in this chapter instead.

chapter

25

Governmental Accounting: The Special-Purpose Funds and Special General Ledger

Deficit spending is simply a scheme for the "hidden" confiscation of wealth.

ALAN GREENSPAN, CHAIRMAN, FEDERAL RESERVE BOARD

LEARNING OBJECTIVES

To Understand

- When to record a transaction in one of the special funds.
- The way to account for transactions in the remaining funds.
- The financial statements to be included in the general-purpose financial statements for *external* reporting.
- The way to *convert* from the *fund-based statements* to the *government-wide statements* for *governmental activities*.

TOPIC OUTLINE

A: THE REMAINING FOUR *GOVERNMENTAL FUNDS*

I. *Special Revenue Funds* (the *second* of the five *governmental funds*)

II. *Capital Projects Funds* (the *third* of the five *governmental funds*)

III. *Debt Service Funds* (the *fourth* of the five *governmental funds*)

IV. Special Assessments (*Not* a Fund)

V. General Capital Assets and General Long-Term Liabilities (*Not* a Fund)

VI. *Permanent Funds* (the *fifth* of the five *governmental funds*)

B: THE PROPRIETARY FUNDS

VII. *Internal Service Funds*

VIII. *Enterprise Funds*

C: THE FIDUCIARY FUNDS

IX. *Agency Funds*

X. *Trust Funds* (Three Types)

D: FINANCIAL REPORTING TO THE PUBLIC: GENERAL-PURPOSE FINANCIAL STATEMENTS

XI. The Seven *Fund-Based* Financial Statements

XII. The Consolidation and *Conversion* Process for Preparing *Government-Wide* Financial Statements

XIII. The Two *Government-Wide* Financial Statements

CHAPTER OVERVIEW

In Chapter 24, we discussed the *General Fund*. In this chapter, we discuss (1) the remaining 10 types of funds, (2) general capital assets, (3) general long-term liabilities, and (4) the manner of preparing *government-wide financial statements*.

Certain governmental revenues, functions, or activities often must be accounted for in a designated fund separate from all others. In some situations, greater accounting control may be obtained by using a separate fund, even though it is *not* required by law. In most cases, the type of fund to be used to account for the specific revenues, functions, or activities is readily determinable. In a few instances, selecting the most appropriate type of fund requires greater scrutiny.

Certain transactions or events require entries in one or more funds. For example, the decision to build a new civic center to be financed by issuing general obligation bonds eventually results in entries being made in a *Capital Projects Fund*, a *Debt Service Fund*, the *General Fund* (in some cases), and the *GCA-GLTL g/l*.

A: THE REMAINING FOUR *GOVERNMENTAL* FUNDS

SECTION OVERVIEW

Recall from Chapter 24 that all *governmental funds* use (1) the *current financial resources measurement focus* and (2) the *modified accrual basis*. Also recall that the following financial statements are used—at the *fund-based* reporting level—for *governmental funds*:

1. A balance sheet.
2. A statement of revenues, expenditures, and changes in fund balances.

Recall further that the operating statement uses an *all-inclusive* format. At this point, we show how *special items*, *extraordinary items*, *and* certain *contributions* (items not addressed in Chapter 24) are reported in a governmental fund operating statement under this all-inclusive format. This format and the sequence required in the operating statement (using assumed amounts) are shown in Illustration 25-1 (we show the remaining line items that were *not* presented in Chapter 24).

ILLUSTRATION 25-1 FORMAT AND SEQUENCE OF THE OPERATING STATEMENT—ALL *GOVERNMENTAL FUNDS*

Statement of Revenues, Expenditures, and Change in Fund Balances

Revenues (shown in detail)	$811	
Total revenues		$ 811
Expenditures (shown in detail)	$800	
Total expenditures		$(800)
Excess (deficiency) of revenues over expenditures		**$ 11**
Other Financing sources and uses, including *transfers* (to be shown in detail)		(5)
Contributions (applies only to *permanent funds*)		4
Special items (unusual *or* infrequent, but *not* both)		2
Extraordinary items (unusual *and* infrequent)		(3)
Net Change in Fund Balance		**$ 9**
Fund Balance—*Beginning* of Year		391
Fund Balances—*End* of Year		**$ 400**

I. *Special Revenue Funds* (the *second* of the five *governmental funds*)

Special Revenue Funds account for the proceeds of **specific revenue sources that are *legally restricted* to expenditure for specified purposes.** *Special Revenue Funds* may be used for (1) small activities, such as the maintenance of a municipal swimming pool or (2) gigantic activities, such as operating a state highway system. Typically, its revenues are obtained primarily from tax and nontax **sources *not* directly related to services rendered or facilities provided for use.** In other words, revenues are *not* obtained primarily from *direct charges to the users* of the services or facilities (which is often an objective of *Enterprise Funds*).

The following activities could be accounted for in either *Special Revenue Funds* or *Enterprise Funds*, depending on the individual facts, circumstances, and operating policies: off-street parking facilities, transportation systems, turnpikes, golf courses, swimming pools, libraries, and auditoriums.

Special Revenue Funds may derive their revenues from one or several sources, commonly, (1) specified property tax levies, (2) state gasoline taxes, (3) licenses, (4) grants, and (5) shared taxes from other governmental units (including federal revenue sharing).

Unless legal provisions specify the contrary, *Special Revenue Funds* are accounted for using the same accounting principles, procedures, and financial statements shown for the *General Fund* in Chapter 24. Accordingly, we do *not* illustrate any journal entries for *Special Revenue Funds*.

Check Point

The operations of a public library receiving the majority of its support from property taxes levied for that purpose should be accounted for in which fund?

a. *General Fund*
b. *Special Revenue Fund*
c. *Enterprise Fund*
d. *Internal Service Fund*
e. None of the above

Answer: b

II. *Capital Projects Funds* (the *third* of the five *governmental funds*)

Capital Projects Funds account for **financial resources to be used for the acquisition or construction of *major* capital facilities** (other than those financed by proprietary funds and trust funds). Examples of major capital facilities are administration buildings, auditoriums, civic centers, and libraries. These funds do *not* account for the purchase of capital assets having comparatively limited lives, such as vehicles, machinery, and office equipment, which are normally budgeted for and acquired through the *General Fund* or a *Special Revenue Fund* and recorded as *expenditures* in those funds.

Capital Projects Funds (more than one can exist) **do *not* account for the capital assets acquired—only for the *construction* of the capital assets.** When construction is completed on a particular capital project, that *particular Capital Projects Fund* is discontinued. The capital assets constructed are accounted for in the *General Capital Assets and Long-Term Liabilities* general ledger (hereafter, the *GCA-GLTL g/l*), discussed later in this chapter. Furthermore, *Capital Projects Funds* do *not* account for the repayment and servicing of any debt obligations issued to raise money to finance the acquisition of capital facilities. Such debt and related servicing is accounted for in a *Debt Service Fund* (discussed shortly).

Recall that the *measurement focus* for *governmental funds* is *current financial resources*. Accordingly, the same two fund financial statements used for the *General Fund* are used for *Capital Projects Funds*. Likewise, the *modified accrual basis* is used.

Establishment and Operation

Capital Projects Funds are usually established on a project-by-project basis because legal requirements may vary from one project to another. (Some governmental units include capital budgets as part of their annual appropriated budget, in which case the annual capital budget is recorded in the general ledgers of the *various Capital Projects Funds*.) Most capital facilities are financed by issuing general obligation bonds, the liability for which is recorded in the *GCA-GLTL g/l* (as discussed in detail later). Often some portion of the cost is paid for with money obtained from the *General Fund* (or possibly a *Special Revenue Fund*), which interfund activity is reported as an **interfund transfer** (discussed in Chapter 24) by both funds (a **transfer in** the *Capital Projects Fund*). Federal and state grants are another major source of resources.

Contracted labor usually constructs major capital facilities. Because *encumbrance accounting procedures* alone are usually deemed sufficient for control purposes, recording the budgeted amounts in the general ledger is usually considered unnecessary. Construction costs incurred are charged to *expenditures*. At each year-end, *expenditures* are closed out to the Unreserved Fund Balance account, as are any inflow amounts recorded in accounts pertaining to bond proceeds and transfers in for the year. Each *Capital Project Fund* is terminated upon completion of the project for which it was created.

At the completion of the project, the cost of the facility is recorded as a capital asset in the *General Capital Assets and Long-Term Liabilities* general ledger. Until then, any costs incurred are shown as Construction in Progress in that general ledger. Thus the year-end closing entry in the *Capital Projects Fund* triggers the recording of an amount in the *GCA-GLTL g/l* equal to the *credit* to the Expenditures account.

Issuing Bonds at a *Premium*

Bond premiums (and discounts, discussed shortly) arise because of adjustments to the interest rate. The bond indenture agreements usually specify that any bond premium is to be set aside in the related *Debt Service Fund*. This is desirable because it removes the incentive to spend more on a project than is authorized merely by raising additional cash by *increasing* the *stated* interest rate. In the *Capital Projects Fund*, the proceeds of the bond offering—including the premium—are reported as Other Financing Sources—Bond Proceeds in the operating statement. The transfer of the premium to *the Debt Service Fund* is reported as a *transfer out* in the *Capital Projects Fund* and a *transfer in* in the *Debt Service Fund*. Regardless of whether the bonds are issued at a premium (or a discount), the bond issue is recorded at its face amount in the *GCA-GLTL g/l* (as discussed more fully later).

Issuing Bonds at a *Discount*

Bond discounts are rare because the *stated* interest rate is usually set high enough so that no discount results. (Many governmental units are legally prohibited from issuing bonds at a discount.) If a discount does result, theoretically there should be a transfer from the related *Debt Service Fund* to the *Capital Projects Fund* to cover the shortfall. In practice, such a transfer may *not* be possible because money may *not* be available in the related *Debt Service Fund* or because of legal restraints. In such cases, the size of the project may be curtailed, or the shortage may be covered by an *interfund transfer* from the *General Fund*.

Investing Excess Cash Until Needed

All the money necessary to pay for the capital project is usually raised at or near the inception of the project, but contractors are paid as work progresses. Excess cash, therefore, may be temporarily invested in high-quality, interest-bearing securities. In such cases, the interest income on the investments is credited to *revenues* in the *Capital Projects Fund*. This inflow of resources may be (1) spent on the project or (2) *transferred* to the *related Debt Service Fund* (a *transfer out*), depending on legal requirements.

Disposing of Cash Remaining at the Completion Date

Any cash remaining at the completion date is disposed of in accordance with legal requirements. In most cases, the remaining cash is *transferred* to the related *Debt Service Fund* (a *transfer out*).

Paying for Cost Overruns

The source of additional money to pay for cost overruns is specified by legal requirements or operating policy. In most cases, an *interfund transfer* is made from the *General Fund* to pay for the cost overrun.

Comprehensive Illustration

Journal Entries and Financial Statements

Assume that Funn City established a *Capital Projects Fund* during the fiscal year ended June 30, 2006, to construct a new city hall. Assumed transactions pertaining to the establishment and operation of the fund, along with the related journal entries, follow:

1. **Fund establishment.** The new city hall is expected to cost $5,000,000. The city obtained a **capital grant** of $1,500,000 from the state government, of which $600,000 was contributed at the inception of the project. The remaining $900,000 is deemed to be *susceptible to accrual*. The *General Fund* contributes $500,000, of which $200,000 was contributed at the inception of the project.

Cash	600,000	
Grant Receivable from State Government	900,000	
Revenues.		1,500,000
To record amounts *received and due from* the state government.		
Cash	200,000	
Due from *General Fund*.	300,000	
Other Financing Sources—Transfers In		500,000
To record amounts received and due from the *General Fund*.		

2. **Bond sales.** The remaining $3,000,000 was obtained from the sale of general obligation bonds at 101. The bond indenture agreement requires any premium to be set aside in the related *Debt Service Fund*.

Cash	3,030,000	
Other Financing Sources—Bond Proceeds		3,030,000
To record the *sale* of general obligation bonds.		
Other Financing Uses—Transfers Out	30,000	
Cash		30,000
To *transfer* bond premium to *Debt Service Fund*.		

Recall that the bond liability must also be recorded in the *GCA-GLTL g/l*. *GAAFR* recommends making the entry at year-end in connection with the preparation of the *government-wide statements*. We illustrate this later.

3. **Construction-related activity.** A construction contract for $4,600,000 is authorized and signed. During the year ended June 30, 2006, *billings* of $2,700,000 were rendered, and *payments* totaling $2,200,000 were made.

ENCUMBRANCES	4,600,000	
BUDGETARY FUND BALANCE RESERVED FOR ENCUMBRANCES		4,600,000
To record encumbrance on construction contract.		

BUDGETARY FUND BALANCE RESERVED FOR ENCUMBRANCES	2,700,000	
ENCUMBRANCES		2,700,000
To *cancel* part of encumbrance for project contract with general contractor for completions to date.		

Expenditures	2,700,000	
Contracts Payable		2,700,000
To record *actual* expenditures to date on contract with general contractor for completions to date.		

Contracts Payable	2,200,000	
Cash		2,200,000
To record *payments* to contractor.		

In addition to the preceding construction contract, $390,000 was incurred for the services of architects and engineers. Of this amount, $310,000 was paid. (For simplicity, we assume that encumbrance accounting procedures were *not* used.)

Expenditures	390,000	
Vouchers Payable		390,000
To record fees for architects and engineers.		

Vouchers Payable	310,000	
Cash		310,000
To record *payment* of architect and engineering fees.		

4. **Closing entries.** The appropriate *closing entries* at June 30, 2006, are as follows:

Revenues	1,500,000	
Other Financing Sources—Bond Proceeds	3,030,000	
Other Financing Sources—Transfers In	500,000	
Expenditures ($2,700,000 + $390,000)		3,090,000
Other Financing Uses—Transfers Out		30,000
Unreserved Fund Balance		1,910,000
To close out *actual* revenues, other financing sources and uses, and expenditures into unreserved fund balance.		

BUDGETARY FUND BALANCE RESERVED FOR ENCUMBRANCES	1,900,000	
ENCUMBRANCES		1,900,000
To *close* encumbrances outstanding at year-end by reversing the entry that previously recorded them.		

Unreserved Fund Balance	1,900,000	
Fund Balance Reserved for Encumbrances		1,900,000
To record *actual* fund balance reserved account to indicate the portion of year-end balance segregated for expenditure upon contractor performance.		

In addition to the preceding closing entries, both the partially completed capital facility and the $3,000,000 bond liability must be reflected in the *GCA-GLTL g/l* at June 30, 2006. These accounts are discussed in detail later in the chapter. For now, you should know that the following entry would be made in the *GCA-GLTL g/l:*

Construction in Progress	3,090,000	
Bond Payable (at *face value*)		3,000,000
Net Assets Invested in Capital Assets, Net of Related Debt		90,000
To record city hall construction in progress.		

Fund-Based Financial Statements

The *fund-based* financial statements that would be prepared for the fiscal year ended June 30, 2006, as a result of the preceding journal entries are shown in Illustrations 25-2 and 25-3.

Completion of Project in Following Year

Assume that the project is completed in the following fiscal year. The journal entries made during the fiscal year ended June 30, 2007, follow.

1. **Reestablishment of budgetary control over outstanding encumbrances.** Budgetary control must be reestablished over outstanding encumbrances on July 1, 2006. This is done by *reversing* the prior year-end closing entries related to encumbrances.

ENCUMBRANCES	1,900,000	
BUDGETARY FUND BALANCE RESERVED FOR ENCUMBRANCES		1,900,000
To *reestablish* budgetary control on remainder of construction contract.		
Fund Balance Reserved for Encumbrances	1,900,000	
Unreserved Fund Balance		1,900,000
To reverse *appropriation* of fund balance made at 6/30/06 relating to *encumbrances* outstanding at 6/30/06, which will be honored during the current year.		

ILLUSTRATION 25-2 CAPITAL PROJECTS FUND—BALANCE SHEET

Funn City
Capital Projects Fund—City Hall
Balance Sheet
June 30, 2006

Assets	
Cash	$ 1,290,000
Grant receivable	900,000
Due from *General Fund*.	300,000
Total Assets	**$2,490,000**
Liabilities and Fund Balance	
Vouchers payable	$ 80,000
Contracts payable	500,000
Total Liabilities.	**$ 580,000**
Fund Balance:	
Reserved for encumbrances	$ 1,900,000
Unreserved	10,000
Total Fund Balance	**$1,910,000**
Total Liabilities and Fund Balance	**$2,490,000**

ILLUSTRATION 25-3 CAPITAL PROJECTS FUND—OPERATING STATEMENT

Funn City
Capital Projects Fund—City Hall
Statement of Revenues, Expenditures, and Changes in Fund Balance
For the Fiscal Year Ended June 30, 2006

Revenues	
Intergovernmental—state grant	$ 1,500,000
Expenditures	
Capital outlay	(3,090,000)
Revenues *under* Expenditures	**$(1,590,000)**
Other Financing Sources (Uses)	
Proceeds of general obligation bonds	$ 3,030,000
Transfer In from *General Fund*	500,000
Transfer Out to *Debt Service Fund*	(30,000)
Total Other Financing Sources (Uses)	$ 3,500,000
Excess of Revenues and Other Sources over Expenditures and Other Uses	**$ 1,910,000**
Fund Balance, July 1, 2005	-0-
Fund Balance, June 30, 2006	**$ 1,910,000**

2. **Cash receipts.** All receivables were collected.

Cash	900,000	
Grant Receivable		900,000
To record *collection* of grant receivable.		
Cash	300,000	
Due from *General Fund*		300,000
To record *collection* of amounts received from the *General Fund*.		

3. **Construction-related activity.** The contractor submitted bills for the remainder of the contract. Additional engineering services totaled $6,000. All liabilities were paid.

BUDGETARY FUND BALANCE RESERVED FOR ENCUMBRANCES	1,900,000	
ENCUMBRANCES		1,900,000
To *cancel* remainder of encumbrance for project contract with general contractor upon completion of contract.		
Expenditures	1,900,000	
Contracts Payable		1,900,000
To record *expenditures* relating to billings on remainder of contract.		
Contracts Payable	2,400,000	
Cash		2,400,000
To record *payments* to contractor.		
Expenditures	6,000	
Vouchers Payable		6,000
To record fees for engineering services.		

Vouchers Payable	86,000	
Cash		86,000
To record *payment* of engineering fees. ($6,000 + $80,000 owed at 6/30/06.)		

4. **Disposition of remaining cash.** After payment of all liabilities, $4,000 of remaining cash was transferred to the *Debt Service Fund.*

Transfers Out	4,000	
Cash		4,000
To record transfer of remaining cash to *Debt Service Fund.*		

5. **Closing entry.** The appropriate closing entry at June 30, 2007, follows:

Unreserved Fund Balance	1,910,000	
Expenditures		1,906,000
Transfers Out		4,000
To *close* expenditures and transfers out into Unreserved Fund Balance.		

In addition to the preceding closing entry, the fully completed capital facility would be reflected in the *GCA-GLTL g/l* at June 30, 2007, as a result of the following entry in these accounts:

Buildings	4,996,000	
Construction in Progress		3,090,000
Net Assets Invested in Capital Assets, Net of Related Debt		1,906,000
To record completed city hall in the *GCA-GLTL g/l.*		

Fund-Based Financial Statements for Year Ended June 30, 2007

Because all liabilities were paid by June 30, 2007, and no assets remained, a balance sheet at June 30, 2007, is unnecessary. The *fund-based* operating statement for the year ended June 30, 2007 is shown in Illustration 25-4.

CHECK POINT

The proceeds of a federal grant to help finance the future construction of an adult training center should be recorded in which fund?

a. *General Fund*
b. *Special Revenue Fund*

ILLUSTRATION 25-4 CAPITAL PROJECTS FUND—OPERATING STATEMENT

Funn City
Capital Projects Fund—City Hall
Statement of Revenues, Expenditures, and Changes in Fund Balance
For the Fiscal Year Ended June 30, 2007

Revenues	$ -0-
Expenditures:	
Capital outlay	(1,906,000)
Excess of Expenditures *over* Revenues	**$(1,906,000)**
Fund Balance, 7/1/06	**1,910,000**
Transfer out to *Debt Service Fund*	(4,000)
Fund Balance, 6/30/07	**$ -0-**

c. *Capital Projects Fund*
d. *Permanent Fund*
e. None of the above

Answer: c

III. *Debt Service Funds* (THE *FOURTH* OF THE FIVE *GOVERNMENTAL FUNDS*)

For discussion purposes, *long-term borrowings* of governmental units may be categorized as follows:

1. **Revenue bonds.** Revenue bonds are issued to finance the establishment or expansion of activities accounted for in *Enterprise Funds*. These bonds are shown as liabilities of the *Enterprise Funds* because their repayment and servicing can come only from money generated from the operations of those funds.
2. **General obligation bonds serviced from *Enterprise Funds*.** General obligation bonds also are issued to finance establishment or expansion of activities accounted for in *Enterprise Funds*. They bear the full faith and credit of the governmental unit. When such bonds are to be repaid and serviced from money generated from the operations of an *Enterprise Fund*, the bonds should be shown as liabilities of the *Enterprise Fund* and as a contingent liability of the governmental unit.
3. **All other long-term borrowings (both bonds and notes).** All long-term borrowing *not* fitting into one of the two preceding categories is (1) classified as *general long-term debt* and (2) recorded as a liability in the *GCA-GLTL g/l*. (Later, we discuss other types of long-term liabilities [*compensated absences*, *claims and judgments*, and *capital lease liabilities*] that are also classified and recorded in this manner.)

Debt Service Funds are created to service debt that (1) arose from *long-term borrowings* and (2) is recorded as a liability in the *GCA-GLTL g/l*. *Debt Service Funds* account for (1) the *matured portion* of and the payment of *principal* on such long-term debt and (2) interest that is *currently due* and the payment thereof on the *entire* unpaid balance of the debt. Although notes payable occasionally are encountered, substantially all long-term *borrowings* of governmental units consist of one of the following two major types of *bonds*:

1. **Term bonds'** principal is repaid in a lump sum at the bonds' maturity date. Such a lump-sum payment is usually made possible by accumulating money in *the Debt Service Fund* on an actuarial basis over the life of the bond issue ("sinking fund"). Term bonds are less prevalent than they once were.
2. The principal of **serial bonds** is repaid at various predetermined dates over the life of the issue. **Regular** serial bonds are repaid in equal annual installments. **Deferred serial bonds** also are repaid in equal annual installments, but the first serial payment is delayed a specified number of years. **Irregular serial bonds** are repaid in other than equal principal repayments.

On the date that a principal payment relating to GLTD is to be made, a liability is established in the *Debt Service Fund* for the amount of the payment. Simultaneously, the amount of the debt as recorded in the *GCA-GLTL g/l* is reduced by a like amount. Thus the liabilities are transferred **at the maturity dates** to a *Debt Service Fund* for their liquidation.

An Unusual Feature

The only unusual feature of *Debt Service Funds* is the method of accounting for interest on the general long-term liabilities. **Interest is *not* reflected as a liability in the *Debt Service Fund* until the date it is due and payable.** This use of the cash basis of accounting is the major exception to the accrual of expenditures in the period to which they relate. As a result, interest for the period from the last payment date to the end of the fiscal year is *not* reflected as a liability at the end of the fiscal year. This is so because governmental units generally budget for interest on the *cash basis* instead of the *accrual basis*.

Debt Service Funds use the *current financial resources measurement focus* and the *modified accrual basis*. The two *fund* financial statements used for the *General Fund* are also used for *Debt Service Funds*.

Establishment and Operation

The legal provisions of a specific debt issue may require the establishment of a separate *Debt Service Fund* solely for that debt issue. In other cases, several debt issues may be accounted for using a single *Debt Service Fund*. Recording budgeted amounts in the general ledger is *not* necessary in those *Debt Service Funds* in which the amounts required to be received and expended are set forth in bond indentures or sinking fund provisions and in which few transactions occur each year. *Encumbrance accounting* is *not* appropriate because contracts are not entered into and purchase orders are not issued.

Sources of Revenues

Debt Service Funds may obtain their revenues from one or several sources. The most common source is *property taxes*. In such cases, a separate rate is levied for each bond issue or group of bond issues; the revenues are recognized on the *modified accrual basis*. (The accounting procedures are identical to those used by the *General Fund* in accounting for *property taxes*.) Revenues obtained from such sources as *shared sales taxes* are recorded when the *eligibility requirements* are met. When money is to be transferred from the *General Fund*, a receivable from the *General Fund* may be recorded at the start of the fiscal year for the amount authorized to be transferred to the *Debt Service Fund*.

Recall from Chapter 24 that *interfund transfers* are reported in the "other financing sources and uses" section of the operating statement at the *fund-based* reporting level for *governmental funds*. Accordingly, a transfer from the *General Fund* would result in (1) the *General Fund* debiting Other Financing Uses—Transfers Out and (2) *the Debt Service Fund* crediting Other Financing Sources—Transfers In. Payments made for principal and interest are recorded as expenditures.

Governmental units commonly use designated fiscal agents to make the payments to the bondholders. In such cases, money is transferred from *the Debt Service Funds* to the fiscal agents, who submit reports and canceled coupons (if used) to the governmental unit. The fee charged for such services is recorded as an expenditure of the *Debt Service Fund*.

The operation of *Debt Service Funds* pertaining to issues of *regular serial bonds* essentially involves collecting revenues and transferring monies to the fiscal agent. Significant accumulations of money requiring investment do *not* occur. In these cases, the journal entries to record the revenues, the expenditures, and the closing of the books parallel those used in the *General Fund*. Accordingly, an illustration of journal entries and financial statements for this type of *Debt Service Fund* is not presented.

The operation of *Debt Service Funds* is more complex *when deferred serial bonds* and *term bonds* are involved. Accumulated money must be invested, and bond premiums and discounts may exist on such investments. Actuarial computations are used to determine additions and earnings. The journal entries and financial statements for a *Debt Service Fund* pertaining to term bonds are illustrated in the following section.

Comprehensive Illustration

Journal Entries and Financial Statements: *Term* Bonds

Assume that Funn City established a *Debt Service Fund* on October 1, 2005, for an 8%, $400,000 general obligation bond issue due in 20 years (the proceeds of which will be used to construct a new civic center). Interest is to be paid *semiannually* on March 31 and September 30. We assume that all required additions to the fund will come from the *General Fund* and a specific tax levy. Assumed transactions pertaining to the operation of the fund for the fiscal year ended June 30, 2006, along with related journal entries, follow:

Transaction or Event	Journal Entry		
The required fund transfer from the *General Fund* is recorded on 10/1/05.	Due from *General Fund*	5,000	
	Other Financing Sources—Transfer In		5,000
The required fund transfer is received from the General Fund.	Cash	5,000	
	Due from *General Fund*		5,000
Property taxes are levied.[a]	Property Tax Receivables	23,000	
	Allowance for Uncollectibles		1,000
	Revenues		22,000
Property taxes are collected.[b]	Cash	20,000	
	Property Tax Receivables		20,000
An investment of $8,500 is made.	Investment	8,500	
	Cash		8,500
Cash is transferred to the fiscal agent for the 3/31/06 interest payment.	Cash with Fiscal Agent	16,000	
	Cash		16,000
Interest of $16,000 and the fiscal agent's fee of $100 is charged as an expenditure on the interest due date of 3/31/06.	Expenditures	16,100	
	Interest Payable		16,000
	Accrued Liability		100
Interest is paid by the fiscal agent, and the fiscal agent's fee is paid.	Interest Payable	16,000	
	Accrued Liability	100	
	Cash with Fiscal Agent		16,000
	Cash		100
Interest earned on investments is accrued at 6/30/06.	Interest Receivable	500	
	Revenues		500
The fiscal year-end closing entry is made.	Other Financing Sources—Transfer In	5,000	
	Revenues	22,500	
	Expenditures		16,100
	Fund Balance Reserved for Debt Service		11,400

[a] For simplicity, we (1) credit *Revenues* initially rather than *Deferred Revenues* and (2) assume that the entire carrying value at year-end will be collected within 60 days.

[b] For simplicity, we ignore the establishment of delinquent accounts at year-end.

Financial Statements

The *fund-based* financial statements that would be prepared for the fiscal year ended June 30, 2006, as a result of the preceding journal entries are shown in Illustrations 25-5 and 25-6.

The following points are important to understand the financial statements:

1. A liability for *interest* for the period April 1, 2006, through June 30, 2006, is *not* reflected in the balance sheet at June 30, 2006, in accordance with *the modified accrual basis*. This interest will be shown as an *expenditure* in the following year when the September 30, 2006, interest payment is due and payable.
2. If all required additions are made on time and earnings on investments earn the rate assumed in the actuarial calculations, $400,000 will be accumulated in the *Debt Service Fund* by the maturity date of the bonds (19 1/4 years from June 30, 2006).
3. At the maturity date of the bonds, the entire $400,000 is recorded as a liability in the *Debt Service Fund* by *debiting* the Expenditures account and *crediting* Bonds Payable. Simultaneously, this debt is removed from the *GCA-GLTL g/l.*
4. Making all required additions and earning interest at rates at least equal to the actuarially assumed interest rate is critical to the accumulation of the $400,000 required to redeem the bonds. If a *lower* interest rate is actually earned, additional money must be contributed to the fund to

ILLUSTRATION 25-5 DEBT SERVICE FUND—BALANCE SHEET

Funn City
***Debt Service Fund*—Civic Center**
Balance Sheet
June 30, 2006

Assets	
Cash	$ 400
Property tax receivables	3,000
Less: Allowance for uncollectible taxes	(1,000)
Investments	8,500
Interest receivable	500
Total Assets	**$11,400**
Fund Balance	
Fund balance reserved for debt service	**$11,400**[a]

[a] The actuarial requirement at 6/30/06 is $10,200.

ILLUSTRATION 25-6 DEBT SERVICE FUND—OPERATING STATEMENT

Funn City
***Debt Service Fund*—Civic Center**
Statement of Revenues, Expenditures, and Changes in Fund Balance
For the Fiscal Year Ended June 30, 2006

Revenues	
Property taxes	$ 22,000
Interest on investments	500
Total Revenues	$ 22,500
Expenditures	
Interest on bonds	$ 16,000
Fiscal agent's fees	100
Total Expenditures	$ 16,100
Revenues *over* Expenditures	**$ 6,400**
Other Financing Sources	
Transfer In from *General Fund*	5,000
Excess of Revenues and Other Sources over Expenditures	**$11,400**[a]
Fund Balance, 7/1/05	-0-
Fund Balance, 6/30/06	**$11,400**

[a] The actuarial requirement for the year was $9,300.

make up the shortage. To the extent that earnings *exceed* the actuarially assumed rate, future contributions may be *reduced* accordingly.

5. The following essential disclosures for *Debt Service Funds* pertain to term bonds: (a) the actuarially computed amount that should exist in the Fund Balance account as of the statement of financial position date and (b) the actuarially computed amount of earnings that should have been earned during the current fiscal year.

IV. SPECIAL ASSESSMENTS (*NOT* A FUND)

Some government activities involve constructing **public improvements that benefit a specific geographical area rather than the community as a whole.** The most common examples are residential streets, sidewalks, street lighting, and sewer lines. In these cases, governmental units usually charge all or most of the costs of the improvements directly to the owners of the properties benefited. In most cases, money is collected from the appropriate property owners in installments over a period of years. In some cases, the *General Fund* contributes monies for part of the improvements. Such transfers are operating transfers.

Although construction may be started after all the necessary money has been collected, it is more common to (1) borrow money (usually by issuing bonds), (2) use the borrowed funds to pay for the improvements, (3) collect money in installments from property owners in succeeding years, and (4) use the collected money to make principal and interest payments on the borrowings. In these cases, the borrowings are generally serial bonds, which may be *either special assessment bonds* or *general obligation bonds*. The *former* may be repaid only from assessments made against the applicable properties benefited, whereas the *latter* bear the full faith and credit of the governmental unit. To pay for the interest on outstanding bonds, the assessment payers are charged interest in installments.

Manner of Accounting

The accounting for special assessments is set forth by GASB *Statement No.* 6, "Accounting and Financial Reporting for Special Assessments." *GAS 6* requires that special assessments be accounted for in one or more of the existing funds and the *GCA-GLTL g/l*.

Construction Activity

Under *GAS 6*, all construction activity is accounted for and reported as any other capital improvement—**in a Capital Projects Fund.** No illustrations of entries are provided here because they would be identical to those shown earlier for *Capital Projects Funds*. The capital improvements (depending on their nature) may have to be reported in the *GCA-GLTL g/l*.

Financing Activity: The Critical Determinant Is the Government's Obligation to Assume the Debt

The manner of accounting for Special Assessment Receivables from the property owners and the Special Assessment Bonds depends on whether the governmental unit is "obligated in some manner" to make good the repayment of the special assessment bonds in the event of default by the assessed property owners. According to *GAS* 6,

> The phrase obligated in some manner as used in this Statement is intended to include all situations other than those in which (a) the government is prohibited (by constitution, charter, statute, ordinance, or contract) from assuming the debt in the event of default by the property owner or (b) the government is not legally liable for assuming the debt and makes no statement, or gives no indication, that it will, or may, honor the debt in the event of default.[1]

In the vast majority of cases, the governmental unit is obligated in some manner. We discuss these situations in the following paragraphs. In the section on *Agency Funds* later in the chapter, we discuss the situation in which the governmental unit is not obligated in any manner (and, consequently, the financing activity must be accounted for in an *Agency Fund*).

[1] Governmental Accounting Standards Board, *GAS* 6, "Accounting and Financial Reporting for Special Assessments" (Norwalk, CT: Governmental Accounting Standards Board), para. 19. Copyright by Financial Accounting Foundation. Reprinted with permission.

When the Government *Is* Obligated in Some Manner

In situations in which the governmental unit *is* obligated in some manner, *GAS 6* requires that a *Debt Service Fund* be used to account for (1) the servicing of any Special Assessment debt and (2) the collection of Special Assessment Receivables. The Special Assessment debt is initially recorded in the *GCA-GLTL g/l.* To the extent that such debt is to be repaid from Special Assessment Receivables, a special classification, Special Assessment Debt with Governmental Commitment, is to be used in the *GCA-GLTL g/l.* Other than this special designation, accounting and reporting for this debt are the same as for general obligation debt recorded in the *GCA-GLTL g/l* and serviced through a *Debt Service Fund.*

The accounting procedures for Special Assessment Receivables in *a Debt Service Fund* are nearly the same as for other property tax receivables accounted for in *Debt Service Funds* (illustrated earlier). **The one significant difference is that the deferred portion of the assessment cannot be recognized as revenues until later periods because the amounts are *not* "available to pay current period liabilities"** (the revenue-recognition criteria discussed in Chapter 24). To illustrate, assume that a street lighting project has an estimated cost of $500,000. On July 1, 2005, certain property owners are assessed $500,000 to be collected in *five* equal installments of $100,000 per year beginning April 1, 2006. Interest at 12% is to be charged on the deferred portion of the assessment ($400,000). Also on July 1, 2005, special assessment bonds having a face value of $500,000 are issued at par, with interest at 8% to be paid annually. The entries pertaining to the assessment (but not the bonds) for the years ended June 30, 2006, and June 30, 2007, follow.

For the year ended June 30, 2006:

Special Assessment Receivables—Current	100,000	
Special Assessment Receivables—Deferred	400,000	
Revenues		100,000
Deferred Revenues		400,000
To record levy of assessments on 7/1/05.		
Cash	100,000[a]	
Special Assessment Receivables—Current		100,000
To record collection of current assessment receivables due on 4/1/06.		

[a] These proceeds would be used to retire a portion of the special assessment bonds.

For the year ended June 30, 2007:

Special Assessment Receivables—Current	100,000	
Special Assessment Receivables—Deferred		100,000
To reflect the current portion at 7/1/06.		
Deferred Revenues.	100,000	
Revenues		100,000
To recognize revenues.		
Cash	148,000[a]	
Special Assessment Receivables—Current		100,000
Revenues		48,000
To record collection of current assessment receivables due on 4/1/07 along with interest of $48,000 ($400,000 × 12%).		

[a] These proceeds would be used to retire a portion of the special assessment bonds and pay related interest.

Manner of Recording Interest

Recall from the discussion of *Debt Service Funds* that (1) they are used to service debt recorded in the *GCA-GLTL g/l* and (2) interest is recognized *when due* rather than in the period to which the interest relates. Because of this manner of accounting for interest, *GAS 6* allows interest on Special Assessment Receivables to be recognized *when due* because the amounts usually offset each other approximately. If the amounts do *not*, interest is to be recognized in the period to which it relates.

Service-Type Special Assessments

Governmental units provide many routine services that are financed from general revenues, such as street cleaning and snow plowing. Sometimes these services are provided at more frequent intervals or provided outside the normal service area. In these cases, the affected property owners may be assessed for the *incremental* services. Under *GAS 6*, such assessment revenues and the related expenditures (expenses) for which the assessments were levied are to be accounted for and reported

> in the fund type that best reflects the nature of the transactions, usually the *General Fund*, a *Special Revenue Fund*, or an *Enterprise Fund*, giving consideration to the "number of funds" principle. . . .[2]

CHECK POINT

Receipts from taxes levied in connection with a special assessment for sidewalk improvements (involving a bond issuance for which the governmental unit has guaranteed repayment) should be accounted for in which fund?

a. *Special Revenue Fund*
b. *General Fund*
c. *Internal Service Fund*
d. *Capital Projects Fund*
e. *Debt Service Fund*

Answer: e

V. GENERAL CAPITAL ASSETS AND GENERAL LONG-TERM LIABILITIES (*NOT* A FUND)

Recall from Chapter 24, that a special general ledger is used to record certain capital assets and certain long-term liabilities—the "*General Capital Assets* and *General Long-Term Liabilities*" general ledger (hereafter, the *GCA-GLTL g/l*). The difference between its assets and liabilities is recorded in the *Net* Assets account (reported in the financial statements in three subaccount categories). As mentioned in Chapter 24, the *GCA-GLTL g/l* only contains *"real"* accounts (*assets* and *liabilities*)—it does *not* contain any *"nominal"* accounts (*revenues* and *expenses*). Because the *GCA-GLTL g/l* is *not* a *fund*, it does *not* have cash as an asset and, therefore, *cannot* be used to record receipts and payments. The *GCA-GLTL g/l*'s amounts are only presented in the *government-wide* statements—which use the *economic resources measurement focus* and *accrual basis* (more on these statements shortly).

---

[2] *GAS* 6, par. 14.

General Capital Assets

The *GCA-GLTL g/l* accounts for a governmental unit's *capital assets* that are *not* properly reportable in (1) proprietary funds (*Internal Service Funds* and *Enterprise Funds*) or *(2) Trust Funds*. Such assets are called **"general capital assets."**

Accordingly, the *GCA-GLTL g/l* accounts for the following types of capital assets: Land, Land Improvements, Easements, Buildings, Building Improvements, Equipment, Vehicles, Machinery, Historical Treasures, Works of Art and Infrastructure (such as bridges, streets, and sewer systems), and all other tangible and intangible assets that are (1) used in operations and (2) have initial useful lives extending beyond a single reporting period.

Recall that because of the use of the *current financial resources measurement focus* in *governmental funds*, capital assets are *not* reported as *assets* in any of the governmental funds.

Also recall that *depreciation expense* is *not* reported in the *operating statements* of any of the governmental funds. Recall further that when capital assets are acquired by *a governmental fund* (typically a *Capital Projects Fund*, the *General Fund*, or a *Special Revenues Fund*), the *Expenditures* account is charged—*not* an asset account. To report the capital assets acquired by these *governmental funds*, it, therefore, is necessary to track and account for them *outside* the governmental funds.

CHECK POINT

A new fire truck was purchased out of a city's *General Fund*. An entry is also required in which of the following?

a. *Permanent Fund*
b. *Capital Projects Fund*
c. *Special Revenue Fund*
d. *GCA-GLTL g/l*
e. None of the above

Answer: d

Depreciating General Capital Assets

In the *government-wide* financial statements, general capital assets (other than land, land improvements, certain infrastructure assets, and works of art and historical treasures that are inexhaustible) must be depreciated over their estimated useful lives in a systematic and rationale manner.

Infrastructure Assets—The "Modified Approach"

If *two* conditions exist, infrastructure assets that are part of a "*network*" (assets that *provide a particular type of service*, such as all of a government's highways and roads) or a "*subsystem of a network*" (assets that make up a similar portion or segment of a network of assets, for example, both highways and roads could each be considered a subsystem of the network of highways and roads) *need not* be depreciated. The two conditions are:

1. Use of an asset management system that has three specific characteristics: (a) maintaining an up-to-date inventory of eligible infrastructure assets, (b) performing condition assessments *at least every three years* (either internally or by contract), (c) and estimating yearly the annual amount needed to maintain and preserve the eligible infrastructure assets at the condition level established and disclosed by the government.
2. Documentation that the eligible infrastructure assets are being preserved approximately at (or above) the condition level established and disclosed.

CHECK POINT

A city sells an unused fire station previously accounted for in its *GCA-GLTL g/l*. An entry is also required in which of the following?

a. *General Fund*
b. *Special Revenue Fund*
c. *Trust Fund*
d. *Debt Service Fund*
e. None of the above

Answer: a

General Long-Term Liabilities

The *GCA-GLTL g/l* also accounts for a governmental unit's liabilities that (1) have **a maturity date of *more than one year* at the time of their incurrence** and (2) are *not* properly reportable in (1) proprietary funds (*Internal Service Funds* and *Enterprise Funds*) or *(2) Trust Funds*. Such debts are called **"general long-term liabilities."** They are reported in the *GCA-GLTL g/l* right up to their *maturity dates*, at which time the liabilities are transferred to either (1) the appropriate *Debt Service Fund* (if the liability arose from a *borrowing* [bonds and notes]) or (2) the *General Fund* (if the liability arose from other than a borrowing [compensated absences, claims, and judgments, and capitalized lease liabilities]. Thus because the liabilities are *not* removed from the *GCA-GLTL g/l* until their *maturity date*, the *GCA-GLTL g/l* includes the portion of long-term liabilities that is *due and payable in the coming fiscal year*. Thus it has both the *current* and the *long-term* portions.

General long-term liabilities are *not* reported in any of the *fund-based* financial statements pertaining to *governmental activities*. They are reported, however, in the *government-wide* financial statements. Later in the chapter, we show the procedures used to include these liabilities in preparing the *government-wide* financial statements for *governmental activities*.

Consolidating the *GCA-GLTL g/l* Amounts

Later in the chapter, we show the consolidation worksheet procedures used to include the *general capital assets* and *general long-term liabilities* in the *government-wide* financial statements for *governmental activities*. These procedures involve both a *consolidation* process and a *conversion* process (converting the governmental fund *fund-based statements* to reflect (1) the *economic resources measurement focus* and (2) the *accrual basis*).

Making Entries in the *GCA-GLTL g/l*

As to record-keeping for the *GCA-GLTL g/l*, *GAAFR* illustrates a procedure in which the general ledger balances are updated **at each year-end** in connection with this consolidation/ conversion process. Accordingly, this is the procedure we later illustrate.

CHECK POINT

A transaction in which a city issues *general obligation serial bonds* to finance the construction of a fire station requires accounting recognition in which of the following?

a. *General Fund*
b. *Capital Projects Fund* and *General Fund*
c. *Capital Projects Fund* and the *GCA-GLTL g/l*
d. *General Fund* and the *GCA-GLTL g/l*
e. None of the above

Answer: c

VI. *Permanent Funds* (The *Fifth* of the Five *Governmental Funds*)

Permanent Funds are for endowment-type situations. These funds are used to report resources that are legally restricted to the extent that only their earnings—*not* their principal—may be used for purposes that support the reporting government's programs—that is, for the **benefit of the reporting government or its citizenry**. (An example is a cemetery perpetual-care fund that provides income for the ongoing maintenance of a public cemetery.)

Unique Aspects

The only unique aspects of *Permanent Funds are as follows:*

1. *Endowment contributions* (both *permanent* and *temporary* endowments) are reported as "contributions" in the same section of the operating statement as (a) special items (unusual *or* infrequent items but *not* both), (b) extraordinary items (unusual *and* infrequent), and (c) interfund transfers. Thus endowment contributions are *not* reported as *revenues*.
2. *Temporary endowments* are reported in *Permanent Funds* right up until their expiration dates, at which time the resources are transferred to the appropriate fund (usually the *General Fund*), where they may be spent.
3. *Investment income* is usually the only revenue inflow.

As with all governmental funds, *Permanent Funds* (1) use the *current financial resources measurement focus* and (2) the *modified accrual basis*. Accordingly, they are required to present (1) a balance sheet and (2) a statement of revenues, expenditures, and changes in fund balances. Because of their simplicity, we do *not* illustrate any transactions or their financial statements.

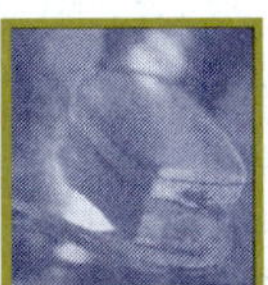

Check Point

A city received a temporary endowment. The cash received must be invested. Both the *income* and the *principal* must be used for street improvements. This transaction is recorded in which of the following?

a. *Capital Projects Fund*
b. *Private-Purpose Trust Fund*
c. *Permanent Fund*
d. *Investment Trust Fund*
e. None of the above

Answer: c

B: The Proprietary Funds

SECTION OVERVIEW

In this section, we discuss the two *proprietary types* of funds: *Internal Service Funds* and *Enterprise Funds*, the accounting for which parallels that used in the *private sector*. *Internal Service Funds* **provide services to *departments within a governmental unit*** (or to related governmental units). In contrast, *Enterprise Funds* **provide services primarily to the *general public*.**

Recall from Chapter 24 that *proprietary funds* use (1) the *economic resources measurement focus* and (2) the *accrual basis*. Recall also that the following financial statements are used—at both the *fund-based* reporting level and the *government-wide* reporting level:

1. A balance sheet (which includes *all* the fund's assets and liabilities).
2. A statement of revenues, expenses, and changes in net assets (or equity).
3. A statement of cash flows.

The Operating Statement

The operating statement uses an *all-inclusive* format. This format and the exact sequence required in the operating statement (using assumed amounts) are shown in Illustration 25-7.

The Balance Sheet

The only unique aspect of the balance sheet for proprietary funds is the categories used to describe the difference between assets and liabilities. Recall from Chapter 24 that *proprietary funds* use the following three ***accessibility-based*** categories in the net assets sections of their balance sheets—at *both* the *fund-based* and *government-wide* reporting levels:

Net Assets:
Invested in capital assets, net of related debt
Restricted for debt service
Unrestricted.

Assume that at December 31, 2005, a *proprietary fund* reported (1) capital assets of $800,000 and (2) debt of $600,000 that had been incurred to construct those capital assets. The difference of $200,000 is reported for the "Invested in Capital Assets, Net of Related Debt" category at year-end. Assume further that in 2006, (1) $40,000 of the debt was paid off and (2) the capital assets were depreciated by $7,000. At December 31, 2006, the "Invested in Capital Assets, Net of Related Debt" balance would be adjusted *upward* by $33,000 ($40,000 – $7,000), and the Unrestricted Net Assets balance would be adjusted *downward* by $40,000 (to reflect the decrease in cash).

ILLUSTRATION 25-7 FORMAT AND SEQUENCE OF OPERATING STATEMENT—ALL PROPRIETARY FUNDS

Statement of Revenues, Expenses, and Change in Fund Net Assets

Operating revenues (shown in detail)	$223	
Total operating revenues		$ 223
Operating expenses (shown in detail)	$200	
Total operating expenses		(200)
Operating income (loss)		**$ 23**
Nonoperating revenues and expenses (detailed)		
Investment earnings (for example)	$ 10	
Interest expense (for example)	(7)	3
Income before (describe items, listed below, if any)		**$ 26**
Capital contributions (grants, developers, and other)	$ 15	
Additions to *permanent* and *term* endowments	40	
Special items (unusual *or* infrequent, but *not* both)	–	
Extraordinary items (unusual *and* infrequent)	–	
Interfund transfers	(60)	(5)
Increase (decrease) in Net Assets		**$ 21**
Net Assets—*Beginning* of Year		119
Net Assets—*End* of Year		**$ 140**

VII. *Internal Service Funds*

Various departments of a governmental unit usually require common services. Each department may hire people to perform these services, or it may contract with outside vendors. It is usually cheaper, however, for the governmental unit to establish one or more separate operations to provide these services to its various departments. *Internal Service Funds* account for each of these separate operations in a manner that charges the total cost of an operation to the various user departments. *Internal Service Funds* commonly are established for motor pool operations, central purchasing and stores, maintenance services, printing and reproduction services, and data processing services.

The objective of an *Internal Service Fund* is to recover the total cost of an operation from billings to the various user departments. Generally, billings are set at levels intended to break even. (Any excess or deficiency is closed at year-end to fund's *Net Assets* account.) The accounting principles and procedures used in the *private sector* also lend themselves to use with *Internal Service Funds*, even though billings are *not* made to independent third parties. Accordingly, the *economic resources measurement focus* and the *accrual basis* are used.

Simply because all costs are recovered through billings, it does not automatically follow that the services are being provided at a lower cost than would be incurred if an *Internal Service Fund* were *not* used. This determination may be made only by comparing (1) the total cost incurred with (2) amounts that would have been incurred if the *Internal Service Fund* had *not* been established.

Establishment and Operation of *Internal Service Funds*

Internal Service Funds are normally established by money transferred from the *General Fund*. Recall from Chapter 24 that this type of interfund transaction is a *transfer*. Recall also from Chapter 24 that if an *interfund loan* is made by the *General Fund* (rather than a *transfer*), the *General Fund* records a receivable (Due from *Internal Service Fund*), and the *Internal Service Fund* records a liability (Due to *General Fund*). Cash is then used to purchase materials, parts, supplies, and equipment as needed to fulfill the fund's objectives.

A significant managerial accounting issue is that of developing a cost accounting system for charging the various user departments for the costs of the operation as reflected in the operating statement. When billings *exceed* costs, some or all of the excess may need to be transferred to the *General Fund*. When billings are *below* costs, the deficiency may be made up through (1) additional charges to the user departments or (2) a transfer from the *General Fund*. As explained shortly, however, any excess or deficiency is *eliminated* (via an allocation process) in preparing the *government-wide statements*.

Comprehensive Illustration

Journal Entries and Financial Statements

Assume that Funn City established a Central Printing and Reproduction Fund during the fiscal year ended June 30, 2006. Assumed transactions pertaining to the establishment and operation of the fund, along with related journal entries, follow:

1. **Establishment of the fund.** A transfer of $40,000 from the *General Fund* established the fund.

Cash	40,000	
Transfers In		40,000
To record transfer received from the *General Fund*.		

2. **Purchase and depreciation of equipment.** Equipment costing $30,000 was acquired on July 3, 2005. The equipment is assigned a 10-year life and no salvage value.

Equipment	30,000	
Vouchers Payable		30,000
To record purchase of equipment.		

Operating Expenses	3,000	
Accumulated Depreciation		3,000
To record depreciation expense.		

3. **Purchase and use of supplies inventory.** Supplies costing $65,000 were acquired. A physical inventory taken on June 30, 2006, was valued at $11,000.

Inventory of Supplies	65,000	
Vouchers Payable		65,000
To record purchase of supplies.		
Operating Expenses	54,000	
Inventory of Supplies		54,000
To record cost of supplies used.		

Note that inventories are accounted for in the same manner as in a private corporation.

4. **Incurrence of operating expenses and payment of liabilities.** Various operating expenses were incurred. Of these expenses, $7,000 represented charges from the city's electric utility (an *Enterprise Fund*).

Operating Expenses	67,000	
Vouchers Payable		60,000
Due to *Electric Utility Fund*		7,000
To record operating expenses.		
Vouchers Payable	138,000	
Due to *Electric Utility Fund*	5,000	
Cash		143,000
To record partial payment of liabilities.		

5. **Billings and collections.** Billings to the city's various departments totaled $125,000. Of this amount, $9,000 pertained to services performed for the city's electric utility, and $5,000 pertained to services performed for the city's central garage (an *Internal Service Fund*).

Due from *General Fund*	111,000	
Due from *Electric Utility Fund*	9,000	
Due from *Central Garage Fund*	5,000	
Operating Revenues		125,000
To record billing to departments for services rendered.		
Cash	110,000	
Due from *General Fund*		102,000
Due from *Electric Utility Fund*		5,000
Due from *Central Garage Fund*		3,000
To record partial collection of amounts due from other funds.		

Because closing entries are identical to those made in the *private sector*, they are *not* shown.

Financial Statements

The balance sheet and operating statement prepared for the fiscal year ended June 30, 2006, are shown in Illustrations 25-8 and 25-9.

Allocation Process Required in Preparing *Government-Wide Statements*

In preparing *government-wide financial statements* for the *governmental funds*, however, the *Internal Service Fund* financial statement amounts are "consolidated" with those of the *governmental*

ILLUSTRATION 25-8 INTERNAL SERVICE FUND—BALANCE SHEET

Funn City
Central Printing and Reproduction Fund
Balance Sheet
June 30, 2006

Assets	
Cash	$ 7,000
Due from *General Fund*	9,000
Due from Electric Utility Fund	4,000
Due from Central Garage Fund	2,000
Inventory of supplies	11,000
Equipment	30,000
Accumulated depreciation	(3,000)
Total Assets	**$60,000**
Liabilities and Net Assets	
Vouchers payable	$ 17,000
Due to Electric Utility Fund	2,000
Total Liabilities	**$19,000**
Net Assets—Unrestricted	**$41,000**
Total Liabilities and Net Assets	**$60,000**

ILLUSTRATION 25-9 INTERNAL SERVICE FUND—OPERATING STATEMENT

Funn City
Central Printing and Reproduction Fund
Statement of Revenues, Expenses, and Changes in Fund Net Assets
For the Year Ended June 30, 2006

Operating revenues:	
Charges for services	$125,000
Operating expenses:	
Supplies	$ 54,000
Salaries and wages	42,000
Lease expense	18,000
Utilities	7,000
Depreciation	3,000
Total operating expenses	$124,000
Operating income	**$ 1,000**
Transfers in from *General Fund*	40,000
Net Assets, 7/1/05	-0-
Net Assets, 6/30/06	**$ 41,000**

Note: A statement of cash flows would also be prepared.

funds (which they serve). Recall that in preparing the *government-wide statements* for *governmental funds*, a "conversion" is made to the *economic resources measurement focus* and the *accrual basis* (the same as that used for *Internal Service Funds*) as well.

When an operating income or loss is reported by an *Internal Service Fund* (the usual case), the profit or loss element must be eliminated in the consolidation process. Thus when an *operating loss* exists, the deficiency is allocated to user departments of the *governmental* funds (as though additional billings were made to cover the shortfall). When an *operating income* exists, the operating expenses of the user departments must be reduced (as though an adjustment was made for "overbilling"). We show this allocation process later when we illustrate the preparation of the *government-wide statements*.

CHECK POINT

A data processing center established by a governmental unit to service all agencies within the unit should be accounted for in which fund?

a. *Capital Projects Fund*
b. *Internal Service Fund*
c. *Agency Fund*
d. *Trust Fund*
e. *Enterprise Fund*

Answer: b

VIII. *ENTERPRISE FUNDS*

Enterprise Funds **must** be used when the full cost of providing services (including *depreciation expense* and *interest expense*) is to be recovered through fees and charges because of (1) legal requirements or (2) management policy. Otherwise, *Enterprise Funds* **may** be used to report **any activity for which a fee is charged to external users for goods or services**—regardless of whether the intent is to recover the cost of the goods or services provided. *Enterprise Funds* evaluate operations from a "profit-and-loss" perspective.

The most common type of activity accounted for in an *Enterprise Fund* is the *public utility* providing water services, electricity, or natural gas. Other activities commonly accounted for in *Enterprise Funds* are off-street parking facilities, recreational facilities (principally golf courses and swimming pools), airports, hospitals, and public transit systems. In practice, many activities are accounted for in *Enterprise Funds*, even though they come no where near recovering their costs (most common are public transit systems [some recover only 15%]).

Although evaluated from a profit-and-loss perspective, the activities accounted for in *Enterprise Funds* are *not* engaged in to maximize profits, as in *the private sector*. Instead, the intent is to raise sufficient revenues either to (1) recover costs to break even or (2) generate profits so that capital is effectively raised to finance expansion of operations.

Establishment and Expansion

Some of the more common ways to establish an operation to be accounted for as an *Enterprise Fund* or to expand the operations of an existing *Enterprise Fund* follow:

1. **Transfer from the *General Fund*.** Money transferred from the *General Fund* is reported as an interfund transfer. Accordingly, the *Enterprise Fund* debits the Cash account and credits the Transfers In account.
2. **Loan from the *General Fund*.** When the *General Fund* makes a loan, it debits the Due from *Enterprise Fund* account and credits the Cash account. The *Enterprise Fund* debits Cash and credits Due to *General Fund* (a liability account). If interest is paid on the loan, the *Enterprise Fund* has interest expense and the *General Fund* has interest revenue.
3. **Issuance of revenue bonds.** Revenue bonds are issued by an *Enterprise Fund* and are repayable, with interest, only from the earnings of the operations accounted for in the *Enterprise Fund*. (If the bonds also have a security interest in the fixed assets of the *Enterprise Fund*, they are called mortgage revenue bonds.) Revenue bonds require accounting entries only in the *Enterprise Fund*. Bond indenture agreements frequently restrict the use of bond proceeds to specific capital projects; therefore, the bond proceeds are deposited in a separate checking account called,

for example, Construction Cash. Using a separate account provides greater accounting control to ensure that the proceeds are spent only on authorized projects. The offsetting credit is to the Revenue Bonds Payable account.

4. **Issuance of general obligation bonds.** General obligation bonds are issued by a governmental unit with its full faith and backing. The proceeds are transferred to the *Enterprise Fund*, which uses the cash in accordance with the bond indenture agreement. General obligation bonds fall into the following two categories, based on the source of their repayment and payment of related interest:
   a. **Repayable from earnings of the enterprise.** When the governmental unit intends to repay the principal and related interest from *Enterprise Fund* earnings, the GASB *Codification* recommends that such debt be reflected as a liability in the *Enterprise Fund*.
   b. **Repayable from taxes and general revenues.** When the bonds and related interest are to be repaid from taxes and general revenues of the governmental unit, the bond liability is shown as a liability of the *GCA-GLTL g/l*. The *Enterprise Fund* treats the money received as an *interfund transfer* and credits the Transfers In account. Thus a liability is *not* reflected in the *Enterprise Fund*.

Unique Features of Financial Statements

Because the financial statements of *Enterprise Funds* are similar to those of private enterprises engaged in comparable activities, typical transactions, related journal entries, and a complete set of illustrative financial statements are *not* presented. Instead, we discuss the unique features of *Enterprise Fund* financial statements. (The balance sheet has certain unique classification features.)

1. **Restricted assets.** Assets restricted as to use are shown separately. The most common examples are these:
   a. **Construction cash.** Construction cash is not available for normal operating purposes, and it must be identified as usable only for its designated purpose—for example, plant expansion.
   b. **Customer deposits.** For public utilities that require their customers to make deposits to ensure payment of final statements, the deposits constitute restricted assets that are not available for normal operations. When such deposits are invested in allowable investments, the investments should also be shown as restricted assets.
   c. **Debt-related accumulations.** Some bond indenture agreements require that certain amounts of cash provided from operations be set aside in separate accounts for retiring and servicing bonds. In some cases, monies must be set aside to cover potential future losses.
2. **Appropriation of net assets.** When money relating to retiring debt and servicing bonds has been set aside pursuant to bond indenture agreements, it may be necessary to appropriate a portion of the net assets as being restricted for debt service. The appropriation indicates that a portion of the net assets is *not* available for normal operations, internal expansion, or cash transfers to the *General Fund*; that is, cash that might otherwise be used for such purposes has been set aside for other purposes. This practice differs from customary practice in the *private sector*, where showing the *restricted assets* separately is deemed sufficient disclosure.

   Technically, at any balance sheet date, the appropriation should equal only the amounts set aside to cover (a) future interest expense, (b) future principal payments (above and beyond amounts deemed to have been generated from operations to date), and (c) potential future losses.
3. **Depreciation expense.** For public utilities, depreciation expense is usually a major expense because of the large capital investment required. Depreciation expense is customarily shown on a separate line of the operating statement.
4. **Income taxes.** Because governmental units do *not* pay income taxes, no income tax expense is shown in the statement of revenues and expenses.
5. **Payments to the *General Fund*.** Payments to the *General Fund* in lieu of taxes are **services used** transactions, which were discussed in Chapter 24. Accordingly, such payments are recorded as *expenses* in the *Enterprise Fund* and as revenues in the *General Fund*. Payments to the *General Fund not* in lieu of taxes but to finance *General Fund* expenditures are *interfund transfers*.

6. ***Inverted* balance sheet format.** Some governmental utilities use an *inverted format* for their balance sheets. (Many state public utility commissions require the *inverted format*.) Under this presentation, capital assets, long-term debt, and net assets are shown *before* current items to emphasize the relative importance of the investment in fixed assets and the related financing sources. The *conventional format*, which places current items first, is still more prevalent, however, than the *inverted format*.

No need exists to illustrate transactions for an *Enterprise Fund* because they would be identical in nature to those illustrated for an *Internal Service Fund*. Accordingly, we do *not* present illustrative entries for typical transactions. Later in the chapter, however, we show a full set of *Enterprise Fund* financial statements in discussing the basic financial statements to be furnished for *external* financial reporting purposes. (See Illustrations 25-12, 13, and 14 on pages 876, 877, and 879.)

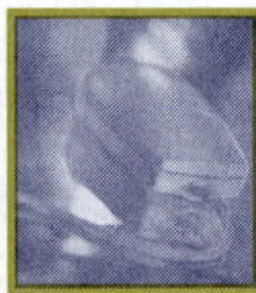

CHECK POINT

Recreational facilities run by a governmental unit and financed on a user-charge basis most likely would be accounted for in which fund?

a. *General Fund*
b. *Trust Fund*
c. *Enterprise Fund*
d. *Capital Projects Fund*
e. *Special Revenue Fund*

Answer: c

C: THE FIDUCIARY FUNDS

SECTION OVERVIEW

In this section, we discuss the four types of *fiduciary funds*. Trust Funds and *Agency Funds* are used to report assets that (1) are held in a trustee or agency *capacity for others and* (2) ***cannot* be used to support the government's own programs or activities** (any income on the assets benefits *others*). Thus these assets are *held* but *not* owned. Assets are deemed to be *held* if the government either (1) is performing investment functions or (2) has *significant* administrative involvement (beyond the mere remittance of predetermined amounts to a third party).

The four types of fiduciary funds and their functions are as follows:

1. ***Agency Funds***—Used for instance when **resources are held in a purely custodial capacity** (*assets* equals *liabilities*). Also, certain *special assessments* must be accounted for in *Agency Funds*, as discussed shortly. Typically involve only the receipt, temporary investment, and remittance of fiduciary resources to third parties (individuals, private organizations, or other governments).
2. **Pension (and other employee benefit) Trust Funds**—Used to account for employer and employee retirement *contributions*, the *investment* of such contributions, and the *payments* to retired employees. (*Most* governments have these.)
3. **Investment Trust Funds**—Used for situations in which the government (a) manages external investment pools on behalf of *other governments* or (b) holds individual investments or "investment accounts" on behalf of *other governments*. Thus a government's investments of *internal* cash *cannot* be accounted for in this trust fund. (*Few* governments have these—a discussion of them is beyond the scope of this text.)
4. ***Private*-Purpose Trust Funds**—Used for all trust arrangements *not* properly reported in *Pension Trust Funds* or *Investment Trust Funds*, under which both the *principal* and *income* benefit

third parties (individuals, private organizations, or other governments). The key factor is that an "**absence of a *public* purpose**" must exist.

Thus *endowments* received that benefit specified individuals are accounted for in private-purpose trust funds. Such funds usually do *not* have *capital assets*.

Recall from Chapter 24 that *fiduciary funds* use (1) the *economic resources measurement focus* and (2) the *accrual basis*. Recall also that the following financial statements are used at both the *fund-based* reporting level and the *government-wide* reporting level:

1. A statement of fiduciary net assets.
2. A statement of changes in fiduciary net assets (or equity).

IX. *Agency Funds*

Agency Funds act as conduits for the transfer of money. Thus they are **purely custodial in nature.** Money deposited with such a fund is generally disbursed shortly after receipt to authorized recipients, such as other governmental funds, other governmental units, and private corporations. Common examples of *Agency Funds* are tax collection funds and employee benefit funds.

1. **Tax collection funds.** When overlapping governmental units collect tax revenues from the same source, it is usually more practical and economical for only one of the governmental units to collect the taxes and then to distribute them to the various taxing authorities. Counties commonly collect all property taxes and then distribute amounts collected to the various cities, school districts, water districts, and any other special districts.
2. **Employee benefit funds.** When governmental employees have premiums for medical and dental insurance plans withheld from their paychecks, the withholdings are deposited in such funds. Periodically, the governmental unit makes a lump-sum payment from these funds to an insurance company. (The alternative to using employee benefit funds is to set up liabilities in the appropriate funds.)

Agency Funds have no unusual operating characteristics or unique accounting issues. Usually, cash is the only asset, which is completely offset by liabilities to the authorized recipients. Thus the Net Assets category does *not* exist. Because cash disbursements are made frequently, on many occasions throughout the year these funds have no assets or liabilities at all. *Agency Funds* do *not* report operations. Thus they are presented in only one financial statement—the statement of fiduciary net assets.

In light of their simplicity, we do *not* illustrate transactions for *Agency Funds* beyond the journal entries shown in the following discussion of special assessment debt for which the governmental unit is *not* obligated in any manner.

Special Assessment Debt for Which the Government Is *Not* Obligated in Any Manner

If the governmental unit is *not* obligated in any manner to pay off special assessment debt in the event of a default by the property owners, *Agency Fund* must be used to account for both (1) the collection activity pertaining to the special assessment receivables and (2) the debt service activity pertaining to the special assessment debt. The rationale is that the governmental unit is acting merely as an agent for the assessed property owners and the debtholders. Accordingly, the special assessment debt is *not* reflected as a liability in the financial statements of the governmental unit. Nor is the special assessment levy accrued as a receivable in the governmental unit's financial statements. Only the cash collections of the levy and the disbursement of this money to the debtholders are recorded in the *Agency Fund*.

To illustrate, the entries related to the collection of the first annual installment of $100,000 due April 1, 2006, from the property owners (the same information used earlier in the chapter in the discussion and illustration of special assessments) are as follows:

Cash	100,000	
Due to Special Assessment Bondholders		100,000
To record collection of first annual installment from property owners.		

Due to Special Assessment Bondholders	100,000	
Cash		100,000
To distribute money to bondholders.		

Because the bonds are *not* reported as a liability in the governmental unit's financial statements, *GAS 6* requires that the source of funds in the *Capital Projects Funds* be identified by a description such as "contribution from property owners"—*not* as "bond proceeds." Later in the chapter (in Illustration 25-15 on page 880), we present a statement of fiduciary net assets for an *Agency Fund* in discussing the basic financial statements presented for *external* financial reporting purposes. (Recall that *Agency Funds* do *not* have an *operating statement*.)

CHECK POINT

A city collects property taxes for the local sanitary, park, and school districts and periodically remits collections to these units. This activity should be accounted for in which fund?

a. *Agency Fund*
b. *General Fund*
c. *Internal Service Fund*
d. *Special Revenue Fund*
e. *Trust Fund*

Answer: a

X. TRUST FUNDS (THREE TYPES)

Most Trust Funds involve investing and using money in accordance with stipulated provisions of trust indenture agreements or statutes.

Pension (and Other Employee Benefit) Trust Funds

Public employee pension and retirement trust funds have the same operation characteristics and accounting issues as *private* pension and retirement plans that are funded with a trustee. Accordingly, journal entries for typical transactions are *not* illustrated. As mentioned in Chapter 24, a major shortcoming of many pension trust funds is the lack of a sound actuarial basis in accounting for contributions to meet retirement payments. Later in the chapter (in Illustration 25-15 on page 880), we present the financial statements of a pension trust fund in discussing the basic financial statements presented for *external* financial reporting purposes.

Private-Purpose Trust Funds

The key factor for using this trust fund is that an "absence of a *public* purpose" must exist—*not* that of a substantial *private* benefit occurring. Accordingly, it is appropriate to account for *some types of endowments* in this trust fund.

Most Private-Purpose Trust Funds have investments as their largest asset. Recall from Chapter 24 that (1) all investments are valued at their *fair value* and (2) all unrealized gains and losses are recognized *currently* in the operating statement.

Later in the chapter (in Illustration 25-15 on page 880), we present the financial statements of Private-Purpose Trust Fund in discussing the basic financial statements presented for *external* financial reporting purposes.

Investment Trust Funds

Investment trust funds (which usually exist only at the *state level*) are used to report the external portion of investment pools reported by the sponsoring government. We do *not* discuss these funds.

CHECK POINT

The activities of a municipal employees' retirement and pension system should be recorded in which fund?

a. *General Fund*
b. *Special Revenue Fund*
c. *Debt Service Fund*
d. *Agency Fund*
e. *Trust Fund*

Answer: e

D: FINANCIAL REPORTING TO THE PUBLIC: GENERAL-PURPOSE FINANCIAL STATEMENTS

SECTION OVERVIEW

The annual financial report for governmental units is called the comprehensive annual financial report (CAFR). The financial statements required therein are a **complete, integrated set of basic financial statements** structured as follows:

1. **Government-wide financial statements (two statements)**
   A. **Purpose of these statements:** To present an overall picture of "operational accountability" (so as to show the extent to which the government (1) has met their operating objectives efficiently and effectively, *using all resources available for that purpose*, and (2) can continue to meet their objectives for the foreseeable future).
   B. **Measurement focus:** *Economic resources* (same as in the *private* sector—thus depreciation expense *is* reported).
   C. **Basis of accounting:** *Accrual basis.*
   D. **Activities to be reported:** Governmental activities (includes *Internal Service Funds*), business-type activities (*Enterprise Funds*), and nonfiduciary component units. Fiduciary activities are *excluded.*
   E. **The *two* required financial statements:** A statement of net assets (assets, followed by liabilities, followed by net assets) and a statement of activities (in a unique "net cost" format). The statement of net assets includes (1) general capital assets and (2) general long-term liabilities. The statement of activities includes depreciation expense. (Much more on these statements later.)

2. **Fund-based financial statements** (seven or nine statements depending on whether ***component units*** exist)
   A. **Purpose of these statements:** To show "fiscal accountability" (shows whether the government has complied with public decisions concerning the raising and spending of public moneys *in the short term*).
   B. **Measurement focus:** ***Governmental Funds***—*current financial resources* (excludes depreciation expense); ***Proprietary Funds***—*economic resources;* ***Fiduciary Funds***—*economic resources.*
   C. **Basis of accounting:** ***Governmental Funds***—*modified accrual basis;* ***Proprietary Funds***—*accrual basis;* ***Fiduciary Funds***—*accrual basis.*
   D. **Funds to be reported:** *Governmental funds* (and *nonfiduciary component units*), *business-type funds*, and *fiduciary funds*. For the *governmental funds* and the Enterprise Funds among the proprietary funds, the presentation is **by major funds**—*not* by *fund types*. Because the statements for the governmental funds are *fund-based*, they *exclude* (1) general capital assets, (2) general long-term liabilities, and (3) depreciation expense. *Internal Service Funds* are exempt from the major fund reporting requirement. For the *fiduciary funds*, the presentation is **by fund type** (thus Fiduciary Funds are exempt from the major fund reporting requirement).
   E. **The *seven* required financial statements (exclusive of component units):** *Two* traditional-type *fund-based* statements for *governmental funds* (a Balance Sheet and a Statement of Revenues, Expenditures, and Changes in Fund Balances); *three* traditional-type fund statements for *proprietary funds* (a Balance Sheet, a Statement of Revenues, Expenses, and Changes in Fund Equity, and a Statement of Cash Flows); and *two* traditional-type fund statements for fiduciary activities (a Statement of Fiduciary Net Assets and a Statement of Changes in Fiduciary Net Assets). Certain formatting requirements exist.
3. **Linking the *fund-based* financial statements to the *government-wide* financial statements** (necessary only for *governmental activities* because the measurement focuses and bases of accounting differ)
   A. **The summary reconciliation of total *governmental funds* fund balances** (in the *fund-based* Balance Sheet) **to the total *governmental activities* net assets** (in the *government-wide* Statement of Net Assets). (The two major reconciling items are (1) general capital assets and (2) general long-term liabilities.)
   B. **The summary reconciliation of total change in *governmental funds* fund balances** (in the governmental activities *fund-based* Statement of Revenues, Expenditures, and Changes in Fund Balances) **to total changes in *government activities* net assets** (in the *government-wide* Statement of Activities. (The three major reconciling items are (1) bond proceeds, (2) repayment of bond principal, and (3) the excess of capital expenditures over depreciation expense [or vice-versa].)

   Requiring these reconciliations (1) shows how the various financial statements form a single, integrated model and (2) emphasizes that the *fund-based financial statements* provide useful information in understanding the *government-wide financial statements*. ***These reconciliations must appear (1) at the bottom of the fund-based financial statements or (2) in an accompanying schedule.***

Additional Reporting Requirements

The following items must also be reported:

> **Required supplementary information (RSI).** RSI takes on a greatly expanded role in the new financial reporting model. RSI consists of (1) budgetary comparison financial statements for the *General Fund* and major *Special Revenue Funds* (which may be presented *either* as the *third* of the basic governmental fund financial statements *or* as a schedule in RSI) and (2) an interpretive narrative by management called **Management's Discussion and Analysis (MD&A).**

> **Supplementary information.** These items consist of certain specified combining financial statements.

Building Up Approach

In the CAFR, the *government-wide* statements always precede the *fund-based* statements. For instructional purposes only, however, we use the approach of (1) *first* presenting the *fund-based statements* (with which you are already familiar) in Illustrations 25-10 through 25-15, (2) illustrating the ***consolidation* and *conversion* process** necessary for certain of those statements to arrive at the *government-wide statements* (Illustration 25-16 on pages 882–885), and (3) presenting the *government-wide statements* last (Illustrations 25-17 and 25-18 on pages 887 and 890–891, respectively).

XI. THE SEVEN *FUND-BASED* FINANCIAL STATEMENTS

The Governmental Activities Balance Sheet

The balance sheet is the basic statement of position for *governmental funds*. Illustration 25-10 shows balance sheets for **all** *governmental funds*—**by major funds.**

Review Points for Illustration 25-10.

1. **Display of major funds.** A separate column is reported for each major individual *governmental fund*. A single column aggregating all remaining governmental funds—regardless of fund type—is required.
2. **Criteria for "major" funds.** The *General Fund* is always considered to be a major fund. Other funds (excluding *Internal Service Funds* and *Fiduciary Funds*) are considered to be major if they meet *both* of the following criteria:
   (a) The fund has at least 10% of the total assets, liabilities, revenues, or expenditures/expenses of the corresponding element total (assets, liabilities, and so forth) of all funds within its category (governmental or enterprise).
   (b) The same element that meets the preceding 10% test also is at least 5% of the total assets, liabilities, revenues, or expenditures/expenses of governmental and *Enterprise Funds* combined.
3. **The first mandatory reconciliation to the government-wide statements.** A Total column for all governmental funds is required. The *total governmental fund balances* in this Total column must be reconciled to the *total net assets* for *governmental activities* reported in the *government-wide* **Statement of Net Assets** (shown later in Illustration 25-17 on page 887).

The *Governmental Funds* Statement of Revenues, Expenditures, and Changes in Fund Balances

Governmental funds retain their traditional "operating statement" under the new financial reporting model. Illustration 25-11 (page 874) shows a statement of revenues, expenditures, and changes in fund balances for **all** *governmental activities*—**by major fund.**

Review Points for Illustration 25-11 (on pages 874–875).

1. **Display of major funds.** A separate column is reported for each major individual *governmental fund*. A single column aggregating *all* remaining governmental funds—regardless of fund type—is required.
2. **The *second* mandatory reconciliation to the government-wide statements.** A Total column for all governmental funds is required. The ***net** change in fund balance* in this Total column must be reconciled to the ***total** change in net assets* for *governmental activities* reported in the *government-wide* **Statement of Activities** (shown later in Illustration 25-18 on pages 890–891).

ILLUSTRATION 25-10 FUND-BASED STATEMENT: GOVERNMENTAL FUNDS—BALANCE SHEET

City of Hope
Governmental Funds—Balance Sheet (*by major fund*)
December 31, 2006
(In thousands)

	GENERAL FUND	HUD PROGRAMS	COMMUNITY REDEVELOP-MENT	ROUTE 7 CONSTRUCTION FUND	OTHER GOVERNMENTAL FUNDS	TOTAL GOVERNMENTAL FUNDS
ASSETS						
Cash and cash equivalents	$ 3,418	$ 1,237			$ 5,607	$ 10,262
Investments			$ 13,263	$ 10,467	3,485	27,215
Receivables, net	3,645	2,953	353	11	10	6,972
Receivable from other funds	1,371					1,371
Receivable from other governments		119			1,596	1,715
Liens receivable	792	3,196				3,988
Inventories	183					183
Total Assets	**$9,409**	**$7,505**	**$13,616**	**$10,478**	**$10,698**	**$ 51,706**
LIABILITIES						
Accounts payable	$ 3,409	$ 130	$ 190	$ 1,104	$ 1,075	$ 5,908
Payable to other funds		25				25
Payable to other governments	94					94
Deferred revenue	4,251	6,274	250	11		10,786
Total Liabilities	**$7,754**	**$6,429**	**$ 440**	**$ 1,115**	**$ 1,075**	**$ 16,813**
FUND BALANCES						
Reserved for:						
Inventories	$ 183					$ 183
Liens receivable	792					792
Encumbrances	40	$ 41	$ 119	$ 5,793	$ 1,814	7,807
Debt service					3,832	3,832
Other purposes					1,405	1,405
Unreserved, reported in:						
General Fund	640					640
Special Revenue Funds		1,035			1,331	2,366
Capital Projects Funds			13,057	3,570	1,241	17,868
Total Fund Balances	**$1,655**	**$1,076**	**$13,176**	**$ 9,363**	**$ 9,623**	**$ 34,893**
Total Liabilities and Fund Balances	**$9,409**	**$7,505**	**$13,616**	**$10,478**	**$10,698**	

Reconciliation to Government-Wide Statement:

(1) **Capital assets** used in *governmental activities* are *not* financial resources and therefore are *not* reported in the funds	161,083
(2) **Other long-term** assets are *not* available to pay for current-period expenditures and therefore are *deferred* in the funds	9,349
(3) ***Internal Service Funds*** are used by management to charge the costs of certain activities, such as insurance and telecommunications, to individual funds. The assets and liabilities of the *Internal Service Funds* are included in *governmental activities* in the Statement of Net Assets	2,995
(4) **Long-term liabilities**, including bonds payable, are *not* due and payable in the current period and therefore are *not* reported in the funds	(84,760)
Net Assets of Governmental Activities (as shown in Illustration 25-17)	**$123,560**

Source: GASB *Statement No. 34*, "Basic Financial Statements—and Management's Discussion and Analysis—for State and Local Governments," (Norwalk, CT: Governmental Accounting Standards Board, 1999), Appendix C, Illustration C-1, adapted.

The Proprietary Funds Balance Sheet

The balance sheet is the basic statement of position for proprietary funds. Illustration 25-12 on page 876 shows a balance sheet for **all** proprietary funds—**by major fund.**

ILLUSTRATION 25-11 FUND-BASED STATEMENT: STATEMENT OF REVENUES, EXPENDITURES, AND CHANGES IN FUND BALANCES

City of Hope
Statement of Revenues, Expenditures, and Changes in Fund Balances (*by major fund*)
For the Year Ended December 31, 2006
(In thousands)

	GENERAL FUND	HUD PROGRAMS	COMMUNITY REDEVELOP-MENT	ROUTE 7 CONSTRUCTION FUND	OTHER GOVERNMENTAL FUNDS	TOTAL GOVERNMENTAL FUNDS
REVENUES:						
Property taxes	$ 51,174				$ 4,680	$ 55,854
Franchise & public service taxes	13,025					13,025
Fees and fines	607				0	607
Licenses and permits	2,288				0	2,288
Intergovernmental	6,120	$ 2,578			2,831	11,529
Charges for services	11,374				31	11,405
Investment earnings	552	87	$ 550	$ 270	364	1,823
Miscellaneous	882	66		3		951
Total Revenues	**$86,022**	**$2,731**	**$ 550**	**$ 273**	**$ 7,906**	**$ 97,482**
EXPENDITURES:						
Current operating:						
General government	$ 8,630		$ 418	$ 17	$ 121	$ 9,186
Public safety	33,730					33,730
Public works	4,976				3,720	8,696
Health and sanitation	8,076					8,076
Culture and recreation	11,412					11,412
Community development		$ 2,954				2,954
Education—payment to school district	21,893					21,893
Debt service:						
Principal					3,450	3,450
Interest and other charges					5,215	5,215
Capital outlay			2,247	11,281	3,192	16,720
Total Expenditures	**$88,717**	**$2,954**	**$ 2,665**	**$ 11,298**	**$15,698**	**$121,332**
Excess (deficiency) of Revenues over Expenditures	**$ (2,695)**	**$ (223)**	**$ (2,115)**	**$(11,025)**	**$ (7,792)**	**$ (23,850)**
OTHER FINANCING SOURCES (USES):						
Proceeds of refunding bonds					$ 38,045	$ 38,045
Proceeds of long-term capital debt			17,529		1,300	18,829
Payment to bond refunding escrow agent					(37,284)	(37,284)
Transfers *in*	129				5,551	5,680
Transfers *out*	(2,164)	(348)	(2,273)		(219)	(5,004)
Total Other Financing Sources and Uses	**$ (2,035)**	**$ (348)**	**$15,256**	**$ –**	**$ 7,393**	**$ 20,266**
SPECIAL ITEM:						
Proceeds from sale of park land	3,477					3,477
Net Change in Fund Balances	**$ (1,253)**	**$ (571)**	**$13,141**	**$(11,025)**	**$ (399)**	**$ (107)[a]**
Fund Balances—*Beginning*	2,908	1,647	35	20,388	10,022	35,000
Fund Balances—*Ending*	**$ 1,655**	**$1,076**	**$13,176**	**$ 9,363**	**$ 9,623**	**$ 34,893**

[a] The required reconciliation of this amount to the Government-Wide Statement of Activities is on page 875.

ILLUSTRATION 25-11 FUND-BASED STATEMENT: STATEMENT OF REVENUES, EXPENDITURES, AND CHANGES IN FUND BALANCES (*CONTINUED*)

Reconciliation to Government-Wide Statement (Illustration 25-18)

Net change in fund balances—total *government funds* (per preceding page)	$ (107)
Amounts reported for *governmental activities* in the *statement of activities* (Illustration 25-18) differ because:	
(1) *Governmental* ***funds*** report **capital outlays** as *expenditures* while *governmental* ***activities*** report *depreciation expense* to allocate those expenditures over the life of the assets. This is the amount by which *capital outlays* exceeded *depreciation expense* in the current year.	14,040
(2) In the *Statement of Activities*, only the **gain on the sale of the park land** is reported, while in the *governmental* ***funds***, the *proceeds from the sale* increase financial resources. Thus the *change in net assets* differs from the *change in fund balance* by the cost of the land sold.	(823)
(3) **Revenues** in the *Statement of Activities* that do *not* provide *current financial resources* are *not* reported as *revenues* in the *governmental* ***funds***.	1,921
(4) **Bond proceeds** provide current financial resources to *governmental* ***funds***, but issuing debt increases long-term liabilities in the *Statement of Net Assets*. Repayment of bond principal is an *expenditure* in the *government* ***funds***, but the repayment reduces long-term liabilities in the *Statement of Net Assets*. This is the amount by which ***proceeds*** exceeded ***repayments***.	(16,140)
(5) Some **expenses** reported in the *Statement of Activities* do *not* require the use of *current financial resources*, and therefore they are *not* reported as *expenditures* in the *governmental* ***funds***.	(1,246)
(6) ***Internal Service Funds*** are used by management to charge the costs of certain activities, such as telecommunications and insurance to individual funds. The net revenue (expense) of the *Internal Service Funds* is reported with *governmental activities*.	(759)
Change in Net Assets of Governmental Activities (as shown in Illustration 25-18)	**$ (3,114)**

Source: Adapted from GASB, *Governmental Accounting Statement No. 34*, "Basic Financial Statements—and Management's Discussion and Analysis—for State and Local Governments," (Norwalk, CT: Governmental Accounting Standards Board, 1999), Appendix C, Illustration C-2.

Review Points for Illustration 25-12 (on page 876).

1. **Display of major funds.** A separate column is reported for each major individual *Enterprise Fund*. A single column aggregating all remaining *Enterprise Funds*—regardless of fund type—is required.
2. **Separate column of *Internal Service Funds*.** *Internal Service Funds*—which use the same measurement focus and basis of accounting as *Enterprise Funds*—are presented in a single column (aggregated).
3. **Terminology in the equity section.** Equity on the balance sheet is the difference between assets and liabilities—it must be reported either as "net assets" or "fund equity."
4. **Consistent subclassifications in the equity section.** The same subclassifications used on the *government-wide* **Statement of Net Assets** ("invested in capital assets net of related debt," "restricted," and "unrestricted") must be used.
5. **Automatic tie-in to the government-wide Statement of Net Assets.** Because of the use of the same measurement focus and basis of accounting, the total assets, total liabilities, and total net assets automatically tie into the business-type activities amounts in the *government-wide* **Statement of Net Assets** (shown in Illustration 25-17 on page 887), except for the $175,000 interfund item discussed in Note 2.

The Proprietary Funds Statement of Revenues, Expenses, and Changes in Net Assets

Proprietary funds retain their traditional "operating statement" under the new financial reporting model. Illustration 25-13 on page 877 shows a Statement of Revenues, Expenditures, and Changes in Net Assets for **all** proprietary funds—**by major fund**.

ILLUSTRATION 25-12 FUND-BASED STATEMENT: PROPRIETARY FUNDS—BALANCE SHEET

City of Hope
Proprietary Funds—Balance Sheet (*by major fund*)
December 31, 2006
(in thousands)

	BUSINESS-TYPE ACTIVITIES			GOVERNMENTAL ACTIVITIES
	SEWER	WATER AND PARKING FACILITIES	TOTALS	INTERNAL SERVICE FUNDS (1)
ASSETS				
Current assets:				
Cash and cash equivalents	$ 8,417	$ 369	$ 8,786	$ 3,336
Investments				150
Receivables, net	3,565	4	3,569	158
Due from other governments	41		41	
Inventories	127		127	140
Total Current Assets	**$ 12,150**	**$ 373**	**$ 12,523**	**$ 3,784**
Noncurrent assets:				
Restricted cash and cash equivalents		$ 1,493	$ 1,493	
Capital assets:				
Land	$ 813	3,022	3,835	
Distribution and collection systems	39,504		39,504	
Buildings and equipment	106,136	23,029	129,165	$ 14,722
Less accumulated depreciation	(15,329)	(5,787)	(21,116)	(5,782)
Capital assets, net	**$131,124**	**$ 20,264**	**$151,388**	**$ 8,940**
Total Assets	**$143,274**	**$ 22,130**	**$165,404**	**$ 12,724**
LIABILITIES				
Current liabilities:				
Accounts payable	$ 447	$ 304	$ 751	$ 780
Due to other funds (2)	175		175	1,171
Compensated absences	113	9	122	238
Claims and judgments				1,688
Bonds, notes, and loans payable	3,945	360	4,305	249
Total Current Liabilities	**$ 4,680**	**$ 673**	**$ 5,353**	**$ 4,126**
Noncurrent Liabilities:				
Compensated absences	$ 451	$ 35	$ 486	
Claims and judgments				$ 5,603
Bonds, notes, and loans payable	54,452	19,544	73,996	
Total Noncurrent Liabilities	**$ 54,903**	**$ 19,579**	**$ 74,482**	**$ 5,603**
Total Liabilities	**$ 59,583**	**$ 20,252**	**$ 79,835**	**$ 9,729**
NET ASSETS				
Invested in capital assets, net of related debt	$ 72,728	$ 360	$ 73,088	$ 8,691
Restricted for debt service		1,452	1,452	
Unrestricted	10,963	66	11,029	(5,696)
Total Net Assets	**$ 83,691**	**$ 1,878**	**$ 85,569**	**$ 2,995**
Total Liabilities and Net Assets	**$143,274**	**$ 22,130**	**$165,404**	**$ 12,724**

1. The amounts in this column are included in the governmental activities column in Illustration 25-17 on page 887. This manner of reporting *Internal Service Funds* (proprietary funds) (1) enables the "Totals" column on this statement to flow directly to the "Business-Type Activities" column on the statement of net assets in Illustration 25-17 and (2) avoids the need for a reconciliation on this statement.
2. The $175,000 Due to Other Funds is classified in the Assets section in the statement of net assets in Illustration 25-17. Thus the total assets and the total liabilities here differ by $175,000 from those shown in Illustration 25-17.

Source: Adapted from GASB, *Governmental Accounting Statement No. 34*, "Basic Financial Statements—and Management's Discussion and Analysis—for State and Local Governments," (Norwalk, CT: Governmental Accounting Standards Board, 1999), Appendix C, Illustration D-2.

ILLUSTRATION 25-13 FUND-BASED STATEMENT: PROPRIETARY FUNDS—STATEMENT OF REVENUES, EXPENSES, AND CHANGES IN NET ASSETS

City of Hope
Proprietary Funds—Statement of Revenues, Expenses, and Changes in Net Assets (*by major fund*)
For the Year Ended December 31, 2006
(in thousands)

	BUSINESS-TYPE ACTIVITIES			GOVERNMENTAL ACTIVITIES
	SEWER	WATER AND PARKING FACILITIES	TOTALS	INTERNAL SERVICE FUNDS (1)
Operating Revenues:				
Charges for services	$ 11,330	$ 1,340	$ 12,670	$ 15,256
Miscellaneous		4	4	1,067
Total Operating Revenues	$ 11,330	$ 1,344	$ 12,674	$ 16,323
Operating Expenses:				
Personal services	$ 3,401	$ 762	$ 4,163	$ 4,157
Contractual services	344	96	440	584
Utilities	754	101	855	215
Repairs and maintenance	747	65	812	1,961
Other supplies and expenses	498	17	515	234
Insurance claims and expenses				8,004
Depreciation	1,163	542	1,705	11,708
Total Operating Expenses	**$ 6,907**	**$ 1,583**	**$ 8,490**	**$16,863**
Operating Income (Loss)	**$ 4,423**	**$ (239)**	**$ 4,184**	**$ (540)**
Nonoperating Revenues (Expenses):				
Interest and investment revenue	$ 454	$ 147	$ 601	$ 135
Miscellaneous revenue		105	105	21
Interest expense	(1,601)	(1,167)	(2,768)	(42)
Miscellaneous expense		(47)	(47)	(176)
Total Nonoperating Revenue (Expenses)	**$ (1,147)**	**$ (962)**	**$ (2,109)**	**$ (62)**
Net income (loss) before contributions and transfers	$ 3,276	$ (1,201)	$ 2,075	$ (602)
Capital contributions	1,646		1,646	18
Transfers out	(290)	(211)	(501)	(175)
Change in net assets	**$ 4,632**	**$ (1,412)**	**$ 3,220**	**$ (759)**
Total Net Assets—*Beginning*	79,059	3,290	82,349	3,754
Total Net Assets—*Ending*	**$83,691**	**$ 1,878**	**$85,569**	**$ 2,995**

(1) The amounts in this column are included in the governmental activities column in Illustration 25-18 on pages 890–891. This manner of reporting *Internal Service Funds* (proprietary funds) (1) enables the "Totals" column on this statement to flow directly to the "Business-type Activities" amounts on the statement of activities in Illustration 25-18 (with interest expense and miscellaneous expense being reclassified to "expenses") and (2) avoids the need for a reconciliation on this statement.

Source: Adapted from GASB, *Governmental Accounting Statement No. 34*, "Basic Financial Statements—and Management's Discussion and Analysis—for State and Local Governments," (Norwalk, CT: Governmental Accounting Standards Board, 1999), Appendix C, Illustration D-3.

Review Points for Illustration 25-13.

1. **Display of major funds.** A separate column is reported for each major individual *Enterprise Fund.* A single column aggregating all remaining *Enterprise Funds* is used.
2. **Automatic tie-in to the government-wide statement of activities.** Because of the use of the same measurement focus and basis of accounting, the $3,220 total change in net assets in the Business-Type Activities Totals column automatically ties into the Change in Net Assets for

Business-Type Activities amount in the *government-wide* **Statement of Net Assets** (shown in Illustration 25-18 on pages 890–891).

The Proprietary Funds Statement of Cash Flows

The required statement of cash flows for *proprietary activities* has the same columnar headings as the previous two statements required for *proprietary funds*. Some key points are:

1. **Mandatory use of the *direct method*.** The use of the *direct method* is mandatory.
2. **New reconciliation required.** A reconciliation between "net cash provided by (used for) operating activities" and "operating income (loss)" is required.

See Illustration 25-14 for a statement of cash flow for **all** *proprietary funds*—**by major fund.**

The Fiduciary Funds Statements

Two statements are required: (1) a *Statement of Fiduciary Net Assets* for Trust Funds and Agency Funds, and (2) a Statement of *Changes in Fiduciary Net Assets* for Trust Funds. Illustration 25-15 on page 880 shows the required fiduciary statements—**by major fund.**

XII. THE CONSOLIDATION AND *CONVERSION* PROCESS FOR PREPARING *GOVERNMENT-WIDE* FINANCIAL STATEMENTS

To obtain amounts for the *government-wide* financial statements for *governmental activities*, **five steps** are needed in what is both a *consolidation* and *conversion* process (all steps can be performed on a *single* worksheet):

1. ***Consolidation* of *Internal Service Fund* Assets and Liabilities.** The combined assets and liabilities for all *Internal Service Funds* are consolidated with the assets and liabilities for *governmental funds*—this is merely a summing across process on the worksheet.
2. ***Elimination* of *Internal Service Fund* Profit or Loss Element.** The combined income or loss for all *Internal Service Funds* is allocated to the various user departments so that the income or loss is eliminated. Accordingly, (1) additional expenses are charged to the user departments in the event of a *loss*, and (2) amounts already reported as expenditures by the user departments as a result of *Internal Service Fund* billings are reduced in the event of *income*. Certain items are *excluded*, however, in determining the income or loss to be allocated. These items are (1) *Investment Income*, (2) *Transfers (In and Out)*, and (3) *Contributions to Permanent and Term Endowments* (received). They are *excluded* from the determination of the amount to be allocated because these amounts can be and are *consolidated* with the comparable items reported for the *governmental funds*.
3. ***Consolidation* of General Long-Term Assets and Liabilities.** The balances in the *GCA-GLTL g/l* are consolidated with the combined assets and liabilities for the *governmental funds*—this consolidation is merely a summing across process on the worksheet. Because entries are made in this general ledger only at *year-end* as a result of the conversion entries prepared (discussed in step 5 below), the balances shown on the worksheet are **"beginning of year"** amounts. (We show the *year-end* adjusting entry for this general ledger later.)
4. **Reclassifications and Elimination of *Intra*governmental Balances.** Certain *fund-based* accounts are reclassified to conform to the reporting format used in the *government-wide* statements. For example, the fund balance amounts in the *fund-based statements*—both reserved and unreserved—are reclassified to the appropriate categories used in the *government-wide statements* (*Invested in Capital Assets, Net of Related Debt*, *Restricted*, and *Unrestricted*). Also, any unset-

ILLUSTRATION 25-14 FUND-BASED STATEMENT: PROPRIETARY FUNDS—STATEMENT OF CASH FLOWS

City of Hope
Proprietary Funds—Statement of Cash Flows
For the Year Ended December 31, 2006
(in thousands)

	BUSINESS-TYPE ACTIVITIES			GOVERNMENTAL ACTIVITIES
	SEWER	WATER AND PARKING FACILITIES	TOTALS	INTERNAL SERVICE FUNDS (1)
CASH FLOWS FROM OPERATING ACTIVITIES:				
Receipts from customers	$ 11,400	$ 1,345	$ 12,745	$ 15,326
Payments to suppliers	(2,725)	(365)	(3,090)	(2,812)
Payments to employees	(3,360)	(751)	(4,111)	(4,210)
Internal activity—payments to other funds	(1,297)		(1,297)	
Claims paid				(8,482)
Other receipts (payments)	(2,325)		(2,325)	1,061
Net cash provided by operating activities	**$ 1,693**	**$ 229**	**$ 1,922**	**$ 883**
CASH FLOWS FROM *NONCAPITAL FINANCING* ACTIVITIES:				
Operating subsidies and transfers to other funds	**$ (290)**	**$ (211)**	**$ (501)**	**$ (175)**
CASH FLOWS FROM *CAPITAL AND RELATED FINANCING* ACTIVITIES:				
Proceeds from capital debt	$ 4,041	$ 8,661	$ 12,702	
Capital contributions	1,646		1,646	
Purchases of capital assets	(4,194)	(145)	(4,339)	$ (400)
Principal paid on capital debt	(2,178)	(8,895)	(11,073)	(954)
Interest paid on capital debt	(1,480)	(1,166)	(2,646)	42
Other receipts (payments)		19	19	131
Net cash (used) by capital and related financing activities	**$(2,165)**	**$(1,526)**	**$ (3,691)**	**$(1,181)**
CASH FLOWS FROM *INVESTING* ACTIVITIES:				
Proceeds from sales/maturities of investments				$ 16
Interest and dividends	$ 455	$ 144	$ 599	130
Net cash provided by investing activities	**455**	**$ 144**	**$ 599**	**$ 146**
Net (decrease) in cash and cash equivalents	**$ (307)**	**$(1,364)**	**$ (1,671)**	**$ (411)**
Balances—*Beginning* of year	8,724	1,733	10,457	3,747
Balances—*End* of year	**$ 8,417**	**$ 369**	**$ 8,786**	**$ 3,336**
Reconciliation *of operating income (loss)* to net cash provided (used) by operating activities:				
Operating income (loss)	**$ 4,423**	**$ (239)**	**$ 4,184**	**$ (540)**
Adjustments:				
Depreciation expense	1,163	542	1,705	1,708
Changes in assets and liabilities:				
Receivables, net	652	1	653	32
Inventories	3		3	40
Accounts and other payables	(297)	(87)	(384)	475
Accrued expenses	(4,251)	12	(4,239)	(831)
Net cash provided by *operating* activities	**$ 1,693**	**$ 229**	**$ 1,922**	**$ 883**

tled *intra*governmental balances (reported in "Due to" and "Due from" accounts) between (1) the various *governmental funds* and (2) the *Internal Service Funds* are eliminated.

5. ***Conversion* Entries** (to convert from the *current financial resources measurement focus* and the *modified accrual basis* to the *economic resources measurement focus* and the *accrual basis*).

ILLUSTRATION 25-15 FUND-BASED STATEMENT: FIDUCIARY FUNDS—STATEMENT OF FIDUCIARY NET ASSETS AND CHANGES IN FIDUCIARY NET ASSETS

City of Hope
Fiduciary Funds—Statement of Fiduciary Net Assets
December 31, 2006
(in thousands)

	EMPLOYEE RETIREMENT PLAN	PRIVATE-PURPOSE TRUSTS	AGENCY FUNDS
ASSETS			
Cash and short-term investments	$ 2	$ 1	$ 45
Receivables:			
Interest and dividends	$ 508	$ 1	
Other receivables	7		$ 83
Total receivables	$ 515	$ 2	$ 183
Investments, at fair value:			
U.S. government obligations	$ 13,056	$ 80	
Municipal bonds	6,528		
Corporate bonds	16,320		
Corporate stocks	26,112		
Other investments	3,264		
Total Investments	$ 65,280	$ 80	
Total Assets	**$65,797**	**$82**	**$228**
LIABILITIES			
Accounts payable		$ 1	
Refunds payable and other	$ 1		228
Total Liabilities	**$ 1**	**$ 1**	**$228**
NET ASSETS			
Held in trust for pension benefits and other purposes	**$65,796**	**$81**	

Statement of Changes in Fiduciary Net Assets
For the Year Ended December 31, 2006 (in thousands)

	EMPLOYEE RETIREMENT PLAN	PRIVATE-PURPOSE TRUSTS
ADDITIONS		
Contributions:		
Employer	$ 2,721	
Plan members	1,421	
Total Contributions	$ 4,142	
Investment income:		
Net appreciation (depreciation) in fair value of investments	$ (272)	
Interest	2,461	$ 5
Dividends	1,445	
Total Investment Earnings	$ 3,634	$ 5
Less investment expense	(216)	
Net Investment Income	$ 3,418	$ 5
Total Additions	**$ 7,560**	**$ 5**
DEDUCTIONS		
Benefits	$ 2,453	$ 4
Refunds of contributions	465	
Administrative expenses	88	1
Total Deductions	**$ 3,006**	**$ 5**
Change in Net Assets	**$ 4,554**	**$-0-**
Net Assets—*Beginning* of the Year	61,242	81
Net Assets—*End* of the Year	**$65,796**	**$81**

Source: Adapted from GASB, *Governmental Accounting Statement No. 34*, "Basic Financial Statements—and Management's Discussion and Analysis—for State and Local Governments," (Norwalk, CT: Governmental Accounting Standards Board, 1999), Appendix C, Illustration E-2.

Entries are made for such items as (1) recording depreciation, (2) capitalizing the amount reported as *expenditures* for *general capital assets*, (3) reporting as a *liability* the amount reported for *Proceeds from Borrowings*.

Refer to Illustration 25-16 on pages 882–885 for a consolidation and conversion worksheet used to obtain amounts for the *government-wide statements* for *governmental activities*. Part A is for the operating statement. Part B is for the balance sheet/statement of net assets. The various entries shown therein are described below.

Allocation Needed to Eliminate the Internal Service Fund *Loss*

In Illustration 25-13 (page 877), the *Internal Service Funds* (in total) had a *loss* of $719,000 for 2006—exclusive of (1) *investment income* of $135,000 and (b) *transfers out* of $175,000 (the change in net assets is a decrease of $759,000; $759,000 – $175,000 + $135,000 = $719,000). Accordingly, an additional $719,000 of costs must be allocated to the various user departments. The allocable amounts (listed below) along with the $135,000 of *investment income* and the $175,000 of *transfers out* are shown in the Internal Service Funds column of Part A of Illustration 25-16. The departments to which the additional $719,000 was allocated follow:

General government	$135,000
Public safety	271,000
Public works	135,000
Health and sanitation	68,000
Culture and recreation	68,000
Interest	42,000
Total	$719,000

Reclassifications and Elimination of *Intra*governmental Balances

Explanations for the entries shown in the "Reclassifications and Interfund eliminations" column of Illustration 25-16 (pages 882–885) are as follows:

Entry	
	Balance Sheet/Statement of Net Assets:
a	To reclassify *receivables* into one account.
b	To eliminate *interfund* receivables and payables.
c	To reclassify *payables* into one account.
d	To reclassify the *fund balances* classification amounts to the appropriate net assets categories used in the *Statement of Net Assets*.
	Operating Statement:
e	To eliminate intragovernmental transfers.
f	To reclassify certain *inter* governmental revenues into the program categories used in the *Statement of Activities*.
g	To reclassify certain revenues into charges for services.

Conversion Entries to Change *Measurement Focus* and *Basis of Accounting*

The entries shown in the "Conversion" columns of Illustration 25-16 are as follows:

Entry	Description of Conversion Entries (*amounts are in thousands*)		
A	To **capitalize** the amount reported for **capital outlay** in the *governmental funds:*		
	Buildings and Equipment	16,720	
	Expenditures		16,720

(continued on page 886)

ILLUSTRATION 25-16 PART A CONSOLIDATION AND CONVERSION WORKSHEET—OPERATING STATEMENT

City of Hope
Consolidation and Conversion Worksheet
For the Year Ended December 31, 2006 (in thousands)

Source:	TOTAL GOVERNMENTAL FUNDS Illus. 25-11	INTERNAL SERVICE FUNDS (see text expl.)	GENERAL CAPITAL ASSETS AND L-T LIABILITIES n/a
REVENUES:			*(No nominal) accounts exist in this general ledger.)*
Property taxes	$ 55,854		
Franchise and public service taxes	13,025		
Fees and fines	607		
Licenses and permits	2,288		
Intergovernmental	11,529		
Operating grants and contributions			
Capital grants and contributions			
Charges for services	11,405		
Investment earnings	1,823	$ 135	
Miscellaneous	951		
Gain on sale of park land			
Total Revenues	**$ 97,482**	**$ 135**	**$ –**
EXPENDITURES/EXPENSES:		*(Allocated amounts)*	
Current operating:			
General government	$ 9,186	$ 135	
Public safety	33,730	271	
Public works	8,696	135	
Health and sanitation	8,076	68	
Culture and recreation	11,412	68	
Community development	2,954		
Education—payment to school district	21,893		
Debt service:			
Principal	3,450		
Interest and other charges	5,215	42	
Capital outlay	16,720		
Total Expenditures/Expenses	**$121,332**	**$ 719**	**$ –**
Excess (deficiency) of Revenues over Expenditures/Expenses	$ (23,850)	$ (584)	$ –
OTHER FINANCING SOURCES (USES):			
Proceeds of refunding bonds	38,045		
Proceeds of long-term capital debt	18,829		
Payment to bond refunding escrow agent	(37,284)		
Transfers in	5,680		
Transfers out	(5,004)	(175)	
Total Other Financing Sources/Uses	**$ 20,266**	**$ (175)**	**$ –**
Special Item—Proceeds on sale of land	3,477		
Net Change for the Year	**$ (107)**	**$ (759)**	**$ –**

ILLUSTRATION 25-16 PART A CONSOLIDATION AND CONVERSION WORKSHEET—OPERATING STATEMENT (*CONTINUED*)

RECLASSIFICATIONS AND INTERFUND ELIMINATIONS		CONVERSION ENTRIES				STATEMENT OF ACTIVITIES
		DR.			CR.	
				D	566	$ 56,420
						13,025
(607)	g					–
(2,288)	g					–
(10,071)	f					1,458
5,176	f					5,176
4,895	f					4,895
2,961	g			D	1,355	15,721
						1,958
(66)	g					885
				C	2,654	2,654
$ –						**$ 102,192**
		275	B	G	25	$ 9,571
		330	B			34,845
		514	G			
		1,316	B	G	18	10,129
		654	B	G	24	8,774
		65	B	G	12	11,533
		40	B			2,994
						21,893
				F	3,450	–
		811				6,068
				A	16,720	–
$ –						**$ 105,807**
		–			–	$ (3,615)
		38,045	E			–
		18,829	E			–
				F	37,284	–
(5,179)	e					501
5,179	e					–
$ –						
		3,477	C			–
$ –		**64,356**	**CF**	**CF**	**62,108**	**$ (3,114)**

CF = Carried Forward to Part B on page 885.

ILLUSTRATION 25-16 PART B CONSOLIDATION AND CONVERSION WORKSHEET—BALANCE SHEET/STATEMENT OF NET ASSETS

City of Hope
Consolidation and Conversion Worksheet
For the Year Ended December 31, 2006 (in thousands)

Source:	TOTAL GOVERNMENTAL FUNDS Illus. 25-10	INTERNAL SERVICE FUNDS Illus. 25-12	GENERAL CAPITAL ASSETS AND L-T LIABILITIES *General Ledger*
ASSETS			*(These are the beginning of year balances.)*
Cash and cash equivalents	$ 10,262	$ 3,336	
Investments	27,215	150	
Receivables, net	6,972	158	
Due from other funds	1,371		
Due from other governments	1,715		
Liens receivable	3,988		
Inventories	183	140	
Capital Assets:			
LAND AND INFRASTRUCTURE, NET			120,463
BUILDINGS AND EQUIPMENT, NET		8,940	27,403
Total Assets	**$ 51,706**	**$12,724**	**$147,866**
LIABILITIES			
Accounts payable	$ 5,908	$ 780	
Due to other funds	25	1,171	
Due to other governments	94		
Deferred revenue	10,786		(7,428)
Long-term liabilities:			
BONDS AND NOTES PAYABLE		249	48,428
COMPENSATED ABSENCES		238	5,537
CLAIMS AND JUDGMENTS		7,291	8,070
Total Liabilities	**$ 16,813**	**$ 9,729**	**$ 54,607**
FUND BALANCES/NET ASSETS			
Reserved for:			
Inventories	$ 183		
Liens receivable	792		
Encumbrances	7,807		
Debt service	3,832		
Other purposes	1,405		
Unreserved, reported in:			
General fund	640		
Special revenue funds	2,366		
Capital projects funds	17,868		
Invested in capital assets, net of related debt		$ 8,691	$ 85,194
Restricted—reserved for:			
Capital projects			
Debt service			
Community development projects			
Other purposes			
Unrestricted		(5,696)	8,065
AMOUNTS BROUGHT FORWARD FROM PART A			
Total Fund Balances/Net Assets	**$ 34,893**	**$ 2,995**	**$ 93,259**
Total Liabilities & Fund Balance/Net Assets	**$ 51,706**	**$12,724**	**$147,866**
Proof of postings			

ILLUSTRATION 25-16 PART B CONSOLIDATION AND CONVERSION WORKSHEET— BALANCE SHEET/STATEMENT OF NET ASSETS (*CONTINUED*)

RECLASSIFICATIONS AND INTERFUND ELIMINATIONS		CONVERSION ENTRIES DR.			CONVERSION ENTRIES CR.	STATEMENT OF NET ASSETS
						$ 13,598
						27,365
5,703	a					12,833
(1,196)	b					175
(1,715)	a					–
(3,988)	a					–
						323
						–
				C	823	118,620
				B	1,020	
		16,720	A	B	1,660	51,403
$ (1,196)		**$16,720**			**$3,503**	**$ 224,317**
94	c					$ 6,782
(1,196)	b					–
(94)	c					–
		1,921	D			1,437
						–
		40,734	F	E	56,874	64,817
				G	6,585	12,360
						15,361
$ (1,196)		**$42,655**			**$63,459**	**$ 100,757**
(183)	d					–
(792)	d					–
(7,807)	d					–
(3,832)	d					–
(1,405)	d					–
						–
(640)	d					–
(2,366)	d					–
(17,868)	d					–
						–
9,826	d					$ 103,711
						–
11,706	d					11,706
3,021	d					3,021
4,811	d					4,811
3,214	d					3,214
2,315	d	5,339	G			(2,903)
		64,356	BF	BF	$62,108	
$ –		**$69,695**			**$62,108**	**$ 123,560**
$ (1,196)		**$112,350**			**$125,567**	**$ 224,317**
		129,070			129,070	

BF = Brought Forward from Part A on page 883.

Entry	Description of Conversion Entries (*amounts are in thousands*)		
B	To **depreciate** governmental *general capital assets:*		
	Depreciation Expense—General Government	275	
	Public Safety	330	
	Public Works	1,316	
	Health and Sanitation	654	
	Culture and Recreation	65	
	Community Development	40	
	Accumulated Depreciation		2,680
C	To (1) *eliminate* the amount reported for proceeds from **sale of park land**, (2) eliminate the land's cost from the *GCA-GLTL g/l*, and (3) *report* the gain on the sale of the park land:		
	Proceeds from Sale of Park Land	3,477	
	Land		823
	Gain on Sale of Park Land		2,654
D	To report the *increase* in **deferred revenues** as revenues in the *government-wide Statement of Activities* (because the "available-at-year-end" criterion used in the *modified accrual basis* is *not* used in the *accrual basis*).		
	Deferred Revenues	1,921	
	Revenues—Property Taxes		566
	Revenues—Licenses and Fines		1,355
E	To eliminate the "proceeds from borrowing" and reflect such borrowings as long-term liabilities in *the government-wide Statement of Net Assets.*		
	Proceeds of Refunding Bonds	38,045	
	Proceeds of Long-Term Debt	18,829	
	Bonds and Notes Payable		56,874
F	To reclassify **payments made to retire debt** (reported as *expenditures* in the *fund-based statements*) and reflect as a liability reduction in the *government-wide Statement of Net Assets.*		
	Long-Term Liabilities	40,734	
	Expenditures—Debt Repayment		40,734
G	To (1) reflect **additional liabilities for expenses** that could *not* be recorded in the *fund-based statements* (because the amounts would *not* be paid from "current financial resources") and (2) adjust net assets at *the beginning of the year* for the amount of those liabilities existing at that time:		
	Net Assets—Beginning of Year	5,339	
	Expenses (*debit* or *credit* as appropriate)—General Government		25
	Public Safety	514	
	Public Works		18
	Health and Sanitation		24
	Culture and Recreation		12
	Community Development	811	
	Accumulated Depreciation		6,585

Year-End Adjusting Entry to the *GCA-GLTL g/l*

Recall that the *GCA-GLTL g/l* only has "real" accounts—no "nominal" accounts. Accordingly, the adjusting entry at year-end to update the balances therein for the year's activity is entirely to *asset* accounts, *liability* accounts, and *net assets*. The appropriate year-end adjusting entry is developed from the asset and liability amounts shown in the preceding *conversion entries*. That entry is **shown in sequential order of the preceding conversion** entries and is as follows:

Account	Debit	Credit
Buildings and Equipment (*from Entry **A***)	16,720	
Accumulated Depreciation (*from Entry **B***)		2,680
Land (*from Entry **C***)		823
Deferred Revenues (*from Entry **D***)	1,921	
Bonds and Notes Payable (*from Entry **E***)		56,874
Bonds and Notes Payable (*from Entry **F***)	40,734	
Long-Term Liabilities (*from Entry **G***)		6,585
Net Assets (*from Entry **G***)	5,339	
Net Assets (**to balance**)	2,248	
Proof of postings	***66,962***	***66,962***

XIII. THE TWO GOVERNMENT-WIDE FINANCIAL STATEMENTS

The Statement of Net Assets

The basic government-wide statement of position is the *Statement of Net Assets*. Either a *net assets format* (assets – liabilities = net assets [a vertical sequencing with *assets* at the *top*]) or the traditional *balance sheet format* (assets = liabilities + net assets) is allowed. In both cases, however, the term *net assets* must be used rather than *equity*. Furthermore, the assets and liabilities may be presented in either an *unclassified* format or a *classified* format (distinguishing between *current* and *noncurrent* amounts).

Illustration 25-17 shows a *Statement of Net Assets* using the *unclassified* format.

ILLUSTRATION 25-17 GOVERNMENT-WIDE STATEMENT: STATEMENT OF NET ASSETS (NET ASSETS FORMAT—UNCLASSIFIED)

City of Hope
Statement of Net Assets
December 31, 2006 (in thousands)

	PRIMARY GOVERNMENT			
	GOVERNMENTAL ACTIVITIES	BUSINESS-TYPE ACTIVITIES	TOTAL	COMPONENT UNITS
Assets				
Cash and cash equivalents	$ 13,598	$ 10,279	$ 23,877	$ 304
Investments	27,365		27,365	7,429
Receivables (net)	12,833	3,610	16,443	4,042
Internal balances	175	(175)		
Inventories	323	127	450	84
Capital assets:				
Land and infrastructure	118,620	34,788	153,408	751
Buildings, property, and equipment, net	51,403	116,600	168,003	36,994
Total Assets	**$224,317**	**$165,229**	**$389,546**	**$49,604**
Liabilities				
Accounts payable	$ 6,782	$ 751	$ 7,533	$ 1,803
Deferred revenue	1,437		1,437	39
Long-term liabilities:				
Due within one year	11,439	4,427	15,866	1,427
Due in more than one year	81,099	74,482	155,581	27,106
Total Liabilities	**$100,757**	**$ 79,660**	**$180,417**	**$30,375**
Net Assets				
Invested in capital assets, net of related debt	$ 103,711	$ 73,088	$ 176,799	$ 15,907
Restricted for:				
Capital projects	11,706		11,706	492
Debt service	3,021	1,452	4,473	
Community development projects	4,811		4,811	
Other purposes	3,214		3,214	
Unrestricted (deficit)	(2,903)	11,029	8,126	2,830
Total Net Assets	**$123,560**	**$ 85,569**	**$209,129**	**$19,229**

Note: In the "net assets" format, amounts are *not* shown for "total liabilities and total net assets."

Source: Adapted from GASB, *Governmental Accounting Statement No. 34*, "Basic Financial Statements—and Management's Discussion and Analysis—for State and Local Governments" (Norwalk, CT: Governmental Accounting Standards Board, 1999), Appendix C, Illustrations A-1 and A-2.

Review Points for Illustration 25-17.

1. **Scope.** This statement (a) *excludes* fiduciary activities and (b) *includes* nonfiduciary component units.
2. **Separation.** *Governmental activities* must be reported separately from *business-type activities*—even though both are presented using the *same* measurement focus and basis of accounting. *Internal Service Fund* assets and liabilities are reported in the *governmental activities* category; thus *business-type activities* consist only of *Enterprise Fund* assets and liabilities.
3. ***Combining* funds and general capital assets and general long-term liabilities.** The *governmental activities* column reports both (1) all assets and liabilities related to *governmental funds* (including *Internal Service Funds*) and (2) assets and liabilities currently reported in the *GCA-GLTL g/l*.
4. **Mandatory** total column. A total column for the *primary government* is mandatory—it can*not* be labeled "memorandum only."
5. **Elimination of *interfund account balances.*** Within each categorical column, interfund account balances must be eliminated (thus each categorical column is a consolidated column). Likewise, intercategorical balances must be eliminated (as shown on the Internal balances line) in arriving at amounts in the total column.
6. **Categories for displaying *net assets.*** Net assets must be reported in the *three* categories shown. The Restricted category is used to reflect constraints placed on net assets by *external* parties (such as creditors, grantors, contributors, and laws or regulations of other governments).

The Statement of Activities

This statement uses a "net cost" format because the statement (1) first directs a reader's attention to the cost of a government's various functions and programs, (2) then shows how a portion of the cost of some functions or programs may be financed by charges for services or by restricted grants and contributions. The difference between these two elements is then reported as the net cost that must be financed through a government's own resources (such as taxes and non-program-specific grants).

Illustration 25-18 on pages 890–891 shows a *Statement of Activities*.

Review Points for Illustration 25-18.

1. **Scope.** Similar to the *Statement of Net Assets*, the *Statement of Activities* (a) *excludes* fiduciary activities and (b) *includes* nonfiduciary component units.
2. **Separation.** Similar to the *Statement of Net Assets*, the *Statement of Activities* reports governmental activities *separately* from *business-type activities* even though both use the *same* measurement focus and basis of accounting.
3. **Depreciation.** Expenses must include depreciation on all the government's capital assets—including those reported in the *GCA-GLTL g/l* for internal record-keeping purposes.
4. **Mandatory** total column. A total column for the primary government is mandatory—it *cannot* be labeled "memorandum only."
5. **Elimination of interfund transactions.** Within each of the net expenses (revenues) categorical columns, interfund transactions must be eliminated. Likewise, intercategorical amounts must be eliminated (as shown on the Transfers line near the bottom) in arriving at amounts in the Total column. If elimination of transactions distorts the amount of a functional cost/program, however, elimination is *not* appropriate.

Required Supplementary Information (RSI)

The term "required supplementary information" is used to describe information that (1) is required to accompany audited financial statements for fair presentation in conformity with GAAP, but (2) has not itself been subject to audit (auditors are required, however, to perform certain limited procedures in connection with RSI).

Under the current reporting model, RSI is limited to information pertaining to pension reporting and public-entity risk pools. As stated earlier, RSI takes on a greatly expanded role under the new reporting model. The RSI requirements consist of (1) budgetary comparison statements for (a) the *General Fund* and (b) each major *Special Revenue Fund* (both the *original* budget and any *amended* budget must be reported in RSI), and (2) management's discussion and analysis (MD&A), something the Securities and Exchange Commission has required for *publicly owned* companies for nearly 30 years.

Management's Discussion and Analysis

The MD&A typically will be located before the basic financial statements. MD&A requirements include:

- An explanation of the objectives of the government-wide statements and the fund-based statements.
- Condensed government-wide statements.
- An analysis of significant variations between original and final budget, and between actual and final budget for the *General Fund*.
- A discussion of **whether the government's financial position has improved or deteriorated.**
- A description of currently known facts, decisions, or conditions that have had, or are expected to have, a material effect on financial position or results of operations.

End-of-Chapter Review

Summary of Key Points

Illustration 25-19 on page 892 summarizes the major key points of this chapter.

Assignment Material

Review Questions

1. When is a *Special Revenue Fund* used instead of the *General Fund*?
2. What is the relationship between a Capital Projects Fund and the *GCA-GLTL g/l*?
3. Do *general capital assets* include *all* capital assets? Why or why *not*?
4. What is the relationship between the *Debt Service Funds* and the *GCA-GLTL g/l*?
5. What is the difference in meaning of the term *general long-term liabilities* as used in government and as used in private industry?
6. Do *General Long-Term Liabilities* include *all* long-term debt? Why or why *not*?
7. What determines whether special assessment receivables are recorded in a *Debt Service Fund* or in an *Agency Fund*?
8. Which fund is used to account for construction activity to be financed from a special assessment to certain property owners?
9. What is the distinction between an *Agency Fund* and a *Trust Fund*?
10. What are the *three* types of *Trust Funds*?
11. In what way are *Enterprise Funds* and *Internal Service Funds* similar to commercial operations?

ILLUSTRATION 25-18 GOVERNMENT-WIDE STATEMENT: STATEMENT OF ACTIVITIES

City of Hope
Statement of Activities
For the Year Ended December 31, 2006 (in thousands)

		PROGRAM REVENUES			NET (EXPENSE) REVENUE AND CHANGES IN NET ASSETS			
					PRIMARY GOVERNMENT			
	EXPENSES	CHARGES FOR SERVICES	OPERATING GRANTS AND CONTRIBUTIONS	CAPITAL GRANTS AND CONTRIBUTIONS	GOVERN-MENTAL ACTIVITIES	BUSINESS-TYPE ACTIVITIES	TOTAL	COMPONENT UNITS
PRIMARY GOVERNMENT: *(by functions/programs):*								
Government Activities:								
General government	$ 9,571	$ 3,147	$ 843		$ (5,581)		$ (5,581)	
Public safety	34,845	1,199	1,308	$ 62	(32,276)		(32,276)	
Public works	10,129	1,555		2,253	(6,321)		(6,321)	
Health and sanitation	8,774	5,825	575		(2,374)		(2,374)	
Culture and recreation	11,533	3,995	2,450		(5,088)		(5,088)	
Community development	2,994			2,580	(414)		(414)	
Education (payment to school district)	21,893				(21,893)		(21,893)	
Interest on long-term debt (*excludes* direct interest expense reported in functions)	6,068				6,068		(6,068)	
Total Governmental Activities	**$105,807**	**$15,721**	**$5,176**	**$4,895**	**$ (80,015)**		**$ (80,015)**	
Business-Type Activities *(by different identifiable activities):*								
Water	3,596	4,159		1,160		$ 1,723	1,723	
Sewer	4,912	7,171		486		2,745	2,745	
Parking facilities	2,797	1,344				(1,453)	(1,453)	
Total Business-Type Activities	**$ 11,305**	**$12,674**	**$ –**	**$1,646**		**$ 3,015**	**$ 3,015**	
Total Primary Government	**$117,112**	**$28,395**	**$5,176**	**$6,541**	**$ (80,015)**	**$ 3,015**	**$ (77,000)**	
COMPONENT UNITS: *(by functions/programs)*								
Landfill	$ 3,382	$ 3,858		$ 11				$ 487
Public school system	31,187	706	$ 3,937					(26,544)
Total Components Units	**$ 34,569**	**$ 4,564**	**$3,937**	**$ 11**				**$ (26,057)**

(continued)

ILLUSTRATION 25-18 GOVERNMENT-WIDE STATEMENT: STATEMENT OF ACTIVITIES (*CONTINUED*)

	NET (EXPENSE) REVENUE AND CHANGES IN NET ASSETS			
	PRIMARY GOVERNMENT			
	GOVERN-MENTAL ACTIVITIES	BUSINESS-TYPE ACTIVITIES	TOTAL	COMPONENT UNITS
General revenues:				
Real estate taxes	$ 56,420		$ 56,420	
Franchise and public service taxes	13,025		13,025	
Payments from City of Hope				$ 21,893
Grants and contributions *not* restricted to specific programs	1,458		1,458	6,462
Investment earnings	1,958	$ 601	2,559	882
Miscellaneous	885	105	990	22
Special Item—Gain on sale of park land	2,654		2,654	
Transfers In (Out)	501	(501)	0	
Total General Revenues, Special Items, and Transfers	**$ 76,901**	**$ 205**	**$ 77,106**	**$ 29,259**
Change in Net Assets	**$ (3,114)**	**$ 3,220**	**$ 106**	**$ 3,202**
Net Assets—Beginning	**126,674**	**82,349**	**209,023**	**16,027**
Net Assets—Ending	**$123,560**	**$85,569**	**$209,129**	**$ 19,229**

Source: Adapted from GASB, *Governmental Accounting Statement No. 34*, "Basic Financial Statements—and Management's Discussion and Analysis—for State and Local Governments" (Norwalk, CT: Governmental Accounting Standards Board, 1999), Appendix C, Illustration B-1. Copyright © 1999 by Financial Accounting Foundation. Reprinted with permission.

ILLUSTRATION 25-19 SUMMARY COMPARISON OF ALL FUNDS

Fund Type	Measurement Focus	Basis of Accounting	Records Annual Budget in General Ledger	Uses Encumbrances Accounting	Reports Capital Assets and Long-Term Debt in Its Own Balance Sheet	Does *Not* Have a Net Assets Category
Governmental Funds—* Fund Based *Statements:						
General Fund	CFR	MA	X	X		
Special Revenue Funds	CFR	MA	X	X		
Capital Projects Funds	CFR	MA	(1)	X		
Debt Service Funds	CFR	MA	(1)			
Permanent Funds	CFR	MA	(1)			
***Governmental Funds—* Government-Wide *Statements:*[a]**						
General Fund	ER	A	n/a	n/a	(2)	
Special Revenue Funds	ER	A	n/a	n/a	(2)	
Capital Projects Funds	ER	A	n/a	n/a	(2)	
Debt Service Funds	ER	A	n/a	n/a	(2)	
Permanent Funds	ER	A	n/a	n/a	(2)	
Proprietary Funds—* (Fund-Based *and* Government-Wide *Statements):						
Internal Service Funds	ER	A			X	
Enterprise Funds	ER	A			X	
Fiduciary Funds—* Fund-Based *Statements:						
Agency Funds	n/a	A				X
Pension Trust Funds	ER	A			X	
Investment Trust Funds	ER	A			n/a	
Private-Purpose Trusts	ER	A			X	

[a] The balances in the *fund-based* **Statement of Net Assets** for *Internal Service Funds* are consolidated with the *governmental funds* in preparing the *government-wide* **Statement of Net Assets** for *governmental funds*. Also, any profit or loss element that exists for the *Internal Service Funds* is eliminated in consolidation.

(1) This depends on whether the governmental unit has legally adopted an annual budget for this fund—some governmental units do and some do *not*.

(2) The balances in the *GCA-GLTL g/l* are consolidated with the balances in the governmental funds in arriving at the amounts reported in the *government-wide* **Statement of Net Assets.**

Code: CFR = Current Financial Resources
ER = Economic Resources
MA = Modified Accrual
A = Accrual

12. What significance may be attributed to the fact that the billings of an *Internal Service Fund* or an *Enterprise Fund* exceed its costs and expenses?
13. What two major reporting level categories of financial statements exist?
14. What two financial statements exist at the *government-wide* reporting level?
15. What is the *measurement focus* and *basis of accounting* for the *government-wide financial statements*?
16. What two major categories of activities are reported in the *government-wide financial statements*?
17. What six financial statements exist in the *fund financial statements* reporting level?

18. What is the *measurement focus* and *basis of accounting* at the *fund financial statements* reporting level?

19. What two major categories of activities are reported in the *fund financial statements* reporting level?

20. Which two items in the *fund financial statements* must be reconciled to which two items in the *government-wide financial statements*?

21. Where must the required reconciliations in Question 20 be shown?

22. How are *Internal Service Funds* reported?

23. How are *Fiduciary Funds* reported?

24. How are *General Capital Assets* and *General Long-Term Liabilities* reported?

25. How is depreciation of General Capital Assets handled under GASB's new reporting model?

26. What is the definition of *Required Supplementary Information*?

27. What information is reported as *Required Supplementary Information*?

Exercises

E 25-1 **GLTL: Preparing Journal Entries** The following transactions occurred during Bondsville County's fiscal year ended 6/30/06:

1. On 10/1/05, general obligation term bonds having a face value of $1,000,000 and an 8% interest rate were issued. Interest is payable semiannually on April 1 and October 1. The $980,000 proceeds were used to construct a new courthouse.
2. On 1/1/06, the county transferred $16,000 from the *General Fund* to a *Debt Service Fund* for sinking fund purposes.
3. The *Debt Service Fund* immediately invested this money, and by 6/30/06, the county's fiscal year-end, $1,000 of interest had been earned on these investments.
4. On 3/27/06, $40,000 was transferred from the *General Fund* to the *Debt Service Fund* to meet the first interest payment.
5. On 4/1/06, the *Debt Service Fund* made the required interest payment of $40,000. (A fiscal agent is *not* used.)

Required Prepare the journal entries that should be made in all the appropriate funds for these transactions.

E 25-2 ***Debt Service Fund* and GLTL: Preparing Journal Entries** The city of Promises had the following transactions during its fiscal year ended 6/30/05:

1. General obligation serial bonds having a face value of $100,000 matured during the year, and they were redeemed. Money was transferred from the *General Fund* to the *Debt Service Fund* to redeem this debt.
2. Total interest paid on serial bonds during the year was $80,000. Money was transferred from the *General Fund* to the *Debt Service Fund* to pay this interest.
3. General obligation term bonds having a face value of $500,000 were issued for $505,000. The proceeds are for construction of a new fire station, which is expected to cost $500,000. The $5,000 premium, which will *not* be used for construction purposes, was properly transferred to the *Debt Service Fund*.
4. A cash transfer of $10,000 was made from the *General Fund* to a *Debt Service Fund* in connection with a sinking fund requirement pertaining to general obligation term bonds.

5. Special assessment bonds having a face value of $400,000 were issued at par. The proceeds are for residential street improvements. The city is liable for this debt in the event of default by the assessed property owners.

Required Prepare journal entries for each of these transactions in all appropriate funds. Use the following headings for your workpaper:

Transaction Number	Account Titles and Explanations	Amount		Fund
		Dr.	Cr.	

E 25-3 COMPREHENSIVE: Matching Transactions with Possible Ways to Record Transactions Each item in the *left-hand* column represents various transactions pertaining to a city that uses encumbrance accounting. The *right-hand* column lists possible ways to record the transactions.

Transactions

1. General obligation bonds were issued at par.
2. Approved purchase orders were issued for supplies.
3. These supplies were received and the related invoices were approved.
4. *General Fund* salaries and wages were incurred.
5. The *Internal Service Fund* had interfund billings.
6. Revenues became available from a previously awarded grant.
7. Property taxes were collected in advance.
8. Appropriations were recorded on adoption of the budget.
9. Short-term financing was received from a bank, secured by the city's taxing power.
10. There was an excess of estimated *inflows* over estimated *outflows*.

Possible Ways to Record the Transactions

A. Credit Appropriations.
B. Credit Budgetary Fund Balance—Unreserved.
C. Credit Expenditures.
D. Credit Deferred Revenues.
E. Credit Revenues.
F. Credit Tax Anticipation Notes Payable.
G. Credit Other Financing *Sources*.
H. Credit Other Financing *Uses*.
I. Debit Appropriations.
J. Debit Deferred Revenues.
K. Debit Encumbrances.
L. Debit Expenditures.

Required For each of the transactions, what is the appropriate recording of the transaction? A method to record the transactions may be selected once, more than once, or *not* at all.

E 25-4 COMPREHENSIVE: Matching Funds and Items with Possible Accounting and Reporting Methods Each item in the *left-hand* column is a fund or item. The *right-hand* column lists possible accounting and reporting methods.

Funds and Items

1. *Enterprise Fund* Capital Assets.
2. *Capital Projects Fund*.
3. General Capital Assets.
4. Infrastructure Assets.
5. *Enterprise Fund* Cash.
6. *General Fund*.
7. *Agency Fund* Cash.
8. General Long-Term Liabilities.
9. *Special Revenue Fund*.
10. *Debt Services Fund*.

Possible Accounting and Reporting Methods

A. Accounted for in a fiduciary fund.
B. Accounted for in a proprietary fund.
C. Accounted for in a permanent fund.
D. Accounted for in a special general ledger.
E. Accounted for in a special assessment fund.
F. Accounts for major construction activities.
G. Accounts for property tax revenues.
H. Accounts for payment of interest and principal on tax-supported debt.
I. Accounts for revenues from earmarked sources to finance designated activities.
J. Reporting is optional.

Required For each of the city's funds or items, what is the appropriate accounting and reporting method? Each method may be selected once, more than once, or *not* at all.

E 25-5 Determining Reportable Total Assets in the *Statement of Net Assets* The following data were obtained from Salsa City's 12/31/06 financial records and statements:

Total Assets—governmental activities (*excluding* both General Capital Assets and *Internal Service Fund* assets)	$900,000
Total Assets—business-type activities	500,000
Total Assets—*Internal Service Funds*	200,000
Total Assets—fiduciary funds	100,000
Total Assets—component units	400,000
General Capital Assets	600,000

Required For each categorical column in the *government-wide* statement of net assets, what amounts appear on the total assets line?

E 25-6 Reconciling to Net Assets in the *Statement of Net Assets* The following data were obtained from Selso City's 12/31/06 financial records and statements:

Total fund balances—governmental activities	$330,000
Total net assets—business-type activities	70,000
Total net assets—component units	100,000
Total net assets—*Internal Service Funds*	50,000
Total fund balances—fiduciary funds	200,000
General capital assets	900,000
General long-term liabilities	800,000
Proceeds of bond offering	120,000
Expenditures for general capital assets	110,000

Required Prepare the required reconciliation to the *government-wide* statement of net assets.

E 25-7 Understanding the Interrelationship of the Funds and the *GCA-GLTL G/L—Capital Assets*

1. A city built a new city hall, the construction of which was accounted for in a *Capital Projects Fund*. Entries relating to the new building are also required in which of the following?
   a. *General Fund*
   b. *Enterprise Fund*
   c. *Permanent Fund*
   d. *GCA-GLTL g/l*
   e. None of the above

2. A city's water utility, which is accounted for in an *Enterprise Fund*, acquired some new capital assets. An entry is also required in which of the following?
   a. *Agency Fund*
   b. *Internal Service Fund*
   c. *General Fund*
   d. *GCA-GLTL g/l*
   e. No additional entry is required

3. A city's purchasing and stores department is properly accounted for in an *Internal Service Fund*. When capital assets are acquired for this department, accounting entries are required in which of the following?
   a. *GCA-GLTL g/l*
   b. *Internal Service Fund*
   c. *Internal Service Fund* and the *GCA-GLTL g/l*
   d. *General Fund* and the *GCA-GLTL g/l*
   e. *Enterprise Fund*
   f. *Enterprise Fund* and the *GCA-GLTL g/l*

E 25-8 Understanding the Interrelationship of the Funds and the *GCA-GLTL G/L—Debt*

1. A transaction in which a municipal electric utility issues bonds (to be repaid from its own operations) requires accounting recognition in which of the following?
   a. *Enterprise Fund*
   b. *Debt Service Fund*

c. *Enterprise* and *Debt Service Funds*
d. *Enterprise Fund*, a *Debt Service Fund*, and the *GCA-GLTL g/l*
e. None of the above

2. The liability for *general obligation bonds* issued for the benefit of a municipal electric company and serviced by its earnings should be recorded in which of the following?
a. *Enterprise Fund*
b. *General Fund*
c. *Enterprise Fund* and the *GCA-GLTL g/l*
d. *Enterprise Fund* and disclosed in a note to the financial statements
e. None of the above

3. The liability for *special assessment bonds* that carry a *secondary pledge* of a city's general credit should be recorded in which of the following?
a. *Debt Service Fund*
b. *GCA-GLTL g/l*
c. *Agency Fund*
d. Only disclosure would be made in a note to the financial statements.
e. None of the above

4. The liability for *special assessment bonds* when the city is *not* obligated in any manner in the event of default by the property owners should be recorded in which of the following?
a. *Debt Service Fund*
b. *GCA-GLTL g/l*
c. *Agency Fund*
d. Only disclosure would be made in a note to the financial statement.
e. None of the above

5. Several years ago, a city established a sinking fund to retire an issue of general obligation bonds. This year, the city made a $50,000 contribution to the sinking fund from general revenues and realized $15,000 in revenue from sinking fund securities. The bonds due this year were retired. These transactions require accounting recognition in which of the following?
a. *General Fund*
b. *Debt Service Fund* and the *GCA-GLTL g/l*
c. *Debt Service Fund*, the *General Fund*, and the *GCA-GLTL g/l*
d. *Capital Projects Fund*, a *Debt Service Fund*, the *General Fund*, and the *GCA-GLTL g/l*
e. None of the above

E 25-9 Familiarity with General-Purpose Financial Statements

1. In the CAFR (Comprehensive Annual Financial Report), the *government-wide Statement of Net Assets* includes which of the following funds?

	Governmental	Enterprise	Internal Service	Fiduciary
a.	Yes	Yes	Yes	Yes
b.	Yes	Yes	Yes	No
c.	Yes	Yes	No	Yes
d.	Yes	Yes	No	No
e.	Yes	No	No	No
f.	Yes	No	No	Yes

2. In the CAFR, the *government-wide Statement of Activities* includes which of the following funds?

	Governmental	Enterprise	Internal Service	Fiduciary
a.	Yes	Yes	Yes	Yes
b.	Yes	Yes	Yes	No
c.	Yes	Yes	No	Yes

d.	Yes	Yes	No	No
e.	Yes	No	No	No
f.	Yes	No	No	Yes

3. In the CAFR, the *Statement of Revenues, Expenditures, and Changes in Fund Balances* includes which of the following funds?

	Governmental	Enterprise	Internal Service	Fiduciary
a.	Yes	Yes	Yes	Yes
b.	Yes	Yes	Yes	No
c.	Yes	Yes	No	Yes
d.	Yes	Yes	No	No
e.	Yes	No	No	No
f.	Yes	No	No	Yes

4. In the CAFR, the *Statement of Cash Flows* includes which of the following funds?

	Governmental	Enterprise	Internal Service	Fiduciary
a.	No	Yes	Yes	Yes
b.	No	Yes	Yes	No
c.	Yes	Yes	No	Yes
d.	Yes	Yes	Yes	No
e.	Yes	No	No	No
f.	Yes	Yes	Yes	Yes

Problems

P 25-1 **Capital Projects Fund: Preparing Journal Entries and Financial Statements** On 8/1/05, the City of Atlantis authorized the issuance of 6% general obligation serial bonds having a face value of $8,000,000. The proceeds will be used to construct a new convention center estimated to cost $8,300,000. Over the past several years, the Unreserved Fund Balance account in the city's *General Fund* has been approximately $300,000 higher than is prudently needed. Accordingly, this excess accumulation will be used to pay for the remainder of the construction cost. A *Capital Projects Fund*, designated the *Convention Center Construction Fund*, was established to account for this project.

The following transactions occurred during the fiscal year ended 6/30/06:

1. On 8/4/05, a $180,000 payment was made from the *General Fund* to Ace Architecture Company for the design of the convention center. (This $180,000 for architect's fees was part of the $8,300,000 total estimated cost of the convention center.) The *Expenditures* account was charged on the books of the *General Fund*.

2. On 9/5/05, a $8,100,000 construction contract was entered into with Nautilus Construction Company.

3. On 10/2/05, the city deposited $120,000 ($300,000 – $180,000 paid to the architect) to the *Convention Center Construction Fund*.

4. On 12/1/05, one-half of the authorized bond issue was sold at 101. The bond premium was properly transferred to a *Debt Service Fund*.

5. On 4/30/06, Nautilus submitted a $2,100,000 bill for work completed to date. Only $1,900,000 was *paid*.

6. On 6/1/06, the first semiannual interest payment on the bonds was made. (Principal payments are deferred until 12/1/07.)

7. On 6/20/06, the city was awarded an irrevocable federal grant totaling $1,000,000 to help finance the cost of the convention center. Payment will be received within 60 days. The city had applied for this grant in May 2005, with slight expectation of receiving it. Accordingly, it obtained authorization for a bond issue of $8,000,000 instead of $7,000,000.

Additional Information

1. The city intends to use a *Special Revenue Fund* to account for the operations of the convention center upon completion of the project.
2. The city does *not* record budgets for capital projects in *Capital Projects Funds.*

Required

1. For these transactions, prepare the entries that should be made in the *Convention Center Construction Fund* for the year ended 6/30/06. (Also, show the appropriate *General Fund* entry for items 1 and 3.)
2. Prepare the appropriate closing entries at 6/30/06.
3. Prepare a Balance Sheet at 6/30/06.
4. Prepare a Statement of Revenues, Expenditures, and Changes in Fund Balance for the year ended 6/30/06.

P 25-2 ***Debt Service Fund*: Preparing the Operating Statement from Selected Information** The following information relating to the City of Debtville's *Debt Service Fund* is provided for the year ended 12/31/06:

Interest	
Interest owed at 12/31/05 (none past due)	$ 160,000
Interest payments made at due dates during 2006	700,000
Interest owed at 12/31/06 (none past due)	130,000
Cash received from the *General Fund* to pay interest	700,000
Property Taxes	
Property tax assessments made in 2006 (to be collected by the *Debt Service Fund*)	566,000
Property tax collections by the *Debt Service Fund*	550,000
Allowance for uncollectible accounts	
12/31/05	4,000
12/31/06	5,000
Accounts written off during 2006 (from 2005 assessments)	2,000
Property tax receivables	
12/31/05	26,000[a]
12/31/06	40,000[b]
General Long-Term Liabilities	
Cash received from the *General Fund* to pay for the retirement of debt principal	400,000
GLTL that matured during 2006 and was paid off	1,000,000
Miscellaneous	
Gain on sale of investments	11,000
Interest on investments	75,000
Fund balance, 12/31/05 (all reserved for debt service)	621,000

[a] At 12/31/05, the entire *net realizable amount* of the property tax receivables was expected to be collected within 60 days, the time period the city uses to determine whether revenues are "available."

[b] At 12/31/06, $25,000 of the *net realizable amount* of the property tax receivables are expected to be collected after 60 days.

Required Prepare a Statement of Revenues, Expenditures, and Changes in Fund Balance for 2006. (Hint: Use T accounts for calculations pertaining to property tax revenues.)

P 25-3 **Special Assessments: Preparing Journal Entries and Financial Statements** Sunn City had the following transactions pertaining to street improvements for which a special assessment was made:

1. On 9/1/05, a special assessment levy of $200,000 was made against properties on Main Street for street improvements. The $200,000 is to be paid in four annual installments beginning 3/1/06. No uncollectible accounts are expected. Concurrently, a $200,000 bond issue was authorized, which carries a secondary pledge by the city. The proceeds can be used only on the project.
2. On 10/1/05, $203,000 was received from the sale of 10% special assessment serial bonds. The bond indenture requires any premium to be set aside for servicing the bonds.

3. On 10/5/05, a construction contract for $195,000 was signed with a general contractor who is to be paid at the completion of the work.

4. On 12/5/05, the contractor completed the work and was paid in full.

5. In February 2006, the first installment of the special assessment levy was collected in full.

6. On 3/31/06, the city retired $50,000 of the special assessment bonds and made the $10,000 semiannual interest payment. The city council authorized all interest payments on the bonds to be the responsibility of the *General Fund*.

Required

1. Prepare the journal entries that should be made in all the appropriate *funds* for these transactions.
2. Prepare any appropriate year-end adjusting entries.
3. Prepare Statements of Revenues, Expenditures, and Changes in Fund Balance for the fiscal year ended 6/30/06—omit the *General Fund*.
4. Prepare balance sheets at 6/30/06 for all funds—omit the *General Fund*. (Assume that the city follows customary practice in reporting street improvements.)
5. Prepare the entry to close the books at year-end for each fund.

P 25-4 Capital Projects Fund and *Debt Service Fund*: Preparing Journal Entries and Financial Statements

River City, whose citizens were troubled by the lack of recreational facilities for its youth, entered into the following transactions during its fiscal year ended 12/31/05:

1. On 1/3/05, a $600,000 serial bond issue having an 8% stated interest rate was authorized to acquire land and construct a youth recreation center thereon. The bonds are to be redeemed in 10 equal annual installments beginning 2/1/06.

2. On 1/10/05, the city made a $50,000 nonrefundable deposit on the purchase of land for the youth recreation center. The contracted price for the land is $150,000, which is $40,000 below the city's estimate.

3. On 3/1/05, the city issued serial bonds having a $450,000 face value at 102. The bond indenture requires any premium to be set aside for servicing bond indebtedness. The *General Fund* was repaid $50,000.

4. On 3/10/05, the city paid the remaining amount on the land contract and took title to the land.

5. On 3/17/05, the city signed a $400,000 construction contract with Rover Construction Company.

6. On 7/10/05, the contractor was paid $200,000 for work completed to date.

7. On 9/1/05, a semiannual interest payment was made on the outstanding bonds. (The source of the money was the *General Fund*.)

8. On 12/1/05, the city issued serial bonds having a $100,000 face value at par.

9. On 12/2/05, the contractor completed the recreation center and submitted a final billing of $210,000, which includes $10,000 of additional work authorized by the city in October 2005. The $210,000 was paid to the contractor on 12/12/05.

10. Through 12/10/05, the city had invested excess cash (from the bond offering) in short-term certificates of deposit. The amount collected on these investments totaled $12,000. (For this item, you need to make an entry only for the investment income.)

Required

1. Prepare the journal entries for the preceding transactions for all the funds.
2. Prepare any appropriate year-end adjusting entries.
3. Prepare Statements of Revenues, Expenditures, and Changes in Fund Balance for 2005—omit the *General Fund*.
4. Prepare Balance Sheets for all funds at 12/31/05—omit the *General Fund*.

P 25-5 ***Internal Service Fund*: Preparing Journal Entries and Financial Statements** The City of Paradise had the following transactions relating to its newly established Central Printing *Internal Service Fund* during the fiscal year ended 6/30/05:

1. It received a $100,000 transfer from the *General Fund* to establish the *Internal Service Fund.*
2. Machinery and equipment costing $80,000 were purchased and paid for by the *Internal Service Fund*. These items were placed in service on 1/4/05, and they have an estimated useful life of 10 years. (All machinery and equipment is depreciated using a 10-year life.)
3. Materials and supplies of $18,000 were ordered using purchase orders. For $14,000 of these purchase orders, the materials and supplies were *received* at a cost of $14,300. *Payments* totaling $9,500 were made on these billings.
4. Total billings for the year were $60,000. Of this amount, $7,000 was billed to the city's water utility, which is operated in an *Enterprise Fund.* The remaining amount was billed to various departments in the *General Fund.* Of these billings, $32,000 was *collected* from the *General Fund* and $5,500 from the water utility.
5. Salaries and wages totaling $49,000 were *paid.*
6. The city's electric utility, operated as an *Enterprise Fund*, billed the *Internal Service Fund* $900. Of this amount, $700 was *paid.*
7. Materials and supplies on hand at 6/30/05 were counted and costed at $3,800.
8. A $5,000 subsidy was received from the *General Fund* near the end of the fiscal year, recognizing that the first year of operations was a start-up year at a loss. In addition, $10,000 was received from the *General Fund* near the end of the fiscal year as a temporary advance to be repaid (without interest) during the following fiscal year.

Required

1. Prepare the appropriate journal entries for these transactions in the *Internal Service Fund.*
2. Prepare the year-end closing entry.
3. Prepare a Balance Sheet at 6/30/05.
4. Prepare a Statement of Revenues, Expenses, and Changes Net Assets for the year ended 6/30/05.

P 25-6 ***Enterprise Fund*: Preparing Journal Entries** The following activities pertain to *Enterprise Funds*:

1. **City A** contributed $1,000,000 to a newly established *Enterprise Fund* formed to provide off-street parking facilities.
2. **City B** established an *Enterprise Fund* to account for the building of a municipal golf course using the $3,000,000 proceeds of general obligation bonds to be repaid from golf course earnings. The bonds were issued at a $50,000 premium.
3. **City C** established an *Enterprise Fund* to account for its municipal swimming pools to be built using the $2,000,000 proceeds of general obligation serial bonds to be repaid from taxes and general revenues. The bonds were issued at a $25,000 *discount.*
4. **City D** operates a water utility in an *Enterprise Fund.* To expand operations, the city issued $5,000,000 of revenue bonds at a $40,000 *premium.*
5. **City E** operates an electric utility in an *Enterprise Fund*, which made a $500,000 payment in lieu of taxes to the city's *General Fund.*
6. **City F** operates an airport in an Enterprise Fund, which made a $600,000 payment to the city to finance *General Fund* expenditures.
7. **City G** discontinued its municipal golf course, which was accounted for in an *Enterprise Fund.* It sold the land to a residential home developer. All outstanding liabilities were paid, and the remaining $750,000 cash was disbursed to the *General Fund.*

8. **City H** operates a public transit system in an *Enterprise Fund.* The transit system usually recovers approximately 60% of its costs and expenses from user charges. During the current year, the *Enterprise Fund* received an $800,000 subsidy from the *General Fund.*

9. **City I** operates an electric utility in an *Enterprise Fund.* During the year, the city redeemed $500,000 of its electric utility's revenue bonds.

10. **City J** operates a gas utility in an *Enterprise Fund.* During the year, the city redeemed $1,000,000 of its general obligation serial bonds issued many years ago to finance the gas utility expansion. The bonds were to be repaid from taxes and general revenues.

Required For each transaction, prepare the necessary journal entries for all the funds and account groups involved. Use the following headings for your workpaper:

Transaction Number	Account Titles and Explanations	Amount		Fund or Special General Ledger
		Dr.	Cr.	

P 25-7 ***Agency Fund*** **(Resulting from a Special Assessment)** On 1/2/05, the city council of Walkerville approved a six-year special assessment project for a sidewalk improvement program. Transactions during 2005 and other information pertaining to this project follow:

1. 1/2/05: Issued 10% serial bonds having a face amount of $500,000 at their face amount. (The city is *not* obligated in any manner in the event of default.)
2. 1/2/05: Signed a construction contract having a fixed price of $600,000.
3. 1/2/05: Levied special assessments totaling $660,000, of which $60,000 is expected to be uncollectible. Beginning 7/1/05, interest at 10% is to be charged on the deferred installments of $550,000, of which $110,000 is due annually each July 1 beginning 7/1/06, along with accrued interest.
4. 7/1/05: Collected $101,000 on the current portion of the $110,000 assessment that became due.
5. 7/1/05: Disbursed $100,000 to the Capital Projects Fund.

Required Prepare the entries required in the *Agency Fund* for 2005.

P 25-8 **Comprehensive: (All Funds and the *GCA-GLTL g/l*) Preparing Journal Entries for Typical Transactions** The Village of Starville had the following transactions for the year ended 12/31/05:

1. Property taxes of $500,000 were levied. Of this amount, $100,000 was a special levy for servicing and retiring serial bonds issued 15 years ago to construct a fire station. Of the total amount levied, 2% was estimated to be uncollectible. An *Agency Fund* was used.
2. The village received its share of state sales taxes on gasoline. The $33,000 share can be used only for street improvements and maintenance. During the year, the village spent $31,000 for this purpose. (The village used its own workforce.)
3. On 3/31/05, general obligation bonds bearing 6% interest were issued in the face amount of $500,000. The proceeds were $503,000, of which $500,000 was authorized to be spent on a new library. The remaining $3,000 was set aside for the eventual retirement of the debt. The bonds are due in 20 years, with interest to be paid each year on March 31 and September 30.
4. A $490,000 construction contract was entered into with Booker Construction Company to build the new library. Of the $240,000 bill submitted, $216,000 was paid.
5. On 9/30/05, the interest due on the library bonds was paid using money from the *General Fund.*
6. On 11/30/05, the fire station serial bonds referred to in item 1 were paid off ($60,000), along with interest due at that time ($36,000).

7. On 7/31/05, 8% special assessment bonds having a face value of $90,000 were issued at par; the proceeds will be used for a street lighting project. Interest is paid annually each July 31. (The village has pledged to pay off these bonds in the event that the assessed property owners default.)
8. Assessments of $100,000 were levied for a residential street lighting project; the village contributed $7,000 from the *General Fund* as its share. Of the $100,000 assessed, $10,000 was collected, with the remaining $90,000 to be collected in succeeding years.
9. An $8,000 *General Fund* transfer was made to establish an *Internal Service Fund* to provide for a central purchasing and stores function.
10. During the year, the *Internal Service Fund* purchased various supplies costing $6,500. Of this amount, $4,400 was billed to the city's various departments at $5,500.
11. A *Capital Projects Fund* having a $2,000 fund balance was terminated. The cash was sent to the *General Fund* as required.
12. A local resident donated marketable securities with a market value of $80,000 (the resident's cost was $44,000) under the terms of a trust agreement. The principal is to remain intact. Earnings on the principal are to be used for improving city sidewalks. Revenues earned during 2005 totaled $7,500, of which $7,000 was disbursed for sidewalk improvements.
13. The village water utility billed the *General Fund* $6,600.
14. A *new* fire truck costing $22,000 was ordered, received, and paid for. The *old* fire truck (which had cost $8,000) was sold for $1,500.

Required For each transaction, prepare the necessary journal entries for all the appropriate funds involved. Use the following headings for your workpaper:

Transaction Number	Account Titles and Explanations	Amount		Fund
		Dr.	Cr.	

P 25-9 Additional Requirement for Problem 24-8 in Chapter 24 (pages 837–838)

Required Prepare the entries that would be made in the other funds **and the *GCA-GLTL g/l*** in Problem 25-8 to account properly for the items that should *not* be accounted for in the *General Fund*.

P 25-10 Comprehensive: Preparing Balance Sheets from Trial Balances Following is the trial balance of all the funds and general ledger accounts for Nerf City at 6/30/05, just *prior to the adjusting and closing entries*. All depreciation adjustments have been made.

General Fund

Cash	$ 150,000	Vouchers Payable	$ 75,000
Taxes Receivable—Current	130,000	Due to *Internal Service Fund*	15,000
Inventory	20,000	BUDGETARY FUND BALANCE RESERVED FOR ENCUMBRANCES	30,000
ESTIMATED REVENUES	900,000	BUDGETARY FUND BALANCE	100,000
ENCUMBRANCES	30,000	Unreserved Fund Balance	50,000
Expenditures	770,000	APPROPRIATIONS	800,000
		Revenues	930,000
	$2,000,000		$2,000,000

New Fire Station Capital Projects Fund[a]

Cash	$ 10,000		
Expenditures	90,000	Unreserved Fund Balance	$100,000
	$100,000		$100,000

[a] This project was completed by year-end. The money raised can be spent only on the fire station.

New Fire Station Debt Service Fund

Cash	$22,000	Revenues	$ 2,000
Investments	20,000	Unreserved Fund Balances	40,000
	$42,000		$42,000

Internal Service Fund

Cash	$ 85,000	Revenues	$ 90,000
Due from *General Fund*	15,000	Accumulated Depreciation	50,000
Equipment	200,000	Net Assets	260,000
Expenses	100,000		
	$400,000		$400,000

Pension Trust Fund and Agency Fund

Cash	$ 50,000	Investment Income	$ 30,000
Investments	300,000	Liability to Federal Government	14,000
Expenses	10,000	Liability to State Government	6,000
		Net Assets—Restricted	310,000
	$360,000		$360,000

General Capital Assets and General Long-Term Liabilities

Buildings	$390,000	Bonds Payable	$350,000
Equipment	50,000	Invested in Capital Assets, net	
Construction W.I.P.	60,000	of related debt	150,000
	$500,000		$500,000

Required Prepare a schedule that shows the adjusted balances for assets, liabilities, fund balances, and net assets for all funds ***and* general capital assets and general long-term liabilities** at 6/30/05.

P 25-11 **Reconciling to the *Changes* in Net Assets** For 2005, Carso City had the following items relating to its governmental activities:

Change (an *increase*) in fund balances, as reported in its *fund-based* operating statement	$500,000
Expenditures for *general capital assets*	160,000
Depreciation expense on *general capital assets*	90,000
Carrying value of *general capital assets* abandoned	20,000
Carrying value of *general capital assets* sold for $55,000 cash	40,000
Fair value of *general capital assets* received from donors (donors' cost basis was $66,000)	100,000

Required Prepare the required reconciliation to the *government-wide statement of activities.*

P 25-12 **Reconciling to the Changes in Net Assets** The following changes and other items were obtained from Suba City's 12/31/05 financial records and financial statements:

	Increase (Decrease)
Net Change In:	
Total fund balances—governmental activities	$700,000
Total net assets—business-type activities	(90,000)
Total net assets—component units	80,000
Total net assets—*Internal Service Funds*	60,000
Total fund balances—fiduciary funds	(40,000)
General Fixed Assets	190,000
General Long-Term Debt	520,000
Other Items:	
Expenditures for general capital assets	390,000
Depreciation expense recognized on general capital assets	50,000
Carrying value of general capital assets abandoned	30,000
Proceeds from sale of general capital assets having a carrying value of $120,000	140,000
Proceeds of bond offering (for new City Hall)	620,000
Repayment of general long-term liabilities bond principal	400,000
Lawsuit liability recognized in 2005—expected settlement is in 2007	300,000
Interest paid in 2005 on general long-term liabilities	70,000

Required Prepare the required reconciliation to the *government-wide* Statement of Activities.

P 25-13 **Conversion Entries** Information for Citrus City's year ended 6/30/05 follows:

1. Depreciation of *general capital assets* totaled $90,000.
2. Capital equipment expenditures totaled $222,000, as follows:

General Fund	$200,000
Enterprise Funds	20,000
Internal Service Funds	2,000

3. Bond proceeds recorded in *Capital Projects Funds* totaled $300,000. Payments to retire bonds being serviced by *Debt Service Funds* totaled $400,000. Interest owed on bonds being serviced by *Debt Service Funds* at 6/30/05 *increased* by $50,000 (from $500,000 on 6/30/04). Deferred revenues relating to property taxes at 6/30/05 *decreased* by $60,000 (from $600,000 at 6/30/04).
4. An employee who was injured during the year filed a lawsuit. A settlement was made that requires the city to pay $70,000 annually for 10 years *beginning* 8/1/05.
5. Vacation pay owed at year end *increased* as follows:

	6/30/04	6/30/05
Expected to be paid shortly after year-end in year of incurrence	$10,000	$ 12,000
Not expected to be paid shortly after year-end in year of incurrence	80,000	88,000
Total	$90,000	$100,000

Required
1. Prepare the conversion entries to be recorded on the consolidation/conversion worksheet at 6/30/05.
2. Prepare the entry to adjust the *general capital assets and general long-term liabilities ledger* at 6/30/05.

THINKING CRITICALLY

Cases

C 25-1 **Expenditure Recognition on Construction Contract** On 1/1/05, the city council of Centersville approved the construction of a new civic center. It immediately signed a construction contract having a fixed price of $10,000,000. The terms of the contract follow:

1. A $2,000,000 payment is to be made to the contractor at the time of the signing. (The city made the payment.)
2. Progress billings are to be made each December 20 based on the percentage of completion multiplied by $7,000,000.
3. Progress payments are to be made within 10 days after bills are submitted.
4. Upon completion of the project, the $1,000,000 final payment is to be made. On 12/20/05, the contractor submitted a progress billing for $2,800,000 (40% of $7,000,000). The city paid it on 12/30/05.

Required
1. What amount should the city report for expenditures in its *Capital Projects Fund* for 2005?
2. Assuming that the contractor uses the percentage of completion method of accounting, what amount should the contractor report for sales for 2005?
3. Explain the disparity between requirements 1 and 2.

C 25-2 **Accounting for *General Fund* Overhead Allocation to an *Enterprise Fund*** Crystal City has an Electric Utility *Enterprise Fund*. The city believes that some of its general overhead (accounted for in the *General Fund*) should be allocated to the Electric Utility *Enterprise Fund* because it obtains benefits. If the utility were a private corporation, its overhead would be higher than it is now. A cash payment will be made from the Electric Utility *Enterprise Fund* to the *General Fund* for the amount of the overhead allocation.

Required How should the overhead allocation and cash payment be reported in each fund's financial statements?

chapter

26

Not-for-Profit Organizations: Introduction and *Private* NPOs

The important thing is to not stop questioning.

ALBERT EINSTEIN

LEARNING OBJECTIVES

To Understand

> The types of not-for-profit organizations (NPOs) that exist.

> The salient characteristics of NPOs.

> The uniform manner of reporting contributions and valuing investments required for all *private* NPOs.

> The types of long-lived assets that *private* NPOs must depreciate or need *not* depreciate.

> The unique, uniform manner to display financial information in financial statements for all *private* NPOs.

TOPIC OUTLINE

Appendices can be found at http://www.pahler.swlearning.com

CHAPTER OVERVIEW

We begin this chapter by describing (1) the various types of not-for-profit organizations (NPOs) that exist, (2) the unique characteristics of NPOs, and (3) certain aspects of *nongovernmental* NPOs. Nongovernmental NPOs (hereafter *private* NPOs) fall under the jurisdiction of the Financial Accounting Standards Board (FASB) and must follow its guidance.

Governmental NPOs (hereafter *public* NPOs), however, fall under the jurisdiction of the Governmental Accounting Standards Board (GASB) and must follow GASB guidance. This chapter discusses FASB guidance. GASB guidance for *public* NPOs is discussed in detail in Appendix 26B. The major substantive financial reporting differences between the FASB guidance and the GASB guidance exist primarily for only one type of NPO—colleges and universities—and are discussed in Appendix 26C.

Concerning the FASB guidance discussed in this chapter, we discuss (1) reporting contributions (a major source of funds for many NPOs); (2) recognizing depreciation on long-lived assets; (3) presenting in the financial statements amounts used for external reporting purposes; and (4) valuing investments in debt and equity securities, investments that are often quite sizable for many NPOs.

Determining Whether an NPO Is a *Private* or *Public* Organization

In some cases, it may *not* be readily apparent whether an NPO is a *private* or *public* organization. Accordingly, the AICPA's "**Not-for-Profit Organizations**" audit and accounting guide (discussed later) contains a definition of a *public* (governmental) organization that is to be used in making this determination. A *public* organization is one that has one or more of the following characteristics:

a. Popular election of officers or appointment (or approval) of a controlling majority of the members of the organization's governing body by officials of one or more state or local governments;
b. The potential for unilateral dissolution by a government with the net assets reverting to a government; or
c. The power to enact and enforce a tax levy.[1]

Thus NPOs *not* having at least one of the preceding characteristics are *private* organizations.

A: INTRODUCTION

I. TYPES OF NOT-FOR-PROFIT ORGANIZATIONS

Traditionally, NPOs have been grouped into the following four categories:

> Health care organizations (HCOs).
> Colleges and universities (C&Us).
> Voluntary health and welfare organizations (VHWOs).
> Certain (or "all other") nonprofit organizations (CNOs).

Category 1: Health Care Organizations

This category includes hospitals (other than those at the federal level, such as veterans hospitals), health maintenance organizations, nursing homes, continuing care retirement communities, intermediate care facilities, medical group practices, clinics, and other ambulatory care organizations.

1 "Not-for-Profit Organizations" (New York: American Institute of Certified Public Accountants, 1996), para. 1.03.

Category 2: Colleges and Universities

This category includes all state and private colleges and universities, as well as two-year colleges. Commercial business and technical schools—"for-profit" enterprises—are excluded.

Category 3: Voluntary Health and Welfare Organizations

This category includes NPOs that provide a broad range of public services in the areas of health, social welfare, and community services. Such organizations include the American Red Cross, the American Cancer Society, the American Heart Association, the United Way of America, Goodwill Industries, the Salvation Army, the Girl Scouts, the Boy Scouts, and many others dedicated to serving human needs and the public good. In terms of the size of VHWOs, more than 90% of them are almost minuscule in comparison to the large VHWOs, such as the United Way or the American Red Cross.

Category 4: Certain Not-for-Profit Organizations

This category includes cemetery organizations, civic and community organizations, fraternal organizations, performing arts organizations, private and community foundations, professional associations,[2] political parties, political action committees, public broadcasting stations, religious organizations, research and scientific organizations, social and country clubs, trade associations, and zoological and botanical societies.

Excluded Entities

Excluded from the CNO category are entities whose purpose is to serve the economic interests of their owners, members, participants, or trust beneficiaries by paying dividends, lowering costs, or providing other economic benefits directly and proportionately to these parties. Examples of such excluded entities are credit unions, employee benefit and pension plans, mutual insurance companies, mutual banks, farm and rural cooperatives, and trusts.

II. Characteristics of Not-for-Profit Organizations

NPOs usually possess the following characteristics (in varying degrees) that distinguish them from commercial business enterprises:

> An absence of an ownership interest such as that for business enterprises.
> A mission to provide services to their users, patients, society as a whole, or members—but *not* at a profit.
> A dependence on significant levels of contributions (from resource providers who do *not* expect commensurate or proportionate monetary return) to carry out the stated mission.
> A significant level of assets that are restricted as to their use as a result of donor stipulations—something that has major financial reporting implications.
> Tax-exempt status (avoids income taxes **and** enables many NPOs to obtain greater contributions than otherwise possible).

[2] In accounting, the professional organizations are the Financial Accounting Standards Board (FASB), the American Institute of Certified Public Accountants (AICPA), the Institute of Management Accountants (IMA), the Government Finance Officers Association (GFOA), the American Accounting Association (AAA), the National Association of College and University Business Officers Organization (NACUBO), and Beta Alpha Psi (BAP).

Absence of an Outside Ownership Interest

NPOs are *not* owned by an individual proprietor, partners, or common and preferred stock investors but by the general public or the NPO's members. Accordingly, success is *not* measured by achieving acceptable rates of profitability on an equity interest as it is for business enterprises.

Converting to a For-Profit Entity or Going Out of Existence

Private NPOs sometimes (1) convert to a for-profit business, (2) are acquired by a *private* for-profit business (many *private* hospitals were acquired by health maintenance organizations in the last few years), or (3) cease their activities and go out of existence. Under state laws, such NPOs must (1) give their remaining assets to an appropriate governmental unit or (2) donate their remaining assets to a public charity or public purpose. (See the Case in Point below.)

CASE IN POINT

In 1994, Blue Cross of California converted to a for-profit health maintenance organization, Wellpoint Health Systems. Under California state law, Blue Cross had to donate the $2.3 billion value of its net assets to a charitable or public purpose. Blue Cross's plan was to donate this amount to a new nonprofit foundation that would give millions annually to health charities.

Financial Reporting for *Private* NPOs

Because managements of *private* NPOs are *not* responsible to shareholders (who do *not* exist), they are responsible instead to (1) the NPO's board of directors or board of trustees and (2) state agencies (which require annual reports to be filed).

The Mission to Provide Services

Because the mission is to provide services rather than maximize stockholders' equity, a comparison of revenues with costs and expenses does *not* have the same meaning to NPOs as it does for *business enterprises*. For *business enterprises*, revenues are compared with costs and expenses to determine *net income*. Furthermore, a causal relationship exists between these items for *business enterprises* because costs and expenses are incurred to generate revenues.

For NPOs, however, no such causal relationship exists between costs and expenses incurred and revenues. Accordingly, the *gross profit* and *operating profit* indicators are meaningless. Additional factors that cause these indicators to be meaningless are (1) the diversity of funding sources, (2) the providing of services at prices *not* intended to recover the entire cost, and (3) for *public* colleges and universities, the political nature and uncertain timing of the funding sources.

Even though revenues of NPOs are *not* "earned" as is the case for *business enterprises*, it is still just as important to compare revenues with costs and expenses. Such a comparison merely tells a different story—that is, **the extent to which the NPO is covering its costs and expenses incurred to provide services during the period.** To prevent any potential misunderstanding that an NPO's *operating statement* is an *income statement*, *private* NPOs are required to call their operating statement a *statement of activities*. (*Public* NPOs also use this or other descriptive titles to describe the operating statement to avoid any implication that it is an *income statement*.)

Dependence on Contributions (More Important for Some NPOs Than Others)

The amounts charged to the users of NPO services often are *less* than the costs and expenses incurred to provide the services. For example, many hospitals and *private* C&Us *cannot* meet their operating costs and expenses from patient fees and student tuition alone. The difference must be provided by private and public funding, such as that from federal and state governments, philanthropic organizations, and individuals. These *external providers* perceive the NPO as a public-service agency accomplishing goals for the public good.

The type of NPO that depends most heavily on contributions is by far the VHWO. Most of their financial resource inflows are from others who do *not* receive direct benefits. Their principal financial resource inflows are public contributions made either directly to them or through the United Way[3] and government grants. Collectively, these inflows from *outside sources* are commonly referred to as *outside money*, as contrasted with inflows from *investment earnings* and *user fees*, which collectively are commonly referred to as *inside money*. Many NPOs, however, receive no contributions, most notably the majority of CNOs, which serve their members.

Assets Restricted as to Use

An NPO's assets may be restricted by (1) stipulations that donors impose (*external* restrictions) or (2) actions of the NPO's board of directors (*internal* restrictions).

Donor Restrictions

Many contributors to NPOs stipulate (1) the specific program or manner in which the contributed asset is to be used, (2) the time period in which the contributed asset is to be used, or (3) the specific program for which the income earned on the contributed asset (for contributed assets required to be invested) is to be used. **Donor-imposed restrictions** limit management's ability to (1) use the NPO's assets as management pleases and (2) respond to unexpected needs and opportunities—something the FASB refers to as an NPO's **"financial flexibility."**

Donor restrictions must be fully disclosed. These disclosures are so important that *FAS 117* requires that the format of the financial statements themselves (shown shortly) rather than the notes reveal these restrictions.

Donor-Restricted Endowment Funds

Often donors stipulate that the contributed asset (whether received by gift or bequest) *cannot* be expended either (1) in perpetuity or (2) for a specified period. For control purposes, the NPO must account for the donated asset(s) separately to comply with the donor's stipulations in future periods. Accordingly, it is said that the donor has created an endowment fund. An **endowment fund** is merely an established fund of cash, securities, or other assets that is accounted for separately from all other assets either by using (1) separate general ledger accounts or (2) a separate set of books. *Private* C&Us usually have quite sizable donor-restricted endowment funds.

CASE IN POINT

Harvard University's Endowment Fund

Harvard University has 22 billion in its donor-restricted endowment fund.

Historically, such assets usually have been accounted for in separate sets of books for control purposes (doing so results in fund accounting), although this is *not* absolutely necessary unless the donor so stipulates.

Board-Designated Endowment Funds

Far less sizable and prevalent than donor-restricted endowments are **board-designated endowments** (often called *quasi-endowments*). These endowments are created by action of the NPO's board of directors, such as a board designation that certain assets be set aside and used only for a capital addition project. Board-designated assets may be disclosed in the financial statements **or** in the notes.

---

[3] As a condition of granting money, the United Way almost always requires recipient VHWOs to (1) be audited and (2) follow GAAP.

Tax-Exempt Status

Most *private* NPOs of any size seek and receive tax-exempt status from the IRS.[4] Upon determination that the NPO is a qualifying organization (such as a charity, an educational institution, a religious organization), the IRS sends a letter stating that the entity qualifies as a Section 501(c) corporation of the Internal Revenue Code. A tax-exempt *private* NPO for income tax–reporting purposes (1) pays no income taxes on the excess of its revenues (including its contribution revenues) over its costs and expenses (with certain exceptions discussed shortly) and (2) files annually with the IRS an information return on Form 990, 990A, or 990PF. Also, most states allow *private* NPOs that have 501(c) status to be exempt from paying (1) *state income* taxes, (2) *state sales taxes*, and (3) *property taxes*. More than 800,000 NPOs file tax returns with the IRS annually. In general, only NPOs having annual revenues of *more than* $25,000 must file federal tax returns (churches are exempt). (The IRS may revoke an NPO's tax-exempt status if the IRS's "reasonable compensation" rules are violated.)

Scores of *private* colleges and hospitals have changed to nonprofit status over the years to greatly increase their ability to obtain federal grants and donor contributions that are tax deductible only if made to an NPO qualifying as such for tax-reporting purposes. (Of course, *not* having to pay income taxes is an additional bonus.)

Currently, nearly 1.3 million tax-exempt NPOs exist in the United States, with the number growing at the rate of more than 40,000 annually. These NPOs raise over $700 billion of revenue annually and control an estimated 11% of the gross national product.

What If Some of the *Private* NPOs Activities Are *Business Related*?

If some of a *private* NPO's activities are business related or if any of an NPO's investments are *not* passive in nature, however, the NPO must report such business-related income on a separate tax return and pay income taxes on that income at the *highest* corporate rate. For example, assume a symphony NPO sells tickets to (1) concerts that it presents and (2) events that others present. The activities associated with selling tickets to the other events are *business related*. (Note that having *business-related* activities requires allocating costs and expenses to those business-related activities.)

Allowable Exceptions

The IRS regulations contain **two** allowed exceptions to the taxability of unrelated business income:

1. **The items sold must satisfy the "substantially related" test.** For example, the sale of books and supplies by college bookstores satisfies this test because those items are substantially related to the colleges' educational purposes. Thus there must be a **"substantial causal relationship"** between (1) the NPO's business activities and (2) the NPO's exempt purpose. **The business activity must "contribute importantly" to the achievement of the NPO's exempt purpose.** If there is *not* a sufficient connection, the NPO will be charged as having unrelated business taxable income (UBTI in tax jargon).
2. **The items sold must satisfy the "convenience test."** For example, a college bookstores' sales to students and college employees of wearing apparel, toiletries, and snack food satisfy this test because such items are for the convenience of the students and employees. (Sales to alumni would *not* qualify.) The sale of computers to students and faculty, however, is not as clear.

---

[4] Internal Revenue Code Section 501(c) classifies NPOs into 25 categories, each of which is dealt with in a separate subsection. Some of the NPOs may be eligible for tax-deductible donations under Section 170 of the Code. NPOs exempt under Section 501(c)(3) receive the largest part of tax-deductible donations. These are NPOs whose purpose is charitable, educational, religious, scientific, or related to public safety testing. Their activities are restricted in that they must further one or more of these exempt purposes. Examples of these NPOs include public charities, nonprofit hospitals, nonprofit universities and schools, youth organizations, community fund-raising campaigns, and environmental support groups. They are also restricted from activities to influence legislation, and they *cannot* participate in any political campaign on behalf of, or in opposition to, any candidate for political office.

In contrast, donations to 501(c)(4) "social welfare organizations" are *not* tax-deductible. Such NPOs **can** lobby, so long as the principal purpose of the lobbying is to advance social welfare. (The biggest 501(c)(4) is the American Association of Retired Persons [AARP], which is also the biggest nonprofit lobby.) Many 501(c)(3) NPOs create 501(c)(4) units to skirt lobbying restrictions.

In practice, tax law on this subject is somewhat vague, and thus it leaves wide latitude for interpretation as to whether a specific activity is taxable. Further complicating the matter is that the tax law has several categories of NPOs, each of which has its own rules. Thus social welfare organizations and charities are held to different standards.

Overall, more than 50% of the total revenues of all NPOs comes from the sale of goods, services, and endorsements, as opposed to donations, bequests, and members' dues. Often, these sales are in direct competition with *private* for-profit businesses, which often claim that they "suffer from unfair competition."

The Internal Revenue Service (1) audits roughly 11,000 of the 1.3 million tax-exempt NPOs each year and (2) assesses roughly $125 million of taxes and penalties.

CASE IN POINT

The American Association of Retired Persons (AARP), a lobby for the nation's older people and one of Washington's most formidable lobbies, is a tax-exempt NPO. Roughly 45% of its 1994 revenues of $382 million (excluding federal grants) came from endorsing products of commercial companies.

These commercial operations, which AARP claims should be *non*taxable, have been so successful that AARP is currently embroiled in a dispute with the IRS. In 1994, AARP paid the IRS $135 million to resolve claims over tax returns for 1985–1993.

III. FASB Guidance versus GASB Guidance

Because C&Us and HCOs exist widely in both the *private sector* and the *public sector*, the different reporting requirements of the FASB and the GASB are easily dealt with by sequencing our remaining discussion of NPOs as follows:

Chapter 26 (FASB Guidance)	Appendix 26B & 26C (GASB Guidance)
Private HCOs	Public HCOs
Private C&Us	Public C&Us
VHWOs	
CNOs	

Furthermore, the major substantive financial reporting difference between the FASB guidance and the GASB guidance concerns C&Us—*not* both HCOs *and* C&Us. These differences are discussed in detail in Appendix 26C.

B: *Private* NPOs

IV. The FASB's 1993 Standards for *Private* NPOs—A Historic Achievement in Bringing About Uniformity, Simplification, and Proper Focus

In 1993, the FASB completed two major projects that addressed the primary financial reporting issues for private NPOs: (1) *when* and *how* to report contributions received and (2) whether to present financial statements for external reporting purposes that focus on (a) the NPO as a whole (an *aggregated* basis) or (b) individual funds (a *disaggregated* basis). The completion of these projects resulted in the 1993 issuance of the following two FASB financial reporting standards:

1. FASB *Statement No. 116*, "Accounting for Contributions Received and Contributions Made."
2. FASB *Statement No. 117*, "Financial Statements of Not-for-Profit Organizations."

These standards (1) eliminated numerous financial reporting inconsistencies between the various types of *private* NPOs, (2) require financial statement reporting that focuses on the NPO as a whole (*aggregated*) rather than on a fund-by-fund basis (*disaggregated*), and (3) apply to all *private* NPOs. By concluding that differences in organizational structure, purpose, or legal form do *not* justify different standards for recognizing and measuring assets and liabilities, the FASB both (1) maximized comparability among different kinds of NPOs and (2) thereby enhanced the understandability and decision usefulness of not-for-profit financial statements.

Even though these standards constitute a giant step forward in financial reporting for *private* NPOs, the manner of reporting fund-raising costs for VHWOs is another important reporting issue to financial statement users that warrants addressing.

Revisions to the AICPA's Four Old NPO Audit and Accounting Guides

The AICPA published two new audit and accounting guides in 1996 that (1) are based on the four FASB NPO standards (*Nos. 93*, *116*, *117*, and *124*) and (2) superseded four of its old NPO audit guides. (Both of these guides were revised in 2003.)

A unique aspect of the AICPA audit guides is that *FAS 117* allows them to provide more detailed guidance than that set forth in *FAS 117*. Accordingly, the specific guidance in these audit guides can and does differ from that in *FAS 117*. The major differences that exist for HCOs—both *private* and *public*—are discussed in Appendix 26B. (The differences for other types of NPOs are *not* significant.)

The NPO Audit and Accounting Guide (Excluding HCOs)

This guide is titled "Not-for-Profit Organizations"; it superseded three of the AICPA's old NPO audit guides (the C&U audit guide issued in 1975, the VHWO audit guide issued in 1988, and the CNO audit guide issued in 1987) concerning *private* NPOs.

The HCO Audit and Accounting Guide

This guide is titled "Health Care Organizations"; it superseded the AICPA's old HCO audit guide issued in 1990 concerning *all* HCOs—that is, for-profit HCOs, *private* not-for-profit HCOs, and *public* HCOs (automatically not-for-profit).

V. ACCOUNTING FOR CONTRIBUTIONS

FAS 116, "Accounting for Contributions Received and Contributions Made," which encompasses contributed services, requires *private* NPOs to (1) report almost all *unrestricted* and *restricted* contributions, including contributions that establish endowments, as contributions in the Revenues, Gains, and Other Support category of the statement of activities **when received** and (2) value both the contributions revenue and the related contribution receivables at their fair value when received.

Contributions Defined

In *FAS 116*, *contributions* are defined as shown on the following page.

> An *unconditional* [emphasis added] transfer of cash or other assets to an entity or a settlement or cancellation of its liabilities in a voluntary nonreciprocal transfer by another entity acting other than as an owner.[5]

For clarification purposes, *unconditional* means with no conditions (or strings) attached. *Nonreciprocal transfers* are transactions in which value is *not* received or given in exchange. Therefore, transfers of assets under contract that are in substance the purchase of goods or services are outside the scope of *FAS 116*.

What Does Transfer Mean?

The preceding definition of *contributions* implies that the transfer of cash or other assets must have been made to qualify as a contribution. However, **unconditional promises**[6]—which may be written or oral—**to give** cash or other assets in the future are considered to be unconditional transfers. Accordingly, such unconditional promises to give can be accrued as Contributions Receivable in the balance sheet **when received** and thus can be concurrently recognized in the statement of activities as revenues from contributions. (Other terms used to describe promises to give are *awards*, *grants*, *subscriptions*, and *appropriations*.)

To recognize unconditional promises in the financial statements, however, sufficient evidence in the form of verifiable documentation that a promise was made and received must exist. A communication that is unclear as to whether it constitutes an unconditional promise is deemed an unconditional promise if it is legally enforceable.

Note that besides cash, the preceding definition of contributions includes the transfer of **other assets**, defined in *FAS 116* as follows:

> securities, land, buildings, use of facilities or utilities, materials and supplies, intangible assets, services, and unconditional promises to give those items in the future.[7]

Conditional Promises to Give

The conceptual opposite of the unconditional promise to give is the **conditional promise to give**, which depends on the occurrence of a specified future and uncertain event that must occur to bind the promisor and thus transform the promise from conditional to unconditional status. For example, the promisor may stipulate that the NPO must first raise at least 50% of the $1 million needed for the expansion project. Being conditional, such promises to give automatically fall outside the definition of contributions. If the possibility that the condition will *not* be met is remote, such promises are considered unconditional.

If assets have been received and the retention and use of such assets is conditional on a future event, the offsetting credit is made to the Refundable Advance account (in the Liabilities section of the balance sheet) until the conditional future event occurs.

Check Points

Under *FAS 116*, promises to give cash for which stipulations exist as to the use of the cash are recorded as which of the following?

a. Revenues or other support when received.
b. Revenues or other support when collected.
c. Revenues or other support when the expenditures are made to satisfy the intended purpose.
d. Direct additions to equity.

Answer: a

---

[5] *Statement of Financial Accounting Standards No. 116*, "Accounting for Contributions Received and Contributions Made" (Norwalk, CT: Financial Accounting Standards Board, 1993), p. 67.

[6] The four nonprofit AICPA audit guides that predate *FAS 116* use the term *pledge* instead of *contribution*. *FAS 116* does *not* use *pledge* because that term describes not only promises to give but also plans or intentions to give that are *not* promises.

[7] *FAS 116*, para. 5.

Under *FAS 116*, recognition in the statement of activities of the receipt of a conditional promise to give is which of the following?

a. Mandatory
b. Prohibited
c. Optional
d. Depends on the probability of the condition occurring

Answer: d

Contributions of Monetary and Nonmonetary Assets

With certain limited exceptions, contributions of monetary and nonmonetary assets are recognized as revenues when received. (The exceptions are [1] assets received on conditional status for which the possibility of the conditional future event occurring is remote, as mentioned previously, and [2] collection items that are *not* recognized in the financial statements, which are discussed in detail later.)

Measurement at Fair Value

Contributions of monetary and nonmonetary assets are valued at the fair value of the assets received, which may require (1) obtaining quoted market prices (usually the best evidence of fair value, if available), (2) using independent appraisals, or (3) using other appropriate methods, such as determining the present value of estimated future cash flows—for unconditional promises to give expected to be collected over *more than* one year. When present value procedures are used, the subsequent recognition of the interest element is reported as *contribution income* by the donee—*not* as interest income. Allowances for uncollectibles should be recorded as necessary so that the contribution revenues and related receivables are both valued at their fair value.

The journal entry to recognize unconditional promises of $5,000 cash that (1) are estimated to be 80% collectible and (2) can be spent for any purpose, is as follows:

Contributions Receivable	5,000	
Allowance for Uncollectibles.		1,000
Contribution Revenues—Unrestricted[a]		4,000

[a] This unrestricted designation is explained more fully shortly.

CHECK POINT

On 1/1/06, a *private* NPO received the gift of an office building having an estimated useful life of 10 years and no salvage value. The donor's cost was $300,000, and the fair value at the donation date was $500,000. The building cannot be sold for five years. What amount should be reported for depreciation expense for 2006?

a. $–0–
b. $30,000
c. $50,000
d. $60,000
e. $100,000

Answer: c

Contributions of Services

Contributed services are recognized as revenues in the period received if

> the services received (a) **create or enhance nonfinancial assets** [emphasis added] or (b) **require specialized skills** [emphasis added], are provided by individuals possessing those skills, and

> would typically need to be purchased if not provided by donation. Services requiring specialized skills are provided by accountants, architects, carpenters, doctors, electricians, lawyers, nurses, plumbers, teachers, and other professionals and craftsmen. Contributed services and promises to give services that do not meet the above criteria shall not be recognized.[8]

For contributed services, disclosures must be made of (1) the nature and extent of the contributed services received during the period, (2) the amount recognized as revenues in the financial statements, and (3) the programs or activities in which those services were used. When the conditions for recognition are *not* satisfied, *FAS 116* encourages disclosures of the fair value of contributed services received that have *not* been recognized in the financial statements, if practicable.

Measurement at Fair Value

Recognizable contributed services that do *not* create or enhance nonfinancial assets, such as a CPA performing a free audit or a lawyer giving free legal advice, are recorded at the fair value of the services contributed. For recognizable contributed services that create or enhance nonfinancial assets, such as refurbishing a building by either lay volunteers or volunteer carpenters, the fair value of the asset or asset enhancement may be recognized instead of the fair value of the contributed services.

A journal entry to recognize the $4,000 fair value of free legal services follows:

Expenses—Management and General	4,000	
Contribution Revenues—Unrestricted		4,000

Note that the result is the same as if (1) the lawyer had contributed $4,000 cash to the NPO and (2) the NPO used the $4,000 cash to pay the lawyer for the legal services.

CHECK POINT

Under *FAS 116*, which of the following types of contributed services would *not* be reported in the statement of activities?

a. A CPA performs the NPO's annual audit at no charge.
b. A board member of the NPO is a lawyer, and that member performs some legal work for the NPO at no charge.
c. An employee of the NPO having an annual salary of $40,000 per year for working 2,000 hours works 2,300 hours, volunteering the 300 extra hours.
d. A plumber makes free repairs to the NPO facility.

Answer: c

Contributed Works of Art, Historical Treasures, and Similar Assets Received (Collection Items)

Collection items received **need** *not* be capitalized as assets and concurrently recognized as revenues in the statement of activities. Specifically, collection items need not be capitalized if all the following conditions are satisfied:

> **a.** [They] are held for public exhibition, education, or research in furtherance of public service rather than financial gain
> **b.** [They] are protected, kept unencumbered, cared for, and preserved
> **c.** [They] are subject to an organizational policy that requires the proceeds from sales of collection items to be used to acquire other items for collections.[9]

---

[8] *FAS 116*, para. 9.

[9] *FAS 116*, para. 11.

If a *private* NPO chooses to capitalize and recognize such collections, however, either **retroactive capitalization** or **prospective capitalization** is permitted—selective capitalization is *not* permitted.

CHECK POINT

Under *FAS 116*, the recognition of contributed **collection items** is which of the following?
a. Mandatory
b. Prohibited
c. Optional

Answer: c

Reporting Contributions in the *Statement of Activities*

As discussed in more detail shortly, *FAS 117* requires a *Statement of Activities* that shows the changes in three categories of net assets (or equity):

1. Unrestricted net assets.
2. Temporarily restricted net assets.
3. Permanently restricted net assets.

Accordingly, contributions relating to each category must be displayed separately in the *Statement of Activities.*

Unrestricted Contributions

Contributions received *without* donor restrictions increase unrestricted **net assets.** Accordingly, in the statement of activities, such contributions are reported in the Unrestricted category.

Restricted Contributions

A restriction on the use of contributed assets can result from either (1) a donor's explicit stipulations or (2) the circumstances surrounding the contribution that clearly show the donor's intent to restrict use of the contributed assets. In the statement of activities, such contributions are reported in one of the restricted categories (*temporarily restricted* or *permanently restricted*, as appropriate).

As a practical matter, however, donor-restricted contributions whose conditions are *fulfilled in the same period in which the contribution is recognized* may be reported in the Unrestricted category provided that the entity (1) consistently follows this policy and (2) discloses it.

For simplicity, we hereafter usually use the following abbreviations for these three net asset categories:

1. For unrestricted net assets: *UR net assets.*
2. For temporarily restricted net assets: *TR net assets.*
3. For permanently restricted net assets: *PR net assets.*

CHECK POINTS

A *private* NPO received promises of $600,000 in 2006 from local citizens, half of which were payable in 2006, the other half payable in 2007 for use in 2007. Only 90% of the amount is expected to be collectible. What amount should be reported for Contribution Revenues (in total) for 2006?
a. $-0-
b. $270,000

c. $540,000
d. $600,000

Answer: c

What amount should be reported for Contribution Revenues—Unrestricted for 2006?
a. $-0-
b. $270,000
c. $540,000
d. $600,000

Answer: b

Permanently Restricted Contributions

Contributions having stipulations that prohibit spending the contributed asset (the principal) in perpetuity create **permanent endowments.**

Reporting Income Earned on Invested Principal

As to income earned on the invested principal, the donor may stipulate that it be used for (1) any purpose (thus being classified in the Unrestricted category), (2) certain purposes (thus being classified in the Temporarily Restricted category), (3) increasing the principal, for example, to maintain purchasing power or reach a specified dollar amount (thus being classified in the Permanently Restricted category), or (4) any combination of these.

Temporarily Restricted Contributions

A donor may stipulate that the contributed asset be expended (1) on a specific program or activity, (2) in a later time period, or (3) to acquire fixed assets. Thus unlike a permanently restricted asset, the **temporarily restricted** contributed asset eventually will be expended (or used up for depreciable fixed assets) as the donor intended. The following items are also usually classified as temporarily restricted contributions:

1. **Promises with future payment dates.** Sometimes donors make unconditional promises to give with payments due over several periods. To the extent that future payments have been recorded as Contributions Receivable, the offsetting credit is usually reported as increasing ***temporarily restricted*** **net assets** (or equity). The unavailability of the funds usually means that the use of the asset is effectively restricted to the future period(s). If the donor intended the contribution to be used to support activities of the current period (whether by explicit stipulations or circumstances surrounding the receipt of the promise), however, the contribution may be shown as increasing ***UR*** *net assets.*
2. **Term endowments.** The principal of term endowments may be expended at some future point in time.

Check Point

Under *FAS 116*, contributions that are **endowments** are recorded as which of the following?
a. Revenues or other support when received.
b. Revenues or other support when collected.
c. Revenues or other support when the expenditures are made to satisfy the intended purpose.
d. Direct additions to equity.

Answer: a

Classifying Contributions of Fixed Assets: It Depends on Donor Stipulations or on the NPO's Accounting Policy

Explicit Donor Stipulations Exist

When a donor stipulates that the contributed fixed asset must be used for a specified time period, the contribution is reported as increasing either ***TR** net assets* or ***PR** net assets*, as appropriate. For example, land contributed for use as an open space preserve to be held in perpetuity is reported as increasing ***PR** net assets*. Assuming that the land has a fair value of $600,000, the journal entry is

Land	600,000	
Contribution Revenues—Permanently Restricted		600,000

On the other hand, a depreciable fixed asset that must be held for at least 10 years is classified as increasing ***TR*** **net assets**. After the tenth year, a **reclassification** from ***TR*** **net assets** to ***UR*** **net assets** must be reported separately in the statement of activities. (More about this shortly.)

Explicit Donor Stipulations Do *Not* Exist

In the absence of explicit donor stipulations, each NPO must establish an accounting policy as to whether an implied time restriction exists. If the NPO's accounting policy is to imply a time restriction, the contribution of a fixed asset is reported as though the donor had stipulated a time period restriction. Such policy is based on the presumption that the donor intended to have the NPO use the fixed asset over its useful life.

If the NPO's policy is *not* to imply a time restriction, the contribution of a fixed asset is reported as increasing unrestricted net assets. Such a policy is based on the presumption that the donor most likely did *not* intend to prevent the NPO from selling or disposing of the fixed asset at any point in time if it was in the best interest of the NPO; thus the NPO has the financial flexibility to dispose of the fixed asset at will.

If a donor contributes a fixed asset with the intent to have the NPO sell it and use the proceeds for any purpose, its contribution is always reported as increasing ***UR** net assets* (or equity).

Expiration of Donor-Imposed Time or Purpose Restrictions

As expenditures are made according to a donor's stipulations (for a specific purpose or in a specific time period), the NPO fulfills the donor's wishes. Accordingly, the donor's restrictions "expire." The statement of activities must reflect the expiration of a donor-imposed restriction. This is done by showing separately from other transactions a *reclassification* in the statement of activities between (1) the *temporarily restricted* category (a decrease) and (2) the *unrestricted category* (an increase). The journal entry to reflect the expiration of a $70,000 *purpose* restriction follows (we use the account descriptions illustrated in the AICPA's 1996 audit guide for NPOs as abbreviated for simplicity):

TR Net Assets—Transfer Out	70,000	
UR Net Assets—Transfer In		70,000

Note: These amounts, which are displayed as reclassifications in the statement of activities as shown later, are closed to the appropriate equity accounts when the accounts in the statement of activities are closed to the equity accounts at year-end.

A *purpose* restriction is deemed to have expired when an expense has been incurred for that purpose, regardless of whether unrestricted resources are also available for that expense. In other words, a liability could be incurred and cash might *not* be available at that time to pay the liability, but the purpose restriction is still deemed to have expired when the liability was incurred.

Expiration of Restrictions on Long-Lived Assets

Restrictions on contributed long-lived assets classified as temporarily restricted net assets (due either to donor stipulations or the NPO's accounting policy of implying a time restriction) expire over the estimated useful lives of the assets as they are exhausted or used up. Thus as depreciation expense is recognized on such *temporarily restricted* assets, a reclassification between the ***TR*** *Net Asset* category (a decrease) and the ***UR*** *Net Asset* category (an increase) must be reflected or recognized in the statement of activities. Assuming that the annual depreciation expense is $12,000, the year-end journal entry to reflect such a restriction expiration is as follows:

TR Net Assets—Transfer Out.	12,000	
UR Net Assets—Transfer In		12,000

Assume also that (1) a building having a fair value of $360,000 at the time of the donation had to be kept for 10 years, (2) it is depreciated over 30 years, and (3) its carrying value is $240,000 at the end of the tenth year. The journal entry at the end of the tenth year to reflect this restriction expiration is as follows:

TR Net Assets—Transfer Out.	240,000	
UR Net Assets—Transfer In		240,000

In the absence of donor-imposed restrictions or an accounting policy specifying how long contributed long-lived assets must be used, restrictions on long-lived assets and cash to acquire them expire when the long-lived assets are placed in service.

Distinguishing Contributions from *Exchange Transactions*

Recall that contributions are **nonreciprocal transfers**. In contrast, **exchange transactions** are *reciprocal* transfers in which each party receives and sacrifices something of approximately equal value. Determining the proper reporting classification of certain inflows may require judgment. (Detailed guidance is set forth in Chapter 5 of the AICPA's 1996 *Not-for-Profit Organizations* audit and accounting guide.) Furthermore, a given inflow may be *part contribution* and *part exchange transaction*. For example, some NPOs receive membership dues that have elements of *both* a *contribution* and an *exchange transaction* because members receive tangible or intangible benefits from their membership in the NPO. If the NPO has annual dues of $300 and the only benefit the members receive is a monthly newsletter with a fair value of $100, the remaining $200 is a *contribution*. The $100 is an exchange transaction (and must be recognized as revenues as the earnings process is completed).

Manner of Reporting Contributions Raised for Others

FASB *Statement No. 136*, "Transfers of Assets to a Not-for-Profit Organization or Charitable Trust That Raises or Holds Contributions for Others" (1999), requires NPOs that raise contributions that are designated for others (collectively referred to as "umbrella charity groups") to report those contributions as *liabilities*—**not** as *contribution revenues*. Only the portion of the contributions that the NPO can keep (roughly 10% for many NPOs) can be reported as *contributions revenues*. United Way, for instance, normally charges a processing fee equal to about 10% of designated donations. In addition, *FAS 136* requires that if an NPO discloses a ratio of *fundraising expenses* to *amounts raised*, it must also disclose how it computed the ratio.

VI. Recognizing Depreciation on Long-Lived Assets

FASB *Statement* No. 93, "Recognition of Depreciation by Not-for-Profit Organizations," requires that (1) **long-lived tangible assets be depreciated,** (2) the depreciation method(s) and expense for the period be disclosed, and (3) information on the major classes of depreciable assets and accumulated depreciation be disclosed.

Works of Art or Historical Treasures

Works of art or historical treasures *need not* be depreciated so long as certain conditions are met. In this respect, *FAS 93* states:

> Consistent with the accepted practice for land used as a building site, depreciation need not be recognized on individual works of art or historical treasures whose economic benefit or service potential is used up so slowly that their estimated useful lives are extraordinarily long. A work of art or historical treasure shall be deemed to have that characteristic only if verifiable evidence exists demonstrating that (a) the asset individually has cultural, aesthetic, or historical value that is worth preserving perpetually and (b) the holder has the technological and financial ability to protect and preserve essentially undiminished the service potential of the asset and is doing that.[10]

VII. Financial Statements for External Reporting

Required Financial Statements: A Focus on the Organization as a Whole

Unlike *FAS 116* (contributions), which focuses on recognition and measurement issues, *FAS 117* (financial statements of NPOs) specifies (1) **what** financial statements to present for external reporting purposes and (2) **what specific information, as a minimum, to show in those statements.** *Private* NPOs are required to present financial statements that focus on the **organization as a whole**; these are

> A statement of financial position.
> A statement of activities (the "operating" statement).
> A statement of cash flows.

Substantial Formatting Latitude Allowed

FAS 117 imposes no more stringent reporting standards than those for commercial for-profit entities. Thus even though these statements must include certain minimum information (discussed later), it neither prescribes nor prohibits particular formats for the financial statements. No requirement exists to distinguish "operating" items from "nonoperating" items. Thus *FAS 117* allows the same formatting flexibility in preparing financial statements that for-profit entities have.

---

[10] *FAS 93*, "Recognition of Depreciation by Not-for-Profit Organizations" (Norwalk, CT: Financial Accounting Standards Board, 1987), para. 6.

Accordingly, if an NPO desires to report an intermediate measure of "operations" (for example, the excess of operating revenues over operating expenses), it may do so under *FAS 117*. (*FAS 117* requires that such measure be reported, however, in a statement that at a minimum reports the change in ***UR** net assets* for the period.)

Providing More Relevant Information and Achieving Improved Understandability and Comparability

Donors make financial decisions in the context of NPOs as a whole, not of their individual parts. Accordingly, reporting on a fund-by-fund basis does **not** provide the most relevant information for external users to assess an NPO's ability to take appropriate actions to alter the amounts and timing of cash flows, often in response to rapidly changing needs and opportunities. For this reason, *FAS 117* emphasizes providing financial information for the entity as a whole.

Requiring Classifications Based on Donor-Imposed Restrictions

To provide information on financial flexibility, *FAS 117* requires classifications of an entity's net assets (equity) based on (1) **whether donor-imposed restrictions exist** and (2) **the type of donor-imposed restrictions.** Accordingly, the required statement of financial position must display three classes of net assets (or equity)—which are the same as those discussed earlier in the section on contributions: (1) **unrestricted,** (2) **temporarily restricted,** and (3) **permanently restricted.** Likewise, the statement of activities must display information showing the changes in these three classes of net assets (equity).

Donors' stipulations pertaining to endowments *usually* permit the NPO to (1) pool the donated assets with other assets and (2) sell or exchange the donated assets and make other suitable investments (providing that the economic benefits of the donated assets are *not* consumed or used for a purpose that does *not* comply with the donors' stipulations). Consequently, the terms **PR** *net assets* and **TR** *net assets* as used in the Net Assets section of the balance sheet generally refer to amounts of *net assets* restricted by donors—***not* to *specific* assets.** If a donor stipulated that a **specific** asset (such as shares of XYZ common stock) be held in perpetuity, however, the ***PR** net assets* amount *does* relate to a *specific* asset.

Standard Format for the Statement of Cash Flows

The required statement of cash flows is to be formatted in a manner consistent with the provisions of *FAS 95*, "Statement of Cash Flows," and with the other statements and accompanying notes that assist external users in assessing a private NPO's

- Liquidity and financial flexibility.
- Ability to meet its obligations.
- Management in discharging its stewardship responsibilities.

VIII. Illustrated Financial Statements

The Statement of Financial Position

The minimal display requirements for the statement of financial position follow:

- The statement should focus on the NPO as a whole and show amounts for its **total assets, total liabilities,** and **total net assets** (or equity).
- The net assets/equity section should show total amounts for each of the three classifications of net assets: **unrestricted, temporarily restricted,** and **permanently restricted.**
- The nature and amounts of **donor-imposed restrictions** should be disclosed.

> Information about **liquidity** should be shown in any of several ways in the statement and in its notes.

Illustration 26-1 presents a sample statement of financial position that meets the minimum disclosure requirements of *FAS 117*.

Review Points for Illustration 26-1. Note the following:

1. Like the balance sheets of for-profit business enterprises, the statement format assists the user in assessing **liquidity**. For ease of understanding, we show a **classified** statement of financial position, that is, with current and noncurrent asset and liability categories. An allowable alternative (the one illustrated in *FAS 117*) is to use an **unclassified** format with assets and liabilities sequenced based on relative liquidity.
2. The statement **purposely does *not* use the description "Fund Balance."** *FAS 117* does **not** use this description because it is considered appropriate only for reporting on a *fund-by-fund* basis,

ILLUSTRATION 26-1 STATEMENT OF FINANCIAL POSITION

The Foundation for the Needy
Statement of Financial Position
December 31, 2006

ASSETS	
Current Assets	
Cash and cash equivalents	$ 42,000
Accounts and interest receivable	51,000
Inventories and prepaid expenses	41,000
Contributions receivable	33,000
Short-term investments	24,000
Total *Current* Assets	$ 191,000
Noncurrent Assets	
Long-term investments	1,420,000
Land, buildings, and equipment	583,000
Assets restricted to investment in land, buildings, and equipment	36,000
Total Assets	$2,230,000
LIABILITIES	
Current Liabilities	
Accounts payable	$ 32,000
Refundable advance	3,000
Grants payable	2,000
Notes payable	14,000
Total Current Liabilities	$ 51,000
Noncurrent Liabilities	
Annuity obligations	11,000
Long-term debt	45,000
Total Liabilities	$ 107,000
NET ASSETS (OR EQUITY)	
Unrestricted[a]	**$ 990,000**
Temporarily restricted[a] **(Note A)**	**373,000**
Permanently restricted[a] **(Note B)**	**760,000**
Total Net Assets (Equity)	$2,123,000
Total Liabilities and Net Assets (Equity)	$2,230,000

[a] This is an *actual* general ledger account—*not* merely a classification category. Amounts shown in the applicable column of the *statement of activities* in Illustration 26-3 (discussed shortly) were closed to this account.

not on an *overall organization basis.* (Also, the term is more appropriate for *governmental* NPOs whether they report on an overall basis or a *fund-by-fund* basis.)

3. The unique feature of this statement relates to the three categories shown in the Net Assets (or Equity) section. (More about these categories shortly.)
4. Although not shown in the illustrated statement, a private NPO could also disclose **board-designated assets** in this statement by subdividing the unrestricted category into a board-designated category and an undesignated category. Such disclosures could also be made in the notes.

Important *Required* Notes to the Statement of Financial Position

Important financial statement notes concerning the ***TR* net asset** and **PR net asset** categories in the statement of financial position are shown in Illustration 26-2.

The Statement of Activities

The minimal information to be shown in the statement of activities—certain exceptions apply to HCOs, as discussed later—follows:

> Revenues, gains, and other support **by category** (unrestricted, temporarily restricted, or permanently restricted).
> Revenues, gains, and other support in the unrestricted category unless donor-imposed requirements limit the use of the assets. Contributions are presumed to be unrestricted in the absence

ILLUSTRATION 26-2 STATEMENT OF FINANCIAL POSITION

Key Notes for the Statement of Financial Position

Note A

Temporarily restricted net assets are restricted to the following:

Spending only for the following purposes or periods	
Community services	$111,000[a]
Public education	109,000[a]
Acquisition of buildings and equipment	26,000[b]
For community services after 2005 (pursuant to a **term endowment**)	20,000[a]
For any purpose after 12/31/06	6,000[a]
	$272,000
Buildings and equipment (already acquired)	101,000[b]
	$373,000

Note B

Permanently restricted net assets are restricted to the following:

Perpetual endowments for which the principal must be invested in perpetuity, the income from which is expendable for the following purposes	
Community services	$211,000
Public education	89,000
Any activities of the organization	422,000
	$722,000
Perpetual endowment requiring income to be added to the original gift until the principal is $50,000	33,000
Land required to be used as a public recreation area that by donor stipulation *cannot* be sold	5,000
	$760,000

[a] As funds are expended in accordance with the wishes of donors, these restrictions expire.

[b] As depreciation is recognized over the useful lives of these assets (the assets substantively being used up), these restrictions expire because the assets are being used in accordance with the donors' intent. During 2006, $12,000 depreciation expense was recognized on net assets restricted to investment in buildings and equipment.

of explicit donor stipulations or particular circumstances that indicate a donor's implicit restrictions on use.

> Other events that simultaneously increase one class of net assets while decreasing another—**expirations of restrictions**—reported separately from revenues, gains, expenses, and losses.
> **All expenses** in the unrestricted category.
> **Expenses by functional classification (such as major classes of program services and supporting activities)**, unless shown in notes to the financial statements. Reporting expenses by natural classification in a supplementary schedule is optional, except for VHWOs, which must also report by natural classifications (such as salaries, rent, utilities, interest expense, depreciation) in a matrix format in a separate financial statement.
> For the organization as a whole, the amount of change in ***UR** net assets*, ***TR** net assets*, and ***PR** net assets*.
> **Gross amounts for revenues and expenses**—including special events that often are ongoing and major activities, as opposed to being peripheral or incidental transactions. (However, investment revenues may be shown net of custodial fees and investment advisory fees.)

An example of a statement of activities meeting these minimum information disclosure requirements is shown in Illustration 26-3.

ILLUSTRATION 26-3 STATEMENT OF ACTIVITIES—SEPARATE COLUMNS FORMAT

The Foundation for the Needy
Statement of Activities
For the Year Ended December 31, 2006

	UNRESTRICTED	TEMPORARILY RESTRICTED	PERMANENTLY RESTRICTED	TOTAL
Revenues, Gains, and Other Support				
Contributions	$ 137,000	$ 32,000	$ 13,000	$ 182,000
Fees	64,000			64,000
Investment income (interest and dividends):				
Endowments	38,000	22,000	2,000	62,000
Other than endowments	23,000	16,000		39,000
Investment gains (realized and unrealized), net:				
Endowments	41,000	29,000	44,000	114,000
Other than endowments	27,000			27,000
Miscellaneous	16,000			16,000
	$ 346,000	$ 99,000	$ 59,000	$ 504,000
Net Assets Released from Restrictions as a Result of:				
Program expenditures	**76,000**	**(76,000)**		**–0–**
Equipment acquisitions	**11,000**	**(11,000)**		**–0–**
Time expirations	**26,000**	**(26,000)**		**–0–**
Total Revenues, Gains, and Other Support	$ 459,000	$ (14,000)	$ 59,000	$ 504,000
Expenses and Losses				
Community services	$(122,000)			$ (122,000)[a]
Public education	(84,000)			(84,000)[a]
Research	(52,000)			(52,000)[a]
Management and general	(94,000)			(94,000)[a]
Fund-raising	(23,000)			(23,000)[a]
Total Expenses	$(375,000)	$ –0–	$ –0–	$ (375,000)
Hurricane loss	(18,000)			(18,000)
Actuarial loss on annuity obligations		(3,000)		(3,000)
Total Expenses and Losses	$(393,000)	$ (3,000)	$ –0–	$ (396,000)
Change in Net Assets	**$ 66,000**	**$(17,000)**	**$ 59,000**	**$ 108,000**
Net assets—12/31/05	924,000	390,000	701,000	2,015,000
Net assets—12/31/06	$ 990,000	$ 373,000	$760,000	$2,123,000

[a] The breakdown of this amount by *"natural classification"* is shown in Illustration 26-5 on page 929.

Review Points for Illustration 26-3. Note the following:

1. The statement of activities is in **columnar format**. A **"layering" format** (not illustrated here) is also acceptable.
2. Contributions are assumed to have been received for all three net asset categories (the typical situation for most NPOs). The $13,000 contribution in the Permanently Restricted column is to **establish an endowment.**
3. Investment income from interest and dividends on endowments is also reported in all three net asset categories. All but $2,000 of the $62,000 of income earned on the endowments, however, **may be expended.** (Endowments are the bulk if not all of the $760,000 of permanently restricted net assets at year-end.) The $2,000 reported in the Permanently Restricted column signifies that this amount is being used either to (1) maintain purchasing power of some portion of the endowment principal or (2) increase the amount of some portion of the endowment principal for other reasons stipulated by a donor(s).
4. Expirations of donor-imposed **temporary restrictions** are reflected or recognized by showing separately **a reclassification** between the temporarily restricted category and the unrestricted category.
5. The statement shows expenses as decreases only in the Unrestricted column. Expenses are shown by function.
6. By requiring a format that shows the change in an NPO's net assets, the FASB has effectively required NPOs to present the **equivalent of *a statement of comprehensive income*** for a commercial for-profit entity. Such statement was discussed and illustrated in Chapter 15 (reporting foreign operations).
7. This operating statement format *cannot* be used by *private* HCOs. Instead, a substantially different format is required (as briefly discussed and illustrated later).

The Statement of Cash Flows

To assess the ability of an NPO to continue to provide services, users must have a complete set of financial statements, including a statement of cash flows. *FAS 117* amends *FAS 95*, "Statement of Cash Flows," so that it is also applicable to *private* NPOs. This statement can be prepared using the **direct** method (the preferred method) or the **indirect** method. An example of a cash flow statement for a private NPO using the direct method is shown in Illustration 26-4.

ILLUSTRATION 26-4 STATEMENT OF CASH FLOWS (DIRECT METHOD)

The Foundation for the Needy
Statement of Cash Flows
For the Year Ended December 31, 2006

Cash Flows from Operating Activities		
Cash collected from contributors	$ 171,000	
Cash collected from fees charged to service recipients	61,000	
Cash received from interest and dividends	54,000	
Miscellaneous receipts	14,000	
Cash paid to employees and suppliers	(323,000)	
Grants paid	(7,000)	
Interest paid	(4,000)	
Net Cash Used by Operating Activities		$ (34,000)
Cash Flows from Investing Activities		
Proceeds from sales of investments	$ 122,000	
Purchase of investments	(81,000)	
Purchase of equipment	(6,000)	
Insurance proceeds from hurricane loss	3,000	
Net Cash Obtained by Investing Activities		$ 38,000

ILLUSTRATION 26-4 STATEMENT OF CASH FLOWS (DIRECT METHOD) (*CONTINUED*)

Cash Flows from Financing Activities		
Proceeds from contributions restricted for the following:		
Investment in endowments	$ 13,000	
Investment in equipment	6,000	
	$ 19,000	
Other financing activities		
Cash received for interest and dividends which is restricted for reinvestment	$ 2,300	
Payments of principal on notes payable	(4,000)	
Payments of principal on long-term debt	(5,000)	
Payments of annuity obligations	(300)	
	$ (7,000)	
Net Cash Obtained by Financing Activities		$ 12,000
Net *Increase* in Cash and Cash Equivalents		**$ 16,000**
Cash and Cash Equivalents at 12/31/05		**26,000**
Cash and Cash Equivalents at 12/31/06		**$ 42,000**
Supplemental data for items *not* reportable in this statement:		
Gifts of equipment received		$ 4,000
Gift of paid-up life insurance, cash surrender value		5,000

Schedule to Statement of Cash Flows—
Reconciliation of *Change in Net Assets*
to *Net Cash Used by Operating Activities*

Change [Increase] in Net Assets (per Illustration 26-3)	**$108,000**
Adjustments to reconcile change in net assets to net cash used by operating activities:	
+ Depreciation expense	22,000[b]
+ Hurricane loss	18,000[a]
+ Actuarial loss on annuity obligations	3,000[a]
− Increase in accounts and interest receivable	(6,000)[b]
+ Decrease in inventories and prepaid expenses	5,000[b]
− Increase in contribution receivable	(12,000)[b]
+ Increase in accounts payable	1,000[b]
− Decrease in refundable advance	(9,000)[b]
− Decrease in grants payable	(8,000)[b]
− Contributions restricted for long-term investment	(13,000)[a]
− Interest and dividends restricted for long-term investment	(2,000)[a]
− Net unrealized and realized gains on long-term investments	(141,000)[a]
Net Cash Used by Operating Activities	**$ (34,000)**

[a] Amount ties into statement of activities in Illustration 26-3.

[b] An assumed amount inasmuch as a comparative balance sheet at 12/31/05 is *not* presented in Illustration 26-1.

Note: This schedule shows the extent to which the change in the NPO's net assets for 2006 was the result of cash flows from operating activities versus all other items. We believe a more understandable format is as follows:

Net Cash Used by Operating Activities	**$ (34,000)**
+ Net changes in receivables, payables, accruals, supplies, prepaids, and refundable advances	29,000
Subtotal	$ (5,000)
− Noncash flow items that decreased net assets:	
Depreciation expense	(22,000)
Hurricane loss	(18,000)
Actuarial loss	(3,000)
+ Other Cash and Noncash flow items that increased net assets:	
Contributions restricted for long-term investment	13,000
Interest and dividends restricted for long-term investment	2,000
Net unrealized and realized gains on long-term investments	141,000
Change *[Increase]* in Net Assets (per Illustration 26-3)	**$108,000**

The Statement of Functional Expenses—*Required* Only for *VHWOs*

Illustration 26-5 shows a statement of functional expenses that all VHWOs must furnish (VHWO regulators and watchdog groups lobbied heavily for this requirement). Many critics believe this statement should be required for all NPOs because (1) it is the single most important statement users look at and (2) the matrix makes very clear how the money is being used because it is so simple, direct, and easy to understand. The FASB, however, was apparently convinced by the arguments of *non* VHWO NPOs who claimed that furnishing such a statement would be (1) expensive and (2) **not** particularly useful to their financial statement users.

Note that requiring this statement does *not* solve the thorny joint-cost allocation problem of allocating costs between (1) **program activities** and (2) **fund-raising activities.** The statement does, however, give donors information that might indicate the existence of a problem.

CHECK POINTS

During 2006, a *private* NPO (1) incurred an $8,000 charge for printing its annual report and (2) spent $22,000 for merchandise sent to potential contributors on an unsolicited basis. What amount should be classified as fund-raising costs for 2006?

a. $-0-
b. $8,000
c. $22,000
d. $30,000

Answer: c

During 2006, a labor union incurred (1) $50,000 of administrative costs, (2) $2,000 of fund-raising costs, (3) $30,000 of labor negotiation costs, and (4) $4,000 of membership development costs. What amount should be reported for program services for 2006?

a. $30,000
b. $32,000
c. $34,000
d. $36,000
e. $80,000

Answer: a

Special Operating Statement Format *Required* for HCOs

For HCOs, however, the operating statement is presented quite differently (it resembles that used by **commercial** [for-profit] entities). This special manner of reporting for *private* HCOs exists because of the specific guidance set forth in the AICPA's 2003 HCO audit guide, discussed in detail in Appendix 26B. Specifically, the statement must:

1. Be called a *statement of operations* (rather than a *statement of activities*).
2. Report a *measure of operations*, such as *operating income or loss*. (In practice, it is common in the HCO industry to refer to items as being reported either "*above* the line" or "*below* the line.")
3. Report amounts only for the *unrestricted* category of net assets. (Receipts of *restricted* contributions are reported separately in a *statement of changes in net assets* [which is similar to a *statement of changes in stockholders' equity* used by *commercial* entities].)
4. Report *unrestricted* net asset inflows relating to expirations of restrictions in one of **two** specified categories, as appropriate:
   A. Expirations pertaining to *operations* (reported "*above* the line"). Report as a separate line item in the *revenues* section using the caption "net assets released from restrictions used for operations."

ILLUSTRATION 26-5 STATEMENT OF FUNCTIONAL EXPENSES

The Foundation for the Needy
Statement of Functional Expenses
For the Year Ended December 31, 2006

	PROGRAM SERVICES				*SUPPORTING* SERVICES			
	COMMUNITY SERVICES	PUBLIC EDUCATION	RESEARCH	SUBTOTAL—PROGRAM SERVICES	MANAGEMENT AND GENERAL	FUND-RAISING	SUBTOTAL—SUPPORTING SERVICES	TOTAL EXPENSES
Salaries	$ 55,000	$22,000	$18,000	$ 95,000	$53,900	$ 9,000	$ 62,900	$157,900
Employee benefits	6,500	3,200	2,200	11,900	7,700	1,300	9,000	20,900
Payroll taxes	4,500	2,400	1,800	8,700	6,300	1,100	7,400	16,100
Total Payroll Costs	$ 66,000	$27,600	$22,000	$115,600	$67,900	$11,400	$ 79,300	$194,900
Professional services	3,300	8,800	7,000	19,100	7,700	800	8,500	27,600
Supplies	1,400	2,600	2,100	6,100	1,300	300	1,600	7,700
Telephone	2,300	2,900	1,400	6,600	1,400	3,800	5,200	11,800
Occupancy	6,700	4,200	3,300	14,200	6,500	1,700	8,200	22,400
Equipment rental	4,300	1,400	2,600	8,300	1,600		1,600	9,900
Depreciation	2,200	1,600	1,100	4,900	3,800	600	4,400	9,300
Conferences	1,300	1,900	11,700	14,900	900		900	15,800
Printing and postage	3,400	33,000	800	37,200	2,900	4,400	7,300	44,500
Food and meals	31,100			31,100			0	31,100
Total Expenses	$122,000	$84,000	$52,000	$258,000	$94,000	$23,000	$117,000	$375,000

B. **Expirations pertaining to *fixed asset contributions* (reported "*below* the line").** Report as a separate line item *below* the measure of operations line using the caption "net assets released from restrictions used for purchase of property and equipment."

Illustration 26-6 shows the special reporting format for *private* HCOs.

IX. *FUND ACCOUNTING* FOR INTERNAL PURPOSES

Prior to the issuance of the FASB's NPO Standards in 1993, *private* NPOs used fund accounting internally and reported **externally** on a *fund-by-fund basis* (pursuant to the requirements of then existing GAAP). Because *external* financial reporting now requires information on an *aggregated basis*, this question is raised: Have *private* NPOs continued to use fund accounting for *internal* record-keeping purposes?

Unless mandated by donors (rarely done) or the board of directors for internal control purposes, no requirements exist to use *fund accounting*. Furthermore, *FAS 117* neither encourages nor discourages the continued use of *fund accounting* because this is an **internal** bookkeeping matter.

Knowledgeable individuals associated with finance officers of colleges and universities have indicated to us that (1) fund accounting is slowly fading away and (2) some NPOs that installed new accounting information systems have designed their new chart of accounts to conform with the external reporting requirements of *FAS 117* rather than tailoring them to *fund accounting*. Certainly,

ILLUSTRATION 26-6 STATEMENT OF OPERATIONS FOR AN HCO

Clean Sheets Samaritan Hospital
Statement of Operations
For the Years Ended December 31, 2006 and 2005
(excludes amounts pertaining to restricted items)

	2006	2005
Revenues:		
Net patient service charges	$64,400,000	$61,100,000
Other revenues	3,300,000	3,100,000
Net assets released from restrictions used for operations	**1,200,000**	**600,000**
Total Revenues	$68,900,000	$64,800,000
Expenses:		
Salaries and benefits	$46,100,000	$43,300,000
Medical supplies and drugs	4,600,000	4,100,000
Insurance	3,300,000	3,200,000
Other supplies	4,400,000	4,600,000
Provision for bad debts	3,500,000	3,100,000
Depreciation and amortization	3,600,000	3,500,000
Interest	1,700,000	1,600,000
Total Expenses	$67,200,000	$63,400,000
OPERATING INCOME	**$1,700,000**	**$1,400,000**
Other Income:		
Investment income (interest, dividends, and realized gains and losses, net)[a]	440,000	410,000
EXCESS OF REVENUES AND OTHER INCOME OVER EXPENSES	**$2,140,000**	**$1,810,000**
Change in net unrealized gains (losses) on other than trading securities	(90,000)	170,000
Net assets released from restrictions used for purchase of property and equipment	**400,000**	**200,000**
Contribution from Funn Foundation for property acquisitions	1,000,000	–0–
Transfers to parent		(100,000)
INCREASE IN *UNRESTRICTED* NET ASSETS	**$3,450,000**	**$2,080,000**

[a] If the HCO holds trading securities, the AICPA's 2003 HCO audit guide requires any *unrealized* gains and losses on them to be reported in this category as well.

externally imposed stipulations, internal control, practicality, and economic cost considerations are key factors in determining the extent to which *fund accounting* continues to be used *internally*.

Does *Fund Accounting* Entail Physical Segregation of Assets?

The use of fund accounting for **internal** record-keeping purposes does *not* mean that the various assets accounted for in each of the separate funds must be physically segregated from assets accounted for in the other funds. Often the assets accounted for in the various funds are *not* kept separate. For example, it is common to use only one checking account for cash reported in several funds, thereby eliminating the need to prepare multiple bank account reconciliations each month. The fact that the assets are commingled suggests that NPOs may discontinue fund accounting.

Complying with *FAS 117* When Using *Fund Accounting*

If fund accounting is used for **internal** record-keeping purposes, however, some form of "aggregating worksheet" (similar in concept to a consolidated worksheet) to determine the aggregated amounts to present in the financial statements issued for **external** reporting purposes must be prepared.

Furthermore, footnote 5 to *FAS 117* does *not* preclude the presentation of **disaggregated** data (by fund groups) so long as the required **aggregated** information is presented (a presentation we have not seen any NPOs use). Some funds will fall entirely within one of the three net asset categories. Other funds may have to be split into two or more of the three net asset categories to arrive at the required **aggregated** data.

X. ACCOUNTING FOR INVESTMENTS—IN GENERAL

Under *FAS 124*, "Accounting for Certain Investments Held by Not-for-Profit Organizations," the following investments of *private* NPOs must be valued at their fair value **in the statement of financial position:**

1. Investments in **equity securities** that have a **readily determinable fair value** (excluding investments accounted for under the **equity method**).
2. All investments in **debt securities.**

Interest, dividends, and other investment income on all investments are reported in the statement of activities as revenues (1) in the periods in which they are **earned** and (2) as increasing **UR** *net assets*, **TR** *net assets*, or **PR** *net assets*, as appropriate.

Gains and losses—both realized and unrealized—on all investments are reported in the statement of activities as investment gains and losses (1) in the periods in which they *occur* and (2) as increases or decreases in ***UR*** *net assets* **unless their use is temporarily or permanently restricted by explicit donor stipulations or by law** (which applies only if *no* donor stipulations exist).

See the Appendix for a detailed illustration of accounting for investments.

Disclosures

FAS 124 also requires a variety of disclosures, including the following:

1. The methods and significant assumptions used to estimate the fair values.
2. The basis for determining the carrying value of investments that are *not* required to be valued at fair value.
3. The aggregate carrying value of the investments by major type (for example, equity securities, U.S. Treasury securities, corporate debt securities, mortgage-backed securities, oil and gas, and real estate).

4. The aggregate amount of the shortfall in the fair value of donor-restricted endowment funds below the amount required to be maintained by donor stipulations or law.
5. The composition of return on investment.
6. A reconciliation of the investment return to amounts reported in the statement of activities in certain situations.

Other investment-related FASB standards that also apply to all *private* NPOs are FASB *Statement No. 107*, "Disclosures About Fair Value of Financial Instruments," and FASB *Statement No. 133*, "Accounting for Derivative Instruments and Hedging Activities."

Recall that the Business Perspective in Chapter 4 (pages 104–105) discusses how an accounting instructor at a small private college (1) questioned one of the college's investments and (2) subsequently uncovered a massive fraud perpetrated on scores of C&Us and VHWOs.

XI. Other Professional Pronouncements Specific to NPOs

Several other professional pronouncements also apply to NPOs. A detailed discussion of all of them, however, is beyond the scope of this chapter. We do briefly discuss one of them in some detail because of its importance.

1. **AICPA *Statement of Position 98-2*, "Accounting for Costs of Activities of Not-for-Profit Organizations and State and Local Governmental Entities That Include Fund Raising."** External users of NPO financial statements, including donors and other resource providers, want NPOs to (1) *maximize* spending on causes they exist to support (program activities) and (2) ***minimize*** spending on (a) fundraising (soliciting contributions) and (b) management and general activities (administration). Consequently, NPO managers have a built-in bias to (1) *overreport* the costs of program activities and (2) *underreport* the costs of fund-raising activities and administrative expenses. Historically, this has been a troublesome area with many abuses because of loose accounting rules.

   SOP 98-2 provides improved, detailed guidance by containing criteria (including a function test) for determining whether the joint costs an NPO incurs in activities that involve fund-raising should be (1) reported *entirely* as fund-raising costs or (2) *allocated* among (a) fund-raising and (b) other functions, such as program and management and general. *SOP 98-2* (85 pages, including 9 appendices, a 2-page flowchart, and detailed descriptions of commonly used allocation methods) is somewhat complex, and a more detailed discussion is beyond the scope of this chapter.

   In a nutshell, when an NPO makes a solicitation that includes elements of other activities, such as (1) program activities (for example, enclosing literature about drug prevention) or (2) management and general activities, *SOP 98-2* requires that such a solicitation be considered a *joint activity*. For an NPO to report any costs of a joint activity as functions *other than* fund-raising, the criteria of (1) **purpose**, (2) **audience**, and (3) **content** must be satisfied. If a joint activity satisfies *all three* criteria, joint activity costs are reported as follows:

   A. **Identifiable costs:** Costs that can be identified with a particular function are charged to that function.
   B. **Nonidentifiable costs:** Costs that *cannot* be identified with a particular component of the activity are allocated between (1) fund-raising and (2) the appropriate program or the management and general function. Allocation methods (to be determined by management) must be rational, systematic, and reasonable.
2. **AICPA *Statement of Position 93-7*, "Reporting on Advertising Costs."** *SOP 93- 7* sets forth guidance on accounting for advertising costs and requires all NPOs to make certain disclosures, including total costs for the period.

3. **AICPA *Statement of Position 94-2*, "The Application of the Requirements of Accounting Research Bulletins, Opinions of the Accounting Principles Board, and Statements and Interpretations of the Financial Accounting Standards Board to Not-for-Profit Organizations."** *SOP 94-2* requires NPOs to follow the guidance in these pronouncements—**unless** a pronouncement explicitly exempts them.
4. **AICPA *Statement of Position 94-3*, "Reporting of Related Entities by Not-for-Profit Organizations."** *SOP 94-3* provides reporting guidance concerning the consolidation of related NPOs.

End-of-Chapter Review

Summary of Key Points

A. Contributions:

1. With certain specified exceptions, contributions (including endowments) are to be recognized **in the statement of activities when received.**
2. Contributions affecting a particular class of net assets recognized in the statement of activities must be reported as unrestricted support or restricted support **in that class** of net assets.
3. Contributions received are to be measured at their **fair values.** Receivables for **long-term (beyond one year) unconditional promises to give** may be reported at the **present value** of the estimated cash inflows.
4. **Unconditional promises to give** with payments due in future periods are reported as restricted support unless the contribution is intended to support unrestricted operations in the period in which the promise is received.
5. **Conditional promises to give** are *not* recognized in the financial statements until the conditional promise becomes **unconditional.**
6. Contributions received **to acquire long-lived assets** are reported as restricted support. Contributions of long-lived assets are reported as **restricted support** or **unrestricted support,** depending on (a) donor stipulations or, in the absence of donor restrictions, (b) the NPO's accounting policy regarding an implied time period restriction.
7. **Expirations of donor-imposed time and purpose restrictions** are reflected in the statement of activities by showing a reclassification of amounts between the temporarily restricted category (a decrease) and the unrestricted category (an increase).
8. **For long-lived depreciable assets classified as part of temporarily restricted net assets,** a time-period restriction expiration is reported in the statement of activities over the depreciable life of the assets.
9. **Contributed services** are recognized only if they (1) create or enhance nonfinancial assets or (2) are obtained from individuals or organizations possessing specialized skills and typically would otherwise be purchased.
10. **Contributed works of art, historical treasures,** and similar assets (collection items) received need not be capitalized in the balance sheet and concurrently recognized in the statement of activities.

B. Depreciation of Long-Lived Assets:

1. Depreciable long-lived tangible assets **must be depreciated,** and depreciation expense for the period must be disclosed.
2. Individual works of art and historical treasures **need *not* be depreciated,** if the NPO can demonstrate that verifiable evidence exists that the asset (1) is and can be maintained by the NPO in a manner that preserves its value and (2) the asset individually has cultural, aesthetic, or historical value worth preserving perpetually.

C. Financial Statements:

1. **Specified financial statements.** *FAS 117* specifies that for external reporting purposes, private NPOs must present for the organization as a whole (a) a statement of **financial**

position, (b) a statement of **activities,** and (c) a statement of **cash flows.** (Thus this is an aggregated reporting manner as though a single set of books were used rather than several sets of books as in fund accounting.)
2. **Reporting specified financial statement information.** For the statement of financial position, total assets, total liabilities, and total net assets (or equity) for the NPO as a whole must be reported.
3. **Classified reporting.** For the statement of financial position, the **total net assets** (or equity) must be classified based on **donor-imposed restrictions.** For the statement of activities, **all accounts—except expenses—**are also to be classified on this basis.
4. ***Required* classification categories.** Three classification categories are to be used: **unrestricted, temporarily restricted,** and **permanently restricted.**
5. The statement of activities must report the **changes** in each of the three classes of equity or net assets. This is done either by "layering" or using separate columns.
6. The standards specify only minimal information and category display requirements, thus allowing flexibility in the use of reporting formats.

D. Investments:
1. Investments in equity securities that have a **readily determinable fair value** and all investments in debt securities are to be valued **at their fair value.**
2. Interest, dividends, and other investment income are reported as revenues **in the statement of activities when earned** as increases in the appropriate category of net assets.
3. Gains and losses on investments are reported as gains and losses **in the statement of activities (a) when they occur** and (b) as increases or decreases, respectively, to the appropriate category of net assets.

Glossary of New Terms

Board-designated endowment An endowment created as the result of the board of directors' action (classified as unrestricted net assets in the statement of financial position). Also called a quasi-endowment.

Conditional promise to give "A promise to give that depends on the occurrence of a specified future and uncertain event to bind the promisor."*

Contribution "An unconditional transfer of cash or other assets to an entity or a settlement or cancellation of its liabilities in a voluntary nonreciprocal transfer by another entity acting other than as an owner."*

Donor-imposed condition "A donor stipulation that specifies a future and uncertain event whose occurrence or failure to occur gives the promisor a right of return of the assets it has transferred or releases the promisor from its obligation to transfer its assets."*

Donor-imposed restriction "A donor stipulation that specifies a use for the contributed asset that is more specific than broad limits resulting from the nature of the organization, the environment in which it operates, and the purposes specified in its articles of incorporation or bylaws or comparable documents for an unincorporated association. A restriction on an organization's use of the asset contributed may be temporary or permanent."*

Endowment A type of restricted contribution in which the donor stipulates that the principal be maintained intact either in perpetuity or for a specified period. Thus only the income from the investment of the principal (the corpus) may be spent. Endowments require the establishment of endowment funds.

Endowment fund An established fund of cash, securities, or other assets accounted for separately from all other assets for control purposes either by (1) using separate general ledger accounts or (2) a separate set of books.

Exchange transactions Reciprocal transfers in which each party receives and sacrifices something of approximately equal value.

Financial flexibility The freedom to use assets (resources) for various purposes to be able to respond to unforeseen events and opportunities.

---

* Definition quoted from *FAS 116*, Appendix D.

Nonreciprocal transfer "A transaction in which an entity incurs a liability or transfers an asset to another entity (or receives an asset or cancellation of a liability) without directly receiving (or giving) value in exchange."*

Permanent endowment A type of restricted contribution in which the principal must remain intact in perpetuity (classified as permanently restricted net assets in the statement of financial position).

Permanent restriction "A donor-imposed restriction that stipulates that resources be maintained permanently but permits the organization to use up or expend part or all of the income (or other economic benefit) derived from the donated assets."*

Permanently restricted net assets "The part of the net assets of a not-for-profit organization resulting (a) from contributions and other inflows of assets whose use by the organization is limited by donor-imposed stipulations that neither expire by passage of time nor can be fulfilled or otherwise removed by actions of the organization, (b) from other asset enhancements and diminishments subject to the same kinds of stipulations, and (c) from reclassifications from (or to) other classes of net assets as a consequence of donor-imposed stipulations (*Concepts Statement* 6, paragraph 92)."*

Promise to give "A written or oral agreement to contribute cash or other assets to another entity. A promise to give may be either conditional or unconditional."*

Restricted support "Donor-restricted revenues or gains from contributions that increase either temporarily restricted net assets or permanently restricted net assets."*

Temporarily restricted net assets "The part of the net assets of a not-for-profit organization resulting (a) from contributions and other inflows of assets whose use by the organization is limited by donor-imposed stipulations that either expire by passage of time or can be fulfilled and removed by actions of the organization pursuant to those stipulations, (b) from other asset enhancements and diminishments subject to the same kinds of stipulations, and (c) from reclassifications to (or from) other classes of net assets as a consequence of donor-imposed stipulations, their expiration by passage of time, or their fulfillment and removal by actions of the organization pursuant to those stipulations" (*Concepts Statement* 6, paragraph 93).*

Temporary restriction "A donor-imposed restriction that permits the donee organization to use up or expend the donated assets as specified and is satisfied either by the passage of time or by actions of the organization."*

Term endowment A type of restricted contribution in which the principal becomes expendable at a future date (classified as temporarily restricted net assets in the statement of financial position).

Unconditional promise to give "A promise to give that depends only on passage of time or demand by the promisee for performance."*

Unrestricted net assets "The part of net assets of a not-for-profit organization that is neither permanently restricted nor temporarily restricted by donor-imposed stipulations" (*Concepts Statement* 6, paragraph 94).*

Unrestricted support "Revenues or gains from contributions that are not restricted by donors."*

Assignment Material

Review Questions

1. What are the four categories of NPOs?
2. What are the five main characteristics of NPOs?
3. When a *private* NPO ceases its operations, what happens to its remaining assets after all liabilities are settled?
4. Is it appropriate to compare an NPO's revenues with its costs and expenses? Why or why not?
5. What title is used for the operating statement of *private* NPOs? Why is this title used instead of statement of income?

6. What does the term *financial flexibility* mean?
7. How does an entity *officially* become an NPO?
8. What are the two categories of restrictions used in *FAS 116* and *FAS 117*?
9. How are contributions of works of art, historical treasures, and similar assets accounted for under *FAS 116*?
10. How are *contributed (donated) services* accounted for under *FAS 116*?
11. Why are certain contributed (donated) services *not* recognized in the statement of activities under *FAS 116*?
12. Under what conditions are gifts of long-lived assets *not* reported as *restricted support* under *FAS 116*?
13. How are *conditional promises to give* reported under *FAS 116*?
14. How are investments in debt and equity securities valued under *FAS 124*?
15. Which long-lived assets must be depreciated under *FAS 93*?
16. What are the three classifications of net assets required in the statement of financial position under the *FAS 117*?
17. How is the expiration of a *temporary restriction* reported in the statement of activities under *FAS 117*?
18. Revenues and expenses are generally reported at their *gross* amounts in the statement of activities. Under what exception may revenues be reported *net* of related expenses under *FAS 117*?

Exercises

E 26-1 **Manner of *Reporting* Contributions** Each of the items in the *left column* represents various contribution transactions pertaining to a *private* NPO. The *right column* lists possible manners of reporting.

Contribution Transactions

1. Receipt of a conditional promise to give.
2. Receipt of a contributed fixed asset.
3. Receipt of an unconditional cash contribution.
4. Receipt of cash to use for a specific purpose.
5. Receipt of an art collection.
6. Receipt of a long-term unconditional promise to give.
7. Receipt of free legal services.
8. Receipt of services from volunteer fund-raisers.

Possible Manners of Reporting

A. Recognize when received.
B. Recognize when collected.
C. Recognize at a later date.
D. Recognize when received or do not recognize at all.
E. Recognize in the balance sheet but not in the statement of activities.
F. Do not recognize at all.
G. Recognize when placed in service.

Required What is the appropriate manner to report each of these transactions? A reporting manner may be selected once, more than once, or not at all.

E 26-2 **Manner of *Recording* Contributions** Each of the items in the *left column* represents various contribution transactions pertaining to a *private* NPO. The *right column* lists possible manners of recording.

Contribution Transactions

1. A donor contributed cash.
2. A donor contributed cash, specifying that it be used for medical research.

Possible Manners of Reporting

A. Credit Fund Balance.
B. Credit Contribution Revenues—Unrestricted.

Contribution Transactions

3. A donor contributed cash, specifying that it be used for operating purposes in the following year.
4. A donor contributed cash, specifying that it be used for medical research in the following year.
5. A donor contributed cash, specifying that only the income earned on the investment of the cash can be spent.
6. A donor contributed cash, specifying that it is to be used for adding a new wing to the hospital.
7. A lawyer gives free legal advice.

Possible Manners of Reporting

C. Credit Contribution Revenues—Restricted.
D. Credit Contribution Revenues—Temporarily Restricted.
E. Credit Contribution Revenues—Permanently Restricted.
F. Credit Deferred Contribution Revenue.
G. No entry.

Required What is the proper manner to record each of these transactions? A reporting manner may be selected once, more than once, or not at all.

E 26-3 **Classifying Transactions in the *Statement of Activities*** Each of the items in the *left column* represents various transactions. The *right column* lists possible—both appropriate and inappropriate—reporting categories in the statement of activities.

Transactions

1. Transfer of cash from an unrestricted fund to a restricted fund to repay debt.
2. Transfer of cash from an unrestricted fund to a restricted fund to pay interest on debt.
3. Recording depreciation.
4. Receipt of cash to establish an endowment fund.
5. Receipt of cash for fixed asset additions.
6. Receipt of cash for operations.
7. Expenditure of cash received in the prior year designated for fixed asset additions.
8. Receipt of free legal advice from a lawyer.

Category of Presentation in the Statement of Activities

A. Revenues, Gains, and Other Support.
B. Net Assets Released from Restrictions.
C. Interfund Transfers.
D. Expenses and Losses.
E. Residual Equity Transfers.
F. Between Net Assets at Beginning of Year and Net Assets at End of Year.
G. Operating Transfers.
H. As Expenses and Losses and as Revenues, Gains, and Other Support (offsetting debits and credits).
I. None of the above.

Required What is the appropriate category in the statement of activities in which to report each transaction? A category may be selected once, more than once, or not at all.

E 26-4 **Categorizing Transactions in the *Statement of Activities*** Each of the items in the *left column* represents various transactions. The *right column* lists possible—both appropriate and inappropriate—classification categories in the statement of activities.

Transactions

1. Transfer of cash from an unrestricted fund to a restricted fund to repay debt.
2. Transfer of cash from an unrestricted fund to a restricted fund to pay interest on debt.
3. Recording depreciation on a fixed asset contributed to the NPO.
4. Receipt of cash to establish an endowment fund.
5. Receipt of cash for fixed asset additions.
6. Receipt of cash for operations.
7. Expenditure of cash received in the prior year designated for fixed asset additions.

Classification Category in the Statement of Activities

A. Unrestricted.
B. Temporarily Restricted.
C. Permanently Restricted.
D. Interfund Transfers.
E. Unrestricted and Temporarily Restricted.
F. Unrestricted and Permanently Restricted.
G. None of the above.

Required For each transaction, in which classification category or categories in the statement of activities should an amount be reported? A classification category may be selected once, more than once, or not at all.

E 26-5 ***Private* C&U: Determining Whether Certain Fund Accounting Transactions Are Reported under *FAS 117*** A *private* university that uses fund accounting had the following transactions during 2006:

1. A $900,000 cash disbursement was made from the Current Unrestricted Fund to the Retirement of Indebtedness Fund.
2. The Retirement of Indebtedness Fund retired $200,000 of its bonded indebtedness.
3. The Retirement of Indebtedness Fund disbursed $700,000 cash on 9/30/06 in payment of interest on its bonds.

Required Should these transactions be reported in the 2006 *statement of activities*?

E 26-6 ***Private* HCO: Determining Whether Certain Fund Accounting Transactions Are Reported under *FAS 117*** A *private* hospital that uses *fund accounting* had the following transactions during 2006:

1. Pursuant to the board of directors' authorization, $100,000 was disbursed from the General Fund to the Plant Replacement and Expansion Funds.
2. The investments of a term endowment established by a donor were sold at the termination date. All cash on hand ($222,000) was transferred to the General Fund.
3. The Specific-Purpose Funds reimbursed the General Fund $300,000 in connection with spending on donor-stipulated purposes.

Required How should these transactions be reported in the 2006 statement of activities?

Problems

P 26-1 ***Private* C&U: Recording Transactions and Preparing a *Statement of Activities*** During 2006, Ivory Tower College, a *private* NPO, had the following transactions and events:

1. A wealthy citizen donated $500,000 cash, which can only be invested. Net investment income (dividends and interest) can be used only for granting scholarships.
2. Investment income (interest) on the investment in item 1 totaled $33,000. Of this amount, $21,000 was expended on scholarships. Investment advisory fees of $1,000 were paid.
3. A wealthy citizen donated 10,000 shares of BT&T common stock. The citizen's cost basis was $12 per share. The market price was $30 per share at the donation date. The common stock cannot be sold for 10 years. After 10 years, the university has total discretion as to investing or spending the proceeds from the sale of the stock.
4. Concerning the donation in item 3, dividends of $44,000 were declared, of which $22,000 was collected by year-end. The investment income (dividends) can be used for any purpose.
5. Concerning the donation in item 3, the common stock had a market price of $35 per share at year-end.
6. Interest of $6,000 was earned on an investment made with a $100,000 cash donation in the prior year that is *permanently restricted*. None of the income can be spent until the market value of the investment reaches $200,000.
7. The college's engineering school employs a retired engineer who teaches engineering classes and who is paid a nominal stipend of $3,000 per year. Other faculty in the engineering school are paid $60,000 per year.

8. Cash of $80,000 from contributions in the preceding year and restricted as to a specific program purpose was expended as intended.

9. Cash of $90,000 received from contributions in the preceding year solely to buy new equipment was expended as intended.

Required

1. Prepare the journal entries to record these transactions. Assume that fund accounting is not used.
2. Prepare the revenues, gains, and other support section of the 2006 *statement of activities* (including restriction expirations) using the columnar format. (Code your amounts to the related transaction number.)

P 26-2 ***Private* VHWO: Recording Transactions and Preparing a Statement of Activities** During 2006, Free Food Foundation, a VHWO serving needy families, had the following transactions or events:

1. Cash contributions of $111,000 were received.

2. Unconditional promises to give, which are legally enforceable, total $22,000 at the end of 2006. The promissors made no stipulations regarding when or how the money could be spent. At the end of 2005, $16,000 of unconditional promises existed, all of which were collected in 2006.

3. At year-end, a citizen promised in writing to contribute $30,000 cash if the local baseball team, which finished in last place in 2006, wins the World Series in 2007.

4. A wealthy citizen donated a van to deliver meals to disabled citizens. Its fair value is $24,000. If the van is not used as intended, it must be returned to the donor.

5. A wealthy citizen donated $500,000 cash with the stipulation that it can only be invested. Income on the investment can be spent only to provide counseling.

6. During 2006, income (interest and dividends) on the investment in item 5 totaled $36,000. Investment advisory fees totaling $1,000 were paid.

7. A gift of common stock received on 12/30/05 (valued at $200,000) appreciated in value by $22,000 in 2006. Investment income and appreciation gains beyond what is needed to maintain the original economic value can be spent for any purpose. Inflation in 2006 was 5%. Dividends of $72,000 were declared on this stock in 2006, of which $54,000 had been collected by year-end.

8. A local CPA audited the NPO's 2006 financial statements at no charge, which normally would have been $8,000.

9. A biannual special fund-raising event resulted in $660,000 of cash contributions. The event incurred costs of $60,000. The board of directors designated $300,000 for spending in 2007 (the following year).

10. For the $300,000 in item 9 that could be spent in 2006, $280,000 was spent.

11. Depreciation expense of $4,000 on the van in item 4 was recognized.

12. Volunteers contributed 1,200 hours of time delivering meals to elderly people. Assume that the minimum wage is $5.

Required

1. Prepare the journal entries to record these transactions. Assume that fund accounting is *not* used.
2. Prepare the revenues, gains, and other support section of the 2006 *statement of activities* (including restriction expirations) using the columnar format. (Code your amounts to the related transaction number.) Show multiple lines for contribution revenues for ease of coding the transactions.

P 26-3 ***Private* HCO: Recording Transactions and Preparing a Statement of Activities** During 2006, Clean Sheets Hospital, a *private* NPO, had the following transactions or events:

1. Cash of $110,000 received in the preceding year and restricted to salaries for a specific program purpose was expended.
2. In connection with desired expansion plans, a prominent citizen purchased land adjacent to the hospital at a cost of $220,000 and donated it to the hospital to use as it pleases consistent with its mission.
3. A wealthy citizen donated $300,000 cash that can only be invested. Income earned on the investment in excess of $10,000 can be used for any purpose. The first $10,000 must be reinvested.
4. The cash received in item 3 was invested; it earned $14,000 (interest and dividends).
5. Local citizens volunteered 10,000 hours as candy-stripers (working at the hospital's information desk, gift shop, and nurses stations). The minimum wage is $5 per hour.
6. On 12/28/06 a wealthy citizen donated $600,000 cash, of which $500,000 is to be used to establish a kidney dialysis unit. The remaining $100,000 is to be used to run the unit.
7. Depreciation of $700,000 was recognized. Of this amount, $75,000 pertained to equipment that had been donated to the hospital two years ago on the condition that the equipment be used for at least seven years. The remaining depreciation pertains to assets acquired with unrestricted funds.
8. A wealthy citizen donated $800,000 cash to be used for any purpose.

Required

1. Prepare the journal entries to record these transactions. Assume that fund accounting is not used.
2. Prepare the 2006 operating statement. (Code your amounts to the related transaction number.) **Reminder:** This entity is an HCO.

P 26-4 ***Private* VHWO: Manner of Reporting Certain Transactions**

1. The board of directors designated $600,000 to refurbish one of its buildings.
2. An endowment fund had an $80,000 unrealized gain on one of its common stock investments. The donor stipulated that any holding gains need *not* be added to the principal—they could be spent for any purpose. Accordingly, the VHWO sold a sufficient number of shares of the common stock holding to obtain $80,000 cash that it could spend.
3. A building having a $700,000 carrying value was sold at a $90,000 gain.
4. An endowment fund created by a board designation had a market valuation loss of $44,000.
5. A common stock investment, which must be held in perpetuity and which is classified as *permanently restricted*, decreased in value by $55,000 during the year.

Required How should each of these transactions be reported in the *statement of activities*?

THINKING CRITICALLY

Cases

C 26-1 **Determining How to Report Aggregated and Disaggregated Data** *FAS 117* emphasizes reporting for the organization as a whole, not by fund.

Required How might a *private* NPO present *disaggregated* data on a fund basis for the statement of financial position and still comply with the requirement to show *aggregated* data?

C 26-2 **Evaluating Continued Use of Fund Accounting for Internal Record-Keeping Purposes** *FAS 117* does *not* address how a private NPO should internally maintain its books and records.

Required If you were the controller of a private NPO, would you continue to use fund accounting internally? Why or why not?

Index

A

D

G

H

I

O

P

Q

R

S

T

U

V

W

X

Z

Checklist of Key Figures

Chapter 1

E 1-1 1 and 4: B,D,E; 7: C,D,E
E 1-3 a, b, d
E 1-4 e, b, d
E 1-5 Debit APIC for $300,000
E 1-6 Debit APIC for $495,000
E 1-7 1. $20,000
2. $–0–

P 1A-1 Debit Home Office Capital (preclosing) $120,000

Chapter 2

E 2-1 Cost: $300,000 or any lower amount; Equity: $250,000
E 2-2 Equity: 2006: Debit Equity in Net Loss $90,000
E 2-3 1. $250,000
2. $140,000
E 2-4 $100,000
E 2-5 2. Debit Retained Earnings 1/1/05 $210,000
E 2-6 1. Cost: $200,000; Equity: $680,000
2. Cost: 2005: $(400,000); 2006: $40,000 Equity: 2005: $(650,000); 2006: $770,000
E 2-7 1. Cost: $200,000; Equity: $680,000
2. Cost: 2005: $(400,000); 2006: $40,000 Equity: 2005: $(600,000); 2006: $720,000
E 2-8 1. Cost: $30,000; Equity: $190,000
2. Cost: 2007: $(70,000); 2008: $40,000 Equity: 2007: $(150,000); 2008: $280,000
E 2-9 2. $750,000
3. $123,000
4. Subsidiary's 2007 loss, $(14,000)
E 2-10 2. $550,000
3. $64,000
4. Consolidated 2007 net income, $120,000

P 2-1 2. Consolidated net income, $75,000; Consolidated assets, $785,000
P 2-2 3. Consolidated net income, $75,000; Consolidated assets, $785,000
P 2-3 2. Consolidated net income, $130,000; Consolidated assets, $790,000
P 2-4 3. Consolidated net income, $130,000; Consolidated assets, $790,000
P 2-5 Consolidated net income, $80,000; Consolidated assets, $920,000
P 2-6 2. $113,000
3. $136,000
4. $381,000
5. $120,000
6. $381,000
8. Credit Equity in Net Loss $23,000
P 2-7 2. $180,000
3. $229,000
4. $500,000
5. $80,000
6. $240,000

Chapter 3

E 3-1 1. $144,000
2. $155,000 ($11,000 to NCI)
E 3-2 2. Debit Equity in Net Income $28,000
E 3-3 A. $366,000; B. $122,000; C. $21,000; D. $90,000
E 3-4 Debit Equity in Net Income $63,000; Credit NCI in Net Income $21,000
E 3-5 1. G, 2. G, 3. G
E 3-6 1. C, 2. A, 3. C, 4. D

P 3-1 3. NCI in net income, $10,000; CI in net income, $65,000; Consolidated assets, $797,000
P 3-2 2. CI in net income, $127,000; Consolidated assets, $794,000
P 3-3 1. Equity: E, N/A, C, E, E, D, A, A, A, A, A, A, N/A
Cost: N/A, E, C, E, E, D, A, A, D, D, A, D, E
2. 14. $4,000
15. $25,000
16. $115,000
18. $79,000 ($115,000 – $36,000)

E 3A-1 Debit NCI in Net Income $12,000; Credit NCI in Net Assets $33,000
E 3A-2 A. $90,000; B. $600,000; C. $306,000; D. $360,000; E. $40,000; F. $800,000

P 3A-1 2. NCI in net income, $10,000; CI in net income, $65,000; Consolidated assets, $797,000
P 3A-2 2. CI in net income, $127,000; Consolidated assets, $794,000

E 3B-1 1. $18,000 ($6,000 current)
E 3B-2 1. $72,000 ($36,000 current)

Chapter 4

P 4-1 8. Retained Earnings, $660,000
P 4-2 8. Retained Earnings, $300,000
P 4-3 8. Retained Earnings, $300,000

Chapter 5

E 5-1 Total cost, $2,700,000
E 5-2 Total cost, $2,772,000
E 5-3 Total cost, $1,000,000
E 5-4 1. Total cost, $3,200,000
E 5-5 1. Total cost, $4,200,000
E 5-6 Goodwill, $120,000
E 5-7 Bargain purchase element, $100,000
E 5-8 1. Goodwill, $65,000

P 5-1 3. Goodwill, $370,000
P 5-2 1. Bargain purchase element, $110,000
2. Land revaluation, $155,000
P 5-3 1. Bargain purchase element, $80,000
2. Equipment revaluation, $(100,000)
P 5-4 2. Consolidated assets, $960,000
P 5-5 2. Consolidated assets, $920,000
P 5-6 1. Total cost, $935,000
3. Consolidated assets, $8,100,000
P 5-7 1. Goodwill, $210,000
P 5-8 1. Parent's cost at 12/31/06, $330,000; Goodwill, $77,000 at 12/31/06

E 5A-1 1. Goodwill, $220,000
E 5A-2 1. Goodwill, $220,000

P 5A-1 1. Total cost, $935,000
3. Combined assets, $8,100,000

E 5B-1 1. Goodwill, $55,000
E 5B-2 1. Goodwill, $82,000

Chapter 6

E 6-2 1. $1,012,000
2. $200,000
3. Equity: $112,000
E 6-3 3. Credits to Investment account: $190,000 and $175,000; $229,000 and $223,000
E 6-4 3. Credits to Investment account: $334,000 and $359,000; Debits to Investment account: $42,000 and $39,000
E 6-5 1. $30,000
2. $260,000
5. $130,000
E 6-6 NCI in net income, $150,000; CI in net income, $1,420,000
E 6-7 1. Stane: NCI in net income, $30,000; CI in net income, $243,000
Steele: NCI in net income, $20,000; CI in net income, $72,000
2. Stane: NCI in net income, $20,000; CI in net income, $162,000
E 6-8 1. NCI in net income, $15,000; CI in net income, $295,000
2. NCI in net income, $15,000; CI in net income, $292,000
E 6-9 1. NCI in net income, $50,000; CI in net income, $926,000
3. $126,000
E 6-10 Goodwill, $30,000; Investment balance, $240,000 + $(21,000); NCI in net assets, $160,000
E 6-11 Goodwill, $28,000; Investment balance, $147,000 + $56,000; NCI in net assets, $63,000
E 6-12 1. $110,000
2. Retained earnings column, $60,000

P 6-1 3. Consolidated assets, $990,000
P 6-2 3. Consolidated assets, $950,000
P 6-3 1. Bargain purchase element, $50,000
2. Total cost at 12/31/06, $239,000
4. Consolidated net income, $310,000; Consolidated assets, $928,000
P 6-4 2. Investment balance at 12/31/06, $650,000 + $282,000
5. Consolidated net income, $466,000; Consolidated assets, $9,025,000
P 6-5 1. Total investment cost, $470,000
3. Total investment cost at 12/31/06, $378,000 + $124,000
5. Consolidated net income, $552,000; Consolidated assets, $4,522,000
P 6-6 1. Goodwill, $16,000
3. Consolidated assets, $998,000
P 6-7 1. Goodwill at 12/31/06, $16,000; Investment balance at 12/31/06: Equity method, $172,000 + $100,000
3. NCI in net income, $12,000; CI in net income, $100,000; Consolidated assets, $1,023,000
P 6-8 1. Long-term debt, $32,000
3. Consolidated assets, $980,000
P 6-9 1. NCI in net assets at 12/31/06, $57,000; Investment balance at 12/31/06: Equity method, $228,000 + $(28,000)
3. NCI in net income, $14,000; CI in net income, $158,000; Consolidated assets, $996,000

P 6-10 1. Goodwill at 1/1/06, $48,000
2. Goodwill at 12/31/06, $48,000; Investment balance at 12/31/06, $405,000 + $186,000
5. NCI in net income, $84,000; CI in net income, $1,296,000; NCI in net assets, $270,000; Consolidated assets, $9,719,000

P 6-11 3. Parent's separate earnings, $172,000
4. Consolidated retained earnings, $380,000

P 6-12 1. Total investment cost, $552,000
3. Investment balance at 12/31/06, $440,000 + $116,000
5. NCI in net income, $12,000; CI in net income, $532,000; Consolidated assets, $5,934,000; NCI in net assets, $110,000

P 6-13 1. Investment balance at 12/31/06, $302,000; Goodwill at 12/31/06, $74,500; NCI in net assets, $22,000

P 6-14 1. Investment balance at 4/1/06, $887,000; Goodwill at 4/1/06, $122,000; NCI in net assets at 12/31/06, $280,000
4. Debit Goodwill $122,000

Chapter 7

E 7-1 1. Reval. Capital, $300,000 increase

P 7-1 1. Reval. Capital, $600,000 increase
P 7-2 1. Reval. Capital, $110,000 increase
P 7-3 1. APIC, $340,000 decrease
P 7-4 1. Reval. Capital, $135,000 increase
P 7-5 1. APIC, $110,000 increase, net
P 7-6 1. Reval. Capital, $285,000 increase
P 7-7 3. Consolidated assets, $990,000
P 7-8 2. $237,500
3. $47,500
P 7-9 1. Goodwill, $70,000

Chapter 8

E 8-5 1. Adjusted book balances, $77,000
E 8-6 1. $90,000
2. $85,000

P 8-1 1. Adjusted book balances, $340,000
2. Parr: Intercompany-acquired inventory, $45,000
3. Unrealized profit, $3,000

P 8-2 1. Intercompany royalty fee in year-end inventory, $20,000

P 8-3 2. Credit Cost of Sales $7,000
3. Consolidated net income, $72,000; Consolidated assets, $722,000

Chapter 9

E 9-1 1. Unrealized profit $9,000
E 9-2 1. Unrealized profit, $60,000
E 9-3 Total intercompany cost of sales, $400,000
E 9-4 Total intercompany gross profit, $105,000; Unrealized profit, $25,000
E 9-5 1. $30,000 + $123,000 = $153,000
E 9-6 1. $20,000 + $125,000 = $145,000
E 9-7 1. $1,850,000
2. $1,080,000
E 9-8 1. $4,500,000
2. $1,597,000
E 9-9 3. $15,000 at 12/31/06 and 07
E 9-10 $10,000
E 9-11 $37,000
E 9-13 1. Unrealized profit, $10,000
2. Intercompany profit *deferral* $10,000; Investment in subsidiary, $560,000
3. Equity in net income, $63,000; Investment in subsidiary, $563,000
E 9-14 Situation 1: $24,000; Situation 2: $22,000

P 9-1 1. Unrealized profit, $6,000
3. Consolidated assets, $694,000

P 9-2 1. Unrealized profit, $10,000
3. NCI in net income, $6,000; CI in net income, $114,000; NCI in net assets, $21,000

P 9-3 Unrealized profit, $12,000; Credit Cost of Sales $52,000

P 9-4 1. Unrealized profit, $10,000
3. Consolidated net income, $79,000; Consolidated assets, $940,000

P 9-5 1. Unrealized profit, $5,000
3. NCI in net income, $7,000; CI in net income, $128,000; NCI in net assets, $34,000; Consolidated assets, $753,000

P 9-6 1. Sano's 2007 net income, $54,000
2. Unrealized profit at 12/31/06, $6,000
3. Unrealized intercompany profit at 12/31/07, $5,000 ($8,000 – $3,000 LCM adj.)

E 9A-1 2. Debit Cost of Sales $96,000
3. Unrealized profit at 12/31/06, $3,000
E 9A-2 3. Debit Intracompany Profit *Deferred* $14,800
E 9A-3 2. Debit Cost of Sales $54,000
4. Credit Cost of Sales $9,000
E 9A-4 Home Office's cost of beg. inventory, $15,000

P 9A-1 1. Debit Home Office Capital (*preclosing*) $140,000;
Total assets, $1,330,000
3. Debit Cost of Sales $149,000

P 9A-2 3. Debit Intracompany Profit *Deferred* $16,000
5. Debit Home Office Capital (*preclosing*) $130,000;
Total assets, $1,396,000;
Credit Cost of Sales $16,000

Chapter 10

E 10-3 1. $23,000 depreciation expense

E 10-4 1. Net book value, $500,000
2. Net book value, $525,000

E 10-5 1. $20,000 intercompany loss
2. $200,000, $75,000

E 10-6 1. $16,000 intercompany gain
2. $100,000, $80,000

E 10-7 Credit Accum. Depr. $108,000

E 10-8 Credit Accum. Depr. $104,000

E 10-9 $19,000 gain

E 10-10 1. $14,000 loss

E 10-11 1. $44,000 gain

E 10-12 1. $29,500 loss

P 10-1 1. $72,000
2. $42,000 intercompany gain
4. Credit Accum. Depr. $33,000

P 10-2 2. Credit Accum. Depr. $27,000
3. Consolidated net income, $168,000;
Consolidated assets, $868,000

P 10-3 3. NCI in net income, $13,000;
CI in net income, $256,000;
Consolidated assets, $552,000

P 10-4 1. $150,000
2. $120,000 intercompany loss

P 10-5 2. Credit Accum. Depr. $2,000
3. NCI in net income, $10,000;
CI in net income, $80,000;
Consolidated assets, $792,000;
NCI in net assets, $39,000

P 10-6 2. Debit Depreciation Expense $4,000
3. NCI in net income, $17,000;
CI in net income, $303,000;
Consolidated assets, $851,000;
NCI in net assets, $43,000

P 10-7 2. Credit Depreciation Expense $5,000
3. NCI in net income, $18,000;
CI in net income, $92,000;
Consolidated assets, $978,000;
NCI in net assets, $57,500

P 10-8 1. Parent's net income, $1,850,000;
Subsidiary's net income, $305,000

P 10-9 1. $96,000 loss

P 10-10 1. $120,000 loss

Chapter 11

E 11-1 Debit Investment account $33,000 and $17,000

E 11-2 Debit Investment account $50,000

E 11-3 Retained Earnings decrease of $160,000

E 11-4 No changes

E 11-5 1. $15,000/$25,000 = 60%; $2.80
2. $16,000/$25,000 = 64%; $2.82

E 11-6 1. $75,000/$100,000 = 75%; $13.75
2. $85,000/$100,000 = 85%; $14.25

P 11-1 $23,000 of goodwill results

P 11-2 1. Decrease in parent's interest, $90,000
3. Reclassify $90,000 to Excess Cost elements

P 11-3 1. Increase excess cost $120,000
2. Debit Excess Cost $120,000

P 11-4 1. Decrease excess cost $48,000
2. Credit Gain on Sale $292,000

P 11-5 1. Decrease excess cost $52,000 at disposal date
2. Credit Gain on Sale $31,000

P 11-6 1. Parent's dilution, $225,000

P 11-7 1. Parent's accretion, $40,000

P 11-8 1. Investment balance at 12/31/06: MODULE 1, $705,000; MODULE 2, $705,000
5. NCI in net income, $71,000;
CI in net income, $864,000;
Consolidated assets, $2,446,000;
Consolidated Ret. Earnings, $612,000;
NCI in net assets, $235,000

P 11-9 Cash flow from Operations, $138,000;
Investing, $(90,000); Financing, $2,000

P 11A-1 1. NCI: At 12/31/05, $134,000; At 12/31/06, $136,000
2. Debit NCI in Net Income $14,000 at 12/31/05

P 11A-2 1. NCI: At 12/31/06, $324,000; At 12/31/07, $346,000
2. Debit NCI in Net Income $3,000 at 12/31/06

E 11B-1 2. $38,000

E 11B-2 2. $207,000

E 11B-3 2. $31,000

E 11B-4 1. $9,977,480
2. $1,132,520

E 11B-5 1. $580,000 and $20,000
2. $567,391 and $32,609

P 11B-1 1. $592,000
2. $33,000

P 11B-2 1. $1,080,700
2. $21,800

P 11B-3 1. $687,600
2. $21,400

P 11B-4 1. $878,000 and $10,000
2. $868,352 and $19,648

P 11B-5 1. $450,000 and $40,000
2. $430,851 and $59,149
4. Balances at 12/31/06: CI, $1,157,533; NCI, $205,447

Chapter 12

E 12-1 Segments 1, 2, 4, and 7 exceed $150 million

E 12-2 Segments 2, 4, and 6 exceed $980,000

E 12-3 Segments 2, 3, and 5; 75% test is satisfied

E 12-4 Consolidated revenues, $4,100,000; Consolidated pretax income, $700,000

E 12-5 Measure of profit, $160,000

P 12-1 2. Threshold amount, $400,000,000
3. Threshold amount, $2,550,000,000

P 12-2 1. Test #2: Segments 2, 3, 5, and 7 exceed $24 million
All tests: 2, 3, 4, 5, and 7

P 12-3 1. Test #2: Segments 3 and 4 exceed $288 million
All tests: Segments 1, 3, and 4

P 12-4 Consolidated revenues, $5,000,000,000; Consolidated pretax income, $260,000,000

P 12-5 Revenues, $5,000,000,000; Long-lived assets, $2,750,000

Chapter 13

E 13-1 1. Direct rate at 12/31/06, 1 peso equals $.50

E 13-3 1. $78,000
2. $5,000 FX loss

E 13-4 1. $210,000
2. $20,000 FX loss

P 13-1 Vendor A: $400 FX loss at 7/10/06, plus $2,400 FX gain at 7/31/06;
Customer A: $500 FX loss at 7/20/06, plus $1,600 FX loss at 7/30/06

P 13-2 Vendor A: $1,000 FX gain at 6/30/06 and $2,000 FX gain at 7/15/06;
Customer A: $1,400 FX loss at 6/30/06 and $600 FX loss at 7/10/06

P 13-3 FX loss: 12/31/06, $57 and $126; 1/5/07, $156 and $66

P 13-4 1. Expected rate at 12/31/06: $.525
2. *Nominal* change $.075 (decrease)
3. *Real* change $.015 (increase)

E 13A-1 1. E 2. A, B, E

E 13A-2 1. D 2. A, C, D

E 13A-3 c. $10,000

E 13A-4 a. $–0–

Chapter 14

E 14-1 2. Call, hedge; 5. Call, speculation; 7. Put, hedge

E 14-2 1. $.4864

E 14-3 1. Neither, sell, sell, neither, neither, sell

E 14-4 1. Buys, speculation; 4. Buys, hedge; 7. Sells, hedge

E 14-5 3. Exporting hedge; 6. Importing hedge

E 14-6 4. Recognize currently; 5. Recognize in OCI

P 14-1 $1,300 FX gain at 12/31/06 on option

P 14-2 $9,300 FX gain at 12/31/06 on option

P 14-3 $39,000 FX gain at 12/31/06 on option

P 14-4 1. 12/31/06: $1,200 FX gain on forward; 1/15/07: $200 FX loss on forward

P 14-5 1. 12/31/06: $700 FX gain on forward; 1/15/07: $300 FX loss on forward

P 14-6 1. 6/30/06: $6,000 FX loss on forward; 8/2/06: $1,000 FX gain on forward

P 14-7 1. Capitalized cost of equipment, $530,000

P 14-8 1. FX Contract Value—Forward at 12/31/06, $17,000 (favorable)

P 14-9 FX Contract Value—Forward at 12/31/06, $12,000 (favorable);
Credit cash for $11,000 at 4/30/07

P 14-10 1. Time value, $16,000
2. 6/30/06: $65,000 FX gain on option; $39,000 recognized in earnings under Assumption C;
12/31/06: $41,000 FX loss on option

P 14-11 1. Intrinsic value, $10,000; Time value, $7,000
2. 6/30/06: $27,000 FX gain on option; $21,600 recognized in earnings;
12/31/06: $14,000 FX loss on option

Chapter 15

E 15-1 Debit Retained Earnings (B-O-Y) for $60,000

E 15-2 2. Credit Retained Earnings (B-O-Y) for $160,000

E 15-3	$(10,000)—Adverse
E 15-4	$(100,000)—Adverse
E 15-7	2. $42,000; $13,000—Favorable
E 15-8	1. Parent records $9,000 loss 2. Subsidiary records 100,000 loss in LCUs
E 15-9	1. Dividend receivable, $2,700,000 2. FX Gain, $300,000
E 15-10	1. Debit Land—Revaluation 100,000 LCUs 2. Credit Deferred Income Taxes Payable 5,000 LCUs
P 15-1	Credit Retained Earnings (B-O-Y) $20,000 (Without Taxes) and $12,000 (With Taxes)
P 15-2	1. Translation adjustment, $(157,000) 2. Net income, $72,000 5. Loss on sale, $129,000
P 15-3	1. Translation adjustment, $195,000 favorable 2. Net income, $420,000 5. Gain on sale, $110,000
P 15-4	1. Parent records $200,000 loss 2. Subsidiary records 166,667 loss in pounds 3. $40,000 7. $2,000
P 15-5	1. $45,000 FX gain
P 15-6	1. Current year translation adjustment, $(79,000) 2. Ending Retained Earnings, $583,000 3. Parent records $22,000 FX loss 4. Defer $62,000 of intercompany profit 8. Consolidated net income, $1,436,000; Consolidated assets, $5,007,000
P 15-7	1. Settle up at $60,000
P 15-8	2005: Credit OCI $6,000 ($10,000 – $4,000)

Chapter 16

E 16-1	Brazil, Net *monetary liability* position; Mexico, Net *monetary asset* position; Belgium, Net *liability* position; Ireland, Net *asset* position
E 16-2	1. $25,000—Favorable 2. $(10,000)—Adverse
E 16-3	1. $500,000—Favorable 2. $(100,000)—Adverse
E 16-6	2a. $30,000 2b. $63,000
E 16-7	1. $8,000 2. $(40,000)
E 16-8	1. $180,000 2. $200,000
E 16-9	1 and 2. Sell, neither, neither, sell 3. Neither, buy, buy, neither
P 16-1	3. Decrease in cash of $100,000
P 16-2	1. Gain from remeasurement, $220,000 2. Net income, $201,000
P 16-3	1. Loss from remeasurement, $(305,000) 2. Net income, $313,000
P 16-4	1. Cash at 1/1/06, 700,000 pesos (forced out) 2. Net *decrease* in cash, $(148,000)
P 16-6	2. Credit Deferred Income Taxes Payable 2,500 LCUs
E 16A-1	Debit Investment in Subsidiary $140,000
E 16A-2	Credit Deferred Income Taxes Payable—foreign $15,000
P 16A-1	1. Debit Income Tax Expense $90,000 2. $240,000
P 16A-2	1. Debit Income Tax Expense $50,000
P 16A-3	1. Debit Income Tax Expense $120,000
P 16A-4	1. Debit Income Tax Expense $30,000
E 16B-1	Correct economic reporting result: 3. $(20,000) 5. $20,000 *real* gain 6. no effect
E 16B-2	Correct economic reporting result: 1. $25,000 *nominal* gain 4. $25,000 *nominal* gain 5. no effect
E 16B-3	Situation 2: favorable (a *real* gain) Situation 4: unfavorable (an *imaginary* loss)
E 16B-4	$943,000 for PPP approach
E 16B-5	$.525
P 16B-1	3. $2,000,000
P 16B-2	1. and 2. Balance, 12/31/06, $1,641,600
P 16B-3	1. $634,000 increase in equity 2. $22,000 nominal gain

Chapter 17

E 17-3	$60,000 each quarter
E 17-4	$1,100,000
E 17-5	Expense in second quarter
P 17-1	First quarter bonus expense, $16,000 or $10,000; Second quarter bonus expense, $5,000 or $2,000
P 17-2	First quarter income tax expense, $200,000; Second quarter income tax expense, $220,000

P 17-3 3. Revised estimated annual tax rate, 42.36%;
Second quarter income tax expense, $170,160

Chapter 18

There are no key figures for Chapter 18.

Chapter 19

E 19-1 Gain on discharge of debt, $7,000,000
E 19-2 Gain on discharge of debt, $2,500,000
E 19-3 $156,000 available to unsecured creditors

P 19-1 1. Gain on debt discharge, $284,000; Increase in APIC, $136,000
3. Decrease in APIC, $266,000 ($566,000 – $300,000)
P 19-2 1. Discount, $19,773,720;
Gain on discharge of debt, $254,773,720
2. First-year interest expense, $42,033,942 (15% × $280,226,280)
P 19-3 1. Deficiency to unsecured creditors, $18,200
P 19-4 1. Deficiency to unsecured creditors, $41,000

Chapter 20

E 20-1 1. Divide equally
E 20-2 1. Monte, $89,000
E 20-3 1b. Bunn, $(2,800)
1c. Bunn, $(14,000)
E 20-4 1b. Agee, $30,000
1c. Agee, $(21,000)
E 20-5 1b. Agee, $34,000
E 20-6 1. Booker's capital, $130,000; Page's capital, $220,000
2. Booker's tax basis, $170,000; Page's tax basis, $280,000

P 20-1 2. Horn, $104,000
5. Horn, $105,100
P 20-2 1. Archer's profit, $54,250
2. Credit Archer's capital, $3,800
P 20-3 1. Credit Altoe's capital, $99,000;
Credit Sopra's capital, $80,000
2. Bass to contribute $900; Sopra to withdraw $4,550
P 20-4 1. Profit, $88,300
2. Arby's share of profits, $35,840
P 20-5 Capital balances (adjusted): Arfee, $40,870; Barker, $60,242
P 20-6 Profit, $18,272; Total assets (adjusted), $77,067

E 20A-1 1. Evers' tax basis, $74,000; Marsh's tax basis, $13,000
4. Taxable gain, $10,000
E 20A-2 1. Teller's ending tax basis, $75,000
2. Teller's ending tax basis, $83,000

Chapter 21

E 21-1 1. $75,000
E 21-2 1. Goodwill, $24,000
E 21-3 Bonuses given: Cord, $6,000; Stringer, $4,000
E 21-4 1. Goodwill, $20,000
2. Dunes receives bonus of $2,400
E 21-5 2. Goodwill of $40,000
5. Ball gives bonus of $1,000
6. Goodwill, $2,500; Credit Glover's capital, $12,500
E 21-6 1. and 2. Cash distribution to Oakley, $61,200
E 21-7 1. Gain on sale of interest, $30,000
4. Taxable gain, $50,000

P 21-1 2. Bonus given by Mounds, $7,500
P 21-2 2. Bonus given to Arbee, $16,000
3. Implied goodwill, $80,000
P 21-3 1. Credit to Y's capital, $49,000
2. Credit to X's capital, $58,800;
Net bonus to A,B,C, and D, $2,400
P 21-4 1. Debit Goodwill $65,000
2. Bonus given by Klubb, $11,000
P 21-5 1. Debit Goodwill $100,000
2. Bonus given to Cowes, $40,000
P 21-6 Goodwill, $85,000; Bonus given by Douglas, $35,000;
Capital: Ash, $702,470; Cherry, $489,770

P 21A-1 2. Rook's tax basis, $74,000
6. Taxable gain, $27,000 ($150,000 – $123,000)
P 21A-2 2. Kingmee's tax basis, $57,000
4. Checker's taxable gain, $10,000

Chapter 22

E 22-1 Cash distribution: Lane, $1,000; Tower, $3,000
E 22-2 Cash distribution: Singer $9,000
E 22-3 Cash distribution: Kross, $12,000
E 22-4 Cash distribution: Deere, $1,000
E 22-5 4.
E 22-6 Cash distribution: Deeds, $6,000; Grant, $3,000; Trusty, $11,000
E 22-7 Cash distribution: Sumner, $28,800; Winters, $41,200

E 22-8	Cash distribution: Queen, $20,000
P 22-1	Cash distribution: Stone, $2,400; Rockne, $600
P 22-2	Cash distribution: Noble, $16,000; Prince, $8,000
P 22-3	Personal payment from Ryley to Wheatman, $6,400
P 22-4	Cash distribution: Brown, $26,600; Cox, $18,400
P 22-5	Final cash distribution: Barley, $44,300; Rice, $1,550
P 22-6	1. First $3,000 to Steele; next $2,500 to Steele and Woods 3:2
P 22-7	First $9,000 to Beltmore; next $5,000 to Beltmore and Tanner 3:2
P 22-8	Final cash distribution: Arbuckle, $41,500; Beltmore, $26,400; Tanner, $8,600; August cash distribution: Beltmore, $4,000

Chapter 23

P 23-1	Principal balance, $210,000; Income balance, $1,000; Original principal, $397,400; Legacies paid or delivered, $176,000
P 23-2	Principal balance, $414,950; Income balance, $6,725; Original capital, $501,550; Legacies paid or delivered, $19,900
P 23-4	3. Principal balance, $293,550; Income balance, $6,470

Chapter 24

E 24-1	Credit Budgetary Fund Balance $80,000
E 24-2	$4,000 ($33,000 – $27,000 – $2,000)
E 24-3	6. Credit Expenditures $66,000
E 24-4	$775,000 ($700,000 + $75,000 expected within 60 days)
E 24-5	Credit Deferred Revenues $6,000
E 24-6	1. Credit Revenues $300,000
E 24-7	Fund Balance at 6/30/06, $155,000
E 24-8	$42,000 favorable variance
E 24-9	$10,000 favorable variance
E 24-10	Credit Budgetary Fund Balance $21,000; Credit Unreserved Fund Balance $9,000
P 24-1	2. Total expenditures, $899,000; Total revenues, $977,000 ($767,000 + $210,000)
P 24-2	1. Revenues, $880,000; Expenditures, $830,000; Total fund balance at 6/30/06, $260,000 2. Unreserved Fund Balance at 6/30/06, $180,000
P 24-3	2. Credit Unreserved Fund Balance $32,000 3. 6/30/06 Fund balance, $102,000
P 24-4	2. Credit Unreserved Fund Balance $89,000 3. 6/30/06 Fund balance, $189,000
P 24-5	3. Credit Unreserved Fund Balance $34,000 4. Total assets, $158,000; total fund balance, $142,000
P 24-6	3. Total expenditures, $832,000; 6/30/06 Fund balance, $188,000
P 24-7	3. Excess of revenues over expenditures, $40,000; 6/30/06 Fund balance, $260,000
P 24-8	5. 7/1/05 Fund balance (corrected retroactively), $80,000; 6/30/06 Fund balance (corrected), $88,000

Chapter 25

E 25-3	1. G, 2. K, 3. L, 4. L, 5. E, 6. J, 7. D, 8. A, 9. G, 10. A, B
E 25-4	1. B, 2. F, 3. D, 4. D, 5. B, 6. G, 7. A, 8. D, 9. I, 10. H
E 25-5	Governmental activities, $1,700,000
E 25-6	Total net assets, $480,000
E 25-7	1. D, 2. E
E 25-8	1. A, 2. D
E 25-9	1. B, 2. B
P 25-1	3. Fund balance at 6/30/06, $3,020,000
P 25-2	Revenues (under) expenditures, $(1,076,000); Fund balance at 12/31/06, $645,000
P 25-3	3. Fund balance at 6/30/06: Capital Projects Fund, $–0–; Debt Service Fund, $8,000
P 25-4	3. Total other financing sources and uses: Capital Projects Fund, $548,000; Debt Service Fund, $29,000
P 25-5	4. Increase in net assets, $100,600
P 25-7	Only 4 and 5 require entries
P 25-9	Debit Expenditures $100,000 and Credit OFS Transfer In $100,000 in Debt Service Fund
P 25-10	Total Equity: GF, $210,000; DS, $52,000; CP, $–0–; IS, $250,000; T&AF, $330,000; GCA, $590,000; GLTL, $350,000
P 25-11	Net change (an increase) in net assets, $610,000
P 25-12	Net change (an increase) in net assets, $430,000

Chapter 26

E 26-1	D, A, B, B, D, A, A, F
E 26-2	B, D, D, D, E, D, B
E 26-3	I, I, D, A, A, A, B, H
E 26-4	G, G, A [E], C, B, A, G [E]

P 26-1 2. Unrestricted category, $292,000;
Temporarily restricted category, $191,000

P 26-2 2. Unrestricted category, $883,000;
Temporarily restricted category, $61,000

P 26-3 2. Total revenues, $985,000;
Total expenses, $810,000;
Increase in unrestricted net assets, $399,000

P 26-4 2. $80,000 unrealized gain (**UR**)
4. $44,000 loss (**UR**)
5. $55,000 loss (**PR**)

P 26A-1 Balances at 12/31/07: **UR**, $5,000,000; **TR**, $22,000; **PR**, $700,000

E 26B-1 1. E, A, C, A, A, D

E 26B-2 Revenues, $6,400,000; Expenses $905,000

E 26B-3 1. Credit Other Revenues $3,000

E 26B-4 3. Credit **TR** Fund Balance $900,000
5. $500,000 in the **PR** column of Statement of Changes in Fund Balances

E 26C-1 Net tuition revenues, $7,100,000

E 26C-2 Gifts received, $950,000 (nonoperating revenues)

E 26C-3 1. Investment income, $1,300,0000
2. Credit Unrestricted Net Assets $250,000

P 26C-1 1. Net nonoperating revenues, $46,100,000
2. Credit Unrestricted Net Assets $47,240,000

P 26C-2 1. Net nonoperating revenues, $890,000
2. Credit Restricted Net Assets—Expendable $726,000
2. Credit Unrestricted Net Assets $153,000